INTERNATIONAL MARKETING

SIXTH EDITION

INTERNATIONAL STUDENT VERSION

Masaaki Kotabe

Temple University

Kristiaan Helsen

Hong Kong University of Science and Technology

WILEY

DEDICATION

To Lorraine, Akie, Euka, and Hiro
—M.K.

For my mother and A.V.
—K.H.

ABOUT THE AUTHORS

 **Masaaki "Mike" Kotabe** holds the Washburn Chair Professorship in International Business and Marketing at the Fox School of Business at Temple University. Prior to joining Temple University in 1998, he was Ambassador Edward Clark Centennial Endowed Fellow and Professor of Marketing and International Business at the University of Texas at Austin. Dr. Kotabe also served as the vice president of the Academy of International Business in the 1997–1998 term. He received his Ph.D. in Marketing and International Business at Michigan State University. Dr. Kotabe teaches international marketing, global sourcing strategy (R&D, manufacturing, and marketing interfaces), and Asian business practices at the undergraduate and MBA levels and theories of international business at the Ph.D. level. He has lectured widely at various business schools around the world, including Austria, Germany, Finland, Norway, Brazil, Colombia, Mexico, China, Japan, Korea, Indonesia, and Turkey. For his research, he has worked closely with leading companies such as AT&T, Kohler, NEC, Nissan, Philips, Sony, and Seven & I Holdings (parent of 7-Eleven stores), and served as advisor to the United Nations' and World Trade Organization's Executive Forum on National Export Strategies.

Dr. Kotabe has written many scholarly publications. His numerous research articles have appeared in such journals as *Journal of Marketing, Journal of International Business Studies, Strategic Management Journal*, and *Academy of Management Journal*. His books include *Global Sourcing Strategy: R&D, Manufacturing, Marketing Interfaces* (1992), *Japanese Distribution System* (1993), *Anticompetitive Practices in Japan* (1996), *MERCOSUR and Beyond* (1997), *Marketing Management* (2001), *Market Revolution in Latin America: Beyond Mexico* (2001), *Emerging Issues in International Business Research* (2002), *Global Supply Chain Management* (2006), and *SAGE Handbook of International Marketing* (2009).

He currently serves as the editor of the *Journal of International Management*, and also serves and/or has served on the editorial boards of *Journal of Marketing, Journal of International Business Studies, Journal of International Marketing, Journal of World Business, Journal of the Academy of Marketing Science, Advances in International Management, Journal of Business Research*, and *Thunderbird International Business Review*, among others. Dr. Kotabe was elected a Fellow of the Academy of International Business for his significant contribution to international business research and education.

 **Kristiaan Helsen** has been an associate professor of marketing at the Hong Kong University of Science and Technology (HKUST) since 1995. Prior to joining HKUST, he was on the faculty of the University of Chicago for five years. He has lectured at Nijenrode University (Netherlands), the International University of Japan, Purdue University, the Catholic University of Lisbon, and CEIBS (Shanghai). Dr. Helsen received his Ph.D. in Marketing at the Wharton School of the University of Pennsylvania.

His research areas include promotional strategy, competitive strategy, and hazard rate modeling. His articles have appeared in journals such as *Marketing Science*, *Journal of Marketing*, *Journal of Marketing Research*, and *European Journal of Operations Research*, among others. He also co-edited the *Handbook of International Marketing* with Masaaki Kotabe. Dr. Helsen is on the editorial board of the *International Journal of Research in Marketing*.

PREFACE

Four Fundamental Issues Addressed in the Sixth Edition

We have continued to receive many letters and e-mail messages as well as user reviews on Amazon.com from instructors and business executives around the world who used the previous editions of our *International Marketing*. Their comments have been unanimously favorable. Thanks to the increased desire in many parts of the world for access to our book in their own languages, our book has been translated into Chinese, Japanese, Portuguese, and Spanish. However, we just cannot sit on our laurels. As the world around us has been constantly changing, the content and context of our book also have to change to reflect the *climate of the time*. As we all know, the Great Recession of 2009—the worst global financial crisis since the Great Depression of 1929—brought the global economy to a screeching halt and changed the global marketing environment completely. The continued global economic growth that many of us had taken for granted for many years proved to be a false assumption. Along with the global recession also came some serious doubts about the virtue of freer trading environments and unfettered global competition, and increased awareness about corporate social responsibility. This recessionary environment has since persisted particularly in many traditionally developed countries including the United States, those in Europe, and Japan, while emerging economies led by Brazil, Russia, India, and China (commonly referred to as BRIC) have continued to grow rapidly. Consequently, the balance of economic power, and thus importance to the world economy, has been rapidly shifting from traditionally developed markets to emerging markets in recent years. In a way, it is an exciting period with so many changes occurring. We are fortunate enough to capture various changes in the marketplace and describe them in this sixth edition of our book.

In our mind, the role of a textbook is not only to describe today's realities but also to extrapolate from them on how the future will unfold. After all, that is how marketing executives have to act and make *correct* decisions based on the facts they have gathered. Today's realities are a serendipitous product of past realities, and the future will be an uncharted course of events lying ahead of us. We constantly strive to help you better understand state-of-the-art marketing practices on a global basis with relevant historical background, current marketing environments, and logical explanations based on a massive amount of knowledge generated by marketing executives as well as by academic researchers from around the world.

Therefore, the sixth edition of our book builds on four major changes that have taken place in the last decade or so. *First*, the landscape of the global economy has changed drastically, particularly as a result of the global financial crisis and the ensuing global recession. The emergence of Brazil, Russia, India, and China, among others, as economic superpowers has occurred during the same period. For example, China's role as the world's factory is well established; India's increased role in information technology development is obvious; and Brazil and Russia are still rich in mineral resources that are becoming scarce around the world.

Second, the explosive growth of information technology tools, including the internet and electronic commerce (e-commerce), has had a significant effect on the way we do business internationally. This continues to be an evolving phenomenon that we need to investigate carefully. On the one hand, everyone seems to agree that business transactions will be faster and more global early on; this is very true. As a result, marketing management techniques such as customer relationship management and global account management have become increasingly feasible. On the other hand, the more deeply we have examined this issue, the more convinced we have become that certain things will not change, or may even become more local as a result of globalization that the internet and e-commerce bestow on us.

Third, it is an underlying human tendency to desire to be different when there are economic and political forces of convergence (often referred to as globalization). When the globalization argument (and movement) became fashionable in the 1980s and 1990s, many of us believed that globalization would make global marketing easier. As we explain later in the text, marketing beyond national borders, indeed, has become easier, but it does not necessarily mean that customers want the same products in countries around the world. Just think about many new countries being born around the world as well as the regional unifications take place simultaneously. Another example is that while e-commerce promotion on the internet goes global, product delivery may need to be fairly local in order to address local competition and exchange rate fluctuations as well as the complexities of international physical distribution (export declarations, tariffs, and nontariff barriers). From a supply-side point of view, globalization has brought us more products from all corners of the world. However, from a demand-side (marketing-side) point of view, customers have a much broader set of goods and services to *choose from*. In other words, marketers now face all the more divergent customers with divergent preferences—far from a homogeneous group of customers.

Fourth, if not last, we have become increasingly more aware of various consequences of corporate action, ranging from environmental pollution to global warming, and from food safety to unsafe work environments around the world. Companies realize that they must consider the impact of their decisions and policies on a wide range of stakeholders besides their shareholders. To be successful in the long term, a company must create value for its shareholders and customers but also local communities and society at large. While the idea that a company has societal obligations has been around for many decades, corporate social responsibility (CSR) has never been more prominent on the corporate agenda.

Indeed, these changes we have observed in the last decade or so are more than extraordinary. In this sixth edition, we have expanded on these issues in all chapters, wherever relevant. We have added many new examples that have occurred in this period. However, we do not sacrifice logical depth in favor of brand-new examples. This revision required a lot of work, as it did in the past. But it was well worth the effort because we are confident as to how satisfied and enlightened readers like you will become.

We strongly believe that cases provide students not only with lively discussions of what goes on with many companies but also provides an in-depth understanding of many marketing-related concepts and tools as used by those companies. In this revision, we have added a number of new cases as well as keeping several cases from the earlier editions that were voted as *favorites* by our textbook users and their students. We have more than 15 long cases as well as 45 short end-of-chapter cases to go with this edition. The cases represent many products and services and many regions and countries as well as many nationalities. These cases are placed on the textbook website for easy download.

Many users of the previous editions continue to commend us for writing a book that is academically rigorous and conceptually sound, yet also full of lively examples that students can easily identify with in order to drive important points across. We combine the academic rigor and relevance (and fun of reading) of materials to meet both undergraduate and MBA educational requirements. We keep this tradition in our sixth edition.

Our Pedagogical Orientation

Marketing in the global arena is indeed a dynamic discipline. Today, there are many international or global marketing management books vying for their respective niches in the market. It is a mature market. As you will learn in our book, in a mature market, firms tend to focus closely—maybe, too closely—on immediate product features for sources of differentiation and may inadvertently ignore the fundamental changes that are reshaping the industry. Often, those fundamental changes come from outside the industry. The same logic applies to the textbook market. Whether existing textbooks are titled international marketing or global marketing, they continue to be bound by the traditional bilateral view of competition. While any new textbook has to embrace the traditional coverage of existing textbooks, we intend to emphasize the multilateral (global) nature of marketing with local sensitivity throughout our book.

Some textbooks have replaced the word *international* with *global*. Such a change amounts to only a repackaging of an existing product we often see in a mature product market, and it does not necessarily make the textbook globally-oriented. We need some paradigm shift to accomplish the task of adding truly global dimensions and complex realities to a textbook. You might ask, "What fundamental changes are needed for a paradigm shift?" and, "Why do we need fundamental changes to begin with?"

Our answer is straightforward. Our ultimate objective is to help you prepare for the new century and become an effective manager overseeing global marketing activities in an increasingly competitive environment. You may or may not choose marketing for your career. If you pursue a marketing career, what you will learn in our book will not only have direct relevance but will also help you understand how you, as a marketing manager, can affect other business functions for effective corporate performance on a global basis. If you choose other functional areas of business for your career, then our book will help you understand how you can work effectively with marketing people for the same corporate goal. Our book is organized as shown in the flowchart.

We believe that our pedagogical orientation not only embraces the existing stock of useful marketing knowledge and methods but also sets itself apart from the competition in a number of fundamental ways, as follows.

Global Orientation

As we indicated at the outset, the term *global* epitomizes the competitive pressure and market opportunities from around the world and the firm's need to optimize its market performance on a global basis. Whether a company operates domestically or across national boundaries, it can no longer avoid competitive pressure and market opportunities. For optimal market performance, the firm should also be ready and willing to take advantage of resources on a global basis, and at the same time respond to different needs and wants of consumers. In a way, global marketing is a constant struggle with economies of scale and scope needs of the firm and its responsiveness and sensitivity to different market conditions. While some people call it a *glocal* orientation, we stay with the term *global* to emphasize marketing flexibility on a global basis.

Let us take a look at a hypothetical U.S. company exporting finished products to Europe and Japan. Traditionally, this export phenomenon has been treated as a bilateral business transaction between a U.S. company and foreign customers. However, in reality, to the executives of the U.S. company, this export transaction may be nothing more than the last phase of the company's activities they manage. Indeed, this company procures certain components from long-term suppliers in Japan and Mexico, other components in a business-to-business (B2B) transaction on the internet with a supplier in Korea, and also from its domestic sources in the United States, and assembles a finished product in its Singapore plant for export to Europe and Japan as well as back to the United States. Indeed, a Japanese supplier of critical components is a joint venture

International Marketing, 6th ed.
(2015)

Globalization

1. Globalization

Global Marketing Environment

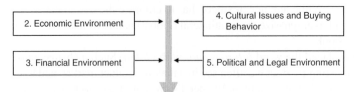

2. Economic Environment

4. Cultural Issues and Buying Behavior

3. Financial Environment

5. Political and Legal Environment

Development of Competitive Strategy

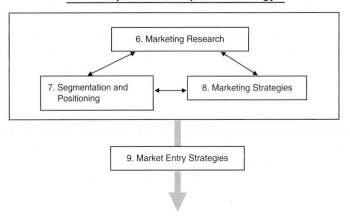

6. Marketing Research

7. Segmentation and Positioning

8. Marketing Strategies

9. Market Entry Strategies

Global Marketing Strategy Development

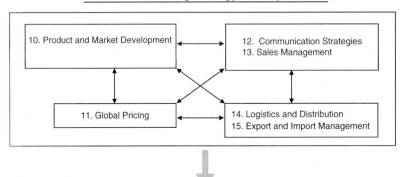

10. Product and Market Development

12. Communication Strategies
13. Sales Management

11. Global Pricing

14. Logistics and Distribution
15. Export and Import Management

Managing Global Operations

16. Planning, Organization, and Control of Global Marketing Operations

17. Marketing in Emerging Markets

18. Sustainable Marketing in the Global Marketplace

majority-owned by this American company, while a Mexican supplier has a licensing agreement with the U.S. company that provides most of technical know-how. A domestic supplier in the United States is in fact a subsidiary of a German company. In other words, this particular export transaction by the U.S. company involves a joint venture, a licensing agreement, a B2B transaction, subsidiary operation, local assembly, and R&D—all managed directly or indirectly by the U.S. company. On top of that, add the realities of market complexities arising from diverse customer preferences in European, Japanese, and North American markets. Think about how these arrangements could affect the company's decisions about product policy, pricing, promotion, and distribution channels.

Many existing textbooks have focused on each of these value-adding activities as if they could be investigated independently. Obviously, in reality, they are not independent of each other, and cannot be. We emphasize this multilateral realism by examining these value-adding activities as holistically as possible.

At the same time, we are fully aware of the increased importance of the roles that emerging markets and competitive firms from those markets play in fundamentally reshaping the nature of global competition. In this sixth edition, we have expanded Chapter 17 to highlight various marketing issues related to emerging markets.

Furthermore, we also recognize the importance of the sustainability of global marketing. We would like you to be knowledgeable about, and act on, not only ethical but also environmental implications of marketing activities on a global basis. In this sixth edition, we have added Chapter 18 to address various issues related to global corporate social responsibility.

Interdisciplinary Perspective

To complement our global orientation, we offer an interdisciplinary perspective in all relevant chapters. We strongly believe that you cannot become a seasoned marketing executive without understanding how other functional areas interface with marketing. The reverse is also true for nonmarketing managers. Some of the exemplary areas in which such a broad understanding of the interface issues is needed are product innovation, designing for manufacturability, product/components standardization, and product positioning. In particular, Japanese competition has made us aware of the importance of these issues, and leading-edge business schools have increasingly adopted such an integrated approach to business education. Our book strongly reflects this state-of-the-art orientation.

Proactive Orientation

Market orientation is a fundamental philosophy of marketing. It is an organizational culture that puts customers' interests first in order to develop a long-term profitable enterprise. In essence, market orientation symbolizes the market-driven firm that is willing to constantly update its strategies using signals from the marketplace. Thus, marketing managers take market cues from the expressed needs and wants of customers. Consequently, the dominant orientation is that of a firm reacting to forces in the marketplace in order to differentiate itself from its competitors. This reactive outside-in perspective is reflected in the typical marketing manager's reliance on marketing intelligence, forecasting, and market research.

While not denying this traditional market orientation, we also believe that marketing managers should adopt an inside-out perspective and capabilities to shape or drive markets. This aspect of the link between strategic planning and marketing implementation has not been adequately treated in existing textbooks. For example, recent trends in technology licensing indicate that it is increasingly used as a conscious, proactive component of a firm's global product strategy. We believe that it is important for marketers to influence those actions of the firm that are some distance away from the customer in the value chain, because such actions have considerable influence on the size of the market and customer choice in intermediate and end product markets.

Cultural Sensitivity

A book could not be written that was not influenced by its authors' background, expertise, and experiences around the world. Our book represents an amalgam of our truly diverse backgrounds, expertise, and experiences across the North and South America, Asia, and Western and Eastern Europe. Given our respective upbringing and work experience in Asia, Western Europe, and Latin America, as well as our educational background in the United States, we have been sensitive not only to cultural differences and diversities but also to similarities.

Realistically speaking, there are more similarities than differences across many countries. Many times, most of us tend to focus either too much on cultural differences rather than on similarities, or vice versa, ignoring differences and focusing on similarities. If you look only at cultural differences, you will be led to believe that country markets are uniquely different, thus requiring marketing strategy adaptations. If, on the other hand, you do not care about, or care to know about, cultural differences, you may be extending a culture-blind, ethnocentric view of the world. Either way, you may not benefit from the economies of scale and scope accruing from exploiting cultural similarities—and differences.

Over the years, two fundamental counteracting forces have shaped the nature of marketing in the international arena. The same counteracting forces have been revisited by many authors in such terms as "standardization vs. adaptation" (1970s), "globalization vs. localization" (1980s), "global integration vs. local responsiveness" (1990s), and more recently—let us add our own—"online scale vs. offline market sensitivity." Terms have changed, but the quintessence of the strategic dilemma that multinational companies (MNCs) face today has not changed and will probably remain unchanged for years to come. Forward-looking, proactive firms have the ability and willingness to accomplish both tasks simultaneously. As we explain later in the text, Honda, for example, developed its Accord car to satisfy the universal customer needs for reliability, drivability, and comfort, but marketed it as a family sedan in Japan, as a commuter car in the United States, and as an inexpensive sports car in Germany, thereby addressing cultural differences in the way people of different nationalities perceive and drive what is essentially the same car.

With our emphasis on global and proactive orientations, however, we will share with you how to hone your expertise to be both culturally sensitive and able to see how to benefit from cultural similarities and differences.

Research Orientation

We strongly believe that theory is useful to the extent that it helps practices. There are many useful theories for international marketing practices. Some of the practical theories are a logical extension of generic marketing theories you may have encountered in a marketing course. Others are, however, very much unique to the international environment.

Many people believe—erroneously—that international or global marketing is just a logical extension of domestic marketing, and that if you have taken a generic marketing course, you would not need to learn anything international. The international arena is like a Pandora's box. Once you move into the international arena, there are many more facts, concepts, frameworks, and even climate differences you need to learn than you ever thought of in order to become a seasoned marketing manager working globally. To assist you in acquiring this new knowledge, various theories provide you with the conceptual tools that enable you to abstract, analyze, understand, predict phenomena, and formulate effective decisions. Theories also provide you with an effective means to convey your logic to your peers and bosses convincingly.

We also apply those theories in our own extensive international work, advising corporate executives, helping them design effective global strategies, and teaching our students at various business schools around the world. Our role as educators is to convey sometimes complex theories in everyday language. Our effort is reflected well in this textbook. This leads to our next orientation.

Practical Orientation

Not only is this book designed to be user-friendly, it also emphasizes practice. We believe in experiential learning and practical applications. Rote learning of facts, concepts, and theories is not sufficient. A good marketing manager should be able to put these to practice. We use many examples and anecdotes as well as our own observations and experiences to vividly portray practical applications. This book also contains real-life, lively cases so that you can further apply your newly acquired knowledge to practice and experience for yourself what it takes to be an effective international marketing manager.

Therefore, this book has been written for both upper-level undergraduate and MBA students who wish to learn practical applications of marketing and related logic and subsequently work internationally. Although we overview foundation materials in this book, we expect that students have completed a basic marketing course.

To further enhance your learning experience, Professor Syed Anwar of West Texas A&M University kindly shares his excellent international marketing one-stop search website, *Marketing & International Links*[1] with you.

Internet Implications

As we stated earlier, we extensively address the implications of the internet and e-commerce in global marketing activities. E-commerce is very promising, but various environmental differences—particularly differences in culture and law as well as consumer needs—are bound to prevent it from becoming an instantaneous freewheeling tool for global marketing. What we need to learn is how to manage *online scale and scope economies* and *offline sensitivities to different market requirements.* We try our best to make you become internet-savvy. These issues are addressed in all the chapters where relevant. We admit that there are many more unknowns than knowns about the impact of the internet on global marketing activities. That is why we point out areas in which the internet is likely to affect the way we do business and have you think seriously about the imminent managerial issues that you will have to deal with upon graduation.

Not only is this book designed to be user-friendly, it also emphasizes practice. We believe in Instructor Support Materials. To accomplish our stated goals and orientations, we have made a major effort to provide the instructor and the student with practical theories and explanations using examples, anecdotes, and cases to maximize the student's learning experience. Some of the specific teaching features are:

• **Global Perspectives**, boxed cases that bring concrete examples from the global marketing environment into the classroom. They are designed to highlight some of the hottest global topics that students should be aware of and may actually act on in their career. The instructor can use these inserts to exemplify theory or use them as mini-cases for class discussion.

---

[1] http://wtfaculty.wtamu.edu/~sanwar.bus/otherlinks.htm#Marketing_&_International_Business_Links.

- **Questions.** This section contains two types: Questions that help students test themselves with, and summarize, the facts, concepts, theories, and other chapter materials in their own words, and questions that help students apply the specific knowledge they learned in each chapter to actual business situations.

Book Companion Site Resources (www.wiley.com/college/kotabe)

- **End-of-Chapter Short Cases** that are designed to address various specific issues explained in the chapters. Short cases at the end of each chapter are useful for showing students how relevant newly learned subject matter can be, as well as for open class discussion with the students. These end-of-chapter short cases are placed on the textbook website for easy download.

- **Long Cases** that are designed to challenge students with real and current business problems and issues. They require in-depth analysis and discussion of various topics covered in the chapters and help students experience how the knowledge they have gained can be applied in real-life situations. These long cases are placed on the textbook website for easy download.

- **Maps** that provide economic geography of the world. Students should be knowledgeable about where various economic resources are available and how they shape the nature of trade and investment and thus the nature of global competition. Global marketing could not be appreciated without understanding economic geography.

- **Instructor's Manual** provides major assistance to the instructor while allowing flexibility in the course scheduling and teaching emphasis. Reserved for professors teaching the course and password-protected on the BCS:
  - **Test Bank:** A test bank consists of short essay questions and multiple-choice questions. This test bank is also computerized and available to adopters on IBM compatible computer diskettes.
  - **Power Point Slides:** Available online to assist the instructor in preparing presentation materials.
  - Global Marketing Management System Online, 4.0 (GMMS04)—developed by Dr. Basil J. Janavaras, professor of International Business at Minnesota State University, is a Web-based global marketing management research and planning program. If you are interested in using the GMMSO for your class project, register online (free trial and free with adoption for Instructors) at www.gmmso4.com or contact: Dr. Basil J. Janavaras, Janavaras & Assoc. International, Inc., (JAI), www.janavaras.com e-mail: basilj@janavaras.com Ph. (507) 382–0304.

Finally, we are delighted to share our teaching experience with you through this book. Our teaching experience is an amalgam of our own learning and knowledge gained through our continued discussion with our colleagues, our students, and our executive friends. We would also like to learn from you, the instructor and the students, who use our book. Not only do we wish that you learn from our book but we also believe that there are many more things that we can learn from you. We welcome your sincere comments and questions. Our contact addresses are as follows:

Masaaki Kotabe

Ph. (215) 204-7704

e-mail: mkotabe@temple.edu

Kristiaan Helsen

Ph. (852) 2358-7720

e-mail: mkhel@ust.hk

ACKNOWLEDGEMENTS

This book would not have ever materialized without guidance, assistance, and encouragement of many of our mentors, colleagues, students, and executives we have worked with and learned from over the years. We are truly indebted to each one of them. We also thank the many reviewers for their constructive comments and suggestions which helped us improve our argument and clarity and raise the quality of our book.

Syed Anwar, West Texas A&M

David Borker, Manhattanville College

Susan Carder, Northern Arizona University

Sang Choe, University of Southern Indiana

Shannon Cummins, University of Nebraska-Lincoln

Anthony Di Benedetto, Temple University

Lawrence Duke, Drexel University

Ruth Lumb, Minnesota State University Moorhead

Mike Mullen,Florida Atlantic University

Louis Nzegwu, University of Wisconsin-Platteville

Sekar Raju, Iowa State University

Alok Saboo, Pennsylvania State University

Surinder Tikoo, SUNY New Paltz

Srdan Zdravkovic, Bryant University

The first co-author would like to extend thanks to his colleagues around the world. At Temple University, Dean Moshe Porat at the Fox School of Business and Management is acknowledged for emphasizing international business education and research as the school's primary focus of excellence, providing enormous opportunities for this co-author to meet with and discuss with leading practitioners/executives of international business those emerging issues that are shaping and re-shaping the way business is conducted around the world. A good deal of credit also goes to Dan Zhang and Primidya Soesilo for having educated me with so many fascinating business examples and cases from around the world throughout the revision process.

Various colleagues outside Temple University have helped the first co-author in the writing process. Tim Wilkinson (Montana State University) offered an interesting insight into the workings of the European Union and its marketing peculiarities. Amal Karunaratna (University of Adelaide, Australia) assisted in providing interesting examples from Down Under. Taro Yaguchi (Omori & Yaguchi Law Firm, Philadelphia) offered an update on ever-changing laws and treaties that affect firms marketing internationally. Sae-Woon Park (Changwon National University, Korea), who has many years of export management and export financing practices, assisted in documenting the most up-to-date and state-of-the-art export practices in use today.

The second co-author would like to extend his thanks to MBA students at the University of Chicago, Nijenrode University, Hong Kong University of Science and Technology, and MIM students at Thammasat University (Bangkok). He also acknowledges the valuable comments on Chapter 13 from Chris Beaumont and John Mackay, both with McCann-Erickson, Japan. Professor Niraj Dawar (University of WesternOntario, Canada) offered helpful insights on marketing in emerging markets. A word of gratitude for their feedback and encouragement is given to two colleagues who spent their sabbatical at HKUST: Jerry Albaum (University of Oregon) and Al Shocker (University of Minnesota), and to Romualdo Leones for some of the photo materials used in the new edition.

Finally and most importantly, we are deeply grateful to you, the professors, students, and professionals for using this book. We stand by our book, and sincerely hope that our book adds to your knowledge and expertise. We would also like to continuously improve our product in the future.

As we indicated in the Preface, we would like to hear from you as you are our valued customers. Thank you!

CONTENTS

1 GLOBALIZATION 1

Why Global Marketing Is Imperative 3
Globalization of Markets: Convergence and Divergence 8
   International Trade versus International Business 11
   Who Manages International Trade? 12
Evolution of Global Marketing 13
   What Is Marketing? 13
   Domestic Marketing 16
   Export Marketing 16
   International Marketing 17
   Multinational Marketing 18
   Global Marketing 18
   The Impact of Economic Geography and Climate on Global Marketing 19
Appendix: Theories of International Trade and the Multinational Enterprise 21
Summary 27

2 ECONOMIC ENVIRONMENT 28

Intertwined World Economy 30
   Foreign Direct Investment 31
   Portfolio Investment 33
Country Competitiveness 35
   Changing Country Competitiveness 35
   Human Resources and Technology 35
Emerging Economies 37
Evolution of Cooperative Global Trade Agreements 40
   General Agreements on Tariffs and Trade 40
   World Trade Organization 41
Information Technology and the Changing Nature of Competition 45
   Value of Intellectual Property in the Information Age 46
   Proliferation of E-Commerce and Regulations 47
Regional Economic Arrangements 48
   Free Trade Area 48
   Customs Union 51
   Common Market 51
   Monetary Union 52
   Political Union 52
Multinational Corporations 52

3 FINANCIAL ENVIRONMENT 56

Historical Role of the U.S. Dollar 57

Development of Today's International Monetary System 58
  The Bretton Woods Conference 58
  The International Monetary Fund 59
  The International Bank for Reconstruction and Development 61
  Fixed versus Floating Exchange Rates 61
  Currency Blocs 62

Foreign Exchange and Foreign Exchange Rates 64
  Purchasing Power Parity 64
  Forecasting Exchange Rate Fluctuation 65
  Coping with Exchange Rate Fluctuations 66
  Spot versus Forward Foreign Exchange 68
  Exchange Rate Pass-Through 69

Balance of Payments 71
  The Internal and External Adjustments 73

Economic and Financial Turmoil around the World 74
  Asian Financial Crisis and Its Aftermath 74
  The South American Financial Crisis and Its Aftermath 76
  The U.S. Subprime Mortgage Loan Crisis and the Subsequent Global Financial Crisis 77
  Financial Crises in Perspective 77
  Responses to the Regional Financial Crises 79

Marketing in the Euro Area 82
  Historical Background 82
  Ramifications of the Euro for Marketers 85

4 CULTURAL ISSUES AND BUYING BEHAVIOR 89

Meaning of Culture 91

Elements of Culture 92
  Material Life 92
  Language 93
  Social Interactions 96
  Aesthetics 98
  Religion 102
  Education 104
  Value Systems 106

Cross-Cultural Comparisons 108
  High- versus Low-Context Cultures 108
  Hofstede's Classification Scheme 109
  GLOBE Project 111
  World Value Survey (WVS) 113

Adapting to Cultures 114

Culture and the Marketing Mix 116
  Product Policy 118
  Pricing 119
  Distribution 119
  Promotion 120

5   POLITICAL AND LEGAL ENVIRONMENT   123

Political Environment—Individual Governments   124
  Home Country versus Host Country   124
  Structure of Government   126
  Government Policies and Regulations   128
Political Environment—Social Pressures and Political Risk   136
  Social Pressures and Special Interests   136
  Managing the Political Environment   139
Terrorism and the World Economy   143
International Agreements   144
  Group of Seven (G7), Group of Eight (G8), and Group of Eight Plus Five (G8 + 5)   145
  Wassenaar Arrangement   146
International Law and Local Legal Environment   147
  International Law   147
  Local Legal Systems and Laws   147
  Jurisdiction   151
Issues Transcending National Boundaries   151
  ISO 9000 and 14000   151
  Intellectual Property Protection   152
  International Treaties for Intellectual Property Protection   157
  Antitrust Laws of the United States   160
  Antitrust Laws of the European Union   162
  U.S. Foreign Corrupt Practices Act of 1977   162

6   MARKETING RESEARCH   167

Research Problem Formulation   170
Secondary Global Marketing Research   172
  Secondary Data Sources   172
  Problems with Secondary Data Research   174
Primary Global Marketing Research   176
  Focus Groups   176
  Survey Methods for Cross-Cultural Marketing Research   177
  Observational Research   183
Leveraging the Internet for Global Market Research Studies   184
Market Size Assessment   186
  Method of Analogy   187
  Trade Audit   188
  Chain Ratio Method   188
  Cross-Sectional Regression Analysis   190
New Market Information Technologies   191
Managing Global Marketing Research   193
  Selecting a Research Agency   193
  Coordination of Multicountry Research   194

7   SEGMENTATION AND POSITIONING   198

Reasons for International Market Segmentation   199
  Country Screening   199

Global Marketing Research   200
Entry Decisions   200
Positioning Strategy   201
Resource Allocation   201
Marketing Mix Policy   202

International Market Segmentation Approaches   203

Segmentation Scenarios   204

Bases for International Market Segmentation   207
Demographics   207
Socioeconomic Variables   208
Behavior-Based Segmentation   209
Lifestyle and Values   209

International Positioning Strategies   212
Uniform versus Localized Positioning Strategies   214
Universal Positioning Appeals   215

Global, Foreign, and Local Consumer Culture Positioning   217

Appendix   220

8   MARKETING STRATEGIES   223

Information Technology and Global Competition   224
Real-Time Management   224
Online Communication   225
Electronic Commerce (E-Commerce)   225
E-Company   227
Faster Product Diffusion   228
Global Citizenship   228

Global Strategy   228
Global Industry   228
Competitive Industry Structure   231
Competitive Advantage   233
Hypercompetition   238
Interdependency   238

Global Marketing Strategy   239
Benefits of Global Marketing   240
Limits to Global Marketing   242

R&D, Operations, and Marketing Interfaces   244
R&D/Operations Interface   245
Operations/Marketing Interface   246
Marketing/R&D Interface   248

Regionalization of Global Marketing Strategy   249
Cross-Subsidization of Markets   251
Identification of Weak Market Segments   252
Use of the "Lead Market" Concept   252
Marketing Strategies for Emerging Markets   254

Competitive Analysis   256

9 **MARKET ENTRY STRATEGIES** **259**

Country Selection   260
Scale of Entry   263
Choosing the Mode of Entry   264
  Decision Criteria for Mode of Entry   *264*
Exporting   268
Licensing   270
  Benefits   *271*
  Caveats   *271*
Franchising   272
  Benefits   *273*
  Caveats   *273*
Expanding through Joint Ventures and Alliances   274
  Benefits   *276*
  Caveats   *276*
  Drivers behind Successful International Joint Ventures   *278*
Wholly Owned Subsidiaries   280
  Benefits   *280*
  Caveats   *280*
  Acquisitions and Mergers   *281*
  Greenfield Operations   *284*
Dynamics of Entry Strategies   284
Timing of Entry   285
Exit Strategies   287
  Reasons for Exit   *288*
  Risks of Exit   *289*
  Guidelines   *290*
Appendix A   292
Appendix B   293

10 **PRODUCT AND MARKET DEVELOPMENT** **295**

Global Branding Strategies   296
  Global Branding   *296*
  Local Branding   *300*
  Global or Local Branding?   *301*
  Brand-Name Changeover Strategies   *306*
Management of Multinational Product Lines   309
Product Piracy   312
  Strategic Options against Product Piracy   *313*
Country-of-Origin (COO) Effects   316
  Country-of-Origin (COO) Influences on Consumers   *317*
  Strategies to Cope with COO Stereotypes   *318*
Global Marketing of Services   321
  Challenges in Marketing Services Internationally   *321*
  Opportunities in the Global Service Industries   *322*
  Global Service Marketing Strategies   *323*

11   GLOBAL PRICING   326

Drivers of Foreign Market Pricing   327
Company Goals   327
Company Costs   328
Customer Demand   329
Competition   330
Distribution Channels   331
Government Policies   332
Managing Price Escalation   332
Pricing in Inflationary Environments   334
Global Pricing and Currency Fluctuations   336
Currency Gain/Loss Pass Through   336
Currency Quotation   340
Transfer Pricing   340
Determinants of Transfer Prices   340
Setting Transfer Prices   341
Minimizing the Risk of Transfer Pricing Tax Audits   342
Global Pricing and Anti-dumping Regulation   344
Price Coordination   345
Global-Pricing Contracts (GPCs)   347
Aligning Pan-Regional Prices   347
Implementing Price Coordination   349

12   COMMUNICATION STRATEGIES   351

Global Advertising and Culture   352
Language Barriers   352
Other Cultural Barriers   354
Communication and Cultural Values   354
Setting the Global Advertising Budget   355
Percentage of Sales Method   358
Competitive Parity   358
Objective-and-Task Method   358
Resource Allocation   358
Creative Strategy   359
The "Standardization" versus "Adaptation" Debate   359
Merits of Standardization   361
Barriers to Standardization   363
Approaches to Creating Advertising Copy   364
Global Media Decisions   366
Media Infrastructure   366
Media Limitations   366
Recent Trends in the Global Media Landscape   367
Advertising Regulations   369
Choosing an Advertising Agency   372
Other Communication Platforms   374
Sales Promotions   374

Direct Marketing   376
Global Sponsorships   377
Mobile (Brand-in-the-Hand) Marketing   379
Trade Shows   380
Product Placement   381
Viral Marketing   383
Global Public Relations (PR) and Publicity   383
Globally Integrated Marketing Communications (GIMC)   384

13   SALES MANAGEMENT   387

Market Entry Options and Salesforce Strategy   389
Role of Foreign Governments   392
Cultural Considerations   392
Personal Selling   392
Cultural Generalization   393
Corporate (Organizational) Culture   394
Relationship Marketing   394
Myers–Briggs Type Indicator   396
Impact of Culture on Sales Management and Personal Selling Process   398
Salesforce Objectives   400
Salesforce Strategy   400
Recruitment and Selection   401
Training   402
Supervision   403
Evaluation   405
Cross-Cultural Negotiations   405
Stages of Negotiation Process   406
Cross-Cultural Negotiation Strategies   406
Expatriates   409
Advantages of Expatriates   410
Difficulties of Sending Expatriates Abroad   410
The Return of the Expatriate—Repatriation   414
Generalizations about When Using Expatriates Is Positive or Negative   414

14   LOGISTICS AND DISTRIBUTION   416

Definition of Global Logistics   418
Managing Physical Distribution   419
Modes of Transportation   420
Warehousing and Inventory Management   422
Third-Party Logistics (3PL) Management   425
Logistical Revolution with the Internet   426
Managing Sourcing Strategy   427
Procurement: Types of Sourcing Strategy   428
Outsourcing of Service Activities   432
Free Trade Zones   436
International Distribution Channel   438
Channel Configurations   438

Channel Management   439
International Retailing   440
Private-Label Branding (Store Brands)   442
"Push" versus "Pull"   444
On-Time Retail Information Management   444
Retailing Differences across the World   446
Appendix: Maquiladora Operation   451

15   EXPORT AND IMPORT MANAGEMENT   453

Organizing for Exports   454
Research for Exports   454
Export Market Segments   455
Indirect Exporting   456
Direct Exporting   458
Mechanics of Exporting   459
Legality of Exports   459
Export Transactions   461
Terms of Shipment and Sale   461
Payment Terms   463
Currency Hedging   464
Role of the Government in Promoting Exports   464
Export–Import Bank   466
Tariff Concessions   467
Export Regulations   468
Managing Imports—The Other Side of the Coin   470
Mechanics of Importing   471
Import Documents and Delivery   472
Import Duties   473
Gray Markets   474

16   PLANNING, ORGANIZATION, AND CONTROL OF GLOBAL MARKETING OPERATIONS   483

Global Strategic Marketing Planning   484
Bottom-Up versus Top-Down Strategic Planning   484
Pitfalls   484
Key Criteria in Global Organizational Design   485
Environmental Factors   485
Firm-Specific Factors   486
Organizational Design Options   487
International Division Structure   487
Global Product Division Structure   487
Geographic Structure   488
Matrix Structure   492
The Global Network Solution   493
Organizing for Global Brand Management   495
Global Branding Committee   495

Brand Champion   495
Global Brand Manager   496
Informal, Ad Hoc Branding Meetings   496
Life Cycle of Organizational Structures   496
Control of Global Marketing Efforts   498
Formal ("Bureaucratic") Control Systems   498
Informal Control Methods   500
"Soft" versus "Hard" Levers   501

17   MARKETING IN EMERGING MARKETS   504

Emerging Markets   505
Definition   505
Characteristics of Emerging Markets   506
Competing with the New Champions   509
The New Champions   510
Competing against the Newcomers   513
Targeting/Positioning Strategies in Emerging Markets—BOP or No BOP?   515
Entry Strategies for Emerging Markets   518
Timing of Entry   518
Entry Mode   518
Product Policy   519
Product Innovation   519
Branding   521
Packaging   522
Pricing Strategy   523
The Distribution Challenge   524
Creating Distribution Systems   524
Managing Distributor Relationships   525
Communication Strategies for Emerging Markets   526
Push versus Pull Activities   526
Mass Media versus Non-Traditional Marketing Approaches   526

18   SUSTAINABLE MARKETING IN THE GLOBAL MARKETPLACE   530

Global Corporate Citizenship   531
Scope of CSR   531
Major Areas of CSR   533
Corruption/Graft   533
Environmental Concerns   535
Supply Chain Accountability   537
Commitment toward Customers   538
Community Support (Cause-Related Marketing)   539
The Case for Sustainability   540
Challenges for Sustainability Strategies   541
Cultural Tensions   542
Sustainability Image   543
Poor Infrastructure   545

Sustainable Marketing and Global Consumers   545

Developing and Implementing a Sustainable Strategy   547

Step 1: Set Objectives and Targets   547

Step 2: Understand the Operating Environment   548

Step 3: Specify Strategic Sustainability Initiatives   548

Step 4: Implement   550

Step 5: Develop Metrics for Monitoring and Reporting   551

Global Stakeholder Engagement Programs   553

Sustainable Marketing Mix Policy for the Global Marketplace   555

Developing Sustainable Products and Services   555

Sustainable Pricing   556

Communication and Sustainability   557

Sustainability and Distribution Channels   559

Crisis Management and Consumer Boycotts   560

Crisis Management   560

Consumer Boycotts   562

SUBJECT INDEX   565

NAME INDEX   584

COMPANY INDEX   591

GLOBALIZATION

1

CHAPTER OVERVIEW

1. Why global marketing is imperative

2. Globalization of markets: convergence and divergence

3. Evolution of global marketing

4. Appendix: theories of international trade and the multinational enterprise

Marketing products and services around the world, transcending national and political boundaries, is a fascinating phenomenon. The phenomenon, however, is not entirely new. Products have been traded across borders throughout recorded civilization, extending back beyond the Silk Road that once connected East with West from Xian to Rome on land and the recently excavated sea trade route between the Roman Empire and India that existed 2,000 years ago. However, since the end of World War II, the world economy has experienced a spectacular growth rate never witnessed before in human history, largely led by large U.S. companies in the 1950s and 1960s, then by European and Japanese companies in the 1970s and 1980s, and most recently joined by new emerging market firms, such as Lenovo, Mittal Steel, and Cemex. In particular, recent competition from the so-called BRIC countries (Brazil, Russia, India, and China) has given the notion of global competition an extra touch of urgency and significance that you see almost daily in print media such as the *Wall Street Journal*, the *Financial Times*, *Nikkei Shimbun*, and *Folha de São Paulo*, as well as TV media such as the BBC, NBC, and CNN. With a few exceptions, such as Korea's Samsung Electronics (consumer electronics) and China's Haier (home appliances), these emerging-market multinational companies are not yet household names in the industrialized world, but from India's Infosys Technologies (IT services) to Brazil's Embraer (light jet aircrafts), and from Taiwan's Acer (computers) to Mexico's Cemex (building materials), a new class of formidable competitors is rising.[1]

In this chapter, we will introduce you to the complex and constantly evolving realities of global marketing. The term *global marketing* refers to a strategy to achieve one or more of four major categories of potential globalization benefits: cost reduction, improved quality of products and programs, enhanced customer preference, and increased competitive advantage on a global basis. The objective is to make you think beyond exporting and importing. As you

---

[1]"The Global Emergence of the 'New Champions,'" *BusinessWeek*, November 12, 2008, p. 11; and also read Martin Roll, *Asian Brand Strategy: How Asia Builds Strong Brands* (New York: Palgrave Macmillan, 2006).

will learn shortly, despite wide media attention, exporting and importing are a relatively small portion of what constitutes international business. We are not saying, however, that exporting and importing are not important.

It was conventional wisdom that world merchandise trade would on average grow by twice the annual growth rate of global GDP. It was so until 2008. Total merchandise trade volume reached $16.3 trillion in 2008, compared to $6 trillion in 2000.[2] Since the aftermath of the devastating September 11, 2001, terrorist attacks in the United States, the improved market conditions in the United States and Europe as well as strong growth in the emerging markets, including China and India, had steadily improved the world economy. However, the unprecedented global recession triggered by the subprime mortgage crisis in the United States in 2008–2009, the aftermath of the U.S.-led war against global terrorism, and high oil prices, among other things, continue to keep the world economy from making a full-fledged recovery. As a result of the worst recession since the Great Depression of 1929–1932, world trade volume shrank in 2009 for the first time in over 25 years. Despite the sharp drop of world merchandise exports down to $12.5 trillion in 2009, total merchandise trade volume bounced back to US$15.2 trillion in 2010 and grew steadily to US$18.2 trillion in 2011—a growth of 46 percent in two years. Exports of commercial services also grew 21 percent from US$3.4 trillion in 2009 to US$4.1 trillion in 2011.[3]

At the time of this writing at the end of 2012, however, the world economy has come into an uncertain and vulnerable period as Europe's financial turmoil has caused contagion effects for developing and other high-income countries. Europe seems to have entered recession, while some major developing countries (Brazil, India, Russia, South Africa, and Turkey) have experienced slower growth than earlier in the recovery. The World Bank predicts another growth slowdown in world trade from an estimated of 6.6 percent in 2011 to 4.7 percent in 2012, before strengthening again to 6.8 percent in 2013. The global economy is expected to grow to 2.5 percent and 3.1 percent in 2012 and 2013, respectively.[4]

Whenever the growth of the global economy slows down, however, the specter of economic nationalism—each country's urge to protect domestic jobs and keep capital at home instead of promoting freer international trade—tends to hamper further globalization.[5] Although sometimes bumpy, it is expected that the drive for globalization will continue to be promoted through more free trade; more internet commerce; more networking of businesses, schools, and communities; and more advanced technologies.[6]

[2]*The World Factbook 2011*, https://www.cia.gov/library/publications/the-world-factbook/index.html.

[3]*WTO International Trade Statistics 2012*, www.wto.org.

[4]World Bank, *Global Economic Prospect*, January 2012, www.worldbank.org/gep2012.

[5]Occupy Wall Street and other "Occupy" *movements* that happened in many cities around the world in 2001–2012 demonstrated the general public's concerns about large companies and the global financial system controling the world economy and benefiting a few, undermining democracy. Also read "Capitalism and its Critics: Rage against the Machine," *Economist*, October 22, 2011.

[6]The reader needs to be cautioned that there may be limits to the benefit of globalization for two primary reasons. First, firms in poor countries with very weak economic and financial infrastructure may not be able to (afford to) adjust fast enough to the forces of globalization. Second, poor countries could be made worse off by trade liberalization because trade tends to be opened for high-tech goods and services exported by rich countries—such as computers and financial services—but remains protected in areas where those poor countries could compete, such as agricultural goods, textiles or construction. See, for example, Joseph E. Stiglitz, *Globalization and Its Discontents* (New York: W.W. Norton & Co., 2003). For an excellent treatise on various paradoxes of globalization, refer to Terry Clark, Monica Hodis, and Paul D'Angelo, "The Ancient Road: An Overview of Globalization," in Masaaki Kotabe and Kristiaan Helsen, ed., *The SAGE Handbook of International Marketing* (London: Sage Publications, 2009), 15–35.

Why Global Marketing Is Imperative

We frequently hear terms such as *global markets*, *global competition*, *global technology*, and *global competitiveness*. In the past, we heard similar words with *international* or *multinational* instead of *global* attached to them. What has happened since the 1980s? Are these terms just fashionable concepts of the time without some deep meanings? Or has something inherently changed in our society?

Saturation of Domestic Markets

First and at the most fundamental level, the saturation of domestic markets in the industrialized parts of the world forced many companies to look for marketing opportunities beyond their national boundaries. The economic and population growth in developing countries also gave those companies an additional incentive to venture abroad. Now companies from emerging economies, such as Korea's Samsung and Hyundai and Mexico's Cemex and Grupo Modelo, have made inroads into the developed markets around the world. The same logic applies equally to companies from developed countries, such as Australia and New Zealand, geographically isolated from the other major industrialized parts of the world. Dôme Coffees Australia is building a multinational coffee shop empire by expanding into Asia and the Middle East. Inevitably, the day will come when Starbucks from the United States and Dôme Coffees from Australia will compete head-on for global dominance.[7]

Emerging Markets

During the twentieth century, the large economies and large trading partners have been located mostly in the **Triad Regions** of the world (North America, Western Europe, and Japan), collectively producing over 80 percent of world GDP with only 20 percent of the world's population.[8] However, in the next 10 to 20 years, the greatest commercial opportunities are expected to be found increasingly in 10 Big Emerging Markets (BEMs)—the Chinese Economic Area, India, the Commonwealth of Independent States (Russia, Central Asia, and Caucasus states), South Korea, Mexico, Brazil, Argentina, South Africa, Central European countries, Turkey, and the Association of Southeast Asian Nations (Indonesia, Brunei, Malaysia, Singapore, Thailand, the Philippines, and Vietnam). Accordingly, an increasing number of competitors are expected to originate from those 10 emerging economies. In the past 20 years, China's real annual GDP growth rate has averaged 9.5 percent a year, while India's has been 5.7 percent, compared to the average 3 percent GDP growth in the United States. Clearly, the milieu of the world economy has changed significantly, and over the next two decades, the markets that hold the greatest potential for dramatic increases in U.S. exports are not the traditional trading partners in Europe, Canada, and Japan, which now account for the overwhelming bulk of the international trade of the United States. Instead, they will be those BEMs and other developing countries that constitute some 80 percent of the "bottom of the pyramid."[9] As the traditional developed markets have become increasingly competitive, such emerging markets promise to offer better growth opportunities to many firms.

Unfavorable Domestic Economy

The ongoing global economic downturn has forced businesses to outsmart unfavorable economies in their domestic markets and to venture abroad to fast-growing markets in some regions of the world, such as Asia, in search of marketing opportunities. Large-scale business such as Yum! Brands, the proprietor of KFC and Pizza Hut, which operated 2,497

---

[7]"Bean Countess," *Australian Magazine*, December 9–10, 2000, p. 50+.

[8]L. Bryan, *Race for the World: Strategies to Build A Great Global Firm* (Boston: Harvard Business School Press, 1999).

[9]C.K. Prahalad, *The Fortune at the Bottom of the Pyramid: Eradicating Poverty through Profits* (Philadelphia: Wharton School Publishing, 2004).

stores in China in 2009 (compared with 5,253 in the United States), reached soaring global total sales of 31 percent in 2008 in China, helping the company shrug off the U.S. recession.[10] This global expansion decision has not only been the priority of large businesses, but also of small businesses. The declining value of U.S. dollars in 2008 forced small businesses to think globally as the decline actually provided an opportunity to take advantage of the exchange rate. In 2010, a total of 286,661 small businesses with less than 500 employees exported from the United States, accounting for 97.8 percent of all U.S. exporters.[11]

Global Competition

We believe something profound has indeed happened in our view of competition around the world. About 30 years ago, the world's greatest automobile manufacturers were General Motors, Ford, and Chrysler. Today, companies like Toyota, Honda, BMW, Renault, and Hyundai, among others, stand out as competitive nameplates in the global automobile market. Similarly, personal computers used to be almost synonymous with IBM, which dominated the PC business around the world. Today, the computer market is crowded with Dell and Hewlett-Packard (HP) from the United States, Sony and Toshiba from Japan, Samsung from Korea, Acer and ASUS from Taiwan,[12] and so on. Indeed, Lenovo, a personal computer company from China, acquired the IBM PC division in 2005, and now sells the ThinkPad series under the Lenovo brand. The deal not only puts Lenovo into the industry's third place, but also challenges the world top players, Dell and HP/Compaq, respectively.[13] Even in a low-tech area, creative firms from emerging economies are expanding overseas. For example, the VietMac burger from Vietnam has taken the country by storm. Made from two rice patties over your choice of additive-free meat and salad, the meal is touted as a healthy alternative to its bread-bun rivals such as McDonald's and Burger King. Just one year after the first restaurant opened, VietMac has 12 outlets nationwide and is already going global with a franchise opening in Germany in 2012.[14] In the not-so-distant future, VietMac may pose a major competitive threat to the global giants of the fast food industry. In a similar vein, a startup video game company from Kenya, Planet Rackus, released Ma3Racer, a video game in which a gamer maneuvers a homicidal minibus swerving around potholes, seldom signaling and using its iffy brakes only at the last second with the sole goal of not hitting pedestrians in congested and chaotic Nairobi, Kenya's capital. Within a month, a quarter of a million people in 169 countries had downloaded the game. Its success differs from its Silicon Valley sisters in that this Kenyan company has designed the game for mobile phones rather than for computers. Kenya is still a poor country with very limited computer ownership but almost 75 percent of Kenyans have mobile phones.[15]

As many firms in emerging economies have gained their competitive advantage based on "frugal innovations" that emphasize value for the money, firms in traditionally developed countries also have to learn to develop similar products. Whether developed-country firms market frugal products or not in their own markets, emerging-market firms will. For example, India's Mahindra & Mahindra now markets many small garden tractors to American hobby farmers, forcing John Deere, a dominant U.S. farming equipment company, to do the same with its small tractors emphasizing value for the money.[16] Nike is a U.S. company with a truly all-American shoe brand, but its shoes are all made by its contract manufacturers in foreign countries

---

[10]Todd Guild, "Think Regionally, Act Locally: Four Steps to Reaching the Asian Consumer," *McKinsey Quarterly*, September 2009, pp. 25–35.

[11]http://www.trade.gov/mas/ian/smeoutlook/tg_ian_001925.asp, accessed March 25, 2013.

[12]"Why Taiwan Matters: The Global Economy Couldn't Function without It, but Can It Really Find Peace with China?" *Business Week*, May 16, 2005, pp. 74–81.

[13]"Can China's Lenovo Brand in the Land of Dell?" *B to B*, October 10, 2005, pp. 1 and 45.

[14]"Viet Burger Chain Goes Global,"*InsideRetail.Asia*, April 15, 2012, http://www.insideretail.asia/InsideRetailAsia/InsideRetailAsianews/Viet-burger-chain-goes-global-4678.aspx.

[15]"Upwardly Mobile: Kenya's Technology Start-Up Scene is About to Take Off," *Economist*, August 25, 2012, p. 53.

[16]"Frugal Ideas Are Spreading from East to West," *Economist*, March 24, 2012, p. 68.

and exported to many countries. Pillsbury (known for its Betty Crocker recipes and Häagen-Dazs ice cream brand) and 7-Eleven convenience stores are two American institutions owned and managed, respectively, by Diageo from the United Kingdom and Seven & i Holdings Co. from Japan. On the other hand, the world of media, led by U.S. media giants, has become equally global in reach. MTV has more than 150 TV channels worldwide targeting teenagers in 162 countries in 33 languages around the world, and a large part of its local channel contents are made locally.[17]

Global Cooperation

Global competition also brings about global cooperation. In the industrial engine markets, for example, Rolls Royce Group (the global power systems company) and Daimler (the global automotive company) formed a 50:50 joint venture to secure 100 percent of Tognum (a German engine and drive system specialist company). With this acquisition, Rolls Royce and Daimler intend to establish a leading supplier of complete industrial engine system.[18] Starbucks—the world's largest coffee shop chain (based in Seattle)—agreed to collaborate with Tata Global Beverage—an Indian, Kolkata-based beverage company—to open at least 50 stores in India by the end of 2012.[19] Global cooperation also frequently occurs in higher education. Manchester University (U.K.) has been partnering with Penn State University (U.S.) and Nanyang Technological University (Singapore) in a offering Master of Science program in Project Management.[20]

Internet Revolution

The proliferation of the internet and **e-commerce** is wide-reaching. The number of internet users in the world reached 2.41 billion in June 2012, which amounts to five times the number in 2000. According to internet World Statistics, 44.8 percent of internet users are from Asia, followed by 21.5 percent and 11.4 percent from Europe and North America, respectively. Latin America represents 10.4 percent. Although Africa and Middle East account for only 7.0 percent and 3.7 percent, respectively, these two regions represent the top two regions in their usage growth with 36 times and 26 times, respectively, between 2000 and 2012.[21] Although it is difficult to obtain precise statistics measuring internet usage due to the fact that different sources use different methods and definitions of e-commerce activities, Cisco Systems, for example, predicts global e-commerce will reach $1.4 trillion in 2015, increasing at 13.5 percent annually for the next four years.[22]

Compared to business-to-consumer (B2C) e-commerce, business-to-business (B2B) e-commerce is larger, growing faster, and has less unequal geographical distribution globally.[23] Increases in the freedom of movement of goods, services, capital, technology, and people coupled with rapid technological development has resulted in an explosion of global B2B e-commerce. The share of the global B2B e-commerce a country is likely to receive, on the other hand, depends upon country-level factors such as income and population size, the availability of credit, venture capital, telecom and logistical infrastructure, tax and other incentives, tariff/non-tariff barriers, government emphasis on

---

[17]http://en.wikipedia.org/wiki/MTV_Networks, accessed January 25, 2013.

[18]See Daimler Annual Report 2012, http://www.daimler.com/Projects/c2c/channel/documents/2287152_Daimler_Annual_Report_2012.pdf.

[19]"Starbucks to Open First Indian Store This Autumn," *New York Times*, January 31, 2012, http://www.nytimes.com.

[20]"University Gives Project Managers a Boost with Joint Masters Course," University of Manchester, http://www.manchester.ac.uk/aboutus/news/archive/list/item/?id=7480&year=2011&month=10.

[21]http://www.internetworldstats.com/stats.htm, accessed March 27, 2013.

[22]"Global e-Commerce Reach $1.4 Trillion in 2015," Internet Retailer, www.internetretailer.com/, June 7, 2011.

[23]*B2B* and *B2C*, among others, have become trendy business terms in recent years. However, they are fundamentally the same as more conventional terms, consumer marketing and industrial marketing, respectively, except that B2B and B2C imply the use of the internet, intranet, customer relationship management software, and other information technology expertise. In our book, we will not use these trendy terms unless they are absolutely necessary in making our point.

the development of human capital, regulations to influence firms' investment in R&D, organizational level politics, language, and the activities of international agencies.[24]

Who could have anticipated the e-commerce companies of today, including Amazon, eBay, and Google in the United States; QXL Ricardo and Kelkoo in Europe; Rakuten and 7Dream in Japan; and Baidu in China? The internet opened the gates for companies to sell direct-to-consumers easily across national boundaries. Many argue that e-commerce is less intimate than face-to-face retail, but it could actually provide more targeted demographic and psychographic information.

Manufacturers that traditionally sell through the retail channel may benefit the most from e-commerce. Most importantly, the data allow for the development of relevant marketing messages aimed at important customers and the initiation of loyal relationships on a global basis.[25] With the onset of satellite communications, consumers in developing countries are also as familiar with global brands as consumers in developed countries, and as a result, there is tremendous pent-up demand for products marketed by multinational companies (which we also refer to as MNCs).[26]

What's more, the internet builds a platform for a two-way dialogue between manufacturers and consumers, allowing consumers to design and order their own products from the manufacturers. The customized build-to-order business model is already an established trend. Dell Computer is a pioneer that does business globally by bypassing traditional retail channels. It accepts orders by phone, fax, or going online.[27] General Motors started providing a build-to-order Web service for its Brazilian customers in 2000. Mazda's Web Tune Factory site, one of the first Japanese auto build-to-order models, allows consumers to choose their own engine specifications, transmission type, body color, wheel design, and interior and exterior equipment.[28] However, we would also like to stress as a caveat that the proliferation of e-commerce and satellite communications does not necessarily mean that global marketing activities are going culture- and human contact-free. Learning foreign languages will likely remain as important as ever.

An examination of the 100 largest companies in the world also vividly illustrates the profound changes in the competitive milieu and provides a faithful mirror image of broad economic trends that we have seen over the past 30-some years (see **Exhibit 1-1**). The last decade in particular was characterized by the long-term recession in Japan and a resurgence of the U.S. economy that had once been battered by foreign competition in the 1980s. Take Japan, which has suffered several recessions since 1995 and many political changes, as an example. The number of Japanese companies on the list fell from 23 in 2000 to 12 in 2012. The number of U.S. and European firms in the largest 100 has stayed relatively stable since 1990. Although the United States boasts the largest number of firms in the top 100 list, the list of countries with large firms is getting more decentralized. One of the biggest changes since 1990 has been the emergence of China.[29] As economic reform has progressed and Chinese companies have improved their accounting standards, their presence has grown steadily. Ten Chinese companies are on the 2012 *Fortune Global 100* list. The current world economy has changed so drastically from what it was merely two decades ago.

The changes observed in the past 40 years simply reflect that companies from other parts of the world have grown in size relative to those of the United States despite the resurgence of the U.S.

---

[24]Nikhilesh Dholakia, "Determinants of the Global Diffusion of B2B E-commerce," *Electronic Markets*, 12 (March 2002), pp. 120–129.

[25]Andrew Degenholtz, "E-Commerce Fueling the Flame for New Product Development," *Marketing News*, March 29, 1999, p. 18.

[26]D. J. Arnold, and J. Quelch, "New Strategies in Emerging Markets," *Sloan Management Review*, 40(1), 1998, pp. 7–20.

[27]However, Dell's direct sales on the internet fails to work in some emerging markets, particularly where customers want to see products before they buy. Such is the case in small cities in China. See "Dell May Have to Reboot in China," *Business Week*, November 7, 2005, p. 46.

[28]Setsuko Kamiya, "Mazda lets buyers fine-tune Rodster," The Japan Times Online, www.japantimes.co.jp, January 5, 2002.

[29]See "The China Price," *Business Week*, December 6, 2004, pp. 102–120; "How China Runs the World Economy," *Economist*, July 30, 2005, p. 11.

Exhibit 1-1 Change in the World's 100 Largest Companies and Their Nationalities

Country	1970	1980	1990	2000*	2012*
United States**	64	45	33	36	29
Japan	8	8	16	23	12
Germany**	8	13	12	10	11
China	0	0	0	3	10
Britain**	9	7	8	6	4
Italy**	3	4	4	3	4
Spain	0	0	2	1	3
South Korea	0	0	2	0	2
Netherlands**	4	5	3	6	2
Switzerland	2	3	3	4	2
Brazil	0	1	1	0	2
Russia	0	0	0	0	2
India	0	0	0	0	2
Mexico	0	1	1	1	1
Norway	0	0	0	0	1
Luxembourg	0	0	0	0	1
Malaysia	0	0	0	0	1
Venezuela	0	1	1	1	1
Taiwan	0	0	0	0	1
Thailand	0	0	0	0	1
Belgium	0	1	1	1	0
Finland	0	0	1	0	0
Sweden	0	0	2	0	0
Austria	0	0	1	0	0
South Africa	0	0	1	0	0
Canada	0	2	0	0	0
Australia	1	0	0	0	0
Total	102	103	102	103	101

Source: Fortune, various issues up to 2012.

* Fortune Global 500 criteria changed to include services firms (including retailing and trading).

** Includes joint nationality of firms (joint nationality has been counted for both the countries), so the total may exceed 100.

economy in the 1990s. In other words, today's environment is characterized not only by much more competition from around the world but also by more fluid domestic and international market conditions than in the past. As a result, many U.S. executives are feeling much more competitive urgency in product development, materials procurement, manufacturing, and marketing internationally. It does not necessarily mean that U.S. companies have lost their competitiveness, however. The robust economy in the United States in the late 1990s began to slow down by 2000 due to the crash of the dotcom bubble economy, and was worsened by the terrorist attacks on September 11, 2001. But strong consumer demand has saved the U.S. economy. On the other hand, many Asian countries have recovered from the 1997 Asian financial crisis (see Chapter 3 for detail).

The same competitive pressure equally applies to executives of foreign companies. For example, while its Japanese home market shrank in the 1990s, Toyota's new strategy has been to de-Japanize its business and make the U.S. market its corporate priority. By 2001, Toyota had already accomplished its goal by selling more vehicles in the United States (1.74 million) than in Japan (1.71 million), with almost two-thirds of the company's operating profit coming from the U.S. market. Now Toyota's top U.S. executives are increasingly local hires. As Mark Twain once wrote, "if you stand still, you will get run over." This maxim holds true in describing such competitive pressure in an era of global competition.

It is not only this competitive force that is shaping global business today. Particularly in the past 20 years, many political and economic events have affected the nature of global competition. The demise of the Soviet Union, the establishment of the European Union and the North American Free Trade Agreement, deregulation, and privatization of state-owned industries have also changed market environments around the world. Furthermore, the emerging markets of Eastern Europe and the rapidly re-emerging markets of Southeast Asia also add promises to international businesses.

The fluid nature of global markets and competition makes the study of global marketing not only interesting but also challenging and rewarding. The term *global* epitomizes both the competitive pressure and the expanding market opportunities all over the world. It does not mean, however, that all companies have to operate globally like IBM, Sony, Philips, or Samsung. Whether a company operates domestically or across national boundaries, it can no longer avoid competitive pressure from around the world. Competitive pressure can also come from competitors at home. When Weyerhaeuser, a forest products company headquartered in Seattle, Washington, began exporting newspaper rolls to Japan, it had to meet the exacting quality standard that Japanese newspaper publishers demanded—and it did. As a result, this Seattle-based company now boasts the best newspaper rolls and outperforms other domestic companies in the U.S. market. Even smaller firms could benefit from exacting foreign market requirements. When Weaver Popcorn Co. of Van Buren, Indiana, started to export popcorn to Japan, Japanese distributors demanded better quality and fewer imperfections. This led to improvements in Weaver's processing equipment and product, which helped its domestic as well as international sales.[30] Furthermore, e-commerce comes in handy to those smaller firms with international marketing ambitions. Therefore, even purely domestic companies that have never sold anything abroad cannot be shielded from international competitive pressure. The point is that when we come across the term *global*, we should be aware of both this intense competitive pressure and expanding market opportunities on a global basis.

Globalization of Markets: Convergence and Divergence

When a country's per capita income is less than $10,000, much of the income is spent on food and other necessity items and very little disposable income remains. However, once per capita income reaches $20,000 or so, the disposable portion of income increases dramatically because the part of the income spent on necessities does not rise nearly as fast as income increases. As a result, one billion people, constituting some 16 percent of the population, with per capita income of $20,000 and above, have considerable purchasing power. With this level of purchasing power, people, irrespective of their nationality, tend to enjoy similar educational levels, academic and cultural backgrounds, and access to information. As these cultural and social dimensions begin to resemble each other in many countries, people's desire for material possessions, ways of spending leisure time, and aspirations for the future become increasingly

---

[30]Doug LeDuc, "Overseas Markets Spur Growth for Van Buren, Ind.–Based Popcorn Maker," *News-Sentinel*, April 19, 1999.

similar. Even deeply rooted cultures have begun to converge.[31] In other words, from a marketing point of view, those people have begun to share a similar "choice set" of goods and services originating from many parts of the world. What does it mean?

In one sense, we see young people jogging, wearing Nike shoes (an American product made in China), listening to Gotye (an Australian-Belgian male artist) or Kimbra (a New Zealand female artist) on Apple's iPhone (an American product assembled by Foxconn, a Taiwanese company, in Shenzhen, China with a microprocessor made by Korea's Samsung in Austin, Texas) in Hong Kong, Philadelphia, São Paulo, Sydney, and Tokyo. Similarly, Yuppies (young urban professionals) in Amsterdam, Chicago, Osaka, and Dallas share a common lifestyle, driving a BMW (a German car assembled in Toluca, Mexico) to the office, listening to Sumi Jo's and Sissel Kyrkjebø's new albums (purchased on their business trips to Korea and Norway, respectively), using a Dell notebook computer (an American product assembled by Quanta in Taiwan) at work, signing important documents with an exquisite Parker Pen (made by a French-based company owned by a U.S. company), and having a nice seafood buffet at Mövenpick (a Swiss restaurant chain) on a Friday evening. In the evenings, these people spend their spare time browsing around various websites using the Google search engine (an American internet company) to do some "virtual" window-shopping on their PCs (powered by a microprocessor made in Malaysia by Intel, an American company). The convergence of consumer needs in many parts of the world translates into tremendous business opportunities for companies willing to risk venturing abroad.

The *convergence* of consumer needs at the macro level may be true, but it does not necessarily mean that individual consumers will adopt all the products from around the world. Globalization does not suffocate local cultures, but rather liberates them from the ideological conformity of nationalism.[32] As a result, we have become ever more selective. Therefore, you find one of your friends at school in the United States, driving a Chevrolet Aveo (a subcompact car made by Daewoo in Korea, owned by General Motors), enjoying Whoppers at a Burger King fast food restaurant (an ex-British company and now an American), and practicing capoeira (a 400-year-old Brazilian martial art), and another friend in Austria driving a Peugeot 107 (a French car made by Toyota in the Czech Republic; also marketed as Citroën 1 as well as Toyota Aygo), enjoying sushi at a sushi restaurant (a Japanese food), and practicing karate (an ancient Japanese martial art), as well as a cousin of yours driving a Ford Escape (an American sports utility vehicle), munching on pizzas (an American dish of Italian origin), and practicing soccer (a sport of English origin, known as "football" outside the United States). In other words, thanks to market globalization, not only have we become more receptive to new things, but we also have a much wider, more divergent "choice set" of goods and services to choose from to shape our own individual preferences and lifestyles. This is true whether you live in a small town in the United States or a big city in Europe. Yet web-based marketing communications that have seemingly flattened the world still reflect cultural differences.[33] In other words, the *divergence* of consumer needs and cultural preferences exists at the same time. For example, Pollo Campero, a Latin American fried chicken chain from Guatemala, has been catching on quietly in the United States, the land of KFC, to cater to Americans' increased appetite for a different kind of chicken.[34] From a marketing point of view, it is becoming more difficult—not easier—to pinpoint consumers' preferences in any local market around the world.[35]

As presented in **Global Perspective 1-1**, the European Union (EU) market offers a vivid example of how market forces of convergence and divergence are at work. One thing is clear: there is no such a thing as a static market in an era of globalization.

---

[31]For an excellent story about global cultural convergence, read "Global Culture" and "A World Together," *National Geographic*, *196* (August 1999), pp. 2–33.

[32]Mario Vargas Llosa, "The Culture of Liberty," *Foreign Affairs*, issue 122, January/February 2001, pp. 66–71.

[33]Daniel Baack and Nitish Singh, "Culture and Symbol Systems: An Investigation of the Link Between Culture and Web Communications," *Journal of Business Research*, 60 (3), 2007, pp. 181–188.

[34]"Invasion of the Guatemalan Chicken," *Business Week*, March 22, 2010, pp. 72–73. (ch2).

[35]"Globalism Has Made Local More Important," *Advertising Age*, February 20, 2012, p. 11.

Global Perspective 1-1

Market Convergence and Divergence at Work in the European Union

Will Euroland survive? Rejection of the proposed EU Constitution by France and the Netherlands in 2005 caused anguish for political and EU economic elites. An "ever closer union" had been seen—until the no vote called it into question (see Chapter 2 for details)—as the European answer to globalization, political security, and economic growth. European leaders aren't the only ones concerned. Insightful American and Japanese business managers are also worried because, contrary to popular belief, the chief economic beneficiaries of European integration are American and Japanese multinational corporations.

Historically, Europe, due to national, cultural, and ethnic differences, has had heterogenous and fragmented markets. These markets produced small to mid-sized firms capable of adapting to, and prospering in, highly differentiated environments. Even the largest European companies tended to operate at the national, rather than Pan-European, level, avoiding the many encumbrances of functioning across borders where market conditions were so dissimilar. For instance, for many years Unilever sold a fabric softener in 10 countries under 7 different brand names, using a variety of marketing strategies and bottle shapes.

Typical European firms pursued niche strategies, emphasizing craftsmanship, specialization, and networks of relationships. Europe, with its myriad laws, languages, and customs, historically constituted a market environment with significant entry and operating barriers. Foreign firms could not use economies of scale or scope inherent in large homogenous markets; they were unable to compete on the basis of low cost or low price. High labor costs, heavy taxation to support welfare states, and high expectations of European retailers and consumers, all worked together to shape an environment that favored the creation of specialized, premium products rather than mass consumption products. This put U.S. multinationals in Europe at a competitive disadvantage.

The traditional European advantage was based on the notion that a less homogenous market place requires a more individualized marketing strategy. This approach is at odds with the strategy of many American firms—the ability to reduce costs through economies of scale and scope. Historically, market fragmentation shielded Europe from U.S. competition. Such fragmentation constituted location-specific advantages which were either costly to overcome, or were simply impenetrable for many smaller U.S. companies. However, the creation of the European Union changed the rules of the game.

One major purpose of the EU is to create extensive homogeneous markets in which large European firms are able to take advantage of economies of scale and therefore are better able to compete with their U.S. counterparts. EU reformers hope to create an economy analogous to the United States, in which low inflation coexists with high growth, thereby leading to low unemployment.

The formation of the EU has resulted in extremely large levels of U.S. and Japanese foreign direct investment (FDI) in Europe. Why? First, it was feared that the EU would become Fortress Europe through the implementation of significant protectionist measures against firms from outside the EU. Under these circumstances FDI constitutes tariff jumping in anticipation of negative actions that may or may not occur in the future. Second, the elimination of internal borders creates a single market, amenable to the large economies of scale and scope preferred by U.S. and Japanese multinationals.

Numbers tell the story. The average foreign direct investment inflows into the European Community (as the EU was then known until November 1, 1993) amounted to $65.6 billion from 1985 to 1995. The inflow in 1999 (the year the euro, a new currency adopted by 11 EU member countries, was launched) was $479.4 billion—a 700 percent increase. By 2000 Japanese investment in the EU was roughly six times more than EU investment in Japan. In 1980 the total FDI stock of European Community was $216 billion; by 2009 it was $3,844 billion.

Four and a half decades ago the French intellectual, J.J. Servan-Schreiber complained bitterly about the U.S. presence in Europe in a best-selling book entitled, *The American Challenge* (1967). The Europeans now face similar competitive dynamics. Ironically, in their quest for economic competitiveness, they may have made themselves more vulnerable to the ambitions of U.S. and other foreign multinationals.

What can European firms do to cope with the onslaught of U.S. and other foreign multinationals? Large European firms can counter U.S. competitors by exporting or investing directly in the United States and other markets. Red Bull, the Austrian company that created the energy drink category, expanded throughout Europe after the Maastricht Treaty came into force in 1993. In 1997 it was big enough to take on the American market, and by 1999 its sales were $75 million. Today, Red Bull is popular around the world. In 2011, 4.6 billion cans were sold in over 160 countries and the company sales amounted to 4.25 billion euros. On March 24, 2008, Red Bull introduced its first foray into the cola market with a product named Simply Cola. Mergers and acquisitions resulting from unification also enhance the ability of EU firms to enter the United States. For example, in June of 2000 the French firm Publicis Group acquired Saatchi & Saatchi, the U.K.-based advertising firm, as a means of strengthening its position in the American market.

Smaller European firms are likely to consider pursuing a universal niche market strategy. For instance, Iona Technologies PLC, an Irish software firm, has successfully internationalized by pursuing a global niche market strategy.

Finally, there remain EU customers who continue to prefer the more expensive, high-quality European products. Keeping this market segment from being eroded by U.S. and other foreign competitors is key in retaining the viability of the EU market. The irony is that, if the failure of the EU Constitution is just the first event in a cascade of reversals for the integrationists, the newly refragmented markets may once again play a major role in strengthening the competitive position of smaller European firms.

Source: Lance Eliot Brouthers and Timothy J. Wilkinson, "Is the EU Destroying European Competitiveness?" *Business Horizons*, 45 (July-August 2002), 37–42; *EU Foreign Direct Investment Yearbook 2008*, Luxembourg: Office for Official Publications of the European Communities, 2007; "Buyers Bullish on Red Bull, Sales Up," *New Europe*, February 25, 2008, Issue 770, http://www.neurope.eu/articles/83145.php, accessed August 10, 2008; "United Europe Celebrates Ethnic Diversity," *CNN.com*, November 20, 2008; and European Commission, *Eurostat*, http://epp.eurostat.ec.europa.eu/statistics_explained/index.php/Foreign_direct_investment_statistics, accessed April 10, 2012.

International Trade versus International Business

The United States, which enjoys one of the highest per-capita income levels in the world, has long been the most important single market for both foreign and domestic companies. As a result of its insatiable demand for foreign products, the United States has been running a trade deficit since 1973—for four consecutive decades (more on this in Chapter 2). In the popular press, the trade deficits have often been portrayed as a sign of the declining competitiveness of the United States. This assumes—rather erroneously—that U.S. companies engaged only in exports and imports and that international trade takes place between independent buyers and sellers across national boundaries. In order to appreciate the complexities of global competition, the nature of international trade and international business has to be clarified first, followed by a discussion of who manages international trade.

First of all, we have to understand the distinction between international trade and international business. Indeed, **international trade** consists of exports and imports, say, between the United States and the rest of the world. If U.S. imports exceed U.S. exports, then the nation would register a trade deficit. If the opposite were the case, then the United States would register a trade surplus. On the other hand, **international business** is a broader concept and includes international trade and foreign production. U.S. companies typically market their products in three ways. First, they can export their products from the United States, which is recorded as a U.S. export. Second, they can invest in their foreign production on their own and manufacture those products abroad for sale there. This transaction does not show up as a U.S. export, however. And third, they can contract out manufacturing in whole or in part to a company in a foreign country, either by way of licensing or joint venture agreement. Of course, not all companies engage in all three forms of international transaction. Nonetheless, foreign manufacture on its own or on a contractual basis is a viable alternative means to exporting products abroad. Although it is not widely known, foreign production constitutes a much larger portion of international business than international trade.

The extensive international penetration of U.S. and other companies has been referred to as *global reach*.[36] Since the mid-1960s U.S.-owned subsidiaries located around the world have produced and sold three times the value of all U.S. exports. Although more recent statistics are not available, this 3:1 ratio of foreign manufacture to international trade had remained largely unchanged in the 1980s and 1990s, and it becomes much more conspicuous if we look at U.S. business with the European Union, where U.S.-owned subsidiaries sold more than six times the total U.S. exports in 1990. Similarly, European-owned subsidiaries operating in the United States sold five times as much as U.S. imports from Europe.[37] This suggests that experienced companies tend to manufacture overseas much more than they export. On the other hand, Japanese companies did not expand their foreign manufacturing activities in earnest until about 30 years ago. According to one estimate, more than 90 percent of all the cases of Japanese foreign direct investment have taken place since 1985.[38] Despite their relative inexperience in international expansion, Japanese subsidiaries registered two-and-a-half times as much foreign sales as all Japanese exports worldwide by 1990.[39]

Who Manages International Trade?

As just discussed, international trade and foreign production are increasingly managed on a global basis. Furthermore, international trade and foreign production are also intertwined in a complex manner. Think about Honda Motors, a Japanese automobile manufacturer. Honda initially exported its Accords and Civics to the United States in the 1970s. By the mid-1980s the Japanese company began manufacturing those cars in Marysville, Ohio, in the United States. The company currently exports U.S.-made Accord models to Japan and elsewhere and boasts that it is the largest exporter of U.S.-made automobiles in the United States. Recently Honda started manufacturing its "world car" in Thailand, Brazil, and China due to the low cost, and then exported to Europe and Japan. It is expected in a matter of time that Honda cars sold in Japan will eventually all be produced and imported from aboard.[40] Similarly, Texas Instruments has a large semiconductor manufacturing plant in Japan, marketing its semiconductor chips not only in Japan but also exporting them from Japan to the United States and elsewhere. In addition to traditional exporting from their home base, those companies manufacture their products in various foreign countries both for local sale and for further exporting to the rest of the world, including their respective home countries. In other words, multinational companies (MNCs) are increasingly managing the international trade flow within themselves. This phenomenon is called **intra-firm trade**.

Intra-firm trade makes trade statistics more complex to interpret, since part of the international flow of products and components is taking place between affiliated companies within the same corporate system, transcending national boundaries. Although statistical information is scarce, one United Nations official report shows that in 1999, 34 percent of world trade was intra-firm trade between MNCs and their foreign affiliates and between those affiliates, and that an additional 33.3 percent of world trade was exports by those MNCs and their affiliates. In other words, two-thirds of

[36]Richard J. Barnet and R. E. Muller, *Global Reach: The Power of the Multinational Corporations* (New York: Simon and Schuster, 1974).

[37]Peter J. Buckley and R. D. Pearce, "Overseas Production and Exporting by the World's Largest Enterprises," *International Executive* 22 (Winter), 1980, pp. 7–8; Dennis J. Encarnation, "Transforming Trade and Investment, American, European, and Japanese Multinationals Across the Triad," a paper presented at the Academy of International Business Annual Meetings, November 22, 1992.

[38]Masaaki Kotabe, "The Promotional Roles of the State Government and Japanese Manufacturing Direct Investment in the United States," *Journal of Business Research, 27* (June 1993), pp. 131–46.

[39]Encarnation, "Transforming Trade and Investment."

[40]"Honda To Re-Important 'World Car' Produced in Thailand," *Nikkei Interactive Net*, www.nni.nikkei.co.jp, December 18, 2001; "Honda Could Bring a Small Car to Europe from Thailand," *Automotive News Europe*, December 13, 2004, p. 3.

world trade is managed one way or another by MNCs.[41] These trade ratios have been fairly stable over time.[42]

Although few statistics are available, service industries are going through the same evolution as manufacturing industries on a global basis. Following the global recession in 2010, world exports of commercial services grew by 9 percent, reaching US$3.7 trillion. Although demonstrating a global rebound, service exports still fall below the level achieved before the financial and economic crisis. Surprisingly, the most rapid growth has been in Asia, led by India and China, with 22 percent of growth in service exports. Nevertheless, among the top global service exporters and importers, the United States was still ranked the largest exporter, providing US$578 billion of services to the rest of the world. The United States was also the top importer of services, receiving US$391 billion worth of services in 2011.[43] Indeed, some similarities exist in intra-firm trade of services. Today, approximately 16 percent of the total value of U.S. exports and imports of services were conducted across national boundaries on an intra-firm basis.[44] Government deregulation and technological advancement have facilitated the tradability of some services globally and economically.

Evolution of Global Marketing

What Is Marketing?

Marketing is essentially the activity, set of institutions, and processes for creating, communicating, delivering, and exchanging offerings that have value for customers, clients, partners, and society at large.[45] Marketing is not only much broader than selling, it also encompasses the entire company's *market orientation* toward customer satisfaction in a competitive environment. In other words, marketing strategy requires close attention to both customers and competitors.[46] Quite often marketers have focused excessively on satisfying customer needs while ignoring competitors. In the process, competitors have outmaneuvered them in the marketplace with better, less-expensive products. It is widely believed that in many cases, U.S. companies have won the battle of discovering and filling customer needs initially, only to be defeated in the competitive war by losing the markets they pioneered to European and Japanese competitors.[47]

---

[41]Khalil Hamdani, "The Role of Foreign Direct Investment in Export Strategy," presented at 1999 Executive Forum on National Export Strategies, International Trade Centre, the United Nations, September 26–28, 1999.

[42]United Nations Center on Transnational Corporations, *Transnational Corporations in World Development: Trends and Perspectives* (New York: United Nations, 1988); Organization for Economic Cooperation and Development, *Intra-Firm Trade* (Paris, OECD, 1993); William J. Zeile, "U.S. Affiliates of Foreign Companies," *Survey of Current Business*, August 2005, pp. 198–214; and OECD, *OECD Handbook on Economic Globalisation Indicators 2010*, September 2010.

[43]*WTO International Trade Statistics 2012*, www.wto.org.

[44]Janet Y. Murray and Masaaki Kotabe, "Sourcing Strategies of U.S. Service Companies: A Modified Transaction-Cost Analysis," *Strategic Management Journal* 20, September 1999, 791–809; Kotabe, Masaaki and Janet Y. Murray, "Global Procurement of Service Activities by Service Firms," *International Marketing Review* 21 (6), 2004, 615–633; for detailed statistics, see Michael A. Mann, Laura L. Brokenbaugh, and Sylvia E. Bargas, "U.S. International Services," *Survey of Current Business*, 80, October 2000, pp. 119–161.

[45]This is the definition of marketing adopted by the American Marketing Association in October 2007, and is strongly influenced by Drucker's conception of two entrepreneurial functions—marketing and innovation—that constitute business. Recent thinking about marketing also suggests the task of the marketer is not only to satisfy the current needs and wants of customers, but also to innovate on products and services, anticipating and even creating their future needs and wants. See Peter F. Drucker, *The Practice of Management* (New York: Harper & Brothers, 1954), pp. 37–39; and also Frederick E. Webster, Jr., "The Changing Role of Marketing in the Corporation," *Journal of Marketing*, 56 (October 1992), pp. 1–16.

[46]Janet Y. Murray, Gerald Yong Gao, and Masaaki Kotabe, "Market Orientation and Performance of Export Ventures: The Process through Marketing Capabilities and Competitive Advantages," *Journal of the Academy of Marketing Science*, 39 (April), 2011, pp. 252–269.

[47]Robert M. Peterson, Clay Dibrell, and Timothy L. Pett, "Whose Market Orientation Is Longest: A Study of Japan, Europe, and the United States," *Enhancing Knowledge Development in Marketing*, 1999 American Marketing Association Educators' Proceedings, Summer 1999, p. 69.

It is increasingly difficult for companies to avoid the impact of competition from around the world and the convergence of the world's markets. As a result, an increasing number of companies are drawn into marketing activities outside their home country. However, as previously indicated, different companies approach marketing around the world very differently. For example, Michael Dell established Dell Computer because he saw a burgeoning market potential for IBM-compatible personal computers in the United States. After his immediate success at home, he realized a future growth potential would exist in foreign markets. Then his company began exporting Dell PCs to Europe and Japan. In a way this was a predictable pattern of foreign expansion. On the other hand, not all companies go through this predictable pattern. Think about a notebook-size Macintosh computer called the PowerBook 100 that Apple Computer introduced in 1991. In 1989, Apple enlisted Sony, the Japanese consumer electronics giant, to design and manufacture this notebook computer for both the U.S. and Japanese markets.[48] Sony has world-class expertise in miniaturization and has been a supplier of disk drives, monitors, and power supplies to Apple for various Macintosh models. In an industry such as personal computers, where technology changes quickly and the existing product becomes obsolete in a short period of time, a window of business opportunity is naturally limited. Therefore, Apple's motivation was to introduce the notebook computer on the markets around the world as soon as it could before competition picked up.

Companies generally develop different marketing strategies depending on the degree of experience and the nature of operations in international markets. Companies tend to evolve over time, accumulating international business experience and learning the advantages and disadvantages associated with complexities of manufacturing and marketing around the world.[49] As a result, many researchers have adopted an evolutionary perspective of internationalization of the company just like the evolution of the species over time. In the following pages we will formally define and explain five stages characterizing the evolution of global marketing. Of course, not all companies go through the complete evolution from a purely domestic marketing stage to a purely global marketing stage. An actual evolution depends also on the economic, cultural, political, and legal environments of various country markets in which the company operates, as well as on the nature of the company's offerings. A key point here is that many companies are constantly under competitive pressure to move forward both *reactively* (responding to the changes in the market and competitive environments) and *proactively* (anticipating the change). Remember, "If you stand still, you will get run over . . ."

Therefore, knowing the dynamics of the evolutionary development of international marketing involvement is important for two reasons. First, it helps in the understanding of how companies learn and acquire international experience and how they use it for gaining competitive advantage over time. This may help an executive to be better prepared for the likely change needed in the company's marketing strategy. Second, with this knowledge, a company may be able to compete more effectively by predicting its competitors' likely marketing strategy in advance.

As shown in **Exhibit 1-2**, there are five identifiable stages in the evolution of marketing across national boundaries.[50] These evolutionary stages are explained below.

---

[48]"Apple's Japanese Ally," *Fortune*, November 4, 1991, pp. 151–52.

[49]Anna Shaojie Cui, David A. Griffith, S. Tamer Cavusgil, "The Influence of Competitive Intensity and Market Dynamism on Knowledge Management Capabilities of Multinational Corporation Subsidiaries," *Journal of International Marketing*, 13 (3), 2005, pp. 32–53.

[50]This section draws from Balaj S. Chakravarthy and Howard V. Perlmutter, "Strategic Planning for a Global Business," *Columbia Journal of World Business* (Summer 1985), pp. 3–10; Susan P. Douglas and C. Samuel Craig, "Evolution of Global Marketing Strategy: Scale, Scope and Synergy," *Columbia Journal of World Business*, 24 (Fall 1989), pp. 47–59.

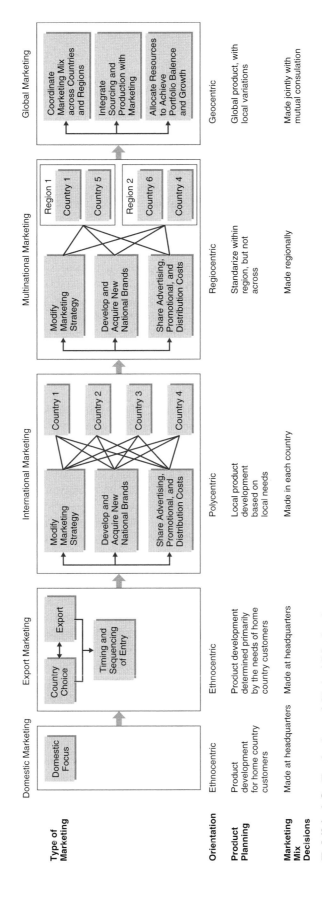

Exhibit 1-2 Evolution of Global Marketing

Sources: Constructed from Susan P. Douglas and C. Samuel Craig, "Evolution of Global Marketing Strategy: Scale, Scope and Synergy," *Columbia Journal of World Business, 24* (Fall 1985), p. 50; and Balai S. Chakravarthy and Howard V. Perlmutter, "Strategic Planning for a Global Business," *Columbia Journal of World Business, 20* (Summer 1985), p. 6.

Domestic Marketing

The first stage is **domestic marketing**. Before entry into international markets, many companies focus solely on their domestic market. Their marketing strategy is developed based on information about domestic customer needs and wants; industry trends; and economic, technological, and political environments at home. When those companies consider competition, they essentially look at domestic competition. Today, it is highly conceivable that competition in a company's home market is made up of both domestic competitors and foreign competitors marketing their products in the home market. Domestic marketers tend to be *ethnocentric* and pay little attention to changes taking place in the global marketplace, such as changing lifestyles and market segments, emerging competition, and better products that have yet to arrive in their domestic market. *Ethnocentrism* is defined here as a predisposition of a firm to be predominantly unconcerned with its viability worldwide and to think of its legitimacy only in its home country[51]—that is, where all strategic actions of a company are tailored to domestic responses under similar situations. As a result, they may be vulnerable to the sudden changes forced on them by foreign competition. For example, U.S. automakers suffered from this ethnocentrism in the 1960s and 1970s as a result of their neglect of imminent competition from Japanese automakers with more fuel-efficient cars that would eventually seize a market opportunity in the United States as a result of the two major oil crises in the 1970s.

Export Marketing

The second stage is export marketing. Usually, initial **export marketing** begins with unsolicited orders from foreign customers. When a company receives an order from abroad, it may reluctantly fill it initially, but it gradually learns the benefit of marketing overseas. In general, in the early stage of export marketing involvement, the internationalization process is a consequence of incremental adjustments to the changing conditions of the company and its environment, rather than a result of its deliberate strategy. Such a pattern is due to greater uncertainty in international business, higher costs of information, and the lack of technical knowledge about international marketing activities. At this early export marketing stage, exporters tend to engage in *indirect exporting* by relying on export management companies or trading companies to handle their export business.

Some companies progress to a more involved stage of internationalization by *direct exporting* once three internal conditions are satisfied. First, the management of the company obtains favorable expectations of the attractiveness of exporting based on experience. Second, the company has access to key resources necessary for undertaking additional export-related tasks. Such availability of physical, financial, and managerial resources is closely associated with firm size. Particularly, small companies may have few trained managers, and little time for long-term planning as they are preoccupied with day-to-day operational problems, and consequently find it difficult to become involved in exporting. Third, management is willing to commit adequate resources to export activities.[52] The company's long-term commitment to export marketing depends on how successful management is in overcoming various barriers encountered in international marketing activities. An experienced export marketer has to deal with difficulties in maintaining and expanding export involvement. These difficulties include import/export restrictions, cost and availability of shipping, exchange rate fluctuations, collection of money, and development of distribution channels, among others. Overall, favorable experience appears to be a key component in getting companies involved in managing exports directly without relying on specialized outside export handlers. To a large degree an appropriate measure of favorableness

---

[51]Chakravarthy and Perlmutter, pp. 3–10.
[52]S. Tamer Cavusgil, "On the Internationalization Process of Firms," *European Research*, 8 (November 1980), pp. 273–79.

for many companies consists of profits. An increase in profits due to a certain activity is likely to increase the company's interest in such activity.[53]

External pressures also prod companies into export marketing activities. Saturated domestic markets may make it difficult for a company to maintain sales volume in an increasingly competitive domestic market; it will become much more serious when foreign competitors begin marketing products in the domestic market. Export marketers begin paying attention to technological and other changes in the global marketplace that domestic marketers tend to ignore. However, export marketers still tend to take an ethnocentric approach to foreign markets as being an extension of their domestic market and export products developed primarily for home country customers with limited adaptation to foreign customers' needs.

International Marketing

Once export marketing becomes an integral part of the company's marketing activity, it will begin to seek new directions for growth and expansion. We call this stage **international marketing**. A unique feature of international marketing is its *polycentric* orientation with emphasis on product and promotional adaptation in foreign markets, whenever necessary.[54] *Polycentric orientation* refers to a predisposition of a firm to the existence of significant local cultural differences across markets, necessitating the operation in each country being viewed independently (i.e., all strategic decisions are thus tailored to suit the cultures of the concerned country). As the company's market share in a number of countries reaches a certain point, it becomes important for the company to defend its position through local competition. Because of local competitors' proximity to, and familiarity with, local customers, they tend to have an inherent "insider" advantage over foreign competition. To strengthen its competitive position, the international marketer could adapt its strategy, if necessary, to meet the needs and wants of local customers in two alternative ways. First, the company may allocate a certain portion of its manufacturing capacity to its export business. Second, because of transportation costs, tariffs, and other regulations, and availability of human and capital resources in the foreign markets, the company may even begin manufacturing locally. BMW has been exporting its cars to the United States for many years. In 1992, the German company invested a manufacturing plant in South Carolina in order to be more adaptive to changing customer needs in this important market and to take advantage of rather inexpensive resources as a result of the dollar depreciation against the euro. Accordingly, BMW South Carolina has become part of BMW Group's global manufacturing network and is the exclusive manufacturing plant for all Z4 Roadster and X5 Sports Activity Vehicles.[55]

If international marketing is taken to the extreme, a company may establish an independent foreign subsidiary in each and every foreign market and have each of the subsidiaries operate independently of each other without any measurable headquarters control. This special case of international marketing is known as **multidomestic marketing**. Product development, manufacturing, and marketing are all executed by each subsidiary for its own local market. As a result, different product lines, product positioning, and pricing may be observed across those subsidiaries. Few economies of scale benefits can be obtained. However, multidomestic marketing is useful when customer needs are so different across different national markets that no common product or promotional strategy can be developed. Even Coca-Cola, which used to practice a globally standardized marketing strategy, changed its strategy when it found that its structure had

[53]Masaaki Kotabe and Michael R. Czinkota, "State Government Promotion of Manufacturing Exports: A Gap Analysis," *Journal of International Business Studies*, 23 (Fourth Quarter 1992), pp. 637–58.

[54]Warren J. Keegan, "Multinational Product Planning: Strategic Alternatives," *Journal of Marketing*, 33 (January 1969), pp. 58–62.

[55]http://www.bmwusa.com/, accessed January 20, 2013.

become too cumbersome and that it was insensitive to local markets. In 2000, the company decided to return to a more multidomestic marketing approach and to give more freedom to local subsidiaries. Local marketing teams are now permitted to develop advertising to local consumers and even launch new local brands.[56]

Multinational Marketing

At this stage, the company markets its products in many countries around the world. We call this stage **multinational marketing**. Management of the company comes to realize the benefit of economies of scale in product development, manufacturing, and marketing by consolidating some of its activities on a regional basis. This *regiocentric* approach suggests that product planning may be standardized within a region (e.g., a group of contiguous and similar countries), such as Western Europe, but not across regions. Products may be manufactured regionally as well. Similarly, advertising, promotional, and distribution costs may also be shared by subsidiaries in the region. In order for the company to develop its regional image in the marketplace, it may develop and acquire new regional brands to beef up its regional operations. General Motors has a regional subsidiary, Opel (headquartered in Germany), to market both GM and Opel cars with a strong European distinction. In more recent years, GM, unable to sell its way into Japan for a long time, has quietly formed a network of equity alliances with Japanese auto makers to expand into this once-impenetrable market and to serve as a platform for its Asian expansion. Even when having difficulty occupying a market, a firm may think out of the box regarding an alliance or partnership that can lead it into the market.

Global Marketing

The international (country-by-country) or multinational (region-by-region) orientation, while enabling the consolidation of operations within countries or regions, will tend to result in market fragmentation worldwide, nonetheless. Operational fragmentation leads to higher costs. As many Japanese companies entered the world markets as low-cost manufacturers of reliable products in the 1970s, well-established U.S. and European multinational companies were made acutely aware of the vulnerability of being high-cost manufacturers. Levitt,[57] an arduous globalization proponent, argues:

> *Gone are accustomed differences in national or regional preference. Gone are the days when a company could sell last year's models—or lesser versions of advanced products—in the less developed world. . . . The multinational and the global corporation are not the same thing. The multinational corporation operates in a number of countries, and adjusts its products and practices in each—at high relative costs. The global corporation operates with resolute constancy—at low relative cost—as if the entire world (or major regions of it) were a single entity; it sells the same things in the same way everywhere.*

Global marketing refers to marketing activities by companies that emphasize the following:

1. *Standardization efforts*—standardizing marketing programs across different countries particularly with respect to product offering, promotional mix, price, and channel structure. Such efforts increase opportunities for the transfer of products, brands, and other ideas across subsidiaries and help address the emergence of global customers.

---

[56]Isabelle Schuiling and Jean-Noë Kapferer, "Real Differences between Local and International Brands: Strategic Implications for International Marketers," *Journal of International Marketing*, 12 (4), 2004, pp. 97–112.

[57]Theodore Levitt, "The Globalization of Markets," *Harvard Business Review*, 61 (May–June) 1983, pp. 92–102.

2. *Coordination across markets*—reducing cost inefficiencies and duplication of efforts among their national and regional subsidiaries.

3. *Global integration*—participating in many major world markets to gain competitive leverage and effective integration of the firm's competitive campaigns across these markets by being able to subsidize operations in some markets with resources generated in others and responding to competitive attacks in one market by counterattacking in others.[58]

Although Levitt's view is somewhat extreme, many researchers agree that global marketing does not necessarily mean standardization of products, promotion, pricing, and distribution worldwide, but rather it is a company's proactive willingness to adopt a global perspective instead of a country-by-country or region-by-region perspective in developing a marketing strategy. Clearly, not all companies adopt global marketing. For example, Black & Decker, a U.S. hand tool manufacturer, adopted a global perspective by standardizing and streamlining components such as motors and rotors while maintaining a wide range of product lines, and created a universal image for its products. In this case, it was not standardization of products per se but rather the company's effort at standardizing key components and product design for manufacturability in manufacturing industry and core and supplementary services in service industry to achieve global leadership in cost and value across common market segments around the world. Some regions with their distinctive characteristics require even seasoned global companies to adopt different approaches in reaching their consumers.

The Impact of Economic Geography and Climate on Global Marketing

Global marketing does not necessarily mean that products can be developed anywhere on a global basis. The economic geography, climate, and culture, among other things, affect the way in which companies develop certain products and consumers want them. First, the availability of resources is a major determinant of industry location. The U.S. automobile industry was born at the dawn of the twentieth century as a result of Henry Ford having decided to locate his steel-making foundry in Detroit, located midway between sources of iron ore in the Mesabi Range in Minnesota and sources of bituminous coal in Pennsylvania. Similarly, in the last quarter of the twentieth century, Silicon Valley in and around Palo Alto, California, and Silicon Hill in Austin, Texas, emerged as high-tech meccas as a result of abundant skilled human resources (thanks to leading universities in the areas), aided by warm, carefree environments—a coveted atmosphere conducive to creative thinking. For the same reason, Bangalore in India has emerged as an important location for software development. Brazil boasts that more than half of the automobiles on the road run on 100 percent pure alcohol, thanks to an abundant supply of ethanol produced from subsidized sugar cane. Even bananas are produced in abundance in Iceland, thanks to nature-provided geothermal energy tapped in greenhouses.[59] Because Germans consume the largest amount of bananas, about 33 lbs (or 15 kg) on a per capita basis, in the European Union, Iceland could become an exporter of bananas to Germany![60]

Obviously, the availability of both natural and human resources is important in primarily determining industry location as those resources, if unavailable, could become a bottleneck. It is to

---

[58]Shaoming Zou and S. Tamer Cavusgil, "The GMS: A Broad Conceptualization of Global Marketing Strategy and its Effect on Firm Performance," *Journal of Marketing*, 66, October 2002, pp. 40–56.

[59]"Wait, bananas grow in Iceland?!" *Christian Science Monitor*, June 8, 2010, http://www.csmonitor.com/The-Culture/The-Home-Forum/2010/0608/Wait-bananas-grow-in-Iceland-!.

[60]Paul Sutton, "The Banana Regime of the European Union, the Caribbean, and Latin America," *Journal of Interamerican Studies and World Affairs*, 39, Summer 1997, pp. 5–36.

be stressed that consumer needs are equally important as a determinant of industry location.[61] As the Icelandic banana example shows, the fact that Germans consume a large amount of bananas gives Icelandic growers a logistical advantage. Ask yourself why cellular phones have been most widely adopted in Finland, and fax machines and bubble-jet printers in Japan. In Finland and other Scandinavian countries, it snows heavily in winter but it is very damp snow owing to the warm Gulf Stream moderating what could otherwise be a frigid climate. The damp snow frequently cuts off powerlines. Thus, Scandinavians had always wished for a mobile means of communication such as CB radio and cellular phones. Companies such as Nokia in Finland and Ericsson in Sweden became early world-class suppliers of cellular technology.[62] Similarly, Japanese consumers always wanted machines that could easily produce and reproduce complex characters in their language. Thus, Japanese companies such as Canon, Epson (a subsidiary of Seiko Watch), and Fujitsu have emerged as major producers of fax and bubble-jet printers. For outdoor activity-loving Australians, surfing is a national sport. No wonder that Quiksilver, an Australian company that knows functional as well as aesthetic designs for sportswear quite well, has conquered the European market from skate boarders beneath the Eiffel Tower to snowboarders in the Swiss Alps and surfers in Spain.[63] Similarly, Billabong, another Australian surfing goods retailer with a keen eye on what outdoor sports lovers want to wear, has been expanding into the U.S. market with a broad range of leisure-related products following the acquisition of Element, a U.S. skateboarding clothing company, Von Zipper, a U.S. sunglasses and snow goggles brand, and more recently RVCA, a Southern California-based hippy apparel brand.[64] Indeed, as the old proverb says, "Necessity is the mother of invention."

The point is that what companies can offer competitively may be determined either by the availability of natural and human resources or by the unique consumer needs in different countries or regions or by both. Global marketers are willing to exploit their local advantages for global business opportunities. Then ask yourself another question about an emerging societal need around the world: environmental protection. Where are formidable competitors likely to originate in the near future? We think it is Germany. Germans have long been concerned about their environmental quality represented by the cleanliness of the Rhine River. When the Rhine got polluted by phosphorus—a major whitening agent in laundry detergent—the German government was the first in the world to ban its use. Now German companies are keen on developing products that are fully recyclable. In a not-too-distant future, recyclable products will become increasingly important. Naturally, marketing executives need to have an acute understanding of not only the availability of various resources but also emerging consumer and societal needs on a global basis.

So far we focused on complex realities of international trade and investment that have characterized our global economy in the past twenty years. The more statistics we see, the more befuddled we become by the sheer complexities of our global economy. Naturally, we wish the world had been much simpler. Luckily enough, however, economists and business researchers have tried over the years to explain the ever-increasing complexities of the global economy in simpler terms. A simplified yet logical view of the world is called a **theory**. Indeed, there are many different ways—theories—of looking at international trade and investment taking place in the world. For those of you interested in understanding some orderliness in the complex world of international trade and investment, we encourage you to read the appendix to this chapter. Some theoretical understanding will not only help you appreciate the competitive world in which we live, but also help you make better strategy decisions for a company you may join shortly or a company you may own.

---

[61]Michael E. Porter, *The Competitive Advantage of Nations*, New York: Free Press, 1990.

[62]Lilach Nachum, "Does Nationality of Ownership Make Any Difference and If so Under What Circumstances," *Journal of International Management*, 9, 2003.

[63]"Global Surfin' Safari: Quiksilver Rides Wave In Europe and Far East," *Women's Wear Daily*, June 30, 2005, pp. 1–8.

[64]"Skateboarding Springs into Billabong," *The Australian*, July 4, 2001, p. 21; "Billabong Acquires RVCA," *Transworld Business*, http://business.transworld.net/37851/features/billabong-acquires-rvca/, accessed July 11, 2010.

SUMMARY

World trade has grown from $200 billion to more or less $15 trillion in the last 40 years. Although world trade volume is significant in and of itself, international business is much more than trade statistics show. Companies from Western Europe, the United States, and Japan collectively produce probably more than three times as much in their foreign markets as they export. And about a third of their exports and imports are transacted on an intra-firm basis between their parent companies and their affiliated companies abroad or between the affiliated companies themselves.

What this all means is that it is almost impossible for domestic company executives to consider their domestic markets and domestic competition alone. If they fail to look beyond their national boundaries, they may unknowingly lose marketing opportunities to competitors that do. Worse yet, foreign competitors will encroach on their hard-earned market position at home so fast that it may be too late for them to respond. International markets are so intertwined that separating international from domestic business may be a futile mental exercise.

Historically, international expansion has always been a strategy consideration after domestic marketing, and has therefore been reactionary to such things as a decline in domestic sales and increased domestic competition. Global marketing is a proactive response to the intertwined nature of business opportunities and competition that know no political boundaries. However, global marketing does not necessarily mean that companies should market the same product in the same way around the world as world markets are converging. To the extent feasible, they probably should. Nonetheless, global marketing is a company's willingness to adopt a global perspective instead of country-by-country or region-by-region perspective in developing a marketing strategy for growth and profit.

What companies can offer competitively may be determined either by the availability of natural and human resources or by the unique consumer needs in different countries or regions or by both. Global marketers should be willing to exploit their local advantages for global marketing opportunities. The proliferation of e-commerce on the internet accelerates such global marketing opportunities.

QUESTIONS

1. What is the nature of global competition?

2. Why are consumption patterns similar across industrialized countries despite cultural differences?

3. How is the internet reshaping the nature of global marketing?

4. Why do you think a company should or should not market the same product in the same way around the world?

5. Merchandise trade today accounts for less than 2 percent of all the foreign exchange transactions around the world. Can one deduce that merchandise plays an insignificant role in today's economies? Why or why not?

6. Globalization involves the organization-wide development of a global perspective. This global perspective requires globally thinking managers. Although the benefits of globalization have received widespread attention, the difficulties in developing managers who think globally has received scant attention. Some senior managers consider this to be a significant stumbling block in the globalization efforts of companies. Do you agree with the concerns of these managers? Would the lack of truly globally thinking managers cause problems for implementing a global strategy? And how does the proliferation of e-commerce affect the way these managers conduct business?

Appendix: Theories of International Trade and the Multinational Enterprise

Theories are a simplification of the complex realities one way or another. A few important theories will be explained here. Each of the theories provides a number of fundamental principles, with which you can not only appreciate why international trade and investment occur but also prepare for the next impending change you will probably see in the not-so-distant future. These theories are arranged chronologically so that you can better understand what aspect of the ever-increasing complexities of international business each theory was designed to explain.

Comparative Advantage Theory

At the aggregate level, countries trade with each other for fundamentally the same reasons that individuals exchange products and

services for mutual benefit. By doing so, we all benefit collectively. Comparative advantage theory is an arithmetic demonstration made by the English economist, David Ricardo, almost 190 years ago that a country can gain from engaging in trade even if it has an absolute advantage or disadvantage. In other words, even if the United States is more efficient in the production of everything than China, both countries will benefit from trade between them by specializing in what each country can produce relatively more efficiently.

Let us demonstrate comparative advantage theory in its simplest form: the world is made up of two countries (the United States and China) and two products (personal computers and desks). We assume that there is only one PC model and only one type of desk. We further assume that labor is the only input to

Exhibit 1-3
Comparative
Advantage at Work

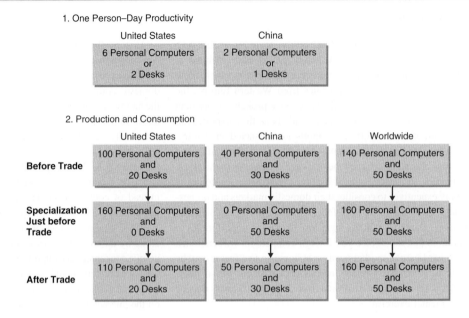

1. One Person–Day Productivity

	United States	China
	6 Personal Computers or 2 Desks	2 Personal Computers or 1 Desks

2. Production and Consumption

	United States	China	Worldwide
Before Trade	100 Personal Computers and 20 Desks	40 Personal Computers and 30 Desks	140 Personal Computers and 50 Desks
Specialization Just before Trade	160 Personal Computers and 0 Desks	0 Personal Computers and 50 Desks	160 Personal Computers and 50 Desks
After Trade	110 Personal Computers and 20 Desks	50 Personal Computers and 30 Desks	160 Personal Computers and 50 Desks

produce both products. Transportation costs are also assumed to be zero. The production conditions and consumption pattern in the two countries before and after trade are presented in **Exhibit 1-3**. As shown, U.S. labor is assumed to be more productive absolutely in the production of both personal computers (PC) and desks than Chinese labor.

Intuitively, you might argue that because the United States is more productive in both products, U.S. companies will export both PCs and desks to China, and Chinese companies cannot compete with U.S. companies in either product category. Furthermore, you might argue that as China cannot sell anything to the United States, China cannot pay for imports from the United States. Therefore, these two countries cannot engage in trade. This is essentially the **absolute advantage** argument. Is this argument true? The answer is no.

If you closely look at labor productivity of the two industries, you see that the United States can produce PCs more efficiently than desks compared to the situation in China. The United States has a three to one advantage in PCs, but only a two to one advantage in desks over China. In other words, the United States can produce three PCs instead of a desk (or as few as one-third of a desk per PC), while China can produce two PCs for a desk (or as many as a half desk per PC). Relatively speaking, the United States is comparatively more efficient in making PCs (at a rate of three PCs per desk) than China (at a rate of two PCs per desk). However, China is comparatively more efficient in making desks (at a rate of half a desk per PC) than the United States (at a rate of one third of a desk per PC). Therefore, we say that the United States has a **comparative advantage** in making PCs, while China has a comparative advantage in making desks.

Comparative advantage theory suggests that the United States should specialize in the production of PCs, while China should

specialize in the production of desks. As shown in **Exhibit 1-3**, the United States produced and consumed 100 PCs and 20 desks, and China produced and consumed 40 PCs and 30 desks. As a whole, the world (the United States and China combined) produced and consumed 140 PCs and 50 desks. Now as a result of specialization, the United States concentrates all its labor resources on PC production, while China allocates all labor resources to desk production. The United States can produce 60 more PCs by giving up on 20 desks it used to produce (at a rate of three PCs per desk), resulting in a total production of 160 PCs and no desks. Similarly, China can produce 20 more desks by moving its labor from PC production to desk production (at a rate of half a desk per PC), with a total production of 50 desks and no PCs. Now the world as a whole produces 160 PCs and 50 desks.

Before trade occurs, U.S. consumers are willing to exchange as many as three PCs for each desk, while Chinese consumers are willing to exchange as few as two PCs for each desk, given their labor productivity, respectively. Therefore, the price of a desk acceptable to both U.S. and Chinese consumers should be somewhere between two and three PCs. Let us assume that the mutually acceptable price, or **commodity terms of trade** (a price of one good in terms of another), is 2.5 PCs per desk. Now let the United States and China engage in trade at the commodity terms of trade of 2.5 PCs per desk. To simplify our argument, further assume that the United States and China consume the same number of desks after trade as they did before trade, that is, 20 desks and 30 desks, respectively. In other words, the United States has to import 20 desks from China in exchange for 50 PCs (20 desks times a price of a desk in terms of PCs), which are exported to China from the United States. As a result of trade, the United States consumes 110 PCs and 20 desks, while China consumes 50 PCs and 30 desks.

Given the same amount of labor resources, both countries respectively consume 10 more PCs while consuming the same number of desks. Obviously, specialization and trade have benefited both countries.

In reality, we rarely exchange one product for another. We use foreign exchange instead. Let us assume that the price of a desk is $900 in the United States and 6,300 yuan in China. Based on the labor productivity in the two countries, the price of a PC should be $300 (at a rate of a third of a desk per PC) in the United States and 3,150 yuan (at a rate of half a desk per PC) in China. As we indicated earlier, U.S. consumers are willing to exchange as many as three PCs for each desk worth $900 in the United States. Three PCs in China are worth 9,450 yuan. Therefore, U.S. consumers are willing to pay as much as 9,450 yuan to import a $900 desk from China. Similarly, Chinese consumers are willing to import a minimum of two PCs (worth 6,300 yuan in China) for each desk they produce (worth $900 in the United States). Therefore, the mutually acceptable exchange rate should be:

$$6,300 \text{ yuan} \leq \$900 \leq 9,450 \text{ yuan, or}$$

$$7.0 \text{ yuan} \leq \$1 \leq 10.5 \text{ yuan.}$$

An actual exchange rate will be affected also by consumer demands and money supply situations in the two countries. Nonetheless, it is clear that exchange rates are primarily determined by international trade.

From this simple exercise, we can make a few general statements or **principles of international trade**.

Principle 1: Countries benefit from international trade.

Principle 2: International trade increases worldwide production by specialization.

Principle 3: Exchange rates are determined primarily by traded goods.

By now you might have wondered why U.S. workers are more productive than Chinese workers. So far we have assumed that labor is the only input in economic production. In reality, we do not produce anything with manual labor alone. We use machinery, computers, and other capital equipment (capital for short) to help us produce efficiently. In other words, our implicit assumption was that the United States has more abundant capital relative to labor than China does. Naturally, the more capital we have relative to our labor stock, the less expensive a unit of capital should be relative to a unit of labor. The less expensive a unit of capital relative to a unit of labor, the more capital we tend to use and specialize in an industry that requires a large amount of capital. In other words, the capital–labor endowment ratio affects what type of industry a country tends to specialize in. In general, a capital-abundant country (e.g., the United States) tends to specialize in capital-intensive industry and export capital-intensive products (personal computers), and import labor-intensive products (desks). Conversely, a labor-abundant

country (China) tends to specialize in labor-intensive industry and export labor-intensive products (desks), and import capital-intensive products (personal computers). This refined argument is known as **factor endowment theory** of comparative advantage.

The factor endowment theory can be generalized a bit further. For example, the United States is not only capital-abundant but also abundant with highly educated (i.e., skilled) workers. Therefore, it is easy to predict that the United States has comparative advantage in skill-intensive industries such as computers and biotechnology and exports a lot of computers and genetically engineered pharmaceutical products around the world, and imports manual labor-intensive products such as textiles and shoes from labor-abundant countries such as China and Brazil.

Now you might have begun wondering how comparative advantage arguments will help businesspeople in the real world. Suppose that you work as a strategic planner for Nike. Shoe manufacturing is extremely labor intensive, while shoe designing is becoming increasingly hi-tech (i.e., skill-intensive). The United States is a relatively skill-abundant and labor-scarce country. Therefore, the country has a comparative advantage in skill-intensive operations but has a comparative disadvantage in labor-intensive operations. There are two ways to use your knowledge of comparative advantage arguments. First, it is easy to predict where competition comes from. Companies from countries like China and Brazil will have a comparative advantage in shoe manufacturing over Nike in the United States. Second, you can advise Nike to establish shoe-manufacturing plants in labor-abundant countries instead of in the labor-scarce United States. As we said earlier, shoe designing has become increasingly hi-tech, involving computer-aided designing and development of light, shock-absorbent material, which requires an extremely high level of expertise. Therefore, based on the comparative advantage argument, you suggest that product designing and development be done in the United States, where required expertise is relatively abundant. Indeed, that is what Nike does as a result of global competitive pressure, and has exploited various countries' comparative advantage to its advantage. Nike has product designing and development and special material development conducted in the United States and has manufacturing operations in labor-abundant countries like China and Brazil.

The comparative advantage theory is useful in explaining inter-industry trade, say computers and desks, between countries that have very different factor endowments. It suggests efficient allocation of limited resources across national boundaries by specialization and trade, but hardly explains business competition, because computer manufacturers and desk manufacturers do not compete directly. Further, it fails to explain the expansion of trade among the industrialized countries with similar factor endowments. Trade among the twenty or so industrialized countries now constitutes almost 60 percent of world trade, and much of it is intra-industry in nature. In other words, similar products are differentiated either physically or only in the customers' minds and traded across countries. Thus, BMW exports its sports cars to Japan, while Honda exports its competing models to Germany. BMW and Honda compete directly within the same automobile industry. This type of intra-industry competition cannot be explained by comparative advantage theory.

International Product Cycle Theory

When business practitioners think of competition, they usually refer to intra-industry competition. Why and how does competition tend to evolve over time and across national boundaries in the same industry? Then, how does a company develop its marketing strategy in the presence of competitors at home and abroad? **International product cycle theory** addresses all these questions.

Several speculations have been made.[65] First, a large domestic market such as the United States makes it possible for U.S. companies to enjoy **economies of scale** in mass production and mass marketing, enabling them to become lower-cost producers than their competition in foreign countries. Therefore, those low-cost producers can market their products in foreign markets and still remain profitable. In addition, an **economies of scope** argument augments an economies of scale argument. Companies from a small country can still enjoy economies of scale in production and marketing by extending their business scope beyond their national boundary. For example, Nestlé, a Swiss food company, can enjoy economies of scale by considering European, U.S., and Japanese markets together as its primary market. Second, technological innovation can provide an innovative company a competitive advantage, or **technological gap**, over its competitors both at home and abroad. Until competitors learn about and imitate the innovation, the original innovator company enjoys a temporary monopoly power around the world. Therefore, it is technological innovators that tend to market new products abroad. Third, it is generally the per-capita income level that determines consumers' **preference similarity**, or consumption patterns, irrespective of nationality. Preference similarity explains why intra-industry trade has grown tremendously among the industrialized countries with similar income levels.

Combining these forces with the earlier comparative advantage theory, international product cycle theory was developed in the 1960s and 1970s to explain a realistic, dynamic change in international competition over time and place.[66] This comprehensive theory describes the relationship between trade and investment over the product life cycle.

One of the key underlying assumptions in the international product cycle theory is that "Necessity is the mother of invention." In the United States, where personal incomes and labor costs were the highest in the world, particularly in the 1960s and 1970s, consumers desired products that would save their labor and time and satisfy materialistic needs. Historically, U.S. companies developed and introduced many products that were labor- and time-saving or responded to high-income consumer needs, including dishwashers, microwave ovens, automatic washers and dryers, personal computers, and so on. Similarly, companies in Western Europe tend to innovate on material- and capital-saving products and processes to meet their local consumers' needs and lifestyle orientation. Small and no-frill automobiles and recyclable products are such examples. Japanese companies stress products that conserve not only material and capital but also space to address their local consumers' acute concern about space limitation. Therefore, Japanese companies excel in developing and marketing small energy-efficient products of all kinds.[67]

International product cycle theory suggests that new products are developed primarily to address the needs of local consumers, only to be demanded by foreign consumers who have similar needs with a similar purchasing power. As the nature of new products and their manufacturing processes becomes widely disseminated over time, the products eventually become mass-produced standard products around the world. At that point, the products' cost competitiveness becomes a determinant of success and failure in global competition. Your knowledge of comparative advantage theory helps your company identify where strong low-cost competitors tend to appear and how the company should plan production locations.

As presented in **Exhibit 1-4**, the pattern of evolution of the production and marketing process explained in the international product cycle consists of four stages: introduction, growth, maturity, and decline. Let us explain the international product cycle from a U.S. point of view. It is to be reminded, however, that different kinds of product innovations also occur in countries (mostly developed) other than the United States. If so, a similar evolutionary pattern of development will begin from those other industrialized countries.

In the *introductory stage*, a U.S. company innovates on a new product to meet domestic consumers' needs in the U.S. market. A few other U.S. companies may introduce the same product. At this stage, competition is mostly domestic among U.S. companies. Some of those companies may begin exporting the product to a few European countries and Japan where they can find willing buyers similar to U.S. consumers. Product standards are not likely to be established yet. As a result, competing product models or specifications may exist on the market. Prices tend to be high. In the *growth stage*, product standards emerge, and mass production becomes feasible. Lower prices spawn price

[65]Mordechai E. Kreinin, *International Economics: A Policy Approach*, 5th ed. (New York: Harcourt Brace Jovanovich, 1987), pp. 276–78.
[66]See, for example, Raymond Vernon, "International Investment and International Trade in the Product Cycle," *Quarterly Journal of Economics*, 80 (May 1966), pp. 190–207; "The Location of Economic Activity," *Economic Analysis and the Multinational Enterprise*, John H. Dunning, ed. (London: George Allen and Unwin, 1974), pp. 89–114; and "The Product Cycle Hypothesis in a New International Environment," *Oxford Bulletin of Economics and Statistics*, 41 (November 1979), pp. 255–67.

[67]Vernon, 1979.

Exhibit 1-4 International Product Cycle

	Introduction	Growth	Maturity	Decline
Demand Structure	Nature of demand not well understood Consumers willing to pay premium price for a new product	Price competition begins Product standard emerging	Competition based on price and product differentiation	Mostly price competition
Production	Short runs, rapidly changing techniques Dependent on skilled labor	Mass production	Long runs with stable techniques Capital intensive	Long runs with stable techniques Lowest cost production needed either by capital intensive production or by massive use of inexpensive labor
Innovator Company Marketing Strategy	Sales mostly to home-country (e.g., U.S.) consumers Some exported to other developed countries (e.g., Europe and Japan)	Increased exports to the other developed countries (e.g., Europe and Japan)	Innovator company (e.g., U.S.) begins production in Europe and Japan to protect its foreign market from local competition	Innovator company (U.S.) may begin production in developing countries
International Competition	A few competitors at home (e.g., U.S.)	Competitors in developed countries (e.g., Europe and Japan) begin production for their domestic markets They also begin exporting to the United States	European and Japanese companies increase exports to the United States They begin exporting to developing countries	European and Japanese competitors may begin production in developing countries Competitors from developing countries also begin exporting to the world

Source: Expanded on Louis T. Wells, Jr., "International Trade: The Product Life Cycle Approach," in Reed Moyer, ed., *International Business: Issues and Concepts* (New York: John Wiley, 1984), pp. 5–22.

competition. U.S. companies increase exports to Europe and Japan as those foreign markets expand. However, European and Japanese companies also begin producing the product in their own local markets and even begin exporting it to the United States. In the *maturity stage*, many U.S. and foreign companies vie for market share in the international markets. They try to lower prices and differentiate their products to outbid their competition. U.S. companies that have carved out market share in Europe and Japan by exporting decide to make a direct investment in production in those markets to protect their market position there. U.S. and foreign companies also begin to export to developing countries, because more consumers in those developing countries can afford the product as its price falls. Then, in the *decline stage*, companies in the developing countries also begin producing the product and marketing it in the rest of the world. U.S., European, and Japanese companies may also begin locating their manufacturing plants in those developing countries to take advantage of inexpensive labor. The United States eventually begins to import what was once a U.S. innovation.

The international product cycle argument holds true as long as we can assume that innovator companies are not informed about conditions in foreign markets, whether in other industrialized countries or in the developing world. As we amply indicated in Chapter 1, such an assumption has become very iffy. Nor can it be safely assumed that U.S. companies are exposed to a very different home environment from European and Japanese companies. Indeed, the differences among the industrialized countries are reduced to trivial dimensions. Seeking to exploit global scale economies, an increasing number of companies are likely to establish various plants in both developed countries and developing countries, and to crosshaul between plants for the manufacture of final products. As an explanation of international business behavior, international product cycle theory has limited explanatory power. It does describe the initial international expansion (exporting followed by direct investment) of many companies, but the mature globetrotting companies of today have succeeded in developing a number of other strategies for surviving in global competition.

Internalization/Transaction Cost Theory

Now that many companies have established plants in various countries, they have to manage their corporate activities across national boundaries. Those companies are conventionally called multinational companies. It is inherently much more complex and difficult to manage corporate activities and market products across national boundaries, rather than from a domestic base. Then why do those multinational companies invest in foreign manufacturing and marketing operations instead of just exporting from their home base? International product cycle theory explains that companies invest abroad reactively once their foreign market positions are threatened by local competitors. Thus, the primary objective of foreign direct investment for the exporting companies is to keep their market positions from being eroded. Are there any proactive reasons for companies to invest overseas?

To address this issue, a new strand of theory has been developed. It is known as **internalization** or **transaction cost theory**. Any company has some proprietary expertise that makes it different from its competitors. Without such expertise no company can sustain its competitive advantage. Such expertise may be reflected in a new product, unique product design, efficient production technique, or even brand image itself. As in the international product cycle argument, a company's expertise may eventually become common knowledge as a result of competitors copying it or reverse-engineering its product. Therefore, it is sometimes to an innovator company's advantage to keep its expertise to itself as long as possible in order to maximize the economic value of the expertise. A company's unique expertise is just like any information. Once information is let out, it becomes a public good—and free.

In other words, the multinational company can be considered an organization that uses its internal market to produce and distribute products in an efficient manner in situations where the true value of its expertise cannot be assessed in ordinary external business transactions. Generating expertise or knowledge requires the company to invest in research and development. In most circumstances, it is necessary for the company to overcome this appropriability problem by the creation of a monopolistic internal market (i.e., internalization) when the knowledge advantage can be developed and explored in an optimal manner on a global basis.[68] The motive to internalize knowledge is generally strong when the company needs to invest in business assets (e.g., manufacturing and marketing infrastructure) that have few alternative uses, uses those assets frequently, and faces uncertainty in negotiating, monitoring, and enforcing a contract. Such a situation suggests a high level of transaction costs due to specific assets and contractual uncertainty involved.[69]

Resource-Based View and Appropriability Theory

Now that many companies have established subsidiaries and other affiliates in various countries, they have to manage their far-flung corporate operations to their competitive advantage. The **resource-based view** of the firm suggests that companies can be conceived of as controlling bundles of various resources, also called capabilities. These capabilities are developed through previous experience and over time. When resources are *valuable, rare, difficult to imitate* (inimitable), and *non-substitutable*, they can lead to sustainable competitive advantage.[70] Resources and capabilities do not include only physical assets but also skills, technologies, and more intangible endowments, such as productive routines and other organizational competencies as well. An individual subsidiary as a resource node or bundle of resources and capabilities with its own unique resource profile plays a significant role in maintaining the multinational company's competitive advantage. Furthermore, its subsidiary's intraorganizational linkages give rise to competitive advantages due to scope and scale economies and other relational benefits.

However, the company's organizational resources can only be sources of sustained competitive advantage if competitors that do not possess these resources cannot obtain them easily. The company's expertise can be channeled through three routes to garner competitive advantage: appropriability regime, dominant design, and operational/marketing capabilities.[71] **Appropriability regime** refers to aspects of the commercial environment that govern a company's ability to retain its technological advantage. It depends on the efficacy of legal mechanisms of protection, such as patents, copyrights, and trade secrets. However, in today's highly competitive market, legal means of protecting proprietary technology have become ineffective as new product innovations are relatively easily reverse-engineered, improved upon, and invented around by competitors without violating patents and other proprietary protections bestowed on them. It is widely recognized that the most effective ways of securing maximum returns from a new product innovation are through lead time and moving fast down the experience curve (i.e., quickly resorting to mass production).[72] Obviously, the value of owning technology has lessened drastically in recent years as the inventor company's temporary monopoly over its technology has shortened.

Dominant design is a narrow class of product designs that begins to emerge as a "standard" design. A company that has won a dominant design status has an absolute competitive advantage over its competition. In an early stage of product development,

---

[68]Alan M. Rugman, ed., *New Theories of the Multinational Enterprise* (London: Croom Helm, 1982).

[69]Oliver E. Williamson, "The Economics of Organization: The Transaction Cost Approach," *American Journal of Sociology*, 87 (1981), pp. 548–77.

[70]Jay B. Barney, "Firm Resources and Sustained Competitive Advantage," *Journal of Management*, 17(1) (1991), pp. 99–120.

[71]David J. Teece, "Capturing Value from Technological Innovation: Integration, Strategic Partnering, and Licensing Decisions," in Bruce R. Guile and Harvey Brooks, eds., *Technology and Global Industry: Companies and Nations in the World Economy* (Washington, D.C.: National Academy Press), pp. 65–95.

[72]Richard C. Levin, Alvin K. Klevorick, Richard R. Nelson, and Sidney G. Winter, "Appropriating the Returns from Industrial Research and Development," *Brookings Papers on Economic Activity*, 3 (1987), pp. 783–831.

many competing product designs exist. After considerable trial and error in the marketplace, a product standard tends to emerge. A good case example is Sony's Betamax format and Panasonic's VHS format for VCRs. The Betamax format was technologically superior with better picture quality than the VHS format, but could not play as long to record movies as the VHS. Although the Sony system was introduced slightly earlier than the Panasonic system, the tape's capability to record movies turned out to be fatal to Sony as the VHS tape was increasingly used for rental home movies and home recording of movies. Thus, the VHS emerged as the worldwide standard for videocassette recording.

Was it simply the act of the "invisible hand" in the marketplace? The answer is clearly no. Panasonic actively licensed its VHS technology to Sanyo, Sharp, and Toshiba for production and supplied VHS-format videocassette recorders to RCA, Magnavox, and GTE Sylvania for resale under their respective brand names.[73] When Philips introduced a cassette tape recorder, a similar active licensing strategy had been employed for a quick adoption as a dominant standard around the world. Despite various government hurdles to stall the Japanese domination of emerging HDTV technology, Sony is currently trying to make its format a standard by working its way into Hollywood movie studios. It is clear that a wide adoption of a new product around the world, whether autonomous or deliberated, seems to guarantee it a dominant design status.

Operational and marketing ability is in almost all cases required for successful commercialization of a product innovation. The issue here is to what extent this ability is specialized to the development and commercialization of a new product. Indeed, many successful companies have highly committed their productive assets to closely related areas without diversifying into unrelated businesses. This commitment is crucial. Take semiconductor production for example. A director at SEMATECH (a U.S. government-industry semiconductor manufacturing technology consortium established in Austin, Texas, to regain U.S. competitive edge in semiconductor manufacturing equipment from Japanese competition) admits that despite and because of a rapid technological turnover, any serious company wishing to compete on a state-of-the-art computer chip with the Japanese will have to invest a minimum of a billion dollars in a semiconductor manufacturing equipment and facility. General Motors has invested more than $5 billion for its Saturn project to compete with the Japanese in small car production and marketing. A massive retooling is also necessary for any significant upgrade in both industries. Furthermore, the software side of the manufacturing ability may be even more difficult to match, as it involves such specialized operational aspects as JIT (just-in-time) manufacturing management, quality control, and components sourcing relationships. Irrespective of nationality, those multinational companies that are successful in global markets tend to excel not only in product innovative ability but also in manufacturing and marketing competencies.[74] It is clear that innovative companies committed to manufacturing and marketing excellence will likely remain strong competitors in industry.

These three sources of competitive advantage are not independent of each other. Given the relative ease of learning about competitors' proprietary knowledge without violating patents and other legal protections, many companies resort to mass production and mass marketing to drive down the cost along the experience curve. To do so requires enormous investment in manufacturing capacity. As a result, the efficacy of appropriability regime is highly dependent on investment in manufacturing and marketing ability. Similarly, a wide acceptance of a product is most likely necessary for the product to become a dominant design in the world for a next generation of the product. Thus, mass production and marketing on a global scale is likely to be a necessary, if not sufficient, condition for a company to attain a dominant design status for its product.

It is apparent that patents, copyrights, and trade secrets are not necessarily optimal means of garnering competitive advantage unless they are strongly backed by strengths in innovative manufacturing and marketing on a global basis. Likewise, companies strong in manufacturing without innovative products also suffer from competitive disadvantage. In other words, it takes such an enormous investment to develop new products and to penetrate new markets that few companies can go it alone anymore. Thus, to compete with integrated global competitors, an increasing number of companies have entered into strategic alliances so as to complement their competitive weaknesses with their partner's competitive strengths.

SUMMARY

Three theories that cast some insight into the workings of international business have been reviewed. These theories are not independent of each other. Rather, they supplement each other. Comparative advantage theory is useful when we think broadly about the nature of industrial development and international trade around the world. International product cycle theory helps explain why and how a company initially extends its market horizons abroad and how foreign competitors shape global competition over time and place.

Internalization or transaction cost theory provides some answers to how to manage multinational operations in a very competitive world.

There are other theories to supplement our understanding of international business. However, they are beyond the scope of this textbook and are probably unnecessary. Now you can appreciate how international business has expanded in scope over time. With understanding of these theories, we hope you can better understand the rest of the book.

[73]Richard S. Rosenbloom and Michael A. Cusumano, "Technological Pioneering and Competitive Advantage: The Birth of VCR Industry," *California Management Review*, 29 (Summer 1987), pp. 51–76.

[74]Masaaki Kotabe, "Corporate Product Policy and Innovative Behavior of European and Japanese Multinationals: An Empirical Investigation," *Journal of Marketing*, 54 (April 1990), pp. 19–33.

2

ECONOMIC ENVIRONMENT

CHAPTER OVERVIEW

1. Intertwined world economy

2. Country competitiveness

3. Emerging economies

4. Evolution of cooperative global trade agreements

5. Information technology and the changing nature of competition

6. Regional economic arrangements

7. Multinational corporations

At no other time in economic history have countries been more economically interdependent than they are today. Although the second half of the twentieth century saw the highest-ever sustained growth rates in **Gross Domestic Product** (GDP) in history, the growth in international flows in goods and services (called international trade) has consistently surpassed the growth rate of the world economy. Simultaneously, the growth in international financial flows—which includes foreign direct investment, portfolio investment, and trading in currencies—has achieved a life of its own. Thanks to trade liberalization heralded by the General Agreement on Tariffs and Trade (GATT) and the **World Trade Organization (WTO)**, the GATT's successor, the barriers to international trade and financial flows keep getting lower.

However, the first decade of the 21st century has been beset with a recessionary world economy. For example, growth in the value of the United States' trade decelerated throughout 2001. Western Europe's merchandise exports and imports increased by a meager 2 percent during the same period. Overall, the year 2001 witnessed the first decline in the volume of world merchandise trade since 1982 and the first decrease in world merchandise output since 1991. Then again, the severe global recession in 2008 decelerated the global economy. Despite this adverse world market environment, the emerging economies recorded an outstanding trade growth performance. A rapid growth of leading emerging economies such as China, India, and Brazil, and a further strengthening of trade and investment links between the European Union and Central and Eastern Europe contributed largely to this outcome. Africa and the Middle East also expanded their imports despite unstable prices of oil and other commodities. Overall, during the first decade of the twenty-first century, world GDP grew 27.7 percent while the total merchandise export grew 49.9 percent (see **Exhibit 2-1**).[1]

[1] *World Trade Report 2012*, www.wto.org, Geneva: World Trade Organization, 2012.

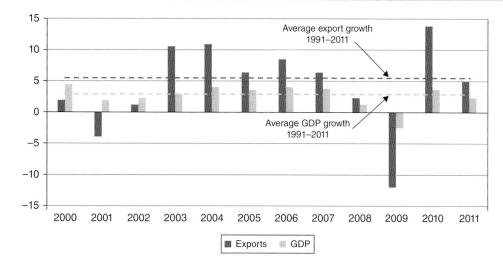

Exhibit 2-1 Growth (in Percent) in the Volume of World Merchandise Trade and Gross Domestic Product (GDP), 2000–2011

Source: World Trade Report 2012, www.wto.org, World Trade Organization, 2012.

Although the initial recovery after the 2008 global recession was quite amazing, we still see some precarious long-term recovery prospects for the world economy as evidenced by the world GDP growing by 3.6 percent in 2010 but only 2.4 percent in 2011 and the total merchandise export growth leaping 14.5 percent in 2010 but dropping to 5 percent in 2011. The World Bank (at the time of this writing) predicted that the global GDP growth would slow down to 2.5 percent in 2012 and 3.1 percent in 2013.[2] Economic growth was expected to decline for developing countries from a resilient 7.9 percent in 2007 to 5.4 percent in 2012, while high income countries are expected to experience a slowdown to 1.4 percent, with –0.3 percent for the Euro Area.[3]

Expanding world markets will likely remain a key driving force for the twenty-first century economy. However, the severe slump in Asia in the late 1990s, the renewed financial crisis in South America, and the slump in the U.S. and European economies in early 2000s, and now the current global recession (2008–present in 2012)—the worst since the 1930s—point out the vulnerabilities to the global marketplace, making the long-term trends of fast-rising trade and rising world incomes uncertain.

Since the second half of the 1990s, there have been some strong antiglobalization movements for various reasons including economics, environmental concern, and American cultural hegemony, among others. Let us focus just on economics here. Some in developed countries argue that globalization would result in increased competition from low-income countries, thus threatening to hold down wages, say, in the United States. However, real wages in the United States increased at a 1.3 percent annual rate in the 1990s, much faster than the 0.2 percent annual gain of the 1980s.[4]

Globalization has helped improve the economies of emerging and developing countries more than those of developed countries. The gap in real GDP growth rate between emerging countries and developed countries widened from zero in 1991 to about 5 percentage points in 2008. Helping poorer countries catch up economically has long been among the benefits touted for globalization. Unfortunately, the 2008 global recession has caused exactly the reverse—the economic downturn has been sharpest in

[2]"World Bank Slashes Global GDP Forecasts, Outlook Grim", http://www.reuters.com/article/2012/01/18/us-worldbank-outlook-idUSTRE80H04S20120118, January 8, 2012.

[3]World Bank, *Global Economic Prospect,* January 2012, www.worldbank.org/gep2012.

[4]"Restating the '90s," *Economist,* April 1, 2002, pp. 51–58.

countries that opened up most to world trade, especially East Asian countries. For example, Singapore's exports were over 200 percent of GDP, but its economic growth fell to –0.8 percent in 2009, following the 2008 global recession.[5]

Despite the current global recession, most countries in the twenty-first century have not shunned globalization and are likely to continue their globalization trend. It has been protected by the belief of firms in the efficiency of global supply chains. But like any chain, these are only as strong as their weakest link. A dangerous miscalculation could occur if firms should decide that this way of organizing production and marketing has had its day.[6] Regardless, even a firm that is operating in only one domestic market is not immune to the influence of economic activities external to that market. The net result of these factors has been the increased interdependence of countries and economies, increased competitiveness, and the concomitant need for firms to keep a constant watch on the international economic environment.

Intertwined World Economy

There is no question that the global economy continues to become more intertwined. Whether the world economy was in a growth mode or is in a severe recession mode, the 2008 global recession has made all of us aware that countries are ever more interdependent of each other. The United States is a $15.7 trillion economy in 2012, and its U.S. trade deficit of $735 billion is 4.7 percent of the U.S. GDP. In 2012, about 15 percent of what Americans consumed was imported in the United States (measured based on the ratio of the country's imports to its GDP). The United States is relatively more insulated from external shocks than Britain or Thailand. In 2012, the imports/GDP ratios for Britain and Thailand were about 26.3 percent and 59.6 percent, respectively.[7] Nonetheless, the U.S. economy, too, is getting increasingly intertwined with the rest of the world economy.

The importance of international trade and investment cannot be overemphasized for any country. In general, *the larger the country's domestic economy, the less dependent it tends to be on exports and imports relative to its GDP.*[8] Let's compute trade dependence ratios (total trade/GDP) using the available statistics. For the United States (GDP=$15.7 trillion in 2012), international trade in goods (sum of exports and imports) rose from 10 percent of the GDP in 1970 to 25 percent in 2012. For Japan (GDP=$6.0 trillion), with about one-third of the U.S. GDP, its trade dependence ratio forms 27 percent in 2012. For Germany (GDP = $3.4 trillion), trade forms about 79 percent of the GDP. For the Netherlands (GDP = $773 billion), trade value exceeds GDP, for as high as 131 percent of GDP (due to re-export); and for Singapore (GDP = $277 billion), trade is 293 percent of its GDP![9] These trade statistics are relative to the country's GDP. In absolute dollar terms, however, a small relative trade percentage of a large economy still translates into large volumes of trade (see **Exhibit 2-2**). As shown in the last column for exports and imports in **Exhibit 2-2**, the per capita amount of exports and imports is another important statistic for marketing purposes as it represents, on average, how involved or dependent each individual is on international trade.

[5]World Bank Data, http://data.worldbank.org/indicator/NY.GDP.MKTP.KD.ZG, accessed May 10, 2012.

[6]Ibid.

[7]Computed from trade statistics in U.S. Central Intelligence Agency, *The World Factbook 2012*, https://www.cia.gov/library/publications/the-world-factbook/.

[8]In other words, smaller economies are more susceptible than larger economies to various external shocks in the world economy, such as the recession in the United States that would import less, sudden oil price surges, and exchange rate fluctuations. Read "Restoring the Balance: The World Economy is Still Growing Rapidly, but Is Also Out of Kilter," *Economist,* September 24, 2005, p. 13.

[9]Computed from trade statistics in U.S. Central Intelligence Agency, *The World Factbook 2012*, https://www.cia.gov/library/publications/the-world-factbook/.

Exhibit 2-2 Top 10 Exporters and Importers in World Merchandise Trade, 2012

Rank	EXPORTERS	Value ($billion)	Export Dependence[*] (%)	Value per capita ($)	Rank	IMPORTERS	Value ($billion)	Import Dependence[**] (%)	Value per capita ($)
1	China	1,904	16.6	1,417	1	United States	2,236	14.6	7,124
2	European Union	1,791	11.4	3,555	2	European Union	2,000	12.8	3,970
3	United States	1,497	9.8	4,770	3	China	1,743	15.2	1,298
4	Germany	1,408	44.9	17,313	4	Germany	1,198	38.2	14,734
5	Japan	788	17.5	6,187	5	Japan	808	18.0	6,347
6	France	587	26.1	8,946	6	France	689	30.7	10,491
7	South Korea	557	35.4	11,390	7	United Kingdom	640	27.9	10,143
8	Netherlands	552	77.4	32,981	8	Italy	556	29.7	9,082
9	Italy	524	28.0	8,552	9	South Korea	524	33.3	10,733
10	Russia	521	21.6	3,655	10	Netherlands	493	69.2	29,473

[*] Exports/GDP × 100

[**] Imports/GDP × 100

Source: Computed from trade statistics in Central Intelligence Agency, *World Factbook 2012,* https://www.cia.gov/library/publications/the-world-factbook/.

For instance, individuals (consumers and companies) in the United States and Japan—the world's two established developed economies—tend to be able to find domestic sources for their needs because their economies are diversified and extremely large. The U.S. per capita value of exports and imports was $4,770 and $7,124 in 2012, respectively. For Japan, its per capita value of exports and imports was $6,187 and $6,347, respectively. On the other hand, individuals in smaller and rich economies tend to rely more heavily on international trade, as illustrated by the Netherlands with per capita exports and imports of $32,981 and $29,473, respectively. Although China's overall exports and imports amounted to $1.9 trillion and $1.7 trillion, respectively, the per capita exports and imports amounted to only $1,417 and $1,298, respectively, in 2012. One implication of these figures is that the higher the per capita trade, the more closely intertwined is that country's economy with the rest of the world. Intertwining of economies by the process of specialization due to international trade leads to job creation in both the exporting country and the importing country.

However, beyond the simple figure of trade as a rising percentage of a nation's GDP lies the more interesting question of what rising trade does to the economy of a nation. A nation that is a successful trader—that is, it makes goods and services that other nations buy and it buys goods and services from other nations—displays a natural inclination to be competitive in the world market. The threat of a possible foreign competitor is a powerful incentive for firms and nations to invest in technology and markets in order to remain competitive. Also, apart from trade flows, foreign direct investment, portfolio investment, and daily financial flows in the international money markets profoundly influence the economies of countries that may be seemingly completely separate.

Foreign Direct Investment

Foreign direct investment—which means investment in manufacturing and service facilities in a foreign country with an intention to engage actively in managing them—is another facet of the increasing integration of national economies. As shown in **Exhibit 2-3**, the overall world inflow of

Exhibit 2-3 Foreign
Direct Investment
Inflows (in US$
billion), 1980–2011
Source: UNCTAD, World
Investment Report 2012,
http://www.unctad.org/,
accessed January 30, 2013.

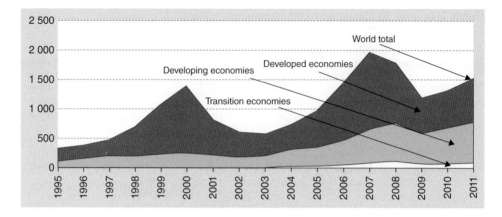

foreign direct investment (FDI) increased twenty-five-fold from 1980 to 2000 when it peaked at $1.41 trillion. Then the global recession that ensued after the September 11, 2001, terrorist attacks on U.S. soil dampened FDI flows significantly for a few years. Since 2004, global FDI inflows have continued growing, reaching the highest level ever recorded of $1.83 trillion in 2007. The 2008 worldwide financial and economic crisis along with the sudden appreciation of the U.S. dollar has changed the FDI situation drastically. In 2008, FDI flows declined by more than 20 percent, followed by continuing decline in 2009 to $1.19 trillion. Global FDI has not fully recovered to its pre-crisis level yet; however, figures of 2011 showed a positive sign of future improvement. Although still standing 25 percent below the pre-crisis average, global FDI rose quite moderately to $1.5 trillion in 2011.[10]

Two things should be noted. In the past, foreign direct investment was considered as an alternative to exports in order to avoid tariff barriers. However, these days, foreign direct investment and international trade have become complementary.[11] For example, Dell Computer uses a factory in Ireland to supply personal computers in Europe instead of exporting from Austin, Texas. Similarly, Honda, a Japanese automaker with a major factory in Marysville, Ohio, is the largest exporter of automobiles from the United States. As firms invest in manufacturing and distribution facilities outside their home countries to expand into new markets around the world, they have added to the stock of foreign direct investment. Second, although not shown in the exhibit, the composition of FDI has shifted from manufacturing to services in all regions. FDI in services increased from being one-quarter of the world inflow FDI stock in the 1970s to 49 percent in 1990, and to 62 percent with an estimated value of $6 trillion in 2005. Most notably, although FDI outflows in services are still dominated by developed countries, they are no longer controlled by firms from the United States, but much more evenly distributed among developed countries. By 2002, Japan and the European Union had emerged as significant sources of outward FDI in service sectors. Developing countries' outward FDI in services had also grown gradually since the 1990s.[12] Unfortunately, however, following the world recession in 2008, the global outward FDI in the service sector did not look as promising, and it indeed declined by more than 20 percent from $630 billion in 2009 to $490 in 2010, although it bounced back up to $570 billion in 2011. In the same period, FDI projects in manufacturing showed a continuous rise from $510 billion in 2009

[10]UNCTAD, World Investment Report 2012.
[11]"Trade by Any Other Name," *Economist*, October 3, 1998, pp. 10–14.
[12]UNCTAD, *World Investment Report 2008.*

to $620 billion and $660 billion in 2010 and 2011, respectively. This picture is quite different from the pre-crisis period 2005–2007.[13]

The increase in foreign direct investment is also promoted by efforts by many national governments to woo multinationals and by the leverage that the governments of large potential markets such as China and India have in granting access to multinationals. For example, in 2006, China's FDI inflow still reached $69 billion, even though this was the first time it had declined in seven years due mainly to reduced flows to financial services. Meanwhile, China gradually became a source of outward FDI. China's FDI outflows increased by 32 percent to $16 billion in 2006, and its outward FDI stock reached $73 billion, the sixth-largest in the developing world.[14] In 2010, China recorded a historical high of $68 billion in FDI outflows with FDI outward stock reaching $298 billion. In successfully implementing its outward foreign direct investment (OFDI), China has experienced evolutionary changes in government policies—starting from a very strict, highly regulated OFDI policy (e.g. strict OFDI approval process, remittance requirement for profit earned abroad, and $10 million cap of project investment value, etc.) to a more relaxed policy concerning foreign exchange regulations, to a "Going Global" policy that provides strong national public endorsement for any institutions that foster FDI.[15] The Chinese government has transformed from a regime that intervenes in business decisions to a government that influences and directs the market through rules and administrative bodies. Currently, the Chinese government provides financial support (such as single corporate income tax principle), as well as credit support (such as provision of credit funds and discounted bank loans in China), to enterprises going abroad.

Fluctuation of FDI (i.e., increase or decrease in direct investment) is affected by policy measures taken by national governments. These policy measures can be related to investment liberalization or restrictions. In 2010, a total of 149 measures related to FDI around the world: 101 measures were related to liberalization while 48 measures dealt with the introduction of restrictions to investment.[16] For example, Indonesia partially liberalized construction services, film, and health services, and parts of electricity generation; Guatemala allowed foreign insurance companies to establish branches in the country; through its 2010 FDI policy, Bhutan allowed 100 percent foreign ownership in certain activities such as education, luxury hotels and resorts, and specialized health services. On the other hand, Australia rejected the Singapore Exchange's offer (US$8.3 billion) to take over the Australian Securities Exchange; while Canada blocked Australian mining company "BHP Billiton's" takeover of Potash Corp. (a Canadian fertilizer and mining company).[17]

Portfolio Investment

An additional facet to the rising integration of economies has to do with **portfolio investment** (or **indirect investment**) in foreign countries and with money flows in the international financial markets. *Portfolio investment* refers to investments in foreign countries that are withdrawable at short notice, such as investment in foreign stocks and bonds. In the international financial markets, the borders between nations have, for all practical purposes, disappeared.[18] The enormous quantities of money that get traded on a daily basis have assumed a life of their own. When

[13]UNCTAD, *World Investment Report 2012*.

[14]UNCTAD, *World Investment Report 2007*.

[15]Yadong Luo, Qiqzhi Xue, and Binjie Han, "How Emerging Market Governments Promote Outward FDI: Experience from China," *Journal of World Business*, 45 (January), 2010, pp. 68–79.

[16]UNCTAD, Presidential Regulation No. 36, 2010.

[17]UNCTAD, Australian Treasury, Foreign Investment Decision, April 8, 2011; Ministry of Industry Press Release, November 3, 2010.

[18]Kenichi Ohmae, *The Borderless World* (New York: Harper Collins Books, 1990).

trading in foreign currencies began, it was as an adjunct transaction to an international trade transaction in goods and services—banks and firms bought and sold currencies to complete the export or import transaction or to hedge the exposure to fluctuations in the exchange rates in the currencies of interest in the trade transaction. However, in today's international financial markets, traders trade currencies most of the time without an underlying trade transaction. They trade on the accounts of the banks and financial institutions they work for, mostly on the basis of daily news on inflation rates, interest rates, political events, stock and bond market movements, commodity supplies and demand, and so on. As mentioned earlier, the weekly volume of international trade in currencies exceeds the annual value of the trade in goods and services.

The effect of this proverbial tail wagging the dog is that all nations with even partially convertible currencies are exposed to the fluctuations in the currency markets. A rise in the value of the local currency due to these daily flows vis-à-vis other currencies makes exports more expensive (at least in the short run) and can add to the trade deficit or reduce the trade surplus. A rising currency value will also deter foreign investment in the country and will encourage outflow of investment.[19] It may also encourage a decrease in the interest rates in the country if the central bank of that country wants to maintain the currency exchange rate and a decrease in the interest rate would spur local investment. An interesting example is the Mexican meltdown in early 1995 and the massive devaluation of the peso, which was exacerbated by the withdrawal of money by foreign investors. And more recently, the massive depreciation of many Asian currencies in the 1997–1999 period, known as the Asian financial crisis, is also an instance of the influence of these short-term movements of money.[20] Unfortunately, the influences of these short-term money flows are nowadays far more powerful determinants of exchange rates than an investment by a Japanese or German automaker.

Another example is provided by Brazil, which was a largely protected market until 1995. Liberalization is on the way as a result of the formation in 1994 of the Southern Common Market (Mercado Común del Sur, or MERCOSUR), to be explained later in the chapter. Since the debt crisis of 1982, Brazil had suffered a chronic hyperinflation that ruined its economy and competitiveness. Brazil's new currency, real, was launched in 1994 both as the instrument and as the symbol of a huge effort for Brazil to catch up with the developed world. Financial markets first attacked the Brazilian real in March 1995, in the wake of Mexico's peso devaluation. Brazil responded by adopting a pegged exchange rate, under which the real devalued by 7.5 percent a year against the U.S. dollar. Then, the Asian financial crisis and the crash of many Asian currencies (with as much as 75 percent in the case of Indonesian currency, the rupiah, in a matter of a few weeks) in 1998 reverberated again in Brazil and Mexico as well, because portfolio investors started viewing all emerging markets in a negative light. Worse yet, in 2002, Argentina caused another financial crisis in Latin America, triggered by one of the largest government debt defaults ever. The Brazilian real was under pressure, falling from R1/US$ in July 1994 to R3.63/US$ in October 2002—a whopping 72 percent depreciation since its introduction. The central bank had to sell dollars and buy real to shore up the value of the real. This led to a credit crunch, causing a slowdown in export growth, only to be temporarily stabilized by the International Monetary Fund's $30 billion rescue loan to Brazil in 2002.[21] There were also adverse effects on the Indian stock markets. The point is that, at least in the short run, these daily international flows of money have dealt a blow to the notion of economic independence and nationalism.

---

[19]"Beware of Hot Money," *Business Week*, April 4, 2005, pp. 52–53.

[20]Masaaki Kotabe, "The Four Faces of the Asian Financial Crisis: How to Cope with the Southeast Asia Problem, the Japan Problem, the Korea Problem, and the China Problem," *Journal of International Management*, 4 (1), 1998, 1S–6S.

[21]"A Matter of Faith—Will a big bail–out led by the IMF allow Brazil to avoid defaulting?" *Economist*, August 15, 2002; the Brazilian economy has since stabilized and started growing again, which is reflected in the real's appreciation to R2.28/US$ as of late 2005.

Country Competitiveness

Country competitiveness refers to the productiveness of a country, which is represented by its firms' domestic and international productive capacity. Human, natural, and capital resources of a country primarily shape the nature of corporate productive capacity in the world, and thus the nature of international business. As explained in the appendix to Chapter 1, a country's relative endowment in those resources shapes its competitiveness.

Changing Country Competitiveness

Country competitiveness is not a fixed thing. The dominant feature of the global economy is the rapid change in the relative status of various countries' economic output. In 1830, China and India alone accounted for about 60 percent of the manufactured output of the world. Since then, the share of the world manufacturing output produced by the twenty or so countries that are today known as the rich industrial economies moved from about 30 percent in 1830 to almost 80 percent by 1913.[22] In the 1980s, the U.S. economy was characterized as "floundering" or even "declining," and many pundits predicted that Asia, led by Japan, would become the leading regional economy in the 21st century. Then the 1997–1999 Asian financial crisis changed the economic milieu of the world (to be explained in detail in Chapter 3). Since the September 11, 2001, terrorist attacks, the U.S. economy has grown faster than any other developed country at an annual rate of 3–4 percent. However, even the U.S. economic growth rate pales in comparison to China and India, two leading emerging economic powers in the last decade or so. China and India have grown at an annual rate of 7–10 percent and 4–7 percent, respectively, since the dawn of the twenty-first century.[23] Obviously, a decade is a long time in the ever-changing world economy, and indeed, no single country has sustained its economic performance continuously.

Human Resources and Technology

Although wholesale generalizations should not be made, the role of human resources has become increasingly important as a primary determinant of industry and country competitiveness as the level of technology has advanced. As shown in **Exhibit 2-4**, according to World Economic Forum's *Global Competitiveness Report*, Singapore, one of the four Asian Tigers, consistently ranked among the world's top 10 economies. In fact, for the past three consecutive years, Singapore has always been in the top five of the global competitiveness ranking. This achievement is largely due to Singapore's competitive advantage in education, healthcare, and good government—all with only 19 percent consumption of GDP. Unlike China, which often sees foreign investment as a route to learn and acquire technology, Singapore opens its door widely to investors by providing an environment equipped with excellent infrastructure, low taxes, a well-educated taskforce, and open trade routes.[24] Another one of the four Asian Tigers, Taiwan, also ranked within the top 20 for the past three consecutive periods (from 2008/09 to 2011/12). These two Asian countries have virtually no natural resources to rely on for building their competitiveness. Clearly, human resources are crucial for the long-term economic vitality of natural resource-poor countries. All of the top 10-ranked countries, with the exception of the United States and Canada, are scarce in natural resources.

---

[22]Paul Bairoch, "International Industrialization Levels from 1750 to 1980," *Journal of European Economic History*, 11 (1982), pp. 36–54.
[23]United Nations Conference on Trade and Development, *Trade and Development Report 2005*, Geneva: United Nations.
[24]"Go East, Young Bureaucrat: Emerging Asia Can Teach the West a Lot about Government," *Economist*, Special Report, March 17, 2011.

Exhibit 2-4 Global Competitiveness Ranking[25]

Country	Score	Rank in 2011/12	Rank In 2008/09	Country	Score	Rank in 2011/12	Rank In 2008/09	Country	Score	Rank in 2011/12	Rank in 2008/09
Switzerland	5.74	1	2	Hong Kong	5.36	11	11	Malaysia	5.08	21	21
Singapore	5.63	2	5	Canada	5.33	12	10	Israel	5.07	22	23
Sweden	5.61	3	4	Taiwan	5.26	13	17	Luxembourg	5.03	23	25
Finland	5.47	4	6	Qatar	5.24	14	26	South Korea	5.02	24	13
United States	5.43	5	1	Belgium	5.20	15	19	New Zealand	4.93	25	24
Germany	5.41	6	7	Norway	5.18	16	15	China	4.90	26	30
Netherlands	5.41	7	8	Saudi Arabia	5.17	17	27	United Arab Emirates	4.89	27	31
Denmark	5.40	8	3	France	5.14	18	16	Brunei Darussalam	4.78	28	39
Japan	5.40	9	9	Austria	5.14	19	14	Ireland	4.77	29	22
United Kingdom	5.39	10	12	Australia	5.11	20	18	Iceland	4.75	30	20

Source: World Economic Forum, *Global Competitiveness Report 2008–2009; 2009–2010;* and *2011–2012*, http://www.weforum.org/.

Similarly, three of the top 10 countries in 2011–2012 are Nordic countries, led by Sweden and followed by Finland and Denmark. Although the rankings change to some extent, Norway and Iceland also kept within top 20 and top 30, respectively. Nordic countries share a number of characteristics that make them extremely competitive, such as very healthy macroeconomic environments and highly transparent and efficient public institutions, with general agreement within society on the spending priorities to be met in the government budget. While the business communities in the Nordic countries point to high tax rates as a potential problem area, there is no evidence that these are adversely affecting the ability of these countries to compete effectively in world markets, or to provide to their respective populations some of the highest standards of living in the world. Indeed, the high levels of government tax revenue have delivered world-class educational establishments, an extensive safety net, and a highly motivated and skilled labor force.[26]

Although the United States kept its top positions of No. 2 and No.1 in the reports of 2005–2006 and 2008–2009, respectively, the prognosis for future U.S. competitiveness might not be as good as it currently appears. Seemingly contradictory to the current U.S. situation, the U.S. Council on Competitiveness[27] reported in 1999 that U.S. technological competitiveness had peaked in 1985 and that the United States might be living off its historical assets that were not being renewed (see **Exhibit 2-5** showing the change in the innovative capability of leading countries over the years). Although a more recent country innovativeness report is not available, this report clearly pointed to the rise of Finland as a technological powerhouse. Other conclusions include that although the United States and Switzerland had been the most innovative in the last three decades, other OECD nations have been increasingly catching up to U.S. and Swiss levels. In particular, Denmark and Sweden have registered major gains in innovative capacity since the mid-1980s. Another interesting observation is that despite its economic slowdown in the 1990s, Japan has maintained its innovative capacity over the years

---

[26]World Economic Forum, *Global Competitiveness Report 2011–2012*, http://www.weforum.org/.
[27]Michael E. Porter and Scott Stern, *The Challenge to America's Prosperity: Findings from the Innovation Index*, Washington, D.C.: Council on Competitiveness, 1999.

Exhibit 2-5 Change in Country Innovativeness: A Key to a Country's Long-Term Competitiveness

Rank Year	1980	1986	1993	1995	1999	2005 (projected)
1	Switzerland	Switzerland	Switzerland	U.S.A.	Japan	Japan
2	U.S.A.	U.S.A.	Japan	Switzerland	Switzerland	Finland
3	Germany	Japan	U.S.A.	Japan	U.S.A.	Switzerland
4	Japan	Germany	Germany	Sweden	Sweden	Denmark
5	Sweden	Sweden	Sweden	Germany	Germany	Sweden
6	Canada	Canada	Denmark	Finland	Finland	U.S.A.
7	France	Finland	France	Denmark	Denmark	Germany
8	Netherlands	Netherlands	Canada	France	France	France
9	Finland	Norway	Finland	Canada	Norway	Norway
10	U.K.	France	Australia	Norway	Canada	Canada
11	Norway	Denmark	Netherlands	Netherlands	Australia	Australia
12	Denmark	U.K.	Norway	Australia	Netherlands	Austria
13	Austria	Australia	U.K.	Austria	Austria	Netherlands
14	Australia	Austria	Austria	U.K.	U.K.	U.K.
15	Italy	Italy	New Zealand	New Zealand	New Zealand	New Zealand

Source: Adapted from Michael E. Porter and Scott Stern, *The New Challenge to America's Prosperity: Findings from the Innovation Index*, Washington, D.C.: Council on Competitiveness, 1999, pp. 34–35.

with little sign of weakening. The recovery of the Japanese economy seemed to underscore its technological strengths, among other things.[28] Finally, although not shown in **Exhibit 2-5**, Singapore, Taiwan, South Korea, India, Israel, and Ireland have upgraded their innovative capacity over the past decade, becoming new centers of innovative activity.[29]

One major lesson here is that we should not be misled by mass media coverage of the current economic situations of various countries. While mass media coverage is factual and near-term focused, it may inadvertently cloud our strategic thinking. In other words, the current performance of the U.S. economy should not erroneously lull us into believing that U.S. companies are invincible in the global economy.[30]

Emerging Economies

In much of the twentieth century, large economies and large trading partners had been located mostly in the **Triad Regions** of the world (North America, Western Europe, and Japan). However, in the next 10 to 20 years, the greatest commercial opportunities are expected to be found increasingly in 10 **Big Emerging Markets** (BEMs)—the Chinese Economic Area (CEA: including China, Hong Kong region, and Taiwan), India, the Commonwealth of Independent States (Russia, Central Asia, and the Caucasus states), South Korea, Mexico,

---

[28]"The Viagra Economy," A Survey of the World Economy Economist, September 24, 2005, 12–14; and "Japan: The Sun Also Rises," *Economist,* October 6, 2005, pp. 3–6.

[29]Michael E. Porter and Scott Stern, *The Challenge to America's Prosperity: Findings from the Innovation Index*, Washington, D.C.: Council on Competitiveness, 1999, p. 7.

[30]Paul Krugman, "America the Boastful," *Foreign Affairs*, 77 (May/June 1998), pp. 32–45.

Brazil, Argentina, South Africa, Central European countries,[31] Turkey, and the Association of Southeast Asian Nations (ASEAN: including Brunei, Cambodia, Indonesia, Laos, Malaysia, Myanmar, the Philippines, Singapore, Thailand, and Vietnam). For instance, in the past 20 years, China's real annual GDP growth rate has averaged 9.5 percent a year, while India's has been 5.7 percent, compared to the average 3 percent GDP growth in the United States. Companies like Hewlett-Packard (HP) have benefited a lot from BEMs. For example, growth in such markets as Brazil, Russia, India, and China helped HP shrug off the effects of a slowdown in the United States and prompted the company to raise its sales forecast in 2008–2010. However, we should also realize that an increasing number of competitors are expected to originate from those emerging economies.

Accordingly, an increasing number of competitors are also expected to originate from those emerging economies. According to trade statistics compiled in *World Factbook 2012*, published by the U.S. Central Intelligence Agency (see **Exhibit 2-2**), the world's nine largest exporting countries accounted for more than half of the world merchandise trade in 2011: China ($1.91 trillion), the United States ($1.50 trillion), Germany ($1.41 trillion), Japan ($788 billion), France ($587 billion), South Korea ($556 billion), Netherlands ($552 billion), Italy ($524 billion), and Russia ($521 billion). A look at the trade data from recent years turns out three notable changes attesting to the globalization of the markets. First, China has successfully proven to be the leading exporter for three years in a row (2009–2011), surpassing the United States and Germany. This signifies that its economy has grown strong and will likely continue strengthening for the foreseeable future. Second, after taking over the United States as the largest exporting country for the first time in 2004, Germany maintained its position as the second leading single exporting country for eight consecutive years until 2011 when it was again surpassed by the United States. Third, Korea and Russia have reached the top 10 exporting country group.

As a result, over the next two decades, the markets that hold the greatest potential for dramatic increases in U.S. exports are not the traditional trading partners in Europe and Japan, which now account for the overwhelming bulk of the international trade of the United States, but will instead be the BEMs. Already, there are signs that in the future the biggest trade headache for the United States may not be Japan but China and India.[32] China's trade surplus with the United States ballooned from $86 billion in 2000 to $295.5 billion in 2011; it had already surpassed Japan's trade surplus position with the United States by 2000.[33] India has increasingly become a hotbed for information technology (IT), communications, software development, and call centers, particularly for many U.S. multinationals. Russia is extremely rich in natural resources, including oil and natural gas, that are dwindling in the rest of the word. It has gradually warmed up to international commerce, and will potentially become a major trading nation. Brazil is not only natural resources-rich but also boasts some complex technologies including jet engine and aircraft manufacturing. As these four leading emerging economies, among others, are likely to reshape the nature of international business in the next decade, the profiles of these countries will be highlighted here (see **Exhibit 2-6** for summary country profile).

---

[31]Poland, Czech Republic, Slovakia, Slovenia, Hungary, Estonia, Latvia, Lithuania, Romania, and Bulgaria. See an excellent article, "The Rise of Central Europe," *Business Week*, December 12, 2005, pp. 50–56.
[32]The economic role of smaller emerging economies cannot be ignored. Read, for example, "Good Morning, Vietnam: Intel' Deal to Build a Factory is Likely to Spur More Western Investment," *Business Week*, March 13, 2006, pp. 50–51.
[33]*Statistical Abstract of the United States, 2012*, http://www.census.gov/compendia/statab/2012edition.html.

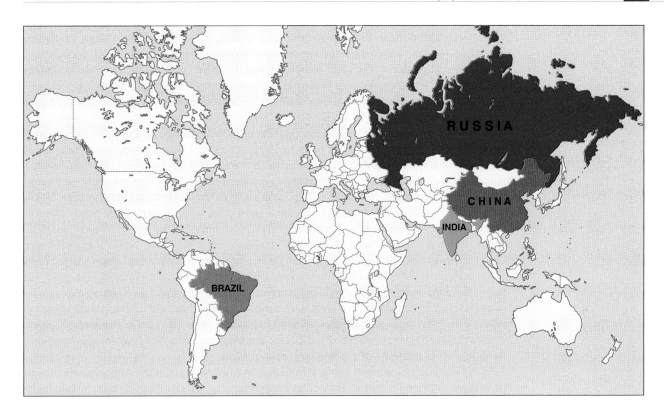

Marketing in emerging markets is contextually different from marketing in developed countries. Companies that have succeeded in developed countries may or may not be able to approach those emerging markets the same way. When they enter huge emerging markets in rapidly developing economies, Western companies typically bring with them U.S., Japanese, or Western European quality standards, dismissing local goods as inferior. They know there is a great hunger in those countries for Western goods of the same quality that developed-country consumers and businesses might buy in New York, London, or Tokyo. However, they forget

Exhibit 2-6   Leading Emerging Economies in 2011

	Brazil	China	India	Russia
Population	206 million	1,343 million	1,205 million	138 million
Population Growth Rate	1.10%	0.48%	1.31%	−0.48%
GDP in current US$	$2.52 trillion	$6.99 trillion	$1.84 trillion	$1.79 trillion
GDP in current US$ based on purchasing power parity	$2.28 trillion	$11.29 trillion	$4.46 trillion	$2.38 trillion
GDP per capita based on purchasing power parity	$11,600	$8,400	$3,700	$16,700
GDP real growth rate	2.8%	9.2%	7.8%	4.3%
Inflation rate	6.9%	5.4%	6.8%	8.9%
Fixed Investment (% of GDP)	19.0%	54.2%	30.7%	21.1%
Current account balance	−$63.5 billion	$280.6 billion	−$62.96 billion	$90.51 billion

Sources: Compiled from IMF statistics and U.S. Central Intelligence Agency, *The World Factbook 2012*, https://www.cia.gov/library/publications/.

that, in spite of the lust for high-quality Western goods, relatively few developing-country customers can afford them. In terms of price and quality, most developing-country customers weigh more on the former and choose not-up-to-Western-standards but good enough and inexpensive local products. The local companies making these "good enough" products costing up to 75 percent less than Western brands are actually serious challengers to their developed-country rivals, especially given that they will finally produce ever-better products as they gain scale, lower costs, and invest in R&D.

Take Nokia, one of the world's largest suppliers of mobile phones, for example. This Finnish company entered the Chinese market early in 1991. As most Western companies usually do, it conducted market research and identified distributors in the wealthiest cities and sold them product "by the container load." By 1999, the company outperformed any other domestic or foreign companies and became the No.1 with a 30 percent share of the handset market. However, Nokia did not realize that while it was focusing on the biggest cities with Western-grade handsets, local challengers were gradually taking up the populous countryside by selling "good enough" handsets. Soon Nokia and local challengers' positions were reversed. Nokia's market share fell from 30 percent in 1999 to the low teens in 2003, and the local challengers' share jumped from just 2.5 percent in 1999 to nearly 30 percent. Undoubtedly, Nokia was paying the price for focusing its China strategy on the high-end market. The large loss woke up Nokia to renovate its strategy: it set up its own distribution and sales network across China and introduced cheaper new handsets with fewer bells and whistles, quickly expanding from 10 cities to hundreds of cities. This reinvention of strategy worked. By 2005, the company created a new peak of sales by selling 51 million—or 35 percent—of the handsets sold in China.[34]

Like Nokia, many developed-country firms fail to fully understand the competitive environment in those emerging markets. They enter these emerging markets ready to sell existing high-end products to increasingly prosperous city dwellers. It might work for a while, but not forever. A valuable lesson from the Nokia example is to have the right products at the right price. There is no doubt about the attractiveness and potential of the emerging markets. To succeed, however, developed-country companies need a new reference. We will further explore issues related to the emerging markets in Chapter 16.

Evolution of Cooperative Global Trade Agreements
General Agreements on Tariffs and Trade

In the aftermath of World War II, the then-big powers negotiated the setting up of the **General Agreements on Tariffs and Trade** (GATT), with the objective of ensuring free trade among nations through negotiated lowering of trade barriers. GATT provided a forum for multilateral discussion among countries to reduce trade barriers. Nations met periodically to review the status of world trade and to negotiate mutually agreeable reductions in trade barriers.

The main operating principle of GATT is the concept of **Normal Trade Relations** (NTR) status (formerly known as **Most Favored Nation** or MFN status). The NTR status meant that any country that was a member state to a GATT agreement and that extended a reduction in tariff to another nation would have to automatically extend the same benefit to all members of GATT. However, there was no enforcement mechanism, and over time many countries negotiated bilateral agreements, especially for agricultural products, steel, textiles, and automobiles. GATT was successful in lowering trade barriers to a substantial extent (e.g., developed countries' average tariffs on manufactured goods from around 40 percent down to a mere 4 percent) during

---

[34]Harold Sirkin and Jim Hemerling, "Price Trumps Quality in Emerging Markets," *BusinessWeek.com,* June 4, 2008, http://www.businessweek.com/.

its existence from 1948 to 1994. However, some major shortcomings limited its potential and effectiveness. The initial rounds of GATT concentrated only on the lowering of tariff barriers. As trade in services expanded faster than the trade in goods and GATT concentrated on merchandise trade, more and more international trade came to reside outside the purview of GATT. Second, GATT tended to concentrate mostly on tariffs, and many nations used non-tariff barriers, such as quota and onerous customs procedures, to get around the spirit of GATT when they could not increase tariffs. Finally, as developed nations moved from manufacturing-based economies to services- and knowledge-based economies, they felt the need to bring intellectual property within the purview of international agreements, because that was where the competitive advantage lay for firms in the developed nations.

World Trade Organization

The World Trade Organization (WTO) was created in the eighth round of GATT talks—called the **Uruguay Round**—that lasted from 1986 to 1994. The WTO took effect on January 1, 1995. The WTO has statutory powers to adjudicate trade disputes among nations to oversee the smooth functioning of the multilateral trade accords agreed upon under the Uruguay Round. *Its main function is to ensure that trade flows as smoothly, predictably, and freely as possible.* As of March 2, 2013, the WTO had 159 member countries.[35] The Uruguay Round was successful in bringing many agricultural products and textiles under the purview of GATT. In particular, this Round ensured the ultimate harmonization of the overall customs process and the fundamental determinations that are made for all goods crossing an international border: admissibility, classification, and valuation.[36] It also included provisions for trade in intellectual property for the first time and provided for many services.

Then, the WTO's ninth and latest round–called the **Doha Development Agenda** (**Doha Round**, for short)–was launched in Doha, Qatar, in November 2001. Most notably, the inaugural meeting at the Doha Round also paved the way for China and Taiwan to get full membership in the WTO[37] (see **Global Perspective 2-1** on the accession of China in 2001 and then Russia in 2011 to the WTO). This new round places the needs and interests of developing countries at the heart of its

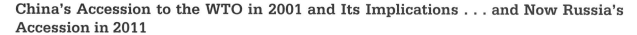

Global Perspective 2-1

China's Accession to the WTO in 2001 and Its Implications . . . and Now Russia's Accession in 2011

After 15 years of arduous negotiation, China joined the World Trade Organization (WTO) in December 2001. The United States reached a bilateral agreement with China on WTO accession that secures broad-ranging, comprehensive, one-way trade concessions on China's part, in which China made specific commitments to open its market to U.S. exports of industrial goods, service, and agriculture to a degree unprecedented in the modern era. For example, China promised to reduce import tariffs from an average of 24.6 percent to 9.4 percent within three to five years. The United States also offered extension of permanent Normal Trade Relations (NTR) to China, as China entered the WTO. The

---

[35]World Trade Organization, http://www.wto.org/english/thewto_e/whatis_e/tif_e/org6_e.htm, accessed July 1, 2012.

[36]Paulsen K. Vandevert, "The Uruguay Round and the World Trade Organization: A New Era Dawns in the Private Law of International Customs and Trade," *Case Western Reserve Journal of International Law*, 31 (Winter 1999), pp. 107–138.

[37]Anne McGuirk, "The Doha Development Agenda," *Finance & Development*, 39 (September 2002), 4–7.

House vote was called one of the most important trade and foreign policy decisions the United States had made in many years. Because of the accession, the markets of WTO members were also opened to China.

Trade officials from the United States, Europe, and Japan have portrayed China's entry into the WTO as an antidote to their growing trade deficits with China. But the reality is that China's agreement to reduce tariffs, phase out import quotas, open new sectors of its economy to foreign investment, and otherwise follow WTO rules will not reverse this imbalance in trade. China's accession to the WTO has begun to boost its economic reforms in the world's most populous nation. There is no doubt that China and its 1.3 billion people benefit tremendously from its WTO accession. It has allowed China to expand trade, attract foreign investment, and give private firms a greater role in the economy, but more importantly, it has increasingly integrated China with the rest of the world economy. According to the United Nations Conference on Trade and Development (UNCTAD), although global inflows of foreign direct investment (FDI) declined from 2001 to 2003, China experienced an increased trade inflow of 14 percent ($53 billion in 2003) and became the world's largest FDI recipient. China is actively attracting FDI in manufacturing and service sectors from multinational corporations. Multinational corporations have found China's workforce not only cheap and vast but also educated and disciplined. Meanwhile, as an emerging FDI outward investor, firms in China have invested in neighboring countries and in Africa, Latin America, North America, and Europe to access natural resources, markets, and strategic assets such as technology and brand names. In 2002, China's outward investment flows exceeded $35 billion, reaching more than 160 countries.

Entry into the WTO membership followed Beijing winning the right to host the 2008 Olympic Games and Shanghai hosting the Asia Pacific Economic Cooperation (APEC) leaders' summit. Driven by the government's open policy to foreign investment since 1980s and accession by the WTO as an important trade partner to the world, China is emerging as the virtual factory of the world, driving a profound shift in global investment flows.

How has this affected other economies such as the United States, Japan, and Europe? With China's increased trade surplus with the United States, the deflationary crisis in Tokyo, as well as European manufacturers becoming vulnerable to the MADE IN CHINA shock, should China be blamed for the rich countries' economic problems? On the one hand, China has presented business opportunities for firms to offshore manufacturing and services jobs to its low-waged, skilled workforce, and has also lowered its import tariffs since its entry into the WTO; on the other hand, China has caused some firms to lose global market share and job opportunities by conducting cheap-currency strategy.

Now 10 years after China's accession to the WTO, Russia also became the most recent addition to the WTO in December 2011 after 18 years of negotiations. Some estimates suggest Russian membership will help to boost its economy by tens of billions of dollars each year. Russia is Europe's third-largest export market, while Russia's own exports have been dominated by oil and gas. Over time, competitive forces will help improve allocation of resources from less competitive to more competitive industries within the country. Furthermore, Russia has to bring its laws into conformity with WTO rules and regulations that will address the very issues that foreign investors usually complain about, such as corruption, the protection of minority shareholders, and the independence of the judiciary. Other WTO members will also benefit from a near-term reduction in tariffs on their exports. As has been the case with the accession of China into the WTO community, another major transformation of the world economy with Russia as a WTO member is likely to unfold in the next decade and beyond.

Sources: Nicholas R. Lardy, "Sweet and Sour Deal," *Foreign Policy,* March/April 2002, 20–21; Bill Powell, "It's All Made in China Now," *Fortune,* March 4, 2002; "Tilting at Dragons," *Economist.* October 25, 2003, pp. 65–66; "The China Price," *Business Week,* December 6, 2004, pp. 102–124; and "Russia Becomes WTO Member after 18 Years of Talks," *BBC News,* December 18, 2011.

work (**Exhibit 2-7** gives an idea of the "intended" scope of the Doha Round). Agricultural tariffs are five times higher on average than those for industrial products. High tariffs undermine the ability of developing countries to trade their way out of poverty—it is estimated that two-thirds of the world's poorest people are dependent on agriculture. The United States currently spends up to $19 billion on farm-production subsidies, which heavily distort trade. The EU spends over

Exhibit 2-7 Agenda for the Doha Round

- Market access for agriculture
- Market access for services
- Market access for non-agricultural products
- Trade-related aspects of intellectual property rights (TRIPS)
- Relationship between trade and investment
- Interaction between trade and competition policy
- Transparency in government procurement
- Trade facilitation
- WTO rules: antidumping
- WTO rules: subsidies
- WTO rules: regional trade agreements
- Dispute Settlement Understanding
- Trade and environment
- Electronic commerce
- Small economies
- Trade, debt, and finance
- Trade and transfer of technology
- Technical cooperation and capacity building
- Least-developed countries
- Special and differential treatment
- Organization and management of the work program

Source: World Trade Organization, http://www.wto.org/english/thewto_e/minist_e/min01_e/mindecl_e.htm, accessed January 25, 2013.

$75 billion.[38] The reluctance of some of the world's richest countries to substantially reduce high farm tariff and non-tariff barriers stymied the opportunity to secure other reforms that would have delivered huge benefits to the world trading regime. Broadly speaking, the United States was under pressure to reduce trade-distorting farm subsidies, while Europe and India tried to keep too many farm products from deeper tariff cuts, and some developing countries were under pressure to reduce industrial tariffs further and faster. The agenda also included new trade talks—an action program to resolve developing countries' complaints about the implementation of Uruguay Round agreements, and an accord on **Trade Related Aspects of Intellectual Property Rights** (TRIPS) ensuring that patent protection does not block developing countries' access to affordable medicines. As these countries eventually failed to come to an agreement on farm product issues, the Doha Round of multilateral trade talks did not make much progress in other areas and eventually collapsed on July 29, 2008.[39]

Incidentally, the WTO is not simply an extension of GATT. The GATT was a multilateral agreement with no institutional foundations. The WTO is a permanent institution with its own secretariat. The GATT was applied on a provisional basis in strict legal terms. WTO commitments are full and permanent and legally binding under international law. Although GATT was restricted to trade in merchandise goods, WTO includes trade in services and trade-related aspects of intellectual property. It is to be noted that GATT lives on within WTO. Some of the major issues and agendas in WTO are highlighted below.

Dispute Settlement Mechanism

The WTO dispute settlement mechanism is faster, more automatic, and therefore much less susceptible to blockages than the old GATT system. Once a country indicates to WTO that it has a complaint about the trade practices of another country, an automatic schedule kicks in. The two countries have three months for mutual "consultations" to iron out their differences. If the

---

[38]"A Stopped Clock Ticks Again," *Economist,* October 13, 2005, pp. 76–79.
[39]"So Near and Yet So Far: Trade Ministers Have Come Too Close to a Deal to Let the Doha Round Die," *Economist,* August 2, 2008, p. 14; and "After Doha," *Economist,* September 6, 2008, pp. 85–86.

disputants cannot come to a mutually satisfactory settlement, then the dispute is referred to the Dispute Settlement Mechanism of WTO, under which a decision has to be rendered within six months of the setting up of the panel to resolve the dispute. The decision of the panel is supposed to be legally binding. However, trade experts have revealed deep ambivalence about the WTO's experiment with binding adjudication, and there is little clear sense of where the system should go from here. Litigation draws on different skills, resources, and even cultural attitudes than does diplomacy, with a possibility placing certain nations at a real disadvantage.[40]

Finally, although WTO is a global institutional proponent of free trade, it is not without critics. In December 1999, WTO launched what would have become the beginning of a ninth round of negotiations inaugurated in Seattle, the United States. However, its Seattle meeting was only to be greeted by jeers and riots triggered by labor unions, environmentalists, and other on-lookers who were opposed to free trade for various reasons. As a result, the meeting was postponed until 2001 under so much uncertainty, which resulted in the Doha Round mentioned earlier. Indeed, contrary to the globalization forces at work, antiglobalization sentiment has been building over the years (see **Global Perspective 2-2**).

Global Perspective 2-2

Antiglobalization Movement

Opposition to corporate and economic globalization has been growing for many years, but has received media attention only since the late 1990s. The antiglobalization movement, launched by a French farmer, quickly spread the network to other parts of the world. The growing trend toward antiglobalization activism is directed, first, against multinational corporate power and, second, against global agreements on economic growth made by international trade institutions, such as the World Trade Organization (WTO), the World Bank, and the International Monetary Fund (IMF).

The movement is often described as "multi-generational, multi-class, and multi-issue." Participants protest against capitalism, free trade, international investment (especially from the West to the Third World), cultural and economic globalization, wars, and Western politics. During the last decade, massive antiglobalization protests have accompanied international meetings in cities such as Seattle, Quebec City, Genoa, and Washington, D.C. The antiglobalization movement became front-page stories when its protesters gathered during the WTO meeting in Seattle in late 1999, when the activists almost disrupted the meeting. Later

protests focused on the World Bank and IMF. Their main slogan is "Here, another world is possible."

There are two kinds of people in the movement: Reformists and Radicals. Reformists are often engaged in a serious exchange of ideas and proposals on socioeconomic and environmental changes, which ask for broader international participation in decision-making. Protests organized by radicals often become violent and disruptive. Campaigners cyberattacked international businesses' websites, burned their properties, and destroyed international meetings. Multinational companies are often accused of social injustice, unfair labor practices—including slave labor wages, living, and working conditions—as well as a lack of concern for the environment, mismanagement of natural resources, and ecological damage.

Sources: "Anti-Globalization: A Spreading Phenomenon," *Perspectives* (Canadian Security Intelligence Report # 2000/08), http://www.csis-scrs.gc.ca/eng/miscdocs/200008_e.html; Sean Higgins, "Anti-Globalization Protesters Discover New Enemy: Israel," *Investor's Business Daily*, April 23, 2002, p.A16; James Petras, "Porto Alegre 2002: A Tale of Two Forums—Correspondence; Anti-Globalization Social Forum," *Monthly Review* 53, April 1, 2002, p.56; Neil Thomas, "Global Capitalism, the Anti-Globalisation Movement and the Third World," *Capital & Class*, Summer 2007, pp. 45–78.

---

[40]Susan Esserman and Robert Howse, "The TWO on Trial," *Foreign Affairs*, 82 (January/February 2003), pp. 130–140.

Trade Related Aspects of Intellectual Property Rights (TRIPS)

Trade Related Aspects of Intellectual Property Rights (TRIPS) Agreement, concluded as part of the GATT Uruguay Round, mandates that each member country accord to the nationals of other member countries the same treatment as its nationals with regard to intellectual property protection (see Chapter 5 for details). However, it is not an international attempt to create a universal patent system. In March 2002, the WTO's TRIPS Council started work on a list of issues at the November 2001 Ministerial Conference in Doha. These include specific aspects of TRIPS and public health, geographical indications, protecting plant and animal inventions, biodiversity, traditional knowledge, the general review of the TRIPS Agreement, and technology transfer. One hot issue is to find a solution to the problems countries may face in making use of compulsory licensing if they have too little or no pharmaceutical manufacturing capacity. During a special session, WTO members also embarked on a two-phase program for completing negotiations on a multilateral registration system for geographical indications for wines and spirits.[41]

Global E-Commerce

Due to an explosive use of the internet, a global effort to regulate international e-commerce has become increasingly necessary (see Chapter 17 for the impact of the internet on various marketing activities). According to the Internet World Statistics, the number of internet users reached 2.4 billion by June 30, 2012, a six-time increase from 2000 to 2012.[42] To address this issue, the WTO's Work Program on Electronic Commerce has been working on how to define the trade-related aspects of electronic commerce that would fall under the parameters of WTO mandates. The Work Program submitted a report to the organization's General Council on March 31, 1999, in which it sought to define such services as intellectual barriers to trade in the context of electronic commerce. Probably the best thing the WTO can do to assist the development of electronic commerce in global trade is to meet its stated goal of assisting in the creation of an environment in which electronic commerce can flourish. According to WTO documents, such an environment requires liberalized market policies and predictable trade regimes that encourage the massive investments in technology that is required for electronic commerce to work.[43]

The United States has been taking the lead in bringing e-commerce-related issues to the table. A U.S. document that was presented to the Work Program's general meeting on March 22, 1999, clearly outlined both the issues raised by the introduction of e-commerce in international trade and the importance of e-commerce to the global economy. The U.S. also proposed the WTO examine services that may emerge as more viable in terms of international trade through e-commerce. For example, with widespread use of the internet, has the notion of retailing across borders—previously inhibited by different time zones and the high cost of international communications—now become commercially viable? Now that networked appliances are used increasingly, will remote monitoring, testing, and diagnostics of such devices become increasingly important? Much has yet to be clarified and resolved.

Information Technology and the Changing Nature of Competition

As the nature of value-adding activities in developed nations shifts more and more to information creation, manipulation, and analysis, developed nations have begun taking an increased interest in

---

[41]Compiled from TRIPS Material on the WTO Website, http://www.wto.org/english/tratop_e/trips_e/trips_e.htm; "Patently Problematic," *Economist,* September 14, 2002, pp.75–76; and Donald Richards, "Trade-Related Intellectual Property Rights," *Review of International Political Economy,* 12, August 2005, pp. 535–551.

[42]Internet World Stats, http://www.internetworldstats.com/stats.htm, accessed November 12, 2012.

[43]David Biederman, "E-Commerce and World Trade," *Traffic World,* 258 (April 26, 1999), p. 22.

international intellectual property protection measures. This shift is comparable to the industrial evolution from agriculture to manufacturing we experienced in the twentieth century. Although the importance of farm products to humankind did not change over the years, the portion of the economy allocated to agriculture has consistently declined, and so have the margins for the agricultural sector. Therefore, farmers moved into manufacturing, or at least into food processing, to maintain margins.

An analogous situation faces a content maker for **information-related products** such as software, music, movies, newspapers, magazines, and education in the late-twentieth century headed into the twenty-first century. In an early civilization, people just knew how to do things, and learning and transferring knowledge to other people was costly and not easy at all. Then people later learned to document their knowledge in written media such as books and drawings. Copying and passing on intellectual property became easier and less costly. In more recent years, we use tapes, discs, and other electronic media.

Value of Intellectual Property in the Information Age

Now with the advent of the Information Age, **electronically represented intellectual property** can be freely copied anywhere in the world, and knowledge transfer has become virtually instantaneous. Because more and more of value creation in developed nations is coming from the development and sale of such information-based intellectual property, it is no surprise that developed nations are highly interested in putting strong international intellectual property laws in place. It is costly for corporations to protect their intellectual property, and to adjust for losses in productivity and perceived damage to corporate brand and share price.[44] The U.S. insistence on the inclusion of provisions relating to intellectual property in the WTO's TRIPS agreement is a direct consequence, and is understandable as cyber crime affects all parties with intellectual property. Technology-based protection of electronic information through hardware, software, or a combination thereof in the form of encryption and digital signatures has been suggested as the means of circumventing the problem of unauthorized copying.

Controlling copies (once created by the author or by a third party), however, becomes a complex challenge. A firm can either control something very tightly, limiting distribution to a small, trusted group, or it can rest assured that eventually its product will find its way to a large non-paying audience—if anyone cares to have it in the first place. But creators of content on the internet still face the eternal problem: the value of their work generally will not receive recognition without wide distribution. Only by attracting broad attention can an artist or creator hope to attract high payment for copies.

The trick may be to control not the copies of the firm's information product but instead a relationship with the customers—subscriptions or membership. And that is often what the customers want, because they see it as an assurance of a continuing supply of reliable, timely content. Thus, the role of marketing may be expected to assume increasing importance. A firm can, of course, charge a small amount for mass copies. Metering schemes will allow vendors to charge—in fractions of a penny, if desired—according to usage or users rather than copies. However, it will not much change the overall approaching-zero trend of content pricing. At best, it will make it much easier to charge those low prices.

Other hurdles exist for content creators with the emergence of electronic commerce (e-commerce). In the past, comparing and contrasting the price and quality of products and services was a time-consuming endeavor. Now, e-commerce operators make it easy for prospective customers to make such a comparison. These vendors even offer customer ratings. E-commerce represents a truly efficient market for information. Information has become transparent. As a result, content creators can no longer maintain a monopolistic advantage for long. This transformation in

---

[44]DeeDee Doke, "Sniffing Out the Evidence," *Personnel Today*, May 11, 2004, pp. 20–22.

the form of value creation and ease of dissemination implies a jump in economic integration as nations become part of an international electronic commerce network. Not only money but also products and services will flow faster.

The other consequence of fungible content, information products, and electronic networks is an additional assault on the power of national governments to regulate international commerce. Ford uses a product design process whereby designers at Dearborn, Michigan, pass on their day's work in an electronic form to an office in Japan, which then passes the baton along to designers in Britain, who pass it back to Dearborn the next day. When the information represented in the design crosses borders, how do the governments of the United States, Japan, and Britain treat this information? How will such exchanges be regulated? Less-open societies like China and Malaysia, recognizing the power of electronic networks, are already attempting to regulate the infrastructure of and access to the electronic network.

Proliferation of E-Commerce and Regulations

A similar problem applies to electronic commerce. The rapid proliferation of e-commerce led by internet and e-commerce providers, such as Amazon and E*Trade as well as by traditional marketers that have gone into e-commerce, such as Dell Computer, Victoria's Secret, and Nokia, has spawned a type of international commerce and transactions that countries' regulations have not kept pace with. In terms of e-commerce, how do countries control online purchases and sales? If one looks at Europe, each country has different tax laws and internet regulations, as well as consumer protection laws. In addition, import and export formalities still apply to goods bought electronically. How to monitor electronic commerce transactions remains a problem for most national governments.[45]

One such example is illustrated by the launch of Viagra by Pfizer in 1998. The company celebrated the most successful drug launch in history with the introduction of Viagra, the first pill that allows effective oral treatment for men who suffer from erectile dysfunction (impotence). The internet attracted the portion of patients from all over the world who are not willing to talk about their problem even to their doctors. The internet quickly filled up with virtual pharmacies that promised to supply Viagra via a mouse click. Internet pharmacies sometimes try to conceal their location, set up in offshore locations, and sell their items in a gray area of doing business. Customers who are not willing to disclose their erectile dysfunction can easily order Viagra without consultation of their physician, but run the risk of becoming victims of fraud.

Pfizer and counterfeiting experts have warned the public not to buy from internet pharmacies.[46] In reputable pharmacies, cases of fraud usually do not occur, but there are tens of other fraud websites that will exploit the patient's unwillingness to talk about impotence. The Federal Trade Commission (FTC) is in charge of cases where entities are trying to mislead potential customers and commit fraud. The FTC sent out some warnings about products that claim to be related to Viagra, and no prescription is necessary. The warnings advise people to check credentials of suppliers. Fraud on the internet can be found in reports where businesses set up to sell counterfeit pills managed to have about 150,000 customers in about a year. The owner of these "enterprises" advertised pills under names similar to Viagra, like Viagrae. Pfizer sued, and the FTC was able to find that this name was only one small part in a larger fraud to distribute large amounts of phony pills.[47]

Regulating international e-commerce obviously requires cross-border cooperation. The rising problems resulted in numerous international treaties. For example, in May 2001, the Council of

---

[45]Kim Viborg Andersen, Roman Beck, Rolf T. Wigand, Niels Bjùrn-Andersen, and Eric Brousseau, "European e-Commerce Policies in the Pioneering Days, the Gold Rush and the Post-Hype Era," *Information Polity*, 9 (3–4), 2004, pp. 217–232.

[46]"Black Market Filled Phony Viagra Tablets," www.cafecrowd.com, accessed August 10, 1999.

[47]See "FTC: Watch for Viagra Knock-Offs," at www.msnbc.com/news/2090, accessed August 10, 1999.

Europe, working with Canada, Japan, South Africa, and the United States, approved the 27th draft of the Convention on cyber crime—the first international treaty on crime in cyberspace. The treaty requires participating countries to create laws regarding various issues including digital copyrights and computer-related fraud. It offers international businesses the best hope for legal recourse if they become the victim of cyber crime in e-commerce. The United Nations Commission on International Trade Law (UNCITRAL), the core legal body within the United Nations system in the field of international trade law, formed a Working Group on Electronic Commerce to re-examine these treaties in 1997, which has since convened more than 45 times.[48]

Regional Economic Arrangements

An evolving trend in international economic activity is the formation of multinational trading blocs. These blocs take the form of a group of countries (usually contiguous) that decide to have common trading policies for the rest of the world in terms of tariffs and market access but have preferential treatment for one another. Organizational form varies among market regions, but the universal reason for the formation of such groups is to ensure the economic growth and benefit of the participating countries. Regional cooperative agreements have proliferated after the end of World War II. There are already more than 120 regional free trade areas worldwide. Arguably, among the best known ones existing today are the European Union and the North American Free Trade Agreement. Some of the other major ones include the MERCOSUR (Southern Common Market) and the Andean Group in South America, the Association of South East Asian Nations (ASEAN), the Gulf Cooperation Council in the Arabian Gulf region (GCC), and the South Asian Agreement for Regional Cooperation in South Asia (SAARC), among others. The existence and growing influence of these multinational groupings implies that nations need to become part of such groups to remain globally competitive. To an extent, the regional groupings reflect the countervailing force to the increasing integration of the global economy—it is an effort by governments to control the pace of the integration.

Market groups take many forms, depending on the degree of cooperation and inter-relationships, which lead to different levels of integration among the participating countries. There are five levels of formal cooperation among member countries of these regional groupings, ranging from free trade areas to the ultimate level of integration—which is political union.

Before the formation of a regional group of nations for freer trade, some governments agree to participate jointly in projects that create economic infrastructure (such as dams, pipelines, roads) and that decrease the levels of barriers from a level of little or no trade to substantial trade. Each country may make a commitment to financing part of the project, such as India and Nepal did for a hydroelectric dam on the Gandak River. Alternatively, they may share expertise on rural development and poverty alleviation programs, or may lower trade barriers in selected goods such as in SAARC, which comprises India, Pakistan, Sri Lanka, Bangladesh, Nepal, the Maldives, and Bhutan. This type of loose cooperation is considered a precursor to a more formal trade agreement.

Free Trade Area

A **Free Trade Area** has a higher level of integration than a loosely formed regional cooperation and is a formal agreement among two or more countries to reduce or eliminate customs duties and non-tariff trade barriers among partner countries. However, member countries are free to maintain individual tariff schedules for countries that do not belong to the free trade group. One

---

[48]United Nations Commission on International Trade Law, http://www.uncitral.org/uncitral/en/commission/working_groups/4Electronic_Commerce.html, accessed April 30, 2012.

fundamental problem with this arrangement is that a free trade area can be circumvented by nonmember countries that can export to the nation having the lowest external tariff in a free trade area, and then transport the goods to the destination country in the free trade area without paying the higher tariff applicable if it had gone directly to the destination country. In order to stem foreign companies from benefiting from this tariff-avoiding method of exporting, *local content laws* are usually introduced. Local content laws require that in order for a product to be considered "domestic," thus not subject to import duties, a certain percentage or more of the value of the product should be sourced locally within the free trade area. Thus, local content laws are designed to encourage foreign exporters to set up their manufacturing locations in the free trade area.

The North American Free Trade Agreement (NAFTA) is the free trade agreement among Canada, the United States, and Mexico. It provides for the elimination of all tariffs on industrial products traded between Canada, Mexico, and the United States within a period of 10 years from the date of implementation of the NAFTA agreement—January 1, 1994. NAFTA was preceded by the free trade agreement between Canada and the United States, which went into effect in 1989. The United States has a free trade area agreement with Israel as well. Canada signed a trade deal with the Andean Group in 1999 as a forerunner to a possible free trade agreement.[49] Mexico also established a formal trans-Atlantic free trade area agreement with the European Union without U.S. involvement in 2000,[50] and with Japan in 2005.[51] On the other hand, the United States reached a free trade agreement with Chile on December 11, 2002,[52] formed the Central American–Dominican Republic Free Trade Agreement (CAFTA–DR) with Costa Rica, the Dominican Republic, El Salvador, Guatemala, Honduras, and Nicaragua, effective on January 1, 2006,[53] and concluded another free trade agreement with Colombia on February 27, 2006.[54] Most recently, the United States also reached and officially signed a free trade agreement with South Korea, Panama, and Colombia on October 21, 2011, cited as "the biggest package" in almost two decades.[55]

Another free trade group is the European Free Trade Association (EFTA) comprising Iceland, Liechtenstein, Norway, and Switzerland. Although Austria, Finland, and Sweden used to be EFTA member countries, they have joined the European Union (EU) and Switzerland has been negotiating with the EU to become a member.[56] It appears that some, if not all, of the remaining EFTA members may gradually merge into the European Union (which we discuss later). In the meantime, the EFTA states currently have 24 free trade agreements (covering 33 countries), in addition to the 27 members states of the European Union. At the time of this writing in mid- 2012, EFTA states are engaged in negotiations on free trade agreements with Algeria, Bosnia and Herzegovina, Central American States, India, Indonesia, Russia, Belarus, Kazakhstan, and Thailand.[57] MERCOSUR is a free trade area consisting of Brazil, Argentina, Uruguay, and Paraguay with Chile, Bolivia, Peru, and Venezuela as associate members,[58] with the intention to lower internal trade barriers and the ultimate goal of the creation of a customs union.[59]

---

[49]"Canadian Companies Get Andean Boost," *World Trade*, 12 (September 1999), p. 14.

[50]"Mexico Turns To Europe," *Europe*, July–August 2001, pp. 18–19.

[51]Joseph P. Whitlock, "US Has Stake in Japan-Mexico FTA," *Journal of Commerce*, 6 (23), June 6, 2005, pp. 34–34.

[52]"U.S. and Chile Reach Free Trade Accord," *New York Times*, http://www.nytimes.com, December 11, 2002.

[53]"CAFTA-DR to Build Options over Time," *Marketing News*, February 1, 2006, pp. 13–14.

[54]"United States and Colombia Conclude Free Trade Agreement," U.S. Department of State, http://www.state.gov/p/wha/rls/62197.htm, accessed August 20, 2008.

[55]"Obama Signs Trade Deals With South Korea, Panama, Colombia," *Bloomberg News*, October 21, 2011.

[56]Sieglinde Gstöhl, "Scandinavia and Switzerland: Small, Successful and Stubborn towards the EU," Journal of European Public Policy, 9 (August 2002), pp. 529–549.

[57]Official Site for EFTA, http://www.efta.int/free-trade/free-trade-agreements.aspx.

[58]At the time of this writing in July 2012, Venezuela's entry as a full member is still pending ratification by Brazil and Paraguay.

[59]Maria Cecilia Coutinho de Arruda and Masaaki Kotabe, "MERCOSUR: An Emergent Market in South America," in Masaaki Kotabe, *MERCOSUR and Beyond: The Imminent Emergence of the South American Markets* (Austin, TX: The University of Texas at Austin, 1997).

One of the most ambitious free trade area plans ever initiated by the United States is the Free Trade Area of the Americas (FTAA). It was proposed in December 1994, by 34 countries in the region as an effort to unite the economies of the Western Hemisphere into a single free trade agreement. However, because of various political oppositions and reluctance from some major countries, such as Brazil and Venezuela, the negotiations for the agreement were stalled at the Fourth Summit of the Americas on November 4–5, 2005.[60] If completed, however, the FTAA agreement would encompass an area from the Yukon to Tierra del Fuego with over 900 million people and well over $20 trillion in combined GDP, making it the most significant regional trade initiative pursued by the United States. Regional cooperative agreements in the 1990s such as NAFTA and MERCOSUR have made trading within the continent much easier, but the South America markets are still less open than those of East Asia.

Japan had not been keen on regional free trade area agreements as it preferred a broader multilateral free trade regime as espoused by WTO. However, under pressure from an increasing number of successful regional trade agreements, Japan has also decided to join the fray, aiming to offset the economic challenges posed by the EU and the NAFTA zones by having formed a free trade agreement with Singapore, recently another with Mexico,[61] and having resumed free trade area talks with the ASEAN. Immediately after the collapse of the Doha Round of multilateral trade negotiations in late July 2008, India also reached a free trade agreement with the ASEAN. The ASEAN also announced another regional free trade deal with Australia and New Zealand.[62] On January 1, 2010, the world's largest free trade area in terms of population came into effect: the agreement between the ASEAN and China, which covers around 2 billion people. This agreement is the third-largest agreement after the EU and NAFTA, from an economic value standpoint.[63] Such regional free trade agreements are clearly on the rise (see **Global Perspective 2-3** on the push for free trade areas in Asia).

Global Perspective 2-3

Free Trade Areas in Asia

The global trend of forming strategic trade blocs is accelerating, given the success of the EU and NAFTA. The United States, with NAFTA already under its belt, is now creating a trans-Pacific trade area. Because the United States and European countries now have entered the final stages of creating huge economic zones, Japan has figured that it is time to catch up.

In January 2002, the Japanese government, having criticized and opposed free trade areas (FTAs) for years, had its first-ever free trade agreement with Singapore. Now it is part of a much larger free trade area initiative led by the ASEAN, referred to as a Regional Comprehensive Economic Partnership (RCEP), covering the 10 ASEAN members plus China, Japan, South Korea, India, Australia, and New Zealand. The RCEP is designed to liberalize trade in goods, services, and investments in the region, with $19 trillion in combined GDP and a population of 3.4 billion. The trade representatives from these countries hope to complete negotiations of the 16-country free-trade pact by 2015, when the envisioned pan-Asian economic community is scheduled to be fully implemented.

The proposed pan-Asian free trade agreement is seen as ASEAN's response to the U.S.-led Trans-Pacific Partnership

---

[60]"Hemisphere Meeting Ends without Trade Consensus," New York Times, November 6, 2005.

[61]Joseph P. Whitlock, "US Has Stake in Japan-Mexico FTA," *Journal of Commerce*, 6 (23), June 6, 2005, p. 34.

[62]"Regional Trade Agreements: A Second-Best Choice," *Economist,* September 6, 2008, p. 16.

[63]"Ajar for Business: More Breadth than Depth," *Economist*, January 7, 2010, http://www.economist.com/node/15211682.

(TPP) trade agreement that would group 11 trading partners in the Asia-Pacific region, including Brunei, Chile, Singapore, New Zealand, the United States, Australia, Peru, Vietnam, Malaysia, Mexico, and Canada. Parallel to this ASEAN-led free-trade initiative, Japan, China, and South Korea have also agreed to start negotiations for a trilateral free trade area.

Although it is a complex web of regional free trade negotiations, these initiatives will eventually lead toward the possibility of streamlining rules on customs procedures and tax systems, which vary widely among Asian countries, and consider ways to use capital in the private sector more effectively. The proposal is aimed at facilitating economic integration in the Asia-Pacific region to build the foundations for the region's role as a global growth hub.

Sources: Yoshikuni Sugiyama, "Economic Forum—Japan Does About-Face on Asia FTAs," *Yomiuri Shimbun*, September 11, 2001; "East Asian Free Trade Area: Bank on It," East Asia Forum, December 11, 2011, http://www.eastasiaforum.org/; and "Ministers of ASEAN, 6 Regional Partners Agree to Start FTA Talks," Nikkei.com, August 30, 2012.

Customs Union

The inherent weakness of the free trade area concept may lead to its gradual disappearance in the future, though it may continue to be an attractive stepping-stone to a higher level of integration. When members of a free trade area add common external tariffs to the provisions of the free trade agreement then the free trade area becomes a **customs union**.

Therefore, members of a customs union not only have reduced or eliminated tariffs among themselves, but they also have a common external tariff to countries that are not members of the customs union. This prevents nonmember countries from exporting to member countries that have low external tariffs with the goal of sending the exports to a country that has a higher external tariff through the first country that has a low external tariff. The ASEAN (Brunei, Cambodia, Indonesia, Laos, Malaysia, Myanmar, the Philippines, Singapore, Thailand, and Vietnam) is a good example of a currently functional customs union with the goal of a common market. The Treaty of Rome of 1958, which formed the European Economic Community, created a customs union between West Germany, France, Italy, Belgium, Netherlands, and Luxembourg.

Common Market

As cooperation increases among the countries of a customs union, they can form a **common market**. A common market eliminates all tariffs and other barriers to trade among members of the common market, adopts a common set of external tariffs on nonmembers, and removes all restrictions on the flow of capital and labor among member nations. The 1958 Treaty of Rome that created the European Economic Community had the ultimate goal of the creation of a common market—a goal that was substantially achieved by the early 1990s in Western Europe.

The **Maastricht Treaty**, which succeeded the Treaty of Rome, entered into force on November 1, 1993, calling for the creation of a union (and hence the change in name to European Union). At a historic summit on December 13, 2002, the EU agreed to add 10 new member countries, creating the 25-member **European Union** effective on May 1, 2004, with a total economy larger than that of the United States.[64] In 2007, two countries, Bulgaria and Romania, became new additional members of the EU, expanding the total number of EU members to 27.[65] Those new members are mostly Eastern and Central European countries once part of the Soviet empire. Now German banks can freely open branches in Poland, and Portuguese workers can live and work in Luxembourg.

---

[64]As of the beginning of 2006, the European Union consists of 25 countries including Austria, Belgium, Cyprus, the Czech Republic, Denmark, Estonia, Finland, France, Germany, Greece, Hungary, Ireland, Italy, Latvia, Lithuania, Luxembourg, Malta, Poland, Portugal, Slovakia, Slovenia, Spain, Sweden, the Netherlands, and the United Kingdom.
[65]http://europa.eu/index_en.htm, accessed on March 1, 2009.

Monetary Union

The Maastricht Treaty also laid down rules for, and accomplished, the creation of a **monetary union** with the introduction of the euro—a new European currency—in January 1999, which began its circulation in January 2002. As per the Maastricht Treaty, seventeen of the EU's member countries have adopted the euro so far, with Estonia being the last one to adopt in 2011.[66] The United Kingdom, Denmark, and Sweden have not accepted the third stage, and the three EU members still use their own currency today. A monetary union represents the fourth level of integration with a single common currency among politically independent countries. In strict technical terms, a monetary union does not require the existence of a common market or a customs union, a free trade area, or a regional cooperation for development. However, it is the logical next step to a common market, because it requires the next-higher level of cooperation among member nations.

Political Union

The culmination of the process of integration is the creation of a **political union**, in other words, a nation. The ultimate stated goal of the Maastricht Treaty is a political union with the adoption of a constitution for an enlarged European Union. However, the member countries have varying levels of concern about ceding any part of their sovereignty to any envisaged political union. In 2005, France and the Netherlands shocked the whole of Europe by voting against the EU constitution by a decisive margin. According to the analysts, the rejections by the Dutch and French are a terrible blow to the morale of true believers in political union in the EU. In order for the constitution to come into force, all members of EU must ratify it. Because France has always been politically central to the EU, as one of the six founders and one of the twelve members that have joined the European currency, it is extremely difficult for the EU to handle the divided opinion. Previously some political leaders had urged voters to approve the constitution to make Europe more efficient, dynamic, and democratic. However, the French consider the constitution as a means for the EU members to impose "Anglo-Saxon" free market policies on them. They voted against the constitution to protect their jobs, employment rights, and social benefits from low-cost, low-tax, deregulated countries.[67]

Multinational Corporations

Although no steadfast definition of **multinational corporations** (MNCs) exists, the U.S. government defines the multinational company for statistical purposes as a company that owns or controls 10 percent or more of the voting securities, or the equivalent, of at least 1 foreign business enterprise. Many large multinationals have many subsidiaries and affiliates in many parts of the world. As shown in **Exhibit 2-8**, the outward FDI stock reached $21.2 trillion in 2011—a little more than a tenfold increase since 1990 ($2 trillion). Outward FDI stock has shown a steady growth since the 1990s. After plunging in 2009, sales of foreign affiliates rebounded in 2010 and continued to grow in 2011 with sales rising by 9 percent, hitting a record $28 trillion. Employment by foreign affiliates also continued to expand from 21 million people in 1990 to an average of 52 million people in 2005–2007, to 69 million people in 2011.

Although FDI stock in manufacturing had experienced a consecutive decline over 15 years since 1990, world inflow FDI stock in services had climbed from 49 percent of the region's total

---

[66]As of March 2012, the euro member countries are Belgium, Germany, Ireland, Spain, France, Italy, Luxembourg, the Netherlands, Austria, Portugal, Finland, Greece, Slovenia, Cyprus, Malta, Slovakia, and Estonia.

[67]"Dead, but Not Yet Buried," *Economist*, June 4, 2005, pp. 47–48.

Exhibit 2-8 Selected Indicators of Foreign Direct Investment and International Production, 1990–2011

Item	1990	2005–2007 pre-crisis average	2009	2010	2011
FDI inflows	207	1 473	1 198	1 309	1 524
FDI outflows	241	1 501	1 175	1 451	1 694
FDI inward stock	2 081	14 588	18 041	19 907	20 438
FDI outward stock	2 093	15 812	19 326	20 865	21 168
Income on inward FDI	75	1 020	960	1 178	1 359
Rate of return on inward FDI	*4.2*	*7.3*	*5.6*	*6.3*	*7.1*
Income on outward FDI	122	1 100	1 049	1 278	1 470
Rate of return on outward FDI	*6.1*	*7.2*	*5.6*	*6.4*	*7.3*
Cross-border M&As	99	703	250	344	526
Sales of foreign affiliates	5 102	20 656	23 866	25 622	27 877
Value added (product) of foreign affiliates	1 018	4 949	6 392	6 560	7 183
Total assets of foreign affiliates	4 599	43 623	74 910	75 609	82 131
Exports of foreign affiliates	1 498	5 003	5 060	6 267	7 358
Employment by foreign affiliates (thousands)	21 458	51 593	59 877	63 903	69 065
Memorandum:					
GDP	22 206	50 411	57 920	63 075	69 660
Gross fixed capital formation	5 109	11 208	12 735	13 940	15 770
Royalties and licence fee receipts	29	156	200	218	242
Exports of goods and non-factor services	4 382	15 008	15 196	18 821	22 095

Source: World Investment Report 2012, UNCTAD, http://www.unctad.org/, accessed January 25, 2013.

inward stock in 1990 to 62 percent in 2005, with an estimated value of $6 trillion. During the same period, world inflow FDI stock in manufacturing fell from 41 percent to 30 percent. Outward FDI in services continues to be dominated by developed countries, although FDI is more evenly distributed among them than before. By 2002, Japan and the European Union had emerged as significant sources of outward FDI in service sectors. Developing countries' outward FDI in services has also grown gradually since the 1990s.[68] Although not shown in Exhibit 2-8, all three sectors of production (primary, manufacturing, and services) experienced rises in FDI flows in 2011. After falling sharply in 2009 and 2010, service-sector FDI rebounded in 2011 to reach some $570 billion. Primary sector investment also rebounded from the negative trend of the previous two years at $200 billion. The share of both sectors rose slightly at the expense of manufacturing.[69]

The forces of economies of scale, lowering trade and investment barriers, the need to be close to markets, internalization of operations within the boundaries of one firm, and the diffusion of technology will continue to increase multinationals' influence in international trade and investment. The sovereignty of nations will perhaps continue to weaken due to multinationals and the increasing integration of economies. Some developing countries harbor negative feelings about the sense of domination by large multinationals, but the threat to sovereignty may not assume the proportions alluded to by some researchers.[70] Although

---

[68]World Investment Report 2008, http://www.unctad.org/, accessed March 1, 2009.

[69]World Investment Report 2012, http://www.unctad.org/, accessed December 1, 2012.

[70]Raymond Vernon, *Sovereignty At Bay,* New York: Basic Books, 1971.

established multinationals' sheer size may appear hegemonic and have some monopolistic power in smaller economies, they have yet to solve the problem associated with their large size. Current trends indicate that beyond a certain size firms tend to become complacent and slow, and they falter against competition. They are no longer able to remain focused on their businesses and lack the drive, motivation, and can-do attitude that permeates smaller firms. Those firms that do focus on their core businesses shed unrelated businesses as the latter tend to be less profitable or even to incur losses.[71] For example, Novartis, the Swiss pharmaceutical group, recently sold off its Swedish Wasa biscuits and crackers subsidiary to the Italian food company, Barilla, in order to concentrate on its health science products.[72] Thus, the nation-state, while considerably weaker than its nineteenth century counterpart, is likely to remain alive and well.

Currency movements, capital surpluses, faster growth rates, and falling trade and investment barriers have all helped multinationals from many countries join the cross-border fray. In today's world it is not unusual for a startup firm to become global at its inception. Those firms are known as "born global."[73] It is now easier than ever for small firms to be in international business through exports and imports and through electronic commerce (e-commerce). A major survey of companies with fewer than 500 employees by Arthur Andersen & Co. and National Small Business United, a trade group, found that exporters averaged $3.1 million in revenue, compared with $2.1 million for all companies in the survey in 1996, and also reported that exporters' profits increased 4.4 percent while the overall average was 2.6 percent. Exporters are also more technology-savvy: 92 percent have computers (vs. 79 percent overall) and 70 percent use the internet (vs. 44 percent overall).[74]

SUMMARY

The severe global recession since late 2008 has slowed down the world economy. Nevertheless, the world economy is increasingly intertwined, and virtually no country is immune from the economic events in the rest of the world. It is almost as if participation in the international economy is a *sine qua non* of economic growth and prosperity—a country has to participate in the world economy in order to grow and prosper—but participation is not without its risks. Events outside one country can have detrimental effects on the economic health of that country. The Asian financial crisis that started in 1997 with a precipitous depreciation of Thailand's baht, Indonesia's rupiah, Malaysia's ringgit, and Korea's won, among others, is an example of a situation where withdrawal of funds by portfolio investors caused a severe economic crisis. In effect, participating in the international economy imposes its own discipline on a nation, independent of the policies of the government of that nation. This is not to suggest that countries should stay outside the international economic system because of the risks. Those countries that have elected to stay outside the international economic system—autarkies like Burma and North Korea—continue to fall farther behind the rest of the world in terms of living standards and prosperity.

Various forces are responsible for this increased integration. Major emerging economies have begun to reshape the nature of international trade and investment. Growth in international trade continuously outpaces the rise in national outputs. The nature of value-adding activities is changing in the advanced countries from manufacturing to services and information manipulation. Such changes are a result of and force behind the rapid advancement in telecommunications and computers. Even developing nations, regardless of their political colors, have realized the importance of telecommunications and e-commerce, and are attempting to improve their infrastructure. The capital markets of the world are already integrated for all practical purposes, and this integration affects exchange rates, interest rates, investments, employment, and growth across the world. Multinational corporations have truly become the global operations in name and spirit that they were envisaged to be. Even smaller companies are leapfrogging the gradual expansion pattern of traditional multinational companies by adopting e-commerce that has no national boundaries. In short, to repeat an old maxim, the world is becoming a global village.

---

[71]John A. Doukas and L.H.P. Lang, "Foreign Direct Investment, Diversification and Firm Performance," *Journal* of *International Business Studies*, 34 (March 2003), pp. 153–172.

[72]Paul Betts, "Barilla Pays SFr475m for Wasa Biscuits," *Financial Times* (April 27, 1999), p.33.

[73]Alex Rialp, Josep Rialp, Gary A. Knight, "The Phenomenon of Early Internationalizing Firms: What do We Know after a Decade (1993–2003) of Scientific Inquiry?" *International Business Review*, 14 (April 2005), pp. 147–166.

[74]"Export Energy," *Business Week*, November 17, 1997.

QUESTIONS

1. What is GATT, and what is its role in international transactions?

2. In what ways have U.S. foreign direct investment and trade patterns changed over the past decade?

3. Do current measures of balance of payments accurately reflect a country's transactions with the rest of the world? What are the concerns?

4. What are some of the forces influencing the increase in size of multinational corporations? Are there any forces that are influencing them to downsize?

5. A justification of developing countries against product patents for pharmaceutical products has been that if they were enforced, life-saving drugs would be out of reach for all but the very rich. A similar argument is being used in a populist move in the U.S senate for reducing the patent lives of innovative drugs, in a bid to reduce health care costs. Some senators and the pharmaceutical industry leaders claim that this move would discourage medical innovation and slow down the development of drugs for the cure of such diseases as AIDS and cancer, and thereby increase the costs of taking care of current and future patients. How would you react to the arguments and counterarguments for reducing patent lives, and what would be your stance on this issue? In your opinion, what would be the international repercussions if this bill were to pass? How do you think other developed and developing countries would react?

6. Information technology is having significant effects on the globalization activities of corporations. Texas Instruments is now developing sophisticated chips in India. Motorola has set up programming and equipment design centers in China, India, Singapore, Hong Kong, Taiwan, and Australia. Similarly, a large number of U.S. and European corporations are looking at ways to transfer activities such as preparing tax returns, account statements, insurance claims, and other information processing work to Asia. Although until now it was only blue-collar employees in the industrialized countries who faced the threat of competition from low-wage countries (which could be countered to some extent through direct and indirect trade barriers), this new trend in movement of white-collar tasks may be a cause for concern to industrialized countries, as the sophistication of these tasks increases. This movement of white-collar jobs could be a cause for social concern in the near future. Do you foresee social pressures in developed countries having the potential to reverse the trend of movement of white-collar tasks to developing countries? Given the intangibility of information, are there any effective ways of controlling the movement of information across borders?

7. Electronic commerce (e-commerce) blurs the distinction between a good and a service. Under the WTO, goods tend to be subject to tariffs—services are not—but trade in services is limited by restrictions on "national treatment" or quantitative controls on access to foreign markets. For example, a compact disc sent from one country to another is clearly a good, and will be subject to an import tariff as it crosses the national border. But if the music on the disc is sent electronically from a computer in one country to another on the internet, will it be a good or a service? Customized data and software, which can be put on CD, are usually treated as services. What kind of confusion would you expect with the WTO overseeing increased transactions on the internet?

3 FINANCIAL ENVIRONMENT

CHAPTER OVERVIEW

1. Historical role of the U.S. dollar

2. Development of today's international monetary system

3. Foreign exchange and foreign exchange rates

4. Balance of payments

5. Economic and financial turmoil around the world

6. Marketing in the euro area

When international transactions occur, foreign exchange is the monetary mechanism allowing for the transfer of funds from one nation to another. The existing international monetary system always affects companies as well as individuals whenever they buy or sell products and services traded across national boundaries. For example, due to the stronger yen compared to the U.S. dollar in early 2008, Japanese multinational corporations, such as Toyota, reported a reduction in their profits as these companies' overseas businesses in the United States collect sales in U.S. dollars but report profit in Japanese yen. Every 1 yen increase in the Japanese currency relative to the U.S. dollar is expected to trim Toyota's operating profit by around 35 billion yen (which would amount to a whopping $350 million at 105 yen/$).[1] It is obvious that the current international monetary system has a profound impact not only on individuals and companies but also on the U.S. balance of payments at the aggregate level.

This chapter examines international trade in monetary terms. In fact, the international monetary system has changed rather drastically over the years. Given the drastic realignment in recent years of the exchange rates of major currencies, including the U.S. dollar, the European **euro**, and the Japanese yen, the current international monetary system may well be in for a major change. The adoption of the euro as a common currency in the European Union in 1999 is just one example of the many changes to come. Although international marketers have to operate in a currently existing international monetary system for international transactions and settlements, they should understand how the scope and nature of the system has changed and how it has worked over time. Forward-looking international marketers need to be aware of the dynamics of the international monetary system.

---

[1]"The Yen Also Rises," *Economist*, May 19, 2008.

Since the last decade—particularly, the second half of the last decade—of the twentieth century, the global financial market has been anything but stable. Indeed, this time period has proven to be one of the most turbulent periods in recent history. The seemingly unstoppable rapid economic growth of Asia came to a screeching halt in 1997, and the introduction of the euro in the European Union in 1999 has drastically changed the European economic environment. The beginning of the twenty-first century has not been smooth, either. As described in Chapter 2, the financial crisis in South America and the slump in the U.S. and European economies since 2001 have also made us aware of how vulnerable the global economy can be. The worst of such vulnerability manifested itself again in an unprecedented global recession triggered by the U.S. subprime mortgage loan-led credit crisis that has quickly spread around the world since late 2008. These events profoundly affect international marketing practices. We are convinced that these epoch-making events need your special attention and that your understanding of them will allow you to become seasoned marketing decision-makers in crucial areas such as product development, brand management, and pricing, among others, when developing marketing strategy on a global basis. It is another way to tell you that you have to be up-to-the-minute with ever-changing events that could affect your understanding of the class material, let alone your future career. In this chapter, we also provide a special detailed examination of the implications of the Asian and South American financial crises and marketing in the Euro Area.

Historical Role of the U.S. Dollar

Each country also has its own currency through which it expresses the value of its products. An international monetary system is necessary because the vast majority of countries have their own monetary unit or currency that serves as a medium of exchange and store of value. The absence of a universal currency means that we must have a system that allows for the transfer of purchasing power between countries with different national currencies. For international trade settlements, the various currencies of the world must be exchanged from one to another. This is accomplished through foreign exchange markets.

Periodically, a country must review the status of its economic relations with the rest of the world in terms of its exports and imports, its exchange of various kinds of services, and its purchase and sale of different types of capital assets and other international payments, receipts and transfers. In the post–World War II period, a number of institutions came into existence to monitor and assist countries as necessary in keeping their international financial commitments. As a result, a new system of international monetary relations emerged, which promoted increased international trade through the 1950s and 1960s. In the early 1970s, however, a weakening U.S. dollar caused the existing system to show strains and eventually break down.

The U.S. trade deficit has pushed the value of the U.S. dollar downward in the last 40 years. Since 1960, the dollar has fallen by approximately two-thirds against the euro (using Germany's currency as a proxy before 1999) and the Japanese yen.[2] Despite this long-term trend, the value of the dollar also fluctuates up and down significantly in the short and intermediate term, and it remains stronger than commonly expected. Whether a strong dollar is in the best interest of the United States or not is debatable, but a strong dollar certainly reflects global confidence in U.S. economic leadership. However, the dollar could become an overvalued currency and make the current account deficits unsustainably large. A sharp downward shift of dollar value could have an

---

[2]"The Passing of the Buck?" *Economist*, December 4, 2004. pp. 71–73.

enormous impact on the global economy. During the annual G8 Summit meetings in June 2002, one of the most urgent issues was whether enough had been done to cushion against a collapse of the dollar.[3]

For example, within two years after the euro's introduction in 1999, the dollar appreciated 20 percent against the euro. Although the U.S. dollar appreciated slightly against the euro between 2009 and 2011, the dollar has kept depreciating against the euro in the long run by as much as 60 percent because of the weak U.S. economy, uncertainty about the aftermath of a U.S.-led war in the Middle East, and rising oil prices.

The monetary stability of the world became unsettled beginning with the 1970s and continuing into the early 1980s. As the 1980s advanced, the U.S. economy stabilized, and the value of the dollar against other currencies climbed to an all-time high. This caused U.S. exports to become costlier, and foreign imports to become cheaper, resulting in an adverse trade balance. In the fall of 1985, leading industrialized countries joined the United States' effort to intervene in the foreign exchange markets to decrease the value of the dollar. The dollar had steadily fallen and remained weak since mid-1980s. However, the current severe global recession has demonstrated an unexpected aspect of the dollar: When the global economy is in an unprecedented level of turmoil as it has been since late 2008, the world still considers the U.S. dollar as a last-resort currency to hold on to. As a result, the dollar has since appreciated dramatically against most other foreign currencies but depreciated against the Japanese yen. For example, as of February 4, 2009, the U.S. dollar appreciated 15 percent against the euro, 39 percent against the Australian dollar, and a whopping 46 percent against the Korean won, and depreciated almost 20 percent against Japanese yen from a year earlier. Clearly, the currency market has been far from stable.

Development of Today's International Monetary System
The Bretton Woods Conference

Post–World War II developments had long-range effects on international financial arrangements, the role of gold, and the problems of adjustment of balance-of-payments disequilibria. Following World War II, there was a strong desire to adhere to goals that would bring economic prosperity and hopefully a long-term peace to the world. The negotiations to establish the postwar international monetary system took place at the resort of Bretton Woods in New Hampshire in 1944. The negotiators at Bretton Woods recommended the following:[4]

1. Each nation should be at liberty to use macroeconomic policies for full employment.

2. Free floating exchange rates could not work. Their ineffectiveness had been demonstrated in the interwar years. The extremes of both permanently fixed and floating rates should be avoided.

3. A monetary system was needed that would recognize that exchange rates were both a national and international concern.

In order to avoid both the rigidity of a **fixed exchange rate** system and the chaos of freely floating exchange rates, the **Bretton Woods Agreement** provided for an adjustable peg. Under this system, currencies were to establish par values in terms of gold, but there was to be little, if any, convertibility of the currencies for gold. Each government was responsible for monitoring its own currency to see that it did not float beyond 1 percent above or below its established par value.

---

[3]Jesper Koll, "Dangers of a Falling Dollar," *Wall Street Journal*, June 12, 2002.
[4]Carlo Cottarelli and Curzio Giannini, *Credibility without Rules? Monetary Framework in the Post-Bretton Woods Era*, Washington, D.C.: International Monetary Fund, 1997.

As a nation's currency attained or approached either limit, its central bank intervened in the world financial markets to prevent the rate from passing the limit.

Under this system, a country experiencing a balance-of-payments deficit would normally experience devaluation pressure on its current value. The country's authorities would defend its currency by using its foreign currency reserves, primarily U.S. dollars, to purchase its own currency on the open market to push its value back up to its par value. A country experiencing a balance-of-payments surplus would do the opposite and sell its currency on the open market. An institution called the **International Monetary Fund** (IMF) was established at Bretton Woods to oversee the newly agreed-upon monetary system. If a country experienced a fundamental or long-term disequilibrium in its balance of payments, it could alter its peg by up to 10 percent from its initial par value without approval from the International Monetary Fund. Adjustment beyond 10 percent required IMF approval.

In the 1960s, the United States began to experience sequential balance of payments deficits, resulting in downward pressure on the dollar. Because the U.S. government was obligated to maintain the dollar at its par value, it had to spend much of its gold and foreign currency reserves in order to purchase dollars on the world financial markets. In addition, the U.S. dollar was the reserve currency, convertible to gold under the Bretton Woods Agreement; the U.S. Treasury was obligated to convert dollars to gold upon demand by foreign central banks.

Furthermore, many central banks engaged in massive dollar purchases on the foreign exchange markets to counteract the downward pressure on the dollar and related upward pressure on their own currencies. The continued defense of the dollar left central banks around the world with massive quantities of dollars. These countries, knowing that the dollars they held were in fact convertible to gold with the U.S. Treasury, attempted to hold back, demanding gold in exchange. However, it became clear by 1971 that the dollar was quite overvalued, and devaluation of the dollar versus gold was inevitable. Central banks increasingly presented U.S. dollar balances to the U.S. Treasury for conversion to gold, and gold flowed out of the U.S. vaults at an alarming rate.

This situation led President Richard Nixon to suspend the convertibility of the dollar to gold on August 15, 1971. This effectively ended the exchange rate regime begun at Bretton Woods more than 25 years earlier.

The International Monetary Fund

The International Monetary Fund (IMF) oversees the international monetary system. The IMF was a specialized agency within the United Nations, established to promote international monetary cooperation and to facilitate the expansion of trade, and in turn to contribute to increased employment and improved economic conditions in all member countries.

Its purposes are defined in the following terms:[5]

> To promote international monetary cooperation through a permanent institution, providing the machinery for consultations and collaboration on international monetary problems.
>
> 1. To facilitate the expansion and balanced growth of international trade, and to contribute thereby to the promotion and maintenance of high levels of employment and real income, and to the development of the productive resources of all members as primary objectives of economic policy.
>
> 2. To promote exchange stability, to maintain orderly exchange arrangements among members, and to avoid competitive exchange depreciation.

---

[5]International Monetary Fund, *The Role and Function of the International Monetary Fund* (Washington, D.C.: International Monetary Fund, 1985).

3. To assist in the establishment of a multilateral system of payments in respect to current transactions between members and in the elimination of foreign exchange restrictions that hamper the growth of world trade.

4. To give confidence to members by making the general resources of the fund temporarily available to them under adequate safeguards, thus providing them with the opportunity to correct maladjustments in their balance of payments without resorting to measures destructive of national or international prosperity.

5. In accordance with the above, to shorten the duration and lessen the degree of disequilibrium in the international balance of payments to members.

Today the IMF has 188 members.[6] Its accomplishments include sustaining a rapidly increasing volume of trade and investment and displaying flexibility in adapting to changes in international commerce. To an extent, the IMF served as an international central bank to help countries during periods of temporary balance of payments difficulties, by protecting their rates of exchange. This helped countries avoid the placement of foreign exchange controls and other trade barriers.

As time passed, it became evident that the IMF's resources for providing short-term accommodation to countries in monetary difficulties were not sufficient. To resolve the situation, and to reduce upward pressure on the U.S. dollar by countries holding dollar reserves, the fund created special drawing rights in 1969. **Special drawing rights (SDRs)** are special account entries on the IMF books designed to provide additional liquidity to support growing world trade. The value of SDRs is determined by a weighted average of a basket of four currencies: the U.S. dollar, the Japanese yen, the European Union's euro, and the British pound. Although SDRs are a form of fiat money and not convertible to gold, their gold value is guaranteed, which helps to ensure their acceptability.

Participant nations may use SDRs as a source of currency in a spot transaction, as a loan for clearing a financial obligation, as security for a loan, as a swap against a currency, or in a forward exchange operation. A nation with a balance of payment problem may use its SDRs to obtain usable currency from another nation designated by the fund. By providing a mechanism for international monetary cooperation, working to reduce restrictions to trade and investment flows, and helping members with their short-term balance of payment difficulties, the IMF makes a significant and unique contribution to economic stability and improved living standards throughout the world.

In the wake of the 1997–1998 Asian financial crisis, the IMF worked on policies to overcome or even prevent future crises. After 1997, the external payments situation was stabilized through IMF-led aid programs, and financial packages were being geared to encourage the adoption of policies that could prevent crises in selected developing countries. Backed by an IMF quota increase of $90 billion, the IMF would make a contingent short-term line of credit available before a crisis broke out, but only if a country adopted certain policies that would limit its vulnerability. The line of credit is expected to be of short term and to charge interest rates above market rates to discourage misuse.[7] In September 2002, the IMF also approved $30 billion in emergency loans to Brazil battered by the financial crisis in Argentina. The announcement pushed various developing market currencies higher as investors welcomed both the vote of confidence in Brazil and the broader implications of the loan announcement for emerging market assets. Now as the global financial crisis has spread since late 2008, net capital inflows into emerging markets, which were $929 billion in 2007, fell to a meager $165 billion in 2009. Again, the IMF is channeling a massive amount of capital to those countries to stem any precipitous collapse not only of their economies

---

[6]International Monetary Fund Homepage, www.imf.org, accessed March 28, 2013.

[7]Suk H. Kim and Mahfuzul Haque, "The Asian Financial Crisis of 1997: Causes and Policy Response," *Multinational Business Review*, 10 (Spring 2002), pp. 37–44; and Ramon Moreno, "Dealing with Currency Crises," *FRBSF Economic Letter*, Number 99–11, April 2, 1999.

but also of the global trading regime itself.[8] These loans signal that there is still a commitment by international organizations to countries with major financial problems.

The International Bank for Reconstruction and Development

Another creation of the Bretton Woods Agreement was the International Bank for Reconstruction and Development, known as the **World Bank**. Although the International Monetary Fund was created to aid countries in financing their balance of payment difficulties and maintaining a relatively stable currency, the World Bank was initially intended for the financing of postwar reconstruction and development, and later for infrastructure building projects in the developing world. More recently, the World Bank has participated actively with the IMF to resolve debt problems of the developing world, and it has also played a major role in bringing a market economy to the former members of the Eastern bloc. Each year the World Bank lends US$15–20 billion to developing country governments to support projects for economic development and poverty reduction. The World Bank is the largest external fund provider for education and HIV/AIDS programs, strongly supports debt relief, and is responding to the voices of poor people. The organization greatly supports developing country governments to build schools and health centers, provide water and electricity, fight disease, and protect the environment.[9]

Fixed versus Floating Exchange Rates

Since the 1970s all major nations have had floating currencies. An IMF meeting in Jamaica in 1976 reached consensus on amendments to the IMF Articles of Agreement that accepted floating rates as the basis for the international monetary system. The amended agreement recognized that real rate stability can only be achieved through stability in underlying economic and financial conditions. Exchange rate stability cannot be imposed by the adoption of pegged exchange rates and official intervention in the foreign exchange markets.

There are two kinds of currency floats, and these are referred to as free or managed or as clean or dirty. The **free (clean) float** is the closest approximation to perfect competition, because there is no government intervention and because billions of units of currency are being traded by buyers and sellers. Buyers and sellers may change sides on short notice as information, rumors, or moods change, or as their clients' needs differ.

A **managed float** allows for a limited amount of government intervention to soften sudden swings in the value of a currency. If a nation's currency enters into a rapid ascent or decline, that nation's central bank may wish to sell or buy that currency on the open market in a countervailing movement to offset the prevailing market tendency. This is for the purpose of maintaining an orderly, less-volatile foreign exchange market.

In March 1973, the major currencies began to float in the foreign exchange markets. Advocates for the floating exchange regime argued that it would end balance of payments disequilibria because the value of each currency would float up or down to a point where supply equaled demand. It has not worked that way, at least in part due to the reluctance of governments to permit extreme changes in the value of their currencies. Governments have intervened in the currency markets to moderate or prevent value changes. In reality, however, the supposed benefits of floating exchange rates have not been borne to date. For example, floating exchange rates were supposed to facilitate balance of payments adjustments. However, not only have imbalances not

---

[8]"Supersizing the Fund," *Economist*, February 5, 2009; also see "2008–2009 Global Financial Crisis" at http://wtfaculty. wtamu.edu/~sanwar.bus/otherlinks.htm#GlobalFinCrisis, an excellent website maintained by Professor Syed Anwar of West Texas A&M University.

[9]The World Bank, http://www.worldbank.org/, accessed December 20, 2005.

disappeared, they have become worse, as attested to by the recent Asian and Latin American financial crises.

1. Currency speculation was expected to be curtailed. But speculation has since been greater than ever. Similarly, short-term speculations worsened the Asian and Latin financial crises.

2. Market forces, left to their own devices, were expected to determine the correct foreign exchange rate balance. But imbalances have become greater than ever, as have fluctuations in rates.

3. Autonomy in economic and monetary policy was hoped to be preserved, allowing each country free choice of its monetary policy and rate of inflation. But this has also not materialized.

As a result, international marketers have had to cope with the ever-fluctuating exchange rates (see **Exhibit 3-1**). Refer back to the enormous change in Toyota's operating profits as a result of a small change in the yen/dollar exchange rate illustrated in the opening paragraph of this chapter. Even a small fluctuation in exchange rates cannot be ignored, since it has an enormous impact on a company's operating profit.

Currency Blocs

Although currencies of most countries float in value against one another, those of many developing countries are pegged (or fixed) to one of the major currencies or to a basket of major currencies such as the U.S. dollar, Special Drawing Rights, or some specially chosen currency mix. In general, developing countries that depend on their trading relationships with a major country, such as the United States, for economic growth tend to use the currency of the principal country.

For example, the Chinese currency, renminbi (yuan), had been pegged to the U.S. dollar for a decade at 8.28 yuan to the dollar. Based on its growing trade surplus with the United States as well as its sustained real GDP growth in the past 20 years of 9.5 percent, China has been accused of pursuing a cheap-yuan policy and has been pressured to revalue its currency. In the past, in order to prevent the yuan from rising against the dollar, the Chinese central bank had to buy huge amounts of U.S. Treasury securities. The Chinese government believed that the fixed exchange rate would provide stability to the Chinese economy as it relied so much on trade with the United States. However, as the dollar continued to fall against other key currencies, the Chinese central bank decided on July 21, 2005, to abandon the yuan's peg to the dollar in favor of a link to a basket of several currencies, including the euro and the yen, and revalued the yuan by 2.1 percent against the dollar. On September 23, 2005, the Chinese central bank further decided to let the yuan float against the major currencies by up to 3 percent a day against the euro, yen, and other non-dollar currencies, compared with 1.5 percent previously. Daily movements against the dollar, meanwhile, remained limited to only 0.3 percent.[10] On May 16, 2007, however, China again took steps to let its currency trade more freely against the dollar and to cool its sizzling economy and its soaring trade surplus.[11] The yuan is now allowed to fluctuate against the dollar by 0.5 percent a day, up from 0.3 percent. The renminbi exchange rate rose from 8.28 yuan/$ in July 2005 to 6.84 yuan/$ in February 2009, a jump of 21 percent in three years. In March 2012, the renminbi exchange rate rose again to 6.21 yuan/$.

Today, the global economy is increasingly dominated by three major **currency blocs**. The U.S. dollar, the EU's euro, and the Japanese yen each represent their "sphere of influence" on the currencies of other countries in their respective regions (i.e., North and South America, Europe,

---

[10]"Yuan Step at a Time," *Economist*, January 22, 2005, p. 74; and "Patching the Basket," *Economist*, October 1, 2005, p. 71.

[11]"China Eases Controls to Allow Yuan Float Freely against Dollar," *SeekingAlpha.com*, August 30, 2007.

Exhibit 3-1 Foreign Exchange Rate Fluctuations Over the Past 30+ Years (Foreign Currency Units/U.S. Dollar)

Year	Deutsche Mark	French Franc	Japanese Yen	Swiss Franc	British Pound
1980	1.96	4.55	203	1.76	0.42
–	–	–	–	–	–
1985	2.46	7.56	201	2.08	0.69
–	–	–	–	–	–
1990	1.49	5.13	134	1.30	0.52
1991	1.52	5.18	125	1.36	0.53
1992	1.61	5.51	125	1.46	0.66
1993	1.73	5.90	112	1.48	0.68
1994	1.55	5.35	100	1.31	0.64
1995	1.43	4.90	103	1.15	0.65
1996	1.50	5.12	94	1.24	0.64
1997	1.73	5.84	121	1.45	0.64
1998	1.82	6.10	139	1.53	0.60
1999	0.94 euro*		108	1.69	0.66
2000	1.08		108	1.69	0.66
2001	1.12		122	1.69	0.69
2002	1.06		125	1.55	0.67
2003	0.88		116	1.35	0.61
2004	0.80		108	1.24	0.55
2005	0.80		116	1.24	0.55
2006	0.79		113	1.24	0.54
2007	0.68		111	1.13	0.50
2008	0.72		91	1.07	0.62
2009	0.72		92	1.09	0.62
2010	0.78		91	1.08	0.67
2011	0.75		82	0.92	0.65
2012	0.78		80	0.94	0.63
2013**	0.75		99	0.92	0.64

* *Sources:* International Monetary Fund, *Balance of Payments Statistics Yearbook* (Washington, D.C.: U.S. Government Printing Office); and Internal Revenue Service, *Yearly Average Currency Rates.*
* The euro was introduced in 1999 and completely replaced the currencies of member countries in 2002.
** Exchange rate as of August 22, 2013.

and East Asia, respectively).[12] After its launch in 1999, the euro immediately became the world's second-leading international currency, although a recent financial crisis across a number of euro member countries casts some doubt about the stability, or even long-term viability, of the euro.[13] The U.S. dollar is still likely to remain the dominant international currency for the time being. However, the current financial crisis in the United States also seems to indicate that companies

---

[12]Michael H. Moffett, Arthur I. Stonehill, and David K. Eiteman, *Fundamentals of Multinational Finance*, 2nd ed., Reading, Mass.: Addison-Wesley, 2006.
[13]"Special Report: Europe and Its Currency," *Economist*, November 12, 2011, pp. 3–16.

based in countries with more stable currencies than the U.S. dollar, such as Japan, have seriously started to move away from the U.S. dollar as the international transaction currency.[14]

Although the U.S. dollar has lost some of its role as the international transaction currency, it remains the currency of choice that many Latin American companies use for operating purposes. The Japanese yen has increasingly become a regional transaction currency in Asia. In other words, U.S. companies will find it easier to do business with companies in Latin America as business planning and transactions are increasingly conducted in dollar denominations. On the other hand, those U.S. companies will increasingly have to accept yen-denominated business transactions in Asia and euro-denominated transactions in Europe, thus being susceptible to exchange rate fluctuations. Considering increased trade volumes with Asian and European countries as well as with Latin American countries, it has become all the more important for U.S. marketing executives to understand the dynamic forces that affect exchange rates and predict the exchange rate fluctuations as the changes in currency values affect costing and pricing, and even firms' product positioning strategy.

Foreign Exchange and Foreign Exchange Rates

Foreign exchange, as the term implies, refers to the exchange of one country's money for that of another country. When international transactions occur, foreign exchange is the monetary mechanism allowing the transfer of funds from one nation to another. In this section, we explore the factors that influence exchange rates over time and how these exchange rates are determined.

Purchasing Power Parity

One of the most fundamental determinants of the exchange rate is **purchasing power parity (PPP)**, whereby the exchange rate between the currencies of two countries makes the purchasing power of both currencies equal. In other words, the value of a currency is determined by what it can buy.

The following formula represents the relationship between inflation rates and the exchange rate, say, in the United States and Europe's eurozone:

$$R_t = R_0 * \frac{(1 + Infl_{euro})}{(1 + Infl_{US})}$$

where

R = the exchange rate quoted in euro/\$,

$Infl$ = inflation rate,

t = time period.

For example, if the inflation rate in the eurozone were 2 percent a year and U.S. inflation were 5 percent a year, the value of the dollar would be expected to decline by the difference of 3 percent, so that the real prices of goods in the two countries would remain fairly similar. If the current exchange rate (R_0) is 0.757 euro to the dollar (€ 0.757/\$), then

$$R_t = 0.757 * \frac{(1 + .02)}{(1 + .05)} = €0.735/\$.$$

[14]"Japan Firms Rethink Using Dollar as Settlement Currency," NikkeiNet Interactive, www.nni.nikkei.co.jp, October 9, 2008.

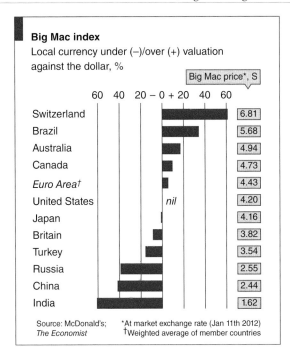

Big Mac index

Local currency under (−)/over (+) valuation against the dollar, %

Big Mac price*, S

		60 40 20 − 0 + 20 40 60	
Switzerland			6.81
Brazil			5.68
Australia			4.94
Canada			4.73
Euro Area†			4.43
United States	nil		4.20
Japan			4.16
Britain			3.82
Turkey			3.54
Russia			2.55
China			2.44
India			1.62

Source: McDonald's; The Economist
*At market exchange rate (Jan 11th 2012)
†Weighted average of member countries

Exhibit 3-2 The Big Mac Index

Source: "Big Mac Index," *Economist*, January 12, 2012. © The Economist Newspaper Ltd. All rights reserved. Reprinted with permission. www.economist.com.

In other words, the dollar is expected to depreciate from €0.757/$ to €0.735/$ in a year. The U.S. dollar will be able to buy slightly fewer euro. Or, stated in reverse, the euro will be able to buy slightly more U.S. dollars.

In fact, the *Economist* publishes a PPP study every year based on McDonald's Big Mac hamburger, sold all over the world. It is known as the Big Mac Index to show whether currencies are at their "correct" exchange rate. Look at the recent Big Mac Index to see how actual exchange rates "deviate" from the Big Mac Index (see **Exhibit 3-2**). The average price for a Big Mac was $4.20 in the United States in 2012, while in Switzerland, the same sandwich cost $6.80. According to the theory of purchasing power parity, this implies that the Swiss franc is 62 percent overvalued. The exchange rate that would equalize a Swiss Big Mac with an American Big Mac is SFr 1.55/US$1, whereas the actual exchange rate is 0.96. India serves as an example of the cheapest burger in the chart. Although Big Macs are not available in India, the Maharaja Mac that is made with chicken is used as a substitute. Using the Big Mac Index, the Indian rupee is 60 percent undervalued. In July 2011, the euro was 21 percent overvalued as compared to the 2012 index that shows a mere 6 percent overvaluation. Theoretically, over the long run, exchange rates tend to move in the direction of the PPP index. If the dollar is overvalued relative to a foreign currency (i.e., the foreign currency is undervalued relative to the dollar), people using that foreign currency will find it more expensive to buy goods from the United States. Conversely, people living in the United States will find it cheaper to import goods from a country with an undervalued currency.

Forecasting Exchange Rate Fluctuation

Actual exchange rates can be very different from the expected rates. Those deviations are not necessarily a random variation. As summarized in **Exhibit 3-3**, many interrelated factors influence the value of a floating currency. In particular, the nation's inflation rate relative to its trading partners, its balance of payments situation, and world political events are the three most fundamental factors.

Exhibit 3-3   Factors Influencing Foreign Exchange Rates

Macroeconomic Factors

1. **Relative Inflation:** A country suffering relatively higher inflation rates than other major trading partners will cause depreciation of its currency.
2. **Balance of Payments:** Improvement (deterioration) in the balance of payments for goods and services is an early sign of a currency appreciation (depreciation).
3. **Foreign Exchange Reserves:** A government may intervene in the foreign exchange markets to either push up or push down the value of its currency. The central bank can support (depreciate) the domestic currency by selling its foreign currency reserves to buy its own currency (selling its domestic currency to buy foreign currency).
4. **Economic Growth:** If the domestic economy is growing fast relative to major trading partners, the country's imports tend to rise faster than exports, resulting in deterioration of the trade balance and thus depreciation of its currency. However, if the domestic economic growth attracts a large amount of investment from abroad, it could offset the negative trade effect, thus potentially resulting in appreciation of the domestic currency.
5. **Government Spending:** An increase in government spending, particularly if financed through deficit spending, causes increased inflationary pressures on the economy. Inflation leads to domestic currency depreciation (as in 1).
6. **Money Supply Growth:** Many countries' central banks attempt to stave off recession by increasing the money supply to lower domestic interest rates for increased consumption and investment. An increase in money supply usually leads to higher inflation rates and subsequently currency depreciation.
7. **Interest Rate Policy:** As in 6, the central bank may also control its discount rate (interest rate charged to banks) to raise domestic lending rates so as to control inflation. Higher interest rates discourage economic activity and tend to reduce inflation and also attract investment from abroad. Reduced inflation and increased investment from abroad both lead to currency appreciation.

Political Factors

1. **Exchange Rate Control:** Some governments have an explicit control on the exchange rate. The official rate for domestic currency is artificially overvalued, thereby discouraging foreign companies from exporting to such a country. However, as long as there is a genuine domestic demand for imported products, the black market tends to appear for foreign currency. Black market exchange rates for a domestic currency tend to be much lower than the government-imposed artificial rate. Thus, a wide spread between the official exchange rate and the black market rate indicates potential pressures leading to domestic currency devaluation.
2. **Election Year or Leadership Change:** Expectations about imminent government policy change influence exchange rates. In general, pro-business government policy tends to lead to domestic currency appreciation as foreign companies are willing to accept that currency for business transactions.

Random Factors

Unexpected and/or unpredicted events in a country, such as assassination of political figures or a sudden stock market crash, can cause its currency to depreciate for fear of uncertainty. Similarly, events such as sudden discovery of huge oil reserves and gold mines tend to push up the currency value.

Source: Developed from a discussion in Chapter 3 of David K. Eiteman, Arthur I. Stonehill, and Michael H. Moffett, *Multinational Business Finance*, 9th ed., New York: Addison-Wesley, 2001.

Although accurately predicting the actual exchange rate fluctuations is not possible and it is not related directly to marketing executives' jobs, seasoned marketers can benefit from such knowledge. Exchange rate fluctuations have an enormous direct impact on the bottom line for the company—profitability.

Coping with Exchange Rate Fluctuations

When the fast-food operator KFC opens new restaurants in Mexico, for example, it often imports some of the kitchen equipment, including fryers, roasters, stainless steel counters, and other items for its stores from U.S. suppliers.

In order to pay for these imports, the Mexican subsidiary of KFC must purchase U.S. dollars with Mexican pesos through its bank in Mexico City. This is necessary because Mexican pesos are not a readily accepted form of currency in the United States. Most likely, KFC–Mexico will pay for the imported merchandise via a bank cashier's check from its local bank in Mexico City, denominated in U.S. dollars. If the exchange rate on the date of purchase is 10.19 Mexican pesos per U.S. dollar and their debt is $10,000 dollars, then KFC–Mexico must pay 101,900 pesos, plus a commission to the bank, for the dollars it sends to the U.S. supplier. The bank in Mexico acquires the dollars on the open foreign exchange market or through other banks for the purpose of satisfying the foreign exchange needs of its customers.

This is the case when currency is freely convertible with minimal government foreign exchange controls, as has been true in Mexico. However, this is not always the case. Governments have often limited the amount of domestic currency that can leave a country, in order to avoid capital flight and decapitalization. One example of this was South Africa in the 1980s, where it was illegal to buy foreign currency or take domestic currency out of the country without government approval. If a company in South Africa required foreign manufactured goods, it had to solicit authorization for the purchase of foreign exchange through the national treasury in order to make payment.

Even more rigid exchange controls existed in the former Soviet Union and other Eastern bloc countries prior to the fall of communism, where trade in foreign currency was a crime bringing harsh punishment. The problem with such tight exchange controls is that often they promote a black market in unauthorized trade in the controlled currency. In such cases, the official rate of exchange for a currency will tend to be overvalued, or in other words, possess an officially stated value that does not reflect its true worth. The black market will more likely reflect its true worth on the street.

Another issue affecting foreign exchange concerns fluctuation in the rates of exchange, whereby currencies either appreciate or depreciate with respect to one another. Since the 1970s most of the world's currencies have been on a floating system, often fluctuating with wide variations. For example, in 1976, the Mexican peso traded at an exchange rate of 12.5 per dollar, but in 1993 it had fallen to 3,200 pesos per dollar.

This peso depreciation reflected much greater inflation in Mexico compared to the United States, and the fear of political/financial instability in Mexico prompted Mexican residents to buy dollars for security. In 1993, the Mexican government dropped three zeroes off the currency, creating a new peso (nuevo peso) worth 3.2 pesos per dollar. This rate climbed again with the depreciation that began in December 1994 to the 12.76 pesos per dollar range by 2012. On the other hand, in the early 1980s, the Japanese yen traded at approximately 250 yen per dollar, but by 1996 had appreciated to 94 yen per dollar before losing value to 125 yen per dollar in 2002. Since then the Japanese yen has continued to appreciate against the U.S. dollar to 82 yen per dollar in 2012. This long-term depreciation of the dollar against the yen reflects continuing U.S. trade deficits with Japan, as well as an increasingly stagnant U.S. economy.

Many countries attempt to maintain a lower value for their currency in order to encourage exports. The reason for this is that if the dollar depreciates against the Japanese yen, for example, U.S. manufactured goods should become cheaper to the Japanese consumers, who find that their supply of yen suddenly purchases a greater quantity of dollars; and Japanese and other foreign goods become more expensive to Americans. The depreciation of the U.S. dollar should then help to reduce the United States' deficit with its trading partners by increasing exports and reducing imports, in the absence of other countervailing factors.

Directly related to the issue of floating currency is the concept of transaction gain or loss on the import or export of merchandise. Returning to the example of KFC–Mexico's import of $10,000 in kitchen equipment, if that company ordered the equipment in January 2008 (when the exchange rate was 10 pesos per dollar) for payment in June 2009 (when the exchange rate had fallen to 11.5 pesos per dollar), they would have incurred a foreign exchange transaction loss. This happens because the company would have to buy dollars for payment in the month of June at a depreciated rate, thus paying more pesos for every dollar purchased. Only if they had the foresight (or good luck) to buy the dollars in January 2008 at the more favorable rate could they avoid this foreign exchange loss. A more detailed illustration follows:

Cost of imported equipment in pesos at exchange rate in effect at order date (10 pesos per dollar)	100,000 pesos
Cost of imported equipment in pesos at exchange rate in effect at payment date (11.5 pesos per dollar)	115,000 pesos
Foreign exchange loss in pesos	15,000 pesos

Conversely, if the peso were to appreciate prior to the payment date, KFC–Mexico would have a transaction gain in foreign exchange.

Spot versus Forward Foreign Exchange

If payment on a transaction is to be made immediately, the purchaser has no choice other than to buy foreign exchange on the **spot (or current) market**, for immediate delivery. However, if payment is to be made at some future date, as was the case in the KFC–Mexico example, the purchaser has the option of buying foreign exchange on the spot market or on the **forward market**, for delivery at some future date. The advantage of the forward market is that the buyer can lock in on an exchange rate and avoid the risk of currency fluctuations; this is called **currency hedging**, or protecting oneself against potential loss.[15]

The sound management of foreign exchange in an environment of volatile floating rates requires an astute corporate treasurer and effective coordination with the purchasing or marketing functions of the business.[16] If they see their national currency or the currency of one of their subsidiaries declining, they may purchase a stronger foreign currency as a reserve for future use. Often, if the corporation's money managers are savvy enough, significant income can be generated through foreign exchange transactions beyond that of normal company operations.[17] However, in recent years, many companies seem to be reducing hedging because exchange rate fluctuations have become so erratic and unpredictable. According to a survey conducted by the University of Pennsylvania's Wharton School and Canadian Imperial Bank of Commerce, only one-third of large U.S. companies engage in some kind of foreign-currency hedging.[18]

For example, Merck, a pharmaceutical giant, hedges some of its foreign cash flows using one- to five-year options to sell the currencies for dollars at fixed rates. Merck argues that it can protect against adverse currency moves by exercising its options or enjoy favorable moves by not exercising them. But many well-established companies see no strong need to hedge for protection against currency risk. The reason is that fluctuations in the underlying business can spoil the hedge's effectiveness. For companies with a strong belief in hedging, the sustained rise in the dollar over the past several years proved a serious test. Coca-Cola hopes to limit the negative impact of unfavorable currency swings on earnings to 3 percent annually over the long term.

---

[15]Alternatively, there is **operational hedging**, which is to shift production and procurement abroad to match revenues in foreign currency when exchange rate fluctuations are very difficult to predict (i.e., successful currency hedging is increasingly difficult). For example, by producing abroad all of the products a company sells in foreign markets, this company has created an "operational hedge" by shielding itself from fluctuating exchange rates. See, for example, Christos Pantzalis, Betty J. Simkins, Paul A. Laux, "Operational Hedges and the Foreign Exchange Exposure of U.S. Multinational Corporations," *Journal of International Business Studies,* 32 (4), 2001, pp. 793–812.

[16]Raj Aggarwal and Luc A. Soenen, "Managing Persistent Real Changes in Currency Values: The Role of Multinational Operating Strategies," *Columbia Journal of World Business* (Fall 1989), pp. 60–67.

[17]Stephen D. Makar and Stephen P. Huffman, "Foreign Currency Risk Management Practices in U.S. Multinationals," *Journal of Applied Business Research*, 13, Spring 1997, pp. 73–86.

[18]Peter Coy, De'Ann Weimer, and Amy Barrett, "Perils of the Hedge Highwire," *Business Week*, October 26, 1998, p. 74.

However, Coca-Cola's profits from foreign sales were knocked off by 10 percent due to the stronger dollar in 1998, instead. Eastman Kodak used to use an aggressive hedging strategy, but abandoned such practice recently as it realized that hedging was not necessary because the ups and downs of currencies would even out in the long run.[19]

However, it does not necessarily mean that currency hedging is less important to any company. Who should consider financial hedging more seriously? For an export-oriented economy, which is heavily dependent on the export of dollar-based products, such as Norway, currency hedging strategies remain vital.[20] While more young companies have started getting involved with international imports or exports, currency hedging has also become more accessible to them, thanks to a growing number of services offered by large banks as well as business-to-business websites. Currency hedging allows small business owners to greatly reduce or eliminate the uncertainties attached to any foreign currency transaction.

Forward currency markets exist for the strongest currencies, including the EU's euro, the British pound, Canadian dollar, Japanese yen, Swiss franc, and U.S. dollar. The terms of purchase are usually for delivery of the foreign currency in either 30, 60, or 90 days from the date of purchase. These aforementioned currencies are often called hard currencies, because they are the world's strongest and represent the world's leading economies.

Traditionally weaker currencies, such as the Indian rupee or the Colombian peso, are rarely used in forward currency markets, because there is no worldwide demand for such a market; nearly all international transactions are expressed in terms of a hard currency. **Exhibit 3-4** illustrates the daily quotes for foreign exchange on the spot and forward markets. In the second column, the foreign currency is expressed in terms of how many U.S. dollars it takes to buy one unit of foreign currency. The third column indicates the inverse, or how many units of a foreign currency it would take to purchase one dollar. For example, on August 22, 2013, one Japanese yen was worth $0.01013; more conventionally, the value of the yen was expressed as 98.72 yen per dollar. Similarly, on the same day, one euro was worth $1.3356, or conversely, one U.S. dollar could buy 0.7487 euro.

Exchange Rate Pass-Through

The dramatic swings in the value of the dollar since the early 1980s have made it clear that foreign companies charge different prices in the United States from those in other markets.[21] When the dollar appreciated against the Japanese yen and the German mark in the 1980s, Japanese cars were priced fairly low in the United States, justified by the cheaper yen, while German cars became far more expensive in the United States than in Europe. In the 1990s, when the dollar began depreciating against the yen and the mark, Japanese and German auto makers had to increase their dollar prices in the United States. Japanese auto makers did not raise their prices nearly as much as German competitors. Obviously, they "price to market."[22] As a result, Japanese car makers did not lose as much U.S. market share as did German car makers.

One of the success factors for many Japanese companies in the U.S. markets seems to be in the way they used dollar-yen exchange rates to their advantage, known as the **target exchange rate**. Japanese companies, in particular, are known to employ a very unfavorable target exchange rate (i.e., hypothetically appreciated yen environment) for their costing strategy to make sure they will

---

[19]Ibid.

[20]Ranga Nathan and Nils E. Joachim Hoegh-Krohn, "Norwegian Institutional Investors: Currency Risk," *Derivatives Quarterly*, 6 (Fall 1999), pp. 59–63.

[21]Terry Clark, Masaaki Kotabe, and Dan Rajaratnam "Exchange Rate Pass-Through and International Pricing Strategy: A Conceptual Framework and Research Propositions," *Journal of International Business Studies*, 30 (Second Quarter 1999), pp. 249–268.

[22]"Pricing Paradox: Consumers Still Find Imported Bargains Despite Weak Dollar," *Wall Street Journal* (October 7, 1992), p. A6.

Exhibit 3-4 FOREIGN EXCHANGE RATES

Monday, August 22, 2013
U.S.-dollar foreign-exchange rates in late New York trading

	IN US$	PER US$		IN US$	PER US$
Americas			**Europe**		
Argentina peso	0.1781	5.6138	Czech Rep. koruna	0.05196	19.246
Brazil real	0.4108	2.4344	Denmark krone	0.1790	5.5855
Canada dollar	0.9508	1.0517	Euro Area euro	1.3356	0.7487
Chile peso	0.001952	512.30	Hungary forint	0.00445892	224.27
Colombia peso	0.0005187	1928.01	Norway krone	0.1637	6.1070
Ecuador US dollar	1	1	Poland zloty	0.3144	3.1806
Mexico peso	0.0764	13.0907	Romania leu	0.3009	3.3237
Peru new sol	0.3553	2.8142	Russia ruble	0.03026	33.051
Uruguay peso	0.04645	21.5270	Sweden krona	0.1534	6.5198
Venezuela b. fuerte	0.15748031	6.3500	Switzerland franc	1.0832	0.9232
			Turkey lira	0.5015	1.9941
Asia-Pacific			UK pound	1.5589	0.6415
Australian dollar	0.9007	1.1103			
China yuan	0.1633	6.1225	**Middle East/Africa**		
Hong Kong dollar	0.1289	7.7556	Bahrain dinar	2.6531	0.3769
India rupee	0.01552	64.41495	Egypt pound	0.1431	6.9873
Indonesia rupiah	0.0000906	11033	Israel shekel	0.2785	3.5909
Japan yen	0.01013	98.72	Jordan dinar	1.4127	0.7079
Malaysia ringgit	0.3014	3.3174	Kenya shilling	0.01141	87.650
New Zealand dollar	0.7829	1.2774	Kuwait dinar	3.5141	0.2846
Pakistan rupee	0.00965	103.580	Lebanon pound	0.0006612	1512.45
Philippines peso	0.0226	44.175	Saudi Arabia riyal	0.2666	3.7504
Singapore dollar	0.7799	1.2822	South Africa rand	0.0973	10.2806
South Korea won	0.0008930	1119.81	UAE dirham	0.2723	3.6730
Taiwan dollar	0.03321	30.113			
Thailand baht	0.03121	32.039	SDR[*]	1.52	0.66
Vietnam dong	0.00005	21105			

*Special Drawing Rights (SDR); from the International Monetary Fund; based on exchange rates for U.S., British, and Japanese currencies.
Sources: Wall Street Journal, August 22, 2013; and International Monetary Fund, www.imf.org, August 22, 2013.

not be adversely affected should the yen appreciate. Therefore, despite close to a twofold appreciation of the yen vis-à-vis the dollar from 240 yen/$ to 110 yen/$ in a decade, the dollar prices of Japanese products have not increased nearly as much. The extent to which a foreign company changes dollar prices of its products in the U.S. market as a result of exchange rate fluctuations is called **exchange rate pass-through**. Although accurately estimating the average increase in dollar prices of Japanese products is almost impossible, our estimate suggests about 30 percent price increase, or pass-through, over the same period. If this estimate is accurate, Japanese companies must have somehow absorbed more than 70 percent of the price increase. This cost absorption could result from smaller profit margins and cost reductions as well as

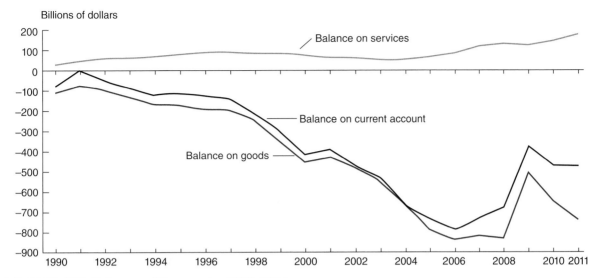

Exhibit 3-5 U.S. Balance of Payments, 1990–2011

Source: Constructed from *Statistical Abstract of the United States 2012*, Washington, DC: U.S. Census Bureau, 2012; and U.S. Bureau of Economic Analysis, *U.S. Economy at a Glance: Perspective from the BEA Accounts*, http://www.bea.gov/newsreleases/glance.htm, accessed May 1, 2012.

effective use of the unfavorable target exchange rate for planning purposes. According to Morgan Stanley Japan Ltd.'s estimate in the 1990s,[23] Toyota could break even at an unheard-of 52 yen to the dollar. In other words, as long as the Japanese currency does not appreciate all the way to 52 yen to the dollar, Toyota is expected to earn windfall operating profits.

The emergence of the internet as a global purchasing tool also brings a whole new aspect to the concept of pass-through, particularly in the retail setting. Now that retailers can sell to the world through one website, it is increasingly difficult for them to set different prices for each country. One can already see this with software purchased and downloaded online. Consumers in England will not pay 120 pounds for a software program that they know sells for $100 in the United States. Online commerce will limit price flexibility in foreign markets. This pass-through issue will be elaborated on in Chapter 11.

Balance of Payments

The balance of payments of a nation summarizes all the transactions that have taken place between its residents and the residents of other countries over a specified time period, usually a month, quarter, or year. The transactions contain three categories: current account, capital account, and official reserves. There is also an extra category for statistical discrepancy. **Exhibit 3-5** shows the balance of payments for the United States 1990–2011.

The balance of payments record is made on the basis of rules of credits (transactions that result in an inflow of money) and debits (transactions that result in an outflow of money), similar to those in business accounting. Exports, like sales, are outflows of goods, and are entered as credits to merchandise trade. Imports, or inflows of goods, are represented by debits to the same account. These exports and imports are most likely offset by an opposite entry to the capital account, reflecting the receipt of cash or the outflow of cash for payment.

---

[23]Valerie Reitman, "Toyota Names a Chief Likely to Shake Up Global Auto Business," *Wall Street Journal* (August 11, 1995), p. A1, A5.

When a German tourist visits the United States and spends money on meals and lodging, it is a credit to the U.S. trade in services balance reflecting the U.S. rendering of a service to a foreign resident. On the other hand, this transaction would represent a debit to the trade in services account of Germany, reflecting the receipt of a service from a U.S. resident (or company) by a resident of Germany. If the foreign resident's payment is made in cash, the credit to trade in services is offset by a debit (inflow) to short-term capital. On the other hand, if a foreign resident purchases land in the United States, paying cash, this is represented on the United States balance of payments as a debit to short-term capital (representing the inflow of payment for the land) and a credit to long-term capital (representing the outflow of ownership of real estate).

This is based on the principle of double entry accounting, so theoretically every debit must be offset by a credit to some other account within the balance of payments statement. In other words, the balance of payments statement must always balance, because total debits must equal total credits. A deficit (debit balance) in one account will then be offset by a surplus (credit balance) in another account. If the statement does not balance, an entry must be made as statistical discrepancy. But in reality, there is no national accountant making accounting entries for every international transaction. In the United States, the Department of Commerce, which prepares the balance of payments statement, must gather information from a variety of sources, including banks and other business entities, concerning the inflow and outflow of goods, services, gifts, and capital items.

The **balance of payments on goods** (also known as **trade balance**) shows trade in currently produced goods. Trade balance is the most frequently used indicator of the health of a country's international trade position. The **balance of payments on services** shows trade in currently transacted services. The **balance of payments in current account** (**current account balance**, for short) shows trade in currently produced goods and services, as well as unilateral transfers including private gifts and foreign aid. The goods or merchandise account deals with tangibles such as autos, grain, machinery, or equipment that can be seen and felt, as well as exported and imported. The services account deals with intangibles that are sold or bought internationally. Examples include dividends or interest on foreign investments, royalties on trademarks or patents abroad, food or lodging (travel expenses), and transportation. Unilateral transfers are transactions with no quid pro quo; some of these transfers are made by private individuals and institutions and some by governments. These gifts are sometimes for charitable, missionary, or educational purposes, and other times they consist of funds wired home by migrant workers to their families in their country of origin. The largest unilateral transfers are aid, either in money or in the form of goods and services, from developed to developing countries.

Although not shown in Exhibit 3-5, the mirror image of the balance of payments in current account (goods, services, and unilateral transfers), as a result of double entry accounting, is the capital account. The balance of payments in capital account (**capital account**) summarizes financial transactions and is divided into two sections, short- and long-term capital accounts. Long-term capital includes any financial asset maturing in a period exceeding one year, including equities. Subaccounts under long-term capital are direct investment and portfolio investment.

Direct investments are those investments in enterprises or properties that are effectively controlled by residents of another country. Whenever 10 percent or more of the voting shares in a U.S. company are held by foreign investors, the company is classified as a U.S. affiliate of a foreign company and therefore a foreign direct investment.[24] Similarly, if U.S. investors hold 10 percent or more of the voting shares of a foreign company, the entity is considered a foreign affiliate of a U.S. company.

---

[24]Department of Commerce, *U.S. Direct Investment Abroad* (Washington, D.C.: Bureau of Economic Analysis, 2012).

Portfolio investment includes all long-term investments that do not give the investors effective control over the investment. Such transactions typically involve the purchase of stocks or bonds of foreign investors for investment. These shares are normally bought for investment, not control, purposes.

Short-term capital includes only those items maturing in less than one year, including cash. The official reserves account registers the movement of funds to or from central banks.

A key point to remember here is that the deficit or surplus is calculated based not on the aggregate of all transactions in the balance of payments, but on the net balance for certain selected categories.

There are three particularly important balances to identify on the balance of payments statement of a country, including the balance of the merchandise trade account, the current account (including merchandise trade, trade in services, and unilateral transfers), and the basic balance (the current account and long-term capital). Everyone knows about the U.S. deficit in merchandise trade, but what is less commonly known is that the U.S. regularly runs a surplus in trade in services. This surplus offsets a small part of the deficit in the merchandise account.

Many observers have commented that since the 1980s, the United States has been able to continue its import binge via the sale of long-term investments, including real estate and ownership in companies. This belief was heightened by the high-profile sale of such U.S. landmarks as the legendary Hollywood studio MGM to Sony of Japan in 2005 and Anheuser-Busch to InBev of Belgium in 2008. These foreign companies invested in U.S. capital assets, paying in cash that was then recycled in payment for merchandise imports by U.S. residents. The criticism was made that the U.S. was selling off capital assets for short-term merchandise imports like a wealthy heir who sells off the family jewels to finance a profligate lifestyle. Meanwhile, others viewed the increase in foreign investment in the United States as proof of the nation's vitality and long-term attractiveness to investors.

The Internal and External Adjustments

According to the theory of international trade and balance of payments, a surplus or deficit in a country's basic balance should be self-correcting to some extent. This self-correction is accomplished through the internal and external market adjustments. The market adjustment mechanisms bring a nation's deficit or surplus within the basic balance back into equilibrium. This is a natural event where the economy of a nation corrects its prior excesses by moving back toward the middle.[25]

The **internal market adjustment** refers to the movement of prices and incomes in a country. The following is a hypothetical example of such an adjustment process in the case of a current account surplus country, such as Japan.

1. As Japan continues to export more than it imports resulting in a surplus in the current account, its internal money supply grows, the result of receiving payment from foreigners for their purchases of goods, services, and investments originating in Japan. The payments are made to Japanese residents and may be deposited in banks either in Japan or abroad, either in yen or in foreign currency. But wherever and however payment is made, it becomes an asset of a Japanese resident.

2. As Japan's money supply increases, domestic residents of Japan spend more, because they have more money available to spend. Japan's money supply is increasing because foreigners are buying Japanese goods in greater quantities than Japanese are buying foreign goods.

3. As local residents in Japan spend more (i.e., have greater demand for products and services), domestic prices rise. In other words, inflation occurs.

---

[25]Mordechai E. Kreinin, *International Economics: A Policy Approach,* Mason, OH: Thomson South-Western, 2006, pp. 241–252.

4. As domestic prices increase, Japanese residents find that foreign goods are relatively cheaper.

5. Because the Japanese find foreign goods cheaper, they import more goods from abroad. This begins to reduce Japan's current account surplus and bring it back into balance.

The **external market adjustment** concerns exchange rates or a nation's currency and its value with respect to the currencies of other nations. The following is a hypothetical description of the application of the external adjustment to a surplus nation, in this case again, Japan.

Japan exports more than it imports, resulting in a surplus in its current account. So, foreigners must pay Japanese residents for the goods they purchase from Japan. Payment will likely be made in Japanese yen.

1. Because Japanese residents export more than they import, there is more demand for yen by foreigners than demand for dollars by Japanese residents. This excess in relative demand for yen causes it to appreciate in value with respect to other currencies. Remember, it appreciates because foreigners must pay Japanese suppliers for their goods and services.

2. The appreciated yen causes Japanese goods, services, and investments to be more expensive to foreign residents who convert prices quoted in yen to their local currencies.

3. All other things being equal, this should cause foreigners to buy fewer Japanese goods and thus shrink Japan's trade surplus.

However, other factors, such as a country's taste for foreign goods and general habits of consumption, must be taken into account, as well as the quality and reputation of a country's manufactured goods. Many other factors beyond domestic prices and foreign exchange values affect Japan's trade balance with the United States, and these have become a topic of serious discussion between the governments of these two nations.

Economic and Financial Turmoil around the World

Since the last few years of the twentieth century we have observed some unprecedented economic and financial crises in some parts of the world that have caused significant slowdowns in the growth of the world economy and international trade and investment. Excessive borrowing by companies, households, or governments lie at the root of almost every economic crisis of the past two decades from East Asia to Russia and to South America, and from Japan to the United States. In this section, we highlight the Asian financial crisis of 1997–1998, the South American financial crisis of 2002 that spread out of Argentina to other parts of South America, and most recently the severe global recession triggered by the U.S. subprime mortgage loan crisis in 2008–2009, to illustrate the global ripple effect of local and regional economic downturn.

Asian Financial Crisis and Its Aftermath

Chronologically speaking, China's devaluation of its currency, the yuan, from 5.7 yuan/$ to 8.7 yuan/$ in 1994, set the stage for an on-going saga of the Asian financial crisis. The mechanism of how the Asian financial crisis occurred is summarized in **Exhibit 3-6**.

The currency devaluation made China's exports cheaper in Southeast Asia where most currencies were virtually pegged to the U.S. dollar. According to Lawrence Klein, a Nobel Laureate in economics, the Southeast Asian countries' strict tie to the U.S. dollar cost them between 10 and 20 percent of export loss spread over three or four years.[26]

---

[26]"Panel Discussion One: An Overview of the Crisis," *Journal of International Management*, Supplement, 4 (1), 1998, pp. 7S–17S.

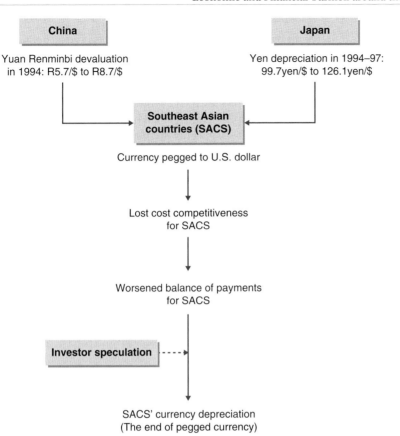

Exhibit 3-6
Mechanism of the
Asian Financial
Crisis

Separately, Japan's post-bubble recession also caused its currency to depreciate from 99.7 yen/$ in 1994 to 126.1 yen/$ in 1997, resulting in a two-pronged problem for Southeast Asian countries. First, recession-stricken Japan reduced imports from its Asian neighbors; second, the depreciated yen helped Japanese companies increase their exports to the rest of Asia. Consequently, Southeast Asian countries' trade deficits with China and Japan increased abruptly in a relatively short period. Southeast Asian countries' trade deficits were paid for by their heavy borrowing from abroad, leaving their financial systems vulnerable and making it impossible to maintain their currency exchange rates vis-à-vis the U.S. dollar. The end result was the sudden currency depreciation by the end of 1997. For example, Thailand lost almost 60 percent of its baht's purchasing power in dollar terms in 1997. The Malaysian ringgit lost some 40 percent of its value in the same period. The Korean won was similarly hit toward the end of 1997 and depreciated 50 percent against the U.S. dollar in less than two months. The worst case was Indonesia whose rupiah lost a whopping 80 percent of its value in the last quarter of 1997. In a way, it would amount to a U.S. dollar bill becoming worth only 20 cents in three months!

The Asian financial crisis in the latter half of the 1990s had escalated into the biggest threat to global prosperity since the oil crisis of the 1970s. The region's once booming economies were fragile, liquidity problems hurt regional trade, and losses from Asian investments eroded profits for many Japanese companies. Similarly, among Western companies, quite a few U.S. companies that had large investments in Asia reported less than expected earnings. Others feared that the Asian crisis would wash ashore to seemingly unrelated regions of the world, including the

United States and Europe.[27] For example, the unsettling ups and downs of the Dow Jones Industrial Average reflected the precarious nature of U.S. investments in Asia. Economists blamed Asia for nipping the world's economic growth by one percentage point in 1998–1999.[28]

Now that the Asian market has recovered from the crisis, the acceleration of Asia's economic growth since 2000 can be credited to the gradual recovery of the Japanese economy.[29] In 2003, Asia's GDP grew at 3.5 percent, exceeding the average growth rate for the 1990s. By 2010, Asia's GDP grew at 8.2 percent. Asia's power in crisis recovery has been enviable: led by India and China, exports rose by 22 percent in 2010, the most rapid growth compared to the rest of the world. Activity in Asia remained solid, although somewhat moderated in the first half of 2011 due to temporary disruption in supply chains caused by a massive Japanese earthquake and tsunami. Asian developing countries' GDP grew at 9.5 percent in 2010. China's growth was forecasted to average about 7.8 percent in 2012, while India's growth being 4.9 percent, but expected to bounce back to 8.2 percent and 6 percent in 2013, respectively. In general, growth is expected to remain strong in the years ahead with weaker external demand offset by domestic demand.[30]

The South American Financial Crisis and Its Aftermath

Starting from the end of 2001, we have witnessed the largest debt default in Argentina. Unlike the Asian financial crisis, Argentina's problems took a long time to develop, giving enough signs to investors and analysts.[31] However, the trouble has turned out to be much worse than anyone would have imagined. By April 2002, Argentine currency had lost nearly 40 percent of its value since the government freed it from the dollar in December 2001. The unemployment rate reached about 25 percent, and bank accounts remained frozen. Several presidents failed to slow down the recession. The economy contracted by 1 percent in 2001, and a whopping 8 percent in 2002.[32] In December 2001, the government stopped payment on much of its $141 billion in foreign debt— the biggest government default in history. Thousands of commercial establishments were closed in a week.

The first reason behind the crisis lies in Argentina's own monetary system. For a decade, the Argentine government fixed the peso at one U.S. dollar, which overvalued the currency and caused a lack of competitiveness when other currencies depreciated. Three months after the peso was freed from the dollar, the rate became 3 pesos to the dollar, with a depreciation of 67 percent.[33] The second reason is the unbelievable government debt. Argentina has years of chronic government deficit spending. The debt sent the interest rate up and caused many businesses to close. As more companies closed and more people were laid off, the government's tax income shrank and increased the debt burden. Finally, as the IMF refused to make an advance payment on a previously agreed loan to allow Argentina to make its next debt payment, the economy became paralyzed. The Argentina crisis inevitably hurt its neighbors, such as Brazil, South America's largest economy that conducts nearly one-third of its trade with Argentina. The Mexican peso had weakened 5 percent within two months since the end of March 2002. The Brazilian real had

---

[27]"Europeans, Despite Big Stakes Involved, Follow U.S. Lead in Asia Financial Crisis," *Wall Street Journal*, January 16, 1998, A11.

[28]This section builds on Masaaki Kotabe, "The Four Faces of the Asian Financial Crisis: How to Cope with the Southeast Asia Problem, the Japan Problem, the Korea Problem, and the China Problem," *Journal of International Management*, 4 (1), 1998, 1S–6S.

[29]"The Sun Also Rises," *Economist*, October 8, 2005, pp. 3–6.

[30]International Monetary Fund, "World Economic Outlook 2012: Coping with High Debt and Sluggish Growth," October 2012, www.imf.org.

[31]Martin Crutsinger, "Shock Waves from Argentina Crisis Could Yet Reach U.S. Economy," *AP Newswire* (April 28, 2002).

[32]Terry L. Mccoy, "Argentine Meltdown Threatens to Derail Latin Reforms," *The Orlando Sentinel,* April 22, 2002, p.A15.

[33]Ian Campbell, "As IMF Fiddles, Argentina Burns," *United Press International* (March 28, 2002).

retreated 6.4 percent over the same period, and several other regional currencies had also slid while their counterparts from Asia and Europe were in their 12-month high. After the Argentine crisis, both international bank loans and capital inflows in Latin America declined. International financial flows to Latin America have declined substantially since the crisis in Argentina.[34]

The U.S. Subprime Mortgage Loan Crisis and the Subsequent Global Financial Crisis

The property boom in the United States since the early 1990s and the availability of easy mortgage loans through the Federal Reserve's loose monetary policy helped pump up the property bubble, much like what had happened in Japan a decade earlier. In the process, a huge amount of easy mortgage loans were offered to the subprime mortgage market—that is, those customers who could otherwise not afford to purchase houses. Easy money and loose regulations allowed banks to securitize the expected cash flows from a pool of underlying assets such as home mortgages and sell those securities on the open market. Not only domestic but also foreign—particularly, European and Japanese—banks and securities companies purchased them. Then an onslaught of defaults in the subprime mortgage market in the United States in recent years snowballed into a global credit crisis, causing the collapse of the securities market around the world.[35] The current global recession is the worst of its kind since the Great Depression of 1929–1932.

As the credit market has dried up, businesses that rely on consumer credit have suffered dearly. For example, when the credit crisis became evident by the end of 2009, the December sales of cars and light trucks in the United States fell by 36 percent compared with a year ago; in France, car sales were down by 16 percent despite government incentives designed to prop up the market; in Spain, car sales were off by almost 50 percent; and in Japan, by 22 percent.[36] Car sales have since continued to decline. Toyota, now the world's largest and most profitable automaker, reduced domestic production by 40 percent in January 2009 as its exports dropped almost 60 percent from a year earlier.[37] You can see the severity of the current global recession as such a precipitous sales decline is extraordinary by any standard.

Financial Crises in Perspective

There are some common factors across the recent financial problems facing Asian and South American countries and in how they could affect businesses and consumers in the region. The Asian financial crisis has to be placed properly in perspective as showing that the "economic miracles" of the East and Southeast Asian countries have already shifted the pendulum of international trade from cross-Atlantic to cross-Pacific in the last decade. Companies from the United States and Japan, in particular, have been helping shape the nature of the cross-Pacific bilateral and multilateral trade and investment. Today, as a result, North America's trade with these five Asian countries alone exceeds its trade with the European Union by upwards of 20 percent. The trend is irreversible. Although the recent stock market turmoil and the subsequent depreciation of the foreign exchange rates of many Asian countries may have set back their economic progress temporarily, the fundamental economic forces are likely to remain intact.

---

[34]Patricia Alvarez-Plata and Mechthild Schrooten, "Latin America after the Argentine Crisis: Diminishing Financial Market Integration," *Economic Bulletin*, 40, December 2003, pp. 431–436.

[35]"Ruptured Credit," *Economist*, May 15, 2008.

[36]"The Big Chill," *Economist*, January 15, 2009.

[37]"Toyota, Nissan Japan Output Drop As Exports Sink," NikkeiInteractive.net, February 25, 2009, http://www.nni .nikkei.co.jp/.

Now we are in the midst of a severe global recession. Again and again, unbridled asset appreciation, whether it is stock prices or property values, and the availability of easy credit appear to lead to an eventual collapse of a financial system. The United States is no exception. As we discussed in Chapter 2, the fundamental source of easy money in the United States is the persistent current-account deficits in the United States, matched by surpluses in emerging markets, notably China. In other words, the United States has been living beyond its economic means by borrowing money from foreign creditors. It is a stark reminder to the rest of the world that no country can sustain its livelihood for good on borrowed money.[38]

In order for countries to sustain their strong economic performance, the importance of several necessary conditions needs to be stressed. Those include strong financial institutions—commercial and investment banks, stock exchanges; transparency in the way the institutions do business; financial reporting systems that are consistent with free markets where capital and goods flow competitively; and supply of a managerial pool to shepherd these economies through very difficult transitional periods. While the Asian countries remain strong and attractive with respect to their economic fundamentals, recent events have demonstrated that the institutional environment of the countries needs reforms (see **Global Perspective 3-1** for a new lurking problem in emerging economies).

Global Perspective 3-1

Inflation Surges in Emerging Economies

Inflation has been a concern in the recovery of the world economy. The threat of rising prices has preoccupied policymakers and the public as the slow process of economic recovery continues throughout the world. Concerns are the greatest in the emerging economies. For example, in December 2010, the inflation rate in China reached 4.6 percent, while it almost hit 10 percent in India. Consumer prices in China increased by 5.4 percent in March 2011, the biggest hike since July 2008.

In the Euro Area, inflation hit 2.4 percent in January 2011. Britain's inflation stood at 3.7 percent in December 2010, which was expected to rise even higher to 4–5 percent in January 2011, according to warnings from the governor of the Bank of England. In May 2011, the world inflation rate was up to 4.7 percent from 4.5 percent in the previous year; while in the main emerging countries, inflation was up to 6.6 percent. Even in the United States, where inflation has been historically low, it rose to 1.5 percent at the end of 2010.

The thing that needs to be worried about is the far-too-loose global monetary conditions due to low interest rates and bloated central bank balance sheets in the rich countries and the emerging economies' inability or unwillingness to tighten monetary and fiscal policy in response. Inflation could run out of control if this combination is not corrected appropriately. Concerns about inflation manifest in various ways in different parts of the world. In emerging markets, while technocrats fear overheating economies, politicians worry about social unrest. Worries are rising as well among central bankers in rich economies as reflected by a vote for an immediate rise in interest rates by the Bank of England's policy committee in January 2011.

Although inflation has been up, it is hardly high in rich economies. In the eurozone, core inflation was steady at 1.1 percent, and prices are rising much more slowly than in 2008. In most rich countries, inflation expectations have risen from very low to low—and thus have not set off the alarm. Acting as a blessing in disguise, the high unemployment rate keeps workers from demanding higher pay. With no higher wages, rising food and fuel prices will cut into consumer spending that eventually suggests lower inflation.

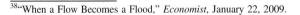

[38]"When a Flow Becomes a Flood," *Economist*, January 22, 2009.

The story is different in emerging economies. With the monetary condition a lot looser than in 2008, most of emerging countries are racing along. This poses a real risk of a persistent inflation problem. Low interest rates in the rich economies cause problems for policymakers in the emerging economies. If they raise interest rates, they would attract more foreign capital, and thus, fuel more inflation. In China, household inflation expectations are rising to their highest levels in over a decade. Signs of growing wage pressure persist. Higher wages are not always bad; however, the danger comes when loose monetary conditions and an overheating economy exist. This would mean that prices and wages would chase each other upward.

Sources: "Parsing Prices: Rising Inflation Is Not as Worrisome as It Appears, at Least for Now," *Economist*, February 3, 2011; "Greater Expectations? Inflation Is Rising, but Worries Are Overstated," *Economist*, February 3, 2011; and "Emerging Markets Inflation Surges," *Financial Times*, April 15, 2011.

Responses to the Regional Financial Crises

For illustrative purposes, let us use the Asian financial crisis of 1997–1998 and explain how domestic and foreign companies coped with the sudden recessionary environment brought about by the crisis. Such implications apply to any regional and global financial crisis.

Reeling from the initial shock of the financial crisis, marketing executives have begun to cope with the realities of marketing their products in a completely changed world—from the world that was once believed to continue growing with ever increasing prosperity to a world that has decimated the burgeoning middle class by snapping more than 50 percent of consumers' spending power. Marketers are facing two dire consequences of the crisis: declining markets and increased competition from existing competitors. Their major task is to figure out how to keep current customers and gain new ones and maintain profitability in the long run.

Although Asia's current recession caused by its financial crisis is a serious one, other countries or regions have also experienced economic slumps over the years. *Recession* is usually defined as an economic situation in which the country's GDP has shrunk for two consecutive quarters. Based on this definition, the United States has experienced 29 recessions since 1894, approximately once every four to five years. First, we examine how consumers react to an economic slump. Second, we show different ways in which competing companies cope with the recession and the changed consumer needs.

Consumer Response to the Recession

As we all know from our own personal experiences, we tend to become more selective in choosing products and stay away from impulse buying in a recessionary period. In other words, consumers begin to spend their money more wisely and emphasize value for the money. We may consume less of some products, but we may even consume more of certain other products. General changes in the consumption pattern in an economic downturn are summarized in **Exhibit 3-7**.

Although a recession alters the mood of a country, it does not necessarily affect consumption of all products in the same way. If you now travel to any major city in Asia, such as Kuala Lumpur in Malaysia, you will hardly notice any change in shopping behavior at first glance. Finding a parking spot at One Utama, a large shopping mall on the outskirts of Kuala Lumpur, is as difficult now as it was a year ago. Young Malaysian couples shop for groceries and kitchenware, while moviegoers flock to a cinema multiplex showing Columbia Pictures' *Spider-Man*. The coffee houses such as Starbucks are successful as ever, teeming with trendy customers, and high-tech aficionados are trying out the latest PalmPilots. In sharp contrast, if you visit the huge upscale Meladas Casa Mobili store, you will see few middle-class families buying its exquisite Italian

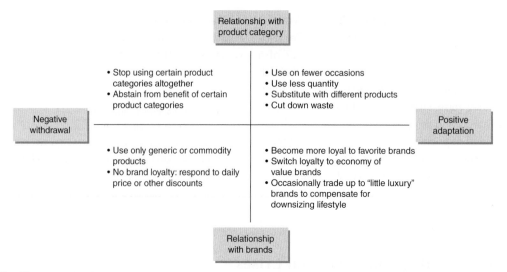

Exhibit 3-7   Changes in Consumption Patterns During a Recession

Source: Adapted from James Chadwick, "Communicating through Tough Times," *Economic Bulletin*, August 1998, p. 27.

furniture there. Indeed, the items most susceptible to a recessionary downturn usually are big ticket items, such as cars, home furnishings, large appliances, and travel. Those relatively unaffected are alcohol, tobacco, small appliances, packaged goods, and computer items.[39]

Corporate Response to the Recession

Different companies have reacted in various ways to the recession, based on their different corporate objectives. In general, there are short-term and long-term orientations in crisis management. Short-term orientation dictates that the corporate goal is to maximize year-to-year profit (or minimize loss), whereas long-term orientation tolerates some short-term loss for the benefit of future gains. Although any definitive value judgment should not be made of the two different orientations, short-term orientation tends to serve stockholders' speculative needs, while long-term orientation tends to cater to customer needs. A short-term-oriented solution is to pull out of the market, at least temporarily as long as the markets remain in a recession. Long-term oriented solutions are to modify marketing strategies in various ways to address the consumer needs that were completely changed during the recession.

- **Pull-out.** Pulling out of the market is an easy way out, at least financially, in the short run. Immediately after Indonesia's rupiah depreciated by almost 80 percent in a couple of months, J.C. Penny and Wal-Mart simply left the Indonesian market without second thought. Similarly, Daihatsu, a small Japanese automobile manufacturer, decided to pull out of Thailand. While the pull-out strategy may be the least painful option in the short run, it could cause some irreparable consequences in the long run, and particularly so in many Asian countries where long-term, trustworthy, and loyal relationships are a vital part of doing business and short-term financial sacrifices are revered as an honorable act. A better strategy would be to cut the planned production volume and maintain corporate presence on the market as General Motors did in Thailand.[40]

---

[39]James Chadwick, "Communicating through Tough Times in Asia," *Economic Bulletin*, August 1998, pp. 25–29.
[40]"Asia's Sinking Middle Class," *Far Eastern Economic Review*, April 9, 1998, p. 12.

- **Emphasize a product's value.** Weary consumers become wiser consumers. In a prosperous time, middle-class consumers may have resorted to some impulse buying and conspicuous consumption. But during the current recession, they want to maintain their current lifestyle and standard of living. However, they want to feel vindicated that the product or service they purchase is worth the money they pay for it. Marketers will have to develop a promotion that emphasizes the value contained in the product. For example, Procter & Gamble's new Pantene shampoo line, which sells for $2.20 to $7.30, is one of the most expensive shampoos available in Hong Kong. Its advertising campaign promotes Pantene's extra moisturizers and other high-tech ingredients to clearly convey the benefits of Pantene over other less expensive brands.[41]

  Another way to add value is to enhance the perceived quality image of a product. For example, in Thailand, an advertising campaign for a relatively cheap Clan MacGregor scotch whiskey made locally under license emphasizes the product value: "Even if you have to buy something cheap, you are getting something of real value." This is stated in reference to three times more expensive imported Johnnie Walker Black Label whiskey. This ad helps enhance Clan MacGregor's quality image in the minds of consumers.[42]

- **Change the product mix.** If a company has a wide array of product lines, it can shift the product mix by pushing relatively inexpensive product lines while de-emphasizing expensive lines. This strategy is suited to riding over a slump by generating sufficient cash flow not only to cover the fixed costs of business operations but also to maintain the corporate presence on the market. Particularly in Asia, the company's dedication to the market as perceived by local customers will win many favorable points in the long run. For example, Burberry's, a British fashion retailer, has replaced its expensive jackets in window displays with relatively inexpensive T-shirts, stressing that everyone can still afford some luxury even in hard times.[43]

- **Repackage the goods.** As stated earlier, middle-class consumers want to maintain their lifestyle and quality of life as much as possible. This means that they will keep buying what they have been buying but consume less. Companies like Unilever are repackaging their products to suit consumers' declining purchasing power. Unilever has reduced the size of its Magnum brand ice cream packs and made it cheaper, has begun to offer giveaways on its Lux soaps (buy six, get one free), and is marketing its detergents in smaller and cheaper refillable packs.[44]

- **Maintain stricter inventory.** Japanese companies have long taught us that their just-in-time inventory management practices not only reduce unnecessary inventory but also improve their product assortment by selling only what customers want at the moment. Even if companies are not practicing just-in-time inventory management, it would make a lot of sense to keep inventory low. Essentially, inventory is a tied-up capital of unsold merchandise that can be costly to the company. For example, the Kuala Lumpur store of Swedish furniture retailer, Ikea, has not restocked certain slow-selling items.[45]

- **Look outside the region for expansion opportunities.** Asia's recession is still a regional problem although there is some risk that it will bring down the rest of the world with it to cause a global economic crisis. Nevertheless, market opportunities can be found outside the recession-stricken part of Asia. This strategy is not only a part of geographical diversification to spread out the market risk but also an effective way to take advantage of cheaper Asian currencies, which translate to lower prices in other foreign countries. For instance, Esprit, the Hong Kong–based

[41]"Multinationals Press On in Asia Despite Perils of Unstable Economies," *Asian Wall Street Journal*, September 4–5, 1998, p. 12.
[42]"Asia's Sinking Middle Class," p. 12.
[43]"Asia's Sinking Middle Class," p. 13.
[44]"Asia's Sinking Middle Class," p. 12.
[45]"Asia's Sinking Middle Class," p. 13.

retailer, is now marketing very aggressively in Europe. Despite the Asian slump, its revenues increased 52 percent during fiscal 1998 with most of the gain coming from the European market.[46]

Hewlett-Packard and Dell Computer, among others that depend heavily on now less expensive components made in Asia, have begun to trim the prices of their products.[47]

- **Increase advertising in the region.** It sounds somewhat antithetical to the strategy stated above. However, there is also a strong incentive to introduce new products now. It is a buyer's market for advertising space. Television stations are maintaining advertising rates but giving bonus airtime, effectively cutting advertising costs. As a result, Unilever can better afford to reach the large middle-class market segment in Hong Kong that its SunSilk shampoo targets. American Express is launching the Platinum card for the first time in Malaysia, and it is targeted at the highest-income consumers whose wealth has been cushioned by investment overseas.[48]

  Historical evidence also suggests that it is usually a mistake to cut advertising budgets during a recession.[49]

  For example, Oxy, a South Korean household products manufacturer, like many other hard-hit companies, slashed its advertising budget by a third, while its competitors halted their advertising completely. Before the slump, Oxy had commanded an 81 percent of the closet dehumidifier market with its Thirsty Hippo model. Now instead of losing sales, Oxy boosted its market share to 94 percent at the expense of its rivals.[50]

- **Increase local procurement.** Many foreign companies operating in Asian countries tend to procure certain crucial components and equipment from their parent companies. Now that Asian currencies have depreciated precipitously, those foreign companies are faced with those imported components and equipment whose prices have gone up enormously in local currencies. Companies with localized procurement were not affected easily by fluctuating exchange rates. As a result, many companies scurried to speed steps toward making their operations in Asian countries more local. Japanese companies seemed to be one step ahead of U.S. and European competitors in this localization strategy. Since the yen's sharp appreciation in the mid-1980s, Japanese manufacturers have moved to build an international production system that is less vulnerable to currency fluctuations by investing in local procurement.[51]

Marketing in the Euro Area
Historical Background

Initially, the European Union (formerly, the European Economic Community) consisted of 6 countries, including Belgium, Germany, France, Italy, Luxembourg, and the Netherlands. Denmark, Ireland, and the United Kingdom joined in 1973; Greece in 1981; Spain and Portugal in 1986; Austria, Finland, and Sweden in 1995. The European Union consisted of 15 developed European countries until 2004, when 10 more countries joined the European Union—Cyprus, the Czech Republic, Estonia, Hungary, Latvia, Lithuania, Malta, Poland, Slovakia, and Slovenia. In 2007, two more countries, Bulgaria and Romania, became new members of the European Union (EU), expanding the total number of EU member countries to 27. These 12 central and eastern European countries are, in general, less developed than the previous 15 countries. Hence, due to

---

[46]"With Asia in collapse, Esprit pushes aggressively into Europe," *Asian Wall Street Journal*, January 4, 1999, p. 2.

[47]"Asia Crisis May Benefit U.S. Companies," *New York Times on the Web*, January 19, 1998, at www.nytimes.com.

[48]"Multinationals Press On in Asia Despite Perils of Unstable Economies," p. 12.

[49]James Chadwick, "Communicating through Tough Times in Asia," pp. 26–28.

[50]Karene Witcher, "Marketing Strategies Help Asian Firms Beat a Downturn," *Asian Wall Street Journal*, December 7, 1998, p. 9.

[51]"Manufacturers Reshape Asian Strategies," *Nikkei Weekly*, January 12, 1998, pp. 1 and 5.

The Eurozone

■ EU members in the eurozone

▨ EU members not in the eurozone

FINLAND

SWEDEN

ESTONIA

LATVIA

BRITAIN

LITHUANIA

DENMARK

IRELAND

NETHER-
LANDS

POLAND

GERMANY

BELGIUM

LUX.

CZECH REPUBLIC

SLOVAKIA

AUSTRIA HUNGARY

FRANCE

SLOVENIA

ROMANIA

BULGARIA

PORTUGAL

ITALY

SPAIN

GREECE

MALTA

CYPRUS

Exhibit 3-8
17 Eurozone
Countries (As of
January 1, 2012)

the great differences in per capita income and historic national animosities, the European Union faces difficulties in devising and enforcing common policies.

On January 1, 1999, 11 countries (Austria, Belgium, Finland, France, Germany, Ireland, Italy, Luxembourg, Portugal, Spain, and the Netherlands) embarked on a venture that created the world's second-largest economic zone (officially the **Euro Area** and more commonly the eurozone) after the United States. Later, six countries (Cyprus, Greece, Malta, Slovakia, Slovenia, and Estonia)[52] joined the eurozone with a total membership of 16 countries as of January 1, 2009 (see **Exhibit 3-8**). The seeds for the euro had been planted almost exactly three decades ago. In 1969, Pierre Werner, a former prime minister of Luxembourg, was asked to

---

[52]Eurozone membership years are as follows: Greece in 2001, Slovenia in 2007, Cyprus and Malta in 2008, Slovakia in 2009, and Estonia in 2011.

chair a think tank on how a European monetary union (EMU) could be achieved by 1980. The Werner report published in October 1970 outlined a three-phase plan that was very similar to the blueprint ultimately adopted in the Maastricht Treaty, signed on February 7, 1992. Just like the Maastricht Treaty, the plan envisioned the replacement of local currencies by a single currency. However, the EMU was put on hold following the monetary chaos created by the first oil crisis of 1973. The next step on the path to monetary union was the creation of the European monetary system (EMS) in the late 1970s. Except for the United Kingdom, all member states of the European Union joined the Exchange Rate Mechanism (ERM). The ERM determined bilateral currency exchange rates. Currencies of the then-nine member states could still fluctuate but movements were limited to a margin of 2.25 percent. The EMS also led to the European currency unit (ecu)—in some sense the predecessor of the euro. Note that this newly-bred currency never became a physical currency.

The foundations for monetary union were laid at the Madrid summit in 1989 when the EU member states undertook steps that would lead to free movement of capital. The Maastricht Treaty, signed shortly afterward, spelled out the guidelines toward the EMU. The monetary union was to be capped by the launch of a single currency by 1999. This treaty also set norms in terms of government deficits, government debt, and inflation rate that applicants had to meet in order to qualify for EMU membership. As stated earlier, there are now 16 member countries in the eurozone. Monetary policy for this group of countries is run by the European Central Bank headquartered in Frankfurt, Germany. Three of the developed EU member states, namely the United Kingdom (not surprisingly), Sweden, and Denmark, decided to opt out and sit on the fence. The new EU members may choose to adopt the euro in the future when they meet the EU's fiscal and monetary standards and the member states agreement. The eurozone economies combined represent about a third of world's gross domestic product and 20 percent of overall international trade, with a population of roughly 320 million people. Each of these countries has committed itself to adopting a single currency, the euro, designated by the € symbol.

On January 1, 2002, the euro notes and coins began to replace the German mark, the Dutch guilder, and many other currencies. By July 1, 2002, the local currencies ceased to exist. Those of you who traversed Europe before 2002 may remember the financial strains of exchanging one European currency for another one. Now this hassle became a thing of the past. The creation of the euro has been described as "the most far-reaching development in Europe since the fall of the Berlin Wall."[53] According to the Economic and Monetary Union (EMU), it has already helped create a new culture of economic stability in Europe, to weather the recent slowdown in the world economy, and to avoid damaging intra-European exchange rate tension. With the euro in place, the citizens of Euro Area countries are now looking forward to the benefits of increased price transparency, more intense competition in the market place, and greater financial integration in Europe.[54] Although some of the benefits of the euro to firms and consumers are clear, many policy questions are still left unanswered.

Now, in order to protect all the member states, the EU has made agreements to maintain economic stability within the eurozone and avoid any financial crisis. For example, under the Europe's Stability and Growth Pact, the EU's executive body would recommend that public warnings be issued to any country that fell afoul of European deficit control agreements. Some countries such as France have complained that there was too much stress on budget stability and not enough on growth, thus seeking to loosen the constraints imposed on national budgets.[55]

---

[53]"The Long and Arduous Ascent of Euro-Man," *Financial Times*, December 15, 1998, p. 4.

[54]"Three and a Half Years on the Benefits of the Single Currency Are Evident," The European Commission, Brussels, June 19, 2002.

[55]"France Challenges EU Deficit Pact," *CNN News*, http://www.cnn.com/, June 18, 2002.

Ramifications of the Euro for Marketers

Will the euro be the final stage leading to a "United States of Europe"? What opportunities does the euro create for firms operating in the eurozone? What are the possible threats? Answers to these and many other euro-related questions are murky at best.

What is clear is that the switch to the euro has a wide-ranging impact on companies doing business in the eurozone. There have been gains but also plenty of pain. Massive investments in computer infrastructure and logistical expenses have been needed to put the changeover in place. For example, Allianz, the German insurance group, spent $124 million in euro-related data processing and devoted the equivalent of 342 years' worth of extra manpower into its euro-changeover enterprise. DaimlerChrysler pumped $120 million into its euro-conversion projects.[56] A consensus estimate was that the euro-switch would cost companies around $65 billion.[57] On top of these upfront investments, there was also the cost of lost revenues from price harmonization within the eurozone. Apart from these immediate bottom-line effects, EMU also has a strategic impact on companies' operations. For marketers, the key challenges include:

- **Price Transparency.** Before the introduction of the euro, drug prices varied as much as 250 percent within Europe, and German cars in Italy cost up to 30 percent less than in their home market.[58]

  Conventional wisdom says that prices will slide down to the same level throughout the Eurozone. The reason for this is that the single currency makes markets more transparent for consumers and corporate purchase departments. Now that retailers in different eurozone member states display their prices in euro, price differentials have become clear to the consumer. Customers can then easily compare prices of goods across countries.[59]

  Savvy shoppers will bargain-hunt cross-border or search the internet for the best deal. Significant price gaps will also open up arbitrage opportunities leading to parallel imports from low-priced to high-priced markets. Ultimately, manufacturers are forced to make their prices more uniform. While the logic of this argument sounds strong, there is some skepticism about whether the greater transparency achieved via the euro will really push prices downwards. For one thing, one could argue that anyone capable of browsing the internet or handling a pocket calculator already enjoys the benefits of full price transparency. Hence, whether a single currency will enlighten shoppers a great deal is debatable. For many goods and services, cross-border transaction costs (e.g., shipping bulky goods), cost differentials (e.g., labor, energy), standard differences (e.g., televisions in France), and different tax regimes will still justify significant price gaps. Shrewd companies can also find ways to "localize" their products by offering different features or product configurations. One important point to remember is that transparency is two-way. For many firms, not only will the cost of their end-product become more comparable but also the cost of supplies sourced from within the eurozone.[60]

  In fact, in a 1997 survey of 2,100 companies within the European Union, 65 percent of the respondents viewed "greater price transparency" as one of the key areas of cost saving (ranked second behind "reduction of exchange risks or costs").[61]

  Pricing implications of the euro will be discussed further in Chapter 11.

- **Intensified Competitive Pressure.** Many analysts predict that competitive pressure will intensify in scores of industries following the launch of the euro. Pressure to lower prices has increased. Most likely, the single currency spurs the pace of cross-border competition. But then again, intensified competition should be seen as the outcome of an ongoing process of

---

[56]"The Euro: Are You Ready?" *Business Week*, December 14, 1998, p. 35.

[57]"The Euro: Are You Ready?" p. 35.

[58]"When the Walls Come Down," *Economist*, July 5, 1997, p. 69.

[59]John Paul Quinn, "The Euro: See-Through Pricing Arrives," *Electrical Wholesaling*, April 2002, pp. 22–24.

[60]"US Sop Giants' Million-$ Chances to Score," *Financial Times*, December 16, 1998, p. 4.

[61]www.euro.fee.be/Newsletter.

which the euro is only one single step. The euro plays a role, but it is surely not the sole driver that accelerates rivalry within the European Union. To prepare their defenses, several companies have taken measures to lower their costs. This desire to cut costs has also spurred a wave of mergers and acquisitions to build up economies of scale. The Dutch supermarket chain Ahold, for example, is scouting opportunities in Britain, France, Germany, and Italy. By building up muscle, Ahold will be able to negotiate better prices with its suppliers.

- **Streamlined Supply Chains.** Another consequence of the euro is that companies will attempt to further streamline their supply channels. When prices are quoted in euro, singling out the most efficient supplier becomes far easier. Cutting back the number of suppliers is one trend. Numerous firms also plan to build up partnerships with their suppliers. Xerox, for instance, is cutting its supplier base by a factor of 10.[62]

- **New Opportunities for Small and Medium-Sized Companies.** The euro is most likely also a boon for small and medium-sized enterprises (SMEs). So far, many SMEs have limited their operations to their home markets. One motivation for being provincial has often been the huge costs and hassle of dealing with currency fluctuations. According to one study, currency volatility has deterred almost a third of German SMEs from doing business abroad.[63]

- **Adaptation of Internal Organizational Structures.** The euro also provides multinational companies (MNCs) an incentive to rethink their organizational structure. In the past, firms maintained operations in each country to match supply and demand within each country, often at the expense of scale economies. Given that currency volatility, one of the factors behind such setups, significantly lessens with the introduction of the euro, many MNCs doing business on the continent are trimming their internal operations.[64]

  For instance, Michelin, the French tire-maker, closed down 90 percent of its 200 European distribution sites. The pharmaceutical concern Novartis streamlined its European production and eliminated overlapping operations.[65]

  In the long run, firms like Michelin and Novartis will enjoy tremendous benefits of economies of scale. Once again, the euro should be viewed here as a catalyst stimulating a trend that has been ongoing for a number of years rather than a trigger.

- **EU Regulations Crossing National Boundaries.** As the EU matures and the member governments expand its authority, Europeans have found that the EU has increasingly become a force for social regulation that crosses ethnic and national boundaries. Its officials are regulating what people can eat, how they can travel, even how they incinerate their trash. Many cases have been filed for national violations of EU farming, fishing, educational, fiscal, consumer, transportation, taxation, and environmental policies. Countries stand accused of failing to enact laws that conform to EU policies, or of failing to enforce such laws.[66] Companies have been struggling through the EU's complex regulatory process. As a result, various industry associations are now trying to clarify exactly where EU-wide rules end and member state laws begin. For example, a workshop organized by an international food and nutrition policy consultancy, European Advisory Services (EAS), in February 2008, aimed to guide companies toward developing multi-country strategies and successfully introducing food supplements and functional ingredients into the European market.[67]

---

[62]"Business Performance Will Need Sharper Edge," *Financial Times*, November 5, 1998, p. VIII; and John K. Ryans, "Global Marketing in the New Millennium," *Marketing Management*, 8 (Winter 1999), pp. 44–47.

[63]"When the Walls Come Down," *Economist*, July 5, 1997, p. 70.

[64]"Faster Forward," *Economist*, November 28, 1998, p. 84.

[65]"The euro," *Business Week*, April 27, 1998, p. 38.

[66]Jeffrey Smith, "EU Rules Leave a Bad Taste in Italians' Mouths," *Washington Post*, August 7, 2000, p. A01.

[67]"EAS Clarifies EU and National Boundaries for Companies Launching Food Supplements," WNII, whatsnewiningredients.com, February 14, 2008.

SUMMARY

The international financial environment is constantly changing as a result of income growth, balance of payments position, inflation, exchange rate fluctuations, and unpredictable political events in various countries. The International Monetary Fund and World Bank also assist in the economic development of many countries, particularly those of developing countries, and promote stable economic growth in many parts of the world. In most cases, the change in a county's balance of payments position is an immediate precursor to its currency rate fluctuation and subsequent instability in the international financial market.

Thanks to the huge domestic economy and the international transaction currency role of the U.S. dollar, many U.S. companies have been shielded from the changes in the international financial market during much of the postwar era. However, as the U.S. economy depends increasingly on international trade and investment for its livelihood, few companies can ignore the changes.

Having been more dependent on foreign business, many European and Japanese companies have honed their international financial expertise as a matter of survival, particularly since the early 1970s. Accordingly, European countries and Japan have been better able to cope with foreign exchange rate fluctuations than the United States.

International marketers should be aware of the immediate consequences of exchange rate fluctuations on pricing. As increased cost pressure is imminent in an era of global competition, cost competitiveness has become an extremely important strategic issue to many companies. Astute companies have even employed an adverse target exchange rate for cost accounting and pricing purposes. Although accurate prediction is not possible, international marketers should be able to guesstimate the direction of exchange rate movements in major currencies. Some tools are available.

The Asian and South American financial crises, the recent unprecedented global recession triggered by the U.S. subprime mortgage loan crisis, as well as the introduction of the euro in the European Union are highlighted. We do not mean to imply that other issues, such as the collapse of the Russian economy, the recession in the United States and the EU, and global warming, are not equally important and do not have many business implications. We are sure that you are convinced of the importance of keeping constantly abreast of events around you to understand and cope with the ever-changing nature of international business.

We expect that companies from various Asian countries will become ever leaner and more astute competitors in many different ways. South America is also expected to recover.[68] U.S. and other foreign companies doing business in Asia and South America should not pull out of the Asian markets simply because it is very difficult to do business there. Doing so will likely damage corporate reputation and customer trust. U.S. and other foreign companies should have longer-term orientation in dealing with Asian and Latin American consumers and competitors by developing strategies that emphasize value and reducing operational costs thereby reducing susceptibility to occasional financial upheavals.

On the other hand, the European Union (EU) is going through a different kind of economic and political metamorphosis. The EU's new common currency, the euro, has begun to change the way companies do business in Europe. Price comparison across European countries has become easier than ever before. The ease of doing business across countries will permit small and medium-sized companies to go international in the region. Competitive pressure is bound to increase. European companies can also enjoy broader economies of scale and scope, making themselves more competitive in and outside the EU. Again, U.S. and other foreign companies should not take for granted the changing face of the EU market and competition originating from it.

---

[68]Masaaki Kotabe and Ricardo Leal, *Market Revolution in Latin America: Beyond Mexico*, New York: Elsevier Science, 2001.

QUESTIONS

1. Which international currency or currencies are likely to increasingly assume a role as the international transaction currency in international trade? Why?

2. Discuss the primary roles of the International Monetary Fund and World Bank.

3. How does a currency bloc help a multinational company's global operations?

4. Describe in your own words how knowledge of the spot and forward exchange rate market helps international marketers.

5. Define the four types of balance of payments measures.

6. What are the advantages and disadvantages of having the euro as a common currency in the European Union?

7. Fujitsu, a Japanese computer manufacturer, was recently quoted as taking various steps to prevent wild foreign exchange fluctuations from affecting the company's business. One step being taken is the balancing of export and import contracts. In 2001, the company entered into $3.4 billion of export contracts and $3.2 billion of import contracts. For the year 2002, these

figures were expected to be balanced. Explain how this measure would help the firm. What are the advantages and disadvantages of this measure? Are there any alternate courses of action that would give the same end results?

8. In July 2005, China dropped its decade-long currency peg to the U.S. dollar, and instead repegged to a basket of currencies. China reevaluated the yuan to make the currency effectively 2.1 percent stronger against the U.S. dollar. On May 16, 2007, China again took steps to let its currency trade more freely against the dollar and to cool its sizzling economy and contain its soaring trade surplus with the United States. The yuan was allowed to fluctuate further against the dollar by 0.5 percent a day, up from 0.3 percent. Under the new currency system, China has not yet surrendered control of the currency. It has moved away from a fixed exchange rate but not all the way to a flexible or free-floating one. American manufacturers and labor unions hope the yuan's reevaluation will help U.S. factory sales and jobs by making U.S. goods more affordable abroad. For China, the currency move will make Chinese exports a little more expensive abroad. Many Asian countries have been trying to compete with China's low-cost manufacturing, and after China's yuan reevaluation, Malaysia announced it would drop its peg to the U.S. dollar as well. In the short run, the change in China's currency management system could be almost unnoticeable. In the longer run, however, the impact on trade and on the world financial system could be huge. Based on what you have learned from this chapter, what would be the impacts on the world's economy if China and other Asian countries truly allowed their currencies to float, or, instead, kept holding them within narrow bands against the dollar?

CULTURAL ISSUES AND BUYING BEHAVIOR

4

CHAPTER OVERVIEW

1. Meaning of culture
2. Elements of culture
3. Cross-cultural comparisons
4. Adapting to cultures
5. Culture and the marketing mix

In the Western hemisphere, people have a long tradition of engaging in outdoor leisure activities. However, it was not until 1995 that the first outdoor product store opened in China. The North Face, a leading U.S.-based supplier of outdoor sports gear and apparel products, entered the Chinese market in 2007. When it first arrived, the firm had to surmount several obstacles. Differences in body shapes, styles, and tastes meant that products needed to be adapted for Chinese consumers. However, Chinese outdoor activists also differ from their Western counterparts in terms of their mindset. For instance, in China the sense of community and group outdoor activities is much more important than in the West, where people tend to focus on individual achievements and activities. In collaboration with its advertising agency, North Face developed a series of campaigns to foster outdoor leisure activities. The "Go Wild" campaign which the firm ran in 2012 invited city dwellers to break free from their stressful urban lifestyle by engaging in thrilling experiences in the great outdoors. The campaign centered on an online documentary series consisting of four short movies directed by a renowned Chinese director. One of the movies showed the founder of a local magazine hiking with his grown son through the harsh mountains of Tibet.[1] By 2012, five years after entering China, North Face's business has grown sevenfold, well beyond the firm's expectations. The company sees a huge market potential in China: whereas in South Korea 25 percent of the people are outdoor sports enthusiasts, the share is only 0.5 percent in China.[2]

As the North Face's experience in China illustrates, cultural norms and values can often have a major impact on the success of a company's marketing strategy in the host country. In

---

[1]"The North Face and O&M Shanghai Inspire Chinese to 'Go Wild,'" http://www.ogilvy.com/News/Press-Releases/March-2012-The-North-Face-and-Ogilvy-Shanghai-Inspire-Chinese-to-Go-Wild.aspx.
[2]"Outdoor Success," http://europe.chinadaily.com.cn, accessed August 27, 2013.

general, consumers' cultures are a key driver of their buying motivations, attitudes toward the brand or marketing campaign, and their ultimate buying behavior.[3]

At the same time, cultural mistakes are easily made. To celebrate the United Arab Emirates' (UAE) 40th birthday in December 2011, Puma launched a limited edition shoe draped in the colors of the country's flag. The promotion sparked anger among UAE citizens. As one Emirati businessman commented: "The flag is a very sacred symbol for the UAE. It cannot be trivialized, especially not as footwear."[4] On the other hand, when Italian carmaker Fiat introduced a limited-edition 500 model decked out in the colors of the American flag in spring 2012 it created no controversy in the U.S. market.[5] German pen maker Montblanc had to withdraw a special edition $25,000 "Gandhi" fountain pen in India after the product sparked a furor over the use of the spiritual leader's name for commercial purposes.[6] Both the Puma and Montblanc examples show that trivializing the host country's cultural symbols and heritage can be disastrous.

Managers running a company in a foreign country need to interact with people from different cultural environments. Culture clashes among international joint venture partners or between local and headquarters management can often undermine the best intentions. For instance, Japan's slow-moving, consensus-driven culture was partly blamed for former Sony CEO Howard Singer's failure to restore the fortunes of the Japanese consumer electronics giant.[7]

To be able to grasp the intricacies of foreign markets, it is crucial to get a thorough understanding of cultural differences. From a global marketing perspective, the cultural environment matters for two reasons. First and foremost, cultural forces are a major factor in shaping a company's global marketing mix program. Global marketing managers constantly face the thorny issue of finding out to what extent their marketing mix programs should address cultural differences. Cultural blunders can easily become a costly affair for MNCs. Some of the possible liabilities of cultural gaffes include embarrassment, lost customers, missed opportunities, and a tarnished brand or corporate reputation.[8] Second, cultural analysis can often signal new market opportunities. A company that recognizes cultural values that its rivals have so far ignored often can gain a competitive edge. For instance, several Japanese diaper makers were able to steal market share away from Procter & Gamble by selling diapers that were much thinner than the ones marketed by P&G, thereby better meeting the desires of Japanese mothers.[9]

Evolving trends, as mapped out by changes in cultural indicators, also lead to market opportunities that savvy marketers can leverage. Consider for a moment the opportunities created by China's one-child policy. Children in China impact consumption patterns in three ways: (1) they have spending power, (2) they have "pester power," and (3) they act as change agents. Giving pocket money to children is increasingly common in China. Chinese children

[3]For a good overview of recent research insights on how cultural backgrounds impact consumer decision making, see Donnel A. Briley and Jennifer L. Aaker, "Bridging the Culture Chasm: Ensuring That Consumers Are Healthy, Wealthy, and Wise," *Journal of Public Policy & Marketing*, 25 (2006), pp. 53–66.

[4]"UAE Flags Cultural Sensitivity of Puma Shoes," http:// www.brandchannel.com, accessed March 1, 2012.

[5]http://www.autoblog.com/2012/03/06/2012-fiat-500-america-geneva-2012/, accessed August 27, 2013.

[6]"Montblanc's $25,000 Gandhi Pen Stirs Controversy," http://www.usatoday.com, accessed Jan. 20, 2012.

[7]"Sony: Channels to Choose," http://www.ft.com, accessed March 1, 2012.

[8]Tevfik Dalgic and Ruud Heijblom, "International Marketing Blunders Revisited—Some Lessons for Managers," *Journal of International Marketing* 4, no. 1 (1996): 81–91.

[9]Alecia Swasy, *Soap Opera: The Inside Story of Procter & Gamble* (New York: Random House, 1993). Japanese homes usually have far less space than European or American ones.

are being doted on not just by their parents but also by two sets of grandparents. Moreover, Chinese children can also have a tremendous amount of "pester power." For that reason, they are often referred to as "little emperors." Finally, children are important change agents for scores of new consumer products because they are often the first ones to be exposed (via friends, television) to the innovation. To capitalize on the rising importance of children within Chinese society, multinationals have developed goods and services that cater toward their needs. Disney, for instance, set up a chain of language schools in major cities to teach English to Chinese children using Disney-inspired learning materials. The program—branded Disney English—uses a combination of story-telling, sing-alongs, and role-playing.[10]

Within a given culture, consumption processes can be described via a sequence of four stages—access, buying behavior, consumption characteristics, and disposal:

1. *Access.* Does the consumer have physical and/or economic access to the product/service?
2. *Buying behavior.* How do consumers make the decision to buy in the foreign market?
3. *Consumption characteristics.* What factors drive the consumption patterns?
4. *Disposal.* How do consumers dispose of the product (in terms of resale, recycling, etc.)?[11]

Consumers' cultural values and norms will impact each of these four stages.

This chapter deals with the cultural environment of the global marketplace. First we describe the concept of culture. We then explore various elements of culture. Cultures differ a great deal, but they can also overlap. We will discuss several schemes that can be used to compare cultures. As a global business manager, you should be aware of your own cultural norms and other people's cultural mindset. To that end, we will discuss several ways to adapt to foreign cultures. The final part of this chapter will discuss how the host country's culture can influence the company's marketing mix strategy.

Meaning of Culture

The literature offers a host of definitions of culture. The Dutch social scientist Hofstede, for instance, defines culture as "the collective programming of the mind which distinguishes the members of one group or category from those of another."[12] Daphna Oyserman, a social psychologist at the University of Michigan, describes culture as "that which goes without saying; the right way to be, do, and feel."[13]

Human life is embedded within one's culture. Human culture provides acceptable working solutions to three basic problems of survival: sustaining the group over time, organizing relationships, and facilitating individual welfare.[14] These solutions are "good enough," meaning they are not necessarily the most efficient ones. For instance, a harsh climate could have led the group to adopt a particular diet, house construction style, and dress code to cope with the elements. These solutions then become part of the group's culture. Once a solution has been established, it will usually persist even when other solutions become available or the environment changes. As a result, cultures tend to be fairly stable over time. Changes are typically very slow, even glacial.

---

[10]http://china.disneycareers.com/en/about-disney-china/disney-english/?rlang=en, accessed August 27, 2013.

[11]P. S. Raju, "Consumer Behavior in Global Markets: The A-B-C-D Paradigm and Its Applications to Eastern Europe and the Third World," *Journal of Consumer Marketing*, 12 (5), 1995, pp. 37–56.

[12]Geert Hofstede, *Cultures and Organizations: Software of the Mind* (London: McGraw-Hill, 1991), p. 5.

[13]Daphna Oyserman (University of Michigan), seminar at HKUST, March 5, 2012.

[14]S.Schwartz, "Universals in the Content and Structure of Values: Theoretical Advances and Empirical Tests in 20 Countries," *Advances in Experimental Social Psychology*, 25 (1992): 1–65.

Despite the wide variety of definitions, there are common elements that span the different formulations. First of all, people *learn* culture.[15] In other words, people do not inherit their culture. A society's culture is passed on ("cultivated") by various peer groups (family, school, youth organizations, and so forth) from one generation to the next. Second, culture consists of many different parts that are all *interrelated*. One element (say, one's social status) of a person's culture does have an impact on another part (say, the language that this person uses). So, a person's cultural mindset is not a random collection of behaviors. In a sense, culture is a very complex jigsaw puzzle in which all the pieces fit together. Finally, culture is *shared* by individuals as members of society. These three facets—cultures being learned, shared, and composed of interrelated parts—spell out the essence of culture.

Cultures may be defined by national borders, especially where countries are isolated by natural barriers. Examples are island nations (e.g., Japan, Ireland, Australia) and peninsulas (e.g., Korea, Thailand). However, most cultures cross national boundaries. In addition, most nations contain different subgroups (subcultures) within their borders. These subgroups could be defined along linguistic (Flemish versus Walloons in Belgium) or religious lines (Buddhist Sinhalese versus Hindu Tamils versus Muslims in Sri Lanka). Few cultures are homogeneous. Typically, most cultures contain subcultures that often have little in common with one another. Needless to say, the wide variety of cultures and subcultures creates a tremendous challenge for global marketers.

Elements of Culture

Culture consists of many components that interrelate with one another. Knowledge of a culture requires a deep understanding of its different parts. In this section, we describe those elements that are most likely to matter to international marketers: material life, language, social interactions, aesthetics, religion, education, and values.

Material Life

A major component of culture is its material aspect. Material life refers primarily to the technologies that are used to produce, distribute, and consume goods and services within society. Differences in the material environment partly explain differences in the level and type of demand for many consumption goods. For instance, energy consumption is not only much higher in developed countries than in developing nations but also relies on more advanced forms such as nuclear energy. To bridge material environment differences, marketers are often forced to adapt their product offerings. Consider, for instance, the soft drink industry. In many countries outside the United States, store shelf space is heavily restricted, and refrigerators have far less capacity (smaller kitchens) compared to the United States. As a result, soft drink bottlers sell one- or one-and-a-half liter bottles rather than two-liter bottles. In markets like Kenya, Vietnam, and India, transportation infrastructure is extremely poor, making distribution of products a total nightmare. In Brazil, Nestlé sails a supermarket barge down the Amazon river to reach 800,000 potential customers in that region. The vessel carries 300 different goods including chocolate, ice cream, and juices.[16]

Technology gaps also affect investment decisions. Poor transportation conditions, unreliable power supply, and distribution infrastructure in many emerging markets force companies to improvise and look for alternative ways to market and deliver their products. In rural areas of

---

[15]Some biologists have made a compelling case that culture is not a uniquely human domain in the sense that animals (especially primates) can also possess a culture. A good introduction to this perspective is Frans de Waal, *The Ape and the Sushi Master* (London: Penguin Books, 2001).

[16]http://www.bloomberg.com/news/2010-06-17/nestle-navigates-amazon-rivers-to-reach-cut-off-consumers-before-unilever.html

countries like India, conventional media are incapable of reaching the whole universe of consumers. Global marketers in such countries need to come up with innovative ways to access rural consumers. Governments in host nations often demand technology transfers as part of the investment package. Companies that are not keen on sharing their technology are forced to abandon or modify their investment plans. When the Indian government asked Coca-Cola to share its recipe, Coke decided to jump ship and left the India marketplace in 1977. The soft drink maker returned to India in 1992.

Language

In developing a line of talking dolls targeted at children in China, a major hurdle for Fisher-Price engineers was the Mandarin "sh" sound, which involves a soft hiss that was difficult to encode on sound-data chips. In the end, Fisher-Price was able to resolve the issue of recording the phrase "It's learning time" in Mandarin.[17]

The Fisher-Price problem is just one example of scores of language-related challenges that international marketing managers need to confront. Two facets of language have a bearing on marketers: (1) the use of language as a communication tool within cultures and (2) the huge diversity of languages across and often within national boundaries.

Let us first consider the communication aspect. As a communication medium, language has two parts: the spoken and the so-called silent language. The spoken language consists of the vocal sounds or written symbols that people use to communicate with one another. Silent language refers to the complex of nonverbal communication mechanisms that people use to get a message across. Edward Hall identified five distinctive types of silent languages: space, material posses-sions, friendship patterns, time, and agreements. Space refers to the conversation distance between people: close or remote. The second type, material possessions, relates to the role of possessions in people's esteem of one another. Friendship patterns cover the notion and treatment of friends. Perceptions of time also vary across cultures. Differences exist about the importance of punctuality, the usefulness of "small talk," and so forth. The final type refers to the interpretation of agreements. People in some cultures focus on the explicit contract itself. In other cultures, negotiating parties put faith in the spirit of the contract and trust among one another.

Not surprisingly, a given gesture often has quite different meanings across cultures. In Japan, scribbling identifying cues on business cards is a major violation of basic business etiquette. On the other hand, foreigners (*gaijin*) are not expected to engage in the bowing rituals used for greeting people of various ranks.[18] In countries such as the United States, the hand gesture made by connecting the thumb and the forefinger in a circle and holding the other fingers straight signals an "okay." The same hand gesture could mean "money" in Japan, "zero" in Russia, and a gross insult in Brazil and parts of Southern Europe.

People from different cultures also read facial expressions differently. One recent cross-cultural study found that East Asian subjects focused mostly on the eyes while Western participants scanned the whole face, including the eyes and the mouth. In the study, East Asians were more likely than Western people to read the expression for "fear" as "surprise" and "disgust" as "anger."[19] These cross-cultural variations are reflected in differences between Eastern and Western emoticons—the pictorial representations used to express a person's mood in online messaging or text messages: Eastern emoticons focus on the eyes whereas Western ones also include the mouth (see **Exhibit 4-1**). Other examples abound of silent language forms that are harmless in one society and tactless or even insulting in others. It is imperative that managers

---

[17]"Fisher-Price Talks Mandarin," *The Wall Street Journal*, June 2, 2008, p. 28.

[18]"When Fine Words Will Butter No Parsnips," *Financial Times*, May 1, 1992.

[19]Rachael E. Jack, Caroline Blais, Christoph Scheepers, Philippe G. Schyns, and Roberto Caldara, "Cultural Confusions Show That Facial Expressions Are Not Universal," *Current Biology* 19 (August 2009): 1543–1548.

Exhibit 4-1   East–West Differences in Emoticons

Emotion	West	East
"Happy"	:-)	(^_^)
"Sad"	:-(	(;_;) or (T_T)
"Surprise"	:-o	(o.o)

Source: http://news.bbc.co.uk/2/hi/8199951.stm.

familiarize themselves with the critical aspects of a foreign culture's hidden language. Failure to follow this rule will sooner or later lead to hilarious or embarrassing situations.

The huge diversity of languages poses another headache to multinational companies. Language is often described as the mirror of a culture. The number of "living" languages is estimated to be 6,912, though most of these are spoken by very few people.[20] Differences exist across and within borders. Not surprisingly, populous countries contain many languages. In India, Hindi, spoken by 30 percent of the population, is the national language but there are 14 other official languages.[21] Papua New Guinea, an island nation in the southern Pacific Ocean, has around 715 indigenous languages. Even small countries show a fair amount of language variety. Switzerland, with a population of nearly 7.5 million people, has four national languages: German (spoken by 63.7 percent of the population), French (20.4 percent), Italian (6.5 percent), and Romansch (0.5 percent).[22]

Even within the same language, meanings and expressions vary a great deal among countries that share the language. A good example is English. English words that sound completely harmless in one English-speaking country often have a silly or sinister meaning in another Anglo-Saxon country. Until 1990, Snickers bars were sold under the brand name Marathon in the United Kingdom. Mars felt that the Snickers name was too close to the English idiom for female lingerie (knickers).[23] Cert, a London-based consultant, offers a few rules of thumb about talking to non-native English speakers in English:

1. *Vocabulary*. Go for the simplest words (e.g., use the word *rich* instead of *loaded*, *affluent*, or *opulent*). Treat colloquial words with care.

2. *Idioms*. Pick and choose idioms carefully (for instance, most non-U.S. speakers would not grasp the meaning of the expression *nickel-and-diming*).

3. *Grammar*. Express one idea in each sentence. Avoid subclauses.

4. *Cultural references*. Avoid culture-specific references (e.g., "Doesn't he look like David Letterman?").

5. *Understanding non-native English speakers*. This will be a matter of unpicking someone's accent. If you do not understand, make it seem that it is you, not the other party, who is slow.

Language blunders easily arise as a result of careless translations of advertising slogans or product labels. Toshiba once had a commercial jingle in China that went "Toshiba, Toshiba." Unfortunately, in Mandarin Chinese, Toshiba sounds a lot like "let's steal it" (*tou-chu-ba*). The English version of a newspaper ad campaign run by Electricité de France (EDF), the main electricity supply firm in France, said that the company offered "competitive energetic solutions"

---

[20]http://gamma.sil.org/ethnologue, accessed September 12, 2008.

[21]These are Bengali, Telugu, Marathi, Tamil, Urdu, Gujarati, Malayalam, Kannada, Oriya, Punjabi, Assamese, Sindhi, and Sanskrit. Hindustani, a mixture of Hindi and Urdu, is not an official language, though widely spoken.

[22]Romansch descends from Vulgar Latin, the language that was spoken in the Roman Empire. It is spoken by less than 1 percent of the Swiss population. Note though that only German, French, and Italian are official languages, https://www.cia .gov/library/publications/the-world-factbook/, accessed August 27, 2013.

[23]Masterfoods recently launched a new energy bar in the United States under the Snickers Marathon brand name.

Exhibit 4-2 How Not to Sell Abroad

Company/Brand	Original wording	Mistranslation
Parker Pen	The Quink pen "won't leak and embarrass you"	Spanish: *embarazar* you—make you pregnant.
Toyota	MR 2 Sports Car	French: "M-R deux" sounded like *merde*, a common expletive.
Bacardi	Pavane, an upscale drink	German: Pavane sounded like *Pavian* (baboon).
Coors	Slogan: "Turn it loose"	Spanish: "Get loose bowels."
IKEA	Gutvik children's bed	German: *Gutvik* sounded very close to "good f . . . "
General Motors	Buick LaCrosse	Québécois French: *La crosse* is slang for self-gratification. GM renamed the car The Allure for the Canadian market.
Hershey	La Dulceria Thalia, a treat filled with caramel cream ("cajeta," in ads)	Spanish: Hershey's targeted its ad campaign at the Mexican market, but in other Spanish-speaking countries such as Argentina, *cajeta* is slang for female genitalia.
Calpis Co.	Calpis is a Japanese soft drink with a milky flavor	English: *Calpis* sounds similar to cow piss. In some English-speaking countries such as the United States the drink was renamed Calpico.
Motorola	"Hello Moto" slogan	Hindi: The campaign "Hello Moto" did nothing for Motorola in India because *moto* means fatty in Hindi.

Source: Based on "Found in Translation: Avoiding Multilingual Gaffes," money.cnn.com, accessed on May 7, 2012.

and was "willing to accompany your development by following you on all of your sites in Europe and beyond."[24] **Exhibit 4-2** lists a few other examples of "unfortunate" translations. Certain concepts are unique to a particular language. For example, an expression for the Western concept of romance does not exist in languages such as Chinese, Thai, Malay, and Korean.[25]

Mistranslations may create the impression that the company does not care about its customers abroad. Several techniques can be used to achieve good translations of company literature. With **back translation**, a bilingual speaker—whose native tongue is the target language—translates the company document first in the foreign language. Another bilingual translator—whose native tongue is the base language—then translates this version back into the original language. Differences between the versions are then resolved through discussion until consensus is reached on the proper translation.

Firms doing business in multilingual societies need to decide what languages to use for product labels or advertising copy. Multilingual labels are fairly common now, especially in the pan-European market. Advertising copy poses a bigger hurdle. To deal with language issues in advertising copy, advertisers can rely on local advertising agencies, minimize the spoken part of the commercial, or use subtitles. We will revisit these issues in much more detail in the global advertising and promotion chapter (Chapter 12).

In markets such as China, marketers also need to decide whether to keep the original brand or company name or whether to adopt a localized brand identity. Many multinationals in China have localized their brand names by creating equivalent names that sound like their global name with a positive meaning in Chinese. Hewlett-Packard, for instance, adopted *Hui-Pu* as its Chinese brand name. Hui means "kindness" and Pu means "universal." Other companies take a different track and translate their name using characters that do not necessarily have the same

---

[24]"The Case of the Misleading Coffin," *Financial Times*, June 21, 1999, p. 12.

[25]Jocelyn Probert and Hellmut Schütte, "De Beers: Diamonds Are for Asia," INSEAD-EAC, Case Study 599-011-1 (1999).

◆ ◆

Global Perspective 4-1

Kit Kat in Japan: *Kitto Katsu*

Kit Kat, the candy brand owned by Swiss multinational Nestlé, has become the leading confectionary brand in Japan (Kit Kat is made under license by Hershey in the U.S. market). The road to the top spot took some very clever, creative marketing. A number of years ago, Nestlé, the Swiss multinational food company, discovered a sharp spike in the sales of Kit Kat candy bars during exam periods. Apparently, Japanese parents would place Kit Kat bars as a treat in their children's lunch boxes, especially during exam season. In addition, studious pupils were buying Kit Kats for themselves as a reminder that they were going to give these exams their best shot. Kit Kat had become a lucky charm for Japanese students cramming for their exams.

One reason for Kit Kat's success has to do with the ring of its brand name: the "Kit Kat" name sounds very much like the expression "kitto katsu," a Japanese exam-season mantra that literally means "I'll do my best to make sure I succeed." To leverage the brand name's symbolic meaning, Nestlé partnered with Japan Post to create "Kit Kat Mail," a postcard like product available only at the post office. These items could be mailed to students as an edible good-luck charm. Nestlé also decorated post offices with a cherry blossom theme, as Japan's annual exam period overlaps with the celebration of the country's cherry-blossom season.

Using the postal service as a distribution channel provided Nestlé with the further advantage of no competition—unlike convenience stores or supermarkets.

To cater to the taste of Japanese consumers, Nestlé offers a wide variety of flavors. Just as in the rest of the world, the firm sells its staple chocolate flavors. But it does not end there. Other flavors reflect specialties from regions across Japan such as sweet potatoes from Okinawa, melons from Hokkaido, strawberries from Tochigi, green tea from Kyoto, and soy sauce from Tokyo. Other even more exotic flavors include wasabi (green horse-radish), chili, miso (a traditional Japanese seasoning), cherry, and lemon or strawberry cheesecake. Many of these special flavors are introduced for a limited time only to encourage shoppers to try something new, and are then subsequently taken off the market. Excess inventory is collected and used to create "Happy Bags" that are sold during gift-giving periods such as New Year.

Sources: "Kit Kat Takes on Japanese Tastes," http://www.independent .co.uk/life-style/food-and-drink/kit-kat-takes-on-japanese-tastes-1901867. html; and "Soy-sauce-flavored Kit Kats? In Japan, They're No. 1," http:// adage.com/article/global-news/marketing-nestle-flavors-kit-kat-japan-markets/142461/.

---

sound as the original name. In 2002, Oracle, following a brainstorming session with its Chinese executives, adopted the name *Jia Gu Wen*. The literal translation means the recording of data and information—a nice fit with Oracle's core business. Apparently, the meaning of the phrase stems from a time when tortoise shells were used to record the prophecies from an oracle during the Shang dynasty. **Global Perspective 4-1** discusses how Nestlé leveraged the Japanese sound of the Kit Kat candy brand name.

Social Interactions

The movie *Iron & Silk* is a neat illustration of the cultural misunderstandings that arise in cross-cultural interactions. The movie is based on the true-life story of Mark Salzman, a Yale graduate who, after his studies, went to China to teach English in a small village. During his first day of class, his students, out of respect for their teacher, insist on calling him "Mister Salzman." Mark prefers to be addressed on a first-name basis. Ultimately, students and teacher settle on "teacher Mark" as a compromise.

A critical aspect of culture is the social interactions among people—the manner in which members of society relate to one another. Probably the most crucial expression of social interactions is the concept of kinship. This concept varies dramatically across societies. In most Western countries, the family unit refers to the **nuclear family**, being the parents and the children. The relevant family unit in many developing countries is the **extended family**, which often comprises a much wider group of only remotely related family members. The way families are structured has important ramifications. Family units fulfill many roles, including economic and psychological support. For instance, in Chinese society, many parents believe that having a son is a vital element for their old age. Views on marriage and the role of husband and wife can also be unique to a particular culture. Attitudes toward love and marriage in China are far more materialistic than in other countries. Marriage is seen as a partnership toward achieving success. Chinese women often select prospective husbands based on financial status and career prospects rather than love, which is considered a luxury. Role expectations are very traditional: the man should be provider and protector; the woman should do the cooking, be a good mother, and be virtuous.[26] In countries where extended families are the norm, major purchase decisions are agreed upon by many individuals. Within such communities, members of an extended family will pool their resources to fund the purchase of big-ticket items (e.g., sewing machines, washing machines).

Identifying the key influencers within a given culture is often critical for a targeting strategy to succeed. A few years ago, Procter & Gamble had to tackle a major issue for its Gillette brand in India: most Indian men did not like to shave. However, Gillette's research showed that 77 percent of Indian women prefer clean-shaven men. This insight inspired the "Women Against Lazy Stubble" (WALS) campaign. The campaign began in 2009 on Facebook and then quickly expanded to other media, including mock news-reports and lifestyle TV shows. Sales of Gillette's Mach3 brand skyrocketed as a result of the WALS campaign.[27]

In Chinese cultures, **guanxi** refers to the network of interpersonal ties among people or companies. Within a business context, *guanxi* opens dialogue, builds trust, and facilitates exchanges of favors.[28] When formal mechanisms fail, *guanxi* can provide a solution. Although firms can benefit from their managers'*guanxi*, companies should be aware of *guanxi*'s dark side. The biggest risk could emerge if *guanxi* obligations overburden the firm by forcing the company to reciprocate favors it may not be able to deliver. To buffer against such liabilities, some firms in China maintain a rotation system to ensure that key executives do not stay in the same place for more than two years.[29] **Exhibit 4-3** spells out five rules that are helpful in successfully cracking the *guanxi* code.

Countries also vary in terms of the scope of the decision-making authority. A study by Asia Market Intelligence (AMI), a Hong Kong–based research firm, looked at the decision-making influence of husbands and wives on grocery shopping. The study showed that even in Asia's most conservative societies, men are heavily involved in grocery shopping. The reasons for the rising number of men doing the family grocery shopping vary, including more women entering the workforce and changing attitudes toward gender roles.[30]

Another important aspect of social interactions is the individual's reference groups—the set of people to whom an individual looks for guidance in values and attitudes. As such, reference groups will have an enormous impact on people's consumption behavior patterns. The consumer

[26]Probert and Schütte, "De Beers: Diamonds Are for Asia," p. 11.

[27]"Brand of the Year. Gillette India," *Campaign* (January 2011): 81.

[28]Robert E. Hoskisson, Lorraine Eden, Chung M. Lau, and Mike Wright, "Strategy in Emerging Economies," *Academy of Management Journal* 43, no. 3 (2000): 246–267.

[29]Flora F. Gu, Kineta Hung, and David K. Tse, "When Does *Guanxi* Matter? Issues of Capitalization and Its Dark Sides," *Journal of Marketing* 72, no. 3 (July 2008): 12-28.

[30]"As More Women Enter Work Force, More Men Enter the Supermarket," *Asian Wall Street Journal,* March 8, 2001, pp. N1, N7.

Exhibit 4-3   Rules for Cracking the *Guanxi* Code in China

1. Be prepared to carry stacks of business cards, but don't waste time trying to swap one with every person in the room. *Guanxi* is about building trust, not a personal database.
2. Never pass up an invitation to play golf or other sports with the locals. Wine tastings and art auctions are good places to network.
3. When someone promises to "open doors" for you, be suspicious. Increased transparency in China means that everybody has to jump through the same hoops.
4. Tap into your own alma mater's alumni associations in China. Even consider enrolling in local executive MBA programs.
5. In traditional *guanxi*, if someone does you a favor, one day you will have to repay (in *The Godfather* fashion). These days, however, people are more willing to give without expecting something in return.

Source: "You Say *Guanxi*, I Say Schmoozing," *BusinessWeek*, November 19, 2007, p. 85.

research literature identifies three kinds of reference groups:[31] membership groups—those to which people belong; anticipatory groups—groupings of which one would like to be a part; and dissociative groups—groups with which individuals do not want to be associated. Reference groups are especially influential for consumer products that are socially visible, such as most status goods and luxury items. Knowledge about reference group patterns can provide input in formulating product positioning strategies and devising advertising campaigns. A good example is a campaign that Allied Domecq developed to reposition Kahlúa in Asia. During the Asian recession in the late 1990s, Allied Domecq wanted to revamp Kahlúa, a Mexican coffee liqueur brand, as the brand of choice among young Asians. To reach out to its target audience, Allied Domecq sponsored a dance program on MTV Networks Asia called "Party Zone Mixing with Kahlúa." The prime motivation behind the sponsorship was that "Young adults throughout Asia look to MTV as a trendsetter and representative of their lifestyle."[32] The "chav" phenomenon in Britain is a good illustration of the importance of dissociative reference groups. Chavs belong to a social underclass of young, white, undereducated, and mostly unemployed people. Chavs have adopted the classic Burberry fashion-brand as their clan plaid, though most of what they purchase is counterfeit. Not surprisingly, Burberry is not very pleased with the popularity of its label among chavs.[33]

Aesthetics

Aesthetics refers to the ideas and perceptions that a culture upholds in terms of beauty and good taste. For many products or services, satisfying consumers' aesthetic or sensory needs (visual, taste, smell, sound) can often be at least as important as meeting more basic needs. Cultures differ sharply in terms of their aesthetic preferences, though variations are mostly regional, not national. As a result, multinational firms must often customize the design or look of products to meet cross-cultural differences in consumers' aesthetic perceptions and preferences. To win over Japanese customers, in 2011 Samsonite introduced a new range of products designed, made, and sourced in Japan, Asia's largest luggage market. The top end of this "made in Japan" series included limited edition small bags priced at around $700 each.[34] However, in Korea, China, and other Asian countries, Samsonite launched the Samsonite RED label—a line of sleek, casual-looking luggage targeted at young professionals.

---

[31]James F. Engel, Roger D. Blackwell, and Paul W. Miniard, *Consumer Behavior* (Hinsdale, IL: Dryden, 1986), pp. 318–24.
[32]"Kahlua Gets New Sales Face in Asia," *Advertising Age International*, March 8, 1999, pp. 5–6
[33]"Burberry Admits that Chav Effect Checked Sales over Christmas," http://www.telegraph.co.uk, accessed August 27, 2013.
[34]"Samsonite Makes Its Case for Japan," http://www.ft.com, accessed May 1, 2012.

Aesthetics plays a major role in designing the visual aspects of the product, including elements such as the packaging and the logo. For instance, one study of the design of brand logos in Singapore and China suggested that companies should select logo designs that are elaborate (complex, depth, active), harmonious (symmetry, balance), and natural.[35]

One important element of a product's visuals is its color imagery. Not surprisingly, color perceptions and preferences can vary enormously across cultures. This is illustrated in **Exhibit 4-4**, which shows car color preferences in different countries/regions. As you can

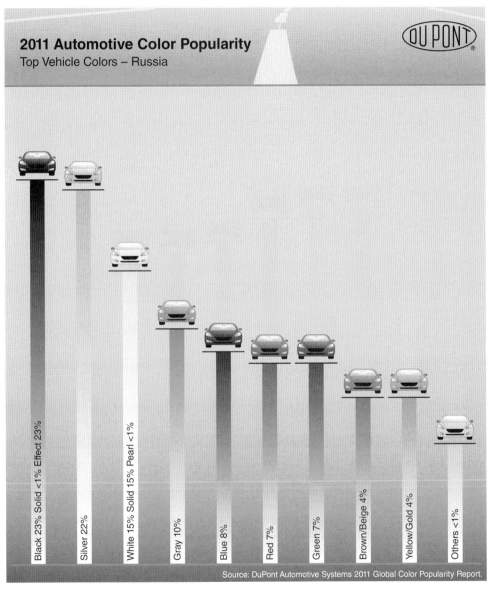

2011 Automotive Color Popularity
Top Vehicle Colors – Russia

DUPONT

Black 23% Solid <1% Effect 23%
Silver 22%
White 15% Solid 15% Pearl <1%
Gray 10%
Blue 8%
Red 7%
Green 7%
Brown/Beige 4%
Yellow/Gold 4%
Others <1%

Source: DuPont Automotive Systems 2011 Global Color Popularity Report.

Exhibit 4-4 2011 Car Color Preferences

[35]Pamela W. Henderson, Joseph A. Cote, Siew Meng Leong, and Bernd Schmitt, "Building Strong Brands in Asia: Selecting the Visual Components of Image to Maximize Brand Strength," *International Journal of Research in Marketing*, 20 (December 2003), pp. 297–313.

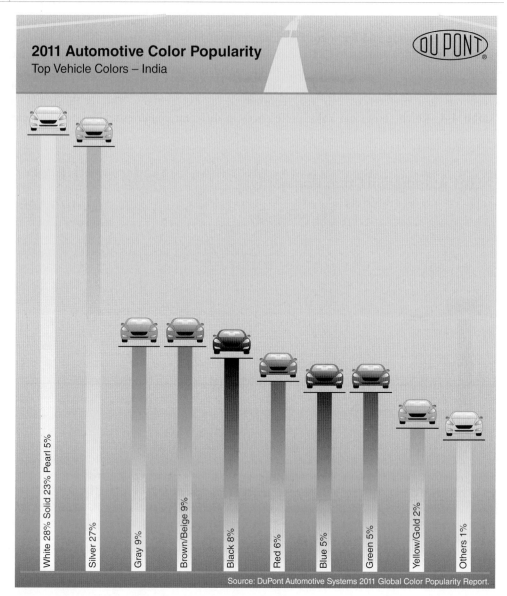

Exhibit 4-4   (*continued*)

see, there are clearly sharp contrasts in people's color preferences. White is the top choice in most Asian countries (e.g., Japan: 26%, India: 28%), North America (23%), and Mexico (25%). However, black is popular in Europe (25%) and Russia (23%). Silver is preferred in China (26%), Brazil (30%), and Korea (30%).

In Chinese cultures, red is perceived as a lucky color. During the Beijing 2008 Olympics, many multinationals in China draped their brands in red. Even Pepsi changed its iconic blue can into a red-painted can for the occasion.[36] Yellow, on the other hand, is perceived as pleasant and

---

[36]http://www.youtube.com/watch?v=dzFuIQe88jU, accessed October 30, 2008.

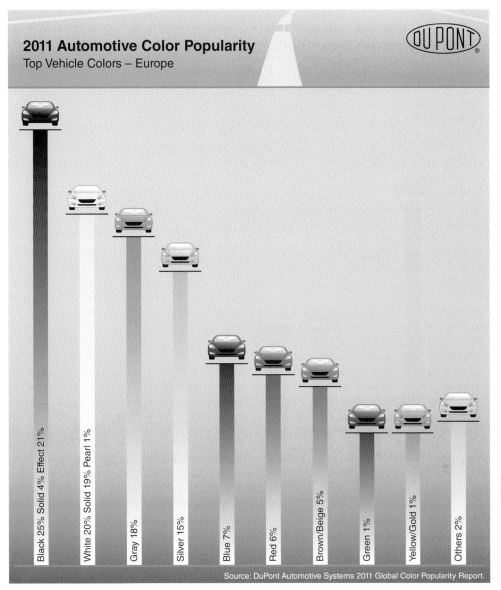

2011 Automotive Color Popularity
Top Vehicle Colors – Europe

DUPONT

Black 25% Solid 4% Effect 21%

White 20% Solid 19% Pearl 1%

Gray 18%

Silver 15%

Blue 7%

Red 6%

Brown/Beige 5%

Green 1%

Yellow/Gold 1%

Others 2%

Source: DuPont Automotive Systems 2011 Global Color Popularity Report.

Exhibit 4-4 (*continued*)

associated with authority. In Japan, pastel tones, expressing softness and harmony, are preferred to bright colors.[37] Given that colors may invoke different meanings, it is important to realize how the colors of a particular package, product, or brand are perceived in the host culture.

Other forms of aesthetics relate to attitudes and preferences toward music, food (e.g., spicy foods), physical beauty (e.g., preference for white skin in many Asian countries), and fashion.

---

[37]Bernd H. Schmitt, "Language and Visual Imagery: Issues in Corporate Identity in East Asia," *Journal of World Business* (Winter 1995): 28–36.

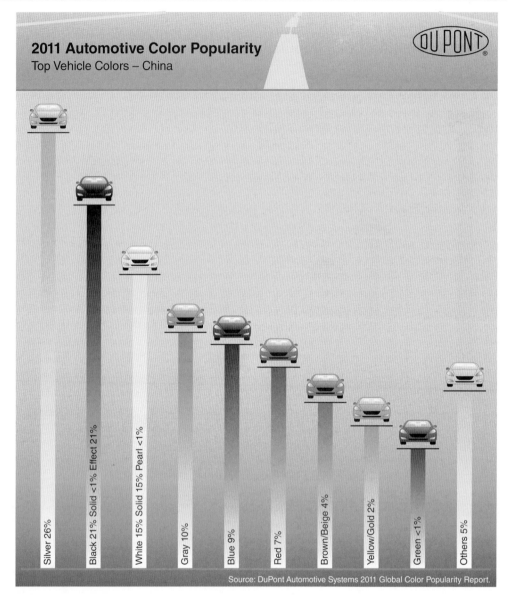

Exhibit 4-4 (*continued*)
Source: http://www2.dupont.com/Media_Center/en_US/color_popularity/.

Religion

Religion refers to a belief in supernatural agents. Religions embrace three distinct elements: explanation (e.g., God seen as a first cause behind the creation of the universe), a standardized organization (e.g., priests, churches, rituals), and moral rules of good behavior.[38] Religion plays a vital role in many societies. To appreciate people's buying motives, customs, and practices, awareness and understanding of their religion is often crucial. For instance, in India the concept of *karma* with its emphasis on long-term consequences for one's actions and deeds is well

---

[38]Jared Diamond, "The Religious Success Story," *New York Review of Books*, November 7, 2002, pp. 30–31.

established. One recent study showed that belief in karma causes consumers to set higher expectations on the quality of a product or service.[39]

In Islamic societies, companies can broaden the appeal of their brands and grow their business by engaging with Muslim consumers. For GlaxoSmithKline (GSK), gaining *halal* (religiously "pure") status for its Ribena and Lucozade beverages was an important step to gain clout in Muslim communities.[40]

Religious taboos often force companies to adapt their marketing mix program. When designing a reading toy called "Storybook Rhymes" aimed toward Turkish children, Fisher-Price ran into difficulties.[41] The toy featured a traditional Turkish poem paired with an illustration of a pig. As the pig was deemed inappropriate for a Muslim country, Fisher-Price replaced the illustration with a picture of cats. Along the same lines, many advertisers in China were forced to remove pig characters from their ads to celebrate the Chinese New Year of the Pig in 2007 when Chinese TV stations banned such advertising. The reason for the ban was that Chinese authorities did not want to offend the country's Muslim minorities.[42]

In Asian countries with large Chinese ethnic communities, the ancient philosophy of *feng shui* (wind-water) plays an important role in the design and placement of corporate buildings and retail spaces. According to *feng shui*, the proper placement and arrangement of a man-made structure and its interior objects will bring good fortune to its residents and visitors. Good *feng shui* allows the cosmic energy to flow freely throughout the building and hinders evil spirits from entering the structure.[43] For instance, Disney decided to shift the angle of the front entrance gate to Hong Kong Disneyland by 12 degrees after consulting a Chinese *feng shui* master. Other measures included placing cash registers close to corners or along walls, no fourth-floor buttons in elevators (4 is bad luck in Chinese), a ballroom measuring exactly 888 square meters (8 symbolizes prosperity in Chinese cultures), and burning ritual incense whenever a building was finished.[44]

Religion also shapes the holiday calendar in many countries. A country like Sri Lanka, with several officially recognized religions (Hinduism, Buddhism, Islam), forces a careful examination of one's calendar whenever meetings are to be scheduled. On the other hand, religious holidays often steer advertising campaigns or may open up untapped market opportunities. In many Western European countries, Saint Nicholas Day (December 6) is the key event for toy companies and candy makers. The holy month of Ramadan (the ninth month of the Muslim calendar) is also becoming increasingly commercialized. In major Islamic cities such as Cairo and Jakarta, Ramadan has a Christmas-like atmosphere these days.[45] During the 2008 Ramadan Coca-Cola ran a 60-second TV commercial dubbed "Iftar Street"[46] in sixteen Muslim countries.[47] The spot featured two male actors being caught in a traffic jam. When they spot a Coke delivery truck, the two begin distributing Coke bottles among the rest of the commuters. As the sun sets, the group begins eating and drinking to celebrate the end of the fasting day.[48] In many Muslim countries Coca-Cola also decorates Coke cans with a crescent moon and star, well-recognized

---

[39]Praveen K. Kopalle, Donald R. Lehmann, and John U. Farley, "Consumer Expectations and Culture: The Effect of Belief in Karma in India," *Journal of Marketing Research* 37, no. 3 (August 2010): 251–63.

[40]"Muslims offer a new Mecca for marketers," *Financial Times*, August 11, 2005, p. 6.

[41]"Fisher-Price Talks Mandarin," *Wall Street Journal*, June 2, 2008, p. 28.

[42]"Ban Thwarts 'Year of the Pig' Ads in China," www.npr.org, accessed March 12, 2012.

[43]Bernd Schmitt and Alex Simonson, *Marketing Aesthetics: The Strategic Management of Brands, Identity, and Image* (New York: The Free Press, 1997), pp. 275–76.

[44]"Disney bows to *feng shui*," *International Herald Tribune*, April 25, 2005, pp. 1, 6.

[45]"Parts of Mideast Are Split between Ramadan as Time for Prayer and Partying," *Asian Wall Street Journal*, December 5, 2002, pp. A1, A8.

[46]*Iftar* refers to the evening meal for breaking the fast during the Ramadan holiday.

[47]http://541aesthetic.wordpress.com/2008/09/16/media-hong-kong-mccann-indonesia-launches-global-coke-tvc-drive-for-ramadan/, accessed October 30, 2008.

[48]http://hk.youtube.com/watch?v=I7bsW4zdYKo, accessed October 30, 2008, shows the Indonesian version of Coca-Cola's 2008 Ramadan TVC.

symbols in Islam, to celebrate Ramadan. Even in countries that are relatively secular, religious holidays can create ample market opportunities. A good example is Japan where Kentucky Fried Chicken has managed to turn eating its chicken meals into a holiday tradition during the Christmas season.

The role of women in society is sometimes largely driven by the local religion. In Islamic societies, conducting market research that involves women is extremely difficult. For instance, mixing men and women in focus groups is prohibited in Saudi Arabia. Likewise, UPS, the courier firm, only hires men in India to make delivery rounds in deference to local cultural sensibilities.[49]

Religious norms can also influence advertising campaigns. In Iran, all ads need to be cleared by Islamic censors. This approval process can take up to three months. Iranian authorities frowned on one print ad created for Chiquita because they considered showing only three bananas on a full-page ad a waste of space.[50] Also in Iran, Gillette's local advertising agency had a hard time placing an ad for the Gillette Blue II razor. Islam dictates that its followers refrain from shaving. Ultimately, Gillette's account executive was able to convince the advertising manager of one local newspaper by using the argument that shaving sometimes becomes necessary, such as in the case of head injuries resulting from a car accident.[51] In Egypt, Coca-Cola's business was hampered by rumors that its logo read "no Mohammed, no Mecca" when read backwards and in Arabic script—a heresy for local Muslims. Coke called on Egypt's Grand Mufti, the country's most senior authority on Sunni Islam, to issue a religious opinion. The Mufti ruled that Coke was *halal*.[52] Hush Puppies, the U.S.-based shoe brand, lost market share in Malaysia when consumers there discovered that its shoes contained pigskin.[53]

Education

Education is one of the major vehicles for channeling culture from one generation to the next. Two facets of education that matter to international marketers are the level and the quality of education. The level of education varies considerably between countries. Most developed countries have compulsory education up to the late teens. In some countries, however, education is largely the preserve of males. As a consequence, males are often far better-educated than females in such societies. One powerful indicator of the education level is a country's illiteracy rate. In countries with low literacy levels, marketers need to exercise caution in matters such as product labeling, print ads, and survey research. Gerber Foods used to market baby foods in some parts of Africa by putting a cut baby face on the labels of its jars. Sales were very dismal: apparently many local people thought that the jars contained ground-up babies.[54]

Companies are also concerned about the "quality" of education. Does education meet business needs? Chinese software companies produce less than 1 percent of the world's software, despite the presence of many skilled programmers. One reason for the slow development of China's software industry is cultural. Managers able to supervise large-scale projects are scarce: "Chinese people individually are very, very smart but many, many people together are sometimes stupid."[55] Many multinationals doing business in China also face a severe shortage of talent. For instance, Unilever had over 30,000 local applicants for 100 places in its management trainee program in China. Unfortunately, only 80 of them were qualified.[56] High-tech companies operating in India

---

[49]"Late to India, UPS Tries to Redraw Its Map," *Wall Street Journal*, January 25/27, 2008, p. 4.

[50]"Multinationals Tread Softly While Advertising in Iran," *Advertising Age International*, November 8, 1993, p. I-21.

[51]"Smooth Talk Wins Gillette Ad Space in Iran," *Advertising Age International*, April 27, 1992, p. I-40.

[52]"U.K. Supermarket Sainsbury Travels Mideast's Rocky Road," *Advertising Age International*, July 2000, p. 19.

[53]"Muslim Market Minefield," *Media*, February 8, 2002, pp. 16–17.

[54]David A. Ricks, *Blunders in International Business*, (Cambridge, MA: Blackwell Publishers, 1993).

[55]"China Takes Pivotal Role in High-Tech Production," *International Herald Tribune*, December 5, 2002, p. 2.

[56]"Fighting for the Next Billion Shoppers," http://www.economist.com/node/21557815?zid=293&ah=e50f636873b4236 9614615ba3c16df4a.

Exhibit 4-5 Cross-Country Performance Mathematics Skills Among High School Students (PISA 2009)

Country	Score on the mathematics scale	Score on the science scale
OECD average	496	501
China (Shanghai)	600	575
Singapore	562	542
Korea	546	538
Taiwan	543	520
Finland	541	554
Switzerland	534	517
Japan	529	539
Canada	527	529
Netherlands	526	522
New Zealand	519	532
Jordan	387	415
Brazil	386	405
Colombia	381	402
Albania	377	391
Tunisia	371	401
Indonesia	371	401
Qatar	368	379
Peru	365	369
Panama	360	376
Kyrgyzstan	331	330

Source: OECD PISA 2009 database

face similar problems. Indian colleges produce plenty of engineering graduates but 85 percent of them according to one estimate are not ready for work after graduation.[57]

PISA is a study conducted by the OECD every three years that assesses skills in reading, science, and mathematics of 15-year old students in participating countries.[58] Sixty-five countries took part in the 2009 survey.[59] **Exhibit 4-5** shows how countries compare in their mathematics and science skills. As you can see, there are some huge differences, even among countries with a similar level of economic development. Among the top scorers are mostly Far Eastern countries such as China (including Hong Kong and Taipei), Singapore, Korea, and Japan. U.S. students rank in the middle with scores of 487 and 502 on the mathematics and science scales, respectively —higher than their Russian counterparts (468 for math; 478 for science) but below most Far Eastern and European students.

Shortages in certain fields often force companies to bid up against one another for the scarce talent that is available. Many companies try to build up a local presence by hiring local people.

---

[57]"Wanted: Employees for India's Tech Sector," *Wall Street Journal*, July 17, 2008, p. 28.

[58]PISA stands for the Programme for International Student Assessment. You can visit the project's website, www.pisa.oecd.org, for further information about the project and additional datasets.

[59]A further ten countries carried out the exercise in 2010.

However, a shortage of qualified people in the local market usually forces them to rely on expatriates until local employees are properly trained. Scarcity often also leads to high turnover rates among staff.

People's thought processes also differ across cultures. Richard Nisbett, a social psychologist at the University of Michigan, has done extensive research in this area. The work is summarized in his book *Geography of Thought*. One of the experiments that Nisbett ran would show a picture of a chicken, a cow, and grass. Participants were then asked to group these objects into two categories. Western people would put chicken and cow in the same category; Asians would join cow and grass into one category. The difference arises because Western people tend to think in terms of objects (e.g., animals versus non-animals) while Asians tend to focus on relationships ("cows eat grass"). In general, East Asians (i.e., Chinese, Japanese, Koreans) tend to focus on the big picture, make little use of categories, and stress change. East Asians also appear to accept multiple perspectives and contradictions, and search for a "middle way" or compromise. Western people, however, are more analytical in their thought processes, relying on rules, paying attention to categories and very specific objects. Their thinking and behavior is much more rule-based (*Ten steps to . . .*) than that of East Asians.

Value Systems

All cultures have value systems that shape people's norms and standards. These norms influence people's attitudes toward objects and behavioral codes. Value systems tend to be deeply rooted. Core values are intrinsic to a person's identity and inner self. One study of the decision-making process made by executives from China showed that even after almost four decades of communist philosophy, traditional Chinese values (e.g., saving face, long-term exchange relationships, respect for leaders) heavily influence market entry and product decisions.[60] **Exhibit 4-6** is an excerpt of a study commissioned by Dentsu, a Japanese advertising agency, on the beliefs and attitudes of Asian citizens. Note that the data were gathered between November 1996 and January 1997—prior to the start of the Asian financial crisis. The figures show that talk about "Asian values" may be a bit premature—there appears to be little common ground among Asian citizens. For instance, 85 percent of Mumbai citizens agree that children should look after aged parents, compared to a mere 15 percent agreement for Tokyo citizens.

For marketers, a crucial value distinction is a culture's attitude toward change. Societies that are resistant to change are usually less willing to adopt new products or production processes. Terpstra and David (1991) suggest several useful guidelines that are helpful to implement innovations in cultures hostile toward changes:[61]

1. Identify roadblocks to change.

2. Determine which cultural hurdles can be overcome.

3. Test and demonstrate the innovation's effectiveness in the host culture.

4. Seek out those values that can be used to back up the proposed innovation.

---

[60]David K. Tse, Kam-hon Lee, Ilan Vertinsky, and Donald A. Wehrung, "Does Culture Matter? A Cross-Cultural Study of Executives' Choice, Decisiveness, and Risk Adjustment in International Marketing," *Journal of Marketing* 52, no. 4 (October 1988): 81–95.

[61]Terpstra and David, *The Cultural Environment of International Business,* pp. 124–125.

Exhibit 4-6 Dentsu Lifestyle Survey

	Beijing	Mumbai	Tokyo	Singapore	Bangkok
Beliefs (% who agree with statement)					
Children should look after aged parents	67%	85%	15%	77%	78%
Parents should not rely on their children	21	11	39	9	8
Cannot say	12	5	46	14	14
Men work, women stay at home	20	37	21	26	24
Concerns (% agree)					
Personal safety	73	38	*	*	*
Economic development	70	62	48	67	87
Cost of living	60		56	50	62
Education and culture	46	49	*	39	49
Moral civilization	38	*	*	*	*
Health and welfare	*	48	68	55	49
Pollution	*	*	46	*	39
Employment	*	*	37	*	*
Citizens' rights	*	*	*	35	*
National security	*	50	*	*	*
Image as a nation (% agree)					
Hard working	86	59	65	65	**
Takes good care of family	63	**	**	21	31
Funny	**	53	**	**	**
Polite	41	47	30	29	38
Bad at negotiating	**	**	45	**	**
Loyal to company	**	**	42	**	**
Closed society	**	**	36	**	**
Clean	**	**	**	37	**
Appreciates nature	**	**	**	**	**
What the state must do (% agree)					
Adopt policies according to public opinion	65	56	68	50	67
Grant full social benefits	68	68	65	56	63
Regulate individual rights for greater good	47	67	11	42	51
Promote competition based on ability	33	26	25	26	38
Adopt Western systems	21	38	8	24	36
Have a strong leader push social reform	11	35	5	18	14

* Not among top five concerns.
** Not among top 10 concerns.
Source: Dentsu Institute for Human Studies.

From an international marketer's vantage point, a society's value system matters a great deal. Local attitudes toward foreign cultures will drive the product positioning and design decisions. In many countries, goods with American roots are strongly valued. U.S. companies are able to leverage on such sentiments by using Americana as a selling point. McIlhenny sells Tabasco with the same product label and formulation worldwide, emphasizing its American roots.

Cross-Cultural Comparisons

Cultures differ from one another but usually share some aspects. Getting a sense of the similarities and dissimilarities between your culture and the host country's culture is useful for a wide array of reasons. Cultural classifications allow the marketing manager to see how much overlap is possible between the marketing programs to be implemented in different markets. Furthermore, most cultural traits tend to be regional instead of national. For example, Walloons in French-speaking Belgium have much more in common, culture-wise, with the French than with the Flemish of northern Belgium. This section gives you an overview of the most common classification schemes.

High- versus Low-Context Cultures

One of the characters in the movie *Chan Is Missing* is a lawyer who describes a confrontation between her client who was involved in a traffic accident and a policeman at the scene of the accident. The client is a recent immigrant from mainland China. The policeman asks her client whether or not he stopped at the stop sign, expecting a yes or no for an answer. The Chinese immigrant instead starts talking about his driving record, how long he has been in the United States, and other matters that he feels are relevant. The policeman, losing his patience, angrily repeats his question. The events described in the movie are a typical example of the culture clash that arises when somebody from a high-context culture (China) is faced with a person from a low-context culture (United States).

The notion of cultural complexity refers to the way messages are communicated within a society. The anthropologist Edward Hall makes a distinction between **high-context** and **low-context** cultures.[62] The interpretation of messages in high-context cultures rests heavily on contextual cues. Little is made explicit as part of the message. What is left unsaid is often as important (if not more) as what is said. Examples of contextual cues include the nature of the relationship between the sender and receiver of the message (for instance, in terms of gender, age, balance of power), the time and venue of the communication. Typical examples of high-context societies are Confucian cultures (China, Korea, Japan) and Latin America. Outsiders often find high-context cultures completely mystifying.

Low-context cultures have clear communication modes. What is meant is what is said. The context, within which messages are communicated, is largely discounted. The United States, Scandinavia, and Germany are all examples of low-context cultures. In many areas of international marketing, the distinction between high- and low-context cultures does matter. For example, in the field of personal selling, many U.S. companies like to rotate salespeople across territories. In high-context societies, where nurturing trust and rapport with the client plays a big role, firms might need to adjust such rotation policies. In the field of international advertising, campaigns that were developed with a high-context culture in mind are likely to be less effective when used in low-context cultures, and vice versa.

Research in social psychology also reveals key cultural differences between East (high-context) and West (low-context) in how people perceive reality and reasoning.[63] For instance, one study contrasted the eye movements of Chinese and American students scanning pictures of objects placed within surroundings. American students focused on the central object while Chinese students spent more time on the background, putting the object in context. An analysis of crime reports in newspapers found that English-language papers focus on the personality traits of perpetrators while Chinese papers stress the context (e.g., the perpetrators' background).

---

[62]Edward T. Hall, *Beyond Culture* (New York: Doubleday, 1977).
[63]"Where east can never meet west," *Financial Times*, October 21, 2005, p. 8.

High- and low-context cultures also differ on their view of logic. Westerners have a deep-seated distaste for contradictions. Easterners, however, tend to accept them.[64]

Hofstede's Classification Scheme

The Dutch scholar Geert Hofstede developed another highly useful cultural classification scheme.[65] His grid is based on a large-scale research project he conducted among employees of more than sixty IBM subsidiaries worldwide. This research led to four cultural dimensions with a fifth one added based on follow-up work. The first dimension is labeled **power distance**. It refers to the degree of inequality among people that is viewed as being acceptable. Societies that are high in power distance accept and expect relatively high social inequalities within institutions (e.g., the family, school) or organizations (e.g., the company). Everyone has his or her rightful place in society; status symbols play a vital role; the ideal boss is a benevolent dictator or a good patriarch. Members of such societies accept wide differences in income and power distribution. Examples of high power distance countries are Malaysia (PD score = 104), the Philippines (94), Latin American countries such as Mexico (81) and Venezuela (81), Arab countries (80), India (77), and West Africa (77). Low power distance countries include the United States (40), Germany (35), Great Britain (35), Scandinavia (e.g., Norway and Sweden score: 31, Denmark: 18), and Israel (13). Low power distance societies tend to be more egalitarian. IKEA, the Sweden-based furniture chain, illustrates the notion of low power distance. The company is obsessed with the concept of "lista," which roughly translates as "making do." IKEA staff travel coach and never stay in luxury hotels. Ingvar Kamprad, the company's founder, once declared: "We don't need flashy cars, impressive titles, uniforms, or other status symbols. We rely on our strength and our will!"[66] At IKEA's headquarters, staff dress informally, offices are open plan, and the managing director works in a small room with glass panels to ensure accessibility.[67]

The second dimension is labeled **uncertainty avoidance**, referring to the extent to which people in a given culture feel threatened by uncertainty and rely on mechanisms to reduce it. Societies with strong uncertainty avoidance prefer rigid rules and formality that structure life. What is different is threatening; extreme uncertainty creates intolerable anxiety. Examples of countries that score high on uncertainty avoidance are Greece (112), Portugal (104), Japan (92), France (86), and Spain (86). In low uncertainty avoidance cultures, people tend to be more easygoing, innovative, and entrepreneurial. What is different is intriguing. Some low uncertainty avoidance countries are India (40), Malaysia (36), Great Britain (35), Sweden (29), and Singapore (8).

The third dimension is called **individualism**. As the label suggests, this criterion describes the degree to which people prefer to act as individuals rather than as group members ("me" versus "we" societies). In societies that are high on individualism, the focus is on the individual's own interests and those of the immediate family; one's identity is based on one's personal achievements. In such cultures, a child early on realizes that one day he or she will need to stand on his or her own feet. There is little need for loyalty to a group. **Collectivism** refers to the extent to which individuals see themselves as interdependent and part of a larger group or society. In collectivist societies, the interests of the group take center stage. Members in such societies differentiate between in-group members who are part of its group and all other people. They expect protection from the group and remain loyal to their group throughout their lives. One negative consequence of collectivism is in the domain of graft: one study found that countries with a high degree of collectivism tend to have a higher incidence of bribery. The reason is that collectivism lowers

---

[64]See also, Richard Nisbett, *The Geography of Thought* (New York: Free Press, 2004.)

[65]Geert Hofstede, *Cultures and Organizations* (New York: McGraw-Hill, 1991).

[66]Lauren Collens, "House Perfect," *The New Yorker* (October 3, 2011): 54–65.

[67]"The Gospel According to IKEA," http://www.guardian.co.uk/g2/story/0,3604,336379,00.html.

individuals' perceived responsibility for their action.[68] High-scoring individualist countries include the United States (91), Australia (90), and Great Britain (89). Collectivist countries are South Korea (18), Taiwan (17), Indonesia (14), and Venezuela (12).

The fourth distinction, **masculinity**, considers the importance of "male" values such as assertiveness, status, success, competitive drive within society, and achievement versus "female" values like being people-oriented, solidarity, and quality of life. "Masculine" societies are those in which values associated with the role of men prevail. Cultures where people favor values such as solidarity, preserving the environment, and quality of life, are classified as "feminine." Not surprisingly, Japan (95) is a very masculine society. Other high scorers include Austria (79), Italy (70), and Mexico (69). At the other end of the scale are countries such as Thailand (34), Chile (28), the Netherlands (14), and Sweden (5) that score relatively low on the masculinity trait.

Follow-up research on Hofstede's work in Asia led to a fifth dimension: **long-termism**.[69] This criterion refers to the distinction between societies with a pragmatic, long-term orientation and those with a short-term focus. People in long-term-oriented societies tend to have values that center around the future (e.g., perseverance, thrift). On the other hand, members of short-term-oriented cultures are concerned about values that reflect the past and the present (e.g., respect for tradition). These are typically markets with a "live now, pay later" mindset where consumers buy expensive consumer durables on credit. China (118), Hong Kong (96), Japan (80), and South Korea (75) score high on the long-term dimension. However, the United States (29), Great Britain (25), Canada (23), and the Philippines (19) score very low on this criterion.

Exhibit 4-7 (**A** and **B**) portrays how different countries score on the various dimensions. One must be cautious when applying these schemes to global buyer behavior. It is important to bear in mind that the five dimensions and the respective country scores that were derived in Hofstede's work were not determined in a consumption context. In fact, questions have been raised about the ability of these values to make meaningful predictions about consumption patterns.[70] Countries with the same scores may have entirely different buying behaviors. Similarly, countries that have completely different scores on a given cultural dimension could have very similar consumption patterns.[71]

Several researchers have looked at the influence of culture on consumption patterns. Luxury articles are often used as a badge of one's success. They are more appealing to members of masculine cultures than to people in feminine cultures. Indeed, one study found that the masculinity of a culture correlates positively with the ownership of expensive (more than $1500) watches ($r = 0.56$) or multiple (>4) watches ($r = 0.53$), sales of jewelry ($r = 0.44$), and the ownership of a suit or dress priced over $750 ($r = 0.68$).[72] These findings are also confirmed by further anecdotal evidence. According to a study done by Morgan Stanley Dean Witter, Japanese customers (including those traveling overseas) represent 88 percent of the sales of Louis Vuitton, 48 percent of Gucci, and 38 percent of Hermès. One in three Japanese women and one in three men own a Vuitton product. Many Japanese teenage girls want Louis Vuitton because "everyone has it."[73]

---

[68]Nina Mazar and Pankaj Aggarwal, "Greasing the Palm: Can Collectivism Promote Bribery?" *Psychological Science* 22, no. 7 (2011): 843–848.

[69]Geert Hofstede and Michael H. Bond, "The Confucius Connection: From Cultural Roots to Economic Growth," *Organizational Dynamics* 16, no. 4 (Spring 1988): 4–21.

[70]Marieke de Mooij, *Advertising Worldwide* (New York: Prentice-Hall, 1994), p. 159.

[71]See Daphna Oyserman, "Culture as Situated Cognition: Cultural Mindsets, Cultural Fluency, and Meaning Making," *European Review of Social Psychology* 22 (2011): 164–214, for a further discussion of these limitations.

[72]Marieke de Mooij and Geert Hofstede, "Convergence and Divergence in Consumer Behavior: Implications for International Retailing," *Journal of Retailing* 78 (2002): 61–69.

[73]"Addicted to Japan," Newsweek International (October 14, 2002), p. 44.

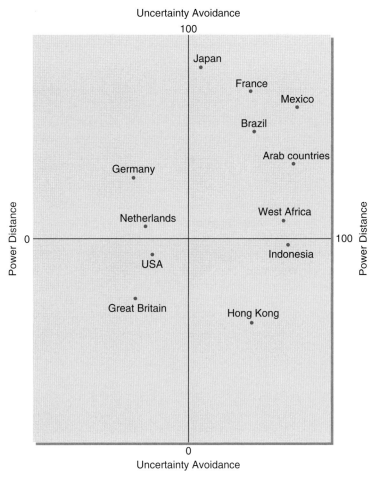

Exhibit 4-7a   Uncertainty Avoidance versus Power Distance

GLOBE Project

GLOBE (Global Leadership and Organizational Behavior Effectiveness) is a large-scale research program involving the efforts of a team of 160 scholars. The study explored cultural values and their impact on organizational leadership in around 60 countries.[74] The GLOBE study developed a scale of nine cultural dimensions based on a survey of 17,000 middle managers in three industries: banking, food processing, and telecommunications. These nine dimensions are:

1. *Collectivism I (institutional):* The degree to which organizational and societal institutional practices encourage and reward collective distribution of resources.

2. *Collectivism II (in-group):* The degree to which individuals express pride, loyalty, and cohesiveness in their organizations or families.

3. *Gender egalitarianism:* The degree to which an organization or society minimizes gender role differences and gender discrimination.

---

[74]Robert J. House, Paul J. Hanges, Mansour Javidan, Peter W. Dorfman, and Vipin Gupta, *Culture, Leadership, and Organizations: The GLOBE Study of 62 Societies* (SAGE Publications, 2004).

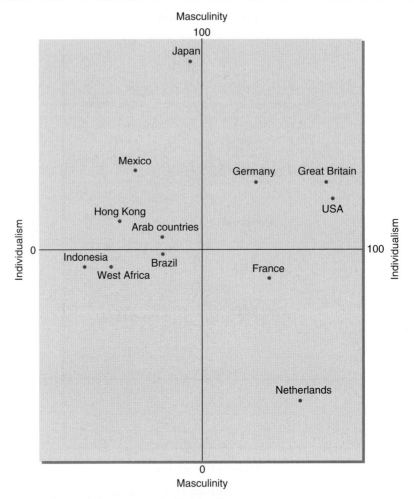

Exhibit 4-7b Masculinity versus Individualism

Source: Based on: Geert Hofstede, "Management Scientists Are Human," *Management Science* 40, No. 1 (January 1994): 4–13.

4. *Assertiveness:* The extent to which individuals are assertive, confrontational, and aggressive in social relationships.

5. *Performance orientation:* The extent to which a society encourages and rewards group members for performance improvement and excellence.

6. *Humane orientation:* The extent to which a culture encourages and rewards people for being fair, altruistic, generous, caring, and kind to others.

7. *Uncertainty avoidance:* The extent to which members of an organization or society strive to avoid uncertainty by reliance on social norms, rituals, and bureaucratic practices.

8. *Power distance:* The degree to which members of a society expect and agree that power should be unequally shared.

9. *Future orientation:* The degree to which individuals engage in future-oriented activities such as planning and investing in the future, delaying gratification.

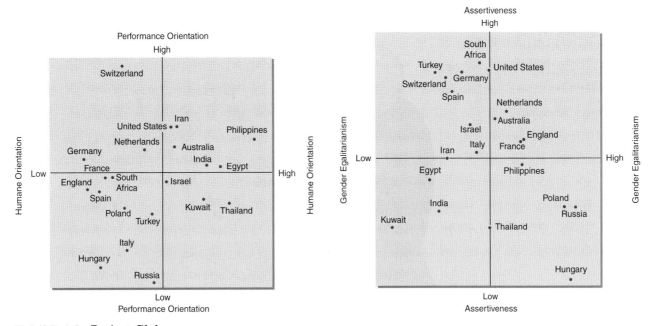

Exhibit 4-8 Project Globe

Data compiled from special issue of *Journal of World Business*. 37, no. 1 (Spring 2002).

Exhibit 4-8 maps a subset of the countries on four of the dimensions. GLOBE has some overlap with the Hofstede scheme that we discussed earlier. In fact, three of the dimensions are the same (power distance, uncertainty avoidance, and long-term/future orientation). The individualism/collectivism construct is split into two separate ones; the masculinity dimension is replaced with four components: assertiveness, performance orientation, gender balance, and humane orientation. However, there are some notable differences. The study and the measurements are far more recent—in fact, the project is still ongoing. The project also assigned scores to each country on the nine cultural dimensions from two angles: cultural practices or "As Is," and values or "What Should Be." (**Exhibit 4-7** is based on the *As Is* part.)[75]

World Value Survey (WVS)

The **World Value Survey** (WVS) is a global study of sociocultural changes conducted by a network of social scientists at leading universities worldwide.[76] This survey assesses people's values and beliefs and covers nearly 90 percent of the world's population. The first wave of the survey was carried out in 1981; the sixth wave was ongoing in 2012. The WVS scheme differs from the other schemes in two major respects. First, the surveys have been done multiple times, thereby showing how cultural values have changed over the last three decades. Second, the population covered by the sample is much broader than in other similar studies. For instance, the sixth data-collection phase covers 50 countries.

The chart in **Exhibit 4-9** shows how cultural attitudes in the surveyed countries stack up against one another. Most of the cross-cultural variations (70 percent) can be captured by two dimensions. The first one is the Traditional/Secular-rational dimension (vertical axis in **Exhibit 4-9**). This

---

[75]See Geert Hofstede, "The GLOBE Debate: Back to Relevance," *Journal of International Business Studies* 41 (October–November 2010): 1339–1346 for a critical assessment of the GLOBE study.

[76]See the project's website for further background information: http://www.worldvaluessurvey.org/

Exhibit 4-9 World Value Survey (WVS)

Source: Ronald Inglehart and Christian Welzel, "Changing Mass Priorities: The Link Between Modernization and Democracy," *Perspectives on Politics* 8, no. 2 (June 2010): 554.

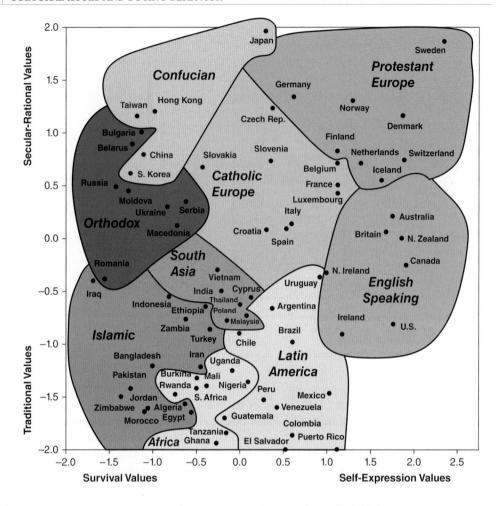

measure captures the relative importance of religious values as opposed to secular norms within society. Societies with a traditionalist orientation stress family values, parent–child ties, and deference to authority. The second category is the Survival/Self-expression dimension (horizontal axis in **Exhibit 4-9**). At one end of the spectrum are the survival values related to economic and physical security. At the other end are the self-expression values. Usually, as countries grow wealthier and modernize, the emphasis is on moving from Traditional toward Secular orientation and from Survival toward Self-expression values. Not all countries obey this rule though: countries such as the United States, Portugal, Ireland, and Mexico uphold Traditional values and Self-expression values at the same time (the lower-right quadrant in Exhibit 4-9).

Adapting to Cultures

An American businessman gave four antique clocks wrapped in white paper to a prospective client in China. The executive did not realize that the words in Mandarin for clock and the number 4 sound very much like the word for death; further, white is a funeral color in Chinese cultures. The symbolism was so powerful that the American lost the deal.[77] This anecdote underscores the importance of understanding the host country's culture. To succeed in

---

[77]"Going Global, Stateside," http://www.nytimes.com/2010/03/09/business/global/09training.html?pagewanted=print.

the global marketplace, you need to become sensitive to cultural biases that influence your thinking, behavior, and decision making. Given the diversity of cultures, cultural mishaps easily arise when global marketers interact with members of a "foreign" culture. Some of these cultural gaffes are relatively harmless and easily forgiven. Unfortunately, many cultural mistakes can put the company and its products in an unpleasant situation or can even create permanent damage. There are numerous firms whose globalization efforts have been hampered by cultural blunders.

In today's global digital environment, companies also need to be sensitive on how cultural adaptations in one market may affect their image in other markets. In 2009 an online Microsoft advertisement in Poland had replaced a black man with a Caucasian man. The apparent reason was that there are few black men in Poland. However, an Asian man who appeared in the original advertisement had survived the editing job. However, a portion of the black man's hand still remained in the ad. Not surprisingly, the photoshopped ad received a lot of publicity back in the United States. The Swedish furniture IKEA ran into similar trouble when images of women were skillfully removed from the Saudi Arabia version of its online catalog. IKEA attributed the gaffe to the franchisee which runs its Saudi operation. Still, the "sanitized" catalogue received a lot of negative publicity back in Sweden and elsewhere. Sweden's trade minister stated that "You can't remove or airbrush women from reality." The furniture retailer issued an apology saying: "We should have reacted and realized that excluding women from the Saudi Arabian version of the catalog in conflict with the IKEA Group values."[78]

Lack of cultural sensitivity takes many forms. Most of us hold cultural stereotypes that distort cultural assessments. Cultural gaffes are especially likely to happen when people move to a culture that seems very similar to the culture (e.g., same language) of their home-country as they are least prepared then to anticipate differences. Unfortunately, companies usually only become aware of cultural misunderstandings after the fact. Whether a large multinational or a small business, companies need to have a solid understanding of the culture they operate in.

Cultural adaptation can be hampered by the tendency to use a **self-reference criterion (SRC)**, a term coined by J. A. Lee, a cultural anthropologist. The SRC refers to people's unconscious tendency to resort to their own cultural experience and value systems to interpret a given business situation. Lee outlined a four-step procedure that allows global marketers to identify cross-cultural differences and take the necessary actions to cope with them. The four-step correction mechanism goes as follows:[79]

Step 1: Define the business problem or goal in terms of your own cultural traits, customs, or values.

Step 2: Define the business problem or goal in terms of the host culture's traits, customs, or values.

Step 3: Isolate the SRC influence in the problem and examine it scrupulously to see how it interferes with the business problem.

Step 4: Redefine the business problem, but this time without the SRC influence, and solve for the "optimal" business goal situation.

The following example illustrates the power of SRC and how it can be fixed. A mining company based in Britain had been unsuccessful in trying to win business from an American firm. The proposal turned off the Americans because it began with 10 pages listing all the risks of the venture and how much failure would cost. The American company considered the proposal as being negative and unenthusiastic; the British—being culturally more risk averse—viewed the

---

[78]"IKEA Regrets Cutting Women from Saudi Ad," http://online.wsj.com, accessed October 18, 2012.
[79]J. A. Lee, "Cultural Analysis in Overseas Operations," *Harvard Business Review* (March–April 1966): 106–14.

Americans as unrealistic. When the British rewrote the proposal with a positive spin, they clinched the deal the next day.[80]

Another bias that can wreak havoc is the tendency to overgeneralize when observing an unfamiliar culture. Research in social psychology has documented the so-called **out-group homogeneity bias**: people's tendency to believe that out-group members (say, the members of the host culture) are more alike and less diverse than members of one's own group.[81] For instance, one mistake people sometimes make is to paint Muslims with the same brush and view and them as ultraconservative and extremely religious. In reality, there are enormous differences in Muslim consumer attitudes across countries and even within the same country. Pakistan is a good illustration. Advertising in Pakistan on the whole focuses on images of youth, vitality, and modernity, without a *burqa* in sight. Northern Pakistan, however, is much more conservative than other parts of Pakistan. For this region, advertisers often must replace female models with male ones or simply use product shots in their ads.[82]

Companies can rely on several tools to prepare managers for cross-cultural differences.[83] Intensive foreign-language training is one of the more common tools to foster cultural sensitivity. Language skills, however, are not sufficient to become a successful international manager. Other qualities such as humility—a willingness to accept the fact that you will not be as competent as in your own environment—also play an important role.[84] Numerous resources exist to familiarize managers with other aspects of the host country's cultural environment. These days most multinationals offer cultural training for their outbound employees. Such cross-cultural training seminars typically last one or two days and cost around $5,000. They usually provide practical information about the assigned country (e.g., business customs, dining protocol, negotiation strategies) and make comparisons with the home country's culture. Several companies now also provide online tools for employees who do not have the time or the budget for formal in-person training. Examples of such online tools include Dean Foster Associates' "Culture Guides-to-Go" (http://www.deanfosterassociates.com/learn-about-cultures/guides/) and RW's[3] CultureWizard (http://rw-3.com/). Some resources are also available now as iPad or iPhone apps. Two excellent ones—both free—are the "Lonely Planet"[85] (www.lonelyplanet.com) and the "World Customs and Cultures"[86] apps. The latter, for example, provides valuable insights on local mores covering areas such as greetings, eye contact, gender issues, gestures, personal space, and taboos. While such pre-departure training programs and resources can help in smoothing the effects of culture shock, their value should not be overestimated as employees cannot be expected to master all of the nuances of cross-cultural communication in such a short time span.

Culture and the Marketing Mix

Culture is a key pillar of the marketplace. The success of international marketing activities is to a large extent driven by the local culture. These cultural variables may act as barriers or opportunities. In this section we show how culture and the firm's marketing mix interact. **Global Perspective 4-2** shows how the global health organization Population Services International (PSI) adapts marketing tools to local Burmese tastes to make condoms acceptable in Myanmar.

---

[80]"Going Global, Stateside."

[81]Alex Haslam, Penny Oakes, John Turner, and Craig McGarty (1996). Richard Sorrentino and Edward Higgins, eds., "Social identity, self-categorization, and the perceived homogeneity of ingroups and outgroups: The interaction between social motivation and cognition," *Handbook of motivation and cognition: The interpersonal context* (New York: Guilford Press) **3**: pp.182–222.

[82]"Meet the New Muslim Consumer," *Campaign Asia-Pacific* (October 2010: 60–66.

[83]Howard Tu and Sherry E. Sullivan, "Preparing Yourself for an International Assignment," *Business Horizons* (January–February 1994): 67–70.

[84]"Culture Shock for Executives," *Financial Times*, April 5, 1995, p. 12.

[85]http://itunes.apple.com/app/lonely-planet-travel-guides/id317165182?mt=8.

[86]http://itunes.apple.com/us/app/world-customs-cultures/id337842349?mt=8.

Global Perspective 4-2

Preventing HIV/ AIDS in Myanmar

Condoms were seldom used in Myanmar (Burma) just a decade ago. Yet, today they are one of the country's fastest-growing consumer goods—more than 40 million were purchased in 2005. This compares to only 4.4 million in 1997 (see table). This rapid increase reflects increased awareness of HIV/AIDS among the local population. HIV/AIDS rates in Myanmar among high-risk groups are among the highest in the region now: up to 2.2 percent of adult Burmese have been infected.

The surge in sales of condoms is largely the result of Population Services International (PSI). PSI is a non-profit organization based in Washington, D.C. For the first 16 years after its founding in 1970, PSI concentrated on the area of family planning through social marketing. In the late 1980s, PSI has also entered the areas of malaria and HIV/AIDS prevention. The group, which had a 2005 budget of $297 million, has program offices in almost 70 countries.

PSI launched its social marketing campaign in Myanmar in 1996, despite criticism by pro-democracy groups. PSI supplies about 75 percent of all the condoms used in Myanmar. Heavy subsidies allow them to be sold for one-third of the production cost. Guy Stallworthy, PSI's Myanmar country director, points out that "Price is the number one issue here—you are not going to get a mass market with an expensive product. . . . Consumers don't have much money but they are discerning and want to buy quality things . . . if you can somehow make quality affordable, you are bound to be a winner in this country."

Apart from pricing, promotion is a major challenge. When PSI first imported condoms in Myanmar, the brand name was written in Burmese. However, PSI found out that the Burmese associated Burmese-language packaging with inferior quality. In 1998, PSI changed to *Aphaw* ("trusted companion") in English, with usage instructions in Burmese.

Condoms Distributed in Myanmar since the Launch of Aphaw (in millions)

Year	Private Sector	Public Sector	PSI Social Marketing	Total Condom Market
1997	1.4	1.2	1.8	4.4
1998	2.2	2.1	3.3	7.6
1999	2.8	2.0	6.8	11.6
2000	7.0	1.5	7.9	16.4

Source: www.psi.org, accessed February 22, 2006

PSI built up its own national distribution network, with 28 sales representatives and 50 wholesalers. Aphaw condoms are available in every town and major village. PSI developed its own advertising mascot: a chameleon (a "pothinnyo") wearing a traditional sun hat. These days, PSI's mascot has an 82 percent recognition among urban Burmese. PSI collaborated with cultural troupes to produce traveling theatrical performances to educated communities about the risks of HIV/AIDS. It also produced soap operas and feature films to stem the spread of HIV/AIDS. In 2005, PSI's mascot made its TV debut when PSI sponsored the broadcast of English Premier League soccer matches on local television. At 0.8 per capita per year, condom use is still minimal compared to Thailand or Cambodia. PSI's goal is to raise condom use to one per capita per year by 2008.

Sources: "A Golden Opportunity: Preventing HIV/AIDS in Myanmar," http://www.psi.org/resources/pubs/myanmar_profile.pdf, accessed February 22, 2006; and "A Chameleon Enlists in War on Aids," *Financial Times*, February 20, 2006, p. 6.

Product Policy

The Powerpuff Girls is an animated karate superheroes show aired on the Cartoon Network with a huge following among American preteens. When in 2001 the show debuted in Japan with a "Japanese look" it failed miserably. To boost its appeal, Cartoon Network decided to revamp the characters. Toei, a well-established Japanese animation house, was brought in to assist with the overhaul. The characters Blossom, Buttercup, and Bubbles were given Japanese names, more realistic outfits (e.g., miniskirts, hip-hugging belts), and the lives of Japanese junior-high-school students. As Japanese kids prefer more narrative plots, the shows were made 15 to 20 minutes long (compared to the 7 to 11 minute shows in the United States). They also introduced new themes in line with Japanese girls' expectations such as love themes and acceptance of people who are different ("Monsters can be anyone who is different from us. If we change our attitude, they can become our friends"). The show became successful not just among Japanese girls but also attracted animation-obsessed adult men (*otaku*). As a result, the Cartoon Network launched special items tied to the show such as bookmarks and pop music targeting the show's adult Japanese fans.[87]

To adapt to local cultural norms, some companies may even change brand visuals such as their logo. In Saudi Arabia, the mermaid in the center of Starbucks's logo was judged to be morally reprehensible. When Starbucks entered the country in 2000, it removed the signature mermaid from its logo and only left the crown over waves.

In recent years, doughnuts have been catching on in Asia as a luxury treat.[88] International doughnut chains such as Dunkin' Donuts and Krispy Kreme have modified their product offerings in the region to cater toward Asian palates. Dunkin' Donuts Taiwan, for instance, offers localized flavors such as green tea and honeydew melon. In pork-loving China, where donuts are not a mainstream breakfast item, the company catered to local tastes by adding donuts with shredded pork to its menu.[89] Doughnut chains also lowered the sugar content as most Asians have a lower preference for sweet foods. As both examples show, scores of products and services must be tailored to local values and preferences to make them more appealing in the host market.

The sale of some products or services can also be banned or heavily restricted due to cultural reasons. In March 2004, the government of Saudi Arabia banned the import and sale of mobile phones with cameras after reports of "misconduct" (photographing of women) by owners of such phones.[90]

The implied meanings of brand names also exemplify the role of culture in global marketing. Sometimes the brand name can hurt sales as P & G experienced with its Ariel laundry detergent in Middle Eastern countries like Egypt. Many Egyptians mistakenly believed that the detergent had ties with Ariel Sharon, Israel's former prime minister.

Cultural norms sometimes open up new product opportunities. In most Asian countries, white skin is associated with positive values that relate to beauty, class, and an upscale lifestyle. Dark skin is linked with hard labor and toil. In India, the skin whitener market has been growing at an annual rate of around 20 percent. Launched in 1978, Fair & Lovely has become one of Unilever's most popular brands in India with the promise of an "unmatched radiant fairness in just four weeks." The brand was rolled out across Asia, the Middle East, and Africa in the 1980s and spawned scores of imitators.[91] Almost all major cosmetics companies now market skin whitening

---

[87]"Cartoon Characters Get Local Makeovers in Asia," *Wall Street Journal*, October 16, 2007, p. 28.
[88]"Doughnuts Catching on in Asia as a High-end Western Treat," *International Herald Tribune*, June 13, 2007, p. 12.
[89]"Dunkin' Aims at China with Pork Donuts, LeBron James," www.reuters.com, accessed May 6, 2012.
[90]"Saudi ministries picture the future as embargo on mobiles draws in King Fahd," *Financial Times*, November 23, 2004, p. 7.
[91]"The Face of Asian Beauty," *Campaign Asia-Pacific* (November 2011): 38–41.

products in Asia.[92] On the other hand, in many Western countries a tan symbolizes good health and a life of leisure holidays spent in exotic places.

Pricing

Customers' willingness to pay for your product will vary across cultures. Products that are perceived as good value in one culture may have little or no value in other cultures. In Western countries, a high price is often seen as a signal of premium quality for many product categories. Such beliefs sometimes also exist in less developed markets. For instance, multinational pharmaceuticals such as Pfizer benefit from a belief in much of the developing world that branded medicines are worth paying a premium because of the perception that generic drugs are less safe and/or less effective. In Venezuela, a monthly standard dose of Lipitor, Pfizer's cholesterol-lowering drug, costs between $100 and $125, compared to less than $50 for a generic drug.[93]

One example of how pricing and culture interact is the practice of odd pricing in which prices end with 9 (or 5) ($19.99 instead of $20). Specific price points like End-9 prices are known to increase unit sales substantially. This sales effect is due to the fact that these "magic prices" signal good value to the customers. In Chinese-speaking cultures, however, the price points used often end with 8 instead of 9.[94] In Chinese cultures, the number 8 is associated with prosperity and good luck. This symbolism stems from the fact that the number 8's pronunciation in Chinese, *ba*, sounds a lot like the Mandarin word for "getting rich."[95]

Distribution

Cultural variables may also dictate distribution strategies. In the wake of China's all-out ban on direct selling in 1998, companies like Amway and Avon were forced to drop their core business model in that market. Amway set up retail stores to comply with the government regulations— something it had done in no other country. However, the company then found that these stores were very useful, as Chinese consumers prefer a brand with premises they can visit in case of problems. These days, China is Amway's biggest market.[96]

Retailers must often fine-tune their practices when entering foreign markets. Wal-Mart learned this lesson the hard way in Germany, a market that the mega-retailer was never able to crack. Grocery bagging turned out to be a no-no for German shoppers, as they do not like strangers handling their groceries. When clerks followed orders to smile, male customers took that as a come-on.[97] After many years of sustained losses, Wal-Mart sold its 85 German stores to its German rival Metro in July 2006.

Especially in emerging markets, multinationals often must tweak their distribution model, even when their model is a key success factor in more mature markets. A good example is Dell's direct

---

[92]Here is a sample of some of the whitening brands launched in Asia-Pacific: L'Oréal White Perfect Fairness Control; Yves Saint Laurent White Mode Repair Whitening Night Cream; Clarins White Plus HP; Chanel Blanc Pureté; Shiseido White Lucent.

[93]"Drug Firms See Poorer Nations as Cure for Sales Problems," *Wall Street Journal Asia*, July 8, 2009, pp. 14–15.

[94]Lee C. Simmons and Robert M. Schindler, "Cultural Superstitions and the Price Endings Used in Chinese Advertising," *Journal of International Marketing* 11, no. 2 (2003): 101–111.

[95]Note that the Beijing Olympics 2008's opening date was August 8, 2008 (8-8-08).

[96]"Street Smarts Needed to Thrive in China," http://www.ft.com/intl/cms/s/0/49b7809c-5c80-11e0-ab7c-00144feab49a. html#axzz1mWvLejY5.

[97]"Wal-Mart: Local Pipsqueak," *BusinessWeek*, April 11, 2005, pp. 25–26.

sales model, which has long been a key part of the computer maker's success. In countries like Russia, Dell is pushing into traditional retailing by opening company-owned retail stores. Russia lacks the basic infrastructure needed to support Dell's direct sales and customers have little experience with e-commerce.[98] In China, where face-to-face contact is important when selling computers, Dell overhauled its direct-sales model when it announced a deal in September 2007 to sell computers through Gome, a leading Chinese electronics retailer.[99] McDonald's offers another example.[100] In many developing world cities, McDonald's now offers home delivery service. The model works well in traffic-congested cities with cheap labor. In Egypt, where the delivery setup originated in 1995, deliveries account for 27 percent of McDonald's revenue.

Promotion

Of the four marketing mix elements, promotion is the most visible one. People who do not buy your product for whatever reason may still be exposed to your promotion activities. Culture will typically have a major influence on a firm's communication strategy. At the same time, advertising can often be a powerful tool to change cultural mindsets or behaviors of local consumers. For instance, in 2011 Unilever ran a very creative online campaign in China to convince young Chinese men to adopt Lynx deodorant as part of their grooming repertoire in a country where men traditionally had never been expected to smell good.

The manner in which customers process marketing communications often hinges on their cultural values. One study found that North Americans are persuaded more by promotion-focused information (benefits to be gained) whereas Chinese consumers are driven by prevention-focused messages (problems that can be avoided).[101] Advertising styles that are effective in certain cultures can be counterproductive in other cultures. In high-context cultures (e.g., Spain, Italy, Japan), communication styles tend to be more indirect and subtle, making use of less copy and more symbols. In low-context cultures (e.g., Germany, Scandinavia), on the other hand, advertising uses more copy, factual data, and reasoning.[102] Advertising in countries such as the United States and the United Kingdom often uses a lecture-format style in which a celebrity "lectures" the audience about the good points of the product being advertised. Cultures in these countries are low in power distance and high in individualism. One study compared the reactions of Chinese and U.S. subjects to different advertising appeals. Not surprisingly, the study found that Chinese consumers favored a collectivistic appeal, whereas their U.S. counterparts preferred an individualistic appeal.[103]

Country of origin strategies may also need to be customized across countries. In collectivist cultures, local brands are likely to benefit from touting their local roots. However, one study suggests that in individualist countries, country of origin appeals will be beneficial only when the local brand is superior.[104] Therefore, buy-local campaigns in highly

[98]BusinessWeek, *October 8, 2007, p. 78.*

[99]"China Chapter of Dell's Retail Adventure Opens," *Financial Times,* September 25, 2007, p. 7.

[100]"Knock Knock, It's Your Big Mac," *BusinessWeek,* July 23, 2007, p. 36.

[101]Donnel A. Briley and Jennifer L. Aaker, "When Does Culture Matter? Effects of Personal Knowledge on the Correction of Culture-Based Judgments," *Journal of Marketing Research,* 18 (2006), pp. 395–408.

[102]Marieke de Mooij, *Global Marketing and Advertising. Understanding Cultural Paradoxes* (Thousand Oaks, CA: SAGE Publications, 1998), pp. 157–158.

[103]Yong Zhang and James P. Neelankavil, "The Influence of Culture on Advertising Effectiveness in China and the USA. A Cross-Cultural Study," *European Journal of Marketing* 31 (1997): 134–149.

[104]Gürhan-Canli, Zeynep, and Durairaj Maheswaran, "Cultural Variations in Country of Origin Effects," *Journal of Marketing Research* 37 (August 2000): 309–317.

individualist countries such as Australia and the United States may be counterproductive unless the product has superior quality.

Local cultural taboos and norms also influence advertising styles. In the United States, Gidget, a talking Chihuahua, was the advertising mascot for Taco Bell, a Mexican-style fast-food chain owned by Yum! Brands.[105] However, Gidget never featured in Taco Bell's Singapore ads. Singapore's large Muslim population was the main motivation for dropping Gidget—Muslims view dogs as unclean animals.[106]

SUMMARY

Culture is an intrinsic part of any society; a powerful force that will affect the level of market demand for your product, consumer behavior and preferences in the local market, as well as the behavior and attitudes of the local managers. Cultural diversity brings along an immense richness. Cultural changes may open up new market opportunities. In Chinese culture, for instance, the Year of the Dragon is an auspicious year in the lunar calendar as it is associated with wealth and power. As a result of this superstition, dragon years typically spur a 5 percent rise in the number of births.[107] This every-12-year baby spike is a big market opportunity for the makers of infant-related products such as Danone, Procter & Gamble, and Mead Johnson.[108] At the same time, cultural diversity also poses enormous challenges to international marketers and managers in general. In a sense, cultural differences can be seen as entry barriers; these can be surmounted with the right dose of cultural sensitivity, hard work, and a great product or service.

Failure to respect the local culture can create resentment and may severely damage the company's reputation in the host market. Companies like Coca-Cola and KFC learned this lesson the hard way in India. When Coca-Cola reentered India in 1992 after a long absence, it acquired Thums Up, a leading local brand. It subsequently tried to promote its global brand by piggybacking Thums Up's distribution network, at the expense of the local brand. Loyal customers of Thums Up were not pleased. In the end, Coke decided to promote Thums Up rather than substitute it with its global core brand.

Nuggets of wisdom such as "When in Rome . . . ," are nice catch phrases but unfortunately, it is seldom easy to learn what it means to "do as the Romans do." There simply are no magic bullets or shortcuts. In fact, overconfidence in one's familiarity with the host culture is a common error, especially when one mistakenly believes that the host culture is very similar to the culture in the home country. A good illustration is Colgate's experience with the launch of Cleopatra, a premium soap brand, in Québec. The brand had been hugely successful in France. However, in Québec, Canada's sole French-speaking province, the brand flopped. Even though both markets have a "French" culture, there were some major cultural variations in grooming rituals that the company had overlooked.

In this chapter we analyzed what is meant by culture. We examined several elements of culture in detail. Cultures have differences but also share certain aspects. We examined several frameworks that you can use to analyze and classify different cultures. Once you are aware of the differences and parallels, the next and most formidable task is to become sensitive to the host culture. We discussed some of the procedures and tools that managers can access to smooth the adjustment to unfamiliar cultures. Cross-cultural training is one route toward cultural adaptation. The ideal, however, is to immerse oneself in the foreign culture through intensive language training, prolonged visits, or other means. Finally, we looked at the interface between culture and the marketing mix instruments. In general, culture will affect the implementation of a marketing mix strategy ("how things are done") rather than strategy development.

---

[105]The Chihuahua is a breed associated with Mexico as is the food served at Taco Bell. Gidget died in 2009.

[106]"As Taco Bell Enters Singapore, Gidget Avoids the Ad Limelight," Ad Age International, January 11, 1999, pp. 13–14. "A Campaign Too Far for Carlsberg," *Financial Times*, August 11, 1998, p. 8.

[107]The most recent Year of the Dragon was 2012. Famous people born in previous dragon years include Joan of Arc, Bruce Lee, Sigmund Freud, and John Lennon.

[108]"A Dragon May Give China's Economy a Lift," *Bloomberg Businessweek*, December 18, 2011, pp. 35, 36.

QUESTIONS

1. Describe the importance of reference groups in international marketing.

2. How do high-context cultures differ from low-context ones?

3. Yum! Brands plans to make Taco Bell, the company's Mexican-inspired fast food brand, its next big global brand, following the footsteps of Pizza Hut and KFC. In June 2010, the company opened its first Taco Bell restaurant in Bangalore, India. Just as it did for the earlier introduced KFC and Pizza Hut restaurants, Yum! Brands tailors its foods such as tacos and burritos for Indian consumers, making them spicier and making half the menu vegetarian. Prices start as low as 35 cents. How do you assess Yum! Brands' decision to pick India as one of its early markets for Taco Bell's globalization effort? What cultural challenges could Taco Bell face, and how could these be resolved?

4. The Ogilvy/Noor index is a construct that measures the appeal of global brands to Muslim consumers. The index is based on a sample drawn of consumers in the Muslim-majority markets of Saudi Arabia, Egypt, Pakistan, and Malaysia. The higher the score, the more Muslim-friendly the brand is perceived. Thirty-five brands were evaluated. The table below shows the ten highest and lowest ranked brands.

Ogilvy Noor Index—Top/Bottom Ranked Brands

Brand	Ogilvy Noor Index	Brand	Ogilvy Noor Index
Lipton	131	Axe	88
Nestlé	130	Emirates	85
Nescafe	122	Red Bull	78
Nido	118	Etihad Airways	77
Kraft	117	Singapore Airlines	63
Maggi	117	Cathay Pacific	62
Mirinda	110	Citibank	59
Pringles	110	Standard Chartered	54
Lays	110	HSBC	51
7 Up	109	Royal Bank of Scotland	47

Source: www.campaignasia.com.

Note that even though banks such as Citibank, HSBC, and Standard Chartered offer Islamic financial services that comply with Islamic law (*shariah*) they score very low. What could be the reason(s) for their low rankings? What other conclusions can be drawn from the results?

POLITICAL AND LEGAL ENVIRONMENT

5

CHAPTER OVERVIEW

1. Political environment—individual governments

2. Political environment—social pressures and political risk

3. Terrorism and the world economy

4. International agreements

5. International law and local legal environment

6. Issues transcending national boundaries

Business has been considered an integral part of economic forces. Indeed, economics was once called political economy, and as such, business could not be conducted devoid of political and legal forces. Although we tend to take political and legal forces for granted most of the time in doing business domestically, they could become central issues in international business and cannot be ignored. It is human nature that we tend to look at other countries' political and legal systems as peculiar because they differ from ours. We might even make some value judgment that our own country's political and legal system is superior to other countries' and that they should change their system to our way. This ethnocentrism, however, hinders our proper understanding of, and sensitivity to, differences in the system that might have major business implications. By the very nature of their jobs, international marketers cannot afford to be ethnocentric as they interact with a multitude of political and legal systems, including their own at home.

International marketers should be aware that the economic interests of their companies can differ widely from those of the countries in which they do business and sometimes even from those of their own home countries. There are various international agreements, treaties, and laws already in place for them to abide by. Furthermore, there is an increased level of visible distrust of multinational firms around the world, calling for creating codes of conduct for them.[1]

In this chapter, we will examine political and legal forces that affect the company's international marketing activities from the following three perspectives: the political and legal climates of the host country; those of the home country; and the international agreements, treaties, and laws affecting international marketing activities transcending national

---

[1]S. Prakash Sethi, *Setting Global Standards: Guidelines for Creating Codes of Conduct in Multinational Corporations* (Hoboken, NJ: Wiley, 2003); and also see International Labor Organization's effort at http://actrav.itcilo.org/actrav-english/telearn/global/ilo/guide/main.htm, 2012.

boundaries. Although political and legal climates are inherently related and inseparable, because laws are generally a manifestation of a country's political processes, we will look at political climate first, followed by legal climate.

Political Environment—Individual Governments

Government affects almost every aspect of business life in a country. First, national politics affect business environments directly, through changes in policies, regulations, and laws. The government in each country determines which industries will receive protection in the country and which will face open competition. The government determines labor regulations and property laws. It determines fiscal and monetary policies, which then affect investment and returns. We will summarize those policies and regulations that directly influence the international business environment in a country.

Second, the political stability and mood in a country affect the actions a government will take—actions that may have an important impact on the viability of doing business in the country. A political movement may change prevailing attitudes toward foreign corporations and result in new regulations. An economic shift may influence the government's willingness to endure the hardships of an austerity program. We will discuss the strategic importance of understanding political risk in an international business context.

Home Country versus Host Country

Whenever marketing executives do business across national boundaries, they have to face the regulations and laws of both the home and host countries. A **home country** refers to a country in which the parent company is based and from which it operates. A **host country** is a country in which foreign companies are allowed to do business in accordance with its government policies and within its laws. Therefore, international marketing executives should be concerned about the host government's policies and their possible changes in the future, as well as their home government's political climate.

Because companies usually do not operate in countries that have been hostile to their home country, many executives tend to take for granted the political environment of the host country in which they currently do business. Sweeping political upheavals, such as the Cuban crisis in the 1960s, the Iranian Revolution in the 1980s, the breakup of the Soviet Union in the late 1980s, the Persian Gulf War in the 1990s, the Kosovo crisis in Yugoslavia[2] in 1999, the suicide bombings in Indonesia during the last several years, and more recently, the U.S.-led wars in Iraq and Afghanistan have already made many business executives fully aware of dire political problems in some regions, and many companies have since stayed away from those areas. Despite the fact that those major political upheavals provide the largest single setting for an economic crisis faced by foreign companies, what most foreign companies are concerned about on a daily basis should be a much larger universe of low-key events that may not involve violence or a change in government regime but that do involve a fairly significant change in policy toward foreign companies.[3] The end of apartheid in South Africa in 1994 signaled foreign companies' cautious yet optimistic attitude toward resuming business relations with this African country.[4] Similarly,

---

[2]As a result of a series of ethnic tensions since 1980, the former Yugoslavia is now divided into seven independent states: Serbia, Croatia, Bosnia and Herzegovina, Kosovo, Macedonia, Slovenia, and Montenegro.

[3]Stephen J. Kobrin, "Selective Vulnerability and Corporate Management," in Theodore H. Moran, ed., *International Political Risk Assessment: The State of the Art, Landegger Papers in International Business and Public Policy*, Georgetown University, Washington, D.C. 1981, pp. 9–13.

[4]"2011 Investment Climate Statement—South Africa," U.S. Department of State, Diplomacy in Action, March 11, 2011, http://www.state.gov/e/eb/rls/othr/ics/2011/157358.htm., accessed June 10, 2012.

Vietnam has begun to attract foreign direct investment to spur its domestic economic growth and shift toward a more market-based economy.[5]

The intertwined nature of home and host government policies is illustrated by the U.S.–China diplomatic relationship having been re-established in the mid-1970s under the Nixon administration. As a result, the Chinese government finally opened its economy to foreign direct investment—mostly through joint ventures—in the 1980s. The first pioneer foreign companies stood to gain from the host government policies designed to protect the domestic producers they teamed up with in China. Thus, the United States' Chrysler, Germany's Volkswagen, and France's Peugeot, with their respective Chinese partner companies, were such beneficiaries. However, the U.S.–China relationship has since been anything but smooth. The United States, in particular, has been openly critical of China's human rights "violations" since the Tiananmen Square massacre of 1989 and has tried to make its trade policy with China contingent upon measurable improvements in China's human rights policy.

When China entered the World Trade Organization (WTO) in December 2001, the United States also offered extension of permanent Normal Trade Relations to China. The U.S. government needs to do more to help China change its legal and political system to meet the challenges of its accession to the WTO. The wrenching social changes—including increased unemployment in large cities—caused by the opening of China's economy carry the risk of serious political instability. Besides, the current government and Communist Party leadership, when mixed with the politics of WTO implementation, could create systemic instability in China. Despite China's continued spectacular economic growth, foreign companies operating in, or contemplating entry into, China may experience undue uncertainties in the future.[6]

The emergence of the internet could also pose issues for Chinese trade relations. Though China seeks to free its markets in response to global pressure, particularly from the United States, the internet undermines China's general censorship policies. This dilemma was recently shown when the Chinese government ordered all new computers sold in China be installed with the government's Green Dam censoring software, but the idea was abandoned after international protests.[7] Nonetheless, encouraged by reformist leaders, internet use is growing explosively. In 1997, only 640,000 Chinese were connected. By June 30, 2012, China's internet users reached a total of 538 million individuals—more than double the 2008 amount and representing 50 percent of internet users in Asia. China ranks first in the world of top internet using countries, surpassing the United States.[8] Today e-commerce has become a strong driver of China's market economy by expanding with annual sales rising at 40 percent. According to statistics from China E-Business Research Center, China's online transactions volume reached 4.5 trillion yuan ($684 billion) in 2010.[9] Included in its plan for national economic and social development, China is vigorously promoting e-government, which includes a taxation management information system, a customs management information system, a financial management information system, an agricultural management information system, and a quality supervision management information system. E-commerce is on the development agenda and China is eager to expedite the application of information technology in such key areas as foreign trade, petrochemicals, metallurgy, and machinery.[10]

In a similar vein, Russia's recent accession into the WTO membership in December 2011 should be noted. Although many uncertainties remain, it is also expected to usher in a new era in

---

[5]"Vietnam Development Report 2012: Market Economy for A Middle-Income Country," The World Bank, http://www.worldbank.org/en/news/feature/2012/01/12/vietnam-development-report-2012-an-overview, accessed August 23, 2013.

[6]"Is China Edging towards Political and Economic Uncertainty?" Institute for Defense Studies and Analyses, March 20, 2012, http://www.idsa.in/.

[7]"Internet Censorship in China," About.com, Chinese Culture, http://chineseculture.about.com/, accessed June 10, 2012.

[8]Internet World Stats, http://www.internetworldstats.com/stats3.htm#asia, accessed January 25, 2013.

[9]"China 2010 E-Commerce Market Reaches RMB 4.5 Trillion," China E-Business Research Center, January 20, 2011, http://www.marbridgeconsulting.com/, accessed June 10, 2012.

[10]"Report on China's Economic and Social Development Plan," *Xinhua*, March 16, 2005.

global trading relationships as has been the case with China's WTO membership (see **Global Perspective 2-1** in Chapter 2).

International marketers must understand the fluid nature of the host country political climate in relation to the home country policies. Some countries are relatively stable over time; other countries experience different degrees of political volatility that make it difficult for international marketers to predict and plan ahead. Nonetheless, there are a few crucial political factors international executives should know that determine the nature of the host country's political climate.

Structure of Government

Ideology

One way to characterize the nature of government is by its political ideology, ranging from **communism** and socialism to capitalism. Under strict communism, the government owns and manages all businesses, and no private ownership is allowed. As the breakup of the Soviet Union shows, strict government control not only strips its people of private incentives to work but is also an inefficient mechanism for allocating scarce resources across the economy. On the other hand, **capitalism** refers to an economic system in which free enterprise is permitted and encouraged along with private ownership. In a capitalistic society, free-market transactions are considered to produce the most efficient allocation of scarce resources. However, capitalism is not without critics. Even the Wall Street financier, George Soros, has called attention to the threat that the values propagated by global laissez-faire capitalism pose to the very values on which open and democratic societies depend. Without social justice as the guiding principle of civilized life, life becomes a survival of the fittest.[11] For example, capitalism, if unfettered, may result in excessive production and excessive consumption, thereby causing severe air and water pollution in many parts of the world, resulting in global warming, as well as depleting the limited natural resources. Government roles would be limited to those functions that the private sector could not perform efficiently, such as defense, highway construction, pollution control, and other public services. An interesting example can be found in Japan. Although Japanese companies perfected an efficient just-in-time (JIT) delivery system, frequent shipments have caused increased traffic congestion and air pollution in Japan, and thus may not be as efficient in delivering social well-being.[12] Now the Japanese government is trying to regulate the use of JIT production and delivery systems. **Socialism** generally is considered a political system that falls in between pure communism and pure capitalism. A socialistic government advocates government ownership and control of some industries considered critical to the welfare of the nation.[13]

After the breakup of the Soviet Union in 1991, most Central and East European countries converted to capitalistic ideology.[14] Similarly, China has been in a transition stage, although some uncertainties still remain. There remain few countries that adhere to an extreme communist doctrine other than North Korea and Cuba. While many countries cherish capitalism and democracy, the extent of government intervention in the economy varies from country to country. (Both capitalistic and socialistic countries in which government planning and ownership play a major role are also referred to as **planned economies**.)

---

[11]George Soros, *The Crisis of Global Capitalism* (New York: PublicAffairs, 1998).

[12]Kamran Moinzadeh, Ted Klastorin, and Emre Berk, "The Impact of Small Lot Ordering on Traffic Congestion in a Physical Distribution System," *IIE Transactions* 29 (August 1997): 671–679.

[13]Refer to an excellent classic treatise on capitalism, socialism, and communism by Joseph A. Schumpeter, *Capitalism, Socialism, and Democracy* (New York: Harper & Brothers, 1947).

[14]Tom Diana, "Steady Economic Progress in Central and Eastern Europe," *Business Credit* 107 (June 2005): 54–57.

Political Parties

The number of political parties also influences the level of political stability. A one-party regime does not exist outside the communist country. Most countries have a number of large and small political parties representing different views and value systems of their population. In a **single-party-dominant country**, government policies tend to be stable and predictable over time. Although such governments provide consistent policies, they do not always guarantee a favorable political environment for foreign companies operating in the country. A dominant party regime may maintain policies, such as high tariff and non-tariff barriers, foreign direct investment restrictions, and foreign exchange controls, that reduce the operational flexibility of foreign companies. For example, in Mexico a few political parties have always existed, but one party, called the Institutional Revolutionary Party (PRI), had been dominant in the past seventy years. However, since 2000, Mexico's ruling party had lost its firm grip on its politics to the National Action Party (PAN). In July 2012, Mexicans elected the PRI candidate for President, and the party that had ruled Mexico for more than 70 years appears ready for a comeback. Although the opening of the Mexican political system may eventually lead to a stronger democracy over time, drug-related crime and rampant violence in recent years have battered Mexico's sense of public security and economic stability.[15]

The trauma followed by the collapse of one-party-dominant systems can be large, as experienced by the breakup of the Soviet Union. In the early 1970s, PepsiCo had cultivated ties with Soviet leaders that led to a deal providing the Soviet Union and its East European allies with Pepsi concentrate and state-of-the-art bottling technology in return for the inside track to the huge unexploited soft-drink market within the Soviet Empire. However, when the Soviet Union collapsed in 1991, PepsiCo was devastated. Almost overnight, all the hard-earned skills and nepotism that PepsiCo had developed for operating in a centralized command economy counted for nothing. Making matters worse, PepsiCo was seen to be connected with the discredited former regime. Archrival Coca-Cola almost immediately launched a drive for market share. The results were striking. In Hungary, for example, PepsiCo's market share tumbled from 70 percent to 30 percent almost overnight.[16]

In a **dual-party system**, such as the United States and Britain, the parties are usually not divided by ideology but rather have different constituencies. For example, in the United States, the Democrats tend to identify with working-class people and assume a greater role for the federal government while the Republicans tend to support business interests and prefer a limited role for the federal government. Yet both parties are strong proponents of democracy. In such a dual-party system, the two parties tend to alternate their majority position over a relatively long period. In 1995, the Democrats finally relinquished control of Congress to the Republican majority after many years. We have since seen some sweeping changes in government policy, ranging from environmental protection to affirmative action as well as frequent political stalemates between the party lines bickering over budget issues.[17]

The other extreme situation is a **multiple-party system** without any clear majority, found in Italy and more recently in Japan and Taiwan. The consistency of government policies may be compromised as a result. Because there is no dominant party, different parties with differing policy goals form a coalition government. The major problem with a coalition government is a lack of political stability and continuity, and this portends a high level of uncertainty in the business climate. In Japan, because career bureaucrats, who are not political appointees, used to be in virtual control of government policy development and execution, the changes in government leadership did not seem to pose any measurable policy change until

---

[15]"Growing Instability in Mexico Threatens U.S. Economy and Border Security," The Heritage Foundation, http://www.heritage.org/, February 12, 2009.

[16]Hugh D. Menzies, "Pepsico's Soviet Travails," *International Business* (November 1995): 42.

[17]"America's Economy: Which Way America?" *Economist*, May 25, 2012.

recently. However, in recent years owing to Japan's prolonged recession, those non-political elite bureaucrats have lost clout, and instead a succession of prime ministers has tried, mostly in vain, to initiate many economic and financial reforms for Japan's resurgence.[18] Indeed, at the time of writing in late December 2012, the Democratic Party of Japan that came to power three years ago has lost its majority position back to the Liberal Democratic Party that had almost continuously ruled Japan since 1955. Again, major policy changes are expected.[19]

Besides the party system, foreign businesses also have to pay attention to the local government structure. Some governments are very weak and hardly have any control at the local level. For example, Indonesia, whose government used to be very centralized and straightforward, now has been steadily releasing power to local communities. This means that foreign businesses now have to deal with local government and political system in each of its 33 provinces.[20]

Government Policies and Regulations

It is the role of government to promote a country's interests in the international arena for various reasons and objectives. Some governments actively invest in certain industries that are considered important to national interests. Other governments protect fledgling industries in order to allow them to gain the experience and size necessary to compete internationally. In general, reasons for wanting to block or restrict trade are as follows:

1. National security
   - Ability to produce goods necessary to remain independent (e.g., self-sufficiency)
   - Not exporting goods that will help enemies or unfriendly nations

2. Developing new industries
   - Idea of nurturing nascent industries to strength in a protected market

3. Protecting declining industries
   - To maintain domestic employment for political stability

For example, Japan's active industrial policy by the Ministry of International Trade and Industry (MITI) in the 1960s and 1970s is well known for its past success and has also been adopted by newly industrialized countries (NICs), such as Singapore, South Korea, and Malaysia.[21] Governments use a variety of laws, policies, and programs to pursue their economic interests. More recently, the Baltic States of Estonia, Latvia, and Lithuania, controlled by the Soviet regime until the late 1980s, have liberalized their economies significantly by opening up their economies to international trade and foreign direct investment as well as treating foreign companies no differently from domestic companies. As a result of their rapid transition to open market economies, they were formally inducted into the European Union in 2004.[22]

This section focuses on describing those government programs, trade and investment laws, and macroeconomic policies that have an immediate and direct impact on the international business in a country. We will discuss laws regulating business behavior—such as antitrust laws and antibribery laws—in a subsequent section on international legal environments. Later sections of this chapter will discuss the legal systems that produce and enforce a country's laws.

---

[18]"Japan's Nostalgia for Leadership: The 21st-Century Samurai," *Economist*, March 17, 2012.

[19]"Japan Voters Sweeps in New Leader,"*Wall Street Journal*, December 16, 2012.

[20]John McBeth, "Power to the People," *Far Eastern Economic Review*, August 14, 2003, pp. 48–50.

[21]Masaaki Kotabe, "The Roles of Japanese Industrial Policy for Export Success: A Theoretical Perspective," *Columbia Journal of World Business* 20 (Fall 1985): 59–64; Mark L. Clifford, "Can Malaysia Take That Next Big Step?" *Business Week*, February 26, 1996, pp. 96–106.

[22]"The External Sector: Capital Flows and Foreign Debt," *Country Profile. Estonia*, 2005, pp. 43–45.

Incentives and Government Programs

Most countries use government loans, subsidies, or training programs to support export activities and specific domestic industries. These programs are important for host-country firms, as well as for firms considering production in one country for export to others. In the United States, the International Trade Administration (ITA) has a national network of district offices in every state, offering export promotion assistance to local businesses. Furthermore, in light of federal budget cuts and as a supplement to the ITA's trade promotion efforts, state governments have significantly increased their staff and budgets, not only for export assistance, particularly in nurturing small local businesses,[23] but also for attracting foreign direct investment to increase employment in their respective states.[24] Thus, the major objectives of any state government support are (1) job creation and (2) improving the state balance of trade (as in any country).

The state government's export promotion activities are more systematic, while its investment attraction activities are characterized by their case-by-case nature. Foreign investment attraction activities generally consist of seminars, various audio-visual and printed promotional materials, and investment missions, among others. Of these, investment missions and various tax and other financial incentives appear to play the most important role in investment promotional efforts. Investment missions are generally made by government officials, particularly by the governor of the state, visiting with potential investors. One study has shown that whether or not they participate in foreign investment attraction activities, state governments that are active in export promotion tend to attract more foreign companies' direct investment in their states than those state governments that are not active.[25] For example, export-active states may be more politically favorable and receptive to foreign companies operating there. A well-known example is that to attract a Nissan plant, Tennessee spent $12 million for new roads to the facility, and provided a $7 million grant for training plant employees and a $10 million tax break to the Japanese company in 1985.[26] Alabama provided a $253 million package of capital investments and tax breaks to lure Mercedes-Benz's sports utility vehicle production facility to the state in the early 1990s.[27] Similarly, to encourage Japanese automakers to produce in Thailand, the Thai government provides cheap labor, an eight-year tax holiday, and virtually eliminated excise taxes on domestic pickup sales.[28] Since the mid-1980s, the Chinese government has offered preferential tax rates to attract foreign companies' investment in China. On average, the income tax rate for domestic companies is 33 percent while foreign companies pay half of that. Statistics show that foreign companies used to get an annual tax break of approximately US$50 billion in China. But the tax honeymoon for foreign companies investing in China ended with the implementation of a new corporate income tax law from January 1, 2008. In the new tax regime, the unified tax rate is set at 25 percent for both the Chinese and foreign firms, creating a competitive environment for both domestic and foreign investors. While putting an end to many preferential tax policies and incentives enjoyed by foreign firms, the new law retains some favorable terms for companies whose development is in line with the nation's strategic priorities, such as the 20 percent

---

[23]Masaaki Kotabe and Michael R. Czinkota, "State Government Promotion of Manufacturing Exports: A Gap Analysis," *Journal of International Business Studies* 23 (Fourth Quarter 1992): 637–658; and for a recent comprehensive study, see Timothy J. Wilkinson, Bruce D. Keillor, and Michael d'Amico, "The Relationship between Export Promotion Spending and State Exports in the U.S.," *Journal of Global Marketing* 18 nos. 3/4 (2005): 95–114.

[24]J. Myles Shaver, "Do Foreign-Owned and U.S.-Owned Establishments Exhibit the Same Location Pattern in U.S. Manufacturing Industries?" *Journal of International Business Studies* 29 (Third Quarter 1998): 469–492.

[25]Masaaki Kotabe, "The Promotional Roles of the State Government and Japanese Manufacturing Direct Investment in the United States," *Journal of Business Research*, 27 (June 1993): 131–46.

[26]"Tennessee's Pitch to Japan," *New York Times*, February 27, 1985. pp. D1 and D6.

[27]"Tax Freedom Day Index Would Be Keen Indicator," *Orlando Sentinel*, May 8, 1994, p. D1.

[28]"In a World of Car Builders, Thailand Relies Heavily on a Pickup," *New York Times*, June 16, 2005.

preferential rate for small enterprises with small profit margins and also a 15 percent rate for high-tech companies.[29]

Most governments subsidize certain industries directly. Direct government subsidies are an important international consideration. In Europe, Airbus Industries was established with joint government subsidies from the governments of Britain, France, Germany, and Spain in 1970 to build a European competitor in the jet aircraft industry once dominated by U.S. companies, including Boeing and McDonnell-Douglas-Lockheed. The United States is no exception. When threatened by Japanese competition in the semiconductor industry in the 1980s, the Reagan administration launched a Japanese-style government-industry joint industrial consortium known as SEMATECH (Semiconductor Manufacturing Technology) in 1987, with the federal government subsidizing half of its $200 million operating budget.[30] Thanks to SEMATECH, the U.S. semiconductor industry finally recaptured the leading market share position by 1995, long lost to Japanese in the 1980s.

The point is to recognize how government support for particular industries or for exporting in general will affect which industries are competitive and which are not. International businesses can benefit by planning for and utilizing home-country and host-country government programs.

Government Procurement

The ultimate government involvement in trade is when the government itself is the customer. It engages in commercial operations through the departments and agencies under its control. As the U.S. government accounts for a quarter of the total U.S. consumption, the government has become the largest single consuming entity in the United States. Thus, the government procurement policy has an enormous impact on international trade. In the United States, the Buy American Act of 1933 gives a bidding edge to domestic suppliers, although the U.S. Congress has recently begun to open certain government procurements to goods and services from countries that are parties to various international trade agreements that the United States also belongs to.[31] For foreign suppliers to win a contract from a U.S. government agency, their products must consist of at least 50 percent U.S.-made parts, or they must undercut the closest comparable U.S. product by at least 6 percent.[32] This "buy domestic" policy orientation is not limited to the United States, but applies to all other nations. In other words, when a U.S. company tries to sell to any foreign government agency, it should always expect some sort of bidding disadvantage relative to local competitors.

Trade Laws

National trade laws directly influence the environment for international business. Trade controls can be broken into two categories—economic trade controls and political trade controls. Economic trade controls are those trade restraints that are instituted for primarily economic reasons, such as to protect local jobs. Both **tariffs** and **nontariff** barriers (NTBs) work to impede imports that might compete with locally produced goods (see **Exhibit 5-1**). Tariffs tax imports directly, and also function as a form of income for the country that levies them. In industrialized

---

[29]Jim Yardley, "China Moves to End Tax Breaks for Foreign Businesses," *International Herald Tribune*, March 8, 2007; "Tax Burdens Equalized for Chinese, Foreign Firms," *Beijing*, April 15, 2007, http://www.btmbeijing.com; and Bi Xiaoning, "Businesses Positive about Corporate Tax Law," *China Daily*, April 11, 2008.

[30]Due to the U.S. government's gradual budget cut, SEMATECH became a technology consortium funded solely by member companies in 1998.

[31]William T. Woods, "Federal Procurement: International Agreements Result in Waivers of Some U.S. Domestic Source Restrictions," GAO-05-188, *GAO Reports*, January 26, 2005, pp. 1–24.

[32]Robert Fryling, "Buy American Act: Help for United States Manufacturers," *Contract Management Magazine* 42 (April 2002): 42-43; and "Part 25.001: The Buy American Act," Federal Acquisitions Regulation, http://www.acquisition.gov/far/loadmainre.html, accessed August 23, 2013.

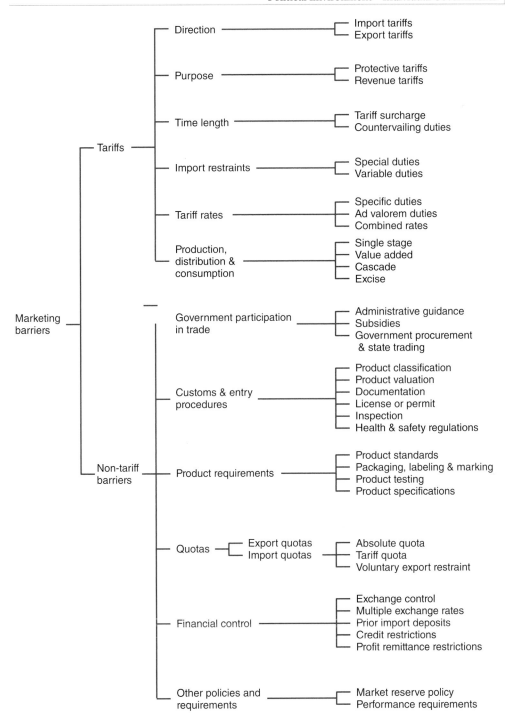

Exhibit 5-1 Tariff and Nontariff Barriers
Source: Adapted from Sak Onkvist and John J. Shaw, "Marketing Barriers in International Trade," Business Horizons 31 (May–June 1988): 66.

countries today, average tariff rates on manufactured and mining products are about 5–6 percent. Tariff protection for agricultural commodities is higher than for manufactured products, both in industrial and in developing countries. However, in industrialized countries the average tariff rate on agriculture is almost double the tariff for manufactured products. Tariffs on labor-intensive products also largely surpass the average for industrial goods. Compared to industrial products as a whole, labor-intensive products are again more protected in industrialized countries than in developing countries, by an estimated one-third.[33]

Nontariff barriers include a wide variety of quotas, procedural rules for imports, and standards set upon import quality that have the effect of limiting imports or making importing more difficult. For example, European carmakers are facing challenges from nontariff barriers in South Korea. Rather than adopting internationally harmonized standards, South Korea sets a series of complicated domestic regulations on noise, emissions, safety belts, and other issues that have prevented many European firms from entering the market. In 2007, European carmakers only managed to sell 15,000 vehicles in South Korea, generating revenue of $650 million. In contrast, Korean automakers exported slightly more than 74,000 cars to Europe with revenue of $3,900 million.[34] By May 2012, Korea's exports to Western Europe rose by 70 percent, while the EU exports to Korea just by 15 percent.[35]

Embargoes and **sanctions** are country-based political trade controls. Political trade restraints have become an accepted form of political influence in the international community. They are coercive or retaliatory trade measures often enacted unilaterally with the hopes of changing a foreign government or its policies without resorting to military force. Embargoes restrict all trade with a nation for political purposes. The United States maintains an economic embargo on Cuba today in an effort to change the country's political disposition. Sanctions are more narrowly defined trade restrictions, such as the U.S. government's decision in May 2012 to impose a tariff of more than 31 percent on Chinese solar panels as a result of the U.S. Commerce Department ruling that Chinese manufacturers were guilty of dumping solar panels in the U.S. market for less than it cost to produce them.[36]

A trade war waged by the U.S. government could make such seemingly unrelated items as Scottish cashmere sweaters, Pecorino cheese (but only the soft kind), German coffee makers, and French handbags scarce on American store shelves.[37]

Export license requirements are product-based trade controls. All exports officially require a specific **export license** from the Export Administration of the Department of Commerce. However, most products that are not sensitive to national security or are in short supply in the country may be sent to another country using only a general license. The application process for more sensitive products, including much high-technology exports, is quite extensive and can include review by numerous government agencies (see Chapter 15 for export control).

International businesses have a number of reasons to be concerned with trade restrictions. First, trade restrictions may completely block a company's ability to export to a country. Even if the company can export its goods, restrictions such as quotas or local modification requirements may make the product so expensive that an otherwise lucrative market is eliminated. Some companies attempt to benefit from import restrictions by establishing production facilities inside the foreign market country. For example, Brazil suddenly raised a tariff on imported cars from 20 percent to 70 percent in late 1994. As a result, foreign auto makers Fiat and Ford, with operating plants in Brazil, enjoyed a definite cost advantage over Chrysler, Toyota, Volvo, and others that exported cars to the country. Naturally, those late comers decided to begin production in Brazil to avoid its hefty import tariffs. This is one illustration of strategic reasons why firms sometimes have plants in various countries rather than relying solely on exporting from home. In this manner those companies, domestic or foreign, already manufacturing in the market can access the desired market with little competition from external producers.

---

[33] *Global Economic Prospects and the Developing Countries 2002* (Washington, D.C.: World Bank, 2002) (see Chapter 2).

[34] Lawrence J. Speer, "Talks Aim to Ease Access to Korean Market," *Automotive News Europe*, May 12, 2008.

[35] John Reed, "Ford Europe hits at EU-Korea trade deal," *Financial Times*, May 1, 2012.

[36] "U.S. Imposes Tariffs on China Solar Panels," *Wall Street Journal*, May 18, 2012.

[37] "Trade Fight Spills Over into Handbags, Coffee Makers," CNN Interactive, www.cnn.com, March 3, 1999.

However, trade restrictions are not necessarily good, even for companies inside a protected country. Trade restrictions often block companies from purchasing needed inputs at competitive prices. For example, in 1992 the U.S. International Trade Commission levied an import tariff on the flat panel display screens used in laptop computers in response to a complaint that foreign companies were dumping the screens below cost on the U.S. market. Although local producers of computer screens benefited from the protection from competition, U.S. producers of laptop computers, which relied mostly on imported screens, could no longer compete. Many laptop producers were forced to ship their assembly plants overseas in order to stay in the market.

At a more macro level, if trade laws harm other countries, they are likely to provoke retaliation. For example, the European Union (EU) recently applied a law that would require any airlines to pay for carbon emissions on flights to and from Europe, which would come into effect in April 2013. In response to the law, the Chinese government has put on hold a plan for Chinese airlines to buy 45 Airbus aircraft worth at least $14 billion. Similarly, at the time of this writing, the EU is also facing a potential retaliation by the United States as the former U.S. Secretary of State Hillary Clinton said in a letter to the EU in December 2011 that the U.S. "will be compelled to take appropriate action" if the EU goes ahead with the scheme. The diplomatic spat over the European carbon emission tax comes at a sensitive time for Airbus as it is currently negotiating the future of its Tianjin factory deal with its Chinese partners that is due to expire in 2016.[38] One thing is clear—government trade laws have a complex and dynamic impact on the environment for international business.

Trade war can have positive consequences, however, if it leads to freer trade instead of more restricted trade. The Association of South East Asian Nations (ASEAN) nations are slashing tariffs among themselves to compete with China. A pact to drop tariffs on goods traded within the 10-nation group to 5 percent or less now makes it possible for Procter & Gamble (P&G) to export to most of Asia out of its single remaining shampoo factory in Bangkok. Before the pact, P&G had to buy new production gear for separate plants in Thailand, Indonesia, and the Philippines.[39]

Investment Regulations

International investments have been growing at a much faster pace than international trade. Foreign direct investments are explained in terms of various market imperfections, including government-imposed distortions, but governments also have a significant role in constructing barriers to foreign direct investment and portfolio flows. These barriers can broadly be characterized as ownership and financial controls.

Ownership Controls. Most countries feel that some assets belong to the public—there is a sense of "national ownership." In a highly nationalistic country, this sentiment could apply to the ownership of any company. In many countries, the natural resources (e.g., the land and mineral wealth) are viewed as part of the national wealth, not to be sold to foreigners. For example, Kuwait has a constitutional ban on foreign ownership of its oil reserves. Recently, there was a heated debate as to whether or not state-owned Kuwait Petroleum Corp. (KPC) had the right to sign agreements with foreign oil companies to produce local oil. The government argued that KPC was allowed under existing laws to forge foreign participation accords in return for cash incentives. But its efforts to advance the plan repeatedly came under attack by opposition members of parliament who argued that foreign companies' provision of cash incentives would amount to foreign direct investment, thus foreign control.[40] In a similar vein, Russia has decided to revive its

---

[38]"EU Court Forces US Airlines to Pay for Emissions," *Spiegel Online International*, December 21, 2011; and "UPDATE: Airlines, Airbus Renew Criticism of EU CO2 Scheme," *Wall Street Journal*, May 24, 2012.

[39]Michael Shar, "A New Front in the Free-Trade Wars," *Business Week*, June 3, 2002.

[40]Jeanne M. Perdue, "Kuwait Gets Green Light to Invite Majors," *Petroleum Engineer International* 72 (September 1999): 7.

ailing auto industry—which is rapidly losing market share to Western and Japanese imports and locally assembled foreign models—through direct state intervention. The Russian government seized control of General Motors' pioneering joint venture with Russia's largest automaker, OAO Avtovaz in early 2006.[41]

The United States has very few restrictions on foreign ownership; however, for reasons of national security, limitations do exist. For example, the Federal Communications Commission limits the control of U.S. media companies to U.S. citizens only. This was one of the motivating factors for Rupert Murdoch to relinquish his Australian citizenship for U.S. citizenship in order to retain control of his media network, Fox Television. Similarly, the U.S. Shipping Act of 1916 limits noncitizen ownership of U.S. shipping lines. The Federal Aviation Act requires airlines to be U.S. citizens (defined as one where 75 percent of the voting rights of the firm are owned and controlled by U.S. citizens) in order to hold U.S. operating rights. The International Banking Act of 1978 limits interstate banking operations by foreign banks. Consequently, foreign banks cannot purchase or take over U.S. banks with interstate operations.

Financial Controls.   Government-imposed restrictions can serve as strong barriers to foreign direct investments. Some common barriers include restrictions on profit remittances, and differential taxation and interest rates. Restrictions of profit remittances can serve as a disincentive to invest, because returns cannot be realized in the home currency of the parent company. Although government controls on profit remittance are drawbacks in attracting investment, some governments also use such restrictions as a way to encourage foreign companies to increase exports from the host country. For example, Zimbabwe permits higher profit remittance rates—up to 100 percent—to foreign companies operating in that country that export significantly.[42]

Various multinational companies have been able to exploit legal loopholes to circumvent this problem to some extent. Tactics include currency swaps, parallel loans, countertrade activities, and charging for management services, among others. Also, various countries treat operations of foreign companies differently from those of local companies. Two means through which local companies are supported are lower tax rates and lower interest rates for loans secured from local financial institutions. These differences can put foreign companies at a significant disadvantage relative to domestic companies in that particular market, and can also act as a deterrent to foreign direct investments.

Macroeconomic Policies

Companies search internationally for stable growing markets where their profits will not be deteriorated by exchange loss or inflation. Government policies drive many economic factors such as the cost of capital, levels of economic growth, rates of inflation, and international exchange rates. Governments may directly determine the prime lending rate, or they may print or borrow the funds necessary to increase the money supply. Governments may fix their currencies' exchange rates, or they may decide to allow the international currency market to determine their exchange rates. The monetary and exchange policies a government pursues will affect the stability of its currency—which is of critical concern to any company doing business abroad. In the early 1990s, Mexico kept the peso's exchange rate artificially high despite its increasing trade deficit. One primary objective for such an exchange rate policy was to make it relatively easy for Mexico to import capital goods, such as machinery, from the United States for economic development. When Mexico's trade deficit rose to well over 8 percent of the country's GNP by 1994, Mexico could no longer hold on to an artificially high value of the peso and let it loose in December 1994. How serious was Mexico's trade deficit? Think, for a moment, that the United States had registered the

---

[41]"GM Venture in Russia Hits Snag Following Kremlin Involvement,"*Wall Street Journal,* February 18, 2006, p. A7.
[42]"International Tax: Zimbabwe Highlights 2012," Deloitte, www.deloitte.com, 2012.

large trade deficit of $172 billion in 1987, which once ushered in a doomsday prophecy of the decline of U.S. competitiveness. Yet, the U.S. trade deficit was no more than 3 percent of the country's GDP then! By 2008, the U.S. trade deficit had increased to $813 billion, or about 6 percent of U.S. GDP, although it came down to $803, or 5.3 percent of U.S. GDP, in 2011 due to the recession. As we discussed in Chapter 3, the U.S. trade deficit could not keep growing without a possibility of more ominous consequences than the current unprecedented recession. Today, the United States is the world's largest debtor, with Japan and China being the two largest creditor nations.[43] A sharp reversal in Japan's and China's appetite for U.S. Treasury bonds could send U.S. interest rates soaring.[44] The U.S. government needs to develop policies to reduce the country's trade deficit.

Government fiscal policies also strongly influence macroeconomic conditions. The types of taxes a government employs will influence whether a particular type of business is competitive within a country. For example, if a government lowers long-term capital gains taxes or allows accelerated depreciation of corporate capital assets, it will encourage investment in manufacturing facilities. The Japanese government has been known for its pro-business tax abatement and depreciation policies that helped develop the world's leading manufacturing industries in Japan, ranging from steel and shipbuilding in the 1960s and 1970s, to machine tools, automobiles, and consumer electronics in the 1970s and 1980s, and to semiconductor and semiconductor manufacturing equipment in the 1980s and 1990s.

Although a government can play a role in a thriving economy and creating accessible capital, a number of other factors also determine a country's political environment. Historical considerations, social and political pressures, and the interests of particular constituencies will affect the political environment in important ways. For example, during the early 1990s China was enjoying an unprecedented economic boom. However, companies that tried to take advantage of China's open market policy have met with mixed results.[45] When China joined the WTO in December 2001, it agreed to open up its financial industry, but only gradually. Foreign companies are not yet permitted to become majority owners. In banking, foreigners' stakes are limited to 15 percent, and it was not until 2006 that foreigners could conduct local-currency business with Chinese citizens in banking.[46]

India, on the other hand, still has some restrictions on foreign investment over the years. One example is Press Note 18, which requires any investor with previous or existing joint ventures or technology agreements to seek approval from the Foreign Investment Promotion Board (FIPB) for new direct investments in the same or a related field. Applicants must prove that the new proposal will not jeopardize the interest of the existing joint venture or technology partner. The Press Note 18 is intended to protect the interests of shareholders, public financial institutions, and workers. Although many foreign investors complain about the policy, influential government officials do not want to abandon the guidelines because they consider their domestic industry not strong enough to face direct competition from foreign firms in selected sectors. Under the guidelines, Suzuki, a small Japanese automaker, had to include Maruti Udyog, its existing joint venture, in its plans to make new investments for a car assembly plant and a diesel engine plant. According to Suzuki, the governmental regulations have become a tool of the Indian partners to demand unrealistic and opportunistic exit valuations or to create more barriers for foreign competitors.[47]

---

[43]"United States Largest Foreign Debtor; Japan Largest Creditor," *Economics in Pictures*, http://www.economicsinpictures.com/, accessed August 2, 2011.

[44]"World Bank Warns Global Recovery Has Peaked," *Wall Street Journal*, April 7, 2005, p. A2.

[45]"To Enter or Not to Enter?" *Country Monitor*, January 28, 2002, p. 5.

[46]"Strings Attached," *Economist*, March 8, 2003, pp. 67–68.

[47]"Can They Let Go?" *Business India Intelligence*, October 16, 2004, pp. 1–2.

Political Environment—Social Pressures and Political Risk

Foreign companies also have to consider social factors as part of the political environment of host countries. The political environment in every country is regularly changing. New social pressures can force governments to make new laws or to enforce old policies differently. Policies that supported international investment may change toward isolationism or nationalism. In order to adequately prepare for international business or investment, the environment in each target country should be analyzed to determine its level of economic and political risk and opportunity.

Social Pressures and Special Interests

Governments respond to pressures from various forces in a country, including the public at large, lobbyists for businesses, religious organizations, non-governmental organizations (NGOs), and sometimes the personal interests of the members of the government. In order to assess the political stability of a country, it is critical to evaluate the importance of major forces on the government of the country. Many developing countries have undertaken significant liberalization programs since the 1980s.[48] Although these programs have been regularly promoted by the International Monetary Fund (IMF), their success during recent years must be attributed to a larger social acceptance of the potential benefits of necessary austerity measures. For example, one study has shown that the IMF's Structural Adjustment Program helped improve the economic efficiency of both domestic and foreign companies operating in Nigeria in the 1980s.[49] The benefits of liberalization extend beyond the borders of the countries involved. Consider the liberalization in Mexico, where the privatization of the state telephone company (TelMex) led to large investments by Southwestern Bell. Similarly, private companies are moving rapidly to finance other large public projects. An international consortium composed of Mexico's Grupo Hermés, the United States' AES Corp., and the Japanese firm Nichimen constructed Mexico's first independent power-producing plant in Yucatán State.[50] While liberalization may provide unprecedented opportunities, the forces of special interests or the backlash of public sentiment may also cause governments to limit or curtail entirely certain international business operations.

Feelings of national interest can act as a deterrent to international business. For example, in mid-September 2012, the sovereignty dispute that had been going on for decades between Japan and China over the Senkaku Islands (known as Diaoyu in China) escalated—following the Japanese government's purchase of three of the uninhabited islands formerly owned by the Kurihara family for 2.05 billion yen (or some $26 million). Japan's gesture triggered heated protests and anti-Japan demonstrations by the Chinese both in China and in some foreign countries. In China, more than 60,000 Chinese citizens staged anti-Japanese rallies in at least 24 cities—the largest anti-Japan demonstration since the normalization of diplomatic relations between the two countries in 1972. Some of the rallies turned violent, as Japanese brand cars were vandalized and Japanese-owned businesses and factories in China were looted and temporarily shut down. About 30–40 percent of Chinese tourist trips to Japan were cancelled. Obviously, this has brought an adverse impact on China–Japan business relationships, and the picture is not good for both countries. Not only has China become Japan's largest trading partner in recent years (with total trade between the two reaching $345 billion), it also has become the top trading partner of most Southeast Asian countries—a position that China uses as leverage in the

---

[48]Kate Gillespie and Hildy J. Teegen, "Market Liberalization and International Alliance Formation," *Columbia Journal of World Business* 31 (Winter 1996): 40–54.

[49]Sam C. Okoroafo and Masaaki Kotabe, "The IMF's Structural Adjustment Program and Its Impact on Firm Performance: A Case of Foreign and Domestic Firms in Nigeria," *Management International Review* 33, no. 2 (1993): 139–156.

[50]"Mexico's Energy Infrastructure Expanding to Match Growth," *NAFTA Works* (February 1997): 1–2.

disputes. The idea of putting economic sanctions on Japan was voiced although, at the time of this writing, no sanctions have been implemented. It is arguable who would be worse off, but both economies would definitely suffer—China relies heavily on Japanese investment capital and technology, while China is also the biggest customer for Japan's heavy machinery and high-tech gear. The collateral damage resulting from the China–Japan trade war could spread beyond the two countries, affecting the supply chain for everything from iPads to automobiles.[51]

The boycotting of Japanese products by Chinese consumers seems to be an expected consequence of the worsening tension. Interestingly, however, product boycotts may also threaten other products that are not directly related to the confronting countries. Apple received a boycott threat from furious Chinese microbloggers from Weibo, a famous Chinese micro-blogging site, following the news that in Japan, the newly released iPhone 5 listed a set of disputed islands as part of Japan in its Apple Map application. Despite clarification by the map provider's senior official to an official Chinese media that the Diaoyu Islands were marked as Chinese territory in iPhone 5, the Chinese microbloggers claimed that search results for the Diaoyu Islands showed up only on the previous models, which had been updated to the latest iOs 6 maps and sold in China, but not for its counterparts across the world. When typing "Diaoyu Islands" into Apple maps, the result shows only the latitude and longitude of the location. On the contrary, when typing "Senkaku Islands," a corresponding position with a "Senkaku Islands" label would come up. Thus, not only does political tension affect businesses; businesses can also trigger political tension.[52]

Besides such outcries from local customers, large-scale strikes organized by labor unions could equally harm businesses across national boundaries. For example, in March 2012, several large airlines including Lufthansa, Air Berlin, and Air Canada scrapped hundreds of international flights because of strikes by baggage handlers, security staff, and ground crew workers. 80 percent of the 435 flights were cancelled by Lufthansa, with another 29 flights cancelled by Air Berlin. Canada's passenger air system was in chaos as dozens of flights from Toronto International Airport to the United Kingdom, the United States, Japan, and Germany were cancelled, leaving thousands of travelers stranded.[53]

Furthermore, in recent years, the emergence of nongovernmental organizations (NGOs) as organizational manifestations of broader social movements has dramatically altered the global political-economic landscape. NGOs are relatively informal organizations established by "concerned people" who participate in global value creation and governance. Sometimes, NGOs are antigovernment or anti-MNCs, trying to address societal and environmental issues that they feel are ignored.[54] The ExxonMobil case presented in **Global Perspective 5-1** vividly illustrates the social pressures from NGOs affecting government and corporate policies.

How should a manager evaluate the opportunities and risks a country presents? A manager should certainly consider the political history of the country, as well as the history of similar industries within the country. In the following section, we will discuss a number of factors that international managers should consider when determining the economic and political risks associated with a country.

---

[51]"What's at Stake in China-Japan Spat: $345 Billion to Start,"ChinaRealTimeReport, *Wall Street Journal*, September 17, 2012, http://blogs.wsj.com/chinarealtime/; "Senkaku row reverberates across Southeast Asia," Japan Times, September 27, 2012, http://www.japantimes.co.jp/.

[52]"China's and Japan's Diaoyu/Senkaku-Islands Dispute: The iPhone 5 Factor," *The Atlantic*, September 24, 2012, http://www.theatlantic.com/.

[53]"Lufthansa, Air Berlin Drop Flights Amid Airport Walkouts," *Bloomberg Businessweek*, March 27, 2012; and "Wildcat Strike: Canada's Passenger Air System Is in Chaos," *USA Today*, March 23, 2012.

[54]Hildy Teegen, Jonathan P. Doh, and Sushil Vachani, "The Importance of Nongovernmental Organizations (NGOs) in Global Governance and Value Creation: An International Business Research Agenda," *Journal of International Business Studies* 35 (November 2004): 463-483.

Global Perspective 5-1

Social Pressures Affecting Government and Corporate Policies: A Role of NGOs

ExxonMobil, the world's largest corporation by revenue, has been building a 660-mile pipeline from the oil fields of Chad, in the geographic heart of Africa, to the coast of Cameroon. The pipeline, three feet underground, cuts through forests and farmlands as it makes its way to the sea. Besides local governments to deal with, ExxonMobil has to confront various NGOs for the environmental concerns. Under pressure from activists, ExxonMobil has been forced to take on the unlikely role of development agency, human-rights promoter, de facto local government, and even environmental watchdog.

Using the internet and mass media as cudgels, NGOs such as Greenpeace, Human Rights Watch, and Friends of the Earth, have grown increasingly adept at singling out multinationals. The oil company offers a particularly ripe target. Companies like ExxonMobil are big, which NGOs readily translate as "bad." The oil company cannot choose where oil deposits are located, and it increasingly operates in countries with unsavory rulers, sensitive environments and impoverished populations. Its power tends to dwarf that of its host countries. ExxonMobil's 2011 revenues were $486.4 billion, compared with Chad's GDP of $9.6 billion.

The solution is a complex, four-way agreement between ExxonMobil, the host governments, activists, and the World Bank. In keeping with its mission of alleviating poverty, the World Bank will lend $93 million to the governments of Chad and Cameroon so they could participate as equity investors in the project. By standing between ExxonMobil and its worst critics, and between ExxonMobil and the troublesome host governments, the World Bank could serve as a moral buffer, providing ExxonMobil with invaluable political insurance. While reassuring people about its skills and technology, ExxonMobil has helped oversee a $1.5 million initiative in which the oil company has built schools, funded health clinics, dug wells, advised local entrepreneurs, fielded an AIDS-education van, and distributed 32,000 antimalarial mosquito nets. It has also paid for prostitute focus groups, gorilla habitat studies, even ritual chicken sacrifices.

The company also promised to help create an environmental foundation, two national parks in Cameroon, and an "Indigenous Peoples Plan" for the Pygmies, local minorities in Africa. ExxonMobil will also offer compensation to owners of every mango tree, bean plant, and cotton field, on a plant's expectancy, annual yield, local fruit prices, and so forth.

To complicate matters for ExxonMobil, the demands of Western NGOs often conflict directly with the wishes of locals. The NGOs want Cameroon's rain forests untouched; local farmers plead for ExxonMobil to clear them with chain saws. The NGOs want roads routed around villages; villagers sneak out at night to move road markers closer to their homes and stores, so that they will have more compensation money to improve their lives.

It still remains a question whether the local Chad government can be trusted with ExxonMobil's oil money. Although the World Bank will retain its right to cut off all loans and future aid to Chad, nothing can stop its leader from living high on the hog, paying his army, and ignoring the other seven million people in the country. The last time $25 million was paid to Chad's President, he used $4.5 million to buy weapons.

Indeed, in 2006, the government of Chad blatantly broke its agreement with the World Bank over the development of the Chad/Cameroon pipeline. This presented the company with an unenviable dilemma. It either continues to operate with funds being directed into the government's direct control, destroying the carefully crafted mechanisms designed to ensure that the country's poor benefit from the oil wealth, or seeks to uphold the legal agreement, probably resulting in its operation being closed down.

With the "help" of NGOs, the World Bank, and chicken sacrifice, ExxonMobil is practicing an unfamiliar way of doing business. The traditional way of doing business, getting the oil out of the ground without getting involved in politics, human rights, and the environment, just is not tenable anymore.

Source: Jerry Useem, "Exxon's African Adventure," *Fortune*, April 15, 2002, pp. 50–58; and "Exxon Ponders the Challenge of Chad," Corporate Social Responsibility, March 6, 2006, www.mallenbaker.net.

Exhibit 5-2 Government Policy Areas and Instruments

Policy Instruments	Policy Areas					
	Monetary	Fiscal	Trade	Foreign Investment	Incomes	Sectoral
Legal	• Banking reserve levels	• Tax rates • Subsidies	• Government import controls	• Ownership laws	• Labor laws	• Land tenure laws
Administrative	• Loan guarantee • Credit regulation	• Tax collection	• Import quotas • Tariffs • Exchange rates and controls	• Profit repatriation controls • Investment approvals	• Price controls • Wage controls	• Industry licensing • Domestic content
Direct market operations	• Money creation	• Government purchases	• Government imports	• Government joint ventures	• Government wages	• State-owned enterprises

Source: Adapted from James E. Austin, *Managing in Developing Countries: Strategic Analysis and Operating Techniques* (New York: Free Press, 1990), p. 89.

Managing the Political Environment

International managers must manage the political environment in which the international firm operates. This means, first and foremost, learning to follow the customs of the country in which the firm is operating. But managing the political environment also means knowing which facets of the foreign country must be carefully monitored, and which can be manipulated. If managed correctly, the political environment can become a marketing support system, rather than an inhibitor, for the foreign company.[55]

In order to make informed decisions, the marketing manager must understand the political factors of the country, and also must understand the national strategies and goals of the country. The political factors in a country include political stability, the predominant ideology toward business (and foreign business in particular), the roles that institutions have in the country (including churches, government agencies, and the legal systems), and the international links to other countries' legal and ideological structures.[56]

In order to be welcomed in a host country, the foreign firm has to offer some tangible benefits that the host government desires. Thus, it is critical that a manger recognize what the host country government's motivations and goals are. Most international business activities offer something to all parties involved. If the host country is actively pursuing job creation goals, then a foreign firm that can offer jobs has leverage for obtaining concessions against other problems. The manager will want to understand what national policies are being pursued, and what policy instruments the government typically uses to promote its interests (see **Exhibit 5-2**).

It is important to carefully assess the political power structure and mood in a country before making decisions regarding business operations. By evaluating various environmental factors (see **Exhibit 5-3**), marketing managers can arrive at a more thorough understanding of the likelihood of various problems or opportunities in a country. As shown in **Exhibit 5-4**, managers can also purchase or subscribe to country risk ratings provided by various risk analysis agencies such as the PRS Group's International Country Risk Guide, the Economist Intelligence Unit (EIU), Business Environment Risk Intelligence (BERI), and Business Monitor International (BMI).

---

[55]Michael G. Harvey, Robert F. Lusch, and Branko Cavarkapa, "A Marketing Mix for the 21st Century," *Journal of Marketing Theory and Practice* 4 (Fall 1996): 1–15

[56]James E. Austin, *Managing in Developing Countries: Strategic Analysis and Operating Techniques* (New York: Free Press, 1990).

Exhibit 5-3 Country Risk Assessment Criteria

Index Area	Criteria
Economic Risk	• GDP Per Capita • Real Annual GDP Growth as Annual % Change • Annual Inflation Rate as Annual % Change • Budget Balance as % of GDP • Current Account as % of GDP
Financial Risk	• Foreign Debt as % of GDP • Foreign Debt Service as % of Exports of Goods and Services • Current Account as % of Exports of Goods and Services • International Liquidity as Months of Import Cover • Exchange Rate Stability as % Change
Political Risk	• Government Stability • Socioeconomic Conditions • Investment Profile • Internal Conflict • External Conflict • Corruption • Military in Politics • Religious Tensions • Law and Order • Ethnic Tensions • Democratic Accountability • Bureaucracy Quality

Source: The PRS Group, *International Country Risk Guide,* http://www.prsgroup.com/, accessed January 20, 2009.

Exhibit 5-4 Examples of Country Risk Ratings (70 Selected Countries Ranked by Composite Overall Rating, as of January 2011)

Rank	Country	Composite Risk Measure	Economic Risk	Financial Risk	Political Risk
1	Norway	90.5	46.0	46.5	88.5
2	Singapore	88.5	47.0	45.0	85.0
3	Switzerland	88.0	45.0	45.0	86.0
4	Brunei	87.5	46.0	46.5	82.5
5	Luxembourg	86.8	39.0	43.0	91.5
6	Hong Kong	85.8	48.0	42.0	81.5
6	Taiwan	85.8	45.0	46.5	80.0
8	Sweden	85.0	43.0	40.0	87.0
9	Denmark	84.8	40.5	44.5	84.5
9	Finland	83.8	39.5	36.0	92.0
11	Austria	83.5	39.5	39.0	88.5
11	Germany	83.5	42.5	42.0	82.5
13	Canada	82.8	39.0	40.0	86.5
13	United Arab Emirates	82.8	46.5	40.5	78.5
15	Oman	82.3	45.0	45.5	74.0
16	Kuwait	82.0	46.5	45.5	72.0
16	Netherlands	82.0	39.0	39.0	86.0
16	Qatar	82.0	50.0	41.0	73.0
19	Japan	81.0	39.5	44.0	78.5
20	South Korea	80.5	41.5	41.5	78.0
21	Saudi Arabia	80.3	44.5	46.5	69.5

22	New Zealand	80.0	37.0	35.5	87.5
22	Belgium	80.0	38.5	40.5	81.0
24	Trinidad & Tobago	79.5	38.5	47.5	73.0
25	Malaysia	79.3	42.0	43.0	73.5
26	Botswana	78.8	36.0	47.0	74.5
27	Australia	78.5	39.0	33.5	84.5
28	Chile	78.0	39.5	39.5	77.0
29	United Kingdom	77.3	34.0	39.5	81.0
30	Malta	77.0	31.0	38.0	85.0
30	United States	77.0	35.5	37.0	81.5
30	Uruguay	77.0	39.5	40.5	74.0
33	Czech Republic	76.5	36.5	38.5	78.0
34	Bahamas	75.8	33.0	36.5	82.0
35	Poland	75.5	35.5	36.5	79.0
36	France	75.0	35.5	37.0	77.5
36	China	75.0	39.5	48.0	62.5
38	Panama	74.8	37.0	37.5	75.0
39	Italy	74.5	37.0	36.5	75.5
39	Brazil	74.5	38.0	42.0	69.0
41	Mexico	74.3	37.0	41.0	70.5
42	Azerbaijan	74.0	35.0	48.5	64.5
42	Costa Rica	74.0	34.0	40.5	73.5
44	Israel	73.5	41.0	42.5	63.5
44	Argentina	73.5	41.5	41.0	64.5
46	Russia	72.8	39.0	44.5	62.0
47	Kazakhstan	72.0	39.5	35.0	69.5
47	Estonia	72.0	40.5	30.5	73.0
47	Portugal	72.0	32.5	35.0	76.5
47	Peru	72.0	39.0	42.5	62.5
51	Philippines	71.8	38.0	42.5	63.0
51	Ireland	71.8	29.5	36.5	77.5
53	Hungary	71.5	32.5	34.5	76.0
54	Croatia	70.8	33.0	33.0	75.5
55	Thailand	70.5	41.0	44.0	56.0
56	Spain	70.0	35.0	34.5	70.5
57	Iceland	68.8	27.5	28.0	82.0
57	Colombia	68.8	34.5	40.5	62.5
59	Vietnam	68.5	30.5	41.0	65.5
59	Indonesia	68.5	38.0	40.0	59.0
61	Iran	68.3	37.5	47.5	51.5
62	India	67.3	32.5	43.5	58.5
63	Cuba	66.0	36.5	39.0	56.5
64	Ukraine	64.8	31.5	35.0	63.0
65	Turkey	63.3	35.0	34.5	57.0
66	Greece	61.5	26.5	28.5	68.0
67	Venezuela	59.5	26.5	46.0	46.5
68	Iraq	58.5	31.0	42.5	43.5
69	Pakistan	57.3	30.5	38.5	45.5
70	Somalia	41.5	27.0	32.5	23.5

Note: Lower scores represent higher risk (highest risk = 1, lowest risk = 100)
Source: Compiled from the PRS Group, *International Country Risk Guide,* http://www.prsgroup.com/, accessed July 1, 2012.

Regardless of categories employed in their risk ratings, there are three general types of risks involved in operating in a foreign country: risks associated with changes in company ownership, risks associated with changes in company operations, and risks associated with changes in transfers of goods and money. Changes in ownership structure are usually due to dramatic political changes, such as wars or coups d'état. A company may face the expropriation or confiscation of its property, or it may face the nationalization of its industry. **Expropriation** refers to foreign government's takeover of company goods, land, or other assets, with compensation that tends to fall short of their market value. **Confiscation** is an outright takeover of assets without compensation. **Nationalization** refers to foreign governments' takeover for the purpose of making the industry a government-run industry. In nationalization, companies usually receive some level of compensation for their losses.

To reduce risk of expropriation or confiscation of corporate assets overseas, many companies use joint ventures with local companies or adopt a domestication policy. Joint ventures with local companies imply shared activities and tend to reduce nationalistic sentiment against the company operating in a foreign country. **Domestication policy** (also known as **phase-out policy**) refers to a company gradually turning over management and operational responsibilities as well as ownership to local companies over time.

However, these risks have been reduced in recent years as many countries have realized the need for international support in order to receive the loans and investment they need to prosper. Consequently, the number of privatizations of once-government-owned industries has increased in the last decade.[57] It is well known that government-owned companies generally do not measure up to the performance standard of private companies.[58]

Other changes in operating regulations can make production unprofitable. For example, local-content requirements may force a company to use inputs of higher cost or inferior quality, making its products uncompetitive. Price controls may set limits on the sales price for a company's goods that are too low to recover investments made. Restrictions on the number of foreign employees may force a company to train local citizens in techniques that require years of specialization.

Shifts in regulations on the transfer of goods and money can also dramatically affect the profitability of operating in a country. These changes include exchange rate restrictions or devaluations, input restrictions, and output price fixing. If a country is experiencing a shortage of foreign capital, it may limit the sale of foreign currencies to companies that need to buy some inputs from abroad or repatriate profits back home. Faced with such foreign exchange restrictions, companies have developed creative, if not optimal, means to deal with the foreign exchange restrictions. **Countertrade** is a frequently used method that involves trading of products without involving direct monetary payments. For example, in order to expand its operations in Russia, the Russian subsidiary of PepsiCo needed to import bottling equipment from the United States. However, the Russian government did not allow the company to exchange rubles for dollars, so it exported Russian vodka to the United States to earn enough dollars to import the needed equipment. As a result of the countertrade arrangement, PepsiCo is now considered the most widely available Western consumer product in the Commonwealth of Independent States (ex-Soviet states). Firms that use countertrade are also shifting away from short-term marketing motives, such as disposing of surplus, obsolete, or perishable products, to long-term marketing motives such as establishing relationships with new partners, gaining entry to new or difficult markets, and accessing networks and expertise.[59]

---

[57]Douglas L. Bartley and Michael S. Minor, "Privatization in Eastern Europe: A Field Report," *Competitiveness Review* 6, no. 2 (1996): 31–43; and John Nellis, "Time to Rethink Privatization in Transition Economies," *Finance & Development* 36 (June 1999): 16–19.

[58]Lien-Ti Bei and Cian-Fong Shang, "Building Marketing Strategies for State-Owned Enterprises against Private Ones Based on the Perspectives of Customer Satisfaction and Service Quality," *Journal of Retailing & Consumer Services* 13 (January 2006): 1–13.

[59]Dorothy Paun and Aviv Shoham, "Marketing Motives in International Countertrade: An Empirical Examination," *Journal of International Marketing* 4, no. 3 (1996): 29–47.

Terrorism and the World Economy

Terrorism used to be considered a random political risk of relatively insignificant proportions. However, it seems to have gradually escalated in the last decade or so.[60] It culminated on September 11, 2001, in New York City and Washington, D.C., when massive terrorist attacks occurred. By attacking the World Trade Center and the Pentagon, symbols of financial, economic, and military power, terrorists also disrupted the U.S. economy and affected the global market. The cost of the attack is hard to believe. An IMF study identified the direct loss as totaling about $21.4 billion, or about 0.25 percent of the U.S. GDP.[61] Other studies' estimates are much higher.[62] Short-term lost economic output was estimated at $47 billion and lost stock market wealth at $1.7 trillion.[63] Long-term costs of security spending and antiterrorist activities can also be significant.

The tighter security measures instated after September 11 affect international trade tremendously. Security checks cause delays in shipments of goods, raising concerns among businesses that rely on just-in-time delivery. In the United States after the attack, because of the security check at the Canadian border, Ford Motor and General Motors experienced periodic parts shortages, which delayed production for hours, steel makers slowed production, and office-supply stores in the New York area ran out of ink and paper.

The September 11th attacks, along with the wars in Iraq and Afghanistan and increasing instability in the Middle East, have caused tremendous concern about future oil supplies for economic security. Because Arab oil supplies look shakier than ever, U.S. policy makers and oil companies are working on oil pipelines in Africa and other parts of Asia. An oil pipeline was constructed from Baku through Georgia to the Turkish port of Ceyhan as a vital project for oil security, and has been operational since 2005.[64] However oil pipelines in some parts of Africa are also facing frequent attacks from terrorists. For example, actions of insurgents in recent years have led to a significant reduction of oil production in Nigeria. Thousands of foreign workers have been compelled to leave the country, and two oil refining factories have been closed. In the middle of 2007 regular insurgent attacks had resulted in a 25 percent reduction in Nigeria oil exports.[65]

Two massive terrorist bombings in Bali, Indonesia, on October 12, 2002, and on October 1, 2005, affected many countries, including Australia, South Africa, Ecuador, and Sweden. Australians always thought that given their country's relatively geographically isolated location, they were immune to terrorism. Now even Australian firms and tourists have to think twice about where to invest and travel.[66] Similarly, coordinated terrorist attacks by Islamic extremists struck the heart of Mumbai, India's commercial capital, on November 26–29, 2008, primarily targeted at U.S. and British citizens as well as Jewish people.[67] The growing threat today is from the so-called "global jihad movement," a mixed group inspired by Osama bin Laden. Despite his demise, threats of terrorism would continue to evolve.[68]

As recently as 2006, the U.S. government, sensitive about Middle Eastern terrorism, became embroiled in a heated dispute over port security issues as a result of the proposed purchase of five

[60]Masaaki Kotabe, "Global Security Risks and International Competitiveness," *Journal of International Management* 11 (December 2005): 453–456.

[61]International Monetary Fund, "How Has September 11 Influenced the Global Economy?," *World Economic Outlook* (December 2001): 16.

[62]Jim Saxton, "The Economic Costs of Terrorism Pose Policy Challenges," Joint Economic Committee Press Release, United States Congress, May 1, 2002, www.house.gov/jec/.

[63]Peter Navarro and Aron Spencer, "September 11, 2001: Assessing the Costs of Terrorism," *Milken Institute Review* (Fourth Quarter 2001), p.20.

[64]"Hidden Risks to the Global Economy," *Emerging Market Monitor,* February 13, 2012, pp. 1–3.

[65]"In Nigeria Insurgents Have Damaged Oil Pipeline and Have Killed 11 Militants," http://www.world-terrorism.org/items/date/2008/05, accessed September 1, 2008.

[66]"The Bomber Will Always Get Through," *Economist,* October 8, 2005, pp. 12–13.

[67]"At Least 100 Dead in India Terror Attacks," *New York Times,* November 26, 2008.

[68]"Bin Laden Is Dead, Obama Says,"*New York Times,* May 1, 2011.

U.S. major commercial port operations by Dubai Ports World, a United Arab Emirates–owned company and one of the most globally efficient port operators.[69] Eventually, the U.S. Congress introduced legislation to delay the sale. Clearly, economic efficiency cannot be pursued devoid of international politics.

Terrorist activities and local military skirmishes in various parts of the world disrupt not only international movement of supplies and merchandise but also international financial flow as well as tourism. They threaten the smooth functioning of international marketing activities we had taken for granted in the last thirty years. International marketers should be aware that global strategy based on coordination of various value-adding activities scattered around the world as envisioned in the 1980s and 1990s may need to be replaced (at least on a case-by-case basis) by more locally and regionally based strategies that require increased levels of local procurement and local marketing for the sake of political correctness and local sensitivity.[70]

International Agreements

International politics have always been characterized by the predominance of strong ideological links, centered around, and dominated by, a relatively small number of large powers. After World War II, those links centered on the two contending superpowers, the United States and the former Soviet Union. However, recently the hierarchical structure of world politics has been challenged by two processes.

First, the true independence of previously colonial countries has led to a much larger set of nations playing relatively independently on the international stage, entering into contracts and relations with new political and economic partners. Second, the loosening of the tight bipolarity in world politics, combined with the relative decline of the United States as the economic superpower in the free world and the breakup of the Soviet Union that had once led the communist world, has created an increased level of ambiguity in geopolitical stability.[71]

While most nations guard their independence by maintaining the ability to produce critical products domestically, citizens around the world have learned to expect and demand the lifestyle that international trade provides. Thus, domestic politics cannot be isolated from international politics. Political actions in one country will eventually influence the actions of other countries. For example, Mexico's decision to devalue its currency in late 1994 caused U.S. exports to Mexico to decrease. If the industries that are harmed by the decrease in sales have enough political force, they might ask the U.S. government to pressure Mexico to invest in strengthening its currency or face trade repercussions.

Not only do nations react to each other's actions, they develop relationships that determine their future actions. They form networks for achieving mutual goals, and they develop political and trade histories and dependencies that influence their perceptions of the world. Thus, the international political environment is determined by a dynamic process of the interactions of players each pursuing their own interests and working together for mutual interests. Coordination is required, for example, in order to establish and maintain a trade embargo as a viable alternative to military force. Similarly, coordination is required to avoid harmful currency devaluations or the financial insolvency of governments. The level at which governments rely on each other and are affected by each other's actions also leads to regular conflicts and tensions. Indeed, history has shown that war—an ultimate form of international conflicts and tensions—is less likely to occur between two countries the more trade they engage with each other.[72]

---

[69]"Big Problem, Dubai Deal or Not," *New York Times*, February 23, 2006.

[70]Kotabe, Masaaki, "To Kill Two Birds with One Stone: Revisiting the Integration-Responsiveness Framework," in Michael Hitt and Joseph Cheng, ed., *Managing Transnational Firms* (New York: Elsevier, 2002), pp. 59–69.

[71]Tom Nierop, *Systems and Regions in Global Politics—An Empirical Study of Diplomacy, International Organization and Trade, 1950–1991* (New York: Wiley, 1994).

[72]Edward D. Mansfield, *Power, Trade, and War* (Princeton, NJ: Princeton University Press, 1994).

In the United States, the Congress, not the president, is in charge of international trade negotiations. As a legislative process, any decision made on trade-related issues tends to be slow, and the U.S. government's inaction sometimes becomes a bottleneck to international trade negotiations. As a result, the U.S. government may lose credibility in such negotiations. If Congress sees the benefit of faster trade negotiations, it may grant fast-track trade authority to the President. **Fast-track trade authority** gives the U.S. President a free hand in directly negotiating trade deals with foreign governments. Nevertheless, actual trade negotiations are a very complex political process.

The roles of the General Agreement on Tariffs and Trade (GATT) and the World Trade Organization that succeeded GATT in 1995 were explained in Chapter 2 as part of the economic environment. We limit our discussion to two major international agreements that have shaped and will reshape the political economies of the world.

Group of Seven (G7), Group of Eight (G8), and Group of Eight Plus Five (G8 + 5)

The **G7** is an economic policy coordination group made up of political leaders from Canada, England, France, Germany, Italy, Japan, and the United States. The G7 began during the economic crises of the mid-1970s. The G7 countries continue to play a major role in world economy. For example, during a recent G7 meeting in Rome, Italy in February 2009, the main agenda was to discuss the global financial crisis of 2008–2010, and the group of finance ministers pledged to take all necessary steps to help stem the financial crisis.[73]

Russia joined the G7 in 1997, and the group consisting of the original G7 and Russia is known as the **G8**. Heads of state, senior economic ministers, and heads of central banks typically meet once a year to further economic coordination. G7 meetings have primarily dealt with financial and macroeconomic issues (such as the Asian and Latin American financial crisis), but since Russia's participation, the G8 has included some politically sensitive issues such as an effort to make arrangements for the reconstruction of Kosovo—and indeed of the Balkan states as a whole—after the Kosovo conflict. The recent 38th G8 summit was held in Camp David, in the United States, in May 2012 to discuss how to bolster the struggling global economy and how to deal with possible oil supply disruptions ahead of tough sanctions on Iran, enforced due to suspicions the country is developing a nuclear weapon. One urgent issue that the group discussed was how to deal with an economically weakened Europe and, in particular, a debt-ridden Greece that might be forced to exit the eurozone.[74]

In 2005, a new Group of Eight plus Five (**G8 + 5**) was formed when Tony Blair, then–Prime Minister of the United Kingdom, in his role as host of the 31st G8 summit at Gleneagles, Scotland, invited the leading emerging countries (Brazil, China, India, Mexico, and South Africa) to join the talks. This enlargement aimed to form a stronger and more representative group that would inject fresh impetus into the trade talks at Doha, and underscored the need to achieve a deeper cooperation on climate change. Following the 33rd G8 summit (Heiligendamm 2007), German chancellor Angela Merkel announced the establishment of the "Heiligendamm Process," through which the full institutionalization of the permanent dialogue between the G8 countries and the 5 major emerging economies, which deals with the biggest challenges the global economy is facing today, would be implemented.[75]

---

[73]"A G7 Heart-to-Heart in Rome," Forbes.com, February 13, 2009.

[74]"G-8 Leaders Stare into Economic Unease," *Wall Street Journal*, May 19, 2012.

[75]"Heiligendamm Process," GLOBE INTERNATIONAL, http://www.globeinternational.org/index.php, accessed September 1, 2008.

Wassenaar Arrangement

The **Wassenaar Arrangement** was founded in 1995 as a multilateral export control agreement on conventional arms and dual-use goods and technologies. Australia, Japan, and the NATO countries (except Iceland) are members. It is essentially a successor to the Cold War–era **COCOM (the Coordinating Committee for Multilateral Controls)**. COCOM was founded in 1949 to stop the flow of Western technology to the former Soviet Union. Over time, however, two trends started exerting pressure on the policies adopted by COCOM. First, technologies that had primarily military applications were increasingly finding more civilian applications. Satellites, computers, and telecommunication technologies were prime examples of this trend. Second, the trend of economic liberalization in the newly industrializing and developing countries put further competitive pressures on Western companies to share technologies that were until then privy to the Western world. U.S. firms were particularly adversely affected. Many U.S. companies, including the large telecommunications companies, complained to the government that the restrictions were outdated and that they were losing valuable contracts to competitors from countries without such restrictions.

In 1992, COCOM reevaluated its mission and loosened restrictions on exports of computers, telecommunications equipment, machine tools, and other materials that might assist the newly independent nations of Eastern Europe and the former Soviet Republics in their effort to develop market-driven economies. Due to the changed political and economic environment, the COCOM agreement was terminated in 1994 and replaced by the Wassenaar Arrangement of 1995. However, the spirit of the committee still lives on. The new group of 40 countries includes not only the original COCOM members but also Russia and a few other ex-Soviet republics. Unlike COCOM, recommendations by the group to restrict sensitive exports to specified countries are not binding on the members. Two issues of primary importance for being considered within this multilateral system are nuclear technologies and missile (especially ballistic missile) technologies. Today, the United States and some other industrialized countries forbid the export of such generally available technology as software for encoding electronic messages and semiconductor manufacturing equipment. For example, in 2000, the Japanese government imposed an export control on Sony's PlayStation 2 (PS2) electronic game console. PS2's 128-bit central microprocessor developed by Sony and Toshiba had twice the raw number-crunching power of Intel's most advanced Pentium chip used in professional desktop computers. When coupled with a video camera, PS2 could make an ideal missile-guidance system! The biblical prophecy promising peace to those who turn their swords to ploughshares seems very optimistic in today's world of dual-usage technologies, known as DUTs. Such provocations led the Japanese government to designate the machine a "general-purpose product related to conventional weapons." Under Japan's Foreign Exchange and Foreign Trade Control Law, this requires anyone wishing to take more than 50,000 yen (about $600) worth of such equipment out of Japan to get permission from the Ministry of Economy, Trade and Industry. Violators trying to sneak loads of PS2s abroad could face up to five years in jail.[76] Now think for a moment: Sony's PlayStation 3 (PS3) introduced in 2006, is several times more powerful than the PS2, and is capable of surpassing 250 gigaflops per second, rivaling the best mid-1990s supercomputer.[77] Indeed, the U.S. Department of Defense announced that it would buy an additional 2,200 PS3s to complement a military supercomputer cluster.[78]

---

[76]"War Games," *Economist,* April 22, 2000, p. 60; and Richard Re, "Playstation2 Detonation," *Harvard International Review* 25 (Fall 2003): 46-50.

[77]"Super Cell," *Forbes*, February 14, 2005, p. 46.

[78]"Military Purchases 2,200 PS3s,"SciTechBlogs.CNN.com, December 9, 2009.

International Law and Local Legal Environment

International marketing managers should understand two legal environments—the legal environment in each country in which they do business, and the more general international legal environment. At a macro level, international law and the bodies that evaluate it affect high-level international disputes and influence the form of lower-level arbitration and decisions. Local laws and legal systems directly determine the legal procedures for doing business in a foreign country. Local laws also determine the settlement of most international business conflicts—the country whose laws are used is determined by the jurisdiction for the contract.

International Law

International law, or "the law of nations," may be defined as a body of rules that is binding on states and other international persons in their mutual relations. Most nations and international bodies have voluntarily agreed to subjugate themselves to some level of constraint for the purpose of living in a world in which order, and not chaos, is the governing principle. In short, international law represents "gentlemen's agreements" among countries.

Although, technically speaking, there is no enforceable body of international law,[79] international customs, treaties, and court decisions establish a defined international legal environment. International bodies and policies exist for arbitrating cases that cannot be settled fairly in any given country.

International law comes from three main sources—**customs**, international **treaties**, and national and international **court decisions**. Customs are usages or practices that have become so firmly accepted that they become rules of law. For example, nations have historically claimed sovereignty over the resources in their offshore continental shelves. This historical practice has developed into a consensus that amounts to an international law. Custom-based laws develop slowly.

Treaties and international contracts represent formal agreements among nations or firms that set down rules and obligations to govern their mutual relationships. Treaties and contracts are only binding on those who are signatories to them, but if a great number of treaties or contracts share similar stipulations, these may take on the character of a customer-based law or a general rule.

National courts often make rulings in cases that apply to international issues. When these rulings offer an unusually useful insight into the settlement of international cases, or when they develop into a series of interpretations consistent with other nations' courts, then national rulings may be accepted as international laws. If the issue of conflict is one where a national court is not acceptable to one or both parties, international courts and tribunals may rule. International tribunals may be turned to for **arbitration** if the parties agree to let the case be tried. The International Court of Justice was established by the United Nations to settle international conflicts between nations, not between individual parties (such as firms) across national boundaries. However it must be again noted that international court rulings do not establish precedent, as they might in the United States, but rather apply only to the case at hand.

Local Legal Systems and Laws

Legal systems and the laws they create differ dramatically in countries around the world. Many legal systems do not follow the common law system followed in the United States. We discuss a number of different legal systems and the types of laws that govern contracts and business in each system. We also discuss the issue of jurisdiction, which determines the critical issue of what

---

[79]The government of a sovereign nation stipulates its laws with policing authority. Because no supra-national government exists, no supra-national (i.e., international) laws are binding. Although the United Nations is the most comprehensive political body, made up of more than 100 member nations, it is not a sovereign state, and therefore, does not have enforceable laws that the member nations have to abide by other than voluntarily.

courts, and what laws, are used in deciding a legal question. For most business issues, international law is primarily a question of which national laws apply and how to apply them to cases involving international contracts, shipping, or parties.

The laws that govern behavior within a country, as well as the laws that govern the resolution of international contractual disputes, are primarily local, or municipal, laws. Foreign subsidiaries and expatriate employees live within the legal bounds of their host countries' legal systems. Although U.S. embassy property is considered U.S. territory no matter where it is located, companies and their employees must live within the local country laws. The inability of the U.S. government in 1994 to change the Singapore government's punishment by caning of Michael Fay, an American teenager charged of vandalism there, illustrates a clear example of the sovereignty of each country's laws.[80] The international marketing manager must be aware of the laws that will govern all business decisions and contracts.

Business Practices and the Legal System

Businesses face a myriad of legal issues every day. Questions relating to such issues as pricing policies and production practices must be clearly answered in order to avoid legal rapprochement and punishment. Choices relating to legal industry constraints and various regulations on product specifications, promotional activities, and distribution must be understood in order to function efficiently and profitably. Legal systems in each country deal with these questions differently. For a brief summary of legal issues facing companies, see **Exhibit 5-5**.

For example, in many parts of the world, automobiles with engines larger than 2,000 cc displacement face a much stiffer commodity tax than those with smaller engines. In some

Exhibit 5-5   Legal Issues Facing the Company

Type of Decision	Issue
Pricing decisions	Price fixing
	Deceptive pricing
	Trade discount
Packaging decisions	Pollution regulations
	Fair packaging and labeling
Product decisions	Patent protection
	Warranty requirements
	Product safety
Competitive decisions	Barriers to entry
	Anticompetitive collusion
Selling decisions	Bribery
	Stealing trade secrets
Production decisions	Wages and benefits
	Health and safety requirements
Channel decisions	Dealers' rights
	Exclusive territorial distributorships

Source: Adapted from Philip Kotler and Gary Armstrong, *Principles of Marketing*, 8th ed. (Englewood Cliffs, N.J.: Prentice Hall, 1998.

---

[80]"Singapore's Prime Minister Denounces Western Society," *Wall Street Journal*, August 22, 1994, p. A8.

countries it is illegal to mention a competitor's name in an advertisement. In some countries that follow Islamic law, it is even illegal to borrow money or charge interest! However, businesses need financial resources to grow; thus they must learn how to acquire the resources they need within the legal limits established by the country in which they are operating. For example, in Pakistan, importers and exporters of raw materials rely on a technique that is known as *murabaha* to avoid the ban on interest. In this arrangement, a bank buys goods and sells them to a customer who then pays the bank at a future date and at a markup agreed upon by the bank and its customer. In Indonesia, credit card companies such as Visa and MasterCard receive collateral assets, such jewelry and cattle, which they can sell, from card users instead of charging interest.[81]

In recent years, some countries have started raising legal requirements for environmental protection. In Japan, the famed just-in-time delivery system, such as the one practiced by Toyota and 7-Eleven Japan, has been criticized for causing traffic congestion and air pollution.[82] **Green marketing** has become fashionable in an increasing number of countries. It is marketers' reaction to governments' and concerned citizens' increased calls for reduction of unnecessary packaging materials and increased recycling and recyclability of materials used in the products. Recent developments in the European Union threaten to utilize environmental standards to control internal and external trade in consumer products. In many parts of Asia, consumer awareness and appreciation of environmental protection is also making green issues a crucial part of firms' marketing strategy.[83] Marketers who do not conform may be restricted from participation. Meanwhile, those marketers who do meet the requirements enjoy the benefits of improved product development capabilities, although such capabilities may not automatically translate into improved market share.[84]

Regulations on E-Commerce

Local business laws also affect the use of the internet. While there are no measurable restrictions for e-commerce in the United States, it is not the case in foreign countries. For example, France has regulated that the use of "cookies," software or hardware that identifies the user, should only be allowed when consent is granted.[85] Britain has a set of e-commerce laws designed to protect consumers. Interestingly, however, one study shows that almost half of the U.K.'s top 50 retailers are flouting these laws. For example, one website failed to contain an appropriate data protection consent form. Another website informed users that their personal details would be passed onto other firms unless they sent an e-mail opting out. Both are in direct violation of the British laws. With so much business being done over the internet, it is disconcerting that major retailers are not meeting the letter and the spirit of the laws.[86]

Types of Legal Systems

Three principal legal "systems" are used in the majority of counties: common law systems, code law systems, and Islamic law systems. **Common law** systems base the interpretation of law on

---

[81]Clement M. Henry, ed., "Special Issue: Islamic Banking," in *Thunderbird International Business Review* 41 (July/August and September/October 1999); Ahmed Al Janahi and David Weir, "How Islamic Banks Deal with Problem Business Situations: Islamic Banking as a Potential Model for Emerging Markets," Thunderbird *International Business Review* 47 (July/August 2005): 429–445. For broader regulatory issues on Islamic finance, an excellent treatise is found in Mohammed El Qorchi, "Islamic Finance Gears Up: While Gaining Ground, the Industry Faces Unique Regulatory Challenges," *Finance and Development* 42 (December 2005): 46–49.

[82]Eiji Shiomi, Hiroshi Nomura, Garland Chow, and Katsuhiro Niiro, "Physical Distribution and Freight Transportation in the Tokyo Metropolitan Area," *Logistics and Transportation Review* 29 (December 1993): 335–343.

[83]"Green Marketing Makes Its Asian Debut," *Media: Asia's Media & Marketing Newspaper,* April 3, 2008, p. 22.

[84]William E. Baker and James M. Sinkula, "Environmental Marketing Strategy and Firm Performance: Effects on New Product Performance and Market Share," *Journal of the Academy of Marketing Science* 33 (Fall 2005): 461–475.

[85]John Leyden, "Online Data Protection Incites Worry," *Network News*, May 5, 1999, p.4.

[86]"Half of Top 50 UK Retailers Are Breaking Online Trading Laws," *Computer Weekly*, February 13, 2003, p. 18.

prior court rulings—that is, legal precedents and customs of the time. The majority of the states in the United States follow common law systems (Louisiana is an exception). **Code (written) law** systems rely on statutes and codes for the interpretation of the law. In essence, there is very little "interpretation" in a code law system—the law must be detailed enough to prescribe appropriate and inappropriate actions. The majority of the world's governments rely on some form of code law system. Finally, **Islamic law (Sharia)** systems rely on the legal interpretation of the Koran and the words of Mohammed. Unlike common and code law systems, which hold that law should be man-made and can be improved through time, Islamic legal systems hold that God established a "natural law" that embodies all justice.

Examples of Different Laws

Legal systems address both criminal and civil law. Criminal law addresses stealing and other illegal activities. **Civil law** addresses the enforcement of contracts and other procedural guidelines. Civil laws regulating business contracts and transactions are usually called **commercial law**. International businesses are generally more concerned with differences in commercial laws across different countries. For example, who is responsible if a shipper delivers goods that are not up to standards and the contract fails to address the issue? What if the ship on which goods are being transported is lost at sea? What if the goods arrive so late as to be worthless? What if a government limits foreign participation in a construction project after a foreign company has spent millions of dollars designing the project?

Sometimes the boundary between criminal and civil law will also be different across countries. For example, are the officers of a company liable for actions that take place while they are on duty? When a chemical tank leak in Bhopal, India, killed more than 3,000 Indian citizens in 1984, it was not immediately clear whether the officers of Union Carbide were criminally liable. Since then, some 20,000 people have died from the contamination. It was seven years later in 1991 that the Bhopal court finally issued an arrest warrant for the former CEO of Union Carbide, now living in the United States. Union Carbide was subsequently acquired by Dow Chemical in 2001. In that same year, the same court in Bhopal rejected an attempt by the Indian government to reduce homicide charges to negligence and stepped up demands that the United States extradite the former Union Carbide CEO to stand trial. The issue still lingers on to this day.[87]

Exhibit 5-6 The Number of Lawyers Per 100,000 Residents

United States	365
Britain	175
Germany	134
France	64
Japan	16
China	9

Source: Compiled from Stephen P. Magee, "The Optimum Number of Lawyers," in F. H. Buckley, ed., *The American Illness: Essays on the Rule of Law* (New Haven CT: Yale University Press, 2013).

Cultural Values and Legal Systems

In Japan, legal confrontations are very rare. As shown in **Exhibit 5-6**, Japan's population of lawyers is low, which makes it difficult to obtain evidence from legal opponents. In addition, rules against class-action suits and contingency-fee arrangements make it difficult to bring suit against a person or company. There are disadvantages to Japan's system, but it supports the cultural value of building long-term business ties based on trust.

In the United States, there is a strong belief in the use of explicit contracts and a reliance on the legal system to resolve problems in business. In other countries, such as China, a businessman who tries to cover all possible problems or contingencies in a contract may be viewed as untrustworthy. Chinese culture values relationships (known as *guanxi*) and therefore relies more heavily on trust and verbal contracts than does U.S. culture.[88] In Brazil, however, there is a value system different from both the United States' explicit contractual agreement and China's mutual trust and verbal contract. The Brazilian value system is known as *Jeitinho*, in which people believe

---

[87]Dow Chemical: Liable for Bhopal?"*Business Week,* June 9, 2008, pp. 61–62.

[88]See, for example, Don Y. Lee and Philip L. Dawes, "Guanxi, Trust, and Long-Term Orientation in Chinese Business Markets," *Journal of International Marketing* 13, no. 2 (2005): 28–56; and Henry F.L. Chung, "Performance," Industrial *Marketing Management* 40, no. 4 (2011): 522–533.

that they can always find a solution outside the legal contract on a case-by-case basis.[89] If a culture does not respect the value of following through on an obligation, no legal system, whether written or verbal, will afford enough protection to make doing business easy.

Jurisdiction

Because there is no body of international law in the strictly legalistic sense, the key to evaluating an international contract is by determining which country's laws will apply, and where any conflicts will be resolved.

Planning Ahead

By far the easiest way to assure what laws will apply in a contract is to clearly state the applicable law in the contract. If both a home country producer and a foreign distributor agree that the producer's national laws of contracts will apply to a contract for the sale of goods, then both can operate with a similar understanding of the legal requirements they face. Similarly, to assure a venue that will interpret these laws in an expected manner, international contracts should stipulate the location of the court or arbitration system that will be relied upon for resolving conflicts that arise.

If contacts fail to provide for the jurisdiction of the contract, it is not so clear which laws apply. Courts may use the laws where the contract is made. Alternatively, courts may apply the laws where the contract is fulfilled.

Arbitration and Enforcement

Due to the differences in international legal systems, and the difficulty and length of litigating over a conflict, many international contracts rely on a pre-arranged system of arbitration for settling any conflict. Arbitration may be by a neutral party, and both parties agree to accept any rulings.

However if one of the parties does not fulfill its contracted requirements and does not respond to or accept arbitration, there is little the injured party can do. There is no "international police" to force a foreign company to pay damages.[90]

Issues Transcending National Boundaries
ISO 9000 and 14000

In a bid to establish common product standards for quality management, so as to obviate their misuse to hinder the exchange of goods and services worldwide, the International Standards Organization (based in Geneva, Switzerland) has instituted a set of process standards. Firms who conform to these standards are certified and registered with International Standards Organizations. This common standard is designated **ISO 9000**. The ISO 9000 series was developed by its Technical Committee on Quality Assurance and Quality Management between 1979 and 1986 and was published in 1987. The series has been adopted widely by companies in the United States. The adoption of the ISO 9000 standards by member countries of the European Union has spurred widespread interest in companies worldwide to obtain this certification if they intend to trade with the European Union.

One of the reasons for the spurt of interest in ISO 9000 is the decision by the European Union to adopt ISO standards; the other main reason is the acknowledgment of the importance of

[89]Fernanda Duarte, "Exploring the Interpersonal Transaction of the Brazilian Jeitinho in Bureaucratic Contexts," *Organization* 13 (July 2006): 509–527.

[90]Gerald Aksen, "Reflections of an International Arbitrator," *Arbitration International* 23, no. 2 (2007): 255–259.

quality by companies worldwide. It must be highlighted that ISO 9000 is not only concerned with standardized systems and procedures for manufacturing, but for all the activities of firms. These activities include management responsibility, quality systems, contract reviews, design control, document control, purchasing, product identification and tracking, (manufacturing) process control, inspection and testing, control of nonconforming products and necessary corrective actions, handling, storage, packaging and delivering, recordkeeping, internal quality audits, training, and servicing.

With the growing adoption of the ISO 9000 standards by firms worldwide, an ISO 9000 certification has become an essential marketing tool for firms. The adoption rate of ISO 9000 certifications in U.S. industries has lagged behind that of other developed countries, however. Firms that have it will be able to convince prospective buyers of their ability to maintain strict quality requirements. Firms that do not have ISO 9000 certification could increasingly be at a disadvantage relative to other competitors in the world.[91]

Over the past decade, the need to pursue "sustainable development" has been at the center of discussions of environmental issues and economic development. Attainment of sustainable development was articulated as a goal in 1987 by the World Commission on the Environment and Development (World Commission), a body established by the United Nations. The World Commission defined sustainable development as development that "meets the needs of the present without compromising the ability of future generations to meet their own needs." Sustainable development was the focus of discussion at the United Nations Conference on the Environment and Development held in Rio de Janeiro in 1992, and its attainment was articulated as a goal in the Environmental Side Agreement to the North American Free Trade Agreement (NAFTA). In 1996, the International Organization for Standardization (ISO) named the attainment of sustainable development as a major goal in its new ISO 14000 Series Environmental Management Standards. The ISO 9000 standards are a forerunner to and served as a model for the ISO 14000 series.

The **ISO 14000** standards are receiving significant amounts of attention from business managers and their legal and economic advisors. Business managers view ISO 14000 as a market-driven approach to environmental protection that provides an alternative to "command and control" regulation by government. Businesses view implementation of ISO 14000 as a means to "self-regulate," thereby minimizing their exposure to surveillance and sanctions by the United States Environmental Protection Agency and its state-level counterparts. For example, ISO 14000 is already strengthening chemical companies' relations with plant communities by providing third-party audits of a plant's environmental systems. It is an efficient way to show the community that companies are making environmental improvements. Therefore, any person or organization interested in environmental protection or business management should become familiar with the provisions and potential ramifications of ISO 14000.[92]

Intellectual Property Protection

The term intellectual property refers to a broad range of innovations relating to things such as works of authorship, inventions, trademarks, designs, and trade secrets. Intellectual property rights broadly include patents, trademarks, trade secrets, and copyrights. These ideas typically involve large investments in creative and investigative work to create the product, but fairly low costs of

[91]Thomas H. Stevenson and Frank C. Barnes, "What Industrial Marketers Need to Know Now about ISO 9000 Certification," *Industrial Marketing Management* 31, no. 8 (2002): 695–703.

[92]V. Kanti Prasad and G. M. Naidu, "Perspectives and Preparedness Regarding ISO-9000 International Quality Standards," *Journal of International Marketing* 2, no. 2 (1994): 81–98; and Morgan P. Miles, Linda S. Munilla, and Gregory R. Russell, "Marketing and Environmental Registration/Certification: What Industrial Marketers Should Understand about ISO 14000," *Industrial Marketing Management* 26 (July 1997): 363–370.

manufacturing. As such they are amenable to being duplicated readily by imitators. Imitation reduces the potential returns that would have accrued to the innovator, thereby limiting its ability to appropriate the large investments made. With increasing movements of goods and services across borders, the potential loss of revenues to innovator firms, most of which reside in industrialized countries, is significant.[93]

Few topics in international business have attracted as much attention and discussion in recent years as intellectual property rights. According to the study by Business Action to Stop Counterfeiting and Piracy (BASCAP), the value of counterfeit and pirated products sold world-wide is expected to grow to as much as $1.7 trillion by 2015.[94] Apart from hurting legitimate businesses and trade, intellectual property infringement leads to the loss of government tax revenue.

Piracy is most rampant in the software industry. For example, according to the Business Software Alliance, a global antipiracy watchdog group, global software piracy reached a record figure of $59 billion in 2010. This figure represents a 14 percent increase compared with 2009 and a doubling since 2003. 42 percent of PC software was pirated worldwide in 2010.[95] In percentage terms, the worldwide weighted average software piracy rate was 59.9 percent in 2012. Central/Eastern Europe topped the piracy rate at 62 percent of all software used, followed by Latin America at 61 percent, Asia Pacific at 60 percent, Middle East/Africa at 58 percent, the European Union at 33 percent, and North America at 19 percent.[96] More concerning is the counterfeiting of medicines, which threatens public safety and poses a growing threat around the world. Global sales of counterfeit medicines are estimated to be worth more than $75 billion, having doubled in just five years between 2005 and 2010. Numerous studies have also reported a large number of websites selling prescription drugs without a prescription.[97]

Corporations as well as individual managers have to deal with the growing importance of intellectual property as a significant form of competitive advantage. The laws to deal with this issue are neither uniform across countries, nor are they extended across national boundaries (outside of the government pressure). Even if they are similar, the implementation levels vary significantly. Essentially, protection of intellectual property requires registration in all the countries in which a firm plans to do business. Managers need to be cognizant of this and take proactive measures to counteract any infringements (see **Exhibit 5-7** for the top 60 countries in the ratings for the level of intellectual property protection).

Various anticounterfeiting tools and technologies have been developed by firms to aid others' anticounterfeiting efforts, or to enhance their own. Hewlett-Packard's Specialty Printing Systems, for instance, has expanded its offerings to the pharmaceutical industry with the introduction of a new ink cartridge that allows individual capsules or tablets to be marked. Eastman Kodak Co. developed a Traceless System for anticounterfeiting on its branded rechargeable lithium-ion digital camera batteries supplied by Sanyo Electric. With "forensically undetectable" markers put on printed materials, product packaging or product components, the system can help fight against counterfeiting as only handheld Kodak readers can detect the markers. Also among the firms deploying this anticounterfeiting technology are Donruss Playoff and Liz Claiborne. However, in spite of anticounterfeiting tools

[93]Masaaki Kotabe, "Intellectual Property Protection around the Globe," in Bruce Keillor and Timothy J. Wilkinson, eds., *International Business in the 21st Century*, vol.3, (Praeger, 2011), pp. 95–113.

[94]"Estimating the Global Economic and Social Impacts of Counterfeiting and Piracy," *Business Action to Stop Counterfeiting and Piracy (BASCAP)*, International Chamber of Commerce, www.bascap.com, accessed September 14, 2011.

[95]"Software Piracy Hits Record High of $59 Billion," *CNET News*, news.cnet.com, May 12, 2011.

[96]*2011 Software Piracy Data*, Business Software Alliance, http://www.bsa.org/country/Anti-Piracy/What-is-Software-Piracy.aspx, accessed September 20, 2012.

[97]"Fake Drug Sales Are Increasing on the Internet and Turning Up in Legitimate Supply Chains, Review Finds,"ScienceDaily.com, accessed February 22, 2012.

Exhibit 5-7   Top 60 Countries in Ratings for the Level of Intellectual Property Protection
(Minimum = 0 . . . 10 = Maximum)

Rank	Country	Rating	Rank	Country	Rating	Rank	Country	Rating
1	Finland	8.6	21	South Africa	7.4	39	Greece	6.1
2	Sweden	8.4	22	Taiwan	7.3	42	Estonia	6
2	Denmark	8.4	22	Israel	7.3	42	Saudi Arabia	6
4	Singapore	8.3	24	Italy	7	44	Chile	5.9
4	Switzerland	8.3	25	Portugal	6.9	44	Lithuania	5.9
4	Luxembourg	8.3	25	Hungary	6.9	46	Jordan	5.8
4	Japan	8.3	27	United Arab Emirates	6.8	46	Jamaica	5.8
4	United States	8.3	27	Spain	6.8	48	Oman	5.7
9	Netherlands	8.2	27	Czech Republic	6.8	48	Slovenia	5.7
9	United Kingdom	8.2	27	South Korea	6.8	50	Rwanda	5.6
11	Canada	8.1	31	Poland	6.6	50	Ghana	5.6
11	Germany	8.1	31	Puerto Rico	6.6	50	Bulgaria	5.6
13	New Zealand	8	31	Slovakia	6.6	53	Brazil	5.5
13	Austria	8	34	Iceland	6.5	53	Colombia	5.5
13	Ireland	8	35	Qatar	6.4	55	Panama	5.4
13	Belgium	8	35	Malta	6.4	55	India	5.4
17	France	7.9	37	Trinidad and Tobago	6.3	55	Romania	5.4
18	Norway	7.8	38	Cyprus	6.2	55	Uganda	5.4
18	Australia	7.8	39	Bahrain	6.1	59	Uruguay	5.2
20	Hong Kong	7.6	39	Malaysia	6.1	59	China	5.2

Source: 2012 Report: Intellectual Property Rights Index, http://www.internationalpropertyrightsindex.org/, accessed September 14, 2012.

and technologies, litigation, as well as legislation that we will discuss later in this section, piracy is still rampant around the world.[98]

Now with the convenient online access, it is even more difficult to ensure that copyright rules are not violated in the cyberspace. Recently, Google's books online has been under criticism from the American Publishing Organization, which accuses it of breaching copyright laws. Google aims to put 15 million volumes online from four top U.S. libraries—the libraries of Stanford, Michigan, and Harvard universities, and of the New York Public Library, by 2015. Critics worry that if the people can read a book online for free, they would not bother purchasing it. As easy as a click to download music online to listen to offline, a recent court ruling clearly states that although the copyright of music has lapsed, reproducing and distributing the music is a breach to the copyright law.[99]

Counterfeiting is not restricted to poor countries, either. Milan, Italy, for example, is a leading producer of counterfeit luxury products; the U.S. state of Florida is an international haven for fake aircraft parts; and Switzerland is a big player in pharmaceutical counterfeits production with almost 40 percent of fake medicines seized by the EU. Increasingly, all countries of the World Trade Organization (WTO) are required to implement **Trade Related Aspects of Intellectual Property Rights** (TRIPS) to execute intellectual property protection, and companies are joining together to fight against the violations. (Revisit Chapter 2 for more information on TRIPS.)

---

[98]Jill Jusko, "Counterfeiters Be Gone," *Industry Week* (July 2008): 67–68.

[99]"Court Secures Classical Copyright," *BBC News*, April 6, 2005, http://news.bbc.co.uk/2/hi/entertainment/4415829.stm.

Patent

A patent, if granted, offers a patent holder legal monopoly status on the patented technology and/or process for a certain extended period (usually 15–21 years depending on the country). Patent laws in the United States and Japan provide an example of the differences in laws across countries and their implications for corporations.[100] The most significant difference between the two countries has been on the **"first-to-file"** and **"first-to-invent"** principles. All countries around the world now follow the "first-to-file" principle. Only the United States had followed the "first-to-invent" principle until recently. In September 2011, the U.S. government finally decided to convert to the globally accepted "first-to-file" system from its "first-to-invent," which took effect on March 18, 2013.

In the "first-to-file" system, the patent is granted to the first person filing an application for the patent. In the "first-to-invent" system long used by the United States, however, the patent is granted to the person who first invented the product or technology. Any patents granted prior to the filing of the patent application by the "real" inventor would be reversed in order to protect rights of the inventor. Although the "first-to-file" system took effect in mid-March 2013, it may take a while for American corporate culture based on the long-standing "first-to-invent" principle to make the transition to the new "first-to-file" system.[101] The difference between the two principles has been no small matter (see **Global Perspective 5-2** for far-reaching implications).

The marketing implications of this difference for U.S. companies as well as foreign companies are significant. To protect any new proprietary technologies, U.S. companies must ensure that their inventions are protected abroad through formal patent applications being filed in various countries, especially the major foreign markets and the markets of competitors and potential competitors. For foreign companies operating in the United States, the implications are that they must be extremely careful in introducing any technologies that have been invented in the United States. A "first-to-file" mentality could result in hasty patent applications and significant financial burden in the form of lawsuits that could be filed by competitors that claim to have invented the technology earlier.

In some extreme situations, governments have broken patent law for public health reasons. For example, Brazil's government, after signing an intellectual property protection agreement, announced in August 2001 its plans to break a patent for a drug used to treat AIDS despite the international patent held by Roche, the drug's Swiss-based pharmaceutical company. Federal officials said they were unsuccessful in talks with Roche to lower the prices the country paid for nelfinavir, a drug blocking the HIV virus from replicating itself and infecting new cells.[102] The Brazilian government is not the only one to grab a company's patent rights in the interest of public health. Scared by the anthrax outbreaks in the United States, Canada's health ministry decided that public health came first. It commissioned a generic drug company to make a million doses of ciprofloxacin, a drug used to treat one of the nastier forms of the disease whose patent belongs to German drug giant Bayer.[103]

Copyright

Copyrights protect original literary, dramatic, musical, artistic, and certain other intellectual works. Copyright protection lasts 50 years in the European Union countries and Japan, compared with 95 years in the United States.[104] The difference in the lengths of period of copyright

---

[100]Masaaki Kotabe, "A Comparative Study of U.S. and Japanese Patent Systems," *Journal of International Business Studies* 23 (First Quarter 1992): 147–168.

[101]"Patent Office—'First to File' Bill," *New York Times*, September 9, 2011; "Inventors Race to File Patents," *Wall Street Journal*, March 15, 2013, p. B6.

[102]"Brazil to Break Patent, Make AIDS Drug," *CNN.com*, August 23 2001, http://www.cnn.com/2001/WORLD/americas/08/23/aids.drug0730/index.html.

[103]"Patent Problems Pending," *Economist*, October 27, 2001, p. 14.

[104]"Copyright Revisions Have Japan's Majors Jumping into the Vaults," *Billboard*, April 18, 1998, p. 52; and "Companies in U.S. Sing Blues As Europe Reprises 50's Hits," *New York Times*, January 3, 2003, Late Edition, p. A1.

Global Perspective 5-2

Two Worlds Apart: the "First-to-Invent" Principle vs. the "First-to-File" Principle

Under long-held patent U.S. law, an individual applicant for a patent must prove that he had the idea first, not simply that he won the race to the courthouse. He can assert his priority to the invention at any time; he is entitled to a patent if thereafter he has not "suppressed, abandoned, or concealed" the invention. The U.S. system was established to protect the inventor who lacks the resources to keep up a stream of patent applications merely to invoke their priority.

Supporters of the "first-to-file" system, largely lawyers and corporations, argue that it would better serve the public because it is simpler and conforms to the systems in the rest of the world. Moreover, it would spur inventors to file for patents earlier and to disclose their inventions sooner, thus speeding the progression from idea to finished product. Many supporters also note that most U.S. companies are equipped to act on a first-to-file basis, because they typically apply for patents as soon as inventions are produced. With the adoption of the first-to-file system, this date would also affect patent rights abroad, and thus provide greater reliability for U.S. patents worldwide.

The principal objection to the first-to-file system is that it fosters premature, sketchy disclosure in hastily filed applications, letting the courts work things out later. Although unlikely, it leaves open the possibility of someone stealing the profits of an invention from the true inventor by beating him to the courthouse steps. In the end, the Patent Office could be deluged with applications filed for defensive purposes, as is the case in Japan where this phenomenon is called "patent flooding."

The effect of "first to file" vs. "first to invent" may be best illustrated by the case of the laser, a discovery generally credited to the physicist Charles Townes, who won a Nobel Prize for elucidating the principle of the maser, the theoretical father of the laser. Townes owned the patent on the device. Years later, Gordon Gould, a former graduate student at Columbia University, where Townes taught physics, proved by contemporary notebooks and other means that he had developed the idea long before Townes patented it in 1958.

Gould could not have brought his case to the courts in foreign countries that give priority to the first to file. In the United States, however, the court accepted Gould's evidence of priority and awarded him the basic patents to the laser in 1977 and 1979, ruling that Townes and his employer, at the time AT&T Co., had infringed on Gould's idea. Patlex Corp., of which Gould is a director, now collects fees from laser users throughout the world.

Most recently, the patent infringement dispute between Apple and Samsung (still under way at the time of this writing in August 2013) over various features of smartphones around the world seems to have brought the philosophical differences between the "first-to-file" and the "first-to-invent" systems to the fore. In the "first-to-invent" United States, the court decided in favor of Apple over Samsung, while in "first-to-file" Japan and Korea, the courts decided in favor of Samsung over Apple. Although the details are not yet in the public domain, it is interesting to see how this lawsuit in "first-to-file" Europe and other countries would play out if the patent infringement lawsuits were filed in these markets for smartphones.

However, as stated earlier in the text, although the United States has finally decided to covert to the first-to-file principle, its conversion may not be as smooth once you consider the fact that the Metric Conversion Act of 1975 has failed to convert the country to the metric system from a type of Imperial Measurement System (e.g., pound, ounce, mile, and foot), which is still widely used in the United States.

Source: Lee Edson, "Patent Wars," *Across the Board* 30 (April 1993): 24–29; and Q. Todd Dickinson, "Harmony and Controversy," *IP Worldwide* (September 2002): 22–24; "Patent Office—'First to File' Bill," *New York Times*, September 9, 2011; "Apple vs. Samsung: Swipe, Pinch and Zoom to the Courtroom," *Economist*, September 1, 2012; "South Korean Court Rules Samsung Didn't Copy iPhone," USA Today, August 24, 2012; and "Apple Loses Patent Lawsuit against Samsung in Japan," *Bloomberg Businessweek*, August 31, 2012.

protection could cause tremendous price differences between countries for those products whose copyrights expired in the EU or Japan but are still effective in the United States. This issue will be discussed in detail in the "Gray Markets" section of Chapter 16.

A computer program is also considered a literary work and is protected by copyright. A copyright provides its owner the exclusive right to reproduce and distribute the material or perform or display it publicly, although limited reproduction of copyrighted works by others may be permitted for fair use purposes. In the United States, the use of the copyright notice does not require advance permission, or registration with, the Copyright Office. In fact, many countries offer copyright protection without registration, while others offer little or no protection for the works of foreign nationals.[105]

In the United States, the **Digital Millennium Copyright Act** (DMCA) was passed in 1998 to address a growing struggle in cyberspace between industries supplying digital content and those arguing against strict enforcement of copyright on the internet. The DMCA bans any efforts to bypass software that protects copyrighted digital files. Similar laws have been passed in other countries as well. For example, selling "mod" (modification) chips, a device used to play copied games, tinkering with a game console to play legally and illegally copied software, is a practice that has turned into a legal landmine for the video game sector.

Trademark

A **trademark** is a word, symbol, or device that identifies the source of goods and may serve as an index of quality. It is used primarily to differentiate or distinguish a product or service from another. Trademark laws are used to prevent others from offering a product or service with a confusingly similar mark. In the United States, registration is not mandatory, because "prior use"[106] technically determines the rightful owner of a trademark. However, because determining who used the trademark prior to anyone else is difficult and subject to lawsuits, trademark registration is highly recommended. In most foreign countries, registration is mandatory for a trademark to be protected. In this sense, the legal principle that applies to trademarks is similar to the one that applies to patents: the "first-to-invent" principle used until recently in the United States and the "first-to-file" principle in the rest of the world. Therefore, if companies expect to do business overseas, their trademarks should be registered in every country in which protection is desired.

Trade Secret

A **trade secret** is another means of protecting intellectual property and fundamentally differs from patents, copyright, and trademarks in that protection is sought without registration. Therefore, it is not legally protected. However, it can be protected in the courts if the company can prove that it took all precautions to protect the idea from its competitors and that infringement occurred illegally by way of espionage or hiring employees with crucial working knowledge.

International Treaties for Intellectual Property Protection

Although patent and copyright laws have been in place in many countries for well over a hundred years, laws on trademarks and trade secrets are of relatively recent vintage, having been instituted in the late nineteenth century and beginning of the twentieth century.[107] There are many

---

[105]Subhash C. Jain, "Intellectual Property Rights and International Business," in Masaaki Kotabe and Preet S. Aukakh, eds., *Emerging Issues in International Business Research* (Northampton, MA: Edward Elgar Publishing, 2002): 37-64.
[106]A common law philosophy that defines a rightful owner by use and not by registration.
[107]Bruce A. Lehman, "Intellectual Property: America's Competitive Advantage in the 21st Century," *Columbia Journal of World Business* 31 (Spring 1996): 8–9.

international treaties to help provide intellectual property protection across national boundaries when, in fact, laws are essentially national. Some of the most important treaties are the Paris Convention, the Patent Cooperation Treaty, the Patent Law Treaty, the European Patent Convention, and the Berne Convention.

Paris Convention

The **Paris Convention** for the Protection of Industrial Property was established in 1883, and the number of signatory countries currently stands at 175 in 2013. It is designed to provide "domestic" treatment to protect patent and trademark applications filed in other countries. Operationally, the convention establishes rights of priority that stipulate that once an application for protection is filed in one member country, the applicant has twelve months to file in any other signatory countries, which should consider such an application as if it were filed on the same date as the original application.[108] It also means that if an applicant does not file for protection in other signatory countries within a grace period of twelve months of original filing in one country, legal protection cannot be provided. In most countries, other than the United States, the "first-to-file" principle is used for intellectual property protection. Lack of filing within a grace period in all other countries in which protection is desired could mean a loss of market opportunities to a competitor who filed for protection of either an identical or a similar type of intellectual property. The two new treaties, explained below, are further attempts to make international patent application as easy as domestic patent application.

Patent Cooperation Treaty

The **Patent Cooperation Treaty** (PCT) was established in 1970, amended in 1979, and modified in 1984. It is open to any signatory member country to the Paris Convention. The PCT makes it possible to seek patent protection for an invention simultaneously in each of a large number of countries by filing an "international" patent application. The patent applicant can file his or her international patent application with his or her national Patent Office, which will act as a PCT "Receiving" Office or with the International Bureau of World Intellectual Property Organization (WIPO) in Geneva. If the applicant is a national or resident of a contracting State that is party to the European Patent Convention, the Harare Protocol on Patents and Industrial Designs (Harare Protocol) or the Eurasian Patent Convention, the international application may also be filed with the European Patent Office (EPO), the African Regional Industrial Property Organization (ARIPO), or the Eurasian Patent Office (EAPO), respectively.[109]

Patent Law Treaty

The **Patent Law Treaty** (PLT), adopted in Geneva in June 2000, comes as the result of a World Intellectual Property Organization (WIPO) initiative. Its aim is to harmonize the formal requirements set by patent offices for granting patents, and to streamline the procedures for obtaining and maintaining a patent. Initially, PLT will apply to all European Union countries, the United States, Japan, Canada, and Australia. Eventually it will include virtually all countries in the world. While the PLT is only concerned with patent formalities, many of the provisions will prove extremely useful when the PLT comes into force for a large number of states, providing speedier and less costly procedures for years to come.[110]

---

[108]World Intellectual Property Organization, *Paris Convention for the Protection of Industrial Property*, http://www.wipo.int/treaties/en/ip/paris/, accessed February 20, 2006.

[109]World Intellectual Property Organization, *International Protection of Industrial Property—Patent Cooperation Treaty*, http://www.wipo.int/pct/en/treaty/about.htm, accessed February 20, 2006.

[110]Q. Todd Dickinson, "Harmony and Controversy," *IP Worldwide*, September 2002): 22–24.

European Patent Convention

The **European Patent Convention** is a treaty among 38 European countries (as of August 1, 2012) setting up a common patent office, the European Patent Office, headquartered in Munich, Germany, which examines patent applications designated for any of those countries under a common patent procedure and issues a European patent valid in all of the countries designated. The European Patent Office represents the most efficient way of obtaining protection in these countries if a patent applicant desires protection in two or more of the countries. The European Patent Convention is a party to the Paris Convention, and thus recognizes the filing date of an application by anyone in any signatory country as its own priority date if an application is filed within one year of the original filing date. The European Patent Office receives the application in English. The application will be published 18 months after the filing, consistent with the "first-to-file" principle. Once a patent is approved, registrations in, and translations into the language of, each designated country will be required. The European Patent Convention does not supersede any signatories' pre-existing national patent system. Patent applicants still should file and obtain separate national patents, if they would prefer national treatment (favored over pan-European treatment by individual national courts).[111]

Berne Convention

The **Berne Convention** for the Protection of Literary and Artistic Works is the oldest and most comprehensive international copyright treaty. This treaty provides reciprocal copyright protection in each of the fifteen signatory countries. Similar to the Paris Convention, it establishes the principle of national treatment and provides protection without formal registration. The United States did not join the Berne Convention until 1989.[112]

WIPO Copyright Treaty

The **WIPO Copyright Treaty** is a recent development in international copyright protection established by the World Intellectual Property Organization (WIPO) with 89 member countries in 1996. This treaty addresses copyright protection in the internet era, and updates and supplements the Berne Convention by protecting the rights of authors of literary and artistic works distributed within the digital environment. The treaty clarifies that the traditional right of reproduction continues to apply in the digital environment and confers a right holder's right to control on-demand delivery of works to individuals.[113] In compliance with the WIPO Copyright Treaty, the United States passed the Digital Millennium Copyright Act (DMCA) in 1998, as stated earlier. However, DMCA-type provisions implemented in other member countries, resulting from each respective country's implementation of the WIPO Copyright Treaty, are not uniform because of differences in legal systems, governance, prioritization, and influence of intellectual property rights or merely cultural preference.[114]

Anti-Counterfeiting Trade Agreement (ACTA)

The Anti-Counterfeiting Trade Agreement (ACTA) is the most recent groundbreaking initiative signed in Tokyo on October 1, 2011, by key trading partners[115] to strengthen the

---

[111]Martin Grund and Stacy J. Farmer, "The ABCs of the EPC 2000,"*Managing Intellectual Property* (April 2008): 85–88.

[112]Nancy R. Wesberg, "Canadian Signal Piracy Revisited in Light of United States Ratification of the Free Trade Agreement and the Berne Convention: Is This a Blueprint for Global Intellectual Property Protection?" *Syracuse Journal of International Law & Commerce* 16 (Fall 1989): 169–205.

[113]Amanda R. Evansburg, Mark J. Fiore, Brooke Welch, Lusan Chua, and Phyllis Eremitaggio, "Recent Accessions to WIPO Treaties," *Intellectual Property & Technology Law Journal* 16 (August 2004): 23.

[114]Ross Dannenberg and David R. Gerk, "DMCA Copyright Protections: Uniquely American or Common & Uniform Abroad?" *Intellectual Property & Technology Law Journal* 21 (May 2009): 1–5.

[115]The signatory countries are the United States, Australia, Canada, Korea, Japan, New Zealand, Morocco, and Singapore. Representatives of the remaining ACTA negotiating parties are the European Union, Mexico, and Switzerland, which confirmed their continuing strong support for and preparations to sign the Agreement as soon as practicable.

international legal framework for effectively combating global proliferation of commercial-scale counterfeiting and piracy. In addition to calling for strong legal frameworks, the agreement also includes innovative provisions to deepen international cooperation and to promote strong intellectual property rights enforcement practices. The ACTA marks an important step forward in the international fight against trademark counterfeiting and copyright piracy. The next step in bringing the ACTA into force will be the ratification, acceptance, or approval of measures from each of the signatory countries.[116]

In a similar vein, the G8 summit also declared patent harmonization a topic of high importance, asking for accelerated discussions of the Substantive Patent Law Treaty (SPLT), a proposed international patent law treaty aimed at harmonizing substantive points of patent law. In contrast with the Patent Law Treaty, which only relates to formalities, the SPLT aims at going far beyond formalities to harmonize substantive requirements, such as novelty, inventive step and non-obviousness, industrial applicability and utility, as well as sufficient disclosure, unity of invention, or claim drafting and interpretation.[117]

Antitrust Laws of the United States

The antitrust laws of the United States[118] need to be highlighted as the U.S. government makes extraterritorial applications of its antitrust laws, affecting both U.S. and foreign businesses, not only in the United States but also in foreign countries. The U.S. antitrust laws have their foundation in the Sherman Antitrust Act of 1890, the Clayton Act of 1914, the Federal Trade Commission (FTC) Act of 1914, and the Robinson-Patman Act of 1936. U.S. antitrust laws have been, from the beginning, concerned with maximizing consumer welfare through the prevention of arrangements that increase market power without concurrently increasing social welfare through reduced costs or increased efficiency.

The **Sherman Act** prohibits 1) any conspiracy in restraint of trade or commerce and 2) to monopolize, or attempt to monopolize the trade or commerce. In the *Standard Oil* case of 1911, the courts ruled that an act must be an unreasonable restraint of trade for the Sherman Act to apply. Toward this end, a distinction developed between (1) cases in which a rule of reason should apply and (2) cases considered to be *per se* violations of the law. Sometimes, firms being dominant in the marketplace may be subjected to investigation for a possible Sherman Act violation.[119]

The **Clayton Act** strengthened the U.S. antitrust arsenal by prohibiting trade practices that were not covered by the Sherman Act. It outlaws price discrimination between different purchasers, exclusive dealings, mergers and acquisitions, among others, that substantially lessen competition or tend to create a monopoly. Concurrent with the enactment of the Clayton Act, Congress created the Federal Trade Commission (FTC) in 1914. The **Federal Trade Commission (FTC) Act** is designed to prohibit unfair or deceptive trade practices in commerce, such as false advertising and bait-and-switch pricing. The **Robinson-Patman Act** prohibits anticompetitive practices by companies, specifically price discrimination. It prevents unfair price discrimination for the first time, by requiring that the seller offer the same price terms to customers at a given level of trade.

The U.S. antitrust laws were originally aimed at domestic monopolies and cartels, although the act expressly extends coverage to commerce with foreign nations. In the 1940s, the prosecution of Alcoa (*United States v. Aluminum Company of America*, 148 F.2d 416 (1945)) resulted in a clear

---

[116]Anti-Counterfeiting Trade Agreement, The Office of the United States Trade Representative, http://www.ustr.gov/acta, accessed August 1, 2012.

[117]William New, "G8 Governments Want ACTA Finalized This Year, SPLT Talks Accelerated," Intellectual Property Watch, http://www.ip-watch.org/, accessed July 9, 2008; and "Draft Substantive Patent Law Treaty," World Intellectual Property Organization, http://www.wipo.int/patent-law/en/harmonization.htm, accessed August 1, 2012.

[118]This section draws from Masaaki Kotabe and Kent W. Wheiler, *Anticompetitive Practices in Japan: Their Impact on the Performance of Foreign Firms* (Westport, CT: Praeger Publishers, 1996).

[119]"DOJ begins investigating possible Sherman Act violations by IBM,"Lexology—Association of Corporate Counsel, http://www.lexology.com, accessed October 16, 2009.

extension of U.S. antitrust laws to activities of foreign companies, even if those actions occur entirely outside the United States as long as they have a substantial and adverse effect on the foreign or domestic commerce and trade of the United States.

Successful extraterritorial enforcement, however, depends on effective jurisdictional reach. Detecting, proving, and punishing collusion and conspiracy to restrain trade among foreign companies is extremely difficult. From gathering evidence to carrying out retribution, the complexity of nearly every aspect of antitrust litigation is compounded when prosecuting a foreign entity. Issues of foreign sovereignty and diplomacy also complicate extraterritorial antitrust enforcement. If a foreign entity's actions are required by their own government, they are exempt from prosecution under U.S. law. Prior to the 1990s and the demise of the Soviet Union, U.S. trade and economic matters were typically a lower priority to defense and foreign policy concerns. This was particularly true with Japan. In nearly every major trade dispute over steel, textiles, televisions, semiconductors, automobiles, and so on, the Departments of State and Defense opposed and impeded retaliation against Japanese companies for violations of U.S. antitrust laws. A strong alliance with Japan and the strategic geographic military locations the alliance provided were deemed to be of more importance than unrestricted trade. This arrangement helped Japanese companies improve their competitive position.

The extraterritorial application of U.S. antitrust laws has recently been subject to considerably more debate. In 1977 the Antitrust Division of the Justice Department issued its *Antitrust Guidelines for International Operations*, which, consistent with the precedent established in the Alcoa case, reaffirmed that U.S. antitrust laws could be applied to an overseas transaction if there were a direct, substantial, and foreseeable effect on the commerce of the United States. The Foreign Trade Antitrust Improvements Act of 1982 again reiterated this jurisdiction. There has been controversy, however, over the degree of U.S. commerce to which jurisdiction extends.

The 1977 Justice *Guidelines* suggested that foreign anticompetitive conduct injuring U.S. commerce raises antitrust concerns when either U.S. consumers or U.S. exporters are harmed. Later, in 1992, U.S. Attorney General William Barr announced that Justice would take enforcement action against conduct occurring overseas if it unfairly restricts U.S. exports, arguing that anticompetitive behavior of foreign companies that inhibits U.S. exports thereby reduces the economies of scale for U.S. producers and indirectly affects U.S. consumers through higher prices than might otherwise be possible.

Critics argue that comity concerns and the difficulties in gathering evidence and building a case around conduct occurring wholly within a foreign country make it unrealistic for the Justice Department to attempt such an extraterritorial application of U.S. laws. Perhaps the gravest concern, however, is that the policy may lead to prosecution of foreign business methods that actually promote U.S. consumer welfare, for it is predominantly believed in the U.S. economic and legal community that antitrust laws should be concerned solely with protecting consumer welfare. U.S. public opinion has also traditionally and strongly supported the government's role as the champion of consumer rights against commercial interests. U.S. antitrust laws have always reflected this grassroots backing. Such a tradition has not existed in Japan, and the development of antitrust laws there has been quite different.

Fully cognizant that there were many small- and medium-size firms with exportable products that were not currently being exported, the U.S. Congress passed the Export Trading Company legislation (ETC Act) in 1982 to encourage those firms to join forces to improve their export performance by exempting them from antitrust laws. Patterned after practices in Germany and Japan, the ETC Act also permits banks to own and operate export trading companies (ETCs) so that the export trading companies will have better access to capital resources, as well as market information through their banks.[120] As a result, the ETC Act assists in the formation of shippers' associations to reduce costs and increase efficiency, covers technology-licensing agreements with

---

[120]Charles E. Cobb, Jr., John E. Stiner, "Export Trading Companies: Five Years of Bringing U.S. Exporters Together: The Future of the Export Trading Company Act," *Business America* 10 (October 12, 1987): 2–9.

foreign firms, and facilitates contact between producers interested in exporting and organizations offering export trade services. However, those trading companies are not allowed to join forces in their importing businesses, hence they are called export trading companies. In reality, many manufacturing companies import raw materials and in-process components from abroad and export finished products using those imported materials. Japanese trading companies handle both exports and imports, and have many manufacturing companies as captive customers for both exports and imports. However, in the United States, those trading companies certified as ETCs under the ETC Act may not fully exploit economies of scale in their operation as they cannot collectively handle manufacturing firms' imports.

Antitrust Laws of the European Union

In addition to the United States' antitrust forces, other countries have an organization that settles antitrust cases. The European Union (EU) is no exception. While the EU does not apply its antitrust laws extraterritorially outside the region, its laws are applied not only to EU-member country companies but also to foreign companies as long as their corporate action has antitrust implications within the EU community.

In 2000, the European Commission indicated that it was prepared to block the merger of EMI Group and Time Warner, Inc. unless they came up with concrete proposals to allay concerns that the size of the joint venture would allow it to limit access to its copyrights and raise prices. In September 2000, in an effort to save their proposed music joint venture Warner-EMI, which would be by far the largest music publisher, the two companies submitted to the European Commission a new set of antitrust remedies involving sales of music labels and copyrights. They also offered to sell several catalogs of songs to reduce their huge market shares in music publishing.[121] Similarly, Microsoft faces a tough time in Europe although it prevailed in the United States against the government's efforts to unbundle its code. In 2004, the European regulators forced the company to remove the Media Player software from its Windows operating system. The EU also requested that the company release more of its Windows code to competitors. Further, the EU can levy fines of up to 10 percent, roughly $3.2 billion, of the company's revenue.[122]

To do business in Europe, foreign companies must comply with EU antitrust law, just as European companies must abide by U.S. antitrust law to do business in the United States. In 2001, the European Union formally blocked General Electric's $43 billion purchase of Honeywell International, the first time a proposed merger between two U.S. companies has been prevented solely by European regulators. The veto by the EU's 20 member executive commission was widely expected after the U.S. companies failed to allay European fears that the deal would create an unfairly dominant position in markets for jet liner engines and avionics. The deal had already secured regulatory approval from U.S. antitrust authorities but was blocked by EU.[123]

U.S. Foreign Corrupt Practices Act of 1977

Among the many corrupt practices that international marketers face, bribery is considered the most endemic and murky aspect of conducting business abroad. However, special care must be taken to identify and accommodate the differences between international markets and those in the United States. Laws may vary widely from country to country, and these laws may on occasion conflict with one another, although international organizations such as the International Monetary Fund, the Organization of Economic Cooperation and Development (OECD), have increased global

---

[121]Philip Shishkin and Martin Peers, "EMI Group and Time Warner Submit Concessions to Allay Antitrust Worries," *Wall Street Journal*, September 20, 2000.

[122]"Microsoft Detaches Windows from Media Player in Europe," *Wall Street Journal*, January 25, 2005, p. B3.

[123]Syed Tariq Anwar, "EU's Competition Policy and the GE-Honeywell Merger Fiasco: Transatlantic Divergence and Consumer and Regulatory Issues," *Thunderbird International Business Review* 47 (September/October 2005): 601–626.

efforts to combat corrupt business practices.[124] Several countries in the Asia-Pacific Economic Cooperation (APEC) also joined the OECD Convention criminalizing foreign commercial bribery in 1997.[125] Bribery is a means for one party to get from another party (at the cost of a third party) some special treatment that would otherwise not normally be obtainable. However, what constitutes bribery may also differ, depending on local customs and practices.

In order to create the level playing field for U.S. companies to do business abroad and to establish a high ethical standard to be followed by foreign countries, the United States passed the **Foreign Corrupt Practices Act** (FCPA) in 1977. The FCPA was designed to prohibit the payment of any money or anything of value to a foreign official, foreign political party, or any candidate for foreign political office for purposes of obtaining, retaining, or directing business. For example, in 2005, Monsanto Chemical was fined $1.5 million for violating the FCPA by making illegal cash payment to a senior Indonesian Ministry of Environment official a few years earlier.[126] The long arm of the U.S. law even reaches into the offices of Germany's most important company, Siemens. Because its shares are listed on the New York Stock Exchange and it has extensive operations in the United States, Siemens is subject to the FCPA. Siemens or its employees face accusations that they used bribes to sell medical equipment in China and Indonesia, close deals to provide telecom gear to the Hungarian and Norwegian armed forces, and win a power plant contract in Serbia, to name a few examples. Munich prosecutors, who uncovered evidence that Siemens used bribes to land contracts around the globe, have already extracted $290 million in fines. With $1.9 billion in questionable payments made to outsiders by the company from 2000 to 2006, Siemens is the biggest FCPA case—foreign or domestic—of all time. U.S. authorities see the Siemens case as a perfect opportunity to show they are serious about pursuing foreign companies that violate U.S. anticorruption laws.[127] The FCPA sets a high ethical standard for U.S. firms doing business abroad, but it basically cannot keep foreign firms (in spite of the rare example of its reaching into Siemens mentioned above) from engaging in bribery and other anticompetitive acts in foreign countries.

The FCPA, although silent on the subject, does not prohibit so-called facilitating or grease payments, such as small payments to lower-level officials for expediting shipments through customs or placing a transoceanic telephone call, securing required permits, or obtaining adequate police protection—transactions that simply facilitate the proper performance of duties. These small payments are considered comparable to tips left for waiters. While some companies find such payments morally objectionable and operate without paying them, other companies do not prohibit such payments but require that employees seek advice in advance from their corporate legal counsel in cases where facilitating payments may be involved.[128]

The FCPA does not prohibit bribery payments to nongovernmental personnel, however. Nor does the United States have laws regulating other forms of payment that approach extortion. What constitutes bribery or extortion also becomes less transparent, and international marketers' ethical dilemma increases (see **Global Perspective 5-3**). From an ethical point of view, the major questions that must be answered are:

1. Does such an act involve unfairness to anyone or violate anyone's rights?

2. Must such an act be kept secret, such that it cannot be reported as a business expense?

3. Is such an act truly necessary in order to carry on business?

---

[124]Carolyn Hotchkiss, "The Sleeping Dog Stirs: New Signs of Life in Efforts to End Corruption in International Business," *Journal of Public Policy & Marketing* 17 (Spring 1998): 108–115.

[125]Madeleine K. Albright, "APEC: Facing the Challenge," *U.S. Department of State Dispatch* 8 (December 1997): 3–5.

[126]"Bribe Costs Monsanto $1.5 million," *Chemical & Engineering News*, January 17, 2005, p. 28.

[127]Jack Ewing, "Siemens Braces for a Slap from Uncle Sam," *BusinessWeek.com*, November 15, 2007.

[128]Mary Jane Sheffet, "The Foreign Corrupt Practices Act and the Omnibus Trade and Competition Act of 1988: Did They Change Corporate Behavior?" *Journal of Public Policy and Marketing* 14 (Fall 1995): 290–300.

Global Perspective 5-3

Cultural Relativism/ Accommodation—Selling out?

The following is an excerpt from an anonymous source that circulated via e-mail on the GINLIST:

> Cultural accommodation is an essential element in successful international and cross-cultural relationships. The question faced by the U.S. multinationals is whether to follow the advice, "When in Rome, do as the Romans do." Foreign firms operating in the U.S. are faced with a similar question, "When in America, should you do as the Americans do?" How far does an individual or a company go to accommodate cultural differences before they sell themselves out? . . . I will attempt to answer this question by looking at issues involving my personal core values, bribery and gift giving, and how these relate to the definitions presented. I will also discuss trust and credibility and how these qualities relate to the subject and present a case for marketplace morality.
>
> The primary issue . . . is one of cultural relativism and its place in cross-cultural encounters. Cultural relativism is a philosophical position which states that ethics is a function of culture. . . . Ethical relativism is the belief that nothing is objectively right or wrong, and that the definition of right or wrong depends on the prevailing view of a particular individual, culture, or historical period.
>
> Cultural or ethical relativists will find themselves in a constant state of conflict within their own society. By definition, it would be impossible to reach an agreement on ethical rights and wrongs for the society. An ethical relativist believes that whatever an individual (any individual) believes to be right or wrong is in fact correct. As an example, imagine trying to hold Hitler's Nazi government accountable for their crimes during World War II from this perspective. If ethics is relative and that right and wrong are defined by the prevailing view of a particular individual, culture, or historical period, then Hitler's policies of racial purification were ethically correct. However, according to my ethical beliefs (and those of the world's representatives who presided over the Nuremberg Trials), that conclusion is completely unacceptable. There are some things that are moral and ethical absolutes . . .
>
> As we adapt to the differences in cultures, each individual and culture must still determine where the line is (which defines) the clear violations of moral absolutes. In pursuing this objective, we must come to terms with our core values and how they match up with both the

> company ethos and that of the host and home countries . . .
>
> It is interesting to note the Catch 22 that an international company can find itself in on this subject. In reference to China, if the company tries to avoid the appearance of a bribe by not participating in a culture's gift giving custom and just say[s] "thanks," they may be seen as using the "verbal thanks as getting out of their obligation." The international manager must not only understand and respect the cultural subtleties, but know how to find the limits of the ethical behavior. One specific limit put in place by the U.S. Government is the Foreign Corrupt Practices Act (FCPA). This Act was passed in reaction to a "rash of controversial payments to foreign officials by American business in the 1970s." The Act specifically calls for "substantial fines for both corporations and individual corporate officers who engage in the bribery of foreign government officials."
>
> U.S. firms are restricted from bribing; however, many companies in other countries engage in this practice routinely. American firms allege that restricting them from this practice puts them at a serious disadvantage to other nations' firms. In the short term, this may be true. Consider what would happen if every firm bribed. The cost of a project would be driven up so high that the country itself could no longer afford it. The bribe is not free and is always paid either by a higher contract price or through shortcuts in quality and material which may result in serious social costs. Consider a freeway overpass or a bridge not built to adequate safety standards or with poor quality materials. The result could be a collapsed bridge, resulting in loss of both life and property. The bribe also undermines the competitive process so that the purchaser pays more than the competitive price and erodes the trust in the public officials and the firm.
>
> Is there a morality separate from the individual and from the culture? . . . A multinational corporation doing business in societies with differing moral norms must subscribe to a morality of the marketplace which is based on trust and credibility. Violating such norms would be self defeating. Companies engaging in business practices that result in a loss of trust or credibility will eventually lose their share of the market. . . .
>
> A person who approaches the world from a cultural relativist perspective will change his or her position and standards depending on the prevailing view of the culture or sub-culture that person is in. Trust and

credibility can neither be built nor retained from such a position. International or domestic businessmen want to know who they are dealing with. They want to know if they can trust the person and/or company they are about to join together with . . .

Where is the line drawn that separates accommodation from selling out? In a large part it depends on the individual's value system, since what they're selling out on is really their own core values, trust, and credibility. There are moral absolutes, which, if violated, are always examples of stepping across the line.

Source: An anonymous source, distributed via e-mail on GINLIST, October 11, 1994.

Unless the answer to the first two questions is negative and to the third positive, such an act is generally deemed unethical.[129] It is advised that multinational firms maintain good "corporate citizenship" wherever they do business, because long-term benefits tend to outweigh the short-term benefit gained from bribes for the same reasons just mentioned—for example, corporate contributions to humanitarian and environmental causes, such as the Save the Rain Forest project in Brazil, and moral stands on oppressive governments, such as two European brewers, Carlsberg and Heineken, pulling out from Burma to protest this Asian country's dictatorship regime.[130]

SUMMARY

When doing business across national boundaries, international marketers almost always face what are perceived to be political and legal barriers. It is because government policies and laws can be very different from country to country. In most cases, a foreign company has to accept a host country's government policies and laws, as they are usually outside its control. Some large multinational firms, if backed by their home country government, may sometimes influence the host country's policies and laws. However, such an extraterritorial interference may have negative consequences in the long run for a short-term gain.

Despite various international agreements brought about by such international organizations as the WTO, G8, and WIPO, which collectively strive toward freer and more equitable world trade, every nation is sovereign and maintains its special interests, which may occasionally clash with those of the international agreements. Although the world has been moving toward a freer trade and investment environment, the road has not necessarily been smooth. When considering entry or market expansion in foreign countries, their country risks need to be assessed. Multinational firms need to be aware of political risks arising from unstable political parties and

government structure, changes in government programs, and social pressures and special interest groups in a host country. Political risks are further compounded by economic and financial risks. When disputes arise across national boundaries, they will most likely have to be settled in one country. Therefore, careful planning for establishing the jurisdictional clause in the contract is needed before the contract is entered into.

Although government policies and the laws of a country usually affect business transactions involving that country, increased business activities transcending national boundaries have tested the territoriality of some policies and laws of a country. The United States frequently applies its laws, such as antitrust laws and the Foreign Corrupt Practices Act, outside its political boundaries to the extent that U.S. businesses are affected or to the extent that its legal value system can be extended. On the other hand, despite the importance of intellectual property in international business, protection of intellectual property in foreign countries is granted essentially by registration in those countries. International marketing managers should be aware that domestic protection usually cannot be extended beyond their national boundary.

QUESTIONS

1. What different types of trade controls influence international business? What are their intended objectives?

2. What are the factors that international managers should consider in determining the economic and political risks associated with a country?

3. Briefly describe the various types of local legal systems. How do differences in these legal systems affect international business?

4. Describe the various types of barriers to international trade and investment.

---

[129]Richard T. De George, *Business Ethics*, 4th ed. (Englewood Cliffs, N.J.: Prentice Hall, 1995): 511–512.

[130]"Brewer Decides to Pull Out of Its Business in Burma," *Wall Street Journal*, July 12, 1996, p. A8A.

5. Various foreign companies operating in Russia, especially in the oil and gas exploration business, have had to face the vagaries of Russian legislation, which changes frequently, making it difficult to plan activities. Besides being heavily taxed, foreign firms have had to face a change in export duties of crude oil over a dozen times in the past few years. Yet most companies continue to negotiate for making investments worth billions of dollars. Discuss some of the possible reasons for the actions of these companies. Companies take various steps to manage political risk. If you were representing a company negotiating investments in Russia, what steps would you take to manage (and/or reduce) the political risk associated with these investments?

6. KFC, a fast-food operator, faced immense resistance from some politically active consumer groups when it opened its operations in India. One group proclaimed that opening KFC outlets in the country would propagate a "junk-food" culture. Others proclaimed that this was "the return of imperialistic powers" and was an attempt to "Westernize the eating habits" of Indians. Overzealous local authorities in the city of Bangalore used a city law restricting the use of MSG (a food additive used in the chicken served by KFC) over a certain amount as a pretext for temporarily closing down the outlet, despite the fact that the authorities did not even have the equipment to measure the MSG content in the proportions stated in the law. In the capital city of New Delhi, a KFC outlet was temporarily closed down because the food inspector found a "house-fly" in the restaurant. While both of these issues got resolved through hectic consultations with these consumer groups and through legal orders issued protecting the interests of the outlets, they do reflect how political and social concerns of even a small segment of the population can adversely affect the operations of companies in foreign markets. If you were the country manager of KFC in India, what steps would you have taken to avoid these problems?

7. An extension of the antitrust laws into the arena of international trade has taken the form of antidumping laws, which have been enacted by most Western countries, and which are increasingly being enacted by developing countries. On the surface, most of the antidumping laws across the various countries seem to be similar to each other. However, since much of the content of these laws is open to interpretation, the results of these laws can vary significantly. The bottom line for the initiation of any antidumping investigation is that if a foreign manufacturer gets an "undue" advantage while selling its products (either through pricing its products higher in other protected markets or through government subsidies) in another country relative to the domestic manufacturer and hurts the domestic industry, the company is resorting to unfair competition and should be penalized for it. While large firms are relatively more aware of the nuances of antidumping laws and have the resources, especially legal ones, to deal with this issue, it is the smaller firms, who often depend on governmental export assistance in various forms, that are the most susceptible to it.

One of your friends is planning to start exporting an industrial product to various countries in Europe. To help finance his export endeavor, he plans to utilize concessional export credit provided by the U.S. government to small exporters. This product is highly specialized, and caters to an extremely small niche market. Europe is a large market for this product. There are only two other manufacturers of this product, both based in Europe. One of these manufacturers is a $100 million company, which manufactures various other products besides the product in question. What would be your advice to your friend in terms of the significance of antidumping laws? What specific steps, if any, would you encourage your friend to take, especially in context of his limited financial resources?

MARKETING RESEARCH

6

CHAPTER OVERVIEW

1. Research problem formulation

2. Secondary global marketing research

3. Primary global marketing research

4. Leveraging the internet for global market research studies

5. Market size assessment

6. New market information technologies

7. Managing global marketing research

Lego, the Danish maker of plastic construction sets, has established a leading reputation in the toy industry. In the United States, for instance, Lego reached the $1 billion revenue mark for the first time in 2010. Most of the sales, however, came from sets sold to boys. Lego had had a hard time attracting girls to play with Legos. In the U.S. market, only 9 percent of active Lego households reported that the primary user was a girl. Over the years, Lego had rolled out five sets aimed at girls, but none of these became successful. To crack the girls segment, Lego undertook a global four-year research project. The study spanned four countries—Germany, the U.K., the United States, and South Korea—and recruited 3,500 girls and their moms. Lego's research teams observed and interviewed the participants. The key goal of the project was to understand what would make Lego play more interesting among girls. The key insights were:

- The greatest concern for girls was "beauty." Lego apparently fell short on this dimension. Girls absolutely hated the mini-figures. They like more detailed, realistic figures. They also preferred brighter, friendlier colors.

- Girls favored role-play but they also love construction. However, their building style differed from that of boys. Boys preferred to closely follow the set shown on the box or the manual. Girls, however, liked to try out different scenarios without necessarily finishing the whole model.

- Boys related to the figurines in the third-person, while girls would project their identities on the mini-figs.

These insights inspired the development of Lego Friends, a new line aimed at the girls segment. Lego launched Lego Friends during the 2011–2012 holiday season in France, the U.K., and the United States The new line consists of a set of new female figurines—larger and more detailed than the classical mini-figs. It has five main characters that come with their own names, biographies, and story lines. It also includes six new Lego colors, including azure and lavender. The mini-dolls live in a community named Heartlake City, which includes features such as a vet clinic, a beauty salon, a café (selling cupcakes), and a horse academy.[1] By September 2012, the share of Lego sets primarily bought for girls had risen from 9 to 27 percent in the U.S. market. Lego's sales of the new line were double what the firm had expected.

Oreo cookies, the iconic American cookie brand, were first introduced in China in 1996, more than eighty years after the U.S. launch.[2] In 2005, as sales of Oreos in China had been flat for five years, Kraft decided to refashion the Oreo for the China market. Up to that time Kraft had simply been selling the U.S. version of Oreos. To guide the makeover, Kraft initiated a huge market research project. Kraft learned that Oreos were far too sweet for Chinese consumers. The company tested out twenty prototypes of reduced-sugar Oreos before arriving at the right formulation. Another finding was that a package of 14 Oreos priced at five yuan (about seventy U.S. cents) was too expensive for many Chinese. Kraft launched smaller-sized packages for just two yuan. However, the most radical change was the shape of the cookies. Kraft's researchers found out that sales of wafer cookies were increasing much faster than traditional round cookies. Therefore, in 2006 Kraft introduced a new version of Oreo: a long, narrow, layered stack of crispy wafer filled with vanilla and chocolate cream, all coated with chocolate. The new Oreos were so successful that Kraft decided to sell them in other Asian markets, in Australia, and in Canada.[3]

The Lego and Kraft stories highlight the potentially huge benefits of market research in foreign markets. Given the complexity of the global marketplace, solid marketing research is critical for a host of global marketing decisions. Skipping the research phase in the international marketing decision process can often prove a costly mistake.

Market research assists the global marketing manager in two ways:[4] (1) to make better decisions that recognize cross-country similarities and differences and (2) to gain support from the local subsidiaries or partners (e.g., distributors) for proposed marketing decisions.

To some degree, the procedures and methods that are followed in conducting global marketing research are close to those used in standard domestic research. Most of the marketing research tools and procedures used in the home market (e.g., questionnaire design, focus group research, multivariate techniques such as cluster analysis, conjoint measurement) will also prove very valuable in the global marketplace. Also, the typical sequence of a multicountry market research process follows the familiar pattern used in domestic marketing research. In particular, the steps to be followed to conduct global market research are:

1. Define the decision problem(s).

2. Develop a research design.

3. Determine information needs.

4. Determine the sources of information.

5. Collect the relevant data from secondary and primary sources.

6. Analyze the data, interpret and summarize the results.

7. Communicate the findings to the key decision-makers.

---

[1] "Lego Is for Girls," http://www.businessweek.com, accessed on October 1, 2012.
[2] The brand celebrated its 100th anniversary in 2012.
[3] "Kraft Reinvents Iconic Oreo to Win in China," *The Wall Street Journal*, May 1, 2008, p. 28.
[4] Kamran Kashani, "Beware the Pitfalls of Global Marketing," *Harvard Business Review* (Sept.–Oct. 1989): 97.

Exhibit 6-1 Scope of International Marketing Research

- SINGLE-COUNTRY RESEARCH
  - Market size and growth? Segments?
  - Competition in the foreign market?
  - Consumer needs? Customer perceptions?
  - Will strategy used in country A also work for country B? What adaptations are necessary?

- MULTICOUNTRY RESEARCH

Sequential (e.g., Stage 1: countries A, B & C→ Stage 2: countries D & E)

Simultaneous

Exhibit 6-2 A Multicountry Marketing Research Project at Eli Lilly: Estimating the Market Potential for a Prescription Weight Loss Product

- **Research Problem:**
  Estimate the dollar potential for a prescription weight-loss product in the U.K., Spain, Italy, and Germany.
- **Research Hypothesis:**
  Patients would be willing to pay a premium price for the product even without reimbursement by the government.
- **Secondary Data Research:**
  - Market share of a similar product (Isomeride).
  - Incidence of overweight and obesity in Europe.[5]
- **Primary Data Research:**
  - Sample size: 350 physicians from the U.K., Italy, Spain, and Germany.
  - Sampling procedure: random selection from a high-prescribers doctor list based on company data.
  - Data Collected:
    1. Diary kept by physicians for 2 weeks.
    2. Questionnaires completed by patients who were judged to be prospects for the product by physician.
    3. Pricing study done based on 30 additional phone interviews with physicians in the U.K., Italy, and Spain to measure price sensitivity.

Based on: William V. Lawson, "The 'Heavyweights'—Forecasting the obesity market in Europe for a new compound," *Marketing and Research Today* (November 1995): 270–74.

The scope of international mark research could be either single-country research or multicountry research (see **Exhibit 6-1**). With a multicountry study, implementation can be sequential by running the project first in one set of countries and subsequently in another group. Alternatively, a project could be run simultaneously in all the markets to be studied.

What sets global market research apart from standard market research projects is the added layer of complexity due to cultural and economic differences. This is especially true for multi-country research (as opposed to single-market) and projects run in less developed countries. In the latter, the infrastructure to implement a research project could be lacking or dysfunctional.

A typical example of a multicountry market research project is summarized in **Exhibit 6-2**. The major challenges that global marketing researchers need to confront are:[6]

1. Complexity of research design due to environmental differences.

2. Lack and inaccuracy of secondary data.

---

[5]Overweight: people whose body weight is 25–29 percent over the recommended weight; obese: people whose body weight is more than 30 percent over their ideal weight.

[6]Susan P. Douglas and C. Samuel Craig, *International Marketing Research* (Englewood Cliffs, NJ: Prentice-Hall, 1983).

3. Time and cost requirements to collect primary data.

4. Coordination of multicountry research efforts.

5. Difficulty in establishing comparability across multicountry studies.

In this chapter, you will learn about the major issues that complicate cross-country research. We also suggest ways to cope with these roadblocks. We then describe several techniques that are useful for market demand assessment. Next we discuss how the internet can support global market research studies. During the last two decades new market information technologies have emerged. We discuss the impact of these technological advances on marketing research. Finally, we consider several issues that concern the management of global market research.

Research Problem Formulation

Any market research study begins with a precise definition of the managerial problem(s) to be addressed. The mantra of a well-defined problem being a half-solved problem definitely applies in a global setting. Fancy data-analytical tools will not compensate for poorly defined problems. Once the nature of the managerial problem(s) becomes clear, the issues need to be translated into specific research questions. The scope of market research questions extends to both strategic and tactical marketing decisions. For example, a product positioning study carried out for BMW in the European market centered on the following three issues:

1. What does the motorist in the country concerned demand of his/her car?

2. What does s/he believe s/he is getting from various brands?

3. What does that imply with regard to positioning the BMW brand across borders?[7]

In an international context, the problem formulation is sometimes hindered by the self-reference criterion, that is, people's habit to fall back on their own cultural norms and values (see Chapter 4). This tendency could lead to wrong or narrow problem definitions. In a multicountry research process, the self-reference criterion also makes finding a consensus between headquarters and local staff an immensely formidable task. To avoid such mishaps, market researchers must try to view the research problem from the cultural perspective of the foreign players and isolate the influence of the self-reference criterion. At any rate, local subsidiaries should be consulted at every step of the research process if the study will affect their operations, including the first step of the problem definition.

A major difficulty in defining the problem is the lack of familiarity with the foreign environment. This may lead to making false assumptions, misdefining the problem(s), and, ultimately, misleading conclusions about the foreign market(s). To reduce part of the uncertainty, some exploratory research at the early stage of the research process can often be very helpful. A useful vehicle for such preliminary research is an **omnibus survey**.[8] Omnibus surveys are regularly scheduled surveys that are conducted by research agencies (e.g., Nielsen) with questions from multiple clients. The surveys are administered to a very large sample of consumers, usually a panel created by the agency. The questionnaire contains a plethora of questions on a variety of topics. Each research client can include one or more questions in the survey while sharing demographic information about respondents with the other clients. The prime benefit of an omnibus survey is its cost, as the subscribers to the survey share the expenses. Surveys are typically priced on a per-question basis. Another selling point is speed; results are quickly

[7]Horst Kern, Hans-Christian Wagner, and Roswitha Hassis, "European Aspects of a Global Brand: The BMW Case," *Marketing and Research Today* (February 1990): 47–57.

[8]David A. Aaker, V. Kumar, and George S. Day, *Marketing Research* (New York: John Wiley & Sons, Inc., 1998), p. 237.

available, sometimes within a week when the omnibus is run on a weekly basis. A major disadvantage is that only a limited amount of company-relevant information is obtainable through an omnibus. Also, the panel is not always representative of the firm's target market profile although the client can sometimes select from a target market rather than sample from all respondents.

Still, an omnibus survey is probably the most economical way to gather preliminary information on target markets. An omnibus is particularly suitable when you need to ask a few simple questions across a large sample of respondents. Findings from an omnibus can assist managers and researchers in fine-tuning the decision problem(s) to be tackled. An omnibus is also an option to gauge the market potential for your product in the foreign market when you have only a limited budget. Omnibuses conducted on a regular basis can also be useful as a tracking tool to spot changes in consumer attitudes or behaviors. **Exhibit 6-3** presents key features of Nielsen's Global Omnibus Survey conducted in 2011.

Exhibit 6-3 Nielsen Global Omnibus Survey (2011)

Geographical Coverage & Sample Size:

- 25,000 consumers in 56 countries:
  - Asia-Pacific (15)
  - Europe (26)
  - Africa & Middle East (6)
  - Americas (9)

- Threshold: 60 percent internet penetration or 10 million online population

Timing:

- Two waves:
  - March/April 2011
  - August/September 2011

Survey Method:

- Internet

Examples of Questions:

- At the moment would you consider yourself:

  Very overweight   Somewhat overweight   A little overweight   About the right weight   Underweight

- Which of the following actions are you taking to lose weight?
  1. Doing physical exercise
  2. Changing my diet
  3. Taking diet pills/bars/shakes
  4. Taking prescription medicine
  5. Other
- How well do you understand the nutritional information labels on food packaging?

  Mostly   In part   Not at all

- Thinking about dining out, should restaurants include calorie count and nutritional information on menus?

  Always   Sometimes   Never

Source: http://au.nielsen.com/site/documents/Nielsen-GlobalHealthyEatingReport-Jan2012.pdf.

Once the research issues have been stated, management needs to determine the information needs. Some of the information will be readily available within the company or in publicly available sources. Other information will need to be collected from scratch.

Secondary Global Marketing Research

Assessing the information needs is the next step after the research problem definition. Some pieces of information will already be available. That type of information is referred to as **secondary data**. When the information is not useful, or simply does not exist, the firm will need to collect the data. **Primary data** are data collected specifically for the purpose of the research study. Researchers will first explore secondary data resources, because that kind of information is usually much cheaper and less time consuming to gather than primary data. Both forms of data collection entail numerous issues in an international marketing setting. We first discuss the major problems concerning secondary data research.

Secondary Data Sources

Market researchers in developed countries have access to a wealth of data that are gathered by government and private agencies. Unfortunately, the equivalents of such databases often are missing outside the developed world. Even when the information is available, it may be hard to track down. **Exhibit 6-4** shows the wide variety of secondary data resources that are available to global market

Exhibit 6-4 Resources for Secondary Data

International Trade

- *Yearbook of International Trade Statistics* (United Nations)
- *US Imports* (U.S. Bureau of the Census)
- *US Exports* (U.S. Bureau of the Census)

Country Information (Socioeconomic & Political Conditions)

- *Yearbook of Industrial Statistics* (United Nations)
- *Statistical Yearbook* (United Nations; updated by Monthly Bulletin of Statistics)
- *OECD Economic Survey*
- *The World Competitiveness Yearbook* (IMD)
- *Country Reports* (The Economist Intelligence Unit—www.eiu.com)
- *Demographic Yearbook* (United Nations)
- *Statistical Yearbook* (United Nations)
- *UNESCO Statistical Yearbook*
- *CIA World Fact Book* (https://www.cia.gov/library/publications/the-world-factbook/)

Cultural Background

- Lonely Planet (www.lonelyplanet.com)
- Country reports (www.countryreports.org)

International Commercial Law

- Lex Mercatoria (http://www.jus.uio.no/lm/)

Category-Specific Data

- Euromonitor publications (*www.euromonitor.com*): *European Marketing Data and Statistics, International Marketing Data and Statistics, Consumer Europe,* and *European Advertising Marketing and Media Data*
- www.marketresearch.com
  FINDEX: The Worldwide Directory of Market Research Reports, Studies & Surveys (Cambridge Information Group Directories)

---

researchers. Also, a wealth of international business resources can be accessed via the internet. One very valuable online resource for global business intelligence is globalEDGE (http://globaledge.msu .edu) created by the International Business Center at Michigan State University. This resource is an extremely well-organized directory that provides linkages to hundreds of online international business resources.

Obviously, researchers can also tap information resources available within the company. Many companies have their own libraries that provide valuable data sources. Large companies typically compile enormous databanks on their operations. Government publications sometimes offer information on overseas markets. In the United States, the U.S. Department of Commerce offers detailed country reports and industry surveys. Many countries have a network of government-sponsored commercial delegations (e.g., Chambers of Commerce, the Japanese External Trade Organization[9]—www.jetro.go.jp). These agencies will often provide valuable information to firms that desire to do business in their country, despite the fact that the main charter of most of these agencies is to assist homegrown companies in the foreign market.

Besides government offices, international agencies such as the World Bank, the Organization for Economic Cooperation and Development (OECD), the International Monetary Fund (IMF), and the United Nations gather a huge amount of data. Reports published by these organizations are especially useful for demographic and economic information. Given that most of these documents report information across multiple years, their data can be used to examine trends in socio-economic indicators. Unfortunately, reports published by such international agencies cover only their member states.

Several companies specialize in producing business-related information. Such information is usually far more expensive than government-based data. However, this sort of information often has more direct relevance for companies. Two prominent examples are the Economist Intelligence Unit (E.I.U.) and Euromonitor. Some of the most useful resources put together by the E.I.U. (http://www.eiu.com) are the country reports that appear on a quarterly basis. These country reports give a detailed update on the major political and economic trends in the countries covered. Euromonitor publishes several reports that are extremely useful to global marketers. Two well-known reports are the *European Marketing Data and Statistics* and *International Marketing Data and Statistics*, annual volumes covering Europe and the global marketplace outside Europe, respectively. Euromonitor's databases are also accessible online on a subscription basis (www .euromonitor.com).

Another form of secondary data sources are the so-called **syndicated datasets** sold by market research companies such as Nielsen (www.nielsen.com) and the GfK Group (www.gfk.com). The two main types for syndicated datasets are retail stores and consumer panels. With store data, the research firm gets detailed sales information from retail outlets whose cash registers are equipped with optical scanning equipment. Besides the sales tracking data, store-environment information (e.g., special in-store displays) is also gathered. Big market research suppliers also maintain consumer panels in major markets. Such panels present the second source of information for syndicated data. Consumer panels allow the research firm to track the buying behavior of participating households over time (longitudinal purchase data). The information is recorded either via purchase diaries or—in the more advanced markets—handheld scanners. In the 1980s and 1990s consumer panels were only available in Western countries, given the need for a sophisticated infrastructure and the high expense. However, in recent years the big research firms have set up panels in major emerging markets, including China and India. Nielsen, for example, monitors the shopping behavior of over 250,000 households in 25 countries.[10]

As firms move from government publications to syndicated data, the richness of the information increases enormously. At the same time, the cost of collecting and processing

---

[9]JETRO.

[10]www.nielsen.com, accessed June 30, 2012.

data goes up. Just as in a domestic marketing context, firms planning research in the global marketplace have to decide on the value added of additional information and make the appropriate trade-offs.

Problems with Secondary Data Research

In the global market scene, some of the information sought by market researchers does not exist. When data are missing, the researcher needs to infer the data by using proxy variables or values from previous periods. Even if the datasets are complete, the researcher will usually encounter many problems:

Accuracy of Data

The accuracy of secondary data is often questionable, for various reasons. The definition used for certain indicators often differs across countries. The quality of information may also be compromised by the mechanisms that were used to collect it. Most developed countries use sophisticated procedures to assemble data. Due to the lack of resources and skills, many developing countries have to rely on rather primitive mechanisms to collect data. The purpose for which the data were collected could affect their accuracy. International trade statistics do not cover cross-border smuggling activities. Such transactions are, in some cases, far more significant than legitimate trade. In some countries, statistics agencies might "cook" sensitive data. In China, for instance, GDP data are thought to be "man made," especially at the provincial level where local leaders vie with one another to present a stellar picture. To keep track of real economic growth in China, the following three indicators are preferable over reported GDP data: (1) electricity output, (2) bank loans, and (3) freight hauled by rail.[11]

Age of Data

The desired information may be available but outdated. Many countries collect economic activity information on a far less frequent basis than the United States. The frequency of census-taking also varies from country to country. In many developed countries (e.g., Italy, Spain, Poland, United States) a census is carried out every ten years. In many emerging markets, census-taking seldom takes place. In Saudi Arabia, for instance, the census has been taken only four times since the foundation of the kingdom. Lebanon has not conducted a census since 1932, out of fear that the findings could trigger strife between the country's various religious segments.

Reliability over Time

Often companies are interested in historical patterns of certain variables to spot underlying trends. Such trends might indicate whether a market opportunity is opening up or whether a market is becoming saturated. To track trends, the researcher has to know to what degree the data are measured consistently over time. Sudden changes in the definition of economic indicators are not uncommon. Juggling with economic variable measures is especially likely for variables that have political ramifications, such as unemployment and inflation statistics. For instance, government authorities may adjust the basket of goods used to measure inflation to produce more favorable numbers. One notable example is Argentina. In June 2008, the country's monetary policymakers introduced a new consumer price index to doctor the official inflation rate. According to the new inflation measurement procedure, a product is removed from the index when its price rises too sharply.[12] While INDEC, Argentina's statistics bureau, claims that the current inflation rate is

---

[11]"Chinese GDP Data: How Reliable?" http://blogs.wsj.com/chinarealtime/2011/06/10/chinese-gdp-data-how-reliable/.

[12]"Hocus-pocus," *The Economist*, http://www.economist.com, June 12, 2008.

around 9 percent, private sector economists put the actual rate at almost 25 percent.[13] Market researchers should be aware of such practices and, if necessary, make the appropriate corrections.

Comparability of Data

Cross-country research often demands a comparison of indicators across countries. Different sources on a given item often produce contradictory information. The issue then is how to reconcile these differences. One way to handle contradictory information is to **triangulate**, that is, to obtain information on the same item from at least three different sources and speculate on possible reasons behind these differences.[14] For instance, suppose you want to collect information on the import penetration of wine as a percentage of total consumption in various European countries. Triangulation might show that some of the figures you collected are based on value, while others are based on volume. It might also reveal that some sources include champagne but others do not.

Comparability can also be hindered by the lack of functional or conceptual equivalence.[15] **Functional equivalence** refers to the degree to which similar activities or products in different countries fulfill similar functions. Many products perform very different functions in different markets. In the United States bicycles are used primarily for leisure. In countries such as the Netherlands and China, bicycles are a major means of transportation. Absence of conceptual equivalence is another factor that undermines comparability. **Conceptual equivalence** reflects the degree to which a given concept has the same meaning in different environments. Many concepts have totally different meanings or may simply not exist in certain countries. The concept of "equal rights" for women is unfamiliar in many Muslim societies. Likewise, the notion of "intellectual property" is often hard to grasp in some cultures. Often, what one culture sees as obvious another does not.

The comparison of money-based indicators (e.g., income figures, consumer expenditures, international trade statistics) is hampered by the need to convert such figures into a common currency. The key issues are what currency to use and at what exchange rate (beginning of the year, year-end, or year-average). A further complication is that exchange rates do not always reflect the relative buying power between countries. As a result, comparing economic indicators using market exchange rates can be very misleading.

Lumping of Data

Official data sources often group statistics on certain variables in very broad categories. This compromises the usefulness and the interpretation of such data for international market researchers. Managers should check what is included in certain categories.[16]

Given the hurdles posed by secondary data, it is important to verify the quality of collected information. To assess the quality of data, the researcher should seek answers to the following checklist:

1. When were the data collected? Over what time frame?

2. How were the data collected?

3. Have the variables been redefined over time?

4. Who collected the data?

5. For what purpose were the data gathered?

---

[13]http://www.economist.com/node/21548229.
[14]S.C. Williams, "Researching Markets in Japan—A Methodological Case Study," *Journal of International Marketing* 4, no. 2 (1996): 87–93.
[15]Michael R. Mullen, "Diagnosing Measurement Equivalence in Cross-National Research," *Journal of International Business Studies* 26, no.3 (1995): 573–596.
[16]S.C. Williams, "Researching Markets in Japan," p. 90.

Of course, satisfactory answers to any of these questions may not ensure total peace of mind. Researchers and managers should always be on guard regarding the quality of secondary data.

Primary Global Marketing Research

Seldom do secondary data prove sufficient for international market research studies. The next step in the research process is to collect primary data specifically for the purpose of the research project. Primary data can be collected in several ways: (1) focus groups, (2) survey research, (3) observational research, and (4) test markets. In this section we will concentrate on the first three approaches. The last one, test marketing, is discussed in Chapter 10 on global new product development.

Focus Groups

Before embarking on large-scale quantitative market research projects, most firms will conduct exploratory research. One of the most popular tools at this stage is the focus group. A **focus group** is a loosely structured free-flowing discussion among a small group (8 to 12 people) of target customers facilitated by a professional moderator. Focus groups can be used for many different purposes: to generate information to guide the quantitative research projects, to uncover new product opportunities, to test out new product concepts, and so forth.[17] Early in 2008 focus groups in Stockholm, Tokyo, Zürich, and London were introduced to and asked to comment on digital Sony e-readers and prototype color e-paper displays, less than a millimeter[18] thick. The global focus group test allowed newspaper publishers to identify common drivers and barriers in consumer expectations as well as regional differences.[19]

The rules for designing and running focus groups in a domestic marketing setting apply to global market research projects as well.[20] Hiring well-trained moderators is critical in conducting focus groups for international market research. Moderators should be familiar with the local language and social interaction patterns. In some countries the focus group moderator should be of the same gender as the participants. Cultural sensitivity is an absolute must with focus groups. Japanese consumers tend to be much more hesitant to criticize new product ideas than their Western counterparts.[21] In addition, many Asian societies like Japan are highly collective (see Chapter 4). Strangers outside the group are excluded. As a result, getting the desired group dynamics for focus groups within such cultures is often very hard. To stimulate group dynamics, the following steps should be taken:[22]

- Be precise in recruitment to ensure group homogeneity and ease of bonding.

- Hire moderators who are able to develop group dynamics quickly through warm-ups, humor, and group-playing.

- Hire moderators who can spot and challenge "consensus"-driven behaviors and attitudes.

---

[17]One of the authors recently participated in a focus group for Cathay Pacific, a Hong Kong–based airline. The focus group discussion covered topics such as the launch of a new lounge, Cathay's website, and its in-flight magazine.

[18]One millimeter = 0.393 inches.

[19]http://www.biz-community.com/Article/196/16/25598.html, accessed January 19, 2009.

[20]See, for example, Thomas C. Kinnear and James R. Taylor, *Marketing Research* (New York: McGraw-Hill, Inc., 1996), Chapter 10.

[21]David B. Montgomery, "Understanding the Japanese as customers, competitors, and collaborators," *Japan and the World Economy* 3, no. 1 (1991): 61–91.

[22]Chris Robinson, "Asian culture: The marketing consequences," *Journal of the Market Research Society* 38, no. 1 (1996): 55–62.

When analyzing and interpreting focus group findings, market researchers should also concentrate on the nonverbal cues (e.g., gestures, voice intonations).[23] Information provided by these nonverbal cues is often as important as the verbal content of the focus groups.

Survey Methods for Cross-Cultural Marketing Research

Questionnaires are the most common vehicle to gather primary data in marketing research. Survey research begins with the design of a questionnaire. The next step is to develop a sampling plan to collect the data. Once these two tasks have been accomplished, the researcher moves to the next phase, the physical collection of information to the questionnaires. Each stage may lead to major headaches.

Questionnaire Design

By far the most popular instrument to gather primary data is the questionnaire. Preparing questionnaires for global market research poses tremendous challenges. As in domestic marketing, care should be exercised with the wording and the sequencing of the questions. With multicountry projects, further care is needed to assure comparability of survey-based results across frontiers. Measurement issues in cross-country research center around this question: "Are the phenomena in countries A and B measured in the same way?" Absence of measurement equivalence will render cross-country comparisons meaningless. Earlier we discussed the need for conceptual and functional equivalence of secondary data. The same requirements apply to primary data in order to avoid cultural biases. Cross-country survey research needs to fulfill two further criteria: **translation** and **scalar equivalence**.

The first aspect deals with the translation of the instrument from one language into another one. Cross-cultural research, even within the same country or parent language (e.g., English, Spanish), demands adequate translations from the master questionnaire into other languages. Careless translations of questionnaires can lead to embarrassing mistakes. Good translations are hard to accomplish. Several methods exist to minimize translation errors. Two procedures often used to avoid sloppy translations are back-translation and parallel translation. **Back-translation** is a two-phase process. Suppose a company wants to translate a questionnaire from English into Arabic. In the first step, the master questionnaire is translated into Arabic by a (bilingual) translator whose native language is Arabic, the target language. In the second stage, another bilingual interpreter whose native language is English, the base language, translates the Arabic version back into English. This version is then compared with the original survey to uncover any bugs or translation errors. The process is repeated until an acceptable degree of convergence is achieved. **Parallel translation** uses multiple interpreters who translate the same questionnaire independently. A committee of translators compares alternative versions, and differences are reconciled.

Most surveys typically have a battery of questions or "Agree/Disagree" statements with a scale (e.g., 7-point) to record responses. To make the findings of cross-country market research projects meaningful, it is paramount to pursue **scalar equivalence**: scores from subjects of different countries should have the same meaning and interpretation.[24] The standard format of scales used in survey research differs across countries. Keep in mind that high scores in one country are not necessarily high scores elsewhere. Latin Americans, for example, tend to use the high end of the scale. An unenthusiastic respondent may still give your company a "7" or an "8" score. Asians, on the other hand, tend to use the middle of the scale.[25]

[23]Naresh K. Malhotra, James Agarwal, and Mark Peterson, "Methodological issues in cross-cultural marketing research. A state-of-the-art review," *International Marketing Review* 13, no. 5 (1996): 7–43.

[24]Naresh K. Malhotra, James Agarwal, and Mark Peterson, "Methodological issues in cross-cultural marketing research. A state-of-the-art review," *International Marketing Review*, p. 15.

[25]Jennifer Mitchell, "Reaching across borders," *Marketing News*, May 10, 1999, p. 19.

Very happy

Happy

Not happy
but also
not unhappy

Unhappy

Very unhappy

Exhibit 6-5 The
Funny Faces Scale

Source: C.K. Corder, "Problems
and Pit-falls in Conducting
Marketing Research in Africa,"
in Betsy Gelb, ed., *Marketing
Expansion in a Shrinking
World.* Proceedings of Ameri-
can Marketing Association
Business Conference (Chicago:
AMA, 1978), pp. 86–90.

In some cases, you may also need to adjust the anchors of the scale. One market research study that measured attitudes of Japanese managers adopted scales that included "definitely true," "somewhat true," and "not at all true." A pre-test of the survey showed that the Japanese respondents had trouble with the concept of "agree/disagree."[26] To make cross-country comparisons meaningful, it is advisable to adjust responses in each country by, for instance, taking deviations from country-averages on any given question. By the same token, in some societies people are cued to view "1" as best and the other endpoint of the scale as worst, while in others "1" is considered the worst, regardless of how the scale is designated.

Survey research in developing nations can be further hindered by low levels of education. Specially designed visual scales like the **funny faces scale** shown in **Exhibit 6-5** can be used to cope with illiteracy. This scale uses facial representation instead of numbers to reflect the amount of agreement with a particular statement. In general, in developing countries, market researchers should also try to reduce the verbal content and use visual aids. In countries that are unfamiliar with survey research, it is advisable to avoid lengthy questionnaires or open-ended questions.[27]

Regardless of whether the survey is to be administered in Paris, Texas, or Paris, France, it is absolutely imperative to pre-test the questionnaire. Pre-testing is the only foolproof way to debug the questionnaire and spot embarrassing, and often expensive, mistakes. Speed is often critical when collecting data. However, rushing into the field without a thorough pre-test of the questionnaire is a highly risky endeavor.

Sampling Plan

To collect data, the researcher has to draw a sample from the target population. A sampling plan basically centers around three issues:[28]

- Who should be surveyed? What is our target population (**sampling unit**)?

- How many people should be surveyed (**sample size**)?

- How should prospective respondents be chosen from the target population (**sampling procedure**)?

Decisions on each of these issues will be driven by balancing costs, desired reliability, and time requirements. In multicountry research, firms also need to decide which countries should be researched. There are two broad approaches. The first approach starts off with a large-scale exploratory research project covering many countries. This step might take the form of an omnibus survey. The alternative approach focuses on a few key countries. To choose these countries, a firm might group countries (e.g., along sociocultural indicators) and pick one or two representative members from each cluster. Depending on the findings coming from this first pool of countries, the research process is extended to cover other countries of interest.

The preparation of a sampling plan for multicountry research is often a daunting task. When drawing a sample, the researcher needs a sampling frame, that is, a listing of the target population (e.g., a telephone directory). In many countries, such listings simply do not exist or may be very inadequate. The proportion of individuals meeting the criteria of the target population could vary considerably. This forces the researcher to be flexible with the sampling methods employed in different countries.[29]

---

[26]Jean L. Johnson, Tomoaki Sakano, Joseph A. Cote, and Naoto Onzo, "The Exercise of Interfirm Power and Its Repercussions in U.S.-Japanese Channel Relationships," *Journal of Marketing* 57, no. 2 (April 1993): 1–10.

[27]Kaynak Erderer, *Marketing in the Third World* (New York: Praeger, 1982, Chapter 4).

[28]See, for example, Naresh K. Malhotra, *Marketing Research. An Applied Orientation* (Englewood-Cliffs, NJ: Prentice Hall, 1993, Chapter 13.

[29]D. N. Aldridge, "Multicountry Research," in *Applied Marketing and Social Research*, edited by U. Bradley, 2nd ed. (New York: John Wiley, 1987), pp. 364–365.

Computing the desired sample size in cross-country market research often becomes at best guesswork because the necessary pieces of information are missing. Desired sample sizes may also vary across cultures. Typically, heterogeneous cultures (e.g., India) require bigger samples than homogeneous cultures (e.g., South Korea, Thailand).[30] This is due to the fact that diverse cultures typically have much more variance in the traits to be measured than homogeneous ones.

Most researchers prefer some form of probabilistic sampling that enables them to make statistical inferences about the collected data. The absence of sampling frames and various cultural hurdles (e.g., inapproachability of women in Muslim societies) make a non-probabilistic sampling procedure such as convenience sampling the only alternative, especially in developing countries.

Contact Method

After preparing a sampling plan, you need to decide how to contact prospective subjects for the survey. The most common choices are mail, telephone, or person-to-person interviews (e.g., shopping mall intercepts). These days the internet has also become a viable alternative. Several factors explain why some methods prevail in some countries and are barely used elsewhere. Cultural norms often rule out certain data collection methods. Germans tend to show greater resistance to telephone interviewing than other Europeans.[31] In several countries, landline phones are in decline. In Finland, for instance, about 50 percent of homes only use mobile phones.[32] Daytime phone calls will not work in Saudi Arabia, because social norms dictate that housewives do not respond to calls from strangers.[33] Cost differentials will also make some methods preferable over others. **Exhibit 6-6** shows a market research cost comparison based on a survey conducted by ESOMAR in 2007. The index is a composite score that was calculated using a representative quantitative and qualitative study, where an index value of 100 represents the midpoint. Note that a market research project done in the United States can be more than six times as costly as a similar study conducted in Pakistan.

In many emerging markets, the lack of a well-developed marketing research infrastructure is a major hurdle to conduct market research studies. Lack of decent phone service in many emerging countries creates a challenge for phone surveys. Using the internet to collect questionnaire data can also be hindered due to low internet penetration. In the wake of cost differences and various obstacles, researchers are often forced to use multiple data collection modes in the various countries to conduct a global research project.

Collect the Information

Once the design of your questionnaire and your sampling plan are completed, you need to collect the data in the field. This field will be covered with landmines, some of them fairly visible, others invisible. Primary data collection may be hindered by respondent- and/or interviewer-related biases.

Probably the most severe problem is nonresponse due to a reluctance to talk with strangers, fears about confidentiality, or other cultural biases. In many cultures, the only way to cope with nonresponse is to account for it when determining sample sizes. In China, surveys that are sanctioned by the local authorities will lead to a higher response rate.[34]

Courtesy bias refers to a desire to be polite towards the other person. This bias is fairly common in Asia and the Middle East.[35] The subject feels obliged to give responses that hopefully

---

[30]N. K. Malhotra, et al., "Methodological issues," p. 27.

[31]D. N. Aldridge, "Multicountry Research," p. 365.

[32]http://www.b2binternational.com/b2b-blog/2007/11/15/market-research-prices-a-global-comparison-part-i/, accessed January 16, 2009.

[33]Secil Tuncalp, "The Marketing Research Scene in Saudi Arabia," p. 19.

[34]Henry C. Steele, "Marketing Research in China," p. 160.

[35]Erdener Kaynak, *Marketing in the Third World*, p. 171.

Exhibit 6-6   ESOMAR 2007 Market Research Price Study

Rank	Country	Index
1	Ireland	224
2	USA	220
3	France	204
4	UK	202
5	Belgium	185
6	Germany	181
7	Switzerland	179
8	Japan	176
9	Finland	173
10	Sweden	170
54	Peru	59
55	Cyprus	58
56	Ecuador	57
56	Ukraine	57
58	Egypt	56
59	Panama	54
60	Guatemala	52
61	Bulgaria	46
62	Macedonia	41
63	Pakistan	35

Source: Compiled from data presented at http://www.b2binternational.com/b2b-blog/ 2007/11/15/market-research-prices-a-global-comparison-part-i/.

will please the interviewer. Another snag in survey research are biases towards **yea-saying** or **nay-saying**. Yea-saying is the tendency of respondents to agree with statements regardless of the content. People may do this for several reasons: a desire to please, uncritical reading of items, impulsiveness, deference to the interviewer, or difficulty with the scale itself.[36] Nay-saying on the other hand is the tendency to disagree with items regardless of the content. This may occur due to excessive reserve, hostility toward the researcher, or lack of interest. In some countries, responses may reflect a **social desirability bias** where the subject tries to project a good self-image to others. This type of response behavior is often deliberate, but it can also occur unintentionally due to the respondent's self-deception.[37] A simple way to protect against this bias is to ensure respondent anonymity. When the bias is suspected to be extremely strong, researchers can use a scoring system to measure the degree of socially desirable responding.[38] In settings where there is an

---

[36]Hans Baumgartner and Jan-Benedict E.M. Steenkamp, "Response Tendencies in Marketing Research: A Cross-National Investigation," in Rajiv Grover and Marco Vriens (Eds.), *The Handbook of Marketing Research: Uses, Misuses and Future Advances* (Sage Publications), pp. 143–156.

[37]Jan-Benedict E.M. Steenkamp, Martijn G. De Jong, and Hans Baumgartner, "Socially Desirable Response Tendencies in Survey Research," *Journal of Marketing Research* 47 (April 2010): 199–214.

[38]Gerard J. Tellis and Deepa Chandrasekaran, "Extent and Impact of Response Biases in Cross-National Survey Research," *International Journal of Research in Marketing* 27 (2010): 329–341.

Exhibit 6-7 Cross-Country Comparisons of Survey Response Biases

Country	Mean Yea-Saying	Mean Nay-Saying	Mean Socially Desirable Responding
Australia	0.57	0.41	0.28
Brazil	0.73	0.32	0.58
Canada	0.60	0.47	0.27
China	0.62	0.39	0.75
France	0.58	0.43	0.51
Germany	0.47	0.38	0.49
India	0.68	0.36	0.18
Italy	0.67	0.48	1.24
Japan	0.59	0.51	0.48
South Korea	0.69	0.49	0.60
Netherlands	0.50	0.52	0.58
Singapore	0.54	0.35	1.18
Sweden	0.55	0.44	0.32
U.K.	0.51	0.43	0.39
U.S.	0.61	0.44	0.75

Source: Based on Table 3 in Gerard J. Tellis and Deepa Chandrasekaran, "Extent and Impact of Response Biases in Cross-National Survey Research," *International Journal of Research in Marketing*, 27 (2010): p. 333.

"objective" truth, researchers can offer incentives for unbiased responding.[39] **Exhibit 6-7** summarizes the results of a recent cross-country study that looked into survey response biases. The yea-saying bias is severe in Brazil, India, China, Italy, and South Korea. On the other hand, nay-saying is high in the Netherlands, South Korea and Japan. Respondents from Italy, the United States, Singapore, and China appear to exhibit high levels of socially desirable responding.

Extreme response style (ERS) is another frequently met issue in survey-based global marketing research. This bias refers to the tendency of respondents to favor or avoid using the endpoints of a rating scale, relatively independently of the specific item content.[40] **Exhibit 6-8** illustrates that a country's culture is a key driver behind ERS. In particular, ERS is positively related to individualism (as opposed to collectivism), uncertainty avoidance, and masculinity.[41] When ERS is a potential issue, researchers can add a dedicated scale to measure the extent of the bias.[42]

Another hurdle that global marketing researchers should be aware of is the so-called **anchor contraction effect (ACE)**. This phenomenon refers to the tendency for respondents to report more intense emotions when answering questions using rating scales in a nonnative language than in the native tongue. Nonnative English speakers might experience emotional scale anchors such as "happy" or "sad" in a customer satisfaction survey as *less* intense in English than in their native language. One solution is to use emoticons (e.g., a funny faces scale) or colors as cues for emotional intensity.[43]

---

[39] Steenkamp, De Jong, and Baumgartner, p. 209 – Figure 2 in the article outlines a procedure on how to handle socially desirable response tendencies.

[40] Martijn G. De Jong, Jan-Benedict E.M. Steenkamp, Jean-Paul Fox, and Hans Baumgartner, "Using Item Response Theory to Measure Extreme Response Style in Marketing Research: A Global Investigation," *Journal of Marketing Research* 45 (February 2008): 104–115.

[41] De Jong et al. (2008), p. 114.

[42] See De Jong et al. (2008) for a more advanced model to assess ERS in global marketing research.

[43] Bart De Langhe, Stefano Puntoni, Daniel Fernandes, and Stijn M.J. Van Osselaer, "The Anchor Contraction Effect in International Marketing Research," *Journal of Marketing Research* 48 (April 2011): 366–380.

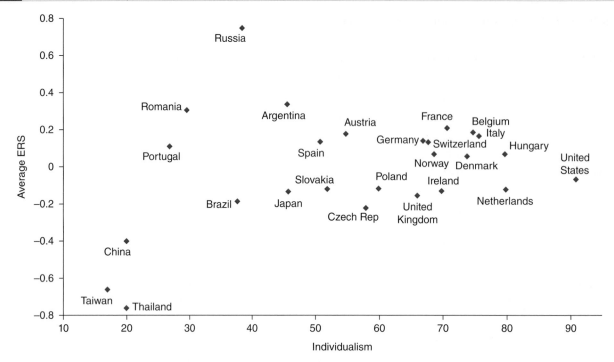

Exhibit 6-8 Individualism and Extreme-Response Style

Source: Martijn G. De Jong, Jan-Benedict E.M. Steenkamp, Jean-Paul Fox, and Hans Baumgartner, "Using Item Response Theory to Measure Extreme Response Style in Marketing Research: A Global Investigation," *Journal of Marketing Research* 45 (February 2008): Figure 3, p. 113.

Topics such as income or sex are simply taboo subjects in numerous countries. Unfortunately, there are no magic bullets to handle these and other biases. Measures such as careful wording and thorough pre-testing of the survey and adequate training of the interviewer will minimize the incidence of such biases. In some cases, it is worthwhile to incorporate questions that measure tendencies such as social desirability. Another option for handling cultural biases is to transform the data first before analyzing them. For instance, one common practice is to convert response ratings or scores to questions into rankings.

House-to-house or shopping mall survey responses could also be scrambled by interviewer-related biases. Availability of skilled interviewers can be a major bottleneck in cross-country research, especially in emerging markets. Lack of supervision or low salaries will tempt interviewers in some countries to cut corners by filling out surveys themselves or ignoring the proper sampling procedure. In many cultures, it is advisable to match interviewers to interviewees. Disparities in cultural backgrounds may lead to misunderstandings.[44] In some societies (e.g., Latin America), local people regard survey-takers with suspicion.[45] Obviously, adequate recruiting, training and supervision of interviewers will lessen interviewer-related biases in survey research. In countries where survey research is still in an early stage and researchers have little expertise, questionnaires should not be overly complex.[46] When developing a survey instrument like a questionnaire for a global market research project, it is also helpful to have **redundancy**: Ask the same question in different

---

[44]D. N. Aldridge, "Multicountry Research," p. 371.

[45]S. P. Douglas and C. S. Craig, *International Marketing Research*, p. 227.

[46]J. Stafford and N. Upmeyer, "Product Shortages," p. 40.

ways and in various parts of the questionnaire. That way, the researcher can crosscheck the validity of the responses.[47]

Observational Research

Besides traditional survey research methods, companies also increasingly rely on less conventional observation-based methods such as **ethnographic research**. With this research approach, field workers (usually cultural anthropologists) embed themselves in the local communities that they are studying. The basic aim of this type of research is to understand how people live by participating in their everyday life. The main task for the researchers involved in such studies is to observe, interact, and ask questions. Part of the data collection exercise often involves videotaping participating consumers in purchase or consumption settings. Techniques such as picture completion or collages are often useful when studying the behavior or feelings of young children.[48] **Global Perspective 6-1** describes how Nokia uses ethnographic research studies to design new mobile phones. Besides Nokia, other major companies that heavily rely on

Global Perspective 6-1

Nokia's Use of Ethnographic Research

Nokia Design is a group of 250 people (psychologists, industrial designers, anthropologists) worldwide that uses human-behavioral research to get insights useful for the design of new mobile phones. Research questions may focus on current behaviors (e.g., "how are early adopters of mobile TV using mobile TV?") or areas where growth is likely in the medium- or long-term.

The process starts with a team of anthropologists and psychologists. These researchers will spend time with local people to better understand how they behave and communicate. Insights gathered from ethnographic research assist Nokia in spotting new behavior patterns and can then be brought into the design process. Nokia also has an advanced design team that looks five to fifteen years out, trying to predict mega-trends in society.

One study looked into how people share objects. For the study, Nokia picked two cultures, Indonesia and Uganda. For the Uganda project, Nokia's researchers wanted to spend time in the capital Kampala, in a remote fishing village, and in villages with no mobile connectivity. The study typically lasted ten to twelve days with a research team that included two or three Nokia people, one or two local guides, and up to six local university students. At each site, Nokia's researchers observed and interviewed around thirty local people.

One surprising finding that emerged from Nokia's research in emerging markets is the challenge of the basic assumption that a mobile phone is owned and used by a single person. Due to the cost barrier, mobile phones in emerging market communities are often shared. As a result, Nokia designed phones (Nokia 1200 and Nokia 1208) with shared use as the top priority. The phones include a shared address book so that users can save their own contacts separately from others and a call tracker that allows people to preset a time or cost limit on each call. Other features include a keypad to protect the phone from dust, a special grip to cope with hot weather conditions, a one-touch flashlight (in case of power outages), and a demo mode to quickly learn how to use a phone.

Sources: "Nokia's Global Design Sense," http://www.businessweek.com, accessed July 31, 2008; and "Nokia's Design Research for Everyone," http://www.businessweek.com, accessed July 31, 2008.

---

[47]Naghi Namakforoosh, "Data collection methods hold key to research in Mexico," *Marketing News*, Aug. 29, 1994, p. 28.
[48]C. Samuel Craig and Susan P. Douglas, "Conducting International Marketing Research in the 21st Century," *International Marketing Review* 18, no. 1 (2001): 80–90.

ethnographic research include Intel and Microsoft. Intel, for example, used ethnographic research to address strategic questions such as: Will television and PC technology converge? Will smartphones take over most of the functions of personal computers? Do baby boomers retain their TV and PC habits as they age, or do they shift to new media?[49]

Leveraging the Internet for Global Market Research Studies

The internet has opened up new avenues for gathering market intelligence about consumers and competitors worldwide. It is without doubt one of the richest and least expensive resources of secondary data available. One shortcoming is that the sheer wealth of data has led to an embarrassment of riches: How does one separate out the useful from the useless information? Where can one find the most reliable information? Advances in search-engine technology will hopefully provide ample solutions.

In terms of primary research, the internet has created stunning possibilities. The lower cost of online survey is clearly a major driver behind the rise of online global market research. ESOMAR's 2007 global market research cost study found that online research was 33 percent cheaper than phone-based research. The same study also showed that online research costs are still declining in many countries such as Australia, Japan, and the United Kingdom.[50] Another major advantage is that marketers can get instant feedback on new product concepts or advertising concepts. Measurement tools that are especially useful in global market research include the following:

- **Online surveys.** For online survey research, three types of methods exist: (1) e-mail surveys, (2) website surveys, and (3) panel website surveys.[51] E-mail surveys are self-administered questionnaires that are sent as an attachment to e-mails to be completed by the addressee. With random website surveys, visitors to a site are asked to fill out a questionnaire. They are directed to the web page on which the survey is posted. Another variant is the pop-up survey that pops up in a new window while the user is browsing a website. These surveys are useful when the target audience is wide. Panel website surveys rely on a panel of respondents where each panel member has an e-mail address. When eligible for a survey, panel members are contacted via e-mail and asked to complete a survey that is accessible only via a password. The different forms have their advantages and disadvantages. Web-based surveys allow a better display of the questionnaire than an e-mail survey. However, e-mail surveys enable better control over who can participate. **Exhibit 6-9** summarizes the pros and cons of using on-line surveys in international marketing research. In many countries, especially those with low internet penetration, getting adequate sample representativeness of the target population is a major hurdle. To remedy this problem, global market research projects can rely on a multimode approach (e.g., web and phone interviews combined with internet surveys).[52] Over time, as technology and internet access improve, the appeal of online surveys is expected to grow.

- **Bulletin boards and chat groups.** Online bulletin boards are virtual corkboards where visitors can post questions, responses, and comments. Chat groups are virtual discussion groups that hold online conversations on a topic of their choice. Companies can monitor and participate in bulletin board and chat group discussions in many countries simultaneously.

---

[49]Ken Anderson, "Ethnographic Research: A Key to Strategy," *Harvard Business Review* (March 2009): 24.

[50]http://www.b2binternational.com/b2b-blog/2007/11/19/market-research-prices-a-global-comparison-part-ii/, accessed on January 16, 2009.

[51]Jonathan Dodd, "Market research on the Internet—threat or opportunity?" *Marketing and Research Today* (February 1998): 60–66.

[52]Janet Ilieva, Steve Baron, and Nigel M. Healey, "Online Surveys in Marketing Research: Pros and Cons," *International Journal of Market Research* 44 (Quarter 3 2002): 361–76.

Exhibit 6-9 Pros and Cons of the Internet as a Tool for Global Marketing Research

Pros:

- Large samples are possible in small amount of time.
- Global access to the internet.
- Cost—in most cases, online surveys can be done much more cheaply than using other methods—also costs are largely scale-independent in the sense that large-scale surveys do not demand far bigger resources than small surveys.
- Anonymity—can be helpful for sensitive topics.
- Data analysis—data can be directly loaded into statistical tools and databases, saving time and resources.
- Short response times.

Cons:

- Infrastructure—in many countries, access to the internet is still fairly limited.
- Sample representativeness—for random website surveys and e-mail surveys, representativeness can be a major issue. Likewise, there is also the risk of a self-selection bias.
- Time necessary to download pages (for website surveys)
- Technological problems such as incorrect e-mail addresses, poor connections.
- Low response rates—response rates can be fairly low; respondents may quit halfway.
- Multiple responses from same respondent.

Source: Jonathan Dodd, "Market research on the Internet—threat or opportunity?" *Marketing and Research Today* (February 1998): 60–67; Cheryl Harris, "Developing online market research methods and tools—Considering theorizing interactivity: models and cases," *Marketing and Research Today* (November 1997): 267–273; and Janet Ilieva, Steve Baron, and Nigel M. Healey, "Online Surveys in Marketing Research: Pros and Cons," *International Journal of Market Research* 44 (Quarter 3, 2002): 361–376.

- **Web visitor tracking.** Servers automatically collect a tremendous amount of information on the surfing behavior of visitors such as the amount of time spent on each page. Marketers can access and analyze this information to see, for instance, how observed patterns relate to purchase transactions.

- **Online (virtual) panels.** An **online panel** is a group of pre-screened respondents who have voluntarily agreed to participate in various online research studies. Prior to joining the online panel, respondents usually complete a profiling questionnaire that gathers information on their demographics, lifestyles, interests, and so forth. Several global market research companies have set up online panels in several countries that can be used to collect data for multicountry market research projects for their clients. One of the largest panels is the Harris Poll Online Panel, which has over six million members from over 125 countries.[53]

- **Focus groups.** An online focus group is set up by selecting participants who meet certain criteria. Subjects are told which chat room to enter and when. The groups are run like ordinary focus groups. Not only can they be administered worldwide, but transcripts of the group discussions are immediately available.

- **Social media.** Social media such as Facebook and Twitter provide companies another platform to conduct online consumer research. Companies increasingly use social media to solicit customer feedback on new products or even as a suggestion box for new product ideas. Frito-Lay, the snack division of PepsiCo, is a good example. To get product ideas for new chip flavors, Frito-Lay runs contests on Facebook in which participants can vote on new flavors and the creator gets a cash award. Overseas contests resulted in flavors like "hot-and-spicy crab" in Thailand and "pickled cucumber" in Serbia.[54] One important advantage of the social media approach compared to more standard consumer panels or focus groups is that they attract a

---

[53]www.harrisinteractive.com, accessed on January 19, 2009.
[54]"Social Media Give Companies a Clue on Catchy Products," *International Herald Tribune*, August 1, 2012, pp, 1, 19.

Exhibit 6-10   Research Methodology Behind the Durex "Sexual Wellbeing" Survey

---

1. **Timing.** August–September 2006.

2. **Research objectives.** To gain global consumer insight into sexual wellbeing and its importance in overall wellbeing; understanding what makes up sexual wellbeing and the importance of each of its attributes; current levels of satisfaction.

3. **Sample size.** Around 26,000 people in 26 countries (Australia, Austria, Brazil, Canada, China, France, Germany, Greece, Hong Kong, Italy, Japan, India, Malaysia, Mexico, Netherlands, New Zealand, Nigeria, Poland, Russia, Singapore, Spain, South Africa, Switzerland, Thailand, United Kingdom, and the United States).

4. **Contact method.** Online with the assistance of the Harris Interactive market research agency. However, for Nigeria, a face-to-face/self completion approach was used due to low use of internet and telephone in this country.

5. **Sampling approach.** Random samples of participants aged 16+ or 18+ were sent an e-mail invitation. Samples were drawn from Harris Interactive's internet panel.

6. **Questionnaire design.** A literature review was undertaken, followed by a series of workshops in local markets to ensure that the survey was culturally relevant. Once a draft was prepared, a two-phase pilot study was run to make sure respondents understood the questionnaire and found it easy to complete. The final draft was also reviewed by field experts.

Source: http://www.durex.com/en-GB/SexualWellbeingSurvey, accessed August 1, 2008.

younger audience. By adding social media to more traditional research platforms, companies can get much wider consumer feedback.

Although online research can produce high-quality market intelligence, it is important that one be aware of its shortcomings. Sample representativeness can be a major issue when internet users are not representative of the target population as a whole. This is especially a concern in countries where internet access is still low. When a sample is to be drawn, online research could be hampered through incorrect or outdated e-mail addresses.

With some of the research methods described (e.g., website surveys), there can also be a self-selection bias. Website visitors might also fill out the same questionnaire multiple times. It is also difficult to find out whether or not respondents are honest. Identity validation can also be an issue, especially when multiple people use the same e-mail address. Despite these limitations, the internet offers some clear advantages for running international market research projects. **Exhibit 6-10** describes the research methodology used by Durex to conduct its annual global "Sexual Wellbeing" survey online.

Market Size Assessment

When deciding whether to enter a particular country, one of the key drivers is the market potential. In most developed countries, a fairly accurate estimate of the market size for any particular product is easily obtainable. For many frequently purchased consumer goods, information suppliers like Nielsen can provide an up-to-date estimate of category volume and market shares based on scanning technology. Such information, however, does not come cheap. Before investing a substantial amount of money, you might consider less costly ways of estimating market demand. For many industries and developing countries, information on market demand is simply not readily available. Under such circumstances, there is a need to come up with a market size estimate, using "simple" ingredients.

Below we introduce four methods that can be fruitfully employed to assess the size of the market for any given product. All of these procedures can be used when very little data are available and/or the quality of the data is dismal, such as is typically the case for many emerging markets. All four methods allow you to make a reasonable guesstimate of the market potential without necessitating intensive data-collection efforts. Market size estimates thus derived prove useful for country selection at the early stage. Countries that do not appear to be viable opportunities are weeded out. After this preliminary screening stage, richer data regarding market size and other indicators are collected for the countries that remain in the pool.

Method of Analogy

The first technique, the **analogy method**, starts by picking a country that is at the same stage of economic development as the country of interest and for which the market size is known. The method is based on the premise that the relationship between the demand for a product and a particular indicator, for instance, the demand for a related product, is similar in both countries.

Let us illustrate the method with a brief example. Suppose that a consumer electronics company wants to estimate the market size for DVD players in the Ukraine. For the base country, it picks a neighboring Central European country, say Poland, for which the firm possesses information on the sales of DVD players. It also needs to choose a proxy variable that correlates highly with the demand for DVD players. One reasonable candidate is the number of color televisions in use. So, in this example, we assume that the ratio of DVD-player sales to color TV ownership in the Ukraine and Poland is roughly equivalent:

$$\frac{\text{DVD Player Demand}_{\text{Ukraine}}}{\text{Color TVs in Use}_{\text{Ukraine}}} = \frac{\text{DVD Player Demand}_{\text{Poland}}}{\text{Color TVs in Use}_{\text{Poland}}}$$

Because the company is interested in the demand for DVD players, it can derive an estimate based on the following relationship:

$$\text{DVD Player Demand}_{\text{Ukraine}} = \frac{\text{Color TVs in Use}_{\text{Ukraine}} * \text{DVD Player Demand}_{\text{Poland}}}{\text{Color TVs in Use}_{\text{Poland}}}$$

For this specific example, we collected the following bits of information (2001 figures):

	Sales	
	Color TV (000s)	DVD Players (000s)
Poland	14,722.64	69.17
Ukraine	15,626.15	???

Plugging in those numbers, we get:

Estimate DVD Player Demand$_{\text{Ukraine}}$ (Annual Retail Sales)

$$= 15{,}626.15 * (69.17/14{,}722.64) = 73.4$$

The critical part is finding a comparable country and a good surrogate measure (in this case, the number of color television sets in use). In some cases, the analogy exists between different time periods. For example, the stage of economic development in country A ten years back could be similar to the current state of the economy in country B. In the same fashion as illustrated above, we can derive an estimate for the product demand in country B, but this time we would apply the ratio between product demand and the surrogate measure in country A that existed ten years ago:

$$M_B{}^{2010} = X_B{}^{2010} * (M_A{}^{2000}/X_A{}^{2000})$$

where

M = the market size for the product of interest

X = the surrogate measure

This variant is sometimes referred to as the longitudinal method of analogy.

Use of either approach produces misleading estimates whenever:[55]

1. Consumption patterns are not comparable across countries due to strong cultural disparities.

2. Other factors (competition, trade barriers) cause actual sales to differ from potential sales.

3. Technological advances allow use of product innovations in a country at an earlier stage of economic development ("leapfrogging").

McDonald's uses a variation of the analogy method to derive market size estimates:[56]

$$\frac{\text{Population of Country } X}{\substack{\text{No. of People per McDonald's} \\ \text{in United States } (22{,}260)}} \times \frac{\text{Per Capita Income of Country } X}{\substack{\text{Per Capita Income in} \\ \text{United States } (\$49{,}000)}} = \substack{\text{Potential} \\ \text{Penetration} \\ \text{in Country } X}$$

This method is illustrated in **Exhibit 6-11**, which contrasts the number of restaurants McDonald's could build with its current (2011) number of outlets for several of the company's markets around the world.[57] As a benchmark, we also included the 2006 numbers. The last column shows the ratio of current restaurants to the estimated market potential.[58] Currently, McDonald's has around 33,000 restaurants in 119 countries and territories serving nearly 68 million people every day.[59] Interestingly, in two of its markets, namely Canada and Australia, McDonald's appears to have saturated the market. However, in numerous other countries, the fast-food chain still has a lot of mileage. Not surprisingly, each one of the four BRIC[60] countries seems to offer tremendous opportunities for McDonald's.

Trade Audit

An alternative way to derive market size estimates is based on local production and import and export figures for the product of interest. A **trade audit** uses a straightforward logic: Take the local production figures, add imports, and subtract exports:

$$\text{Market Size in Country A} = \text{Local Production} + \text{Imports} - \text{Exports}$$

Strictly speaking, one should also make adjustments for inventory levels. While the procedure is commonsensical, the hard part is finding the input data. For many emerging markets (and even developed countries), such data are missing, inaccurate, outdated, or collected at a very aggregate level in categories that are often far too broad for the company's purposes.

Chain Ratio Method

The **chain ratio method** starts with a very rough base number as an estimate for the market size (e.g., the entire population of the country). This base estimate is systematically fine-tuned by applying a string ("chain") of percentages to come up with the most meaningful estimate for total market potential.

To illustrate the procedure, let us look at the potential market size in Japan for Nicorette gum, a nicotine substitute marketed by GlaxoSmithKline. Japan's total population is 127 million.

---

[55]Lyn S. Amine and S. Tamer Cavusgil, "Demand Estimation in Developing Country Environment: Difficulties, Techniques and Examples," *Journal of the Market Research Society* 28, no. 1 (1986): 43–65.

[56]"How Many McDonald's Can He Build," *Fortune*, October 17, 1994, p. 104. Population and per capita income based on estimates reported in http://www.cia.gov/cia/publications/factbook/, accessed on July 20, 2012.

[57]For a complete listing, see http://www.mcdonalds.com/corp/.

[58]Column (2) / Column (4) X 100

[59]http://www.aboutmcdonalds.com/mcd/investors/company_profile.html, accessed July 4, 2012.

[60]Brazil, Russia, India, and China.

Exhibit 6-11 MARKET POTENTIAL ESTIMATES FOR MCDONALD'S

Country	Current Number of Restaurants (2011)	2006 Number of Restaurants	Market Potential	
North America				
Canada	1,419	1,391	1,292	109.8
United States	14,098	13,875		
Europe				
France	1,226	1,084	2,142	57.2
Germany	1,415	1,276	2,862	49.4
Italy	431	343	1,735	24.8
Netherlands	227	220	655	34.6
Russia	310	168	2,152	14.4
Spain	424	372	1,337	31.7
United Kingdom	1,198	1,214	2,115	56.6
Asia/Pacific, Middle East & Africa				
Australia	865	746	823	105.1
China	1,464	784	10,468	14.0
India	242	105	4,088	5.9
Japan	3,298	3,830	4,110	80.2
Malaysia	222	170	409	54.2
Philippines	329	254	390	84.3
South Korea	261	262	1,438	18.1
Thailand	361	345	584	61.8
Latin America				
Argentina	202	181	685	29.5
Brazil	662	540	2,244	29.5
Mexico	398	351	1,560	25.5

Sources: "How Many McDonald's Can He Build?" *Fortune*, October 17, 1994, p. 104; https://www.cia.gov/library/publications/the-world-factbook/ accessed on July 20, 2012, and http://www.aboutmcdonalds.com/mcd/investors/financial_highlights.html, accessed on July 20, 2012.

In 2002, Japan's smoking rate was around 31 percent.[61] Nicorette's target is adult smokers. The 15- to 64-year-old age group is about 67.5 percent of Japan's total population.[62] With the chain ratio method, we can then derive a rough estimate for Nicorette's market potential in Japan as follows:

Japan

Base Number	
Total Population:	127 MM people
Adult population (15–64)	85.6 MM = 0.675 × 127 MM
Adult smokers	26.5 MM = 0.31 × 85.6 MM

---

[61] http://www.jointogether.org/sa/news/summaries/reader/0,1854,554957,00.html.
[62] https://www.cia.gov/library/publications/the-world-factbook/, accessed August 27, 2013.

Obviously, given further information, we can refine this market-size estimate much further. In this case, the company also learned via surveys that 64 percent of adult smokers in Japan would like to quit or cut smoking and 25 percent of them would like to quit immediately.[63] So, Nicorette's market size potential would be approximately 4.2 million smokers (= 0.25 × 0.64 × 26.5 MM adult smokers).

Cross-Sectional Regression Analysis

Statistical techniques such as cross-sectional regression can be used to produce market size estimates. With regression analysis, the variable of interest (in our case "market size") is related to a set of predictor variables. To apply regression, you would first choose a set of indicators that are closely related to demand for the product of interest. You would then collect data on these variables and market size figures for a set of countries (the cross-section) where the product has already been introduced. Given these data, you can then fit a regression that will allow you to predict the market size in countries in your consideration pool.[64]

Again, let us illustrate the procedure with a simple example. Suppose a consumer electronics firm XYZ based in Europe is considering selling DVD players in the Balkan region or the Near East. Five countries are on its shortlist: Croatia, Greece, Israel, Romania, and Turkey. The company has gathered information on the annual sales figures of DVD players in several (mostly Western) European countries. As predictor variables, the firm chose two indicators: per capita GDP (on a purchasing power parity basis) and the number of color TV sets in use. It collected data on these two measures and the (2001) sales of DVD players in fifteen European countries.[65] Using these data as inputs, it came up with the following regression model:

$$\text{Annual Unit Sales DVD Players} = -13.3 + 2.43 \times \text{Per Capita Income}$$
$$+ 1.25 \times \text{Number of Color TVs in Use}[66]$$

Based on this regression, we are now able to predict the yearly unit sales of DVD players in the five countries being considered. We plug in the income and number of color TV sets for the respective countries in this equation, with the following results:[67]

Croatia	3,639
Greece	55,403
Israel	36,774
Romania	5,943
Turkey	34,345

Clearly, at least from a unit sales perspective, Greece seems to be the most promising market. Runner-up countries are Israel and Turkey.

When applying regression to produce a market size estimate, you should be careful in interpreting the results. For instance, caution is warranted whenever the range of one of the

---

[63]"Stubbing Out Japan's Taboo Smoking Habit," *Ad Age Global* (November 2001): 23

[64]For further details, see, for example, David A. Aaker, V. Kumar, and George S. Day, *Marketing Research* (New York: John Wiley & Sons, 1995, Chapter 18.

[65]Our source for the data is http://www.euromonitor.com.

[66]The R^2 equals 0.92; t-statistics are 8.1 and 8.7 for "Per Capita Income" and "Number of Color TVs" respectively. Note that we transformed the data by taking logarithms first.

[67]GDP per capita figures (2001) are Croatia $8,300; Greece $17,900; Israel $20,000; Romania $6,800; Turkey $6,700. Number of color TV sets in use figures (2001, in thousands) are Croatia 1,955; Greece 3,948; Israel 2,088; Turkey 17,262.

predictors for the countries of interest is outside the range of the countries used to calibrate the regression. Having said this, regression is probably one of the handiest tools to estimate market sizes, keeping in mind its constraints.

The methods we just described are not the only procedures you can use. Other more sophisticated procedures exist. Finally, some words of advice. Look at the three estimates for the size of the wallpaper market (in terms of number of rolls) in Morocco, based on different market-size estimation techniques:[68]

Chain Ratio Method:	484,000
Method by Analogy:	1,245,000
Trade Audit:	90,500

You immediately notice a wide gap among the different methods. Such discrepancies are not uncommon. When using market size estimates, keep the following rules in mind:

1. Whenever feasible, use several different methods that possibly rely on different data inputs.

2. Do not be misled by the numbers. Make sure you know the reasoning behind them.

3. Do not be misled by fancy methods. At some point, increased sophistication will lead to diminishing returns (in terms of accuracy of your estimates), not to mention negative returns. Simple back-of-the-envelope calculations are often a good start.

4. When many assumptions are to be made, do a sensitivity analysis by asking what-if questions. See how sensitive the estimates are to changes in your underlying assumptions.

5. Look for interval estimates with a lower and upper limit rather than for point estimates. The range indicates the precision of the estimates.[69] The limits can later be used for market simulation exercises to see what might happen to the company's bottom line under various scenarios.

New Market Information Technologies

These days almost all packaged consumer goods come with a bar code. For each purchase transaction, scanner data can be collected at the cash registers of stores that are equipped with laser scanning technology. The emergence of scanner data, coupled with rapid developments in computer hardware (e.g., workstations) and software has led to a revolution in market research. Although most of the early advances in this information revolution took place in the United States, Europe, and Japan, the rest of the world has rapidly followed suit. Scanning technology has spurred several sorts of databases. The major ones include:[70]

- **Point-of-sale (POS) store scanner data.** Companies like Nielsen and GfK obtain sales movement data from the checkout scanner tapes of retail outlets. These data are processed to provide instant information on weekly sales movements and market shares of individual brands, sizes, and product variants. Shifts in sales volume and market shares can be related to changes in the store environment (retail prices, display, and/or feature activity) and competitive moves. In the past, tracking of sales was based on store audits or warehouse withdrawal. The advantages of POS scanner data over these traditional ways of data gathering are obvious: speedier data access and much more accuracy.[71] The data are

---

[68]Lyn S. Amine and S. Tamer Cavusgil, "Demand Estimation in a Developing Country," Table 4.

[69]Referred to as a "confidence interval" by statisticians.

[70]See, for example, Del I. Hawkins and Donald S. Tull, *Essentials of Marketing Research* (New York: Macmillan Publishing Company, 1994), pp. 115–121.

[71]Gerry Eskin, "POS scanner data: The state of the art, in Europe and the world," *Marketing and Research Today* (May 1994): 107–117.

collected on a weekly basis instead of bi-monthly. Further, they are gathered at a very detailed UPC[72]-level, not just the brand level.

- **Consumer panel data.** Market research companies such as Nielsen and GfK have consumer panels consisting of households that record their purchases. Nielsen, for example, monitors shopping behavior of more than 250,000 households in 25 countries through its consumer panels.[73] There are two approaches to collect household level data. Under the first approach, shopper data are collected via handheld scanners. On returning from each shopping trip, the panel member scans the items bought, and the scanner transmits the data directly to the research company. In less sophisticated markets, the information is gathered through a diary maintained by the panel member.

- **Single-source data.** Single-source data are continuous data that combine for any given household member TV viewing and internet browsing behavior with purchase transaction (product description, price, promotion, etc.) information. TV viewing behavior is tracked at the panel member's home via special monitoring devices. The TV audience measurement system usually requires cooperation of the panel member. Each time the family member watches a program, he or she has to push a button to identify him/herself. More advanced systems involve a camera that records which members of the household are watching TV. Single-source data allow companies to measure, among other things, the effectiveness of their communication strategies.

Household-level scanning data are collected now in most developed countries by research firms such as Nielsen and GfK. Companies like Nestlé also put together their own databases. These innovations in marketing decision support systems have spurred several major developments in the marketing area:

- **Shift from mass to micro marketing.**[74] Better knowledge about shopping and viewing behavior has moved the focus from mass marketing to the individual. New information technologies enable firms to tailor their pricing, product line, advertising, and promotion strategies to particular neighborhoods or even individuals. Database marketing gives companies an opportunity to enter into direct contact with their customers. Nestlé's strategy for its Buitoni pasta brand offers a good example of the power of database marketing in a pan-European context. In the United Kingdom, Nestlé built up a database of people who had requested a free recipe booklet. The next step was the launch of a Casa Buitoni Club. Members of the club receive a magazine and opportunities to win a trip for cooking instruction. The goal of the strategy is to build up a long-term commitment to the Buitoni brand.[75] Likewise, in Malaysia Nestlé built up a database with information on consumption patterns, lifestyle, religion, race, and feelings about specific brands. By building up its database knowledge, Nestlé hopes to do a better job in target marketing and adapting its products to the local market.[76]

- **Continuous monitoring of brand sales/market share movements.** Sales measurement based on scanner data are more accurate and timely than, for instance, data from store audits. In Japan, thousands of new products are launched continuously. Accurate tracking information on new brand shares and incumbent brand shares is crucial information for manufacturers and retailers alike.[77]

---

[72]Universal Product Code.

[73]www.nielsen.com, accessed on July 23, 2012.

[74]David J. Curry, *The New Marketing Research Systems: How to Use Strategic Database Information for Better Marketing Decisions* (New York: John Wiley & Sons, 1994).

[75]Stan Rapp and Thomas L. Collins, *Beyond Maxi-Marketing: The New Power of Caring and Sharing* (New York: McGraw-Hill, 1994).

[76]"Nestlé builds database in Asia with direct mail," *Ad Age International* (January 1998): 34.

[77]H. Katahira and S. Yagi, "Marketing Information Technologies in Japan," p. 310.

- **Scanning data are used by manufacturers to support marketing decisions.** Initially, most scanning data were simply used as tracking devices. This has changed now. Scanning data are increasingly used for tactical decision support. The databases are used to assist all sorts of decisions in inventory management, consumer/trade promotions, pricing, shelf space allocation, and media advertising. Scanning data are also increasingly used for category management.

- **Scanning data are used to provide merchandising support to retailers.** Many manufacturers also employ information distilled from scanning data to help out retailers with merchandising programs (e.g., in-store displays). Such support helps to build up a long-term relationship with retailers. Scanning data help manufacturers to show the "hard facts" to their distributors.

Richer market information should help global marketers to improve marketing decisions that have cross-border ramifications. Scanning data from the pan-European region allows marketers to gauge the effectiveness of pan-European advertising campaigns, branding decisions, distribution strategies, and so forth. The information can also be used to monitor competitors' activities. With the emergence of consumer panel data, marketers are able to spot similarities and differences in cross-border consumer behavior. In short, the consequences of new market research systems are dramatic. Several environmental forces (e.g., single European market, cultural trends) promote the so-called global village or flat world phenomenon with a convergence in tastes, preferences leading to universal segments. On the other hand, the new information technologies will ultimately allow marketers to enter into one-on-one relationships with their individual customers.

Despite the promises of scanner databases, their full potential has not yet been exploited in many countries. Many users still simply view scanner data as an instrument to track market shares. Two factors are behind this state of affairs. One reason is the conservatism of the users of the data. Another factor is the attitude of local retailers toward data access. In countries like the United Kingdom, retailers are reluctant to release their data because they fear that by doing so they might inform their competition. Rivals are not just other retailers but in many cases the manufacturers who compete with the retailer's store brands.

Advances in computer technology have also spurred new data collection techniques such as computer-assisted telephone interviewing (CATI) and computer-assisted personal interviewing (CAPI). Benefits derived from such tools include speed, accuracy, and the ability to steer data collection based on the response. In international marketing research, another material advantage of these techniques is that they can be used to centrally administer and organize data collection for international samples.[78]

Managing Global Marketing Research

Global marketing research projects have to cater to the needs of various interest groups: global and regional headquarters, and local subsidiaries. Different requirements will lead to tension among the stakeholders. In this section we center on two highly important issues in managing global marketing research: (1) who should conduct the research project, and (2) coordination of global marketing research projects.

Selecting a Research Agency

Even companies with in-house expertise will often employ local research agencies to assist with a multicountry research project. The choice of a research agency to run a multicountry research project is made centrally by headquarters or locally by regional headquarters or country affiliates. Reliance on local research firms is an absolute must in countries such as China, both to be close to

---

[78]C. Samuel Craig and Susan P. Douglas, "Conducting International Marketing Research."

the market and to get around government red tape.[79] Local agencies may also have a network of contacts that give access to secondary data sources. Whatever the motive for using a local research agency, selection of an agency should be made based on careful scrutiny and screening of possible candidates. The first step is to see what sorts of research support services are available to conduct the research project. Each year *Marketing News* (an American Marketing Association publication) puts together a directory of international marketing research firms (http://www.marketingpower. com/AboutAMA/Advertising/Pages/MarketingNewsSpecializedDirectories.aspx).

Several considerations enter the agency selection decision. Agencies that are partners or subsidiaries of global research firms are especially useful when there is a strong need for coordination of multicountry research efforts. The agency's level of expertise is the main ingredient in the screening process: What are the qualifications of its staff and its field-workers? The agency's track record is also a key factor: How long has it been in business? What types of research problems has it handled? What experience does the agency have in tackling a particular type of research problem(s)? For what clients has it worked? In some cases, it is worthwhile to contact previous or current clients and explore their feelings about the prospective research supplier.

When cross-border coordination is an issue, companies should also examine the willingness of the agency to be flexible and be a good team player. Communication skills are another important issue. When secrecy is required, it is necessary to examine whether the candidate has any possible conflicts of interest. Does the agency have any ties with (potential) competitors? Does it have a good reputation for keeping matters confidential? Again, a background check with previous clients could provide the answer.

Cost is clearly a crucial input in the selection decision. Global research is usually much more expensive than research done in the United States.[80] The infrastructure available in the United States to do market research is far more economical than in most other parts of the world. However, there are other costs associated with global research that are not incurred with domestic research. Such cost items include the cost of multiple translations, multicountry coordination, and long-distance project management.

Quality standards can vary a lot. One golden rule needs to be observed though: Beware of agencies that promise the world at a bargain price. Inaccurate and misleading information will almost certainly lead to disastrous decisions.

Coordination of Multicountry Research

Multicountry research projects demand careful coordination of the research efforts undertaken in the different markets. The benefits of coordination are manifold.[81] Coordination facilitates cross-country comparison of results whenever such comparisons are crucial. It also can have benefits of timeliness, cost, centralization of communication, and quality control. Coordination brings up two central issues: (1) who should do the coordinating? and (2) what should be the degree of coordination? In some cases, coordination is implemented by the research agency that is hired to run the project. When markets differ a lot or when researchers vary from country to country, the company itself will prefer to coordinate the project.[82]

The degree of coordination centers on the conflicting demands of various users of marketing research: global (or regional) headquarters and local subsidiaries. Headquarters favor standardized data collection, sampling procedures, and survey instruments. Local user groups prefer country-customized research designs that recognize the peculiarities of their

---

[79]H. C. Steele, "Marketing Research in China," p. 158.

[80]Brad Frevert, "Is Global Research Different?" *Marketing Research* (Spring 2000): 49–51.

[81]D. N. Aldridge, "Multicountry Research," p. 361.

[82]"Multicountry research: Should you do your own coordinating?" *Industrial Marketing Digest*, pp. 79–82.

local environment. This conflict is referred to as the emic versus etic dilemma.[83] The **emic** school focuses on the peculiarities of each country. Attitudinal phenomena and values are so unique in each country that they can only be tapped via culture-specific measures. The other school of thought, the **etic** approach, emphasizes universal behavioral and attitudinal traits. To gauge such phenomena requires culturally unbiased measures. For instance, for many goods and services, there appears to be convergence in consumer preferences across cultures. Therefore, consumer preferences could be studied from an etic angle. Buying motivations behind those preferences, however, often differ substantially across cultures. Hence, a cross-country project that looks into buying motivations is likely to require an emic approach.[84]

In cross-cultural market research, the need for comparability favors the *etic paradigm* with an emphasis on the cross-border similarities and parallels. Nevertheless, to make the research study useful and acceptable to local users, companies need to recognize the peculiarities of local cultures. So, ideally, survey instruments that are developed for cross-country market research projects should encompass both approaches—emic *and* etic.[85] There are several approaches to balance these conflicting demands. In a pan-European positioning study conducted for BMW, coordination was accomplished via the following measures:[86]

1. All relevant parties (users at headquarters and local subsidiaries) were included from the outset in planning the research project.

2. All parties contributed in funding the study.

3. Hypotheses and objectives were deemed to be binding at later stages of the project.

4. Data collection went through two stages. First, responses to a country-specific pool of psychographic statements were collected. The final data collection in the second stage used a mostly standardized survey instrument containing a few statements that were country-customized (based on findings from the first run).

The key lessons of the BMW example are twofold. First, *coordination* means that all parties (i.e., user groups) should get involved. Neglected parties will have little incentive to accept the results of the research project. Second, multicountry research should allow some leeway for country peculiarities. For instance, questionnaires should not be over standardized but may include some country-specific items. This is especially important for collecting so-called "soft" data (e.g., lifestyle/attitude statements).

---

[83]S. P. Douglas and C.S Craig, *International Marketing Research*, pp. 132–37.
[84]Malhotra, Agarwal, and Peterson, p. 12.
[85]N. K. Malhotra, J. Agarwal, and M. Peterson, "Methodological issues," p. 12.
[86]H. Kern, H.-C. Wagner, and R. Hassis, "European Aspects of a Global Brand," pp. 49–50.

SUMMARY

Whenever you drive to an unknown destination, you probably use a road map or GPS, ask for instructions to get there, and carefully examine the road signals. If not, you risk getting lost. By the same token, whenever you need to make marketing decisions in the global marketplace, market intelligence will guide you in these endeavors. Shoddy information invariably leads to shoddy decision making; good information facilitates solid decision making. In this day and age, having timely and adequate market intelligence also provides a competitive advantage. This does not mean that global marketers should do research at any cost. As always, examining the costs and the value added of having more information at each step is important. Usually it is not difficult to figure out the costs of gathering market intelligence. The hard part is the benefit component. Views on the benefits and role of market research sometimes differ between cultures. What can marketers do to boost the payoffs of their global marketing research efforts? As always, there are no simple solutions.

The complexities of the global marketplace are stunning. They pose a continual challenge to market researchers. Hurdles are faced in gathering secondary and primary data. Not all challenges will be met successfully. Mistakes are easily made. One American toiletries manufacturer conducted its market research in (English-speaking) Toronto for a bar soap to be launched in (French-speaking) Québec. The whole venture became a sad soap opera with a tragic ending.[87]

In this chapter we discussed the intricacies in developing and implementing a market research project in a cross-national setting. We also reviewed several techniques that prove useful to estimate the market size whenever few or only poor quality data are at your disposal.

To make cross-country comparisons meaningful, companies need to adequately manage and coordinate their market research projects with a global scope. Inputs from local users of the research are desirable for several reasons. When the locals feel that they have been treated like stepchildren, it will be hard to "sell" the findings of the research project. As a result, getting their support for policies based on the study's conclusions becomes a formidable task. Local feedback also becomes necessary to uncover country-specific peculiarities that cannot be assessed with over standardized measurement instruments.

---

[87]Sandra Vandermerwe, "Colgate-Palmolive: Cleopatra," Case Study, Lausanne: IMD, 1990.

QUESTIONS

1. What is the notion of "triangulation" in global market research?

2. Discuss why market size estimates may differ depending on the method being used. How can such differences be reconciled?

3. Contrast the emic versus the etic approach in international marketing research.

4. Refer to Exhibit 6-11, which presents McDonald's market potential based on the formula given on page 195.

   a. Using the same formula, estimate what McDonald's market potential would be for the former Eastern Bloc countries: Bosnia, Bulgaria, Croatia, Czech Republic, Hungary, Poland, Serbia, Slovakia, and Ukraine. Compare these to the most recent actual number of restaurants in each of these countries (the latest figures can be downloaded from a spreadsheet available on McDonald's Investors information website: Go to http://www.aboutmcdonalds.com/mcd/investors/financial_highlights.html and click on "Financial Information."

   b. The formula that McDonald's uses to estimate market potential basically relies on two factors: the country's population and income. What other factors could be relevant besides these two?

5. Company Euronappy sells disposable diapers in Europe. It would like to expand into the Middle East. After some preliminary market research, four countries were put on the short list: Bahrain, Kuwait, Saudi Arabia, and the United Arab Emirates (UAE). Given its limited resources, the company can only enter two of these countries. Your assignment is to come up with a market size estimate for each one of them so that Euronappy can decide which one to enter. You decide to run a regression using data from Euronappy's European market. Three variables are presumed to predict the sales of disposable diapers: population size, per capita GDP, and the birth rate. Data were collected on all three variables (source: http://www.cia.gov/cia/publications/factbook/) for the 19 European countries where Euronappy operates. However, the birth rate did not seem to be a factor. The estimated regression model is:

   $$Y = -630.6 + 0.015 X_1 + 47.15 X_2$$

   Y = annual sales of diapers in millions of units

   X_1 = population in thousands

   X_2 = per capita Gross Domestic Product (GDP – Purchasing Power Parity Basis) in thousands US$

   a. Collect data on the population and per capita GDP for the four countries on the list (Bahrain, Kuwait, Saudi Arabia, and the UAE).

   b. Now use the estimated regression model to predict the yearly sales of disposable diapers for these four countries. Which of these two would you choose?

   c. Suppose the company is also looking at the Arab Spring countries in North Africa, in particular: Egypt, Libya, and Tunisia. Would you advise them to use the same estimated regression model? Why, or why not?

6. Imagine that Nokia plans to expand its market in South America. Use the chain-ratio method to come up with market size estimates for cellular phones in the following four countries: Argentina, Brazil, Chile, and Peru.

7. The ImagePower® Green Brands Survey is an annual global study that assesses consumer perceptions of brands and corporate behavior regarding environmental issues. The survey is sponsored by a partnership of three WPP agencies (Cohn & Wolfe, Landor Associates, and Penn Schoen Berland) and Esty Environmental Partners, an environmental strategy consultancy. The 2011 survey polled more than 9,000 people in eight countries: Australia (1,100 interviews), Brazil (1,106), China (1,102), France (1,100), Germany (1,100), India (1,101), the U.K. (1,200), and the United States (1,200). The

interviews were conducted online with respondents from tier-one cities.[88] Some of the survey's questions are the following:

- Do you think the state of the environment in this country is headed in the right direction?
- Which of the following do you feel is the most important green issue today? (Energy use, climate change, air pollution, water issues, . . .)
- When you think about what brands to buy, how important is it to you that a company is environmentally friendly?
- In the next year, do you plan to spend more, less, or the same amount on green products or services?

---

[88]Tier-one cities are major metropolitan areas in a country.

- What do you think are the biggest challenges to buying green products or services? (too expensive, limited selection, difficult to find, poorly labeled, low quality . . .)

  To access the complete survey and its findings, visit slideshare.net/WPPGreenBrandsSurvey.

a. What do you envision as the key challenges in developing a global survey such as WPP's Green Brands Survey?

b. This survey was conducted online. What are the main benefits of doing the study online compared to more traditional data collection methods? What could be some possible downsides?

c. How could insights from this survey benefit a global consumer multinational like Unilever, Colgate, or Heinz?

7 SEGMENTATION AND POSITIONING

CHAPTER OVERVIEW

1. Reasons for international market segmentation

2. International market segmentation approaches

3. Segmentation scenarios

4. Bases for international market segmentation

5. International positioning strategies

6. Global, foreign, and local consumer culture positioning

In early February 2009 Lenovo, the Chinese computer maker that vaulted onto the international stage four years earlier by buying the personal computers divisions of IBM, reported a loss of $97 million for the fiscal quarter ending December 31, 2008. PC shipments were down 5 percent while revenue had dropped 20 percent compared to the year-earlier quarter. To overhaul its business, Lenovo announced that it would refocus on China and other emerging markets. Lenovo's management also would concentrate on consumers rather than big corporate customers, the mainstay of the former IBM's business.[1]

Few companies can be all things to all people. Instead of competing across the board, most companies will identify and target the most attractive market segments that they can serve effectively. Variation in customer needs is the primary motive for market segmentation. When consumer preferences vary, marketers can design a marketing mix program that is tailored toward the needs of the specific segments that the firm targets. Marketers select one or more segmentation bases (e.g., age, lifestyle) and slice up their prospective customer base according to the chosen criteria. Marketing programs are then developed that are in tune with the particular needs of each of the segments that the company wants to serve.

In global marketing, market segmentation becomes especially critical, given the sometimes incredibly wide divergence in cross-border consumer needs and preferences. In this chapter, we first focus on the motivations for international market segmentation. Given information on the segmentation criteria you plan to use, you can take several country segmentation approaches. We describe in detail several possible segmentation scenarios. We then consider several bases that marketers might consider for country segmentation. Once the company has chosen its target segments, management needs to determine a competitive

---

[1]"Lenovo Refocuses on China," *Wall Street Journal Asia*, February 6–8, 2009, pp. 1, 15.

positioning strategy for its products. The final sections focus on different international positioning strategies that companies can pursue.

Reasons for International Market Segmentation

The goal of market segmentation is to break down the market for a product or a service into different groups of consumers who differ in their response to the firm's marketing mix program. That way, the firm can tailor its marketing mix to each individual segment, and, hence, do a better job in satisfying the needs of the target segments. This overall objective also applies in an international marketing context. In that sense, market segmentation is the logical outgrowth of the marketing concept.[2]

The requirements for effective market segmentation in a domestic marketing context also apply in international market segmentation. In particular, segments ideally should possess the following set of properties:[3]

1. *Identifiable*. The segments should be easy to define and to measure. This criterion can be easily met for "objective" country traits such as socioeconomic variables (e.g., gender, age). However, identifying segment membership based on values or lifestyle indicators is usually much harder.

2. *Sizable*. The segments should be large enough to be worth going after. Note that modern technologies such as flexible manufacturing enable companies to relax this criterion. In fact, many segments that might be considered too small in a single-country context become attractive once they are lumped together across borders.

3. *Accessible*. The segments should also be easy to reach through promotional and distributional efforts. Differences in the quality of the distribution (e.g., road conditions, storage facilities) and media infrastructure (e.g., internet penetration) imply that a given segment might be hard to reach in some countries and easy to target in other marketplaces.

4. *Stability*. If target markets change their composition or behavior over time, marketing efforts devised for these targets are less likely to succeed.

5. *Responsive*. For market segmentation to be meaningful, it is important that the segments respond differently from each other to differentiated marketing mixes.

6. *Actionable*. Segments are actionable if the marketing mix necessary to address their needs is consistent with the goals and the core competencies of the company.

Let us consider now the main reasons why international marketers implement international market segmentation.

Country Screening

Companies usually do a preliminary screening of countries before identifying attractive market opportunities for their product or service. For preliminary screening, market analysts rely on a few indicators for which information can easily be gathered from secondary data sources. At this stage, the international market analyst might classify countries in two or three piles. Countries that meet all criteria will be grouped in the "Go" pile for further consideration at the next stage. Countries

---

[2]Yoram Wind and Susan P. Douglas, "International Market Segmentation," *European Journal of Marketing* 6, no. 1 (1972): 17–25.

[3]Michel Wedel and Wagner A. Kamakura, *Market Segmentation. Conceptual and Methodological Foundations* (Boston: Kluwer Academic Publishers, 1998), Chapters 1 and 2.

that fail to meet most of the criteria will enter the "No Go" pile. The third set includes countries that meet some of the criteria but not all of them. They may become of interest in the future but probably not in the short term.

Companies will use different sets of criteria to screen countries, depending on the nature of the product. Cultural similarity to the domestic market is one criterion on which companies often rely. Other popular screening criteria include market attractiveness in terms of economic prosperity (e.g., per capita GNP), geographic proximity and the country's economic infrastructure.[4]

Global Marketing Research

Country segmentation also plays a role in global marketing research. Companies increasingly make an effort to design products or services that meet the needs of customers in different countries. Certain features might need to be added or altered, but the core product is largely common across countries. Other aspects of the marketing mix program such as the communication strategy might also be similar. The benefits of a standardization approach often outweigh the possible drawbacks. Still, to successfully adopt this approach, companies need to do sufficient market research. Given the sheer number of countries in which many companies operate, doing market research in each one of them is often inefficient. Especially at the early stage, companies are likely to focus on a select few countries. The key question, then, is which countries to choose. One approach is to start grouping prospective markets into clusters of homogeneous countries. Out of each group, one prototypical member is chosen. Research efforts will be concentrated on each of the key members, at least initially. Presumably, research findings for the selected key member countries can then be projected to other countries belonging to its cluster. For example, Heineken chose four countries to do market research for Buckler, a non-alcoholic beer: the Netherlands, Spain, the United States, and France. The Dutch brewer wanted to assess the market appeal of Buckler and the feasibility of a pan-European marketing strategy consisting of a roughly common targeting, positioning, and marketing mix strategy across the continent.[5]

Entry Decisions

When a product or service does well in one country, firms often hope to replicate their success story in other countries. Entering new markets involves major resource commitments. When launching a new product or service, the company must decide on the sequence of countries to enter. Segmentation of countries could support the selection process. The underlying logic is that the penetration patterns (e.g., rapid versus slow penetration) for the new product are likely to show parallels across countries when the demand (e.g., culture) and supply (e.g., regulations) are similar in these countries.[6]

It is important, though, to realize that a host of factors make or break the success of a new product launch. Tabasco sauce is very popular in many Asian countries like Japan with a strong liking for spicy dishes. Hence, McIlhenny, the Louisiana-based maker of Tabasco sauce, might view entering Vietnam and India, two of the emerging markets in Asia with a palate for hot food, as the logical next step for its expansion strategy in Asia. Other factors, however, such as buying power, import restrictions, or the shoddy state of the distribution and media infrastructure could lessen the appeal of these markets.

[4]Debanjan Mitra and Peter N. Golder, "Whose Culture Matters? Near-Market Knowledge and Its Impact on Foreign Market Entry Timing," *Journal of Marketing Research* 39 (August 2002): 350–65.

[5]Sandra Vandermerwe, "Heineken NV: Buckler Nonalcoholic Beer," Case Study, International Institute for Management Development, Switzerland, 1991.

[6]Stefan Stremersch and Aurélie Lemmens, "Sales Growth of New Pharmaceuticals across the Globe: The Role of Regulatory Regimes," *Marketing Science* 21 (July-August 2009): 690–708.

Positioning Strategy

Segmentation decisions will also influence the company's product positioning strategy. Once the firm has selected the target segments, management needs to develop a positioning strategy that will resonate with consumers in the chosen segments. Basically, the company must decide on how it wants to position its products or services in the mind of the prospective target customers. Environmental changes or shifting consumer preferences often force a firm to rethink its positioning strategy. Cathay Pacific's repositioning strategy in the mid-1990s is a good example. The Hong Kong–based airline carrier realized that its product offerings failed to adequately meet the needs of its Asian clients, who represent 80 percent of its customer base. To better satisfy this target segment, the airline repositioned itself in the fall of 1994 to become the preferred airline among Asian travelers. To that end, Cathay wanted to project an Asian personality with a personal touch. Cathay now offers a wide variety of Asian meals and entertainment. Other measures include a new logo (by some people referred to as a shark-fin), new colors, repainted exteriors, and redesigned cabins and ticket counters. To communicate these changes to the public, Cathay launched a heavy advertising campaign with the slogan "The Heart of Asia."[7]

Resource Allocation

Market segmentation will also be useful in deciding how to allocate the company's scarce marketing resources across different countries. **Exhibit 7-1** shows how Nestlé clusters countries using two criteria for Nescafé, its instant coffee brand: per-capita coffee consumption and the market share of in-home soluble coffee of overall coffee consumption. Countries where the share of instant coffee is more than 50 percent are classified as *leader* markets; countries where R&G coffee[8] is dominant are classified as *challenger* markets. Developed markets are those with an annual per-capita consumption of more than 360 cups. Countries below the 360-cups cutoff are developing markets from Nestlé's perspective. A representation such as the one shown in **Exhibit 7-1** offers guidance for an MNC in formulating its strategic objectives and allocating resources across groups of countries in a given region or worldwide. For instance, Nestlé's

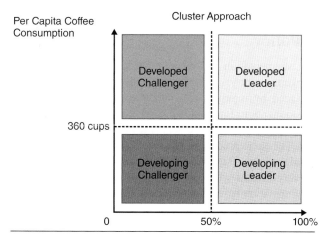

Exhibit 7-1 Market Clustering Approach for Instant Coffee

---

[7]John Pies, former Cathay Pacific executive, private communication.

[8]Roast and ground.

Exhibit 7-2 BCG
Growth-Share
Segmentation

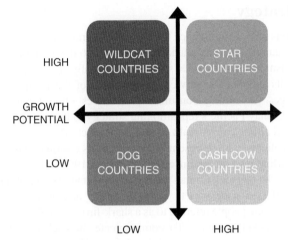

Competitive Strength of Business in Country

managers could decide to concentrate marketing resources in countries that have a low market share but a high per capita consumption to bolster their firm's market share. Alternatively, resources could be allocated to countries where the firm has a strong competitive position but still fairly low coffee consumption. At the same time, managers would probably ponder cutting resources in markets with low coffee consumption and where Nestlé's market share is weak.

A more generalized approach of segmentation-for-resource allocation purposes is the BCG[9] growth-share matrix in an international context (see **Exhibit 7-2**). In this framework, countries are grouped based on two dimensions: (1) the growth potential of the business in the country (e.g., 5-year predicted future growth) and (2) the company's competitive position in the country (e.g., market share). This results in four possible country clusters depending on the relative growth (low versus high) and the company's competitive strength (low versus high). Just as with the standard BCG framework, such groupings can be used to guide marketing resource allocation decisions across countries.

Marketing Mix Policy

In domestic marketing, segmentation and positioning decisions dictate a firm's marketing mix policy. By the same token, country segmentation guides the global marketer's mix decisions. A persistent problem faced by international marketers is how to strike the balance between standardization and customization. International market segmentation could shed some light on this issue. Countries belonging to the same segment might lend themselves to a standardized marketing mix strategy. The same product design, an identical pricing policy, similar advertising messages and media, and the same distribution channels could be used in these markets. Of course, marketers need to be very careful when contemplating such moves. There should be a clear linkage between the segmentation bases and the target customers' responsiveness to any of these marketing mix instruments.

Usually, it is very difficult to establish a linkage between market segments and all four elements of the marketing mix. For instance, countries with an underdeveloped phone infrastructure (e.g., India, China, Sub-Saharan Africa) are typically prime candidates for mobile phone technologies. However, many of these countries dramatically differ in terms of their price sensitivities given the wide gaps in buying power. Therefore, treating them as one group as far as the pricing policy goes

---
[9]Boston Consulting Group

Exhibit 7-3 Johnnie Walker Market Classification for 1997–1998

Classification	Mature	Developing	Emerging
Volume contribution	50%	30%	20%
Markets	Austria, France, Germany, Italy, Japan, UK, USA	Czech Republic, Greece, Mexico, Portugal, South Korea, Spain, Venezuela	Brazil, Chile, Colombia, Indonesia, Poland, Russia, Taiwan, Thailand, Turkey
Character	• Declining, stagnant • Brand proliferation • Price sensitive • Strong retail power • High investment required for advertising and promotional activity • Off-trade* skew	• Growing yet volatile economies • Increased competition • Increasing costs of doing business • Growing retailer power	• Volatile economies • Underdeveloped trade and distribution • Grey channel issues

*Off-trade is the sale of alcoholic beverages for consumption in places other than licensed premises.
Source: Exhibit 2 in Amitava Chattopadhyay and Nina Paavola, "Building the Johnnie Walker Brand," INSEAD Case Study (2006). Copyright © 2006 INSEAD, all rights reserved.

might lead to disastrous consequences. The marketing team behind the Johnnie Walker scotch brand developed a schema classifying countries as "mature" (Western countries and Japan), "developing" (e.g., Spain, Portugal, Mexico, South Korea), or "emerging" (e.g., Brazil, Thailand, Russia, China). Each country group is characterized by different market conditions. For instance, Johnnie Walker faces rising costs of doing business (due to duties increases, product piracy) in "developing" countries and gray-channel situations in "emerging" markets. Depending on the prevailing conditions, different marketing strategies are called for (see **Exhibit 7-3**).[10]

International Market Segmentation Approaches

Global marketers approach the segmentation process from different angles. A very common international segmentation procedure classifies prospect countries geographically on a single dimension (e.g., per capita Gross National Product) or on a set of multiple socioeconomic, political, and cultural criteria available from secondary data sources (e.g., the World Bank, the EU, the OECD). This is known as **country-as-segments** or **aggregate segmentation**. When there are numerous country characteristics being considered for segmenting countries, the segmentation variables are usually first collapsed into a smaller set of dimensions using data reduction techniques such as factor analysis. The countries in the pool are then classified into homogeneous groups using statistical algorithms such as cluster analysis (see the **Appendix** for a brief overview of some of these techniques).

The country-as-segments approach has some major flaws. From a global marketer's perspective, the managerial relevance of geographic segments is often questionable. Country boundaries rarely define differences in consumer response to marketing strategies. Furthermore, it is seldom clear what variables should be included in deriving the geographic segments.

An alternative approach is **disaggregate international consumer segmentation**. Here, the focus is the individual consumer. Just as with domestic marketing, one or more segmentation bases (e.g., lifestyle, demographic, values) are chosen. Consumer segments are then identified in

---

[10]Amitava Chattopadhyay and Nina Paavola, "Building the Johnnie Walker Brand," INSEAD Case Study (2006).

terms of consumer similarities with respect to the chosen bases. The key problem here is that targeting a consumer segment that is geographically dispersed can become a logistical nightmare.

To address the shortcomings of the previous two approaches, **two-stage international segmentation** can offer solace.[11] The first step—**macro-segmentation**—is the classification of countries into different groups on the basis of characteristics deemed to be relevant for marketing purposes. The second phase—**micro-segmentation**—consists of segmenting consumers for each country-cluster identified in the first step. In the first macro-level stage, countries are grouped on general segmentation bases. Some bases are independent of the product or service for which the segmentation is being done. They can be observable (e.g., demographic, socio-economic, cultural) or unobservable (e.g., lifestyle, values, personality) traits. This first step also enables the manager to screen out countries that are unacceptable (e.g., because of high political risk or low buying power) or do not fit the company's objectives. The second micro-level phase is similar to standard segmentation within a given country except that most consumer segments overlap across countries rather than being restricted to one particular country. The candidate micro-level segmentation criteria are similar to the segmentation bases considered for standard market segmentation: demographics (e.g., age, gender, family life-cycle stage), socio-economic measures (e.g., per capita income, social class), lifestyle, values, and benefits sought. The particular bases selected depend on the nature of the goal of the segmentation. Benefit segmentation, for example, is preferred when assessing new product ideas. These disaggregate data then form the ingredients for identifying cross-national segment of consumers within the geographic segment(s) chosen. Note that relatively small segments (e.g., yoga or bowling sports segments for athletic footwear/apparel businesses) within countries could become appealing in terms of scale economies once they are lumped together across countries.

Two-stage segmentation has several benefits. First, compared to purely geographic country-level aggregation, the segments will be more responsive to marketing efforts. The segments are also more in tune with a market-orientation perspective as they focus on consumer needs rather than simply macro-level socioeconomic or cultural variables. Second, as opposed to disaggregate consumer segmentation, the derived segments will be more accessible.[12]

Whichever segmentation approach is chosen, the user should keep in mind that segments can be dynamic over time rather than static. Over time, the size of the derived consumer segments may evolve. Likewise, country segment membership could change over the product life cycle.[13]

Segmentation Scenarios

When a firm segments foreign markets, different scenarios may arise. A common phenomenon is illustrated in **Exhibit 7-4**, where we have one cross-border overlapping segment ("A") and the other segments are either unique to a particular country ("C," "E," and "F") or exist in only two of the three countries ("B" and "D"). Note also that the size of the different segments varies depending on the country.

One possibility is that you uncover so-called **universal** or **global segments**. These are segments that transcend national boundaries. They are universal in the sense that customers belonging to such segments have common needs. Note that this segment could also be a universal niche. A niche is commonly defined as a more narrowly defined group of consumers who seek a

[11] J.-B.E.M. Steenkamp and F. Ter Hofstede, "International Market Segmentation: Issues and Perspectives," *International Journal of Research in Marketing* (September 2002): 185–214.

[12] There are other segmentation approaches that allow for cross-border segments with spatial contiguity. One interesting methodology is outlined in F. Ter Hofstede, M. Wedel, and J.-B.E.M. Steenkamp, "Identifying Spatial Segments in International Markets," *Marketing Science*, 21 (Spring 2002): 160–77.

[13] Aurélie Lemmens, Christophe Croux, and Stefan Stremersch, "Dynamics in the International Market Segmentation of New Product Growth," *International Journal of Research in Marketing* 29, no. 1 (2011): 81–92.

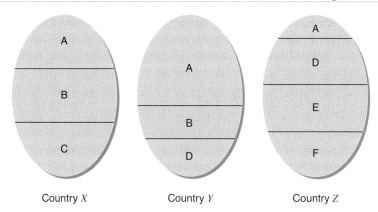

Exhibit 7-4
Different Segment
Scenarios

Country *X* Country *Y* Country *Z*

very special bundle of benefits. Examples of possible universal segments that are emerging include the global youth, international business travelers, and the global elite. One study done at Harvard University looked at consumers' attitudes toward global brands. Based on a survey done with 1,800 respondents in twelve countries, the authors derived the following seven global segments:

- *Global climbers (23.3%)*. These people are extremely conscious of and attracted to brands that suggest global status. They are unimpressed by brands that are linked with countries that have a strong quality reputation for specific products.

- *Civic libertarians (21.5%)*. This group puts heavy emphasis on social responsibility. They are not impressed by brands that are produced in countries with a high reputation in the product category.

- *Multinational fans (15.5%)*. This segment ranks highest on the influence of reputation and global status on brand preference.

- *Antiglobalists (13.1%)*. These people are strongly against brands that express American values and are very cynical about the ethics of companies that own global brands.

- *Global citizens (10.1%)*. This segment values social responsibility.

- *Global agnostics (7.6%)*. These consumers value global brands just as any other brand without using the global dimension as a cue.

- *Pro-West (7.6%)*. These people have a high esteem for American values. Their brand preferences are highly influenced by global status.[14]

How similar customer needs are clearly depends on the product category.[15] Axe,[16] Unilever's brand of male grooming products, shows how one company can successfully market its products to a global segment, in this case global youth. To grab exposure among web-savvy young males worldwide, Unilever developed clever digital marketing ideas around the fragrance. For instance, Axe's marketing team created a series of online games and videos (http://www.theaxeeffect.com) showing the "Axe effect"—women chasing men who used the deodorant.[17]

---

[14]Douglas B. Holt, John A. Quelch, and Earl L. Taylor, "Managing the Global Brand. A Typology of Consumer Perceptions," in *The Global Market*, eds. John Quelch and Rohit Deshpande. (Boston: Harvard Business School Press, 2004): 180–201.
[15]George S. Yip, *Total Global Strategy* (Englewood Cliffs, NJ: Prentice Hall, 1995): 30–32.
[16]The brand is named Lynx in Australia, Ireland, New Zealand, and the United Kingdom.
[17]"Children of the Web," Business Week, July 2, 2007, 51–58.

Commonality of consumer needs is high for high-tech consumer durables and travel-related products (e.g., credit cards, airlines). Redd's, a beer-like brand sold by SABMiller, is an example of a product that is targeted toward a universal segment. The brew, an "apple-infused malt beverage, with a citrus flavor," is aimed specifically at women, a segment that traditionally has been neglected by beer companies. Redd's is sold in packages of five or ten bottles, rather than six- or twelve-packs for typical beer brand. The packs are shaped like a woman's handbag. The brand was first introduced in South Africa and Eastern Europe and then also launched in Latin America.[18] At the other end of the spectrum are food products, where customer needs tend to be very localized. Apart from global segments, you may also encounter **regional segments**. Here the similarity in customer needs and preferences exists at the regional level rather than globally. While differences in consumer needs exist among regions, there are similarities within the region.

With universal or regional segments, the firm still needs to decide the extent to which it wants to differentiate its marketing mix strategy. At one end of the spectrum, management can adopt an undifferentiated marketing strategy that follows a more or less uniform approach world or region wide. An undifferentiated marketing strategy allows the firm to capitalize on scale economies. To a large extent, this is a strategy that suits high-tech companies. For instance, the corporate advertising director of Microsoft remarked in a forum: "The character of the [Microsoft] product is universal. Technology is an English-based thing, so there's a lot of willingness to embrace Western companies."[19] At the other end of the spectrum are firms that tailor their marketing strategy to local markets. Although consumer needs and preferences may be similar, differentiation of positioning and other marketing mix elements might be necessary to cope with variations in local market conditions. A differentiated strategy allows the company to stay better in tune with the local market and to be more flexible.

Unique (diverse) segments are the norm when gaps in cross-country customer needs and preferences are so substantial that it becomes very hard to derive meaningful cross-border segments. Under such a scenario, marketing mix programs must be localized to meet local consumer needs. Rather than going after one common cross-border segment, management picks the most attractive target markets in each individual market. A case in point is the Canon AE-1 camera. When Canon launched this camera, it developed three different marketing programs: one for Japan, one for the United States, and one for Europe. In Japan, Canon targeted young replacement buyers. In the United States, it concentrated on upscale, first-time buyers of 35mm single-lens reflex cameras. In Germany, Canon focused on older and technologically more sophisticated replacement buyers.[20] Jack Daniel's, the Tennessee-based whiskey brand, also pursues diverse target markets. In Australia and New Zealand, the beverage brand pursues young, hip, social drinkers. In China, where a bottle of Jack Daniel's costs much more than in the United States the target is the middle-class consumer.[21]

In most instances, there is a mixture of universal, regional, and country-specific market segments. One final comment to be made here is that markets differ a great deal in terms of their degree of segmentation. Gaps in the degree of segmentation are most visible when contrasting the market structure in a developed country with the one in an emerging market. For most consumer goods, the market structure for a category in the emerging market is often pretty unsophisticated: premium versus economy. Developed countries, on the other hand, have typically many more segments and niches. This is to a large extent due to differences in the degree of market development. Early on in the product life cycle, the market is still relatively undersegmented.

---

[18]"Five-packs for Latinas," *International Herald Tribune*, October 15, 2007, 12–13.

[19]"U.S. Multinationals," *Advertising Age International* (June 1999): 41.

[20]Hirotaka Takeuchi and Michael E. Porter, "Three Roles of International Marketing in Global Strategy," in *Competition in Global Industries*, ed. M. E. Porter (Boston: Harvard Business School Press, 1986): 139–140.

[21]"Jack Daniel's goes down smooth in Australia, New Zealand, China," *Ad Age International* (September 1997): i38–i39.

As consumers grow more sophisticated and demanding and as the category develops, new segments and niches emerge.

Bases for International Market Segmentation

The first step in doing international market segmentation is deciding which criteria to use in the task. Just as in a domestic marketing context, the marketing analyst faces an embarrassment of riches. Literally hundreds of country characteristics could be used as inputs. In a sense, you can pick and choose the variables that you want. However, for the segmentation to be meaningful, the market segments and the response variable(s) the company is interested in should have a linkage. Usually it is not a trivial exercise to figure out *a priori* which of the variables will contribute to the segmentation. Instead, the marketing analyst will need to do some experimentation to find a proper set of segmentation variables. Furthermore, information on several segmentation criteria is typically missing, inaccurate, or outdated for some of the countries to be segmented.

We now briefly discuss different types of country variables that are most commonly used for country segmentation purposes. Most of these criteria can be used for the two segmentation approaches that we discussed earlier. For instance, one could use a socioeconomic variable such as per capita income as a segmentation base to group countries. However, one could also use the income dimension to segment consumers within country first and then derive regional or global segments (e.g., pan-Asian middle class).

Demographics

Demographic variables (e.g., age, gender, family status) are among the most popular segmentation criteria. One reason for their popularity is that they are very easy to measure (recall the "measurability" requirement for effective market segmentation). Moreover, information on population variables is mostly reasonably accurate and readily available.

One segment that marketers often overlook is the elderly. In industrialized countries, the over-60 age segment is expected to rise to a third of the population (over two-fifths in Japan) from 20 percent now. Many of these people are more prosperous and healthier than ever before. Countries with an aging population clearly offer market opportunities for consumer goods and services that cater to the elderly. To gain a foothold within this target market, it is critical to understand the subtleties of marketing to the over-60 group, especially in youth-obsessed cultures. Gerber's launch of a baby-food like product line called Senior Citizen proved to be a failure because older shoppers have no desire to openly show their age.[22] Unilever's low-fat Pro-Activ sub-brand margarine spread,[23] however, was a major success. The product addresses the need for a heart-friendly margarine among aging consumers. Pro-Activ was proven to lower cholesterol levels. As a result, Unilever was able to establish agreements with insurance companies in France and the Netherlands to offer discounts to their insurance customers for consuming Pro-Activ margarine products.[24]

By the same token, countries with high birth rates have similar buying patterns. Examples of goods and services with high potential in such countries include baby food and clothing, toys, prenatal care services, and birth-control devices.

[22]"Over 60 and Overlooked," *The Economist*, August 10, 2002, 51–52.
[23]Pro-Activ is a sub-brand of Unilever's Becel/Flora margarine brand. In the United States the product is sold under the Promise brand name.
[24]"Unilever's Pro-Activ to be Reimbursed By French Insurer," http://www.nutraingredients.com, accessed August 28, 2013.

Socioeconomic Variables

Satellite photos taken of the European continent at night show a blue curve of light that stretches from Manchester, Britain, through the Rhineland down to northern Italy. French journalists labeled this area the *blue banana* ("banane bleue"). It has the largest concentration of big cities worldwide, the densest commercial traffic, and the highest production capacity per square kilometer.[25] The region offers tremendous market opportunities to marketers of luxury goods (e.g., LVMH, BMW), high-end services (e.g., resorts, real estate, mutual funds), and leisure-activity-related goods.

Consumption patterns for many goods and services are largely driven by the consumer wealth or the country's level of economic development in general. Consumers from countries at the same stage of economic development often show similar needs in terms of the per capita amount and types of goods they desire. Not surprisingly, many good marketers view per capita income or a comparable measure as one of the key criteria in grouping international markets. The usual caveats in using per-capita income as an economic development indicator also apply when this measure is used for country segmentation:[26]

- *Monetization of transactions within a country*. To compare measures such as per capita GNP across countries, figures based on a local currency need to be translated into a common currency (e.g., the U.S. dollar or the euro). However, official exchange rates seldom reflect the true buying power of a currency. As a result, income figures based on GNP or GDP do not really tell you how much a household in a given country is able to buy.

- *Gray and black sectors of the economy*. National income figures only record transactions that arise in the legitimate sector of a country's economy. Many countries have a sizable gray sector, consisting of largely untaxed (or under-taxed) exchanges that often involve barter transactions. In cities in the developing world, many professors make ends meet by driving a taxi. In exchange for a dental checkup, a television repairman might fix the dentist's television set. Many communities also thrive on a substantial black sector, involving transactions that are outright illegal. Examples of such activities include the drug trade, smuggling, racketeering, gambling, and prostitution.

- *Income disparities*. Quantities such as the per capita GNP only tell part of the story. Such measures are misleading in countries with wide income inequalities such as Bolivia where the richest 10 percent of the population gets 47 percent share of the country's income, while the poorest 10 percent gets a mere 0.3 percent.[27]

To protect against these shortcomings of standard "per capita income" segmentation exercises, marketers can employ other metrics to group consumers in terms of their buying power.[28] One alternative is to use the PPP (purchasing power parity) as a criterion. PPP reflects how much a household in each country has to spend (in U.S. dollars equivalent) to buy a standard basket of goods. PPP estimates can be found in the *World Bank Atlas* published annually by the World Bank and in the *CIA World Factbook* (https://www.cia.gov/library/publications/the-world-factbook/).

Another alternative to analyze buying power in a set of countries is via a **socioeconomic strata (SES) analysis**. For instance, Strategy Research Corporation applied an SES-analysis for Latin American households using measures like the number of consumer durables in the household, education level, and so on. Each country was stratified into five socioeconomic segments using a

---

[25]http://en.wikipedia.org/wiki/Blue_Banana, accessed on August 28, 2013

[26]Vern Terpstra and Kenneth David, *The Cultural Environment of International Business* (Cincinnati, OH: South-Western Publishing Co., 1991).

[27]https://www.cia.gov/library/publications/the-world-factbook/, accessed January 26, 2009.

[28]Chip Walker, "The Global Middle Class," *American Demographics* (September 1995): 40–46.

Exhibit 7-5   Benefit Segments of Toothpaste Market in the United States, China, and Mexico

	Value Share USA 2004	% Change Share in USA vs. 2000	Value Share China 2004	% Change Share in China vs. 2000	Value Share Mexico 2004	% Change Share in Mexico vs. 2000
Family Anti-Cavity	18.3%	−22.7	28.5%	−29.8	64.8%	−1.9
Kids Anti-Cavity	3.7	−0.1	0.6	+0.5	1.2	+0.1
Premium Multi-Benefit	18.8	+1.5	2.2	−1.1	12.1	+1.5
Sensitivity Relief	7.7	+1.0	0.4	−8.5	3.3	−0.9
Herbal/Natural	1.9	+1.9	15.8	+10.1	2.0	+2.0
TOTAL THERAPEUTIC	53.4	−19.3	82.9	−6.4	87.3	+2.6
Whitening	30.3	+16.4	8.9	+3.8	2.7	−2.2
Freshening	16.3	+2.9	8.2	+2.6	10.0	−0.4
TOTAL COSMETIC	46.4	+19.3	17.1	+6.4	12.7	−2.6
TOTAL MARKET	100.0		100.0		100.0	

Source: Compiled from Exhibits 2B, 7A, and 14 in John A. Quelch and Jacquie Labatt-Randle, "Colgate Max Fresh: Global Brand Roll-Out," Harvard Business School Case Study, 9-508-009, 2007.

letter code: upper class (A), middle-to-upper class (B), middle-class (C), lower class (D), and poverty level (E).

Other schemes broaden the notion of a country's level of development by going beyond standard of living measures. One popular classification schema is based on the Human Development Index (HDI), which is released every year by the United Nations (see http://hdr.undp.org/en/). It covers over 180 UN member countries and territories. HDI widens the notion of economic development by looking at a country's achievements in three areas: life expectancy at birth (a long and healthy life), knowledge (e.g., adult literacy), and a decent standard of living (per capita in PPP). The highest scorers in the 2011 report were Norway (HDI of 0.943), Australia (0.929), and the Netherlands (0.91). At the bottom of the list were Burundi (0.316), Niger (0.295), and Congo (0.286).[29]

Behavior-Based Segmentation

As with domestic marketing, segments can also be formed based on behavioral response variables. Behavioral segmentation criteria include degree of brand/supplier loyalty, usage rate (based on per-capita consumption), product penetration (that is, the percentage of the target market that uses the product or the brand), and benefits sought after. Just as in domestic marketing, benefit segmentation is often used in global marketing for product positioning, product design, or product adaptation purposes. While benefit segments overlap different countries, their relative size often differs in each market. **Exhibit 7-5** shows the proportionate size and growth rate of benefit segments in the toothpaste category in three countries: the United States, Mexico, and China.

Lifestyle and Values

Marketers can group consumers according to their lifestyle (i.e., their attitudes, opinions, and core values). Lifestyle segmentation relates to how people live, how they spend their money, and how they allocate their time across various activities (e.g., leisure, shopping). Lifestyle (psychographic) segmentation is especially popular in advertising circles. Many lifestyle segmentation schemes

---

[29]In fact, all of the bottom-ten HDI countries were sub-Saharan African.

tend to be very general and not related to a specific product category. Obviously, a classification schema derived for a specific product or service area is much more relevant for marketing managers. Distinctions can also be made between whether a given typology was prepared for a specific country or a given region.

Each year Hakuhodo, one of Japan's largest advertising agencies, conducts its so-called Global HABIT survey in cities around the world as part of its effort to gain new consumer insights. One part of the study identified seven lifestyle segments, in varying proportions, worldwide. The seven segments—ranked in order of their global size—include:[30]

1. *The Invisibles* are not ambitious and have few complaints. They get on with life and accept the world as it is. They are not driven to seek wealth; like to be able to save; prefer established styles and good, basic apparel (29%). This is a large cluster in every city: 30% or more in Hong Kong, Singapore, Taipei, New York, and Frankfurt.

2. *The My Family, My World (18.7%).* Having a happy family is top priority for these people. They are careful in all aspects of life; they tend to be smart price-conscious shoppers; they prefer products from companies that take environmental issues seriously. This cluster is large in Manila, Hong Kong, Singapore, and Tokyo.

3. *Hungry Climbers (15.3%).* Members of this segment are eager to advance and to be envied by others. They are keen for signs of visible affluence; they fear falling behind and want to enjoy life; they enjoy the stimulation of new trendy things; want to be rich; they see money as a symbol of success; their income and education is relatively low; they worry about how others see them; their concern for others is low. This segment is relatively large in Ho Chi Minh City, Moscow, Shanghai, and Frankfurt.

4. *The My Life, My Way (14.9%).* These people have personal enjoyment, with their own unique taste and style, as their number one priority. They want to live as they like; they want to enjoy a fun and interesting life; they are less interested in success at work. This cluster is large in Seoul, Mumbai, and São Paulo.

5. *Doing Well, Doing Good (10.6%).* They want to help those who are weak or in trouble. They like to contribute to society as well as achieve personal success; they seek a good balance in their lives; they enjoy meeting new people; they prefer work that allows self-expression; quality of life is important to them; they are ethical shoppers who are concerned about the countries in which the products they buy are made. This segment is fairly large in New York, Singapore, and Taipei.

6. *Stable Roots (7.5%).* This segment's members stress traditional values; they want to lead stable, healthy lives; cherish relationships with those around them; their ideal is a traditional big family where men go out to work and women stay at home; they want to achieve both social and economic success. This cluster is large in Jakarta (40%), Mumbai, and São Paulo.

7. *First to Crave (4%).* People belonging to this segment are sensitive to what others think about them. They want to succeed and to enjoy life; they are very career-oriented; they enjoy the stimulation of new, trendy things; they are risk takers for whom success matters more than stability. Overall this is the smallest segment; it is sizeable in Kuala Lumpur, Frankfurt, and Moscow.

Exhibit 7-6 shows the cluster distributions for six of the cities where the study was done. Lifestyle and value segmentation studies such as Hakuhodo's Global HABIT survey can help managers in deciding how far they should go with localizing their marketing communication strategies. For instance, members of both the "Doing Well, Doing Good" and the "My Family,

---

[30]Hakuhodo, *Seven Global Clusters. Asian Perspectives.* Global HABIT Survey.

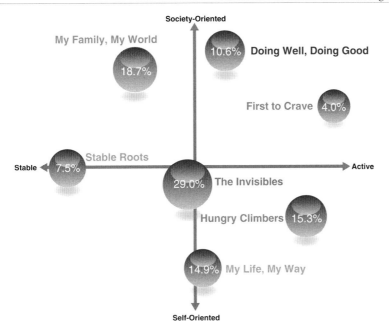

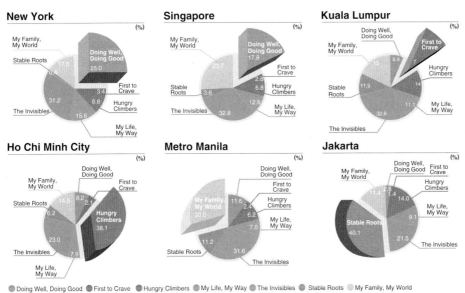

Exhibit 7-6 Hakuhodo Lifestyle Segmentation: Seven Global Clusters

Source: Hakuhodo, Global HABIT Survey. Copyright © Hakuhodo. All rights reserved.

My World" segments are society-oriented. They worry about social and environmental issues and want to help people in need. However, "society" has a different meaning for the two clusters. For members of the "My Family, My World" segment, "society" has a relatively local meaning: their relatives, immediate neighborhood, local community. People belonging to the "Doing Well, Doing Good" cluster, on the other hand, have a broader sense of society: they are more cosmopolitan and are also worried about global environmental and humanitarian concerns. Therefore, a communication strategy that targets these groups by focusing on society-oriented issues must be tweaked depending on which of these two segments is being pursued.

Lifestyle segmentation has been applied for the positioning of new brands, repositioning of existing ones, identifying new product opportunities, and developing brand personalities.[31] Practitioners and academics alike have raised major concerns about the use of lifestyle segmentation:

- Values are too general to relate to consumption patterns or brand choice behavior within a specific product category. As a result, lifestyle segmentation is not very useful as a tool to make predictions about consumers' buying responsiveness. Obviously, this criticism only applies to the general value schemes.

- Value-based segmentation schemes are not always "actionable." Remember that one of the requirements for effective segmentation is actionability. Lifestyle groupings do not offer much guidance in terms of what marketing actions should be taken. Demographic segmentation can easily assist the manager in deciding which type of gender- or age-group-based media outlets to use for a particular communication campaign. With a value-based segmentation schema, the guidance in terms of what marketing actions to pursue is usually much less clear (e.g., what magazines or TV programs would be popular with introverts or "hungry climbers"?). Also, many of the typologies have too many different types to be useful for practical purposes.

- Value segments are not stable because values typically change over time.

- Their international applicability is quite limited because lifestyles, even within the same region, often vary from country to country.[32]

Aside from the criteria discussed here, many other dimensions could form the basis for segmentation. The proper criteria largely depend on the nature of the product and the objectives of the segmentation exercise.

International Positioning Strategies

Segmenting international markets is only part of the game. Once the multinational company has segmented its foreign markets, the firm needs to decide which target markets to pursue and what positioning strategy to use to appeal to the chosen segments. Some marketing scholars refer to positioning as the fifth P in the marketing mix in addition to product, price, promotion, and place. Developing a positioning theme involves the quest for a unique selling proposition (USP). In the global marketing scene, the positioning question boils down to a battle for the mind of your target customers, located not only within a certain country but also in some cases across the globe. The global positioning statement for AXA, the French insurance company, is shown in **Exhibit 7-7**. The formulation of a positioning strategy—be it local or global—moves along a sequence of steps:

1. Identify a relevant set of competing products or brands. What is the competitive frame?

2. Determine current perceptions held by consumers about your product/brand and the competition.

3. Brainstorm to generate possible positioning themes.

4. Screen the positioning alternatives and select the most appealing one.

5. Develop a marketing mix strategy that will implement the chosen positioning strategy.

---

[31]Marieke de Mooij, *Advertising Worldwide*, 2nd ed. (Prentice Hall, 1994).
[32]Peter Sampson, "People Are People the World Over: The Case for Psychological Market Segmentation," *Marketing and Research Today* (November 1992): 236–44.

Exhibit 7-7   Axa's Brand Positioning

AXA's ambition is to become the preferred company in the industry. To achieve this we work toward a global vision of 'redefining standards.'
AXA's brand positioning is "The financial protection company that continuously proves it is worth trusting."
AXA has outlined three attitudes to deliver trust to its customers:

1. Available—we are there when you need us and we listen to you, truly.
2. Reliable—we say what we do and do what we say, we deliver and keep you informed, so you can trust us.
3. Attentive—we treat you with empathy and consideration, look after your best interests and reward your loyalty.

Source: http://www.axa.co.uk/about-us/brand, accessed August 8, 2012.

6. Over time, monitor the effectiveness of your positioning strategy. If it is not working, check whether poor results are due to bad execution or the wrong strategy.

Global Perspective 7-1 discusses the rebranding process that AXA undertook that led to the new "redefining/standards" positioning theme.

Global Perspective 7-1

Repositioning AXA Insurance—"Redefining/Standards"

In 2005, AXA, the French insurer, had become a world market leader in the insurance industry. Henri de Castries, the group's CEO, aspired to turn AXA into the preferred choice among the group's various stakeholders (customers, employees, commercial partners) in its fields of insurance and asset management. AXA's challenge was how to differentiate itself from its key competitors. Up to that point, AXA's slogan had been "Be Life Confident." However, this message had lost its appeal among customers and employees alike. In 2007, customers perceived the brand as cold; employees did not know how to help customers to become "life confident."

To tackle the repositioning challenge, the company set up the multidisciplinary Brand Spirit taskforce. This taskforce gathered and then analyzed opinions from executives, customers, and employees. For instance, AXA employees worldwide were asked to share concerns and offer new ideas via an online rebranding forum. Fifty-five thousand employees worldwide participated in the forum.

In early 2008, the taskforce concluded that AXA could win customers' trust through three core attribute: being "available," "attentive," and "reliable" (see Exhibit 7-7). The

taskforce also proposed a new slogan: "redefining/standards" for the group. To ensure that the three core attributes were not just abstract concepts, the taskforce formulated customer-facing behaviors backed up by action plans and monitoring tools that would help AXA staff to implement these values in customer encounters. For example, employees were told what being available or attentive meant in practice when dealing with customers or colleagues.

The task force also suggested making the new brand motto flexible so that it could easily be adapted to different business needs. As a result, the new slogan "redefining/standards" could be refashioned as "redefining/pensions" or "redefining/car insurance" while still maintaining the underlying theme.

While the success of the rebranding strategy is difficult to assess, some indicators signaled that it was effective. Customer satisfaction measures improved in the wake of the campaign; AXA was also the highest-ranked insurance brand in the 2009 and 2010 Interbrand rankings.

Source: Stefan Michel, "Define and Implement a New Brand," *Financial Times*, March 10, 2011.

Exhibit 7-8 Global
Positioning and
Segmentation
Strategies

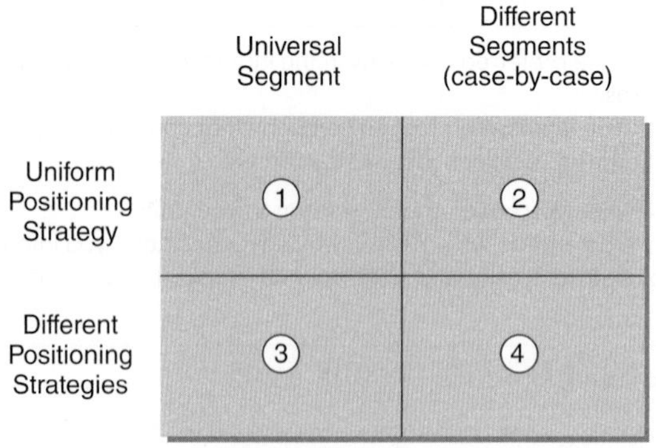

Uniform versus Localized Positioning Strategies

Several global brands such as Nokia ("Connecting people") and Kit Kat ("Have a Kit Kat break") have followed **uniform positioning** themes that are consistent worldwide. Other brands have localized their positioning themes. For global marketers, a key question is to what degree a uniform positioning strategy can be used. Clearly, one key driver here is the target market to be pursued. Roughly speaking, MNCs have two choices: target a universal segment across countries or pursue different segments in the different markets. When focusing on a uniform segment, management needs to decide whether to use the same positioning worldwide or positioning themes that are tailored to individual markets. If the firm decides to opt for different segments on a country-by-country basis, the norm is to also customize the positioning appeals. Other factors that could lead toward localized positioning strategies include local regulations/laws, perceptions about the brand created in the past in the host country, product life cycle differences, local competition, and environmental differences. Mondelez's Halls cough drop brand is an example of localized positioning due to different environmental conditions. In colder climates, Halls is sold as a cold relief product; in hotter or drier countries (e.g., Brazil, Philippines, Thailand) it is pitched as refreshing candy.[33] **Exhibit 7-8** gives an overview of the different strategic options.

When target customers are very similar worldwide, sharing common core values and showing similar buying patterns, a uniform positioning strategy will probably work. By adopting a common positioning theme, the company can project a shared, consistent brand or corporate image worldwide. The need to have a consistent image is especially urgent for brands that have worldwide exposure and visibility. In 2001 Samsung, the leading South Korean consumer electronics conglomerate, announced its intent to obtain the world number-one position in all its main product markets by 2005. To achieve this goal, it positioned its brand as being at the leading edge of digital technology, using an aggressive advertising campaign and developing a whole range of nifty, digital products (e.g., interactive televisions, DVD players, third-generation mobile phones and later also smartphones).[34] Having the same positioning theme also enables the firm to make use of global media. Samsung, for instance, sponsors highly visible, global sports events such as the Summer Olympics and sports teams such as Chelsea FC, a top-tier English soccer team.

Many firms position a brand that is *mainstream* in its home market as a premium brand in their overseas markets, thereby targeting a narrower segment that is willing to pay a premium for imports. By moving upscale in the host country, the company can support the higher costs of doing business there. A case in point is Pizza Hut. In the United States, Pizza Hut is a mass-market

---

[33]http://www.kraftfoodscompany.com/Brands/largest-brands/brands-H/Pages/halls.aspx.
[34]"Koreans Aim to Create a Sharp Image," *Financial Times*, December 28, 2001, p. 14.

fast-food brand. In China and other overseas markets, however, Pizza Hut has found a new life as a fashionable casual-dining restaurant. Pizza Hut was the first restaurant chain to introduce pizza in China in 1990.[35] Yum! China, the owner of Pizza Hut, now has more than 500 restaurants in China and is still growing.[36] Likewise, Burberry's, the British clothing brand, has lost some of its cachet in Britain especially after it became the outfit of choice for soccer hooligans and "chavs."[37] Yet, in spite of its woes in the home market, Burberry's has been able to maintain an upscale image in Asia. Other examples of brands that are mainstream in their home market but have a premium image in the international marketplace include Heineken, Levi's, and Budweiser. This strategy is especially effective in product categories where the local brands already are very well entrenched (like beer in most countries) and imported brands have a potential to leverage the cachet of being "imported." Local brands usually enjoy a pioneering advantage by the fact of being the first one in the market. Therefore, instead of competing head-on with the local competition, foreign brands (despite the fact that they are a mainstream brand in their home market) are mostly better off by targeting the upscale segment. Though smaller in numbers, this segment is willing to pay a substantial premium price. Note that such positioning strategies are not always successful. Gap, the U.S. casual clothing brand, failed to reinvent itself as a premium brand in Germany. Consumers' image of the brand may also deteriorate over time. A good example is the experience of General Motors China. Initially, GM China was pretty successful in positioning the Buick brand as a prestigious car in China even though the car marque had a dismal reputation in the United States. However, lately, Buick's esteem has dropped in the mind of Chinese car buyers.

While a uniform positioning theme may be desirable, it is often very hard to come up with a good positioning theme that appeals in various markets. Universal themes often run the risk of being bland and not very inspired. Very rarely do positioning themes "travel." Instead, management usually modifies or localizes them. Appeals that work in one culture do not necessarily work in others. Differences in cultural characteristics, buying power, competitive climate, and the product life cycle stage force firms to tailor their positioning platform. Land Rover is an example of a brand where a global positioning strategy is hard to implement.[38] One of the core brand values that Land Rover has cultivated over the years in Europe is "authenticity." This core value is based on Land Rover's heritage of fifty years as a 4×4 brand in Europe. The North American market, which Land Rover only entered in the 1980s, presents a different picture. There, Jeep, the Chrysler 4×4 brand, is perceived as the authentic, original four-wheel drive vehicle. Hence, Land Rover would have a formidable task creating the same image of "authenticity" in North America as it successfully did in Europe.

Universal Positioning Appeals

Universal positioning appeals are positioning themes that appeal to consumers anywhere in the world, regardless of their cultural background. Remember that positioning themes can be developed at different levels:

- Specific product features/attributes

- Product benefits (rational or emotional), solutions for problems

- User category

---

[35]"Brands: Moving Overseas to Move Upmarket," http://www.businessweek.com, accessed October 31, 2008.

[36]http://yum.com/brands/china.asp.

[37]"Chavs" refers to an underclass of British society known for its aggressive and vulgar behavior, similar to "white trash" in the United States; http://en.wikipedia.org/wiki/Chav, accessed October 31, 2008. Note that their Burberry's gear is usually counterfeit.

[38]Nick Bull and Martin Oxley, "The search for focus—brand values across Europe," *Marketing and Research Today* (November 1996): 239–247.

- User application

- Heritage

- Lifestyle

Products that offer benefits or features that are universally important would meet the criterion of a universal benefit/feature positioning appeal. In business-to-business markets, where buying behavior is often somewhat less culture-bound than for consumer goods, this is often true. Thus, a promise of superior quality, performance, or productivity for industrial products is one example of a positioning pitch with a universal ring. Benefit- or feature-based positioning can be universal for consumer goods when the core benefit is common worldwide: superior quality or performance appeals for durables like television sets (picture quality), washing machines (cleaning performance), and so forth. However, for products where buying motivations are very culture-bound (for instance, most food and beverage products), coming up with a universal benefit- or feature-related appeal is a much harder task.

Another positioning theme that could be universal is global leadership. Being the most popular brand in the category can be alluring to consumers, especially when the leadership position is worldwide. One good example is Kraft's Oreo cookie brand which is positioned in most countries as "the world's favorite cookie." However, in the United States, Oreo these days is pitched as "milk's favorite cookie."

A special case where universal positioning clearly makes sense is the "global citizen" theme often used with corporate image strategies. Here the positioning strategy stresses a global leadership and/or global presence benefit. This strategy is often successfully used in industries where having a global presence is a major plus (e.g., credit cards, banking, insurance, telecommunications). **Global Perspective 7-2** discusses Swiss banking firm UBS's universal positioning "You and Us" campaign.

Global Perspective 7-2

UBS—The Concept of "Two-Ness"

The wealth management group UBS was formed in 1998 by the merger of two major Swiss banks. It has expanded globally often through acquisitions (e.g., Paine Webber and Warburg in the United States) and now maintains a presence in over fifty countries. Brands that grow by acquiring existing firms face the task of establishing a clear brand identity both internally (employees) and externally (customers). In February 2004, UBS set out to establish a single consistent brand identity across all markets. This led to the "You and Us" advertising campaign. The campaign has two major targets: the high net-worth individual and corporate customers. The focus is the intimacy and strength of UBS's client relationships, backed by the bank's resources. Bernhard Eggli, head of brand management at UBS, noted:

"What we found during research is that there's a lot of similarity in terms of the expectations that our client segments have for their preferred financial services provider, which made it possible for us to move to a single brand. The underlying brand promise works across the globe; the challenge is to find the right execution."

A key task to deliver the universal positioning for the campaign was finding a tagline with global appeal that conveyed UBS's identity. After conducting market research, UBS decided to leave the You and Us tagline in English. "In the attempt to translate the tagline in English, what we have found is that you are losing the simplicity and, to a certain extent, the charm of the tagline," observed Eggli. To underscore the positioning theme, the campaign used images of "two-ness"—two chairs, two cups of coffee, two people, and so on. These images symbolized the intimate relationship between the client and the UBS advisor. To cast actors for the campaign, people were chosen in pairs rather than individually. Background images—skyscrapers, offices—were chosen to reinforce the message that a UBS advisor has the support of a large, powerful institution that can mobilize global resource on behalf of the customer.

Source: http://www.brandchannel.com/features_effect.asp?pf_id=273.

When positioning the product to a specific user category, a uniform approach will often succeed when the user-group shares common characteristics. Avon's "Let's Talk" campaign attests to this rule. The campaign, launched in 26 countries in 2000, was designed to reflect Avon's corporate mission of being a "company for women." To project this positioning, the global campaign highlighted Avon's wide range of beauty products and the company's unique network of 2.8 million sales reps, which facilitates one-on-one customer relationships.[39] Likewise, the global positioning used by Kotex, Kimberly-Clark's feminine protection pad brand, turned out to be highly effective in leveraging a common need among the global women segment. Kotex was positioned as the brand "that is designed to fit and feel better for your body, to help you feel better, more like yourself."[40] Examples where uniform positioning is likely to be futile are appeals that center on the "liberated women" group (e.g., Virginia Slims cigarettes: "You've come a long way, baby"), which is still a very culture-bound phenomenon.

Emotional appeals (e.g., lifestyle positioning) are usually difficult to translate into a universal theme. Values tend to be very culture bound. The trick is to come up with an emotional appeal that has universal characteristics and—at the same time—does not sound dull. One lifestyle survey found that "protecting the family" was seen as a top value in twenty-two countries, including the United States.[41] Therefore, appeals based on family values might be prospective candidates.

Global, Foreign, and Local Consumer Culture Positioning[42]

Brand managers can position their brand as symbolic of a global consumer culture, a "foreign" culture, or a local culture. The first strategy can be described as **global consumer culture positioning (GCCP)**. This strategy tries to project the brand as a symbol of a given global consumer culture. Thereby, buying the brand reinforces the consumer's feeling of being part of a global segment. It also fosters the buyer's self-image as being cosmopolitan, modern, and knowledgeable. Examples of brands that successfully use this strategy are Sony ("My First Sony") and Nike ("Just Do It").

At the other extreme is the **local consumer culture positioning (LCCP)** strategy. Despite the fact that the brand may be global, it is portrayed as an intrinsic part of the local culture. It is depicted as being consumed by local people, and, if applicable, manufactured by locals using local supplies or ingredients. Such brands have achieved a **multi-local status**. A good example

---

[39]"Avon 'Talks' Globally to Women," *Ad Age Global* (October 2001): 43.

[40]"Kotex Wins a Game of Catch-Up," *Ad Age Global* (October 2001): 43.

[41]Tom Miller, "Global segments from 'Strivers' to 'Creatives,'" *Marketing News,* July 20, 1998, p. 11.

[42]Based on Dana L. Alden, Jan-Benedict E.M. Steenkamp, and Rajeev Batra, "Brand Positioning through Advertising in Asia, North America, and Europe: The Role of Global Consumer Culture," *Journal of Marketing* 63 (January 1999):75–87.

is Singer, the maker of sewing machines. Singer was seen as German in Germany, British in the U.K., and American in the United States. In fact, during World War II, German aviators avoided bombing Singer's European factories thinking they were German-owned.[43] When Mercedes launched its mid-price E-class model in Japan, its ad campaign used Japanese scenery and images. The local imagery was underscored with the tagline: "Mercedes and a beautiful country."[44]

A third strategy is **foreign consumer culture positioning (FCCP)**. Here, the goal is to build up a brand mystique around a specific foreign culture, usually one that has highly positive connotations for the product (e.g., Switzerland for watches, Germany for household appliances). In China U.S. jeans maker Lee targets the children of rich Chinese families and young and upcoming executives. In the past, Lee was perceived as a Chinese company based in the United States (Li is a very common family name in China). At the same time, a market research study showed that the Chinese associate jeans with cowboys, the Wild West, freedom, and passion. As a result, the company decided to position Lee jeans as a premium-priced brand with an American heritage. Lee's U.S. roots are highlighted in print materials with the line: "Founded Kansas, USA, 1889."[45] Other American brands such as Nike, Timberland, Cadillac, and Budweiser have been able to position themselves very strongly in their foreign markets as authentic pieces of Americana.

Which positioning strategy is most suitable depends on several factors. One important determinant is obviously your target market. One important element here is the target customers' general **attitudes toward global products (AGP)** and their **attitudes toward local products (ALP)** (e.g., preferring foods/entertainment that are popular around the world versus enjoying your own country's traditional foods/local entertainment). GCC positioning should appeal to consumers high on AGP whereas LCC positioning is more likely to be successful in countries where most consumers are high on ALP.[46] Another driver is the product category. Products that satisfy universal needs and are used in a similar manner worldwide lend themselves more to a GCCP-type approach. High-tech consumer brands (e.g., Siemens, Nokia, Sony) that symbolize modernism and internationalism would qualify. A third factor is the positioning approach used by the local competition. If every player in the local market is using a GCCP strategy, you might be able to break more easily through the clutter by going for an LCCP strategy (or vice versa). A final factor is the level of economic development. In emerging markets that are still in an early stage of economic development, a GCCP approach might be more beneficial than LCCP. In these markets, a brand with a global cachet enhances the owner's self-image and status.

Sometimes local brands fight it out with global brands by using a GCCP or FCCP strategy. For instance, Brand, a local Dutch beer, used a U.S. setting and English language in its advertising. Some brands also use a hybrid approach, by combining ingredients of each of the three strategies. A good example of this approach is the positioning of HSBC, Europe's largest bank, as the "world's local bank." McDonald's is portrayed as a global, cosmopolitan fast-food brand (GCCP) but also as an authentic piece of Americana (FCCP). At the same time, in many countries, McDonald's often highlights its local roots, stressing the fact that it provides local jobs, uses local ingredients, and so forth (LCCP). The fast-food chain localizes its menu, selling salmon sandwiches in Norway, McTeriyaki burgers in Japan, McShawarma and McKebab in Israel, Samurai Pork burgers in Thailand, and so forth.

---

[43]http://www.brandchannel.com/features_effect.asp?pf_id=261.

[44]"Mercedes-Benz Japan drifts down to earth alongside economy," *Ad Age International* (October 1997): 36.

[45]"Lee Plays up US Roots to Target China's Elite," *Media*, May 17, 2002, p. 10.

[46]Jan-Benedict E.M. Steenkamp and Martijn G. de Jong, "A Global Investigation into the Constellation of Consumer Attitudes toward Global and Local Products," *Journal of Marketing* 74 (November 2010): 18–40.

SUMMARY

A common theme in many writings on global marketing is the growing convergence of consumer needs.[47] Colorful phrases have been used to describe this phenomenon, such as "global village," "global mall," and "crystallization of the world as a single place," just to mention a few. This phenomenon of increasing globalization is especially visible for many upscale consumer goods and a variety of business-to-business goods and services that are bought by multinational customers. One director of a global marketing research firm even went so far as to state that "marketers make too much of cultural differences."[48] She advocated her claim with two reasons. First, technology has given consumers worldwide the same reference points. People see the same TV ads, share similar life experiences, and are exposed to the same products and services. Second, technology has also given us common aspirations. According to this school of thought, cultures do differ, but these differences do not have any meaningful impact on people's buying behavior.

In the other camp are people like Nicholas Trivisonno, the former CEO of Nielsen, who noted: "There is no global consumer. Each country and the consumer in each country has different attitudes and different behaviors, tastes, spending patterns."[49]

The truth of the matter is somewhere in between these two extreme opinions. Without proper segmentation of your international markets, it is hard to establish whether the "global consumer" segment is myth or reality.

Global marketers have a continuum of choices to segment their customer base. At one end of the spectrum, the firm might pursue a "universal" segment. Essentially the same product is offered, using a common positioning theme. Most likely there are a few, mostly minor, adaptations of the marketing mix program to recognize cross-border differences. At the other end, the firm might consider treating individual countries on a case-by-case basis. In some circumstances, marketers might be able to offer the same product in each country, provided that the positioning is customized. However, typically, the product will need to be modified or designed for each country separately. In between these two extremes, there are bound to be many other possibilities.

By the same token, your positioning strategy can take different directions. Going after a uniform segment, you can adopt a universal positioning theme or themes that are custom-made. Universal appeals do have benefits. Companies such as UBS, Intel, and Visa have been able to successfully project a uniform, consistent global image. Universal positioning allows the firm to develop a common communication strategy using global or pan-regional media channels. Unfortunately, coming up with a universal message that is appealing often proves to be a herculean task.

[47]Theodore Levitt, "The Globalization of Markets," *Harvard Business Review* 61 (May–June 1983): 92–102.

[48]Luanne Flikkema, "Global marketing's myth: Differences don't matter," *Marketing News*, July 20, 1998, p. 4.

[49]"The global consumer myth," *Financial Times*, April 23, 1991, p. 21.

QUESTIONS

1. What are the major issues in using per capita GDP or GNP as a country segmentation criterion?

2. Sometimes local brands use a global consumer culture positioning approach. Explain.

3. Sergio Marchionne, the CEO of Fiat, describes the company as "Italian based but not an Italian company." In the era of global business, does a company or a brand's national identity still matter? Why or why not?

4. In a host of emerging markets (e.g., India, Brazil, Thailand), more than half of the population is under 25 years old. One marketer observes: "teenagers are teenagers everywhere and they tend to emulate U.S. teenagers" (*Advertising Age International*, October 17, 1994, p. I-15). Is there a global teenager segment? Do teenagers in, say, Beijing really tend to emulate L.A. teenagers? Discuss.

5. Browse through a recent issue of *The Economist*. As you may know, *The Economist* has regional editions. Most of the ads target an international audience (regional or global). Pick four ads and carefully examine each one of them. Who is being targeted in each print ad? What sort of positioning is being used?

Appendix

In this appendix we give an overview of segmentation tools that can be used to do a country segmentation. A huge variety of segmentation methodologies have been developed in the marketing literature. Many of these techniques are quite sophisticated. We will just give you the flavor of two of the most popular tools without going through all the technical nitty-gritty.

When only one segmentation variable is used, classifying countries in distinct groups is quite straightforward. You could simply compute the mean (or median) and split countries into two groups based on the value (above or below) on the criterion variable compared to the mean (or median). When more than two groups need to be formed, one can use other quantiles. Things become a bit more complicated when you plan to use multiple country segmentation variables. Typically, the goal of market segmentation is to relate, in some manner, a battery of descriptive variables about the countries to one or more behavioral response variables:

$$Response = F(Descriptor_1, Descriptor_2, Descriptor_3, \ldots)$$

For instance, the response variable might be the per capita consumption of a given product. The descriptor variables could be the stage in the product life cycle, per capita GNP, literacy level, and so on. We now describe two methods that can help you in achieving this goal: cluster analysis and regression.

Cluster Analysis

Cluster analysis is an umbrella term that embraces a collection of statistical procedures for dividing objects into groups (clusters). The grouping is done in such a manner that members belonging to the same group are very similar to one another but quite distinct from members of other groups.

Suppose information was collected for a set of countries on two variables, X and Y. The countries are plotted in **Exhibit 7-9**. Each dot corresponds to a country. In this case, the clusters are quite obvious. Just by eyeballing the graph, you can distinguish two clear-cut clusters, namely "Cluster 1" and "Cluster 2." Unfortunately, in real-world applications, clustering is seldom so easy. Consider **Exhibit 7-10**. This exhibit plots the values of chocolate volume growth rate and market concentration[50] in eight countries. For this example, it is far less obvious how many clusters there are, let alone how they are composed. In addition, most country segmentations involve many more than two criteria.

Luckily there are many statistical algorithms available that will do the job for you. The basic notion is to group countries together that are "similar" in value for the segmentation bases of interest.

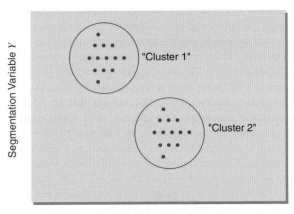

Exhibit 7-9   Principles of Cluster Analysis

Similarity measures come under many guises. The most popular way is to use some type of distance measure:

$$Distance_{country\ A\ vs.\ B} = (X_{country\ A} - X_{country\ B})^2 + (Y_{country\ A} - Y_{country\ B})^2$$

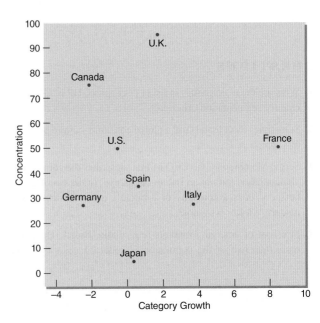

Exhibit 7-10   Plot of Concentration versus Category Growth Chocolate Market

---

[50]Measured via the combined market shares of the three largest competitors—Cadbury, Mars, and Nestlé.

TWO-CLUSTER SOLUTION

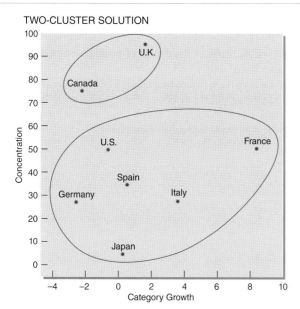

THREE-CLUSTER SOLUTION

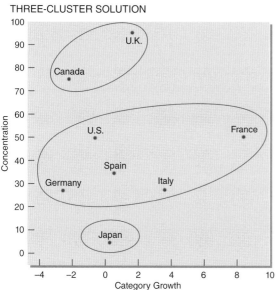

Exhibit 7-11   Cluster Analysis

where X and Y are the segmentation variables. These distances[51] would be computed for each pair of countries in the set. The clustering algorithm takes these distances and uses them as inputs to generate the desired number of country groupings. Most "canned" statistical software packages (e.g., SAS, SPPS-X) have at least one procedure that allows you to run a cluster analysis. **Exhibit 7-11** provides the two- and three-cluster solutions for the chocolate market example.

Regression.   Alternatively, you might consider using regression analysis to classify countries. In regression, one assumes that there exists a relationship between a response variable, Y, and one or more so-called predictor variables, X_1, X_2 and so on:

$$Y = a + b_1 X_1 + b_2 X_2 + b_3 X_3 + \ldots$$

The first term, a, is the intercept. It corresponds to the predicted value of Y when all the Xs are equal to 0. The other parameters, the bs, are the slope coefficients. For example, b_1 tells you what the predicted change in Y will be for a unit change in X_1.

In our context, the dependent variable, Y, would be a behavioral response variable (e.g., per capita consumption), and the predictor variables would be a collection of country characteristics that are presumed to be related to the response measure. For given values of the parameters, you can compute the predicted Y-values, Y. Very seldom, these predicted values will match the observed Ys. The goal of regression is to find estimates for the intercept, a, and the slope coefficients, the bs, that provide the "best" fit by minimizing the prediction errors, Y – Y, between the predicted and observed values of Y. The most common regression procedure, ordinary least squares (OLS), minimizes the sum of the squared differences of these prediction errors.

For each of the parameter estimates, the regression analysis will also produce a standard error. Dividing the parameter estimate by the standard error yields the t-ratio. This ratio tells you whether or not the predictor variable has a "significant" (statistically speaking) relationship with the dependent variable. As a rule of thumb, a t-ratio (in absolute value) larger than 2.0 would indicate a significant effect of the predictor variable on the response variable. The overall goodness of fit is captured via the R^2-statistic. The higher the R^2 value, the better the ability of your regression model to predict your data.

To illustrate the use of regression analysis as a segmentation tool, let us look at a numerical example. Consider a microwave oven maker who wants to explore market opportunities in the European market. Data were collected for several European countries on the penetration of microwave ovens (as percentage of households owning a microwave). Data were also gathered on three potential segmentation variables: income (per capita GDP), participation of women in the labor force, and per capita consumption of frozen foods.[52] Using these data as inputs, the following results were obtained (t-ratios between parentheses):

MICROWAVE OWNERSHIP =

−76.7 − 0.5 FROZEN FOOD + 2.7 WOMEN − 0.03 PER CAP GDP

(−2.2) (−1.3)   (2.9)   (−0.04)

$R^2 = 0.52$

---

[51]Strictly speaking, these are "squared" distances.

[52]The data for this example were collected from the *European Marketing Data and Statistics 1992*, London: Euromonitor.

Note that, apparently, the only meaningful segmentation base is the participation of women in the labor force: microwave ownership increases with the proportion of women in the labor force. Because the microwave is a timesaving appliance, this result intuitively makes sense. The other variables appear to have (statistically speaking) not much of an impact on the adoption of microwave ovens. Somewhat surprisingly, high consumption of frozen foods does not lead to an increased ownership of microwave ovens. There is also no relationship with income. Thus, in this case, the European marketing manager could group countries simply on the basis of the degree of participation of women in the labor force.

Aside from these two commonplace tools, there are many other multivariate statistical procedures that can be used to do country segmentation analysis (e.g., latent class analysis, discriminant analysis, Automatic Interaction Detection).

MARKETING STRATEGIES

8

CHAPTER OVERVIEW

1. Information technology and global competition

2. Global strategy

3. Global marketing strategy

4. R&D, operations, and marketing interfaces

5. Regionalization of global marketing strategy

6. Competitive analysis

On a political map, country borders are clear as ever. But on a competitive map, financial, trading, and industrial activities across national boundaries have rendered those political borders increasingly irrelevant. Of all the forces chipping away at those boundaries, perhaps the most important are the emergence of regional trading blocs (e.g., NAFTA, the European Union, and MERCOSUR), technology developments (particularly in the IT area), and the flow of information.

Today people can see for themselves what tastes and preferences are like in other countries. For instance, people in India watching CNN and Star TV now know instantaneously what is happening in the rest of the world. A farmer in a remote village in Rajasthan in India asks the local vendor for Surf (the detergent manufactured by Unilever) because he has seen a commercial on TV. More than 10 million Japanese traveling abroad every year are exposed to larger-size homes and much lower consumer prices abroad. Such information access creates demand that would not have existed before.

The availability and explosion of information technology such as telecommunications has forever changed the nature of global competition. Geographical boundaries and distance have become less a constraint in designing strategies for the global market. The other side of the coin is that not only firms that compete internationally but also those whose primary market is home-based will be significantly affected by competition from around the world.

The firm is essentially a collection of activities that are performed to design, procure materials, produce, market, deliver, and support its product. This set of interrelated corporate activities is called the **value chain**. In this chapter, we explain the nature of global competition and examine various ways to gain competitive advantage along the value chain for the firm facing global competition.

Information Technology and Global Competition

The development of transportation technology, including jet air transportation, cold storage containers, and large ocean carriers, changed the nature of world trade in the 50 years after the Second World War. Since the 1980s, the explosion of information technology, particularly telecommunications, and more recently, electronic commerce (e-commerce), has forever changed the nature of competition around the world. Geographical distance has become increasingly less relevant in designing global strategy.

Real-Time Management

Information that managers have about the state of the firm's operations is almost in real time. Routinely, the chief executive officer of a firm can know the previous day's sales down to a penny, and can be alerted to events and trends now instead of in several months, when it may be too late to do anything about them.

In the mid-1990s, Volvo faced a classic supply chain dilemma. For whatever reason—perhaps just capricious consumer tastes—halfway through the year the company found itself with an excess inventory of green cars. The sales and marketing team responded appropriately by developing an aggressive program of deals, discounts, and rebates to push green vehicles through the distribution channel. The program worked well, and green Volvos began to move out off dealer lots. However, back at the factory, manufacturing planners also noted the surge in sales of green cars. Unfortunately, they were unaware of the big push taking place on the sales and marketing side and assumed that customers had suddenly developed a preference for the color green. So they responded by increasing production of green cars. The company soon found itself caught in a feedback loop that resulted in an even bigger surplus of green Volvos at the end of the year. This story is typical of the kind of disconnect that is far too common in manufacturing companies, especially those that rely on multi-tier distribution. This inability or failure to share real-time data or knowledge with partners can result in erroneous assumptions and costly errors in decision making. In order to prevent the problem, companies need to use information technology to link all parts of the organization into a real-time enterprise.[1]

Top retailers such as Wal-Mart and Toys "R" Us get information from their stores around the world every two hours via telecommunications. Industry analysts say that former leader K-Mart fell behind due to its delay in installing point-of-sale information technology, which would have enabled it to get faster and more accurate information on inventories and shelf movement of products.[2] Such access is now possible because advances in electronic storage and transmission technology have made it possible to store twenty-six volumes of *Encyclopedia Britannica* on a single chip and transmit that material in a second; the computing power is expected to double every two years (known as Moore's Law).

The combination of information technology, access tools, and telecommunication has squeezed out a huge chunk of organizational slack from corporate operations that were previously inherent due to the slow and circuitous nature of information flow within the firm, with holdups due to human "switches." Ordering and purchasing components, which was once a cumbersome, time-consuming process, is now done by Electronic Data Interchange (EDI), reducing the time involved in such transactions from weeks to days and eliminating a considerable amount of paperwork. Levi-Strauss uses LeviLink, an EDI service for handling all aspects of order and delivery. Customers can even place small orders as needed, say, every week, and goods are delivered within two days. One of Levi-Strauss' customers, Design p.l.c., with a chain of sixty

---

[1]"Does Everyone Have the Same View in Your Supply Chain?" *Frontline Solutions* 3 (July 2002): 27–30.
[2]Julia King, "OLAP Gains Fans among Data-Hungry Firms," *Computerworld* 30 (January 8, 1996): 43, 48.

stores, was able to entirely eliminate its warehouses, which were used as a buffer to deal with the long lead times between order and delivery.[3]

In fact, some companies not yet having become globally recognizable household names, such as Uniqlo (a clothing retailer), Saizeriya (an Italian fastfood chain), and Daiso (a dollar store chain), operating in the Japanese economy that has been battered by a decade-long recession are revolutionizing management of the value chain by getting directly involved both physically and via EDI in the whole process from materials procurement, manufacturing, and retailing. By doing so, they are able to control cost and quality as well as reduce what the Japanese call "muda," or waste, throughout the process.[4]

Online Communication

Sales representatives on field calls who were previously, in effect, tied to the regional or central headquarters due to lack of product information and limited authority are now able to act independently in the field, because laptop computers, faxes, and satellite uplinks enable instant access to data from the company's central database. Changes in prices due to discounts can now be cleared online from the necessary authority. This reduces reaction time for the sales representative and increases productivity. Monitoring problems for the firm are also reduced, as is paperwork.

Multiple design sites around the world in different time zones can now work sequentially on the same problem. A laboratory in California can close its day at 5 pm local time when the design center in Japan is just opening the next day. That center continues work on the design problem and hands it over to London at the end of its day, which continues the work and hands over the cumulated work of Japan and London back to California. Finally, the use of telecommunications improves internal efficiency of the firm in other ways. For instance, when Microsoft came up with an upgrade on one of its applications that required some customer education, a customer, using video conferencing on its global information network, arranged a single presentation for the relevant personnel, dispersed across the world, obviating travel and multiple presentations.

Electronic Commerce (E-Commerce)

Since the 1990s we have seen the explosive growth of e-commerce on the internet, beginning with the United States. In 1995, only 4 percent of Americans used the internet every day. In June 2012, the figure was 78.1 percent and still growing fast.[5] The total global e-commerce market size topped $1 trillion in 2012.[6] Developed countries led by the United States are still leading players in this field, while developing countries like China are emerging with a huge number of internet users, becoming an important force in the global e-commerce market.[7] The number of internet users reached 2.4 billion by June 2012, which amounts to 5.6 times that of December 2000. The growth rate during the 2000–2012 period was 566 percent.[8]

There is no other marketing channel than e-commerce where revenues are growing at this pace. There is no other way a business can grow unimpeded by the need to build commercial space and hire sales staff. While traditional mass-retailers, such as Wal-Mart in the United States, Carrefour

---

[3]Sidney Hill, Jr., "The Race for Profits," *Manufacturing Systems* 16 (May 1998): II–IV+.

[4]If interested in these Japanese companies, see, for example, "As U.S. Retailers Retreat, a Japanese Chain Sees an Opening," *New York Times*, May 22, 2012 (for Uniqlo); "Saizeriya," Wikipedia, http://en.wikipedia.org/wiki/Saizeriya; and "Daiso," http://en.wikipedia.org/wiki/Daiso.

[5]Internet usage statistics for the Americas, http://internetworldstats.com/stats2.htm#americas, accessed March 27, 2013.

[6]"Ecommerce Sales Topped $1 Trillion for First Time in 2012," *eMarketer*, http://www.emarketer.com/, February 5, 2013.

[7]*2010 World Digital Economy — E-Commerce and M-Commerce Trends*, http://www.budde.com.au/Research/2010-World-Digital-Economy-E-Commerce-and-M-Commerce-Trends.html, accessed August 30, 2012.

[8]www.internetworldstats.com, accessed March 27, 2013.

in France, and Metro in Germany, will not disappear any time soon, the internet has fundamentally changed customers' expectations about convenience, speed, comparability, price, and service. Even the traditional mass retailers are benefiting from e-commerce. In 2007, traditional chain retailers accounted for 39.9 percent of online sales among the Top 500 retailers, with a growing rate of 18 percent.[9] Online sales are predicted to increase to $22 billion in 2016, up from $7.9 billion in 2010.[10]

For example, Wal-Mart, the largest U.S. company, even creatively tried hiring TV stars so as to increase its online sales. It has been expanding its online section abroad. As a crucial part of the U.S. retailer's growth strategy in Brazil, the retail giant declared in April 2008 that it was branching out into electronic commerce in Latin America's largest country, where it invested $723 million to keep up with fast-growing consumer demand.[11] Brazil's online retail market is expected to increase by a compound annual growth rate of 17.5 percent over the next five years. Likewise, Dell Computer rocketed to the top of the personal computer business in the United States by selling directly to consumers online. As Mike George, the chief marketing officer and general manager of its consumer business unit, commented, "if Dell changes prices on its website, its customers' buying patterns change literally within a minute." Many consumers are well-researched and knowledgeable about their prospective purchase from the internet before they arrive at a showroom or a retail store.[12] Those new expectations will reverberate throughout the world, affecting every business, domestic or global, in many ways.

Marketing beyond the home country has always been hampered by geographical distance and the lack of sufficient information about foreign markets, although transportation and communications technology has reduced, if not eliminated, many difficulties of doing business across the national boundary. Thanks to an explosive growth of e-commerce on the internet, those difficulties are increasingly becoming a thing of the past. In other words, product life cycle is becoming shorter and shorter. E-commerce breaks every business free of the concept of geographic distance. No longer will geography bind a company's aspirations or the scope of its market. Traditional bookstores used to be constrained to certain geographical areas, probably within a few miles in radius of their physical locations. Now, Amazon.com and BarnesandNoble.com can reach any place on earth whether you are in Amsterdam or Seoul as long as you have access to the internet. For every early e-commerce mover to eliminate the geographic boundaries of its business, there will be dozens of companies that lose their local monopolies to footloose online businesses.

Although Japan was somewhat slower in adopting personal computers than the United States, the internet has also taken off in the world's third-largest economy. For example, Dell Computer and other U.S. computer manufacturers arguably were the first to market their products directly to Japanese consumers over the internet. Dell Computer Japan reported that 75 percent of the total number of computers it sold to individual buyers was bought online in Japan. Rakuten Ichiba, Japan's largest internet shopping site with more than 11,000 registered businesses, averages more than 21 million page views a day.[13] Sales grew from $26 million in 2000 to $4.24 billion in 2010, and net profits reached $428 million in 2010.[14] Despite net loss due to the temporary stalls in the Japanese economy as a result of the great earthquake and tsunami in 2011, Rakuten's nine-months

---

[9]"Chain Stores Ignore Online Retailing at Their Own Peril," InternetRetailer.com, http://www.internetretailer.com/, June 12, 2008.

[10]Forrester Research, Inc., http://www.internetretailer.com/trends/sales/, accessed August 1, 2012.

[11]"Wal-Mart 2008 Financial Review," Wal-Mart Stores 2008 Annual Report; and "Wal-Mart Eyes e-Commerce in Fast-Growing Brazil," http://www.freshplaza.com/, accessed September 15, 2008.

[12]"Crowned at Last," *Economist*, April 2, 2005, pp. 3–6.

[13]"Rakuten Deploys Foundry Networks' Industry-Leading Ethernet Switching to Power Its E-Commerce Site," Foundry Networks Press Release, http://www.thefreelibrary.com/Rakuten+Deploys+Foundry+Networks'+Industry-Leading+Ethernet+Switching...-a0131702150, accessed September 11, 2013.

[14]Rakuten Ichiba, Annual Report, http://global.rakuten.com/investor/documents/annual.html, accessed August 1, 2012.

consolidated statement ending in September 30, 2012, showed profits of $335 million on $5 billion sales, demonstrating an optimistic rebound.[15]

The same explosive internet growth is being experienced in countries that are still catching up technologically to developed countries such as the United States and Japan. For example, China has already become one of the world's largest internet markets. The internet community in China increased by 24 times from 2000 to 2012, soaring from just 22.5 million users in 2000 to 538 million by June 2012.[16] Some large portals in China such as Netease, Sina, Sohu, and Tom have been making a healthy profit since 2003. Online gaming is fast growing and is one of the three largest money-makers for internet companies, with the other two being e-finance and e-education. Unlike other high internet usage countries, the majority of gamers play at the internet cafes in China, rather than at home, and it is estimated that China had 144,000 internet cafes in 2011. China's largest e-game operator, Shanda Games Limited, has grown by operating licensed South Korean online games and has accumulated a huge amount of wealth within a few years. In 2012, Shanda Games had a monthly average of 19–20 million users. In 2011, Shanda reported net revenues of 1.4 billion yuan (over US$220 million), representing an increase of 8.7 percent from a year earlier.[17]

E-Company

The ultimate effect of information networks within the multinational firm is expected to be on the nature of its organizational structure. As information flows faster across the organization and the number of "filtering" points between the source of information (e.g., point-of-sale information or market and industry analysis) and the user of the information (e.g., the brand manager or the chief executive officer) decreases, the nature of the organization chart in the multinational firm changes drastically. An increasing number of multinational firms have begun to use their intranet (internal web servers on the internet) to facilitate communications and transactions among employees, suppliers, independent contractors, and distributors.[18]

Many companies today realize the key to this change is e-business. Siemens, for example, spent €1 billion to turn itself into an **e-company**. Siemens is enabling itself to connect the different parts of its far-flung empire into a more coherent whole. In practice, Siemens plans to utilize its information technology to enhance knowledge management, online purchasing, change the company's value chain, and efficiently deal with its customers. Now customers can click on "Buy from Siemens" on the company's home page and place orders. Inevitably, the Siemens demand chain is going smoothly from customers, through Siemens, and then to its suppliers.[19] Similarly, an assembly-line worker in a Procter & Gamble plant knows from his computer that stores have been selling a particular brand of facial cream more briskly than anticipated. Having this information, he can change production scheduling on his own by giving the computer necessary instructions to cut down on some other brands and to increase the production of the brand in question. The foreperson and the section manager of a conventional plant are no longer required.

---

[15]Rakuten Ichiba, Consolidated Financial Report Q3 2012, http://global.rakuten.com/corp/investors/documents/results/, accessed September 11, 2013.

[16]www.internetworldstats.com.

[17]Shanda Games, http://www.shandagames.com/web/.

[18]John A. Quelch and Lisa R. Klein, "The Internet and International Marketing," *Sloan Management Review* 37 (Spring 1996): 60–75.

[19]Herbert Heinzel, "Siemens—The e-Company: In Its Quest to Become an e-Business Company, Siemens Is Pursuing a Comprehensive Approach That Goes Far Beyond the Mere Selling of Products over the Internet," *Supply Chain Management Review* (March 2002).

Faster Product Diffusion

The obvious impact of information technology is the more rapid dispersion of technology and the shorter product life cycles in global markets than ever before. It suggests that the former country-by-country sequential approach to entering markets throughout the world, described in the international product cycle model in Chapter 1, is increasingly untenable.

This trend is already reflected in many product markets. In the 1970s, the diffusion lag for color television between the United States on one hand and Japan and Europe on the other was six years. In the 1990s, with compact discs the household penetration rates had come down to one year. Now for Intel Core i-based computers, Taiwan-, India-, Japan-, and U.S.-based companies released computers at about the same time in their respective national markets. Thus, a firm selling personal computers would have to launch a new product on a worldwide basis in order not to fall behind in the global sweepstakes.[20]

Global Citizenship

Another important contributing factor in the globalization of markets is the spread of English as the language of international business. **Global citizenship** is no longer just a phrase in the lexicon of futurologists. It has already become every bit as concrete and measurable as changes in GNP and trade flows. In fact, conventional measures of trade flows may have outlived their usefulness, as we will discuss later.

The global environment thus demands a strategy that encompasses numerous national boundaries and tastes, and that integrates a firm's operations across the national borders. This strategy is truly global in nature and has gone beyond the home-country-focused ethnocentric orientation or the multicountry-focused polycentric orientation of many multinational firms in the twentieth century. The firm thus needs to adopt a geocentric orientation that views the entire world as a potential market and integrates firm activities on a global basis.[21]

Global Strategy

The acid test of a well-managed company is being able to conceive, develop, and implement an effective global strategy. A **global strategy** is to array the competitive advantages arising from location, world-scale economies, or global brand distribution, namely, by building a global presence, defending domestic dominance, and overcoming country-by-country fragmentation. Because of its inherent difficulties, global strategy development presents one of the stiffest challenges for managers today. Companies that operate on a global scale need to integrate their worldwide strategy, in contrast to the earlier multinational or multidomestic approach. The earlier strategies would be categorized more truly as multidomestic strategies rather than as global strategies. In the section below, we approach the issue of global strategy through five conceptualizations: 1) global industry, 2) competitive industry structure, 3) competitive advantage, 4) hypercompetition, and 5) interdependency.

Global Industry

The first conceptualization is that of a **global industry**.[22] Global industries are defined as *those where a firm's competitive position in one country is affected by its position in other countries, and*

---

[20]Shlomo Kalish, Vijay Mahajan, and Eitan Muller, "Waterfall and Sprinkler New-Product Strategies in Competitive Global Markets," *International Journal of Research in Marketing* 12 (July 1995): 105–119.

[21]Shaoming Zou and S. Tamer Cavusgil, "The GMS: A Broad Conceptualization of Global Marketing Strategy and Its Effect on Firm Performance," *Journal of Marketing* 66 (October 2002): 40–56.

[22]Michael E. Porter, ed., *Competition in Global Industries* (Boston: Harvard University Press, 1986).

vice versa. Therefore, we are talking about not just a collection of domestic industries, but also a series of interlinked domestic industries in which rivals compete against one another on a truly worldwide basis. For instance, 30 years after Honda began making cars in the first Japanese transplant in Marysville, Ohio, the automaker is increasingly relying on the U.S. market. It has boosted its North American production capacity 40 percent by 2014.[23] Today, more than half the passenger sedans sold in the United States are import brands, and more than half the vehicles sporting foreign nameplates are made in the United States. It is foreign players that are reinvigorating America's automobile business and turning the United States into the center of a global industry.

Therefore, the first question that faces managers is the extent of globalization of their industry. Assuming that the firm's activities are indeed global or, alternatively, that the firm wishes to grow toward global operations and markets, managers must design and implement a global strategy. This is because virtually every industry has global or potentially global aspects—some industries have more aspects that are global and more intensely so. Indeed, a case has been made that the globalization of markets has already been achieved, that consumer tastes around the world have converged, and that the global firm attempts, unceasingly, to drive consumer tastes toward convergence.[24] Four major forces determining the globalization potential of industry are presented in **Exhibit 8-1**.

Exhibit 8-1 Industry Globalization Drivers

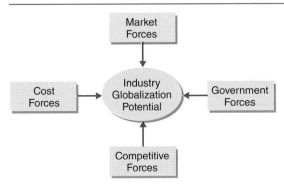

Market Forces

Market forces depend on the nature of customer behavior and the structure of channels of distribution. Some common market forces are:

- Per capita income converging among industrialized nations
- Emergence of rich consumers in emerging markets such as China and India
- Convergence of lifestyles and tastes (e.g., McDonald's in Moscow and Stolichnaya vodka in America)
- Revolution in information and communication technologies (e.g., personal computer, fax machines, and the internet)
- Increased international travel creating global consumers knowledgeable about products from many countries
- Organizations beginning to behave as global customers
- Growth of global and regional channels (e.g., America's Wal-Mart, France's Carrefour/Promodès, Germany's Metro, and Japan' 7-Eleven)
- Establishment of world brands (e.g., Coca-Cola, Microsoft, Toyota, and Nestlé)
- Push to develop global advertising (e.g., Saatchi and Saatchi's commercials for British Airways)
- Spread of global and regional media (e.g., CNN, MTV, Star TV in India)

(continued)

---

[23]"Honda Revs Up outside Japan," *Wall Street Journal,* December 21, 2011.
[24]Theodore Levitt, "The Globalization of Markets," *Harvard Business Review,* 61 (May–June 1983): 92–102.

Exhibit 8-1   (*Continued*)

Cost Forces

Cost forces depend on the economics of the business. These forces particularly affect production location decisions, as well as global market participation and global product development decisions. Some of these cost forces are:

- Push for economies of scale and scope, further aided by flexible manufacturing
- Accelerating technological innovations
- Advances in transportation (e.g., FedEx, UPS, DHL, and Yamato Transport)
- Emergence of newly industrializing countries with productive capabilities and low labor costs (e.g., China, India, and many Eastern European countries)
- High product development costs relative to shortened product life cycle

Government Forces

Rules set by national governments can affect the use of global strategic decision-making. Some of these rules/policies include:

- Reduction of tariff and nontariff barriers
- Creation of trading blocs (e.g., European Union, North American Free Trade Agreement, and MERCOSUR—a common market in South America)
- Establishment of world trading regulations (e.g., World Trade Organization and its various policies)
- Deregulation of many industries
- Privatization in previously state-dominated economies in Latin America
- Shift to open market economies from closed communist systems in China, Eastern Europe and the former Soviet Union

Competitive Forces

Competitive forces raise the globalization potential of their industry and spur the need for a response on the global strategy levels. The common competitive forces include:

- Increase in world trade
- More countries becoming key competitive battlegrounds (e.g., Japan, Korea, China, India, and Brazil)
- Increased ownership of corporations by foreign investors
- Globalization of financial markets (e.g., listing of corporations on multiple stock exchanges and issuing debt in multiple currencies)
- Rise of new competitors intent on becoming global competitors (e.g., Japanese firms in the 1970s; Korean firms in the 1980s; Taiwanese firms in the 1990s; Brazilian, Chinese, and Indian firms in the 2000s; and probably Russian firms in the 2010s)
- Rise of "born global" internet and other companies
- Growth of global networks making countries interdependent in particular industries (e.g., electronics and aircraft manufacturing)
- More companies becoming geocentric rather than ethnocentric (e.g., Stanley Works, a traditional U.S. company, moved its production offshore; Uniden, a Japanese telecommunications equipment manufacturer has never manufactured in Japan)
- Increased formation of global strategic alliances

Source: Adapted from George S. Yip, *Total Global Strategy II*, Upper Saddle River, N.J.: Prentice Hall, 2003, pp. 10–12.

The implications of a distinction between multidomestic and global strategy are quite profound. In a multidomestic strategy, a firm manages its international activities like a portfolio. Its subsidiaries or other operations around the world each control all the important activities necessary to maximize their returns in their area of operation independent of the activities of other subsidiaries in the firm. The subsidiaries enjoy a large degree of autonomy, and the firm's activities in each of its national markets are determined by the competitive conditions in that national market. In contrast, a global strategy integrates the activities of a firm on a worldwide basis to capture the linkages among countries and to treat the entire world as a single, borderless market. This requires more than the transferring of intangible assets between countries.

In effect, the firm that truly operationalizes a global strategy is a geocentrically oriented firm. It considers the whole world as its arena of operation, and its managers maintain equidistance from all markets and develop a system with which to satisfy its needs for both global integration for economies of scale and scope *and* responsiveness to different market needs and conditions in various parts of the world (to be discussed in Chapter 14 in the context of sourcing strategy). In a way, the geocentric firm tries to "kill two birds with one stone."[25] Such a firm tends to centralize some resources at home, some abroad, and distributes others among its many national operations, resulting in a complex configuration of assets and capabilities on a global basis.[26]

This is in contrast to an ethnocentric orientation, where managers operate under the dominant influence of home country practices, or a polycentric orientation, where managers of individual subsidiaries operate independently of each other—the polycentric manager in practice leads to a multidomestic orientation, which prevents integration and optimization on a global basis. Until the early 1980s the global operations of Unilever were a good example of a multidomestic approach. Unilever's various country operations were largely independent of each other, with headquarters restricting itself to data collection and helping out subsidiaries when required. Unilever started adding some geocentric dimensions to its global strategy when the CEO, Patrick Cescau, kicked off an ambitious restructuring program in 2005. Under his direction, the "One Unilever" plan was implemented in which unnecessary complexity was removed. One formulation, one packaging design, and one marketing strategy replaced the fragmented approach.[27]

Sometimes, however, marketing in emerging markets may need a different approach from all previously known ones. In emerging countries such as China, India, Brazil, and other large nations, is not enough to approach with a country-level strategy. A more detailed approach such as a city-clusters approach would be needed to pursue growth in these markets.

Competitive Industry Structure

Competitive industry structure is the second conceptualization that is useful in understanding the nature of global strategy. A conceptual framework that portrays the multidimensional nature of competitive industry structure is presented in **Exhibit 8-2**. It identifies the key structural factors that determine the strength of competitive forces within an industry and consequently industry profitability. Competition is not limited to the firms in the same industry. If firms in an industry collectively have insufficient capacity to fulfill demand, the incentive is high for new market entrants. However, such entrants need to consider the time and investment it takes to develop new or additional capacity, the likelihood of such capacity being developed by existing competitors, and the possibility of changes in customer demand over time. Indirect competition also comes from suppliers and customers, as well as substitute products or services.

1. **Industry competitors** determine the rivalry among existing firms.

2. **Potential entrants** may change the rules of competition but can be deterred by entry barriers. For example, Shanghai Jahwa Co., Ltd., its predecessor founded in 1898, became the largest cosmetics and personal care products company in China by 1990.[28] Shanghai Jahwa owns such successful brands as Maxam, Liushen, Ruby, and G.LF, among others, and is making gradual inroads into markets outside China. Although not yet known to the Western world, its brands

---

[25]Masaaki Kotabe, "To Kill Two Birds with One Stone: Revisiting the Integration-Responsiveness Framework," in Michael Hitt and Joseph Cheng, ed., *Managing Transnational Firms*, New York: Elsevier, 2002, 59–69.

[26]Christopher A. Bartlett and Sumantra Ghoshal, *Managing across Borders*. Boston, MA: Harvard Business School Press, 1989.

[27]Kerry Capell, "Unilever Lathers Up", *BusinessWeek.com*, February 15, 2008.

[28]Based on the first author's visit to Shanghai Jahwa based in Shanghai, China, August 2002.

Exhibit 8-2 Nature
of Competitive
Industry Structure

Source: Reprinted with the
permission of the Free Press,
a division of Simon &
Schuster from
COMPETITIVE STRATEGY:
Techniques for Analyzing
Industries and Competitors
by Michael E. Porter, p. 4.
Copyright © 1980 by The
Free Press.

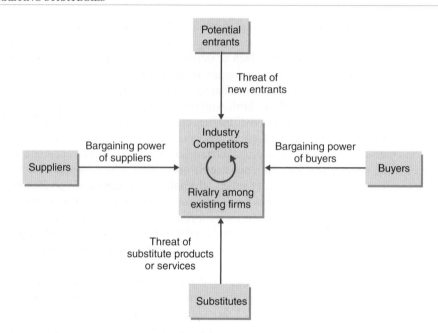

may someday pose a major competitive threat to Clinique, Estée Lauder, Lancôme, Maxfactor, SKII, and other well-known brands and may change the nature of competition in the cosmetics and personal care products industry.

3. The **bargaining power of suppliers** can change the structure of industries. Intel has become a dominant producer of microprocessors for personal computers. Its enormous bargaining power has caused many PC manufacturers to operate on wafer-thin profit margins, making the PC industry extremely competitive.

4. The **bargaining power of buyers** may affect the firm's profitability. It is particularly the case when governments try to get price and delivery concessions from foreign firms. Similarly, Nestlé, whose subsidiaries used to make independent decisions on cocoa purchase, has centralized its procurement decision at its headquarters to take advantage of its consolidated bargaining power over cocoa producers around the world. Given its bargaining power, Nestlé has further completed a trial of a ground-breaking supply chain project that allows suppliers to view its production information and ensure it can meet fluctuations in demand for its products by removing about 20 percent of excess stock from its supply chain.[29]

5. The **threat of substitute products or services** can restructure the entire industry above and beyond the existing competitive structure. For example, the rising consumer interest in car sharing services has reshaped the industry of "vehicle ownerships." Car sharing has become an attractive alternative to owning a vehicle. Pioneered in Switzerland and Germany, the growth of car sharing is springing up in cities in North America and Europe for general hassle, car cost, and gasoline price surge reasons, with Zipcar the biggest North American operator.[30] Another example is demonstrated in the film entertainment industry that has been touched by the presence of digital rental services such as Netflix. As revenues from subscription of online rental services are increasing, sales of feature films on iTunes have slowed down, as well as DVD rental and online film buying.[31]

---

[29]"Nestlé Links SAP Systems to Allow Suppliers to View Production Data," *Computer Weekly*, October 21, 2003, p. 8.
[30]Bernard Simon, "City Pick-Up-and-Go Fleets Wean Drivers off Ownership," *Financial Times*, August 14, 2006.
[31]"Hopes for Hollywood Cloud Darken," *Financial Times*, May 31, 2012.

Competitive Advantage

Competitive advantage is a third conceptualization that is of use in developing and understanding a strategy on a global scale. Companies may adopt different strategies for different competitive advantage. The firm has a competitive advantage when it is able to deliver the same benefits as competitors but at a lower cost, or deliver benefits that exceed those of competing products. Thus, a competitive advantage enables the firm to create superior value for its customers and superior profits for itself.[32] Simply stated, competitive advantage is a temporary monopoly period that a firm can enjoy over its competitors. To prolong such a monopolistic period, the firm strives to develop a strategy that would be difficult for its competitors to imitate.

The firm that builds its competitive advantage on economies of scale is known as one using a **cost leadership** strategy. Customized flexible manufacturing as a result of CAD/CAM (computer-aided design and computer-aided manufacturing) technology has shown some progress. However, it proved to be more difficult operationally than was thought, so economies of scale still remain the main feature of market competition. The theory is that the greater the economies of scale, the greater the benefits to those firms with a larger market share. As a result, many firms try to jockey for larger market shares than their competitors. Economies of scale come about because larger plants are more efficient to run, and their per-unit cost of production is less as overhead costs are allocated across large volumes of production. Further economies of scale also result from learning effects: the firm learns more efficient methods of production with increasing cumulative experience in production over time. All of these effects tend to intensify competition. Once a high level of economies of scale is achieved, it provides the firm strong barriers against new entrants to the market. In the 1970s and early 1980s, many Japanese companies became cost leaders in such industries as automobiles and consumer electronics. However, there is no guarantee that cost leadership will last. In addition, the cost leadership strategy does not necessarily apply to all markets. According to a recent study, implementation of a cost-leadership strategy by developed-country multinational companies (MNCs) actually is rarely effective in emerging markets. In order to achieve high performance, therefore, MNCs that benefit from cost leadership strategy may try using different strategies in different markets instead of a single generic strategy globally.[33]

Until flexible manufacturing and customized production becomes fully operational, cost leaders may be vulnerable to firms that use a **product differentiation** strategy to better serve the exact needs of customers. Although one could argue that lower cost will attract customers away from other market segments, some customers are willing to pay a premium price for unique product features that they desire. Uniqueness may come in the form of comfort, product performance, and aesthetics, as well as status symbol and exclusivity. Despite the Japanese juggernaut in the automobile industry (primarily in the North American and Asian markets) in the 1970s and 1980s, BMW of Germany and Volvo of Sweden (currently owned by China's Geely Automobile), for example, managed to maintain their competitive strengths in the high-end segments of the automobile market. Indeed, Japanese carmakers have struggled for years to make a dent in the European market, and they are finally seeing a turnaround after releasing a spate of new models that European drivers want to buy—small cars with spacious cabins—the type that European firms have yet to make, such as Honda's Jazz (known as the Fit in Japan), Toyota's Yaris (known as the Vitz in Japan), and Mazda's Mazda 6 (known as the Atenza in Japan).[34] While high oil prices are causing pain for U.S. carmakers, such as GM and Ford, Japanese small cars are welcomed by the U.S. consumers. In May 2008, for example, the sales of Toyota's Camry and

---

[32]Michael E. Porter, *Competitive Advantage: Techniques for Analyzing Industries and Competitors* (New York: The Free Press, 1980).

[33]Daniel W. Baack and David J. Boggs, "The Difficulties in Using a Cost Leadership Strategy in Emerging Markets," *International Journal of Emerging Markets* 3 (April 2008): 125–139.

[34]Japanese Carmakers Make European Dent," *Japan Times Online*, December 31, 2002, http://www.japantimes.co.jp/.

Corolla for the first time exceeded Ford's F-150 pick-up, one of the U.S.'s traditional favorite vehicles.[35]

Smaller companies may pursue a limited differentiation strategy by keeping a niche in the market. Firms using a **niche** strategy focus exclusively on a highly specialized segment of the market and try to achieve a dominant position in that segment. Again in the automobile industry, Porsche and Saab maintain their competitive strengths in the high-power sports car enthusiast segment. However, particularly in an era of global competition, niche players may be vulnerable to large-scale operators due to sheer economies of scale needed to compete on a global scale.

First-Mover Advantage vs. First-Mover Disadvantage

For many firms, technology is the key to success in markets where significant advances in product performance are expected. A firm uses its technological leadership for rapid innovation and introduction of new products. The timing of such introductions in the global marketplace is an integral part of the firm's strategy. However, the dispersion of technological expertise means that any technological advantage is temporary, so the firm should not rest on its laurels. The firm needs to move on to its next source of temporary advantage to remain ahead. In the process, firms that are able to continue creating a series of temporary advantages are the ones that survive and thrive. Technology, marketing skills, and other assets that a firm possesses become its weapons to gain advantages in time over its competitors. The firm now attempts to be among the pioneers, or first movers, in the market for the product categories that it operates in.[36] Sony offers an excellent example of a company in constant pursuit of **first-mover advantage** with Trinitron color television, Betamax video recorder, Walkman, 8mm video recorder, DVD (digital video disc), and Blue-ray disc technology although not all of its products, such as the MiniDisc, succeeded in the market.

Indeed, there could even be some first-mover disadvantages.[37] Citigroup's recent case vividly raises the possibility of first-mover disadvantages. To establish its foothold in the growing Chinese economy, Citigroup recently entered into an alliance with Shanghai Pudong Development Bank in China targeting the country's credit card market. About 10 million cards with revolving credit have already been issued in China. Some experts argue that Chinese credit services would be risky for first-mover companies given that the country has no nationwide credit-rating system and a lack of adequate risk management technology.[38]

In general, stable markets favor the first-mover strategy while market and technology turbulence favor the follower strategy. Followers have the benefit of hindsight to determine more preciously the timing, form, and scale of their market entry. It is therefore important for the firm to clearly assess the key success factors and the resulting likelihood of success for achieving the ultimate targeted position in the highly competitive global business environment.[39]

A firm's competitive advantage lies in its capability to effectively anticipate, react to, and lead change continuously and even rhythmically over time. Firms should "probe" into the unknown by taking many small steps to explore their environments. These probes could take the form of a number of new product introductions that are "small, fast, and cheap," and can be supplemented by using experts to contemplate the future, making strategic alliances to explore new technologies, and

---

[35]"Crisis? What Oil Crisis?" *Economist*, June 7, 2008, pp. 73–74.

[36]Gerard J. Tellis and Peter N. Golder, "First to Market, First to Fail? Real Causes of Enduring Market Leadership," *Sloan Management Review* 37 (Winter 1996): 65–75; and Richard Makadok, "Can First-Mover and Early-Mover Advantages Be Sustained in an Industry with Low Barriers to Entry/Imitation?" *Strategic Management Journal* 19 (July 1998): 683–696.

[37]Marvin B. Lieberman and David B. Montgomery, "First-Mover (Dis)advantages: Retrospective and Link with the Resource-Based View," *Strategic Management Journal* 19 (December 1998): 1111–1125.

[38]"Risks in Credit Card Business," *China Daily*, January 10, 2005.

[39]Gerard J. Tellis and Peter N. Golder, "First to Market, First to Fail? Real Causes of Enduring Market Leadership," *Sloan Management Review* 37 (1996): 65–75; and Dean Shepherd and Mark Shanley, *New Venture Strategy: Timing, Environmental Uncertainty and Performance* (Thousand Oaks, CA: Sage Publications, 1998).

holding meetings where the future is discussed by management. To compete on the edge, firms need to understand that:

1. Advantage is temporary. In other words, firms need to have a strong focus on continuously generating new sources of advantages.

2. Strategy is diverse, emergent, and complicated. It is crucial to rely on diverse strategic moves.

3. Reinvention is the goal. It is how firms keep pace with a rapidly changing marketplace.

4. Live in the present, stretch out the past, and reach into the future. Successful firms launch more experimental products and services than others, while they exploit previous experiences and try to extend them to new opportunities.

5. Grow the strategy and drive strategy from the business level. It is important for managers to pay attention to the timing and order in which strategy is grown and agile moves at the business level.

6. To maintain sustainable power in fast-paced, competitive, and unpredictable environments, senior management needs to recognize patterns in firms' development and articulate a semi-coherent strategic direction.[40]

With these strategic flexibilities in mind, we could think of two primary approaches to gaining competitive advantage. The competitor-focused approaches involve comparison with the competitor on costs, prices, technology, market share, profitability, and other related activities. Such an approach may lead to a preoccupation with some activities, and the firm may lose sight of its customers and various constituents. Customer-focused approaches to gaining competitive advantage emanate from an analysis of customer benefits to be delivered. In practice, finding the proper links between required customer benefits and the activities and variables controlled by management is needed. Besides, there is evidence to suggest that listening too closely to customer requirements may cause a firm to miss the bus on innovations, because current customers might not want innovations that require them to change how they operate.[41]

Competitor-Focused Approach

Black & Decker, a U.S.-based manufacturer of hand tools, switched to a global strategy using its strengths in the arenas of cost and quality and timing and know-how. In the 1980s Black & Decker's position was threatened by a powerful Japanese competitor, Makita. Makita's strategy of producing and marketing globally standardized products worldwide made it into a low-cost producer and enabled it to steadily increase its world market share. Within the company, Black & Decker's international fiefdoms combined with nationalist chauvinism to stifle coordination in product development and new product introductions, resulting in lost opportunities.

Then, responding to the increased competitive pressure, Black & Decker moved decisively toward globalization. It embarked on a program to coordinate new product development world-wide in order to develop core standardized products that could be marketed globally with minimum modification. The streamlining of R&D also offered scale economies and less duplication of effort, and new products could be introduced faster. Its increased emphasis on design made it into a global leader in design management. It consolidated its advertising into two agencies worldwide in an attempt to give a more consistent image worldwide. Black & Decker also strengthened the functional organization by giving the functional manager a larger role in coordinating with the country management. Finally, Black & Decker purchased General Electric's

---

[40]Shona L. Brown and Kathleen M. Eisenhardt, *Competing on the Edge* (Boston: Harvard Business Press, 1998).

[41]See, for example, John P. Workman, Jr. "Marketing's Limited Role in New Product Development in One Computer Systems Firm," *Journal of Marketing Research* 30 (November 1993): 405–421.

small appliance division to achieve world-scale economies in manufacturing, distribution, and marketing. The global strategy initially faced skepticism and resistance from country managers at Black & Decker. The chief executive officer took a visible leadership role and made some management changes to start moving the company toward globalization. These changes in strategy helped Black & Decker increase revenues and profits by as much as 50 percent in the 1990s.[42] In order to meet further cost competition, Black & Decker's new global restructuring project plans to reduce manufacturing costs by transferring additional power tool production from the United States and England to low-cost facilities in Mexico, China, and a new leased facility in the Czech Republic and by sourcing more manufactured items from third parties where cost advantages are available and quality can be assured. Its global restructuring plan resulted in global sales increase from $5.4 billion in 2005 to $11 billion by 2011. In 2012, Black & Decker expects to see 51 percent of its global revenue from emerging markets.[43]

A word of caution is in order. Although a company's financial resources provide durability for its strategy, regulatory and other barriers could prove to be overwhelming even in a very promising market such as China. As presented in **Global Perspective 8-1**, AOL Time-Warner's expansion into China illustrates this difficulty.

Customer-Focused Approach

Estée Lauder is one good corporate example that superbly used cost and quality, timing and know-how, strongholds, and financial resources to its advantage. Estée Lauder has grown from a small, woman-owned cosmetics business to become one of the world's leading manufacturers and marketers of quality skin care, makeup, fragrance, and hair care products. Its brands include Estée Lauder, Aramis, Clinique, Prescriptives, Origins, M·A·C, La Mer, Bobbi Brown, and Tommy Hilfiger, among others.

How did Estée Lauder accomplish such a feat? The answer lies in its ability to reach consumers in nearly every corner of the world, in its internal strengths, and the diversity of its portfolio of brands. Since the beginning of its international operations, the company has always conducted in-depth research to determine the feasibility and compatibility of its products with each particular market, which has led to its high quality image. Another reason for the company's success lies in its focus on global expansion before its competitors. Estée Lauder's international operations started in 1960. Because of its strong visibility in Europe, it served as a springboard to other European markets. Shortly thereafter, the company made its foray with the Estée Lauder brand into new markets in the Americas, Europe, and Asia. In the late 1960s the Aramis and Clinique brands were founded, and a manufacturing facility was established in Belgium. In the 1970s, Clinique was introduced overseas, and Estée Lauder began to explore new opportunities in the former Soviet Union. During the 1980s, the company made considerable progress in reaching markets that were still out of reach for many American companies. For example, in 1989 Estée Lauder was the first American cosmetic company to enter the former Soviet Union when it opened a perfumery in Moscow. The same year, it established its first free-standing beauty boutique in Budapest, Hungary. In 1990s the firm moved further into untapped markets such as China. Recently, Clinique established a presence in Vietnam. The company is focusing further on China and the rest of Asia. In addition, there are still many opportunities in Europe. The company will continue to look to Latin America for expansion but with caution, due to economic circumstances and political instability. One more reason for the company' success is its use of financial resources to further strengthen brand value. Since 1989, the firm has opened some of its free-standing stores overseas because it could not find the right channels of distribution to maintain the brand's standards. Estée Lauder has built strong brand equity all over the world with each brand having a

---

[42]Black & Decker, various annual reports.

[43]Black & Decker, Investor Relations, 2011 and 2012 Annual Report.

Global Perspective 8-1

"Rome" Could Not Be Built in a Day . . . Even by AOL Time-Warner in China

AOL, a Time-Warner company, made a foray into China in 2001. AOL partnered with Lenovo (previously known as Legend), China's largest computer-maker, to tackle the world's most promising internet-service market, and became the first foreign broadcaster allowed onto a Chinese cable-TV service. However, AOL realized that it would take years to turn a profit. In China, any vendor or operator that wants to come into the internet space needs deep pockets to last at least five years or more for anything to happen. It takes so many regulatory hurdles to just get approval to start offering internet service in China. Furthermore, because China has a lot of competition, the margins have come down so much and internet-service providers cannot become profitable instantly. But AOL could not wait that long. Because of its continued losses in Japan, AOL closed its Japanese venture. AOL's new portal had many problems. It was not even as good as similar services from money-losing portals like sina.com or sohu.com. Furthermore, Lenovo is essentially a hardware company without much experience in telecom operations. Thus, this partnership lacked a distribution channel for AOL services. As a result, the business failed to go anywhere, and Lenovo finally pulled out of its legacy relationship with Time-Warner in 2004. So far, the only places where internet-service providers make money are in protected markets like South Korea or Taiwan, or where a firm blows out its competition early, as AOL did in the United States. In competitive markets such as Hong Kong, Singapore, and China, price competition for basic services tends to leave everyone unprofitable.

As for television, AOL and other foreign broadcasters still face many regulatory obstacles. Though CCTV has been granted "landing rights," it can only reach a very small part of Guangdong province, and its competitors include established programmers like Hong Kong's TVB and ATV. Meanwhile, AOL's other channels also have problems. Warner Music faces piracy issues: about 95 percent of all music and movie CDs in China are pirated; Time's two flagship news publications—*Time* and *Fortune*—officially sell fewer than 2,000 copies each in China, although *Fortune China* published through a licensee is helping establish the brand name. As for movies, China promises to double the number of overseas films it allows to be released each year, but that still means only 20 films, distributed among all of the world's film studios, the potentials are not good enough for Time-Warner. All these obstacles take a long time to improve, which means that Time-Warner needs to have the patience and financial resources as well as a strong commitment to the Chinese market, hoping that it will be the first player once China opens its door to foreign media companies.

Sources: "Lenovo Reaches for New Direction," CRN, December 3, 2004, http://www.crn.com; "AOL's Mobile Ambitions," *BusinessWeek.com*, September 26, 2007; and "AOL Closes China R&D Base as Economy Slides," PCWorld, March 11, 2009, www.pcworld.com.

---

single, global image. The company's philosophy of never compromising brand equity has guided it in its selection of the appropriate channels of distribution overseas. In the United States and overseas, products are sold through limited distribution channels to uphold the particular images of each brand.

At the same time, Estée Lauder has successfully responded to the needs of different markets. In Asia, for example, a system of products was developed to whiten the skin. This ability to adapt and create products to specific market needs has contributed greatly to the company's ability to enter new markets. Estée Lauder currently has manufacturing facilities in the United States, Canada, Belgium, Switzerland, and the United Kingdom, and research and development laboratories in the United States, Canada, Belgium, and Japan. Estée Lauder's global strategies have paid off. In 2011, 43 percent of net sales came from the Americas (as compared to 61 percent in 2001), 36 percent from

Europe, the Middle East, and Africa (as compared to 26 percent in 2001), and 19 percent from Asia Pacific (as compared to 13 percent in 2001). The proportion of its global net sales increased to 62 percent of its total net sales, from $3.81 billion in 2007 to $5.5 billion in 2011.[44]

Hypercompetition

Hypercompetition, a fourth conceptualization, refers to the fact that all firms are faced with a form of aggressive competition that is tougher than oligopolistic or monopolistic competition, but is not perfect competition where the firm is atomistic and cannot influence the market at all. Hypercompetition is pervasive not just in fast-moving high-technology industries like computers and deregulated industries like airlines, but also in industries that have traditionally been considered more sedate, like processed foods. The central thesis of this argument is that no type of competitive advantage can last—it is bound to get eroded.

In any given industry, firms jockey among themselves for better competitive position, given a set of customers and buyers, the threat of substitutes, and the barriers to entry in that industry. However, the earlier arguments represent the description of a situation without any temporal dimension; there is no indication as to how a firm should act to change the situation to its advantage. For instance, it is not clear how tomorrow's competitor can differ from today's. A new competitor can emerge from a completely different industry given the convergence of industries. Ricoh, once a low-cost facsimile and copier maker, has now come up with a product that records moving images digitally, which is what a camcorder and a movie camera do using different technologies. This development potentially pits Ricoh as a direct competitor to camcorder and movie camera makers, emphasizing differentiation by providing unique technical features —something not possible ten or twenty years ago.

Such a shift in competition is referred to as creative destruction. This view of competition assumes continuous change, where the firm's focus is on disrupting the market. In a hyper-competitive environment, a firm competes on the basis of price, quality, timing, and know-how, creating strongholds in the markets it operates in (this is akin to entry barriers), and financial resources to outlast one's competitors.[45]

Interdependency

A fifth aspect of global strategy is **interdependency** of modern companies. Recent research has shown that the number of technologies used in a variety of products in numerous industries is rising.[46] Because access to resources limits how many distinctive competencies a firm can gain, firms must draw on outside technologies to be able to build a state-of-the-art product. Because most firms operating globally are limited by a lack of all required technologies, it follows that for firms to make optimal use of outside technologies, a degree of components standardization is required. Such standardization would enable different firms to develop different end products, using, in a large measure, the same components.[47] Research findings do indicate that technology intensity—that is, the degree of R&D expenditure a firm incurs as a proportion of sales—is a primary determinant of cross-border firm integration.[48]

---

[44]Estée Lauder, 2011 Annual Report.

[45]Richard D'Aveni, *Hypercompetition: Managing the Dynamics of Strategic Maneuvering* (New York: The Free Press, 1994).

[46]Aldor Lanctot and K. Scott Swan, "Technology Acquisition Strategy in an Internationally Competitive Environment," *Journal of International Management* 6 (Autumn 2000): 187–215.

[47]Masaaki Kotabe, Arvind Sahay, and Preet S. Aulakh, "Emerging Roles of Technology Licensing in Development of Global Product Strategy: A Conceptual Framework and Research Propositions," *Journal of Marketing* 60 (January 1996): 73–88.

[48]Stephen Kobrin, "An Empirical Analysis of the Determinants of Global Integration," *Strategic Management Journal* 12 (1991): 17–31.

The computer industry is a good instance of a case in which firms use components from various sources. HP/Compaq, Dell, and Acer all use semiconductor chips from Intel, AMD, or Cyrix, hard drives from Seagate Western Digital, Maxtor, or Hitachi, and software from Microsoft. The final product—in this case, the personal computer—carries some individual idiosyncrasies of Compaq, Dell, or Acer, but at least some of the components are common and, indeed, are portable across the products of the three companies.

In the international context, governments also tend to play a larger role and may, directly or indirectly, affect parts of the firm's strategy. Tariffs and nontariff barriers such as voluntary export restraints and restrictive customs procedures could change cost structures so that a firm could need to change its production and sourcing decisions. As presented in Chapter 2, the creation of the World Trade Organization in 1995, which launched the Doha Round of trade negotiations in 2001, is an encouraging sign because it leads to greater harmonization of tariff rules and less freedom for national governments to make arbitrary changes in tariff and non-tariff barriers and in intellectual property laws.

Global Marketing Strategy

Multinational companies increasingly use global marketing and have been highly successful—for example, Nestlé with its common brand name applied to many products in all countries, Coca-Cola with its global advertising themes, Xerox with its global leasing policies, and Dell Computer's "sell-direct" strategy. But global marketing is not about standardizing the marketing process on a global basis. Although every element of the marketing process—product design, product and brand positioning, brand name, packaging, pricing, advertising strategy and execution, promotion and distribution—may be a candidate for standardization, standardization is only one part of a **global marketing strategy**, and it may or may not be used by a company, depending on the mix of the product-market conditions, stage of market development, and the inclinations of the multinational firm's management. For instance, a marketing element can be global without being 100 percent uniform in content or coverage. **Exhibit 8-3** illustrates a possible pattern.

Let us take an instance from **Exhibit 8-3** and look at distribution with a magnitude of less than 50 percent on both coverage of world market and extent of uniform content. If we assume that the firm in question (represented in the diagram) does not have a manufacturing facility in each of the markets it serves, then to the extent that various markets have a uniform content, and presumably

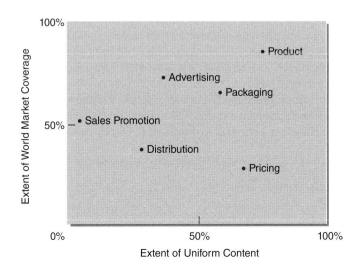

Exhibit 8-3
Variation in Content and Coverage of Global Marketing
Source: Adapted from George S. Yip, *Total Global Strategy: Managing for Worldwide Competitive Advantage* (Englewood Cliffs, NJ: Prentice Hall, 1992), p. 136.

similar operations, there is a requirement for coordination with manufacturing facilities elsewhere in the firm's global network. Also, where content is not uniform, any change requirements for the non-uniform content of distribution require corresponding changes in the product and/or packaging. Thus, a global marketing strategy requires more intimate linkages with a firm's other functions, such as research and development, manufacturing, and finance.[49]

In other words, a global marketing strategy is but one component of a global strategy. For an analogy, you may think of a just-in-time inventory and manufacturing system that works for a single manufacturing facility to optimize production. Extend this concept now to finance and marketing, and include all subsidiaries of the firm across the world as well. One can imagine the magnitude and complexity of the task when a manager is attempting to develop and implement a global strategy. One implication is that without a global strategy for R&D, manufacturing, and finance that meshes with the various requirements of its global marketing strategy, a firm cannot best implement that global marketing strategy.

Benefits of Global Marketing

Global marketing strategy can achieve one or more of four major categories of potential globalization benefits: cost reduction, improved quality of products and programs, enhanced customer preference, and increased competitive advantage.[50] General Motors and Ford approach global marketing somewhat differently; such a strategic difference suggests that the two U.S. automakers are in search of different benefits of global marketing (see **Case Study 8-1**).

Cost Reduction

When multiple national marketing functions are consolidated, personnel outlays are reduced through avoidance of duplicating activities. Costs are also saved in producing global advertisements and commercials and producing promotional materials and packaging. Savings from standardized packaging include reduction in inventory costs. With typical inventory carrying costs at 20 percent of sales, any reduction in inventory can significantly affect profitability. With the availability of a global span of coverage by various forms of modern communication media, multicountry campaigns capitalizing on countries' common features would also reduce advertising costs considerably. ExxonMobil's "Put a Tiger in Your Tank" campaign and the Tiger in many other forms offer a good example of a campaign that used the same theme across much of the world, taking advantage of the fact that the tiger is almost universally associated with power and grace.[51]

Owning a website on the internet and marketing to consumers is another way to reduce costs of conducting global marketing. It benefits both consumers, who can order to their own specifications everything from cars to swimsuits, and manufacturers in helping avoid inventory buildups. It also allows companies to have direct contact with consumers from different parts of the world, giving them deeper insight into market trends at a fraction of the cost incurred in traditional marketing. Cost savings can also translate into increased program effectiveness by allowing more money and resources into a smaller number of more focused programs. Disney, for example, is trying to break out of its traditional marketing methods with some alternative media. Now the company is launching a multi-player online game—Virtual Magic Kingdom—intended to drive kids to Disney resorts.[52]

---

[49]Masaaki Kotabe, *Global Sourcing Strategy: R&D, Manufacturing, and Marketing Interfaces* (New York: Quorum Books, 1992).

[50]George S. Yip, Total *Global Strategy: Managing for Worldwide Competitive Advantage* (Englewood Cliffs, N.J.: Prentice Hall, 1992): 21–23.

[51]If interested in the history of the Esso (ExxonMobil) tiger, probably one of the most recognized mascots in the world in the last 100 years, read "Esso and the Tiger," at ExxonMobil's website, http://www.exxonmobil.com/UK-English/about_history_esso_tiger.aspx, accessed August 10, 2012.

[52]Disney's Virtual Magic Kingdom, http://vmk.disney.go.com/.

Improved Products and Program Effectiveness

This may often be the greatest advantage of a global marketing strategy. Good ideas are relatively scarce in the business arena. Thus a globalization program that overcomes local objections to allow the spread of a good marketing idea can often raise the effectiveness of the program when measured on a worldwide basis. Traditionally, R&D has been concentrated in the headquarters country of a global company. This has sometimes circumscribed a possible synergy from amalgamation of good ideas from around the world.

Procter & Gamble has solved this problem by setting up major R&D facilities in each of its major markets in the Triad—North America, Japan, and Western Europe—and by putting together the pertinent findings from each of the laboratories. As in the saying, "Necessity is the mother of invention," different needs in different parts of the world may lead to different inventions. For example, Procter & Gamble's Liquid Tide laundry detergent was an innovative product developed in an innovative way by taking advantage of both the company's technical abilities and various market requirements in the key markets around the world. Germans had been extremely concerned about polluting rivers with phosphate, a key whitening ingredient in the traditional detergent. To meet the German customer demand, Procter & Gamble in Germany had developed fatty acid to replace phosphate in the detergent. Similarly, Procter & Gamble Japan had developed surfactant to get off grease effectively in tepid water that Japanese use in washing their clothes. In the United States, Procter & Gamble in Cincinnati, Ohio, had independently developed "builder" to keep dirt from settling on clothes. Putting all these three innovations together, the company introduced Liquid Tide and its sister products (e.g., Ariel) around the world.

Three benefits followed from this multiple R&D location strategy. By being able to integrate required product attributes from three separate markets, P&G was able to introduce a much better product than would otherwise have been possible and increase its chances of success. Second, its development costs were spread over a much larger market—a market that was more inclined to receive the product favorably because of the incorporation of the product features described. Third, it increased the sources from which product ideas are available to it. Thus, not only does P&G have immediate returns, but also it has secured for itself a reliable resource base of future products.

Enhanced Customer Preference

Awareness and recall of a product on a worldwide basis increase its value. A global marketing strategy helps build recognition that can enhance customer preferences through reinforcement. With the rise in the availability of information from a variety of sources across the world and the rise in travel across national borders, more and more people are being exposed to messages in different countries. Thus a uniform marketing message, whether communicated through a brand name, packaging, or advertisement reinforces the awareness, knowledge, and attitudes of people toward the product or service. Pepsi has a consistent theme in its marketing communication across the world—that of youthfulness and fun as a part of the experience of drinking Pepsi anywhere in the world.

Increased Competitive Advantage

By focusing resources into a smaller number of programs, global strategies magnify the competitive power of the programs. Although larger competitors might have the resources to develop different high-quality programs for each country, smaller firms might not. Using a focused global marketing strategy could allow the smaller firm to compete with a larger competitor in a more effective manner. However, the most important benefit of a global strategy may be that the entire organization gets behind a single idea, thus increasing the chances of the success of the idea. Avis created a global campaign communicating the idea that "We are number two, therefore we try harder," not only to customers, but also to its employees. As a result the entire organization pulled together to deliver on a global promise, not just in marketing but also in all activities that directly or indirectly affected the company's interface with the customer.

Equally, if not more, important are the benefits of market and competitive intelligence provided by the increased flow of information due to the worldwide coordination of activities. As the global firm meshes the different parts of the organization into the framework of a focused strategy, information flow through the organization improves and enables the functioning of the strategy. A byproduct is that the organization as a whole becomes much better informed about itself and about the activities of its competitors in markets across the world.

Limits to Global Marketing

Although national boundaries have begun losing their significance both as a psychological and as a physical barrier to international business, the diversity of local environments, particularly cultural, political, and legal environments, still plays an important role not as a facilitator, but rather as an inhibitor, of optimal global marketing strategy development. Indeed, we still debate the very issue raised more than thirty years ago: counteracting forces of "unification versus fragmentation" in developing operational strategies along the value chain. As early as 1969, John Fayerweather wrote emphatically:

> What fundamental effects does (the existence of many national borders) have on the strategy of the multinational firm? Although many effects can be itemized, one central theme recurs; that is, their tendency to push the firm toward adaptation to the diversity of local environments which leads toward fragmentation of operations. But there is a natural tendency in a single firm toward integration and uniformity that is basically at odds with fragmentation. Thus the central issue . . . is the conflict between unification and fragmentation—a close-knit operational strategy with similar foreign units versus a loosely related, highly variegated family of activities.[53]

Many authors have since revisited the same counteracting forces in such terms as "standardization vs. adaptation" (1960s–1970s), "globalization vs. localization" (1970s–1980s), "global integration vs. local responsiveness" (1980s–1990s), and most recently, "scale versus sensitivity" (2000s). Today, we may even add another variant, "online scale versus offline market sensitivity." Basically, the left-side concept (i.e., unification, standardization, globalization, global integration, scale, and online scale) refers to a supply-side argument in favor of the benefits of economies of scale and scope, while the right-side concept (i.e., fragmentation, adaptation, localization, local responsiveness, sensitivity, and offline market sensitivity) refers to a demand-side argument addressing the existence of market differences and the importance of catering to the differing market needs and conditions. Terms have changed, but the quintessence of the strategic dilemma that those multinational firms face today has not changed and will probably remain unchanged for years to come.[54]

Now the question is to what extent successful multinational firms can circumvent the impact of local environmental diversity. In some industries, product standardization may result in a product that satisfies customers nowhere. For processed foods, for example, national tastes and consumption patterns differ sufficiently to make standardization counterproductive. In Latin America, a variety of canned spicy peppers, such as jalapeño peppers, is a national staple in Mexico, but is virtually unheard of in Brazil and Chile. Obviously, firms cannot lump together the whole of Latin America into one regional market for condiments.

---

[53]John Fayerweather, *International Business Management: Conceptual Framework* (New York: McGraw-Hill, 1969), pp. 133–34.

[54]Masaaki Kotabe, "To Kill Two Birds with One Stone: Revisiting the Integration-Responsiveness Framework," in Michael Hitt and Joseph Cheng, eds., *Managing Transnational Firms* (New York: Elsevier, 2002), pp. 59–69.

The internet is global in nature and so are the websites. Being on the web arguably translates into reaching customers in many corners of the world from day one. However, it does not mean that e-commerce can be developed without any need for local and regional adaptation. To effectively target and reach global consumers online, many companies still need to approach them in their languages, conforming to their cultural value systems.[55] Indeed, one recent study clearly shows that local websites of India, China, Japan, and the United States not only reflect cultural values of the country of their origin, but also differ significantly from each other on cultural dimensions.[56]

On the other hand, Merck, the world's second-largest pharmaceutical company, faces a different kind of problem with global marketing. The company can market the same products around the world for various ailments, but cultural and political differences make it very difficult to approach different markets in a similar way. Merck, which operates internationally as MSD, has to increase public awareness of health care issues in Mexico, Central America, and much of South America by bringing top journalists from these countries together on a regular basis to meet with health care experts ranging from physicians to government officials. The company is trying to change the way it does business in the Pacific Rim. It used to operate through local distributors and licensees without learning the local quirks of pharmaceutical business. Now, the company is creating subsidiaries in nearly all main Asian countries, including Korea, China, the Philippines, Taiwan, Singapore, and Malaysia, to learn what goes on inside those markets. In Eastern Europe, Merck is starting from scratch, because its entry had been previously barred under the region's strict communist control. For example, in Hungary, the company devoted its initial investment to establishing resource centers that are affiliated with local hospitals and universities in order to create a special image for Merck.[57] Even in supposedly similar cultures, there can be huge differences in what are effective marketing campaigns. The Body Shop found this out when it took a successful ad campaign in Britain and brought it to the United States, assuming it would have the same appeal. The ad showed the naked buttocks of three men and completely misfired in the U.S. market. In the words of Body Shop founder Anita Roddick, "We thought it was funny and witty here, but women in New Hampshire fainted."[58]

However, despite such cultural and political constraints in the markets, Nestlé, for example, has managed to integrate procurement functions to gain bargaining power in purchasing common ingredients such as cocoa and sugar. In other industries, such as computers and telecommunications, consumption patterns are in the process of being established and the associated cultural constraint is getting less prominent. Also, the simultaneous launch of most products in these categories across the world precludes large differences. For these products, governments frequently attempt to exert national control over technological development, the products or the production process.[59] However, while it is the multinational firms that are the vehicle through which technology, production, and economic activity in general are integrated across borders, *it is the underlying technology and economic activity that should be globally exploited for economies of scale and scope*. National markets, regardless of how they are organized economically, are no

---

[55]E. James Randall and L. Jean Harrison-Walker, "If You Build It, Will They Come? Barriers to International e-Marketing," *Journal of Marketing Theory & Practice* 10 (Spring 2002): 12–21; and Kendall Goodrich and Marieke de Mooij, "New Technology Mirrors Old Habits: Online Buying Mirrors Cross-National Variance of Conventional Buying," *Journal of International Consumer Marketing* 23, no. 3/4 (2011): 246–259.

[56]Nitish Singh, Hongxin Zhao, and Xiaorui Hu, "Analyzing the Cultural Content of Web Sites: A Cross-National Comparison of China, India, Japan, and US," *International Marketing Review* 22, no. 2 (2005): 129–145.

[57]Fannie Weinstein, "Drug Interaction: Merck Establishes Itself, Country by Country, in Emerging Markets," *Profiles,* (September 1996): 35–39; and Richard T. Clark, "Standing Behind Our Core Values," *Vital Speeches of the Day*, January 15, 2006, pp. 220–224.

[58]Ernest Beck, "Body Shop Gets a Makeover to Cut Costs," *Wall Street Journal*, January 27, 1999, p. A18.

[59]C. K. Prahalad and Yves L. Doz, *The Multinational Mission* (New York: The Free Press, 1987).

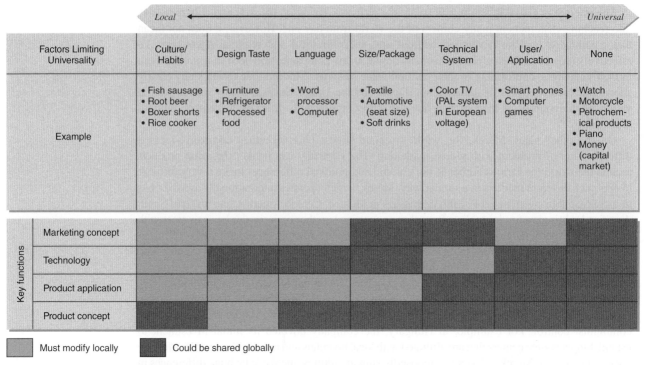

Exhibit 8-4 Degree of Standardizability of Products in World Markets

Source: Adapted from Kenichi Ohmae, *Triad Power: The Coming Shape of Global Competition* (New York: The Free Press), p. 193.

longer enough to support the development of technology in many industries. See **Exhibit 8-4** for some generalizations about the degree of product standardization around the world.

R&D, Operations, and Marketing Interfaces

Marketing managers cannot develop a successful marketing strategy without understanding how other functional areas, such as R&D and operations, influence the degree of their marketing decision making as well as how those functions may be influenced by them. In this section, we focus on the three most important interrelated activities in the value chain: R&D (e.g., technology development, product design, and engineering), operations (e.g., manufacturing), and marketing activities. Marketing managers should understand and appreciate the important roles that product designers, engineers, production managers, and purchasing managers, among others, play in marketing decision making. Marketing decisions cannot be made in the absence of these people.[60] Management of the **interfaces**, or linkages, among these value-adding activities is a crucial determinant of a company's competitive advantage. A recent study also shows that marketing not only plays a pivotal role but affects firm performance more than R&D and operations.[61] See **Exhibit 8-5** for an outline of a basic framework of management of R&D, operations, and marketing interfaces. Undoubtedly, these value-adding activities should be examined as holistically as

---

[60]David B. Montgomery and Frederick E. Webster, Jr., "Marketing's Interfunctional Interfaces: The MSI Workshop on Management of Corporate Fault Zones," *Journal of Market Focused Management* 2 (1997): 7–26.

[61]Alexander Krasnikov and Staish Jayachandran, "The Relative Impact of Marketing, Research-and-Development, and Operations Capabilities on Firm Performance," *Journal of Marketing* 72 (July 2008): 1–11.

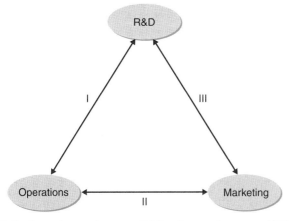

I. R&D/MANUFACTURING INTERFACE
• Product innovation
• Designing for manufacturability
• Manufacturing process innovation
• Components sourcing

II. OPERATIONS/MARKETING INTERFACE
• Product and component standardization
• Product modification

III. MARKETING/R&D INTERFACE
• New product development
• Product positioning

Exhibit 8-5 Interfaces Among R&D, Operations, and Marketing

possible, by linking the boundaries of these primary activities. Linking R&D and operations with marketing provides enormous direct and indirect benefits to companies operating in a highly competitive environment.

R&D/Operations Interface

Technology is broadly defined as know-how. It can be classified based on the nature of know-how composed of product technology (the set of ideas embodied in the product) and process technology (the set of ideas involved in the manufacture of the product or the steps necessary to combine new materials to produce a finished product). However, executives tend to focus solely on product-related technology as the driving force of the company's competitiveness. Product technology alone may not provide the company a long-term competitive edge over competition unless it is matched with sufficient manufacturing capabilities.[62]

Consider the automobile industry as an example. R&D is critical today for automakers because manufacturers are under tremendous pressure to provide more innovative products. Customers continue to raise the bar with respect to styling, quality, reliability, and safety. At the same time, manufacturers face difficult technical challenges on the energy and environmental front. They must make continual improvements in vehicle fuel economy and reductions in tailpipe emissions everywhere in the world. Although more improvement can be squeezed out of the conventional internal combustion engine, manufacturers are looking ahead to hybrid vehicle technology and, ultimately, to a hydrogen-based fuel-cell vehicle. The development costs and infrastructure changes necessary to take the step to fuel cell technology are staggering, so it makes sense for auto manufacturers to team up and share knowledge in order to move the industry as a whole ahead faster.

To reduce the R&D costs, General Motors is working with its alliance partners on more than 50 joint technology development projects ranging from pedestrian protection and 42-volt electrical architecture to all-wheel drive and clean diesel engines. Besides cooperating with other manufacturers, GM has formed research partnerships with suppliers, universities, and governmental agencies. These research alliances cover such areas as advanced internal combustion engine development, fuel cell technology, advanced chassis systems, and electronics and communications

---

[62]Bruce R. Guile and Harvey Brooks, eds., *Technology and Global Industry: Companies and Nations in the World Economy* (Washington, D.C.: National Academy Press, 1987).

systems. They are truly global, involving companies and universities in Canada, Europe, Japan, China, and the Middle East.

By pulling together the talents and resources from this global R&D network, GM has been able to reduce redundancy, accelerate ongoing development, and jump-start new development. Of course, to launch such collaboration successfully requires that the companies involved overcome differences in culture, language, business practices, engineering, and manufacturing approaches.[63] This example suggests that manufacturing processes should also be innovative. To facilitate the transferability of new product innovations to manufacturing, a team of product designers and engineers should strive to design components such that they are conducive to manufacturing without the requirement of undue retooling. Low levels of retooling requirements and interchangeability of components are necessary conditions for efficient sourcing strategy on a global scale. If different equipment and components are used in various manufacturing plants, it is extremely difficult to establish a highly coordinated sourcing plan on a global basis.

Operations/Marketing Interface

A continual conflict exists between manufacturing operations and marketing divisions. It is to the manufacturing division's advantage if all products and components are standardized to facilitate standardized, low-cost production. The marketing division, however, is more interested in satisfying the diverse needs of customers, requiring broad product lines and frequent product modifications, which add cost to manufacturing. How have successful companies coped with this dilemma?

Recently, an increasing amount of interest has been shown in the strategic linkages between product policy and manufacturing—long ignored in traditional considerations of global strategy development. With aggressive competition from multinational companies emphasizing corporate product policy and concomitant manufacturing, many companies have realized that product innovations alone cannot sustain their long-term competitive position without an effective product policy linking product and manufacturing process innovations. The strategic issue, then, is how to design a robust product or components with sufficient versatility built in across uses, technology, and situations.[64]

Four different ways of developing a global product policy are generally considered effective means to streamline manufacturing operations, thus lowering manufacturing cost, without sacrificing marketing flexibility: (1) core components standardization, (2) product design families, (3) universal product with all features, and (4) universal product with different positioning.[65]

Core Components Standardization

Successful global product policy mandates the development of universal products, or products that require no more than a cosmetic change for adaptation to differing local needs and use conditions. For example, Seiko, a Japanese watchmaker, offers a wide range of designs and models, but they

[63]Larry J. Howell and Jamie C. Hsu, "Globalization within the Auto Industry," *Research Technology Management* 45 (July/August 2002): 43–49.

[64]K. Scott Swan, Masaaki Kotabe, and Brent Allred, "Exploring Robust Design Capabilities, Their Role in Creating Global Products, and Their Relationship to Firm Performance," *Journal of Product Innovation Management* 22 (March 2005): 144–164; and also see a special issue on "Product Design Research and Practice: Past, Present, and Future" in *Journal of Product Innovation Management* 28 (May 2011), compiled by K. Scott Swan and Michael Luchs.

[65]Hirotaka Takeuchi and Michael E. Porter, "Three Roles of International Marketing in Global Strategy," in Michael E. Porter, ed. *Competition in Global Industries* (Boston: Harvard Business School Press, 1986): 111–146.

are based on only a handful of different operating mechanisms. Similarly, the best-performing German machine tool–making companies have a narrower range of products, use up to 50 percent fewer parts than their less successful rivals, and make continual, incremental product and design improvements with new developments passed rapidly on to customers.

Product Design Families

A variant of core components standardization involves product design families. It is also possible for companies marketing an extremely wide range of products due to cultural differences in product-use patterns around the world to reap economies of scale benefits. For example, Toyota offers several car models based on a similar family design concept, ranging from Lexus models to Toyota Avalons, Camrys, and Corollas. Many of the Lexus features well received by customers have been adopted into the Toyota lines with just a few minor modifications (mostly downsizing). In the process, Toyota has been able to cut product development costs and meet the needs of different market segments. Similarly, Electrolux, a Swedish appliance manufacturer, has adopted the concept of "design families," offering different products under four different brand names, but using the same basic designs. A key to such product design standardization lies in standardizing components, including motors, pumps, and compressors. Thus, two Electrolux subsidiaries, White Consolidated in the United States and Zanussi in Italy, have the main responsibility for component production within the group for worldwide application.

Universal Product with All Features

As just noted, competitive advantage can result from standardization of core components and/or product design families. One variant of components and product standardization is to develop a universal product with all features demanded anywhere in the world. Japan's Canon has done so successfully with its AE-1 cameras and newer models. After extensive market analyses around the world, Canon identified a set of common features customers wanted in a camera, including good picture quality, ease of operation with automatic features, technical sophistication, professional looks, and reasonable price. To develop such cameras, the company introduced a few breakthroughs in camera design and manufacturing, such as an electronic integrated circuitry brain to control camera operations, modularized production, and standardization and reduction of parts.

Universal Product with Different Positioning

Alternatively, a universal product can be developed with different market segments in mind. Thus, a universal product can be positioned differently in different markets. This is where marketing promotion plays a major role to accomplish such a feat. Product and/or components standardization, however, does not necessarily imply either production standardization or a narrow product line. For example, Japanese automobile manufacturers have gradually stretched out their product line offerings, while marketing them with little adaptation in many parts of the world. This strategy requires manufacturing flexibility. The crux of global product or component standardization, instead, calls for proactive identification of homogeneous segments around the world, and is different from the concept of marketing abroad a product originally developed for the home market. A proactive approach to product policy has gained momentum in recent years as it is made possible by intermarket segmentation.[66] In addition to clustering countries and identifying homogeneous segments in different countries, targeting different segments in different countries with the same products is another way to maintain a product policy of standardization.

---

[66]Theodore Levitt, "The Globalization of Markets," *Harvard Business Review* 61 (May-June 1983): 92–102.

For example, Honda marketed almost identical Accord cars around the world by positioning them differently in the minds of consumers from country to country. Accord has been promoted as a family sedan in Japan, a relatively inexpensive sports car in Germany, and a reliable commuter car in the United States. In recent years, however, Honda has begun developing some regional variations of the Accord. Through a flexible global platform, Honda now offers Accords of different widths, heights, and lengths in the United States, Europe, and Japan. In addition, from the same platform, a minivan, a sport utility vehicle (SUV), and two Acura luxury cars have been developed. From a practical standpoint, the platform is the most expensive and time-consuming component to develop. The global platform allows Honda to reduce the costs of bringing the three distinct Accords to market by 20 percent, resulting in a $1,200 savings per car. Honda clearly adheres to a policy of core component standardization so that at least 50 percent of the components, including the chassis and transmission, are shared across the variations of the Accord.[67]

Marketing/R&D Interface

Both R&D and manufacturing activities are technically outside the marketing manager's responsibility. However, the marketing manager's knowledge of consumers' needs is indispensable in product development. Without a good understanding of the consumers' needs, product designers and engineers are prone to impose their technical specifications on the product rather than fitting them to what consumers want. After all, consumers, not product designers or engineers, have the final say in deciding whether or not to buy the product.

Japanese companies, in particular, excel in management of the marketing/R&D interface.[68] Indeed, their source of competitive advantage often lies in marketing and R&D divisions' willingness to coordinate their respective activities concurrently. In a traditional product development, either a new product was developed and pushed down from the R&D division to the manufacturing and marketing divisions for sales, or a new product idea was pushed up from the marketing division to the R&D division for development. This top-down or bottom-up new product development takes too much time in an era of global competition, in which a short product development cycle is crucial to meet constant competitive pressure from new products introduced by rival companies around the world.

R&D and marketing divisions of Japanese companies are always on the lookout for the use of emerging technologies initially in existing products to satisfy customer needs better than their own existing and their competitors' products. This affords them an opportunity to gain experience, debug technological glitches, reduce costs, boost performance, and adapt designs for worldwide customer use. As a result, they have been able to increase the speed of new product introductions, meet the competitive demands of a rapidly changing marketplace, and capture market share.

In other words, *the marketplace becomes a virtual R&D laboratory for Japanese companies to gain production and marketing experience, as well as to perfect technology.* This requires close contact with customers, whose inputs help Japanese companies improve upon their products on an ongoing basis. In the process, they introduce new products one after another.

Another example worth noting is the exploitation of so-called fuzzy logic by Hitachi and others.[69] When fuzzy logic was conceived in the mid-1960s by Lotfi A. Zadeh, a computer science

---

[67]"Can Honda Build a World Car?," *Business Week,* September 8, 1997, pp. 100–108; and "The Also-Rans," *Economist,* February 21, 2004, pp. 61–62.

[68]X. Michael Song and Mark E. Parry, "A Cross-National Comparative Study of New Product Development Processes: Japan and the United States," *Journal of Marketing* 61 (April 1997): 1–18.

[69]Larry Armstrong, "Why 'Fuzzy Logic' Beats Black-or-White Thinking," *Business Week*, May 21, 1990, pp. 92–93.

professor at the University of California at Berkeley, nobody other than several Japanese companies paid serious heed to its potential application in ordinary products. The fuzzy logic allows computers to deal with shades of gray or something vague between 0 and 1—no small feat in a world of the binary computers. Today, Hitachi, Panasonic, Mitsubishi, Sony, and Nissan Motors, among others, use fuzzy logic in their products. For example, Hitachi introduced a "fuzzy" train that automatically accelerates and brakes so smoothly that no one reaches for the hanging straps. Panasonic began marketing a "fuzzy" washing machine with only one start button that automatically judges the size and dirtiness of the load and decides the optimum cycle times, amount of detergent needed, and water level. Sony introduced a palm-size computer capable of recognizing written Japanese, with a fuzzy circuit to iron out the inconsistencies in different writing styles. Now fuzzy circuits are put into the autofocus mechanisms of video cameras to get constantly clear pictures.[70]

The continual introduction of newer and better designed products also brings a greater likelihood of market success.[71] Ideal products often require a giant leap in technology and product development, and naturally are subject to a much higher risk of consumer rejection. The Japanese approach of incrementalism not only allows for continual improvement and a stream of new products, but also permits quicker consumer adoption. Consumers are likely to accept improved products more quickly than very different products, because the former are more compatible with the existing patterns of product use and lifestyles. Indeed, recent research reinforces the importance of information sharing between R&D and marketing departments as a way to reduce uncertainty in the highly volatile environment of new product development, whether in Japan, China, or the United States.[72]

Regionalization of Global Marketing Strategy

Some firms, such as General Motors, may have difficulty in organizing, or may not be willing to organize, operations to maximize flexibility and encourage integration across national borders. Beyond various cultural, political, and economic differences across national borders, organizational realities also impair the ability of multinational firms to pursue global marketing strategies. Not surprisingly, integration has often been opposed by foreign subsidiaries eager to protect their historical relative independence from their parent companies.

In finding a balance between the need for greater integration and the need to exploit existing resources more effectively, many companies have begun to explore the use of regional strategies in Europe, North America, and the Pacific Rim. Regional strategies can be defined as the cross-subsidization of market share battles in pursuit of regional production, branding, and distribution advantages.[73] Regional strategies in Europe and North America have been encouraged by the economic, political, and social pressures resulting from the development of regional trading blocs, such as the European Union, the North American Free Trade Agreement (NAFTA), and the Southern Common Market (MERCOSUR).[74]

---

[70]Robert J. Crawford, "Reinterpreting the Japanese Economic Miracle," *Harvard Business Review* 76 (January/February 1998): 179–84.

[71]Michael R. Czinkota and Masaaki Kotabe, "Product Development the Japanese Way," *Journal of Business Strategy* 11 (November/December 1990): 31–36.

[72]X. Michael Song and R. Jeffrey Thieme, "A Cross-National Investigation of the R&D–Marketing Interface in the Product Innovation Process," *Industrial Marketing Management* 35 (April 2006): 308–322.

[73]Allen J. Morrison and Kendall Roth, "The Regional Solution: An Alternative to Globalization," *Transnational Corporations* 1 (August 1, 1992): 37–55; and Gerald Millet, "Global Marketing and Regionalization—Worlds Apart?" *Pharmaceutical Executive,* 17 (August 1997): 78–81.

[74]Alan M. Rugman, "Regional Strategy and the Demise of Globalization," *Journal of International Management* 9, no. 4 (2003): 409–417.

Regional trading blocs have had two favorable effects. First, the volatility of foreign exchange rates within a bloc seems to be reduced.[75] Second, with the growing level of macroeconomic integration within regions, the trend is also toward greater harmonization of product and industry standards, pollution and safety standards, and environmental standards—among other things.[76] These regional commonalities further encourage firms to develop marketing strategies on a regional basis.[77] Global marketing strategy cannot be developed without considering competitive and other market forces from different regions around the world. To face those regional forces proactively, three additional strategies need to be considered at the firm level. These are cross subsidization of markets, identification of weak market segments, and the lead market concept.[78] See also **Global Perspective 8-2** for an example of global competition among Sony PlayStation, Microsoft Xbox, and Nintendo GameCube employing these three strategies on an ongoing basis.

◆ ◆

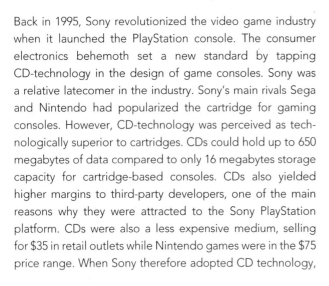

Global Perspective 8-2

Sony, Microsoft, and Nintendo Battling for Global Dominance in the Video Game Industry

Back in 1995, Sony revolutionized the video game industry when it launched the PlayStation console. The consumer electronics behemoth set a new standard by tapping CD-technology in the design of game consoles. Sony was a relative latecomer in the industry. Sony's main rivals Sega and Nintendo had popularized the cartridge for gaming consoles. However, CD-technology was perceived as technologically superior to cartridges. CDs could hold up to 650 megabytes of data compared to only 16 megabytes storage capacity for cartridge-based consoles. CDs also yielded higher margins to third-party developers, one of the main reasons why they were attracted to the Sony PlayStation platform. CDs were also a less expensive medium, selling for $35 in retail outlets while Nintendo games were in the $75 price range. When Sony therefore adopted CD technology,

the firm created the impression that the PlayStation would become the wave of the future in the video game industry. Nintendo steadfastly refused to adopt this new technology even when it released its 64-bit N64. Nintendo's lack of enthusiasm for the CD-platform was mainly due to the fact that it *owned* the cartridge technology and, therefore, was reluctant to abandon this platform. Nintendo's slow response in the wake of new technologies proved to be a recipe for disaster.

Five years later in 2000, the second generation of PlayStation, known as PlayStation 2 (PS2), which Sony introduced, instantly became dominant in the global gaming market. PS2 was the first video game system to use the Digital Video Disc (DVD) format. The DVD platform allowed the PS2 to hold much more information than rival video game systems.

[75]Alan David MacCormack, Lawrence James Newmann, and Donald B. Rosenfield, "The New Dynamics of Global Manufacturing Site Location," *Sloan Management Review* 35 (Summer 1994): 69–80; and Masaaki Kotabe, "To Kill Two Birds with One Stone: Revisiting the Integration-Responsiveness Framework," in Michael Hitt and Joseph Cheng, eds., *Managing Transnational Firms*, New York: Elsevier, 2002, pp. 59–69.

[76]Edmund W. Beaty, "Standard Regionalization: A Threat to Internetworking?" *Telecommunications*, Americas Edition 27 (May 1993): 48–51.

[77]Maneesh Chandra, "The Regionalization of Global Strategy," A paper presented at 1997 Academy of International Business Annual Meeting, Monterrey, Mexico, October 8–12, 1997.

[78]Gary Hamel and C.K. Prahalad, "Do You Really Have a Global Strategy?" *Harvard Business Review* (July–August 1985): 139–148.

Another solid feature of PS2 is that it is able to play most of the original PlayStation games. Due to the blockbuster success of the first generation PS, PS2 penetrated the video game market very easily.

The good times for the video game industry did not last forever. According to analysts, 2002 was the peak of the cycle, and the market cooled off gradually till the seventh generation of consoles began appearing in late 2005 when Microsoft Xbox 360 was introduced. On November 11 2006, Sony launched PlayStation 3 (PS3), the successor to the PlayStation 2 as part of the PlayStation series. Eight days later, the Wii, the fifth home video game console by Nintendo, was released as the direct successor to the Nintendo GameCube.

In the competition of the seventh-generation video game consoles, Nintendo Wii is definitely the winner, with 95.9 million units sold in 2012 (four times increase since 2008), beating Microsoft Xbox's 67.2 million and Sony PS3's 63.9 million units sold as of March 31, 2012. The key for its success lies in its broader demographic target, which benefits from the console's distinguishing feature, the wireless controller known as the Wii Remote. The remote can be used as a handheld pointing device and detect movement in three dimensions, resulting in a revolution in the way video games are played. Another significant feature is WiiConnect24, which enables it to receive messages and updates over the internet while in standby mode. Its low price of $249 is also an important reason for its popularity.

The Sony-Microsoft-Nintendo competition is being played out globally and particularly in the Triad regions of North America, Japan, and Europe. The following table shows the launch dates and the sales volumes for Sony PS3, Microsoft Xbox, and Nintendo Wii.

	Launch Date		
	Sony PlayStation 3	**Microsoft Xbox**	**Nintendo Wii**
Japan	November 11, 2006	December 10, 2005	December 2, 2006
United States	November 17 2006	November 22, 2005	November 19, 2006
Europe (U.K.)	March 23, 2007	December 2, 2005	December 8, 2006
Unit Sales since Launch (as of March 31, 2012)	63.9 million	67.2 million	95.9 million

Sources: "Sony's PS3 Problems Cast a Long Shadow," *BusinessWeek. com*, May 16, 2007; "How the Wii Is Winning," *BusinessWeek.com*, September 12, 2007; "Bringing PlayStation Back to Basics," *Business-Week.com*, September 24, 2007; "More Delays for PlayStation," *BusinessWeek.com*, April 22, 2008; "Consolidated Sales Transition by Region," Nintendo, http://www.nintendo.co.jp/, April 25, 2012; "Global Xbox 360 Sales Down Nearly 50 percent Year-on-Year," Eurogamer, www.eurogamer.net, April 25, 2012; and "PlayStation3 Worldwide Hardware Unit Sales," Sony Computer Entertainment, http://www.scei.co.jp/, April 25, 2012.

Cross-Subsidization of Markets

Cross-subsidization of markets refers to multinational firms using profits gained in a market where they have a strong competitive position to beef up their competitive position in a market where they are struggling to gain foothold. For example, Michelin used its strong profit base in Europe to attack the home market of Goodyear in the United States. Reducing prices in its home market (by Goodyear) would have meant that Goodyear would have reduced its own profits from its largest and most profitable market without substantially affecting Michelin's bottom line, because Michelin would have exposed only a small portion of its worldwide business by competing with Goodyear in the United States. Goodyear chose to strike back by expanding operations and reducing prices in Europe.

Kodak's classic rivalry with Fuji Film in the photographic film market in the 1990s provides another example of the importance of not permitting a global competitor unhindered operation in its home market. Kodak did not have a presence in Japan until the early 1980s. In this omission, Kodak was making the same mistake that many other Western companies have made—avoiding

Japan as unattractive on a stand-alone basis, while not seeing its strategic importance as the home base of a global competitor and a source of ideas.[79]

Identification of Weak Market Segments

The second strategy that firms should always keep an open eye for is the identification of **weak market segments** not covered by a firm in its home market. Japanese TV makers used small-screen portable TVs to get a foot in the door of the large U.S. market for TVs. RCA and Zenith did not think this segment attractive enough to go after. Another classic example is Honda's entry into the U.S. motorcycle market in the 1960s. Honda offered small, lightweight machines that looked safe and cute, attracting families and an emerging leisure class with an advertising campaign, "You can meet the nicest people on a Honda." Prior to Honda's entry, the U.S. motorcycle market was characterized by the police, military personnel, aficionados, and scofflaws like the Hell's Angels and the Devil's Disciples. Honda broke away from the existing paradigms about motorcycles and the motorcycle market, and successfully differentiated itself by covering niches that did not exist before.[80] Once the Japanese companies were established in this small niche, they had a base to expand on to larger and more profitable product lines. More recently in 1997, Labatt International of Canada took advantage of freer trade relationships under NAFTA and awakened Canadian consumers to things Mexican by importing a Mexican beer, Sol, brewed by Cerveceria Cuauhtemoc Moctezuma, to fill a newly found market segment in Canada. Thus, firms should avoid pegging their competitive advantage entirely on one market segment in their home market.

What directions can this lead to in terms of a global product strategy—or a worldwide distribution, pricing, or promotion strategy? We discuss some aspects of a global product strategy for an automobile company. Suppose market data tell the managers that four dozen different models are required if the company desires to design separate cars for each distinct segment of the global market, but the company has neither the financial nor the technological resources to make so many product designs. Also, no single global car will solve the problems for the entire world. The United States, Japan, and Europe in the Triad region are different markets, and so are emerging markets, with different mixes of needs and preferences. Japan requires right-hand drive cars with frequent government-required inspections, while many parts of Europe need smaller cars as compared to the United States, and lower-priced fuel-efficient cars are needed for an emerging mass market in China, India, and other emerging economies. The option of leaving out a Triad market or emerging markets would not be a good one. The company needs to be present in all of these markets with good products.

Use of the "Lead Market" Concept

The solution may be to look at the main requirements of each lead market in turn. A **lead market** is a market where unique local competition is nurturing product and service standards to be adopted by the rest of the world over time. A classic case is facsimile (fax) technology. Siemens in Germany had developed a considerable technological advantage in fax technology in the 1970s. However, because of lukewarm reaction from its domestic market, the German company abandoned the fax and concentrated on improving the telex system. In the meantime, sensing a strong demand for this technology, Japanese companies invested continuously in fax technology and introduced a stream of improved and affordable fax machines in Japan and abroad. Backed by the strength of the local markets, the Japanese bandwagon, led by Sharp and Ricoh, spread over to

---

[79]Yoshi Tsurumi and Hiroki Tsurumi, "Fujifilm-Kodak Duopolistic Competition in Japan and the United States," *Journal of International Business Studies* 30 (4th Quarter 1999): 813–830.

[80]Richard P. Rumelt, "The Many Faces of Honda," *California Management Review* 38 (Summer 1996): 103–111; and Richard D. Pascale, "Reflections on Honda," *California Management Review* 38 (Summer 1996): 112–117.

the rest of the world, displacing the telex system eventually. In retrospect, Siemens should have introduced fax machines in Japan as the lead market instead.[81]

Another example is the recent development of smartphones in the United States. In the first decade of the twenty-first century, Canada's RIM Blackberry was the most dominant smartphone device. Then came Google's Android and Apple's iOS operating systems in the U.S. market. As recently as 2011, they were already the world's leading smartphone operating systems, owning a little over half the market. In 2012 (at the time of this writing), their market share had already surpassed the 80 percentage mark. Of the 152.3 million smartphones shipped in the first quarter of 2012, 59 percent had Android on them and 23 percent ran Apple iOS, with the remainder of the market left to Symbian (6.8 percent), RIM Blackberry (6.4 percent), Linux (2.3 percent), and Windows 7/Mobile (2.2 percent). Android and iOS gains during the period were largely at the expense of Symbian and Blackberry smartphones.[82] Any new developments, such as application software (apps) development, observed in the U.S. market may set the tone for the rest of the world.

Emerging markets could also increasingly serve as potential lead markets. One such interesting example is Mahindra & Mahindra, a major Indian tractor manufacturer, which in 2002 began marketing its basic tractors in a so-called recreational farmers market segment in the United States that U.S. tractor manufacturers had largely ignored. Deere & Co., a U.S. company known for its heavy-duty farm equipment and large construction equipment, opened its R&D facility in Pune, India in 2001 to develop farm equipment suitable for the Indian market. Deere tractors marketed in India were so basic that the U.S. company had never even contemplated selling them in the United States until Mahindra's entry into the recreational farmers market. Now Deere, taking a cue from Mahindra, has begun marketing a slightly modified version of the Indian line of tractors (with softer seats and higher horsepower) to hobbyists and bargain hunters in the United States. As a result, India is fast becoming a lead market for developing stripped-down tractors for India and other emerging markets, which double as recreational tractors for hobbyists in the United States.[83]

As indicated earlier, this is a strategic response to the emergence of lead countries as a market globalization driver. Each can be a lead country model—a product carefully tailored to meet distinct individual needs. With a short list of lead country models in hand, minor modifications may enable a fair amount of sales in other Triad markets and elsewhere. This will halve the number of basic models required to cover the global markets and, at the same time, cover a major proportion of sales with cars designed for major markets. Additional model types could be developed through adaptation of the lead country models for specific segments. This approach in each of the largest core markets permits development of a pool of supplemental designs that can be adapted to local preferences.

In line with our earlier example of Procter & Gamble, it is not necessary that the design and manufacture of a lead country model be restricted to one R&D and manufacturing facility. Ford has now integrated the design and manufacturing process on a global basis. It has design centers at Dearborn in the United States, and sites in England, Italy, and Japan, which are connected by a satellite uplink. Designers using fast workstations and massively parallel computers simulate a complete model and the working of the model for various conditions. Separate parts of the car are simulated at different facilities. Thereafter, the complete design for a lead country is integrated in the facility assigned for the purpose. For instance, the complete design for the new Ford Mustang was put together in Dearborn, but it incorporated some significant changes in body design that were made in England based on designs of Jaguar, which Ford used to own.[84] Similarly, different

[81]Marian Beise and Thomas Cleff, "Assessing the Lead Market Potential of Countries for Innovation Projects," *Journal of International Management* 10 (October 2004): 453–477.

[82]"Android, Apple Own 80% of Global Smartphone Market: Microsoft's Share, 2.2%," *PCWorld*, http://www.pcworld.com, May 24, 2012.

[83]"John Deere's Farm Team," *Fortune,* April 14, 2008, pp. 121–126.

[84]Ford sold Jaguar Land Rover to India's Tata Motors in 2008.

components of an automobile may be sourced from different parts of the global network of the firm or even from outside the firm. As firms move toward concentrating on developing expertise in a few core competencies,[85] they are increasingly outsourcing many of the components required for the total product system that constitutes the automobile.

This increase in outsourcing raises another question for firms that practice it.[86] How can firms ensure uninterrupted flow of components and the quality of products when the component makers are independent companies? The answer to this question and the set of issues that it raises takes us into the area of cooperation between firms and strategic alliances, which will be discussed in Chapter 15.

Marketing Strategies for Emerging Markets

As stated earlier in Chapters 1 and 2, one salient aspect of the globalization of markets is the importance of the emerging markets, known as ten Big Emerging Markets (BEMs) including China, India, Indonesia, Russia, and Brazil. Four hundred midsize emerging-market cities, many unfamiliar in the West, will generate nearly 40 percent of global growth over the next 15 years. The 10 fastest-growing economies during the years ahead will all be in emerging markets, according to the International Monetary Fund. IBM expects to earn 30 percent of its revenues in emerging markets by 2015, up from 17 percent in 2009. At Unilever, emerging markets make up 56 percent of the business already. Aditya Birla Group, a multinational conglomerate based in India, now has operations in 40 countries and earns more than half its revenue outside India.[87]

As multinational companies from North America, Western Europe, and Japan search for growth, they have no choice but to compete in those big emerging markets despite the uncertainty and the difficulty of doing business there. A vast consumer base of hundreds of millions of people—the middle class market, in particular—is developing rapidly. When marketing managers working in the developed countries hear about the emerging middle class markets in China or Brazil, they tend to think in terms of the middle class in the United Sates or Western Europe. In the United States, households that earn an annual income of between $50,000 and $100,000 are generally considered middle class.[88] In China, for example, while there is no official "middle-class" as Chinese do not use the concept, a household income considered to be middle-class in China would be somewhere between $10,000 and $60,000 a year.[89] A rule of thumb is a household with a third of its income for discretionary spending is considered middle-class. Obviously, the concept of the middle class market segment differs greatly between developed and emerging countries, and so does what they can afford to purchase.[90]

Consumers in big emerging markets are increasingly aware of global products and global standards, but they often are unwilling—and sometimes unable—to pay global prices. Even when those consumers appear to want the same products as sold elsewhere, some modification in marketing strategy is necessary to reflect differences in product, pricing, promotion, and distribution. Some unnecessary frills may need to be removed from the product to reduce price, while still maintaining its functional performance; packaging may need to be strengthened as the

---

[85]C. K. Prahalad and Gary Hamel, "The Core Competence of the Corporation," *Harvard Business Review* 68 (May–June 1990): 79–91.

[86]See, for example, Masaaki Kotabe, Michael J. Mol, Janet Y. Murray, and Ronaldo Parente, "Outsourcing and Its Implications for Market Success: Negative Curvilinearity, Firm Resources, and Competition," *Journal of the Academy of Marketing Science* 40, no. 2 (2012): 329–346.

[87]Martin Dewhurst, Jonathan Harris, and Suzanne Heywood, "The Global Company's Challenge," *McKinsey Quarterly*, www.mckinseyquarterly.com, June 2012.

[88]"American Middle Class," Wikipedia, en.wikipedia,org, accessed August 10, 2012.

[89]"China's Middle Class Boom," CNNMoney, money.cnn.com, accessed June 26, 2012.

[90]C.K. Prahalad and Kenneth Lieberthal, "The End of Corporate Imperialism," *Harvard Business Review* 76 (July–August 1998): 69–79.

distribution problems in emerging markets, such as poor road conditions and dusty air, hamper smooth handling. Promotion may need to be adapted to address local tastes and preferences. As these emerging markets improve their economic standing in the world economy, they tend to assert their local tastes and preferences over existing global products. Further, access to local distribution channels is often critical to success in emerging markets because it is difficult and expensive for multinational companies from developed countries to understand local customs and to deal with a labyrinthine network of a myriad of distributors in the existing channel.

If a vote were taken for the foreign company that has changed most in the Chinese market, the winner might be Amway, the U.S.-based direct sales company. It had to re-engineer its China network when its original method was virtually outlawed by China as unsuitable to national characteristics. It owns and runs some 200 retail outlets in China, but when it arrived in China in the early 1990s, it had none. It is churning out advertising campaigns featuring some of the world's most well-known athletes, while for most part of its history, its only marketing strategy was to depend on word of mouth. When it comes to pricing globally, Amway keeps a different price policy based on the local conditions of each country or regional market. In Southeast Asian markets, where currency levels are more fluid, prices are adjusted every couple of years. In China, raising prices seemed unavoidable in 2008 too, as Amway needed to offset the inflation in almost every aspect of business—from labor to materials.[91]

Despite these operational complexities, many foreign companies are actually making BEMs a corporate priority. Take two retail giants as examples. Many of us tend to think that Wal-Mart is one of the most global corporations. However, only 10 percent of its sales are generated outside its core NAFTA market, compared to Carrefour, which generates more than 20 percent of sales outside Europe. What is more, in the all-important emerging markets of China, South America, and the Pacific Rim, Carrefour outpaces Wal-Mart in actual revenue. Take China, the land of a billion-plus consumers, as an example. Carrefour became the first foreign retailer to tap into the attractive Chinese market in 1997. By 2005, Carrefour had opened 62 stores and was planning to open between 12 and 15 new hypermarkets each year, with one-third of them located in central and western areas of China. On December 27, 2012, Carrefour China opened its 215th hypermarket: the Bayuquan Hudiequan store, which is located in the province of Liaoning, following its 2 openings on Christmas day of 2012.[92] Wal-Mart entered the Chinese market and opened its first supercenter and Sam's Club in Shenzhen in 1996. Although its expansion in China had been slow initially, Wal-Mart recently raised the stakes in China by acquiring Trust-Mart, the top retail chain of 100 stores that sell everything from food to electronics in the country, for about $1 billion, in 2011. Despite Trust-Mart's reputation for mediocre management, Wal-Mart would gain massive scale through the acquisition for it to more than double its retail presence. By purchasing an entire chain rather than opening new stores, Wal-Mart has been able to bypass cumbersome Chinese red tape: each city has its own requirements for new stores. By acquiring existing stores, Wal-Mart can avoid the complexities of land acquisition.[93] By December 2012, Wal-Mart's total retail units in China had reached 384 stores—outperforming Carrefour in terms of the number of stores.[94] Wal-Mart needed to expand the number of outlets quickly in order to lower costs and capitalize on the growing affluence among China's urban customers before Carrefour and other rivals got a chance to further establish themselves. Being no. 2 risks being doomed for failure, as Wal-Mart had learned to its cost in South Korea when it had sold its eight-year-old operation there to the domestic market leader, Shinsegae, in May 2006.

European companies like Unilever have also broadened the scope of their market by addressing these issues and also competing for the low-income classes. In Indonesia, Unilever does brisk

---

[91]You Nuo, "Amway's Way," *ChinaDaily.com*, May 12, 2008.
[92]www.carrefour.com, accessed January 25, 2013.
[93]"Wal-Mart Trumps Carrefour in China," *Forbes.com*, October 16, 2006.
[94]www.walmartstores.com, accessed January 25, 2013.

business by selling inexpensive, smaller-size products that are affordable to everyone and available anywhere. For instance, it sells Lifebuoy soap with the motto: "With a price you can afford." Unilever's subsidiary in India, Hindustan Lever, approaches the market as one giant rural market. It uses small, cheap packaging, bright signage, and all sorts of local distributors. In fact, Unilever has been so successful and profitable in Indonesia that its biggest rival, P & G, is now trying to follow suit.

Local companies from those emerging markets are also honing their competitive advantage by offering better customer service than foreign multinationals can provide. They can compete with established multinationals from developed countries either by entrenching themselves in their domestic or regional markets or by extending their unique home-grown capabilities abroad. For example, Honda, which sells its scooters, motorcycles, and cars worldwide on the strength of its superior technology, quality, and brand appeal, entered the Indian market. Competing head-on with Honda's strength would be a futile effort for Indian competitors. Instead, Bajaj, an Indian scooter manufacturer, decided to emphasize its line of cheap, rugged scooters through an extensive distribution system and a ubiquitous service network of roadside-mechanic stalls. Although Bajaj could not compete with Honda on technology, it has been able to stall Honda's inroads by catering to consumers who looked for low-cost, durable machines. Similarly, Jollibee Foods, a family-owned fast-food company in the Philippines, overcame an onslaught from McDonald's in its home market by not only upgrading service and delivery standards but also developing rival menus customized to local Filipino tastes. In additional to noodle and rice meals made with fish, Jollibee developed a hamburger seasoned with garlic and soy sauce, capturing more than half of the fast-food business in the Philippines. Using similar recipes, this Filipino company has now established dozens of restaurants in neighboring markets and beyond, including Hong Kong, the Middle East, and as far as the United States with 25 stores in 2012.[95]

In an era when manufacturing, customer service, and increasingly, the bulk of new sales are coming from Asia, a growing number of U.S. and European companies are starting to look east to India, China, and other emerging markets for their next generation of board leadership. Goldman Sachs, which is investing in Indian industry, named steel magnate Lakshmi Mittal a director on June 29, 2008. Novartis, Procter & Gamble, and Deere are among the handful of other U.S. and European companies that have recruited Chinese and Indian natives to their boards. Given demand by an emerging middle class of consumers in India, China, and the Middle East for laptops and cell phones—as well as the need for those countries' industries to modernize their computer systems—technology companies, such as Hewlett-Packard, IBM, and Cisco Systems, are natural candidates to diversify their boards. Directors who hail from emerging markets can stand toe to toe with management on decisions about how to proceed in Asia, help the Western companies gauge the impact of decisions made in home countries on customers in host counterparts, and make more fit marketing strategies to make the companies be more compelling to customers in these fast growing regions.[96]

Competitive Analysis

As we have discussed so far, a firm needs to broaden the sources of competitive advantage relentlessly over time. However, careful assessment of a firm's current competitive position is also required. One particularly useful technique in analyzing a firm's competitive position relative to its competitors is referred to as **SWOT (Strengths, Weaknesses, Opportunities, and Threats) analysis**. A SWOT analysis divides the information into two main categories (internal factors and external factors) and then further into positive aspects (strengths and opportunities) and negative aspects (weaknesses and threats). The framework for a SWOT analysis is illustrated in **Exhibit 8-6**. The internal factors that may be viewed as strengths or weaknesses depend on their impact on the firm's positions; that is, they may

---

[95]Niraj Dawar and Tony Frost, "Competing with Giants. Survival Strategies for Local Companies in Emerging Markets," *Harvard Business Review* 77 (March–April 1999): 119–129; "Fast Food from Asia," *U.S. News & World Report*, February 26, 2001, p. 48; and Jollibee USA, http://www.jollibeeusa.com, accessed August 10, 2012.

[96]"For Corporate Boards, a Global Search," *BusinessWeek.com*, July 21, 2008.

SWOT Analysis

External Factors \ Internal Factors	Strengths	Weakness
	Brand name, human resources, management know-how, technology, advertising, etc.	Price, lack of financial resources, long product development cycle, dependence on independent distributors, etc.
Opportunities — Growth market favorable investment environment, deregulation, stable exchange rate, patent protection, etc.	**S*O Strategy** — Develop a strategy to maximize strengths and maximize opportunities	**W*O Strategy** — Develop a strategy to minimize weaknesses and maximize opportunities
Threats — New entrants, change in consumer preference, new environmental protection laws, local content requirement, etc.	**S*T Strategy** — Develop a strategy to maximize strengths and minimize threats	**W*T Strategy** — Develop a strategy to minimize weaknesses and minimize threats

Exhibit 8-6   SWOT Analysis

represent a strength for one firm but a weakness, in relative terms, for another. They include all of the marketing mix (product, price, promotion, and distribution strategy) as well as personnel and finance. The external factors, which again may be threats to one firm and opportunities to another, include technological changes, legislation, sociocultural changes, and changes in the marketplace or competitive position.

Based on this SWOT framework, marketing executives can construct alternative strategies. For example, an S*O strategy may be conceived to maximize both the company's strengths and market opportunities. Similarly, an S*T strategy may be considered in such a way as to maximize the company's strengths and minimize external threats. Thus, a SWOT analysis helps marketing executives identify a wide range of alternative strategies to think about.

You should note, however, that SWOT is just one aid to categorization; it is not the only technique. One drawback of SWOT is that it tends to persuade companies to compile lists rather than think about what is really important to their business. It also presents the resulting lists uncritically, without clear prioritization, so that, for example, weak opportunities may appear to balance strong threats. Furthermore, using the company's strengths against its competitors' weaknesses may work once or twice but not over several dynamic strategic interactions, as its approach becomes predictable and competitors begin to learn and outsmart it.

The aim of any SWOT analysis should be to isolate the key issues that will be important to the future of the firm and that subsequent marketing strategy will address.

SUMMARY

Market-oriented firms, facing increased competitiveness in world markets, find it essential to assume a global perspective in designing and implementing their marketing strategies. Cost containment, rising technology costs and the dispersal of technology, a greater number of global competitors in many industries, and the advent of hypercompetition in many markets mean that international business practices need to undergo continuous refinement in order to keep them aligned with company goals. The explosive growth of e-commerce has added urgency to competitive analysis, involving not only established multinational firms but also an increasing number of entrepreneurial start-ups leapfrogging geographical constraints via the internet.

Strategic planning and the integration of the global activities into one coherent whole needs to be implemented for a firm to maximize its activities and for the firm to remain a viable player in international markets. In doing so, the multinational firm needs to mesh in information technology and telecommunications with its global operations in order to make relevant data available to managers in real time. In the end, a global strategy of any kind has to resolve a number of apparent contradictions. Firms have to respond to national needs yet seek to exploit know-how on a worldwide basis, while at all times striving to produce and distribute goods and services globally as efficiently as possible.

In recent years, however, as a result of the formation of regional trading blocs, an increasing number of companies have begun to organize their marketing strategies on a regional basis by exploiting emerging regional similarities. Globally minded, proactive firms increasingly exploit their competitive position in some regions by funneling abundant resources and regionally successful marketing programs to other regions where they do not necessarily occupy a strong market position. SWOT analysis helps isolate the key issues that will be important to a firm's competitiveness and that its subsequent marketing strategy will address.

QUESTIONS

1. What are the various factors/forces/drivers that determine the globalization potential of industries? How do global industries differ from multidomestic industries?

2. How are the concepts of interdependency and standardization related? What are the implications for global strategy?

3. What are the benefits and limitations of global marketing strategies?

4. In the summer of 1995, Procter & Gamble, the U.S. multinational giant, modified its global operational structure. Its new structure would include a top-tier management team consisting of four vice-presidents, each representing a particular region, namely North America, Europe (and also to include the Middle East and Africa), Asia (and Pacific Rim), and Latin America. One of the main reasons cited for this organizational change was the elimination of duties and regulations that now allows P&G to distribute its products to foreign consumers more cheaply and quickly. While acknowledging that over 50 percent of the company's sales come from North America, and so, too, a bulk of its profits, the top management mentioned that it took care not to emphasize a particular region over the other. But competing globally with mature brands in saturated markets posed continued challenges. In 1999, a belt-tightening initiative called Organization 2005 was launched. Since then, a host of marginal and mature brands have been eliminated, and a quarter of P&G's brand managers have left the company. Yet, there is no doubt that most of the company's new products originated in the United States. Few dominant products and brands have been originated from its foreign subsidiaries. There are, however, examples of brands, such as Tide, that involved the cross-fertilization of ideas and technologies from its operations around the world. Based on the facts provided, and any popular press information about P&G you have been exposed to, what would you consider to be P&G's predominant international strategy—global (integrated on a worldwide basis), regional (integrated on a regional level), ethnocentric (predominantly influenced by its operations in North America), or polycentric (primarily independent and autonomous functioning of its international subsidiaries)?

5. One of the many advantages of globalization that have been suggested is economies of scale and scope. There is, however, a counterargument to this advantage. Mass customization production techniques could lead to erosion of scale and scope economies with the added advantage of being able to customize products, if not for individual customers, definitely for individual markets. Discuss the strengths and weaknesses of this counterargument.

6. Since 2005, McKinsey has conducted annual consumer surveys in China, interviewing a total of more than 60,000 people in upwards of 60 cities. Those surveys provide insights to help focus on the future. Some of the findings serve as useful lenses to understand the profile of Chinese consumers in 2020. The per-household disposable income of urban Chinese consumers will double between 2010 and 2020, from about $4,000 to about $8,000. While income is expected to rise across China, some cities and regions are already significantly wealthier than others. Today, about 85 percent of mainstream consumers live in the 100 wealthiest cities.

Some of the key trends in China for the next decade are: high growth in discretionary categories, the tendency to trade up as consumers spend some of their discretionary income on better goods and services, and the emergence of a senior market. A propensity to trade up is driven by the aspiration to improve themselves, the way they live, and their perceived social standing. They judge themselves and others by what they buy. The 2011 survey found that the Chinese seniors were more inclined to saving and less willing to spend on discretionary items.

Knowing these characteristics of Chinese consumers in 2020, discuss how they will have an impact on multinational companies targeting China as their next target market. Pick a hypothetical product and discuss how you would enter and tap this market.

MARKET ENTRY STRATEGIES

9

CHAPTER OVERVIEW

1. Country selection

2. Scale of entry

3. Choosing the mode of entry

4. Exporting

5. Licensing

6. Franchising

7. Expanding through joint ventures and alliances

8. Wholly owned subsidiaries

9. Dynamics of entry strategies

10. Timing of entry

11. Exit strategies

In 1996, Danone, a French food and beverage conglomerate, signed an agreement with the Hangzhou Wahaha Group ("Wahaha"), a Chinese beverage company, to set up a series of joint ventures in China in which Danone would hold a 51 percent stake. The partnership was established to market bottled water, tea, and juices under the *Wahaha* brand name (*Wahaha* means "laughing children" in Chinese). Ultimately, the agreement would result in thirty-nine joint ventures. At the time, *Forbes* magazine hailed the partnership as a "showcase" for joint ventures in China.[1] Danone left most of the day-to-day management in the hands of Wahaha's founder and longtime chairman, Zong Qinghou, one of China's wealthiest business tycoons. The joint venture was hugely profitable as the Wahaha brand name became a household name in China. In spite of all these successes, the relationship turned sour in 2007. After a lengthy investigation, Danone suspected that Zong had set up copycat operations that were stealing revenue of the Sino-French partnership. Danone alleged that Zong was selling similar products under the Wahaha brand name outside of the joint venture. Danone filed a slew of lawsuits in several countries around the world seeking control of the $2.4 billion Wahaha brand. Zong claimed that Danone knew all along what was happening and was simply trying to get hold of his companies on the cheap. He also argued that Danone had violated the spirit of

---

[1]http://en.wikipedia.org/wiki/Wahaha_Joint_Venture_Company, accessed on September 29, 2012.

the agreement by setting up joint ventures with other companies in China. Zong struck back by orchestrating a campaign against the French multinational in the Chinese media, comparing Danone's tactics with the bullying of Western powers during the Opium War era. Local distributors and employees strongly came out in support of Zong, some even calling for a boycott of Danone products. The nationalist backlash in the Chinese media threatened to damage Danone's reputation in China.[2] The yearlong dispute was finally resolved when the two companies reached an "amicable settlement" with the support of both the Chinese and French governments. As part of the settlement, Danone dropped all legal proceedings and sold its entire 51 percent stake to the Wahaha Group for an undisclosed sum (rumored to be €300 million).[3] Several factors were behind the breakdown of the partnership. Zong resented the fact that Danone was just collecting the money while he did all the hard work. He also argued that Danone put up roadblocks when he wanted to develop the business further. Danone's lack of supervision and hands-off management style most likely also contributed a great deal to the derailment of the tie-up. The Danone/Wahaha joint venture breakdown illustrates some of the challenges multinational marketers can face in developing and managing international entries.

We can hardly overstate the need for a solid market entry strategy. Market-entry decisions are some of a firm's most risky strategic choices as international market entry requires a major commitment of scarce resources. Companies on the globalization path must make several important entry-related decisions, including: (1) country selection, (2) the time of entry, (3) the mode of entry, (4) the scale of entry, and (5) the level of adaptation and standardization of the marketing mix strategy. This chapter covers the major decisions that constitute market entry strategies. It starts with the target market selection decision. Next, we will look at the scale of entry decision. We then consider the different criteria that will impact the entry mode choice. Following that, we will concentrate on the various entry strategy options that MNCs might look at. Each of these will be described in some detail and evaluated. The final two issues that we consider deal with timing of entry and divestment decisions.

Country Selection

A crucial step in developing a global expansion strategy is the selection of potential target markets to enter. Companies adopt many different approaches to select countries. A flowchart for one of the more elaborate approaches is given in **Exhibit 9-1**.

To identify market opportunities for a given product (or service) the international marketer usually starts off with a large pool of candidate countries (say, all central European countries). To narrow down this pool of countries, the company will typically do a preliminary screening. The goal of this exercise is twofold: you want to minimize the mistakes of (1) ignoring countries that offer viable opportunities for your product and (2) wasting time on countries that offer little or no potential. Those countries that pass the first filter are scrutinized further to determine the final set of target countries. The following describes a four-step procedure that a firm can employ for the initial screening process.

---

[2]"Danone Exits Chinese Venture with Wahaha after Years of Legal Dispute," http://www.nytimes.com/2009/10/01/business/global/01danone.html.

[3]"Danone, Wahaha Reach a Settlement in Beverage Dispute," http://www.chinadaily.com.cn, accessed on October 17, 2012."Danone Exits Chinese Venture with Wahaha after Years of Legal Dispute," http://www.nytimes.com/2009/10/01/business/global/01danone.html.

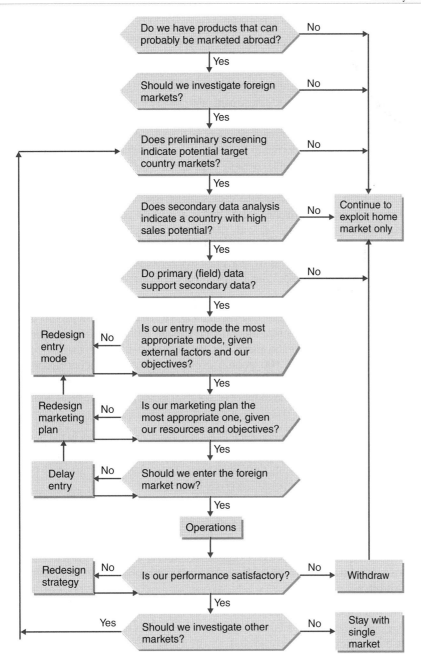

Exhibit 9-1 A Logical Flowchart of the Entry Decision Process

Source: Reprinted with permission from Franklin R. Root, *Entry Strategies for International Markets.* Copyright © 1994 Jossey-Bass Inc., Publishers. First published by Lexington Books. All rights reserved.

Step 1. *Indicator selection and data collection.* First, the company needs to identify a set of socioeconomic and political indicators it believes are critical. The indicators that a company selects are to a large degree driven by the strategic objectives spelled out in the company's global mission. Colgate-Palmolive views per capita purchasing power as a major driver behind market opportunities.[4] Starbucks looks at economic indicators, the

---

[4]"Tangney is bullish on L. America," *Advertising Age International*, May 17, 1993, p. I-23.

size of the population, and whether the company can locate good joint-venture partners.[5] When choosing markets for a particular product, indicators will also depend on the nature of the product. P&G chose Malaysia and Singapore as the first markets in Asia (ex-Japan) for the rollout of Febreze, a fabric odor remover.[6] Not only were both markets known for "home-proud" consumers, but people there also tend to furnish their homes heavily with fabrics. A company might also decide to enter a particular country that is considered a *trendsetter* or *lead market* (see Chapter 8) in the industry. Sany, one of China's flagship machinery groups, established a presence in Germany precisely for this reason. Sany's management argued that if the company can be successful in Germany, a country with the strictest regulatory norms in the industry, it should be able to easily expand into other markets.[7]

Information on macro-economic and political country indicators can easily be gathered from publicly available data sources (see Chapter 6). Typically, countries that do well on one indicator (say, market size) rate poorly on other indicators (say, market growth). For instance, with rising incomes and increasing acceptance of beer, India's beer market is expected to grow rapidly. However, India's per capita beer consumption (1.6 liters) is still a very small fraction of the levels in the United States (75.6 liters) or even China's (35.5 liters).[8] Not every indicator will be equally important. This brings us to the next step.

Step 2. *Determine the importance of country indicators*. The second step is to determine the importance weights of each of the different country indicators that were identified in the previous step. One common method is the "constant-sum" allocation technique. This method simply allocates 100 points across the set of indicators according to their importance in achieving the company's goals (e.g., market share), so, the more critical the indicator, the higher the number of points it is assigned. The total number of points should add up to 100.

Step 3. *Rate the countries in the pool on each indicator*. Next, each country in the pool is assigned a score on each of the indicators. For instance, you could use a 10-point scale (1 meaning very unfavorable; 10 meaning very favorable). The better the country does on a particular indicator, the higher the score it receives.

Step 4. *Compute overall score for each country*. The final step is to derive an overall score for each prospect country. To that end, the weighted scores that the country obtained on each indicator in the previous step are simply summed. The weights are the importance weights that were assigned to the indicators in the second step. Countries with the highest overall scores are the ones that are most attractive. An example of this four-step procedure is given in **Exhibit 9-2**.

Other more sophisticated methods exist to screen target markets. Kumar and colleagues, for example, developed a screening methodology that incorporates multiple objectives a firm could have (instead of just one), resource constraints, and its market expansion strategy.[9] We present one alternative screening procedure in **Appendix A**.

Over time, companies sometimes must fine-tune their market selection strategy. Grolsch, the Dutch premium beer brewer, used to export to emerging markets like China and Brazil. In the

---

[5]"Coffee Talk," *Asia Inc* (March 2005): 16–17.

[6]"Grey Showers Febreze over Southeast Asia," *Ad Age Global* (May 2002): 18.

[7]"Chinese Push into Germany's Heart and Soul," http://www.ft.com, accessed on October 1, 2012.

[8]"SABMiller Loses to Kingfisher in Battle over India's Beer Market: Retail," http://www.bloomberg.com/news/2012-03-02/sabmiller-loses-to-kingfisher-in-battle-over-india-s-beer-market-retail.html.

[9]V. Kumar, A. Stam, and E. A. Joachimsthaler, "An interactive multicriteria approach to identifying potential foreign markets," *Journal of International Marketing* 2, no. 1 (1994): 29–52; see also Lloyd C. Russow and Sam C. Okoroafo, "On the way towards developing a global screening model," *International Marketing Review* 13, no. 1 (1996): 46–64.

Exhibit 9-2 Method for Prescreening Market Opportunities: Example

Country	Per capita Income	Population	Competition	Political Risk	Score
A	50	25	30	40	3400*
B	20	50	40	10	3600
C	60	30	10	70	3650
D	20	20	70	80	3850
Weight	25	40	25	10	

$^{*}(25 \times 50) + (40 \times 25) + (25 \times 30) + (10 \times 40) - 3400$

wake of flagging profits, Grolsch[10] decided to focus on mature beer markets where buying power is high and the premium segment is growing. Markets that met those criteria included the United States, the United Kingdom, Canada, Australia, and continental Europe.[11]

Scale of Entry

Lack of scale was one of the key problems that Wal-Mart encountered in two of the countries where the company failed, South Korea and Germany. In South Korea, with a presence of sixteen stores for the whole country, most Koreans had never heard of Wal-Mart. In Seoul, a sprawling area of 10 million people, Wal-Mart just had one single store. Likewise, in Germany, Wal-Mart had acquired relatively small existing chains with undesirable locations (e.g., the Wiesbaden outlet had a couple of sex shops nearby). In both countries, lack of scale ultimately led to the retailer's inability to effectively compete with incumbent discounters, like the Aldi and Lidl chains in Germany and E-Mart in Korea. In contrast, Wal-Mart started big in its more successful markets like Mexico, where it bought Cifra, Mexico's largest and best-run local retailer.[12] Japan's Fast Retailing opened more than 20 Uniqlo stores in Britain when it first entered the market in 2001. Having been hugely successful in Japan, the casual fashion retailer thought that it was ready to join the global competition in Britain. Poor sales forced the firm to close down 18 of its stores barely two years later.[13] Fast Retailing also initially struggled in the U.S. retail market. In 2005, it opened three Uniqlo stores in New Jersey shopping malls. Failing to get attention for an unfamiliar brand, the company closed them one year later.[14]

Entry scale is a very important element of a firm's globalization strategy.[15] For instance, a retailer like Wal-Mart must decide how many outlets to establish and the stores' size in the new host country. At one extreme, a company could enter with a very small footprint, especially when it sees the entry as a move to test the waters. Based on the initial performance, the firm could widen its scale over time. At the other extreme, a firm could enter the host market on a large scale.

Obviously, access to resources—monetary and human—is one big constraint that determines the scale decision. Typically, most companies are hesitant to commit major resources to a new host market given the huge uncertainty of such entries and the fact that investments are largely sunk.

[10]In November 2007, SABMiller, one of the world's largest brewers, offered €816 million to buy Grolsch. The takeover was completed in March 2008.

[11]"Grolsch targets mature markets," *Financial Times*, February 10, 1999, p. 20.

[12]"Wal-Mart Finds That Its Formula Doesn't Fit Every Culture," http://www.nytimes.com/2006/08/02/business/world-business/02Wal-Mart.html?pagewanted=all.

[13]"Uniqlo Retreats from British Fashion Market," http://www.guardian.co.uk/money/2003/mar/08/business.japan.

[14]"Doing It Their Way," http://www.time.com, accessed on October 19, 2012.

[15]Katrijn Gielens, Kristiaan Helsen, and Marnik G. Dekimpe, "International Entry Strategies," in Venkatesh Shankar and Gregory S. Carpenter, eds., *Handbook of Marketing Strategy*, Cheltenham, U.K.: Edward Elgar, 2012), pp. 391–411.

Companies may decide to take a prudent approach and initially enter the market with a limited presence, especially when there is a lot of uncertainty. When Home Depot, the world's largest home improvement retailer, entered China in 2006 it acquired Home Way, a relatively small local chain with 12 stores in 6 cities. On the other hand, by entering with a big splash, a firm can send a strong signal to local consumers, distributors, and competitors about its commitment and sincerity to the market. In some industries, a large-scale entry can also generate economies of scale.

Researchers have identified a variety of reasons that may cause a positive relationship between entry scale and post-entry performance. First, large-scale entry may induce volume-driven cost advantages. Second, in industries or services where location matters, large-scale entry (e.g., with many outlets) can lead to a lock-up of the more attractive locations.[16] Third, existing players are less likely to respond aggressively when the entrant has made substantial investments. By the same token, large-scale entry could deter other prospective players from entering the country afterwards.

Choosing the Mode of Entry
Decision Criteria for Mode of Entry

Several decision criteria will influence the choice of entry mode. Roughly speaking, two classes of decision criteria can be distinguished: internal (firm-specific) criteria and external (environment-specific) criteria. Let us first consider the major external criteria.

Market Size and Growth

In many instances, the key determinant of entry choice decisions is the size of the market. Large markets justify major resource commitments in the form of joint ventures or wholly owned subsidiaries. Market potential can relate to the current size of the market. However, future market potential as measured via the growth rate is often even more critical, especially when the target markets include emerging markets.

Risk

Another major concern when choosing entry modes is the risk factor. The role of risk in global marketing is discussed in Chapter 5. Risk relates to the instability in the political and economic environment that may impact the company's business prospects. Generally speaking, the greater the risk factor, the less eager companies are to make major resource commitments to the country (or region) concerned. Obviously, the level of country risk changes over time. In Bolivia, for example, the election of Evo Morales, a left-leaning indigenous former coca farmer, created enormous uncertainty for foreign investors in that country.[17] Many companies opt to start their presence with a liaison office in markets that are high-risk but, at the same time, look very appealing because of their size or growth potential. For instance, MetLife, the insurance company, opened a liaison office in Shanghai and Beijing while it was waiting for permission from the Chinese government to start operations. A liaison office functions as a low-cost listening post to gather market intelligence and establish contacts with potential distributors and/or clients.

Government Regulations (Openness)

Government regulations are also a major consideration in entry mode choices. In scores of countries, government regulations heavily constrain the set of available options. A good example

---

[16]Apart from geographic location, pre-emption could also occur in the mind of consumers—perceptual space. See Marvin B. Lieberman and David B. Montgomery, "First-mover Advantages," *Strategic Management Journal* 19 (Summer 1988): 1111–1125 for further discussion.

[17]http://lapaz.usembassy.gov/commercial/2005InvestClimateStat.pdf.

is the regulation of India's retail industry. Until recently, foreign retailers such as Wal-Mart or Tesco were not allowed to enter India with a majority stake out of fear that opening the country's retail industry would hurt India's peasants and small shop owners. In September 2012, India's government relaxed the rules. Under the new retail policy, India's 29 state governments can decide to open up or block their realm to foreign retail chains.[18] In the car industry, local content requirements in countries such as France and Italy played a major role in the decision of Japanese carmakers like Toyota and Nissan to build up a local manufacturing presence in Europe.

Competitive Environment

The nature of the competitive situation in the local market is another driver. The dominance of Kellogg Co. as a global player in the ready-to-eat cereal market was a key motivation for the creation in the early 1990s of Cereal Partners Worldwide, a joint venture between Nestlé and General Mills. The partnership gained some market share (compared to the combined share of Nestlé and General Mills prior to the linkup) in some of the markets, though mostly at the expense of lesser players like Quaker Oats.[19] By the same token, the acquisition by SABMiller, one of the world's largest beer brewers, of Colombia-based Bavaria in a $7.8 billion deal brought the company near-monopoly control in four South American countries: Peru, Colombia, Ecuador, and Panama.[20] The take-over enabled SABMiller to bolster its position in a region which traditionally had been a stronghold of its arch rival AB-InBev.

Cultural Distance

Some scholars argue that the cultural distance between countries also has an impact on entry mode choice decisions. Opinions about the nature of the relationship differ. Some argue that through higher percentages of equity ownership, firms are able to bridge differences in cultural values and institutions. Others note that by relying on joint ventures instead of wholly owned subsidiaries, companies are able to lower their risk exposure in culturally distant markets. A comprehensive analysis of a wide range of studies in the literature found no clear-cut evidence in favor of either argument.[21]

Local Infrastructure

The physical infrastructure of a market refers to the country's distribution system, transportation network and communication system. In general, the poorer the local infrastructure, the more reluctant the company is to commit major resources (monetary or human).

The combination of all these factors determines the overall market attractiveness of the countries being considered. Markets can be classified in five types of countries based on their respective market attractiveness:[22]

1. *Platform* countries that can be used to gather intelligence and establish a network. Examples include Singapore and Hong Kong.

2. *Emerging* countries in which the major goal is to build up an initial presence, for instance, via a liaison office. Vietnam and the Philippines are examples.

---

[18]"Skepticism and Caution Greet India's New Policy on Retailers," http://www.nytimes.com, accessed on October 1, 2012.
[19]Quaker Oats was acquired by PepsiCo in August 2001.
[20]"SABMiller to Raise Its Glass to Loyalty," *Financial Times*, July 25, 2005, p. 16.
[21]Laszlo Tihanyi, David A. Griffith, and Craig J. Russell, "The Effect of Cultural Distance on Entry Mode Choice, International Diversification, and MNE Performance: A Meta-Analysis," *Journal of International Business Studies* 36 (2005): 270–283.
[22]Philippe Lasserre, "Corporate strategies for the Asia Pacific region," *Long Range Planning* 28, no. 1 (1995): 13–30.

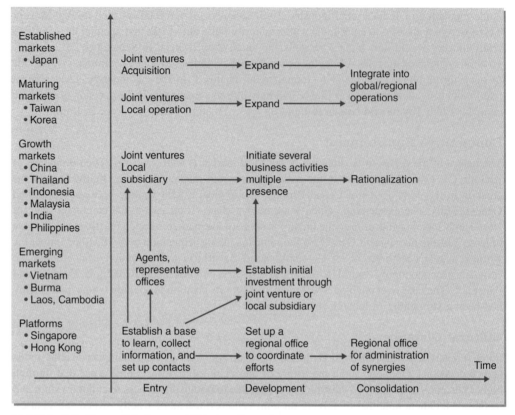

Exhibit 9-3   Entry Modes and Market Development

Source: Reprinted from Philippe Lasserre, "Corporate Strategies for the Asia Pacific Region," *Long Range Planning* 28 (1), p. 21. Copyright 1995, with kind permission from Elsevier Science Ltd., The Boulevard, Langford Lane, Kidlington OX5 1GB UK.

3. *Growth* countries offer early mover advantages that often push companies to build a significant presence to capitalize on future market opportunities as in China and India.

4. *Maturing* and *established* countries like South Korea, Taiwan, and Japan. These countries have far fewer growth prospects than the other types of markets. Often local competitors are well entrenched. On the other hand, these markets have a sizable middle class and solid infrastructure. The prime task here is to look for ways to further develop the market via strategic alliances, major investments, or acquisitions of local or smaller foreign players. A case in point is General Electric, the U.S. conglomerate. In the hope of achieving big profits in Europe, GE has invested more than $10 billion from 1989 through 1996, half of it for building new plants and half for almost 50 acquisitions despite the fact that Europe is a fairly mature market.[23]

Different types of countries require different expansion paths, although deviations cannot be ruled out (see **Exhibit 9-3**). We now give an overview of the key internal criteria.

Company Objectives

Corporate objectives are a key influence in choosing entry modes. Firms that have limited aspirations will typically prefer entry options that entail a minimum amount of commitment (e.g.,

---

[23]"If Europe's dead, why is GE investing billions there?" *Fortune*, September 9, 1996.

licensing). Proactive companies with ambitious strategic objectives, on the other hand, will usually pick entry modes that give them the flexibility and control they need to achieve their goals. InBev, a Belgian-Brazilian beverage company, needed a strong foothold in the U.S. market to become the leading beer brewer worldwide. In June 2008, InBev made an offer for Anheuser-Busch, which accepted the offer a month later after InBev raised the offer price.[24] By merging the two firms, InBev's CEO Carlos Brito hoped to create a "stronger, more competitive global company with an unrivaled worldwide brand portfolio and distribution network."[25] The company has become the world's largest brewer with the number 1 market share spot in most key beer markets.[26]

Need for Control

Most MNCs would like to possess a certain amount of control over their foreign operations. Control may be desirable for any element of the marketing mix plan: positioning, pricing, advertising, the way the product is distributed, and so forth. Caterpillar, for instance, prefers to stay in complete control of its overseas operations to protect its proprietary know-how. For that reason, Caterpillar avoids joint ventures.[27] To a large degree, the level of control is strongly correlated with the amount of resource commitment: the smaller the commitment, the lower the control. Most firms face a trade-off between the degree of control over their foreign operations and the level of resource commitment they are willing to make.

Internal Resources, Assets and Capabilities

Companies with tight resources (human and/or financial) or limited assets are constrained to low-commitment entry modes such as exporting and licensing that are not too demanding on their resources. Even large companies should carefully consider how to allocate their resources between their different markets, including the home market. In some cases, major resource commitments to a given target market might be premature given the amount of risk. On the other hand, if a firm is overly reluctant to commit resources, it could miss the boat by sacrificing major market opportunities. Internal competencies also influence the choice-of-entry strategy. When the firm lacks certain skills that are critical for the success of its global expansion strategy, it can try to fill the gap by forming a strategic alliance.

Flexibility

An entry mode that looks very appealing today will not necessarily be attractive 5 or 10 years down the road. The host country environment changes constantly. New market segments emerge. Local customers become more demanding or more price conscious. Their preferences may change over time. Local competitors become more sophisticated. To cope with these environmental changes, global players need a certain amount of flexibility. The flexibility offered by the different entry mode alternatives varies a great deal. Given their very nature, contractual arrangements like joint ventures or licensing tend to provide very little flexibility. When major exit barriers exist, wholly owned subsidiaries are hard to divest and, therefore offer very little flexibility compared to other entry alternatives.

Although some of the factors listed above favor high-control entry modes, other criteria suggest a low-control mode. The different entry modes can be classified according to the degree of control they offer to the entrant and the amount of risk involved. At one end of the spectrum is exporting, which offers the lowest degree of control, but also the lowest level of risk. Licensing, franchising, and

---

[24]After the merger the company was renamed Anheuser-Busch Inbev.
[25]"InBev Bags Anheuser-Busch," *Forbes*, http://www.forbes.com/, accessed August 22, 2008.
[26]http://www.ab-inbev.com/pdf/AB_InBev_AR11_OurTopTenMarkets.pdf, accessed on October 1, 2012.
[27]"Engine Makers Take Different Routes," *Financial Times*, July 14, 1998, p. 11.

various forms of joint venture relationships provide a progressively increasing degree of control for the firm—coupled with higher risk levels. At the other end of the spectrum are high-commitment ownership-based entries that entail the highest control but also the greatest risk.

To some extent, the appropriate entry-mode decision boils down to the issue of how much control is desirable. Ideally, the entrant would like to have as much control as possible. However, entry modes that offer a large degree of control also impose substantial resource commitments and huge amounts of risk. Therefore, the entrant faces a tradeoff between the benefits of increased control and the costs of resource commitment and risk. Researchers have developed various frameworks to study foreign entry mode decisions. Appendix B gives an overview of the three main theoretical perspectives.

An empirical study of entry decisions made by the 180 largest MNCs over a 15-year period found that MNCs are most likely to enter with wholly owned subsidiaries when one of the following conditions holds:[28]

- The entry involves a R&D-intensive line of business.

- The entry involves an advertising-intensive line of business (high brand-equity).

- The MNC has accumulated a substantial amount of experience with foreign entries.

On the other hand, MNCs are most likely to prefer a partnership when one of these holds:

- The entry is in a highly risky country.

- The entry is in a socioculturally distant country.

- There are legal restrictions on foreign ownership of assets.

Exporting

Most companies start their international expansion by exporting. For many small businesses, exporting is very often the sole alternative for selling their goods in foreign markets. A fair number of Fortune 500 companies, such as Boeing and Caterpillar, still generate a major part of their global revenues via export sales.

Chapter 16 discusses export and import management matters in detail. In this chapter we will give you a snapshot overview of exporting as an entry mode. Companies that plan to engage in exporting have a choice between three broad options: indirect, cooperative, and direct exporting. **Indirect exporting** means that the firm uses a middleman based in its home market to handle the exporting. With **cooperative exporting**, the firm enters into an agreement with another company (local or foreign) where by the partner will use its distribution network to sell the exporter's goods. **Direct exporting** means that the company sets up its own export organization and relies on a middleman based in a foreign market (e.g., a foreign distributor).

Indirect Exporting

Indirect exporting happens when the firm decides to sell its products in the foreign market through independent intermediaries. An **export merchant** is a trading company that will buy the firm's goods outright and then resell them in the foreign markets. The exporter merchant usually specializes in a particular line of products and/or in a certain geographical region. An **export agent** is a trading company that acts for local manufacturers, usually representing a

---

[28]Hubert Gatignon and Erin Anderson, "The multinational corporation's degree of control over foreign subsidiaries: An empirical test of a transaction cost explanation," *Journal of Law, Economics, and Organization* 4, no. 2 (Fall 1988): 305–36.

number of non-competing manufacturers. They seek and negotiate foreign purchases. In return for obtaining an export order, the export agent receives a commission. Unlike the export merchant, the agent does not become the owner of the goods and therefore does not assume the risk of not being able to sell profitably overseas. The use of an **export management company (EMC)** is very popular among small businesses. An EMC is an independent firm that acts as the exclusive export sales department for non-competing manufacturers. EMCs come in all shapes and sizes. Some act as an agent, soliciting orders in foreign markets in the name of the manufacturer. Other EMCs act as a distributor on a "buy-sell" basis: the EMC buys from the firm at a set price and resells to the foreign customers at prices set by the EMC. Indirect exporting offers several advantages to the exporting company compared to other entry modes. The firm gets instant foreign market expertise. The indirect exporters are professionals. They can handle all the details involved in processing exporting orders. They also can appraise market opportunities for the manufacturer. Other strengths are their know-how in selecting agents and/or distributors and management of the distribution network. Often very little risk is involved. Generally speaking, no major resource commitments are required. When the middlemen's profits are based on how successfully they export, they are motivated to do a good job.

Indirect exporting has some downsides. The company has little or no control over the way its product is marketed in the foreign country. Lack of adequate sales support, wrong pricing decisions, or poor distribution channels will inevitably lead to poor sales. Ill-fated marketing mix decisions made by the intermediary could also damage the company's corporate or brand image. The middleman may have limited experience with handling the company's product line. In addition, as they are often relatively small, they may have limited resources to handle tasks such as warehousing or providing credit financing to foreign customers. Often intermediaries will focus their efforts on those products that maximize their profits. As a result, they might not support new product lines or products with low short-term profit potential.

Given the low commitment required, indirect exporting is often seen as a good beach-head strategy for "testing" the international waters: Once the demand for the product takes off, the manufacturer can switch to another, more proactive, entry mode. The decision to develop an export business via an independent middleman centers around three basic questions:[29]

1. Does the firm have the time and know-how to enter export markets?

2. Does the firm have the money and/or specialized personnel needed to develop an export business?

3. Is the foreign business growing at a satisfactory rate?

If the answer to any of these questions is negative, then manufacturers should seriously consider relying on specialized export firms.

Cooperative Exporting

Companies that are unwilling to commit the resources to set up their own distribution organization but still want to have some control over their foreign operations should consider cooperative exporting. One of the most popular forms of cooperative exporting is **piggyback exporting**. With piggybacking, the company uses the overseas distribution network of another company (local or foreign) for selling its goods in the foreign market. Wrigley, the U.S. chewing gum company,[30] entered India by piggybacking on Parrys, a local confectionery firm. Through this tie-up, Wrigley

---

[29]http://www.powerhomebiz.com/vol7/export.htm.

[30]In 2008 Mars acquired Wrigley via a stock offer of around $23 billion.

could plug into Parrys' distribution network, thereby providing Wrigley with immediate access to 250,000 retail outlets. The two major attractions that Parrys' network offered to Wrigley were the overlap in product category and the size of the distribution network.

The quality of the distribution network can also play a role. Gillette tied up with Bangalore-based TTK, an Indian manufacturer of pressure cookers and kitchenware, for the distribution of Braun products, despite the fact that Gillette has its own distribution network in India. Gillette needed department store–type outlets for its Braun product range, precisely the type of distribution channels that TTK uses for the distribution of its merchandise.[31]

Direct Exporting

Under direct exporting, the firm sets up its own exporting department and sells its products via a middleman located in the foreign market. Once the international sales potential becomes substantial, direct exporting often looks far more appealing than indirect exporting. To some degree, the choice between indirect and direct exporting is a "make-or-buy" decision: should the company perform the export task, or is it better off sourcing the task out to outsiders? Compared to the indirect approach, direct exporting has a number of pluses. The exporter has far more control over its international operations. Hence, the sales potential (and profit) is often times much more significant than under indirect exporting. It also allows the company to build up its own network in the foreign market and get better market feedback.

There is a price to be paid, though. Given that the responsibility for the exporting tasks is now in the hands of the company, the demands on resources—human and financial—are much more intense than with indirect exporting. Besides the marketing mix tasks, these tasks involve choosing target markets, identifying and selecting representatives in the foreign market, and scores of logistical functions (e.g., documentation, insurance, shipping, packaging).

Licensing

Companies can also penetrate foreign markets via a licensing strategy. **Licensing** is a contractual transaction where the firm—the **licensor**—offers some proprietary assets to a foreign company—the **licensee**—in exchange for royalty fees. Examples of assets that can be part of a licensing agreement include trademarks, technology know-how, production processes, and patents. Royalty rates range from one-eighth of 1 percent to 15 percent of sales revenue.[32] For instance, Oriental Land Company owns and operates Tokyo Disneyland under license from Disney. In return for being able to use the Disney name, Oriental Land Company pays royalties to Disney. Hasbro, the American toy-maker, used a wide-ranging licensing program to bring some of its iconic toy brands to Europe. For instance, to introduce the Furby character, an interactive robotic toy pet, Hasbro set up a licensing program that covered items such as apparel, back-to-school supplies, food and beverages, home décor, and sporting goods.[33] Another example of global expansion via licensing is Yoplait, the global yogurt brand co-owned by General Mills, the U.S. food conglomerate, and Sodiaal, a French dairy cooperative. Yoplait has a network of 26 licensees around the world.[34]

In high-tech industries, companies often enter **cross-licensing** agreements. Under such an agreement, parties mutually share patents of comparable value without payment of licensing

---

[31]"India—Distribution Overview," IMI960321, U.S. Department of Commerce, International Trade Administration.

[32]"Licensing may be quickest route to foreign markets," *Wall Street Journal*, September 14, 1990, Sec. B, p. 2.

[33]"Furby Sets Sights on Europe," http://www.businesswire.com/news/home/20121017005208/en/FURBY-Sets-Sights-Europe.

[34]http://www.generalmills.com/en/Media/NewsReleases/Library/2011/July/yoplait_finalized.aspx.

fees. One big practitioner of cross-licensing is Microsoft. In August 2008, for instance, Microsoft and Nikon signed a patent cross-licensing agreement that covered digital cameras and other consumer products. The agreement enabled both parties to innovate with each other's technologies.[35]

Benefits

For many companies, licensing has proven to be a very profitable means of penetrating foreign markets. In most cases, licensing is not very demanding on the company's resources. Therefore, it is especially appealing to small companies that lack the resources and wherewithal to invest in foreign facilities. Compared to exporting, another low-commitment entry mode, licensing allows the licensor to navigate around import barriers or get access to markets that are completely closed to imports. For instance, several foreign tobacco companies in China used licensing agreements to avoid the high import tax levied on imported cigarettes.[36] Local governments may also favor licensing over other entry modes.

Companies that use licensing as part of their global expansion strategy lower their exposure to political or economic instabilities in their foreign markets. The only volatility that the licensor faces are the ups and downs in the royalty income stream. Other risks are absorbed by the licensee.

In high-tech industries, technology licensing has two more appeals. In highly competitive environments, rapid penetration of global markets allows the licensor to define the leading technology standard and to rapidly amortize R&D expenditures.[37] In extreme cases, a company might even forgo royalties and offer its product available for free as Google did with its open source Android software, which is the platform for smartphones made by, for instance, Samsung and HTC.

Caveats

Licensing comes with some caveats, though. Revenues coming from a licensing agreement could be dwarfed by the potential income that other entry modes such as exporting could have generated. Another possible disadvantage is that the licensee may not be fully committed to the licensor's product or technology. Lack of enthusiasm on the part of the licensee will greatly limit the sales potential of the licensed product. When the licensing agreement involves a trademark, there is the further risk that misguided moves made by the licensee may tarnish the trademark covered by the agreement. Other risks include the risk of not getting paid, failure to produce in a timely manner or the desired volume, and loss of control of the marketing of the product.[38]

The biggest danger is the risk of opportunism. A licensing arrangement could nurture a future competitor: Today's comrade-in-arms often becomes tomorrow's rival. The licensee can leverage the skills it acquires during the licensing period once the agreement expires.

Companies can make several moves to protect themselves against the risks of licensing arrangements.[39] If possible, the company should seek patent or trademark protection abroad. A

---

[35]http://www.microsoft.com/Presspass/press/2008/aug08/08-27MSNikonPatentPR.mspx.

[36]"Smoke signals point to China market opening," *South China Sunday Post*, October 6, 1996, p. 5.

[37]M. Kotabe, A. Sahay, and P.S. Aulakh, "Emerging role of technology licensing in the development of a global product strategy: conceptual framework and research propositions," *Journal of Marketing* 60, no. 1 (January 1996): 73–88.

[38]Sandra Mottner and James P. Johnson, "Motivations and Risks in International Licensing: A Review and Implications for Licensing to Transitional and Emerging Economies," *Journal of World Business* 35, no. 2 (2000): 171–187.

[39]Franklin R. Root, *Entry Strategies for International Markets*, Chapter 5.

thorough profitability analysis of a licensing proposal is an absolute must. Such an analysis must identify all the costs that the venture ensues, including the opportunity costs that stem from revenues that need to be sacrificed. Careful selection of prospective licensees is extremely important. Once a partner has been chosen, the negotiation process starts. If the negotiations are successful, the partners will sign a licensing contract. The contract will cover parameters such as the technology package, use conditions (including territorial rights and performance require-ments), compensation, and provisions for the settlement of disputes.

Franchising

Scores of service industry companies use franchising as a means for capturing opportunities in the global marketplace. For instance, of the nearly 36,000 Yum! Brands restaurants worldwide,[40] 77 percent are owned by franchisees.[41] **Exhibit 9-4** is a ranking of the top 20 global franchises.

Exhibit 9-4   Top 20 Global Franchises

Company	Industry	Date of Incorporation	Estimated Operating Units	Minimum Initial Franchise Fee (US$)	Min. Royalty (% of Gross Sales)	Country
SUBWAY	Sandwiches	1965	37,335	15,000	8	USA
McDonald's	Fast Food	1955	+33,520	45,000	NA	USA
KFC	Chicken	1939	16,850	45,000	5	USA
7 Eleven	Convenience Stores	1927	44,700	1,000,000	NA	USA
Burger King	Fast Food	1956	12,300	50,000	4.5	USA
Pizza Hut	Pizza	1958	13,430	25,000	6	USA
Wyndham Hotel	Hotel	1990	+7,000	NA*	NA	USA
Ace Hardware	Home Improvement	1928	4,600	5,000	NA	USA
Dunkin' Donuts	Bakery	1954	10,100	40,000	5.9	USA
Hertz	Car Rental	1925	8,500	25,000	10	USA
Snap-on Tools	Automotive Repair	1920	4,800	7,500	NA	USA
Marriott International	Hotels	1967	+3,500	NA	NA	USA
Intercontinental Hotels Group	Hotels	1946	+4,400	NA	NA	UK
GNC Live Well	Wellness Products	1935	7,300	40,000	5	USA
Baskin-Robbins	Ice Cream	1946	6,715	10,000	5.9	USA
Circle K	Convenience Stores	1951	7,450	25,000	4.5	USA
Choice Hotels	Hotels	1963	6,100	NA	NA	USA
Kumon	Child Education	1958	26,000	1,000	NA	Japan
Domino's Pizza	Pizza	1963	9,750	NA	5.5	USA
Tim Hortons	Bakery	1964	4,015	35,000	4.5	Canada

Source: www.franchisedirect.com, accessed on October 2, 2012.

* NA = Not available

---

[40]Yum Brands! restaurant brands in the global arena are primarily Pizza Hut and KFC. The three remaining brands—Taco Bell, Long John Silver's, and A&W—are primarily U.S.-based and have a very marginal presence globally. In 2008 Yum! announced plans to also turn Taco Bell into a global brand.

[41]http://investors.yum.com/phoenix.zhtml?c=117941&p=irol-newsEarnings, accessed on October 2, 2012.

Franchising is to some degree a "cousin" of licensing: It is an arrangement whereby the **franchisor** gives the **franchisee** the right to use the franchisor's trade names, trademarks, business models, and/or know-how in a given territory for a specific time period, normally 10 years.[42] In exchange, the franchisor gets royalty payments and other fees. The package could include the marketing plan, operating manuals, standards, training, financial assistance, territorial rights, and quality monitoring.

For global expansion of a franchise, the method of choice is often **master franchising**. With this system, the franchisor gives a master franchise to a local entrepreneur, who will, in turn, sell local franchises within his territory. The territory could be a certain region within a country or a group of countries (e.g., Greater China). For instance, Domino's Pizza Group plc (DPG) is a U.K.-based master franchisee for the pizza delivery brand with exclusive rights to operate and franchise Domino's Pizza stores in Britain, Ireland, and Germany. Usually, the master franchise holder agrees to establish a certain number of outlets over a given time horizon.

Benefits

The benefits of franchising are clear. First and foremost, companies can capitalize on a winning business formula by expanding overseas with a minimum amount of investment. Just as with licensing, political risks for the rights-owner are very limited. Further, since the franchisees' profits are directly tied to their efforts, franchisees are usually highly motivated. Finally, the franchisor can also capitalize on the local franchisees' knowledge of the local marketplace. They often have a much better understanding of local customs and laws than the foreign firm.

Caveats

Franchising carries some risks, though. Just as in the case of licensing, the franchisor's income stream is only a fraction of what it would be if the company held an equity stake in the foreign ventures. Firms with little or no name recognition typically face a major challenge finding interested partners in the foreign market. Finding suitable franchisees or a master franchisee can be a stumbling block in many markets. Also, in some countries, the concept of franchising as a business model is barely understood.[43] A major concern is the lack of full control over the franchisees' operations and marketing strategies. In 2012, Ikea's franchisee in Saudi Arabia posted a women-free version of the company's catalog on Ikea's Saudi website. Photos of the original Ikea catalog were doctored so that they did not show any images of women. The "sanitized" version was soon discovered by the Swedish press and news about the photo-edits spread rapidly around the world online. Ikea issued an apology and promised to review its "routines" in response to the issue.[44] Given the largely intangible nature of many franchising systems, cultural hurdles can also create problems. In fact, one study showed that cultural and physical proximity are the two most popular criteria used by companies for picking international markets in franchising.[45] **Exhibit 9-5** offers an overview of the key elements for international franchise arrangements with General Nutrition Corporation (GNC), a global specialty retailer of health and wellness products, with over 6,100 outlets in the U.S. and 44 international markets.

---

[42]Albert Kong, "How to Evaluate a Franchise," *Economic Bulletin* (October 1998): 18–20.

[43]Colin McCosker, "Trends and Opportunities in Franchising," *Economic Bulletin,* (October 1998): 14–17.

[44]"Ikea 'Regrets' Removal of Women from Saudi Catalogue," http://www.bbc.co.uk/news/, accessed on October.

[45]John F. Preble and Richard C. Hoffman, "Franchising systems around the globe: A status report," *Journal of Small Business Management* (April 1995): 80–88.

Exhibit 9-5 GNC—International Franchising

Profile of GNC's ideal international franchise candidate

- Financially secure.
- Native to the country being developed.
- Candidate should have the wherewithal to develop a minimum of 25 stores (depending on the country's demographics) within four years.

Initial Investment Needed

- Typically upwards of $1 million.

Ongoing Royalty Fees

- 5 percent of monthly gross sales.

Length of Contract

- The initial term is 10 years, after which the agreement may be negotiated for renewal twice for additional 5-year terms subject to approval.

Training Assistance

- Franchisees must attend a three-phase training program provided by GNC.

Operational Guidance

- Franchisees receive the *GNC International Franchise Operations Manual* to help guide with the day-to-day operations.
- GNC assigns a dedicated International Franchise Consultant to provide technical assistance and help with inventory management and other business needs.

Source: http://www.gncfranchising.com/intl_faq.asp.

Expanding through Joint Ventures and Alliances

For many MNCs who want to expand their global operations, joint ventures prove to be the most viable way to enter foreign markets, especially emerging markets. With a joint venture, the foreign company agrees to share equity and other resources with other partners to establish a new entity in the host country. **Strategic alliances** refer to a broader form of partnerships: a coalition of two or more organizations to achieve strategically significant goals that are mutually beneficial.[46] In some cases, alliance partners will seal the tie-up by investing in one another. One example is U.S. drugstore owner Walgreens's transatlantic alliance with Alliance Boots in 2012, where Walgreens agreed to buy a 45 percent stake in its partner (see **Global Perspective 9-1**). Partnerships may be created between competitors; between suppliers and manufacturers; between companies and distributors; or between firms and government institutions or NGOs.

Many cross-border alliances are marketing-oriented. Firms may use partnerships to improve the effectiveness of their branding strategies; this can take the form of brand alliances, in which the partners put their brand or logo on the same products.[47] Examples of such marketing alliances include Fuji-Xerox, Hero-Honda (an Indian motorbike brand), and the former Sony Ericsson. In some cases, the collaboration could result in a newly created brand name. Nestea, the ready-to-drink tea brand, is one of the best known examples. In 2001, Coca-Cola and Nestlé set up Beverage

---

[46]Edwin A. Murray and John F. Mahon, "Strategic Alliances: Gateway to the New Europe?" *Long Range Planning* (August 1993): 102–111.

[47]Non-Government Organizations.

Global Perspective 9-1

Walgreens's Tie-Up with Alliance Boots: Creating the World's Largest Buyer of Prescription Drugs

In June 2012, U.S. drugstore owner Walgreens and U.K.-based Alliance Boots sealed a transatlantic alliance to create the world's largest buyer of prescription drugs. Walgreens agreed to buy a 45 percent stake in health-and-beauty group Alliance Boots for $6.5 billion paid via a mixture of cash and shares. Alliance Boots is a privately-held pharmaceutical group that consists of a wholesale/distribution business and a health-and-beauty store chain. Boots, the retail portion of the business, has been expanding its global footprint with pharmacies in many European countries, Turkey, and Thailand. Within three years, Walgreens planned to acquire all of Alliance Boots. The combined company would create a global pharmacy chain handling 10 percent of the world's prescription drug volume and delivering products to 170,000 pharmacies, doctors, clinics, and hospitals worldwide.

For Walgreens, which has nearly 8,000 stores in the United States, the deal offered instant access to Alliance Boots's wholesale pharmaceutical business. Gregory Wasson, Walgreens's CEO, declared that the deal would foster Walgreens's global expansion. Prior to the deal, Walgreens had a presence only in the United States. The tie-up would offer Walgreens more clout with suppliers and offer access to its partner's massive global distribution network, especially in emerging markets. In 2007, for instance, Alliance Boots set up a 50-50 joint venture with Guangzhou Pharmaceutical, the third-largest pharmaceutical wholesaler in China. Walgreens sees an enormous opportunity in the so-called pharmerging markets that include Brazil, China, and India. These countries are expected to nearly double their spending on drugs from $194 billion in 2011 to $345 to $375 billion by 2016. Walgreens also anticipated that it could take advantage of the lower-cost environment in emerging markets to develop private-label products for its health-and-beauty business.

Sources: "Walgreens Boots Tie-Up Aims at Global Expansion," *Financial Times*, June 20, 2012, p. 17; "Walgreen to Buy Alliance Boots Stake," *Wall Street Journal*, June 20, 2012, p. 19; "Earth's Drugstore: Walgreen Hedges Obamacare With Global Boots Alliance," http://www.forbes.com, accessed October 22, 2012.

Partners Worldwide as a 50-50 joint venture to expand Nestea in Europe, Canada, and some other markets. By combining forces, the two firms hoped they could compete more effectively against Unilever's Lipton tea brand. Companies could also use cross-border alliances for distributing their goods in the host market(s) or to bolster their global new product development efforts. A case in point is a joint venture that Coca-Cola and Sanofi, a French multinational healthcare company, set up to develop and market health drinks in French pharmacies. Under the partnership, Coca-Cola agreed to develop a new range of healthier beverages under the brand name "Beautific Oenibiol" while Sanofi would oversee the distribution. The new beverages would have well-being benefits such as skin improvement, weight loss, and strengthening of hair and nails.[48]

Depending on the equity stake, three forms of partnerships can be distinguished: majority (more than 50 percent ownership), 50-50, and minority (50 percent or less ownership) ventures. Huge infrastructure or high-tech projects that demand a large amount of expertise and money often involve multiple foreign and local partners. Another distinction is between cooperative and equity joint ventures. A **cooperative joint venture** is an agreement for the partners to collaborate but does not

---

[48]"Coca-Cola, Sanofi Form Pilot Venture to Test 'Beauty Drink,'" http://www.bloomberg.com, accessed on October 17, 2012.

involve any equity investments. For instance, one partner might contribute manufacturing technology whereas the other partner provides access to distribution channels. Cooperative joint ventures are quite common for partnerships between well-heeled multinational companies and local players in emerging markets. A good example of the collaborative approach is Cisco's sales strategy in Asia. Instead of investing in its own sales force, Cisco builds up partnerships with hardware vendors (e.g., IBM), consulting firms (e.g., KPMG), or systems integrators (e.g., Singapore-based Datacraft). These partners in essence act as front people for Cisco. They are the ones that sell and install Cisco's routers and switches.[49] An **equity joint venture** goes one step further. It is an arrangement in which the partners agree to raise capital in proportion to the equity stakes agreed upon.

Benefits

A major advantage of joint ventures compared to lesser forms of resource commitment such as licensing is the return potential. With licensing, for instance, the company solely gets royalty payments instead of a share of the profits. Joint ventures also entail much more control over the operations than most of the previous entry modes discussed so far. MNCs that like to maximize their degree of control prefer full ownership. However, in many instances, local governments discourage or even forbid wholly owned ventures in certain industries. Under such circumstances, partnerships (joint ventures) are a second-best or temporary solution.

Apart from the benefits listed above, the **synergy** argument is another compelling reason for setting up a joint venture. Partnerships not only mean a sharing of capital and risk. Other possible contributions brought in by the local partner include land, raw materials, expertise on the local environment (culture, legal, political), access to a distribution network, personal contacts with suppliers, and relations with government officials. Combined with the foreign partner's skills and resources, these inputs offer the key to a successful market entry. The Sony Ericsson partnership offers an excellent example. The tie-up combined Ericsson's technology prowess and strong links to wireless operators with Sony's marketing skills and expertise in consumer electronics. Each partner stood to gain from helping the other grow in regions where it was weak: Japan for Ericsson and Europe for Sony.[50] In late 2011, almost exactly 10 years after they formed the alliance, the two companies split on good terms when Sony announced it would buy out Ericsson's 50 percent share of the business for $1.5 billion and rename the entity Sony Mobile Communications.[51]

Caveats

For many MNCs, lack of full control is the biggest shortcoming of joint ventures. There are a number of ways for the MNC to gain more leverage. The most obvious way is via a majority equity stake. However, government restrictions often rule this option out. Even when for some reason majority ownership is not a viable alternative, MNCs have other means at their disposal to exercise control over the joint venture. MNCs could deploy expatriates in key line positions, thereby controlling financial, marketing, and other critical operations of the venture. MNCs could also offer various types of outside support services to back up their weaker joint ventures in areas such as marketing, personnel training, quality control, and customer service.[52]

As with licensing agreements, the foreign firm runs the risk that the partner could become a future competitor. Scores of China's most successful domestic companies started off as partners of multinationals. A case in point is Eastcom, a state-owned Chinese manufacturer and distributor of

---

[49]"Cisco's Asian Gambit," *Fortune*, January 10, 2000, pp. 52–54.

[50]"Sony Ericsson: 'In Big Bloody Trouble,'" *Business Week (Asian Edition)*, November 4, 2002, pp. 54–55.

[51]"Sony and Ericsson Part on Good Terms," http://www.ft.com, accessed on October 2, 2012.

[52]Johannes Meier, Javier Perez, and Jonathan R. Woetzel, "Solving the puzzle—MNCs in China," *McKinsey Quarterly* 2 (1995): 20–33.

Exhibit 9-6   Conflicting Objectives in Chinese Joint Ventures

	Foreign Partner	Chinese Partner
Planning	Retain business flexibility	Maintain congruency between the venture and the state economic plan
Contracts	Unambiguous, detailed, and enforceable	Ambiguous, brief, and adaptable
Negotiations	Sequential, issue by issue	Holistic and heuristic
Staffing	Maximize productivity; fewest people per given output level	Employ maximum number of local people
Technology	Match technical sophistication to the organization and its environment	Gain access to the most advanced technology as quickly as possible
Profits	Maximize in long term; repatriate over time	Reinvest for future modernization; maintain foreign exchange reserves
Inputs	Minimize unpredictability and poor quality of supplies	Promote domestic sourcing
Process	Stress high quality	Stress high quantity
Outputs	Access and develop domestic market	Export to generate foreign currency
Control	Reduce political and economic controls on decision making	Accept technology and capital but preclude foreign authority infringement on sovereignty and ideology

Source: Reprinted from M. G. Martinsons and C.-S. Tsong, "Successful Joint Ventures in the Heart of the Dragon," *Long Range Planning,* 28 (5), p. 5. Copyright 1995, with kind permission from Elsevier Science Ltd., The Boulevard, Langford Lane, Kidlington OX5 1GB UK.

telecom equipment. After a 10-year-old collaboration with Motorola, the company launched its own digital cell phone, undercutting Motorola's StarTAC model by $120.[53]

Lack of trust and mutual conflicts turn numerous international joint ventures into marriages from hell. Conflicts can arise over matters such as strategies, resource allocation, transfer pricing, and ownerships of critical assets like technologies and brand names. In 1984, Honda and the Hero Group set up a joint venture to manufacture and sell motorbikes under the Hero Honda brand name in India. Honda would provide the technology while Hero would handle the marketing. Though the Hero Honda brand became one of the leading motorcycle brands in India, the relationship grew increasingly troublesome. For instance, Honda was reluctant to give its Indian partner access to its technological expertise. In 1999 Honda set up a wholly-owned subsidiary; five years later this subsidiary became a direct competitor for Hero Honda motorbikes when it started producing motorbikes. In 2010, following a string of issues, the two partners called it quits.[54]

Often the seeds for trouble with joint ventures or alliances exist from the very beginning of the relationship. **Exhibit 9-6** contrasts the mutually conflicting objectives that the foreign partner and the local Chinese partner may hold when setting up a joint venture in China. Cultural strains between partners often spur mistrust and mutual conflict, making a bad situation even worse. Autolatina, a joint venture set up by Ford Motor Co. and Volkswagen AG in Latin America, was dissolved after seven years in spite of the fact that it remained profitable to the very end. Cultural differences between the German and American managers were a major factor. One participating executive noted that "there were good intentions behind Autolatina's formation but they never really overcame the VW-Ford culture shock."[55]

When trouble undermines the joint venture, the partners can try to resolve the conflict via mechanisms built into the agreement. If a mutually acceptable resolution is not achievable, the joint venture is scaled back or dissolved. For instance, a joint venture between Unilever and AKI

---

[53]"The Local Cell-Phone Boys Get Tough," *Business Week (Asian Edition),* September 20, 1999, p. 24.

[54]"Hero & Honda Technology Pact to Be on till 2014," http://indiatoday.intoday.in/story/hero-&-honda-technology-pact-to-be-on-till-2014/1/122274.html.

[55]"Why Ford, VW's Latin marriage succumbed to 7-year itch," *Advertising Age International,* March 20, 1995, p. I-22.

in South Korea broke up after seven years following disagreements over brand strategies for new products, resource allocation, advertising support, and brand ownership.[56]

Drivers behind Successful International Joint Ventures

There are no magic ingredients to foster the stability of joint ventures. Still, some important lessons can be drawn from academic research of international joint ventures.

Pick the Right Partner

Most joint venture marriages prosper by choosing a suitable partner. That means that the multinational should invest the time to identify proper candidates. A careful screening of the joint venture partner is an absolute necessity. One problem is that it is not easy to sketch a profile of the "ideal" partner. The presence of complementary skills and resources that lead to synergies is one characteristic of successful joint ventures. Prospective partners should also have compatible goals. **Exhibit 9-7** lists the attributes that Starbucks requires.

Some evidence indicates that partners should be similar in terms of size and resources. Partners with whom the firm has built up an existing relationship (e.g., distributors, customers, suppliers) also facilitate a strong relationship.[57] The more balanced the contributions by the partners, the more trusting and harmonious the relationship.[58] One issue that latecomers in a market often face is that the "best" partners have already been snapped up. Note, however, that the same issue arises with acquisition strategies. One study on joint venture performance in China offers five guidelines for partner selection.[59] First, integrate partner selection with your strategic goals. Second, obtain as much information as possible about the candidate (e.g., company brochures, business license). Third, visit the site. Fourth, check whether or not the potential partner shares your investment objective. And, finally, do not put too much emphasis on the rule of *guanxi* (networking).

Exhibit 9-7 Starbucks Coffee's Criteria in Selecting Partners

- Shared values and corporate culture
- Strategic fit
- Seasoned operator of small-box, multi-unit retail
- Sufficient financial and human resources
- Involved and committed top management
- Real estate knowledge and access
- Local business leader
- Strong track record developing new ventures
- Experience managing licensed and premium brands and concepts
- Leverageable infrastructure
- Food and beverage experience

Source: http://www.starbucks.com/aboutus/international.asp, accessed January 30, 2009.

---

[56]"How Unilever's South Korean partnership fell apart," *Advertising Age*.

[57]Karen J. Hladik, "R&D and International Joint Ventures," in P. J. Buckley, ed. *Cooperative Forms of Transnational Corporation Activity*, (London: Routledge, 1994).

[58]Akmal S. Hyder and Pervez N. Ghauri, "Managing International Joint Venture Relationships," *Industrial Marketing Management* 29 (2000): 205–18.

[59]Yadong Luo, "Joint Venture Success in China: How Should We Select a Good Partner," *Journal of World Business* 32, no. 2 (1998): 145–66.

Establish Clear Objectives for the Joint Venture from the Very Beginning[60]

It is important to clearly spell out the objectives of the joint venture from day one. Partners should know what their respective contributions and responsibilities are before signing the contract.[61] They should also know what to expect from the partnership.

Bridge Cultural Gaps

Many joint venture disputes stem from cultural differences between the local and foreign partners. Much agony and frustration can be avoided when the foreign investor makes an attempt to bridge cultural differences. For instance, when setting up joint ventures in China, having an ethnic Chinese or an "old China hand" as a middleman often helps a great deal. The problem is that knowledgeable people who share the perspectives of both cultures are often very hard to find.[62]

Top Managerial Commitment and Respect

Without strong commitment from the parent companies' top management, most international joint ventures are doomed to failure. The companies should be willing to assign their best managerial talent to the joint venture. Venture managers should also have complete access to and support from their respective parent companies.[63]

Incremental Approach Works Best

Rather than being overambitious, an incremental approach towards setting up the international joint venture appears to be much more effective. The partnership starts on a small scale. Gradually, the scope of the joint venture is broadened by adding other responsibilities and activities to the joint venture's charter. The foreign partner often starts off with a minority stake and gradually increases its stake in the joint venture.

A study by a team of McKinsey consultants also advises parent companies to create a launch team during the launch phase—beginning with the signing of a memorandum of understanding and continuing through the first 100 days of operation.[64] The launch team should address the four key joint venture challenges:

1. Build and maintain *strategic alignment* across the separate corporate entities, each of which has its own goals, market pressures, and shareholders.

2. Create a *governance* system that promotes shared decision making and oversight between the parent companies.

3. Manage the *economic interdependencies* between the corporate parents and the joint venture (e.g., compensation of each parent for its contributions).

4. Build the *organization* for the joint venture (e.g., staffing positions, assigning responsibilities).

---

[60]Dominique Turpin, "Strategic alliances with Japanese firms: Myths and realities," *Long Range Planning* 26, no. 4 (1993): 11–16.

[61]Maris G. Martinsons and Choo-sin Tseng, "Successful joint ventures in the heart of the dragon," *Long Range Planning* 28, no. 5 (1995): 45–58.

[62]Martinsons and Tseng, "Successful joint ventures in the heart of the dragon," p. 56.

[63]Turpin, "Strategic alliances with Japanese firms: Myths and realities," p. 15.

[64]James Bamford, David Ernst, and David G. Fubini, "Launching a World-Class Joint Venture," *Harvard Business Review* 82 (February 2004): 90–101.

Wholly Owned Subsidiaries

In September 2008, Coca-Cola offered $2.4 billion in cash to buy China Huiyuan Juice Group. At the time, this was the largest takeover offer ever made by a foreign company to buy a Chinese company. Muthar Kent, Coke's CEO at the time, stated that the acquisition would "provide a unique opportunity to strengthen our business in China, especially since the juice segment is so dynamic and fast growing."[65] In March 2009, the Chinese government rejected the takeover bid due to fears that the acquisition could harm Coca-Cola's smaller competitors and raise consumer prices.[66] If the bid had been approved by the Chinese government,[67] it would have more than doubled Coca-Cola's market share in China's fruit juice market to around 20 percent.[68] Multinational companies often prefer to enter new markets with 100 percent ownership. Ownership strategies in foreign markets can essentially take two routes: acquisitions where the MNC buys up existing companies, or **greenfield operations** that are started from scratch. As with the other entry modes, full ownership entry entails certain benefits to the MNC but also carries risks.

Benefits

Wholly owned subsidiaries give MNCs full control of their operations. It is often the ideal solution for companies that do not want to be saddled with all the risks and anxieties associated with other entry modes such as joint venturing. Full ownership means that all the profits go to the company. Fully owned enterprises allow the foreign investor to manage and control its own processes and tasks in terms of marketing, production, logistics, and sourcing decisions. Setting up fully owned subsidiaries also sends a strong commitment signal to the local market. In some markets—China, for example—wholly owned subsidiaries can be erected much faster than joint ventures with local companies that may consume years of negotiations before their final take-off.[69] The latter point is especially important when there are substantial advantages of being an early entrant in the target market.

Caveats

Despite the advantages of 100 percent ownership, many MNCs are quite reluctant to choose this particular mode of entry. The risks of full ownership cannot be easily discounted. Complete ownership means that the parent company will have to carry the full burden of possible losses. Developing a foreign presence without the support of a third party is also very demanding on the firm's resources. Obviously, a part of the market-related risks, substantial political risks (e.g., expropriation, nationalization) and economic risks (e.g., currency devaluation) must be factored in.

Companies that enter via a wholly owned enterprise are sometimes also perceived as a threat to the cultural and/or economic sovereignty of the host country. When InBev, the Brazilian/Belgian brewer, made a $46.3 billion unsolicited takeover bid for Anheuser-Busch, the leading American beer brewer, several U.S. politicians and journalists were dismayed. Barack Obama, the 2008 Democratic presidential candidate and ultimate victor, stated at a press conference in St. Louis, headquarters of Anheuser-Busch, "I do think it would be a shame if Bud is foreign-owned. I think we should be able to find an American company that is interested in purchasing Anheuser-Busch."[70] Likewise, after Kraft acquired Cadbury and announced the closure of a Cadbury

---

[65]"Coke Eyes Record China Deal," *Financial Times*, September 4, 2008, p. 13.

[66]"Beijing Thwarts Coke's Takeover Bid," online.wsj.com, accessed on July 20, 2009.

[67]Even though Huiyuan Juice is a private company, the deal still had to be approved by the Chinese government.

[68]"Coke to Squeeze More from China," *Financial Times*, September 4, 2008, p. 14.

[69]Wilfried Vanhonacker, "Entering China: An Unconventional Approach," *Harvard Business Review* (March-April 1997).

[70]http://www.flex-news-food.com/pages/17605/Anheuser-Busch/InBev/obama-says-shame-anheuser-busch-sold-inbev. html; ultimately the deal went through and Inbev was renamed Anheuser Busch-InBev.

factory, British parliamentarians accused the company of acting "irresponsibly and unwisely."[71] One way to address hostility to foreign acquisitions in the host country is via "localizing" the firm's presence in the foreign market by hiring local managers, sourcing locally, developing local brands, sponsoring local sports or cultural events, and so forth.[72]

Acquisitions and Mergers

Companies such as Heinz and Coca-Cola have built up strong global competitive positions via cleverly planned and finely executed acquisition strategies. MNCs choose acquisition entry to expand globally for a number of reasons. First and foremost, when contrasted with greenfield operations, acquisitions provide a rapid means to get access to new markets. Geographic expansion was a key motivation for Kraft's takeover of Cadbury, the British confectionary maker, in 2010.[73] With the acquisition, Kraft was able to bolster its position in Europe and gain a foothold in India, a market where it was virtually unknown. In fact, when Kraft introduced Oreo cookies in India in 2011, it used Cadbury instead of Kraft as the umbrella brand.

For relative latecomers in an industry, acquisitions are also a viable option to obtain well-established brand names, instant access to distribution outlets, or technology. Heineken's $7 billion purchase of the beer operations of Femsa, one of the biggest brewers in Mexico, in 2010 was motivated by the firm's desire to revive its fortunes in North America. In the 1990s, Heineken had lost its position as the top import beer brand in the U.S. to Grupo Modelo's Corona.[74] More youthful drinkers preferred the lighter taste and fun lifestyle associated with Corona. The Femsa deal bolstered Heineken's competitive position in Latin America, especially the highly profitable Mexican beer market. As part of the deal, the Dutch brewer also picked up Dos Equis, a Mexican import beer that is becoming increasingly popular among young American beer drinkers.[75]

Cash-rich Chinese companies are also trying to gain a foothold in international markets by buying up foreign firms. The first major such takeover was Lenovo's acquisition of IBM's PC division, as discussed in **Global Perspective 9-2**. Other high-profile deals include Geely's purchase of Ford's Volvo division, heavy-machinery equipment maker Zoomlion's acquisition of Germany's Putzmeister, and Bright Food's takeover of Britain's Weetabix, a cereal maker. Such efforts have not always been successful. Huawei, the Chinese telecom equipment maker, had to drop its bid to buy a major stake in 3Com when U.S. lawmakers raised alarms about Huawei's alleged ties with the People's Liberation Army.[76]

Expansion via **acquisitions or mergers** carries substantial risks. Differences in the corporate culture of the two companies between managers are often extremely hard to bridge. One example of a company that has been plagued with corporate culture disease is Alcatel-Lucent, the telecommunications equipment group that resulted from the 2006 merger of Alcatel and Lucent. Since its creation, the group has been hampered by cultural differences between the American and French arms. As one analyst observed: " . . . Alcatel-Lucent was a merger that sounded good in a PowerPoint presentation. But there have been a lot of serious integration challenges, including cultural issues, that were underestimated and still linger."[77]

---

[71]"A Bitter Taste," *Financial Times*, May 24, 2011, p. 10.

[72]W. Vanhonacker, "Entering China: An Unconventional Approach."

[73]In October 2012, Kraft separated its North American grocery business from its global snacks operation. The domestic business is now known as Kraft Foods Group. The international spinoff was named Mondelez International.

[74]In June 2012, AB InBev, Heineken's arch rival, agreed to merge with Grupo Modelo. The deal was expected to close in early 2013. However, U.S. antitrust regulators were unlikely to clear the proposed merger—"Is A-B InBev's Modelo Merger on the Rocks?" http://www.stltoday.com, accessed on October 13, 2012.

[75]"Heineken's Most Interesting Savior," *Bloomberg Businessweek*, January 9–January 15, 2012, pp. 23–24.

[76]http://www.businessweek.com/globalbiz/blog/eyeonasia/archives/2008/02/huaweis_3com_de.html.

[77]"Culture Clash Hits Home at Alcatel-Lucent," http://www.iht.com/bin/printfriendly.php?id=14867263.

Global Perspective 9-2

THE Lenovo/IBM Deal—A Winning Combination?

The $1.75 billion acquisition of IBM's personal computer business by Lenovo, the Chinese PC maker, marked the dawn of a new era. The cross-border deal gave Lenovo much more than Big Blue's PC business. Lenovo became the first state-controlled Chinese firm to acquire an iconic global brand. "If anyone still harboured any doubts that Chinese corporates were serious players on the global M&A stage those have now totally been dispelled," said Colin Banfield at CSFB.

The talks behind the deal took 18 months. By bringing together China's largest PC maker and IBM's PC division, Lenovo executives hoped they could create a behemoth able to challenge the dominance of Hewlett-Packard and Dell, the market leaders at the time. Lenovo estimated that it could save $200m a year by component cost savings. Lenovo would own IBM's Think trademark and IBM would become Lenovo's "preferred supplier" as part of the deal.

The growth plan spelled out for the "new" Lenovo had three key elements: developing the ThinkPad notebook computer franchise; expanding into emerging markets such as India, Brazil, and Russia; and introducing Lenovo-branded PCs for small business owners in the United States and Europe.

Many observers were skeptical about blending the two very diverse corporate cultures. Michael Dell, the founder and CEO of rival Dell, stated that: "We're not a big fan of the idea of taking companies and smashing them together. When was the last time you saw a successful acquisition or merger in the computer industry? It hasn't happened for a long, long time . . . I don't see this [the IBM-Lenovo merger] as being all that different." Yet, in 2011 Lenovo secured the number two spot in the global PC sales league, overtaking Dell.

There were several motives behind Lenovo's bold acquisition decision. Prior to the purchase of IBM's PC business, the company was already big in the fast-growing Chinese market, where it had a 35 percent market share. Outside of China, Lenovo was barely known. Also, most of Lenovo's sales were in the consumer segment. IBM, on the other hand,

was very strong in the corporate segment. It also had global brand name reputation and valuable technology expertise. With IBM's corporate clientele and global presence, Lenovo was able to instantaneously achieve an ambition that normally would have taken many years to fulfill.

Not surprisingly, the integration of IBM PC and the "old" Lenovo met some hurdles. The focus at the "old" Lenovo was on rules. All employees were expected to clock in and clock out. Employees were forbidden to turn up late for meetings. Where Lenovo had rules, IBM had processes: regular meetings, conference calls, and milestones to keep projects on track. To the Chinese, the focus on processes may have been as alien as the emphasis on rules for former IBM staff. Another cultural gap stemmed from conversational style differences: Americans like to talk; Chinese prefer to listen.

To bridge cross-cultural differences, Lenovo undertook several initiatives. It set up a diversity team to promote respect for different cultures. The working language for the new Lenovo became English as hardly anyone from the IBM side could speak Chinese. Instead of bringing in its "own" people, Lenovo left the IBM management team in place in order to preserve stability. In December 2005, the company hired William Amelio, the former head of Dell's Asia-Pacific division, as CEO. Other steps included staff workshops on cultural sensitivity, respecting time zone differences and key countries' holidays when planning conference calls or key meetings, and discouraging executives from sending e-mails on weekends.

Following the acquisition of IBM's PC division, Lenovo's business outside China had become heavily dependent on the business segment. This focus badly hurt the company during the 2008 financial crisis when most companies sharply cut their IT spending. In February 2009, the company replaced Bill Amelio with Yang Yuanqi, who used to be the company's chairman before the IBM PC division deal. With the new regime in place, Lenovo revamped its strategy, aiming to put more emphasis on the consumer market and emerging markets. Through a string of overseas acquisitions (e.g., Medion Computers in Germany; CCE in Brazil) and aggressive pricing, Lenovo has been able to gain market share. In October 2012, Lenovo overtook Hewlett-Packard to become the world's largest manufacturer of PCs. To reduce its dependence on the PC category, the company is also branching into the smartphone and tablet categories.

Sources: "IBM Brand Loyalty Holds Key for Lenovo," *Financial Times*, December 9, 2004, p. 16; "Deal Divides Opinion Over Future Trends," *Financial Times*, December 9, 2004, p. 16; "Your Rules and My Processes," *Financial Times*, November 10, 2005, p. 10; "Quick-fire Lessons in Globalisation," *Financial Times*, November 11, 2005, p. 8; http://www.businessweek.com/technology/content/dec2005/tc20051221_376268.htm; "Lenovo Close to Passing HP in PCs," http://www.ft.com, accessed on September 30, 2012; "Lenovo Continues Growth with Brazil Purchase," http://www.ft.com, accessed on October 2, 2012; "When East Meets West," *China Daily Asia Weekly*, October 5–11, 2012, p. 24.

A merger or acquisition bid can also be blocked by antitrust rulings if such bid is found to lead to anti-competitive behavior in the country or certain regions.[78] In October 2012, the European Commission objected to a merger deal between UPS, the American courier company, and TNT, its smaller Dutch rival. The Commission feared that the merged company might lead to a lack of competition for certain routes within the European Union.[79]

The assets of the acquisition do not always live up to the expectations of the acquiring company. Outdated plants, tarnished brand names, or an unmotivated workforce are only a few of the many possible disappointments that the acquiring company could face. The local government might also attach certain conditions to the acquisition or expectations in terms of job creation. Failure to live up to such expectations could tarnish the image of the MNC in the host country. In 2005, BenQ, the Taiwanese consumer electronics firm, acquired the mobile phone division of Siemens in the hope of creating a leading brand in the category. Unfortunately, the German branch proved to be an albatross for BenQ, which decided to discontinue manufacturing phones in Germany. This move created a lot of bad feelings among German stakeholders (unions, government) with the suspicion that BenQ only bought the Siemens mobile business for its patents.[80] A careful screening and assessment of takeover candidates can avoid a lot of heartburn on the part of the acquiring company.

As mentioned earlier, open hostility toward foreign companies can also complicate acquisition plans. A joint $10.5 billion bid by Cadbury and Nestlé to buy Hershey Foods, the U.S. chocolate maker, got derailed in part because of strong opposition against a "foreign takeover" from the local community. Another drawback is that acquisition entry can be a very costly global expansion strategy. Good prospects are usually unwilling to sell themselves. If they are, they do not come cheap. Other foreign or local companies are typically interested too, and the result is often a painful bidding war. Heineken, the Dutch beer maker, was forced to raise its bid for Asia-Pacific Breweries (APB), a Singapore group that owns the Tiger Beer brand, from S$5.1 billion to S$5.6 billion (US$4.6 billion) to fend off a challenge from a Thai rival. The new bid meant that Heineken would be paying 35 times APB's earnings. The Dutch brewer was willing to pay such a steep price as control of APB would enable the firm to strengthen its position in the fast-growing Asian beer market.[81]

---

[78]For major mergers, the parties involved may need clearance not just in the country where the merger takes place but also in other jurisdictions. For example, Oracle's takeover of Sun Microsystems needed to be approved not only by U.S. regulators but also by regulators in the European Union, China, and Russia.

[79]"Brussels Objects to UPS and TNT Merger," http://www.ft.com, accessed on October 13, 2012.

[80]"Siemens Strikes Back," http://www.spiegel.de/international/0,1518,440409,00.html.

[81]"Heineken Moves Closer to Gain Control of Asia Pacific Breweries," http://online.wsj.com/article/BT-CO-20120918-713512.html.

Greenfield Operations

Acquisition strategies are not always feasible. Good prospects may already have been nabbed by the company's competitors. In many emerging markets, acceptable acquisition candidates often are simply not available. Overhauling the facilities of possible candidates is sometimes much more costly than building an operation from scratch. In the wake of these downsides, companies often prefer to enter foreign markets through greenfield operations that are established from scratch. Greenfield operations offer the company more flexibility than acquisitions in areas such as human resources, suppliers, logistics, plant layout, or manufacturing technology. Greenfield investments also avoid the costs of integrating the acquisition into the parent company.[82] Another motivation is the package of goodies (e.g., tax holidays) that host governments sometimes offer to whet the appetite of foreign investors. A major disadvantage, though, of greenfield operations is that they require enormous investments of time and capital. Not surprisingly, of all the entry modes we covered, greenfield entries are the most risky ones.

Dynamics of Entry Strategies

Exhibit 9-8 summarizes the pros and cons of the various entry mode alternatives that we discussed in the previous section. Some entry mode choices lead to long-term commitments, especially when they involve binding contractual commitments. Others can be changed very easily. Over time, the drivers that influence a firm's entry strategy will evolve. Indeed, one study that looked at the international expansion path of U.S. service firms found that as their international experience rises, these firms seek out markets that are geographically and culturally more distant from the United States.[83]

Typically, firms adapt their entry mode over time. The drivers that resulted in the initial entry-mode selection tend to change over time. For instance, the host government may loosen ownership restrictions that were imposed on foreign companies. Anecdotal evidence and research studies show that firms often gradually move toward greater control modes over time. For instance, Starbucks initially entered China through three joint ventures covering different regions. Gradually, the firm increased its stake in the three ventures. U.S. chocolate maker Hershey's set up a 51-49 joint venture with an Indian partner, the Godrej Group, in 2007 to boost its business in India. The partnership did not meet Hershey's expectations. It failed to launch major brands from Hershey's portfolio; the only product that was launched was chocolate syrup. Five years later, in September 2012, Hershey bought out its Indian partner and decided to set up its own fully-owned subsidiary. According to Hershey's CEO: "They were good partners. We learned a lot from them, but food is not a core competency for them."[84] Several factors can influence entry mode adaptations. One empirical study that looked at entry decisions in China found that the following characteristics are more likely to result in a conversion of an international joint venture into a wholly owned subsidiary:[85]

- An increase of local market knowledge by the foreign partner.

- A lower level of perceived external risks (e.g., political, legal).

---

[82]Jiatao Li, "Foreign entry and survival: Effects of strategic choices on performance in international markets," *Strategic Management Journal* 16 (1995): 333–351.

[83]Erramilli, M. Krishna, "The Experience Factor in Foreign Market Entry Behavior of Service Firms," *Journal of International Business Studies* 22 (1991): 479–501.

[84]"Hershey CEO Weighs Next Steps in China," http://www.reuters.com, accessed on October 21, 2012.

[85]Jonas F. Puck, Dirk Holtbrügge, and Alexander T. Mohr, "Beyond Entry Mode Choice: Explaining the Conversion of Joint Ventures into Wholly Owned Subsidiaries in the People's Republic of China," *Journal of International Business Studies* 40 (2009): 388–404.

Exhibit 9-8   Advantages and Disadvantages of Different Modes of Entry

Entry Mode	Advantages	Disadvantages
Indirect exporting	• Low commitment (in terms of resources) • Low risk	• Lack of control • Lack of contact with foreign market • No learning experience • Potential opportunity cost
Direct exporting	• More control (compared to indirect exporting) • More sales push	• Need to build up export organization • More demanding on resources
Licensing	• Little or no investment • Rapid way to gain entry • Means to bridge import barriers • Low risk	• Lack of control • Potential opportunity cost • Need for quality control • Risk of creating competitor • Limits market development
Franchising	• Little or no investment • Rapid way to gain entry • Managerial motivation	• Need for quality control • Lack of control • Risk of creating competitor
Contract manufacturing	• Little or no investment • Overcome import barriers • Cost savings	• Need for quality control • Risk of bad press (e.g., child labor) • Diversion to gray and/or black markets
Joint venture	• Risk sharing • Less demanding on resources (compared to wholly-owned) • Potential of synergies (e.g., access to local distribution network)	• Risk of conflicts with partner(s) • Lack of control • Risk of creating competitor
Acquisition	• Full control • Access to local assets (e.g., plants, distribution network, brand assets) • Less competition	• Costly • High risk • Need to integrate differing national/corporate cultures • Cultural clashes
Greenfield	• Full control • Latest technologies • No risk of cultural conflicts	• Costly • Time consuming • High political & financial risks

- A smaller cultural distance between the foreign firm's home country and China.

- A lower perceived complexity of governmental regulations for foreign firms.

Timing of Entry

International market entry decisions also cover the timing-of-entry question: when should the firm enter a foreign market? Numerous firms have been hurt badly by entering markets too early. We already mentioned Uniqlo's ill-timed entries in the United States and Britain. Similarly, Ikea's first foray in Japan in 1974 was a complete fiasco.[86] The Swedish furniture retailer hastily withdrew from Japan after realizing that Japanese consumers were not yet ready for the concept of self-assembly and preferred high quality over low prices. Ikea re-entered Japan in late 2005, but this time using a more service-oriented approach, offering assembly and home delivery.

---

[86]http://www.businessweek.com/magazine/content/05_46/b3959001.htm.

Exhibit 9-9   Timeline of Wal-Mart's International Expansion

Market	Retail Units (as of Aug. 31, 2012)	Date of Entry	Date of Exit
Mexico	2,197 • WS: 216 • SC: 130[87]	Nov 1991	
Canada	337 • WS: 181 • WDC: 156	Nov 1994	
Brazil	349 • WS: 51 • SC: 27	May 1995	
Argentina	88 • WS: 29	Aug 1995	
China	379 • WS: 338 • SC: 7	Aug 1996	
South Korea	16	1998	2006
Germany	85	1998	2006
United Kingdom	547 • SC: 32	Jul 1999	
Japan	427	Mar 2002	
Costa Rica	203 • WS: 7	Sep 2005	
El Salvador	80 • WS: 2	Sep 2005	
Guatemala	201 • WS: 7	Sep 2005	
Honduras	69 • WS: 1	Sep 2005	
Nicaragua	76	Sep 2005	
India (cash-and-carry wholesale)	17	Aug 2007	
Chile	328	Jan 2009	
South Africa[88]	368	2011	

Sources: http://www.corporate.Wal-Mart.com/our-story/locations and http://en.wikipedia.org/wiki/Wal-Mart, accessed October 5, 2012.

   Exhibit 9-9 shows the timeline of Wal-Mart's international expansion strategy. Note that the gap was almost 30 years between the foundation of Wal-Mart by Sam Walton in 1962 and the retailer's first international forays in Mexico (1991). Since then, Wal-Mart has expanded very aggressively. Initially, Wal-Mart concentrated mostly on markets in the Americas. It is only toward the end of the 1990s that the retailer shifted its attention toward Europe and the Asia-Pacific region. As of 2012, Wal-Mart operated more than 10,000 stores in 27 countries

---

[87]WS = Wal-Mart Supercenter; SC = Sam's Club; WDC = Wal-Mart Discount Store

[88]In 2011, Wal-Mart acquired a majority stake in Massmart Holdings, a leading African retailer of general merchandise. Massmart operates in 12 countries in sub-Saharan Africa, including: South Africa (325 units), Botswana (12), Ghana (1), Lesotho (2), Malawi (2), Mozambique (17), Namibia (3), Nigeria (2), Swaziland (1), Tanzania (1), Uganda (1), and Zambia (1).

under 69 banners.[89] Besides retailing, the firm also runs a cash-and-carry wholesale operation in India through a 50-50 joint venture with Bharti Enterprises, an Indian conglomerate.[90] Most recently, in 2011, the group entered sub-Saharan Africa by acquiring a majority stake in Massmart, a South Africa based retailer.

Research on international entry-timing decisions is scarce. One study examined the timing-of-entry decisions of U.S. Fortune 500 firms in China.[91] According to the study's findings, firms tend to enter China earlier:

- The higher their level of international experience;

- The larger the firm size;

- The broader the scope of products and services;

- When competitors had already entered the market;

- The more favorable the risk (political, business) conditions; and

- When non-equity modes of entry (e.g., licensing, exporting, non-equity alliances) are chosen.

In general, companies that entered China relatively late often had an advantage over earlier entrants. A main reason is that latecomers face fewer restrictive business regulations than their predecessors. Companies entering China now have much more flexible ways of setting up their joint ventures. In many industries, companies are now free to set up a wholly owned subsidiary instead of partnering with a Chinese company.[92] Still, some early entrants such as Yum! Brands, the operator of the KFC and Pizza Hut restaurant chain, and Procter & Gamble have been able to leave their competitors in the dust.

One other study looked at the entry-timing pattern for a sample of nineteen multinational firms.[93] This study develops the concept of **near-market knowledge**. Near-market knowledge is defined as the knowledge (cultural, economic) generated in similar markets in which the MNC already operates. The study's key findings are fourfold, namely:

1. Near-market knowledge has an important impact on foreign market entry timing. Near-market knowledge accumulated from successful foreign entries will lead to earlier entry in similar markets.

2. Cultural similarity with the home market is not related to foreign market entry timing. Although cultural similarity with the domestic market may matter for initial foreign entry forays, it turns out not to be critical for later entries.

3. Several economic attractiveness variables matter a great deal. Specifically, countries with wealthier consumers, larger economies, more developed infrastructure, and more easily accessible consumers are likely to be entered earlier.

4. Economic factors are more crucial than cultural factors in entry timing decisions.

Exit Strategies

So far we have concentrated on international entry strategies. In this section we will concentrate on their flipside: exit (or divestment) strategies. Exits in global marketing are not uncommon. In mid-

---

[89]http://corporate.Wal-Mart.com/our-story/locations, accessed on October 20, 2012.

[90]http://Wal-Martstores.com/FactsNews/, accessed February 2, 2009.

[91]Vibah Gaba, Yigang Pan, and Gerardo R. Ungson, "Timing of Entry in International Markets: An Empirical Study of U. S. Fortune 500 Firms in China," *Journal of International Business Studies* 33 (First Quarter 2002): 39–55.

[92]"In China, It May Pay to Be Late," *Asian Wall Street Journal*, February 9, 2004, A1, A6.

[93]Debanjan Mitra and Peter N. Golder, "Whose Culture Matters? Near-Market Knowledge and Its Impact on Foreign Market Entry Timing," *Journal of Marketing Research* 39 (August 2002): 350–365.

2012, Home Depot, the U.S. home improvement retailer, closed all seven of its remaining big-box stores in China after years of losses. The company, which entered China in 2006, conceded that it had misread the country's taste for do-it-yourself products. Instead, China is more of a do-it-for-me culture. Best Buy closed its nine China stores in February 2011.[94] In 2006, Wal-Mart retreated twice in a row: the American mega-retailer first sold its stores in South Korea and then, barely two months later, it also sold its German stores to Metro.[95] Similarly, Nokia, the world's largest mobile phone maker, decided to stop making phones for the Japanese market in 2008.

Reasons for Exit

Decisions to exit or divest a foreign market are not taken lightly. Companies may have multiple good reasons to pull out of their foreign markets:

- *Sustained losses.* Companies usually enter key markets with a long-term perspective. Most companies recognize that an immediate payback of their investments is not realistic and are willing to absorb losses for many years. Still, at some point, most companies have a limit on how long a period of losses they are willing to sustain. A weak sales performance was the key reason why supermarket groups Tesco and Carrefour pulled out of Japan.[96]

- *Difficulty in cracking the market.* A company may also decide to pull the plug when it has difficulty cracking the market in the host country. This was the main reason why Nokia decided to stop making and selling mobile phones for the Japanese market in 2008. The Finnish mobile phone maker never had any luck in gaining traction in Japan since it first entered in 2003. As a senior Nokia executive stated: "In the current global economic climate, we have concluded that the continuation of our investment in Japan-specific, localized products is no longer sustainable."[97]

- *Volatility.* Companies often underestimate the risks of the host country's economic and political environment. Many multinationals have rushed into emerging markets, lured by tempting prospects of huge populations with rising incomes. Unfortunately, countries with high growth potential often are very volatile. Numerous multinational companies pulled out of Argentina and Indonesia in the wake of those countries' economic turmoil. As the then CEO of a major multinational wisecracked during an analyst meeting: "I wish we could just close Argentina."[98]

- *Premature entry.* As we discussed earlier, the entry-timing decision is a crucial matter. Entering a market too early can be an expensive mistake. Entries can be premature for reasons such as an underdeveloped marketing infrastructure (e.g., in terms of distribution, supplies), low buying power, and lack of strong local partners.

- *Ethical reasons.* Companies that operate in countries with a questionable human rights record (e.g., Cuba, Sudan) often draw a lot of criticism in their home-country and/or other markets. The bad publicity engendered by human rights campaigners can tarnish the company's image. Rather than running the risk of ruining its reputation, the company may decide to pull out of the country. Levi Strauss, the San Francisco jeans maker, prides itself on being a company with a conscience. In 1993, Levi Strauss stopped making jeans in China because of human rights

---

[94]"Home Depot Learns Chinese Prefer 'Do-It-for-Me,'" http://www.wsj.com, accessed on October 13, 2012.

[95]"Wal-Mart Gives Up Germany," July 29, 2006, http://www.iht.com/articles/2006/07/28/business/Wal-Mart.php.

[96]"Tesco Puts Japanese Business up for Sale," *Financial Times*, September 1, 2011, p. 16.

[97]http://news.zdnet.co.uk/hardware/0,1000000091,39564647,00.htmexhi.

[98]"Submerged," *Advertising Age*, March 4, 2002, p. 14.

violations. It resumed manufacturing in China in 2000 after finding plants that met its ethical standards.[99]

- *Intense competition.* Intense rivalry is often another strong reason for exiting a country. Markets that look appealing on paper usually attract lots of competitors. The outcome is often overcapacity, triggering price wars, and loss-loss situations for all players competing against one another. Rather than sustaining losses, the sensible thing to do is to exit the market, especially when rival players have competitive advantages that are hard to overcome.

- *Resource re-allocation.* A key element of marketing strategy formulation is resource allocation. A strategic review of foreign operations often leads to a shake-up of the company's country portfolio, spurring the MNC to re-allocate its resources across markets. Of all emerging markets, only China has outgrown the United States in annual economic growth rate over the last three decades. This explains why several European companies such as Unilever, Nestlé, and Reckitt-Benckiser have shifted their focus to North America.[100] Poor results from global operations are often a symptom of overexpansion. For instance, in July 2008 Starbucks decided to close 61 Australian outlets (out of a total of 85)[101] as part of a global overhaul.[102]

Risks of Exit

Obviously, exiting a market is a decision that should be taken carefully. Just as there are barriers to entry, there are exit barriers that may delay or complicate an exit decision. Obstacles that compound divestment decisions include:

- *Fixed costs of exit.* Exiting a country often involves substantial fixed costs. In Europe, several countries have very strict labor laws that make exit very costly (e.g., severance payment packages). It is not uncommon for European governments to cry foul and sue a multinational company when the firm decides to shut down its operations. Long-term contracts that involve commitments such as sourcing raw materials or distributing products often involve major termination penalties.

- *Damage to corporate image.* A negative spillover of a divestment decision could also include damage to the firm's corporate image if plant closures lead to job losses. Nokia's decision to close down its manufacturing operations in Germany and shift them to more cost-friendly sites in Eastern Europe led to calls for a boycott of the firm's phones in Germany. Kurt Beck, the head at the time of the Social Democrats (SPD) told a local newspaper that "As far as I am concerned there will be no Nokia mobile phone in my house."[103]

- *Disposition of assets.* Assets that are highly specialized to the particular business or location for which they are being used also create an exit barrier.[104] The number of prospective buyers may

---

[99]"Levi's Faced Earlier Challenge in China," http://www.wsj.com, accessed on October 26, 2010.

[100]"Western Aggression," *Advertising Age*, March 4, 2002, p. 14.

[101]"Starbucks to Close 61 Australian Outlets," http://business.theage.com.au/business/starbucks-to-close-61-australian-outlets-20080729-3mkm.html.

[102]The company also announced the closure of 600 U.S. stores.

[103]"Germany Threatens Nokia Boycott," http://www.france24.com/france24Public/en/archives/news/business/20080122-Nokia-strike-boycott-germany-backlash-finnish-mobile-company.php.

[104]Michael E. Porter, *Competitive Strategy. Techniques for Analyzing Industries and Competitors* (New York: The Free Press, 1980).

be few, and the price they are willing to pay for these assets will most likely be minimal. Hence, the liquidation value of such assets will be low. Sometimes, assets can be sold in markets where the industry is at an earlier stage in the product life cycle.

- *Signal to other markets.* Another concern is that exiting one country or region may send strong negative signals to other countries where the company operates. Exits may lead to job losses in the host country; customers risk losing after-sales service support; distributors stand to lose company support and may witness a significant drop in their business. Therefore, an exit in one country could create negative spillovers in other markets by raising red flags about the company's commitment to its foreign markets.

- *Long-term opportunities.* Although exit is sometimes the only sensible thing to do, firms should avoid shortsightedness. Volatility is a way of life in many emerging markets. Four years after the ruble devaluation in August 1998, the Russian economy made a spectacular recovery. The country became one of the fastest growing markets worldwide for many multinationals, including Procter & Gamble, L'Oréal, and Ikea.[105] Rather than closing shop, it is often better to pay a price in the short term and maintain a presence for the long haul. Exiting a country and re-entering it once the dust settles comes at a price. Rival companies that stayed in the country will have an edge. Distributors and other prospective partners will be reluctant to enter into agreements. Consumers will be leery about buying the firm's products or services, especially when long-term relationships are involved.

Guidelines

Growing through international expansion is not the right formula for all companies. The lure of emerging markets such as the BRIC countries[106] has titillated many marketing managers. Unfortunately, reality does not always live up to hype. Still, companies should handle exit decisions carefully. Here are a few guidelines that managers should ponder before making an exit decision:

- *Contemplate and assess all options to salvage the foreign business.* Exiting is painful—both for the company and other stakeholders (local employees, distributors, customers). Before making any moves, it is crucial to analyze why results are below expectations and to consider possible alternatives that might save the business. Original targets in terms of market share, return on investment, or payback period may have been too ambitious. Costs could be squeezed by, for instance, sourcing locally rather than importing materials or using local staff instead of expatriates. Repositioning or retargeting the business can offer a solution. Nutra-Sweet's foray into China provides a good example. When NutraSweet's consumer division first entered the Chinese market, it targeted the mass market. Sales were far below expectations. Instead of simply exiting the China market, which was one of the options being contemplated, NutraSweet decided to lower its sales targets, pursue the diabetics niche market, and position its brand as a medical product.

- *Incremental exit.* Short of a full exit, an intermediate option is an incremental exit strategy. Firms could "mothball" their operations and restart them when demand or cost conditions improve.[107]

---

[105]"To Russia with Love," *Business Week (Asian Edition)*, September 16, 2002, 26–27.

[106]Brazil, Russia, India, and China.

[107]David Besanko, David Dranove, and Mark Shanley, *Economics of Strategy* (New York: John Wiley & Sons, 2000), p. 338.

- *Migrate customers.* If exiting proves to be the optimal decision, one delicate matter is how to handle customers who depend on the company for after-sales service support and parts. Obviously, it is important that customers not be "orphaned." One solution is to migrate customers to other vendors who can offer a similar level of service support.

SUMMARY

When a company decides to expand globally, it needs to resolve five entry-related issues: (1) the country selection, (2) the scale of entry, (3) the entry mode, (4) the timing of entry, and (5) the entry marketing mix strategy. In this chapter, we focused on the first four of these decisions; we will address the marketing mix conundrum in the next five chapters. We offered a framework for selecting countries. Deciding on the scale of the entry entails balancing off several considerations. The bulk of the chapter looked at the various entry mode alternatives. Each option has its pros and cons, summarized in **Exhibit 9-8**. Most firms use a combination of entry modes. Starbucks, for instance, employs a mixture of company-owned stores, licensing, and joint ventures. Within the same industry, rivals often adopt different approaches to enter new markets. Cummins Engines, a leading U.S.-based diesel engine maker, uses a strategy based on joint ventures with outside groups—mostly customers but also competitors like Komatsu. Caterpillar, on the other hand, prefers to have total control over its new ventures, using acquisitions as a route to expand overseas.[108] A company's expansion strategies can also vary across regions.

We also noted that companies often adopt a phased entry strategy: they start off with a minimal-risk strategy; once the firm becomes more familiar with the market and the uncertainty drops, it may switch to a higher-commitment mode, such as a wholly owned venture. Caterpillar, Inc., the U.S.-based manufacturer of earth-moving and construction equipment, entered the former Soviet bloc in 1992 via direct exporting to minimize its financial risk exposure. After sales took off, Caterpillar upped the ante by establishing joint ventures with Russian and U.S. firms.[109]

As this chapter discussed, a broad range of variables impact the entry mode choice. The three major dimensions include the resource commitment the firm is willing to make, the amount of risk (political and market) the firm is willing to take, and the degree of control that is desirable. We also discussed the entry timing question. Finally, we looked at market exit (divestment) decisions, the flip side of entry. We surveyed some of the reasons why companies may decide to pull out of a market and ways to go about it.

QUESTIONS

1. What are the possible drawbacks of 50-50 joint ventures?

2. What are the respective advantages and disadvantages of greenfield operations over acquisitions?

3. April 15, 1983, marked the opening of Tokyo Disneyland, the first Disney theme park outside the United States. The theme park is operated under a licensing agreement with Disney by the Oriental Land Company. Under the arrangement, Oriental Land pays royalties and licensing fees to Disney, amounting to 10 percent of admission revenues and 5 percent of food and merchandise sales. Disney's second international theme park was Euro Disney, which was opened in April 1992. The Paris theme park is owned and operated by Disneyland Paris, a company in which slightly less than 40 percent is held by Disney, 10 percent by a Saudi prince, and the remaining 50 percent by other shareholders. The company's stock trades on Paris's Euronext stock exchange. On September 12, 2005, Hong Kong Disneyland was opened, the company's third

international theme park after Tokyo and Paris (Shanghai Disney is scheduled to open in 2016). In contrast to the Tokyo theme park, this one is operated through a joint venture in which Disney holds 43 percent and the Hong Kong government owns the remaining 57 percent. Explain why Disney may have opted for different entry mode alternatives for its international theme parks.

4. Helmut Maucher, former chairman of Nestlé, was quoted as saying: "I don't share the euphoria for alliances and joint ventures. First, very often they're an excuse, and an easy way out when people should do their own homework. Secondly, all joint ventures create additional difficulties—you share power and cultures, and decisions take longer." Comment.

5. **Exhibit 9-10** shows the timeline of Starbucks' global expansion. Discuss Starbucks' entry decisions. Do you see any patterns in its expansion strategy? What could be the underlying reason(s) for the observed patterns?

---

[108]"Engine Makers Take Different Routes," *Financial Times*, July 14, 1998, p. 11.
[109]Avraham Shama, "Entry Strategies of U.S. Firms to the Newly Independent States, Baltic States, and Eastern European Countries," *California Management Review* 37, no. 3 (Spring 1995): 90–109.

Exhibit 9-10   Timeline International Expansion of Starbucks Coffee

1971	First location in Seattle		Hong Kong
1987	Canada (Vancouver, British Columbia)		Qatar
1996	Hawaii		Saudi Arabia
	Japan	2001	Austria
	Singapore		Switzerland
1997	Philippines	2002	China (Shenzhen and Macau)
1998	Malaysia		Germany
	New Zealand		Greece
	Taiwan		Indonesia
	Thailand		Mexico
1999	China (Beijing)		Oman
	Kuwait		Puerto Rico
	Lebanon		Spain
	South Korea	2003	Chile
2000	Australia		Cyprus
	Bahrain		Peru
	China (Shanghai)		Turkey
	Dubai	2004	France

Source: www.starbucks.com.

Appendix A

Alternative Country Screening Procedure.   When the product has already been launched in some regions, the firm may consider using a variant of the country screening procedure described in this chapter. The alternative method leverages the experience the firm gathered in its existing markets. It works as follows: Suppose the MNC currently does business in Europe and is now considering an expansion into Asia.

Step 1: *Collect historical data on European markets*
   Go back to your files and collect the historical data for the European markets on the indicators that you plan to use to assess the market opportunities for the Asian region. Let us refer to these pieces of information as X_{iec}, that is, the score of European country ec on indicator i;

Step 2: *Evaluate the MNC's post-entry performance in each of its existing European markets*
   Assess the MNC's post-entry performance in each European country by assigning a success score (e.g., on a 10-point scale). If performance is measured on just one indicator, say, market-share achieved five years after entry, you could also simply use that indicator as a performance measure. Let us refer to the performance score for country ec as S_{ec}.

Step 3: *Derive weights for each of the country indicators*
   The next step is to come up with importance weights for each of the country indicators. For this, you could run a cross-sectional regression using the European data gathered in the previous two steps. Our dependent variable is the post-entry success score (S_{ec}) while the predictor variables are the country indicators (X_{iec}):

$$S_{ec} = a + w_1 X_{1ec} + w_2 X_{2ec} + \ldots + w_I X_{Iec}$$

$$ec = 1, 2, \ldots, EC$$

By running a regression of the success scores, S_{ec}, on the predictor variables, X_{iec} (i=1, . . . ,I), you can derive estimates for the importance weights of the different indicators.

Step 4: *Rate the Asian countries in the pool on each indicator*
   Each of the Asian candidate markets in the pool is given a score on each of the indicators that are considered: X_{iac}.

Step 5: *Predict performance in prospect Asian countries*
Finally, predict the post-entry performance in the prospective Asian markets by using the weights estimated in the previous step and data collected on each of the indicators (the X_{iac}'s) for the Asian countries. For instance, the regression estimates might look like:

$$\text{Performance} = -0.7 + 6.0\,(\text{Market Size})$$
$$+ 2.9(\text{Growth}) - 1(\text{Competition})$$

By plugging in the ratings (or actual values) for the Asian markets in this equation, you can then predict the MNC's performance in each of these countries.

Appendix B

Mode of Entry Choice—Three Theoretical Perspectives.

This appendix gives a concise overview of three theoretical frameworks that researchers have developed to shed light on how companies make mode of entry decisions.

TRANSACTION-COST ECONOMICS (TCE) A given task can be looked at as a "make-or-buy" decision: either the firm sources the task out to third-party agents or partners (low-control modes such as exporting), or it does the job internally (high control modes such as foreign direct investment). **Transaction-cost economics (TCE)** argues that the desirable governance structure (high- versus low-control mode) depends on the comparative transaction costs, that is, the costs of running the operation. Three factors influence these costs: namely, (1) the degree of specificity of the assets involved in the transaction, (2) the uncertainty surrounding the transaction, and (3) the frequency of the transaction.

In the context of entry mode choice, the TCE perspective treats each entry as a "transaction."[110] The starting premise is that markets are competitive and efficient. Therefore, market pressure minimizes the need for control. Under this utopian scenario, low-control modes such as exporting are preferable because the competitive pressures force the outside partner to comply with his/her contractual duties. When the market mechanism breaks down, however, high-control entry modes become more desirable. From the TCE angle, market failure typically happens when transaction-specific assets become valuable. These are assets that are valuable for only a very narrow range of applications. Examples include brand equity, proprietary technology, and know-how. When these types of assets are highly valuable, the firm may be better off adopting a high-control entry mode in order to safeguard these assets against opportunistic behavior by the foreign partner and uncertainty.[111] The TCE paradigm thus tends to focus on the potential for opportunistic behavior and uncertainty in the new environment and the need for control.

RESOURCE-BASED VIEW (RBV) The **resource-based view (RBV)** focuses on the overall strategic posture of the firm. The RBV starts with the premise that possessing resources is not sufficient for a company to create a competitive advantage: a firm also needs to be organized to take full advantage of its resources. RBV suggests that an entry should be considered in the context of the overall strategic posture of the firm.[112] According to this paradigm, firms with imperfectly imitable resource-based competitive advantages prefer to expand through wholly owned subsidiaries for two reasons. First, through wholly owned entry modes, the firm is better able to protect the value of its resource-based advantages against value erosion (e.g., patent theft). Second, by having a wholly owned subsidiary, the firm can capture and transfer knowledge between the parent and the foreign unit more efficiently.[113] There are three differences between the TCE and RBV perspectives.[114] First, the two theories differ in how they predict different entry modes. Whereas TCE predicts high-control entry modes because of opportunistic behavior of the firm's partner (e.g., licensee), the RBV attributes market failures to other mechanisms: when the multinational has superior capabilities in deploying its know-how and the prospective partner (e.g., licensee) faces challenges in efficiently acquiring and integrating that knowledge, the MNC will prefer high-control entities.[115] Second, while TCE focuses on entries as a one-time event, RBV looks at a sequence of entries as a dynamic process where the MNC is able to learn from and build on its previous entry experience. The third difference relates to the firm-specific advantages: whereas TCE focuses on their exploitation, the RBV stresses both their exploitation and development. The RBV states that market entries are not only "pushed" by the resources held by the MNC, but that the target entry could also help the MNC in developing new advantages.

[110]Erin Anderson and Hubert Gatignon, "Modes of Foreign Entry: A Transaction Cost Analysis and Propositions," *Journal of International Business Studies* 11 (Fall 1986): 1–25.

[111]For a good overview of entry mode choice studies that incorporate the TCA paradigm, see Hongxin Zhao, Yadong Luo, and Taewon Suh, "Transaction Cost Determinants and Ownership-Based Entry Mode Choice: A Meta-Analytical Review," *Journal of International Business Studies* 35 (2004): 524–544.

[112]C. Hill, P. Hwang, and W.C. Kim, "An Eclectic Theory of the Choice of International Entry," *Strategic Management Journal* 9 (1990): 93–104.

[113]Keith D. Brouthers, Lance Eliot Brouthers, and Steve Werner, "Resource-based Advantages in an International Context," *Journal of Management* 34 (April 2008): 189–217.

[114]Mike W. Peng, "The Resource-based View and International Business," *Journal of Management*, 27, no. 6 (2001): 803–829.

[115]A. Madhok, "Cost, Value and Foreign Market Entry Mode: The Transaction and the Firm," *Strategic Management Journal* 18, no. 1 (1997): 39–61.

INSTITUTIONAL THEORY (IT) The **institutional theory (IT)** paradigm focuses on the pressures of the host country's institutional environment in which the firm operates. Each country, with its own institutional environment, prescribes the economic "rules of the game" and shapes the nature of competition. Alliances with local partners are formed in response to pressure stemming from the institutional environment. A firm entering a foreign market in an industry deemed sensitive or strategic by the host government is often forced to enter into an alliance with a local partner. Wal-Mart, for instance, established a joint venture with Bharti Enterprises, an Indian conglomerate, to establish wholesale cash-and-carry stores in India. In countries with weak institutions, a firm may enter an alliance with a local entity to minimize the risks of doing business there. One study showed that in Asian countries that exhibit high institutional environment (e.g., the Philippines), joint ventures had a higher survival rate than wholly owned subsidiaries.[116]

---

[116]Shige Makino and Paul W. Beamish, "Performance and Survival of Joint Ventures with Non-Conventional Ownership Structures," *Journal of International Business Studies* 29, no. 4 (1998): 797–818.

PRODUCT AND MARKET DEVELOPMENT

10

CHAPTER OVERVIEW

1. Global branding strategies

2. Management of multinational product lines

3. Product piracy

4. Country-of-origin (COO) effects

5. Global marketing of services

The detergent division of the German company Henkel has long been committed to a strategy of strong local brands. In Europe Henkel varies its laundry detergent strategy to address regional variations in laundry practices. Southern Europeans traditionally washed their clothes with lower temperatures than their northern counterparts. They prefer less powerful detergents, often used in combination with bleach. People in the north favor powerful detergents and mostly dislike bleach in their laundry. Packaging preferences also differ. People in Northern Europe like compact products, while Southern consumers favor large boxes. To cope with all these variations, Henkel customizes its brand portfolio, positioning, and the product formulations. Henkel's flagship brand is Persil. However, Henkel did not own the Persil brand name in France;[1] it offered a similar product under the brand name Le Chat ("The Cat"). The positioning was also tweaked in different countries. For instance, Persil's whiteness positioning in Germany was replicated for Le Chat in France. In the Netherlands, Persil was positioned as an eco-friendly product. In Italy and Spain, Henkel had not introduced Persil for historical reasons. In Italy, consumers had a strong preference for blue detergents with a stain-fighting capability. This did not fit Persil's core value proposition ("whiteness with care"). Instead, Henkel entered Italy with Dixan, a performance brand. Henkel also entered Spain, another performance-oriented market, by acquiring Wipp, a strong local brand.[2]

The challenges that Henkel addressed—global brand and product line management—are the focal issues in this chapter. Companies that brand their products have various options when they sell their goods in multiple countries. More and more companies see global (or at least regional) branding as a must. Nevertheless, quite a few firms still stick to **local branding** strategies. In between these two extreme alternatives, there are numerous variations. This chapter will consider and assess different branding approaches. Next, we shift our attention to

---

[1] In France the Persil brand name is owned by Unilever.
[2] David Arnold, "Henkel KGaA: Detergents Division," Case Study, Boston: Harvard Business School, 2003.

the managing of an international product line. Multinational product line management entails issues such as: What product assortment should the company launch when it first enters a new market? How should the firm expand its multinational product line over time? What product lines should be added or dropped?

Another concern that global marketers face is the issue of product piracy. In this chapter we will suggest several approaches that can be employed to tackle counterfeiting. A good deal of research has investigated the impact of country-of-origin effects on consumer attitudes towards a product. We will explore the major findings of this research stream and examine different strategies that firms can use to handle negative country-of-origin stereotypes. The balance of this chapter covers the unique problems of marketing services internationally. Services differ from tangible products in many respects. What these differences imply in terms of market opportunities, challenges, and marketing strategies will be discussed in the last section.

Global Branding Strategies

For many firms the brands they own are their most valuable assets. A brand can be defined as "a name, term, sign, symbol, or combination of them which is intended to identify the goods and services of one seller or group of sellers and to differentiate them from those of competitors."[3] Linked to a brand name is a collection of assets and liabilities—the **brand equity** tied to the brand name. These include brand-name awareness, perceived quality, and any other associations invoked by the brand name in the customer's mind. The concerns that are to be addressed when building up and managing brand equity in a multinational setting include:[4]

- How do we strike the balance between a global brand that shuns cultural barriers and one that allows for local requirements?

- What aspects of the brand policy can be adapted to global use? Which ones should remain flexible?

- Which brands are destined to become "global" mega-brands? Which ones should be kept as "local" brands?

- How do you condense a multitude of local brands into a smaller, more manageable number of global (or regional) brands?

- How do you execute the changeover from a local to a global brand?

- How do you build up a portfolio of global mega-brands?

Suffice it to say, there are no simple answers to these questions. In what follows, we will touch on the major issues regarding international branding.

Global Branding

Reflect on your most recent trip overseas and some of the shopping expeditions that you undertook. Several of the brand names that you saw there probably sounded quite familiar: McDonald's, Coca-Cola, Levi Strauss, Canon, Rolex. On the other hand, there were most likely some products that carried brand names that you had never heard of before or that were slight (or even drastic) variations of brand names with a more familiar ring. A key strategic issue that appears on international marketers' agenda is whether or not there should be a **global brand**. What conditions favor launching a product with a single brand name worldwide? The same logo? And

[3]Philip H. Kotler, *Marketing Management* (Upper Saddle River, NJ: Prentice Hall, 2000).
[4]Jean-Noel Kapferer, *The New Strategic Brand Management: Advanced Insights and Strategic Thinking* (London: Kogan Page, 2012).

Exhibit 10-1 World's Most Valuable Brands (2012)

Interbrand Ranking	BrandZ (MillwardBrown) Ranking	Brand	2012 Brand Value (in $millions) (Interbrand)	2012 Brand Value (in $millions) (BrandZ)	Country of Origin
1	6	Coca-Cola	77,839	74,286	USA
2	1	Apple	76,568	182,951	USA
3	2	IBM	75,532	115,985	USA
4	3	Google	69,726	107,857	USA
5	5	Microsoft	57,853	76,651	USA
6	11	GE	43,682	45,810	USA
7	4	McDonald's	40,062	95,188	USA
8	49	Intel	39,385	15.633	USA
9	NA	Samsung	32,893	NA	S. Korea
10	28	Toyota	30,280	21,779	Japan
11	46	Mercedes	30,097	16,111	Germany
12	23	BMW	29,052	24,623	Germany
13	43	Disney	27,438	17,056	USA
14	NA	Cisco	27,197	NA	USA
15	26	HP	26,087	22,898	USA
16	33	Gillette	24,898	19,055	USA
17	21	Louis Vuitton	23,577	25,920	France
18	27	Oracle	22,126	22,529	USA
19	NA	Nokia	21,009	NA	Finland
20	18	Amazon	18,625	34,077	USA
21	NA	Honda	17,280	NA	Japan
22	NA	Pepsi	16,594	NA	USA
23	NA	H&M	16,571	NA	Sweden
24	30	American Express	15,702	20,198	USA
25	22	SAP	15,641	25,715	Germany

Source: Adapted from http://www.interbrand.com/en/best-global-brands/2012/Best-Global-Brands-2012-Brand-View.aspx and http://www.millwardbrown.com/brandz/Top_100_Global_Brands.aspx.

perhaps even the same slogan? When is it more appropriate to keep brands local instead of changing them into global ones? Between these two extremes are several other options. For instance, some companies use local brand names but at the same time put a corporate banner brand name on their products (e.g., "Findus by Nestlé").

Exhibit 10-1 shows two listings of the most valuable brands in the world (in 2008), one put together by Interbrand and one by Millward Brown. The two research companies use somewhat different brand valuation methodologies, hence the sometimes dramatic differences between the two rankings.[5] Interbrand, for instance, assesses the profit stream likely to be generated by

[5]For instance, Google is worth $107,857 million according to Millward Brown as opposed to just $69,726 million based on Interbrand's method. Millward Brown also includes several Chinese brands in its top 50 which do not show up in the Interbrand ranking (e.g., China Mobile at No. 10, China's largest bank ICBC at No. 13, Baidu at No. 25).

products carrying the brand name.[6] Note that both lists are heavily dominated by American brands. This is not too surprising because companies based in the United States have had much more experience with brand management than firms from other countries. It also reflects on the strength of the U.S. domestic market as a springboard for companies with global aspirations.[7]

A truly global brand is one that has a consistent identity with consumers across the world. This means a similar product formulation, the same core benefits and value proposition, the same positioning. Very few brands meet these strict criteria. Even a global marketing juggernaut like Procter & Gamble has only a few brands in its portfolio that can be described as truly global (e.g., Olay, Pantene, Duracell, Gillette). Legal constraints often force the company to market a particular product under two or even more brand names. Lynx/Axe, Unilever's line of male grooming products, is a case in point. The Axe brand was launched in the early 1980s in France by Fabergé, a company bought by Unilever in 1989. In most countries the product is sold under the Axe brand name. However, in several countries such as the United Kingdom and Australia it is named Lynx as the Axe trademark belonged to another firm. For a similar reason, the Burger King fast food giant was forced to rename itself "Hungry Jack's" in Australia as the BK trademark was already registered by a take-away food shop in Adelaide.

What is the case for global branding? One advantage of having a global brand name is obvious: economies of scale. First and foremost, the development costs for products launched under the global brand name can be spread over large volumes. This is especially a bonus in high-tech industries (e.g., pharmaceuticals, computing, chemicals, automobiles) where multi-billion dollar R&D projects are the norm. Scale economies also arise in manufacturing, distribution (warehousing and shipping), and, possibly, promotion of a single-brand product. As we noted in the last chapter, computerized design and manufacturing processes allow companies to harvest the scale benefits of mass production while customizing the product to the needs of the local market. Even then, substantial scale advantages on the distribution and marketing front often strongly favor global branding.

Scale advantage is only one of the reasons for using a global brand name.[8] Part of the task of brand managers is building up brand awareness. By its very nature, a global brand has much more visibility than a local brand. Prospective customers who travel around may be exposed to the brand both in their home country and in many of the countries they visit. Therefore, it is typically far easier to build up brand awareness for a global brand than for a local brand. A global brand can also capitalize on the extensive media overlap that exists in many regions. Cable TV subscribers in Europe and many Asian countries have access to scores of channels from neighboring countries. Having a global brand that is being advertised on one (or more) of these channels can mean more bang for the buck.

A further benefit is the prestige factor. Simply stated, the fact of being global adds to the allure of a brand: It signals that you have the resources to compete globally and the willpower and commitment to support the brand worldwide.[9] The prestige image of being global was also one of the motivations behind Lenovo's decision to develop a global brand: recognition as a global brand would boost the PC maker's image in China, its home market, and thereby create positive spillovers. Those global brands that can claim worldwide leadership in their product category have even more clout: Colgate, Intel, Marlboro, Coca-Cola, and Nike, to mention just a few.

In some cases global brands are also able to leverage the country association for the product: McDonald's is U.S. fast food, L'Oréal is French cosmetics, Swatch is a Swiss watch, Nissin Cup is Japanese noodles, and so on. Brown-Forman, the U.S. distiller, pitches Jack Daniel's, its flagship brand, as a U.S. label. In Romania, Brown-Forman set up a company-sponsored event in

---

[6]You may notice that some major brands like Levi's and Lego appear to be missing. The reason is that Interbrand's calculation method relies on publicly available financial data. Privately-owned companies like Levi Strauss or Lego do not offer sufficient financial information to assess the value of their brand assets.

[7]"Assessing a Name's Worth," *Financial Times*, June 22, 1999, p. 12.

[8]David A. Aaker, *Managing Brand Equity. Capitalizing on the Value of a Brand Name* (New York: The Free Press, 1991).

[9]David A. Aaker, *Building Strong Brands* (New York: The Free Press, 1996).

September 2004 to celebrate the birthday of Jack Daniel. Romanian actors entertained a crowd by dressing up as the Tennessee backwoodsman.[10] A desire to reflect its U.S. roots motivated Disney to change the name for its Paris theme park from Euro Disney to Disneyland Paris.[11] Of course, such positioning loses some of its appeal when your competition has the same heritage. For instance, Marlboro is a U.S. cigarette brand, but so are Camel and Salem. Further, strong ties between the brand and the home country could hurt the brand when relationships between the home and host country become strained. In 2012, a territorial dispute between Japan and China over the control of a group of small uninhabited islands in the East China Sea triggered violent demonstrations across China.[12] Sales of well-known Japanese brands like Toyota, Shiseido, and Honda dropped sharply in the country as a result of the anti-Japanese sentiments stoked by the conflict.

One important question here is also how consumers value global brands. A 2002 study on this issue identified three key dimensions:[13]

1. **Quality signal.** Consumers perceive global brands as being high in quality. A company's global stature signals whether it excels on quality. Consumers often believe that global brands connote better quality and offer higher prestige.[14]

2. **Global myth.** Consumers look at global brands as cultural ideals. The global brand gives its customer a sense of belonging, of being part of something bigger.

3. **Social responsibility.** Consumers also expect global brands to have a special duty to address social issues, to act as good citizens. The playing field is not level. Global players such as Nike and Shell are often held up to higher standards than their smaller counterparts in terms of how they conduct business.[15]

The arguments for global branding listed so far sound very powerful. Note though that, like many other aspects of global marketing, the value of a brand, its brand equity, usually varies a great deal from country to country. A large-scale brand assessment study done by the advertising agency DDB Needham in Europe illustrates this point:[16] brand equity scores for Kodak ranged from 104 in Spain to 130 in the United Kingdom and Italy.[17] Cross-country gaps in brand equity may be due to any of the following factors:

1. **History.** By necessity, brands that have been around for a long time tend to have much more familiarity among consumers than latecomers. Usually, early entrants will also have a much more solid brand image if they have used a consistent positioning strategy over the years.

2. **Competitive climate.** The battlefield varies from country to country. In some countries the brand faces only a few competitors. In others the brand constantly has to break through the clutter and combat scores of competing brands that nibble away at its market share.

3. **Marketing support.** Especially in decentralized organizations, the communication strategy used to back up the brand can vary a great deal. Some country affiliates favor push strategies, using trade promotions and other incentives targeted toward distributors. Others might prefer a

---

[10]"Drinking to the Dollar," *Forbes Global*, April 18, 2005, pp. 34–38.

[11]"The kingdom inside a republic," *The Economist*, April 13, 1996, pp. 68–69.

[12]The islands are referred to as the Senkaku Islands in Japan and the Diaoyu Islands in China.

[13]Douglas B. Holt, John A. Quelch, and Earl L. Taylor, "How Global Brands Compete," *Harvard Business Review* 82 (September 2004): 68–75.

[14]Jan-Benedict E.M. Steenkamp, Rajeev Batra, and Dan L. Alden, "How Perceived Brand Globalness Creates Brand Value," *Journal of International Business Studies* 34, no. 1 (January 2003): 53–65.

[15]"How Model Behavior Brings Market Power," *Financial Times*, August 23, 2004, p. 9.

[16]Jeri Moore, "Building brands across markets: cultural differences in brand relationships within the European Community," in *Brand Equity & Advertising: Advertising's Role in Building Strong Brands*, D. A. Aaker and A. L. Biel, eds., (Hillsdale, NJ: Erlbaum Associates, 1993).

[17]The scores were derived via a multiplication formula: Brand Awareness × Brand Liking × Brand Perception.

pull strategy and thus focus on the end consumers. It is not uncommon for the positioning theme used in the advertising messages to vary from country to country (see Chapter 7).

4. **Cultural receptivity to brands.** Another factor is the cultural receptivity towards brands. Brand receptivity is largely driven by risk aversion. Within Europe, countries such as Spain and Italy are much more receptive to brand names than Germany or France.[18] One recent study looked at the role of brands as signals using survey and experimental data collected in seven countries on purchase behavior for orange juice and personal computers.[19] The study found that the impact of a brand's credibility as a signal of quality on consumers' brand choice is larger in high uncertainty avoidance and high-collectivist cultures.[20,21]

5. **Product category penetration.** A final factor is the salience of the product category in which the brand competes. Because of lifestyle differences, a given category will be established much more solidly in some countries than in others. In general, brand equity and product salience go together: The higher the product usage, the more solid will be the brand equity.

Local Branding

Coca-Cola has four core brands in its brand portfolio (Coke, Sprite, Diet Coke, and Fanta). At the same time, it also owns numerous regional and local brands worldwide. In India, its biggest-selling cola is not Coke but Thums Up, a local brand that Coca-Cola acquired in 1993. In Japan, where carbonated soft drinks are less popular than in most other countries, the ready-to-drink coffee brand Georgia is one of Coca-Cola's best-selling brands. Maytag Corp., the U.S. appliance maker, decided to sell its Chinese appliances using a local name, Rongshida, which originated from its Chinese partner, Hefei Rongshida. The Maytag name was virtually unknown in China. Furthermore, consumer research showed that American appliances were perceived as bulky and big by Chinese consumers. Therefore, rather than selling under the Maytag badge, the company preferred to leverage the image of a long-standing Chinese brand, even though it had come to be seen as somewhat dated.[22] Although the advantages of a global brand name are many, there could also be substantial benefits of using a local brand.

In some cases, a local brand becomes necessary because the name or a very similar name is already used within the country in another (or even the same) product category. Use of a global brand name may also be limited because someone already owns the right for the trademark in the foreign market. Going back to the example we introduced in this chapter, Henkel owns the Persil trademark in most European countries. However, the Persil trademark belongs to Unilever, Henkel's archrival, in the United Kingdom, France, and Ireland.

Cultural barriers also often justify local branding. Without localizing the brand name, the name might be hard to pronounce or may have undesirable associations in the local language. Pocari Sweat, a Japanese sport drink, which is promoted as an "Ion supply drink," never became popular in the West despite its strong popularity in Japan and several Asian countries. Its quaint brand name could have been one explanation. Associations linked to the brand name often lose their relevance in the foreign market.[23] Brand names like Snuggle, Healthy Choice, Weight Watchers, or I Can't Believe It's Not Butter don't mean much in non-English-speaking foreign markets.

---

[18]Jeri Moore, "Building brands across markets: cultural differences in brand relationships within the European Community."

[19]Brazil, Germany, India, Japan, Spain, Turkey, and the United States.

[20]Note though that the collectivism effect was only found for the orange juice data.

[21]Tülin Erdem, Joffre Swait, and Ana Valenzuela, "Brand as Signals: A Cross-Country Validation Study," *Journal of Marketing Research* 70 (January 2006): 34–49.

[22]"Maytag Name Missing in China Ad Effort," *Ad Age Global* (May 2000): 2, 11.

[23]Rajeev Batra, "The why, when, and how of global branding," in *Brand Equity and the Marketing Mix: Creating Customer Value*, Sanjay Sood, ed., Marketing Science Institute, Report No. 95-111, September 1995.

A local linkage can also prove helpful in countries where patriotism and buy-local attitudes matter. Under such circumstances, the local brand name offers a cue that the company cares about local sensitivities. A case in point is the beer industry. Karel Vuursteen, a former chairman of Heineken, said: "There is strong local heritage in the [beer] industry. People identify with their local brewery, which makes beer different from detergents or electronic products."[24] In many emerging markets, once the novelty and curiosity value of Western brands wears off, consumers switch back to local brands. This is partly a matter of affordability. A can of Coca-Cola or a McDonald's Happy Meal is an expensive luxury in most developing countries.

When choosing between the local and foreign product, consumers may also prefer the local alternative because of animosity toward the foreign country.[25] Ariel, P&G's laundry detergent, fell prey to boycott campaigns in the Middle East because of its alleged ties with Ariel Sharon, Israel's prime minister. Mecca Cola is a cola brand that was launched by a French entrepreneur to cash in on anti-American sentiments in Europe and the Middle East. Its bottles bear the none-too subtle slogan "No more drinking stupid, drink with commitment."[26]

If the local brand name stems from an acquisition, keeping the local brand can be preferable to changing it into a global brand name. The brand equity built up over the years for the local brand can often be a tremendous asset. Thus, one motive for sticking with the local brand name is that the potential payoffs from transforming it into a global brand name do not outweigh the equity that would have to be sacrificed. After Mondelēz International (then known as Kraft Foods) acquired the British confectionary company Cadbury, it kept the existing brand name, which was stronger brand equity in markets like Europe and India than the Kraft brand. When Mondelēz introduced its iconic Oreo cookies brand in India, it even used Cadbury as the umbrella brand instead of Kraft. Another motive for keeping the local brand name could be the firm's strategic positioning goals: MNCs may aspire to cover the entire market by having brands positioned at all price points. Often the local brands are positioned at the bottom or medium end while the global brands cover the upper end of the market. Heinz, for example, sells two ketchup brands in Poland: the premium-priced Heinz core brand and Pudliszki, a local brand. This local brand belonged to Poland's largest ketchup maker in which Heinz acquired a controlling stake in 1997.[27]

Global or Local Branding?

Anheuser-Busch InBev, the world's leading beer brewer, has a global portfolio of well over 200 brands. Fourteen of these have retail sales of over $1 billion. The company divides these brands into three categories: (1) global brands, (2) multi-country brands, and (3) local champions. The global brands include Budweiser, Stella Artois, and Beck's. The multi-country brands are two Belgian brands with a long heritage: Leffe, dating from 1240, and Hoegaarden, first made in 1445. **Exhibit 10-2** lists the brands that AB-InBev crowned as its local champions: brands that have established leadership in their respective markets. Most other big multinationals have a portfolio of local, regional, and global brands. By now you probably realize that there are no simple answers to the global-versus-local brand dilemma. In general, a carefully crafted portfolio of local and global brands such as AB-InBev's is preferable to an overemphasis on global brands.[28]

---

[24]"Time for another round," *The Financial Times*, June 21, 1999.

[25]Jill Gabrielle Klein, "Us versus Them, or Us versus Everyone? Delineating Consumer Aversion to Foreign Goods," *Journal of International Business Studies* 33, no. 2 (Second Quarter 2002): 345–363.

[26]"Mecca Cola Challenges US Rival," on http://news.bbc.co.uk/2/hi/middle_east/2640259.stm.

[27]In fact, the Pudliszki brand is so popular in Poland that Heinz also sells it in countries such as the United Kingdom with a large Polish expat community.

[28]Jan-Benedict E. Steenkamp and Martijn G. de Jong, "A Global Investigation into the Constellation of Consumer Attitudes toward Global and Local Products," *Journal of Marketing* 74 (November 2010): 18–40.

Exhibit 10-2 AB-InBev's Local Champions

Brand	Country	Image
Bud Light	United States	The world's best-selling light beer.
Michelob Ultra	United States	Great tasting beer with fewer calories.
Skol	Brazil	Favored by young adults who know how to enjoy life.
Brahma	Brazil	Embodies the Brazilian sensibility, with a dynamic spirit and effortless flair for life.
Antarctica	Brazil	The perfect complement to pleasurable moments and good company.
Quilmes	Argentina	The flavor of getting together.
Jupiler	Belgium	A spirit of courage and adventure.
Hasseröder	Germany	A classic pilsner.
Klinskoya	Russia	Light, refreshing, crisp.
Sibirskaya Korona	Russia	For a rich, satisfying beer experience.
Harbin	China	Nuanced aroma and crisp finish.
Sedrin	China	Enjoyed by friends who share a common bond of excellence.

Source: AB InBev, 2011 Annual Report.
Source: http://www.ab-inbev.com/pdf/AB_InBev_AR11_EN.pdf, accessed December 1, 2012.

The **brand structure** or **brand portfolio** of a global marketer is the firm's current set of brands across countries, businesses, and product-markets.[29] There are basically four main types of branding approaches:[30]

1. *Solo branding.* Each brand stands on its own, with a product or brand manager running it (e.g., Unilever, Procter & Gamble).

2. *Hallmark branding.* The firm tags one brand, usually the corporate one, to all products and services, and does not use any sub-brands (e.g., most banks).

3. *Family (umbrella) branding.* This is a hierarchy of brands that uses the corporate brand as an authority symbol and then has a number of sub-brands under the corporate badge (e.g., Sony PlayStation).

4. *Extension branding.* The idea is to start with one product and then stretch the brand to other categories, as far as possible (e.g., luxury and fashion industries).

A firm's global brand structure is shaped by three types of factors: firm-based drivers, product-market drivers, and market dynamics.[31]

Firm-Based Drivers

The firm's administrative heritage, in particular its organizational structure, is one key factor. Centralized, top-down firms are more likely to have global brands. Decentralized companies where country managers have a large degree of autonomy will have a mish-mash of local and global brands. Another important driver is the company's expansion strategy: Does the firm

---

[29]Susan P. Douglas, C. Samuel Craig, and Edwin J. Nijssen, "Integrating Branding Strategy across Markets: Building International Brand Architecture," *Journal of International Marketing* 9, no. 2 (2001): 97–114.
[30]Lars Göran Johansson, "Electrolux Case Study: The Beginning of Branding as We Know It," in *Global Branding*. MSI Working Paper Series No. 00-114 (2000): 29–31.
[31]Douglas, Craig, and Nijssen, pp. 100–105.

mainly expand via acquisitions or via organic (that is, internal) growth? Ahold, a Dutch retailer, operates its stores using over 10 brand names worldwide (e.g., Albert Heijn in Europe, Hypernova in Slovakia, Pingo Doce in Portugal, Stop & Shop, Peapod, and Giant in the United States, and ICA in Scandinavia).[32] The company started expanding internationally in 1973 by buying established brands. Its policy ever since has been to maintain the local brands, governed by the mantra: "Everything the customer sees, we localize. Everything they don't see, we globalize."[33] Each chain has its own positioning, and the store names and logos vary enormously across countries. This local branding strategy is driven by the belief that all retailing is local as shoppers develop a store loyalty to brands they have known for decades. Obviously, the importance of the firm's corporate identity also plays a major role. Lastly, product diversity is another important factor. For instance, Unilever's product range is far more diverse than Nokia's.

Product-Market Drivers

The second set of brand portfolio drivers relate to product-market characteristics. Three drivers can be singled out here. The first driver is the nature and scope of the target market: How homogeneous are the segments? Are segments global, regional, or localized? The second factor is the degree of cultural embeddedness. Products with strong local preferences (e.g., many foods and beverages) are more likely to succeed as local brands. A final factor is the competitive market structure: Are the key players local, regional, or global competitors?

Market Dynamics

The firm's brand structure is also shaped by the underlying market dynamics. The level of economic integration is the first important driver here. Economic integration typically leads to harmonization of regulations. It also often entails fewer barriers to trade and business transactions within the region. As Europe moved to closer integration in the 1990s, Mars harmonized its confectionary brand names across the continent. The second factor is the market infrastructure in terms of media and distribution channels (e.g., retailing). Finally, consumer mobility (e.g., travel) also plays an important role. With increased mobility, global brands stand to benefit from enhanced visibility.

Apart from the brand structure, the **brand architecture** is another important cornerstone of the firm's international branding strategy. The brand architecture guides the dynamics of the firm's brand portfolio. It spells out how brand names ought to be used at each level of the organization. In particular, the brand architecture establishes how new brands will be treated; to what extent umbrella brands are used to endorse product-level brands; to what degree strong brands will be extended to other product categories (brand extensions) and across country borders. This architecture has three key dimensions (see **Exhibit 10-3**): the level in the organization at which the brand is used, the geographic scope of the brand, and the product scope. Electrolux, the leading maker of kitchen, cleaning, and outdoor appliances, settled on the following guidelines:[34]

- Use the Electrolux brand name as the family brand standing for quality, leadership, and trust.

- Reduce the number of brands. Create bigger, stronger ones.

- Converge to worldwide, consistently positioned brands; both geographically and across product lines.

- Leave to the local manager the burden of proving that his or her local situation should be an exception to the worldwide strategy.

---

[32]"Ahold Promotes Its Many Brands," *Asian Wall Street Journal*, September 28, 2000, p. 26.
[33]"European Consumers Prefer Familiar Brands for Grocers," *Asian Wall Street Journal*, September 3, 2001, p. N7.
[34]"Electrolux Case Study," p. 30.

Exhibit 10-3
Dimensions of
International Brand
Architecture

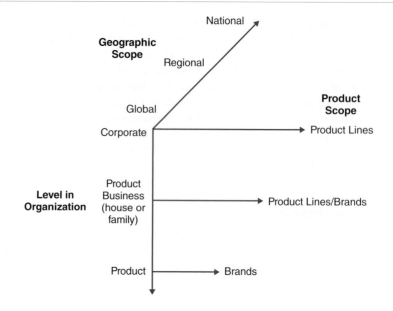

Nestlé provides another example of a company with a well-defined brand architecture. The Swiss food multinational owns nearly 8,000 different brands worldwide. **Exhibit 10-4** shows Nestlé's brand architecture. As you can see, Nestlé's brands are organized in a branding tree. At the root are 10 worldwide corporate brands—brands like Carnation, Nestlé, and Perrier. The next level consists of 45 strategic brands that are managed at the strategic business unit level. Examples include Kit Kat, After Eight, and Smarties. Climbing further, you can spot the regional strategic brands, managed at the regional level. For instance, in the frozen food category, Nestlé markets the Stouffer's brand in America and Asia and the Findus brand in Europe. At the very top of the tree is a multitude of local brands (over 7,000) that are the responsibility of the local subsidiaries.

Although companies often feel driven to build up global brands, there are solid reasons to make an in-depth analysis before converting local brands into regional or global ones. In fact, local brands sometimes can have much more appeal among consumers than their global competing brands. This is especially true when there is not much benefit from being global.

David Aaker, an expert on branding, offers the following checklist for analyzing globalization propositions:[35]

1. What is the cost of creating and maintaining awareness and associations for a local brand versus a global one?

2. Are there significant economies of scale in the creation and running of a communication program globally (including advertising, public relations, sponsorships)?

3. Is there value to associations of a global brand or of a brand associated with the source country?

4. What local associations will be generated by the global name? symbol? slogan? imagery?

5. Is it culturally and legally do-able to use the brand name, symbol, and slogan across the different countries?

6. What is the value of the awareness and associations that a regional brand might create?

---

[35]David A. Aaker, *Managing Brand Equity* (New York: The Free Press, 1991).

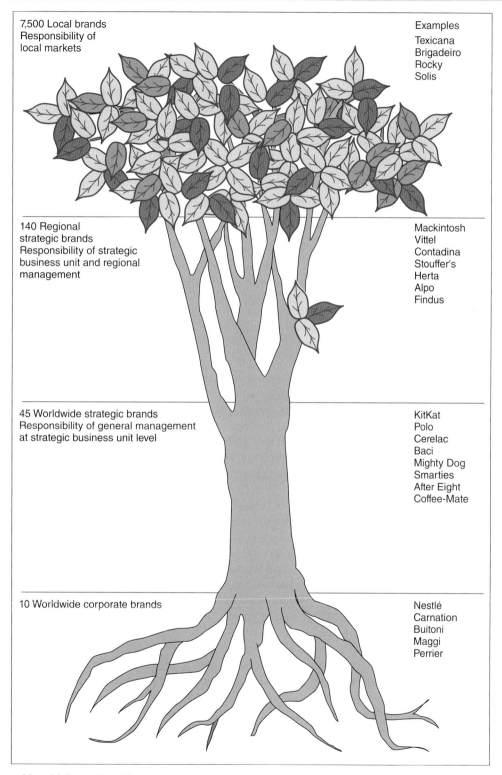

Exhibit 10-4 Nestlé Branding Tree

Brand-Name Changeover Strategies

One of P&G's most popular brands in Germany was a liquid dishwashing detergent named Fairy. Early 2000, the brand had a market share of nearly 12 percent. In the middle of 2000, P&G rechristened the brand using the Dawn global brand name. There was no change in the product formulation. The renamed brand's market share crashed. One year later, Dawn's share stood at 4.7 percent. While Fairy represented a trusted and well-known brand to German consumers, Dawn meant nothing.[36] This bond of trust had been broken with the renaming. It was estimated that P&G sustained a loss in turnover of $8 million. In the end, P&G decided to go back to the old Fairy name. P&G made the same kind of mistake in Austria when it replaced Bold with Dash.[37] Changing the brand name from a local to a global (or regional) brand name is not a trivial matter. Attachments to the existing brand name can be very deep and emotional.

In the global marketplace, several factors might cause a brand name change:

- Pruning of brand portfolio. To realize economies of scale, a company may decide to re-examine its worldwide brand portfolio and merge some of its brands.

- Limited legal rights to a brand name. When a company buys a division from another firm, it will typically have the right to use the acquired brand name(s). However, this right often expires after a certain time span (usually 5 years).

- Legal rights. Often, a company may be forced to create a second brand name for the same product when the trademark to the first name belongs to another firm in the country. Once the firm regains the right to use the trademark it may then decide to unify its existing brand names.

When the case for a transition from a local to a global brand name is made, the firm needs to decide on how to implement the changeover in practice. Four broad strategic options exist:[38] (1) fade-in/fade-out, (2) combine brands via co-branding or under one umbrella brand, (3) **transparent forewarning**, and (4) **summary axing**.

With **fade-in/fade-out**, the new global brand name is somehow tied with the existing local brand name. After a transition period, the old name is dropped. A typical example is the brand name change that Disney implemented for its Paris theme park. It first shrunk the *Euro* part in Euro Disney and added the word *land*. In October 1994 the word *Euro* was dropped altogether and the theme park is now branded as *Disneyland Paris*.[39]

The second route combines the "old" local brand and the global or regional brand in some manner. One tactic that is sometimes employed is to have the global brand as an umbrella or endorser brand. For example, Pedigree was launched in the late 1980s in France as "Pedigree by Pal." Another possibility is **dual branding (co-branding)**. During a transition period, the local and global brand names are kept so that consumers and the trade have sufficient time to absorb the new brand name. When Whirlpool acquired the white goods division of Philips, the company initially employed a dual branding strategy—Philips and Whirlpool. After a transition period, the Philips brand name was dropped. Likewise, Danone used co-branding in South Africa shortly after it bought a stake in the Clover company, South Africa's leading fresh dairy producer. Although Danone is a global brand, at the time the brand name was virtually unknown in South Africa. By using co-branding, Danone was able to leverage the huge brand equity that Clover had in South Africa as well as Clover's strong association with dairy products in the local consumer's mind.[40]

[36]Randall Frost, "Should Global Brands Trash Local Favorites?" www.brandchannel.com, accessed February 9, 2009.

[37]Jean-Noël Kapferer, *The New Strategic Brand Management* (London: Kogan Page, 2008).

[38]Trond Riiber Knudsen, Lars Finskud, Richard Törnblom, and Egil Hogna, "Brand Consolidation Makes a Lot of Economic Sense," *The McKinsey Quarterly* 4 (1997): 189–193.

[39]"The kingdom inside a republic," *The Economist*, April 13, 1996, p. 69.

[40]Russell Abratt and Patience Motlana, "Managing Co-Branding Strategies: Global Brands into Local Markets," *Business Horizons* (Sept.–Oct. 2002): 43–50.

The third approach, transparent forewarning, alerts the customers about the brand name change. The forewarning is typically done via the communication program, in-store displays, and product packaging. A good example is the transition made by Mars in continental Europe for one of its best-selling candy bars. Up to 1991 the candy bar known as Twix in the United States was under the Raider brand name in most of Europe. For various strategic reasons (e.g., economies of scale) Mars decided to drop the Raider name and replace it with the Twix brand name. Given that Raider had very strong brand equity in continental Europe (the second most popular candy bar after Mars), the changeover was not a trivial matter. Mars left no stone unturned in the countries affected by the change: Mars aired a high-impact television ad campaign starring David Bowie highlighting the new Twix packaging, it ran print-ads to signal the change, it used in-store promotions to maximize visibility and awareness, and it also indicated the changeover on the Raider's wrappings with the words "known globally as Twix" during the transition period.[41]

Far less common is the fourth practice, summary axing, where the company simply drops the old brand name almost overnight and immediately replaces it with the global name. This is only appropriate when competitors are rapidly gaining global clout by building up global brands or when the old brand name has weak brand equity.

To manage the transition effectively, several rules should be respected.[42] First, it is critical to conduct consumer research prior to the brand name changeover to understand consumers' perceptions and gauge their response to any modifications (e.g., packaging, logo, brand name). When the brand name is changed gradually, one of the key concerns is the proper length for the transition period. When IBM sold its personal computer division to Lenovo, part of the deal was that Lenovo would have access to the IBM brand name for up to five years. The IBM logo could only be used on Think-family products. When the IBM logo was shown in Lenovo ads, it could only be displayed on the product within the ad. However, ownership of the Think sub-brand (i.e., ThinkPad and ThinkCentre) would be permanent. The timeline agreed between Lenovo and IBM for usage of the IBM name had three phases:[43]

1. *Phase 1 (first 18 months).* Current IBM branding to remain unchanged.

2. *Phase 2 (second 40 months).* The IBM brand name must be less prominent and separate from the Think sub-brand.

3. *Phase 3 (remaining 2 months).* IBM is more like an ingredient or endorsement brand.

In principle, the firm should allow sufficient time for customers to absorb the name change. How long this process will take depends on the product and the strength of the image associated with the old brand name. For some product categories, the purchase cycle matters, too. Sometimes the phase-out can be completed sooner than scheduled. Lenovo, for example, dropped the IBM name two years ahead of schedule.

It is also important that consumers who are exposed to the changeover messages associate the new brand name with the old one. One of the primary goals of Whirlpool's advertising campaign was to maintain awareness of the Philips brand name while building up association with Whirlpool.[44]

To avoid negative spillovers on the global brand name, companies should also ensure that the local products are up to standard before attaching the global brand name to them. Otherwise, the

---

[41]For further details and other examples, see *The New Strategic Brand Management*, London: Kogan Page, 2008.

[42]Marieke de Mooij, *Advertising Worldwide. Concepts, Theories, and Practice of International, Multinational and Global Advertising* (Upper Saddle River, NJ: Prentice Hall, 1994).

[43]John Quelch and Carin-Isabel Knoop, "Lenovo: Building a Global Brand," Case Study, Boston: Harvard Business School, 2006.

[44]Jan Willem Karel, "Brand Strategy Positions Products Worldwide," *The Journal of Business Strategy* (May/June 1991): 16–19.

goodwill of the global brand name could be irreparably damaged. As a result, other products launched under the global brand name might be viewed with skepticism by consumers in the foreign market. Part of Whirlpool's geographic expansion in China involved a joint venture that made air conditioners based on Japanese designs. The air conditioners, sold under a local brand name, Raybo, initially had about half the life expectancy of U.S.-made Whirlpool models. Whirlpool's president at the time declared that his company would not put the Whirlpool name on the product until Raybo's quality problems were fixed.[45]

Finally, companies should monitor the marketplace's response to the brand name change with marketing research. Such tracking studies enable the firm to ensure that the changeover runs smoothly. They also assist firms in determining how long promotional programs that announce the name change should last. Whirlpool tracked brand recognition and buying preference of consumers on a weekly basis during the brand-change period. **Global Perspective 10-1** describes the efforts made by British oil company BP to implement a global corporate makeover.

◆ ◆

Global Perspective 10-1

Beyond Petroleum—BP Amoco's Corporate Makeover

In July 2000, BP Amoco unveiled a global corporate makeover that included a new brand identity and revamped, high-technology service stations. BP spent $7 million of research and design funds to develop the global corporate makeover. The new "exploding sunflower" motif was named the Helios mark after the sun god of ancient Greece. The company ditched the shield logo, which BP had used for 70 years. BP declared: "Our new mark resembles a dynamic burst of energy; bright white at the core with radiant beams of yellow and green light. Our mark's interlocking parts represent the diversity of our people, products and services. Its radiance is a daily reminder of our aspirations and purpose. . . . In a hundred countries across the globe, BP employees bring the world energy in the forms of light, warmth, and mobility."

Although the revamp happened worldwide, the impetus for the change came from BP's U.S. operations. The U.S. market is home to about one-third of BP's 28,000 retail outlets worldwide. After its merger with Amoco and a major acquisition spree, BP owned four separate brands: BP, Amoco, ARCO, and Castrol. BP Amoco recognized the need for a new, unifying image. However, Arco's service station network on the West coast of the United States was not affected by the re-branding exercise as ARCO's existing business has a strong brand identity there.

One reason for the consolidation was to bond BP employees around the world following the merger and acquisitions. However, another key factor was BP's desire to alter the public's perception of BP from a traditional "old economy" British oil company to a global "new economy" energy services group, taking BP into the "Beyond Petroleum" era.

Besides introducing a new logo, BP also upgraded its service stations. New high-tech service stations were rolled out with brightly lit fueling and parking areas. Some of stations are solar-powered and provide internet access to customers. BP spent $7 million on research and design.

Sources: "BP Amoco Unveils Corporate Makeover," *The Financial Times,* July 25, 2000, p. 26; "Oil Group Hopes Helios Will Bring Sunshine," *The Financial Times,* July 25, 2000, p. 26; "BP's Step beyond Petroleum," *The Financial Times,* August 9, 2000, p. 19.

---

[45]"For Whirlpool, Asia is the new frontier," *Wall Street Journal,* April 25, 1996, p. B1.

Management of Multinational Product Lines

Most companies sell a wide assortment of products. The product assortment is usually described on two dimensions: the width and the length of the product mix. The first dimension—width—refers to the collection of different product lines marketed by the firm. For most companies, these product lines are closely related. Some companies, especially major multinationals, market a very broad array of product lines. The second dimension—length—refers to the number of different items that the company sells within a given product line. Thus, the product mix for a particular multinational could vary along the width and/or length dimension across the different countries where the firm operates.

When comparing the product mix in the company's host and home markets, there are four possible scenarios. The product mix in the host country could be (1) an extension of the domestic line, (2) a subset of the home market's product line, (3) a mixture of local and non-local product lines, or (4) a completely localized product line.

Small firms with a narrow product assortment usually simply extend their domestic product line. Bose, the U.S.-based maker of sound systems, has a very limited range of product lines that it markets in all of its overseas markets. On the other hand, larger companies that enter new markets carefully select a subset of their product mix. When Coca-Cola goes into a new market, the focus is obviously first on Coca-Cola. Once the flagship brand is well established, the next introduction is typically Fanta, the flavor line. Fanta is followed by Sprite and Diet Coke (or Coke Zero). Once the infrastructure is in place, other product lines—including local ones—are added over a period of time.[46] Most MNCs have a product mix that is partly global (or regional) and partly local.

Several drivers impact the composition of a firm's international product line. We briefly discuss the key factors:

Customer Preferences

In many product categories, consumer preferences vary from country to country. Especially for consumer-packaged goods, preferences are still very localized. To cater to distinctive customer needs, marketers may add certain items to the individual country's or region product line or fine-tune the line. A good example is Tang, the powdered beverage brand owned by Mondelēz International. Once an American cultural icon, Tang has lost much of its appeal in its home market. Overseas, the brand has become very popular, especially in the developing world where consumers like it for its nutrition and low price. One other factor has been the company's drive to add local flavors and formulas. Customized flavors include mango in the Philippines, soursop in Brazil, horchata in Mexico, and lemon-mint in the Middle East. In countries like Brazil and the Philippines, where kids' diets are short on vitamins and minerals, Tang is fortified with iron as well as other minerals and vitamins.[47]

Exhibit 10-5 lists some of the sandwiches that McDonald's introduced on its menu to cater toward local tastes. Japanese consumers' notorious desire for innovation forces consumer goods marketers in Japan to constantly come up with new product variants. As a result the product variety of many multinational consumer goods company in Japan is much broader than that in other countries. A good example is Nestlé's Kit Kat brand, which has become very popular in Japan, largely due to the similarity of the brand's name to the phrase *kitto katsu* ("you will surely win!"). To cater to its Japanese consumers yearning for novelty, Nestlé has launched an incredible range of flavors (many for a limited time only) including some rather unusual ones such as kiwi, maple syrup, strawberry, banana, green tea, cherry blossom, and cookies & milk.[48] Consumer good multinationals in China

---

[46]www.thecoca-colacompany.com/investors/Divester.html.

[47]'Developing Markets' Growth Rockets Tang to "Billion-Dollar" Status,' http://www.kraftfoodscompany.com/Media-Center, accessed November 5, 2011.

[48]http://www.breaktown.com/, accessed February 12, 2009.

Exhibit 10-5   How McDonald's Customizes Its Menu

Country	Sandwich	Description
France	Croque McDo	A grilled ham and cheese sandwich on toast
India	Maharaja Mac	Two grilled chicken patties with smoke-flavored mayonnaise, onions, tomatoes, and cheddar cheese
Taiwan	Rice Burger	Shredded beef between two rice patties
Japan	Teriyaki Burger	A chicken cutlet patty marinated in teriyaki sauce
Middle East	McArabia Sandwich	A marinated grilled chicken sandwich in flatbread
New Zealand	Kiwi Burger	A hamburger with a fried egg and a slice of pickled beet
Poland	McKielbasa	Kielbasa (Polish sausage) patty topped with ketchup, mustard, and onion.
Pakistan	Spicy McChicken	A chicken sandwich with chutney
Thailand	Samurai Pork Burger	A pork burger flavored with teriyaki sauce
South Korea	Bulgogi Burger	Pork patty marinated in soy-based sauce
Netherlands	McKroket	A deep fried roll containing beef ragout and potato
Greece	Greek Mac	A pita bread sandwich with two beef patties and some yoghurt
Israel	McShawarma	Shawarma served in flatbread

Source: http://en.wikipedia.org/wiki/McDonald%27s_menu_items#Regional_dishes; and "Big Mac's Local Flavor," *Fortune,* May 5, 2008, p. 85.

also need to offer a wide product variety to attract Chinese consumers. The Chinese menu of Dunkin' Donuts includes choices such as dry shredded pork with seaweed and curry beef. In India, on the other hand, Dunkin's menu offers options such as mango doughnuts, mango smoothies, and spicy sandwiches.[49]

Price Spectrum

In emerging markets, companies often compete across the price spectrum by offering premium and budget products. The upscale products are targeted toward wealthy consumers. Budget products are offered as entry-level or value products for other consumers. These low-end products often come in smaller sizes, more economical packaging, and/or cheaper formulations. Nestlé, for instance, launched 29 new ice cream brands in China in March 2005. Many of these were low- and mid-range priced value-for-money products selling for as little as 12¢.[50]

Competitive Climate

Differences in the competitive environment often explain why a company offers certain product lines in some countries but not in others. A telling example is the canned soup industry. In the United States, the wet soup category is basically owned by Campbell Soup: the company has a nearly 70 percent share of the wet soup market.[51] Given the clout of the Campbell brand name, it is virtually impossible to penetrate the U.S. canned soup market. The picture is quite different in the United Kingdom where Campbell was a relative latecomer. In the United Kingdom, the Heinz soup range owns a 56 percent market share.[52] Coca-Cola's product line strategy in Japan is also driven to a large degree by the local rivalry in the Japanese beverage market. One of the pillars of

---

[49]"Dunkin' Brings – What Else – to India," *Wall Street Journal (Asia)*, May 9, 2012, p. 18.
[50]"Nestlé Hits Mainland with Cheap Ice Cream," *Advertising Age*, March 7, 2005., p. 12.
[51]http://www.campbellsoupcompany.com.
[52]http://www.heinz.com.

Exhibit 10-6 Coca-Cola Local Brands in Japan

Brand	Launch Year	Product Description
Ambasa	1981	Noncarbonated, lactic soft drink with familiar smooth taste for everyday use.
Calo	1997	"Functional" soft drink with cocoa taste; helps build healthy bones.
Georgia	1975	Authentic, real coffee drink with variety of flavors sourced from around the world.
Ko Cha Ka Den	1992	Line of blended teas.
Lactia	1996	Lactic, noncarbonated soft drink; offers healthy digestion and quick refreshment.
Perfect Water	1997	Mineral-balanced water; helps restore balance to daily life.
Real Gold	1981	Carbonated, herb-mix flavored drink; provides quick energy.
Saryusaisai	1993	Nonsugar Oolong tea drink.
Seiryusabo	1994	Green and barley tea drinks.
Shpla	1996	Citrus-flavored soft drink; helps overcome mental stress and dullness.
Vegitabeta	1991	Peach-flavored soft drink; helps maintain healthy balance.

Coke's Japan-marketing strategy is to improve on its rivals' products. As a result, Coke sells an incredible variety of beverages in Japan that are not available anywhere else (see **Exhibit 10-6**).

Organizational Structure

Especially in MNCs that are organized on a country-by-country basis, product lines may evolve to a large degree independently in the different countries. The scope of the country manager's responsibility, however, is increasingly being limited in many MNCs (see Chapter 16). Nevertheless, country managers still have a great deal of decision-making autonomy in many functional areas, including product policy.

History

Product lines often become part of an MNC's local product mix following geographic expansion efforts. Companies like Procter & Gamble, Heinz, and AB-InBev penetrate new and existing markets via acquisitions. Some of these acquisitions include product lines that are outside the MNC's core business. Rather than divesting these non-core businesses, a company often decides to keep them. As part of its growth strategy in Central Europe, Heinz acquired Kecskemeti Konzervgyar, a Hungarian canned food company. The company makes a broad range of food products, including baby food, ketchup, pickles—staple items for Heinz—but also products like jams and canned vegetables—items that are not really part of Heinz's core business lines.

Global marketers need to decide for each market of interest which product lines should be offered and which ones are to be dropped. When markets are entered for the first time, market research can be very helpful for designing the initial product assortment. Market research is less useful for radically new products (e.g., frozen yogurt, electric vehicles) or newly emerging markets. In such situations, the company should consider using a "probing-and-learning" approach. Such a procedure has the following steps:

1. Start with a product line that has a minimum level of product variety.

2. Gradually adjust the amount of product variety over time by adding new items and dropping existing ones.

3. Analyze the incoming actual sales data and other market feedback.

4. Based on the market response, fine-tune the product line further.[53]

The gist of this procedure is to use the product line as a **listening post** for the new market to see what product items work best.

By and large, add/drop decisions should be driven by profit considerations. In the global marketing arena, however, it is crucial not to look just at profit ramifications within an individual country. Ideally, the profitability analysis should be done on a regional or even global basis. A good start is to analyze each individual country's product portfolio on a sales turnover basis. Product lines can be categorized as (1) core products, (2) niche items, (3) seasonal products, or (4) filler products.[54] Core products are the items that represent the bulk of the subsidiary's sales volume. Niche products appeal to small segments of the population that might grow. Seasonal products have most of their sales during limited times of the year. Finally, filler products are items that account for only a small portion of the subsidiary's overall sales. These might include "dead-weight" items whose sales were always lackluster or prospective up-and-coming products. From a global perspective, a comparison of the product mix make-up across the various countries provides valuable insights. Such an analysis might provide answers to questions like:

- Could some of our "seasonal" products in country A be turned into "core" items in country B?

- Given our track record in country A, which ones of our filler products should be considered as up and coming in country B, and which ones should be written off as dead-weight products?

- Is there a way to streamline our product assortment in country A by dropping some of the items and consolidating others, given our experience in country B?

Product Piracy

At the 2009 Shanghai auto shows, one of the biggest events was the debut of the Geely Excellence (GE) made by Geely, one of China's leading carmakers. With its winged mascot and huge radiator grill, the GE had a close resemblance to the Rolls-Royce Phantom.[55] However, while a purchaser of the Phantom may have to fork out at least $1 million, the GE clone would set her back only about $60,000.[56] Geely denied any copycatting, but Rolls-Royce considered taking legal action. **Product piracy** is one of the downsides that marketers with popular global brand names face. Any aspect of the product is vulnerable to piracy, including the brand name, the logo, the design, and the packaging. The impact on the victimized company's profits is twofold. Obviously, there are the losses stemming from lost sales revenues. The monetary losses due to piracy can be staggering. Spirits companies estimate that they lose more than $1 billion each year from counterfeit alcohol.[57] In China, Procter & Gamble estimated that 15 percent of the soaps and detergent goods carrying P&G brand names were fakes, costing the firm $150 million a year in foregone sales. Yamaha found that five out of six motorbikes and scooters in China bearing its brand name were fake.[58] Rampant piracy in countries such as China is for many companies also a reason not to enter these markets. A newly worrying trend is the increased export of fake products made in

[53]Anirudh Dhebar, "Using Extensive, Dynamic Product Lines for Listening in on Evolving Demand," *European Management Journal* 13, no. 2 (June 1995): 187–192.

[54]John A. Quelch and David Kenny, "Extend Profits, Not Product Lines, *Harvard Business Review*, (Sept.–Oct. 1994): 153–160.

[55]"A Rolls-Royce Knock-Off from China," www.nytimes.com, accessed May 3, 2009.

[56]http://au.carbage.blogs.topgear.com/2009/04/28/geely-geely-good/.

[57]"Counterfeit Alcohol Problem Takes a Deadly Toll," *Financial Times*, November 5, 2012, p. 16.

[58]"China's Fakes," *Business Week (Asian Edition)*, June 5, 2000, 20–25.

China. Counterfeiters also depress the MNC's profits indirectly. In many markets, MNCs often are forced to lower their prices in order to defend their market share against their counterfeit competitors.

Even more worrisome than the monetary losses is the damage that pirated products could inflict to the brand name. Pirated products tend to be of poor quality. As a result, the piracy scourge often jeopardizes the brand's reputation built over the years. Such risks are especially big in emerging markets where consumers have only recently been exposed to premium branded products and counterfeits often outnumber the real thing by a significant factor.[59] In some categories, counterfeit products can also turn out to be downright dangerous to consumers. The World Health Organization found that 5 to 7 percent of medicines sold were copycat—with too few active ingredients, too many impurities, or labels that cover up expiration dates. Dodgy counterfeit aircraft or car parts can have fatal consequences. According to one study, 10 percent of car spare parts being sold in the EU were reckoned to be counterfeit. Forged aviation parts were the suspected cause of a 2001 American Airlines crash. In September 2012, the Czech Republic banned the sale of hard liquor after at least 20 people died and many others were badly injured from consuming methanol-tainted spirits.[60]

Several factors lie behind the rise of piracy in countries such as China. The spread of advanced technology (e.g., color copying machines, know-how stolen from multinationals by local partners) is one catalyst. Global supply chains also play a key role. Traders often use the web and unauthorized distributors to sell fakes around the world. China's weak rule of law and poor enforcement of existing legislation also contributes to the piracy spread. Finally, profits that can be made from piracy are huge. For instance, profit margins on fake Chinese-made car parts such as shock absorbers can reach 80 percent versus 15 percent for the genuine thing.[61]

Strategic Options against Product Piracy

MNCs have several strategic options at their disposal to combat counterfeiters. **Exhibit 10-7** lists some guidelines to protect intellectual property (IP) in China, which is the source of most of the world's counterfeit goods. Other major weapons at the disposal of MNCs are as follows:

Exhibit 10-7   Guidelines for IP Protection in China

- *Educate your employees.* Employees are the source of most IP losses. IP is still a fairly new concept in China, so education of the workforce on IP is very important. Concentrate on everyday examples.
- *Speedy patent and trademark registration.* Often a Chinese company has already registered a patent or trademark in China to gain an edge against foreign competitors or to sell it back to the foreign firm at a lucrative price. It is important to also register Chinese-language translations of the trademarks.
- *Keep up with best practices.* Information on best practices to protect IP in China is available through trade associations and chambers of commerce. An excellent resource to consult best practices is the website of the Quality Brands Protection Committee (**QBPC**): http://www.qbpc.org.cn/.
- *Put a senior-level executive in charge of IP security.* For effective IP protection, a senior-level executive should be in charge of IP security across the firm.
- *Think globally to protect IP.* A company's strategy to combat IP infringement in China should be global as a leak anywhere could affect the firm's business anywhere in the world.

Source: "Protecting Intellectual Property in China," *Wall Street Journal Asia*, March 10, 2008, p. R8.

---

[59]"Business Faces Genuine Problem of Chinese Fakes," *Financial Times*, April 4, 2000, p. 6.

[60]"Czechs See Peril in a Bootleg Bottle," http://www.nytimes.com, accessed January 4, 2013.

[61]"China's Piracy," pp. 22–23.

Lobbying Activities

Lobbying governments is one of the most common courses of action that firms use to protect themselves against counterfeiting. Lobbyists pursue different types of objectives. One goal is to toughen legislation and enforce existing laws in the foreign market. However, improved intellectual property rights (IPR) protection is more likely to become reality if one can draw support from local stakeholders. For instance, Chinese technology developers increasingly favor a tighter IPR system.[62] In some industries high taxes or duties push people to buy fake products. In that case, affected companies could lobby the host government to lower duties. In Uganda, SABMiller successfully lobbied the local government to lower the excise tax on beers made with all-local ingredients.[63] Another route is to lobby the home government to impose sanctions against countries that tolerate product piracy. Lastly, MNCs might also lobby their home government to negotiate for better trademark protection in international treaties such as the World Trade Organization (WTO) or bilateral trade agreements.

Legal Action

Prosecuting counterfeiters is another alternative that companies can employ to fight product piracy. In China, two big foreign brands, Starbucks and Ferrero Rocher, won highly publicized IPR court cases. In the case of Starbucks, Shanghai company Xingbake Café was using a logo and a name that when translated was similar to that of the global coffee giant. The court ordered Xingbake to pay Rmb500,000 (about $62,000) in damages to Starbucks. Similarly, the British drinks group Diageo successfully sued a local Chinese company that had copied the bottle design and packaging of Johnnie Walker Black Label whiskey.[64] In order to sue infringers, companies need to track them down first. In countries like China foreign firms can hire private agencies to help them with investigations of suspected infringers. Legal action has numerous downsides, though. A positive outcome in court is seldom guaranteed. The whole process is time consuming and costly. Chinese courts and administrative bodies cope with more than 100,000 IP infringement cases per year. The percentage of judgments that are enforced is very low and for most companies winning a case in itself is a victory.[65] Court action can also generate negative publicity.[66] Microsoft's experience in China illustrates this point. When the company sued the Yadu Group, a Beijing company, for using pirated Microsoft software, the Chinese press had a field day bashing Microsoft for going after a local company. The case was dismissed because of a legal technicality. The only party that gained (apart from the lawyers involved) was the defendant whose brand awareness increased enormously because of all the publicity surrounding the case.[67]

Customs

Firms can also ask customs for assistance by conducting seizures of infringing goods. In countries with huge trade flows like China, customs can only monitor a small proportion of traded goods for IP compliance. Customs officers will most likely attach low priority to items such as Beanie Babies or Hello Kitty dolls. However, courtesy calls can be very effective. IP owners can also pinpoint broader concerns to the customs officials such as risks to consumers of fake goods or to the reputation of the host country.[68]

---

[62]Pitman B. Potter and Michel Oksenberg, "A Patchwork of IPR Protections," *China Business Review* (Jan.–Feb. 1999): 8–11.

[63]"Strange Brew: How SABMiller Fights Bootleggers in Africa," http://www.adage.com, accessed February 23, 2011.

[64]"Chinese to Pay Damages over Diageo Designs," *Financial Times*, November 28, 2008, p. 17.

[65]"The Realities of Tackling Corporate Brand Theft in China," *Financial Times*, January 22, 2008, p. 2.

[66]"Counter Feats," *China Business Review* (Nov./Dec. 1994): 12–15.

[67]"Microsoft-Bashing Is Paying off for Software Giant's Foes in China," *Asian Wall Street Journal*, January 3, 2000, pp. 1, 4.

[68]Joseph T. Simone, "Countering Counterfeiters," *China Business Review* (Jan.-Feb. 1999): 12–19.

Product Policy Options

The third set of measures to cope with product piracy covers product policy actions. For instance, software manufacturers often protect their products by putting holograms on the product to discourage counterfeiters. Holograms are only effective when they are hard to copy. Microsoft learned that lesson the hard way when it found out that counterfeiters simply sold MS-DOS 5.0 knockoffs using counterfeit holograms.[69] In 2008 Microsoft initiated a highly controversial initiative to combat software piracy in markets such as China.[70] The firm sent out a security measure through a software update to millions of users of the Windows XP operating system. The update could turn the users' desktop wallpaper black if they were using pirated software.[71] Brown-Forman, the maker of Jack Daniels whiskey, uses anti-refill caps for its larger bottles to prevent criminals from refilling them with counterfeit spirits.[72]

Distribution

Changes in the distribution strategy can offer partial solutions to piracy. When launching Windows XP in China, Microsoft struck a deal with four of China's leading PC makers to bundle the operating system into their computers. Pirated versions of Windows XP were on sale in China for less than $5 shortly after the product was launched in the United States.[73] Some victimized companies have also gone after distributors or B2C websites that were suspected of helping the trade of pirated goods. In February 2010, a court in Paris ordered eBay to pay a fine of €200,000 in damages plus legal fees to Louis Vuitton (LVMH) after the auction site was found guilty of harming the luxury brand's image. The court ruled against eBay for having search terms such as "Louis Viton" or "Wuiton" that could be used to sell counterfeit goods.[74] The suit was the latest in a series of battles between LVMH and eBay. In June 2008, the Commercial Court of Paris fined eBay for failing to stop the sale of fake products allegedly made by LVMH.

Pricing

Marketers can also fight counterfeiters on the price front. Microsoft China, for example, cut the price for its software drastically in October 2008 partly to outmaneuver software piracy competitors: the price for the home and student version of Microsoft Office was lowered from $102 to $30.[75]

Communication Options

Companies also use their communication strategy to counter rip-offs. Through advertising or public relations campaigns, companies warn their target audience about the consequences of accepting counterfeit merchandise. In Japan, LVMH distributed a million leaflets at three airports. The goal of this campaign was to warn Japanese tourists that the importation of counterfeit products is against the law.[76] Anti-counterfeiting advertising campaigns that target end-consumers

---

[69]"Catching Counterfeits," *Security Management* (December 1994): 18.

[70]"Microsoft Stirs Up Pirates," *Wall Street Journal Asia*, October 23, 2008, p. 6.

[71]See also http://www.youtube.com/watch?v=xRsFvmo72_A.

[72]"Counterfeit Alcohol Problem Takes a Deadly Toll," *Financial Times*, November 5, 2012, p. 16.

[73]"Microsoft Victory in China Software Piracy Battle," *Financial Times*, December 7, 2001, p. 6.

[74]"EBay Told to Pay Damages to Unit of LVMH," http://www.online.wsj.com, accessed December 1, 2012.

[75]"Microsoft Stirs Up Pirates."

[76]"Modern day pirates a threat worldwide," *Advertising Age International*, March 20, 1995, pp. I-3, I-4.

could also try to appeal to people's ethical judgments: a "good citizen" does not buy counterfeit goods.[77] The target of warning campaigns is not always the end-customer. Converse, the U.S. athletic shoe brand now owned by Nike, ran a campaign in trade journals throughout Europe alerting retailers to the legal consequences of selling counterfeits.[78]

Country-of-Origin (COO) Effects

Two of the biggest cosmetics companies in the world are Japanese: Kao and Shiseido. While successful in Japan and other Asian countries, Kao and Shiseido have had a hard time penetrating the European and American markets. Apparently, part of the problem is that they are Japanese. In China, however, Shiseido has built up a loyal following. One senior marketing executive of the company observed that: "China and Japan are from the same Asian background, so people think Shiseido is a specialist in Asian skin treatment. They may think it is more suitable for them than Western products."[79] **Exhibit 10-8** shows some of the results of a survey that was done in six cities around the world by the Japanese advertising agency Hakuhodo. The figures show the percentage of respondents in each city who rated a product high quality given its origins. Clearly, Japanese products boast a high-quality image whereas Chinese products, and to a lesser extent Korean, possess a rather poor image. Consumers often rely on a product's **country-of-origin (COO)** as an important cue to assess its quality. This phenomenon can be defined as "the overall perception consumers form of products from such a country, based on their prior perceptions of the country's production and marketing strengths and weaknesses."[80] In this section we explore country-of-origin effects and strategies to cope with them.

Exhibit 10-8   Quality Image of Products Made in Various Countries
(Percent (%) of respondents who rated xxx products as being high quality)

	Hong Kong	Taipei	Seoul	Bangkok	Shanghai	Moscow	Frankfurt
1	Japanese (86.4%)	Japanese (94.3%)	Japanese (29.6%)	Japanese (54.3%)	Japanese (49.6%)	Japanese (70.4%)	European (64.2%)
2	European (74.1%)	European (78.3%)	Korean (28.9%)	U.S. (45.8%)	U.S. (39.2%)	European (42.6%)	Japanese (38.6%)
3	U.S. (60.5%)	U.S. (61.0%)	U.S. (19.3%)	European (34.4%)	Chinese (33.6%)	U.S. (24.8%)	U.S. (24.2%)
4	Korean (38.0%)	Korean (28.3%)	European (11.8%)	Korean (20.3%)	European (26.9%)	Korean (15.4%)	Chinese (9.4%)
5	Chinese (6.0%)	Chinese (2.1%)	Chinese (2.5%)	Chinese (11.6%)	Korean (16.0%)	Chinese (1.0%)	Korean (7.9%)

Source: Hakuhodo Global HABIT 2008 Survey.

---

[77] Alexander Nill and Clifford J. Shultz II, "The Scourge of Global Counterfeiting," *Business Horizons* (Nov.–Dec. 1996), 37–42.

[78] "Converse jumps on counterfeit culprits with ad," *Marketing*, October 21, 1993, p. 11.

[79] "When Chinese Desire Transcends Politics," *Financial Times*, April 1, 2004, p. 9.

[80] Martin S. Roth and Jean B. Romeo, "Matching Product Category and Country Image Perceptions: A Framework for Managing Country-of-Origin Effects," *Journal of International Business Studies* 23 (Third Quarter 1992): 477–497.

Country-of-Origin (COO) Influences on Consumers

In most product categories, the country of origin has a major impact on consumer decision-making. Most of us prefer a bottle of French wine or champagne to a Chinese-made bottle, despite the huge price gap. Consumers hold cultural stereotypes about countries that will influence their product assessments. Academic research studies of COO-effects clearly show that the phenomenon is complex. Some of the key research findings follow:[81]

- *Stability over time.* COO-effects are not stable; perceptions change over time.[82] Country images will change when consumers become more familiar with the country, the marketing practices behind the product improve over time, or when the product's actual quality improves. A classic example is Japanese-made cars, where COO-effects took a 180 degree turn during the last couple of decades, from a very negative to a very positive country image.[83] A similar phenomenon happened more recently for Korean-made cars.

- *Design versus manufacturing.* Research also shows that both the country of design and the country of manufacturing/assembly play a role. Foreign companies can target patriotic consumers by becoming a local player in the host market. For instance, they might set up an assembly base in the country. At the same time, they can capitalize on their country-image to attract those customers who recognize the country's design image. For instance, Toyota pitched its Camry model as "The best car built in America."[84] Apple famously sells its products as "Designed in California, made in China."

- *Willingness to pay.* COO has an impact on how much consumers are willing to pay for a product. Several studies showed that consumers are willing to pay more for branded products that originated from a country with a favorable image.[85] One study using eBay transaction data also found that U.S. retailers were able to command a higher price in an online auction setting.[86]

- *Consumer demographics.* Demographics make a difference. COO influences are particularly strong among the elderly,[87] less educated, and politically conservative consumers.[88] Consumer expertise also makes a difference: novices tend to use COO as a cue in evaluating a product under any circumstances; experts only rely upon COO stereotypes when product attribute information is ambiguous.[89]

---

[81]For an excellent in-depth overview of the literature, see Duhairaj Maheswaran and Cathy Yi Chen, "Nation Equity: Country-of-Origin Effects and Globalization," in *The Sage Handbook of International Marketing* (Masaaki Kotabe and Kristiaan Helsen, eds.) (London: Sage Publications, 2009).

[82]Van R. Wood, John R. Darling, and Mark Siders, "Consumer Desire to Buy and Use Products in International Markets: How to Capture It, How to Sustain It," *International Marketing Review* 16, no. 3 (1999): 231–256.

[83]Akira Nagashima, "A Comparison of Japanese and US attitudes toward foreign products," *Journal of Marketing* (January 1970): 68–74.

[84]Glen H. Brodowsky and J. Justin Tan, "Managing Country of Origin: Understanding How Country of Design and Country of Assembly Affect Product Evaluations and Attitudes toward Purchase," in *American Marketing Association Summer Educators' Conference Proceedings*, Steven Brown and D. Sudharshan, eds., Chicago: American Marketing Association, 1999: 307–20.

[85]Nicole Koschate-Fischer, Adamantios Diamantopoulos, and Katharina Oldenkotte, "Are Consumers Really Willing to Pay More for a Favorable Country Image? A Study of Country-of-Origins Effects on Willingness to Pay," *Journal of International Marketing*, 20 (March 2012): 1–23.

[86]Hu, Ye and Xin Wang, "Country-of-Origin Premiums for Retailers in International Trades: Evidence from eBay's International Markets," *Journal of Retailing*, 86, no. 2 (2010): 200–207.

[87]Terence A. Shimp and Subhash Sharma, "Consumer ethnocentrism: Construction and validation of the CETSCALE," *Journal of Marketing Research* 24, August 1987): 280–89.

[88]Thomas W. Anderson and William H. Cunningham, "Gauging foreign product promotion," *Journal of Advertising Research* (February 1972): 29–34.

[89]Durairaj Maheswaran, "Country of Origin as a Stereotype: Effects of Consumer Expertise and Attribute Strength on Product Evaluations," *Journal of Consumer Research* 21 (September 1994): 354–365.

- *Emotions.* One recent study indicates that emotions consumers experience prior to their product evaluations also play a role: angry consumers are more likely to use COO information in their product evaluations than sad consumers.[90]

- *Culture.* Cultural orientations play a role. One study contrasted COO influences between members of an individualist (United States) and a collectivist culture (Japan).[91] The study's findings showed that individualists evaluated the home country product more favorably only when it was superior to the competition. Collectivists, however, rated the home country product higher regardless of product superiority.[92]

- *Brand name familiarity.* Consumers are likely to use the origin of a product as a cue when they are unfamiliar with the brand name carried by the product.[93]

- *Product category.* Finally, COO-effects depend upon the product category.[94] A 2008 study in fourteen cities[95] that surveyed consumers' opinions about Japanese products recorded high "good quality" scores for digital cameras (28.6%), white goods (28.5%), flat-screen TVs (25.8%), and cars (25.4%).[96] Scores were low for cosmetics (13.6%), skincare products (12.1%), facial cleanser (12.0%), and instant foods (9.7%).[97] As shown in **Exhibit 10-9**, there are four possible outcomes depending on (1) whether there is a match between the product and country and (2) whether or not the (mis-)match is favorable. For each combination, the exhibit also lists some of the strategic implications.

Strategies to Cope with COO Stereotypes

Before exploring strategic options to deal with COO, firms should conduct market research to investigate the extent and the impact of COO stereotypes for their particular product. Such studies would reveal whether the country-of-origin really matters to consumers and to what degree COO hurts or helps the product's evaluation. One useful technique makes use of a dollar preference scale. Participants are asked to indicate how much they are willing to pay for particular brand/country combinations.[98]

Country image stereotypes can either benefit or hurt a company's product. Evidently, when there is a favorable match between the country image and the desired product features, a firm could leverage this match by touting the origin of its product, provided its main competitors do not have the same (or better) origin. Our focus below is on strategies that can be used to counter negative COO stereotypes. The overview is organized along the four marketing mix elements:

---

[90]Durairaj Maheswaran and Cathy Yi Chen, "Nation Equity: Incidental Emotions in Country-of-Origin Effects," *Journal of Consumer Research* 33, no. 3 (Dec. 2006): 370–76.

[91]Zeynep Gürhan-Canli and Durairaj Maheswaran, "Cultural Variations in Country of Origin Effects," *Journal of Marketing Research* 37 (August 2000): 309–317.

[92]See also V. Swaminathan, K. L. Page, and S. Gürhan-Canli, "'My' Brand or 'Our' Brand: The Effects of Brand Relationship Dimensions and Self-construal on Brand Evaluations," *Journal of Consumer Research* 34, no. 2 (2011): 248–59.

[93]Victor V. Cordell, "Effects of consumer preferences for foreign sourced products," *Journal of International Business Studies* (Second Quarter 1992): 251–269.

[94]George Balabanis and Adamantios Diamantopoulos, "Domestic Country Bias, Country-of-Origin Effects, and Consumer Ethnocentrism: A Multidimensional Unfolding Approach," *Academy of Marketing Science Journal* 32 (Winter 2004): 80–95.

[95]Shanghai, Beijing, Hong Kong, Taipei, Seoul, Singapore, Bangkok, Jakarta, Kuala Lumpur, Manila, Ho Chi Minh City, Delhi, Mumbai, and Moscow.

[96]http://www.hakuhodo.jp.

[97]The scores refer to the percentage of respondents in the survey who agreed with the statement, "Japanese products are of good quality."

[98]Usually the respondents are also given an anchor point (e.g., "Amount above or below $10,000?"). For further details, see Johny K. Johansson and Israel D. Nebenzahl, "Multinational production: Effect on brand value," *Journal of International Business Studies* (Fall 1986): 101–26.

Exhibit 10-9 Product-Country Matches and Mismatches: Examples and Strategic Implication

	Country Image Dimensions	
	Positive	**Negative**
Important	I Favorable Match Examples: • Japanese auto •German watch Strategic Implications: • Brand name reflects COO • Packaging includes COO information • Promote brand's COO • Attractive potential manufacturing site	II Unfavorable Match Examples: • Hungarian auto • Mexican watch Strategic Implications: • Emphasize benefits other than COO • Noncountry branding • Joint venture with favorable match partner • Communication campaign to enhance country image
Not Important	III Favorable Mismatch Example: • Japanese beer Strategic Implications: • Alter importance of product category image dimensions • Promote COO as secondary benefit if compensatory choice process	IV Unfavorable Mismatch Example: • Hungarian beer Strategic Implications: • Ignore COO — such information not relevant

(Dimensions as Product Features — row label along left side)

Source: Martin S. Roth and Jean B. Romeo, "Matching Product Category and Country Image Perceptions: A Framework for Managing Country-of-Origin Effects," *Journal of International Business Studies*, Third Quarter 1992, p. 495.

Product Policy

A common practice to cope with COO is to select a brand name that disguises the country-of-origin or even invokes a favorable COO.[99] It is probably no coincidence that two of the more successful apparel retailers based in Hong Kong have Italian-sounding names (Giordano and Bossini). Print ads for Finlandia vodka in U.S. magazines highlight the linkage between the vodka's origin (*Vodka of Finland*) and its ingredients (*Made from pure glacial spring water, untouched, untainted, and unspoiled*). A variant is to pick a non-descriptive brand names (e.g., ZTE, Geely, TCL). Another branding option to downplay negative COO feelings is to use private-label branding. One study that looked at COO influences on prices in the Philippines showed that marketers can overcome negative COO effects by developing brand equity.[100] Sheer innovation and a drive for superior quality will usually help firms to overcome COO biases in the long run. Korean carmaker Hyundai's brand building strategy in the United States is a good illustration. Hyundai entered the U.S. market in 1986 with a single model, the Hyundai Excel. A slew of quality issues promptly made the brand into a favorite joke topic for comedians. The company began investing heavily in quality and design improvement. It launched the industry's first 100,000-mile powertrain warranty and created a program that offered new car buyers to forgive

---

[99]France Leclerc, Bernd H. Schmitt, and Laurette Dubé, "Foreign Branding and Its Effects on Product Perceptions and Attitudes," *Journal of Marketing Research* 31 (May 1994): 263–270.

[100]John Hulland et al., "Country-of-Origin Effects on Sellers' Price Premiums."

loan payments when they lost their jobs due to the 2008 economic crisis. In 2012, its flagship brand, Hyundai Elantra, was named the "North American Car of the Year." J.D. Power's survey also showed that Hyundai had the highest customer retention rate (64 percent) in 2011 beating Ford (60 percent), Honda (60 percent), and BMW (59 percent).[101] Tied with BMW was Hyundai's sibling brand, Kia.

Pricing

Selling the product at a relatively low price will attract value-conscious customers who are not very concerned about the brand's country-of-origin. Obviously, this strategy is only doable when the firm enjoys a cost advantage. At the other end of the pricing spectrum, firms could set a premium price to combat COO biases. This is especially effective for product categories in which price plays a role as a signal of quality (e.g., wines, cosmetics, clothing).

Distribution

Alternatively, companies could influence consumer attitudes by using highly respected distribution channels. Herborist is a skin care line created by Shanghai Jahwa, a major Chinese manufacturer of personal care products. The brand differentiates itself from other cosmetics brands by developing products based on Chinese herbal science. When Shanghai Jahwa considered rolling the brand out beyond China, it needed to surmount the MADE-IN-CHINA stigma. The brand describes itself as MADE-IN-SHANGHAI, a claim that draws on the Chinese city's cosmopolitan image that resonates more easily with premium consumers. To launch the brand in overseas markets, the company also relied on renowned distributors. In France and other European countries, Herborist is distributed through Sephora, an upscale French cosmetics retailer owned by LVMH. Sephora sells the Chinese line both online and in its brick-and-mortar stores, including the chain's Champs Elysées outlet.[102]

Communication

Lastly, the firm's communication strategy can be used to alter consumer's attitudes toward the product. Such strategies could pursue either of two broad objectives: (1) improve the country image or (2) bolster the brand image. The first goal, changing the country image, is less appealing because it can lead to free-rider problems. Efforts carried out by your company to change the country image would also benefit your competitors from the same country of manufacture, even though they don't spend a penny on the country-image campaign. For that reason, country-image-type campaigns are done mostly by industry associations or government agencies. For instance, in the United States, Chilean wines were promoted with wine tastings and a print advertising campaign with the tag line: "It's not just a wine. It's a country." The $2–3 million campaign was sponsored by ProChile, Chile's Ministry of Foreign Affairs' trade group.[103] Likewise, Colombian coffee brands managed to change cultural mindsets about the country's image through aggressive advertising. Corona, on the other hand, became widely popular in developed markets by branding itself as a lifestyle beer while downplaying its Mexican provenance.[104] Tencent, the China-based internet giant, hired the Argentine soccer player Lionel Messi as brand spokesperson in its global ad campaign for the launch of WeChat, an online messaging service. Sponsorship is another potent weapon. ThaiBev, a Thai beer brewer, signed sponsorship deals with soccer teams Everton, Barcelona, and Real Madrid to promote its flagship brand Chang Beer in the West.

---

[101]"Hyundai Maintains Momentum, But How Far Can It Go as Just One Brand?" http://www.brandchannel.com, accessed December 2, 2012.

[102]"'Made in China' Does Not Always Translate Well," *Financial Times*, December 30, 2011, p. 8.

[103]"Non-traditional nations pour into wine market," http://www.adage.com, accessed September 13, 2013.

[104]Rohit Deshpandé, "Why You Aren't Buying Venezuelan Chocolate," *Harvard Business Review* 88 (December 2010): 25–27.

Global Marketing of Services

Most of the discussion in this chapter so far has focused on the marketing of so-called tangible goods. However, as countries grow richer, services tend to become the dominant sector of their economy. In this section we will first focus on the challenges and opportunities that exist in the global service market. We will then offer a set of managerial guidelines that might prove fruitful to service marketers who plan to expand overseas.

Challenges in Marketing Services Internationally

Compared to marketers of tangible goods, service marketers face several unique hurdles on the road to international expansion. The major challenges include:

Protectionism

Trade barriers to service marketers tend to be much more cumbersome than for their physical goods counterparts. Many parts of the world are littered with service trade barriers coming under many different guises. Most cumbersome are the non-tariff trade barriers, where the creative juices of government regulators know no boundaries. In the past, the service sector has received less attention in global trade agreements. The rules of the GATT system, for instance, only applied to visible trade. Its successor, the World Trade Organization (WTO), now expands at least some of the GATT rules to the service sector.[105]

Need for Geographic Proximity with Service Transactions

The human aspect in service delivery is much more critical than for the marketing of tangible goods. Services are performed. This performance feature of services has several consequences in the international domain. Most services are difficult to trade internationally and require a physical presence of the service provider. Given the intrinsic need for people-to-people contact, cultural barriers in the global marketplace are much more prominent for service marketers than for other industries. Being in tune with the cultural values and norms of the local market is essential to be successful in most service industries. As a result, services are typically standardized far less than are tangible products.[106] At the same time, service companies usually aspire to provide a consistent quality image worldwide. Careful screening and training of personnel to assure consistent quality is extremely vital for international service firms. To foster the transfer of know-how between branches, many service companies set up communication channels such as regional councils.

The need for direct customer interface also means that service providers often need to have a local presence. This is especially the case with support services such as advertising, insurance, accounting, law firms, or overnight package delivery. In order not to lose MNC customer accounts, many support service companies are often obliged to follow in their clients' footsteps.

Difficulties in Measuring Customer Satisfaction Overseas

Given the human element in services, monitoring consumer satisfaction is an absolute must for successful service marketing. The job of doing customer satisfaction studies in an international context is often frustrating. The hindrances to conducting market research surveys also apply here. In many countries, consumers are not used to sharing their opinions or suggestions. Instead of

---

[105]Joseph A. McKinney, "Changes in the World Trading System."

[106]B. Nicolaud, "Problems and Strategies in the International Marketing of Services," *European Journal of Marketing* 23, no. 6 (1989): 55–66.

expressing their true opinions about the service, foreign respondents may simply state what they believe the company wants to hear (the "courtesy" bias).[107]

Opportunities in the Global Service Industries

Despite the challenges described above, many international service industries offer enormous opportunities to savvy service marketers. The major ones are given here:

Deregulation of Service Industries

While protectionism is still rampant in many service industries, there is a steady improvement for international service providers in terms of deregulation. In scores of countries, government authorities have privatized services such as utilities (e.g., water, electricity), telecommunications, and mail delivery. The underlying thinking is that private firms can run these services more efficiently and have the resources to upgrade the infrastructure. Further, by shifting these services to the private sector, governments can allocate their resources to other areas (e.g., education, social welfare). Several individual countries are taking steps to lift restrictions targeting foreign service firms. Even sectors that were traditionally off-limits to foreigners are opening up now in scores of countries. India and the Philippines, for example, opened up their telephone industry to foreign companies.[108]

Increasing Demand for Premium Services

Demand for premium quality services expands with increases in consumers' buying power. International service providers that are able to deliver a premium product often have an edge over their local competitors. There are two major factors behind this competitive advantage. One of the legacies of years of protectionism is that local service firms are typically unprepared for the hard laws of the marketplace. Notions such as customer orientation, consumer satisfaction, and service quality are marketing concepts that are especially hard to digest for local service firms that, until recently, did not face any serious competition. For example, local funeral companies in France invested very little in funeral homes. Prior to the de-monopolization of the industry, the funeral business in France was basically a utility: firms bid for the right to offer funeral services to a municipality at fixed prices. Service Corp. International, a leading American funeral company, unveiled plans to gain a foothold in France by selling premium products and upgraded facilities.[109] Despite Malaysia's highly protectionist banking laws, Citibank Malaysia has become one of the country's biggest mortgage lenders through a combination of savvy marketing, an assertive sales force, and a strong customer service orientation.[110]

Global service firms can also leverage their "global know-how" base. A major strength for the likes of Federal Express, Wal-Mart, and AT&T is that they have a worldwide knowledge base into which they can tap instantly.

Increased Value Consciousness

As customers worldwide have more alternatives to choose from and have become more sophisticated, they have also grown increasingly value conscious. Service companies that compete internationally also have clout on this front versus local service providers, because global service

[107]Gaye Kaufman, "Customer satisfaction studies overseas can be frustrating," *Marketing News*, August 29, 1994, p. 34.

[108]"Asia, at your service," *The Economist*, February 11, 1995, 53–54.

[109]"Funereal prospects," *Forbes*, September 11, 1995, 45–46.

[110]"Citibank Expands Niche in Malaysian Mortgages by Courting Customers," *Asian Wall Street Journal*, November 28, 2002, p. A5.

firms usually benefit from scale economies. Such savings can be passed through to their customers. McDonald's apparently saved around $2 million by centralizing the purchase of sesame seeds.[111] In Thailand, Makro, a large Dutch retailer, uses computerized inventory controls and bulk selling to undercut its local rivals.[112] Given the size of its business, Toys 'R' Us, the U.S. discount toy retailer, was able to set up its own direct import company in Japan, allowing the firm to deliver merchandise straight from the docks to its warehouses, thereby bypassing distributors' margins.[113]

Global Service Marketing Strategies

To compete in foreign markets, service firms resort to a plethora of different strategies.

Capitalize on Cultural Forces in the Host Market

To bridge cultural gaps between the home and host market, service companies often customize the product to the local market. Successful service firms grab market share by spotting cultural opportunities and setting up a service product around these cultural forces. Most fast food restaurants in the United States have a drive-through facility. In many Asian and Middle Eastern cities, however, food delivery is commonplace. Home delivery service has become a core part of the growth strategy for both McDonald's and KFC in many Asian countries (e.g., China, Singapore) and the Middle East. For KFC, delivery accounts for a third of sales in Egypt and nearly half in Kuwait. Customers phone in their orders or place them online. Motorbike drivers deliver the food in specially designed boxes. In some countries (e.g., China) customers pay a flat delivery fee while in others the fee is 15 percent to 20 percent of the order price.[114]

Standardize and Customize

As noted in the last chapter, one of the major challenges in global product design is striking the right balance between standardization and customization. By their very nature (service delivery at the point of consumption) most services do not need to wrestle with that issue. Both standardization and adaptation are doable. The core service product can easily be augmented with localized support service features that cater to local market conditions.[115] Customization can sometimes render the service offering almost unrecognizable from the service in the home market. Japan's Wendy's burger restaurants can be described as "fast casual" rather than just fast food places. Service is faster than at table-service restaurants while the quality and ambience is better than at regular fast-food chains like McDonald's. Wendy's restaurants in Japan feature agreeable lighting, free Wi-Fi, and comfortable seating. Menu offerings include the "Foie Gras Rossini"—a hamburger topped with goose liver paté, priced at around 1,280 yen ($16) or about sixteen times the cost of a plain hamburger at McDonald's.[116]

Central Role of Information Technologies (IT)

Information technology forms a key pillar of global service strategies. Service firms add value for their customers by employing technology such as computers, intelligent terminals, and state-of-the-art telecommunications. Many service firms have established internet access to communicate

---

[111]"Big Mac's counter attack," *The Economist*, November 13, 1993, pp. 71–72.

[112]"Asia, at your service," *The Economist*, February 11, 1995, pp. 53–54.

[113]"Revolution in toyland," *Financial Times*, April 8, 1994, p. 9.

[114]"For Fast Food, China Calls McDonald's," *Wall Street Journal*, December 13, 2011, pp. 19–20.

[115]Christopher H. Lovelock and George S. Yip, "Developing Global Strategies for Service Businesses," *California Management Review* 38, no. 2 (Winter 1996): 64–86.

[116]"Hamburger Helper," *Forbes Asia* (December 2012): 96–102.

with their customers and suppliers. IT is especially valued in markets that have a fairly underdeveloped infrastructure. Companies should also recognize the potential of realizing scale economies by centralizing their IT functions via "information hubs."[117] A case in point is HSBC, a leading British bank.[118] HSBC relies on 400 low-cost employees in Hyderabad, India, and Guangzhou, China, to industrialize its simple back-room operations on a global scale, freeing up its UK backrooms for more complicated tasks.

Add Value by Differentiation

Services differ from tangible products by the fact that it is usually far easier to find differentiation possibilities. Service firms can appeal to their customers by offering benefits not provided by their competitors and/or lowering costs. Apart from monetary expenses, cost items include psychic costs (hassles), time costs (waiting time), and physical efforts.[119] Especially in markets where the service industry is still developing, multinational service firms can add value by providing premium features. Safaricom, the Kenyan affiliate of the British mobile service provider Vodafone, developed a unique money transfer system called M-Pesa.[120] The service basically transforms a mobile phone into an electronic wallet: subscribers can store, transfer, or withdraw money through their mobile phone. Given the huge success of the service, Vodafone is rolling out similar schemes elsewhere in Africa as well as in India.

Establish Global Service Networks

Service firms with a global customer base face the challenge of setting up a seamless global service network. One of the key questions is whether the company should set up the network on its own, or use outside partners. Given the huge investments required to develop a worldwide network, more and more companies are choosing the latter route. Trends of firms grouping together to establish global network can be observed service industries like airline travel (e.g., the Star Alliance, One World) and advertising.

---

[117] ibid.
[118] "Bull-terrier Banking," *Forbes Global*, July 24, 2000, pp. 36–38.
[119] "Services go international," *Marketing News*, March 14, 1994, pp. 14–15.
[120] Pesa is Swahili for money.

SUMMARY

Mission statements in annual reports reflect the aspiration of countless companies to sell their products to consumers worldwide. This push toward global expansion raises many tricky questions on the product policy front. Mastering these global product issues will yield success and possibly even worldwide leadership.

Companies need to decide what branding strategies they plan to pursue to develop their overseas business. There is plenty of ammunition to build a case for global brands. At the same time, there are also many arguments that can be put forward in favor of other branding strategies. Developing a global branding strategy involves tackling questions such as:

- Which of the brands in our brand portfolio have the potential to be globalized?

- What is the best route towards globalizing our brands? Should we start by acquiring local brands, develop them into regional brands, and, ultimately, if the potential is there, into a "truly" global brand?

- What is the best way to implement the changeover from a local to a global (or regional) brand?

- How do we foster and sustain the consistency of our global brand image?

- What organizational mechanisms should we as a company use to coordinate our branding strategies across markets? Should coordination happen at the regional or global level?

The ultimate reward of mastering these issues successfully is regional, sometimes even worldwide, leadership in the marketplace.

QUESTIONS

1. Why is the market share of private labels much higher in Europe than in Asia?

2. What factors should MNCs consider when implementing a brand-name facelift in their foreign markets?

3. How can companies counter negative country-of-origin images? How can they leverage favorable ones?

4. Dr. Hans-Willi Schroiff, vice-president of market research at Henkel, a German company, made the following observation about P&G's multinational marketing strategy: "A strict globalization strategy like P&G's [will not be] successful if 'meaningful' local brands are corpses on the battlefield. It caused severe share looses for P&G here in Europe. Consumers do not switch to the global brand, but to another brand that looks more like 'home' to them." Comment on this statement. Do you agree or disagree (and why)?

5. Software piracy in China is a huge problem for Microsoft. In 2008 Microsoft went on the offensive by sending a software update that could turn the desktop wallpaper black when a pirated Windows XP operating system was being used (http://www.youtube.com/watch?v=xRsFvmo72_A). Not surprisingly, this move stirred much controversy in China. Is this the right approach to combat piracy? What are the possible risks? Are there better ways to fight the problem, if so, how?

6. Nestlé, the Swiss food conglomerate, has created a Nestlé Seal of Guarantee that it puts on the back of some of its products (e.g., Maggi sauces). The Seal of Guarantee is not used for many of its other products like pet food and mineral water. What might be Nestlé's motivations for adding or dropping its Nestlé Seal of Guarantee stamp to the brand name?

11 GLOBAL PRICING

CHAPTER OVERVIEW

1. Drivers of foreign market pricing

2. Managing price escalation

3. Pricing in inflationary environments

4. Global pricing and currency fluctuations

5. Transfer pricing

6. Global pricing and anti-dumping regulation

7. Price coordination

Global pricing is one of the most critical and complex issues that multinational firms face. Price is the only marketing mix instrument that creates revenues. All other elements entail costs. Thus, a company's global pricing policy may make or break its overseas expansion efforts. Furthermore, a firm's pricing policy is inherently a highly cross-functional process based on inputs from the firm's finance, accounting, manufacturing, tax, and legal divisions. Predictably, the interests of one group (say, marketing) may clash with the objectives of another group (say, finance).

The basic pricing challenges companies face in domestic marketing (e.g., skimming versus penetration pricing) also apply in global marketing. However, global pricing becomes further complicated due to the very nature of the global marketplace (e.g., currency movements, inflation, cross-border variations in willingness to pay, competition).

One special form of pricing in global marketing is prices set between subsidiaries for goods or services provided by one country affiliate for another one. Pricing such transactions is known as transfer pricing. We will look at different ways to implement transfer pricing.

Multinationals also face the challenge of how to coordinate their pricing policy across different countries. A lack of coordination could create a parallel trade or gray market situation (see Chapter 14). With parallel imports, middlemen make a profit by shipping products from low-priced countries to higher-priced markets. These imports will compete with the high-priced equivalent products offered by the company's authorized distributors. Efforts to trim big price gaps between countries may be hampered by stonewalling attempts of local country managers.

This chapter will focus on global pricing strategies. After presenting an overview of the key drivers of foreign market pricing, we will discuss several strategic international pricing issues. Several of these challenges deal with export price decisions. The final section of the chapter gives an overview of various approaches to implement cross-border price coordination.

Drivers of Foreign Market Pricing

In December 2008, the retail price recorded for a 500 ml bottle of Listerine mouthwash was \$3.60 (4,720 won) in Seoul, \$4.72 in New York, and \$11.27 (€8) in Rome; for a Davidoff cigar cutter the price ranged from \$222 (323,000 won) in Seoul, \$322 in New York, up to \$727 (25,900 baht) in Bangkok.[1] Even within the same geographic area such as the pan-European market, wide cross-border price differences can be very common. **Exhibit 11-1** shows retail price variations for a sample of other products around the world. What lies behind these enormous price variations? A hodgepodge of factors governs global pricing decisions. Some of the drivers are related to the 4 Cs: *Company* (costs, company goals), *Customers* (price sensitivity, segments, consumer preferences), *Competition* (market structure, intensity), and *Channels*. Aside from these, in many countries, multinationals' pricing decisions are often influenced by government policies (price controls, taxes, import duties). We now consider the main drivers that may affect global pricing.

Company Goals

When developing a pricing strategy for its global markets, the firm needs to decide what it wants to accomplish with its strategy. These goals might include maximizing current profits, penetrating

Exhibit 11-1 Retail Price Comparison Across Cities
(Index = Recorded Price/Lowest Price × 100)

Item	New York	Hong Kong	Seoul	Tokyo	Paris	London	Shanghai	Sydney	Date
Nikon D80 SLR Camera	103.9 ($816)	100.0 ($786)	105.2 ($827)	114.9 ($903)	167.4 ($1,316)	129.9 ($1,021)	107.6 ($846)	NA	March 2008
Davidoff Cigar Cutter	145.0 ($322)	164.0 ($364)	100.0 ($222)	202.7 ($450)	137.3 ($305)	124.3 ($276)	164.4 ($365)	154.9 ($344)	December 2008
Listerine Mouthwash	131.1 ($4.72)	121.4 ($4.37)	100.0 ($3.60)	NA	215.3 ($7.75)	164.7 ($5.93)	NA	150.3 ($5.41)	December 2008
iRobot Vacuum Cleaner	100.0 ($324)	182.4 ($591)	115.7 ($375)	232.7 ($754)	130.9 ($424)	109.6 ($355)	NA	122.5 ($397)	October 2008
Prada Nappa Gauffré Antik Handbag	111.8 ($2,915)	100.0 ($2,607)	116.5 ($3,038)	111.9 ($2,918)	NA	NA	112.1 ($2,923)	113.0 ($2,945)	November 2006
TaylorMade Golf Club	127.8 ($216)	100.0 ($169)	NA	174.0 ($294)	NA	NA	NA	140.0 ($236)	November 2006
Jack Daniel's 750 ml Whiskey	106.0 ($25.46)	156.4 ($37.55)	200.0 ($47.96)	126.0[*] ($30.26)	100.0[*] ($24.01)	141.3[*] ($33.94)	NA	NA	November 2006
Sonicare Toothbrush	107.1 ($120)	100.0 ($112)	108.9 ($122)	103.6 ($116)	139.3 ($156)	158.9 ($178)	156.2 ($175)	NA	September 2008
BlackBerry Bold 9000	100.0 ($571)	115.1 ($657)	116.7 ($666)	NA	114.9 ($656)	128.7 ($735)	NA	132.0 ($754)	April 2009
Brita Marella Jug	NA	222.0 ($46.16)	231.5 ($48.13)	207.7 ($43.19)	121.6 ($25.29)	108.4 ($22.54)	NA	100.0 ($20.79)	November 2008

[*] 700 ml

Source: Based on various issues of the Weekend Journal of the *Wall Street Journal* ("Arbitrage").

---

[1] Price data compiled from December 2008 issues in the "Arbitrage" section of the weekend edition of *Wall Street Journal*. Prices include taxes.

the market, projecting a premium image, and so forth. According to one study,[2] the most important pricing objectives of companies doing business in the United States (including foreign-based firms) are (1) to achieve a satisfactory return on investment, (2) to maintain market share, and (3) to meet a specified profit goal (in that order). Company objectives will vary from market to market, especially in multinationals with a large degree of local autonomy. New Balance, the U.S.-based maker of high-tech running shoes, sells its shoes in France as haute couture items rather than simply athletic shoes (as it does in the United States, for instance). To beef up the premium image, the price is about 800 francs (around $130) a pair—almost twice the U.S. price.[3] Company goals are likely to change over time. Initially, when a firm enters a country, it often sets a relatively low price (compared to other countries) to penetrate the market. Once the firm is well entrenched, it may shift its objectives and bring them in line with the goals pursued in other countries.

Company Costs

Company costs figure prominently in the pricing decision. Costs set the floor: the company wants to set at least a price that will cover all costs needed to make and sell its products. Cost differentials between countries can lead to wide price gaps. It is important that management considers all relevant costs of manufacturing, marketing, and distributing the product. Company costs consist of two parts: variable costs, which change with sales volume, and fixed costs (e.g., overheads) that do not vary.

Export pricing policies differ depending on the way costs are treated.[4] Three basic options exist for setting export prices: (1) rigid cost-plus pricing, (2) flexible cost-plus pricing, and (3) dynamic incremental pricing.[5] With **rigid cost-plus pricing**, the export price is set by adding all costs accrued in selling the product to the international market and a gross margin. The second option, **flexible cost-plus pricing**, closely resembles the first method but adjusts prices to market conditions in the host market (e.g., level of competition). The final method, **dynamic incremental pricing**, arrives at a price after removing domestic fixed costs. The premise is that these costs have to be borne anyway, as they are sunk costs, regardless of whether or not the goods are exported. Only variable costs generated by the exporting efforts and a portion of the overhead load (the "incremental" costs) should be recuperated. Examples of exporting-related incremental costs include manufacturing costs, shipping expenses, insurance, and overseas promotional costs. Although the last approach is more suitable from an economic perspective, it comes with certain risks. In the export market, situations where the export list price is far below the domestic price could trigger accusations of dumping, as discussed later.

When demand is highly price sensitive, the company needs to consider how it can reduce costs from a global perspective. Manufacturing scale economies provide an incentive to standardize product offerings or to consolidate manufacturing facilities. In some markets, logistics costs can be trimmed by centralizing distribution centers or warehouse facilities. By the same token, significant marketing costs may prompt a multinational operating in Europe to develop pan-European advertising campaigns. In many developing countries, high price sensitivity is a big hurdle. Hindustan Lever, Unilever's India subsidiary, spends a large amount of its R&D money on developing new technologies to lower production costs.[6] Companies operating in these countries typically try to source mainly from local suppliers. McDonald's in India spent six years to set up a local supply chain even before opening its first restaurant in the country. However, high quality

[2]S. Samiee, "Pricing in Marketing Strategies of U.S.- and Foreign-Based Companies," *Journal of Business Research* 15, 1987): 17–30.
[3]"The Road to Richesse," *Sales & Marketing Management* (November 1999): 89–96.
[4]S. Tamer Cavusgil, "Unraveling the Mystique of Export Pricing," *Business Horizons* 31 (May–June 1988): 54–63.
[5]See for instance, Kristiaan Helsen, "Pricing in the Global Marketplace," in *The SAGE Handbook of International Marketing*, M. Kotabe and K. Helsen (eds.) (London: SAGE Publications, 2009).
[6]See also Chapter 18.

potatoes were unavailable in India. McDonald's and its supplier partner, McCain Foods, worked closely with farmers in India to develop process-grade potato varieties.[7]

Customer Demand

Whereas costs set a floor, the consumers' willingness to pay for your product set a ceiling to the price. Consumer demand is a function of buying power, tastes, habits, and substitutes. These demand conditions will vary from country to country. Buying power is a key consideration in pricing decisions. Countries with low per capita incomes pose a dilemma. Consumers in such countries are far more price sensitive than in developed markets. Therefore, price premiums are often a major hurdle for most consumers in these markets. Foreign companies targeting the masses in emerging markets such as China or India offer cheaper products with lower costs by changing the product formula, packaging, or size. One risk here is brand dilution, where a premium brand loses its cachet when a large number of consumers start using it. Another danger is cannibalization. This occurs when high-income customers switch to the cheaper products in the firm's product line. The marketing of Procter & Gamble's Crest toothpaste in China illustrates how companies can manage these issues. To lure the Chinese middle classes, P&G changed the brand's formulation and packaging to emphasize cavity prevention, a generic benefit. The whitening benefit was reserved for premium Crest products.[8] In Egypt, one of the moves that P&G undertook to revitalize the sales of Ariel, its high suds laundry detergent brand, was to downsize the package size from 200 grams to 150 grams, thereby lowering the cash outlay for ordinary consumers.[9]

Another strategic option is to be a niche player by charging prices in the same range as Western prices and target the upper-end of the foreign market. Marketers such as Starbucks and Häagen-Dazs follow this option in their global strategy. Starbucks charges by and large the same price worldwide, whether its coffee is sold in wealthy Western markets or poorer countries such as Thailand or China. A third option is to have a portfolio of products that cater to different income tiers. In India, Unilever dominates many consumer goods categories by following this road. One final option—which seldom works—is to sell older versions of the product at a lower price in markets with low buying power. For instance, in India, Daimler sold older Mercedes models; United Distillers sold passé brands such as Vat 69. Such a pricing strategy can backfire as it manifests a certain amount of arrogance toward the local population.[10]

Typically, the nature of demand will change over time. In countries that were entered recently, the firm may need to stimulate trial via discounting or a penetration pricing strategy. In more mature markets, the lion's share of customers will be repeat buyers. Once brand loyalty has been established, price will play less of a role as a purchase criterion, and the firm may be able to afford the luxury of a premium pricing strategy. Obviously, the success of such a pricing strategy will hinge on the company's ability to differentiate its product from the competition.

Cultural symbolism can also influence pricing decisions. In Chinese cultures, the number "8" has an auspicious meaning as the word for "eight" (bā) sounds similar to the Chinese word for "wealth" (fā). As a result, special price offers in Chinese cultures often end with at least one 8 digit. Cultural differences could also affect how people judge fairness when the price of an identical good differs across customers (e.g., cross-border differences in prices posted on the internet). Paying a higher price than another customer is usually deemed unfair. However, one study found that Chinese ("collectivist") consumers were more sensitive to price gaps when the price comparisons were made with a friend rather than a stranger. U.S. ("individualist") consumers

---

[7]http://www.mcdonaldsindia.com, accessed on January 13, 2013.
[8]"The Right Way to Appeal to the Masses," *Financial Times*, September 15, 2004, p. 10.
[9]Mahmoud Aboul-Fath and Loula Zaklama, "Ariel High Suds Detergent in Egypt—A Case Study," *Marketing and Research Today* (May 1992): 130–35.
[10]"Slim Pickings for the Global Brand in India," *Financial Times*, October 11, 2000, p. 14.

were relatively less affected by whether the customer paying a lower price was a friend or a stranger.[11]

Competition

Competition is another key factor in global pricing. Differences in the competitive situation across countries will usually lead to cross-border price differentials. The competitive situation may vary for a number of reasons. First, the number of competitors typically differs from country to country. In some countries, the firm faces very few competitors (or even enjoys a monopoly position), whereas in others, the company has to combat numerous competing brands. Also, the nature of competition will differ: global versus local players, private firms versus state-owned companies. Even when local companies are not state-owned, they often are viewed as "national champions" and treated accordingly by their local governments. Such a status entails subsidies or other goodies (e.g., cheap loans) that enable them to undercut their competitors. In some markets, firms have to compete with a knock-off version of their own product. The presence of counterfeit products could force the firm to lower its price in such markets. Microsoft, for instance, slashed the Chinese price of its MS Office software suite by more than 70 percent from Rmb699 to Rmb199 ($29) in 2008 to encourage consumers to purchase genuine software instead of pirated software. The piracy rate for personal computer software in China was estimated to be more than 80 percent in 2007.[12]

In developing countries, especially in rural areas, the nature of competition can also vary. Brands will typically compete for "share-of-wallet" in such countries. An Indian villager is not just choosing between a bottle of Coca-Cola and Pepsi but also between buying one soft drink, a disposable razor, or a tube of toothpaste.

The role of competition can be illustrated by taking a look at the pharmaceutical industry. The data in **Exhibit 11-2** show the average quarterly volume sales and selling price (charged by manufacturers) for three antidepressants (Prozac, Zoloft, Paxil) marketed in the United States, the U.K., France, Italy, and Germany. Looking at the data, you can see that Prozac (from Eli Lilly based in the United States) charges a higher price than Paxil (from GlaxoSmithKline in the U.K.).

Exhibit 11-2 Average Quarterly Sales and Ex-Factory Selling Prices of Antidepressants (1988, Q1—1999, Q1)

Brand	Manufacturer	United States	Germany	Italy	U.K.	France
Prozac	Eli Lilly					
Sales	(U.S.)	162.13	2.47	3.65	18.88	32.92
Price		1.62	1.48	0.99	1.18	0.84
Zoloft	Pfizer (U.S.)					
Sales		140.05	1.99	1.77	7.3	9.47
Price		1.59	1.0	0.92	1.4	0.70
Paxil	GSK (U.K.)					
Sales		110.46	1.66	4.04	16.70	21.94
Price		1.59	1.48	1.20	1.26	0.65

Source: Based on Table 1 (p. 73) of Pradeep K. Chintagunta and Ramarao Desiraju, "Strategic Pricing and Detailing Behavior in International Markets," *Marketing Science* 24 (Winter 2005).
Sales are in standard close equivalents (millions); prices are in dollars.

---

[11]Lisa E. Bolton, Hean Tat Keh, and Joseph W. Alba, "How Do Price Fairness Perceptions Differ across Culture?" *Journal of Marketing Research* 47 (June 2010): 564–576.
[12]"Microsoft Aims to Undercut Chinese Pirates," *Financial Times*, September 24, 2008, p. 22.

However, the reverse is the case in the United Kingdom. An in-depth analysis of this particular industry found that pharmaceutical companies tend to behave much more aggressively toward their competitors in the home market as opposed to foreign markets.[13]

In many markets, legitimate distributors of global brands need to compete with smugglers. Smuggling operations put downward pressure on the price of the affected product. The strength of private labels (store brands) is another important driver. In countries where store brands are well entrenched, companies are forced to accept lower margins than elsewhere.

A company's competitive position typically varies across countries. Companies will be price leaders in some countries and price takers in other countries. Heinz's policy is to cut prices in markets where it is not the leading brand.[14] Finally, the rules of the game usually differ. Non-price competition (e.g., advertising, channel coverage) may be preferable in some countries. Elsewhere, price combats are a way of life. For example, in Western countries, a price war is to be avoided at all costs. In contrast, Chinese companies often see a price war as a strategic weapon to grab market dominance.

Distribution Channels

Another driver behind global pricing is the distribution channel. The pressure exercised by channels can take many forms. Variations in trade margins and the length of the channels will influence the ex-factory price charged by the company. The balance of power between manufacturers and their distributors is another factor behind pricing practices. Countries such as France and the United Kingdom are characterized by large retailers who are able to order in bulk and to bargain for huge discounts with manufacturers. In the pan-European market, several smaller retailers have formed cross-border co-ops to strengthen their negotiation position with their common suppliers. The power of large-scale retailers in Europe is vividly illustrated by the hurdles that several manufacturers faced in implementing every-day-low-pricing (EDLP). With EDLP, the manufacturer offers consistently lower prices to the retailer (and the ultimate shopper) instead of promotional price discounts and trade promotions.[15] Several German supermarket chains de-listed P&G brands like Ariel, Vizir, and Lenor detergent products, and Bess toilet tissue when P&G introduced EDLP in Germany in early 1996.[16] Likewise, Delhaize,[17] a large Belgian grocery chain, removed about 300 Unilever products from its stores claiming that they were priced too high. The banished products included major brands such as Dove soap and Axe deodorant.[18]

Large cross-country price gaps open up arbitrage opportunities that lead to **parallel imports (gray markets)** from low-price countries to high-price ones (see Chapter 14). These parallel imports are commonly handled by unauthorized distributors at the expense of legitimate trade channels. To curtail parallel trade, firms can consider narrowing cross-border price disparities. Thus, pre-emption of cross-border bargain hunting is often times a strong motivation behind a company's pricing practices.

---

[13]Pradeep K. Chintagunta and Ramarao Desiraju, "Strategic Pricing and Detailing Behavior in International Markets," *Marketing Science* 24 (Winter 2005): 67–80.

[14]"Counting costs of dual pricing," *Financial Times*, July 9, 1990, p. 4.

[15]Trade promotions are promotions where the manufacturer offers monetary incentives to the channel (e.g., wholesalers, retailers) as a reward for activities (e.g., in-store displays, price discounts, advertising the manufacturer's product) that will stimulate the sales of the product. The most common trade promotion tools include off-invoice allowances (discount off the list price on the invoice) and extra cases of merchandise for channels who order a minimum amount.

[16]"Heat's on value pricing," *Advertising Age International* (January 1997): I-21, I-22.

[17]Delhaize also operates 1,500 stores in the United States, including the Food Lion chain.

[18]"Belgian Grocer Battles Unilever on Pricing," *Wall Street Journal Asia*, February 12, 2009, p. 16.

Government Policies

Even after the launch of the euro, car prices in the European Union can still vary by up to 50 percent. One of the main reasons for these car price disparities is the sales tax rate for new cars. These vary from as low as 15 percent in Luxembourg up to 200 percent in Denmark. This taxation gap also has an impact on pre-tax car prices. In fact, most carmakers in Europe subsidize the pre-tax prices in high-tax countries by charging more in low-tax countries.[19] Indeed, a 2006 European Commission report found that pre-tax prices were the lowest in Denmark, followed by Hungary. However, when taxes were included, cars in Denmark were the most expensive in Europe.[20]

Government policies can have a direct or indirect impact on pricing policies. Factors that have a direct impact include sales tax rates (e.g., value added taxes), tariffs, and price controls. Sometimes government interference is very blatant. The Chinese government sets minimum prices in scores of industries. The goal is to stamp out price wars and protect the Chinese economy against deflation pressures. Firms that ignore the pricing rules are slapped with hefty fines.[21]

An increase in the sales tax rate will usually lower overall demand. However, in some cases taxes may selectively affect imports. For instance, in the late 1980s, the U.S. government introduced a 10-percent luxury tax on the part of a car's price that exceeds $30,000. This luxury tax primarily affected the price of luxury import cars because few U.S.-made luxury cars sold for more than the $30,000 threshold. Tariffs obviously will inflate the retail price of imports. Another concern is price controls. These affect either the whole economy (for instance, in high-inflation countries) or selective industries. In many countries, a substantial part of the health care costs are borne by the government. Prices for reimbursable drugs are negotiated between the government authorities and the pharmaceutical company. Many pharmaceutical companies face the dilemma of accepting lower prices for their drugs or having their drugs registered on a negative list, which contains drugs that the government will not reimburse.[22] Furthermore, several governments heavily encourage the prescription of generics or stimulate parallel imports from low-price countries to put price pressure on drug companies. In the European Union, governments increasingly benchmark their prices against other member states and adjust them if necessary.[23] To sustain higher prices, manufacturers often launch new drugs in high-price markets first so that prices in these countries can be used as reference points.[24]

Aside from direct intervention, government policies can have an indirect impact on pricing decisions. For instance, huge government deficits spur interest rates (cost of capital), currency volatility, and inflation. The interplay of these factors will affect the product cost. Inflation might also impact labor costs in those countries (e.g., Belgium, Brazil) that have a wage indexation system. Such a system adjusts wages for increases in the cost of living.

Earlier we pinpointed the main factors that will drive global pricing decisions. We now highlight the key managerial issues in global pricing.

Managing Price Escalation

Exporting involves more steps and substantially higher risks than simply selling goods in the home market. To cover the incremental costs (e.g., shipping, insurance, tariffs, margins of various intermediaries), the final foreign retail price will often be much higher than the domestic retail

---

[19]"Car price disparities highlighted," *Financial Times*, January 7, 1999, p. 2.

[20]http://ec.europa.eu/taxation_customs/taxation/other_taxes/passenger_car/index_en.htm.

[21]"So Much for Competition," *Business Week (Asian edition)*, November 30, 1998, pp. 22–23.

[22]Some countries have a "positive" list of drugs from which physicians can prescribe.

[23]Neil Turner, "European Pricing Squeeze," *Pharmaceutical Executive* (October 2002): 84–91.

[24]David Hanlon and David Luery, "The Role of Pricing Research in Assessing the Commercial Potential of New Drugs in Development," *International Journal of Market Research* 44, no. 4 (2002): 423–447.

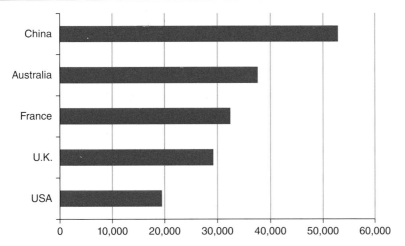

Exhibit 11-3 Retail Price Harley-Davidson Ultra Electric Glide (in US$ Equivalent)

Source: Harley-Davidson websites.

price. This phenomenon is known as **price escalation**. **Exhibit 11-3** provides an example of price escalation for one of Harley-Davidson's popular motorcycle models. Note that the huge price tag for Harleys sold in China is mainly due to the hefty 50 percent import duty. As a result, Harleys can be much more expensive than German luxury sedans manufactured in China. Price escalation raises two questions that management needs to confront: (1) Will our foreign customers be willing to pay the inflated price for our product ("sticker shock")? And (2) will this price make our product less competitive? If the answer is negative, the exporter needs to decide how to cope with price escalation.

There are two broad approaches to deal with price escalation: (1) find ways to cut the export price or (2) position the product as a (super) premium brand. Several options exist to lower the export price:[25]

1. **Rearrange the distribution channel.** Channels are often largely responsible for price escalation, either due to the length of the channel (number of layers between manufacturer and end-user) or because of exorbitant margins. In some circumstances, it is possible to shorten the channel. Alternatively, firms could look into channel arrangements that provide cost efficiencies. In recent years, several U.S. companies have decided to penetrate the Japanese consumer market through direct marketing (e.g., catalog sales, telemarketing, selling through the internet). This allows them to bypass the notorious Japanese distribution infrastructure and become more price-competitive.

2. **Eliminate costly features (or make them optional).** Several exporters have addressed the price escalation issue by offering no-frills versions of their product. Rather than having to purchase the entire bundle, customers can buy the core product and then decide whether or not they want to pay extra for optional features.

3. **Downsize the product.** Another route to dampen sticker shock is downsizing the product by offering a smaller version of the product or a lesser count.[26] This option is only desirable when consumers are not aware of cross-border volume differences. To that end, manufacturers may decide to go for a local branding strategy.

---

[25]S. Tamer Cavusgil, "Unraveling the Mystique of Export Pricing," *Business Horizons* (May–June 1988): 56.
[26]Loyal Coca-Cola cross-border travelers may have noticed can-size differences of their favorite tipple. For instance, for Diet Coke, can sizes range from 325 ml (e.g., Malaysia, Thailand) up to 355 ml (U.S.A.).

4. **Assemble or manufacture the product in foreign markets.** A more extreme option is to assemble or even manufacture the entire product in foreign markets (not necessarily the export market). Closer proximity to the export market will lower transportation costs. To lessen import duties for goods sold within European Union markets, numerous firms have decided to set up assembly operations in EU member states. Due to high tariffs for motorbikes imported in India, Harley-Davidson decided to set up an assembly facility for bikes to be sold in that market. Still, companies need to be careful with relocation decisions. U.S.-based fans of Beck's, a German pilsner, in the United States heavily criticized AB-InBev, the brand's owner, for no longer importing the brand from Germany but instead brewing it locally in St. Louis along with Budweiser. Customers deplored the fact that they have to pay the full-import price for a beer that did not taste as good as the German original.[27]

5. **Adapt the product to escape tariffs or tax levies.** Finally, a company could also modify its export product to bring it into a different tariff or tax bracket. When the United States levied a new 10 percent tax on over $30,000 luxury cars, Land Rover increased the maximum weight of Range Rover models sold in America to 6,019 pounds. As a result, the Range Rover was classified as a truck (not subject to the 10 percent luxury tax) rather than a luxury car.

These measures represent different ways to counter price escalation. Alternatively, an exporter could exploit the price escalation situation and go for a premium positioning strategy. LEGO, the Danish toymaker, sells building block sets in India that are priced between $6 and $223, far more than most other toys that Indian parents can purchase. To justify the premium price, LEGO uses a marketing strategy that targets middle-class parents and stresses the educational value of LEGO toys.[28] Of course, for this strategy to work, other elements of the export marketing-mix should be in tandem with the premium positioning. In Europe and Japan, Levi Strauss sells its jeans mainly in upscale boutiques rather than in department stores.[29]

Pricing in Inflationary Environments

When McDonald's opened its doors in January 1990, a Big Mac meal (including fries and a soft drink) in Moscow cost 6 rubles. Three years later, the same meal cost 1,100 rubles.[30] Rampant inflation is a major obstacle to doing business in many countries. Moreover, high inflation rates are usually coupled with highly volatile exchange rate movements. In such environments, price setting and stringent cost control become extremely crucial. Not surprisingly, in such markets, companies' financial divisions are often far more important than other departments.[31]

There are several alternative ways to safeguard against inflation

1. **Modify components, ingredients, parts, and/or packaging materials.** Some ingredients are subject to lower inflation rates than others. This might justify a change in the ingredient mix. Of course, before implementing such a move, the firm should consider all its consequences (e.g., consumer response, impact on shelf life of the product).

2. **Source materials from low-cost suppliers.** Supply management plays a central role in high inflation environments. A first step is to screen suppliers and determine which ones would be most cost efficient without cutting corners. If feasible, materials could be imported from low-inflation countries. Note, however, that high inflation rates are coupled with a weakening currency. This will push up the price of imports.

[27]"The Plot to Destroy America's Beer," http://www.businessweek.com, accessed January 12, 2013.
[28]"LEGO building its way to China," *Advertising Age International*, March 20, 1995, p. I-29.
[29]"The Levi straddle," *Forbes*, January 17, 1994, p. 44.
[30]"Inflation bits Russians, who still bite into Big Mac," *Advertising Age International*, March 15, 1993, I-3, I-23.
[31]"A rollercoaster out of control," *Financial Times*, February 22, 1993.

3. **Shorten credit terms.** In some cases, profits can be realized by juggling the terms of payment. For instance, a firm that is able to collect cash from its customers within 15 days, but has one month to pay its suppliers, can invest its money during the 15-day grace period. Thus, firms strive to push up the lead time in paying their suppliers. At the same time, they also try to shorten the time to collect from their clients.[32]

4. **Include escalator clauses in long-term contracts.** Many business-to-business marketing situations involve long-term contracts (e.g., leasing arrangements). To hedge their position against inflation, the parties will include escalator clauses that will provide the necessary protection.

5. **Quote prices in a stable currency.** To handle high inflation, companies often quote prices in a stable currency such as the U.S. dollar or the euro.

6. **Pursue rapid inventory turnovers.** High inflation also mandates rapid inventory turnarounds. As a result, information technologies (e.g., scanning techniques, computerized inventory tracking) that facilitate rapid inventory turnovers or even just-in-time delivery will yield a competitive advantage.

7. **Draw lessons from other countries.** Operations in countries with a long history of inflation offer valuable lessons for ventures in other high-inflation countries. Cross-fertilization by drawing from experience in other high inflation markets often helps. Some companies— McDonald's[33] and Otis Elevator International,[34] for example—relied on expatriate managers from Latin America to cope with inflation in the former Soviet Union. Inspired by its experience in Brazil, McDonald's decided to negotiate separate inflation rates with each supplier. These rates were then used for monthly realignments, instead of the government's published inflation figures.

To combat hyperinflation, governments occasionally impose price controls (usually coupled with a wage freeze). For instance, Brazil went through five price freezes over a six-year interval. Such temporary price caps could be selective, targeting certain products, but, in extreme circumstances, they will apply across-the-board to all consumer goods. Price freezes have proven to be very ineffective to dampen inflation—witness the experience of Brazil. Often, expectations of an imminent price freeze start off a rumor mill that will spur companies to implement substantial price increases, thereby setting off a vicious cycle. One consequence of price controls is that goods are diverted to the black market or smuggled overseas, leading to shortages in the regular market.

Companies faced with price controls can consider several action courses:

1. **Adapt the product line.** To reduce exposure to a government-imposed price freeze, companies diversify into product lines that are relatively free of price controls.[35] Of course, before embarking on such a changeover, the firm has to examine the long-term ramifications. Modifying the product line could imply loss of economies of scale, an increase in overheads, and adverse reactions from the company's customer base.

2. **Shift target segments or markets.** A more drastic move is to shift the firm's target segment. For instance, price controls often apply to consumer food products but not to animal-related products. So, a maker of corn-based consumer products might consider a shift from breakfast cereals to chicken-feed products. Again, such action should be preceded by a thorough analysis

---

[32]Ibid.

[33]"Inflation lessons over a Big Mac," *Financial Times*, February 22, 1993.

[34]"Russians up and down," *Financial Times*, October 18, 1993, p. 12.

[35]Venkatakrishna V. Bellur, Radharao Chaganti, Rajeswararao Chaganti, and Saraswati P. Singh, "Strategic Adaptations to Price Controls: The Case of the Indian Drug Industry," *Journal of the Academy of Marketing Science* 13, no. 1 (Winter 1985): 143–159.

of its strategic implications. Alternatively, a firm might consider using its operations in the high-inflation country as an export base for countries that are not subject to price controls.

3. **Launch new products or variants of existing products.** If price controls are selective, a company can navigate around them by systematically launching new products or modifying existing ones. Faced with price controls in Zimbabwe, bakers added raisins to their dough and called it "raisin bread," thereby, at least momentarily, escaping the price control for bread.[36] Also here, the firm should consider the overall picture by answering questions such as: Will there be a demand for these products? What are the implications in terms of manufacturing economies? Inventory management? How will the trade react? Furthermore, if these products are not yet available elsewhere, this option is merely a long-term solution.

4. **Negotiate with the government.** In some cases, firms are able to negotiate for permission to adjust their prices. Lobbying can be done individually, but is more likely to be successful on an industry-wide basis.

5. **Predict incidence of price controls.** Some countries have a history of price freeze programs. Given historical information on the occurrence of price controls and other economic variables, econometric models can be constructed to forecast the likelihood of price controls. Managers can use that information to see whether or not price adjustments are warranted, given the likelihood of an imminent price freeze.[37]

A drastic action course is simply to leave the country. Many consumer goods companies chose this option when they exited their South American markets during the 1980s. However, companies that hang on and learn to manage a high-inflation environment will be able to carry over their expertise to other countries. Furthermore, they will enjoy a competitive advantage (due to entry barriers such as brand loyalty, channel and supplier ties) versus companies that reenter these markets once inflation has been suppressed.

Global Pricing and Currency Fluctuations

Exchange rates reflect how much one currency is worth in terms of another currency. Due to the interplay of a variety of economic and political factors, exchange rates continuously float upward or downward. Given the sometimes-dramatic exchange rate movements, setting prices in a floating exchange rate world poses a tremendous challenge.[38] **Exhibit 11-4** lists several exporter strategies under varying currency regimes.

Currency Gain/Loss Pass Through

Two major managerial pricing issues result from currency movements: (1) How much of an exchange rate gain (loss) should be passed through to our customers? and (2) In what currency should we quote our prices? Let us first address the **pass-through** issue. Consider the predicament of American companies exporting to Japan. In principle, a weakening of the U.S. dollar versus the Japanese yen will strengthen the competitive position of U.S.-based exporters in Japan. A weak dollar allows U.S.-based firms to lower the yen-price of American goods exported to Japan. This enables American exporters to steal market share away from the local Japanese competitors without sacrificing profits. By the same token, a stronger U.S. dollar will undermine the

---

[36]"The Zimbabwean Model," *The Economist*, November 30, 2002, p. 72.
[37]James K. Weekly, "Pricing in Foreign Markets: Pitfalls and Opportunities," *Industrial Marketing Management* 21 (1992): 173–179.
[38]Llewlyn Clague and Rena Grossfield, "Export Pricing in a Floating Rate World," *Columbia Journal of World Business* (Winter 1974): 17–22.

Exhibit 11-4   Exporter Strategies Under Varying Currency Conditions

When Domestic Currency is WEAK . . .	*When Domestic Currency is STRONG . . .*
• Stress price benefits	• Engage in nonprice competition by improving quality, delivery, and aftersale service
• Costly features expand product line and add more	• Improve productivity and engage in vigorous cost reduction
• Shift sourcing and manufacturing to domestic market	• Shift sourcing and manufacturing overseas.
• Exploit export opportunities in all markets	• Give priority to exports to relatively strong-currency countries
• Conduct conventional cash-for-goods trade	• Deal in countertrade with weak-currency countries
• Use full-costing approach but use marginal-cost pricing to penetrate new/competitive markets	• Trim profit margins and use marginal-cost pricing
• Speed repatriation of foreign-earned income and collections	• Keep the foreign-earned income in host country, slow collections
• Minimize expenditures in local, host-country currency	• Maximize expenditure in local, host-country currency
• Buy needed services (advertising, insurance, transportation, etc.) in domestic market	• Buy needed services abroad and pay for them in local currency
• Minimize local borrowing	• Borrow money needed for expansion in local market
• Bill foreign customers in domestic currency	• Bill foreign customers in their own currency

Source: S. Tamer Cavusgil, "Unraveling the Mystique of Export Pricing," reprinted from *Business Horizons* (May–June 1988). Copyright 1988 by the Foundation for the School of Business at Indiana University. Used with permission.

competitive position of American exporters. When the dollar appreciates versus the yen, we have the mirror image of the previous situation: the retail price in yen of American exports goes up. As a result, American exporters might lose market share if they leave their ex-factory prices unchanged. To maintain their competitive edge, they may be forced to lower their ex-factory dollar prices. Of course, the ultimate impact on the exporter's competitive position will also depend on the impact of currency movements on the exporter's costs and the nature of the competition in the Japanese market. The benefits of a weaker dollar could be washed out when many parts are imported from Japan, because the weaker dollar will make these parts more expensive. When most of the competitors are U.S.-based manufacturers, changes in the dollar's exchange rate might not matter.

Let us illustrate these points with a numerical example. Consider the situation in **Exhibit 11-5**, which looks at the trade-offs a hypothetical U.S.-based exporter to Japan faces when the exchange rate between the U.S. dollar and the Japanese yen changes. In the example we assume a simple linear demand schedule:

$$\text{Demand (in units) in Japanese export market} = 2{,}000 - 50 \times \text{price (in millions of yen)}.$$

We also make an admittedly dubious assumption: our exporter does not face any costs (in other words, total revenues equal total profits). Initially, one U.S. dollar equals 100 yen, and the firm's total export revenue is $55.5 million. Suppose now that the U.S. dollar has strengthened by 30 percent versus the Japanese yen, moving from an exchange rate of 100 yen to 1 US$ to a 130-to-1 exchange rate (row 2 in Exhibit 11-5). If the US$ ex-factory price remains the same (i.e., $30,000), Japanese consumers will face a 30 percent price increase. Total demand decreases (from 1,850 units to 1,805 units), and US$ revenue drops by $1.35 m.

Exhibit 11-5   A Numerical Illustration of Pass-Through and Local Currency Stability

Demand in Japan (Units) = 2000 − 50 × Price (in Yen)[*]
Costs = $0.0

Panel A: 100% Pass-through

Exchange Rate	Unit Price in US$	Unit Price in Yen[*]	Units Sold	US$ Revenue[*]
100 yen = $1	$30,000	3.0	1,850	$55.50
130 yen = $1	30,000	3.9	1,805	54.15
70 yen = $1	30,000	2.1	1,895	56.85

Panel B: Local Currency Price Stability (in millions except units sold)

Exchange Rate	Unit Price in US$	Unit Price in Yen[*]	Units Sold	US$ Revenue[*]	Revenue Gain(Loss) vs. 100% PT[*]
100 yen = $1	$30,000	3.0	1,850	$55.50	$0.00
130 yen = $1	23,077	3.0	1,850	42.69	(11.45)
70 yen = $1	42,857	3.0	1,850	79.28	22.45

[*] In millions.

Our American exporter faces the problem of whether or not to pass through exchange rate losses, and if so, how much of the loss he should absorb. If our exporter does not lower the U.S. dollar ex-factory price, he is likely to lose market share to his Japanese (and/or European) competitors in Japan. Thus, to sustain his competitive position, the U.S.-based manufacturer would be forced to lower his ex-factory price. In this situation, American exporters face the trade-off between sacrificing short-term profits (maintaining price) and sustaining long-term market share in export markets (cutting ex-factory price). For example, in the extreme case, the U.S. firm might consider sustaining the yen-based retail price (i.e., 3 million yen). In that case, US$ revenues would decline by $11.45 million.

Generally speaking, the appropriate action will depend on the following factors: (1) customers' price sensitivity, (2) the size of the export market, (3) the impact of the dollar appreciation on the firm's cost structure, (4) the amount of competition in the export market, and (5) the firm's strategic orientation. The higher consumers' price sensitivity in the export market, the stronger the case for lowering the ex-factory price. One route to lower price sensitivity is by investing in brand equity. High brand equity provides a buffer to global price competition. With vast markets such as the United States, firms are usually more inclined to absorb currency losses than with smaller countries. A decline in costs resulting from the strengthening of the U.S. dollar (e.g., when many parts are imported from Japan) broadens the price adjustment latitude. The more intense the competition in the export market, the stronger the pressure to cut prices. The fifth factor is the firm's strategic orientation. Firms could be market-share-oriented or focus on short-term profits. Naturally, market-share-oriented firms would tend to pass through less of the cost increase than their financial performance-oriented counterparts.[39] The bottom row of Exhibit 11-5 shows what happens when the U.S. dollar weakens by 30 percent. In that case we have the mirror picture of the previous scenario.

---

[39]Terry Clark, Masaaki Kotabe, and Dan Rajaratnam, "Exchange Rate Pass-Through and International Pricing Strategy: A Conceptual Framework and Research Propositions," *Journal of International Business Studies* 30 (Second Quarter 1999): 249–268.

Exhibit 11-6 Retail Price Changes During Dollar Appreciations: Japanese and German Exports to the U.S. Market

Model	Real Dollar Appreciation	Real Retail Price Change in U.S. Market
Honda Civic 2-Dr. Sedan	39%	−7%
Datsun 200 SX 2-Dr.	39	−10
Toyota Cressida 4-Dr.	39	6
BMW 320i 2-Dr.	42	−8
BMW 733i 4-Dr.	42	−17
Mercedes 300 TD Sta. Wgn.	42	−39

Note: The dollar appreciation measures the movement of the U.S. producer price index relative to the Japanese and German producer price indices converted into dollars by the nominal exchange rate. The real retail price change measures the movement of the dollar retail price of specific auto models relative to the retail unit value of all domestically produced cars.

Source: Reprinted from Joseph A. Gagnon and Michael M. Knetter, "Markup Adjustment and Exchange Rate Fluctuations: Evidence from Panel Data on Automobile Exports," *Journal of International Money and Finance* 14, no. 2 (1995): 304. Copyright 1995, with kind permission from Elsevier Science Ltd., Langford Lane, Kidlington OX5 IGB, UK.

American exporters might lower their markups much higher in price-conscious export markets than in price-insensitive markets. This type of destination-specific adjustment of markup in response to exchange-rate movement is referred to as **pricing-to-market (PTM).** PTM behaviors differ across source countries. One study of export pricing adjustments in the U.S. automobile market contrasted pricing decisions of Japanese and German exporters over periods where both the Japanese yen and the German mark depreciated against the U.S. dollar.[40] The results of the study showed that there was much more pass-through (and less PTM) by German exporters than by their Japanese rivals (see **Exhibit 11-6**).

Playing the PTM game carries certain risks. Frequent adjustments of prices in response to currency movements will distress local channels and customers. When local currency prices move up, foreign customers may express their disapproval by switching to other brands. On the other hand, when prices go down, it will often be hard to raise prices in the future. Therefore, often, the preferred strategy is to adjust mark-ups in such a way that local currency prices remain fairly stable. This special form of PTM has been referred to as **local-currency price stability (LCPS)**, where markups are adjusted to stabilize prices in the buyer's currency.[41] A case in point is Heineken's pricing policy in the United States. In the three-year period since January 2002, the U.S. dollar lost about a third of its value against the euro. However, the U.S. wholesale price of Heineken and Amstel Light had been increased just twice during the same period, each time by a tiny 2.5 percent. U.S. beer drinkers' gain was Heineken's pain. According to analysts Heineken's annual operating profit from the United States must have fallen from €357 million to €119 million between 2002 and 2006.[42] The bottom panel of **Exhibit 11-5** reports the revenue losses or gains of an exporter who maintains LCPS. To pass through exchange rate gains from U.S. dollar devaluations, U.S.-based exporters could resort to temporary price promotions or other incentives (e.g., trade deals) rather than a permanent cut of the local currency regular price.

---

[40]Joseph A. Gagnon and Michael M. Knetter, "Markup adjustment and exchange rate fluctuations: Evidence from panel data on automobile exports," *Journal of International Money and Finance* 14, no. 2 (1995): 289–310.

[41]Michael M. Knetter, "International Comparisons of Pricing-to-Market Behavior," *American Economic Review* 83, no. 3): 473–486.

[42]"Taking the Hit: European Exporters Find the Dollar's Weakness Is Hard to Counter," *Financial Times* (May 3, 2005): 11.

Currency Quotation

Another pricing concern that ensues from floating exchange rates centers on which currency unit is to be used in international business transactions. Sellers and buyers usually prefer a quote in their domestic currency. That way, the other party will have to bear currency risks. The decision largely depends on the balance of power between the supplier and the customer. Whoever yields will need to cover currency exposure risk through hedging transactions on the forward exchange market. A survey of currency choice practices of Swedish, Finnish, and American firms found that firms using foreign currencies have higher export volumes and transaction values than exporters using their home currency. However, profit margins can suffer.[43] Some firms have decided to use a common currency for all their business transactions, world- or region-wide. In the wake of the euro, companies such as Siemens have switched to a euro-regime both for their internal (e.g., transfer pricing) and external (suppliers and distributors) transactions.

Transfer Pricing
Determinants of Transfer Prices

Most large multinational corporations have a network of subsidiaries spread across the globe. Sales transactions between related entities of the same company can be quite substantial, involving trade of raw materials, components, finished goods, or services. **Transfer prices** are prices charged for such transactions. Transfer pricing decisions in an international context need to balance off the interests of a broad range of stakeholders: (1) parent company, (2) local country managers, (3) host government(s), (4) domestic government, and (5) joint venture partner(s) when the transaction involves a partnership. Not surprisingly, reconciling the conflicting interests of these various parties can be a mind-boggling juggling act.

A number of studies have examined the key drivers behind transfer pricing decisions. One survey of U.S.-based multinationals found that transfer pricing policies were primarily influenced by the following factors (in order of importance):

1. Market conditions in the foreign country

2. Competition in the foreign country

3. Reasonable profit for foreign affiliate

4. U.S. federal income taxes

5. Economic conditions in the foreign country

6. Import restrictions

7. Customs duties

8. Price controls

9. Taxation in the foreign country

10. Exchange controls[44]

---

[43]Saeed Samiee and Patrik Anckar, "Currency Choice in Industrial Pricing: A Cross-National Evaluation," *Journal of Marketing* 62 (July 1998): 112–127.

[44]Jane Burns, "Transfer Pricing Decisions in U.S. Multinational Corporations," *Journal of International Business Studies* 11, no. 2 (Fall 1980): 23–39.

Other surveys have come up with different rankings.[45] However, a recurring theme appears to be the importance of market conditions (especially, the competitive situation), taxation regimes, and various market imperfections (e.g., currency control, custom duties, price freeze). Generally speaking, MNCs should consider the following criteria when making transfer-pricing decisions:[46]

- **Tax regimes.** Ideally, firms would like to boost their profits in low-tax countries and dampen them in high-tax countries. To shift profits from high-tax to low-tax markets, companies would set transfer prices as high as possible for goods entering high-tax countries and vice-versa for low-tax countries. However, manipulating transfer prices to exploit corporate tax rate differentials will undoubtedly alert the tax authorities in the high-tax rate country and, in the worst case, lead to a tax audit. Most governments impose rules on transfer pricing to ensure a fair division of profits between businesses under common control. We will revisit the taxation issue shortly.

- **Local market conditions.** Another key influence is local market conditions. Examples of market-related factors include the market share of the affiliate, the growth rate of the market, and the nature of local competition (e.g., nonprice- versus price-based). To expand market share in a new market, multinationals may initially underprice intra-company shipments to a start-up subsidiary.[47]

- **Market imperfections.** Market imperfections in the host country, such as price freezes and profit repatriation restrictions, hinder the multinational's ability to move earnings out of the country. Under such circumstances, transfer prices can be used as a mechanism to get around these obstacles. Also, high import duties might prompt a firm to lower transfer prices charged to subsidiaries located in that particular country.

- **Joint venture partner.** When the entity concerned is part of a joint venture, parent companies should also factor in the interests of the local joint venture partner. Numerous joint venture partnerships have hit the rocks partly because of disputes over transfer pricing decisions.

- **Morale of local country managers.** Finally, firms should also be concerned about the morale of their local country managers. Especially when performance evaluation is primarily based on local profits, transfer price manipulations might distress country managers whose subsidiaries' profits are artificially deflated.

Setting Transfer Prices

There are two broad transfer-pricing strategies: market-based transfer pricing and non-market-based pricing. The first perspective uses the market mechanism as a cue for setting transfer prices. Such prices are usually referred to as **arm's length prices**. Basically, the company charges the price that any buyer outside the MNC would pay, as if the transaction had occurred between two unrelated companies (at "arm's length"). Tax authorities typically prefer this method to other transfer pricing approaches. Because an objective yardstick is used—the market price—transfer prices based on this approach are easy to justify to third parties (e.g., tax authorities). The major problem with arm's length transfer pricing is that an appropriate benchmark is often lacking, due to the absence of competition. This is especially the case for intangible services. Many services are only available within the multinational. A high-stakes dispute between the U.S. Internal Revenue Service (IRS) and GlaxoSmithKline PLC, the British pharmaceuticals company, vividly illustrates

[45]See, for example, Seung H. Kim and Stephen W. Miller, "Constituents of the International Transfer Pricing Decision," *Columbia Journal of World Business* (Spring 1979): 71.

[46]S. Tamer Cavusgil, "Pricing for Global Markets," *Columbia Journal of World Business* (Winter 1996): 66–78.

[47]Mohammad F. Al-Eryani, Pervaiz Alam, and Syed H. Akhter, "Transfer Pricing Determinants of U.S. Multinationals," *Journal of International Business Studies* 21 (Third Quarter 1990): 409–425.

the issue of valuing intangibles.[48] According to the IRS, Glaxo's U.S. subsidiary overpaid its European parent for the royalties associated with scores of drugs, including its blockbuster Zantac drug. Glaxo allegedly had overvalued the drugs' R&D costs in Britain and undervalued the value of marketing activities in the United States, thereby artificially cutting the U.S. subsidiary's profits and tax liabilities. Glaxo vehemently denied this charge. As you can see, the case centered on the issue of where value is created and where credit is due—on the marketing or on the R&D front?

Non-market-based pricing covers various policies that deviate from market-based pricing, the most prominent ones being **cost-based pricing** and **negotiated pricing**. Cost-based pricing simply adds a markup to the cost of the goods. Issues here revolve around getting a consensus on a "fair" profit split and allocation of corporate overhead. Further, tax authorities often do not accept cost-based pricing procedures. Another form of nonmarket based pricing is negotiated transfer prices. Here conflicts between country affiliates are resolved through negotiation of transfer prices. This process may lead to better cooperation among corporate divisions.[49]

One study showed that compliance with financial reporting norms, fiscal and custom rules, and anti-dumping regulations prompt companies to use market-based transfer pricing.[50] Government-imposed market constraints (e.g., import restrictions, price controls, exchange controls) favor nonmarket-based transfer pricing methods. To the question, "Which procedure works best?" the answer is pretty murky: there is no "universally optimal" system.[51] In fact, most firms use a mixture of market-based and nonmarket pricing procedures.

Minimizing the Risk of Transfer Pricing Tax Audits[52]

Cross-country tax rate differentials encourage many MNCs to set transfer prices that shift profits from high-tax to low-tax countries to minimize their overall tax burden. This practice is sometimes referred to as international tax arbitrage. At the same time, MNCs need to comply with the tax codes of their home country and the host countries involved. Non-compliance may risk accusations of tax evasion and lead to tax audits. In January 2004, GlaxoSmithKline, the pharmaceuticals company, was presented with a $5.2 billion bill for extra taxes and interest by the US government following an investigation of the firm's transfer pricing policies. According to one estimate, the total tax loss in the United States due to "creative" transfer pricing was $53 billion in 2001.[53] Therefore, the issue that MNCs face can be stated as follows: How do we as a company draw the line between setting transfer prices that maximize corporate profits and compliance with tax regulations?

To avoid walking on thin ice, experts suggest setting transfer prices that are as close as possible to the Basic Arm's Length Standard (BALS). This criterion is now accepted by tax authorities worldwide as the international standard for assessing transfer prices. In practice, there are three methods to calculate a BALS price: comparable/uncontrollable price, resale price, and cost-plus. The first rule—comparable/uncontrollable—states that the parent company should compare the transfer price of its "controlled" subsidiary to the selling price charged by an independent seller to an independent buyer of similar goods or services. The problem is that such "comparable products" are often not around. The resale price method determines the BALS by subtracting the gross margin

---

[48]"Glaxo Faces Allegations of Tax Underpayment in U.S.," *Asian Wall Street Journal*, December 8, 2002, p. A7.

[49]R. Ackelsberg and G. Yukl, "Negotiated Transfer Pricing and Conflict Resolution in Organization," *Decision Sciences* (July 1979): 387–398.

[50]M. F. Al-Eryani, et al., "Transfer Pricing Determinants," p. 422.

[51]Jeffrey S. Arpan, "International Intracorporate Pricing: Non-American Systems and Views," *Journal of International Business Studies* (Spring 1972): 18.

[52]This section is based on John P. Fraedrich and Connie Rae Bateman, "Transfer Pricing by Multinational Marketers: Risky Business," *Business Horizons* (Jan.–Feb. 1996): 17–22.

[53]"A Big Squeeze for Governments: How Transfer Pricing Threatens Global Tax Revenues," *Financial Times*, July 22, 2004, p. 11.

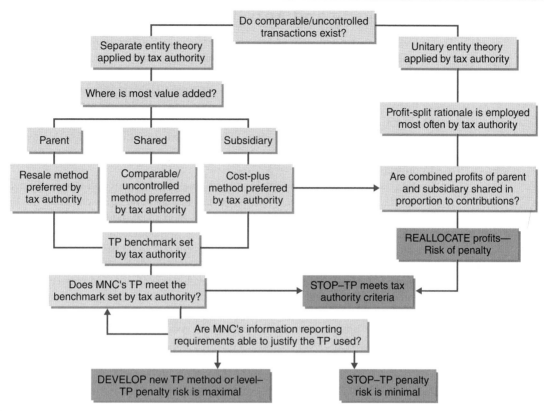

Exhibit 11-7 Decision-Making Model for Assessing Risk of TP Strategy

Source: John P. Fraedrich and Connie Rae Bateman, "Transfer Pricing by Multinational Marketers: Risky Business." Reprinted from *Business Horizon*, January–February 1996 by the Foundation for the School of Business at Indiana University. Used with permission.

percentage used by comparable independent buyers from the final third-party sales price. Finally, the cost-plus method fixes the BALS by adding the gross profit mark-up percentage earned by comparable companies performing similar functions to the production costs of the controlled manufacturer or seller. Note that this rule is somewhat different from the cost method that we discussed earlier because, strictly speaking, the latter method does not rely on mark-ups set by third parties. The OECD has drawn up guidelines on transfer pricing that cover complex taxation issues. The latest version of these rules is presented in *Transfer Pricing Guidelines for Multinational Enterprises and for Tax Administrations.*[54]

Exhibit 11-7 gives a flowchart that can be used to devise transfer-pricing strategies that minimize the risk of tax audits. Decisions center around the following five questions:

1. Do comparable/uncontrolled transactions exist?

2. Where is the most value added? Parent? Subsidiary?

3. Are combined profits of parent and subsidiary shared in proportion to contributions?

4. Does the transfer price meet the benchmark set by the tax authorities?

5. Does the MNC have the information to justify the transfer prices used?

---

[54] A copy (hard or soft) of the guidelines can be ordered at the OECD's website: http://www.oecd.org/tax/transfer-pricing/transfer-pricing-guidelines.htm.

Global Pricing and Anti-dumping Regulation

The anti-dumping laws that most governments use to counter dumping practices present a potential minefield for global pricing policies. **Dumping** occurs when imports are being sold at an unfair price. To protect local producers against the encroachment of low-priced imports, governments may levy countervailing duties or fines. Thus, it is important for exporters to realize that pricing policies, such as penetration pricing, may trigger anti-dumping actions. The number of anti-dumping initiatives has become staggering in recent years. Most of the action takes place in the United States and the European Union. However, anti-dumping cases are increasingly initiated in Japan, India, and other developing countries. Economists often refer to this trend as a rise in protectionism.[55]

Several possible reasons can explain the growing popularity of anti-dumping litigation. The removal of traditional trade barriers (tariffs, quotas) has encouraged several countries to switch to non-tariff barriers such as anti-dumping to protect their local industries. A World Bank study showed that the impact of dumping duties in the U.S. manufactured goods sector has boosted average tariffs in that sector from a nominal 6 percent rate to 23 percent.[56] There is also a huge imbalance between plaintiffs (local producer[s]) and defendants (importer[s]) in anti-dumping cases. Plaintiffs typically face no penalties for frivolous complaints. Moreover, plaintiffs clearly have a home advantage (local legislation, local judge).[57] Anti-dumping action is often utilized as a tactical tool to foster voluntary export restraints (VER). These are limits imposed by the company's home government on the amount of goods that can be exported to the country that wants to protect its local industry. Foreign competitors, faced with the prospect of anti-dumping action, may decide to fall back on VERs as the lesser of two evils.[58] Finally, the concept of a "fair" price is usually pretty murky. U.S. trade law defines dumping to occur when imports are sold below the home-country price (price discrimination) or when the import price is less than the "constructed value" or average cost of production ("pricing below cost"). Either concept can be very vague. In some situations, the imported good is not sold in the home country so that no basis of comparison exists (absence of domestic price).

Anti-dumping actions will persist in the future. Multinationals need to take anti-dumping laws into account when determining their global pricing policy. Aggressive pricing may trigger anti-dumping measures and, thus, jeopardize the company's competitive position. Global companies should also monitor changes in anti-dumping legislation and closely track anti-dumping cases in their particular industry.

To minimize risk exposure to anti-dumping actions, exporters might pursue any of the following marketing strategies:[59]

- **Trading-up.** Move away from low-value to high-value products via product differentiation. Most Japanese carmakers have stretched their product line upwards to tap into the upper-tier segments of their export markets.

- **Service enhancement.** Exporters can also differentiate their product by adding support services to the core product. Both moves—trading up and service enhancement—are basically attempts to move away from price competition, thereby making the exporter less vulnerable to dumping accusations.

---

[55]Jagdish Bhagwati, *Protectionism* (Cambridge: The MIT Press, 1988), Chapter 3.

[56]"Negotiators down in the dumps over US draft," *Financial Times*, November 25, 1993, p. 6.

[57]J. Bhagwati, *Protectionism*, pp.48–49.

[58]James E. Anderson, "Domino Dumping, I: Competitive Exporters," *American Economic Review* 82, no. 1 (March 1992): 65–83.

[59]Michel M. Kostecki, "Marketing Strategies between Dumping and Anti-dumping Action," *European Journal of Marketing* 25, no. 12 (1991): 7–19.

- **Distribution and communication.** Other initiatives on the distribution and communication front of the marketing mix include (1) the establishment of communication channels with local competitors, (2) entering into cooperative agreements with them (e.g., strategic alliances), or (3) reallocation of the firm's marketing efforts from vulnerable products (that is, those most likely to be subjected to dumping scrutiny) to less sensitive products.

Price Coordination

When developing a global pricing strategy, one of the thorniest issues is how much coordination should exist between prices charged in different countries. This issue is especially critical for global (or regional) brands that are marketed with no or very few cross-border variations. Economics dictate that firms should price discriminate between markets such that overall profits are maximized. So, if (marginal) costs were roughly equivalent, multinationals would charge relatively low prices in highly price sensitive countries and high prices in insensitive markets. Unfortunately, reality is not that simple. In most cases, markets cannot be perfectly separated. Huge cross-country price differentials will encourage gray markets where goods are shipped from low-price to high-price countries by unauthorized distributors. Thus, some coordination will usually be necessary. In deciding how much coordination, several considerations matter:

1. **Nature of customers.** When information on prices travels fast across borders, it is fairly hard to sustain wide price gaps. Under such conditions, firms will need to make a convincing case to their customers to justify price disparities. With global customers (e.g., multinational clients in business-to-business transactions), price coordination definitely becomes a must. General Motors applies "global enterprise pricing" for many of the components it purchases. Under this system, suppliers are asked to charge the same universal price worldwide.[60] In Europe, Microsoft sets prices that differ by no more than 5 percent between countries due to pressure from bargain-hunting multinational customers.[61] However, pharmaceutical firms often adopt tiered or differential pricing in developing countries. To make drugs or vaccines affordable in these countries, companies such as GlaxoSmithKline or Sanofi sell their products far below the prices they charge in more developed markets (see **Global Perspective 11-1**).

2. **Amount of product differentiation.** The amount of coordination also depends on how well differentiated the product is across borders. Obviously, the less (cross-border) product differentiation, the larger the need for some level of price coordination and vice versa. Stains in Southern Europe differ from stains in Scandinavia because of different food habits. Also, the spin speed of washing machines varies across Europe. In cold, wet countries (e.g., Great Britain) the average spin speed is 1200 rpm—twice as fast as the 600-rpm speed of washers in Spain.[62] Henkel, the German conglomerate, adjusts the formula for its Persil laundry detergent brand to suit local market conditions. As a result, a detergent sold in one European country may not be suitable for washers elsewhere in Europe. Thus, product differentiation can pose a barrier for cross-border price comparison shopping.

3. **Nature of channels.** In a sense, distribution channels can be viewed as intermediate customers. Thus the same logic as for end consumers applies here: price coordination becomes critical when price information is transparent and/or the firm deals with cross-border distribution channels. Pricing discipline becomes mandatory when manufacturers have little control over their distributors.

---

[60]"GM Powertrain suppliers will see global pricing," *Purchasing*, February 12, 1998.

[61]"European Software-Pricing Formulas, Long Abstruse, Develop a Rationale," *Wall Street Journal*, June 11, 1993.

[62]"A Shopping Contest for the Euro," *Financial Times*, January 5/6, 2002, p. 7.

◆ ◆

Global Perspective 11-1

Glaxosmithkline Adopts Tiered Pricing for Drugs Sold in Africa

Africa has 24 percent of the world's health problems but just 1 percent of the budget. To ensure that drugs and vaccines are widely available to the continent's poor people, pharmaceutical companies such as GlaxoSmithKline (GSK) and Sanofi have adopted "tiered pricing" schemes. This means that these firms set prices for drugs sold to governments in poor African countries far below the prices charged for such drugs in the West.

GSK's least developed countries (LDC) unit charges no more than a quarter of the UK price for the firm's patented drugs. Its off-patent drugs that compete with generics are usually sold at a small premium to the cheapest Indian-made generics. In an interview with Reuters, Duncan Learmouth, the head of GSK's LDC unit, said: "We're real optimists. Not all the least developed countries will be LDCs for ever and

now is a really good time to invest to build a GSK footprint that benefits patients today and benefits our business in the longer term."

The tiered pricing approach brings some challenges. Local African distributors could be reluctant to accept lower profits for the drugs they sell. An ever bigger challenge is that some middlemen might re-export drugs from cheaper African countries to higher-priced markets in the West. Also, governments of richer countries might insist on matching discount for drugs to be sold in their region using the price charged in poor countries as a reference price.

Sources: "GSK to Discount Price of Vaccine in Africa," *Financial Times*, November 19, 2010, p. 19; "Drugmaker GSK Chases Volume over Profit in Africa," http://www.reuters.com, accessed January 13, 2013.

4. **Nature of competition.** In many industries, firms compete with the same rivals in a given region, if not worldwide. Global competition demands a cohesive strategic approach for the entire marketing mix strategy, including pricing. From that angle, competition pushes companies toward centralized pricing policies. On the other hand, price changes made by competitors in the local market often require a rapid response. Should the subsidiary match a given price cut? If so, to what extent? Local subsidiaries often have much better information about the local market conditions to answer such questions than corporate or regional headquarters. Thus, the need for alertness and speedy response to competitive pricing moves encourages a decentralized approach toward pricing decisions.

5. **Market integration.** When markets integrate, barriers to cross-border movement of goods come down. Given the freedom to move goods from one member state to another, the pan-European market offers little latitude for perfect price discrimination.[63] Many of the transaction costs plaguing parallel imports that once existed have now disappeared. In fact, the European Commission imposes heavy penalties against companies that try to limit gray market transactions. The Commission fined Volkswagen (VW) almost $110 million when it accused VW of competition abuses. VW had ordered its Italian dealers not to sell cars to citizens from outside Italy. Austrian and German shoppers tried to buy VW cars in Italy where they were 30 percent cheaper.[64]

---

[63]Wolfgang Gaul and Ulrich Lutz, "Pricing in International Marketing and Western European Economic Integration," *Management International Review* 34, no. 2, (1994): 101–124.
[64]"On the road to price convergence," *Financial Times*, November 12, 1998, p. 29.

Several multinationals doing business in the European Union harmonize their prices to narrow down price gaps between different member states. Mars and Levi Strauss reduced their pan-European price gaps to no more than 10 percent.[65]

6. **Internal organization.** The organization setup is another important influence. Highly decentralized companies pose a hurdle to price coordination efforts. In many companies, the pricing decision is left to the local subsidiaries. Moves to take away some of the pricing authority from country affiliates will undoubtedly spark opposition and lead to bruised egos. Just as with other centralization decisions, it is important to fine-tune performance evaluation systems, as necessary.

7. **Government regulation.** Government regulation of prices puts pressure on firms to harmonize their prices. A good example is the pharmaceutical industry. In many countries, multinationals need to negotiate the price for new drugs with the local authorities. Governments in the European Union increasingly use prices set in other EU member states as a cue for their negotiating position. This trend has prompted several pharmaceutical companies, such as GlaxoSmithKline (GSK), to negotiate a common EU price for new drugs.

Global-Pricing Contracts (GPCs)[66]

Increasingly, purchasers demand **global-pricing contracts** (GPCs) from their suppliers. There are several reasons behind the shift toward GPCs: centralized buying, information technology that provides improved price monitoring, standardization of products or services. GPCs, however, can also benefit suppliers: global customers can become showcase accounts; a GPC can offer the opening toward nurturing a lasting customer relationship; small suppliers can use GPCs as a differentiation tool to get access to new accounts.

However, before engaging in a GPC with a purchaser it is important to do your homework. To achieve successful GPC implementation, Narayandas and his colleague provide the following guidelines:

1. Select customers who want more than just the lowest price.

2. Align the supplier's organization with the customer's. Ideally, the supplier's account-management organization should mirror the client's procurement setup.

3. Hire global account managers who can handle diversity. Get team members who cannot just handle sales, but also market intelligence gathering, problem spotting, contract compliance monitoring.

4. Reward those global-account managers and local sales representatives who make the relationship work.

5. Allow for some price flexibility.

6. Build information systems to monitor the key variables (e.g., cost variations, competitive situation).

Aligning Pan-Regional Prices

In the late 1990s Procter & Gamble was facing a severe parallel imports situation in Russia for its Always feminine protection brand. The price for Always was much higher than in the other

---

[65]"Counting Costs of Dual Pricing in the Run-up to 1992," *Financial Times*, July 9, 1990, p. 4.
[66]This section benefited from Das Narayandas, John Quelch, and Gordon Swartz. "Prepare Your Company for Global Pricing," *Sloan Management Review* (Fall 2000): 61–70.

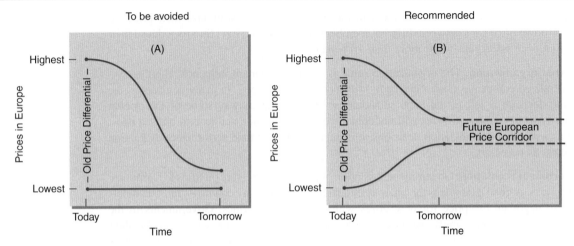

Exhibit 11-8   Pan-European Price Coordination

Courtesy Professor Hermann Simon

Central European countries, especially Poland from which most parallel imports originated. To resolve the problem, P&G lowered the price for Always in Russia and increased it in Poland so that the cross-border price variation became no more than 10 percent. Given the pressure toward increased globalization, some degree of price coordination often becomes very necessary. In some cases, firms set a uniform pricing formula that is applied by all affiliates. Elsewhere, coordination is limited to general rules that only indicate the desired pricing positioning (e.g., premium positioning, middle-of-the road positioning).

Simon and Kucher[67] propose a three-step procedure to align prices in regional markets with arbitrage opportunities. Pressure to narrow down price gaps could lead to two scenarios (see **Exhibit 11-8**). The disaster scenario (panel (A) in Exhibit 11-8) is a situation in which all prices sink to the lowest price. At the other extreme, companies may try to sustain cross-border price gaps. The desired scenario (panel (B) in Exhibit 11-8) tries to find the middle ground by upping prices in low-price countries and cutting them in high-price countries. To pursue this scenario, firms should set a **pricing corridor** within the region.

The procedure works as follows:

Step 1: *Determine optimal price for each country.* Find out what price schedules will maximize overall profits. Given information on the demand schedule and the costs incurred in each market, managers are able to figure out the desirable prices in the respective markets.

Step 2: *Find out whether parallel imports ("gray markets") are likely to occur at these prices.* Parallel imports arise when unauthorized distributors purchase the product (sometimes repackaged) in the low-price market and then ship it to high-price markets. The goal of step 2 is not to pre-empt parallel imports altogether but to boost profits to the best possible degree. Given the "optimal" prices derived in the first step, the manager needs to determine to what extent the proposed price schedule will foster parallel imports. Parallel imports become harmful insofar as they inflict damage on authorized distributors. They could also hurt the morale of the local sales force or country managers. Information is needed on the arbitrage costs of parallel importers. For instance, in the European drug industry, parallel importers target drugs with more than 20 percent price differentials. Conceivably, firms might decide to

---

[67]Hermann Simon and Eckhard Kucher, "The European Pricing Time Bomb—And How to Cope with It," *Marketing and Research Today* (February 1993): 25–36.

abandon (or not enter) small, low-price markets thereby avoiding pricing pressure on high-price markets. MNCs should also consider the pros and cons of non-pricing solutions to cope with parallel imports. Possible strategies include product differentiation, intelligence systems to measure exposure to gray markets, and creating negative perceptions in the mind of the end-user about parallel imports.[68] In 1996 P&G changed the name in Northern Europe for one of its cleaner products from *Viakal* to *Antikal* to fight parallel imports sourced from Italy where the product was 30 percent cheaper.

Step 3: *Set a pricing corridor.* If the "optimal" prices that were derived in Step 1 are not sustainable, firms need to narrow the gap between prices for high-price and low-price markets. Charging the same price across the board is not desirable. Such a solution would sacrifice company profits. Instead, the firm should set a pricing corridor. The corridor is formed by systematically exploring the profit impact from lowering prices in high-price countries and upping prices in low-price countries, as shown in panel (B) of Exhibit 11-8. The narrower the price gap, the more profits the firm has to sacrifice. At some point, there will be a desirable trade-off between the size of the gray market and the amount of profits sacrificed.

Of course, this method is not foolproof. Competitive reactions (e.g., price wars) need to be factored in. Also, government regulations may restrict pricing flexibility. Still, the procedure is a good start when pricing alignment becomes desirable.

Implementing Price Coordination

Global marketers can choose from four alternatives to promote price coordination within their organization, namely:[69]

1. **Economic Measures.** Corporate headquarters are able to influence pricing decisions at the local level via the transfer prices that are set for the goods that are sold to or purchased from the local affiliates. Another option is rationing, that is, headquarters sets upper limits on the number of units that can be shipped to each country. To sustain price differences, luxury marketers like Louis Vuitton set purchase limits for customers shopping at their European boutiques. Louis Vuitton products bought in Europe or Hawaii are often resold in Japan by discount stores as "loss leaders."

2. **Centralization.** In the extreme case, pricing decisions are made at corporate or regional headquarters level. Centralized price decision making is fairly uncommon, given its numerous shortcomings. It sacrifices the flexibility that firms often need to respond rapidly to local competitive conditions.

3. **Formalization.** Far more common than the previous approach is formalization where headquarters spells out a set of pricing rules that the country managers should comply with. Within these norms, country managers have a certain level of flexibility in determining their ultimate prices. One possibility is to set prices within specified boundaries; prices outside these bounds would need the approval from the global or regional headquarters.

4. **Informal Coordination.** Finally, firms can use various forms of informal price coordination. The emphasis here is on informing and persuading rather than prescribing and dictating. Examples of informal price coordination tactics include discussion groups and "best-practice" gatherings.

---

[68]Peggy A. Chaudhry and Michael G. Walsh, "Managing the Gray Market in the European Union: The Case of the Pharmaceutical Industry," *Journal of International Marketing* 3, no. 3 (1995): 11–33.

[69]Gert Assmus and Carsten Wiese, "How to Address the Gray Market Threat Using Price Coordination," *Sloan Management Review* (Spring 1995): 31–41.

Which one of these four approaches is most effective depends on the complexity of the environment in which the firm is doing business. When the environment is fairly stable and the various markets are highly similar, centralization is usually preferable over the other options. However, highly complex environments require a more flexible decentralized approach.

SUMMARY

Two types of mistakes can be made when setting the price in foreign markets: pricing the product too high and pricing it too low. When the price is set too high, customers will stay away from the firm's products. As a result, profits will be far less than they might have been. In India, Procter & Gamble's Ariel detergent brand initially created huge losses, partly because P&G charged a retail price far higher than Unilever's Surf Ultra.[70] Setting prices too low may also generate numerous pains. Local governments may cry foul and accuse the firm of dumping. Local customers may view the low price as a signal of low quality and avoid the product. Local competitors may interpret the low price as an aggressive move to grab market share and start a price war. When the price is far lower than in other markets, distributors (local and nonlocal) may spot an arbitrage opportunity, and ship the product from the low-price to your high-price markets, thereby creating a gray market situation. Making pricing decisions is one of the most formidable tasks that international marketers face. Many different elements influence global pricing decisions. Apart from the roles played by the 4 Cs (customers, competition, channels, and company), marketers also need to factor in the impact (direct or indirect) of local government decisions.

In this chapter, we covered the major global pricing issues that matter to marketers: export price escalation, inflation, currency movements, anti-dumping regulations, and price coordination. Even though pricing is typically a highly decentralized marketing decision, cross-border price coordination becomes increasingly a prime concern. We introduced several approaches through which international marketers can implement price coordination.

---

[70]"Ariel share gain puts P&G India through the wringer," *Advertising Age International*, November 8, 1993, pp. I-3, I-22.

QUESTIONS

1. How does competition in the foreign market affect your global pricing decisions?

2. What measures might exporters consider to protect themselves against anti-dumping accusations?

3. Company Yokurt plans to roll out a new premium yoghurt brand YO in Germany and Poland. Based on a market research study conducted in both countries, the firm found that the demand schedules in the 2 countries for YO would be:

$$\text{Poland}: \quad Q = 100 - 10\,P$$

and

$$\text{Germany}: \quad Q = 150 - 5\,P$$

where Q is the sales in units and P (in euros) is the price

   a. What would be the optimal price (i.e., profit maximizing; you can assume zero costs) for Poland? Germany? (Show all your calculations.)

   b. Suppose parallel importers target dairy products for which the price gap is more than €2. Applying the "pricing corridor" principles, what price would you set for YO in Poland? In Germany? Explain your decisions (e.g., you could sketch the pricing corridor for this example as was done in class—hint: use increments of €2).

   c. What could be the worst case scenario? Show how YO's profits would drop under such a scenario (calculate the profits for the "optimal," "pricing corridor," and "worst case scenario").

4. In Russia, Procter & Gamble markets Tide, its U.S. premium laundry detergent brand, as an economy brand with the slogan "Tide is a guarantee of clean clothes." Except for the brand name and the product category, all aspects of the products (formula, price, positioning) are different between the U.S. and the Russian product. What might be the rationale behind this strategy? Was this strategy a good idea?

COMMUNICATION STRATEGIES

12

CHAPTER OVERVIEW

1. Global advertising and culture

2. Setting the global advertising budget

3. Creative strategy

4. Global media decisions

5. Advertising regulations

6. Choosing an advertising agency

7. Other communication platforms

8. Globally integrated marketing communications (GIMC)

To promote its Temptations range of chocolates in India, Cadbury, the British chocolate maker, put out a print ad that was timed to coincide with India's Independence Day.[1] The ad showed a map of India with the words "Too good to share" printed across the state of Jammu and Kashmir. The reference to Kashmir, which is at the center of a longstanding dispute between India and Pakistan, did not please Hindu nationalists. Cadbury was forced to issue a statement apologizing for the advertisement. One of Procter & Gamble's biggest advertising blunders happened in Japan when the firm introduced its disposable diapers Pampers brand. Around that time, P&G aired a TV commercial in the United States showing an animated stork delivering Pampers diapers at home. P&G's American managers in Japan figured that this could be an excellent piece of advertising they could transplant into the Japanese market to back up the launch of Pampers. The copy was dubbed in Japanese and the Japanese package replaced the American one. Unfortunately, this cute commercial failed to seduce Japanese mothers. After some consumer research, P&G discovered that Japanese consumers were confused about why a bird was delivering disposable diapers. Contrary to Western folklore, storks in Japan are not supposed to deliver babies. Instead, babies allegedly arrive in giant peaches that float on the river to deserving parents.[2] After the blunder, P&G used a more relevant advertising model to promote

---

[1]"Anger over Kashmir Chocolate Ad," http://news.bbc.co.uk, August 21, 2002.

[2]The story goes as follows. A long time ago—in the Japan of the fourteenth century—an old man and his wife had been childless. They were very sad. When the old lady went to a nearby river to do the laundry, she saw a huge "momo" (peach) floating on the river. She brought it back home. And lo and behold, the peach suddenly broke into two halves and a baby came out from inside. They named this baby "Momotaro"—meaning: a boy from a peach.

Pampers to Japanese consumers: the testimonial of a nurse who also happens to be a mother—the "expert mom."[3] As both the Cadbury and the P&G cases illustrate, international advertising can prove to be very tricky.

The first part of this chapter will focus on global advertising. We first cover the cultural challenges that advertisers face. We examine the major international advertising planning decisions that marketers need to address. In particular, we cover budgeting and resource allocation issues, message strategy, and media decisions. One hurdle that advertisers face is the maze of advertising regulations across the world. We highlight the different types of regulations and discuss several mechanisms to cope with them. Next we address another important global advertising concern: advertising agency selection for foreign markets. The second part of this chapter explores other forms of communication tools that global marketers have access to.

Global Advertising and Culture

Advertising is to a large extent a cultural phenomenon. On the one hand, advertising shapes a country's popular culture. At the same time, the host country's culture may also influence the creation of an ad campaign and its effectiveness. As the P&G example in the introduction demonstrated, when advertising appeals are not in sync with the local culture, the ad campaign will falter. In the worst-case scenario, the ad might even stymie the advertised product's sales or damage the brand image. Effective ad campaigns also do a great job in leveraging local cultural phenomena. A TV ad created for Unilever's Vaseline brand in India is an excellent example.[4] The commercial shows the distress of a local woman buying shoes. As the woman prepares to try out a shoe, the salesman spots cracks in her feet and tells her that the shoe is not within her budget. An onscreen message then asks: "Why should someone peep in your life because of cracks in the skin of your feet?" An image of Vaseline cream follows, with the promise that it will soften hard skin and get rid of cracks. The ad cleverly plays on Indian women's embarrassment at (a) having cracked feet and (b) not being able to afford servants. Because most advertising has a major verbal component, we first look at the language barriers.

Language Barriers

Language is one of the most daunting barriers that international advertisers need to surmount. Numerous promotional efforts have misfired because of language-related mishaps. Apart from translation, another challenge is the proper interpretation of ideas. The IBM global slogan "Solutions for a Small Planet" became "small world" in Argentina as "planet" failed to convey the desired conceptual thrust there.[5] Given the bewildering variety of languages, advertising copy translation mistakes are easily made. One can identify three different types of translation errors: simple carelessness, multiple-meaning words, and idioms.[6] Some typical instances of translation blunders that can be ascribed to pure carelessness are the following examples:

Original slogan: "It takes a tough man to make a tender chicken."

Translation: "It takes a sexually excited man to make a chick affectionate."

---

[3]"Even at P&G, only 3 brands make truly global grade so far," *Advertising Age International* (January 1998): 8.

[4]"Vaseline plays on Indian women's embarrassment of not having a servant," http://www.adageglobal.com, accessed December 24, 2002.

[5]David A. Aaker and Erich Joachimsthaler, "The Lure of Global Branding," *Harvard Business Review* (Nov.-Dec. 1999): 144.

[6]David A. Ricks, *Blunders in International Business* (Cambridge, MA: Blackwell Publishers, 1993).

Original slogan: "Body by Fisher."

Translation: "Corpse by Fisher."

Original slogan: "When I used this shirt, I felt good."

Translation: "Until I used this shirt, I felt good."

The second group of translation mishaps relates to words that have multiple meanings. Consider a campaign ran by the Parker Pen Company in Latin America. When entering Latin America, Parker used a literal translation of a slogan the company was using in the United States: "Avoid embarrassment—use Parker Pens." The company translated embarrassed as *embarazada*. However this is a false cognate; *embarazada* does not mean embarrassed, it means pregnant. As a result, Parker was unconsciously advertising its products as a contraceptive.[7]

The third class of language-related advertising blunders stems from idioms or local slang. Idioms or expressions that use slang from one country may inadvertently lead to embarrassing meanings in another country. One U.S. advertiser ran a campaign in Britain that used the same slogan as the one that was used back home: "You can use no finer napkin at your dinner table." Unfortunately, in Britain, the word *napkin* means "diapers."[8] **Exhibit 12-1** lists the different words that Goodyear has singled out for saying *tires* in Spanish.

So, what can be done to overcome language barriers? One obvious solution is to involve local advertising agencies or translators in the development of your promotional campaigns. Their feedback and suggestions are often highly useful.

Another tactic is simply not to translate the slogan into the local language. Instead, the English slogan is used worldwide. The Swiss luxury watchmaker TAG Heuer used the tag line "Don't crack under pressure" without translating it in each of its markets, even Japan, where over 60 percent of the audience had no clue of the slogan's meaning.[9] Other examples of universally used slogans that were left untranslated are "You and us: UBS," "Coke is it," and "United Colors of Benetton." For TV commercials, one can add subtitles in the local language. This is exactly what the U.S. Meat Export Federation (USMEF) did with the "aisareru" beef or "desire beef" campaign in Japan.[10] The campaign was launched in March 2002 by the USMEF to deliver

Exhibit 12-1   Five Different Ways of Saying Tires in Spanish

Spanish Word for Tires	Countries Using Each Word
Cauchos	Venezuela
Cubiertas	Argentina
Gomas	Puerto Rico
Llantas	Mexico, Peru, Guatemala, Colombia, and elsewhere in Central America
Neumaticos	Chile

Source: D. A. Hanni, J. K. Ryans, Jr. and I. R. Vernon, "Coordinating International Advertising—The Goodyear Case Revisited for Latin America." This article originally appeared in *Journal of International Marketing* 3, no. 2 (1995), published by Michigan State University Press, p. 84.

---

[7]David A. Ricks, *Blunders in International Business.*
[8]ibid.
[9]"TAG Heuer: all time greats?" *Director* (April 1994): 45–48.
[10]http://animalrangeextension.montana.edu/Articles/Beef/Q&A2002/Promote.htm.

messages of safety, taste, and nutrition to the Japanese consumers, who had become worried about mad cow disease. The TV commercials featured three U.S. women, working in the U.S. beef industry, who share the concerns of their Japanese counterparts about the safety of the food that they serve to their families.

For radio or TV commercials, voice-overs that use the local slang often become necessary. However, this rule cannot be generalized. For instance, while Egyptian consumers prefer colloquial Egyptian Arabic in their advertising, use of local slang is less advisable for Gulf Arabs.[11] Finally, meticulous copy research and testing should enable advertisers to pick up translation glitches.

Other Cultural Barriers

Many of the trickiest promotional issues occur in the domain of religion. In Saudi Arabia, for example, only veiled women can be shown in TV commercials, except from the back. As you can imagine, such restrictions lead to horrendous problems for haircare advertisers. Procter & Gamble navigated around that constraint by creating a spot for Pert Plus shampoo that showed the face of a veiled woman and the hair of another woman from the back. Early 2007, the start of the "Year of the Pig," CCTV, China's national broadcaster, banned the use of advertising containing pig images out of respect for the country's Muslim minority (2 percent of the population).[12] The ban meant that advertisers would have to re-shoot their Chinese New Year spots. Coca-Cola had prepared two spots—one featuring a piglet and another with a panda bear. After a great deal of pressure CCTV relaxed the ban and decided to review ads on a case-by-case basis.

As Cadbury's Kashmir gaffe described at the beginning of this chapter shows, political sensitivities are also crucial. Canon came under fire in the Chinese media for a promotional CD-ROM that mistakenly referred to Taiwan and Hong Kong as countries—a major affront to China's one-country policy.[13] For similar reasons, Toyota ran into trouble in China with a print ad campaign for the Land Cruiser. One of the print ads showed stone lions saluting a passing Land Cruiser. Stone lions are a symbol of power and authority in China. The campaign caused outrage among the Chinese media and public as it was seen as a display of Japanese imperialism.[14]

Communication and Cultural Values

The effectiveness of a communication campaign often depends on the extent to which the values evoked by the campaign match the cultural values of the target audience. One framework that helps in understanding the influence of culture on advertising is the Hofstede cultural grid discussed in Chapter 4. As you may recall, the schema classifies cultures based on five dimensions: power distance, uncertainty avoidance, individualism/collectivism, masculinity, and long-termism. The schema has been applied in several cross-cultural studies to assess the effectiveness of different advertising approaches. One study explored the link between the values portrayed in Benetton advertising and consumers' values in Norway, Germany, and Italy. The study concludes that when consumers' values match the values expressed by the advertising, the liking for the brand increases.[15] Another study examined the effectiveness of antismoking messages targeted at teenagers in different cultures. According to the study, advertisements that are framed in a negative manner by pointing out the threats of smoking are more effective in

[11]"Peace process forges new Middle East future," *Advertising Age International* April (1996): I13.

[12]"Ban Thwarts 'Year of the Pig' Ads in China, www.npr.org, accessed February 10, 2009.

[13]"China's Paper Tigers Swift to Bite," *Financial Times*, August 23, 2000, p. 9. Part of the animosity stemmed also from the fact that Canon is a Japanese company. Many Chinese still feel very ambivalent toward Japan.

[14]"Toyota Looks for Road to Recovery in China," *Media*, March 12, 2004. p. 19.

[15]Rosemary Polegato and Rune Bjerke, "The Link between Cross-Cultural Value Associations and Liking: The Case of Benetton and Its Advertising," *Journal of Advertising Research* (September 2006): 263–273.

high uncertainty-avoidance (UA) countries than ads with positive messages. However, positively framed anti-smoking ads that stress the benefits of cutting smoking may be more effective in low-UA countries such as Denmark, Russia, the United Kingdom, and the United States.[16] The schema can also be used to assess the effectiveness of comparative advertising within a particular cultural environment. Such ads favorably compare the promoted brand against the competing brand(s) (identified or unidentified). While forbidden or heavily restricted in many countries, comparative advertising is legal in major markets such as the United States and Japan. In group-oriented (collectivist) cultures (e.g., Japan, Thailand), comparison with the competition may not be acceptable because the other party risks losing face. In feminine cultures (e.g., Scandinavia, Thailand), comparative advertising could be viewed as too aggressive and bold. In cultures that are a combination of individualistic and feminine values, comparative advertising could work as long as it is done in a subtle, non-aggressive manner. A good example is the well-known tag line used by the Danish beer brand Carlsberg: "Probably the best beer in the world." Cultures where comparative advertising is likely to be most effective are those that embrace masculinity and individualism as values.[17]

Cultures could also differ in terms of the impact of using celebrities in advertising. One 2008 study found that relative to U.S. consumers, Chinese consumers were much more receptive to ads featuring athletic celebrity endorsers.[18] Celebrity endorsement has become very popular in China. According to one study, 32 percent of the ads in the country used a celebrity spokesperson in 2009 compared to 9 percent globally.[19] Not surprisingly, the rising tide of ads featuring celebrities has led to consumer confusion and apathy. One study that looked at sales pitches featuring Liu Xiang, a Chinese hurdler, found that only Nike was strongly connected with the athlete. Other brands (e.g., Visa, Cadillac) had very low recognition rates as brands promoted by Liu Xiang. Fewer than 20 percent of the people surveyed indicated that an endorsement by the star would make them buy products from any of the companies except Nike.[20]

Setting the Global Advertising Budget

One of the delicate issues that marketers must grapple with when planning their communication strategy centers on the "money" issue. Worldwide advertising spending was over $497.3 billion in 2012 (or $71 per person on the planet), an all-time high. **Exhibit 12-2** ranks the top 20 global advertisers in 2011. Not surprisingly, the biggest spenders are the major multinational consumer goods companies. **Exhibit 12-3** shows that per capita spending is still much higher in the United States than in the BRIC countries. Still, ad spending in all four of these markets has grown very rapidly. For instance, China has come a long way: its spending per person has risen from 9 cents in 1986 to $27 in 2011. **Exhibit 12-4** gives an overview of the 10 biggest advertisers in the BRIC countries.

---

[16]James Reardon, Chip Miller, Irena Vida, and Liza Rybina, "Antismoking Messages for the International Teenage Segment: The Effectiveness of Message Valence and Intensity Across Different Cultures," *Journal of International Marketing* 14, no. 3 (2006): 115–138.

[17]Marieke de Mooij, *Global Marketing and Advertising* (Thousand Oaks, CA: SAGE Publications, 1998), pp. 252–254.

[18]Allen D. Schaefer, R. Stephen Parker, and John L. Kent, "A Comparison of American and Chinese Consumers' Attitudes Toward Athlete Celebrity Endorsers," *Journal of Sport Administration & Supervision* 2 (April 2010): 31–40.

[19]"The Great Fail of China: Celebrity Over-Endorsers Confuse Fans," http://www.brandchannel.com, accessed January 21, 2013.

[20]"Celebrities and China: Marketing Hell," http://www.forbes.com, accessed January, 21, 2013.

Exhibit 12-2 Top 20 Global Advertisers—Measured Media only (2011)

Rank	Company	Home country	Spending amount (billions of $)
1	Procter & Gamble	USA	$11.25
2	Unilever	U.K./Netherlands	$7.36
3	L'Oréal	France	$5.53
4	General Motors	USA	$3.33
5	Nestlé	Switzerland	$2.98
6	Coca-Cola	USA	$2.91
7	Toyota	Japan	$2.83
8	Volkswagen	Germany	$2.82
9	McDonald's	USA	$2.65
10	Reckitt Benckiser	U.K.	$2.62
11	Kraft Foods	USA	$2.49
12	Fiat/Chrysler	Italy/USA	$2.35
13	Mars	USA	$2.25
14	Johnson & Johnson	USA	$2.17
15	Ford Motor	USA	$2.13
16	Comcast	USA	$1.82
17	PepsiCo	USA	$1.80
18	Sony Corp.	Japan	$1.78
19	Pfizer	USA	$1.75
20	Nissan Motor	Japan	$1.75

Source: Compiled from *Advertising Age's* Global Marketers 2012 (December 10, 2012).

The key spending questions for global marketers are threefold: (1) How much should we spend? (2) What budgeting rule shall we use? and (3) How should we allocate our resources across our different markets? Let us first look at the budgeting amount question. Companies rely on different kinds of advertising budgeting rules, notably percentage of sales, competitive parity, and objective-and-task.[21]

Exhibit 12-3 Measured Advertising Spending by Region (2011)

Market	2012 Ad Spending in Billions	Ad Growth 2012 vs. 2000	2012 Ad Dollars Per Person	Share of 2012 Worldwide Ad Spending
USA	$160.8	2.7%	$512	32.2%
Brazil	18.6	215.1	93	3.7
Russia	9.7	1,132.2	68	2.0
India	6.1	409.2	5	1.2
China	36.2	488.9	27	7.3
Worldwide	497.3	29.7	71	100.0

Source: Compiled from *Advertising Age's* Global Marketers 2012 (December 10, 2012).

---

[21]See, for instance, Rajeev Batra, John G. Myers and David A. Aaker, *Advertising Management*, 5th ed. (Upper Saddle River, NJ: Prentice Hall, 1996).

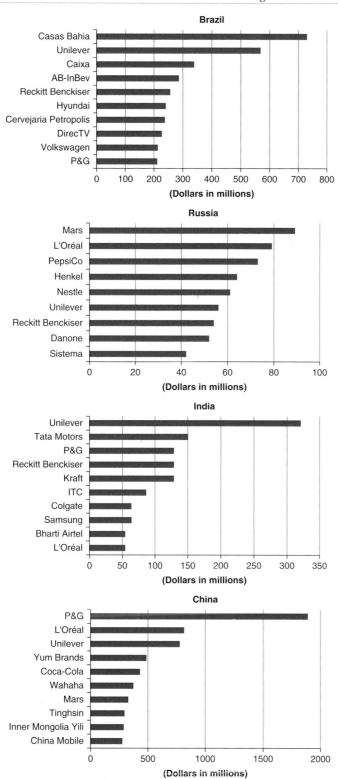

Exhibit 12-4 Top 10 Advertisers in Bric Countries (2011) (Million of Dollars)

Source: Compiled from *Advertising Age's* Global Marketers 2012 (December 10, 2012).

Percentage of Sales Method

The rule based on **percentage of sales** simply sets the overall advertising budget as a percentage of sales revenue. The base is either past or expected sales revenues. The obvious appeal of this decision rule is its simplicity. One nagging question though is what percentage to choose. The biggest downside of this rule is that sales revenue (past or projected) drives advertising spending, whereas the purpose of advertising is to impact sales. The method is clearly not a sound strategy for markets that were recently entered, especially if the percentage base is historical sales revenue.

Competitive Parity

The principle of the **competitive parity** rule is extremely simple: Use your competitors' advertising spending as a benchmark. For instance, a company could simply match its lead competitor's spending amount to get a similar amount of share-of-voice.[22] The rationale for this approach is that the competitors' collective wisdom signals the "optimal" spending amount. It is not surprising that the three biggest global advertising spenders (P&G, Unilever, and L'Oréal) are global rivals. Likewise, six of the largest spenders in the top-20 are car companies: General Motors (4), Volkswagen (6), Toyota (7), Fiat/Chrysler (12), Ford Motor (15), and Nissan Motor (20) (see **Exhibit 12-2**). The competitive parity rule also allows the company to sustain a minimum "share of voice"[23] without rocking the boat. Advertising scholars have pointed out several shortcomings of competitive parity as a budgeting norm. The industry's spending habits may well be very questionable: collective wisdom is not always a given. Also, marketers that recently entered a new market probably should spend far more relative to the incumbent brands to break through the clutter.

Objective-and-Task Method

The most popular budgeting rule is the so-called **objective-and-task** method. Conceptually, this is also the most appealing budgeting rule: it treats promotional efforts as a means to achieve the advertiser's stated objectives. This method was found to be used by almost two-thirds of the respondents in the same survey mentioned earlier.[24] The concept of this budgeting rule is very straightforward. The first step of the procedure is to spell out the goals of the communication strategy. The next step is to determine the tasks that are needed to achieve the desired objectives. The planned budget is then the overall costs that the completion of these tasks will amount to. The objective-and-task method necessitates a solid understanding of the relationship between advertising spending and the stated objectives (e.g., market share, brand awareness). One way to assess these linkages is to use field experiments. With experimentation, the advertiser systematically manipulates the spending amount in different areas within the country to measure the impact of advertising on the key objectives of the campaign (e.g., brand awareness, sales volume, market share).

Resource Allocation

The budgeting process also involves the allocation of resources across the different countries in which the firm operates. **Exhibit 12-5** shows the allocation of advertising dollars (percentage-wise) by the world's top three advertisers in 2007: Procter & Gamble, Unilever, and L'Oréal. Not surprisingly, all three of them allocate a large chunk of their advertising dollars to China and the United States.

There are three approaches that companies use to make advertising allocation decisions. At one extreme are companies like Microsoft and FedEx where each country subsidiary independently

---

[22]Share of voice is a brand's advertising weight as a percentage of the total category advertising.

[23]Share of voice refers to the amount of ad spending on the brand as a proportion of the total category ad-spending amount.

[24]N. E. Synodinos, C. F. Keown, and L. W. Jacobs, "Transnational advertising practices," *Journal of Advertising Research* (April/May 1989): 43–50.

Exhibit 12-5 2007 AD Spending Allocation by 3 Biggest
Advertisers in Key Markets

Country	P&G	Unilever	L'Oréal
Europe			
France	2.4%	NA	12.7%
Germany	3.3	3.9%	6.7
Italy	1.6	2.4	3.3
Russia	2.0	1.6	2.7
Spain	1.8	NA	4.1
United Kingdom	4.9	5.4	6.9
Asia			
China	11.7	8.4	5.7
India	0.8	4.8	1.0
Indonesia	NA	3.8	NA
Thailand	0.6	3.1	1.1
Americas			
Brazil	NA	3.7	NA
Canada	1.9	NA	1.9
Mexico	1.3	1.5	NA
USA	39.5	17.2	22.8
Total Ad Spending Amount (in millions of dollars)	$9,358	$5,295	$3,426

Source: Percentages calculated based on ad spending figures reported in *Advertising Age's Global Marketers*, December 8, 2008, and *Advertising Age Annual 2009*, December 29, 2008.

determines how much should be spent within its market and then requests the desired resources from headquarters. This is known as **bottom-up budgeting**. **Top-down budgeting** is the opposite approach. Here headquarters sets the overall budget and then splits up the pie among its different affiliates. The company puts its budget together centrally and then allocates it depending on regional and local needs. A third approach, which is becoming increasingly more common, takes a regional angle. Each region decides the amount of resources that are needed to achieve its planned objectives and then proposes its budget to headquarters. A survey conducted by *Advertising Age International* in 1995 found that the most favored approaches are bottom-up (28 percent of respondents) and region-up budgeting (28 percent). Only 20 percent of the responses indicated that the headquarters office has direct control over funding decisions. The survey also showed substantial cross-industry differences in resource allocation practices.

Creative Strategy
The "Standardization" versus "Adaptation" Debate

On March 4, 2009, Visa rolled out its first-ever global ad campaign for its debit card.[25] The $140 million campaign, which ran in the United States and 43 countries (e.g., India, Mexico, Japan), was designed to persuade consumers that debit cards are more convenient and safer than cash. The

---

[25]"Visa is Seeking to Usurp Cash as King," *Wall Street Asia*, March 4, 2009, p. 16.

◆ ◆

Global Perspective 12-1

Nissan's Global "Shift" Advertising Campaign

In the past, Nissan Motor's advertising messages varied enormously across markets. In Europe, it had no tagline. In the United States, the tag line was "Driven," and in Japan it used the slogan "Bringing more to your life every day." To beef up its global brand image, Nissan kicked off its global "Shift" campaign in 2002. In the United States, where the campaign coincided with the launch of the Nissan 350Z sports car, the tag line varies, including "Shift passion," "Shift joy," and "Shift forward." One TV ad in the United States shows a baby trying to make its first steps with the tag line "Shift achievement." In Europe, the slogan is "Shift expectations." In Japan, the tag line is "Shift the future."

The "Shift" campaign was born from a cooperative process between Nissan managers from advertising and market-ing divisions worldwide. Brainstorming over a 10-month period spawned hundreds of candidates for a global tagline. One major obstacle was that many of the most common words (e.g., "power," "exciting") were already pre-empted by copyright somewhere. In the end, "Shift" was the winning idea. The "shift" slogan appeared to best convey the sense of change message that Nissan hoped to get across. More-over, it could be easily understood in non-English speaking countries. To give local subsidiaries some amount of control, Nissan allowed local variations for the second half of the tag line.

Source: "Nissan Shifts Focus to Unified Strategy for Its Global Cam-paign," *Asian Wall Street Journal*, October 10, 2002, p. A7.

---

ads promote the use of Visa cards for small purchase transactions: "Our prime objective was to create a campaign that would migrate consumer and business spending from cash and cheques to the better form of electronic payment, Visa. We also wanted a campaign that would work on a global scale while also connecting locally, and 'Go' is one of those few universal words that is broadly understood around the world."[26] In Asia the ads show people from different places enjoying what the world has to offer.[27] **Global Perspective 12-1** discusses the global "Shift" campaign that Nissan Motor started to run in 2002.

One of the thorniest issues that marketers face when developing a communication strategy is the choice of a proper advertising theme. Companies that sell the same product in multiple markets need to establish to what degree their advertising campaign should be standardized. Standardiza-tion simply means that one or more elements of the communication campaign are kept the same. The major elements of a campaign are the message (strategy, selling proposition, platform) and the execution.

The issue of standardize-versus-adapt has sparked a fierce debate in advertising circles. A truly global campaign is uniform in message and often also in execution (at least, in terms of visuals). When necessary, minor changes must be made in the execution to comply with local regulations or to make the ad more appealing to local audiences (voice-overs, local actors). Typically, global campaigns heavily rely on global or pan-regional media channels. "Truly" global campaigns are still relatively rare.

---

[26]"Visa Rolls Out First Global Campaign," www.brandrepublic.asia, accessed March 4, 2009.
[27]See http://www.brandrepublic.asia/Media/The-Workarticle/2009_03/Visa–Visa-Gofesto–Global/34580 for a clip.

Merits of Standardization

What makes the case of standardization so compelling in the eyes of many global marketers? A variety of reasons have been offered to defend global, if not pan-regional, advertising campaigns. The major ones are listed here.

Scale Economies

Of the factors encouraging companies to standardize their advertising campaigns, the most appealing one is the positive impact on the advertiser's bottom line. The savings coming from the economies of scale of a single campaign (as opposed to multiple country-level ones) can be quite eye-catching. Levi Strauss reportedly saved around $2.2 million by shooting a single TV ad covering six European markets.[28] Several factors lie behind such savings. Producing a single commercial is often far cheaper than making several different ones for each individual market. Savings are also realized because firms can assign fewer executives to develop the campaign at the global or pan-regional level.

Consistent Image

For many companies that sell the same product in multiple markets, having a consistent brand image is extremely important. Consistency was one of the prime motives behind the pan-European campaign that Blistex, a U.S.-based lipcare manufacturer, started to run in 1995. Prior to the campaign, advertising themes varied from country to country, often highlighting only one item of Blistex's product line. The entire product range consists of three items, each one standing for a different need. In many of its markets, brand awareness was dismally low. The objectives for the pan-European campaign were (1) to increase brand awareness and (2) to have the same positioning theme by communicating the so-called care-to-cure concept behind Blistex's product line.[29] Campbell's pan-European advertising strategy for the Delacre cookie brand was also driven by a desire to establish a single brand identity across Europe. The brand's platform is that Delacre is a premium cookie brand with the finest ingredients based on French know-how. The same campaign was aired in English reaching 30 million people in more than 20 countries.[30] Message consistency matters a great deal in markets with extensive media overlap or for goods that are sold to global target customers who travel around the world.

Globalization of Media

Another force that drives global communication campaigns is the rise of global media groups. Global conglomerates dominate almost all media forms: television (e.g., Time Warner, News Corp., Viacom), print (e.g., News Corp., Time Warner, Condé Nast, Pearson), cinema (e.g., AMC Cinemas), and outdoor (Clear Channel, JC Decaux).

Global Consumer Segments

Cross-cultural similarities are a major catalyst behind efforts toward a standardized advertising approach. The "global village" argument often pops up in discussions on the merits of global or pan-regional advertising campaigns. The argument of cultural binding especially has clout with respect to product categories that appeal to elites or youngsters as observed by David Newkirk, a consultant with Booz Allen & Hamilton: "The young and the rich have very similar tastes the world over, and that's what's driving the convergences in advertising and media." [31] High-tech and business-to-business products and services typically also have global customer needs. When

---

[28]"A universal message," *Financial Times*, May 27, 1993.

[29]Mark Boersma, Blistex, Personal Communication.

[30]"Rebuilding in a crumbling sector," *Marketing*, February 18, 1993, 28–29.

[31]"A universal message," *Financial Times*, May 27, 1993.

Microsoft launched its new operating system, Vista, the company initiated a $500 million global marketing blitz, which was expected to make 6.6 billion impressions worldwide. According to the software giant, Vista satisfies global needs of its target customers: "They have lots of information on their PCs, they are always on the go, and they need tools which allow them to make decisions quickly."[32]

Creative Talent

Creative talent in the advertising industry is a scarce supply. It is not uncommon that the most talented people within the agency are assigned to big accounts, leaving small accounts with junior staff. The talent issue matters especially in countries that are plagued with a shortage of highly skilled advertising staff. By running a global campaign, small markets can benefit from having the same high-quality, creative ads as larger ones have.

Cross-Fertilization

More and more companies try to take advantage of their global scope by fostering cross-fertilization. In the domain of advertising, cross-fertilization means that marketers encourage their affiliates to adopt, or at least consider, advertising ideas that have proven successful in other markets. This process of exploiting "good" ideas does not even need to be restricted to global brands. Nestlé used the idea of a serialized "soap-mercial" that it was running for the Nescafé brand in the United Kingdom for its Tasters Choice coffee brand in the United States. The campaigns, chronicling a relationship between two neighbors that centered on coffee, were phenomenally successful in both markets. Likewise, a Johnnie Walker campaign ("Pact") developed in China was adapted for other countries in the Asia-Pacific region. The campaign involved a five-part series of spots, shown on television and a designated website, and targeted 25- to 35-year-old males. Its storyline centered on a young architect who pursued his dream to become a film director with the support of his close friends. The use of the "Pact" campaign in other Asian countries was driven by the insight that the themes of personal fulfillment and goal achievement through friendship also resonate in those countries.[33] Coming up with a good idea is typically very time consuming. Once the marketer has hit on a creative idea, it is just common sense to try to leverage it by considering how it can be transplanted to other countries.[34]

In addition to these motivations, there are other considerations that may justify standardized multinational advertising. A survey conducted among ad agency executives found that the uniform brand image factor was singled out as the most important driver for standardizing multinational advertising. Two other critical factors are time pressure and corporate organizational setup.[35] Obviously, developing a single campaign is less time-consuming than creating several ones. The firm's organizational setup also plays a major role, in particular the locus of control. In general, if the multinational's control is highly centralized, it is extremely likely that theme-development is largely standardized. Advertising is usually very localized in decentralized organizations. Also, for many small companies, local advertising is typically the responsibility of local distributors or franchisees. The shift toward regional organizational structures is definitely one of the major drivers behind the growing popularity of regional campaigns.

---

[32]"Vista Unveils Global Blitz," *Media*, February 9, 2007, p. 5.

[33]"Whisky Label Makes Pact," *Media*, March 6, 2008, p. 6. See http://www.youtube.com/watch?v=Vd0mCjsbrgM for a sample spot of the series.

[34]T. Duncan and J. Ramaprasad, "Standardizing Multinational Advertising: The Influencing Factors," *Journal of Advertising* 24, no. 3 (Fall 1995): 55–68.

[35]Ibid.

Barriers to Standardization

Faced with the arguments listed above for standardization, advocates of adaptation can easily bring forward an equally compelling list to build up the case for adaptation. The four major barriers to standardization relate to (1) cultural differences, (2) advertising regulations, (3) differences in the degree of market development, and (4) the "Not Invented Here" (NIH) syndrome.

Cultural Differences

Contrary to the "global village" (or "flat world") cliché, cultural differences still persist for many product categories. Cultural gaps between countries may exist in terms of lifestyles, benefits sought, usage contexts, and so forth. A case in point is the use of references to sex in ad campaigns. While references to sex are not unusual in many Western ads, sex is rarely used in Asia to promote products, due to both regulations and market acceptance. The U.S. version of an ad for personal care brand Herbal Essences, full of sexual innuendo, was also used in Australia. However, the ad was re-shot for Thailand, showing girls having a fun time rather than an erotic experience. Unless it is done in a funny manner, sex is not used in Thai advertising for it runs counter to Buddhist values and Thai culture.[36]

Cultural gaps may even prevail for goods that cater toward global segments. A case in point involves luxury goods that target global elites. The user benefits of cognac are by and large the same worldwide. The usage context, however, varies a lot: in the United States cognac is consumed as a stand-alone drink; in Europe, often as an after-dinner drink; and in China it is consumed with a glass of water during dinner. As a result, Hennessy cognac adapts its appeals according to local customs while promoting the same brand image.[37]

Advertising Regulations

Local advertising regulations pose another barrier for standardization. Regulations usually affect the execution of the commercial. Countries like Malaysia and Indonesia impose restrictions on foreign-made ads to protect their local advertising industries. Ray-Ban had to adapt a pan-Asian campaign in Malaysia by re-shooting the commercials with local talent. In addition, Caucasians were not allowed to appear in Malaysian TV commercials and had to be edited out. In a China, a shot of girl on a table was deemed too sexy.[38] Later in this chapter, we cover the regulations hurdle in more detail.

Market Maturity

Differences in the degree of market maturity also hamper a standardized strategy. Gaps in cross-market maturity levels mandate different advertising approaches. When Snapple, the U.S.-based "New Age" beverage, first entered the European market, the biggest challenge was to overcome initial skepticism among consumers about the concept of "iced tea." Typically, in markets that were entered very recently, one of the main objectives is to create brand awareness. As brand awareness builds up, other advertising goals gain prominence. Products that are relatively new to the entered market also demand education of the customers on what benefits the product or service can deliver and how to use it.

"Not-Invented-Here" (NIH) Syndrome

Finally, efforts to implement a standardized campaign often also need to cope with the NIH-syndrome. Local subsidiaries and/or local advertising agencies could block attempts at

---

[36]"Pushing the Sex Envelope," *Media*, September 20, 2002, pp. 16–17.

[37]"Cachet and Carry," *Advertising Age International*, February 12, 1996, p. I-18.

[38]"Ray-Ban Ogles 16–25 Group in Southeast Asia Blitz," http://adage.com, accessed May 14, 2013.

standardization. Local offices generally have a hard time accepting creative materials from other countries. Later on in this chapter we will suggest some guidelines that can be used to overcome NIH attitudes.

Approaches to Creating Advertising Copy

Marketers adopt several approaches to create multinational ads. At one extreme, the entire process may be left to the local subsidiary or distributor, with only a minimum of guidance from headquarters. At the other extreme, global or regional headquarters make all the decisions, including all the nitty-gritty surrounding the development of ad campaigns. The direction the MNC takes depends on the locus of control and corporate headquarters' familiarity with the foreign market. MNCs that fail to adopt a learning orientation about their foreign markets risk being challenged by the local subsidiaries when they attempt to impose a standardized campaign.[39] In any event, most MNCs adopt an approach that falls somewhere in between a purely standardized and purely localized campaign. McDonald's China, for instance, ran an ad campaign to promote beef that mimicked a famous U.S. TV commercial that featured basketball legends Michael Jordan and Larry Bird. The Chinese version showed a duo of Chinese basketball stars, Yi Jian and Zhu Fang Yu, engaged in a friendly competition. Although the commercials were very similar, local celebrities were used for the Chinese version. Let us look at the main approaches for developing and executing global concepts.

"Laissez-Faire"

With the "laissez-faire" approach, every country subsidiary simply follows its own course developing its own ads based on what the local affiliate thinks works best in its market. There is no centralized decision-making.

Export Advertising

With **export advertising**, the creative strategy is produced in-house or by a centrally located ad agency and then "exported" without inputs from the foreign markets. Usually the ad agency is based in the advertiser's home country. A universal copy is developed for all markets. The same positioning theme is used worldwide. Visuals and most other aspects of the execution are also the same. Minor allowances are made for local sensitivities, but by and large the same copy is used in each of the company's markets. Obviously, export advertising delivers all the benefits of standardized campaigns: (1) the same brand image and identity worldwide, (2) no confusion among customers, (3) substantial savings, and (4) strict control over the planning and execution of the global communication strategy.[40] On the creative front, a centralized message demands a universal positioning theme that travels worldwide. The Visa "More People Go with Visa" 2009 global ad campaign, for instance, tapped in the global need for security and safety. **Exhibit 12-6** offers some other examples of universal appeals. Export advertising is very common for corporate ad campaigns that aim to create awareness, to reposition the company or reinforce an existing company image. It is also very popular when the country of origin is an important part of the brand image.

Prototype Standardization

With **prototype standardization**, the key elements (e.g., the theme, core values, slogan) of the advertisements are the same across countries. However, some flexibility is allowed for language

---

[39]Michel Laroche, V. H. Kirpalani, Frank Pons, and Lianxi Zhou, "A Model of Advertising Standardization in Multinational Corporations," *Journal of International Business Studies* 32, no. 2 (Second Quarter 2001): 249–66.

[40]M. G. Harvey, "Point of view: A model to determine standardization of the advertising process in international markets," *Journal of Advertising Research* (July/August 1993): 57–64.

Exhibit 12-6 Examples of Universal Appeals

- *Superior quality.* Clearly, the promise of superior quality is something that interests any customer. A classic example here is the "Ultimate Driving Machine" slogan that BMW uses in many of its markets.

- *New product/service.* A global rollout of a new product or service is often coupled with a global campaign announcing the launch. One example is the marketing hype surrounding the launch of Windows 8 by Microsoft.

- *Country of origin ("made in").* Brands in a product category with a strong country stereotype often leverage their roots by touting the MADE IN cachet. This positioning strategy is especially popular among fashion and luxury goods marketers.

- *Heroes and celebrities.* Tying the brand to heroes or celebrities is another popular universal theme. A recurring issue on this front is whether advertisers should use "local" or "global" heroes. When sports heroes are used, most advertisers will select local, or at least regional, celebrities. With movie personalities the approach usually differs. Louis Vuitton ran its global 'Core Values' campaign featuring a wide range of celebrities including Mikhail Gorbachev, Keith Richards, Angelina Jolie, and Muhammad Ali.

- *Lifestyle.* The mystique of many global upscale brands is often promoted by lifestyle ads that reflect a lifestyle shared by target customers, regardless of where they live. The execution of the ad may need to be customized for the different markets. A celebrated example is Johnnie Walker's award winning "Keep Walking" campaign that centers on the concept of "progress."

- *Global presence.* Many marketers try to enhance the image of their brands via a "global presence" approach—telling the target audience that their product is sold across the globe. Obviously, such a positioning approach can be adopted anywhere. The "global scope" pitch is often used by companies that sell their products or services to customers for whom this attribute is crucial, though the concept is used by other types of advertisers as well. Warner-Lambert created commercials for its Chiclets chewing gum brand that tried to project the cross-cultural appeal of the brand. One spot showed a young man in a desert shack rattling a Chiclets box. The sound of Chiclets triggers the arrival of a cosmopolitan group of eager customers.

- *Market leadership.* Regardless of the country, being the leading brand worldwide or within the region is a powerful message to most consumers. For products that possess a strong country image, a brand can send a strong signal by making the claim that it is the most preferred brand in its home country or even around the world.[41]

- *Corporate image.* Finally, corporate communication ads that aspire to foster a certain corporate image also often lend themselves to a uniform approach.

(e.g., local voice-over) and cultural barriers. For instance, commercials could be reshot with local celebrities. Typically, advertising instructions are given to the local affiliates concerning the execution of the advertising. These guidelines are conveyed via the company's website, manuals, or multimedia materials (e.g., DVD, CD-ROM). Mercedes used a handbook to communicate its advertising guidelines to the local subsidiaries and sales agents. Instructions are given on the format, visual treatment, print to be employed for headlines, and so on.[42] Likewise, the Swiss watchmaker TAG Heuer had a series of guidebooks covering all the nuts and bolts of their communication approach, including rules on business card design.[43]

Concept Cooperation

With **concept cooperation** headquarters spell out guidelines on the positioning theme (platform) and the brand identity to be used in the ads. Worldwide brand values are mapped out centrally. Responsibility for the execution, however, is left largely to the local affiliates and/or ad agencies. That way, brand consistency is sustained without sacrificing the relevance of the ad campaign to local consumers. Similar to the prototype standardization approach, instructions on proper positioning

---

[41]Note that China's 1995 Advertising Law forbids making such claims.
[42]Rijkens, Rein, *European Advertising Strategies* (London: Cassell, 1992).
[43]"TAG Heuer: all time greats?" pp. 45–48.

themes and concepts are shared with the local agencies and affiliates through manuals, videotapes, or other communication tools. Nestlé's classic "Have a break, have a Kit Kat" campaign is a good illustration of this approach. Originally, the slogan referred to the institutionalized British tea break at 11 a.m. This notion did not apply to consumers in other countries where the "Have a break" concept was extended. Instead, different interpretations of the break concept were developed in the various countries where the campaign was run. One approach that companies and ad agencies increasingly use to strike the balance between thinking global and acting local is the **modular approach**. With this approach, the in-house advertising team or the ad agency develops several variations of the campaign around the same theme. A global Intel campaign that aired in 2005 showed combinations of six celebrities[44] sitting on the laps of ordinary laptop-computer users. Country affiliates could choose which celebrities to use for their campaigns.

Global Media Decisions

Another task that international marketers need to confront is the choice of the media in each of the country where the company is doing business. In some countries, media decisions are much more critical than the creative aspects of the communication campaign. In Japan, for instance, media buying is crucial in view of the scarce supply of advertising space. Given the choice between an ad agency that possesses good creative skills and one that has enormous media-buying clout, most advertisers in Japan would pick the latter.[45]

International media planners have to surmount a wide range of issues. The media landscape varies dramatically across countries or even between regions within a country. Differences in the media infrastructure exist in terms of media availability, accessibility, media costs, and media habits.

Media Infrastructure

Most developed countries offer an incredible abundance of media choices. New media channels emerge continuously. Given this embarrassment of riches, the marketer's task is to decide how to allocate the company's promotional dollars to get the biggest bang for the buck. In other countries, though, the range of media channels is extremely limited. Many of the media vehicles that exist in the marketer's home country (e.g., broadband, digital TV) are simply not available in the foreign market. Government controls in a host of countries can heavily restrict access to mass media options, such as television. In Germany, for instance, TV advertising is only allowed during limited time frames of the day.

The media infrastructure can differ dramatically from country to country, even within the same region. Whereas TV viewers in the West can surf an abundance of 25 TV channels, their Asian counterparts have access, on the average, to a measly choice of 2 to 3 channels. The standard media vehicles such as radio, cinema, and TV are well established in most countries. New media, such as cable, the internet, mobile phones, satellite TV, and pay TV, are steadily growing. Given the media diversity, advertisers are forced to adapt their media schedule to the parameters set by the local environment.

Media Limitations

One of the major limitations in many markets is media availability. The lack of standard media options challenges marketers to use their imagination by coming up with "creative" options. Intel,

---

[44]The six celebrities were actors Tony Leung, John Cleese, and Lucy Liu, skateboarder Tony Hawk, soccer star Michael Owen, and singer Seal.
[45]"The enigma of Japanese advertising," *The Economist*, August 14, 1993, pp. 59–60.

Exhibit 12-7 Average Cost of a Prime-Time
30 Second TV Spot (2007)

Country	Cost of a prime-time ad (in U.S. dollars)	Per capita income (2008E)
China	$23,233	$6,100
Hong Kong	33,555	45,300
India	10,096	2,900
Indonesia	3,226	3,900
Japan	21,693	35,300
Malaysia	2,436	15,700
Philippines	4,548	3,400
Singapore	4,739	52,900
Thailand	5,970	8,700
Vietnam	2,364	2,900

Note: Per capita GDP is in purchasing power parity (PPP) terms.
Sources: MindShare; and https://www.cia.gov/library/publications/the-world-factbook/geos/vm.html, accessed March 4, 2009.

the U.S. computer chip maker, built up brand awareness in China by distributing bike reflectors in Shanghai and Beijing with the words "Intel Inside Pentium Processor." Advertisers in Bangkok have taken advantage of the city's notorious traffic jams by using media strategies that reach commuters. Some of the selected media vehicles include outdoor advertising, traffic report radio stations, and three-wheeled taxis (*tuk-tuks*).[46]

Marketers must also consider media costs. For all types of reasons, media costs differ enormously between countries. **Exhibit 12-7** shows the costs of a prime-time 30-second TV spot in several Asian countries. In general, high costs-per-thousand (CPMs)[47] are found in areas that have a high per capita GNP. Other factors that influence the local media costs include the amount of media competition (e.g., the number of TV stations) and the quality of the media effectiveness measurement systems in place. Advertising rates for free-to-air satellite TV channels in the Arab world are relatively low due to the rapid proliferation of TV stations and the lack of a good television rating system.[48]

A major obstacle in many emerging markets is the overall quality of the local media. Take China, for instance. For many print media, no reliable statistics are available on circulation figures or readership profiles. Print quality of many newspapers and magazines is appalling. Newspapers may demand full payment in advance when the order is booked and ask for additional money later on. There are no guarantees that newspapers will run your ad or TV broadcasters will show your spot on the agreed date. The rise of new technologies, however, is rapidly improving media monitoring in many countries.

Recent Trends in the Global Media Landscape

In the last two decades the global media environment has changed dramatically. Below we pinpoint some of the major trends:

- *Growth of commercialization and deregulation of mass media.* One undeniable change in scores of countries is the growing commercialization of the mass media, especially the

---

[46]"Bangkok is bumper to bumper with ads," *Advertising Age International*, February 20, 1996, p. I-4.

[47]CPM is the cost per thousand viewers of a particular ad.

[48]Morris Kalliny, Grace Dagher, Michael S. Minor, and Gilberto De Los Santos, "Television Advertising in the Arab World: A Status Report," *Journal of Advertising Research* (June 2008): 215–23.

broadcast media. In Belgium, for example, commercial TV was basically non-existent. Advertisers who wanted to air a commercial to promote their goods either had to rely on cinema as a substitute for TV or TV channels from neighboring countries (the Netherlands, Germany, France, and Luxembourg). Following the launch of several commercial TV and radio stations, the media environment is entirely different now. Similar trends toward commercialization and deregulation of the media can be observed in many other countries. Note that this trend is not universal: beginning in January 2009, primetime advertising was banned on all public-broadcasting channels in France.[49]

- *Rise of global and regional media.* One of the most eye-catching developments in the media world has been the proliferation of global and regional media. Several factors explain the appeal of global media to international advertisers. By using such media, advertisers can target customers who would otherwise be hard to reach. International media also facilitate the launch of global or pan-regional ad campaigns. Another major asset is that most international media have well-defined background information on their audience reach and profile. The major barrier to advertising on global media has been the cultural issue. Many satellite TV broadcasters, for instance, initially planned to broadcast the same ads and programs globally. Because of that, viewership for many satellite channels was extremely low. As a result, very few advertisers were interested in airing spots on these channels. Lately, however, more and more satellite networks such as Fox International, ESPN, and MTV have started to customize the content of their programs by adding voice-overs, subtitles, or even local content to their offerings. A push toward localization also exists among many publishing houses of international magazine titles. In Japanese kiosks, magazine racks offer Japanese editions of titles such as *GQ*, *National Geographic*, and *Cosmopolitan*.

- *Growth of non-traditional (NT) interactive media.* One remarkable trend is the growing popularity of non-traditional (NT) interactive media among international advertisers. By coming up with innovative approaches, marketers hope to be able to break through the advertising clutter associated with traditional media and grab the target customer's attention. Interactive media also enable the advertiser to customize the message to the target audience. Obviously, the most visible form is the internet (see Chapter 19). Many other forms of NT marketing tools exist, however. To promote the Xbox videogame player in Europe, Microsoft gave away 2 million DVDs with an interactive commercial.[50] At various points, viewers could click on text or icons to get information about the Xbox or upcoming videogame releases. Targeting 16- to 34-year-old males, the DVDs were distributed by adding them to videogame magazines and holiday catalogs.

- *Improved media monitoring.* To plan a communication campaign, access to high-quality coverage, circulation or viewership data on the media vehicles to be considered are an absolute must. Moreover, companies would also like to be able to track how much, when, and in what media their competitors advertise. In many countries, marketers were plagued with a lack of solid, reliable monitoring systems. Fortunately, the situation is improving rapidly. The advent of new technologies has led to monitoring devices that allow far more precise data collection than in the past, even for very traditional media such as outdoor advertising. Great strides have been made in the area of TV ratings data that measure the viewership for TV programs. Kantar[51] and Nielsen Media Research, two of the major players in this area, now run ratings panels in scores of countries, including China and India. In many countries these firms now collect

---

[49]"France Bans Advertising on State TV during Primetime, www.guardian.co.uk, accessed March 5, 2009.
[50]"Microsoft, Others Target Teenagers Via Interactive DVDs," *Asian Wall Street Journal*, December 30, 2002, p. A5.
[51]Kantar is part of WPP, one of the world's largest advertising companies.

viewing data through top boxes (so-called people meters) that are connected to the panel member's television set.

Advertising Regulations

A Toyota ad that featured Hollywood actor Brad Pitt as a celebrity endorser was banned by the Malaysian government. According to Malaysia's then Deputy Information minister: "Western faces in advertisements could create an inferiority complex among Asians. . . . [The advertisement] was a humiliation against Asians. . . . Why do we need to use [Western] faces in our advertisements? Are our own people not handsome?"[52] Most countries stipulate laws and regulations that the advertising industry must respect. **Exhibit 12-8** lists the key taboos that advertisers in China encounter as spelled out in the 1995 Advertising Law.[53] Furthermore, advertisers need to support any claims with survey data or scientific evidence when describing the superior benefits of their products over competing ones. Ads in China must also use simplified Chinese characters, not the traditional ones used in Taiwan and Hong Kong. Any English text must be translated. While some of China's advertising rules are fairly clear, others can be very murky (e.g., "socially sensitive"). Lack of consistency in implementing the laws has been a major headache for many advertisers in China. Approval of an ad in one Chinese city does not guarantee that the ad will also pass muster in other cities.

Advertising regulations are the rules and laws that limit the way products can be advertised. In many countries government agencies (e.g., the Federal Trade Commission in the United States) supervise the local advertising industry. Often the local advertising industry is also governed by some form of self-regulation. Self-regulation can take various forms.[54] One possibility is that local advertisers, advertising agencies, and broadcast media jointly agree on an ethics code. Although such bodies typically cannot enforce their rules, they can sanction offenders through soft power tools. For instance, the Advertising Standards Authority (ASA) in Great Britain each week

---

Exhibit 12-8　China's 1995 Advertising Law

Ads may not use the following:

- China's national flag, emblem, or anthem, or the name of any state organ or employee.
- Recommendations or endorsements for products that include statements such as "state-approved," "state-level," or "national standard."
- Statements that discriminate by ethnic group, sex, race, or religion.
- Obscenity, superstition, horror, violence, or social evils.
- Content that can be seen injurious to China's environmental conditions or natural resources.
- Statistics or sales figures.
- Superlatives such as "highest level," "best" or "number one."
- The misfortune of others.
- Material not clearly identifiable as advertising. Documentary- or news-like ads must be clearly conveyed as ads and be distinguishable from documentaries or news reports.
- Terms for food, liquor, and cosmetics that can be confused with medical terms.
- Words or phrases that can be interpreted as politically or socially sensitive.
- Disparaging comments with respect to goods or services of other companies.

Source: http://www.saic.gov.cn/english/lawsregulations/Laws/200602/t20060227_55252.html.

---

[52]"Malaysia Bans Toyota Ad," http://www.asiamarketresearch.com, accessed December 20, 2002.
[53]The full English version of the law is posted on the website of China's State Administration for Industry and Commerce (SAIC): http://www.saic.gov.cn/english/lawsregulations/Laws/200602/t20060227_55252.html.
[54]Marieke de Mooij, *Advertising Worldwide*, 2nd ed. (New York: Prentice Hall, 1994).

blacklists violating ads on its website (http://www.asa.org.uk/asa/adjudications/public/). Several reasons lie behind self-regulation of the advertising industry, including protection of consumers against misleading or offensive advertising, protection of legitimate advertisers against false claims, or accusations made by competitors. Another forceful reason to set up self-regulatory bodies is to prevent more stringent government-imposed regulation or control of the advertising industry. This section summarizes the major types of advertising regulations.

Advertising of "Vice Products" and Pharmaceuticals

Tough restrictions, if not outright bans, apply to the advertising of pharmaceuticals and so-called vice products in many countries. Japan, for example, prohibits the use of the word "safe" or "safety" or any derivatives when promoting over-the-counter drugs (e.g., pain relievers, cold medicines).[55] Despite opposition of advertising agencies, advertisers and media channels, rules on the advertising of tobacco and liquor products are becoming increasingly more severe. For instance, in 2006 the Thai government banned all alcohol advertising and sales promotions.

Comparative Advertising

Another area of contention is comparative advertising, where advertisers disparage the competing brand. While such advertising practices are commonplace in the United States, other countries heavily constrain or even prohibit comparative advertising. In China, for instance, advertisers are not allowed to compare their products with their competitors' or to include superlative terms such as "best." Anheuser-Busch, however, was able to air a commercial with Budweiser's slogan that it was "America's favorite beer" after it supported the claim with statistical evidence.[56] In Japan, comparative advertising—though not illegal—is a cultural taboo. It is seen as immodest and underhanded. Often the Japanese side with the competitor![57]

Foreign Made Ads

Several countries also protect their local advertising production industry and acting talent by clamping down on foreign-made ads. For example, Malaysia requires that 80 percent of an ad's production cost should be spent in that country. There are exceptions, though, for campaigns that incorporate global icons (e.g., the cowboy used in Marlboro advertising). One problem is that local talent can be scarce and, as a result, the quality of the locally produced commercials may suffer.[58]

Content of Advertising Messages

The content of advertising messages may be subject to certain rules or guidelines. In Australia, Toyota was forced to withdraw a series of spots advertising the Celica model because of their content. One of the spots was a *Jaws* spoof in which shark-like Celicas speed down a jetty. The ad violated the Advertising Standards Council's guidelines on "dangerous behavior or illegal or unsafe road usage practices."[59] A Volkswagen commercial in Sweden that showed a VW car being driven over lots of food was banned for portraying wasteful behavior.[60]

Ads may also be banned or taken off the air because they are offensive or indecent. A campaign for Unilever's Axe deodorant brand was suspended by the Indian government because of the commercial's steamy nature. The ad showed a man morph into a walking chocolate figure after spraying himself with Axe's Dark Temptation deodorant. Women throw themselves at him, licking

---

[55]John Mackay, McCann-Erickson Japan, private communication.
[56]"China's Rules Make a Hard Sell," *International Herald Tribune*, August 18, 2000, p. 13.
[57]John Mackay, McCann Erickson Japan, private communication.
[58]"Anti-foreign Ad Laws Bite," *Media*, May 18, 2007, p. 5.
[59]"ASC slams brakes on Australian Toyota ads," *Advertising Age International*, May 16, 1994, p. I-6.
[60]http://www.youtube.com/watch?v=xu0hgrKZ66Q.

and biting parts of his body.[61] Many countries also have regulations against sexist advertising or ads with exaggerated claims ("puffery").

Ad campaigns in China are also very vulnerable to censorship due to cultural or political insensitivities. One example of a banned commercial was an ad for Unilever's skincare brand Pond's. Even though the ad had complied with China's censorship regulations, China's television stations pulled the spot off the air because it starred Tang Wei, a leading actress. Tang Wei was blacklisted by SARFT,[62] the agency that supervises China's TV and radio channels, for her role in the controversial movie *Lust, Caution*, in which she displayed full frontal nudity.[63]

Advertising Targeting Children

Another area that tends to be heavily regulated is advertising targeted to children. Korea and Malaysia, for example, ban fast food TV ads targeted toward children, blaming such ads for rising obesity levels among youngsters.[64] In Europe, rules to curb advertising to children are widespread. Greece bans all TV advertising of toys between 7 a.m. and 10 p.m.[65] In Finland, children cannot speak or sing the name of a product in commercials. In Turkey, children are only allowed to watch TV ads with "parental guidance." In Brazil, a consumer protection agency fined McDonald's $1.6 million for a 2010 ad campaign that offered meals with toys from the movie Avatar.[66] China poses a series of rules that advertisers to children need to respect. Contrary to regulations in Western countries, most of the standards center on cultural values: respect for elders and discipline. For instance, one of the rules bans ads that "show acts that children should not be doing alone."[67]

Although many ad regulations often sound annoying or frivolous, having a clear set of advertising rules and restrictions is a boon for consumers and advertisers alike. If no rules govern the advertising environment, the law of the jungle applies. In China, most of the advertising malpractice cases in the past involved ads for drugs, medical services, and food. It was not unusual to have some soaps claim to help people lose weight and some tonics promise to make users smarter.[68]

How should marketers cope with advertising regulations? There are a couple of possible actions:

1. *Keep track of regulations and pending legislation.* Monitoring legislation and gathering intelligence on possible changes in advertising regulations are crucial. Bear in mind that advertising regulations change continuously. In many countries the prevailing mood is in favor of liberalization with the important exception of tobacco and alcohol advertising. European Union member states are also trying to bring their rules in line with EU regulations. Many ad agencies have in-house legal counsel to assist them in handling pending advertising legislation.

2. *Screen the campaign early on.* Given the huge budgets at stake, it is important to get feedback and screen advertisements as early as possible to avoid costly mistakes. In China, TV commercials must be submitted to the local office of the State Administration for Industry and Commerce prior to airing. To be on the safe side, many companies submit their storyboards and script before producing the commercial. Sometimes, however, the media owner (e.g., CCTV, China's main TV channel) wants to review the finished commercial first before airing it.

---

[61]"As the Ads Heat Up, India Tries to Keep Cool," *Wall Street Journal Asia*, September 10, 2008, p. 27.
[62]State Administration for Radio, Film, and Television.
[63]"Director Lee Defends Actor Banned from Chinese Media," http://www.guardian.co.uk/film/2008/mar/11/news.
[64]"Malaysia Bans Fast Food Ads Targeted At Children," *Media*, May 4, 2007, p. 2.
[65]"Kid Gloves," *The Economist*, January 6, 2001, p. 53.
[66]"McDonald's Fined in Brazil for Pushing Happy Meals to Children," http://uk.reuters.com, accessed April 22, 2013.
[67]Louisa Ha, "Concerns about advertising practices in a developing country: An examination of China's new advertising regulations," *International Journal of Advertising* 15 (1996): 91–102.
[68]"China's Rules Make a Hard Sell."

3. *Lobbying activities.* A more drastic action is to lobby local governments or international legislative bodies such as the European Parliament. Lobbying activities are usually sponsored jointly by advertisers, advertising agencies, and the media. CCTV, China's national broadcaster, relaxed a ban on ads containing pig images after a great deal of pressure from ad agencies and their clients.[69] As usual, too much lobbying carries the risk of generating bad publicity, especially when the issues at hand are highly controversial.

4. *Challenge regulations in court.* Advertisers can consider fighting advertising legislation in court. In Chile, outdoor board companies, advertisers and sign painters filed suit in civil court when the Chilean government issued new regulations that required outdoor boards to be placed several blocks from the road.[70] In European Union member states, advertisers have sometimes been able to overturn local laws by appealing to the European Commission or the European Court of Justice. For instance, a host of retailers (including Amazon.com), ad agencies, and media in France filed a complaint with the European Commission in an attempt to overturn a 40-year old French law that bans TV advertising by retailers. They argued that the law runs counter to EU rules.[71]

5. *Adapt marketing mix strategy.* Tobacco marketers have been extremely creative in handling advertising regulations. A widely popular mechanism is to use the brand extension path to cope with tobacco ad bans. For instance, the Swedish Tobacco Co., whose brands have captured more than 80 percent of the Swedish cigarette market, started promoting sunglasses and cigarette lighters under the Blend name, its best-selling cigarette brand, to cope with a complete tobacco ad ban in Sweden.[72] In the United Kingdom, Hamlet, the leading cigar brand, shifted to other media vehicles following the ban on all TV tobacco advertising in the United Kingdom in October 1992. Hamlet started using outdoor boards for the first time, installing them at 2,250 sites. It ran a sales promotion campaign at a horse race where losing bettors got a free Hamlet cigar. It also developed a video with about 20 of its celebrated commercials. The video was made available for purchase or rent.[73] South Korea is the only country where Virginia Slims are pitched as the successful man's cigarette. Why? Because Korean law forbids advertising cigarettes to women and young adults.[74]

Choosing an Advertising Agency

Although some companies like Benetton, Diesel, Avon, and Hugo Boss develop their advertising campaigns in-house, most firms heavily rely on the expertise of an advertising agency. Advertising agencies come in all sizes ranging from small boutique shops to the large multinational groups such as WPP, Omnicom, and Dentsu. Besides providing creative support, agencies could also assist with media planning, dealing with the media, and digital campaigns.

In selecting an agency, the international marketer has several options:

1. Work with the agency that handles the advertising in the firm's home market.

2. Pick a purely local agency in the foreign market.

3. Choose the local office of a large international agency.

4. Select an international network of ad agencies that spans the globe or the region.

[69]"China's Regulation Minefield," *Media*, February 23, 2007, p. 11.

[70]"Chilean fight for outdoor ads," *Advertising Age International*, April 27, 1992, p. I-8.

[71]"Retailers Fight French Law That Bans Advertising on TV," *Asian Wall Street Journal*, February 22, 2001, p. N7.

[72]"Swedish marketers skirt tobacco ad ban," *Advertising Age International*, June 20, 1994, p. I-2.

[73]"Hamlet shifts to other media since TV spots are banned," *Advertising Age International*, April 27, 1992, p. I-8.

[74]"Real Men May Not Eat Quiche... But in Korea They Puff Virginia Slims," *Asian Wall Street Journal*, December 27/28 1996, pp. 1, 7.

When screening ad agencies, the following set of criteria can be used:

- *Market coverage.* Does the agency cover all relevant markets? What is the geographic scope of the agency?

- *Creative talent.* What are the core skills of the agency? Does the level of these skills meet the standards set by the company? Also, is there a match between the agency's core skills and the market requirements? Good creative talent is in short supply in many countries. In most developing markets, expatriates usually take up senior positions at agencies, while locals provide support.

- *Expertise with developing a central international campaign.* When the intent of the marketer is to develop a global or pan-regional advertising campaign, expertise in handling a central campaign becomes essential. One survey suggests, however, the agency's lack of international expertise and coordination ability is still a sore point for many companies.[75] Companies increasingly hire a **global lead agency** to ensure consistency of a global campaign and a roster of local agencies to adapt the campaign to local needs. For instance, in the past BMW's advertising was fragmented when local agencies had full creative freedom. When BMW wanted to make its brand more approachable for a wider audience, it appointed GSD&M to become the driving force behind the new global "Joy" campaign. At the same time, it relied on a network of local agencies to make the campaign relevant for the local audience. These agencies took direction from the global lead agency.[76]

- *Creative reputation.* The agency's creative reputation is often the most important criterion for many advertisers when choosing an ad agency. This relates to the agency's quality of strategic thinking and insight ("theme") as well as the quality of execution.

- *Scope and quality of support services.* Most agencies are not just hired for their creative skills and media buying. They are also expected to deliver a range of support services, like marketing research and developing other forms of communication (e.g., sales promotions, public relations, event-sponsorships).

- *Desirable image ("global" versus "local").* The image—global or local—that the company wants to project with its communication efforts also matters a great deal. Companies that aspire to develop a "local" image often assign their account to local ad agencies. One risk, though, of relying on local agencies is that their creative spark may lead to off-message, provocative advertising. Coke's senior executives were not too amused with an Italian campaign that featured nude bathers on the beach. A Singapore ad made for McDonald's to promote a new Szechuan burger featured a brothel-like "mama-san," not exactly in tune with McDonald's core family values.[77]

- *Size of the agency.* Generally speaking, large agencies have more power than small agencies. This is especially critical for media buying where a healthy relationship between the media outlet and the ad agency is very critical. On the other hand, the creative side of advertising does not always benefit from scale. Many award-winning ad campaigns have been designed by smaller boutique-like agencies.

- *Conflicting accounts.* Does the agency already work on an account of one of our competitors? The risk of conflicting accounts is a major concern to many advertisers. There are two kinds of risks here. First of all, there is the confidentiality issue: marketers share a lot of proprietary data with their advertising agency. Second, there is also the fear that the ad agency might assign superior creative talent to the competing brand's account, especially when that account is bigger.

[75]"Clients and Agencies Split over Ad Superstars," *Ad Age Global* (May 2001): 16.

[76]"Dr Uwe Ellinghaus," *Campaign Asia-Pacific* (November 2010): 48–51.

[77]"A Little Local Difficulty," *Ad Age Global* (February 2002): 4.

Exhibit 12-9
**Advertising Agency
Selection Criteria**

When it comes to choosing
an advertising agency,
marketers based in the
Asia-Pacific region were
asked to rank different
areas in order of
importance.

Source: "Year of Upturn and
Reset for Agencies," *Campaign Asia*, February 2011,
pp. 50–51.

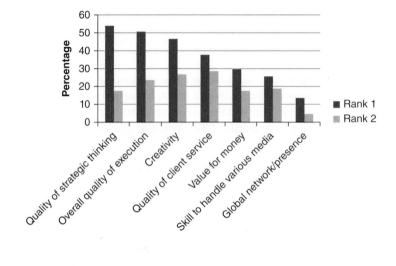

Note that sometimes these criteria may conflict with one another. A characteristic of the Japanese agency industry is that the large agencies service competing brands. Hence, companies that approach a big Japanese ad agency like Dentsu or Hakuhodo may need to accept the fact that the agency also handles the accounts of competing brands. **Exhibit 12-9** shows which areas are most important in choosing an agency based on a 2010 survey of marketers in the Asia-Pacific region.

Other Communication Platforms

For most companies, media advertising is only one part of the communication package. While advertising is the most visible form, the other communication tools play a vital role in a company's global marketing mix strategy. In this section, we discuss the following alternative promotion tools: sales promotions, direct marketing, sponsorships, mobile marketing, trade shows, product placement, and public relations/publicity. Personal selling and internet marketing, both of which can be regarded to some extent as promotion tools, are discussed in later chapters.

Sales Promotions

Sales promotions refer to a collection of short-term incentive tools that lead to quicker and/or larger sales of a particular product by consumers or the trade. There are basically two kinds of promotions: consumer promotions that target end-users (e.g., coupons, sweepstakes, rebates) and trade promotions that are aimed at distributors (e.g., volume discounts, advertising allowances). For most multinationals, the sales promotion policy is a local affair. Several rationales explain the local character of promotions:[78]

- *Economic development.* Low incomes and poor literacy in developing countries make some promotional techniques unattractive but, at the same time, render other tools more appealing. One study of promotional practices in developing countries found above-average use of samples and price-off packs.[79]

---

[78]K. Kashani and J.A. Quelch, "Can sales promotions go global?" *Business Horizons* 33, no. 3 (May-June 1990): 37–43.

[79]J. S. Hill and U. O. Boya, "Consumer goods promotions in developing countries," *International Journal of Advertising* 6 (1987): 249–264.

- *Market maturity variation.* For most product categories, there is a great deal of variation in terms of market maturity. In countries where the product is still in an early stage of the product life cycle, trial-inducing tools such as samples, coupons, and cross-promotions are appropriate. In more established markets, one of the prime goals of promotions will be to encourage repeat purchase. Incentives such as bonus packs, in-pack coupons, and trade promotions that stimulate brand loyalty tend to be favored.

- *Cultural perceptions.* Cultural perceptions of promotions differ widely across countries. Some types of promotions (e.g., sweepstakes) may have a very negative image in certain countries. According to one study, Taiwanese consumers have less-favorable attitudes toward sweepstakes than consumers in Thailand or Malaysia. Nor are Taiwanese concerned about losing face when using coupons. Malaysians, on the other hand, favor sweepstakes over coupons.[80] Shoppers in Europe redeem far fewer coupons than their counterparts in the United States.[81]

- *Trade structure.* One of the major issues companies face is how to allocate their promotional dollars between consumer promotions—which are directly aimed at the end-user ("pull")—and trade promotions ("push")—which target the middlemen. Because of differences in the local trade structure, the balance of power between manufacturers and trade is tilted in favor of trade in certain countries. When Procter & Gamble attempted to cut back on trade promotions by introducing every-day-low-pricing in Germany, several major German retailers retaliated by de-listing P&G brands.[82] Differences in distributors' inventory space and/or costs also play a role in determining which types of promotions are effective.

- *Government regulations.* When C&A, a Brussels-based clothing retailer, offered a 20 percent discount to German customers paying with a credit card instead of cash, it was threatened with huge fines by a German court.[83] C&A's scheme was apparently in violation of a 70-year old German law regulating sales and special offers.[84] By the same token, Lands' End, the U.S. mail order retailer, was forced to withdraw a lifetime guarantee offer in Germany. According to Germany's supreme court, the offer violated the 1932 German Free Gift Act and was anti-competitive.[85] Probably the most critical factor in designing a promotional package is local legislation. Certain practices may be heavily restricted or simply forbidden. In Germany, for instance, coupon values cannot be more than 1 percent of the product's value. Vouchers, stamps, and coupons are banned in Norway.[86] **Exhibit 12-10** shows which promotion techniques are allowed in nine European countries. As you can see, Germany appears to be one of the most restrictive environments for promotion campaigns. The United Kingdom, on the other hand, seems to be very liberal.

Kashani and Quelch suggest that multinational companies appoint an international sales promotion coordinator. The manager's agenda would involve tasks such as these:[87]

- Promote transfer of successful promotional ideas across units.

- Transplant ideas on how to constrain harmful trade promotional practices.

---

[80]Lenard C. Huff and Dana L. Alden, "An Investigation of Consumer Response to Sales Promotions in Developing Markets: A Three-Country Analysis," *Journal of Advertising Research*, (May–June 1998): 47–56.

[81]"Coupon FSIs dropped," *Advertising Age International*, October 11,1993, p. I-8.

[82]"Heat's on value pricing," *Advertising Age International* (January 1997): I-21, I-22.

[83]The purpose of this somewhat unusual promotion was to cut cash register lines during the euro introduction period.

[84]"Defiant C&A reignites debate on German shopping laws," *Financial Times*, January 9, 2002, p. 2.

[85]"Lands' End to File Brussels Complaint," *Financial Times*, January 11, 2000, p. 2.

[86]"Coupon FSIs dropped."

[87]Kashani and Quelch, "Can sales promotions go global?"

Exhibit 12-10   Which Techniques Are Allowed in Europe

Key: Y = permitted X = not permitted ? = may be permitted

Promotion Technique	UK	NL	B	SP	IR	IT	F	G	DK
On-park promotions	Y	Y	?	Y	Y	Y	?	Y	Y
Banded offers	Y	?	?	Y	Y	Y	?	Y	Y
In-pack premiums	Y	?	?	Y	Y	Y	?	Y	?
Multipurchase offers	Y	?	?	Y	Y	Y	?	Y	Y
Extra product	Y	Y	Y	Y	Y	Y	?	?	Y
Free product	Y	?	Y	Y	Y	Y	Y	X	?
Reusable/other use packs	Y	Y	Y	Y	Y	Y	Y	Y	Y
Free mail-ins	Y	Y	?	Y	Y	Y	?	Y	Y
With purchase premiums	Y	?	Y	Y	Y	Y	?	?	?
Cross-product offers	Y	Y	X	Y	Y	Y	?	Y	Y
Collector devices	Y	Y	Y	Y	Y	Y	Y	Y	Y
Competitions	Y	?	?	Y	Y	?	Y	Y	?
Self-liquidating premiums	Y	Y	Y	Y	Y	Y	Y	Y	Y
Free draws	Y	X	?	Y	Y	Y	Y	Y	Y
Share outs	Y	Y	?	Y	Y	?	?	Y	?
Sweepstake/lottery	?	X	?	Y	X	?	?	Y	X
Money off vouchers	Y	Y	Y	Y	Y	Y	Y	?	Y
Money off next purchase	Y	Y	Y	Y	Y	Y	Y	?	Y
Cash backs	Y	Y	Y	Y	Y	X	Y	X	Y
In-store demos	Y	Y	Y	Y	Y	Y	Y	Y	Y

Source: The Institute of Sales Promotion, www.isp.org.uk 2006.

- Gather performance data and develop monitoring systems to evaluate the efficiency and effectiveness of promotions.

- Coordinate relations with the company's sales promotion agencies worldwide.

Direct Marketing

Direct marketing includes various forms of interactive marketing where the company uses media that enable it to get direct access to the end-consumer and establish a one-to-one relationship. The most prominent forms of direct marketing are direct mail, telemarketing, door-to-door selling, internet marketing (see Chapter 18), and catalog selling. In a sense, direct marketing is a hybrid mix of promotion and distribution. For companies such as Avon, Nu Skin, Herbalife, and Amway, direct marketing goes even beyond just being a marketing mix instrument: It is basically a business model for them.

Direct marketing is growing very rapidly internationally. Many of the celebrated firms in the area have been able to successfully transplant their direct marketing model to other markets. About one year after Dell entered China, it managed to become one of the leading PC brands there, despite skepticism that its practice of selling directly would not work in a country where salesmanship centers on connections.[88]

---

[88]"Chasing the China Market," *Asiaweek*, June 11, 1999, p. 46.

Though still rare, some firms have been able to successfully implement global direct marketing campaigns. A good illustration was a campaign run by Unisys, a U.S.-based information technology company. Its "Customer Connection" program was a million-dollar-plus, multilingual program that combined direct mail and telemarketing worldwide. Every quarter, Unisys sent out direct mail to key decision makers in 23 countries. The mailing described product and technology offerings in seven languages and came with a personalized letter signed by a Unisys region or country-manager. Native-speaking telemarketers would then follow up asking if the client managers recalled the mailing, if they had any queries, and if they would like to remain on the mailing list. Follow-up surveys showed that 70 percent of the contacted executives responded positively to the program.[89]

As with other promotion tools, direct marketing may also encounter hurdles in foreign markets. A notorious case was the complete ban on direct selling that the Chinese government imposed in the spring of 1998 due to a series of sales scams and pyramid schemes. Well-established selling companies such as Avon, Amway, and Mary Kay basically had to shut down their operations. As a result, these companies had to rethink their way of doing business in China and focus on retail outlets and sales representatives. Avon, for example, struck a deal with Watson's, a Hong Kong–based drugstore chain, to set up small counters in its stores.[90] In 2005, the Chinese government relaxed its ban on personal selling and instituted a highly monitored licensing schema in which Avon was given the first permit.[91] Direct selling remains heavily regulated in China. The Chinese government allows direct selling for only five product categories.[92] Multi-level marketing practices where agents themselves recruit other sellers and collect commissions from them are strictly forbidden.

Global Sponsorships

Sponsorship is one of the fastest-growing promotion tools. Global spending on sponsorship was projected to amount to around $53 billion in 2013 (see **Exhibit 12-11**).[93] Participating companies typically pay cash to sponsor an event but may sometimes offer value-in-kind services or a mix of the two. The 11 worldwide sponsors (e.g., Coca-Cola, Samsung, Visa) of the London 2012 Olympics paid on average between $80 and $100 million.

Being a sponsor of major global events such as the Olympics or the World Cup has several appeals. First, such events offer companies a platform to raise their profile and build their brand image worldwide and particularly in their key markets. Procter & Gamble, one of the London 2012 Olympics sponsors, used its sponsorship program as an opportunity to reinforce the association in consumer minds between P&G and its internationally well-known brands (e.g., Olay, Pampers, Gillette). Sponsorship of global events can also be very attractive for business-to-business (B2B) companies as a platform to lift their brand name recognition. Dow Chemical viewed its sponsorship of the London 2012 Olympics as the best, easiest, and most visible way to make the Dow brand more widely recognized in China.[94] Second, sponsorship differentiates the firm from the competition. Note, though, that ambush-marketing could dilute this benefit as we will discuss later. Third, the "feel-good" association with big events provides a recruitment and motivational tool for employees. Finally, when the sponsorship involves provision of in-kind

---

[89]"Unisys cuts clear path to int'l recovery," *Marketing News*, September 27, 1999, pp. 4–6.

[90]"Avon scrambles to reinvent itself in China after Beijing's ban on direct selling," *Far Eastern Economic Review*, October 22, 1998, pp. 64–66.

[91]"Avon Given Direct-selling Nod in China," www.chinadaily.com.cn, accessed February 25, 2009.

[92]These are cosmetics, health food, sanitation articles, small kitchen utensils, and healthcare equipment.

[93]http://www.sponsorship.com, accessed January 21, 2013.

[94]"Marketeers Try to Go Distance With Games," *China Daily*, June 27, 2012, p. 14.

Exhibit 12-11
Global Sponsorship
by Region

Source: Based on www.spon-
sorship.com, accessed January 22, 2013.

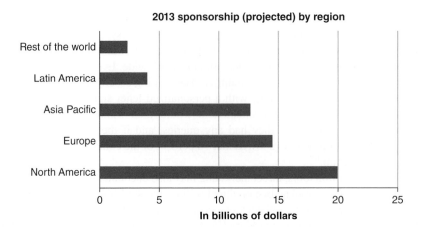

2013 sponsorship (projected) by region

In billions of dollars

services (e.g., information technology) or products (e.g., timing equipment), it gives a global stage for the sponsoring firm to showcase its skills.[95] BMW's Olympic fleet of 4,000 low-emission vehicles enabled the German carmaker to parade its environmental credentials during the 2012 London games.[96]

Ideally, the sponsored event should reinforce the brand image that the company is trying to promote. Red Bull, one of the dominant energy drink brands, is a case in point. From its very launch onwards, Red Bull has strived to promote a daring macho image by sponsoring extreme sports events ranging from wind surfing to hang gliding.[97] In 2004, Red Bull acquired the Jaguar Formula One racing team. With these sponsorships, Red Bull is able to reinforce its image as the beverage that gives "Wings to Body and Mind." Formula One can also help the company to gain more visibility in the United States, the Middle East, and Central America, where its brand is less well established.[98]

Event sponsorship carries four major risks. First, the organizers of the event may sell too many sponsorships, leading toward clutter. Second, the event may be plagued by controversy or scandal. PepsiCo's sponsorship deal of Pakistan's national cricket team was compromised by a spot-fixing scandal. Some prominent team members allegedly had taken bribes from a bookmaker to deliberately underperform during a London test cricket game in 2010. In the end PepsiCo decided to continue its sponsorship. One probable reason for the continued support was that Pakistan's passionate cricket fans rallied behind the accused players.[99] Third, the payback of the sponsorship can prove elusive. A survey of 1,500 Chinese citizens in 2008 found that only 15 percent could name two of the global sponsors and just 40 percent could name one.[100] The fourth risk is known as ambush marketing. With ambush marketing, a company seeks to associate with an event (e.g., the Olympics) without any payments to the event organizer. For instance, 36 women clad in orange outfits attended the 2010 World Cup soccer game between the Netherlands and Denmark to promote Bavaria, a Dutch beer, in spite of Budweiser's sponsorship. The ambusher hereby steals the limelight from its competitor that officially sponsors the event. Sometimes the non-sponsors simply do a far better marketing job than the sponsors. A Nielsen

---

[95]"Olympic Sponsors Seek Podium for Brands," *Financial Times*, September 3/4, 2011, p. 12.

[96]"Olympic Sponsors Seek a Competitive Edge," *Financial Times*, April 13, 2012, p. 15.

[97]"Extreme Sports and Clubbers Fuel Energetic Rise," *Financial Times*, November 23, 2001, p. 10.

[98]"Red Bull Charges into Ailing Jaguar," *Financial Times*, April 22, 2004, p. 16.

[99]"Pakistan Cricket Loses Its Fizz For Pepsi," *Campaign Asia-Pacific* (October 2010): 28.

[100]"Are Olympics Sponsorships Worth It?" http://www.businessweek.com/globalbiz/content/jul2008/gb20080731_125602.htm.

Exhibit 12-12 Guidelines for Event Sponsors to Cope with Ambush Marketing

1. *If an ambush were obvious, it wouldn't be an ambush.* An ambush is unforeseeable. Prior and during the event, sponsoring companies should carefully study the moves of their competitors—major and lessor ones.
2. *Don't always expect the event organizer to look after you.* Sponsorship protection is not always a top priority of event organizers. Sponsors should not simply rely on the event organizer for ambush monitoring.
3. *Don't rely on the government or the legal system to look after you.*
4. *Don't assume that consumers care about ambush marketing.* Many people see ambush marketing as fair game. In fact, local consumers may even side with the offending party especially when it is being seen as an underdog.
5. *Overreaction to an ambush could be viewed as bullying.* Strong actions against the ambusher (e.g., legal action) could create a backlash in the media and among the public.
6. *Sponsorship should be surrounded with meaningful marketing communication efforts.* Event sponsorship should not be a stand-alone activity. To maximize its return on sponsorship investment, the company should treat it as just one weapon in its marketing communication arsenal. Having a sponsorship deal is just a start. To get maximum bang for the buck, the sponsoring firm needs to find a way to activate the deal both prior and during the event. If not, non-sponsors could steal the sponsor's thunder, as we pointed out earlier.

Source: Based on Pitt, Leyland, Michael Parent, Pierre Berthon, and Peter G. Steyn, "Event Sponsorship and Ambush Marketing: Lessons from the Beijing Olympics," *Business Horizons* 53 (2010): 281–290.

study found that campaigns by non-sponsors during the run-up to the 2010 World Cup Soccer tournament overshadowed the marketing efforts of official sponsors. Some of the non-sponsors had created far better ads that led to more buzz online. To stamp out ambush marketing, organizers often place severe restrictions on the marketing activities of non-sponsors. For instance, Heineken handed out green hats to its customers during the Euro 2008 soccer tournament. However, anyone who tried to enter a stadium wearing such a hat was asked to remove it, as Carlsberg was the official sponsor.[101] **Exhibit 12-12** provides a set of guidelines for sponsors of global events faced with ambush threats.

Apart from these four pitfalls,[102] there is also the issue of response measurement. In general, measuring the effectiveness of a particular sponsorship activity is extremely hard. Some firms have come up with very creative procedures to do just that. In Asia, Reebok[103] tested out a campaign on Star TV's Channel V music channel in which the vee-jays wear Reebok shoes. To gauge the impact of the campaign, TV viewers were directed to Reebok's website. At the site, the viewer was able download a coupon that could be used for the next Reebok shoe purchase.[104]

Mobile (Brand-in-the-Hand) Marketing

Mobile phones are part of everyday life for many people around the planet. Worldwide there were around 6 billion mobile phone subscriptions in 2012. China alone is home to

---

[101]"Playing the Game," *The Economist*, July 5, 2008, p. 73.

[102]Note that the sponsored event or sports team also runs certain risks, the main one being that the sponsor can no longer honor the sponsorship commitment due to financial problems or even bankruptcy. Some examples include the sponsorship of the Houston Astros Stadium by Enron, AIG's shirt sponsorship of the Manchester United soccer team, and the shirt sponsorship of Anderlecht, a leading Belgian soccer team, by the Belgian bank Fortis. Luckily, new sponsors emerged in all three cases: Coca-Cola for the Houston stadium (renamed the Minute Maid Park), the insurer Aon for Manchester United, and BNP Paribas (a French bank that took over Fortis) for Anderlecht.

[103]Reebok was acquired by adidas in 2005.

[104]"Reebok sets strategy to get sales on track in fast-growing Asia," *Asian Wall Street Journal*, May 31–June 1, 1996, p. 12.

1 billion subscriptions.[105] In many developed countries 3G-technology is well established, and several countries are planning to launch 4G-technology. The combination of the web and advances in portable device technology has spurred a new communication approach: mobile marketing or brand-in-the-hand marketing. Brand-in-the-hand marketing is a communication strategy that leverages the benefits of mobile devices (at this stage primarily mobile phones) to communicate with the target consumers. One good example is a mobile marketing campaign that BMW ran for its Series 3 car in China during summer 2006. To view the BMW mobile website, customers clicked on BMW banner ads that appeared on the portals of mobile phone carriers such as China Mobile. Within the BMW site, visitors could customize their favorite Series 3 car with preferred colors and features. The site also had a click-to-call feature that enabled visitors to schedule test drive appointments. Tracking results for the 2-month campaign showed more than 500,000 unique visitors and more than 2 million page views.[106]

Mobile marketing differs from traditional communication marketing in two key respects: (1) it can be customized to the consumer's location (e.g., shopping location) or consumption context and (2) the marketer is able to interact with the target customer. Sultan and Rohm recognize three important roles for mobile marketing:

1. Foster top-of-mind brand awareness

2. Increase consumer involvement and interaction (e.g., through content downloads, viral marketing)

3. Directly influence consumer actions[107]

Despite the rich potential of mobile marketing, marketers are still reluctant to embrace mobile marketing due to several issues. One hurdle is the wide regional variation in technology. Most European countries and several Asian markets have a much more advanced mobile phone technology infrastructure than the United States and China. One solution is a phased approach: a company could test a mobile marketing campaign in a country with a highly developed infrastructure (e.g., Korea, Singapore) and then fine-tune it before rolling it out at a later stage in a less advanced but more crucial market (e.g., China, India). Another issue that mobile marketers must grapple with relates to privacy concerns and laws, which can also vary greatly across countries. Finally, the implementation of mobile marketing relies on a series of partners (e.g., wireless carriers) with possibly conflicting interests. Needless to say, setting up such partnerships in different countries can be a daunting task.

Trade Shows

Trade shows (trade fairs) are a vital part of the communication package for many international business-to-business (B2B) marketers. According to one survey, trade shows account for 17 percent of the typical B-to-B marketer's marketing budget.[108] Trade shows have a direct sales effect—the sales coming from visitors of the trade show booth—and indirect impacts on the exhibitor's sales.[109] Indirect sales effects stem from the fact that visitors become more aware of and interested in the

---

[105]http://www.itu.int/dms_pub/itu-d/opb/ind/D-IND-ICTOI-2012-SUM-PDF-E.pdf.

[106]"How to Find Focus Online," *Media*, October 20, 2006, pp. 26–27.

[107]Fareena Sultan and Andrew Rohm, "The Coming Era of 'Brand in the Hand' Marketing," *MIT Sloan Management Review* (Fall 2005): 83–90.

[108]"Study Finds Online, Trade Shows Dominate B-to-B Spending," www.mediapost.com, accessed February, 22, 2009.

[109]S. Gopalakrishna, G. L. Lilien, J. D. Williams, and I. K. Sequeira, "Do trade shows pay off?" *Journal of Marketing* 59 (July 1995): 75–83.

participating company's products. The indirect effects matter especially for new products. Trade fairs are often promoted in trade journals. Government agencies, like the U.S. Department of Commerce, also provide detailed information on international trade fairs.

There are some notable differences between overseas trade shows and North American ones.[110] Overseas fairs are usually much larger than the more regional, niche-oriented shows in the United States. Because of their size, international shows attract a much wider variety of buyers. Hospitality is another notable difference between trade show affairs in the United States and in foreign markets. For instance, even at the smallest booths at German shows, visitors are offered a chair and a glass of orange juice. Larger booths will have kitchens and serve full meals. Empty booths are filled with a coffee table and water cooler. In the United States, trade show events tend to be pure business.

When attending an international trade show, the following guidelines could prove useful:[111]

- Decide on what trade shows to attend at least a year in advance. Prepare translations of product materials, price lists, and selling aids.

- Bring plenty of literature. Bring someone who knows the language or have a translator.

- Send out, ahead of time, direct-mail pieces to potential attendees.

- Find out the best possible space: for instance, in terms of traffic.

- Plan the best way to display your products and to tell your story.

- Do your homework on potential buyers from other countries.[112]

- Assess the impact of trade show participation on the company's bottom line.[113] Performance benchmarks may need to be adjusted when evaluating trade show effectiveness in different countries because attendees might behave differently.[114]

One recent phenomenon is the emergence of "virtual trade shows," which allow buyers to walk a "show floor," view products, and request information without physically being there.[115] An excellent highly informative online resource on international trade shows is the website of Federation of International Trade Associations (FITA): www.fita.org. **Global Perspective 12-2** discusses a non-traditional approach Siemens took to promote its products through a mobile trade show.

Product Placement

Product placement is a form of promotion where the brand is placed in the context of a movie, television show, video game, or other entertainment vehicle. The marketer might pay for the placement or offer the good free of charge (e.g., cars in action movies). One survey estimated that companies spent $7.4 billion globally on paid product placement in 2011.[116] For many

---

[110]"Trading Plätze," *Marketing News*, July 19, 1999, p. 11.

[111]B. O'Hara, F. Palumbo, and P. Herbig, "Industrial trade shows abroad," *Industrial Marketing Management* 22 (1993): 233–237.

[112]"Trading Plätze."

[113]See S. Gopalakrishna and G. L. Lilien, "A three-stage model of industrial trade show performance," *Marketing Science* 14, no. 1 (Winter 1995): 22–42, for a formal mathematical model to assess trade show effectiveness.

[114]Marnik G. Dekimpe, Pierre François, Srinath Gopalakrishna, Gary L. Lilien, and Christophe Van den Bulte, "Generalizing About Trade Show Effectiveness: A Cross-National Comparison," *Journal of Marketing*, 61(October 1997): 55–64.

[115]"All trade shows, all the time," *Marketing News*, July 19, 1999, p. 11.

[116]http://www.pqmedia.com/globalproductplacementforecast-2012.html.

◆ ◆

Global Perspective 12-2

Siemens Exider—A Trade Show on Wheels: "Siemens is Really Cool!"

Siemens AG is a German conglomerate founded more than 150 years ago. The company sells primarily to other businesses. Just like many other firms, the company tried the entire range of traditional advertising campaigns and promotional techniques, but success had been limited. Especially in North America, Siemens has always had to face an uphill task of fighting low brand awareness. So, what to do? In March 2002, Siemens announced a mobile trade show on rails using a train, called "Exider," 1,000 feet long, or 300 meters, with 14 railroad cars. The activity has elements of a multimedia blitz and a traditional trade show. Some cars held Siemens products; others are fitted with video monitors or interactive screens showcasing Siemens products at work. Each wagon is staffed with Siemens experts on hand to explain the technology. The head of the Siemens division behind the project explained: "With the Exider, we want to take our show out to the customers and join them on a trip through the world of modern industrial automation, drive, switching, and installation technology."

The train journey started in Spain. Siemens' market share rose 3 percentage points after the Exider passed through. Other destinations included Britain, China, Singapore, and ultimately the United States. Invitations to visit the train went out to anyone Siemens deemed to be a potential customer. Siemens hoped that people taking the tour would ask questions, pick up brochures, attend technical seminars, and exchange business cards with a Siemens salesperson. For Siemens, the train is a vehicle to bring its technology close to customers, even those in remote areas. A vice president of Polo Ralph Lauren visited the train "to see what other things I might buy from them." Customers on the train were overheard saying that they had never realized that Siemens had such a broad portfolio of solutions in so many industry segments. Some customers looking at a display in one of the coaches said: "Oh? This is really cool!" Stephen Greyser, a Harvard Business School professor, said: "Anyone who steps inside that train becomes a willing collaborator in the process of learning more about what Siemens is and does." Likewise, Michael Watras, a brand consultant, noted: "It's out-of-the-box thinking that positions the brand as cutting-edge."

Sources: "Siemens Makes Tracks toward Higher Profile," *International Herald Tribune*, March 27–28, 2004), p. 11; http://www2.automation.siemens.com/mes/simatic_it/html_76/download/adbv200203215e.pdf.

marketers, product placement can be a very effective tool to target audiences that are less exposed to traditional media advertising. Products that are often featured include cars, luxury goods, consumer electronics, and computers. The none-too-subtle use of product placement in movies such as *Casino Royale* and *I, Robot* has triggered a fair amount of criticism. In terms of product placement as a global marketing tool, one notable example is the 1993 sci-fi movie *Demolition Man*. In the U.S. version of the movie, the hero played by Sylvester Stallone refers to Taco Bell as being the sole survivor of the "franchise wars." In many foreign releases of the movie Taco Bell is replaced with Pizza Hut, which is also owned by Yum! Brands. The reason for the change was that Taco Bell is not present in most of Yum! Brands's non-American markets.

Some recent Hollywood blockbuster movies have also become vehicles to pitch Chinese brands. In *Transformers 3: Dark of the Moon*, Sam, played by Shia LaBoeuf, wears a T-shirt made by Meters/bonwe—a midlevel Chinese clothing brand. A scientist tells Sam to finish his Shuhua Low Lactose Milk—a product marketed by Yili, one of China's largest dairy companies. Brains, one of the robots, transforms itself out of a Lenovo Edge computer. Except for Lenovo's computers, none of these products were available in the United States.[117]

Viral Marketing

Viral marketing refers to marketing tools that try to achieve marketing objectives such as increased brand awareness by boosting a self-replicating viral process through a social network, similar to the spread of a real-world virus. The social network can be virtual (e.g., Facebook, email contacts) or offline (or some combination).[118] Other terms that are sometimes used are buzz marketing and word-of-mouse marketing. The message can be spread through text messages, images, music or video clips, or games. The key for the viral campaign to be effective is twofold: (1) identify people with a high networking influence and (2) create a message that is so compelling that it will be passed on through the network.

Scores of major brands have embraced viral marketing as a communication tool such as Unilever's Axe, Volkswagen, and Carlsberg. Viral marketers must grapple with several challenges. As more and more marketers jump on the bandwagon, the biggest issue is to come up with something that stands out and breaks through the clutter. The creative bar can be much higher than for traditional marketing tools. One consultant points out that a viral marketing campaign has to be "extremely good, absolutely hilarious, or shocking. The trouble is that most companies are not willing to take risks or to break taboos."[119] Another concern is to make sure that the campaign does not offend the global online community by being seen as a blatant commercial infringement. Virtual marketers also have little control over how the message is spread and where it ends up. When a viral message is circulated in a geographic area where the brand is not available, the campaign is wasteful. Netizens could also mock the campaign. When Carlsberg ran a viral e-mail campaign that spoofed its ad slogan during the Euro 2004 soccer campaign,[120] netizens came up with an altered negative version which became much more visible than the original.[121]

Global Public Relations (PR) and Publicity

For global marketers, building up good relationships with various stakeholders (e.g., employees, press, distributors, customers, government authorities) is an important part of their communication strategy. Public relations (PR) consists of managing the flow of information between an organization and its publics.[122] Publicity is spreading information about a product or company to gain awareness. Most of that communication is "free" although most companies will often engage a PR agency to manage the information flow. Effective PR management often leads to high publicity. A well-executed PR campaign needs to fulfill two requirements: (1) it should be creative, and (2) it should be based on insights about the target audience derived from solid research. **Exhibit 12-13** summarizes two well-executed PR campaigns.

[117]"China Brands in Hollywood Placement Push," http://www.ft.com, accessed January 13, 2013.
[118]http://en.wikipedia.org/wiki/Viral_marketing, accessed February 21, 2009.
[119]"Viral Advertisers Play with Fire," *Financial Times*, August 29, 2006, p. 6.
[120]The message was: "Carlsberg don't send e-mails, but if they did they'd probably be the best e-mails in the world."
[121]"Viral Advertisers."
[122]James E. Grunig and Todd Hunt, *Managing Public Relations* (Orlando, FL: Harcourt Brace Jovanovich, 1984).

Exhibit 12-13   Examples of International PR Campaigns

Example 1: Adidas Chinese women's volleyball team

- *Brief:* To strengthen adidas' association with the Chinese women's volleyball team.
- *Target audience:* 14- to 24-year-olds in China.
- *Challenge:* Although the Chinese women's volleyball players were stars in the 1980s with world championship wins, the team had lost its appeal with youth: it was widely perceived as non-feminine and unfashionable.
- *Campaign:* The goal of the campaign was to make women's volleyball "cool." The PR agency launched a yearlong campaign of viral elements and publicity stunts. To change the drab image, glamour shots of the players were taken and angled for various publications, mostly lifestyle media. Stylish video clips of the team were shot and posted online. Adidas organized a "chant" competition to boost enthusiasm and pride in the national team. Adidas' PR agency also set up a blog.
- *Results:* The total media value received was worth Rmb 36 million ($4.6 million), worth more than 13 times the original investment. The blog received more than 20,000 page views on the first day of the launch.

Example 2: Pantene Shine

- *Brief:* To instill the spirit of Pantene shampoo's new platform.
- *Target audience:* 15- to 35-year-old women in India
- *Challenge:* In autumn 2006, P&G launched a new global positioning for Pantene shampoo with a new logo, packaging, and tagline: "Shine, I believe I can."
- *The campaign:* The cornerstone was India's first Pantene Shine Awards. The inaugural award was a high-profile award attended by celebrities from all over India. Six women in the beauty industry were honored at the award show and designated as brand ambassadors, including Bollywood star Sushmita Sen. Pantene's PR agency organized India's first branded chat shows, called *Shine. I believe I can—Sush speaks out.* The brand also launched a reality TV show, inviting entries from women aged 18 to 30 across India to compete for the "dream job" of TV news anchor.
- *Results:* The award show got nearly 500 mentions in print and TV, reaching 90 percent of the target audience.

Source: "Are Clients Ready for Breakthrough Creative?" *Media*, April 20, 2007, p. 8; and "Pantene Rolls Out Reality TV Show," *Media*, May 4, 2007, p. 2.

Globally Integrated Marketing Communications (GIMC)

In a pan-European campaign to promote Sony Ericsson's[123] new T300 mobile phone, hundreds of drooling dogs were walked several times a day during a six-week period in major European cities.[124] The dogs, as well as their walkers, were wearing specially designed branded clothing. The walking activity was part of an integrated campaign centering on the "drooling" theme. Other elements included TV, the internet, posters, viral e-mail, radio, and sponsorships. According to one of Sony Ericsson's European marketing managers: "The drool campaign is about creating lust for THE BAR (the handset's nickname). . . . The entire drool campaign has a real edge to it—something that the target audience (16- to 24-year-olds) all over Europe will relate to."

The North Face, an American outdoor sports product company, faced a great challenge in China where most Chinese had yet to adopt the lifestyle associated with the brand. The goal was to give China's urban dwellers and internet surfers a taste of how great it is to explore new places. The solution was the fully integrated "Conquer China" campaign. The campaign was inspired by

---

[123]The Sony Ericsson joint venture was dissolved in early February 2012 when Sony bought out Ericsson and renamed the entity Sony Mobile Communications.

[124]"Packs of Dogs Provide 'Ad Space' for Euro Launch of Sony T300 Handset," http://www.adageglobal.com, accessed December 16, 2002.

the ritual of explorers laying claim to newly discovered territory by planting a flag. In the campaign, participants would compete to "conquer" China. All they needed was a mobile phone to plant virtual flags at any location they wanted to stake a claim to. The 18-day campaign involved the internet, advertising, in-store promotions, outdoor scoreboards, and live events. There were over 2 million unique visitors to the campaign website. Over 651,000 red flags were planted. The winner had planted over 4,000 flags. Nearly 1.2 million people saw the live events in Beijing and Shanghai. Dealer store sales rose 106 percent.[125]

For most companies, media advertising is only one element of their global communications efforts. As we saw in the previous section, marketers use many other communication tools. In recent years, advertising agencies and their clients have recognized the value of an **integrated marketing communications (IMC)** program—not just for domestic markets but globally. The "drool" campaign is just one example of the push toward IMC. IMC goes beyond taking a screenshot from a TV ad and plastering it everywhere: the core idea should be integrated, not the execution. By coordinating the different communication vehicles—mass advertising, sponsorships, sales promotions, packaging, point-of-purchase displays, and so forth—an IMC campaign can convey one and the same idea to the prospective customers with a unified voice.[126] Instead of having the different promotional mix elements send out a mish-mash of messages with a variety of visual imagery, each and every one of them centers on that single key idea. By having consistency, integration, and cohesiveness, marketers will be able to maximize the impact of your communication tools.

A five-nation survey of ad agencies found that the use of IMC varies a good deal. The percentage of client budgets devoted to IMC activities was low in India (15 percent) and Australia (22 percent). The percentage was far higher in New Zealand (40 percent) and the United Kingdom (42 percent).[127] One study also revealed cross-country differences in the evaluation of the IMC concept: U.S. PR and advertising agencies seem to consider IMC as a way to organize the marketing business of the firm while Korean and U.K. agencies view it as coordination of the various communication disciplines.[128]

A **globally integrated marketing communications (GIMC)** program goes one step further. GIMC is a system of active promotional management that strategically coordinates global communications in all of its component parts, both horizontally (country-level) and vertically (promotion tools).[129]

To run a GIMC program effectively places demands on both the advertiser's organization and the advertising agencies involved. Companies that want to pursue a GIMC for some or all of their brands should have the mechanisms in place to coordinate their promotional activities vertically (across tools) and horizontally (across countries). By the same token, agencies in the various disciplines (e.g., advertising, PR) should be willing to integrate and coordinate the various communication disciplines across countries. GIMC also requires frequent communications both internally and between ad agency branches worldwide.[130] Unfortunately, in many countries it is difficult to find ad agencies that can provide the talent to collaborate on and execute integrated campaigns.

---

[125]"Red Flags, The North Face," *Campaign Asia-Pacific* (December 2010): 15. A short clip on the campaign can be seen on YouTube: http://www.youtube.com/watch?v=0gQ5_F2F2SI.

[126]"Integrated Marketing Communications: Maybe Definition Is in the Point of View," *Marketing News*, January 18, 1993.

[127]Philip J. Kitchen and Don E. Schultz, "A Multi-Country Comparison of the Drive for IMC," *Journal of Advertising Research*, (Jan.-Feb. 1999): 21–38.

[128]Philip J. Kitchen, Ilchul Kim, and Don E. Schultz, "Integrated Marketing Communications: Practice Leads Theory," *Journal of Advertising Research* 48 (December 2008): 531–46.

[129]Andreas F. Grein and Stephen J. Gould, "Globally Integrated Marketing Communications," *Journal of Marketing Communications* 2, no. 3 (1996): 141–158.

[130]Stephen J. Gould, Dawn B. Lerman, and Andreas F. Grein, "Agency Perceptions and Practices on Global IMC," *Journal of Advertising Research* (Jan.–Feb. 1999): 7–20.

SUMMARY

For many marketers, global communications present some of the most daunting challenges. A multitude of decisions need to be carried out on the front of international advertising. This chapter gives an overview of the major ones: creating advertising campaigns, setting and allocating the budget, selecting media vehicles to carry the campaign, choosing advertising agencies, and coordinating cross-country advertising programs. The development of a global advertising plan involves many players—headquarters, regional and/or local offices, advertising agencies—typically making the entire process frustrating. However, the potential rewards of a brilliant and well-executed international advertising strategy are alluring.

One of the front-burner issues that scores of international advertisers face is to what degree they should push for pan-regional or even global advertising campaigns. The arguments for standardizing campaigns are pretty compelling: (1) cost savings, (2) a coherent brand image, (3) similarity of target groups, and (4) transplanting of creative ideas. By now, you should also be quite familiar with the counterarguments: (1) cultural barriers, (2) countries being at different stages of market development, (3) role of advertising regulations, and (4) variations in the media-environment. Most global marketers balance between the two extremes by adopting a compromise solution.[131]

Overall, there seems to be a definite move towards more pan-regional (or even global) campaigns. Numerous explanations have been put forward to explain this shift: the "global" village rationale, the mushrooming of global and pan-regional media vehicles, and restructuring of marketing divisions and brand systems along global or pan-regional lines. Another important development is the emergence of new media outlets, including the internet. While it is hard to gaze into a crystal ball and come up with concrete predictions, it is clear that international advertisers will face a drastically different environment ten years from now.

---

[131]Ali Kanso and Richard Alan Nelson, "Advertising Localization Overshadows Standardization," *Journal of Advertising Research* (Jan.–Feb. 2002): 79–89.

QUESTIONS

1. Discuss the major challenges faced by international advertisers.

2. What factors entice international advertisers to localize their advertising campaigns in foreign markets?

3. What will be the impact of satellite TV on international advertising?

4. What mechanisms should MNCs contemplate to coordinate their advertising efforts across different countries?

5. The allocation of promotional dollars between "pull" (consumer promotions + media advertising) and "push" varies drastically for many advertisers across countries. What are the factors behind these variations?

6. In January 2010, PepsiCo signed a three-year sponsorship deal with Pakistan's cricket team. Cricket in Pakistan is almost like a religion; nobody watches anything else when cricket is on. A few months later, several Pakistani cricket players were being investigated by Scotland Yard for match-fixing following a test match in London. Ultimately, in November 2011, four players of the team were found guilty by a London court and given prison sentences ranging from 6 to 32 months. What options does PepsiCo have to cope with this scandal? How should it react? What factors should it consider in deciding its response?

SALES MANAGEMENT

13

CHAPTER OVERVIEW

1. Market entry options and salesforce strategy

2. Cultural considerations

3. Impact of culture on sales management and personal selling process

4. Cross-cultural negotiations

5. Expatriates

Think of two major markets in Asia: Japan and China. Japan is a well-established developed country similar to the United States, and is the third-largest economy in the world behind China (the second largest) and the United States (the largest). One might assume that foreign firms can sell products pretty much the same way as they do in the United States. Such an assumption may prove to be very wrong! For example, U.S. automakers still have great difficulty making inroads into the Japanese market, although Japan does not impose any tariffs or quotas on foreign cars, and although BMW, Mercedes-Benz, and Volkswagen have become familiar names in Japan. One major, yet little known, reason is in the way cars are sold in Japan. Unlike the United States where customers visit car dealers, a majority of cars are sold by door-to-door salespeople in Japan, in much the same way Avon representatives sell personal care and beauty products. However, now the situation is gradually changing, and Japanese dealers are diversifying. They are investing more money in significantly larger American-style dealership operations and less in door-to-door sales and small one-car show-rooms. The reason for this shift in sales strategies is that Japanese consumers increasingly dislike at-home sales calls, especially women, who today play a major role in new car purchasing decisions. However, traditional door-to-door sales still remain effective in offering a high level of service that continues to determine which cars will eventually be sold, and will not disappear any time soon.[1]

China, on the other hand, is an emerging economic and political giant. Foreign and local companies are fighting an increasingly fierce battle for a slice of the potentially lucrative Chinese market with its 1.3 billion potential consumers. However, it is not easy for foreign enterprises to establish a presence in the unfamiliar, rapidly changing market, where old and

---

[1]Alexandra Harney, "Death of the Salesman Spells Boost for Japan," *Financial Times*, January 5, 1999, p. 6; and Masataka Morita and Kiyohiko G. Nishimura, "Information Technology and Automobile Distribution: A Comparative Study of Japan and the United States," A working paper, University of Tokyo, August 25, 2000.

modern social systems coexist. The truth is that selling products is far more difficult in China than manufacturing them there. Business morals and practices have yet to develop sufficiently in the distribution sector. It is quite common for sales agents to channel products into the black market or for manufacturers' salespeople to discount prices for agents in exchange for secret rebates. Faced with China's labyrinthine sales channels, which even local manufacturers find difficult to manage, foreign businesses are often at a loss as to how to maneuver in them. In such a market, the local salesforce is crucial in penetrating the market. All these examples vividly illustrate the importance of international sales management.

What does the salesperson do in a company? Some salespeople sell products, and others sell services. Some are focused on the immediate sale; some take overall responsibility for all aspects of a global business customer's business—literally on a global basis. Salespeople take orders, deliver products, educate buyers, build relationships with clients, and provide technical knowledge.

In all cases the salesperson is the front line for the company. The customer sees only the salesperson and the product. Through the salesperson, the customer develops an opinion of the company. The success or failure of the company rests largely on the ability of the salesforce. We cannot overstate the importance of making good decisions when those decisions affect the quality and ability of the company's salesforce. This chapter investigates how the processes of sales management and personal selling are changed when taken overseas into another culture.

So what is international about sales management and personal selling? First, we can break international sales management issues into two categories that provide a clarification of the use of the term international: (1) international strategy considerations: issues that analyze more than one country's assets, strengths, and situations, or that deal directly with cross-border coordination; and (2) intercultural considerations: issues that focus on the culture of the foreign country and its impact on operations within that country.

Although these two categories are not mutually exclusive, they help clarify what makes international sales management considerations different from domestic sales management (see **Exhibit 13-1**).

In this chapter, we highlight issues related to the choice of market entry method and the sales management step to setting salesforce objectives. In relating foreign entry choices to sales management, we provide a framework for thinking about the effects of various salesforce management issues. Subsequently, we ask you to carefully consider the cultural generalizations that influence international decisions and interactions. Poor generalizations will produce

Exhibit 13-1   International Sales Strategy and Intercultural Considerations

International Sales Strategy Issues	Intercultural Issues within the Foreign Country
Global/international vs. local account management	Motivation
Salesforce skill availability	Cultural sensitivity
Country image	Ethical standards
Expatriate recruiting	Fairness
Centralized training	Relationship building
Home to host communications	Selling style differences

flawed sales management. Good tools for generalizing about cultures can help the international manager make decisions that accurately take into account cultural differences.

We discuss how cultural differences, in general, affect issues central to sales management. We consider cultural impacts on recruiting, training, supervising, and evaluating salespeople, as well as on the personal sales process. We also examine a special form of cross-cultural interactions: international negotiations.

Finally, we discuss the complex issues involved when a company sends its employees overseas. The successful use of expatriates gives a company significant advantages but requires careful selection, training, supervision, and evaluation.

Market Entry Options and Salesforce Strategy

In the salesforce management "process," we start with setting objectives and strategy. These steps include determining the goals and purposes of the salesforce and the structure that will best meet those goals. To a large extent, these initial steps determine the requirements for the subsequent steps in the process—recruiting, training, supervising, and evaluating.

The question of how to enter the market is central to marketing. As a company decides what form its market entry will take, it is making a decision that limits and defines key underlying aspects of its future salesforce management. For example, if a company decides to sell its products in the United States through a large, integrated distributor, it may only need a small, highly mobile salesforce.

In international sales, the form of entry has even greater implications. The form of entry determines how large the salesforce needs to be and will influence how much training it will require. It also influences whether the salesforce is predominantly local foreign citizens or whether it is primarily expatriates. This composition then influences the compensation scale required. Clearly, the form of entry directly influences many of the downstream sales-force management options. This section reviews various options for entering a foreign market and summarizes the principal implications and questions each option raises.

The entry method we have been referring to is also termed the level of integration in the market. Forward integration suggests greater ownership and control of the distribution channel. For example, a company might begin its foreign sales by exporting through a merchant distributor who takes title to the product and performs all necessary foreign sales functions. Later, the company might integrate forward into the distribution channel by hiring its own commissioned sales agents in the foreign country. Still greater forward integration might consist of the company purchasing a sales subsidiary and establishing product warehouses abroad.[2]

Determining the best level of integration is an issue more appropriate for a chapter on international strategy than sales management. However, in determining the entry form, the company must consider the subsequent influences it will have on their sales management options. In general, greater forward integration is preferred when (1) the operation is large enough to spread out the overhead costs of owning and maintaining infrastructure and training and supervising employees, or (2) an inability to enforce contractual obligations on outside intermediaries or some other need for greater control of the sales process requires a strong presence in the host country. Additionally, (3) sales of a service usually require a presence in the country earlier than would otherwise be considered.

A number of typical entry approaches and the sales management concerns each raises are presented in **Exhibit 13-2**.

---

[2]Saul Kline, Gary L. Frazier, and Victor J. Roth, "A Transaction Cost Analysis Model of Channel Integration in International Markets," *Journal of Marketing Research* 27 (May 1990): 196–208.

Exhibit 13-2   Degree of Involvement and Sales Management Issues

Degree of Involvement	Examples	Description	Sales Management Concerns
Limited Foreign Involvement and Visibility	Export Management Companies (EMC), Export Trading Companies (ETC), direct exporting, licensing	• Concerned with contract for sales from the U.S. • No salesforce or representatives abroad • Little or no control over foreign marketing process	• Goals of the company may not take precedence • Low foreign image and stability • Impossibility of training salesforce
Local Management and Salesforce	Piggybacking, selling through chains	• Little attempt to make foreign sales imitate U.S. sales culture • May "borrow" a salesforce or sell via direct contracts from abroad with multidistributor outlets	• Ineffective customs (lack of influence) • Low product knowledge • Control (trust, commitment) • Poor communications
Expatriate Management and Local Salesforce (Mixed)	Selling through chains with locals, direct selling with locals	• Expatriates oversee sales regions, lead training	• Perceptions of equality and fairness • Cultural interactions
Heavy Reliance on Expatriate Salesforce	Traveling global salesforce, high technology experts	• Client-by-client sales by expatriate salesforce	• Lack of local understanding of insiders and market workings • High cost • Difficulty in recruiting expatriates • Country limits on expatriates or rules, such as taxes, which vary depending on foreign presence

Selling through an Export Management Company (EMC) or an Export Trading Company (ETC) is considered a low-involvement approach to international sales. **Export management companies (EMCs)**, in general, serve the needs of their clients in entering a market or sourcing goods from a market. They are characterized by their "service" nature and their efforts to interact with and meet the needs of the exporter client. Many EMCs have specific expertise in selecting markets abroad and finding customers due to their language capabilities, previous business experience in the country, or a network of their business contacts. The EMC works with an exporter in one of two ways. First, the EMC may act as an agent distributor performing marketing services for the exporter client, responsible primarily for developing foreign business and sales strategies and establishing contact abroad. For this prospecting role, the EMC earns its income from a commission on the products it sells on the exporter's behalf. Second, the EMC can act as a merchant distributor, who purchases products from the domestic exporter, takes title, sells the product in its own name, and consequently assumes all trading risks. The domestic exporter selling directly to the merchant EMC receives its money without having to deal with the complexities and trading risks in the international market. On the other hand, the exporter is less likely to build its own international experience. Many inexperienced exporters use EMC services mainly to test the international arena, with some desire to become direct participants once a foreign customer base has been established.

Since the late 1990s, the rapid growth of the internet and the recent proliferation of e-business have generated threats to the future of EMCs. The impact of e-business on the survival of EMCs has been a subject of serious debate for some time. However, according to recent research, this may not be the case. This study suggests that the primary reason underlying the survival of the EMCs in the past has been their market-based resources and capabilities accumulated over time, and this would also be the primary reason of their survival and reintermediation in the future. By appropriately weaving e-business into their market-based resources and capabilities, the well-established EMCs can acquire a superior position of value creation vis-à-vis their suppliers in their value chains. As a result, the EMCs are expected to continue to play an important mediator role for inexperienced exporters.[3]

Export trading companies (ETCs) are usually large conglomerates that import, export, countertrade, invest, and manufacture in the global arena. The ETC can purchase products, act as a distributor abroad, or offer services. Mitsubishi, Mitsui, Sumitomo, and Marubeni, among others, are major examples of ETCs, which are known in Japan as **sogoshosha** (general trading companies).[4] ETCs utilize their vast size to benefit from economies of scale in shipping and distribution. In the United States, the Export Trading Company Act of 1982 exempted ETCs from antitrust laws.[5] The intent was to improve the export performance of small and medium-sized companies by allowing them joint participation with banks in an ETC. ETCs offer the exporting company a stable, known distributor, but they do not give the exporting company much control over or knowledge about the international sales process.

A recent empirical study, which estimates the determinants of the manufacturing exports demand from 1978 to 2004 to identify the effect of this exemption on the real value of exports, indicates that the program created by the ETC Act to provide limited antitrust immunity for joint export activity appears to have no statistically significant effect on the real value of U.S. exports. However, it also concludes that, although the ETC Act has had limited impact on the country's economy, it does present anecdotal evidence that shows its facilitation on some business cases to increase industry exports.[6]

Licensing also represents a low-involvement approach to foreign sales. The company licenses its product or technology abroad and allows the contracting foreign company to coordinate the production and foreign distribution of the product.

Limited involvement approaches to international market entry simplify sales management greatly by reducing it to a predominantly domestic activity. There is little need to recruit, train, supervise, or evaluate a foreign or expatriate salesforce. However, companies that follow a limited involvement approach sacrifice the benefits that hiring and training their own salesforce can provide. These benefits include the ability to motivate and monitor the salesforce and to train them to better serve the customer, the customer loyalty that a dedicated salesforce can generate, and the perception of permanence and commitment that a dedicated salesforce conveys. Many foreign companies look for such an indication of stability and commitment when selecting suppliers.

Mid-level involvement approaches to foreign sales are those in which the company controls some portion of the distribution process. Thus, the company must employ some management or salesforce abroad. This work force may be either predominantly host country employees, or it may include a large share of expatriates. In either case, the company deals face to face with the foreign culture, and intercultural communication becomes a significant issue. Training can help reduce misunderstandings and miscommunications. For example, training helps the local salespeople better understand the company's policies by reviewing its history and goals. Training also helps the expatriates understand the local market by reviewing the norms of business within their industry and country.

The choice of whether to rely on expatriate involvement is not an easy one. Without expatriate involvement, the company could decide that it is difficult to control the sales process, even though it

---

[3]Varinder M. Sharma, "Export Management Companies and E-Business: Impact on Export Services, Product Portfolio, and Global Market Coverage," *Journal of Marketing Theory & Practice* 13 (Fall 2005): 61–71.

[4]Anne C. Perry, "The Evolution of the U.S. International Trade Intermediary in the 1980s," *Journal of International Business Studies* 21, no. 1 1990): 133–153.

[5]Daniel C. Bello and Nicholas C. Williamson, "The American Export Trading Company: Designing a New International Marketing Institution," *Journal of Marketing* 49 (Fall 1985): 60–69.

[6]Viargaret C. Levenstein, Margaret C. Levenstein, and Valerie Y. Suslow, "The Economic Impact of the U.S. Export Trading Company Act," *Antitrust Law Journal* 74, no. 2 (2007): 343–386.

owns part of the process. With expatriate involvement, local nationals could envy the expatriates' higher levels of pay or resent the limitations on their career opportunities with the company.

High involvement approaches are those in which the company substantially controls the foreign distribution channels. The company could own warehouses to store products and outlets where the products are sold, and it could manage a large, dedicated salesforce abroad. Typically, if a domestic company is highly involved in a foreign market, at least some of that presence will be expatriates. For some companies only the top officer abroad is an expatriate. For others, the expatriate presence is much stronger.

The benefits of controlling distribution include the ability to recruit, train, and supervise a foreign salesforce that can best represent the company abroad. However, controlling distribution requires that the sales volume be large enough to justify the costs, and it also requires enough experience to avoid costly errors.

Role of Foreign Governments

At the time the company is considering its entry strategy, it should consider foreign government rules and practices. Many host country governments design regulations to protect local firms from international competition and ensure that local citizens benefit from experience in management positions at international companies. Thus, governments limit the number of international companies they allow to sell in the market, and they require that foreign companies fill a large number of positions with local citizens. Even the United States follows such practices. The U.S. Citizenship and Immigration Services does not let foreign managers enter the United States to work when it believes that there are U.S. citizens capable of performing the same jobs.[7] Foreign countries also often dictate who can enter, for how long, and for what jobs. These requirements can determine which entry strategy makes sense for a company.

A second issue in deciding the entry approach is the role expected of companies as good "corporate citizens" in the country. If a company sets up a complete sales and distribution subsidiary, it may be expected to build local infrastructure, support local politicians, or take part in local training initiatives. Such considerations will weigh in on the choice of the sales approach.

Cultural Considerations
Personal Selling

At the level of **personal selling** there is little true international selling. The sales task tends to take place on a national basis. Generally, salespeople perform the majority of their sales within one country—probably even within one region or area of a country. A salesperson selling big-ticket items, such as airplanes or dam construction, could sell to many countries. But even then, each sale is a sale within one country, and the entire sales process takes place in one country. Furthermore, despite growing "international sales," salespeople typically work in only one region. Even in the European Union (EU), for example, where close borders and similar economies could encourage salespeople to work over larger areas, personal selling activities still remain bound mostly to a country or a region. Thus, an analysis of international personal selling is a study of how differences in culture impact the forms, rules, and norms for personal selling within each country.[8]

[7]"U.S. Business Leaders Press Senate Panel For More Work Visas," *Wall Street Journal*, July 27, 2011, p. B5.
[8]See, for example, Joel Herche and Michel J. Swenson, "Personal Selling Constructs and Measures: Emic versus Etic Approaches to Cross-National Research," *European Journal of Marketing* 30, no. 7 (1996): 83-97; Ravi Sohi, "Global Selling and Sales Management-Cross Cultural Issues-National Character," *Journal of Personal Selling & Sales Management* 19 (Winter 1999): 80–81; and Nina Reynolds and A. Simintiras, "Toward an Understanding of the Role of Cross-Cultural Equivalence in International Personal Selling," *Journal of Marketing Management* 16 (November 2000): 829–851.

Personal selling is predominantly a personal activity. It requires that the salesperson understands the customer's needs and wants. The salesperson must understand local customs well enough to be accepted and be able to form relationships with the customers. Do customers require a close, supportive relationship where the salesperson regularly checks up on them and knows the names of relatives? Does the customer expect some favors to "lubricate the process"? Each culture has different norms for the process of selling and buying.[9]

Throughout this chapter, we refer to the need to adapt sales and management techniques to the local culture to be successful.[10] It would be wonderful if a diagram were available that could help managers plot the appropriate solutions for each country. Although such a diagram is too much to hope for, we can look at some common generalizations and categorizations of cultural traits and consider how they could affect our sales approach. We must take care, however, not to imply that any culture can be described accurately in a few words or categories.

Cultural Generalization

As an example of a cultural generalization with both helpful insights and misleading oversights, consider the foreign view of Germans. Germans are typically viewed as scientifically exacting and industrious people. We could therefore approach sales in Germany by building a small core of technically trained, independent sales agents. However, if we think Germans look at work the same way Americans do, we will be misguided! The typical German manufacturing workweek is only 30 hours. Also, Germans jealously guard their free time and show little interest in working more to earn more.[11] In fact, Germans get roughly the same amount of work done in fewer hours each week, and with more vacation time than Americans.[12]

We must also be careful not to group people from what may appear to us as very similar cultures, but who consider themselves, and react to situations, in a very distinct manner. Consider, for example, South Korea and Japan. We may think that Koreans would be accustomed to the same bottom-up, consensual decision-making approach for which the Japanese are known. Korean workers, however, tend to work within a top-down, authoritarian leadership structure,[13] and require a higher level of definition in their job structure to avoid suffering from role conflict. A Korean salesperson may accept as normal a short-term position with few prospects for long-term progress, whereas a Japanese salesperson would not dream of it.[14]

Another example is the differences in the orientation of salespeople in Australia and New Zealand. Most of us tend to think that their cultures are very similar. However, salespeople in

[9]Bruce Money, Mary C. Gilly, and John L. Graham, "Explorations of National Culture and Word-of-Mouth Referral Behavior in the Purchase of Industrial Services in the United States and Japan," *Journal of Marketing* 62 (October 1998): 76–87.

[10]Chanthika Pornpitakpan, "The Effects of Cultural Adaptation on Business Relationships: Americans Selling to Japanese and Thais," *Journal of International Business Studies* 30 (Second Quarter 1999): 317–338.

[11]Daniel Benjamin and Tony Horwitz, "German View: You Americans Work Too Hard—And For What?" *Wall Street Journal*, July 14, 1994, p. B1.

[12]"Why Germans Have Longer Vacation Times and More Productivity," *Open Forum*, http://www.openforum.com/, September 28, 2010.

[13]Jiro Usugami and Kyung-Yeol Park, "Similarities and Differences in Employee Motivation Viewed by Korean and Japanese Executives: Empirical Study on Employee Motivation Management of Japanese-Affiliated Companies in Korea," *International Journal of Human Resource Management* 17 (February 2006): 280–294.

[14]Alan J. Dubinsky, Ronald E. Michaels, Masaaki Kotabe, Chae Un Lim, and Hee-Cheol Moon, "Influence of Role Stress on Industrial Salespeople's Work Outcomes in the United States, Japan, and Korea," *Journal of International Business Studies* 23 (First Quarter 1992): 77–99.

New Zealand tend to be more committed to, and generally more satisfied with, their work than their Australian counterparts. Additionally, there are differences in preferences toward compensation (Australians preferring greater security in the form of larger salary) and special incentives (New Zealanders having a much higher preference for travel with other winners and supervisory staff).[15] In a way, salespeople in New Zealand share more similarities in their value system with their Japanese counterparts than their Australian neighbors.

These and other observations suggest that cultural generalizations may be risky even among seemingly similar countries, particularly at the operational level. As explained earlier in Chapter 4, one of the most widely used tools for categorizing cultures for managerial purposes is Hofstede's scale of five cultural dimensions (i.e., power distance; uncertainty avoidance; individualism/collectivism; masculinity/femininity; long-term/short-term orientation). Hofstede's scale uses many questions to determine where countries, not individual people, stand on each dimension.

Corporate (Organizational) Culture

As also explained in Chapter 4, companies also have their own distinct **corporate (organizational) cultures**. The culture at a company helps determine the norms of behavior and the mood at the workplace. This corporate culture acts in conjunction with national or country culture to set the values and beliefs that employees carry in the workplace.

The differences between the cultures of any two companies have been found to be determined significantly by the practices of those already in the company, especially the founders. By contrast, the differences between the cultures of companies in two countries are based more in the ingrained cultural values of the employees.[16] Values are learned earlier in life and are much more difficult to change than practices. Consider an example of the difference in trying to modify each practice. We might expect to initiate novel work practices without strong negative reactions from the employees. For example, we might ask salespeople to report to a group instead of to a boss in an effort to instill a sense of group responsibility. However, if we attempt to change procedures that are strongly rooted in the values of a country's culture, we may be asking for a negative response. Consider the troubles we might encounter if we attempted to integrate men and women in the salesforce in Saudi Arabia. At the very least we would not bring out the best the salesforce has to offer.

Thus, although corporate cultures determine much about the working environment and even the success of an organization, the practices that characterize them are fairly malleable. Country cultures and more specifically, the values people build at an early age in life, also greatly influence which management practices will succeed. However, cultural values are fairly fixed—do not underestimate the importance of cultural values and people's unwillingness to change them.[17]

Relationship Marketing

In the last 20 years, influenced by Japan's vertical *keiretsu* (a closely knit group affiliation among the principal company, upstream suppliers of components and other materials, and

---

[15]William H. Murphy, "Hofstede's National Culture as a Guide for Sales Practices across Countries: The Case of a MNC's Sales Practices in Australia and New Zealand," *Australian Journal of Management* 24 (June 1999): 37–58.

[16]Geert Hofstede, Bram Neuijen, Denise Daval Ohayv, and Geert Sanders, "Measuring Organizational Cultures: A Qualitative and Quantitative Study Across Twenty Cases," *Administrative Science Quarterly* 35 (1990): 286–316.

[17]Ibid.

downstream retailers for its finished products along the value chain), an increasing number of companies, such as Bose, Compaq, and Motorola, have begun to station their engineering personnel in their independent parts suppliers for more effective product development and to station their sales personnel work in the retailer's offices. The principal companies can track demand at store levels directly and place orders on a just-in-time basis. Both upstream and downstream involvements by the principal companies along the value chain can manage information flow from the retailers and customers more effectively and step up the pace of new product development.[18]

This type of buyer-seller relationship is a win-win situation because both sides gain from the deal (although in different ways). Thus, they start out with the intention of producing a mutually beneficial arrangement. An increasing number of organizations have, indeed, come to see the relationship as one of interdependence; the two sides adopt a peer-to-peer relationship.

Indeed, the relationship between a seller and a buyer seldom ends when the sale is made. In an increasing proportion of transactions, the relationship actually intensifies subsequent to the sale. This becomes the critical factor in the buyer's choice of the seller the next time around. How good the seller-buyer relationship is depends on how well the seller manages it.[19] Again, many companies are finding that adoption of the personal computer technology is crucial for their success in maintaining product, pricing, and technical data for effective customer relationships.

It is over a decade and a half since management consultancy Bain & Co carried out its groundbreaking research into the key differences between customer acquisition and customer retention.[20] By considering the real costs and long-term returns, it found that most companies often understated acquisition costs, while cross-selling to an existing customer cost one-sixth of the price of making a sale to a prospect. Bain introduced one of the most famous equations in marketing: a 5 percent increase in customer retention would increase the value of each customer by between 25 and 100 percent. The potential implied in that finding led directly to the development of customer relationship marketing.[21]

Good customer relationships are important by any means in any market. However, they tend to be more conspicuous in high-context cultures, such as Asian and Latin American countries. As discussed in Chapter 4, people in high-context culture countries tend to prefer group-oriented decision-making processes, unlike low-context culture countries, such as the United States and Western and Northern European countries, where decision-making processes are individualistic. In many firms, salespeople are also the primary source of information exchange within a customer-seller relationship and thus play a critical role in the formation and sustainability of customer relationships. To the extent that customer relationship marketing is important, the personal traits of sales managers need to be carefully examined, particularly when they engage in "selling" to corporate clients in other countries. Some examples of selected differences in buyer-seller relationships are presented in **Exhibit 13-3**.

---

[18]Michiel R. Leenders and David L. Blenkhorn, *Reverse Marketing: The New Buyer-Supplier Relationship* (New York: Free Press, 1988).

[19]Gila E. Fruchter and Simon P. Sigué, "Transactions vs. Relationships: What Should the Company Emphasize?" *Journal of Service Research* 8 (August 2005): 18–36.

[20]Frederick Reichheld, *The Loyalty Effect*, Boston, MA: Harvard Business School Press, 1996.

[21]Peter R. Dickson, Walfried M. Lassar, Gary Hunter, and Samit Chakravorti, "The Pursuit of Excellence in Process Thinking and Customer Relationship Management," *Journal of Personal Selling & Sales Management* 29 (Spring, 2009): 111–124.

Exhibit 13-3   Differences in Buyer-Seller Relationships

International Market	Relationship		Nature of Interaction		
	Climate	Importance	Pace	Process	Decision Making
Asian					
Japan	Formal, polite climate with many idiosyncratic nuances	Great importance; long-term relationships are what matter most	Very slow with a lot of initial time spent on relationship building	First all general items are agreed upon, then details are discussed	A total group process with all levels involved in the final decision
China	Bureaucratic climate with an abundance of "red tape"	Very important; traditional, cultural courtesies are expected	Very slow with a lot of initial time spent on relationship building	Discussions are long and repetitive; agreements must be in writing	Usually a group process headed by a senior negotiator
Non-Asian					
USA	Sometimes viewed as an aggressive or confrontational climate	Of less importance; Focus is on achieving desired results	"Time is money"; Effort will be made to expedite the negotiations	Ordered process where each point is discussed in sequence	Can be either an individual or group decision process
Canada	Positive, polite climate; Hard sell will not work here	Of less importance; Focus is on achieving desired results	A little slower than in the USA	Ordered process where each point is discussed in sequence	Can be either an individual or group decision process
Latin America	Positive and hospitable climate	Personal, one-on-one relationships very important	Very relaxed, slow-moving negotiation process	Relationship building through socialization will precede negotiations	Decisions are usually made by a high-level individual
United Kingdom	Traditional, polite climate; Hard sell will not work here	Of less importance; Focus is on achieving desired results	A little slower than in the USA	Ordered process where each point is discussed in sequence	Can be either an individual or group decision process
Germany/ Austria	Rigid, sober climate	Low; Germans remain aloof until negotiations conclude	A little slower than in the USA	Systematic process with emphasis on contractual detail	Even the most routine decisions are made by top-level officials
France/ French Belgium	Formal, bureaucratic climate; Hard sell will not work here	Formal, arms length relationship with attention to etiquette	Slow-paced, deliberative process	French teams use argument to generate discussion	Usually a group process headed by a senior negotiator
Russia	Bureaucratic climate with an abundance of "red tape"	Low; Russians will remain reserved until negotiations conclude	Slow due to importance placed on detail	Cumbersome process due to bureaucratic constraints	Usually a group process headed by a senior negotiator

Source: Adapted from Jeffrey E. Lewin and Wesley J. Johnston, "International Salesforce Management: A Relationship Perspective," *Journal of Business & Industrial Marketing* 12, no. 3/4 1997): 236–352.

Myers–Briggs Type Indicator

All business is personal. Despite all the time that marketing departments put into persuasive press releases and snazzy computer presentations, in the end, people do business with people. One popular tool for characterizing people that addresses their cognitive styles is the **Myers–Briggs Type Indicator (MBTI)** (see **Exhibit 13-4**). The MBTI is based on the following four personal dimensions: (1) extrovert versus introvert, (2) intuitive versus sensing, (3) thinking versus feeling, and (4) judging versus perceiving.

Exhibit 13-4   Myers–Briggs Type Indicator of Personal Characteristics

Personal Dimension	Description
Extrovert vs. Introvert	An extrovert tends to rely on the environment for guidance, be action-oriented, sociable, and communicate with ease and frankness.
	An introvert tends to show a greater concern with concepts and ideas than with external events, relative detachment, and enjoyment of solitude and privacy over companionship.
Sensing vs. Intuitive	A sensing person tends to focus on immediate experience, become more realistic and practical, and develop skills such as acute powers of observation and memory for details.
	An intuitive person tends to value possibility and meaning more than immediate experience, and become more imaginative, theoretical, abstract, and future oriented.
Thinking vs. Feeling	A thinking person tends to be concerned with logical and impersonal decision making and principles of justice and fairness, and is strong in analytical ability and objectivity.
	A feeling person tends to make decisions by weighing relative values and merits of issues, be attuned to personal and group values, and be concerned with human, rather than technical, aspects of a problem.
Judging vs. Perceiving	A judging person tends to make relatively quick decisions, be well planned and organized, and seek closure.
	A perceiving person tends to be open to new information, not move for closure to make quick decisions, and stay adaptable and open to new events or change.

Source: Constructed from Neil R. Abramson, Henry W. Lane, Hirohisa Nagai, and Haruo Takagi, "A Comparison of Canadian and Japanese Cognitive Styles: Implications for Management Interactions," *Journal of International Business Studies* 24 (Third Quarter 1993): 575–587.

Using this scale, Abramsom, Lane, Nagai, and Takagi[22] found significant cognitive distinctions between Canadian and Japanese MBA students. The English-speaking Canadian students preferred intuition, judgment, and thinking, whereas the Japanese students preferred sensing, perceiving, and thinking, but were more feeling-oriented than the Canadian students. In summary, the English-speaking Canadians displayed a logical and impersonal, or objective, style that subordinates the human element. The Japanese displayed a more feeling style, which emphasized the human element in problem solving such as being sympathetic and building trust in human relations. English-speaking Canadians have a tendency to seek decisions quickly and rush to closure on data collection. The Japanese were found to resist quick decision making because of their preference for obtaining large amounts of information. Another study also shows that French-speaking Canadians in Quebec, unlike the English-speaking Canadians, are indeed a bit more similar to the Japanese in terms of their emphasis on trust building.[23] Indeed, Japanese salespeople, who emphasize trust building, use more word-of-mouth referrals in consummating sales more often than their American counterparts.[24]

Although the Myers-Briggs Type Indicator categorizes personal style and traits, there is some similarity to the national culture classification schemes such as Hall's high vs. low context cultures

---

[22]Neil R. Abramson, Henry W. Lane, Hirohisa Nagai, and Haruo Takagi, "A Comparison of Canadian and Japanese Cognitive Styles: Implications for Management Interactions," *Journal of International Business Studies* 24 (Third Quarter 1993): 575–587.

[23]Joseph P. Cannon, Patricia M. Doney, and Michael R. Mullen, "A Cross-Cultural Examination of the Effects of Trust and Supplier Performance on Long-Term Buyer-Supplier Relationships," *Enhancing Knowledge Development in Marketing*, 1999 American Marketing Association Educators' Proceedings, Summer 1999, p. 101.

[24]R. Bruce Money, Mary C. Gilly, and John L. Graham, "Explorations of National Culture and Word-of-Mouth Referral Behavior in the Purchase of Industrial Services in the United States and Japan," *Journal of Marketing* 62 (October 1998): 76–87.

and Hofstede's five components of culture (explained earlier in Chapter 4). People from low-context (individualistic) culture tend to be extrovert, intuitive, thinking, and judging, while those from high-context (group-oriented) culture tend to be introvert, sensing, feeling, and perceiving in orientation. Of course, the interpretation of cultural characteristics at the personal level may border on stereotyping. Rather, think of cultural traits as a general tendency in evaluating personal style and traits.[25]

Differences in style and traits must be taken into consideration whenever two cultures interact. In international sales, cross-cultural interaction takes place between the home office and the subsidiary, between expatriate managers and the salesforce, or between an expatriate salesperson and the customer. If the cultural norms and cognitive styles of both sides are more clearly understood, misconceptions and miscommunications will decrease.

Impact of Culture on Sales Management and Personal Selling Process

In general, the human resource practices of multinational corporations (MNCs) closely follow the local practices of the country in which they operate.[26] These human resource practices include time off, benefits, gender composition, training, executive bonuses, and participation of employees in management. However, human resource practices also depend on the strategy desired, the culture of the company, and even the country from which the company originated.

Thus, although we can say that the sales management process should adapt to the local environment,[27] we acknowledge the difficult give-and-take involved in adapting a company's culture and procedures with the sales and management practices of a foreign country.

> When host-country standards seem substandard from the perspective of the home country (manager), the manager faces a dilemma. Should the MNC implement home country standards and so seem to lack respect for the cultural diversity and national integrity of the host (country)? Or, should the MNC implement seemingly less optimal host country standards?[28]

One recent study suggests that international differences in the effectiveness of different sales management should be incorporated into the design of control systems, should involve local personnel in the decision, and should allow local countries' flexibility to implement control strategy. The transfer of sales management practices across different countries without careful attention to local differences is very risky.[29] To achieve salesforce effectiveness in different countries may require a specific approach, such as the case with China, as presented in **Global Perspective 13-1**.

---

[25]See, for example, William J. Bigoness and Gerald L. Blakely, "A Cross-National Study of Managerial Values," *Journal of International Business Studies* 27 (Fourth Quarter 1996): 739–752; and Kwok Leung, Rabi S. Bhagat, Nancy R. Buchan, Miriam Erez, and Cristina B. Gibson, "Culture and International Business: Recent Advances and their Implications for Future Research," *Journal of International Business Studies* 36 (July 2005): 357–378.

[26]Philip M. Rosenzweig, and Ritin Nohria, "Influences on Human Resource Management Practices in Multinational Corporations," *Journal of International Business Studies* 25 (Second Quarter 1994): 229–251.

[27]One study proves that when management practices are adapted to the national culture of a country in which the company operates, its financial performance tends to improve. See Karen L. Newman and Stanley D. Nollen, "Culture and Congruence: The Fit between Management Practices and National Culture," *Journal of International Business Studies* 27 (Fourth Quarter 1996): 753–779.

[28]Thomas Donaldson, "Multinational Decision-Making: Reconciling International Norma," *Journal of Business Ethics* 4 (1985): 357–366.

[29]Nigel F. Piercy, George S. Low, and David W. Cravens, "Consequences of Sales Management's Behavior- and Compensation-Based Control Strategies in Developing Countries," *Journal of International Marketing* 12, no. 3 (2004): 30–57.

Global Perspective 13-1

Achieving Salesforce Effectiveness in China: Building Pride and Performance

China has been a difficult sales environment for many multinational companies to handle. As much as the expansion of new consumer markets cannot be ignored, many multinational companies are finding it difficult to serve and sell to a market that is characterized with diverse set of sales channels, consumer preferences, and economic strata—spread across a vast region. Another challenge for the multinationals is the shortage of capable salespeople, which forces multinational companies in China to condense sales management training from what normally appears to be 5 years in the United States to as little as 18 months.

Sales representatives in China are confronting a challenging and difficult environment. Annual retail sales have increased more than fifteen-fold from around $100 billion in the 1990s to $1.6 trillion in 2008. With such increases, products from around the world, stretching from as close as Taiwan and Hong Kong to North America and Europe, are vying for consumers' attention. Retail channels are changing and expanding as a result of an exploding number of items offered in the market (e.g., supermarkets are replacing mom-and-pop stores; department stores are proliferating; etc.). Market coverage areas are no longer limited to large urban areas—the Tier 1, Tier 2, Tier 3 cities—but also the more rural and remote areas. For example, only 9 percent of rural households and 72 percent of urban homes had refrigerators in 1998. These numbers increased to 26 percent and 91 percent, respectively, in 2008. Aggressive infrastructure expansion in China has played a major role in fueling this rapid growth.

To succeed and thrive in this challenging environment, sales directors of multinational companies must follow a dual-pronged strategy. First, sales teams must be upgraded by addressing fundamental issues such as recruitment, retention, and advancement—with a sales approach specifically customized for the specific needs of doing business in China. Second, sales leaders must acquire unique skills—pride building skills—to achieve unprecedented team performance by tapping into profound insights about what uniquely drives each individual. Only pride builders can enhance a sales team development strategy sufficiently to transform Chinese sales-people into innovative, driven, and self-starting sales reps who can deftly take on any number of new consumer challenges.

It is difficult to find potentially talented sales reps who speak some English and understand the basic concepts of Western corporate values—that is, who are capable of original, creative, and flexible thinking and problem solving. Thus, multinational companies should hire sales reps who are agile and adaptable in addition to having the traditional sales competencies. As the Chinese consumer sector matures and consumers grow in sophistication, sales reps must become much more adept at creating and cultivating customer relationships, anticipating customer needs, selling and cross-selling products as differentiated from the competition, and tracking and analyzing relevant customer data. Thus, an accelerated and improved salesforce training program is highly crucial, and this can be done by breaking down the walls between the training department and the sales teams, particularly for curriculum development. A training program alone is not enough.

Annual sales position turnover rates often exceed 25 percent in China. In addition to management development and promotion as part of retention strategy, in a high-powered, competitive environment like China, pride building is thought to be effective in retaining and improving sales reps' motivation. While good managers focus on linking individuals' work to the company's mission, pride builders create emotional connections between work and what matters to sales reps. Good managers emphasize results, but pride builders focus on the way or behavior to achieve the results (and on the results as well). While good managers tend to help workers with strong potential, pride builders pay more attention to development needs and opportunities of the entire team. In short, pride builders are able to achieve exceptional results from their teams by fostering deep connections, a feeling of ownership, and a commitment to work. These are what multinational companies operating in China need to concentrate on in order to achieve sales force effectiveness.

Source: Joni Bessler, Niko Canner, and Ilona Steffen, "China Sales Force Effectiveness: Building Pride and Performance," *Booz & Company, Perspective,* January 6, 2010.

The process of salesforce management provides a framework for a closer look at the challenges involved in adapting management practices to a new culture. Salesforce management consists of the following six steps:

1. Setting salesforce objectives

2. Designing salesforce strategy

3. Recruiting and selecting salespeople

4. Training salespeople

5. Supervising salespeople

6. Evaluating salespeople

Salesforce Objectives

Before it can set salesforce objectives, a company must determine its larger, strategic objectives. A company can have the strategic objective of adding value by providing the customer more understanding of a product's use. Or the company may want to enter the market as the low-cost provider. Once such strategic objectives are decided upon, the company can evaluate what roles the salesforce will play in reaching these goals. These roles are the salesforce objectives.

Salesforce objectives will then influence much of the rest of the sales management process. If a salesforce objective is to expand market share, then the salesforce will be designed, recruited, trained, supervised, and evaluated using that objective as a guideline. Salesforce objectives will guide how much salesforce time and effort will be required for digging up leads versus working with existing customers, or how much effort will be placed on new products versus older products, or how much effort will be spent on customer satisfaction compared to sales volume.

Setting salesforce objectives will require a very similar approach internationally as it does domestically. In fact, many "international" salesforce issues are really local issues in a foreign country. However, setting the best international salesforce objectives depends not only on the company goals, but also on an analysis of the culture and values of the country it is entering. The company might use a standardized approach for all countries, or it might customize its salesforce management approach from the ground up for each country. Most companies will probably customize some aspects of each country's salesforce objectives, but will follow previously held beliefs about the purpose of the salesforce to decide most objectives. Once the objectives are known, the company can begin designing the structure of the proposed salesforce.

Salesforce Strategy

Once the salesforce's objectives are set, the company can concentrate on the strategies needed to achieve those objectives. Salesforce strategy addresses the structure, size, and compensation of the salesforce.

The structure determines the physical positioning and responsibilities of each salesperson. A company selling one product to a dispersed client base might consider a territorial salesforce, with each salesperson responsible for a particular area and reporting up the line to a regional sales manager. Another company, with numerous, unrelated, complex products, could consider a product salesforce structure, where each salesperson sells only one product or product line, even when selling to a single customer. A third company, which requires close contact with its customers to keep up with customer needs and build tight relationships, could employ a customer salesforce structure, in which account managers are responsible for particular clients. Each of these approaches has advantages and disadvantages. Choosing the most appropriate international salesforce strategy requires analyzing many of the same considerations as it does domestically. However, additional considerations could arise concerning the lack of capable local salespeople, the cultural expectations of clients, and the dramatically increased costs of maintaining expatriate personnel abroad.

The size of the salesforce depends on the sales structure. The company often calculates how many salespeople are needed by determining how many visits or calls each type of customer should receive and how many salespeople will be needed to make the necessary number of visits. In a foreign culture, customers' distinct expectations may modify the calculations. Although a client in the United States may be satisfied with buying large quantities of a product and hearing from the salesperson every six months, the foreign client may expect a salesperson to be in regular contact and may want to buy smaller quantities more regularly. Such considerations impact the salesforce size. For example, Wal-Mart, the world's largest company, has recognized that the key to its growth lies in rapidly growing China. Unlike Western consumers, Chinese customers tend to buy in smaller quantities and are accustomed to going to the supermarket every one or two days. Thus, Wal-Mart supercenters have to devote more floor space and sales associates to food than to other departments. Furthermore, because Chinese customers need to "feel" the merchandise (put their hands on it) before making the purchase, salesforce assignment needs to be carefully examined in order to cater to Chinese consumers' characteristics.[30]

Salesforce compensation is the chief form of motivation for salespeople. However, companies do not pay salesforces equally in all countries. The purchasing power of the "same" quantity of money may not be the same. And more important, pay expectations, or the going rate, varies dramatically from country to country. The company must carefully consider the social perceptions of its compensation scale. A commission-based compensation might not motivate salespeople in some other countries. For example, while Americans are mostly comfortable with commission-based compensation, their Japanese counterparts may not feel so. The large commission portion of compensation tends to confuse and frustrate most Japanese salespeople. In addition, while financial compensation is the key salesforce motivation in the United States, individual financial incentives are not a recommended way to motivate Japanese salespeople.[31] The company must evaluate the impact that the compensation system will have on employees and then consider what impact the system will then have on the final customer. The pay system must motivate salespeople to leave customers with the appropriate, desired perceptions of the company.

Recruitment and Selection

In order to successfully recruit and select salespeople, the company must understand what it wants in its salespeople and know how to find and attract people with the necessary skills. The first decision is whether the company will recruit from the local, foreign labor force for the jobs it is creating or whether it will fill them by sending domestic employees overseas. The company could find a strong cultural bias against salespeople in the local market and find it difficult to recruit the necessary talent. Even if it can recruit "talented" people, the company may not clearly know what skills and character traits will work the best in the unfamiliar culture. If the company tries to recruit employees at home, it may have a tough time convincing salespeople or managers with the necessary skills to take the time off from the fast track at home.

Complicating the search for talent is the fact that the desired skills and characteristics are not as clear as they appear. Employers might base their expectations for salespeople on their domestic standards. For example, the employer could look for candidates with an outgoing attitude.

---

[30]"The Great Wal-Mart of China," *Fortune*, July 25, 2005, 104–116.

[31]Erin Anderson and Leonard M. Lodish, "Leading the Effective Sales Force: The Asian Sales Force Management Environment," *INSEAD Working Paper Series*, 40, 2006.

However, in some cultures a quieter, more patient approach will truly maximize sales. The skills required for success as a salesperson depend on the culture in which the sales take place.

Finally, the employer must consider the strong influences of tribal, religious, or other group relations within a country. English companies, for instance, might do better to hire Irish salespeople to make sales in Ireland. History could give one group a distinct advantage, especially where they have become accepted as a strong business force. For example, the Parsees in India manage an unusually large portion of the nation's business, and Chinese salespeople, the descendants of Chinese merchant clans, are prominent throughout Asia.[32] A wise sales manager will recruit a salesforce that takes advantage of each country's natural distinctions.

One way for the company to accelerate the difficult process of building a salesforce from scratch is to establish a joint venture or acquire a local company that already has a functional salesforce. For example, when Merck wanted to expand its pharmaceutical business in Japan, it acquired Banyu Pharmaceutical instead of building its subsidiary and distribution channel from scratch. Merck had immediate access to Banyu's field salesforce of more than 1,000. In Japan, where personal relationships probably weigh more in importance than the quality of products per se, personal selling is all the more critical in relationship-building and -maintaining purposes. However, the acquiring company's executives should pay heed to differences in managerial style and consumer behavior in the host country. When Wal-Mart wanted to expand into Europe, its first move in 1997 was to buy out Wertkauf, a German national chain store, in order to have instant distribution channel members working for it and supply channels already established, as well as a beachhead for the rest of Europe. However, Wal-Mart executives' failure to listen to the feedback from its local employees and acknowledge differences in consumer behavior in Germany led to employee frustration, eventually resulting in Wal-Mart's exit from Germany in 2006.[33]

Training

Most sales training takes place in the country where staff reside. The company determines how much technical, product knowledge, company history and culture, or other training its local salesforce requires. However, this country-by-country approach usually fails to develop a globally consistent sales and marketing strategy for MNCs. Therefore, an increasing number of globally oriented companies are now developing a globally consistent sales and marketing program to serve customers and foster long-term partnerships that would engage customers and meet their specific local needs and preferences. For example, BSC, a U.S. manufacturer of medical devices, selected AchieveGlobal, in Tampa, Florida, to train its international sales and marketing staff. The two companies have developed a comprehensive training program, consisting of a three-day sales program for all employees and a two-day coaching seminar for sales managers. The sales training program incorporates product knowledge orientation with needs-satisfaction selling, extensive role playing, and case studies. The session for managers shows them effective ways to coach their teams without handholding. Both companies ensure that BSC's entire sales and marketing staff is trained in the language of their specific country and that the program can be adapted to meet each local culture. This means not only translating the program's language into the local vernacular but also making sure the whole approach meets each country's specific needs. As a result, those sales managers are transferred to local markets with more consistent sales and marketing programs internationally.[34]

---

[32]See an excellent treatise, Min Chen, *Asian Management Systems: Chinese, Japanese and Korean Styles of Business* (London: Routledge, 1995): 69–83.

[33]John Fernie and Stephen J. Arnold, "Wal-Mart in Europe: Prospects for Germany, the UK and France," *International Journal of Retail & Distribution Management*, no. 30 2/3 (2002): 92–102; and Arun Kottolli, "Trans-cultural Business Failure: Wal-Mart Exits Germany," *Thoughts on Marketing, Innovation & Leadership*, http://arunkottolli.blogspot.jp, August 15, 2006.

[34]Slade Sohmer, "Emerging as a Global Sales Success," *Sales & Marketing Management* 152 (May 2000): 124–125.

An additional consideration with regard to international sales training is adapting the training to the needs of the local market. For example, Carrefour, the French retail giant, has created the Carrefour China Institute to train its staff in China to engender the "Carrefour Spirit." Before opening stores in China, the company conducted in-depth research for store location, understanding of the local culture and traditions, and local consumer purchasing behaviors. Inevitably, Carrefour's concepts of "localization management" and "low price and high quality" have worked in the Chinese world. The company was rewarded with $1.9 billion revenue in 2004.[35] The training that the salesforce receives must reflect cultural differences in purchasing patterns, values, and perspective on the selling process.

Although international companies often benefit in the local market by offering their employees better training than local competitors, these companies face the problem of protecting their investment in their employees. Local companies often raid companies with well-trained salesforces for employees. To protect their investments, the MNCs must offer higher compensation and better promotion opportunities than their competitors.

Supervision

Supervising the salesforce means directing and motivating the salesforce to fulfill the company's objectives and providing the resources that allow them to do so. The company can set norms concerning how often a salesperson should call each category of customer, and how much time the salesperson should spend with each of various activities. The company can motivate the salesperson by establishing a supportive, opportunity-filled organizational climate, or by establishing sales quotas or positive incentives for sales. The company often provides the salesperson with tools, such as laptop computers or research facilities, to provide better chances to achieve his or her goals. International sales management addresses how each of these supervising approaches will be received by the salesforce, and what the cultural implications are. For example, cultures that value group identity over individuality will probably not respond well to a sales contest as a motivator.

Motivation and Compensation

Financial compensation is one of the key motivators for employees in all cultures. However, successful sales programs use a wide variety of motivators. The sales manager will want to adapt the incentive structure to best meet local desires and regulations. The use of commissions in motivating salespeople is not publicly acceptable in many countries.[36] Commissions reinforce the negative image of the salesperson benefiting from the sale, with no regard for the purchaser's well-being. Salary increases can substitute for commissions to motivate salespeople to consistently perform highly. However, under certain circumstances, large salary discrepancies between employees are also not acceptable. Strong unions can tie a company's hands in setting salaries. The "collectivist" culture of a country such as Japan cannot accept that one person should earn substantially more than another in the same position. The same collectivist culture makes the "Salesperson of The Month" approach—widely practiced in the United States—ineffective, as it tends to embarrass rather than to motivate the group-oriented Japanese.[37] When financial rewards are not acceptable, the company must rely more heavily on non-financial rewards, such as recognition, titles, and perquisites for motivation.

Foreign travel is another reward employed by international companies. For example, Electrolux rewards winning sales teams in Asia with international trips. When necessary, companies can combine an international trip with training and justify it as an investment in top salespeople.

---

[35]"Carrefour China: A Local Market," *China Business*, April 28, 2005.

[36]Michael, Segalla, Dominique Rouzies, Madeleine Besson, and Barton A. Weitz, "A Cross-National Investigation of Incentive Sales Compensation," *International Journal of Research in Marketing* 23, no. 4 (2006): 419–433.

[37]Bruce R. Money and John L. Graham, "Salesperson Performance, Pay, and Job Satisfaction: Tests of a Model Using Data Collected in the United States and Japan," *Journal of International Business Studies* 30, no. 1 (1999): 149–172.

Management Style

Management style refers to the approach the manager takes in supervising employees. The manager can define the employee's roles explicitly and require a standardized sales pitch or set broad, general goals that allow each salesperson to develop his or her own skills. A number of studies have found that the best management approach varies by culture and country. For example, Dubinsky and colleagues[38] found that role ambiguity, role conflict, job satisfaction, and organizational commitment were just as relevant to salespeople in Japan and Korea as in the United States, and that role conflict and ambiguity have deleterious effects on salespersons in all of the countries. However, specific remedies for role ambiguity, such as greater job formalization (or more hierarchical power, defined rules, and supervision), have varying effects on the salespeople in different countries.

One fair generalization is that greater formalization invokes negative responses from the salesforce in countries in which the power distance is low and the individualism is high (such as in the United States). Greater formalization also invokes positive responses from the salesforce in countries in which the power distance is high and the individualism is low (such as in India).[39]

Ethical Perceptions

Culture, or nationality, also influences salespeople's beliefs about the ethics of common selling practices and the need for company policies to guide those practices. Why is this important? Salespeople need to stay within the law, of course; more importantly to maintain the respect of customers, salespeople must know what is ethically acceptable in a culture. For example, in the United States, giving a bribe is tantamount to admitting that your product cannot compete without help. However, in many cultures, receiving a bribe is seen as a privilege of having attained a position of influence. An understanding of the ethical norms in a culture will help the company maintain a clean image and will also help the company create policies that keep salespeople out of the tense and frustrating situations where they feel they are compromising their ethical standards.

As an example of differences in ethical perceptions, consider the results of a study by Dubinsky and colleagues.[40] The study presented salespeople in Korea, Japan, and the United States with written examples of "questionable" sales situations, as follows:

- Having different prices for buyers for which you are the sole supplier

- Attempting to circumvent the purchasing department and reach other departments directly when it will help sales

- Giving preferential treatment to customers whom management prefers or who are also good suppliers

The salespeople were asked to rate to the extent to which it was unethical to take part in the suggested activity. The results indicated that in general, U.S. salespeople felt that the situations posed fewer ethical problems than did salespeople from Japan and Korea. Another interesting finding of the study—the assumption that Japanese "gift-giving" would extend into the sales realm—was found to be untrue. In fact, Japanese felt salespeople giving gifts to a purchaser was more an ethical problem than did U.S. salespeople. For Koreans, however, gift-giving was less an issue.

[38]Alan J. Dubinsky, Ronald E. Michaels, Masaaki Kotabe, Chae Un Lim, and Hee-Cheol Moon, "Influence of Role Stress on Industrial Salespeople's Work Outcomes in the United States, Japan, and Korea," *Journal of International Business Studies* 23 (First Quarter 1992): 77–99.

[39]Sanjeev Agarwal, "Influence of Formalization on Role Stress, Organizational Commitment, and Work Alienation of Salespersons: A Cross-National Comparative Study," *Journal of International Business Studies* 24 (Fourth Quarter 1993): 715–740.

[40]Alan J. Dubinsky, Marvin A. Jolson, Masaaki Kotabe, and Chae Un Lim, "A Cross-National Investigation of Industrial Salespeople's Ethical Perceptions," *Journal of International Business Studies* 22 (Fourth Quarter 1991): 651–670.

Paradoxically, U.S. salespeople indicated that they wanted their companies to have more policies explicitly addressing these ethical questions. Why? Apparently, salespeople in the United States feel more comfortable when the ethical guidelines are explicitly stated, whereas in other countries (Korea and Japan here), the cultural exchange of living in a more community-oriented society provides the necessary guidelines. Similarly, in countries like Mexico, where power relationships are explicit, salespeople may simply accept and follow management's ethical discretions regardless of their personal ethical standards.[41]

Evaluation

Evaluating salespeople includes requiring them to justify their efforts and provide the company with information about their successes, failures, expenses, and time. Evaluations are important to motivate the salesforce, to correct problems, and to reward and promote those who best help the company achieve its goals. Two types of evaluations are common: quantitative and qualitative evaluations. Examples of quantitative evaluations are comparisons of sales, of sales percents, or increases in sales. Examples of qualitative evaluations include tests of the knowledge and manner of the salesperson. Because net profit is often the company's primary objective, evaluations should serve to promote long-term net profits. In some foreign cultures, however, evaluations could be seen as an unnecessary waste of time, or they may invade the sense of privacy of salespeople.

Evaluations help management keep up on sales progress and help employees receive feedback and set goals. International salesforce evaluations must consider the culture's built-in ability to provide feedback to employees. For example, in Japan the "collectivist" nature of the culture may provide the salesperson with much more sense of performance feedback than the "individualistic" culture in the United States would. Thus, it makes sense that U.S. sales managers use more regular, short-term performance evaluations than Japanese sales managers in order to provide their salesforce with more feedback.[42]

Evaluations in international sales management provide useful information for making international comparisons. Such comparisons can help management identify countries where sales are below average and refine the training, compensation, or salesforce strategy as necessary to improve performance.

Cross-Cultural Negotiations

Conducting successful cross-cultural negotiations is a key ingredient for many international business transactions. International bargaining issues range from establishing the nuts and bolts of supplier agreements to setting up strategic alliances. Negotiation periods can run from a few hours to several months, if not years. Bargaining taps into many resources, skills, and expertise. Scores of books have been devoted to negotiation "dos and don'ts."[43] Cross-cultural negotiations are further complicated by divergent cultural backgrounds of the participants in the negotiation process.[44] In this section, we discuss the cultural aspects of international negotiations and bargaining.

---

[41]William A. Weeks, Terry W. Loe, Lawrence B. Chonko, Carlos Ruy Martinez, and Kirk Wakefield, "Cognitive Moral Development and the Impact of Perceived Organizational Ethical Climate on the Search for Sales Force Excellence: A Cross-Cultural Study," *Journal of Personal Selling & Sales Management* 26 (Spring 2006): 205–217.

[42]Susumu, Ueno and Uma Sekaran, "The Influence of Culture on Budget Control Practices in the U.S. and Japan: An Empirical Study," *Journal of International Business Studies*, 23 (Fourth Quarter 1992): 659–74.

[43]See, for example, Mel Berger, Cross Cultural Team Building: Guidelines for More Effective Communication and Negotiation, New York: McGraw-Hill, 1996.

[44]For those interested in learning more about the complexities of cross-cultural negotiations, see a recent special issue on this topic, edited by Yahir H. Zoubir and Roger Volkema, in *Thunderbird International Business Review* 44 (November/December 2002).

Stages of Negotiation Process

Roughly speaking, four stages are encountered in most negotiation processes:[45] (1) non-task soundings, (2) task-related information exchange, (3) persuasion, and (4) concessions and agreement. Non-task soundings include all activities that are used to establish a rapport among the parties involved. Developing a rapport is a process that depends on subtle cues.[46] The second stage relates to all task-related exchanges of information. Once the information exchange stage has been completed, the negotiation parties typically move to the persuasion phase of the bargaining process. Persuasion is a give-and-take deal. The final step involves concession making, intended to result in a consensus. Not surprisingly, negotiation practices vary enormously across cultures. Japanese negotiators devote much more time to nurturing rapport than U.S. negotiators. For Americans, the persuasion stage is the most critical part of the negotiation process. Japanese bargainers prefer to spend most of their time on the first two stages so that little effort is needed for the persuasion phase. Japanese and American negotiators also differ in the way they make concessions. Americans tend to make concessions during the course of the negotiation process, whereas Japanese prefer to defer this stage to the end of the bargaining.[47] See **Exhibit 13-5** for negotiation styles in five other countries.

Cross-Cultural Negotiation Strategies[48]

Exhibit 13-6 represents a framework of culturally responsive negotiation strategies, driven by the level of cultural familiarity that the negotiating parties possess about one another's cultures. Cultural familiarity is a measure of a party's current knowledge of his counterpart's culture and ability to use that knowledge competently. Depending on the particular situation, eight possible negotiation strategies can be selected. Let us briefly consider each one of them:

Employ an Agent or Adviser

Outside agents, such as technical experts or financial advisors, can be used when cultural familiarity is extremely low. These agents can be used to provide information and to advise on action plans.

Involve a Mediator

Whereas the previous strategy can be used unilaterally, both parties can also jointly decide to engage a mutually acceptable third party as a mediator. Successful mediation depends on maintaining the respect and trust of both parties.

Induce the Counterpart to Follow One's Own Negotiation Script

Effective negotiators proceed along a negotiation script—the rules, conduct, ends they target, means toward those ends, and so forth. When the counterpart's familiarity with your culture is high, it could be feasible to induce the other party to follow your negotiation script. This strategy is especially useful when cultural knowledge is asymmetrical: the other party is knowledgeable about your culture, but you are not familiar with his or hers. Inducement could be via verbal persuasion or subtle cues.

---

[45]John L. Graham and Yoshihiro Sano, "Across the Negotiating Table from the Japanese," *International Marketing Review* 3 (Autumn 1986), 58–71.

[46]Kathleen K. Reardon and Robert E. Spekman, "Starting Out Right: Negotiation Lessons for Domestic and Cross-Cultural Business Alliances," *Business Horizons* (Jan.-Feb. 1994): 71–79.

[47]John L. Graham, "Negotiating with the Japanese (Part 1)," *East Asian Executive Reports*, November 15, 1988, pp. 8, 19–21.

[48]Stephen E. Weiss, "Negotiating with "Romans"—Part 1," *Sloan Management Review* (Winter 1994): 51–61; Stephen E. Weiss, "Negotiating with "Romans"—Part 2," *Sloan Management Review* (Spring 1994): 85–99.

Exhibit 13-5 Negotiation Styles and Guidelines in Five Countries

	France	Poland	Turkey	Russia	Spain
Language	• Younger people: English acceptable • Older people: French—if necessary, agree at early stage to use an interpreter	• English or German • Do not overestimate fluency • Be willing to use an interpreter	• Be careful with terminology; allow extra time for language problems • Be clear and succinct • Avoid being negative	• Do not expect partner speaks English (especially outside big cities); find good interpreter	• Do not assume command of English • Consider using interpreter • Documents and business cards should be in Spanish, not just English
Sequence	• General principles → rough outline → details	• Goal-directed • Little small talk • Prepare for lengthy delays	• Small talk matters a lot • Wait to talk business until host brings it up	• Negotiations can be protracted • Starting times not always respected • Frequent interruptions	
Communication style	• Abstract and elaborate • Relish in logic, battle of wits • Straightness = blunt, rude • Avoid hard sell	• Unemotional • Lack of flexibility of Polish counterparts	• Be flexible to manage delays; factor in unexpected • Avoid bluntness • Stick to main message; avoid weakening arguments with minor points • Listen first, then ask questions; don't put words into counterpart's mouth	• Personal relationships play vital role • Russian partners can be "slow"	• Personal relationships play vital role; regard personal invitations as a partnership investment • Be prepared for delays • Interruptions common • Several people may talk at once • Discussions can be lively • Spanish people rely on quick thinking, spontaneity • Negotiations can be lengthy
Contract	• Very formal, flowery • Fairly brief	• Technical • Very detailed		• Avoid any changes to contracts; if necessary you will need to make a strong case	
Context	• Entertaining matters a great deal but usually done at restaurants • Do not raise issues until end of meal		• Entertaining important, often at host's home	• Usually at restaurants • Toasting important ritual but be careful	• Can invite partner for lunch or dinner • Deals with top executives often agreed during meals, middle managers flesh out details later

Sources: Constructed from "Enjoy a Battle of Wits and a Good Lunch," *Financial Times*, September 11, 2000, p. 9; "Crossing Cultural Barriers," *Financial Times*, September 25, 2000, p. 11 (Poland); "Contacts That Make or Break Turkish Ventures," *Financial Times*, November 6, 2000, p. 14 (Turkey); "A Market Emerging from a Country in Turmoil," *Financial Times*, February 19, 2001, p. 7 (Russia); "Formality, Feasting and Patience," *Financial Times*, October 9, 2000, p. 12 (Spain).

Exhibit 13-6
Culturally
Responsive
Strategies and Their
Feasibility

Reprinted from "Negotiation
with Romans—Part 1," by
Stephen E. Weiss, *Sloan
Management Review* (Winter
1994), pp. 51–61. Copyright
1994 by Sloan Management
Review. All rights reserved.

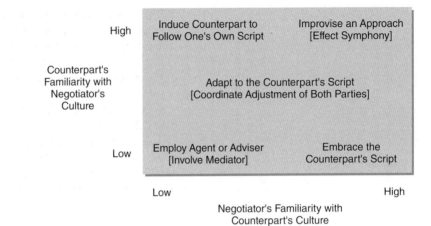

Adapt the Counterpart's Negotiation Script

With moderate levels of familiarity about the counterpart's cultural mindset, it becomes possible to adapt to his negotiation script. Adaptation involves a deliberate decision to adjust some common negotiation rules.

Coordinate Adjustment of Both Parties

When the circumstances lend themselves, both parties can jointly decide to arrive at a common negotiation approach that blends both cultures. Occasionally, they might propose to adopt the negotiation script of a third culture.

Embrace the Counterpart's Script

With this strategy, the negotiator volunteers to adopt the counterpart's negotiation approach. This demands a tremendous effort from the negotiator. It can be effective only when the negotiator possesses a great deal of familiarity with the other party's cultural background.

Improvise an Approach

This strategy constructs a negotiation script over the course of negotiating. This approach is advisable when both parties feel very comfortable with their counterpart's culture. It might be effective when bargaining with members from a high-context culture in which mutual bonding and other contextual cues are at least as important (non-task-related aspects) as the immediate negotiation concerns.

Effect Symphony

The final strategy capitalizes on both parties' high cultural familiarity by creating an entirely new script or by following some other approach atypical to their respective cultures. For instance, the coordination could select parts from both cultures.

The choice of a particular strategy partly depends on how familiar the negotiators are with the other party's culture. To pick a particular strategy, consider the following steps:

1. *Reflect on your culture's negotiation practices.* What negotiation model do you use? What is the role of the individual negotiator? What is the meaning of a satisfactory agreement?

2. *Learn the negotiation script common in the counterpart's culture.* This involves reflecting on questions such as: Who are the players? Who decides what? What are the informal influences

that can make or break a deal?[49] Answers to these questions will help the negotiator to anticipate and interpret the other party's negotiating behaviors. Expectations about the process and the outcome of the bargaining will differ. People can view the process as win-win or win-lose. The approach to building an agreement can focus first on either general principles or specifics. The level of detail required can vary. Perspectives on the implementation of an agreement can also differ. In some cultures renegotiation is frowned upon. In other cultures, an agreement is seen as a starting point of an evolving relationship.[50]

3. *Consider the relationship and contextual clues.* Different contexts necessitate different negotiating strategies. What circumstances define the interaction between the negotiation parties? Contextual clues include considerations such as the life of the relationship, gender of the parties involved, and balance of power.

4. *Predict or influence the counterpart's approach.* Prediction could be based on indicators such as the counterpart's pre-negotiation behavior and track record. In some cases, it is desirable to influence the other party's negotiation strategy via direct means (e.g., explicit request for a negotiation protocol) or through more subtle means (e.g., disclosing one's familiarity with the counterpart's culture).

5. *Choose a strategy.* The chosen strategy should be compatible with the cultures involved, conducive to a coherent pattern of interaction, in line with the relationship and bargaining context, and ideally acceptable to both parties.

Expatriates

Most companies with a salesforce abroad will, at the very least, send a few expatriates as operations begin in a new country. **Expatriates** are home country personnel sent overseas to manage local operations in the foreign market. The general trend among U.S. multinationals since the 1990s has been a decreasing use of expatriate managers overseas and an increasing reliance on local foreign talent.[51] This trend reflects the increasingly international perspective of MNCs, increasing competence of foreign managers, and the relatively increasing competitive disadvantage of the cost of maintaining home country personnel abroad. Despite the relative decline, more employees than ever are involved in international assignments due to the increase in international sales and production. According to a recent study of international assignments, 38 percent of companies surveyed increased the number of international transfers from headquarters in 2004 and 2005. Another 47 percent are still sending the same number abroad. The biggest increases were among companies (both foreign and indigenous) in Asia and Latin America, regions that are home to a new wave of internationally mobile employees. In addition, 44 percent of all firms reported an increase in international transfers between places other than headquarters.[52]

Expatriates have a number of advantages over foreign nationals for companies that sell their products internationally. In general, a successful expatriation starts with a selection of good candidates who are willing to try new things and persist in exhibiting an open-minded and flexible personality to accept the host country's norms. Therefore, firms should select expatriates whose personal values are in line with those of the host countries so that expatriates would have more

---

[49]James K. Sebenius, "The Hidden Challenge of Cross-Border Negotiations," *Harvard Business Review* 80 (March 2002): 76–85.

[50]Sebenius, 2002, p. 84.

[51]Gunter K. Stahl, Edwin L. Miller, and Rosalie L. Tung, "Toward the Boundaryless Career: A Closer Look at the Expatriate Career Concept and the Perceived Implications of an International Assignment," *Journal of World Business* 37 (Autumn 2002): 216–227.

[52]"Travelling More Lightly—Staffing Globalization," *Economist*, June 24, 2006, pp. 77–80.

social interaction with host nationals. For example, when U.S. expatriates possess collective norms that are similar to those of Asian and Latin American cultures, they would have more social interaction with the locals and are more attitudinally attached to the host culture.[53]

Advantages of Expatriates

Jack Welch, the former CEO of General Electric, stated in his speech to GE employees:

> The Jack Welch of the future cannot be me. I spent my entire career in the United States. The next head of General Electric will be somebody who spent time in Bombay (Mumbai), in Hong Kong, in Buenos Aires. We have to send our best and brightest overseas and make sure they have the training that will allow them to be the global leaders who will make GE flourish in the future.[54]

His statement clearly summarizes the importance of expatriates and their international experiences for improved communications between the company's headquarters and its foreign subsidiaries and affiliates, and development of talent within the company.

Better Communication

Expatriates understand the home office, its politics, and its priorities. They are intimately familiar with the products being sold and with previously successful sales techniques. Expatriates can rely on personal relationships with home office management, which increases trust on both sides of the border and can give the expatriate the ability to achieve things that a third-country national or a host country national could not achieve. With an expatriate abroad, communications with the home country will be easier and more precise owing to the groundwork of cultural and corporate understanding. The expatriate will also give the home office the sense that it has someone in place who it is sure understands the company's intent and expectations.

Development of Talent

Sending employees abroad provides the company another advantage that hiring foreign locals may not provide: The company develops future managers and executives who can later use their international perspective in management. For example, the leaders of General Motors, Avon, Campbell Soup, Ford, Gillette, Tupperware, Goodyear, General Mills, Case, and Outboard Marine all have significant overseas experience in their careers.[55] According to research by Gregersen, Morrison, and Black, senior executives of multinationals who have had international assignments indicated that those jobs provided their single most influential leadership experience.[56] Thus, by sending their most promising rising stars overseas, companies are sowing the seeds to harvest the next generation of executives.

Difficulties of Sending Expatriates Abroad

Although the benefits of sending expatriates abroad are clear, difficulties can also arise for various reasons ranging from organizational to personal ones and even to security risk. Some of the major difficulties are as follows.

---

[53]Sunkyu Jun and James W. Gentry, "An Exploratory Investigation of the Relative Importance of Cultural Similarity and Personal Fit in the Selection and Performance of Expatriates," *Journal of World Business*, 40 (February 2005): 1–8.

[54]Mansour Javidan and Robert J. House, "Leadership and Cultures around the World: Findings from GLOBE," *Journal of World Business* 37 (Spring 2002): 3–10.

[55]Mason A. Carpenter and Gerard Sanders, "International Assignment Experience at the Top Can Make a Bottom-Line Difference," *Human Resource Management* 39 (Summer/Fall 2000): 277–285.

[56]Hal B. Gregersen, Allen J. Morrison, and J. Stewart Black, "Developing Leaders for the Global Frontier," *Sloan Management Review* 40 (Fall 1998): 21–32.

Cross-Cultural Training

Training can significantly help in understanding the cultural differences of the foreign country. U.S. companies used to overlook such "cultural sensitivity training"; expatriates were expected to "pick it up as they go." Cultural misunderstandings can have a large impact, however. About 6 percent of expatriate assignments failed prematurely.[57] As a result, **cross-cultural training** has been on the rise in recent years as more globally oriented companies moving fast-track executives overseas want to curb the cost of failed expatriate stints.

According to Expatica's Global Relocation Services' 2008 survey, 67 percent of respondents cited an increase in the expatriate population during 2008. It also reported that 11 percent of all expatriates were new hires and 9 percent of expatriates had previous international experience. Companies are becoming more flexible about the length of international assignments, and are moving away from long-term assignments to a variety of short-term alternatives. The survey found that more companies have embraced a global perception of their entire workforce, therefore utilizing their human resources more effectively, and have chosen to outsource their relocation programs to achieve higher levels of financial return, expatriate performance, and satisfaction. Formal cross-cultural training was mandatory at 23 percent of companies, but 81 percent of them rated it as having great or good value.[58]

Once the expatriate is abroad, it becomes more difficult to provide training, but doing so is even more important. The expatriates are not in constant contact with colleagues and may not be picking up the newest technology in their company's field. They could be missing out on important policy or procedural changes that the company is undertaking. Ongoing training, whether in a foreign or the home country, can make a huge difference in the success of an overseas assignment.

During the first year of the assignment, having an executive coach with deep country-specific experience can add incalculable benefits to the new expatriate. A competent coach is able to provide feedback to executives on how others perceive them, and to provide a local perspective on problem solving that might otherwise not occur to someone who is new to the region.[59] Today, host countries are also taking measures to help foreign expatriates get used to their culture. For example in India, there are end-to-end expatriate-services companies offering a range of relocation and cross-cultural services. A company named Global Adjustments even publishes India's only expatriate cultural monthly magazine called *At a Glance—Understanding India*. Headquartered in Chennai, this company has offices in all six major cities in India (Bangalore, Chennai, Kolkata, Mumbai, Pune, and Delhi) helping expatriates from 74 countries ease the passage to and from India.[60]

However, expatriates must recognize that within an average two- to four-year assignment abroad, they will never internalize enough of the local culture to overcome all social and communication concerns. Even with appropriate training, the expatriates are the product of their home culture. They will eat with a fork when a hand is more polite, shake on a deal and thereby show their lack of faith, or require that a contract with all possible legal contingencies spelled out be signed in triplicate when honor and trust dictate that the deal go through on a shared local drink. These could appear to be small social problems, but such social problems can keep the expatriate out of important deals. As Black and Porter[61] noted in their article title, "a successful manager in Los Angeles may not succeed in Hong Kong." The expatriate could find after some time that the best place to make sales is not at the client's offices but at the bar watching soccer with other executives.

---

[57] *Global Relocation Trends 2008 Survey Report*, www.expatica.com/hr/story/Reporting-on-global-relocation-trends-in-2008.html.

[58] Ibid.

[59] "Preparing Execs for Asia Assignments," *BusinessWeek.com*, April 1, 2008.

[60] "Helping the U.S. and India Work Together," *BusinessWeek.com*, April 29, 2008.

[61] J. Stewart Black and Lyman W. Porter, "Managerial Behaviors and Job Performance: A Successful Manager in Los Angeles May Not Succeed in Hong Kong," *Journal of International Business Studies* 22 (First Quarter 1991): 99–113.

Motivation

Motivating expatriates to accept and succeed at positions abroad requires a combination of carefully planned policies and incentives. Expatriates often express dissatisfaction that their stints abroad hinder their career progress. Companies should set up and publicize career paths that reward and use skills that expatriates acquire overseas. Additionally, while expatriates are overseas, regular communication with the home office will help allay fears that "out of sight, out of mind" will hinder their career progress.[62] Intranet websites for expatriates will help facilitate such communication.

A recent study also shows that employees who choose an expatriate assignment place a high intrinsic value on the overseas experience *per se*, especially on the opportunities it brings for personality development and enrichment of their personal lives. They also believe that their overseas assignment will help improve their professional and management skills and enhance their careers, although not necessarily within their current company.[63]

Compensation

The average cost of maintaining a home-country executive can cost three to five times what it costs to maintain an employee at home.[64] Compensation packages include various premiums including overseas premiums, housing allowances, cost-of-living allowances, tax equalizations, repatriation allowances, all-expense-paid vacations, and performance-based bonuses. Most compensation premiums are paid as a percentage of base salary. Yet despite this, according to Expatica's Global Relocation Trend 2008 Survey, 32 percent of candidates for expatriate posts rated inadequate compensation packages as the most common reason for turning down their assignments.[65]

When it comes to their wallets, worldly expatriates often moan about Tokyo, London, or New York. This is undoubtedly understandable. However, in many other countries such as those in Africa whose living cost people think should be low, expatriates find it even more expensive to work and live there. A recent survey by ECA International, which advises multinational companies how to look after their expatriate staff, rates Harare the most expensive city for such foreigners in the world. Angola's Luanda comes second and Congo's Kinshasa fifth, just behind Oslo and Moscow. Even Gabon's Libreville is deemed more expensive than Tokyo. On the other hand, in cases such as Luanda, where the economy is booming and inflation a mere 12 percent, living costs for foreigners are still incredibly expensive. After decades of war, not much is produced at home, barring oil and diamonds, so most things are imported and command high prices. Foreigners tend to eat at just a handful of restaurants where dinner for two costs more than $150. This make it even more difficult to decide satisfactory compensation packages for expatriates.[66] How much should overseas assignments pay?

One approach has been to pay expatriates a premium for their willingness to live in adverse conditions. Such special "hardship packages" can cause problems, however. Overseas employees could notice the discrepancy in remuneration among expatriates, local nationals, and third-country nationals.[67] An expatriate sales manager in Japan could be motivated by an incentive system through which he or she would earn a higher salary for stellar performance. However, such an

[62]Thomas F. O'Boyle, "Little Benefit to Careers Seen in Foreign Stints," *Wall Street Journal*, December 11, 1989, p. B1, B4.

[63]Gunter K. Sahl, Edwin L. Miller, and Rosalie L. Tung, "Toward the Boundaryless Career: A Closer Look at the Expatriate Career Concept and the Perceived Implications of an International Assignment," *Journal of World Business* 37 (Autumn 2002): 216–227.

[64]Eric Krell, "Evaluating Returns on Expatriates," *HR Magazine* 50 (March 2005): 60–65.

[65]*Global Relocation Trends 2008 Survey Report*, www.expatica.com/hr/story/Reporting-on-global-relocation-trends-in-2008.html.

[66]"Costly Postings," *Economist*, December 16, 2006, p. 48.

[67]So Min Toh and Angelo S. DeNisi, "A Local Perspective to Expatriate Success," *Academy of Management Executive* 19, no. 1 (2005): 132–147.

individual approach would not sit well with Japanese colleagues who subscribe to a collective approach that does not favor standing out of others of similar seniority. Furthermore, expatriates who receive a generous compensation package while abroad may lose motivation on returning home to their previous salary scale.[68] A more recent approach has been to consider the overseas assignment a necessary step for progress within the company.

The company must also consider the impact of the family life cycle on compensation. Expatriates with spouses and children encounter higher needs abroad, including the loss of a spouse's income and the cost of enrolling children in private schools. A program must be flexible enough to adjust to the varying needs of different employees.

Family Discord

The typical candidate for an international assignment is married, has school-age children, and is expected to stay overseas for three years. In this age of two-career families, an international assignment means that a spouse may have to suspend a stateside career. Thus, many employees are reluctant to move abroad. Others who accept transfers grow frustrated as they find that their spouses cannot get jobs or even work permits abroad. Schools where the international assignee's home language is spoken must be found, or children must learn the local language. Concerns about the safety and happiness of family members can keep the candidate from accepting an overseas position. A recent study found that concerns about children and spouses' careers were the two main reasons why employees turned down jobs abroad.[69]

Unsuccessful family adjustment is the single most important reason for expatriate dissatisfaction compelling an early return home. Expatriates as well as their family members are in crisis because of culture shock and stress. As a result, family discord can occur, and marriages can break up.

Thus, international companies try to cut costs by reducing the problems that can hurt expatriates' job satisfaction and performance. Having an experienced and empathetic counselor who can work with all family members in a constructive manner on confusing or negative experiences can greatly improve the chance for success. Many expatriate families in China, for example, isolate themselves from Chinese society because it is intimidating to cope with a steep language barrier as well as unfamiliar cuisine and even unfamiliar transportation or healthcare systems. A guide can give family members the confidence they need to function on their own wherever they are.[70] To help spouses find jobs abroad, Philip Morris Company even hired an outplacement firm to provide career counseling and job leads.[71]

Security Risk

Since the September 11, 2001, terrorist attacks in the United States, security risk has become a serious issue. Particularly, expatriate executives from U.S. companies and their families are not as eager to take on international assignments, especially in countries viewed as security risks. Perceived or real security risk concern requires more development, training, and recruiting of local executives, which in the long run should be beneficial to all.

Despite such an anxiety factor causing some dent in the globalization movement, the forces of market and financial globalization are unlikely to be reversed. In fact, more executives have been trained to believe that international experience is critical to their long-term career success. Because of the increased number of international MBA students in many business schools around the world, they are increasingly being placed in countries in which they fit right in culturally,

[68]Michael Harvey, "Empirical Evidence of Recurring International Compensation Problems," *Journal of International Business Studies* 24 (Fourth Quarter 1993): 785–799.

[69]"Traveling More Lightly - Staffing Globalization," *Economist*, June 24, 2006, pp. 77-80.

[70]"Preparing Execs for Asia Assignments," *BusinessWeek.com*, April 1, 2008.

[71]Carla Johnson, "Relocation Counseling Meets Employees' Changing Needs," *HRMagazine* 43 (February 1998): 63–70.

religiously, and racially. These "indigenized" managers increase the frequency of international travel, cross-border migration, and lower communication costs across national boundaries.[72]

The Return of the Expatriate—Repatriation

Repatriation is the return of the expatriate employee from overseas. Although companies are making efforts to prevent this, many returning expatriates have difficulty finding good job assignments when their foreign positions end. The post-return concern that an overseas assignment can damage a career back home can discourage employees from taking a foreign position. Repatriation is distinct from other forms of relocation. After an average absence of 3.5 years, expatriates themselves have changed, adopting certain values, attitudes, and habits of their host countries. According to Expatica's Relocation Services' 2008 survey, 69 percent of respondents held repatriation discussions, and 77 percent of companies identified new jobs within the company for repatriating employees.[73] This is a far cry from its 2001 survey reporting a deplorable picture that 66 percent of companies surveyed indicated that they offered no post-expatriate employment guarantees.[74] In the past decade, U.S. companies have made a measurable improvement in their repatriation policies.

Expatriates face a long list of difficulties upon returning home. Their standard of living often declines. And they often face a lack of appreciation for the knowledge they gained overseas. Without a clear use for their skills, returned expatriates often suffer from a lack of direction and purpose. New home-side assignments often do not give the repatriated employee the same responsibility, freedom, or respect that they enjoyed overseas. And poor communications with the home office while abroad leave the returnee cut off from the internal happenings and politics of the company, limiting opportunities for career growth.[75]

Expatica's Relocation Services' 2008 survey also reported a number of effective ways to reduce attrition rates. These include providing (1) chances to use international experience, (2) position choices upon return, (3) recognition, (4) repatriation career support, (5) improving performance evaluation, and (6) family repatriation support. Pre-trip training should state the details for the candidate, including future training expected, help the company will provide, and, importantly, the career path that the move will help. The effort and cost of such comprehensive planning sends a strong signal of the importance of foreign assignments to expatriate candidates.

Generalizations about When Using Expatriates Is Positive or Negative

Expatriates are important whenever communication with the home country office is at a premium. Communication is facilitated among managers of the same nationality. Thus, the company is better off with a stronger expatriate base abroad when the overseas situation puts pressure on communications with the home office. Thus, expatriates are especially important in complex operating environments, when elevated political risk requires constant monitoring, or when a high cultural distance separates the home and host countries. On the other hand, in very competitive environments, local nationals could provide important links to the local business community and perhaps play a key strategic role in gaining business.

---

[72]Sevgin Eroglu, "Does Globalization Have Staying Power?" *Marketing Management* 11 (March/April 2002): 18–23.

[73]*Global Relocation Trends 2008 Survey Report*, 2008.

[74]*Global Relocation Trends 2003/2004 Survey Report*, www.nftc.org/default/hr/GRTS%202003-4.pdf.

[75]Aaron W. Andreason and Kevin D. Kinneer, "Bringing Them Home Again," *Industrial Management* 46 (November/December 2004): 13–19.

SUMMARY

No matter how global a company becomes, its salesforce remains its front line. On the other hand, actual sales activities are truly local activities, far detached from decision making at headquarters. Particularly in Latin European, Latin American, and Asian countries, salespeople's ability to build trust with prospective customers prior to sales is extremely important. Effective salesforce management is very elusive, yet crucial to developing a coherent international marketing and distribution strategy.

Because sales activities are local activities, they tend to be strongly affected by cultural differences (e.g., shopping habits, negotiation styles) around the world, making it difficult, if not impossible, for the international marketing manager to integrate overseas sales operations. Many companies rely on merchant distributors at home or sales agents in the foreign market who have more intimate knowledge of the marketplace. As sales increase, these companies begin to increase their commitment to developing their own distribution and salesforce in the foreign market.

The development of an effective sales organization requires salesforce objectives and a salesforce strategy adapted to local differences and calls for careful recruiting, training, supervising, motivating, and compensating local salespeople. We also provided some background on a very complex form of cultural interface: cross-cultural negotiations. Several strategies are introduced to assist you in international bargaining situations.

Furthermore, an increasing number of expatriate managers are sent to overseas posts to directly manage the company's local salesforce. Expatriate managers function as a bridge between headquarters and local operations, and must be culturally adaptive and versatile. Although international assignments have increasingly become a necessary requirement for fast-track managers, cultural adaptability is not always an inborn qualification of many expatriate managers. Cross-cultural training is crucial, because failed expatriate assignments cost the company dearly in terms of lower business performance and dejected employee morale. Use of expatriate managers with personal profiles that fit in well with local cultures is also on the increase for reasons of political correctness. Companies recently have also begun to develop a repatriation program to ease returned expatriates back into their stateside positions. Such a well-organized repatriation program is important to encourage managers to take up expatriate assignments.

QUESTIONS

1. Discuss why mode of entry and sales management are closely related.

2. How could a foreign government affect a company's salesforce management?

3. Discuss why expatriate managers are important to a parent company despite the enormous cost of sending them overseas.

4. Many U.S. companies such as Home Depot, Intel, Kodak, Nike, and Whirlpool have set up sales offices in China. One thing sales managers must be aware of is that the differences in sales styles between the United States and China are vast. For example, relationship building is very important in sales and in hiring salespeople in China. Further, more companies need to figure out what part of the country and what market segments they are to enter. Generally speaking, Chinese consumers are more price conscious than Japanese and Korean consumers. However, Chinese youth are less likely to follow the traditional values of collectivism, restraint, and harmony, but exhibit strong tendencies of individualism and self-reliance. They worship more Western brands in comparison to domestic brands. If U.S.-based companies were to set up sales offices in China, what would be their challenges and opportunities? Given the differences in sales styles between the United States and China, what should the company do to enhance its sales management?

5. Many firms in the past have followed an incremental approach to the sales channels used in international markets. Typically, these companies started by selling in foreign markets through sales agents or distributors. This was followed by opening liaison offices to assist and monitor the activities of the appointed distributors. With subsequent growth in business, the company would set up its own sales subsidiary to manage sales and customer service. This incremental strategy has worked quite effectively for many companies in the past. In your opinion, would the current emphasis on globalization have any bearing on the effectiveness of this incremental strategy? If so, what would this effect be, and why?

14 LOGISTICS AND DISTRIBUTION

CHAPTER OVERVIEW

1. Definition of global logistics

2. Managing physical distribution

3. Managing sourcing strategy

4. Free trade zones

5. International distribution channel

6. International retailing

7. Appendix: maquiladora operation

Companies have to deliver products to customers both efficiently and effectively.[1] First of all, global logistics, also referred to as global supply chain management,[2] has played a critical role in the growth and development of world trade and in the integration of business operations on a worldwide scale. Its primary objective is to develop a cost-efficient delivery mechanism. In fact, the level of world trade in goods and, to some extent, services, depends to a significant degree on the availability of economical and reliable international transportation services. Decreases in transportation costs and increases in performance reliability expand the scope of business operations and increase the associated level of international trade and competition.[3] Second, the use of appropriate distribution channels in international markets increases the

---

[1]For a philosophy of efficiency- vs. effectiveness-seeking in business orientation, see Masaaki Kotabe, "Efficiency vs. Effectiveness Orientation of Global Sourcing Strategy: A Comparison of U.S. and Japanese Multinational Companies," *Academy of Management Executive* 12 (November 1998): 107–119; and Shelby D. Hunt and Dale F. Duhan, "Competition in the Third Millennium: Efficiency or Effectiveness?" *Journal of Business Research* 55 (February), 2002, pp. 97–102.

[2]Some authors (including the authors of this book) use the terms **logistics** and **supply chain** management interchangeably, while others generally define supply chain management somewhat more broadly than logistics. Although, in this chapter, we try not to engage in this definitional debate over what functions are included in each, the Council of Logistics Management offers the following definitions. **Logistics management** typically includes inbound and outbound transportation management, fleet management, warehousing, materials handling, order fulfillment, logistics network design, inventory management of third-party logistics services providers. To varying degrees, the logistics function also includes sourcing and procurement, production planning and scheduling, packaging, and assembly, and customer service. **Supply chain management** is an integrating function with primary responsibility for linking major business functions and business processes within and across companies into a cohesive and high-performing business model. It includes all of the Logistics Management activities noted above, as well as manufacturing operations, and it drives coordination of processes and activities with and across marketing, sales, product design, finance, and information technology.

[3]John H. Dunning, "Reappraising the Eclectic Paradigm in an Age of Alliance Capitalism," *Journal of International Business Studies* 26 (Third Quarter 1995): 461–491.

chances of success dramatically. Its primary objective is to develop a task-effective delivery mechanism for customer satisfaction. Coca-Cola's success relies largely on its global distribution arm, Coca-Cola Enterprises, the world's largest bottler group. It helps Coca-Cola market, produce, and distribute bottled and canned products all over the world. The group also purchases and distributes certain non-carbonated beverages such as isotonics, teas, and juice drinks in finished form from the Coca-Cola company to satisfy the diverse needs of its consumers.[4]

As far back as 1954, Peter Drucker had said that logistics would remain "the darkest continent of business"[5] —the least well understood area of business—and his prediction proved true until well into the twenty-first century. It is not too difficult to demonstrate the importance of the physical handling, moving, storing, and retrieving of material. In almost every product, more than 50 percent of product cost is material related, while less than 10 percent is labor. Yet, over the years this fact has not received much attention. For three consecutive years, from 2006 to 2008, the U.S. total logistics cost stayed at nearly 10 percent of the GDP. In the subsequent years, however, total logistics cost in the United States declined, with the massive slide occurring in 2009 at only 7.9 percent of the GDP. In 2011, the total logistics cost bounced back up to 8.5 percent of GDP.[6] In 2012, the logistics cost in India was as high as 13–14 percent of GDP.[7] In 2011, China's logistic cost reached 18 percent of GDP, according to a report by the China Federation of Logistics and Purchasing (CFLP)—more than double the average in the United States, Japan, and Western Europe.[8]

Since the 1990s, a variety of issues have been driving the increased emphasis on logistics and distribution management. It was epitomized in 1998 by General Motors' lawsuit against Volkswagen over the defection of José Ignacio Lopez, the former vice president of purchasing at General Motors and one of the most renowned logistics managers in the automobile industry.[9] His expertise is said to have saved General Motors several billion dollars from its purchasing and logistic operations, which would directly affect the company's bottom line. The importance of distribution channels is further evidenced by the recent mergers in the auto industry, in which giant multinationals are gobbling up smaller manufacturers with strong brand names, but inadequate global distribution, such as the acquisition of Volvo from Ford by China's Geely.[10]

As firms start operating on a global basis, logistics managers need to manage the shipping of raw materials, components, and supplies among various manufacturing sites at the most economical and reliable rates. Simultaneously, these firms need to ship finished goods to customers in markets around the world at the desired place and time. The development of **intermodal transportation** and electronic tracking technology has caused a quantum jump in the efficiency of the logistic methods employed by firms. Intermodal transportation refers to

[4]Coca-Cola Enterprises, http://www.cokecce.com, accessed March 11, 2009.
[5]Peter F. Drucker, *The Practice of Management* (New York: Harper & Brothers, 1954).
[6]Dan Gilmore, "Supply Chain News: State of the Logistics Union 2012," *Supply Chain Digest*, www.scdigest.com, June 14, 2012.
[7]"India's Logistic Costs Higher than BRIC Nations," *Times of India*, http://timesofindia.indiatimes.com, June 15, 2012.
[8]"Logistics Costs Account for 18% GDP," *China Daily*, www.chinadaily.com.cn, June 8, 2012; and "Chinese Logistics Costs Rise as U.S., Europe Stagnate," *Automotive Logistics*,http://www.automotivelogisticsmagazine.com/data/chinese-logistics-costs-rise-as-us-europe-stagnate, accessed September 20, 2013.
[9]"No Ordinary Car Thief," *U.S. News & World Report*, June 5, 2000, p. 52.
[10]"Geely Buys Volvo. Believe It or Not, It Could Work," *Bloomberg Businessweek*, March 29, 2010.

the seamless transfer of goods from one mode of transport (e.g., aircraft or ship) to another (e.g., truck) and vice versa without the hassle of unpacking and repackaging the goods to suit the dimensions of the mode of transport being used. Tracking technology refers to the means for keeping continuous tabs on the exact location of the goods being shipped in the logistic chain—this enables quick reaction to any disruption in the shipments because (a) the shipper knows exactly where the goods are in real time and (b) the alternative means can be quickly mobilized.

Definition of Global Logistics

Global logistics is defined here as the design and management of a system that directs and controls the flows of materials into, through, and out of the firm across national boundaries to achieve its corporate objectives at a minimum total cost. As shown in **Exhibit 14-1**, global logistics encompasses the entire range of operations concerned with products or components movement, including both exports and imports simultaneously. Global logistics, like domestic logistics, encompasses materials management, sourcing, and physical distribution.[11]

Materials management refers to the inflow of raw materials, parts, and supplies in and through the firm. **Physical distribution** refers to the movement of the firm's finished products to its customers, consisting of transportation, warehousing, inventory, customer service/order entry, and administration. **Sourcing strategy** refers to an operational link between materials management and physical distribution, and deals with how companies manage R&D (e.g., product development and engineering), operations (e.g., manufacturing), and marketing activities. Although the functions of physical distribution are universal, they are affected differently by the tradition, culture, economic infrastructure, laws, and topography, among other factors, in each country and each region. In general, in geographically large countries, such as the United States, where products are transported over a long distance, firms tend to incur relatively more transportation and inventory costs than firms in smaller countries. On the other hand, in geographically concentrated countries, such as Japan and Britain, firms tend to incur relatively more warehousing, customer service/order entry, and general administrative costs than in geographically larger countries. This is so primarily because a wide variety of products with different features have to be stored to meet the varied needs of customers in concentrated areas. Although it is possible to attribute all cost differences to topography, customs, laws of the land, and other factors, the cost differences could also reflect how efficiently or inefficiently physical distribution is managed in various countries and regions.

Exhibit 14-1 Global Logistics

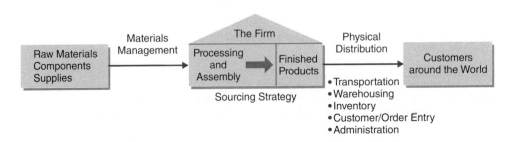

---

[11]Donald J. Bowersox, David J. Closs, M. Bixby Cooper, *Supply Chain Logistics Management, 3rd ed.* (Boston: McGraw-Hill, 2010).

Managing Physical Distribution

Physical distribution is inextricably tied with international trade, multinational manufacturing and sourcing of raw materials, components, and supplies. Physical distribution has become considerably more complex, more costly, and as a result, more important for the success of a firm. A variety of factors contribute to the increased complexity and cost of global logistics, as compared to domestic logistics.

- **Distance.** The first fundamental difference is distance. Global logistics frequently require the transportation of parts, supplies, and finished goods over much longer distances than is the norm domestically. A longer distance generally suggests higher direct costs of transportation and insurance for damages, deterioration, and pilferage in transit and higher indirect costs of warehousing and inventory.

- **Exchange Rate Fluctuation.** The second difference pertains to currency variations in international logistics. The corporation must adjust its planning to incorporate the existence of currencies and changes in exchange rates. For example, in the mid-1990s when the Japanese yen appreciated faster than the U.S. dollar against key European currencies, Honda found it much more economical to ship its Accord models to Europe from its U.S. plant in Marysville, Ohio, rather than from its plants in Japan.

- **Foreign Intermediaries.** Additional intermediaries participate in the global logistics process because of the need to negotiate border regulations of countries and deal with local government officials and distributors. Although home country export agents, brokers, and export merchants work as intermediaries providing an exporting service for manufacturing firms, those home-based intermediaries do not necessarily have sufficient knowledge about the foreign countries' market conditions or sufficient connections with local government officials and distributors. In Asian countries such as Japan, Korea, and China, personal "connections" of who knows whom frequently seem to outweigh the Western economic principle of profit maximization or cost minimization in conducting business.[12] Therefore, working with local distributors has proved very important in building initial connections with the local business community as well as local government regulators.

- **Regulation.** The bulk of international trade is handled by **ocean shipping**. Because the United States is the world's largest single trading country in both exports and imports, and most of its trading partners are located across the Pacific and the Atlantic Oceans, U.S. regulations on ocean transport services directly affect foreign exporters to the United States (as well as U.S. importers of foreign goods) in terms of shipping costs and delivery time. In the United States, the Merchant Marine Act of 1920 (also known as the Jones Act) forbids foreign-owned freighters from transporting passengers and merchandise from one domestic port to another by restricting foreign access to the domestic shipping market. The act requires passengers and merchandise being transported by ship within the United States to travel on U.S.-built, U.S.-owned and U.S.-staffed vessels, while allowing unilateral retaliatory action against restrictions imposed by other countries. In March 2003, more than 50 nations, including Australia, Canada, China, the European Union, and Japan, filed a joint statement with the World Trade Organization calling for the liberalization of international marine transport services during the WTO's new round of multilateral trade negotiations.[13] Until resolved by the WTO, the

---

[12]See, for example, Jean L. Johnson, Tomoaki Sakano, and Naoto Onzo, "Behavioral Relations in Across-Culture Distribution Systems: Influence, Control, and Conflict in U.S.-Japanese Marketing Channels," *Journal of International Business Studies* 21 (Fourth Quarter 1990), 639–655; and Chris Rowley, John Benson, and Malcolm Warner, "Towards an Asian Model of Human Resource Management?: A Comparative Analysis of China, Japan and South Korea," *International Journal of Human Resource Management*, 15 (June/August 2004): 917–933.

[13]"Japan Joins Call for Opening Marine Services Market in WTO Talks," *NikkeiNet Interactive,*http://www.nni .nikkei.co.jp/, March 4, 2003.

barriers imposed by this act continue to add to the costs of logistics in and around the United States.

- **Security.** Security was not an acutely serious concern until September 11, 2001, when the blatant terrorist attacks in the United States awakened the world to the importance of domestic and international security measures. Transportation costs for exporters have increased because of the extra security measures that shipping lines and terminal operators face.[14] However, if the government-imposed user fees or carrier surcharges are too high or come without sufficient advance notice, some exporters could even lose their overseas markets due to increased shipping costs and insurance premiums (refer to "Terrorism and the World Economy" in Chapter 5).

Modes of Transportation

The global logistics manager must understand the specific properties of the different modes of transport in order to use them optimally. The three most important factors in determining an optimal mode of transportation are the value-to-volume ratio, perishability of the product, and cost of transportation. The **value-to-volume ratio** is determined by how much value is added to the materials used in the product. **Perishability** of the product refers to the quality degradation over time and/or product obsolescence along the product life cycle. The **cost of transportation** should be considered in light of the value-to-volume and perishability of the product.

Ocean Shipping

Ocean shipping offers three options. **Liner service** offers regularly scheduled passage on established routes; **bulk shipping** normally provides contractual service for prespecified periods of time; and the third category is for irregular runs. Container ships carry standardized containers that greatly facilitate the loading and unloading of cargo and intermodal transfer of cargo. Ocean shipping is used extensively for the transport of heavy, bulky, or nonperishable products, including crude oil, steel, and automobiles. Over the years, shipping rates have been falling as a result of a price war among shipping lines. For example, an average rate for shipping a 20-foot container from Asia to the United States fell from $4,000 in 1992 to as low as $1,680 by 2009.[15] Although most manufacturers rely on existing international ocean carriers, some large exporting companies, such as Honda and Hyundai, have their own fleets of cargo ships. For example, Honda, a Japanese automobile manufacturer, owns its own fleet of cargo ships not only to export its Japan-made cars to North America on its eastbound journey but also to ship U.S.-grown soybeans back to Japan on its westbound journey. This strategy is designed to increase the vessels' capacity utilization.[16] Indeed, Honda even owns a number of highly successful specialty tofu restaurants in Tokyo frequented by young trendsetters in Japan.[17]

Air Freight

Shipping goods by air has rapidly grown over the last 30 years. Although the total volume of international trade using air shipping remains quite small—it still constitutes less than 2 percent

---

[14]Robert Spich and Robert Grosse, "How Does Homeland Security Affect U.S. Firms' International Competitiveness?" *Journal of International Management* 11 (December 2005): 457–478.

[15]Drewry Independent Maritime Advisor, http://www.drewry.co.uk/, accessed March 15, 2009.

[16]"Engineers Rule," *Forbes*, September 4, 2006, pp. 112–116; and "Honda Mixes Soybeans and Carmaking in U.S.," *New York Times*, April 19, 2005, http://www.nytimes.com/2005/04/18/business/worldbusiness/18iht–honda.html?_r = 0. In 2013, Honda sold its soybean division to Kanematsu, but Honda's fleet of cargo ships continue to be used for westbound shipping of soybeans from the United States.

[17]The first author's personal knowledge.

of international trade in goods—it represents more than 20 percent of the value of goods shipped in international commerce. High-value goods are more likely to be shipped by air, especially if they have a high value-to-volume ratio. Typical examples are semiconductor chips, LCD screens, and diamonds. Perishable products such as produce and flowers also tend to be airfreighted. Changes in aircraft design have now enabled air transshipment of relatively bulky products. Three decades ago, a large propeller aircraft could hold only 10 tons of cargo. Today's jumbo cargo jets carry more than 30 tons, and medium- to long-haul transport planes (e.g., the C-130 and the AN-32) can carry more than 80 tons of cargo. These super-size transport planes have facilitated the growth of global courier services, such as FedEx, UPS, and DHL. Of all world regions, the entire Asia-Pacific is the most popular **air freight** market today, with double-digit, year-on-year growth. Asia has become the world's factory floor to outsource the manufacture of goods and services. The top five commodities moving from the Asia Pacific area to the United States include office machines and computers, apparel, telecom equipment, electrical machinery, and miscellaneous manufactured products. The west-bound (from the United States to Asia/Pacific) commodities mainly include documents and small packages, electrical machinery, and fruits and vegetables. In early 2012, however, air cargo traffic experienced downward pressure due to soaring fuel prices. The demand for air cargo remains weak while sea cargo seems to be favored in world trade.[18]

Intermodal Transportation

More than one mode of transportation is usually employed. Naturally, when shipments travel across the ocean, surface or air shipping is the initial transportation mode crossing national borders. Once on land, they can be further shipped by truck, barge, railroad, or air. Even if countries are contiguous, such as Canada, the United States, and Mexico, for example, various domestic regulations prohibit the unrestricted use of the same trucks between and across the national boundaries. When different modes of transportation are involved, or even when shipments are transferred from one truck to another at the national border, it is important to make sure that cargo space is utilized at full load so that the per-unit transportation cost is minimized.

Managing shipments so that they arrive in time at the desired destination is critical in modern-day logistics management. Due to low transit times, greater ease of unloading and distribution, and higher predictability, many firms use air freight, either on a regular basis or as a backup to fill in when the regular shipment by an ocean vessel is delayed. For footwear firms Reebok and Nike and fashion firms such as Pierre Cardin, the use of air freight is becoming almost a required way of doing business, as firms jostle to get their products first into the U.S. market from their production centers in Asia and Europe. The customer in a retail store often buys a product that may have been airfreighted in from the opposite end of the world the previous day or even the same day. Thus, the face of retailing is also changing as a result of advances in global logistics.

Distance between the transacting parties increases transportation costs and requires longer-term commitment to forecasts and longer lead times. Differing legal environments, liability regimes, and pricing regulations affect transportation costs and distribution costs in a way not seen in the domestic market. Trade barriers, customs problems, and paperwork slow cycle times in logistics across national boundaries. Although this is true, the recent formation of regional trading blocs, such as the European Union, the North American Free Trade Agreement, and the MERCOSUR (The Southern Cone Free Trade Area), is also encouraging the integration and consolidation of logistics in various regions for improved economic efficiency and competition.

---

[18]"Cargo Traffic Remains Soft but Shows Signs of Stabilization," *Cargo Tracker May 2012*, International Air Transport Association, www.iata.org, accessed September 6, 2012.

Warehousing and Inventory Management

A firm's international strategy for logistics management depends, in part, on government policy and on the infrastructure and logistic services environment. The traditional logistics strategy involves anticipatory demand management based on forecasting and inventory speculation.[19] With this strategy, a multinational firm estimates the requirements for supplies as well as the demand from its customers and then attempts to manage the flow of raw materials and components in its worldwide manufacturing system and the flow of finished products to its customers in such a manner as to minimize holding inventory without jeopardizing manufacturing runs and without losing sales due to stockouts.

In the past, the mechanics and reliability of transportation and tracking of the flow of goods was a major problem. With the increasing use of information technology, electronic data interchange, and intermodal transportation, the production, scheduling, and delivery of goods across national borders is also becoming a matter of just-in-time delivery although some structural problems still remain. For instance, current restrictions on U.S.–Canada air freight services and U.S.–Mexico cross-border trucking restrain the speed of goods flow, add to lead times, and are examples of government restrictions that need to be changed to facilitate faster movement of goods across borders.

Despite those restrictions, forward-looking multinational companies can still employ nearly just-in-time inventory management. For example, Sony's assembly plant in Nuevo Laredo, Mexico, just across the Texas border, imports components from its U.S. sister plants in the United States. While cross-border transportation across the U.S.–Mexico international bridges experiences traffic congestion and occasionally causes delays in shipment, Sony has been able to manage just-in-time inventory management with a minimum of safety stock in its warehouse.

Hedging against Inflation and Exchange Rate Fluctuations

Multinational corporations can also use inventory as a strategic tool to deal with currency fluctuations and to hedge against inflation. By increasing inventories before imminent depreciation of a currency instead of holding cash, a firm can reduce its exposure to currency depreciation losses. High inventories also provide a hedge against inflation, because the value of the goods/parts held in inventory remains the same compared to the buying power of a local currency, which falls with a devaluation. In such cases the international logistics manager must coordinate operations with that of the rest of the firm so that the cost of maintaining an increased level of inventories is more than offset by the gains from hedging against inflation and currency fluctuations. Many countries, for instance, charge a property tax on stored goods. If the increase in the cost of carrying the increased inventory along with the taxes exceeds the saving from hedging, increased inventory may not be a good idea.

Benefiting from Tax Differences

Costs can be written off before taxes in creative ways so that internal transit arrangements can actually make a profit. This implies that what and how much a firm transfers within its global manufacturing system is a function of the tax systems in various countries to and from which the transfers are being made. When the transfer of a component A from country B to country C is tax-deductible in country B (as an export) and gets credit in country C for being part of a locally assembled good D, the transfer makes a profit for the multinational firm. Access to and use of such knowledge is the forte of logistics firms that sell these services to the multinational firm interested in optimizing its global logistics.

Logistical Integration and Rationalization

Logistical integration refers to coordinating production and distribution across geographic boundaries—a radical departure from the traditional country-by-country–based structure

---

[19]Louis P. Bucklin, "Postponement, Speculation and the Structure of Distribution Channels," *Journal of Marketing Research* 2 (February 1965): 26–31.

consisting of separate sales, production, warehousing, and distribution organizations in each country. **Rationalization**, on the other hand, refers to reducing resources to achieve more efficient and cost-effective operations. Although conceptually separate, most companies' strategies include both aspects of the logistics strategy.

For example, DuPont expects to save millions annually by centralizing logistics management and consolidating its logistics spending to get better pricing and service from its providers. The company currently uses a wide range of freight carriers, logistics providers, and freight forwarders to handle its shipments. By centralizing its logistical activities, DuPont can optimize its shipments and combine small shipments into larger ones (integration). The company has replaced the disconnected legacy mainframe logistics system used by 70 percent of its individual strategic business units, subsidiaries, joint ventures, and affiliates with Global Logistics Technologies Inc.'s G3 web-based transportation and logistics-management software (rationalization). Since 2001, the company has been able to manage almost all of its operations using the software, including shipments for U.S. domestic, Europe domestic, and some intra-Asia areas. DuPont's logistics management has not only enhanced its product delivery time but also ensured security of shipments, a significant factor because more than 40 percent of what the company ships are classified as hazardous materials. Furthermore, the company has benefited from shortened inventory through improved visibility and standardization of data.[20]

Dramatic economic integration is taking place in the enlarged European Union. However, a word of caution is in order. Remember that although the laws of the European Union point toward further economic integration, there still are and will continue to be political, cultural, and legal differences among countries as well. Similarly, as shown in **Global Perspective 14-1**, the North American Free Trade Agreement is not free of arcane regulations, either. Consequently, despite the promised benefit of logistics integration and rationalization, international marketers as well as corporate planners have to have specialized local knowledge to ensure smooth operations. Customer service strategies particularly need to be differentiated, depending on the expectations of local consumers. For example, German buyers of personal computers may be willing to accept Dell Computer's mail-order service or its website ordering service, but French and Spanish customers could assume that a delivery person will deliver and install the products for them.

E-Commerce and Logistics

Another profound change in the last decade is the proliferation of the internet and electronic commerce ("e-commerce"). The internet opened the gates for companies to sell easily directly to consumers across national boundaries. We stated in Chapter 1 that manufacturers that traditionally sell through the retail channel *can* benefit the most from e-commerce. Furthermore, customer information no longer is held hostage by the retail channel.

We emphasize "can" because logistics cannot go easily as global as e-commerce in reality. This revolutionary way of marketing products around the world is epitomized by Dell Computer, which put pressure on the industry's traditional players with a simple concept: sell personal computers directly on the internet to customers—with no complicated channels. Michael Dell successfully introduced a new way for PC companies to compete—not by technology alone, but by emphasizing customers' needs with an ability to satisfy and serve them quickly and efficiently and above and beyond the traditional national boundary. Now, major PC companies are compressing the supply chain via such concepts as "build to order" rather than "build to forecast." However, order taking can take place globally, but shipping of PCs needs to be rather local or regional for various reasons.

---

[20]"DuPont Streamlines Logistics and IT Costs with Centralized, Web-Based System," *Manufacturing Systems* (April 2004): 52.

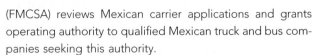

Global Perspective 14-1

Cabotage Rules in the North American Free Trade Agreement

The term *cabotage* refers to the right of a trucker to be able to carry goods in an assigned territory. Traditionally, countries have restricted cabotage rights of foreign truckers. If a U.S. trucking company has a scheduled load to the United States from Toronto, then the truck may carry the load but the driver must be Canadian. Similarly, a U.S. trucker, after delivering goods in Toronto, cannot pick up another load and deliver it in Ottawa—that is a violation of current cabotage rules. Even under the North American Free Trade Agreement (NAFTA), Canada, the United States, and Mexico have varying degrees of—even sometimes confusing—regulations on cabotage rights. In theory, NAFTA should have worked out truly free mobility of goods by allowing the cabotage rights of truckers from Canada, the United States, and Mexico. But the reality is still far from it, although it is improving.

The U.S. government refused to allow Mexican truckers to have full access to the United States until recently. Safety concerns were cited in keeping Mexican trucks from operating throughout the country, although those fears may not be supported by facts. Similarly, the Mexican trucking association, Camara Nacional del Autotransporte de Carga, continues to oppose opening up cabotage to allow point-to-point coverage in Mexico by U.S. trucking companies.

In March 2002, President Bush finally modified the moratorium on granting operating authority to Mexican motor carriers. This action means that the United States has fulfilled its obligations under the North American Free Trade Agreement and that Mexican truck and regular-route bus service into the U.S. interior can begin. As a practical matter, this service is possible only after the U.S. Department of Transportation's Federal Motor Carrier Safety Administration

(FMCSA) reviews Mexican carrier applications and grants operating authority to qualified Mexican truck and bus companies seeking this authority.

The United States does not have coherent cabotage regulations with Canada. The U.S. Immigration and Naturalization Service is going after Canadian drivers who have "violated" cabotage rules by moving trailers within the United States even though U.S. Customs permits such movements. A number of Canadian drivers have had their trucks seized, been fined, and kicked out of the United States. Under an agreement engineered by the Canadian and U.S. trucking associations, Canadian officials have been allowing U.S. drivers to perform cabotage movements in Canada. Now the Canadian government is thinking about retaliating against the United States by mounting a crackdown on U.S. truck drivers entering Canada to parallel the aggressive treatment Canadian drivers are facing from the U.S. Immigration and Naturalization Service.

Despite these arcane regulations still in place in the NAFTA countries, the U.S. Department of Commerce hopes to establish conformity among Canada, Mexico, and the United States in cargo securement regulations in compliance with the North American Cargo Securement Standard Model Regulations.

Source: "U.S. Transportation Department Implements NAFTA Provisions for Mexican Trucks, Buses," FDCH Regulatory Intelligence Database, November 27, 2002; "DOT Eyes Truck Inspection Harmony for All of North America," *Occupational Health & Safety* (December 2002): 10; and John C. Taylor, Douglas R. Robideaux, George C. Jackson, "U.S.-Canada Transportation and Logistics: Border Impacts and Costs, Causes, and Possible Solutions," *Transportation Journal* 43 (Fall 2004): 5–21.

You may ask why most e-businesses do not ship overseas if the web makes any company instantly global. Also, why do more companies not make their internet-powered supply chains globally accessible? The answer is that it remains very difficult to manage the complex logistics, financial, linguistic, and regulatory requirements of global trade. E-businesses operating from one central location could not also address logistical problems associated with local competition and exchange rate fluctuations. For example, in Australia, OzBooks.com sells 1.2 million books and

Dymocks, Australia's largest bookseller, offers just over 100,000 books online. These Australian companies are no comparison in size to Amazon.com with some 5 million books available online. These smaller Australian online booksellers have a competitive advantage over Amazon.com, however. They have a comprehensive offering of books published in Australia while Amazon .com does not. Furthermore, competing on price for international sales without local distribution is tricky as exchange rates fluctuate. When the Australian dollar depreciated during the Asian financial crisis, buying from Amazon.com and other U.S. web retailers became more expensive in Australia, causing Australian consumers to log on to local alternatives such as OzBooks.com instead. As a result, leading e-commerce sites now offer regional websites to handle sales in various parts of the world. For example, Amazon.com now has eight regional websites around the world to cater to these regional and local differences.

Another example is Compaq Computer in Latin America. Since October 1999, the company has been extremely successful in selling computers over the internet throughout Latin America. The company guarantees delivery within 72 hours of placing orders online. Latin Americans shopping online can buy the computers in local currency and do not have to bring the computers through customs. This requires local assembly of Compaq computers. Compaq has assembly plants in Mexico, Ecuador, Argentina, Brazil, Venezuela, Chile, Puerto Rico, Colombia, and Peru.[21]

The web may have dispensed with physical stores, but local adaptation of product offerings and setting-up of local distribution centers remain as crucial as ever. The local competition has forced Amazon.com and other American e-commerce companies to reassess what it means to operate globally on the internet.

Third-Party Logistics (3PL) Management

Good logistics can make all the difference in a company's ability to serve its customers. The crucial factor is not just what the company makes or how the product is made. It is also how quickly the company can get the parts together or shift finished products from its factories to markets. Despite the immense competitive advantage that logistics can generate for the organization, manufacturers often find that logistics operations are usually faster and less expensive if they are outsourced and organized by specialists and professionals who have competence in integrated logistics management and the ability to service multiple clients and products. The 2012 Third-Party Logistics study, citing data from Armstrong and Associates, stated that global expenditure for **third-party logistics (3PL) services** reached a sizable sum of $541 billion. North America's 3PL spending ($149 billion) was slightly lower than that of Asia ($157 billion), while Europe spent $165 billion on the services.[22] The largest 3PL sector is the value-added warehousing and distribution industry. Survey statistics show two important factors: (1) the 3PL industry has a tremendous untapped opportunity for growth with the Fortune 500 companies, and (2) mid-sized companies are making the best use of savings and service advantages that outsourcing can offer.

For example, there is a U.S.-based company called 3PL Worldwide that provides a complete array of order processing, fulfillment services, inventory management, 3PL logistics, call center operations, and warehouse and logistics management to move goods around the world. Its custom-built OrderTrax system processes over a half billion dollars in sales orders annually, and its call center handles hundreds of thousands of customer contacts each month.[23]

Multinational companies also benefit from 3PL arrangements particularly in culturally and/or geographically diverse markets, such as India and China. For example, in India, Whirlpool

---

[21]"IT Watch," *Business Latin America*, September 13, 1999, p7; and "Latin American PC Market Continues to Grow," *World IT Report*, February 19, 2002, p. N.

[22]*2012 Third-Party Logistics Study: The State of Logistics Outsourcing, Results and Findings of the 16th Annual Study*, http://www.3plstudy.com/.

[23]http://www.3plworldwide.com/.

Corporation, a leading U.S. manufacturer of major household appliances, works with Quality Express, whose national delivery network serves over 10,000 retailers and 50,000 construction sites scattered all over India. The result was ERX Logistics, a joint venture that provides Whirlpool with full logistics service for its finished products from warehousing to final delivery. Whirlpool has been able to lower its minimum order quantity from about one-third of a truckload to five or six pieces.[24]

Interestingly, with more companies resorting to 3PL, the range of logistics businesses the express operators are moving into is broadened. In the United States, one service offered by UPS's local branches is a drop-off facility for broken Toshiba laptops. Most laptop owners think that when they have told Toshiba about their problem and put their laptop into a UPS box, it is sent to the Japanese company to be repaired and then returned by UPS. But what really happens is that when the laptop arrives at UPS's Louisville hub, it is taken to a vast estate of warehouses near the airport and mended in a repair shop owned and run not by Toshiba but by UPS. The UPS technicians are trained by Toshiba, and the warehouse holds Toshiba spare parts. Even the people in the Toshiba call-center that deal with inquiries work for UPS. The delivery company has been contracted to provide a complete repair and customer-service operation. Having done this for one company, UPS could capitalize on its investment by providing a similar service for others.

A word of caution is in order. Despite great benefits for both the company and customers, 3PL sourcing comes with risks as well. These risks (as well as the benefits) can be classified as strategy-, finance-, and operation-related. Strategy-related risks may include loss of control over the logistics function, leakage of sensitive information, and loss of customer contact—to name but a few. In the finance-related domain, risks of 3PL outsourcing can range from unrealistic fee structure and financial loss, to cost saving assessment difficulties. Operational-related risks include poor IT capabilities, personnel quality, and customer service; inadequate expertise, and inability to handle special product needs.[25]

Logistical Revolution with the Internet

The trend toward third-party logistics is a result of the internet and the intranet (a specialized secure internet channel established between and within companies) as well as concentrating on core competencies. The internet and the intranet facilitate on-time inventory and distribution coordination without constraints of geographical boundaries. Core competencies refer to the mix of skills and resources that a firm possesses that enable it to produce one set of goods and/or services in a much more effective manner than another firm. Also, competent logistics firms can save money for a multinational firm shipping components between its facilities in different countries, because shipping costs paid internally can vary according to the fluctuation of foreign currencies.

We illustrate how some major companies take advantage of the internet and the intranet for streamlining their logistics. At Dell Computer, the international logistics manager makes certain that the third-party logistics provider has state-of-the-art logistics and keeps it involved in Dell's strategic planning. Dell buys monitors finished and packaged, ready to deliver directly to the customer the world over. It does not add any value to the monitor itself, so Dell tries to avoid handling the monitor, preferring instead to have the logistics provider warehouse it and move it to Dell when the information system link with Dell drops an order into the warehouse computer. This saves Dell inventorying costs and gives it more operational flexibility.[26]

Pharmaceutical giant, Eli Lilly, has gradually outsourced more of its global logistics to Swiss-based Danzas AEI Intercontinental. This e-logistics company's famed "MarketLink" system manages seamless logistics services driven by the real-time flow of data between the company and

---

[24]"India: Logistics Gives the Competitive Edge," *Businessline*, November 5, 2001.

[25]K. Selviaridis, M. Spring, V. Profillidis, and G. Botzoris, "Benefits, Risks, Selection Criteria and Success Factors for Third-Party Logistics Services," *Maritime Economics & Logistics*, no. 104 (2008): 380–392.

[26]Silvia Ascarelli, "Dell Finds U.S. Strategy Works in Europe," *Wall Street Journal*, February 3, 1997, p. A8.

its customers. Danzas AEI was recently put in charge of handling customs and the delivery of Eli Lilly's airborne and ocean imports. Based in the pharmaceutical hub of Basel, Switzerland, Danzas AEI Intercontinental has increasingly specialized in pharmaceutical products, working also with SmithKline Beecham and Hoffman-La Roche.[27]

As the market for third-party logistics has increased substantially since the 1990s, many traditional shippers, such as UPS, Federal Express, Yamato Transport, and DHL, have developed large business units solely devoted to integrated logistics. Many logistic companies are now moving to provide tailored logistic solutions in international markets for their clients. One major player is Roadnet Technologies, which was once called UPS Logistics Group, a subsidiary of United Parcel Service, founded in 1995. Roadnet Technologies offers a full spectrum of supply chain services and logistics expertise throughout the world. Now its operations in North America, Europe, Asia and Latin America include over 500 distribution facilities and strategic stocking locations. The company is composed of industrial engineers, software systems integrators and developers, facility designers, operations managers, high-tech repair technicians, logisticians, and transportation, financial, e-commerce, and international trade experts.[28]

Even online companies, such as Amazon.com, rely increasingly on 3PL services in foreign markets. Amazon.com launched its Canadian website (www.amazon.ca) in July 2002, but logistics is handled by Canada Post Corp. In 2001, more than 250 thousand Canadians ordered products from Amazon's U.S. site, and Canada represents Amazon's largest export market. Now Amazon.ca features bilingual Canadian content and 1.5 million items, and Canada Post handles domestic deliveries. Canada Post's subsidiary, Assured Logistics, handles supply chain services such as warehousing, inventory management, and online fulfillment. This has proved to be mutually beneficial arrangement. Canada Post is establishing itself as a competent player in the online world, and as a result its business is picking up with about 300 Canadian companies now using its online logistical services. On the other hand, Amazon spent US$200 million a year on technology to keep its U.S. operation running, but does not incur that cost in its Canadian operation through Amazon.ca. Furthermore, this arrangement permits Amazon to better cater to the local market needs in Canada.[29]

Some distribution companies even find that the best way to be successful is to create a distribution alliance, and pool their logistics resources together. An example is the global distribution alliance between three international electronics distribution companies: the U.S. company Pioneer-Standard, the British company Eurodis, and Taiwan's World Peace Industrial. The alliance's ability to cover almost the entire globe has enabled it to obtain worldwide exclusive distribution contracts from electronics manufacturers such as Philips Semiconductors.[30] Similarly, six European logistics companies have joined forces to launch Eunique Logistics, a new pan-European alliance that provides customers a single point of contact for a range of distribution and logistics services throughout Europe.[31]

Managing Sourcing Strategy

International logistics covers both the movement of raw materials and components into a manufacturing plant and the movement of finished products from the plant to the firm's customers around the world. Of these aspects of global logistics, it has become imperative for many companies to develop an efficient international sourcing strategy as they attempt to exploit their capabilities in R&D, operations, and marketing globally.

[27]Robert Koenig, "Danzas Expands Pharmaceutical Logistics Business with Eli Lilly," *Journal of Commerce*, December 7, 1998, p.14A; and "Danzas AEI Intercontinental," *Journal of Commerce,* November 25, 2002, p. 32.

[28]http://www.roadnet.com/, accessed September 20, 2012.

[29]"Amazon Lands in Canada, Outsources Logistics," *Computing Canada*, July 5, 2002, p. 6.

[30]"Arrow Hooks US Components Division," *Electronics Weekly*, January 22, 2003, p. 3.

[31]"New European Alliance," *Logistics and Transport Focus*, June 2002, p. 13.

The design of international sourcing strategy is based on the interplay between a company's competitive advantages and the comparative advantages of various countries. **Competitive advantage** influences the decision regarding what activities and technologies a company should concentrate its investment and managerial resources in, relative to its competitors in the industry. **Comparative advantage** affects the company's decision on where to source and market, based on the lower cost of labor and other resources in one country relative to another.[32]

Over the last 30 years or so, gradual yet significant changes have taken place in international sourcing strategy. The cost-saving justification for international procurement in the 1970s and 1980s was gradually supplanted by quality and reliability concerns in the 1990s. Most of the changes have been in the way business executives think of the scope of international sourcing for their companies and exploit various resultant opportunities as a source of competitive advantage. Naturally, many companies that have a limited scope of global sourcing are at a disadvantage over those that exploit it to their fullest extent in a globally competitive marketplace. Six reasons are identified as to why companies adopt an international sourcing strategy.[33] These are:

1. Intense international competition

2. Pressure to reduce costs

3. The need for manufacturing flexibility

4. Shorter product development cycles

5. Stringent quality standards

6. Continually changing technology

Toyota's global sourcing operations illustrate one such world-class case. A Japanese carmaker is equipping its operations in the United States, Europe, and Southeast Asia with integrated capabilities for creating and marketing automobiles. The company gives the managers at those operations ample authority to accommodate local circumstances and values without diluting the benefit of integrated global operations. Thus, in the United States, Calty Design Research, a Toyota subsidiary in California, designs the bodies and interiors of new Toyota models, including the Lexus and Camry. Toyota has technical centers in the United States and in Brussels to adapt engine and vehicle specifications to local needs.[34] Toyota operations that make automobiles in Southeast Asia supply each other with key components to foster increased economies of scale and standardization in those components—gasoline engines in Indonesia, steering components in Malaysia, transmissions in the Philippines, and diesel engines in Thailand. Toyota has also started developing vehicles in Australia and Thailand since 2003. These new bases develop passenger cars and trucks for production and sale only in the Asia-Pacific region. The Australian base is engaged mainly in designing cars, whereas the Thailand facility is responsible for testing them.[35]

Procurement: Types of Sourcing Strategy

Sourcing strategy includes a number of basic choices that companies make in deciding how to serve foreign markets. One choice relates to the use of imports, assembly, or production within the

[32]Bruce Kogut, "Designing Global Strategies: Comparative and Competitive Value-Added Chains," *Sloan Management Review* 26 (Summer 1985): 15–28.

[33]Joseph R. Carter and Ram Narasimhan, "Purchasing in the International Marketplace," *Journal of Purchasing and Materials Management* 26 (Summer 1990): 2–11.

[34]Fumiko Kurosawa and John F. Odgers, "Global Strategy of Design and Development by Japanese Car Makers–From the Perspective of the Resource-Based View," *Association of Japanese Business Studies 1997 Annual Meeting Proceedings*, June 13–15, 1997, pp. 144–146.

[35]"Toyota Design Breaks from Clay and Foam," *Automotive News Europe*, April 4, 2005, p. 38.

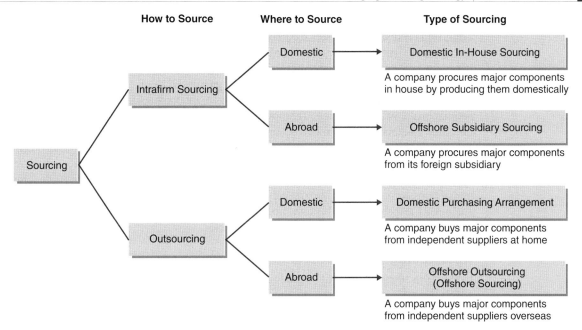

Exhibit 14-2 Types of Sourcing Strategy

country to serve a foreign market. Another decision involves the use of internal or external supplies of components or finished goods.

Sourcing decision making is multifaceted and entails both contractual and locational implications. From a contractual point of view, the sourcing of major components and products by multinational companies takes place in two ways: (1) from the parents or their foreign subsidiaries on an "intra-firm" basis and (2) from independent suppliers on a "contractual" basis. The first type of sourcing is known as **intra-firm sourcing**. The second type of sourcing is commonly referred to as **outsourcing**. Similarly, from a locational point of view, multinational companies can procure components and products either (1) domestically (i.e., domestic sourcing) or (2) from abroad (i.e., offshore sourcing). Therefore, as shown in **Exhibit 14-2**, four possible types of sourcing strategy can be identified.

In developing viable sourcing strategies on a global scale, companies must consider not only the costs of manufacturing and various resources as well as exchange rate fluctuations but also the availability of infrastructure (including transportation, communications, and energy), industrial and cultural environments, ease of working with foreign host governments, and so on. Furthermore, the complex nature of sourcing strategy on a global scale spawns many barriers to its successful execution. In particular, logistics, inventory management, distance, nationalism, and lack of working knowledge about foreign business practices, among others, are major operational problems identified by both U.S. and foreign multinational companies engaging in international sourcing.

Many studies have shown, however, that despite, or perhaps as a result of, those operational problems, *where* to source major components seems much less important than *how* to source them. Thus, when examining the relationship between sourcing and competitiveness of multinational companies, it is crucial to distinguish between sourcing on a "contractual" basis and sourcing on an "intra-firm" basis, for these two types of sourcing will have a different impact on the firm's long-run competitiveness.

Intra-Firm Sourcing

Multinational companies can procure their components in-house within their corporate system around the world. They produce major components at their respective home base and/or at their affiliates overseas to be incorporated in their products marketed in various parts of the world. Thus, trade takes place between a parent company and its subsidiaries abroad, and also between foreign subsidiaries across national boundaries. This is often referred to as intra-firm sourcing. If such in-house component procurement takes place at home, it is essentially **domestic in-house sourcing**. If it takes place at a company's foreign subsidiary, it is called **offshore subsidiary sourcing**. Intra-firm sourcing makes trade statistics more complex to interpret, because part of the international flow of products and components is taking place between affiliated companies within the same multinational corporate system, which transcends national boundaries. In 2009, for example, 30 percent of U.S. exports were attributed to U.S. parent companies transferring products and components to their affiliates overseas, and 48 percent of U.S. imports were accounted for by foreign affiliates exporting to their U.S. parent companies.[36] For both Japan and Britain, intra-firm transactions accounted for approximately 30 percent of their total trade flows (exports and imports combined), respectively.[37] This intra-firm trade also suggests the increased role of foreign affiliates of U.S. multinational firms outside the United States.

Outsourcing (Contract Manufacturing)

In the 1970s, foreign competitors gradually caught up in a productivity race with U.S. companies, which had once commanded a dominant position in international trade. It coincided with U.S. corporate strategic emphasis drifting from manufacturing to finance and marketing. As a result, manufacturing management gradually lost its organizational influence. Production managers' decision-making authority was reduced so that R&D personnel prepared specifications with which production complied and then marketing personnel imposed delivery, inventory, and quality conditions. In a sense, production managers gradually took on the role of outside suppliers within their own companies.[38]

Production managers' reduced influence in the organization further led to a belief that manufacturing functions could, and should, be transferred easily to independent contract manufacturers, depending on the cost differential between in-house and contracted-out production. A company's reliance on domestic suppliers for major components and/or products[39] is basically a **domestic purchase arrangement**. Furthermore, in order to lower production costs under competitive pressure, U.S. companies turned increasingly to outsourcing components and finished products from abroad, particularly from newly industrialized countries including Singapore, South Korea, Taiwan, Hong Kong, Brazil, and Mexico. Initially, subsidiaries were set up for production purposes (i.e., offshore subsidiary sourcing), but gradually, independent foreign contract manufacturers took over component production for U.S. companies. This latter phenomenon is known by many terms, usually called **offshore outsourcing** (or more informally, **offshoring** or outsourcing). For example, Apple and Dell outsource all of their laptop computers to such original design manufacturers as Quanta (a Taiwanese company), Pegatron (a Taiwanese company), and Foxconn (a Chinese company). Dell Computer alone accounts for half of Quanta's sales.[40]

---

[36]Rainer Lanz and Sebastien Miroudot, *Intra-Firm Trade: Patterns, Determinants and Policy Implications,* OECD Trade Policy Papers, No. 114, OECD Publishing, 2011.

[37]United Nations Center on Transnational Corporations, *Transnational Corporations in World Development: Trends and Perspectives* (New York: United Nations, 1988).

[38]Stephen S. Cohen and John Zysman, "Why Manufacturing Matters: The Myth of the Post-Industrial Economy," *California Management Review* 29 (Spring 1987): 9–26.

[39]Rodney Ho, "Small Product-Development Firms Show Solid Growth," *Wall Street Journal*, April 22, 1997, p. 32: This article shows that entrepreneurial companies have begun to fill a void of new product development role as large companies trim their internal R D staff and expenditures in the United States. Although it makes financial sense, at least in the short term, those outsourcing companies will face the same long-term concerns as explained in this chapter.

[40]"The Laptop Trail," *Wall Street Journal*, June 9, 2005, pp. B1 and B8; and "Will Your Next Laptop Be Quanta, Compal, Wistron or Clevo?" CTACS: Callisto Technology and Consultancy Services, October 6, 2012, http://ctacs.weebly.com/.

In recent years, an increasing number of companies has used the internet to develop efficient business-to-business (B2B) procurement (outsourcing) systems on a global scale. On February 25, 2000, General Motors, Ford, and DaimlerChrysler made history by jointly forming Covisint (www.covisint.com), which is probably the largest global online B2B procurement system dedicated to the auto industry. The Big Three have been joined by partners Nissan Motor, Renault, Commerce One, Inc., and Oracle Corp. in an effort to provide procurement, supply-chain, and product-development services to the auto industry on a global scale. The auto industry was an early adopter of the B2B procurement business model for a number of marketing-related reasons. First, automakers could develop products with a relatively short life cycle. Second, they would require a fast response time to market. Third, automakers were early adopters of outsourcing, one primary reason for which is the auto industry's drive for change from a push model to a pull model—their desire to achieve customized make-to-order marketing feasible.[41] However, by 2004, it was clear that Covisint had not been able to build a trust relationship between the participating automakers and their suppliers as it had on paper, and was eventually sold to Compuware Corp. as a messaging data service and portal.[42] Covisint's failure illustrates how difficult it is to manage outsourcing relationships.[43] The near-term benefits of outsourcing are clear. According to a recent survey (see **Exhibit 14-3**), cost reduction, focus on core competencies, access to special expertise, improved financial performance, delivery speed, reduction of resource constrains, and access to new technologies

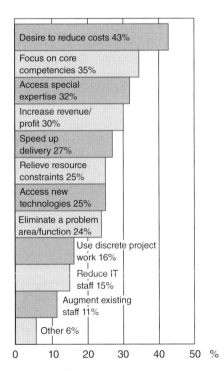

Exhibit 14-3 Major Reasons for Outsourcing

Source: Survey results reported in "Outsourcing: Directions and Decisions for 2003," *2003 Outsourcing Trends*, CIO, http://www.cio.com, accessed February 16, 2006.

---

[41]Beverly Beckert, "Engines of Auto Innovation," *Computer-Aided Engineering* 20 (May 2001): S18–S20.

[42]"Rule of the Road Still Apply to Covisint," *InformationWeek*, February 9, 2004. p. 32.

[43]Martina Gerst and Raluca Bunduchi, "Shaping IT Standardization in the Automotive Industry—The Role of Power in Driving Portal Standardization," *Electronic Markets* 15 (December 2005): 335–343.

are among the most important reasons for outsourcing. However, cultural differences are one of the biggest reasons why offshore outsourcing deals fail or run into problems in the long run.[44]

The short-term benefits of outsourcing are clear. Lower production costs, better strategic focus and flexibility, avoiding bureaucratic costs, and access to world-class capabilities are among the most important reasons for outsourcing. Long-term implications are not so clear, however. In particular, procurement from independent foreign suppliers (i.e., offshore outsourcing) has received quite a bit of attention, for it not only affects domestic employment and economic structure but sometimes also raises ethical issues. Companies using such a strategy have been described pejoratively as **hollow corporations**.[45] It is occasionally argued that those companies are increasingly adopting a "designer role" in global competition by offering innovations in product design without investing in manufacturing and process technology. Revisit some caveats for contract manufacturing discussed in Chapter 9.

Even Covisint, the global B2B procurement business founded by the Big Three automakers, discussed earlier, was not able to generate results that the companies had initially expected. Typical B2B procurement systems, including Covisint, have tended to rely on auctions that emphasize the lowest bids on a global basis. This internet-era emphasis on low cost could border on the cost emphasis of the 1960s and 1970s that ignored the importance of quality, technological superiority, delivery, and other non-cost aspects of competitive advantage. In fact, for superior product development working jointly with external suppliers, automakers need to emphasize the importance of technical collaborations, such as product design, as well as trust-building in supplier-buyer relationships.[46]

Excessive offshore outsourcing practices could indeed have a deleterious impact on companies' ability to maintain their initial competitive advantage based on product innovations.[47] Indeed, keeping abreast of emerging technology through continual improvement in operations and process seems to be essential for the company's continued competitiveness. Take a look at Sony's recent struggles in the consumer electronics market. Sony was once the symbol of technological excellence and product creativity in the highly competitive Japanese electronics industry. Sony's brand image has been tarnished as a result of its excessive outsourcing strategy in the last 10 or so years. Take a look at this Japanese company's recent struggle with its worldwide recall of lithium-ion batteries for notebook computers used by Dell, Apple, and Lenovo and its postponement of the European release of the PlayStation 3 game system due to delays in production of blue laser diodes, a key component of Blu-ray Disc players. One explanation for Sony's recent crises is attributed to the trend of outsourcing to electronic manufacturing services (EMS) companies to cut costs. As a result, Sony has lost consumer confidence.[48]

Outsourcing of Service Activities

In 2011, the United States was the leading exporter and importer of commercial services, providing $578 billion of services to the rest of the world and receiving $391 billion worth of services from abroad.[49] Furthermore, according to a recent government estimate, approximately

---

[44]"Culture Clashes Harm Offshoring," *BusinessWeek.com*, July 17, 2006.

[45]"Special Report: The Hollow Corporation," *Business Week*, March 3, 1986, pp. 56–59; and Robert Heller, "The Dangers of Deconstruction," *Management Today* (February 1993): pp. 14, 17.

[46]Masaaki Kotabe, Xavier Martin, and Hiroshi Domoto, "Gaining from Vertical Relationships: Knowledge Transfer, Relationship Duration, and Supplier Performance Improvement in the U.S. and Japanese Automobile Industries," *Strategic Management Journal* 24 (March 2003): 293–316.

[47]Constantinos Markides and Norman Berg, "Manufacturing Offshore Is Bad Business," *Harvard Business Review* 66 (September-October 1988): 113–120; and Masaaki Kotabe, Michael J. Mol, Janet Y. Murray, and Ronaldo Parente,"Outsourcing and its Implications for Market Success: Negative Curvilineaity, Firm Resources, and Competition," *Journal of the Academy of Marketing Science* 40, no. 2 (2008): 329–346.

[48]"Sony's Technological Leadership in Jeopardy," Nikkei.com, October 7, 2006.

[49]"Trade Growth to Slow in 2012 after Strong Deceleration in 2011," *WTO Press Release 2012*, www.wto.org.

16 percent of the total value of U.S. exports and imports of services were conducted across national boundaries on an intra-firm basis (i.e., between parent companies and their subsidiaries). Increasingly, U.S. companies have expanded their service procurement activities on a global basis in the same way they procure components and finished products. Spending on offshore services is three times higher in North America than in Western Europe, but the gap is closing, with Indian providers becoming more popular in 2007, growing 40 percent in the United States and 60 percent in Europe annually.[50] In 2011, India still occupied the top five most attractive offshoring locations, according to The Global Services Location Index by A.T. Kearney, followed by China, India, Egypt, and Indonesia.[51]

As discussed, firms have the ability and opportunity to procure components/finished goods that have proprietary technology on a global basis. This logic also applies equally to service activities. The technological revolution in data processing and telecommunications (trans-border data flow, telematics, etc.) either makes the global tradability of some services possible or facilitates the transactions economically. Furthermore, because the production and consumption of some services do not need to take place at the same location or at the same time, global sourcing could be a viable strategy.

Thanks to the development of the internet and e-commerce, certain service activities are increasingly outsourced from independent service suppliers. The internet has also accelerated growth in the number of e-workers. This net-savvy and highly flexible corps are able to perform much or all of their work at home, or in small groups close to home, regardless of their locations. International e-workers can also operate in locations far from corporate headquarters. They are part of the growth in intellectual outsourcing. Already such e-workers can write software in India for a phone company in Finland, provide architectural services in Ireland for a building in Spain, and do accounting work in Hong Kong for an insurance company in Vancouver, Canada. Globalization of services through the internet is likely to expand considerably in the future.

Bangalore, India, should particularly be noted. The region is described as the Silicon Valley of that country. Bangalore has rapidly evolved to become the center of offshore programming activities. Many U.S. companies have started outsourcing an increasing portion of software development to companies in Bangalore. Established software vendors, including IBM, Microsoft, Oracle, and SAP, already employ Indian talent no longer just to write software code but also to help design and develop commercial offerings that are higher up in the software design food chain. Increasingly, Indian software entrepreneurs want to put their own companies' brand names on products, at home and abroad, by capitalizing on their country's highly educated and low-cost workforce to build and sell software for everything from back-office programs to customer-facing applications.[52] According to Indian technology industry body, the National Association of Software and Services Companies (NASSCOM), exports of software in the 2011 fiscal year reached $68.7 billion—up from $41 billion in 2008. Growth was expected to be 11–14 percent in the 2012 fiscal year, starting in April to $76 billion to $78 billion. However, the export revenue growth of Indian software companies was expected to moderate due to the economic uncertainties of two major markets: the United States and Europe, which represent almost 90 percent of the revenue.[53] Similarly, China is catching up in this role. Microsoft has four research laboratories located around the globe: Redmond, Washington; Cambridge, UK; Beijing, China, and San Francisco, California, with the goal to invent Microsoft's future by focusing on technologies and technology trends in the next 5–10 year time frame. For example, Microsoft Research (MSR)

---

[50]"Global Outsourcing to Grow 8% in 2008," *BusinessWeek.com*, January 10, 2008.

[51]"Offshoring Opportunities amid Economic Turbulences: The A.T. Kearney Global Services Location Index 2011," AT Kearney Consulting, 2012, www.atkearney.com.

[52]"India's Next Step," *InformationWeek*, August 8, 2005, pp. 34-39.

[53]R. Jai Krishna, "UPDATE: India Software Body Forecasts Lower 2012–13 Export Growth," *Wall Street Journal*, February 8, 2012.

Asia, founded in 1998 in Beijing, has already produced many research results that have been transferred to Microsoft products, including Windows and Office software.[54]

Outsourcing of service activities has been widely quoted in the popular press as a means to reduce costs and improve the corporate focus; that is, concentrating on the core activities of the firm. However, outsourcing may also serve (a) as a means of reducing time to implement internal processes, (b) as a means of sharing risk in an increasingly uncertain business environment, (c) to improve customer service, (d) to get access to better expertise not available in-house, (e) for headcount reduction, and (f) as a means of instilling a sense of competition, especially when departments within firms develop a perceptible level of inertia.[55] Despite its advantages and attractiveness to businesses, offshore outsourcing can bring adverse impact to some other stakeholders—namely, to the workforce in the domestic country. See **Global Perspective 14-2** for some broad issues in offshoring of services.

Global Perspective 14-2

Some Trends and Issues of Service Offshoring

India has been a number one choice for U.S. companies in offshoring their service jobs for years. Outsourcing business grew to about $69 billion in India in 2011. India has substantial advantages in offshoring as there are plenty of English speakers to staff call centers and enough tech talent to run remote data-processing and computer support centers, which cost at about 60 percent discount compared to the U.S. workers. In 2011, however, companies in Latin America and Eastern Europe opened 54 new outsourcing facilities (as opposed to 49 for India), challenging India's prior domination in the service offshoring business.

Hiring an entry-level accountant in Argentina, for example, costs 13 percent less than a similar U.S. worker, while an Indian worker would cost 51 percent less. Getting the lowest wage, however, has not been the main priority in offshoring service jobs anymore because, according to Phil Fersht, chief executive officer of HfS Research, a Boston outsourcing research firm: "The higher-value outsourcing jobs require a greater understanding of business context and a higher amount of interaction with clients." Take Brazil as an example. São Paulo has large groups of young people with engineering and business school degrees who speak English

and possess various exemplary capabilities, from developing video games to analyzing mortgage defaults for U.S. companies. Brazil has the most Java programmers in the world and the second-most mainframe (COBOL) programmers. The Gen Y population in Poland is highly educated—about 50 percent (vs. 10 percent in India) of its 20- to 24-year-olds are in college and prolifically multilingual.

All the exciting stories about the capabilities and the attractiveness of places to offshore the U.S. service jobs do not sound that exciting anymore from the perspective of the U.S. domestic workforce, as well as other workforces of countries that engaged in massive exports of service offshore. Americans have become increasingly concerned about the impact of offshoring on the U.S. economy. The practice of offshoring (i.e. relocating production and service facilities overseas) has increased over the past few years—not only in blue-collar industries, but in white-collar industries as well. The white-collar industries were previously considered to be more stable and less vulnerable to global competition.

In recent years, the United States has outsourced tens of thousands of jobs, ranging from technology support to Wall

---

[54]"Labs: Asia," Microsoft Research, http://research.microsoft.com/aboutmsr/labs/asia/, accessed February 20, 2006.

[55]Maneesh Chandra, "Global Sourcing of Services: A Theory Development and Empirical Investigation," Ph.D. dissertation, University of Texas at Austin, 1999.

Street research. The argument made by corporate executives, politicians, and academics was that there was no choice. Especially with globalization today, it is critical to tap the lower costs and unique skills of labor abroad to remain competitive. This trend has raised fears in the United States that the U.S. economy may be permanently losing certain jobs and job categories. The implications could lead to a hollowing out of the middle class and downward pressure on wages. In his 2004 paper, economist Paul Samuelson, a Nobel Prize winner, stated that "the economic effect of outsourcing is similar to allowing mass immigration of workers willing to compete for service jobs at extremely low wages."

The American workers' fears are quite justified by looking at the following statistics: offshoring has accounted for roughly half a million layoffs during the 2001–2004 period; the number of U.S. jobs outsourced is expected to grow from about 400,000 in 2004 to 3.3 million by 2015; and if this estimate is accurate, offshoring could result in roughly 250,000 layoffs a year. Current labor market data show another justification of those fears: the economy is still millions of jobs short of where it should be at this point in its recovery.

Despite its overall economic gains, offshoring is also redistributive, with affected workers facing possible job loss and wage pressures. McKinsey and Co. conducted a study to estimate redistribution effect. Both the theory and the evidence only give partial answers. The McKinsey study estimates that for every dollar of U.S. services activity that is offshored, there is a global gain of $1.47, suggesting a net gain of 47 cents. India captures 33 cents of the total, leaving the United States with the remaining $1.14. How is this $1.14 distributed? "Reemployed" workers get 47 cents (a substantial reduction), additional exports account for a relatively modest 5 cents, and shareholders and consumers of the firms doing the offshoring gain the other 62 cents. U.S. shareholders and consumers win while U.S. workers lose.

Implications of this matter come in the form of several important challenges. American workers must be capable of competing successfully in the global economy through the acquisition and possession of critical skills. The United States must continue to be viewed as the most attractive location for high value services and manufacturing. What must immediately be followed up is that lawmakers must address the serious challenges faced by permanently displaced workers.

Sources: John Helyar, "Outsourcing: A Passage out of India," *Bloomberg Businessweek*, March 15, 2012; "Outsourcing: Where's Uncle Sam?" The Debate Room, *Bloomberg Businessweek*, http://www.businessweek .com/debateroom/archives/2007/02/outsourcing_wheres_uncle_sam .html#share; "The Impact of Offshoring on the U.S. Economy: Policy Perspectives," Center for American Progress, http://www.realpolice.net/ forums/politics-religion-controversy-74/13032-impact-offshoring-u-s-economy-policy-perspectives.html; and Lael Brainard and Robert E. Litan, "'Offshoring' Service Jobs: Bane or Boon—and What to Do?," *Brookings Institution Policy Brief*, April 2004.

In the case of service companies, the distinction between core and supplementary services is necessary in strategy development. **Core services** are the necessary outputs of an organization that consumers are looking for, while **supplementary services** are either indispensable for the execution of the core service or are available only to improve the overall quality of the core service bundle. Using the healthcare industry as an example, the core service is providing patients with good-quality medical care. The supplementary services may include filing insurance claims, arranging accommodation for family members (especially for overseas patients), handling off-hour emergency calls, and so on. The same phenomenon arises in the computer software industry. When the industry giant, Microsoft, needed help in supporting new users of Windows operating software, it utilized outsourcing with Boston-based Keane, Inc. to set up a help desk with 350 support personnel.

Core services may gradually partake of a "commodity" and lose their differential advantage vis-à-vis competitors as competition intensifies over time. Subsequently, a service provider may increase its reliance on supplementary services to maintain and/or enhance competitive advantage. "After all, if a firm cannot do a decent job on the core elements, it is eventually going to go out of business."[56] In other words, a service firm exists in order to provide good-quality core services to

---

[56]C. H. Lovelock, "Adding Value to Core Products with Supplementary Services," in C. H. Lovelock, ed., *Services Marketing*, 3rd ed. (Englewood Cliffs, NJ: Prentice-Hall, 1996).

its customers; however, in some instances, it simply cannot rely solely on core services to stay competitive. We can expect that core services are usually performed by the service firm itself, regardless of the characteristics of the core service. On the other hand, although supplementary services are provided to augment the core service for competitive advantage, the unique characteristics of supplementary services may influence "how" and "where" they are sourced.[57]

It is important to acknowledge that U.S. consumers exhibit a country of service origin preference. When receiving an offshore service, they consider communication, security, and reliability as the most important service quality attributes.[58] Therefore, it is imperative for U.S. companies (and for other companies across the world considering to offshore their services) to consider and be aware of consumer attitudes and perceptions about countries considered attractive for offshoring. Countries with the highest skilled labor, lowest cost, or geographic closeness to the home country are not necessarily the most preferred ones for service offshoring.

The bottom line is that the quality of the service package that customers experience helps service companies differentiate themselves from the competition. One important category of quality is the variability of the product's or service's attributes—its reliability. As in manufacturing, service companies that choose to differentiate themselves based on reliability must consistently maintain it, or else they will undermine their strategic position by damaging the reputation of their brand name. There is empirical evidence that outsourcing of some service activities for the sake of economic efficiency tends to result in less reliable service offerings.[59] The same concern about the advantages and disadvantages of outsourcing in the manufacturing industry appears to apply in the services industry.

Free Trade Zones

A **free trade zone (FTZ)** is an area located within a nation (say, the United States) but that is considered outside of the customs territory of the nation. The use of FTZs has become an integral part of global sourcing strategy as they offer various tax benefits and marketing flexibility on a global basis.

Many countries have similar programs. In the United States, a free trade zone is officially called a Foreign Trade Zone. FTZs are licensed by the Foreign Trade Zone Board and operated under the supervision of the Customs Service. The level of demand for FTZ procedures has followed the overall growth trend in global trade and investment. Presently, some 700 FTZs are in operation and, as part of their activity, about 540 manufacturing plants are operating with subzone status. Subzones are adjuncts to the main zones when the main site cannot serve the needed purpose and are usually found at manufacturing plants. Across the United States, about 335,000 jobs are directly related to activity in FTZs. Companies operating in FTZs are saving money, improving cash flow, and increasing logistical efficiency.[60] Legally, goods in the zone remain in international commerce as long as they are held within the zone or are exported. In other words, those goods (including materials, components, and finished products) shipped into an FTZ in the United States from abroad are legally considered not having landed in the customs territory of the United States and thus are

[57]Terry Clark, Daniel Rajaratnam, and Timothy Smith, "Toward a theory of international services: Marketing intangibles in a world of nations," *Journal of International Marketing* 4, no. 2 (1996): 9–28; and Janet Y. Murray and Masaaki Kotabe, "Sourcing Strategies of U.S. Service Companies: A Modified Transaction-Cost Analysis," *Strategic Management Journal*, 20 (September 1999): 791–809.

[58]Shawn T. Thelen, Earl D. Honeycutt, Jr., Thomas P. Murphy, "Services Offshoring: Does Perceived Service Quality Affect Country-of-Service Origin Preference?" *Managing Service Quality* 20, no. 3 (2010): 196–212.

[59]C. M. Hsieh, Sergio G. Lazzarini, Jack A. Nickerson, "Outsourcing and the Variability of Product Performance: Data from International Courier Services," *Academy of Management Proceedings*, 2002, pp. G1–G6.

[60]" US Foreign-Trade Zones Boost Employment, Exports," *Journal of Commerce*, September 5, 2005, p. 24.

Exhibit 14-4 Benefits of Using a Foreign Trade Zone (FTZ) in the United States

1. *Duty deferral and elimination*: Duty will be deferred until products are sold in the United States. If products are exported elsewhere, no import tariff will be imposed.
2. *Lower tariff rates*: Tariff rates are almost always lower for materials and components than for finished products. If materials and components are shipped to an FTZ for further processing and finished products are sold in the United States, a U.S. import tariff will be assessed on the value of the materials and components, rather than on the value of the finished products.
3. *Lower tariff incidence*: Imported materials and components that through storage or processing undergo a loss or shrinkage may benefit from FTZ status as tariff is assessed only on the value of materials and components that actually found their way into the product.
4. *Exchange rate hedging*: Currency fluctuations can be hedged against by requesting customs assessment at any time.
5. *Import quota not applicable*: Import quotas are not generally applicable to goods stored in an FTZ.
6. *Made in U.S.A. designation*: If foreign components are substantially transformed within an FTZ located in the United States, the finished product may be designated as MADE IN U.S.A.

not subject to U.S. import tariffs, as long as they are not sold outside the FTZ in the United States (see **Exhibit 14-4**).

An FTZ provides many cash flow and operating advantages as well as marketing advantages to zone users. Even when these goods enter the United States, customs duties can be levied on the lesser of the value of the finished product or its imported components.

Operationally, an FTZ provides an opportunity for every business engaged in international commerce to take advantage of a variety of efficiencies and economies in the manufacture and marketing of their products. Merchandise within the zone can be unpacked and repacked; sorted and relabeled; inspected and tested; repaired or discarded; reprocessed, fabricated, assembled, or otherwise manipulated. It can be combined with other imported or domestic materials; stored or exhibited; transported in bond to another FTZ; sold or exported. Foreign goods can be modified within the zone to meet U.S. import standards and processed using U.S. labor.

Aging imported wine is an interesting way to take advantage of an FTZ. A U.S. wine importer purchases what is essentially newly fermented grape juice from French vineyards and ships it to an FTZ in the United States for aging. After several years, the now-aged French wine can be shipped throughout the United States when an appropriate U.S. import tariff is assessed on the original value of the grape juice instead of on the market value of the aged wine. If tariff rates are sufficiently high, the cost savings from using an FTZ can be enormous.

Another effective use of an FTZ is illustrated by companies such as Ford and Dell Computer. These companies rely heavily on imported components such as auto parts and computer chips, respectively. In such a case, the companies can have part of their manufacturing facilities designated as subzones of an FTZ. This way, they can use their facilities as they ordinarily do, yet enjoy all of the benefits accruing from an FTZ. Furthermore, if foreign components are substantially transformed within an FTZ located in the United States, the finished product may be designated as MADE IN U.S.A. To the extent customers have a favorable attitude toward the MADE IN U.S.A. country-of-origin, such labeling has additional marketing advantage.

At the macro-level, all parties to the arrangement benefit from the operation of trade zones. The government maintaining the trade zone achieves increased investment and employment. The firm using the trade zone obtains a beachhead in the foreign market without incurring all costs normally associated with such an activity. As a result, goods can be reassembled, and large shipments can be broken down into smaller units. Duties could be due only on the imported materials and the component parts rather than on the labor that is used to finish the product.

In addition to free trade zones, various governments have also established export processing zones and special economic areas. Japan, which has had a large trade surplus over the years, has developed a unique trade zone program specifically designed to increase imports rather than exports. The common dimensions of all of these zones are that special rules apply to them, when compared with other regions of the country, and that the purpose of these rules is the desire of governments to stimulate the economy—especially the export side of international trade. Export processing zones usually provide tax- and duty-free treatment of production facilities whose output is destined for foreign markets. The maquiladoras of Mexico are one example (for those interested in Mexico's maquiladoras, see Appendix to this chapter).

For the logistician, the decision of whether to use such zones is framed by the overall benefit for the logistics system. Clearly, transport and retransport are often required, warehousing facilities need to be constructed, and material handling frequency increases. However, the costs could well be balanced by the preferential government treatment or by lower labor costs.

International Distribution Channel

Both consumer and industrial products go through some form of distribution process in all countries and markets. International distribution channels are the link between a firm and its customers in markets around the world. For a firm to realize its marketing objectives, it must be able to make its product accessible to its target market at an affordable price. A firm cannot do this if its distribution structures are inflexible, inefficient, and burdensome. Creating a reliable and efficient international distribution channel can be one of the most critical and challenging tasks that an international marketing manager can face.

Channel Configurations

In essence, companies have two options when it comes to configuring their international distribution systems:

1. A firm may decide to sell directly to its customers in a foreign market by using its own local salesforce or through the internet.

2. A firm may decide to use the resources of independent intermediaries, most often at the local level.

An Australian company, ResMed, a manufacturer of medical respiratory devices, is an example of a firm that uses the first option. Most of ResMed's foreign sales are generated by its own sales staff operation from its own sales offices in the United States, the United Kingdom, and throughout Europe and South-East Asia. Although this direct distribution channel may appear to be the most effective, it is only successful if customers are geographically homogeneous, have similar consumption patterns, and are relatively few.[61] Dell and Hewlett-Packard are two examples of multinational companies in the same personal computer industry with different distribution systems. Dell distributes its PCs directly from its assembly factories to end-users anywhere in the world, while Hewlett-Packard uses international agents and retailers. Dell customers may have to wait several days or weeks to get a PC, whereas Hewlett-Packard customers can walk away from a retailer with a PC immediately. In deciding which distribution channels to adopt, a firm needs to consider the cost of meeting customer needs. Therefore, a firm needs to evaluate the impact on customer service and cost as it compares different international distribution options.

Distribution channels that use intermediaries, agents, or merchants positioned between the manufacturer and customers in a distribution channel can often have several levels and employ

---

[61]Bruce Seifert and John Ford, "Export Distribution Channels," *Columbia Journal of World Business* 24, no. 2 (1989): 15–22.

several intermediaries, each with its own specific purpose within the distribution channel. The use of intermediaries can be a relatively easy, quick and low-cost entry strategy into a new foreign market, therefore their frequent use by many companies, particularly small-to-medium companies that do not have the resources to operate their own marketing and distribution system in a foreign market. **Exhibit 14-5** shows some of the distribution channel configurations.

Within a distribution channel, a firm can elect to go through one or more agent or merchant intermediaries. The basic difference between agent and merchant intermediaries is the legal ownership of goods. An **agent intermediary** does not take title (ownership) to the goods. Rather, it distributes them on behalf of the principal company in exchange for a percentage of the sale price. Merchant intermediaries hold title to the goods they exchange and operate in their own right as independent businesses. The names given to intermediaries can vary from country to country and from industry to industry in the same country.

Apart from meeting customer needs and costs, several other factors influence the choice of distribution channel configuration used by a firm to gain access to its international markets, including the characteristics of the company's customers; the range and choice of intermediaries; competitors; marketing environment; and the strengths and weaknesses of the company itself.[62] However, these factors stand out as being particularly important in selecting a proper distribution channel in terms of market coverage, control, and cost.

Coverage refers to the market segments or geographic area a firm's products are represented in. Although full market coverage may be the company's objective, it is not always possible in a foreign market; nor may it be desirable. In some countries, such as China and Brazil, three or four major cities contain the country's most affluent and viable market segments for foreign products. If a firm wishes to attempt full market coverage, it may have to use several intermediaries.

The more intermediaries in the distribution channel, the more likely that the firm will lose control over all aspects in the marketing of its products. If a firm wishes to have complete control over such aspects of its marketing as establishing prices, the types of outlets where its products should be available, inventory levels and promotion, it has little choice but to develop its own company-controlled distribution system.

Although direct distribution by a firm may allow it to have complete control over all aspects of the marketing of its products, it brings significant cost issues. This is particularly true if the sales base is relatively small. Channel costs include the margins, markups, or commissions payable to the various intermediaries. Although these costs may inflate a product's price in a foreign market, companies may be disappointed if they believe that they can reduce channel costs by using a direct distribution strategy. Local costs associated with maintaining a salesforce, inventory, providing credit, and advertising may offset any cost savings.

In reality, most often, no one factor is more important than another in configuring an international distribution channel. A channel with optimum coverage and control at a minimum cost is the preferred choice, but, in practice, a balance has to be struck.

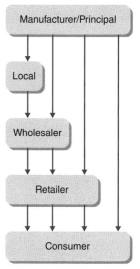

Exhibit 14-5
International Distribution Channel Alternatives

Channel Management

Use of an indirect distribution channel always results in loss of some control over a company's marketing operations. This loss of control can be greater in international distribution channels than in domestic ones because the company has no permanent presence in the foreign market and must rely heavily on the actions of its foreign intermediaries. Differences in expectations and goals between the company and its foreign intermediaries can lead to channel conflict. To deal with this, companies must actively manage the relationship between themselves and their intermediaries,

---

[62]Bert Rosenbloom and Trina L. Larsen, "International Channels of Distribution and the Role of Comparative Marketing Analysis," *Journal of Global Marketing* 4, no. 4 (1991): 39–54.

and often among intermediaries themselves, in order to create a harmonious relationship characterized by loyalty, trust, cooperation, and open communication.[63]

The selection of intermediaries becomes crucial both to the process of maintaining harmonious channel relationships and to a company if it wishes to achieve its foreign sales and other marketing objectives. Some guidelines for selecting and dealing with foreign intermediaries include:[64]

- Search for intermediaries capable of developing markets, not just those with good contacts.

- Regard intermediaries as long-term partners, not as a temporary means of market entry.

- Actively search for and select intermediaries; do not let them select you.

- Support your intermediaries by committing resources such as marketing ideas, funds, and know-how.

- Ensure intermediaries provide the information you need, including up-to-date market information and detailed sales performance data.

- Attempt to maintain as much control as possible over the marketing strategy.

- Try to make links with national intermediaries as soon as possible after entering a foreign market.

In addition, the company should always maintain a genuine interest in both the intermediary and the foreign market, be prepared to adapt to the local competitive conditions, and attempt to minimize disagreements with an intermediary as quickly as possible.

International Retailing

The face of distribution that consumers interact with is the retail store at which they shop. In developed parts of the world, retailing employs between 7 percent and 12 percent of the workforce and wields enormous power over manufacturers and consumers. **International retailing** is any retailing activity that transcends national borders. Over the last two decades, retailers have grown into some of the world's largest companies, rivaling or exceeding manufacturers in terms of global reach. They have been growing much faster abroad than in their domestic markets. The world's top 10 retailers' international operations are summarized in **Exhibit 14-6**.

In search of new opportunities, retailers have not only diversified across geographical market boundaries but also across product boundaries. First, most leading retailers have developed their own private-label product lines as well as sell the products of leading national- and international-brand manufacturers. Second, retailers have increasingly adopted the discount format. As a result, more consumers are getting used to their streamlined no-frills retail format. Third, retailers have also increasingly embraced the virtual store (e-commerce) format.[65]

Take a look at the world's largest discount store chain, Wal-Mart of the United States. Wal-Mart has become the largest company in the United States and the world's largest retailer with annual revenues of about $443.9 billion in 2012. As of January 2012, the company had 3,029 supercenters, 629 discount stores, 196 supermarkets, 14 small formats, and 611 Sam's Club—totaling 4,479 stores in the United States alone. Wal-Mart International operated 5,651 stores, spreading in Mexico (2,088), Canada (333), Brazil (512), Argentina (88), China (370), UK (541),

---

[63]Leonidas C. Leonidou, Constantine S. Katsikeas, and John Hadjimarcou, "Building Successful Export Business Relationships: A Behavioral Perspective," *Journal of International Marketing* 10, no. 3 (2002): 96–115.

[64]David Arnold, "Seven Rules of International Distribution," *Harvard Business Review* 78 (November/December 2000): 131–137.

[65]Katrijn Gielens and Marnik G. Dekimpe, "Global Trends in Grocery Retailing," in Masaaki Kotabe and Kristiaan Helsen, eds., *The SAGE Handbook of International Marketing* (London: SAGE Publications, 2009), pp. 413-428.

Exhibit 14-6 International Operations of the World's Top 10 Retailers

Rank	Company	Country of Origin	2010 Sales (US $billion)	Annual Growth 2005–2010 (%)	Number of Foreign Markets
1	Wal-Mart	United States	419.0	6.0	16
2	Carrefour	France	119.6	3.9	33
3	Tesco	United Kingdom	92.2	9.3	13
4	Metro	Germany	88.9	3.8	33
5	The Kroger Co.	United States	82.2	6.3	1
6	Schwarz (Lidl)	Germany	79.1	9.8	26
7	Costco	United States	76.3	8.0	9
8	Home Depot	United States	68.0	−2.5	5
9	Walgreen Co.	United States	67.4	9.8	2
10	Aldi	Germany	67.1	5.9	18

Source: "2012 Global Powers of Retailing," Deloitte Report.

Japan (419), Costa Rica (200), El Salvador (79), Guatemala (200), Honduras (70), Nicaragua (73), Chile (316), India (15), and Africa (347).[66] The company employs 2.2 million sales associates around the world.[67] Despite its aggressive foreign expansion, however, Wal-Mart experienced continued difficulties in such markets as Argentina and Puerto Rico, pulling out of Germany and South Korea, as well as declining sales in Japan.

Wal-Mart is Procter & Gamble's single largest customer, buying as much as the household product giant sells to Japan. Wal-Mart is extremely successful in the NAFTA region, but is not necessarily the most global retailer. Actually only 10 percent of its sales are generated outside its core NAFTA market, compared to Carrefour, which generates more than 20 percent of sales outside Europe. Wal-Mart's success lies in low tariffs in the NAFTA zone, cheap labor, and low-cost logistics, with savings passed on to consumers.[68] In other foreign markets, however, Wal-Mart's performance has been lackluster, primarily due to its unwillingness to adapt to local market conditions (see, for example, the case study on Wal-Mart operations in Brazil, included in the textbook).

Retailing involves very locally entrenched activities, including stocking an assortment of products that local consumers prefer, catering to local shopping patterns (e.g., shopping frequency, time of shopping, and traffic jams), and seasonal promotion as well as meeting local competition on a daily basis. International retailers that are willing to adapt their strategy to local ways of doing things while taking advantage of their managerial and information technology capabilities seem to be more successful than those that try to extend their ways of doing things abroad. In general, European retailers tend to be more willing to customize their marketing and procurement strategies to various local market peculiarities than are U.S. or Japanese retailers.[69] Wal-Mart, which tended to extend its U.S.-based procurement and product assortment strategies in its earlier foreign expansion, resulting in a huge market adjustment problem, is now moving

[66]Wal-Mart 2012 Annual Report, www.walmartstores.com; and Wal-Mart Stores, Inc. Data Sheet - Worldwide Unit Details January 2012, www.walmartstores.com.

[67]Wal-Mart website: http://corporate.walmart.com/our-story/locations, accessed January 25, 2013.

[68]" How Nafta Helped Wal-Mart Reshape The Mexican Market," *Wall Street Journal*, August 31, 2001, p. A1.

[69]Brenda Sternquist, *International Retailing*, 2nd ed. (New York: Fairchild Publications, 2007).

slowly to convert the stores it has acquired in Europe into retailers unlike anything Americans would recognize as Wal-Marts.[70]

Wal-Mart also began its entry into the difficult Japanese retail market in mid-2002. It increased its equity stake in Seiyu, Japan's fourth-largest supermarket group, paving the way for a low-cost strategy in Japan. However, Wal-Mart is expected to have an upward battle in Japan as quality-conscious Japanese consumers associate its emphasis on "Everyday Low Price" with poor quality, or "*yasu-karou, waru-karou*," which is a Japanese phrase used to express the feeling that "you get what you pay for" or conversely, the more you pay, the better quality you must be getting. Take organic food as one example. Japanese consumers tend to be less tolerant of skin blemishes and lack of size and shape uniformity in organic produce.[71] Consequently, Wal-Mart in Japan suffered continued declining sales and increasing losses in 2007.[72]

On the other hand, Carrefour, as a typical European retailer willing to be more accommodating to local needs and culture, approaches foreign markets differently. With some 10 years of experience in the Chinese market and a good understanding of the Chinese consumer, the French retailer understands that Chinese consumers are eager to learn about Western products and has incorporated numerous signs providing detailed product information in its supermarkets in China. For example, in the bakery department, Carrefour provides detailed explanation regarding the different flours used and their associated benefits. To promote French wine to consumers, Carrefour had a French wine specialist provide advice and offer wine tasting to passing shoppers. The company was a clear market leader in Shanghai and other primary and secondary cities (see **Exhibit 14-7** for Carrefour's SWOT analysis of its China and global operations). After all, it is crucial for retailers to understand that there is no such a thing as a homogenous consumer market. For example, each Asia Pacific market is different and presents a different level of opportunity. Because each consumer has his or her own purchasing habits, there is no one winning Asian retail formula for both retailers and suppliers.[73]

Private-Label Branding (Store Brands)

Retailers increasingly rely on **private-label brands (store brands)** to appeal to price-conscious customers as well as to broaden their product offerings. Worldwide, the share of private labels as a percentage of all consumer packaged goods has grown from 14 to 18 percent.[74] In the food sector, the number is even more astounding: the global market share of private label food products is currently at 25 percent and is expected to continue growing at a staggering 50 percent by 2025.[75] For example, European retail chains such as Tesco sell goods under their own name made by a manufacturer called McBride, based near Manchester, England. McBride is not a household name although European consumers spend nearly $1 billion on household cleaners and personal care goods made by the company.[76]

Private labels come under various guises. At one extreme are the generic products that are packaged very simply and sold at bottom prices. At the other extreme are premium store brands that deliver quality sometimes superior to national brands.

---

[70]Earnest Beck and Emily Nelson, "As Wal-Mart Invades Europe, Rivals Rush to Match Its Formula," *Wall Street Journal Interactive Edition*, http://interactive.wsj.com/, October 6, 1999.

[71]Hatakeyama Noboru, "Highly Demanding Japanese Consumers," *Japan Spotlight Bimonthly* 23 (September/October 2004): 2–5.; and "Wal-Mart to Make Seiyu A Group Company," *NikkeiNet Interactive*, http://www.nni.nikkei.co.jp/, November 2, 2005..

[72]"Wal-Mart Expects Bigger 2007 Loss in Japan," *Wall Street Journal*, February 13, 2008, p. B14.

[73]"Carrefour 2005," Retail Analysis, iReport series, http://www.igd.com/analysis/, accessed February 20, 2006.

[74]Nirmalya Kumar and Jan-Benedict Steenkamp, *Private Label Revolution* (Cambridge: Harvard Business School Press, 2006).

[75]"Private label vs. Brands: An Inseparable Combination," *Rabobank International Food & Agribusiness Research and Advisory 2011 Report*, www.rabobank.com/far.

[76]"The Big Brands Go Begging," *Business Week*, March 21, 2005, pp. 24-25.

Exhibit 14-7   SWOT Analysis of Carrefour's Operations in China and Worldwide

Strengths (in the Chinese Market)

- 10 years of experience in China
- Good understanding of the Chinese consumer
- Clear leader in the Shanghai market
- First mover advantage in many of the primary and secondary cities
- Chinese managers have been trained in its own in-house training center
- Corner on the expatriate and high-end market in primary cities
- Good competition on price, putting pressure on both international and domestic retailers
- Dia Market small-format discount store expansion plans to enable Carrefour to compete in growing convenience market

Weakness (in the Chinese Market)

- Tailored hypermarkets to the upper end of the market, which could be a problem when penetrating less affluent cities
- Received negative media coverage regarding its relationship with the government, local supplier management, and store opening strategy impact on local retailers

Opportunities (in the Global Market)

- Dominant "enlarged home market" position
- Unrivalled international presence and experience of emerging markets
- Multi-format strategy
- Global vision and organization
- World-class merchandising
- Customer knowledge

Threats (in the Global Market)

- Key gaps in international presence (i.e., United States, United Kingdom, and Germany)
- Relatively small turnover in comparison with Wal-Mart
- Slow pace of expansion in some emerging markets
- Lack of scale in Central European markets

Source: "Carrefour 2005," Retail Analysis, iReport series, http://www.igd.com/analysis/, accessed February 20, 2006.

Private labels have made big inroads in several European countries. Switzerland, the United Kingdom, Germany, and Spain were the top four of highest market share countries for private labels, and they will continue to grow steadily. Nielsen's global online survey showed that the private label phenomenon would continue to stay, with 91 percent of more than 27,000 respondents across 53 countries claiming that they would continue to buy private labels even when the economy improves.[77] In Japan and most other Asian countries, on the other hand, store brands are still marginal players. Consumers in this region tend to be extremely brand loyal.[78] In Japan, only top brand manufacturers produce store brand products; there are no store brand—only manufacturers—unlike in the United States and Europe.[79]

---

[77]"Global Private Label Report: The Rise of the Value-Conscious Shopper," The Nielsen Company, *Nielsenwire*, http://blog.nielsen.com/nielsenwire/, March 4, 2011.

[78]"No global private label quake— yet," *Advertising Age International*, January 16, 1995, p. I-26; and Store Brand Success around the World," The Nielsen Company," *Nielsenwire*, http://blog.nielsen.com/nielsenwire/, May 5, 2009.

[79]"Private Brands: A Global Guide to the Rise of Private Label Brands," Interbrand, http://www.interbrand.com/Libraries/Articles/-1_Private_Brands_pdf.sflb.ashx, accessed December 1, 2012.

As a branding strategy, private labeling is especially attractive to MNCs that face well-entrenched incumbent brands in the markets they plan to enter. Under such circumstances, launching the product as a store brand enables the firm to get the shelf space access which it would otherwise be denied.

"Push" versus "Pull"

At the heart of this retailing revolution is the fundamental change in the way goods and services reach the consumer. Previously, the manufacturer or the wholesaler controlled the distribution chain across the world. The retailer's main competitive advantage lay in the merchandising skills of choosing the assortment of goods to sell in the store. The retailer's second advantage—closeness to the customer—was used to beat the rival retailer across the street. The manufacturer decided what goods were available and, in most countries, at what price they could be sold to the public.

That distribution system of earlier times has been turned upside down. The traditional supply chain powered by the manufacturing push is becoming a demand chain driven by consumer pull—especially in the developed countries where the supply and variety of goods is far above base-level requirements of goods and services. In most industrialized countries, resale price maintenance—which allows the supplier to fix the price at which goods can be sold to the final customer—has either been abolished or bypassed. The shift in power in the distribution channel is fundamentally a product of the application of information technology to store management.

Many multinational companies from industrialized countries are now entering markets and developing their distribution channels in developing countries. One study showed that companies from Western countries seem to have difficulty competing with Japanese companies in fast-growing Southeast Asian markets and attributed this to different styles in managing distribution channels.[80] In just three decades, for example, the consumer electronics distribution systems in Malaysia and Thailand have come to be characterized by a striking presence of exclusive dealerships with Japanese multinational manufacturers such as Panasonic, Sanyo, and Hitachi.

For example, Panasonic practices a push strategy with 220 exclusive dealerships in Malaysia and 120 in Thailand. In Malaysia, these exclusive dealerships represent 65 percent of total Panasonic sales, although these numbers represent only 30 percent of the retailers selling Panasonic products. On the other hand, General Electric and Philips use a pull strategy, relying on the multivendor distribution system without firm control of the distribution channel as practiced in Western countries. Competitors from the United States and Europe are feeling locked out of Japanese companies' tightly controlled distribution channels in Southeast Asia. This information suggests that a push strategy is more effective than a pull strategy in emerging markets.

On-Time Retail Information Management

Cutting down on stocks in inventory is a tempting thing to do to achieve cost savings. The chief reason for holding stocks is to smooth out bumps in the supply chain. However one of the biggest sources of inefficiency in logistics occurs exactly because distribution channel members just do so independently of each other. It is known as the "**bullwhip effect**"—after the way the amplitude of a whiplash increases down the length of the whip when it is cracked. Procter & Gamble discovered this effect more than a decade ago. The company noticed an odd thing about the shipment of Pampers, its well-known brand of disposable diapers. Although the number of babies and the demand for diapers remained relatively stable, orders for Pampers fluctuated dramatically. This was because information about consumer demand can become increasingly distorted as it moves

[80]Patricia Robinson, "The Role of Historical and Institutional Context in Transferring Distribution Practices Abroad: Matsushita's Monopolization of Market Share in Malaysia," *The American Marketing Association and the Japan Marketing Association Conference on the Japanese Distribution Strategy*, November 22–24, 1998.

along the supply chain. For instance, when a retailer sees a slight increase in demand for diapers, it orders more from a wholesaler. The wholesaler then boosts its own sales forecast, causing the manufacturer to scale up production. But when the increase in demand turns out to be short-lived, the distribution channel is left with too much stock and orders are cut back.[81]

Computer systems can now tell a retailer instantly what it is selling in hundreds of stores across the world, how much money it is making on each sale, and, increasingly, who its customers are. This information technology has had two consequences.

Reduced Inventory

First, a well managed retailer no longer has to keep large amounts of inventory—the stock burden has been passed upstream to the manufacturer. In addition, the retailer has a lower chance of running out of items. For a company such as Wal-Mart, with more than 60,000 suppliers in the United States alone, keeping everyone informed is critical. The company does this through its Retail Link system, which suppliers can tap into over a secure internet connection. They can check stock levels and sales down to the level of individual stores. Wal-Mart may have a brutal reputation for driving down costs, but its investment in information systems has played a large part in building one of the world's most efficient supply chains, capable of handling more than $300 billion of annual sales.[82] Another good example involves 7-Eleven stores in Japan. The moment a 7-Eleven store customer in Japan buys a soft drink or a can of beer, the information goes directly to the bottler or the brewery and immediately goes into the production schedule and the delivery schedule, actually specifying the hour at which the new supply must be delivered and to which of the 4,300 stores. In effect, therefore, 7-Eleven controls the product mix, the manufacturing schedule, and the delivery schedule of major suppliers such as Coca-Cola or Kirin Breweries. The British retailer Sainsbury's supply chain is geared to provide inputs on demand from the stores with a scheduled truck service to its 350 stores. The stores' ordering cycle is also set to match the loading and arrival of the trucks, which run almost according to a bus schedule.

Further attempts to reduce inventory can also be made jointly by retail chains for their mutual benefit. For example, in February 2000, Sears, Roebuck & Co. and Carrefour, joining the rush to the business-to-business electronic-commerce arena, announced a joint venture to form an online purchasing site where the retailers buy about $80 billion in combined purchases. The venture, called GlobalNetXchange (GNX), creates the industry's largest supply exchange on the internet. GNX is an e-business solution and service provider for the global retail industry. Now suppliers can monitor retailers' sales, reduce inventory levels to a minimum, and better plan manufacturing of products on a hosted platform. It makes money by charging fees to suppliers or retailers using the exchange and is set up as a separate entity with its own management, employees and financing.[83]

Market Information at the Retail Level

Second, the retailer is the one that has real-time knowledge of what items are selling and how fast. This knowledge is used to extract better terms from the manufacturers. This trend in the transfer of power to the retailer in the developed countries has coincided with the lowering of trade barriers around the world and the spread of free-market economies in Asia and Latin America. As a result, retailers such as the U.S.'s Toys 'R' Us, L.L. Bean, and Wal-Mart; Britain's Mark & Spencer and J. Sainsbury; Holland's Mark; Sweden's IKEA; France's Carrefour; and Japan's 7-Eleven stores, Uniqlo, and Muji are being transformed into global businesses.

---

[81]"Shining examples," *Economist*, June 17, 2006, Special Section, pp. 4-6.
[82]Ibid.
[83]"Leading Trading Exchanges Link Together," *Food Logistics* (June 2005): 8.

A firm can use strong logistics capabilities as an offensive weapon to help gain competitive advantage in the marketplace by improving customer service and consumer choice, and by lowering the cost of global sourcing and finished goods distribution.[84] These capabilities become increasingly important as the level of global integration increases, and as competitors move to supplement low-cost manufacturing strategies in distant markets with effective logistic management strategies. This point is well illustrated by Ito-Yokado's takeover in 1991 of the Southland Corporation, which had introduced 7-Eleven's convenience store concept in the United States and subsequently around the world. Seven & I (formerly, Ito-Yokado) of Japan licensed the 7-Eleven store concept from Southland in the 1970s and invented just-in-time inventory management and revolutionized its physical distribution system in Japan. The key to Ito-Yokado's success with 7-Eleven Japan has been the use of its inventory and physical distribution management systems to accomplish lower on-hand inventory, faster inventory turnover, and most importantly, accurate information on customer buying habits. Seven-Eleven Japan[85] now implements its just-in-time physical distribution system in 7-Eleven stores in the United States.[86]

Thus, distribution is increasingly becoming concentrated; manufacturing, by contrast, is splintering. Forty years ago, the Big Three automakers shared the U.S. auto market. Today the market is split among 10—Detroit's Big 3, 5 Japanese car makers, and 5 German car makers. Forty years ago, 85 percent of all retail car sales occurred in single-site dealerships; even three dealership chains were uncommon. Today, a fairly small number of large-chain dealers account for 40 percent of the retail sales of cars.

Given the increased bargaining power of distributors, monitoring their performance has become an important management issue for many multinational companies. Although information technology has improved immensely, monitoring channel members' performance still remains humanistic. In general, if companies are less experienced in international operations, they tend to invest more resources in monitoring their channel members' activities.[87] As they gain in experience, they may increasingly build trust relationships with their channel members and depend more on formal performance-based control.[88]

Retailing Differences across the World

The density of retail and wholesale establishments in different countries varies greatly. As a general rule, industrialized countries tend to have a lower distribution outlet density than the emerging markets. Part of the reason for this difference stems from the need in emerging markets to purchase in very small lots and more frequently because of low income and the lack of facilities in homes to keep and preserve purchased items. At the same time, the advanced facilities available in the developed world allow a much higher square footage of retail space per resident, due to the large size of the retail outlets.

Japan's retail industry has a number of features that distinguish it from retailing in Western countries. The major ones are a history of tight regulation—albeit being increasingly deregulated—less use of cars for shopping, and the importance of department stores in the lives of most people. For

[84]Roy D. Shapiro, "Get Leverage from Logistics," *Harvard Business Review* 62 (May-June 1984): 119–126.

[85]The company is officially known as Seven-Eleven Japan owned by 7&i Holdings, while its stores are known as 7-Eleven stores.

[86]Masaaki Kotabe, "The Return of 7-Eleven . . . from Japan: The Vanguard Program," *Columbia Journal of World Business* 30 (Winter 1995): 70–81.

[87]Esra F. Gencturk and Preet S. Aulakh, "The Use of Process and Output Controls in Foreign Markets," *Journal of International Business Studies* 26 (Fourth Quarter, 1995): 755–786.

[88]Preet S. Aulakh, Masaaki Kotabe, and Arvind Sahay, "Trust and Performance in Cross Border Marketing Partnerships: A Behavioral Approach," *Journal of International Business Studies* 27 (Special Issue 1996): 1005–1032.

more than 40 years until recently, the Large-Scale Retail Store Law[89] in Japan helped to protect and maintain small retail stores (12 retail stores per 1,000 residents in Japan vs. 6 retail stores per 1,000 residents in the United States in 1994) and, partly in consequence, a multilayered distribution system. Consequently, Japan has experienced relatively poor proliferation of megastores and large-scale shopping centers. Because Japan's urban areas are crowded, roads are congested, and parking is expensive or non-existent, many people use public transport to shop. Consequently, shopping is usually within a rather small radius of the home or workplace, and products, especially food, generally are bought in small quantities. Shopping, therefore, is more frequent. This situation is further encouraged by Japanese cooking's requirement for fresh ingredients. Retail stores that not only stay open 24 hours a day throughout the week but also practice just-in-time delivery of fresh perishable foods, such as 7-Eleven and Lawson, are extremely popular in Japan. Even McDonald's in countries like Japan recently introduced McDelivery service (see photo below). Discount stores have also gained in popularity among recession-weary, now price-conscious Japanese consumers. Similarly, department stores are crucial in everyday Japanese life. The variety of goods and services offered by the average department store ranges well beyond that in most retail outlets abroad. Large department stores stock everything from fresh food and prepared dishes, to discount and boutique clothing, and household and garden goods. Many have children's playgrounds and pet centers— some with displays resembling a miniature zoo. Museum-level art and craft exhibitions often are housed on upper floors, and both family and exquisite restaurants usually on the top floor. It is a very different—and often difficult—market for foreign retailers to enter. See **Global Perspective 14-3** for information on international retailers entering the Japanese market.

Global Perspective 14-3

Foreign Retailers and Direct Marketers Entering into Japan En Masse

In Japan, until early 1990s, the Large-Scale Retail Store Law gave small retailers and wholesalers disproportionate influence over the Japanese market by requiring firms planning to open a large store to submit their business plan to the local business regulation council, the local chamber of commerce (made up of those small retailers and wholesalers to be affected), and the Ministry of Economy, Trade and Industry (METI). As a result of this "catch-22" requirement, the process would take between 1 year and 18 months, and was seen by foreign retailers as an almost insurmountable entry barrier.

Under U.S. government pressure, the Large-Scale Retail Store Law was relaxed in 1992 and in 1994. Under the amendments, the task of examining applications for new stores was transferred from the local business regulation council to the Large-Scale Retail Store Council, a government advisory board

under the METI. Consequently, the maximum time required for various applications and approvals is now set at 12 months. These two revisions of the Large-Scale Retail Store Law have contributed to the increase in the number of applications requesting approval to establish a large retail store. According to the Japan Council of Shopping Centers estimate, shopping centers have opened at the rate of more than 100 per year since 1992.

Toys 'R' Us exploited this opportunity and was ultimately successful in cracking the Japanese market. It boasted a total of 37 stores in 1996, and planned to open an average of 10 more per year across the country. Following the success of Toys 'R' Us, other foreign-based retailers have begun to crack the Japanese market. Nearly a dozen other such foreign retailers have opened their stores in Japan in the last decade.

---

[89]Jack G. Kaikati, "The Large-Scale Retail Store Law: One of the Thorny Issues in the Kodak-Fuji Case," *The American Marketing Association and the Japan Marketing Association Conference on the Japanese Distribution Strategy*, November 22–24, 1998.

Foreign firms face more difficulties when opening a general merchandise store than one for a niche product because the large Japanese general merchandise stores, such as Daiei and Ito-Yokado, are well entrenched and dominate the market. Despite such difficulties, Wal-Mart (U.S.), with a partial acquisition of Japan's struggling Seiyu, Carrefour (France), and Metro (Germany) entered the Japanese market. As attested by Carrefour's early departure, whether they can take root there is too early to tell, however.

On the other hand, foreign niche retailers, including Toys 'R' Us, which face few competitors have been fairly successful. For example, U.S.-based Tower Records, U.K.-based HMV, and Virgin Megastores have opened comparably large stores, selling both imported and domestic music tapes and CDs at competitive prices. Specialty retailers of outdoor goods and clothes are other retailers to pour into the Japanese market in the last 10 years. Among them, U.S.-based L.L. Bean and Eddie Bauer are the market leaders.

While Toys 'R' Us and Tower Records have a wholly owned subsidiary in Japan, L.L. Bean and Eddie Bauer teamed up with a well-known Japanese company. L.L. Bean Japan is a Japanese franchise 70 percent owned by Japan's largest retailing group, Seibu, and 30 percent by Panasonic. Eddie Bauer Japan is a joint venture of Otto-Sumitomo, a Sumitomo Group mail-order retailer, and Eddie Bauer USA. In general, forming a joint venture or a franchise allows new entrants to start faster, although they could lose control of the company's operation in Japan. Future would-be entrants should bear in mind that Japan is not an easy place to do business because, in addition to regulations, land and labor costs are extremely high.

On the other hand, direct marketing—another form of retailing—has blossomed into a $20 billion industry despite Japan's continued recession. Ten percent of this market belongs to foreign companies including Lands' End, an outdoor clothing maker, and Intimate Brands, which distributes Victoria's Secret catalogs. "For those companies and individuals who say that Japan is a closed market, I really can't think of an example of an easier market entry than catalog sales," says Cynthia Miyashita, president of mail-order consultant Hemisphere Marketing Inc. in Japan. In high-context cultures like Japan, however, less direct, low-key approaches in which a mood or image is built, in an attempt to build a relationship with the audience, is considered more appropriate in approaching prospect customers than in low-context cultures such as the United States.

Foreign mail-order companies sidestep Japan's notoriously complex regulations, multilevel distribution networks, and even import duties. Here are a few cases in point:

- Japan's post offices are unequipped to impose taxes on the hundreds of thousands of mail-order goods that flood the postal system, making direct marketing products virtually duty-free. Local competitors who import products in bulk have to pay duties, forcing up their prices.
- Many products, such as vitamins and cosmetics, are subject to strict testing regulations in Japan, but those rules do not apply if the products are sold through mail order for personal consumption. That gives direct-mail customers in Japan access to a wide array of otherwise unavailable products.
- Mail costs in the United States are so low that it is more economical to send a package from New York to Tokyo than from Tokyo to Osaka, which reduces overhead costs for direct-mail products.
- Although Japanese companies are not allowed to mail goods from foreign post offices for sale at home, foreign companies face no such restrictions.

Sources: Joji Sakurai, "Firms Challenge Image of Japan's Closed Markets," *Marketing News*, July 20, 1998, p. 2; Jack G. Kaikati, "The Large-Scale Retail Store Law: One of the Thorny Issues in the Kodak-Fuji Case," in Michael R. Czinkota and Masaaki Kotabe, *Japanese Distribution Strategy* (London: Business Press, 2000), pp. 154–163; and "Attitudes toward Direct Marketing and Its Regulation: A Comparison of the United States and Japan," *Journal of Public Policy & Marketing* 19 (Fall 2000): 228–237; and "Wal-Mart to Make Seiyu a Group Company," *NikkeiNet Interactive*, http://www.nni.nikkei.co.jp/, November 2, 2005.

Rules governing shopping hours, such as Sunday shopping, vary quite a bit around the world. In Germany, for example, opening hours have long been restricted through the Ladenschlussgesetz—federal law regulating retail store hours, which was first enacted in 1956, with the latest revision in 2003. The 2003 revision declared that stores must be closed on Sundays and public holidays. Store hours were allowed to open from 6:00 a.m. to 8:00 p.m. during weekdays (Mondays–Fridays), up to 4:00 p.m. on Saturdays, with special rules applied concerning Christmas

Eve (December 24). However, in 2006, the federal government allowed the states to pass their own laws in regulating store hours. Still, Sunday shopping is mostly forbidden in Germany, although there are some exceptions such as gas stations, airports, train stations, and so forth. This situation is quite different from that in the United States, where retail stores may be open seven days a week, 24 hours a day.[90] Keeping stores open in this manner requires very strong logistics management on the part of retailers and the manufacturing firms supplying the retailers. The sending organization, the receiving organization, and the logistics provider (if applicable) have to work very closely together.

In China, basket shopping is still considered the norm for most consumers, and they spend on average $5 per visit. Retailers adjust their store layouts to cope with a large number of basket shoppers. Wal-Mart, for instance, has set up basket-only checkouts in its supercenters to enable faster checkout. Because low price is the most competitive advantage, retailers spread a strong price message throughout most of the stores, in both Chinese and English that promotes both everyday low prices and promotional items throughout food and non-food departments. As a result, high volumes of goods are heavily merchandised by large promotions in bins and in bulk floor stacks. In general, a store flyer is a major marketing tool and is designed to drive foot traffic by presenting discounts for household commodities. Recent research analysts summarized the following key differences between hypermarkets in China and those in the West. In China:

- The majority of hypermarkets are located on two floors, normally with non-food items located on the upper floor and food on the lower.

- Many hypermarkets are located inside shopping centers in the heart of the city.

- They have high staffing levels due to the presence of suppliers' staff working as in-store "merchandisers."

- Retailers provide courtesy buses to bring customers from residential areas into the center city because China has a low car ownership.[91]

E-Commerce and Retailing

Despite those cultural differences and regulations in retailing still in place, countries such as Japan and Germany have warmed up to the same electronic commerce revolution as the United States has already experienced. In Japan, for example, Rakuten Ichiba internet mall (http://www.rakuten.co.jp) has achieved stellar growth since its launch with a mere $500,000 in capital and just 13 stores in May 1997. The mall had increased to over 37,000 stores by December 31, 2010, and generated total sales revenue of $4.27 billion with net profits of $428.9 million in 2010.[92] In Germany, SAP already dominates the market for so-called enterprise software (i.e., enterprise resource planning and customer relationship software). Some 183,000 of the world's largest organizations in more than 130 countries now automate everything from accounting and manufacturing to customer and supplier relations using SAP software, making it by far the leading source of large corporate programs with a record revenue of 14.23 billion euros (or US $17.6 billion) and operating profits of more than 4.88 billion euros (or US$6.0 billion) in 2011.[93]

E-commerce is not limited to developed countries. China is already the fastest growing internet market in Asia. The internet community in China has increased rapidly, soaring from 22.5 million users in 2000 to 538 million users in June 2012, far beyond the United States' 245.2 million as of the same period.[94] As a result of the unfortunate outbreak of the severe acute respiratory syndrome

---

[90]Shopping Hours in Austria, Germany, Switzerland, http://www.german-way.com/shophrs.html.

[91]"Retailing in China," Retail Analysis, iReports, www.igd.com/analysis, accessed January 10, 2006.

[92]Rakuten Ichiba, http://www.rakuten.co.jp/, 2010 Annual Report.

[93]SAP, www.sap.com/corporate-en/investors/pdf/SAP-Fact-Sheet-EN.pdf, accessed January 20, 2013.

[94]Internet Word Stats, http://www.internetworldstats.com/, accessed January 20, 2013.

(SARS) in China in 2003, the Chinese government began to take advantage of the internet to encourage business transactions without unnecessary human contacts. This government effort further helped build the internet market in China.[95] In Brazil, the number of people using the internet grew rapidly from 14 million in 2002 to 88.5 million by June 2012, making it South America's most wired nation, and accounting for 46.6 percent of the region's internet users.[96] A similar growth in entrepreneurial e-commerce operators is expected with the growing internet access.

As explained earlier in this chapter, despite the rapid increase in internet users and e-commerce participants around the world, the need for the local or regional distribution of products remains as important as it was before the internet revolution.

SUMMARY

Logistics, or supply chain management, has traditionally been a series of local issues related to getting goods to the final customer in a local market. However, while the intent of serving the customer remains, retailers have been transformed into global organizations that buy and sell products from and to many parts of the world. At the same time, with the increase in the globalization of manufacturing, many firms are optimizing their worldwide production by sourcing components and raw materials from around the world. Both of these trends have increased the importance of global logistics management for firms.

The relevance of global logistics is likely to increase in the coming years because international distribution often accounts for between 10 percent and 25 percent of the total landed cost of the product. The international logistics manager has to deal with multiple issues, including transport, warehousing, inventorying, and the connection of these activities to the firm's corporate strategy. Inflation, currency exchange, and tax rates that differ across national boundaries complicate these logistics issues, but international logistics managers can exploit those differences to their advantage, which are not available to domestic firms.

Logistics management is closely linked to manufacturing activities, even though logistics management is increasingly being outsourced to third-party logistics specialists. Many companies, particularly those in the European Union, are trying to develop a consolidated production location so that they can reduce the number of distribution centers and market their products from one or a few locations throughout Europe. Firms such as Federal Express, DHL, and TNT have evolved from document shippers to providers of complete logistics functions; indeed, all of these firms now have a business logistics division whose function is to handle the outsourced logistics functions of corporate clients.

Various governments, including the United States, have developed free trade zones, export processing zones, and other special economic zones designed chiefly to increase domestic employment and exports from the zone. Various tax and other cost benefits available in the zones attract both domestic and foreign firms to set up warehousing and manufacturing operations.

In the area of international distribution, marketing managers need to make careful decisions on the configuration of their distribution channels. Issues such as cost, coverage, and control determine how many intermediaries there should be and where. The ongoing management of the distribution channel can be a challenge, with channel conflict being an ever-present issue for many international marketing managers.

Retailing has long been considered a fairly localized activity subject to different customer needs and different national laws regulating domestic commerce. Nevertheless, some significant change is taking place in the retail sector. Information technology makes it increasingly possible for large retailers to know what they are selling in hundreds of stores around the world. Given this intimate knowledge of customers around the world, those retailers have begun to overtake the channel leadership role from manufacturers. The United States' Wal-Mart and Toys "R" Us, Japan's 7-Eleven and Uniqlo, and Britain's Tesco are some of the major global retailers changing the logistics of inventory and retail management on a global basis.

Finally, e-commerce is increasingly dispensing with physical stores. However, local adaptation of product offerings and setting-up of local distribution centers remain as important as it was before the internet revolution. Furthermore, complex international shipping requirements and exchange rate fluctuations hamper smooth distribution of products around the world.

---

[95]"China has World's 2nd Largest Number of Netizens," *XINHUA*, January 16, 2003; and "China takes Steps to Ensure SARS Does Not Hinder Construction Plans," *XINHUA*, May 23, 2003.
[96]Internet Word Stats.

QUESTIONS

1. What factors contribute to the increased complexity and cost of global logistics as compared to domestic logistics?

2. Describe the role of free trade zones (FTZs) in global logistics.

3. How is information technology affecting global retailing?

4. Beginning in 2000 with the announcement by the Big Three automakers of plans for a single online supplier exchange Newco, major manufacturers in at least a half-dozen industries have followed suit. In the wake of the Big Three's announcement, other corporations have come together—on customer-facing and supplier-facing initiatives—to create online joint ventures. Among the most prominent are liaisons between DuPont, Cargill, and Cenex Harvest States Cooperative; Sears and Carrefour; and Kraft, H. J. Heinz Co., and Grocery Manufacturers of America with other major food companies. This represents an enormous shift in online business strategy and raises major challenges for marketers and market makers. The question is will these e-marketplaces be the kind founded by a consortia of manufacturers, by independent, third-party companies, or by a combination of both? At least in the auto industry, there is no question that both material management (supply chains) and distributions (dealerships) are more concentrated, while manufacturing is splintering. What does this imply for

other manufacturing industries, and what does this mean in terms of international marketing strategies?

5. We learned from the text that with the expansion of the European Union in May 2004, traditional distribution hubs in western and central Europe faced tougher competition. For instance, despite integration of all the candidate countries into the systems and practices of the EU, it would take two to three years for those countries to open their road and rail networks under the transition arrangements. Even though governments and the EU have developed programs and initiatives to reduce road congestion and have advised the use of other transport networks as alternatives to roads, companies that operate in Bulgaria, the Czech Republic, Estonia, Hungary, Latvia, Poland, and Slovakia are still concerned about the costs and benefits of transporting goods from roads and the viability of alternative modes of transport. What opportunities and threats does the new EU body offer to transporters, freight-forwarders, and exporters?

6. The concept of "one-stop-shopping" for global logistics is fast catching on. There are now more than 30 large logistic companies, called "mega-carriers," who can provide truly global and integrated logistic services. What are the opportunities and threats that these trends offer to small and large transporters, freight-forwarders, and shippers (exporters)?

Appendix: Maquiladora Operation

The **maquiladora** industry, also known as the in-bond or twin-plant program, is essentially a special Mexican version of a free trade zone. Mexico allows duty-free imports of machinery and equipment for manufacturing as well as components for further processing and assembly, as long as at least 80 percent of the plant's output is exported. Mexico permits 100 percent foreign ownership of the maquiladora plants in designated maquiladora zones.

Mexico's Border Industrialization Program, developed in 1965, set the basis for maquiladora operations in Mexico. It was originally intended to attract foreign manufacturing investment and increase job opportunities in areas of Mexico suffering from chronic high unemployment. Most of them are located along the U.S.–Mexico border, such as Tijuana across from San Diego, Ciudad Juarez across from El Paso, and Nuevo Laredo across from Laredo. Over the years, however, Mexico has expanded the maquiladora programs to industrialized major cities such as Monterrey, Mexico City, and Guadalajara, where more skilled workers can be found. This duty-free export assembly program has helped transform Mexico, once a closed economy, into the world's ninth-largest exporter.[97] Automobile

and electronics product assembly makes up the bulk of maquiladora industries.

The competitive pressures of the world economy forced many large manufacturing companies to abandon their assembly plants in the United States and move to Mexican maquiladoras. Furthermore, to meet local content requirements imposed by NAFTA, foreign firms, too, had expanded their manufacturing operations in maquiladoras. In particular, Asian companies, such as Panasonic, Sanyo, Sony, Samsung, and Daewoo, have invited some of their traditional components suppliers to join them in maquiladoras to increase local procurement.

Mexico had long been an attractive location for labor-intensive assembly because its hourly labor cost declined in dollar terms from $2.96 in 1980 to $1.20 in 1990 and to about $0.50 in 1999. This decline resulted from a series of peso depreciations beginning in 1976, including the devastating depreciation that shook the Mexican economy in late 1994 and 1995. However, since 1999, the Mexican economy has grown rapidly, and the Mexican peso has started appreciating against the U.S. dollar, driving up the costs of maquiladora operations over time. In addition, rising wages are also making maquiladora operations less attractive. Furthermore, as part of the NAFTA agreement, which took effect in 1994, maquiladoras

---

[97] *World Trade Report 2005: Exploring the Link between Trade, Standards, and the WTO*, Geneva, World Trade Organization, 2005.

have also been stripped of many of the tax and tariff exemptions.[98] By 2002, the average labor cost in Mexico had risen to $2.45 per hour, losing cost competitiveness to China, where the average labor cost was 68 cents in the interior region and 88 cents in the eastern coastal region. As recently as 2000, 90 percent of all maquiladora inputs in Mexico came from the United States, 9 percent came from Asia, and China contributed only 1 percent of the total. By 2003, however, the U.S. share of maquiladora inputs had declined to 69 percent, while Asia's share had increased to 28 percent, including 8 percent from China. In other words, instead of manufacturing materials in Mexico's maquiladoras, U.S.-based suppliers (both domestic and foreign companies operating in the United States) are increasingly having their materials partially or completely manufactured in Asia to take advantage of cheaper labor and then sending them to Mexican maquiladoras for final assembly for eventual export to the United States.[99] Although maquiladora exports had continued to grow from $14 billion in 1990 to nearly $105 in 2005, the role of maquiladoras as a cheap manufacturing location is ending. As a result, the only companies that are still operating successfully on the U.S.-Mexican border are high-tech plants. Mexico should become more capital-intensive with efforts toward more value-added production by attracting and retaining high-tech plants, tailored to high-end customers, by offering just-in-timely delivery.[100]

---

[98]The dramatic growth of maquiladoras in Mexico cannot be entirely attributed to Mexico's Border Industrialization Program and inexpensive labor costs. Special U.S. tariff provisions have also encouraged U.S.-based companies to export U.S.-made components and other in-process materials to foreign countries for further processing and/or assembly and subsequently to reimport finished products back into the United States. U.S. imports under these tariff provisions are officially called **U.S. imports under Items 9802.00.60 and 9802.00.80 of the U.S. Harmonized Tariff Schedule** (the 9802 tariff provisions for short).

The 9802 tariff provisions permit the duty-free importation by U.S.-based companies of their materials previously sent abroad for further processing or assembly (i.e., tariffs are assessed only on the foreign value-added portion of the imported products). More specifically, item 9802.00.60 applies to reimportation for further processing in the United States of any metal initially processed or manufactured in the United States that was shipped abroad for processing. Item 9802.00.80 permits reimportation for sale in the United States of finished products assembled abroad in whole or in part made up of U.S.-made components. Therefore, the higher the U.S. import tariff rates, the more beneficial it is for U.S.-based companies to be able to declare U.S. imports under the 9802 tariff provisions. Consequently, many U.S.-based companies have taken full advantage of both the 9802 tariff provisions of the United States and the maquiladora laws of Mexico in pursuit of cost competitiveness.

Under the provisions of NAFTA, however, U.S. import tariffs on products originating from Canada and Mexico continue to be reduced over the next decade or so. As a result, the tariff advantage for products reimported from Mexico into the United States under the 9802 tariff provisions will eventually diminish over time. However, as many items still have 5-, 10-, and some 15-year phase-in periods before elimination of tariffs, the 9802 tariff provisions will remain useful even within NAFTA for the foreseeable future. Keep in mind that these tariff provisions still benefit U.S.-based companies manufacturing *outside of the NAFTA region* as long as U.S.-made materials and components are used in production.

---

[99]"No Rest for the Weary," *Journal of Commerce*, February 21, 2005, pp. 20–22.

[100]"NAFTA Helps Mexico Compete Globally," *Expansion Management*, October 2005, p. 20.

EXPORT AND IMPORT MANAGEMENT

15

CHAPTER OVERVIEW

1. Organizing for exports

2. Indirect exporting

3. Direct exporting

4. Mechanics of exporting

5. Role of the government in promoting exports

6. Managing imports—the other side of the coin

7. Mechanics of importing

8. Gray markets

Exporting is the most popular way for many companies to become international. The main reasons for this are that (1) exporting requires minimum resources while allowing high flexibility, and (2) it offers substantial financial, marketing, technological, and other benefits to the firm. Because exporting is usually the first mode of foreign entry used by many companies, exporting early tends to give them first-mover advantage.[1] However, exporting requires experiential knowledge. Exporters must acquire foreign market knowledge (i.e., clients, market needs, and competitors) and institutional knowledge (i.e., government, institutional framework, rules, norms, and values) as well as develop operational knowledge (i.e., capabilities and resources to engage in international operations).[2] Selling to a foreign market involves numerous high risks arising from the lack of knowledge of and unfamiliarity with foreign environments, which can be heterogeneous, sophisticated, and turbulent. Furthermore, conducting market research across national boundaries is more difficult, complex, and subjective than for its domestic counterpart.

For successful development of export activities, systematic collection of information is critical. Market information can be well-documented and come from public and private data sources, but it can also be so tacit that only seasoned marketing managers with international

---

[1]Yigang Pan, Shaomin Li, and David K. Tse, "The Impact of Order and Mode of Market Entry on Profitability and Market Share," *Journal of International Business Studies* 30 (First Quarter 1999): 81–104.

[2]Kent Eriksson, Jan Johanson, Anders Majkgård, D. Deo Sharma, "Effect of Variation on Knowledge Accumulation in the Internationalization Process," *International Studies of Management and Organization*, 30, (2000): 26–44.

vision and experience could have a "gut-feel" to understand it.[3] Market information helps managers to assess the attractiveness of foreign markets and decide whether to engage in exporting. After a firm has decided to start exporting, it requires information on how to handle the mechanics of it, including how to enter overseas markets and what adaptations to make to the marketing mix elements.[4] A recent study, which compared export leaders (defined as companies that distribute products or services to six or more countries) to export laggards, also shows that the more companies export, the more they spend in information technology. According to the same study, much of the investment the leading export companies make in IT is for e-business, from web-based commerce and supply-chain networks to electronic marketplaces. This focus seems to be paying off.[5]

As presented in Chapter 2, the nature of international exports and imports had also improved from the beginning of this new century until 2007. From 1997 to 2007, global GDP grew more than 30 percent, while total global merchandise exports increased by more than 60 percent. Then since late 2008, U.S. financial turmoil has spread throughout the world, resulting in an unprecedented global recession with plummeting international trade.[6] Weaker demand in the developed countries now provides a less favorable framework for the expansion of international trade than in preceding years.

Although the United States is still relatively more insulated from the global economy than other nations (see Chapter 2), its exports of goods and services combined amounted to $2.1 trillion and represented 13.8 percent of the U.S. GDP in 2011—its highest share ever. The U.S. goods and services exports supported an estimated 9.7 million jobs, with every billion dollars of goods and services exports supporting more than an estimated 5,000 jobs in 2011. In 2009, U.S. manufacturing exports supported an estimated 2.4 million manufacturing jobs—20 percent of all jobs in the manufacturing sector.[7] These facts demonstrate that exports are an important source of U.S. economic growth and job creation. Furthermore, jobs that depend on trade pay between 13 to 18 percent more than the average wage, indicating that these employees generally earn more than others.[8]

This chapter primarily considers the export function; it attempts to explain the import function as the counterpart of the export function, because for every export transaction there is, by definition, an import transaction as well. Aside from some differences between the procedure and rationale for exports and imports, both are largely the same the world over.

Organizing for Exports
Research for Exports

The first step for a firm exporting for the first time is to use available secondary data to research potential markets. Increasingly, international marketing information is available in the form of electronic databases ranging from the latest news on product developments to new material in the academic and trade press. Well over 6,000 databases are available worldwide, with almost 5,000

---

[3]Gary A. Knight and Peter W. Liesch, "Information Internalization in Internationalizing the Firm," *Journal of Business Research* 55 (December 2002): 981–995.

[4]Leonidas C. Leonidou and Athena S. Adams-Florou, "Types and Sources of Export Information: Insights from Small Business," *International Small Business Journal* 17 (April–June 1999): 30-48.

[5]Mary E Thyfault, "Heavy Exporters Spend Big on Leading-Edge IT," *InformationWeek*, April 23, 2001, p. 54.

[6]"World Trade to Shrink in 2009: World Bank," newsroomamerica.com, December 9, 2008.

[7]The Office of The United States Trade Representative, www.ustr.gov.

[8]Council for Economic Education, http://www.councilforeconed.org/; and International Trade Resource Center, Bureau of Export Trade Promotion, http://www.itrc.dti.gov.ph/, accessed September 22, 2013.

available online. The United States is the largest participant in this database growth, producing and consuming more than 50 percent of these database services. When entering a culturally and linguistically different part of the world, managers need to understand a completely new way of commercial thinking that is based on a different culture and works on a different set of premises. Often seasoned managers' flexibility and adaptability acquired through experience and learning prove to be important in building export contracts.[9] It is also to be noted that export research for markets such as China and the former Soviet Republics must still be done largely in the field because very little prior data exist for them, and when they are available, they are often not reliable.[10]

The identification of an appropriate overseas market and an appropriate segment involves grouping by the following criteria:

1. Socioeconomic characteristics (e.g., demographic, economic, geographic, and climatic characteristics)

2. Political and legal characteristics

3. Consumer variables (e.g., lifestyle, preferences, culture, taste, purchase behavior, and purchase frequency)

4. Financial conditions

On the basis of these criteria, an exporter can form an idea of the market segments in a foreign market.[11] First, regions within countries across the world are grouped by macroeconomic variables indicating the levels of industrial development, availability of skilled labor, and purchasing power. For example, from an exporter's point of view the Mumbai–Thane–Pune area in Western India has more in common with the Monterrey area and the Mexico City area in Mexico and the Shanghai–Wuxi area in China than with other areas in India. All three areas already have a well-developed industrial base and purchasing power that is equal to that of the middle class in developed nations. Such economically homogeneous groups across the world are a result of the globalization of markets. These apparently similar markets can, however, differ along political and legal dimensions. An exporter or importer that violates terms has legal recourse in India, and the court of adjudication is in India. Legal recourse is still largely wishful thinking in China. By addressing consumer and macroeconomic variables, the exporter can successfully segment the international market into homogenous segments where similar elements of the marketing mix can be applied.

Data for grouping along macroeconomic criteria are available from international agencies such as the World Bank, which publishes the *World Development Report*. In addition, the United Nations produces a series of statistical abstracts on a yearly basis covering economic, demographic, political, and social characteristics that are very useful for grouping analysis. The International Monetary Fund publishes data on international trade and finance quarterly and annually. Both the Organization for Economic Cooperation and Development (OECD—a group of advanced nations) and the European Union (EU) publish a variety of statistical reports and studies on their member countries.

Export Market Segments

As discussed in Chapter 7, the grouping of countries and regions among countries enables a firm to link various geographical areas into one homogeneous market segment that the firm can cater to in

[9]Amal R. Karunaratna, Lester W. Johnson, and C.P. Rao, "The Exporter-Import Agent Contract and the Influence of Cultural Dimensions," *Journal of Marketing Management* 17 (February 2001): 137–158.

[10]Peter G. P. Walters and Saeed Samiee, "Marketing Strategy in Emerging Markets: The Case of China," *Journal of International Marketing* 11, no. 1 (2003): 97–106.

[11]For a comprehensive review of the export development process, see Leonidas C. Leonidou and Constantine S. Katsikeas, "The Export Development Process: An Integrative Review of Empirical Models," *Journal of International Business Studies* 27 (Third Quarter 1996): 517–551.

meeting its export objectives. The next task is to develop a product strategy for the selected export markets. The export market clusters obtained by clustering regions within different nations would fall into various levels. At the country level would be countries with the same characteristics as the U.S. market. At a regional level within nations, there would be geographical and psychographic segments in many different countries to which the firm can export the same core product it sells in domestic markets without any significant changes. It is a form of market diversification in which the firm is selling a standardized, uniform product across countries and regions.[12] Mercedes-Benz automobiles and Rolex watches sell to the same consumer segment worldwide. Another standardized product that sells worldwide is the soft drink. The Coca-Cola Company markets essentially one Coke worldwide.

Products that can be standardized could satisfy basic needs that do not vary with climate, economic conditions, or culture. A standardized product is the easiest to sell abroad logistically because the firm incurs no additional manufacturing costs and is able to use the same promotional messages across different regions in different countries across the world. If those different regions have comparable logistics and infrastructural facilities, the distribution requirements and expenses would also be similar.

Where it is not possible to sell standardized products, the firm could need to adapt its products for the overseas marketplace. In such instances, either the firm's product does not meet customer requirements, or it does not satisfy the administrative requirements of foreign countries. Such markets can require modification of the product if it is to succeed in the foreign market.[13] Brand names, for example, need to be changed before a product can be sold, because the brand name could mean something detrimental to the product's prospect. Ford once released its new European Ka model in Japan. Ka means "mosquito" in Japanese, a less than popular disease-carrying pest. Analysts called the Ka dead on arrival.[14] Beauty-products giant Estée Lauder found out that its perfume Country Mist would not sell in Germany because *Mist* means "manure" in German. Sometimes, a new product has to be developed from a manufacturing viewpoint because the product is not salable as it is in the export market. For example, room air-conditioner units being exported to Egypt must have special filters and coolers and have to be sturdy enough to handle the dust and heat of Egyptian summer.

Indirect Exporting

Indirect exporting involves the use of independent intermediaries or agents to market the firm's products overseas. These agents, known as export representatives, assume responsibility for marketing the firm's products through their network of foreign distributors and their own salesforce. It is not uncommon for a U.S. producer who is new to exporting to begin export operation by selling through an export representative. Many Japanese firms have also relied on the giant general trading companies known as *sogoshosha*. Use of agents is not uncommon when it is not cost effective for an exporter to set up its own export department. Such firms can initiate export operations through export representatives who know the market and have experience in selling to them. There are several types of export representatives in the United States. The most common are the combination export manager (CEM), export merchant, export broker, export commission house, trading company, and piggyback exporter.

The **combination export manager** (CEM) acts as the export department to a small exporter or a large producer with small overseas sales. CEMs often use the letterhead of the company they

[12]Lloyd C. Russow, "Market Diversification: "Going International," *Review of Business* 17 (Spring 1996): 32–34.

[13]Roger J. Calantone, S. Tamer Cavusgil, Jeffrey B. Schmidt, and Geon-Cheol Shin, "Internationalization and the Dynamics of Product Adaptation—An Empirical Investigation," *Journal of Product Innovation Management* 21 (May 2004): 185–198.

[14]Keith Naughton, "Tora, Tora, Taurus," *Business Week*, April 12, 1999, p. 6.

represent and have extensive experience in selling abroad and in the mechanics of export shipments. CEMs operate on a commission basis and are usually most effective when they deal with clients who have businesses in related lines. Because credit plays an increasingly important role in export sales, CEMs have found it increasingly difficult to consummate export sales on behalf of clients without their credit support. As more and more firms begin exporting on a regular basis, CEMs are becoming a vanishing breed. A list of CEMs can be found in the *American Register of Exporters and Importers* and in the telephone yellow pages.

Export merchants, in contrast to the CEM, buy and sell on their own accounts and assume all responsibilities of exporting a product. In this situation, the manufacturers do not control the sales activities of their products in export markets and depend entirely on the export merchant for all export activities. This loss of control over the export marketing effort is a major drawback to using export merchants. The **export broker**, as the name implies, is someone who brings together an overseas buyer and a domestic manufacturer for the purpose of an export sale and earns a commission for establishing a contact that results in a sale.

Foreign buyers of U.S. goods sometimes contract for the services of a U.S. representative to act on their behalf. This resident representative is usually an **export commission house** that places orders only on behalf of its foreign client with U.S. manufacturers and acts as a finder for its client to get the best buy. A **trading company** is a large organization engaged in exporting and importing. It buys on its own account in one country and exports the goods to another country. Most of the well-known trading companies are Japanese or Western European in origin. Japanese trading companies, known as *sogoshosha*, such as Mitsui, Mitsubishi, Sumitomo, and Marubeni, operate worldwide and handle a significant proportion of Japanese foreign trade. United Africa Company, a subsidiary of Unilever, operates extensively in Africa. Another European trading company is Jardine Matheson in Hong Kong, a major trading force in Southeast Asia. See **Exhibit 15-1** for the major types of trading companies.

Piggyback exporting refers to the practice by which carrier firms that have established export departments assume, under a cooperative agreement, the responsibility of exporting the products of other companies. The carrier buys the rider's products and markets them independently. The rider plays a peripheral role in the export marketing overseas. Piggybacking can be an option to

Exhibit 15-1 Major Types of Trading Companies and Their Countries of Origin

Type	Rationale for Grouping	Some Examples by Country of Origin
General Trading Company	Historical involvement in generalized imports/exports	C. Itoh (Japan), East Asiatic (Denmark), SCOA (France), Jardine Matheson (Hong Kong)
Export Trading Company	Specific mission to promote growth of exporters	Hyundai (Korea), Interbras (Brazil), Sears World Trade (U.S.)
Federated Export Marketing Group	Loose collaboration among exporting companies supervised by a third party and usually market specific	Fedec (U.K.), SBI Group (Norway), IEB Project Group (Morocco)
Trading arm of MNCs	Specific international trading operations in parent company operations	General Motors (U.S.), IBM (U.S.)
Bank-based or affiliated trading group	A bank at the center of a group extends commercial activities	Mitsubishi (Japan), Cobec (Brazil)
Commodity trading company	Long-standing export trading in a specific market	Metallgesellschaft (Germany), Louis Dreyfus (France)

Source: Adapted from Lyn Amine, "Toward a Conceptualization of Export Trading Companies in World Markets," in S. Tamer Cavusgil, ed., *Advances in International Marketing*, vol. 2 (Greenwich, CT: JAI Press, 1987), pp. 199–208.

enter an export market, but is normally avoided by firms who wish to be in exports over the long haul because of the loss of control over the foreign marketing operations.

Direct Exporting

Direct exporting occurs when a manufacturer or exporter sells directly to an importer or buyer located in a foreign market. It requires export managers' full commitment both in their attitudes and in their behavior for export success.[15] Direct exporting can manifest itself in various organizational forms, depending on the scale of operations and the number of years that a firm has been engaged in exporting. In its most simple form, a firm has an export sales manager with some clerical help responsible for the actual selling and directing of activities associated with the export sales. Most of the other export marketing activities (advertising, logistics, and credit, for example) are performed by a regular department of the firm that also handles international trade transactions.

As export activities grow in scale and complexity, most firms create a separate **export department** that is largely self-contained and operates independently of domestic operations. An export department can be structured internally on the basis of function, geography, product, customer, or some other combination. Some firms prefer to have an **export sales subsidiary** instead of an export department in order to keep export operations separate from the rest of the firm. In terms of internal operations and specific operations performed, an export sales subsidiary differs very little from an export department. The major difference is that the subsidiary, being a separate legal entity, must purchase the products it sells in the overseas markets from its parent manufacturer. This means that the parent has to develop and administer a system of transfer pricing. A subsidiary has the advantage of being an independent profit center and is therefore easier to evaluate; it can also offer tax advantages, ease of financing, and increased proximity to the customer.

Instead of a foreign sales subsidiary, a firm also has the option of establishing a **foreign sales branch**. Unlike a subsidiary, a branch is not a separate legal entity. A foreign sales branch handles all sales, distribution, and promotional work throughout a designated market area and sells primarily to wholesalers and dealers. Where it is used, a sales branch is the initial link in the marketing channel in the foreign market. Often the branch has a storage and warehousing facility available so it can maintain an inventory of products, replacement parts, and maintenance supplies.

Indirect exporting and direct exporting are compared in **Exhibit 15-2**. Both have advantages and disadvantages, although over the long term, that is, for a firm desiring a permanent presence in international markets, direct exports tend to be more useful.

Exhibit 15-2   Comparison of Direct and Indirect Exporting

Indirect Exporting	*Direct Exporting*
• Low set-up costs	• High set-up costs
• Exporter tends not to gain good knowledge of export markets	• Leads to better knowledge of export markets and international expertise due to direct contact
• Credit risk lies mostly with the middlemen	• Credit risks are higher especially in the early years
• Because it is not in the interest of the middlemen doing the exporting, customer loyalty rarely develops	• Customer loyalty can be developed for the exporter's brands more easily

---

[15]Rodney L. Stump, Gerard A. Athaide, and Catherine N. Axinn, "The Contingent Effect of the Dimensions of Export Commitment on Exporting Financial Performance: An Empirical Examination," *Journal of Global Marketing* 12, no. 1 (1998): 7–25; and David L. Dean, and Bulent Menguc, "Revisiting Firm Characteristics, Strategy, and Export Performance Relationship," *Industrial Marketing Management* 29 (September 2000): 461–477.

Mechanics of Exporting

The paperwork involved in export declaration forms can be time-consuming, no matter how useful the information provided on the forms may be. In the United States, to expedite the exporting process, the U.S. Commerce Department's Census Bureau launched a new system, the **Automated Export System (AES)**, on October 1, 1999. AES is a computer system that collects Electronic Export Information (EEI), which is the electronic equivalent of the export data formerly collected as Shipper's Export Declaration (SED) information. AES enables exporters to file export information at no cost over the internet; it is part of an effort to make government more efficient and boost U.S. exports.[16]

AES is a joint venture between the U.S. Customs Service, the Foreign Trade Division of the Bureau of the Census (Commerce), the Bureau of Industry and Security (Commerce), the Office of Defense Trade Controls (State), other federal agencies, and the export trade community. It was designed to improve trade statistics, reduce duplicate reporting to multiple agencies, improve customer service, and to ensure compliance with and enforcement of laws relating to exporting. It is the central point through which export shipment data required by multiple agencies is filed electronically on the internet to Customs, using the electronic data interchange (EDI). AES is a completely voluntary system that provides an alternative to filing the paper Shipper's Export Declarations. AES export information is collected electronically and edited immediately, and errors are detected and corrected at the time of filing. AES is a nationwide system operational at all ports and for all methods of transportation.

This internet-based system allows exporters, freight forwarders, and consolidators to file shippers' export declaration information in an automated, cost-free way. AES has the goal of paperless reporting of export information.[17] The new system reduces the paperwork burden on the trade community, makes document storage and handling less costly, improves the quality of export statistics, and facilitates exporting in general. Before AES, the export system was paper bound, expensive, labor intensive, and error prone.

However, a large number of firms still did not want to switch to AES until it was mandatory. Following a three-year standoff, Customs & Border Protection (CBP) and the Census Bureau have resolved their turf war over mandatory filing of export data through the AES. The newly published Foreign Trade Regulations that require electronic filing of export declarations, which took effect on July 1, 2008, brought an end to paper shippers export declaration, and make the AES the only legal means for filing export data.[18]

Legality of Exports

Exporting starts with the search for a buyer abroad. It includes the research to locate a potential market, a buyer, and information concerning the process of closing a sale. We covered the process of getting an order earlier in this chapter. Once an export contract has been signed, the wheels are set in motion for the process that results in the export contract. The first stage has to do with the legality of the transaction. The exporter must determine that the goods can be imported by the importing party; importing country licensing law can halt a transaction unless it is studied in advance.

Standard specifications for products and services are especially important in Europe and Japan as far as U.S. exporters are concerned. As far as export transactions to third-world countries are concerned, the convertibility of the importing country's currency must be determined even in this

---

[16]"Two Major Export Compliance Changes Coming in Early 2006," *Managing Exports & Imports* (October 2005): 1–13.

[17]David Biederman, "AES a Must for Dual-Use Goods," *Traffic World*, January 3, 2000, p. 30.

[18]R. G. Edmonson, "Here Comes Mandatory AES," *Journal of Commerce*, June 9, 2008, p. 21; and "Filing of Export Data via AES Made Mandatory," *Managing Imports & Exports* (August 2008): 1, 10–12.

day of liberalization. If the country's currency is not convertible, the importing party must have permission to remit hard currency. Finally, the exporter must ensure that there are no export restrictions on the goods proposed to be exported from the United States. Security concerns about encryption technology, for example, permit the exports of encryption technology that incorporates no more than 40 bits. All exports from the United States (except those to Canada and U.S. territories) require an **export license**, which can be a general export license or a validated export license. A **general license** permits exportation within certain limits without requiring that an application be filed or that a license document be issued. A **validated license** permits exportation within specific limitations; it is issued only on formal application. Most goods can move from the United States to most countries under a general license. A validated license is required to export certain strategic goods regardless of their destination. For most goods, the license is granted by the U.S. Department of Commerce's Bureau of Industry and Security. For certain specific products, however, the license is granted by other U.S. government agencies (see **Exhibit 15-3**).

As onerous as export validation procedure appears, large companies are proactively dealing with it. For example, Philips, with $4 billion in annual exports to over 150 countries from some 260 U.S. locations, has automated its export process to a significant degree by implementing its PROTECT system, which is a database that permits export managers to simulate their export transaction before it is approved. The PROTECT database includes (1) all Philips products that fall under any type of export control; (2) a full listing of proscribed or sensitive countries and customers; (3) all export control laws and regulations; and (4) concrete instruction on how to act in specific export control matters. In general, the Philips export management system clearly identifies

Exhibit 15-3   U.S. Government Departments and Agencies with Export Control Responsibilities

Licensing Authority	Responsibility
Department of State, Office of Defense Trade Controls (DTC)	Licenses defense services and defense (munitions) articles.
Department of the Treasury, Office of Foreign Assets Control (OFAC)	Administers and enforces economic and trade sanctions against targeted foreign countries, terrorism-sponsoring organizations, and international narcotics traffickers.
Nuclear Regulatory Commission, Office of International Programs	Licenses nuclear material and equipment.
Department of Energy, Office of Arms Controls and Nonproliferation, Export Control Division	Licenses nuclear technology and technical data for nuclear power and special nuclear materials.
Department of Energy, Office of Fuels Programs	Licenses natural gas and electric power.
Defense Threat Reduction Agency—Technology Security	Responsible for the development and implementation of policies on international transfers of defense-related technology, and reviews certain dual-use export license applications.
Department of the Interior, Division of Management Authority	Controls the export of endangered fish and wildlife species.
Drug Enforcement Administration, International Drug Unit	Controls the import and export of listed chemicals used in the production of control substances under the Controlled Substances Act.
Food and Drug Administration, Office of Compliance	Licenses medical devices.
Food and Drug Administration, Import/Export	Licenses drugs.
Patent and Trademark Office, Licensing and Review	Oversees patent filing data sent abroad.
Environmental Protection Agency, Office of Solid Waste, International and Special Projects Branch	Controls toxic waste exports.

Source: Bureau of Industry and Security, U.S. Department of Commerce, http://www.bis.doc.gov/reslinks.htm, accessed March 27, 2013.

who are its customers, how it takes orders, and who is responsible for exports to ensure that export activities follow the company's export compliance guidelines and procedures.[19]

Similarly, exporters from other countries also need to get export licenses in their countries in order to sell their products in foreign markets. For example, although many Chinese automobile companies planned to increase the number of vehicles they export, their efforts were futile because the Chinese government announced that it would limit the number of export licenses available to domestic automotive companies by 2008.[20] Triggered by the safety issues of Mattel toys made in China, the toy industry and the government in China paid a great deal of attention to efforts to correct problems, which led to widespread recalls in 2007. One of the Chinese government's efforts was to revoke export licenses for hundreds of its estimated 3,500 export-oriented toy factories.[21]

Export Transactions

The second pillar of an export transaction involves the logistics of the export transaction, which includes (1) the terms of the sale, including payment mode and schedule, dispute settlement mechanisms, and service requirements (if applicable); (2) monitoring the transportation and delivery of the goods to the assigned party—the assignee in the bill of lading and obtaining proof of delivery—the **customs receipt**; and (3) shipping and obtaining the bill of lading.

When a company has a firm order for exports, it must execute the order by delivering the product or service promised to the overseas customer. A **bill of lading** is a contract between the exporter and the shipping company indicating that the shipping company has accepted responsibility for the goods and will provide transportation in return for payment. A **straight bill of lading** is non-negotiable and is usually used in prepaid transactions. The goods are delivered to a specific individual or company. A **shipper's order bill of lading** is negotiable; it can be bought, sold, or traded while the goods are still in transit (i.e., ownership of the goods can change hands). The customer usually needs the original or a copy of the bill of lading to take possession of the goods (depending on the terms of the export contract).

A **commercial invoice** is a bill for the goods stating basic information about the transaction, including a description of the merchandise, total cost of the goods sold, addresses of the buyer and the seller, and delivery and payment terms. The buyer needs the invoice to prove ownership and to arrange payment terms. Some governments also use commercial invoices to assess customs duties. Other export documentation that may be required includes export licenses, certificates of origin, inspection certification, dock and/or warehouse receipts, destination control certificates (to inform shippers and other foreign parties that the goods can be shipped only to a particular country), shippers' export declaration, and export packaging lists. To ensure that all required documentation is accurately completed and to minimize potential problems, firms entering the international market for the first time with an export order should consider using **freight forwarders** who are shipping agents and specialists in handling export documentation.

Terms of Shipment and Sale

The responsibilities of the exporter, the importer, and the logistics provider should be spelled out in the export contract in terms of what is and what is not included in the price quotation and who owns title to the goods while in transit. **INCOTERMS 2010**, which went into effect on January 1, 2010, and is an acronym for International Commercial Terms, is the internationally accepted

---

[19]"AAEI Conference Highlights: How Microsoft, Philips Meet New Post-9/11 Compliance Requirements," *Managing Exports*, August 2004, pp. 1–4.

[20]Christie Schweinsberg and Sol Biderman, "China Aims to Rein in Auto Exports," *Ward's Auto World*, November 2006, pp. 34–34.

[21]Steve Toloken, "Toy Makers Reaping What They Have Sown," *Plastics News*, February 4, 2008, p. 6.

Exhibit 15-4   Terms of Shipment

RULES FOR ANY MODE OR MODES OF TRANSPORT

EXW—Ex Works (named place of delivery)	The Seller's only responsibility is to make the goods available at the Seller's premises. The Buyer bears the full cost and risks of moving the goods from there to destination.
FCA—FREE CARRIER (. . . named place of delivery)	The Seller delivers the goods, cleared for export, to the carrier selected by the Buyer. The Seller leads the goods if the carrier pickup is at the Seller's premises. From that point, the Buyer bears the cost and risks of moving the goods to destination.
CPT—CARRIAGE PAID TO (. . . named place of destination)	The Seller pays for moving the goods to destination. From the time the goods are transferred to the first carrier, the Buyer bears the risks of loss or damage.
CIP—CARRIAGE AND INSURANCE PAID TO—(. . . named place of destination)	The Seller pays for moving the goods to destination. From the time the goods are transferred to the first carrier, the buyer bears the risks of the loss or damage. The Seller however, purchases the cargo insurance.
DAT—DELIVERED AT TERMINAL (. . . named terminal at the port or place of destination)	The Seller delivers when the goods, once uploaded from the arriving means of transport, are placed at the Buyer's disposal at a named terminal at the named port or place of destination. "Terminal" includes any place, whether covered or not, such as quay, warehouse, container yard or road, rail or air cargo terminal. The Seller bears all risks involved in the bringing of goods to the unloading them at the terminal at the named port or place of destination.
DAP—DELIVERED AT PLACE (. . . named place of destination)	The Seller delivers when the goods are placed at the Buyer's disposal on the arriving means of transport ready for uploading at the named place of destination. The Seller bears all the risks involved in bringing the goods to the named place.
DDP—DELIVERED DUTY PAID (. . . named place)	The Seller delivers the goods—cleared for import—to the Buyer at destination. The Seller bears all the cost and risks of moving the goods to destination, including the payment of Customs duties and taxes.

MARITIME—ONLY TERMS

FAS—FREE ALONGSIDE SHIP (. . . named port of shipment)	The Seller delivers the goods to the origin port. From that point, the Buyer bears all the costs and the risks of loss or damage.
FOB—FREE ON BOARD (. . . named port of shipment)	The Seller delivers the goods on board the ship and clears the goods for export. From that point, the Buyer bears all the cost and risks of loss or damage.
CFR—COST AND FREIGHT (. . . named port of destination)	The Seller clears the goods for export and pays the cost of moving the goods to destination. The Buyer bears all the risks of loss or damage.
CIF—COST INSURANCE AND FREIGHT— (. . . named port of destination)	The Seller clears the goods for export and pays the cost of moving the goods to the port of destination. The Buyer bears all the risks of loss and damage. The Seller however, purchases the cargo insurance.

---

standard definitions for the terms of sale by the International Chamber of Commerce.[22] The terms of shipment are summarized in **Exhibit 15-4**.

The terms of shipment used in the export transaction and their acceptance by the parties involved are important to prevent subsequent disputes. These terms of shipment also have significant implications on costing and pricing. The exporter should therefore learn what terms of shipment importers prefer in a particular market and what the specific transaction requires. A CIF quote by an exporter clearly shows the importer the cost to get the product to a port in a desired country. An inexperienced importer may be discouraged by an EXW quote because the importer may not know how much the EXW quote translates in terms of landed cost at home.

---

[22]http://www.iccwbo.org/incoterms, accessed March 27, 2013.

Exhibit 15-5 Terms of Payment in an Export Transaction

Advance payment	An importer pays exporter first, an exporter sends goods afterwards.
Confirmed irrevocable letter of credit	A letter of credit issued by the importer's bank and confirmed by a bank, usually in the exporter's country. The obligation of the second bank is added to the obligation of the issuing bank to honor drafts presented in accordance with the terms of credit.
Unconfirmed irrevocable letter of credit	A letter of credit issued by the importer's bank. The issuing bank still has an obligation to pay.
Documents against payment (D/P)	An importer pays bills and obtains documents and then goods. Therefore, the exporter retains control of the goods until payment.
Documents against acceptance (D/A)	An importer accepts bills to be paid on due date and obtains documents and then goods. Therefore, the exporter gains a potentially negotiable financial instrument in the form of a document pledging payment within a certain time period.
Open account	No draft drawn. Transaction payable when specified on invoice.
Consignment	A shipment that is held by the importer until the merchandise has been sold, at which time payment is made to the exporter.

Sources: Lakshman Y. Wickremeratne, *ICC Guide to Collection Operations: For the ICC Uniform Rules for Collections* (URC 522) (Paris, International Chamber of Commerce, 1996), pp. 22–26; and "Documentary Collections DC Payment Terms Offer Intermediate Level of Risk for International Collections," *Managing Exports* (December 2002): 4–5.

Payment Terms

The financing and payments of an export transaction constitute the third set of things to do with regard to an export transaction. For example, is export credit available from an Export-Import Bank (discussed later in the chapter) or a local agency supporting exports? What payment terms have been agreed on? Customary payment terms for noncapital goods transactions include advance payment, confirmed irrevocable letter of credit, unconfirmed irrevocable letter of credit, documents against payment (D/P), documents against acceptance (D/A), open account, and consignment basis payments. These terms are explained in **Exhibit 15-5**. The terms of payment between the exporter and the importer are a matter of negotiation and depend on a variety of factors including the buyer's credit standing, the amount of the sale transaction, the availability of foreign exchange in the buyer's country, the exchange control laws in the buyer's country, the risks associated with the type of merchandise to be shipped, the usual practice in the trade, and market conditions (i.e., a buyer's market or a seller's market and payment terms offered by competitors).

When negotiating payment terms with an importer, an exporter must consider the risks associated with the importer and the importer's country, including credit risks, foreign exchange risks, transfer risks, and the political risks of the importer's country. **Credit risk** is the risk that the importer will not pay or will fail to pay on the agreed terms. The exporter must consider this risk. **Foreign exchange risk** exists when the sale is in the importer's currency and that currency can depreciate in terms of the home currency, leaving the exporter with less in the home currency.[23] **Transfer risk** refers to the chances that payment will not be made due to the importer's inability to obtain foreign currency (usually, U.S. dollars) and transfer it to the exporter. **Political risk** refers to the risks associated with war, confiscation of the importer's business, and other unexpected political events.

---

[23]One major study shows that exporters who accept foreign currency as a medium of payment tend to sell a higher volume and have more satisfied customers (i.e., importers) but tend to have lower profit margins than those exporters who accept domestic currency. This is due probably to foreign exchange rate risk. For detail, see Saeed Samiee and Patrik Anckar, "Currency Choice in Industrial Pricing: A Cross-National Evaluation," *Journal of Marketing* 62 (July 1998): 112–127.

If an exporter sells for cash, there is virtually no risk. A sale on a **confirmed irrevocable letter of credit** has slightly more risk. The confirmation places a home bank or other known bank acceptable to the seller; the payment risk assumed by the exporter devolves almost completely to this bank. If the sale is in a foreign currency, the exporter is still exposed to the risk of depreciation of the foreign currency relative to the home currency. An **unconfirmed irrevocable letter of credit** exposes the exporter to the creditworthiness of the buyer's bank in the foreign country because the exporter's home bank is no longer guaranteeing payment. The exporter thus faces the additional risk of a change in the value of the foreign currency (if the sale is not in the exporter's home currency), the risk that the payment cannot be transferred to the exporter's home bank, and the risk that the political conditions in the buyer's country will change to the exporter's detriment.

Documents against payment (D/P) and **documents against acceptance (D/A)** are an importer's IOUs, or promises to pay. These payment terms (D/P and D/A) are much less expensive and easier for both exporters and importers to use than securing letters of credit. D/P and D/A are employed widely around the world but are historically underutilized by U.S. exporters.[24] Exports on a D/P are paid for by an importer when it accepts an exporter's export documents. Exports on a D/A are paid for by an importer on the due date of bill. Relative to a sale on a letter of credit, D/P basis increases the payment risk in an export transaction because no financial institution such as a bank has assumed the risk of payment. A D/A further escalates the risk because the buyer, by "accepting the bill," will receive the title documents and can pick up the goods without payment. Finally, an **open account** sale has no evidence of debt (promissory note, draft, etc.) and the payment may be unenforceable. Usually, conducted only on the basis of an invoice, an open account transaction is recommended only after the exporter and the importer have established trust in their relationship.

Currency Hedging

The fourth task of an exporter is to arrange a foreign exchange cover transaction with the banker or through the firm's treasury in case there is a foreign exchange risk in the export transaction. Such arrangements include reversing the forward currency transaction if required and hedging the foreign exchange risk using derivative instruments in the foreign exchange markets, for example, currency options and futures. In general, customer-oriented exporters tend to use invoicing in foreign currency. Thus, currency hedging becomes all the more important to customer-oriented exporters.[25] When the exporter is receiving some currency other than its domestic currency, covering a trade transaction through forward sales, currency options, and currency futures enables the exporter to lock in the domestic currency value of the export transaction up to a year in the future, thus ensuring more certain cash flows and forecasting. Due care needs to be exercised in the use of currency hedging, because an unwary or uninformed firm can lose large amounts of money (see Chapter 3 for detail).

Role of the Government in Promoting Exports[26]

Government export promotion activities generally comprise (1) export service programs (e.g., seminars for potential exporters, export counseling, how-to-export handbooks, and export financing) and (2) market development programs (e.g., dissemination of sales leads to local

---

[24]"Documentary Collections DC Payment Terms Offer Intermediate Level of Risk for International Collections," *Managing Exports* (December 2002): 4–5.

[25]Patrik Anckar and Saeed Samiee, "Customer-Oriented Invoicing in Exporting," *Industrial Marketing Management* 29 (November 2000): 507–520.

[26]This section draws from Esra F. Gencturk and Masaaki Kotabe, "The Effect of Export Assistance Program Usage on Export Performance: A Contingency Explanation," *Journal of International Marketing* 9, no. 2 (2001): 51–72.

firms, participation in foreign trade shows, preparation of market analysis, and export news letters).[27] In addition, program efforts can be differentiated as to whether the intent is to provide informational or experiential knowledge. Informational knowledge typically is provided through "how-to" export assistance, workshops, and seminars, while experiential knowledge is imparted through the arrangement of foreign buyers' or trade missions, trade and catalog shows, or participation in international market research.

As stated at the beginning of this chapter, export is an important source of economic growth and job creation. Furthermore, jobs that depend on trade pay between 13 to 18 percent more than the average wage. Therefore, government efforts to promote exports seem to make sense. Although exports may be considered a major engine of economic growth in the U.S. economy, many U.S. firms do not export. Many firms, particularly small- to medium-size ones, appear to have developed a fear of international market activities. Their management tends to see only the risks—informational gaps, unfamiliar conditions in markets, complicated domestic and foreign trade regulations, absence of trained middle managers for exporting, and lack of financial resources—rather than the opportunities that the international market can present. These very same firms, however, may well have unique competitive advantages to offer that may be highly useful in performing successfully in the international market.

For example, small- and medium-size firms can offer their customers short response times. If some special situation should arise, there is no need to wait for the home office to respond. Responses can be immediate, direct, and predictable to the customer, therefore providing precisely those competitive ingredients that increase stability in a business relationship and reduce risk and costs. These firms also can often customize their operations more easily. Procedures can be adapted more easily to the special needs of the customer or to local requirements. One could argue that in a world turning away from mass marketing and toward niche marketing, these capabilities may well make smaller-size firms the export champions of the future.

Through the **Export Enhancement Act of 1992**, the U.S. government announced the National Export Strategy, a strategic, coordinated effort to stimulate exports.[28] In pursuit of this objective, the International Trade Administration of the U.S. Department of Commerce has devoted a substantial amount of the tax dollars allocated to it to help U.S. firms export their goods and services. For instance, the Japan Export Information Center (JEIC), established in April 1991, is the primary contact point within the Department of Commerce for U.S. exporters seeking business counseling and commercial information necessary to succeed in the Japanese market. The JEIC's principal function is to provide guidance on doing business in Japan and information on market entry alternatives, market data and research, product standards and testing requirements, intellectual property protection, tariffs, and nontariff barriers. The Japanese External Trade Organization (JETRO), affiliated with Japan's Ministry of Economy, Trade and Industry, has also in recent years switched from promoting Japanese exports to helping U.S. and other foreign companies export and invest in Japan. The new emphasis on import promotion is part of the Japanese government's broader strategy to pull more foreign business into Japan, particularly from small- to mid-size companies.[29]

In the United States, the Department of Commerce (DOC) also has industry specialists and country specialists in Washington, D.C. The industry specialists are available to give exporters information on the current state of the exporter's products overseas; comment on marketing and sales strategies; inform on trade missions, trade shows, and other events; and give other counsel.

[27]William C. Lesch, Abdolreza Eshghi, and Golpira S. Eshghi, "A Review of Export Promotion Programs in the Ten Largest Industrial States," in S. Tamer Cavusgil and Michael R. Czinkota, eds., *International Perspectives on Trade Promotion and Assistance* (New York: Quorum Books, 1990), pp. 25–37.

[28]Richard T. Hise, "Globe Trotting," *Marketing Management* 6 (Fall 1997): 50–58.

[29]Rosalind McLymont, "In an About Face, Japanese Group Provides Help to Foreign Exporters," *Journal of Commerce*, April 19, 1999, p. 5A.

The country specialists are available to give information on the target country, any current trade issues with the United States, customs and tariff information, insight on the business climate and culture, and any other information on a country required by the exporter. For example, Purafil, a company based in Doraville, Georgia, that produces a dry chemical filtration system, benefited handsomely by participating in a DOC-sponsored trade mission to the Middle East for the first time. As part of the trade mission, the DOC provided a venue for Purafil and other companies to network and establish business relationships with prospective clients. One area in which the DOC is particularly helpful is in establishing credibility for the company marketing overseas. As a result, Purafil has been able to increase exports to 60 percent of all its revenues.[30]

Similarly, the DOC's Commercial Service has developed *BuyUSA.gov*, an e-marketplace with a worldwide network of offices and expertise. The service offers online access to U.S. trade specialists who can assist buyers and sellers with exporting issues. For example, J.D. Streett & Company, a small auto lubricant and antifreeze manufacturer based in Maryland Heights, Missouri, spent some $400 to list its products on BuyUSA.com, resulting in major sales to Vietnam in 60 days.[31] Clearly, the government helps exporters find business leads in foreign markets.

Other countries also develop governmental programs to promote exports. For example, China recently raised tax rebates for certain textile and garment exports to help producers cope with the paper-thin profit margins squeezed by the yuan's appreciation and higher costs. Export tax rebates for some textile and garment items are increased by two percentage points to 13 percent from August 1, 2008. The country's textile and clothing exports rose 11.1 percent to US$81.7 billion in the first half of 2008 from a year earlier. The tax rebate would ease pressure and help boost exports.[32] Some governments even proactively engage in attracting inward foreign direct investment in the hope that their countries could increase exports. For example, Argentina, home to one of Latin America's most educated workforces and modern telecommunications, has the potential to become one of the region's leading software exporters. Hoping to lure software makers, the Argentine government enacted a law in 2005, offering technology companies tax benefits. The law has helped draw commitments of new investments of $60 million over the next three years from Intel and Microsoft to develop software in Argentina. Software company executives have lauded Argentina as a potential software-producing leader.[33]

Export–Import Bank

The **Export–Import Bank (Ex-Im Bank)** is an independent U.S. government agency that plays a crucial role in promoting exports and helping finance the sale of U.S. exports primarily to emerging markets throughout the world by providing loans, guarantees, and insurance. For example, in 2012, the Export-Import Bank reported a fourth consecutive record-breaking year of almost $35.8 billion in export financing—about a 9 percent increase from the previous year and more than double the amount from fiscal year 2008. These transactions have supported an estimated 255,000 jobs and over the five-year period (2008–2012), and have enabled more than $170 billion worth of American exports.[34]

The Ex-Im Bank is designed to supplement, but not compete with, private capital. Ex-Im Bank has historically filled gaps created when the private sector is reluctant to engage in export financing. The Ex-Im Bank (1) provides guarantees of working capital loans for U.S. exporters, (2) guarantees the repayment of loans or makes loans to foreign purchasers of U.S. goods and

---

[30]"Clearing the Air," *Export America* 3 (September 2002): 6–7.

[31]"Speeding to New Global Markets," *Export America* 3 (March 2002): 9.

[32]"China Increases Export Tax Rebates for Textile, Garment Product," *ChinaView*, July 31, 2008.

[33]"Argentina Has Potential to be Software Leader," *Reuters*, November 25, 2005.

[34]*The 2012 Annual Report of Export Import Bank of USA*, http://www.exim.gov, accessed January 20, 2013.

services, and (3) provides credit insurance against non-payment by foreign buyers for political or commercial risk. To carry out the U.S. government's strategy for continuing export growth, the Ex-Im Bank is focusing on critical areas such as emphasizing exports to developing countries, aggressively countering the trade subsidies of other governments, stimulating small business transactions, promoting the export of environmentally beneficial goods and services, and expanding project finance capabilities.

The Ex-Im Bank also helps large U.S. companies to win contracts for major infrastructure projects, especially in emerging markets. For example, in 2011, the Ex-Im Bank authorized a long-term loan guarantee of nearly $120 million to support a GE Transportation sale of locomotives to South Africa's Transnet Ltd., a large South African rail, port, and pipeline company headquartered in Johannesburg. Ex-Im Bank financing is facilitating the partnership between GE Transportation Systems, Transnet, and Transnet Rail Engineering (TRE).[35]

The Ex-Im Bank is also combating the "trade distorting" loans of foreign governments through the aggressive use of its Tied Aid Capital Projects Fund. The idea is that the Ex-Im Bank is willing on a case-by-case basis to match foreign tied-aid offers that are commercially viable and pending to be able to preemptively counter a foreign tied-aid offer. For instance, if a highway project in China gets a bid from a European or Japanese consortium of firms that offers to give concessional aid for the project but stipulates that in return for the aid the Chinese should buy machinery and materials from suppliers to be specified by the Europeans (or the Japanese), a U.S. firm bidding for the same project can depend on being able to provide concessional financing through the resources of the Ex-Im Bank. In addition, the U.S. government is no longer shy about openly representing U.S. firms and about being powerful advocates on behalf of U.S. businesses. Cabinet secretaries in the U.S. government have led groups of top business executives to many emerging markets. Accompanying administration officials on foreign missions gives business executives a chance to get acquainted with decision makers in foreign governments that would award many infrastructure projects. The U.S. government lobbied hard to obtain airplane orders for Boeing from Singapore Airlines, Cathay Pacific, and Saudia, all of which were being lobbied hard by the French government to buy from the Airbus–European consortium.

Critics may cavil at this active role of the U.S. government in promoting exports; however, if U.S. firms are to retain their position in existing markets and if they are to gain access to new markets, they must have the same facilities that are available to firms from other nations. The Export-Import Bank of China, the third-largest official credit institution in the world, following Japan Bank for International Cooperation (JBIC) and Export-Import Bank of the United States, inaugurated its Paris office in 2005, which would serve all the French-speaking countries in west Europe, northern Europe, and Africa. The Paris office plays a key role in promoting the bank's official loan business on behalf of the Chinese government to French-speaking countries, those in Africa in particular, under favorable terms.[36] For this reason, the policy of advocacy on behalf of U.S. firms fighting to enter new markets or to retain existing markets is a cornerstone of the national export policy.

Tariff Concessions

Other areas in which the government plays a role in promoting exports include the establishment and maintenance of foreign trade zones (FTZs) and the Export Trading Company Act of 1982.

Foreign Trade Zone

As discussed in detail in Chapter 14, **foreign trade zones** (free trade zones) enable businesses to store, process, assemble, and display goods from abroad without paying a tariff. Once these goods

---

[35]*The 2011 Annual Report of Export Import Bank of USA*, http://www.exim.gov, accessed January 20, 2013.
[36]"Export-Import Bank of China Opens Paris Office," *Peoples' Daily Online*, June 20, 2005.

leave the zone and enter the United States, they are charged a tariff, but not on the cost of assembly or profits. If the product is re-exported, no duties or tariffs apply. Thus, a U.S. firm can assemble foreign parts for a camera in a Florida FTZ and ship the finished cameras to Latin America without paying duty.

American Export Trading Company

The **Export Trading Company Act of 1982** encourages businesses to join together and form export trading companies. The act provides antitrust protection for joint exporting and permits banking institutions to own interests in these exporting ventures. This act makes it practical for small- and medium-size exporting firms to pool resources without the fear of antitrust prosecution and inadequate capitalization. A bank may hold up to 100 percent stock in an export trading company and is exempted from the collateral requirements contained in the Federal Reserve Act for loans to its export trading company.[37]

Export Regulations

Although the U.S. government has become earnest in promoting exports, it also takes a hand in regulating exports. The Foreign Corrupt Practices Act of 1977 (as amended in 1986) imposes jail terms and fines for overseas payoffs that seek to influence overseas government decisions, although payments to expedite events that are supposed to take place under local laws are no longer illegal. Many U.S. exporters, especially exporters of big-ticket items, believe that the Foreign Corrupt Practices Act provides an unfair advantage to exporters from Europe and Japan that have been able to make such payments and get tax write-offs for the payments under export expenses. In 1996, under newly agreed provisions of WTO, firms from other countries were no longer allowed to make such payments without incurring penalties, thus leveling the playing field somewhat for U.S. exporters. Under the Wassenaar Arrangement of 1995 (see Chapter 5), domestic laws also exist that restrict exports of security-sensitive technology such as sophisticated machine tools and encryption technology for computer software and hardware (see **Global Perspective 15-1**).

Antitrust laws prevent U.S. firms from bidding jointly on major foreign projects. Human rights legislation and nuclear nonproliferation policies require that every year the federal government recertify the Normal Trade Relations (NTR)[38] status of major foreign trade partners (e.g., China). These are examples of the U.S. exporting its own rules to other nations under the aegis of WTO. To the extent that such actions result in the same rules for all nations engaging in international trade, such behavior benefits trade; however, such behavior can also be perceived by many nations as an infringement of national sovereignty.

Sometimes the actions of a foreign government can affect exports. These actions relate to tariffs and local laws relating to product standards and classification. For example, computer networking equipment exported from the United States to the European Union is charged a 3.9 percent tariff. A recent EU ruling decided that computer networking equipment (e.g., adapters, routers, and switches) do not crunch data but transport them and so should be classified as telecommunication equipment. Telecommunication equipment, however, carries a higher tariff rate of 7.5 percent, increasing the landed price of these products in Europe.[39] Such actions by foreign governments are usually attempts to provide protection to local industry.

Finally, a government could tax exports with the purpose of satisfying domestic demand first or of taking advantage of higher world prices. For example, in 1998, two typhoons damaged trees in

---

[37]William W. Nye, "An Economic Profile of Export Trading Companies," *Antitrust Bulletin* 38 (Summer 1993): 309–325.

[38]See Chapter 2 for details.

[39]"Europe's Computer Networking Tariffs May Lead to U.S. Complaint to WTO," *Wall Street Journal*, May 1, 1996, p. B7.

Global Perspective 15-1

Export Control in the United States: The Balancing Act between Free Trade and Tight Security

Control of high-tech exports has been regulated under a continuing executive order since 1994 when the Export Administration Act (EAA) of 1979 expired. In the past several years, the technology industry has argued that the current export control regime is outmoded. Current export control rules use a performance rating called "millions of theoretical operations per second" (MTOPS) to determine which microprocessors and computers must apply for export licenses to certain countries. Computing power has become so prolific, however, that it is nearly impossible to regulate by using performance-based controls such as MTOPS.

Indeed, the federal government has had to race with the market over the past several years to keep export control regulations from barring the export of readily available, mass-market computers. For example, as recently as 1999, microprocessors with an MTOPS rating of 1,200 and computers with a rating of 2,000 were subject to controls. Those limits have been raised repeatedly over the past few years. The limits on chips apply to export to certain countries such as China and the former Soviet countries. The limits on computers apply to so-called Tier III countries, which include China, Russia, Israel, Pakistan, and India.

In 2001, key senators introduced the Export Administration Act of 2001, aimed at balancing competing priorities: free trade and tight security. The bill attempted a narrower, more surgical application of controls on dual-use items—commercial exports in aerospace, computers, encryption, and machine tools that could be diverted to military use by overseas companies or countries. The bill would stiffen fines and prison terms for violators, both individual and corporate, in an attempt to bolster control of advanced technologies that are less widely dispersed. The bill also contained a provision that would eliminate the requirement that computer export controls be based on MTOPS levels.

The House of Representatives was unable, however, to pass a similar bill.

The failure of Congress to enact a new EAA requires the president to continue to use his authority under the International Economic Emergency Powers Act (IEEPA) to regulate export controls. The Department of Commerce is currently working to establish a new metric to replace the MTOPS standard for high-performance computers. Meanwhile, the U.S. government raised the MTOPS limit on computers from 85,000 to 190,000 MTOPS in March 2002. This rating would allow for the export of multi-processor servers with up to 32 Intel Itanium CPUs.

Since the September 11th terrorist attacks, U.S. companies have had to adjust to new export control challenges because license applications take longer, are rejected more often, and require more backup information. Microsoft, for instance, has outsourced certain export functions through partnering to achieve export efficiency in all processes. Furthermore, the company has implemented the SAP GTS system to conduct country screening process. Currently, Microsoft is proactively partnering with the U.S. government to secure global supply chains by participating in the C-TPAT (Customers-Trade Partnership Against Terrorism) program. Evidently, Microsoft is not the only company that has to adjust to the post 9/11 export paradigm shift.

Sources: Tam Harbert, "One Step Forward on Export Control," *Electronic Business* (March 2002): 36; "AAEI Conference Highlights: How Microsoft, Philips Meet New Post-9/11 Compliance Requirements," *Managing Exports & Imports* (August 2004): 1-4; "OEE 2005 Enforcement Actions and Fines Expected to Easily Surpass 2005," *Managing Exports & Imports* (May 2005): 8; and William J. Ritchie and Steven A. Melnyk, "The Impact of Emerging Institutional Norms on Adoption Timing Decisions: Evidence from C-TPAT-A Government Antiterrorism Initiative," *Strategic Management Journal*, 33, no. 7 (2012): 860–870.

the northern Philippines, stripping away mature coconuts. Coconut oil shipments during the fourth quarter of 1998 were 60 percent below their normal level. The coconut oil market continued to face production declines and the threat of higher prices. Indonesia, the second-largest producer, continued to impose high export duties on coconut oil.[40] The goal of such measures was to curb exports and try to keep a lid on internal food industry costs as coconut oil prices soared. Similarly, a government could devise a mechanism by which to enforce collection of sales and/or value added tax owed by customers abroad. For instance, Australian exporters like Seawind International are influenced by the export regulations in Australia. One example is that the Australian Tax Office will not allow buyers located in foreign countries to take delivery of their boat and cruise for months before shipping the boat home unless they pay value-added tax.[41]

Managing Imports—The Other Side of the Coin

So far this chapter has been devoted exclusively to exports, and we now turn to imports. For organizations in the United States importing is considerably easier than for most firms in the rest of the world. One of the primary reasons for this is the fact that unlike importers in most of the rest of the world, U.S. importers can pay the seller abroad in their own currency—the U.S. dollar— because the U.S. dollar is an internationally accepted denomination of exchange. Thus, unlike importers in Brazil or Indonesia who must find U.S. dollars (or other hard currencies) to pay for imports, an importer in the United States can manage by shelling out U.S. dollars. About 60 percent of the world's trade is still denominated in U.S. dollars; exporters want dollars in return for the goods or services sold.

However, denomination of trade in dollars is changing, especially in Europe, where the euro has emerged as the currency in which trade is denominated. Most of the time, therefore, a U.S. importer does not have to bother to hedge foreign exchange transactions or try to accumulate foreign currency to pay for imports. On occasion, a U.S. importer does not even need a letter of credit. This same advantage has become available to the European Union (EU) member countries. EU member countries are now able to pay in euros for their imports from other member countries. Similarly, in Asia the Japanese yen is emerging as the currency in which trade is denominated. Japan benefits from this on a more limited geographical basis. Japan is now able to pay in Japanese yen for much of its imports from Southeast Asia.

This is not to suggest that a firm can import anything for sale in the United States. There are restrictions on trade with countries such as Iran, Libya, Cuba, and North Korea. Iran and Libya are thought to be supporters of state-sponsored terrorism. Production and marketing considerations also limit what can be imported and sold profitably in the United States. For soaps and cosmetics, for example, the demand for imports is minimal. However, the United States is a surplus producer of many categories of goods including aircraft, defense equipment, medical electronics, computer software, and agricultural goods.

Importing any good is thus predicated upon the existence of a situation in which the domestic production of the good in question is not sufficient to satisfy demand. For example, annual sales of cut flowers in the U.S. are nearly $10 billion, but domestic production meets only about 30 percent of the demand, with Americans purchasing flowers not just for special occasions but also for sending messages, as a token of friendship, as a get-well wish, or just to convey "have a nice day" to someone. Imports of cut flowers are primarily from Colombia, Mexico, Costa Rica, Ecuador, Peru, and Kenya.[42] The imported flowers must satisfy the selective U.S. consumer and must comply with the U.S. Plant Protection Quarantine Inspection Program and antidumping

---

[40]Jim Papanikolaw, "Coconut Oil Market Tightens Because of Bad Weather in 1998," *Chemical Market Reporter*, January 25, 1999, p. 8.

[41]" . . .But GST Puts a Damper on Exports," *Manufacturers' Monthly*, December 2007, p. 18.

[42]"Say It with Flowers," *New Statesman*, February 16, 2004, pp. 22–23.

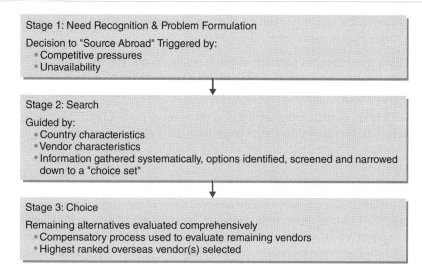

Exhibit 15-6 Model of Importer Buyer Behavior

Source: Neng Liang and Rodney L. Stump, "Judgmental Heuristics in Overseas Vendor Search and Evaluation: A Proposed Model of Importer Buyer Behavior," *International Executive,* Copyright (November, 1996): 779–806. Reprinted by permission of John Wiley & Sons, Inc.

regulations. Because the product is highly perishable, air transportation and rapid transit through customs must be ensured. Thus, the importer of flowers has to go through many hoops to locate a reliable seller and arrange the logistics. Importer behavior will, of course, depend on the category of goods being purchased abroad.

However, importer buyer behavior is a relatively under-researched area in the field of international trade partly because most nations are more interested in maximizing exports rather than imports, and restricting imports is relatively simple as compared to being a successful exporter. The most important of the organizational buying models is the BuyGrid model.[43] Besides elaborating on how the purchasing process evolves and highlighting the role of buyers' search in choice decisions, this framework was the first to categorize buy decisions as (1) straight buys, (2) modified rebuys, and (3) new tasks.

Although this framework was developed primarily for domestic purchases, it is applicable to import decisions as well. Applying the framework for an import decision and taking into account the increased uncertainty in international markets would translate into a procedure presented in **Exhibit 15-6**. This sequence of actions in an import situation appears logical, as it does for exports, but many international supplier relationships start with an "unsolicited export order" in which importers place an order with a selected foreign vendor without any systematic vendor search and evaluation. The lack of a systematic approach to vendor identification and evaluation can stem from difficulty in accessing all relevant information and from the idea of bounded rationality—the notion that due to limited cognitive abilities, humans tend to satisfice, not optimize. Thus, given the information available, which cannot be complete, managers will not be able to make the best decision.[44]

Mechanics of Importing

An import transaction is like looking at an export transaction from the other end of the transaction. Instead of an exporter looking for a prospective buyer, an importer looks for an overseas firm that can supply it the raw materials, components, or finished products that it needs for its business.

---

[43]Patrick J. Robinson, Charles W. Faris and Yoram Wind, *Industrial Buying and Creative Marketing* (Boston: Allyn and Bacon, 1967).

[44]Neng Liang and Rodney L. Stump, "Judgmental Heuristics in Overseas Vendor Search and Evaluation: A Proposed Model of Importer Buyer Behavior," *International Executive* 38 (November/December 1996): 779–806.

Once an importer locates a suitable overseas exporter, it negotiates with the exporter the terms of the sale including, but not restricted to, the following:

- Finding a bank that either has branches in the exporter's country or has a correspondent bank located in the exporter's country and establishing a line of credit with the bank if this has not already been done.

- Establishing a letter of credit with a bank stating the terms of payment and how payment is to be made. This includes terms of clearing the goods from the docks/customs warehouse (sometimes with title for goods going temporarily to the bank), insurance coverage, terms of transfer of title, and so on.

- Deciding on the mode of transfer of goods from exporter to importer and transfer of funds from importer to exporter. Transportation partly provides proof of delivery to the exporter's bank or the exporter. The exporter (or its bank) presents the proof of delivery to the importer's bank (branch in importer's own country/correspondent bank). The importer's bank transfers funds to the exporter's bank and simultaneously debits the importer's account or presents a demand draft to the importer.

- Checking compliance with national laws of the importing country and the exporting country. Import restrictions into the United States include quotas on automobiles, textiles, and steel, quarantine checks on food products, as well as a ban on imports from Cuba, North Korea, and Iran.

- Making allowances for foreign exchange fluctuations by making covering transactions through the bank so that the dollar liability for the importer either remains fixed or decreases.

- Fixing liability for payment of import duties and demurrage (i.e., detention of freight during loading and unloading beyond the scheduled time of departure) and warehousing in case the goods are delayed due to congestion at ports. These payments are normally the responsibility of the importer.

An examination of these mechanics of an import transaction reveals that the transaction is materially the same as an export transaction. The differences that are of interest to managers involved in the import of goods into the United States include these:

- A difference in risk profile, meaning that an exporter faces the risk of receiving no payment due to a variety of factors, whereas nonpayment is not an issue in imports. However, the quality of goods and services imported can be an issue for imports, but this is not usually an issue in exports.

- The facility of being able to pay in its own currency (most of the time), which is not available to importers in almost any other country.

- Everything else being equal, the ease for a U.S. firm to import rather than to export because of the primacy of the U.S. dollar despite the gradual depreciation of the U.S. dollar over time.

Import Documents and Delivery

When a shipment reaches the United States, the consignee (normally the importer) files entry documents with the port director at the port of entry. The bill of lading properly endorsed by the consignor in favor of the consignee serves as the evidence of the right to make entry. The entry documents also include an entry manifest, customs forms, packing lists if appropriate, and the commercial invoice. The entry should be accompanied by evidence that a bond is posted with customs to cover any potential duties, taxes, and penalties that may accrue. A **bond** is a guarantee by someone that the duties and any potential penalties will be paid to the customs of the importing country.

Entry can be for immediate delivery, for ordinary delivery, or for a warehouse or can be unentered for a period of time. Merchandise arriving from Canada and Mexico, trade fair goods, perishable goods, and shipments assigned to the U.S. government almost always utilize the **Special Permit for Immediate Delivery** on Customs Form 3461 prior to the arrival of the goods to enable fast release after arrival. An entry summary must be filed within 10 days of the release of the goods. Imported goods coming in under ordinary delivery use normal channels including Form 7533. Under warehousing, goods are placed in a customs-bonded warehouse if the entry of the imported goods is desired to be delayed. The goods can remain in a bonded warehouse for a period of five years. At any time during the period warehoused goods may be re-exported without payment of duty or may be withdrawn for consumption upon the payment of duty. If the importer fails to enter the goods at the port of entry or the port of destination within five working days after arrival, they may be placed in the general warehouse at the risk and expense of the importer.

Import Duties

Import duties that have to be paid are either ad valorem, specific, or compound. An **ad valorem duty**, which is the one most frequently applied, is a percentage of the value of the merchandise, such as 5 percent ad valorem. Thus, an auto shipment worth $100 million that has an ad valorem rate of 3.9 percent will pay $3.9 million as customs duty. A **specific duty** rate is a specified amount per unit of weight or other quantity, such as 5.1 cents per dozen, 20 cents per barrel or 90 cents per ton. A **compound duty** rate is a combination of an ad valorem rate and a specific rate, such as 0.7 cents per kilogram plus 10 percent as valorem. Average **import duty** rates in the United States (3.5%), the European Union (5.2%), and Japan (5.3%) are relatively low compared to those in many other countries, such as Brazil (31.4%), Mexico (36.1%), and India (48.7%),[45] but used to be much higher. After the Uruguay Round, the major global trade negotiations from 1986 to 1994, developed countries—the most important buyers of developing countries' exports—were opening their markets further. Their import duties for industrial products fell from 6.3 percent on average before the Uruguay Round to 3.8 percent afterward. Also due to the Uruguay Round, significantly more products exported to developed countries will enjoy zero import duties. The entry of imported merchandise into a foreign country is complete after customs clears the goods from the port of entry or the port of destination.

Antidumping import duties are assessed on imported merchandise sold to importers in a foreign country at a price that is less than the fair market value. The fair market value of merchandise is defined under articles of the World Trade Organization as the price at which the good is normally sold in the manufacturer's home market. In the United States, countervailing duties are assessed for some imported goods to counter the effects of subsidies provided by foreign governments, because without the **countervailing duty** the price of these imported goods in the U.S. market would be artificially low, causing economic injury to U.S. manufacturers.

The U.S. importer could even avoid payment of import duties by applying for a **duty-drawback** refund under a Temporary Importation Under Bond (TIB) in the United States. A duty drawback is a refund of up to 99 percent of all ordinary customs duties. It can be a direct identification drawback or a substitution drawback. Direct identification drawback provides a refund of duties paid on imported merchandise that is partially or totally used within five years of the date of import in the manufacture of an article that is exported. Substitution drawback provides a refund of duties paid on designated imported merchandise upon exportation of articles

---

[45]2012 Tariff Profiles, World Trade Organization, www.wto.org.

manufactured or produced with the use of substituted domestic or imported merchandise that is of the same quality as the designated import merchandise.[46] All countries have procedures allowing for the temporary importation of goods across their borders.[47]

As explained in Chapter 14, importing firms can also utilize foreign trade zones profitably. They can set up facilities in an FTZ to import finished goods, component parts, or raw materials for the eventual domestic consumption or import of merchandise that is frequently delayed by customs quota delays or import merchandise that must be processed, generating significant amounts of scrap. An important feature of foreign trade zones for foreign merchants entering the U.S. market is that the goods may be brought to the threshold of the market, making immediate delivery certain and avoiding the possible cancellation of orders due to shipping delays.

Gray Markets

Gray market channels refer to the legal export/import transaction involving genuine products into a country by intermediaries other than the authorized distributors. From the importer's side, it is also known as a **parallel import**. Distributors, wholesalers, and retailers in a foreign market obtain the exporter's product from some other business entity. Thus, the exporter's legitimate distributor(s) and dealers face competition from others who sell the exporter's products at reduced prices in that foreign market. High-priced branded consumer goods (cameras, jewelry, perfumes, watches, and so on) whose production lies principally in one country are particularly prone to gray market imports. Brand reputation is a critical element in gray market goods exports, and the distribution is typically through exclusive wholesalers and distributors.[48]

In the information technology (IT) sector alone, gray market sales accounted for between 5 percent and 30 percent of total IT sales in 2007, with a value of about $58 billion, according to a new report by audit firm KPMG LLP and The Alliance for Gray Market and Counterfeit Abatement.[49] In 2007, 1 million out of 3.75 million iPhones sold are estimated to have been distributed to the gray market.[50] The gray market problem is so serious that multinational companies such as Motorola, HP, DuPont, and 3M devote full-time managers and staff to dealing with gray market issues.[51] Gray market is pervasive across all industries. For example, if purchased on the gray market, a $92,000 brand-new Mercedes-Benz SL55 AMG Convertible, which meets all U.S. safety and pollution control requirements, can be purchased for 20 percent less than the price ($114,580) charged by the local authorized dealer. Similarly, in the luxury boat market, many foreign dealers of U.S. manufacturers are seriously affected by gray market activity. To avoid higher prices abroad, foreign retailers too often come to the United States and purchase their boat from a U.S. dealer, and then arrange their own transportation, circumventing the licensed dealer in their own home country.[52]

---

[46]Michael V. Cerny, "More Firms Establish Drawback Programs as $1.5B Goes Unclaimed," *Managing Exports* (October 2002): pp. 1–6.

[47]Lara L. Sowinski, "Going Global in a Flash," *World Trade* 18 (August 2005): 28–32.

[48]This section draws from Dale F. Duhan and Mary Jane Sheffet, "Gray Markets and the Legal Status of Parallel Importation," *Journal of Marketing* 52 (July 1988): 75–83; Tunga Kiyak, "International Gray Markets: A Systematic Analysis and Research Propositions," A paper presented at 1997 AMA Summer Educators' Conference, August 2–5, 1997; and Michael R. Mullen, C. M. Sashi, and Patricia M. Doney, "Gray Markets: Threats or Opportunity? The Case of Herman Miler vs. Asal GMBH," in Tiger Li & Tamer S. Cavusgil, eds., *Reviving Traditions in Research on International Market* (Greenwich, CT: JAI Press, 2003).

[49]Scott Campbell, "Gray Matter," *VARbusiness*, July 28, 2008, p. 11.

[50]Philip Elmer-DeWitt, "Apple's $300 Million Gray Market Dilemma," *CNNMoney*, January 28, 2008.

[51]Kersi D. Antia, Mark Bergen, and Shantanu Dutta, "Competing with Gray Markets," *Sloan Management Review* 46 (Fall 2004): 63–69.

[52]Frank Reynolds, "Senior Management Apathy Could Sink U.S. Pleasure Boat Exports," *Journal of Commerce*, March 24, 1999, p. 9A.

Although gray market products look similar to their domestic counterparts, they could not be identical and not carry full warranties. Nevertheless, the volume of gray market activities is significant. Three conditions are necessary for gray markets to develop. First, the products must be available in other markets. In today's global markets, this condition is readily met. Second, trade barriers such as tariffs, transportation costs, and legal restrictions must be low enough for parallel importers to move the products from one market to another. Again, under the WTO principles, the trade barriers have been reduced so low that parallel importation has become feasible. Third, price differentials among various markets must be great enough to provide the basic motivation for gray marketers. Such price differences arise for various reasons, including currency exchange rate fluctuations, differences in demand, legal differences, opportunistic behavior, segmentation strategies employed by international marketing managers, and more recently, the World Wide Web's information transparency.

- **Currency fluctuations.** The fluctuating currency exchange rates among countries often produce large differences in prices for products across national boundaries. Gray marketers can take advantage of changes in exchange rates by purchasing products in markets with weak currencies and selling them in markets with strong currencies.

- **Differences in market demand.** Similarly, price differences can be caused by differences in market demand for a product in various markets. If the authorized channels of distribution cannot adjust the market supply to meet the market demand, a large enough price difference could develop for unauthorized dealers to engage in an arbitrage process; that is, buying the product inexpensively in countries with weak demand and selling it profitably in countries with strong demand. For example, Apple Corp.'s international marketing strategy of 3G iPhone attempts to extract different prices from different countries, in which the situation is more attractive as iPhones became better value to Asian gray market entrepreneurs[53]

- **Legal differences.** Different prices across different markets due to different legal systems similarly motivate gray marketing activities. For example, as explained in Chapter 5, copyright protection lasts only 50 years in the European Union and Japan compared with 95 years in the United States. In other words, even if the music recordings were originally made and released in the United States, the recordings made in the early to mid-1950s by such figures as Elvis Presley and Ella Fitzgerald are entering the public domain in Europe, opening the way for any European recording company to release albums that had been owned exclusively by particular labels. Although the distribution of such albums would be usually limited to Europe, online marketers as well as traditional CD stores in the United States routinely sell cheaper foreign imports via gray markets.[54]

- **Opportunistic behavior.** Opportunistic behavior by distributors tends to occur when the distributor's gross margin is disproportionately large relative to the marketing task performed and is particularly attractive if the transaction occurs outside the distributor's assigned territory. For example, if the sale takes place in a neighboring foreign country (i.e., outside the territory), the opportunistic distributor could lower the selling price in that market because the sale is not made at the expense of the distributor's own full markup sales in its domestic market. In other words, this opportunistic behavior typifies the attitude, "Somebody else's problem is not my problem."

- **Segmentation strategy.** Although currency exchange rates and differences in market demand could be beyond the control of international marketing managers, segmentation strategy can result in (1) planned price discrimination and (2) planned product differentiation among various

---

[53]Mark Ritson, "iPhone Strategy: No Longer a Grey Area," *Marketing*, June 11, 2008, p. 21.
[54]"Companies in U.S. Sing Blues as Europe Reprises 50's Hits," *New York Times*, January 3, 2003, Late Edition, p. A1.

markets. Even for an identical product, different pricing strategy can be adopted for various reasons, including differences in product life cycle stage, customer purchase behavior, and price elasticity across different markets. Different prices across different markets motivate gray marketers to exploit the price differences among the markets.

- **The World Wide Web.** As an information medium, the World Wide Web raises a customer's awareness of special offers that were initially designed to be limited to specific regions, countries, or classes of customers. Gray-market sales are growing with the popularity of the internet. Web-based gray marketers can also advertise merely by using the product's brand name or model number on their websites and waiting for search engines to direct consumers there. The internet greatly stimulates gray market activity by presenting different price quotations from multiple merchants. Gray marketers can pay for presence on shopping bots, such as mysimon.com, cnet.com, shopping.yahoo.com, or bottomdollar.com as well as amazon.com and eBay.com. If you look closely at Amazon's website, you will see that the site sells Seiko (not authorized Seiko retailers) at or below dealer cost. If you click the SAS (Southern Audio Services) name on eBay (not authorized SAS retailers), it will come up thousands of times and sell SAS at 30 percent discounts or more. The explosion of unauthorized e-commerce has hit many sectors, including pharmaceuticals, electronics, and software.[55]

Alternatively, the product can be modified to address the specific needs of different markets. Contrary to common sense, adaptation of individual products for a specific market also leads to substantially more gray marketing. This occurs for two reasons. First, when, for example, a stripped version of the product is marketed in Europe and an enhanced version is marketed in the United States, some U.S. consumers, who may not be willing to pay for the enhanced model with too many refinements, import the simpler, less expensive version from an unauthorized distributor through a gray marketing channel. Second, some consumers simply want to purchase the product models that are not available in their domestic markets to differentiate themselves from the rest of the consumers. This is increasingly likely as markets around the world become more homogeneous.[56]

The unauthorized sales of goods and services in a gray market have been condemned for several reasons. There are at least five significant, intertwined consequences—each is closely tied to and feeds off the other—for manufacturers as follows:[57]

1. *The dilution of exclusive rights to distribute a particular product:* Authorized distributors, which should have been the only distributors allowed to distribute the product, become one of many other sources. Drop in margins as the result of competing for the same market is likely to be followed by complaints from authorized distributors to the manufacturers to take significant actions.

2. *The threat of "free riding" by authorized distributors in their effort to indirectly give pressure to the manufacturers:* In free riding, authorized dealers would start skimping on services they would normally provide, such as salesperson training, consumer education on product attributes, and presale services. These are all done in an effort to cut cost so that dealers' prices would match the gray marketers' prices.

---

[55]Steven Sagri, "Don't Give Press Play to Amazon's "Gray Market" Watch Sales," *National Jeweler* (June 2007): 18; and Mina Kimes, "How Middlemen Can Discredit Your Goods," *FSB: Fortune Small Business* (May 2008): 75–78.

[56]Matthew B. Myers, "Incidents of Gray Market Activity among U.S. Exporters: Occurrences, Characteristics, and Consequences," *Journal of International Business Studies* 30 (First Quarter 1999): 10–126.

[57]Kersi D. Antia, Mark Bergen, and Shantanu Dutta, "Competing with Gray Markets," *Sloan Management Review* 46 (Fall 2004): 63–69.

3. ***Damage to channel relationship:*** It is perhaps the biggest cost of gray marketing to manufacturers. When manufacturers are greatly dependent on one or a few authorized channel members, the impact of the gray market can be costly to the relationship between the manufacturers and their authorized channel members. Imagine how serious the consequences would be if an authorized dealer who has invested more than $2 million to set up a new showroom and has been assured that its exclusive territory would make up for the investment later finds out that the same products it sells are being sold at prices 15–20% lower by gray marketers, in the same area.

4. ***Undermining segmented pricing schemes:*** Spoiling segmented pricing schemes otherwise would potentially increase margins for the manufacturers. In multinational operating strategy, a segmented pricing scheme is applied as prices are set at levels each local market can hold up. With the tumbling trade barriers combined with increased availability of information as well as enhanced logistical capabilities, the gray marketing comes into action. Eventually, it would slowly lead manufacturers to adopt a single universal pricing as adopted by LVMH—the producer of luxury brands such as Tag Heuer, Louis Vuitton, and Christian Dior. By choosing instead to price their products the same worldwide, those companies will have to forego the profit-making opportunities that arise from pricing for local markets.

5. ***Loss of reputation and legal liability:*** Any manufacturer would stand behind its products and take control of it; however, that is not the case with the gray marketed products. In the gray market case, manufacturers lose control of their products as they were bought and resold by unauthorized distributors around the world. In the pharmaceutical industry, prescription drugs sold through the gray market are sometimes approaching or even have passed their expiration dates. In 2000, Motorola received a complaint from New Jersey Parking Authorities when 70 of its two-way radios meant for markets in Asia were sold by unauthorized distributors to the New Jersey Parking Authorities. The radios were not FCC-approved for use in the United States and as such, failed to work properly. The company had to replace the radios; nevertheless, the damage to the brand had already been done.

Gray marketing activity can also bring about some beneficial effects to manufacturers. Parallel channels foster intrabrand competition that can force authorized channels to do a better job serving their local customers and lead to improved customer satisfaction. It is conceivable that manufacturers can add gray marketers to the authorized channel or even acquire them, provided that such actions do not lead to increased conflict with existing authorized distributors. In industries with high fixed costs where capacity utilization and economies of scale are important, manufacturers may require the incremental sales generated by parallel channels to sustain high production volumes.[58]

A key question for the manufacturer of branded products is whether a gray market will cause a global strategy to become less desirable. Closer control and monitoring of international marketing efforts can certainly reduce the threat of gray market goods to negligible levels. As rule of thumb, firms using independent distributors (e.g., commission agents and merchant distributors) tend to suffer most from gray market activity while firms with ownership-based control over distribution channels (e.g., joint venture partners, wholly owned subsidiaries, and direct sale of exports to end users) offer more control over the final sale of the product. As presented in **Exhibit 15-7**, international marketers not only try to confront existing gray markets reactively but also are increasingly developing more proactive approaches to gray market problems before they arise.

---

[58]Michael R. Mullen, C. M. Sashi and Patricia M. Doney, "Gray Markets: Threats or Opportunity? The Case of Herman Miler vs. Asal GMBH," in Tiger Li & Tamer S. Cavusgil, eds., *Advances in International Marketing* (Greenwich, CT: JAI Press, 2003): 77–105.

Exhibit 15-7 How to Combat Gray Market Activity

A. Reactive Strategies to Combat Gray Market Activity

Type of Strategy	Implemented by	Cost of Implementation	Difficulty of Implementation	Does It Curtail Gray Market Activity at Source?	What Relief Does It Provide Authorized Dealers?	Long-Term Effectiveness	Legal Risks to Manufacturers or Dealers	Company Examples
Strategic confrontation	Dealer with manufacturer support	Moderate	Requires planning	No	Relief in the medium term	Effective	Low	Creative merchandising by Caterpillar and auto dealers
Participation	Dealer	Low	Not difficult	No	Immediate relief	Potentially damaging reputation of manufacturer	Low	Dealers wishing to remain anonymous
Price cutting	Manufacturer and dealer jointly	Costly	Not difficult	No, if price cutting is temporary	Immediate relief	Effective	Moderate to high	Dealers and manufacturers remain anonymous
Supply interference	Either party	Moderate at the wholesale level; high at the retail level	Moderately difficult	No	Immediate relief or slightly delayed	Somewhat effective if at wholesale level; not effective at retail level	Moderate at wholesale level; low at retail	IBM; Hewlett-Packard; Lotus Corp.; Swatch Watch USA; Charles of the Ritz Group, Ltd.; Leitz, Inc.; NEC Electronics
Promotion of gray market product limitations	Jointly, with manufacturer leadership	Moderate	Not difficult	No	Slightly delayed	Somewhat effective	Low	Komatsu, Seiko, Rolex, Mercedes-Benz IBM
Collaboration	Dealer	Low	Requires careful negotiations	No	Immediate relief	Somewhat effective	Very high	Dealers wishing to remain anonymous
Acquisition	Dealer	Very costly	Difficult	No	Immediate relief	Effective if other gray market brokers don't creep in	Moderate to high	No publicized cases

B. Proactive Strategies to Combat Gray Market Activity

Type of Strategy	Implemented by	Cost of Implementation	Difficulty of Implementation	Does It Curtail Gray Market Activity at Source?	What Relief Does It Provide Authorized Dealers?	Long-Term Effectiveness	Legal Risks to Manufacturers or Dealers	Company Examples
Product/service differentiation and availability	Jointly with manufacturer leadership	Moderate to high	Not difficult	Yes	Medium to long term	Very effective	Very low	General Motors, Ford, Porsche, Kodak
Strategic pricing	Manufacturer	Moderate to high	Complex; impact on overall profitability needs monitoring	Yes	Slightly delayed	Very effective	Low	Porsche
Dealer development	Jointly, with manufacturer leadership	Moderate to high	Not difficult; requires close dealer participation	No	Long term	Very effective	None	Caterpillar, Canon
Marketing information systems	Jointly, with manufacturer leadership	Moderate to high	Not difficult; requires dealer participation	No	After implementation	Effective	None	IBM, Caterpillar, Yamaha, Hitachi, Komatsu, Lotus Development, Insurance companies
Long-term image reinforcement	Jointly	Moderate	Not difficult	No	Long term	Effective	None	Most manufacturers with strong dealer networks
Establishing legal precedence	Manufacturer	High	Difficult	Yes, if fruitful	No	Uncertain	Low	COPIAT, Coleco, Charles of the Ritz Group, Ltd.
Lobbying	Jointly	Moderate	Difficult	Yes, if fruitful	No	Uncertain	Low	COPIAT, Duracell, Porsche

Note: Company strategies include, but are not limited to, those mentioned here.
Source: S. Tamer Cavusgil and Ed Sikora, "How Multinationals Can Counter Gray Market Imports," *Columbia Journal of World Business*, 23 (Winter 1988), pp. 75–85.

Gray marketing is a legal trading transaction. On the other hand, smuggling and black market refer to the illegal importation and sales of either otherwise legal goods or illegal products. Although such illegal transactions are outside the scope of this book, we address these issues in **Global Perspective 15-2** to introduce you to some ethical dilemmas that multinational companies can face concerning the smuggling and black market activities by independent distributors of what would otherwise be legal products.

◆ ◆

Global Perspective 15-2

Smuggling and Black Markets: An Ethical Dilemma for Multinational Companies Selling Lawful Products

Conventional wisdom has it that trade liberalization (i.e., adopting freer trade policy) in many emerging markets would reduce smuggling and black market phenomena because it reduces unnecessary and artificial price differences across countries. Economists call this tendency the "Law of One Price." However, in a seminal work on smuggling in 1996, Kate Gillespie and Brad McBride found quite the opposite: These countries are likely to see the resurgence of organized smuggling and black-market distribution as a result of trade liberalization. A number of reasons may be considered. First, liberalization is rarely complete, and smugglers can still take advantage of evading income, sales, and other taxes as well as tariffs. Second, as the reduced price differences (thanks indeed to trade liberalization) make it difficult for casual smugglers to make enough money, smugglers need to be larger and better organized in pursuit of "economies of scale" in their operations. As a result, smuggling shifted to organized crime and takes on a more sinister aspect. Third, evidence indicates that both the evolution of smuggling into organized crime and the use of smuggling as a way to launder money for international drug cartels and possibly terrorist organizations are increasing.

Smuggling is an illegal importation of either legal products (e.g., TVs, computers, music CDs) or illegal products (e.g., narcotics and child pornographic material). We focus only on smuggling of legal products here. What does smuggling have to do with multinational companies that engage in the business of selling legal products internationally? Nothing directly.

In June 2000, U.S. Customs estimated the global volume of money laundering, much of which is related to the illicit trade in narcotics, to total more than $600 billion a year or between 2 and 5 percent of the world's GDP. The problem is that money is fungible (simply stated, money is money wherever it comes from). U.S. exports are often purchased with narcotics dollars. Those exports include otherwise lawful goods, including household appliances, consumer electronics, liquor, cigarettes, used auto parts, and footwear. The connection between money laundering and smuggled consumer products has been a major concern of U.S. Customs for several years particularly after the government cracked down on money laundering through U.S. banks.

This is how the system works. A drug cartel in a Latin American country exports narcotics to the United States where they are sold for U.S. dollars. The cartel in this Latin American country contacts a third party—a peso broker—who agrees to exchange pesos in the country for the U.S. dollars that the cartel controls in the United States. The peso broker uses contacts in the United States to place the drug dollars purchased from the cartel into the U.S. banking system. Latin American importers then place orders for items and make payments through the peso broker who uses contacts in the United States to purchase the requested items from U.S. manufacturers and distributors. The peso broker pays for these goods with cash or drafts drawn on U.S. bank accounts. The purchased goods are shipped to some Caribbean or South American destinations, sometimes via Europe or Asia, and are then smuggled into this Latin American country. The Latin American importer avoids paying high tariffs, and the peso broker profits by charging both the cartel and the importers for services rendered.

The U.S. multinational companies that sell these products have routinely denied having any idea that they were involved in money laundering. Beginning in June 2000, however, a group of corporate executives began a series of meetings at the Justice Department. The companies included Hewlett-Packard, Ford Motor, Whirlpool, General Motors, Sony, Westinghouse, and General Electric (GE). With the exception of GE, the companies called to participate had products appearing in the black market in a Latin American country. GE was invited as the example of a good corporate citizen that was successfully cleaning up the smuggling of its goods into South America. However, GE's shutting down smuggling came at a fairly steep price to the company and to

the benefit of those competitors that kept their eyes closed on the fact. Between 1995 and 2000, General Electric estimated that its good corporate citizenship policy cost the company about 20 percent of its sales to South America.

Sources: Kate Gillespie and J. Brad McBride, "Smuggling in Emerging Markets: Global Implications," *Columbia Journal of World Business* 31 (Winter 1996): 40–54; and Kate Gillespie, "Smuggling and the Global Firm," *Journal of International Management* 9, no. 3 (2003): 317–333.

SUMMARY

The national government has a variety of programs to support exports, although many government policies—which are sometimes dictated by political compulsions—also hinder exports. Export markets provide a unique opportunity for growth, but competition in these markets is usually fierce. With the rise of the big emerging markets (Brazil, China, and India), competition is likely to intensify even more.

Procedurally, exporting requires locating customers, obtaining an export license from the federal government (a general or validated license); collecting export documents (such as the bill of lading, commercial invoice, export packing list, insurance certificate); packing and marketing; shipping abroad; and receiving payment—most of the time through a bank. Conversely, importing requires locating a seller, obtaining an import license, usually establishing a letter of credit, turning over import documents (the bill of lading, etc.) to indicate receipt of goods, and making payment through the banking system. Methods of payment include advance payment, open account, consignment sale, documents against payment (D/P), documents against acceptance (D/A), and letters of credit. Of these, the last two are the most popular. Depending on the nature of the payment terms and the currency of payment, the

exporter could need to make foreign exchange hedging transactions. The U.S. government is now taking a more active role in promoting the exports of U.S. firms as they bid for big-ticket items in the emerging markets.

Imports are the obverse of exports. A U.S. importer can make payments in U.S. dollars unlike an importer in many other countries. Any good coming in through a U.S. port must pass through customs and pay the appropriate duty and be authorized by customs at the port of entry or the port of destination for entry. Unlike an exporter who faces a payment risk, the importer's risks are associated with delivery schedules and product quality. Foreign exchange risk is common to both imports and exports. Entry of some goods into a country is restricted by bilateral and multilateral quotas as well as by political considerations.

Finally, globalization of markets has spawned gray marketing activities by unauthorized distributors taking advantage of price differences that exist among various countries due to currency exchange rate fluctuations, different market demand conditions, and price discrimination, among other factors. For companies marketing well-known branded products, gray markets have become a serious issue to be confronted proactively as well as reactively.

QUESTIONS

1. What are the factors that influence the decision of the exporter to use a standardized product strategy across countries and regions?

2. Terms of payment represent an extremely important facet of export transactions. Describe the various terms of payments in increasing order of risk.

3. What is the role of government (home country) in export activities? Explain in the context of U.S. exporters.

4. What are gray markets? What factors led to the development of gray markets?

5. You are the manager for international operations of a manufacturer of steel in the United States. You have received an offer to purchase at a very attractive price 5,000 metric tons of wire rods (used to draw wires for the manufacture of nails) from a large nail manufacturer located in developing country X. What would you deem to be the most appropriate choice of export terms of payment and terms of shipment, given the following information

(include any precautions that you would take to ensure the successful execution of the order):

a. The prospective importer has its account at a local bank. Local government rules stipulate making payments only through this bank.

b. The local bank does not have any international operations/branches.

c. The currency of country X has been extremely unstable, with its value having depreciated by more than 20 percent recently.

d. The interest rates are extremely high in this country.

e. The legal system in this country is weak, but the firm that is willing to place the order has a good reputation based on past experience with other international manufacturers.

f. Rain and summer heat can cause the product to deteriorate if kept unused for a time longer than necessary.

g. This country exports a larger amount by the sea route than it imports. Hence, many ships have to go empty to get cargo from this country to the United States.

6. The internet has become a powerful place for products, information, and everything you can think of today, and internet retailing has become increasingly accepted by most consumers. While consumers are surfing for the best prices, it is difficult for them to tell a legitimate, authorized dealer from a gray marketer. Assuming that you are a consultant of a famous computer company, what are your recommendations for the firm to be able to combat gray market activities? Could the company continually attract bargain-seeking consumers by informing consumers of the dark side of gray market retailing?

PLANNING, ORGANIZATION, AND CONTROL OF GLOBAL MARKETING OPERATIONS

16

CHAPTER OVERVIEW

1. Global strategic marketing planning

2. Key criteria in global organizational design

3. Organizational design options

4. Organizing for global brand management

5. Life cycle of organizational structures

6. Control of global marketing efforts

The capstone of a company's global marketing activities will be its strategic marketing plan. To implement its global plans effectively, a company needs to reflect on the best organizational setup that enables it to successfully meet the threats and opportunities posed by the global marketing arena. Organizational issues that the global marketer must confront cover questions like:

- What is the proper communication and reporting structure?

- Who within our organization should bear responsibility for each of the functions that need to be carried out?

- How can we as an organization leverage the competencies and skills of our individual subsidiaries?

- Where should the decision-making authority belong for the various areas?

   We consider the major factors that will influence the design of a global organizational structure. Multinational companies (MNCs) can choose from a wide variety of organizational structures. In this chapter, we discuss the major alternative configurations. We also highlight the central role played by country managers within the firm's organization. More and more companies try to build up and nurture global brands. We look at several organizational mechanisms that firms can adopt to facilitate such efforts. Because change requires flexibility, this chapter explores different ways that MNCs can handle environmental changes. MNCs must also decide where the decision-making locus belongs. The challenge is to come up with a structure that bridges the gap between two forces: being responsive to local conditions and integrating global marketing efforts. The final section focuses on control mechanisms companies can utilize to achieve their strategic goals.

Global Strategic Marketing Planning

The vast majority of multinational companies prepare a **global strategic marketing plan** to guide and implement their strategic and tactical marketing decisions. Such plans are usually developed on an annual basis and look at policies over multiple years. The content of a global strategic marketing plan can be very broad in scope but usually covers at least four areas:[1]

1. *Market situation analysis.* A situation analysis on a global basis of the company's customers (market segments, demand trends, etc.), the competition (SWOT[2] analysis), the company itself, and the collaborators (e.g., suppliers, distribution channels, alliance partners).

2. *Objectives and targets.* For each country or region, management states goals that are achievable and challenging at the same time. Sometimes, companies peg their sales and profit forecasts to the health of the global economy. In 2010, Philips, the Dutch electronics conglomerate, aimed to grow its top line at least 2 percent faster than worldwide GDP. Siemens, the German engineering group, set a growth target of double global GDP expansion.[3]

3. *Strategies.* Once the objectives have been determined, management needs to formulate marketing strategies for each country to achieve the set goals, including resource allocation.

4. *Action plans.* Strategies need to be translated into concrete actions that will implement those strategies. Specific actions are to be spelled out for each marketing mix element.

Although these are the core areas of a global strategic marketing plan, such a plan will also discuss anticipated results and include contingency plans.

Bottom-Up versus Top-Down Strategic Planning

International planning can be top-down (centralized) or bottom-up (decentralized). Obviously, hybrid forms that combine both options are also possible. With **top-down planning**, corporate headquarters guides the planning process. **Bottom-up planning** is the opposite. Here, the planning process starts with the local subsidiaries and is then consolidated at headquarters level. The bottom-up approach has the advantage of embracing local responsiveness. Top-down planning, on the other hand, facilitates performance monitoring. A centralized approach also makes it easier to market products with a global perspective. One survey of large multinational corporations found that pure bottom-up planning was most popular (used by 66 percent of the companies surveyed). Only 10 percent of the interviewed companies, on the other hand, relied on a pure top-down planning process. The balance used a hybrid format (11 percent) or no planning at all (12 percent).[4]

Pitfalls

Marketing plans can go awry. One survey identified the following obstacles as the main problems in preparing strategic plans for global markets:

1. Lack of information of the right kind (39 percent of the respondents).

2. Too few courses of action; too little discussion of alternatives (27 percent).

---

[1]See, for instance, Douglas J. Dalrymple and Leonard J. Parsons, *Marketing Management* (New York: John Wiley & Sons, 2000), Chapter 16.

[2]SWOT analysis is the method used to evaluate the strengths, weaknesses, opportunities, and threats that the company is facing.

[3]"Philips to Set Growth Targets by Global Economy," http://www.ft.com, accessed September 15, 2010.

[4]Myung-Su Chae and John S. Hill, "The Hazards of Strategic Planning for Global Markets," *Long Range Planning* 29, no. 6 (1996): 880–891.

3. Unrealistic objectives (22 percent).

4. Failure to separate short/long-term plans (20 percent).

5. Lack of framework to identify strengths/weaknesses (19 percent).

6. Too many numbers (17 percent).

7. Lack of framework to define marketplace threats and opportunities (15 percent).

8. Senior management de-emphasizing or forgetful about strategic/long-range plans (15 percent).

9. Too little cooperation between headquarters/subsidiaries or among subsidiaries (10 percent).

10. Too much information of the "wrong kind" (4 percent).

11. Too much planning jargon (1 percent).[5]

Obviously, external factors can also interfere with the strategic planning process. Changes in the political and the economic environment can upset the finest strategic plans. China's sudden clampdown on direct selling created upheaval for Avon, Amway, and Mary Kay, among other companies. The 2008–2009 global economic downturn wreaked havoc on the strategic plans of multinationals around the globe. McDonald's, for example, had finalized a three-year strategic plan by October 2008. However, as the global economy worsened, the company revisited its plan in December. McDonald's pressed its managers around the world to closely monitor cost items and data on customer traffic, buying patterns, and the general economic situation (e.g., unemployment rate).[6] As a result, McDonald's U.K. began running more ads for its value-priced Little Tasters menu and McDonald's China slashed prices by up to 33 percent. Other external factors that can hamper strategic marketing planning include changes in the competitive climate (e.g., deregulation), technological developments (e.g., 3G wireless technology), and consumer-related factors.

Key Criteria in Global Organizational Design

As is true of most other global managerial issues, there is no magic formula that offers the "ideal" organizational setup under a given set of circumstances. Yet there are some factors that companies should consider when engineering their global organizational structure. In the following discussion, we make a distinction between environmental and firm-specific factors. We start with a look at the major environmental factors.

Environmental Factors

Competitive Environment

Global competitive pressures force MNCs to implement structures that facilitate quick decision making and alertness. In industries where competition is highly localized, a decentralized structure where most of the decision making is made at the country level is often appropriate. Nevertheless, even in such situations, MNCs can often benefit substantially from mechanisms that allow the company to leverage its global knowledge base.

Rate of Environmental Change

Drastic environmental change is a way of life in scores of industries. New competitors or substitutes for a product emerge. Existing competitors form or disband strategic alliances.

---

[5]Ibid.

[6]"McDonald's seeks way to keep sizzling," *Wall Street Journal Asia*, March 11, 2009, pp. 14–15.

Consumer needs worldwide constantly change. Businesses that are subject to rapid change require an organizational design that facilitates continuous scanning of the firm's global environment and swift alertness to opportunities or threats posed by that environment.

Regional Trading Blocs

Companies that operate within a regional trading bloc (e.g., the European Union, NAFTA, MERCOSUR) usually integrate their marketing efforts to some extent across the affiliates within the block area. A case in point is the European Union. In light of European integration, numerous MNCs decided to streamline their organizational structure. Many of these companies still maintain their local subsidiaries, but the locus of most decision making now lies with the pan-European headquarters. As other trading blocs such as Asia's APEC and South America's MERCOSUR evolve towards the European model, one can expect similar makeovers in other regions.

Nature of Customers

The company's customer base also has a great impact on the MNC's desired organizational setup. Companies such as DHL, IBM, and Citigroup, which have a "global" clientele, need to develop structures that permit a global reach and at the same time allow the company to stay "close" to their customers.

These are the major external drivers. We now turn to the prime firm-specific determinants.

Firm-Specific Factors

Strategic Importance of International Business

Typically, when overseas sales account for a very small fraction of the company's overall sales revenues, simple organizational structures (e.g., an export department) can easily handle the firm's global activities. As international sales grow, the organizational structure will evolve to mirror the growing importance of the firm's global activities. For instance, companies may start with an international division when they test the international waters. Once their overseas activities expand, they are likely to adopt an area-type (country- and/or region-based) structure.

Product Diversity

The diversity of the company's foreign product line is another key factor in shaping the company's organization. Companies with substantial product diversity tend to go for a global product division configuration.

Company Heritage

Differences in organizational structures within the same industry can also be explained via corporate culture. Nestlé and Unilever, for example, have always been highly decentralized MNCs. A lot of the decision-making authority has always been at the local level. When Unilever realized that its marketing efforts required a more pan-European approach to compete with the likes of Procter & Gamble, the company transformed its organization and revised its performance measures to provide incentives for a European focus. One of Unilever's senior executives, however, noted that the changeover "comes hard to people who for years have been in an environment where total business power was delegated to them."[7] As long as a given formula works, there is little incentive for companies to tinker with it. Revamping an organization to make the structure more responsive to new environmental realities can be a daunting challenge.

---

[7]"Unilever adopts clean sheet approach," *Financial Times,* October 21, 1991.

Skills and Resources within the Company

Decentralization could become a problem when local managerial talents are missing. Granted, companies can bring in expatriates, but this is typically an extremely expensive remedy that does not always work out. For instance, expatriate managers may find it hard to adjust to the local environment. Figuring out the rights structure also depends on the geographic spread of the skills and resources needed to operate the business. Another critical factor is how competent people within the organization are working across geographies. If cooperation skills are limited or there is resistance to rotating people across countries, structures along geographies or product lines would be more suitable.[8]

Organizational Design Options

The principal designs that firms can adopt to organize their global activities are:

- **International division.** Under this design, the company basically has two entities: the domestic division, which is responsible for the firm's domestic activities, and the international division, which is in charge of the company's international operations.

- **Product-based structure.** With a product structure, the company's global activities are organized along its various product divisions.

- **Geographic structure.** This is a setup where the company configures its organization along geographic areas: countries, regions, or some combination of these two levels.

- **Matrix organization.** This is an option where the company integrates two approaches—for instance, the product and geographic dimensions—with a dual chain of command.

We will now consider each of these options in greater detail. At the end of this section, we will also discuss the so-called **networked** organization model.

International Division Structure

Most companies that engage in global marketing initially start by establishing an export department. Once international sales reach a threshold, the company might set up a full-blown international division. The charter of the international division is to develop and coordinate the firm's global operations. The unit also scans market opportunities in the global marketplace. In most cases, the division has equal standing with the other divisions within the company.

This option is most suitable for companies that have a product line that is not too diverse and does not require a large amount of adaptation to local country needs. It is also a viable alternative for companies whose business is still primarily focused on the domestic market. Over time, as international marketing efforts become more important to the firm, most companies tend to switch to a more globally oriented organizational structure.

Global Product Division Structure

The second option centers around the company's different product lines or strategic business units (SBUs). Each product division, being a separate profit center, is responsible for managing worldwide the activities for its product line. This alternative is especially popular among high-tech

---

[8]Nirmalya Kumar and Phanish Puranam, "Have You Restructured for Global Success?" *Harvard Business Review* 89 (October 2011): 123–128.

Exhibit 16-1

Organizational Structure of John Deere of a Global Product Structure

Source: http://www.deere.com/en_US/docs/Corporate/investor_relations/pdf/financialdata/reports/2013/2012_annual_report.pdf.

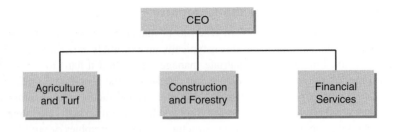

companies with highly complex products or MNCs with a very diversified product portfolio. Ericsson and John Deere are some of the companies that have adopted this structure. **Exhibit 16-1** shows how John Deere organizes its company.

Several benefits are associated with a global product structure. The product focus offers the company a large degree of flexibility in terms of cross-country resource allocation and strategic planning. For instance, market penetration efforts in recently entered markets can be cross-subsidized by profits generated in developed markets. In many companies, a global product structure goes in tandem with consolidated manufacturing and distribution operations. This approach is exemplified by Honeywell, the U.S. maker of control tools, which has set up centers of excellence that span the globe.[9] That way, an MNC can achieve substantial scale economies in the area of production and logistics, thereby improving the firm's competitive cost position. Another appeal is that global product structures facilitate the development of a global strategic focus to cope with challenges posed by global players.[10]

The shortcomings of a product division are not insignificant. Lack of communication and coordination among the various product divisions can lead to needless duplication of tasks. A relentless product-driven orientation can distract the company from local market needs. The global product division system has also been criticized for scattering the global resources of the company.[11] Instead of sharing resources and creating a global know-how pool, international resources and expertise get fragmented. A too narrow focus on the product area will lead to a climate where companies fail to grasp the synergies that might exist between global product divisions.

Geographic Structure

The third option is the geographic structure, where the MNC is organized along geographic units. The units might be individual countries or regions. In many cases, MNCs use a combination of country-based subsidiaries and regional headquarters. There are other variants. Heinz, for instance, has three major regions, each one of them being further divided into subregions, as is shown in **Exhibit 16-2**. Area structures are especially appealing to companies that market closely related product lines with very similar end-users and applications around the world.

Country-Based Subsidiaries

Scores of MNCs set up subsidiaries on a country-by-country basis. To some degree, such an organization reflects the marketing concept. By setting up country affiliates, the MNC can stay in

---

[9]Honeywell, *1995 Annual Report.*

[10]W. H. Davidson and P. Haspeslagh, "Shaping a global product organization," *Harvard Business Review* (July-August 1982): 125–132.

[11]Davidson and Haspeslagh, "Shaping a global product organization," p. 129.

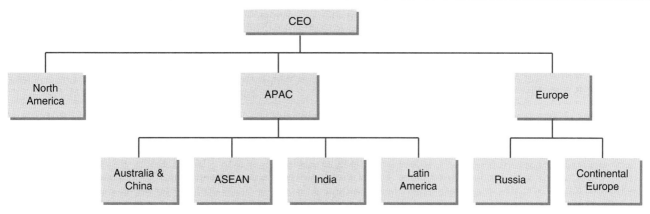

Exhibit 16-2 Heinz Company: Example of a Geographic Structure

Source: http://www.heinz.com/data/pdf/FY12_Heinz_Corporate_Fact_Sheet.pdf.

close touch with local market conditions. The firm can thereby easily spot new trends and swiftly respond to local market developments.

Country-focused organizations have several serious handicaps, however. They tend to be costly. Coordination with corporate headquarters and among subsidiaries can easily become extremely cumbersome. A country-focus often leads to a "not-invented-here" mentality that hinders cross-border collaboration and support. Some critics of the country-model derisively refer to the country-model as a mini–United Nations with a multitude of local fiefs run by scores of country managers.[12]

New Role of Country Managers

Corporate strategy gurus such as Ohmae foresee the demise of the country manager. Major companies have already cut down the role of their country managers within the organization, with power being transferred to a new breed, the "product champion." Often these days, country managers fulfill administrative duties and are described as "hotel managers." Companies such as P&G and Dow Chemical created global business divisions to handle investment strategic decisions. Oracle cut down its country managers to size when the company realized that its country-based organization had become a patchwork of local fiefs that did not communicate with each other: Oracle's logo in France differed from the one in the U.K., global accounts like Michelin were treated as different customers, and so forth.[13] Several forces are held responsible for this shift away from strong country managers:[14]

- The threats posed by global competitors who turn the global marketplace into a global chess game.

- The growing prominence of global customers who often develop their sourcing strategies and make their purchase decisions on a global (or pan-regional) basis.

- The rise of regional trading blocs that facilitate the integration of manufacturing and logistics facilities but also open up arbitrage opportunities for gray marketers.

- Knowledge transparency. The internet and other information technologies allow customers and suppliers to become better informed about products and prices across the globe.

---

[12]Though some of the major MNCs operate in more countries than the number of UN member states.

[13]"From Baron to Hotelier," *The Economist*, May 11, 2002, pp. 57–58.

[14]John A. Quelch, "The new country managers," *McKinsey Quarterly* no. 4 (1992): 155–165.

At the same time, several developments create a need for strong country managers.[15] Nurturing good links with local governments and other entities (e.g., the European Union) becomes increasingly crucial. Local customers still represent the lion's share of most companies' clientele. Local competitors sometimes pose a far bigger threat than global rivals. In many emerging markets, strong local brands (e.g., the Baidu search engine in China; the fast food restaurant Jollibee in the Philippines) often have a much more loyal following than regional or global brands. Many winning new-product or communication ideas come from local markets rather than regional or corporate headquarters. Also, if the role of local management is reduced to pen pushing and paperwork, it becomes harder to hire talented people. For these reasons, several firms have increased the clout of their country managers. A good example is 3M. In 1991, 3M set up 30 product-based units. To cut costs, 3M centralized procurement, production, distribution, and service centers (e.g., human resources). However, a decade later, 3M decided to hand power back to its country managers as they can provide a local perspective on group policies. The country managers also play a valuable role in establishing contacts with local customers and spotting opportunities for new businesses.[16]

To strike the balance between these countervailing forces, country managers of the twenty-first century should fit any of the following five profiles depending on the nature of the local market:[17]

1. The *trader* who establishes a beachhead in a new market or heads a recently acquired local distributor. Traders should have an entrepreneurial spirit. Their roles include sales and marketing, scanning the environment for new ideas, and gathering intelligence on the competition.

2. The *builder* who develops local markets. Builders are entrepreneurs who are willing to be part of regional or global strategy teams.

3. The *cabinet member* who is a team player with profit-and-loss responsibility for a small- to medium-sized country. Teamwork is key here, because marketing efforts may require a great deal of cross-border coordination, especially for global and pan-regional brands. Major strategic decisions are often made at the regional level rather than by the country subsidiary.

4. The *ambassador* who is in charge of large and/or strategic markets. Responsibilities include handling government relations, integrating acquisitions and strategic alliances, and coordinating activities across SBUs. In this role, the country manager can provide hands-on parenting for local markets that need more attention than they can get from the global product division. Ideally a seasoned manager, the ambassador should be somebody who is able to manage a large staff. For instance, Asea Brown Boveri, a Swiss/Swedish consortium, views the tasks of its Asia-based country managers as "to exploit fully the synergies between our businesses in the countries, to develop customer based strategies, to build and strengthen relationships with local customers, governments, and communities."[18]

5. The *representative* in large, mature markets whose tasks include handling government relations and legal compliance and maintaining good relations with large, local customers. Dow Chemical, for example, realized that it needed to have strong local management in Germany who can talk shop with the German government authorities.

Whatever role is decided upon for the country manager, the main requirement is to clearly define the scope of the job. Some companies are now combining the two jobs of country manager

---

[15]John A. Quelch and Helen Bloom, "The return of the country manager," *McKinsey Quarterly* no. 2 (1996): 30–43.
[16]"Country Managers Come Back in from the Cold," *Financial Times*, September 24, 2002.
[17]J. A. Quelch and H. Bloom, "The return of the country manager," pp. 38–39 in Michael Goold and Andrew Campbell, *Designing Effective Organizations* (San Francisco, CA: Jossey-Bass, 2002).
[18]Gordon Redding, "ABB—The battle for the Pacific," *Long Range Planning* 28, no. 1 (1995): 92–94.

Exhibit 16-3 Job Description of Japan Country Manager at Twitter

Responsibilities

- Lead all Twitter business operations in Japan.
- Identify, partner, and collaborate with local strategic partner(s) in Japan to drive higher and sustained adoption for Twitter.
- Work closely with Japanese strategic partner to localize/internationalize the Twitter service.
- Construct a working road map for localization, define hiring plan, and create a dashboard for Twitter usage and trends in Japan.
- Become the go-to person for all matters concerning Japan Twitter strategy, localization road map, and execution.
- Budgetary responsibility and profit/loss leadership over Twitter investments in Japan.
- Liaison between Product and the Japanese Twitter Product, modeling changes and strategies based on analytical reasoning.
- Become a leading and vocal evangelist for the Japanese user base.
- Support the Business Development team in Twitter by identifying, evaluating, and testing revenue-generating strategies for the Japanese Twitter Product.
- Support the internationalization initiatives for Twitter in other regions.

Source: Adapted from twitter.jobscore.com, accessed March 11, 2009.

and product champion.[19] This new breed of hybrid manager, referred to by some as a *country prince*, is based in a country that is seen as strategically important for the product category. Paris-based Nexans, the world's biggest maker of electric cables, adopted this approach. Nexans has three country princes. For instance, one heads the global product division for ship cables and is country manager for South Korea. **Exhibit 16-3** shows the job description for the Japan country manager at Twitter, the San Francisco-based social networking service.

Regional Structures

Many MNCs that do not feel entirely comfortable with a pure country-based organization instead opt for a region-based structure with regional headquarters. A typical structure has divisions for North America, Latin America, Asia-Pacific, and EMEA.[20] To some extent, a regional structure offers a compromise between a completely centralized organization and the country-focused organization. The intent behind most region-based structures is to address two concerns: lack of responsiveness of headquarters to local market conditions and parochialism among local country managers. In more and more industries, markets tend to cluster around regions rather than national boundaries. In some cases, the regions are formal trading blocs like the European Union or NAFTA that allow almost complete free movement of goods across borders. In other cases, the clusters tend to be more culture-driven.

A survey done in the Asia-Pacific region singles out five distinct roles for regional headquarters (RHQs):[21]

1. **Scouting.** The RHQ serves as a listening post to scan new opportunities and initiate new ventures.

2. **Strategic stimulation.** The RHQ functions as a "switchboard" between the product divisions and the country managers. It helps the SBUs in understanding the regional environment.

---

[19]"The Country Prince Comes of Age," *Financial Times* (August 9, 2005): 7.

[20]Europe, the Middle East, and Africa.

[21]Philippe Lasserre, "Regional headquarters: The spearhead for Asia Pacific markets," *Long Range Planning* 29 (February 1996): 30–37.

3. **Signaling commitment.** By establishing an RHQ, the MNC signals a commitment to the region that the company is serious about doing business there.

4. **Coordination.** Often the most important role of the RHQ is to coordinate strategic and tactical decisions across the region. Areas of cohesion include developing pan-regional campaigns in regions with a lot of media overlap; price coordination, especially in markets where parallel imports pose a threat; consolidation of manufacturing; and logistics operations.

5. **Pooling resources.** Certain support and administrative tasks are often done more efficiently at the regional level instead of locally. RQH might fulfill support functions like after-sales services, product development, and market research.

Matrix Structure

Imposing a single-dimensional (product-, country-, or function-based) management structure on complex global issues is often a recipe for disaster. In the wake of the serious shortcomings of the geographic or product-based structures, several MNCs have opted for a matrix organization. The matrix structure explicitly recognizes the multi-dimensional nature of global strategic decision making. With a matrix organization, two dimensions are integrated in the organization. For instance, the matrix might consist of geographic areas and business divisions. The geographic units are in charge for all product lines within their area. The product divisions have worldwide responsibility for their product line. As a result, the chain of command is often dual with managers reporting to two superiors. **Exhibit 16-4** shows an example of a matrix-like organization. Sometimes, the MNC might even set up a three-dimensional structure (geography, function, and business area). The various dimensions do not always carry equal weight. For instance, at Siemens the locus of control is shifting more and more toward the business areas, away from the geographic areas.

The matrix structure has two major advantages.[22] First, matrices reflect the growing complexities of the global market arena. In most industries MNCs face global *and* local competitors; global *and* local customers; global *and* local distributors. In that sense, the matrix structure facilitates the MNC's need to "think globally and act locally"—to be glocal—or, in Unilever's terminology, to be a multi-local multinational. The other appeal of the matrix organization is that, in principle at least, it fosters a team spirit and cooperation among business area managers, country managers, and/or functional managers on a global basis.

In spite of these benefits, companies, such as BP and Philips have disbanded their matrix structure. Others, such as IBM and Dow Chemical, have streamlined their matrix setup.[23] Matrix structures have lost their appeal among many MNCs for several reasons. Dual (or triple) reporting and profit responsibilities frequently lead to conflicts or confusion. For instance, a product division might concentrate its resources and attention on a few major markets, thereby upsetting the country managers of the MNC's smaller markets. Another shortcoming of the matrix is bureaucratic bloat. Very often, the decision-making process gets bogged down, thereby discouraging swift responsiveness toward competitive attacks in the local markets. Overlap among divisions often triggers tension, power clashes, and turf battles.[24]

The four organizational structures that we covered so far are the standard structures adopted by most MNCs. The simplicity of the one-dimensional structures and the shortcomings of the matrix model have led several companies to look for better solutions. Below, we discuss one of the more popular forms: the **networked organization**.

---

[22]Thomas H. Naylor, "The international strategy matrix," *Columbia Journal of World Business* (Summer 1985): 11–19.

[23]"End of a corporate era," *Financial Times,* March 30, 1995, p. 15.

[24]Christopher A. Bartlett and Sumantra Ghoshal, "Matrix management, not a structure, a frame of mind," *Harvard Business Review* (July–August 1990): 138–45.

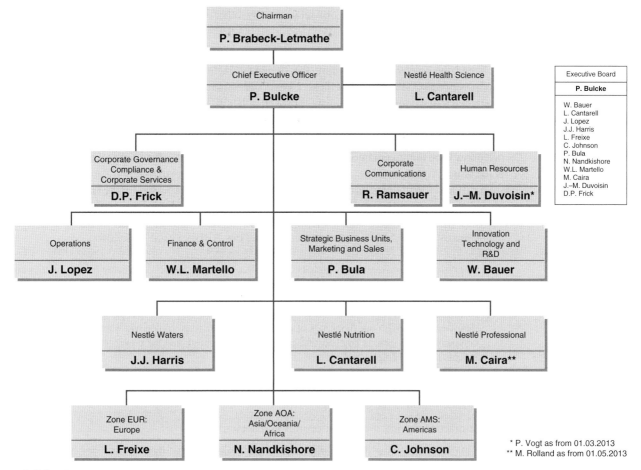

Exhibit 16-4 Nestle's Organizational Setup

Source: http://www.nestle.com/asset-library/Documents/Library/Documents/Corporate_Governance/Oganisation_generale_externe_december_2012.pdf, accessed January 31, 2013.

The Global Network Solution

Global networking is one solution that has been suggested to cope with the shortcomings associated with the classical hierarchical organization structures. The network model is an attempt to reconcile the tension between two opposing forces: the need for local responsiveness and the wish to be an integrated whole.[25] Strictly speaking, the network approach is not a formal structure but a mindset. That is, a company might still formally adopt, say, a matrix structure, but at the same time develop a global network. The networked global organization is sometimes also referred to as a **transnational**.[26] Several features characterize network structures:

- There is much less power at the center of the network than at the top of a hierarchical structure. Ideally, decisions are made through collaboration instead of being imposed from the top.

- Units relate as equals in status and power even though they fulfill different roles.

[25]Christopher A. Bartlett and Sumantra Ghoshal, "Organizing for Worldwide Effectiveness: The Transnational Solution," *California Management Review* (Fall 1988): 54–74.

[26]Christopher A. Bartlett and Sumantra Ghoshal, "Organizing for Worldwide Effectiveness: The Transnational Solution."

- The units that form the network relate to any other unit as necessary; they have multiple relationships.

- Within a network, units of similar size or function can perform very different tasks. They may change the role they play within the organization in response to local market needs and opportunities.[27] Flexibility is key. Networked organizations employ a wide portfolio of strategies and approaches so that they can quickly learn and grasp new opportunities in different regional markets.[28]

According to advocates of the network model, MNCs should develop processes and linkages that allow each unit to tap into a global knowledge pool. A good metaphor for the global network is the atom. At the center is a common knowledge base. Each national unit can be viewed as a source of ideas, skills, capabilities, and knowledge that can be harnessed for the benefit of the total organization.[29] Asea Brown Boveri (ABB), the Swiss-Swedish engineering consortium, is often touted as a prime example of a global networking.[30] Percy Barnevik, former CEO and one of the major forces behind ABB's transformation, describes ABB's vision as follows:

> Our vision was to create a truly global company that knows no borders, has many home countries and offers opportunities for all nationalities. While we strived for size to benefit from economies of scale and scope, our vision was also to avoid the stigma of the big company with a large headquarters and stifling bureaucracy, countless volumes of instructions, turf defenders and people working far from their customers. With our thousands of profit centers close to customers we wanted to create a small company culture with its huge advantages of flexibility, speed, and the power to free up the creative potential of each employee.[31]

Some sample mechanisms to foster cross-border organizational integration without full centralization include the following:

- Best-practice sharing via formal or informal networks.

- Rotating key people within functions from one country to another.

- Training managers who can hold responsibilities over and above those of their main job.

- Developing common work patterns and ethics that facilitate cross-border cooperation. ABB, for instance, uses a company "bible" to tie together the different units within its organization. Its bible describes the firm's mission and values, long-term objectives, and guidelines on how to behave internally.[32] Another well-known example is "The Toyota Way."

- Creating a corporate academy. McDonald's "Hamburger University,"[33] which was founded in 1961, is a celebrated example.[34]

Technological advances have also spurred the creation of so-called virtual teams within more and more companies. Spread around the globe, these teams communicate through e-mail, Skype,

---

[27]David Arnold, *The Mirage of Global Markets. How Globalizing Companies Can Succeed as Markets Localize* (Upper Saddle River, NJ: Pearson Education, 2004), pp. 200–201.

[28]"Do Multinationals Really Understand Globalization?" http://www.businessweek.com, accessed October 16, 2010.

[29]Christopher A. Bartlett, "Building and Managing the Transnational: The New Organizational Challenge," in *Competition in Global Industries*, Michael E. Porter, ed. (Boston: Harvard Business School Press, 1986), pp. 367–401.

[30]William Taylor, "The Logic of Global Business: An Interview with ABB's Percy Barnevik," *Harvard Business Review* (March–April 1991): 91–105.

[31]Asea Brown Boveri, *1995 Annual Report*, p. 5.

[32]Manfred F.R. Kets de Vries," Making a Giant Dance," *Across the Board* (October 1994): 27–32.

[33]See http://www.aboutmcdonalds.com/mcd/corporate_careers/training_and_development/hamburger_university.html.

[34]Giancarlo Ghislanzoni, Risto Penttinen, and David Turnbull, "The Multilocal Challenge: Managing Cross-border Functions," *McKinsey Quarterly* no. 2 (2008): 70–81.

Exhibit 16-5   Guidelines on Global Virtual Teamwork

Tips for Top Performance

- Start with face-to-face meeting to kick off trust building.
- Keep the team as small as practical
- Have a code of practice on how to communicate and behave (e.g., how to respond to e-mails)
- Communicate regularly, but don't overdo it
- Ensure everyone understands each other's role
- Have a supportive sponsor who represents their interests at a senior level within the organization.
- Keep strong links with the parent organization.
- Reward results, not how people work.

Source: " 'Virtual Teams' Endeavor to Build Trust," *Financial Times*, September 9, 2004, p. 8.

or video conferences rather than on a face-to-face basis. **Exhibit 16-5** lists guidelines for global virtual teams to be effective.

Organizing for Global Brand Management

Global branding is the rage for more and more companies. However, to foster and nurture global brands, companies often find it useful to put organizational mechanisms in place. This is especially so for decentralized companies where local decisions involve global branding strategies. Several options exist: (1) a global branding committee, (2) a brand champion, (3) global brand manager, and (4) informal, ad hoc brand meetings. Let us look at each one of these in detail.

Global Branding Committee

Global branding committees are usually made up of top-line executives from corporate (or regional) headquarters and local subsidiaries. Their charter is to integrate and steer global and local branding strategies. Visa International's "Global Branding Marketing Group" exemplifies this approach.[35] The group's goal is to establish better communications among regions and to leverage global media buying power. It is made up of the heads of marketing from each region. HP created a "Global Brand Steering Committee" in 1998. Its primary tasks include brand positioning and vision.[36]

Brand Champion

The **brand champion** is a top-line executive (sometimes a CEO) who serves as the brand's advocate.[37] The approach works well for companies whose senior executives have a passion and expertise for branding. One practitioner of brand championship is Nestlé. The company has a brand champion for each of its 12 corporate strategic brands. The brand champion approves all brand and line extension decisions,[38] monitors the presentation of the brand worldwide, and spreads insights on best practices within the organization.[39]

---

[35]"U.S. Multinationals," *Advertising Age International* (June 1999): 44.

[36]Ibid.

[37]David A. Aaker and Erich Joachimsthaler, "The Lure of Global Branding," *Harvard Business Review* (Nov.-Dec. 1999): 142.

[38]A brand extension is using the same brand for a new product in another product category; a line extension is launching new varieties (e.g., a new flavor, a new package format) of the brand within the same product category.

[39]Ibid., p. 142.

Global Brand Manager

The **global brand manager** is a steward of the brand whose main responsibility is to integrate branding efforts across countries and combat local biases. In the corporate hierarchy, the position is usually just below top-line executives. The position is most suitable for organizations where top management lacks marketing expertise, as is often the case with high-tech firms. For the global brand manager to be effective, the following conditions should hold:[40]

- Commitment to branding at the top of the organization. Top-line executives—though most likely lacking a marketing background—should share the vision and a belief in strong branding.

- Need to create and manage a solid strategic planning process. Country managers should adopt the same format, vocabulary, and planning cycle.

- Need to travel to learn about local management and best practices and to meet local customers and/or distributors.

- Need for a system to identify, mentor, and train prospects that can fill the role.

Informal, Ad Hoc Branding Meetings

Even if for some reason a company decides against a formal structure, it could still find it worthwhile to have informal mechanisms to guide global branding decisions. This usually takes the form of ad-hoc branding meetings. A good example is Abbott International, a U.S.-based pharmaceutical company. Whenever a new product is planned, international executives meet with local staff to discuss the global brand. The ad-hoc committee reviews patents and trademarks for each country to decide whether or not to use the U.S. name in the other countries.[41]

Life Cycle of Organizational Structures

In December 2008 Dell announced plans to reorganize the company around three major customer segments: namely, (1) large enterprise, (2) public (government, education, health care, and the environment), and (3) small and medium businesses. According to Michael Dell, the changeover resulted from listening to customers and responding to their desire for faster innovation and globally standardized products and services: "Customer requirements are increasingly being defined by how they use technology rather than where they use it. That's why we won't let ourselves be limited by geographic boundaries in solving their needs."[42] Organization structures are not set in stone. Change occurs and is not always welcomed by the local staff. Companies need to adapt their organization for several reasons.[43] First, existing structures may have become too rigid or complex with too many divisions and layers of management. A second reason is that the environment changes. To cope with these dynamics, the organization may need an overhaul. Third, managers learn new skills, or new senior management is brought in from outside the firm. Fad-prone managers are often attracted to new theories or paradigms, regardless of whether they actually serve the organization's purpose. Fourth, a key event such as a merger or major acquisition could force a company to rethink its organizational structure. A good example is Lenovo's takeover of IBM's PC division. The acquisition meant a higher emphasis for Lenovo on international markets and the corporate segment, and led to an overhaul of its organization.

---

[40]Ibid., p. 142.

[41]"U.S. Multinationals," p. 44.

[42]http://www.dell.com/content/topics/global.aspx/corp/pressoffice/en/2008/2008_12_31_rr_000?c = us&l = en&s = corp.

[43]Michael Goold and Andrew Campbell, *Designing Effective Organizations* (San Francisco: Jossey-Bass, 2002), pp. 88–89.

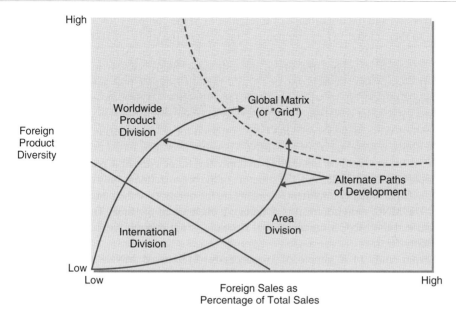

Exhibit 16-6
Stopford-Wells
International
Structural Stages
Model

Source: Reprinted by permission of Harvard Business School Press. From Christopher A. Barlett, "Building and Managning the Transnational: The New Organizational Challenge," in *Competition in Global Industries*, ed. M.E. Porter (Boston, MA: Harvard University Presss, 1987), p. 368. Copyright (c) 1986 by the President and Fellows of Harvard College.

Finally, the pursuit of new strategic opportunities or directions often demands a change in the organization.

Regardless of the reasons, successful restructuring takes time, planning, and resources. Change may imply new relationships, new responsibilities, or even downsizing. Not surprisingly, restructuring is often met with resistance by employees who think they "know better." Hence, apart from the "physical" changes, restructuring often requires a fundamental cultural change.[44]

In some cases companies have moved from one extreme to another before finding a suitable configuration. A case in point is Kraft General Foods Europe (KGFE).[45] In the early 1980s, KGFE tried to impose uniform marketing strategies across Europe. This attempt led to so much ill will among KGFE's local units that Kraft soon abandoned its centralized system. It was replaced by a loose system where country managers developed their own marketing strategies for all Kraft brands, including the regional (e.g., Miracoli pasta) and global brands (e.g., Philadelphia cream cheese). Not surprisingly, this system created a great deal of inconsistency in the marketing strategies used. In the 1990s Kraft was split into a North American and an international division with two chief executives, though the biggest product categories had "global councils" to cover best practices. Still, Kraft was struggling. In 2004, the dual structure was swept away in order to make Kraft truly global, cut costs, and ramp up innovation. The overhaul led to the creation of five global product units (beverages, snacks, cheese and dairy, convenient meals, and grocery) backed by two regional commercial units (one for North America, one for everywhere else). Kraft also set up global units handling support functions such as supply chain and product development.[46]

Several management theorists have made an attempt to come up with the "right" fit between the MNC's environment (internal and external) and the organizational setup. One of the more popular schemas is the stages model shown in **Exhibit 16-6**, which was developed by Stopford and Wells.[47] The schema shows the relationship between organizational structure, foreign

---

[44]"Be Principled for a Change," *Financial Times*, August 23, 2004, p. 9.
[45]"Cross-border Kraftsmen," *Financial Times*, June 17, 1993.
[46]"Search for the Right Ingredients," *Financial Times*, October 7, 2004, p. 8.
[47]John M. Stopford and Louis T. Wells, Jr., *Managing the Multinational Enterprise: Organization of the Firm and Ownership of the Subsidiary* (New York: Basic Books, 1972).

product diversity, and the importance of foreign sales to the company (as a share of total sales). According to their model, when companies first explore the global marketplace they start off with an international division. As foreign sales expand without an increase in the firm's foreign product assortment diversity, the company will most likely switch to a geographic area structure. If instead the diversity of the firm's foreign product line substantially increases, it might organize itself along global product lines. Finally, when both product diversity and international sales grow significantly, MNCs tend to adopt a two-dimensional matrix structure.

The Stopford-Wells staged model has been criticized for several reasons. First, the model is a purely descriptive representation of how MNCs develop over time based on an analysis of U.S.-based MNCs. So, it would be misleading to apply the framework in a prescriptive manner, as several people have done.[48] Second, the structure of the organization is only one aspect of a global organization. Other, equally important, elements are the mindsets of the managers and managerial processes. The MNC's environment is dynamic; it changes all the time. Thus, a fit between the environment and the MNC's organizational structure is not enough. Global organizations also need flexibility.[49]

An in-depth study of a sample of 10 successful U.S.-based MNCs showed that the key challenge for MNCs is building and sustaining the right management process instead of looking for the proper organizational structure.[50] According to the study, the installation of such a process moves through three stages. The first step is to recognize the complexity of the MNC's environment. Country and regional managers must look at strategic issues from multiple perspectives—a **glocal mindset**, so to speak. During the second stage, the company introduces communication channels and decision-making platforms to facilitate more flexibility. In the final stage, the MNC develops a corporate culture that fosters collaborative thinking and decision making. Such an agenda could include activities such as formulating common goals and values, developing reward systems and evaluation criteria that encourage a cooperative spirit, and providing role models.

Control of Global Marketing Efforts

To make global marketing strategies work, companies need to establish a control system. The main purpose of controls is to ensure that the behaviors of the various parties within the organization are in line with the company's strategic goals. We will first concentrate on formal control methods. We will then turn to less formal means to implement control: establishing a corporate culture and management development.

Formal ("Bureaucratic") Control Systems

Any formal control system consists of basically three building blocks: (1) the establishment of performance standards, (2) the measurement and evaluation of performance against standards, and (3) the analysis and correction of deviations from standards.

Establishing Standards (Metrics)

The first step of the control process is to set standards (metrics). These standards should be driven by the company's corporate goals. There are essentially two types of standards: behavior- and

[48]Christopher A. Bartlett, "Building and Managing the Transnational: The New Organizational Challenge," in *Competition in Global Industries*, M.E. Porter, ed. (Boston: Harvard Business School Press, 1986), pp. 367–401.

[49]Sumantra Ghoshal and Nitin Nohria, "Horses for courses: Organizational Forms for Multinational Corporations," *Sloan Management Review* (Winter 1993): 23–35.

[50]Christopher A. Bartlett, "MNCs: Get off the reorganization merry-go-round," *Harvard Business Review* (March–April 1983): 138–146.

outcome-based. Behavior-based control involves specifying the actions that are necessary to achieve good performance. Managers are told through manuals/policies how to respond to various scenarios. Rewards are based on whether the observed behavior matches the prescribed behavior. Examples of behavior-based standards include distribution coverage, branding policies, pricing rules, and R&D spending. Output-based control depends on specific standards that are objective, reliable, and easy to measure. Outcome standards focus on very specific outcome-oriented measures such as profit-loss statements, return on investment (ROI), market share, sales, and customer satisfaction.

When applied too rigorously, behavior-based standards restrain local management's ability to respond effectively to local market conditions. An example is Johnson & Johnson's experience in the Philippines.[51] In the early 1990s, J&J's managers found out that young Philippine women used J&J's baby talcum to freshen their makeup. To cater toward their needs, local management developed a compact holder for the talcum powder. However, a few days before the planned launch of the new product, corporate headquarters asked the local managers to drop the product, claiming that the cosmetics business is not a core business for J&J. Only after the local marketing head made a personal plea for the product at J&J's headquarters was the subsidiary given the green light. The product became a big hit, though it was never launched in other markets because J&J did not want to run the risk of being perceived as a cosmetics maker. Output-based standards such as profits can also create problems. For instance, a change in the company's transfer pricing rules[52] could distort profits of the local subsidiary, even though its performance does not change.[53] Likewise, a high sales volume target could encourage a country subsidiary to get involved with the gray market in order to boost its numbers.

For most companies, the two types of standards matter. Here is a simple illustration. Imagine that headquarters wants country A to increase its market share by 3 percentage points over a one-year period. Country A could take different approaches to achieve this target. One path is to do a lot of promotional activities—couponing, price promotions, trade deals, and so on. Another route is to spend more on advertising. Both paths could achieve the desired outcome. However, with the first option—heavy dealing—the company risks tarnishing its brand image. With the second option, the subsidiary would invest in brand equity. Thus, the same outcome can be realized through two totally different behaviors, one of which can ruin the long-term viability of the company's brand assets.

Ideally, standards are developed via a bottom-up and top-down planning process of listening, reflecting, dialoguing, and debating between headquarters and the local units. Standards should also strike a delicate balance between long- and short-term priorities.[54]

Measuring and Evaluating Performance

Formal control systems also need mechanisms to monitor and evaluate performance. The actual performance is compared against the established standards. In many instances, it is fairly straightforward to measure performance, especially when the standards are based on within-country results. To make global or pan-regional strategies work, MNCs also need to assess and reward individual managers' contributions to the "common good." For example, two-thirds of the bonuses payable to Unilever's senior executives in Europe are driven by Unilever's performance in that region.[55] In practice, however, it is tremendously hard to gauge managers' contributions to the regional or global well-being of the firm.

---

[51]Niraj Dawar and Tony Frost, "Competing with Giants: Survival Strategies for Local Companies in Emerging Markets," *Harvard Business Review* (March–April 1999): 119–129.

[52]The transfer price is the price charged by one country subsidiary to another country affiliate for delivered goods or services to that affiliate (see also Chapter 12).

[53]Robert D. Hamilton III, Virginia A. Taylor, and Roger J. Kashlak, "Designing a Control System for a Multinational Subsidiary," *Long Range Planning* 29, no. 6 (1996): 857–868.

Analyzing and Correcting Deviations

The third element is to analyze deviations from the standards and, if necessary, make the necessary corrections. If actual performance does not meet the set standard, the company needs to analyze the cause behind the divergence. If necessary, corrective measures will be taken. This part of the control system also involves devising the right incentive mechanisms—checks and balances—that make subsidiary managers "tick." While proper reward systems are crucial to motivate subsidiary managers, one study has shown the key role played by the presence of due process.[56] Due process encompasses five features: (1) the head office should be familiar with the subsidiaries' local situation; (2) global strategy development should involve a two-way communication; (3) the head office is relatively consistent in making decisions across local units; (4) local units can legitimately challenge headquarters' strategic views and decisions; and (5) subsidiary units receive explanations for final strategic decisions.

Informal Control Methods

Apart from formal control mechanisms, most MNCs also establish informal control methods. Below we cover the two most common informal control tools, namely, corporate culture and human resource development.

Corporate Culture

For many MNCs with operations scattered all over the globe, shared cultural values are often a far more effective "glue" to bond subsidiaries than formal bureaucratic control tools. Corporate cultures can be clan-based or market-based.[57] **Clan cultures** have the following distinguishing features: they embody a long socialization process; strong, powerful norms; and a well-defined set of internalized controls. **Market cultures** are the opposite: norms are loose or absent; socialization processes are limited; and control systems are purely based on performance measures. For most global organizations where integration is an overriding concern, a clan-like culture is instrumental in creating a shared vision.

Corporate values are more than slogans that embellish the company's annual report. To shape a shared vision, cultural values should have three properties:[58]

1. **Clarity.** The stated values should be simple, relevant, and concrete.

2. **Continuity.** Values should be stable over time and long-term-oriented, not flavor-of-the-month—type values.

3. **Consistency.** To avoid confusion, everyone within the organization should share the same vision. Everybody should speak the same language. Everyone should pursue the same agenda.

Human Resource Development

Another major informal control tool is a company's program for management development. These programs have three critical roles.[59] First and foremost, training programs can help managers worldwide in understanding the MNC's mission and vision and their part in pursuing them.

---

[56]W. Chan Kim and Renée A. Mauborgne, "Making Global Strategies Work," *Sloan Management Review* (Spring 1993): 11–24.

[57]David Lei, John W. Slocum, Jr., and Robert W. Slater, "Global Strategy and Reward Systems: The Key Roles of Management Development and Corporate Culture," *Organizational Dynamics* (Winter 1989): 27–41.

[58]Christopher A. Bartlett and Sumantra Ghoshal, "Matrix Management: Not a Structure, a Frame of Mind," *Harvard Business Review* (July–August 1990): 138–145.

[59]David Lei and colleagues, "Global Strategy and Reward Systems: The Key Roles of Management Development and Corporate Culture," p. 39.

Second, such programs can speed up the transfer of new values when changes in the company's environment dictate a "new" corporate mentality. Finally, they can also prove fruitful in allowing managers from all over the world to share their best practices and success stories.

"Soft" versus "Hard" Levers

A joint research project conducted by the Stanford Business School and McKinsey aimed to uncover what sort of tools multinationals rely on to resolve global vs. local tensions.[60] The project, dubbed the "Globe Project," studied 16 multinational companies through in-depth interviews, questionnaires, and network analysis. Based on company interviews, the researchers identified seven management tools or "levers" that companies use to resolve the global/local trade-offs:

1. *Organizational structure*. Creating formal positions and lines of authority.

2. *Process*. Defining workflows and procedures.

3. *Incentives*. Reward systems that encourage outcomes in line with the desired balance between global and local priorities.

4. *Metrics*. Measurement systems that focus on desired outcomes.

5. *Strategy*. The extent to which the central strategy guides local decisions.

6. *Networks*. Building personal relationships that help resolve disputes and encourage sharing of knowledge and resources.

7. *Culture*. Shared values that encourage a common approach among all members of the organization.

As you can see, there is some overlap between these levers and the control methods we discussed earlier. Three of the tools—process, incentives, and metrics—are hard levers; three other tools—strategy, networks, and culture—are soft levers (formal versus informal methods). Structure is a hybrid. The study scored each company that participated in the project on each of these levers. Depending on the score, a company could be classified as a "hard" or "soft" firm. 3M, the conglomerate with its unique innovation culture, leans very heavily toward soft levers. Toyota, on the other hand, with its heavy focus on quality control, is a prototypical "hard" company.

---

[60]"Corporations with Hard and Soft Centres," *Financial Times*, February 20, 2002, p. 11.

SUMMARY

Running a multinational organization is a tremendous challenge. Local managers need empowerment so that the local unit is able to respond rapidly and effectively to local market threats, grab opportunities, and stay in tune with local market developments. Yet, a "laissez-faire" situation will easily evolve into a patchwork of local barons who will inevitably jeopardize the interests of the group as a whole. Too much centralization, however, will straitjacket the country manager, create resentment, and stifle local creativity and responsiveness. This global (integration, scale) versus local (market responsiveness) tension needs to be addressed. In this chapter, we discussed the structures and control mechanisms that MNCs can use to shape a global organization. Companies can pick from a variety of structures, ranging from a single international division to a global network operation. Formal and informal (culture, management development) control mechanisms are available to run global operations. However, the dynamics of the global marketing arena mean that building a global organization is much more than just choosing the "right" organizational configuration and control systems. Global players constantly need to reflect on how to strike the balance between centralization *and* decentralization, local responsiveness *and* global integration, center *and* periphery. As with many other challenges in global marketing, there are no one-size-fits-all solutions. In their search for the proper structure and strategic coherence, countless MNCs have come up with schemes that led to confusion, frustration, and ill will among subsidiary managers. We can, however, offer some pieces of advice, though:

- **Recognize the need for business asymmetry.** Due to relentless environmental changes, power sharing between the center and the periphery will vary over time, over business units, and even across activities (product development, advertising, pricing) within business units. Different business units within the organization have different needs for responsiveness and global coordination.[61] Especially widely diversified companies should recognize that each business unit needs a different format, depending on its particular circumstances and needs. For instance, Asea Brown Boveri has businesses that are superlocal (e.g., electrical installation) and superglobal (e.g., power plant projects). P&G's model treats countries differently based on their income. In high-income countries, the business unit is in charge of resource allocation; in low-income countries (e.g., China, Eastern Europe) the region is responsible. The reason is that low-income countries are more challenging and less-familiar business environments. However, the global product unit makes production and marketing decisions for products such as Pantene shampoo, which are global in nature—in terms of consumer buying habits and usage.[62]

- **Adopt a bottom-up approach.** Getting the balance right also requires democracy. When building up a global organization, make sure that every country subsidiary has a "voice." Subsidiaries of small countries should not be concerned about getting pushed over by their bigger counterparts.

- **Importance of a shared vision.** Getting the organizational structure right—the "arrows" and "boxes" so to speak—is important. Far more critical, though, is the organizational "psychology."[63] People are key in building an organization. Having a clear and consistent corporate vision is a major ingredient in getting people excited about the organization. To instill and communicate corporate values, companies should also have human resource development mechanisms in place that will facilitate the learning process.

- **Invest heavily in horizontal communication channels and information flows.** Very often multinational corporations focus primarily on vertical communication channels going from the country unit to corporate (or regional) headquarters but neglect horizontal information flows among the different country affiliates. As a result, country units become isolated and try to achieve their own profit goals instead of the overall company profit.[64]

- **Ensure that somebody has a global overview of each product line or brand.** Global oversight of a product line or brand is needed to facilitate transfer of learning and knowledge among markets and to leverage new product and marketing mix programs. The central hub could be corporate or regional headquarters or the lead market with the category's most sophisticated customers and/or distributors and in which most product innovations debut.[65] Lenovo's global marketing hub is located in Bangalore: Lenovo's India team develops global marketing campaigns targeted for dozens of countries, including the United States, France, and Brazil.

- **Need for a good mix of specialists of three types—country, functional, business.** There is no such a thing as a transnational manager. Companies should breed specialists of three different kinds: country, functional, and global business (SBU). Country managers in particular—once feared to become part of the endangered species list—play a key role. As we discussed earlier in this chapter, the country manager's skills and role will differ from country to country. Some subsidiaries need a "trader"; others need an "ambassador."

- **Moving unit headquarters abroad seldom solves the organization's problems.** In recent years, several companies (e.g., IBM, HP, and Siemens) have moved business unit headquarters abroad. Several of these moves were done for very sensible reasons: getting closer to the customer or supplier, being in the big guys' backyard, cutting costs. For instance, the Japanese company Hoya, one of the world's largest makers of spectacle lenses, moved the headquarters of its vision care business to the Netherlands. The move was prompted by Europe's technological prowess in this sector.[66] Unfortunately, in many cases the relocation typically turns out to be mere window-dressing in a drive to become more global-oriented. Sometimes transfers can even be counterproductive, weakening the corporate identity or the "authenticity" of the brand when it is strongly linked to the firm's home country.[67]

[61]"Fashionable federalism," *Financial Times*, December 18, 1992.

[62]"From Baron to Hotelier," *The Economist*, May 11, 2002, pp. 57–58.

[63]Christopher A. Bartlett and Sumantra Ghoshal, "Matrix Management: Not a Structure, a Frame of Mind," *Harvard Business Review* (July-August 1990): 138–145.

[64]David Arnold, *The Mirage of Global Markets. How Globalizing Companies Can Succeed as Markets Localize* (Upper Saddle River, NJ: Pearson, 2004), pp. 205–206.

[65]Ibid.

[66]"A European Move with Global Vision," *Financial Times*, January 12, 2006, p. 10.

[67]"Home Is Not Always Where the Heart Is," *Financial Times*, January 10, 2005, p. 6.

QUESTIONS

1. Describe how external environmental drivers influence the organizational design decision.

2. What mechanisms can companies use to foster a global corporate culture?

3. In his book, *The End of the Nation State* (New York: The Free Press, 1995), Kenichi Ohmae makes the following observations about country-based organization structures:

> One of the prime difficulties of organizing a company for global operations is the psychology of managers who are used to thinking by country-based line of authority rather than by line of opportunity. Lots of creative ideas for generating value are overlooked because such managers are captive to nation-state–conditioned habits of mind. Once that constraint is relaxed . . . a nearly infinite range of new opportunities comes into focus: building cross-border alliances, establishing virtual companies, arbitraging differential costs of labor or even services. . . . I strongly believe that, as head-to-head battles within established geographies yield less and less incremental value, changing the battleground from nation to cross-border region will be at the core of 21st-century corporate strategy.

Do you agree or disagree with these comments? Why?

17 MARKETING IN EMERGING MARKETS

CHAPTER OVERVIEW

1. Emerging markets

2. Competing with the new champions

3. Targeting/positioning strategies in emerging markets—BOP or no BOP?

4. Entry strategies for emerging markets

5. Product policy

6. Pricing strategy

7. The distribution challenge

8. Communication strategies for emerging markets

As developed countries are getting saturated, multinationals have increasingly set their sights on the fast-growing emerging markets (EMs) in Asia, Latin America, the former Eastern Bloc countries, and Africa. McDonald's restaurant in central Moscow's Pushkin Square is the chain's busiest one in the world.[1] Mars sells more cat food in Russia than anywhere else in the world.[2] Russia has also become the largest market for Danish beer brewer Carlsberg, accounting for nearly 40 percent of both sales and profits.[3] Jakarta, the capital of Indonesia, has more BlackBerry users than anywhere else in the world.[4] Otis, the world's leading manufacturer of escalators and elevators, moved its business development office from Connecticut to China, because elevator sales there dwarf the entire North American market.[5] China passed the United States in 2009 to become the world's largest car market and still has room to grow. While 627 in 1,000 in the U.S. market own a car, according to the World Bank, in China, the car ownership is merely 44 in 1,000. GM, already the top foreign car maker in China, hopes to increase sales by about 75 percent by 2015 to $5 million.[6] China's vehicle market has also expanded rapidly at the top end. Of the 1,602 Lamborghinis sold worldwide in 2011, 342 were in China, where a top-of-the-line model starts at about $1 million.[7]

---

[1]"Russia's Consumers Come of Age," www.ft.com, accessed April 2, 2009.
[2]"Brands Make a Dash into Russia," www.ft.com, accessed April 2, 2009.
[3]"Carlsberg: Trouble Brewing in Russia," http://www.ft.com, accessed September 27, 2012.
[4]"The N11 in Focus," *Campaign Asia-Pacific* (February 2011): 38–41.
[5]"Ready for Takeoff," *Forbes Asia* (February 2013): 24–26.
[6]"GM Said to Seek Deals in China to Reach 5 Million Goal," http://www.bloomberg.com, accessed February 6, 2013.
[7]"China Learns 'Lamborghini Way,'" *Advertising Age*, December 10, 2012, p. 22.

Given their growing middle classes and rising incomes, the siren call of emerging markets is hard to resist. Several large Western multinationals now derive the bulk of their revenues from such markets. The global economic downturn has spurred companies even more to explore prospects in that part of the globe. Still, MNCs face daunting obstacles when doing business in these countries. At the same time, a more recent phenomenon has been the steady but undeniable emergence of strong local companies. Several of these firms have been able to prove their mettle in competing with the big multinationals in their home countries. In this chapter we focus on emerging markets. We first highlight the key characteristics of emerging markets. We then turn to the competitive landscape: we look at how companies from these countries have been able to compete successfully against the big multinationals in their home markets and also in the global market place. Next we explore targeting and positioning strategies for emerging markets. In particular, we discuss strategies to reach the so-called bottom-of-the-pyramid segments. The remainder of the chapter examines how the characteristics of emerging markets can influence marketing strategies.

Emerging Markets
Definition

The term **emerging markets** (EMs) refers to economies that are in the process of rapid growth and industrialization.[8] The "emerging markets" moniker was first introduced in 1981 by Antoine van Agtmael at an investor conference in Thailand. Van Agtmael, who at that time was a deputy director at the World Bank's IFC, thought that the term would resonate more with prospective investors in Thailand than the "Third World" label. Today it is not entirely clear which countries qualify as emerging markets. Loosely speaking, the countries that fall under the rubric are those that can be neither classified as developing, nor as developed. Morgan Stanley's Emerging Market Index currently consists of 21 countries.[9] The list includes the usual suspects, such as Brazil, China, Indonesia, and India, but also a few countries that could be easily classified as developed economies (e.g., Taiwan, Israel, Korea) given that their per capita income is at least $20,000.[10] The London-based FTSE Group distinguishes between four types of countries, namely: (1) Developed (e.g., most Western countries, Japan, South Korea), (2) Advanced Emerging (e.g., Brazil, Hungary, Mexico, South Africa), (3) Secondary Emerging, which largely overlaps with the MSCI group, and (4) Frontier countries (e.g., Bahrain, Kenya, Serbia, Vietnam). Another term that is gaining some traction is **transition economies**: countries that are changing from a centrally planned economy to a free market economy.[11] The International Monetary Fund classified 25 countries as transition economies. Most of these are countries that belonged to the former Eastern Bloc but the list also includes four Asian countries, namely Cambodia, China, Laos, and Vietnam.[12] However, for the purpose of this chapter we stick with the emerging market label. Among the emerging markets, for many global marketers the most promising and exciting ones are the four that constitute the **BRIC**, namely: Brazil, Russia, India, and China.[13] By 2007, the BRIC nations already accounted for 15 percent of global GDP.[14] Jim O'Neill, a Goldman Sachs

---

[8]http://en.wikipedia.org/wiki/Emerging_markets#cite_note-1, accessed September 23, 2013.

[9]http://www.msci.com/products/indices/country_and_regional/em/, accessed September 23, 2013.

[10]The complete list consists of the following countries: Argentina, Brazil, Chile, China, Colombia, the Czech Republic, Egypt, Hungary, India, Indonesia, Israel, Jordan, Korea, Malaysia, Mexico, Morocco, Pakistan, Peru, Philippines, Poland, Russia, South Africa, Taiwan, Thailand, and Turkey.

[11]http://en.wikipedia.org/wiki/Transition_economy, accessed September 23, 2013.

[12]http://www.imf.org/external/np/exr/ib/2000/110300.htm, accessed September 23, 2013.

[13]The BRIC is a term coined in 2001 by Jim O'Neill, the chief economist at investment bank Goldman Sachs.

[14]"When Are Emerging Markets No Longer 'Emerging,'" knowledge.wharton.upenn.edu, accessed March 19, 2009.

economist who coined the BRIC acronym, predicts that the BRIC economies combined will be larger than the G7, the Group of Seven (G7) industrialized nations,[15] by 2027.[16] In 2005, Goldman Sachs introduced the concept of the **Next Eleven (N-11)**. These are 11 countries that, as the acronym suggests, will follow in the footsteps of the BRIC in rivaling the G7. The eleven countries are a very diverse mix that includes Bangladesh, Egypt, Indonesia, Iran, Mexico, Nigeria, Pakistan, Philippines, South Korea, Turkey, and Vietnam.[17] Although they are grouped together, these countries are at very different levels of economic development.

Characteristics of Emerging Markets

As we hinted above, the term "emerging markets" has lost some of its meaning given the wide mix of countries that are often classified as such. As a result, it is hard to find common ground among emerging markets. Even classifying them as high-growth countries has become questionable in recent years. During the Asian financial crisis in 1997–1998, many of the so-called Asian Tigers stopped roaring. The economies of some of them rebounded a bit after the crisis, but most of them never fully recovered. More recently, the global economic downturn did not spare the emerging markets: except for China and maybe a few other emerging markets, most of their economies became very weak and started submerging with negative growth rates. Still emerging markets share certain characteristics. In particular, they seem to have the following properties:

1. *Low per capita incomes but rapid pace of economic development.* Per capita incomes are still much lower in most EMs than in developed nations (see column 3 of **Exhibit 17-1**). Obviously, low incomes pose an upper limit on purchases. Still, the incomes in most of these countries are surging rapidly, as shown in **Exhibit 17-1** (column 4), leading to a strong and growing middle-class population. Goldman Sachs estimates that the global middle class, defined as people with annual incomes ranging from $6,000 to $30,000, is growing by 70 million per year. The bank foresees that another 2 billion people will join the group by 2030.[18]

2. *High income inequalities.* The last column of **Exhibit 17-1** shows the Gini index, a statistic often used to measure the degree of income inequality in a country. The higher the value of the Gini coefficient, the more income inequality.[19] As you can see, most EM countries register much higher values for the Gini index than developed nations.

3. *Chronic shortage of resources.* Except for mineral-rich countries such as Russia and Brazil, most emerging markets face a shortage of skilled labor, raw materials, and utilities (electricity, running water). As a result production as well as consumption tend to be constrained.[20]

4. *Huge diversity within market.* Many emerging markets, especially the larger ones, are very diverse. India and China are often described as a "collection of countries," not unlike the European Union. In many of these countries huge differences exist between urban and rural areas. While in local villages and small townships, many consumers may be illiterate, big city dwellers are often very sophisticated and comparable in many respects to their counterparts in major Western cities. As a result of these differences, a uniform marketing strategy approach will not work. A solid understanding of local customs and nuances is necessary to succeed.

---

[15]The G7 consists of Canada, France, Germany, Italy, Japan, the United Kingdom, and the United States.

[16]Jim O'Neill, "The New Shopping Superpower," *Newsweek*, March 30, 2009, p. 17.

[17]http://www2.goldmansachs.com/ideas/brics/BRICs-and-Beyond.html.

[18]"The Expanding Middle: The Exploding World Middle Class and Falling Global Inequality," Goldman Sachs, Global Economics Paper No: 170, July 7, 2008.

[19]http://en.wikipedia.org/wiki/Gini_coefficient.

[20]Jagdish N. Sheth, "Impact of Emerging Markets on Marketing: Rethinking Existing Perspectives and Practices," *Journal of Marketing* 74 (July 2011): 166–182.

Exhibit 17-1 Economic and Demographic Comparison of Emerging Markets versus G7 Countries

Countries	Population Growth (2012 est.) (%)	Median Age (2012 est.)	Per Capita GDP—PPP* (2012 est.) (US$)	GDP—Real Growth Rate (2012 est.) (%)	Gini Index
Emerging Market Countries					
Argentina	1.00	30.7	18,200	2.6	45.8 (2009)
Bangladesh	1.58	23.6	2,000	6.1	33.2 (2005)
Brazil	0.86	29.6	12,000	1.3	51.9 (2012)
Burma	1.07	27.2	1,400	6.2	NA
China	0.48	35.9	9,100	7.8	48 (2009)
Colombia	1.13	28.3	10,700	4.3	56 (2010)
Egypt	1.92	24.6	6,600	2	34.4 (2001)
India	1.31	26.5	3,900	5.4	36.8 (2004)
Indonesia	1.03	28.5	5,000	6	36.8 (2009)
Iran	1.25	27.4	13,100	−0.9	44.5 (2006)
Malaysia	1.54	27.1	16,900	4.4	46.2 (2009)
Mexico	1.09	27.4	15,300	3.8	51.7 (2008)
Morocco	1.05	27.3	5,300	2.9	40.9 (2007)
Nigeria	2.55	17.9	2,700	7.1	43.7 (2003)
Pakistan	1.55	21.9	2,900	3.7	30.6 (2008)
Philippines	1.87	23.1	4,300	4.8	45.8 (2006)
Poland	−0.07	38.8	21,000	2.4	34.2 (2008)
Russia	−0.01	38.8	17,700	3.6	42
South Africa	−0.41	25.3	11,300	2.6	65 (2005)
Thailand	0.54	34.7	10,000	5.6	53.6 (2009)
Turkey	1.20	28.8	15,000	3	40.2 (2010)
Vietnam	1.05	28.2	3,500	5.1	37.6 (2008)
G7 countries					
Canada	0.78	41.2	41,500	1.9	32.1 (2005)
France	0.5	40.4	35,500	0.1	32.7 (2008)
Germany	−0.2	45.3	39,100	0.9	27 (2006)
Italy	0.38	43.8	30,100	−2.3	31.9 (2011)
Japan	−0.08	45.4	36,200	2.2	37.6 (2008)
United Kingdom	0.55	40.2	36,700	−0.1	34 (2005)
USA	0.9	37.1	49,800	2.3	45 (2007)

* PPP = Purchasing power parity.

Source: Based on figures reported on https://www.cia.gov/library/publications/the-world-factbook/, accessed February 2, 2013.

5. *Weak and highly variable infrastructure.* The infrastructure (e.g., logistics, distribution, media, banking) in many of the countries is underdeveloped. Transportation networks such as roads, airports, and railroads are low in coverage and fragile. An exception is China, which has a rapidly expanding high-speed railroad network. Likewise, basic utilities such as water supply and electricity are in short supply. Telecommunications networks and internet access often lag far behind the grids of mature markets in terms of coverage and technology.

6. *Unbranded competition.* In many emerging markets, the bulk of consumption is of unbranded services and products.[21] There are three important reasons for this situation. First, many branded goods are still not accessible in rural markets. Second, a household is often not just a consumption unit but also a production unit. Finally, unbranded products are often "good enough" for most consumers. Unilever, for instance, failed to succeed in India's tea market given the prevalence of unbranded loose tea.[22] In many countries, very often the biggest competition comes from the used goods market.

7. *Technology is underdeveloped.* Most of the countries also lag behind mature markets in the area of technology. This is the case both on the supply side (infrastructure, innovation) and the demand side (adoption of new technologies). On the supply side, most R&D spending and innovation are still centered in developed countries. This is especially true in high-tech industries such as information technology, biotech, and telecommunications. However, without the legacy of old technologies, companies doing business in the countries often can leapfrog old technologies. Indeed, one study that analyzed the mobile technology in various countries found that the BRIC countries appear to lead in mobile technology service breadth through innovation and the introduction of a wider variety of services than developed nations.[23]

8. *Weak distribution channels and media infrastructure.* Compared to developed countries, distribution and media infrastructures in EM countries are largely underdeveloped. Especially in rural areas, distribution is often very inefficient. Lack of adequate distribution channels means that companies often have to set up their own distribution. However, the distribution environment is changing dramatically, even in the poorer emerging markets. For instance, the shopping mall phenomenon that originated in the United States is, for better or worse, spreading to scores of emerging markets. Nine of the 10 largest shopping malls in the world are located in emerging markets: four in China, one in Malaysia, one in Turkey (the biggest mall in Europe), and three in the Philippines (see **Exhibit 17-2**).[24] Other infrastructure components (e.g., market research firms, advertising agencies) that support marketers to

Exhibit 17-2 The World's Largest Shopping Malls

Ranking	Name	Location	Gross Leaseable Area (in million sq. feet)	Year Opened
1	South China Mall	Dongguan, China	7.1	2005
2	Golden Resources Shopping Mall	Beijing, China	6.6	2004
3	SM Mall of Asia	Pasay City, Philippines	4.2	2006
4	Cevahir Istanbul	Istanbul, Turkey	3.8	2005
5	West Edmonton Mall	Edmonton, Canada	3.8	1981
6	SM Megamall	Mandaluyong City, Philippines	3.6	1991
7	Berjaya Times Square	Kuala Lumpur, Malaysia	3.4	2005
8	Beijing Mall	Beijing, China	3.4	2005
9	Zhengjia Plaza	Guangzhou, China	3	2005
10	SM City North Edsa	Quezon City, Philippines	3	1985

Source: Compiled from "World's 10 Largest Shopping Malls," www.forbes.com

[21]Jagdish Sheth, "Impact of Emerging Markets," p. 169.

[22]"MNCs Look to Build Real Equity in Rural Market," *Campaign Asia-Pacific* (June 2012): 22–23.

[23]Alina Chircu and Vijay Mahajan, "Revisiting Digital Divide: An Analysis of Mobile Technology Depth and Service Breadth in the BRIC Countries," University of Texas Austin, working paper, 2007.

[24]"The World's Largest Malls," www.forbes.com, accessed March 26, 2009.

Exhibit 17-3   Challenges in Myanmar's Business Environment

- **Electricity shortages and other utility problems.** Inconsistent power supplies interrupt economic activities such as production and sales. Only 34 percent of rural dwellers have access to constant electricity supply. Inadequate water and phone service and slow internet also hamper production.
- **Sheer poverty.** Per capita GDP in 2010 was only $876 according to United Nations statistics.[25] Around a third of Myanmar's population lives below the poverty line. The Asian Development Bank expects that GDP growth to hover around 6 percent in the near future and per capita GDP could reach $2,000 to $3,000 by 2030. Other analysts are more skeptical and think that it will take Myanmar 50 years to catch up with Thailand.
- **Tight import and export controls.** Most imports and exports require licenses. In many sectors, licenses are restricted to those with good government connections. Myanmar places heavy tariffs on many items. Customs officials often refuse to release goods until tariffs and bribes have been paid.
- **Insufficient, sparse, and costly transport infrastructure.** Transport infrastructure in Myanmar is outdated. This increases the time needed to ship goods and raises the costs of doing business in the country.
- **Corruption.** Small bribes to speed up or complete a government function are common—from clearing goods through customs to obtaining licenses.

Source: "Promise and Pitfalls in Myanmar," *Campaign Asia-Pacific* (November 2012): 40–43.

understand local consumers and communicate with local audiences are lacking or inadequate. As one respondent to a survey pointed out, "You can't buy a report on consumer behavior in Kenya, because it does not exist."[26] Multinationals doing business in these areas need to come up with smart solutions to cope with these kinds of infrastructure weaknesses.

Most of these characteristics are numbers-based (income, population, and so forth). However, we would like to add one final element that relates to a country's institutional framework: EMs are economies that are coming of age as they evolve from a system based on informal relationships to a more formal system with rules that are transparent and apply equally to all market players.[27] This involves strong economic, political, and legal institutions with rigorous regulatory controls (e.g., antitrust, intellectual property rights), rule of law, corporate governance, and contracts that are binding and enforced. **Exhibit 17-3** summarizes the main challenges that companies face in Myanmar (Burma), the most recent member of the EM club.

Competing with the New Champions

Conventional wisdom tells us that as trade barriers crumble and emerging economies take off, multinationals can grab opportunities in these countries and prosper. The boons of these markets include cheap labor, rising incomes, and weak local competitors. These days, however, in many rapidly developing countries the competitive environment does not always live up to this premise. Local players have been able to keep multinationals at bay. One telling sign is the growing number of companies that are rooted in that part of the world showing up in the *Fortune Global 500* ranking. In the 2012 ranking, 73 companies hailed from China, 8 from India, 8 from Brazil, 3 from Mexico, and 7 from Russia.[28]

A more worrying development for multinationals based in the developed world is that several of the so-called new champions are also wielding their clout outside their home market. In this section

---

[25]http://unstats.un.org/unsd/pocketbook/pdf/2011/myanmar.pdf.

[26]Sofie Van den Waeyenberg and Luc Hens, "Overcoming Institutional Distance: Expansion to Base-of-the-Pyramid Markets," *Journal of Business Research*, 65 (2012): 1692-1699.

[27]"When Are Emerging Markets No Longer 'Emerging'?" knowledge.wharton.upenn.edu, accessed March 27, 2009.

[28]http://money.cnn.com/magazines/fortune/global500/2012/full_list/index.html.

we first look at strategies used by local companies in emerging markets. We then examine how multinationals can bolster their competitive position against the onslaught of the new champions.

The New Champions

In the Philippines, many lunch crowd people longing for a burger do not head to a McDonald's or a Burger King restaurant. Instead, they buy their fast food at Jollibee's, a local chain with a cute-looking bee as a mascot. The company, which started with two Manila ice cream parlors in 1978, now dominates the fast food scene in the Philippines. In 2012, it controlled 18 percent of the Metro Manila area, compared to 10 percent for McDonald's. It has become popular by creating the image of a warm, friendly, family-bonding place. In 1986, it opened its first store overseas, in Taiwan. Today, Jollibee outlets can be found across Asia (e.g., Brunei, Hong Kong, Indonesia, Vietnam), the Middle East (e.g., Saudi Arabia, Qatar) as well as in the United States.[29] Jollibee is just one example of a so-called **new champion**, a company created in an emerging market that has been able to humble multinationals. Looking at China, the fastest growing EM, local champions throw their weight in dozens of industries. In the IT industry alone, some of the highfliers that are leaders in their respective fields include Baidu for online search, Alibaba for e-commerce, Youku for online video-sharing, Sina for microblogging, and Tencent for online social networking.

Dozens of the new champions have also become credible challengers outside their home market. Haier is the world's leading appliance maker by sales volume and one of China's most famous brands. In China, its home market, the company has a 25 percent market share. It has also been highly successful beyond China. In the United States, 30 percent of households own a Haier product. Haier has also made inroads in Europe, doubling its market share over a five-year period. Rather than targeting the low end of the market as Chinese firms typically do, Haier decided to compete for the middle to upper end. With a German-sounding name,[30] many of its customers did not realize that the company behind the brand name is Chinese. It set itself apart from other Chinese companies by focusing on brand building instead of simply selling products, competing on value-for-money rather than just low prices. Its strategy for going global followed a "first difficult, then easy" mindset. It set even higher quality standards than the stringent industrial norms applied by Japanese firms. To support its global expansion, Haier set up global research and development centers and created localized designs. This led to a string of innovative products such as air-conditioners that take pictures of intruders and refrigerators with a pizza drawer for the U.S. market. Haier has also won several design awards.[31]

Other EM-based challengers have made forays overseas by buying up global brands. Some high-profile examples include the purchase of the Miller beer brand by South African brewer SAB and the Budweiser brand by Brazil's InBev,[32] the acquisition of IBM's PC division by Chinese computer maker Lenovo, and the purchase of the Jaguar and Land Rover luxury car brands by India's Tata Motor. Some also have made strides in the global arena through global ad campaigns or multimillion dollar sponsorship deals: in 2004 Emirates Air, the Dubai-based airline, signed a £100 million ($140 million) deal to name the new stadium of English soccer team Arsenal;[33] India's Tata Consultancy Services became a sponsor of the Formula One Ferrari team for the 2009 season.[34]

What makes emerging-markets firms so successful? Bhattacharya and Michael identified six strategies that the new champions employ to stave off multinational companies:[35]

---

[29]"A Filipino Sting for McDonald's," *International Herald Tribune*, May 31, 2005, p. 10.

[30]Based in the seaside town of Qingdao, the company's name stems from the Chinese character for "sea."

[31]"China's Haier Plans to Plug into Europe," *Financial Times*, June 19, 2012, p. 21.

[32]Strictly speaking, InBev is a Belgium/Brazil company, but the CEO and key managers are Brazilian. After the Anheuser-Busch acquisition, InBev changed its name to Anheuser-Busch InBev.

[33]http://news.bbc.co.uk/sport2/hi/football/teams/a/arsenal/3715678.stm.

[34]http://news.bbc.co.uk/sport2/hi/motorsport/formula_one/7788830.stm.

[35]Arindam K. Bhattacharya and David C. Michael, "How Local Companies Keep Multinationals at Bay," *Harvard Business Review* 86 (March 2008)): 84–95.

1. *Create customized offerings.* Savvy local companies have often built up an intimate knowledge of their customers. By leveraging their customer information, these firms have been able to develop customized products or services that appeal to their clients. A case in point is Shenzhen-based Tencent and its QQ online messaging service. With a registered user base of 150 million, Tencent dominates China's messaging and social networking site (SNS) market. Foreign internet brands, such as MSN, Yahoo!, and MySpace, lag far behind.[36] Apart from investing very heavily in building up the QQ-brand name, another reason for QQ's dominance is features such as digital avatars that can be personalized. These avatars allow users to personalize their online messaging presence, thereby tapping into Chinese people's desire for freedom of expression. By the same token, Jollibee localized its burgers to taste like stronger-flavored meatballs instead of pure beef patties, which Filipinos find too bland. The chain's menu also includes favorite Filipino items such as sweet spaghetti, palabok (vermicelli noodles), and arroz caldo (a chicken rice dish).[37]

2. *Develop business models to overcome obstacles.* Local champions are adept in identifying key challenges and then developing business models to surmount them. Multinational firms can always copycat them, but savvy local players always sustain their edge by honing their first-mover advantage. A good example is the computer gaming industry in China. For companies such as Sony and Microsoft, product piracy is a key challenge in China. Shanda and other Chinese players have developed a thriving business by developing multiplayer online role-playing games where the issue of piracy is moot. Another important obstacle is the lack of a credit card culture. Shanda overcame that stumbling block by introducing off-line payment mechanisms such as pre-paid cards.

3. *Deploy latest technologies.* Given that local players are typically still very young companies, they are not hampered by the legacy of old technologies and can leapfrog to the latest technologies instead. This enables them to keep their operating costs low and to provide good-quality products or services. Some of these companies have also become very innovative. Safaricom is Kenya's leading mobile phone service provider. The company developed a virtual currency system called M-Pesa that allows clients to transfer money via SMS and handle their mobile phone as an electronic wallet. Users can store cash on their phone and use it to shop, pay bills or transfer money to others. Launched in 2007, M-Pesa was used by 7 in 10 Kenyan adults by late 2012. The success of M-Pesa in Kenya led to the launch of similar mobile money trials such as India and Tanzania, though only a few of these were successful.[38]

4. *Take advantage of cheap labor and train staff in-house.* Labor costs in most emerging markets are still much lower than in developed countries. Rather than relying on capital-intensive modes of business, many of the new champions have developed business models that leverage the cheap labor cost advantage in their home country. Huawei and ZTE, two leading Chinese telecom infrastructure firms, have been able to undercut the likes of Cisco and Alcatel/Lucent in international markets because of their access to a massive pool of Chinese engineers who are willing to accept salaries far lower than their Western counterparts. By the same token, BYD, the biggest Chinese manufacturer of rechargeable batteries, claims that its "human resource advantage" is the key element of its strategy.[39] The company's business model relies on a huge army of migrant workers to assemble its products instead of the robotic arms used on Japanese assembly lines. BYD employs about 10,000 engineers who come from China's best schools. The firm can afford to recruit so many of them because salaries are only $600 to $700 a month. In addition, companies from emerging markets are often much more capable of dealing with the

---

[36]Facebook is banned in China.
[37]"A Filipino Sting for McDonald's."
[38]"M-Pesa's Cautious Start in India," *Financial Times*, December 28, 2012, p. 8.
[39]"Buffett Takes Charge," *Fortune Asia Edition*, April 27, 2009, pp. 36–42.

bare minimum of resources than their rivals from the developed world, a skill that Carlos Ghosn, the head of Renault-Nissan, describes as "frugal engineering."

5. *Scale up rapidly.* Many homegrown champions distinguish themselves by building up scale very quickly. Typically, this happens through a combination of organic growth and absorbing smaller rivals. Several new champions go a step further and take their innovative business models to other emerging markets or sometimes even the Western world. A case in point is Pearl River Piano, China's largest piano manufacturer. The company grew over the last 30 years by out-investing local rivals. Currently, the company has the world's largest piano factory with a capacity of 100,000 pianos per year. In 2000, the firm bought up Rittmuller, a German piano maker, to boost its reputation and to broaden its price points.[40] The firm is now the leader at the low end of the U.S. upright piano market.

6. *Invest in talent to sustain growth.* The new challengers also grow by their willingness to invest in managerial talent. Several of their top executives left senior positions with multinationals to join them. Even though the salaries may not always match those paid by multinationals, there are other ways to attract talent: the prospect of rapid career advancement, the joy of being part of an entrepreneurial culture, shares in the company.

One challenge that the emerging-market champions face is whether they should focus on their home market or expand into the global marketplace. When such companies plan to expand globally, they must also decide on which regions to concentrate. Yingli is a leading Chinese solar panel maker. Initially the company focused on the United States and the European Union. However, the economic downturn, coupled with rising protectionism in these areas, pushed the company to change gears and expand instead into emerging markets such as Turkey, Israel, and South America. Such forays have not always been successful. For example, Li Ning is a leading China-based athletic wear company that decided to globalize. In January 2010, the company opened a flagship store in Oregon (near Nike's home turf), but closed the store the following month.

Deciding which strategy to pursue hinges on two parameters: the strength of globalization pressures and the degree to which a company's assets can be transferred internationally.[41] Combining these two parameters generates a set of four strategic options, as depicted in **Exhibit 17-4**. If globalization pressures are high in the industry but the company's assets are only valuable in its home market, then the best course of action is to enter into a joint venture or sell out to a multinational. This option is the dodging strategy. For instance, Little Sheep, a leading restaurant chain of Mongolian hot-pot eateries in China, was bought by Yum! Brands, owner of KFC and Pizza Hut, in 2011. Yum planned to explore with Little Sheep to introduce the hot-pot concept to a wider global audience. If a company's assets are transferable, it can use its success at home as a platform for expansion in foreign markets. Under this scenario, the company can compete head on with the large multinationals and become a contender. To overcome the first-mover status of established multinationals, the contender should start by benchmarking the global players to search for ways to innovate. The insights derived from the benchmarking exercise can then be used to navigate around the leading global players. This could be done by tapping into niches that have been neglected by the existing multinationals so far.[42] The switch to greener technologies in the car industry gives newcomers from emerging markets an opening to compete with incumbent carmakers. In particular, BYD, a Chinese battery maker, can leverage its expertise in battery design to compete in the electric car niche. By the same token, India's Tata Group aspires to launch its super-cheap fuel-efficient Tata Nano car in Europe and the United States. In

[40]www.pearlriverusa.com.

[41]Niraj Dawar and Tony Frost, "Competing with Giants: Survival Strategies for Local Companies in Emerging Markets," *Harvard Business Review* (March–April 1999): 119–129.

[42]Christopher A. Bartlett and Sumantra Ghoshal, "Going Global: Lessons from Late Movers," *Harvard Business Review* (March–April 2000): 133–142.

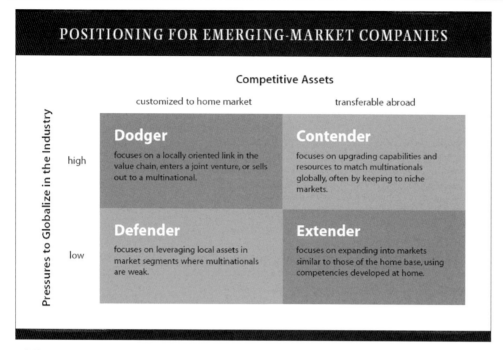

Exhibit 17-4 Strategic Options for Emerging-Market Companies

Tata's case, a key transferable asset is the company's expertise in developing ultra-cheap cars. When there is little pressure to globalize and the company's assets are not transferable, the firm should focus on defending its home turf advantage. Companies finding themselves in such a situation are defenders. Li Ning, a Chinese athletic wear company, may be an example of such a company. One of the firm's assets is Mr. Li Ning, the founder and former gymnast, who personifies the brand. While Li Ning is well recognized in China,[43] the brand personality does not resonate with sports fans outside China. Furthermore, given the size of China's athletic apparel market, there is very little pressure for Li Ning to globalize. The fourth scenario arises when globalization pressures are weak but the company's assets are transferable. Under such circumstances, the company can generate extra revenues and scale economies by leveraging its asset in markets similar to its home market. A case in point is Lenovo, the Chinese personal computing firm. With its dominance of the PC market in China, Lenovo has learned how to effectively compete in emerging markets. Lenovo's strategy is to expand aggressively in emerging markets, including the other three BRIC countries, by transferring its China business model.[44]

Competing against the Newcomers

Multinationals from the United States, Europe, and Japan can fight off the challenge posed by emerging-market newcomers but it may take some innovative thinking. Usually, the established multinationals defend themselves against emerging giants by focusing on the high-end segments of the market. Such a move may allow them to sustain margins but at the expense of lower

---

[43]Li Ning lit the Olympic flame during the opening ceremony of the 2008 Beijing Summer Olympics.

[44]"Lenovo Ousts CEO, Returns to Roots," www.wsj.com, accessed March 28, 2009.

Exhibit 17-5   Powering Growth in Emerging Markets: The Four A's of Heinz

First A: Applicability
Make sure the product suits the local culture.

- The dominant condiment in China is soy sauce, not ketchup; in Indonesia the big sellers are soy and chili sauces.
- Korean people put ketchup on their pizza.

Second A: Availability
Make sure you sell in channels that are relevant to the local people.

- While modern trade (e.g., modern grocery stores, hypermarkets) prevails in the United States and Europe, its share is much lower in many emerging markets.
- In Indonesia, less than one-third of the population buys food in modern grocery stores; people shop in small stores or open-air markets.

Third A: Affordability
Make sure local people can afford the product. Don't price yourself out of the market.

- Small packets of soy sauce in Indonesia.

Fourth A: Affinity
Understand how local people live.

- Reliance on local managers.
- "Emerging Markets Capability Team"—group of senior executives from Western countries—that travels around to coach local staff.

Source: Based on Bill Johnson, "The CEO of Heinz on Powering Growth in Emerging Markets," *Harvard Business Review* (October 2011): 47–50.

volumes. Another option is to take a leaf out of the new champions' book and try to beat them at their own game by pursuing value-for-market strategies. The competitive response that IBM delivered to the onslaught by India-based firms on its service business provides a good illustration of this approach. A threesome of Indian outsourcing upstarts, Tata Consulting Services, Infosys, and Wipro, posed a serious threat to IBM's service business. To fight off the assault, IBM bought Daksh, a smaller rival of the trio, and built it into a large business to compete on cost and quality with its Indian rivals.[45] Heinz's strategy for emerging markets centers on what Bill Johnson, the company's CEO, refers to as the Four A's: Applicability, Availability, Affordability, and Affinity (see **Exhibit 17-5**). In general, multinationals can choose from five strategic alternatives to fend off threats from the emerging giants in their industry:[46]

1. *Go beyond low-cost sourcing in emerging markets.* Western multinationals should view developing countries as more than cheap manufacturing bases. They should examine the entire value chain from R&D to customer service support and see which stages would warrant relocation to emerging markets. For example, Nokia Siemens Network, a joint venture between Nokia and Siemens, set up an innovation center in China to develop software technologies for the telecom industry.

2. *Develop products in emerging markets and bring them home.* Companies could launch in their developed markets new products that were developed by their subsidiaries in emerging

---

[45]"A Special Report on Globalization," *The Economist*, September 20, 2008.
[46]Peter J. Williamson and Ming Zeng, "Value-for-Money Strategies for Recessionary Times," *Harvard Business Review* 87 (March 2009): 66–75.

markets. The reason is that these affiliates often have an intimate knowledge of value-oriented consumers and, thereby, have honed their skills for this segment. Unilever views its Indian subsidiary Hindustan Unilever as a major font for innovative ideas. Pureit, a cheap home water purification system that Hindustan Unilever introduced in 2008, is one example of a brilliant innovation that Unilever plans to transplant to other markets.[47] M-Pesa is an innovative mobile payment solution developed by Safaricom, Kenya's leading mobile phone carrier. Vodafone, the British mobile communications group and a partner of Safaricom, is now taking the breakthrough service to other countries.

3. *Copy branding tactics used in emerging markets.* Emerging giants often use cost-effective tactics to build up their brand image. Western companies could learn from such promotion strategies and emulate such tactics to get more bang for their promotion buck.

4. *Team up with the new emerging giants.* Traditionally, multinationals would form a joint venture with a local firm to penetrate the host market. The local partner would help the multinational through its distribution knowledge or knowledge of local consumers. A more radical approach is to tie up with a new emerging giant and harness its capabilities in delivering value-for-money (cost innovation). This would allow the multinational to share the risks with the local partner and to grow in tandem with the partner. To create an affordable Windows smartphone for Africa, Microsoft joined forces with Huawei, a Chinese telecom equipment maker. Huawei has strong skills in developing low-cost, good quality cellphones. In addition, Africa is one of Huawei's strongest markets outside China.[48]

5. *Invest in growing mass markets in developing countries.* Most Western multinationals focus on the high-end segments of the market when competing in developing countries and leave the mass markets to their local competitors. However, such a strategy enables local players to build up scale and experience. To pre-empt them, multinationals must broaden their scope and also go for the mass markets.

Targeting/Positioning Strategies in Emerging Markets—BOP or No BOP?

Just as with developed markets, choosing the right target markets is one of the key strategic issues multinationals grapple with in emerging markets. As income levels in most of these countries tend to be low, MNCs doing business in this part of the world have typically focused on wealthy consumers and businesses while ignoring the rest of the population. These days, however, several MNCs realize that there could also be huge market opportunities at the so-called bottom of the pyramid. The **bottom of the pyramid (BOP)** is defined as the 4 billion people living on less than $2 per day.

Catering to the BOP in EMs can be very rewarding for MNCs. Some of the benefits of targeting BOP markets include the following:[49]

1. Some BOP markets are large and attractive as stand-alone entities.

2. Innovations developed for a BOP segment in one particular region can be leveraged in other markets, thereby creating a global opportunity for such innovations.

3. Some innovations that originate in BOP markets can also be launched in the MNC's developed markets. In the wake of the 2008 economic downturn, companies have increasingly borrowed innovations from their emerging markets for their Western regions. Many Western consumers,

[47]"Unilever CEO Looking at India for Growth Tips," http://www.business-standard.com, accessed March 29, 2009.
[48]"Microsoft and Huawei to Sell Windows Smartphones in China," http://www.nytimes.com, accessed February 6, 2013.
[49]Ibid., Chapter 3.

faced with lower budgets, have been trying to cut corners by choosing better-value-for-money products.

4. The learning experience from the BOP markets can also benefit the MNC. Pursuing the BOP forces an MNC to deliver value for money, which requires relentless cost discipline. Cost discipline goes beyond cost cutting techniques. To succeed in a BOP market, the MNC should pursue **cost innovation**, meaning, innovation efforts that focus on re-engineering cost structures (instead of new functions or features) so that the firm can offer the same or even much more value at a lower cost for consumers.[50]

In a nutshell, to excel in marketing to BOP consumers, a company needs to come up with a business model that (1) meets the needs and wants of these customers, (2) at a price they can afford, (3) while still generating decent profits for the company. In some cases, this may imply rethinking the entire value supply chain. In Africa, for example, SABMiller, the global drinks group, invests heavily in local sourcing and developing products tailored to local tastes. One result of these efforts was Eagle, a Ugandan beer made from sorghum. Likewise, in Latin America PepsiCo sells a range of potato chip products made from cassava and yam grown by small local farmers that suit local tastes. The company also set up a research facility in Peru to develop new potato varieties.[51]

One fallacy marketers often make is that value for the BOP consumers means low price. Low-income consumers have similar perceptions and needs as their richer neighbors. They are often attracted to international brands due to their perceived quality image. One market researcher in the region notes: "A low-income mother sending her child to school may see the fact that he or she has a very clean white shirt as the only way she can express love. So she will choose her soap powder brand in a much more considered way than a middle-income mother who can afford to express her love in other ways."[52] A new smartphone developed for Africa also illustrates this point. In sub-Saharan Africa, 10 percent of the 445 million cellphone users had smartphones by 2012, but that share was expected to rise rapidly as operators upgrade their networks. Microsoft teamed up with Huawei, a Chinese telecommunications manufacturer, to develop a low-price smartphone targeted at Africa's middle-class consumers. The result of the collaboration was the "Huawei 4 Afrika" with a price tag of only $150. The phone debuted in early 2013 in five African countries (Nigeria, Kenya, Egypt, South Africa, and Ivory Coast). It uses the Windows Phone 8 operating system and is sold with apps designed for African consumers (e.g., African soccer results). Fernando de Sousa, the general manager for Microsoft Africa, noted: "Africans are generally quite conscious of brand, quality, and image. We are being very clear that we are not going to be building something cheap for this market. What we want to do is deliver real quality innovation at an affordable price."[53] Likewise, the Philips umbrella brand name helped to market a new solar lighting product branded "Uday" to rural consumers in Ghana because they recognized the brand from the media and trips to the city.[54]

One fundamental difference between developed countries and the EMs is that segments are usually much coarser in the latter markets. Most categories in developed countries are highly segmented, catering to a wide variety of preferences or tastes. Such a high level of product differentiation tends to be very costly for most product categories. Given the low incomes in most EMs, such a finely refined level of segmentation is not effective. Also, the targeted media (e.g., niche cable channels) that enable highly refined segmentation simply do not exist in many EMs. **Global Perspective 17-1** discusses some of the strategies being used by Hindustan Unilever to conquer India's BOP market.

---

[50]"Value-for-Money Strategies," pp. 68–70.

[51]"Old Roots Tap New Consumers," http://www.ft.com, accessed February 27, 2010.

[52]"A Fresh Look at the Low Earner," *Media*, March 9, 2007, p. 8.

[53]"Microsoft and Huawei to Sell Windows Smartphones in Africa," http://www.nytimes.com, accessed February 6, 2013.

[54]Sofie Van den Waeyenberg and Luc Hens, "Overcoming Institutional Distance: Expansion to Base-of-the-Pyramid Markets," *Journal of Business Research* 65 (2012): 1692–1699.

Global Perspective 17-1

Hindustan Unilever—Straddling the Pyramid

In 2008, Hindustan Unilever Ltd (HUL), Unilever's subsidiary in India, celebrated its 75th anniversary. The company is the largest soap and detergent manufacturer in India. India's current socioeconomic structure looks like a pyramid: a narrow top of high-income households—the "affluent," a broader middle layer of middle-income people—the "aspirers," and huge bottom layer of low-income households, the "strivers." However, HUL foresees that the shape of India's society will evolve from a pyramid to a diamond by 2013 (see Table 1A). Furthermore, India has a very young population.

Table A: India's Changing Income Pattern—From a Pyramid to a Diamond

Socioeconomic class	Number of households in 2003 (in millions)	Number of households projected by 2013 (in millions)
Rich Classes	3	11
Aspiring Classes	46	124
Strivers (BOP)	131	96
Total	181	231

Source: National Council of Agriculture & Economic Research

Instead of simply selling premium brands to the top end of the pyramid, HUL grows its business by "straddling the pyramid." This vision involves offering premium brands to the affluent, value-for-money brands to middle-income consumers, and affordable pricing to low-income consumers. HUL recognizes that India's BOP consumers do not simply look for cheap products but quality products that are affordable.

To straddle the pyramid, HUL's marketing strategy rests on six pillars:

1. An unmatched brand portfolio to serve the many Indias
2. Innovation and R&D capabilities
3. A track record of building large and profitable mass markets

4. A versatile distribution network that is capable of handling both traditional and modern trade
5. A good record of devising strategies that aid rural development in India
6. A strong local talent base.

For each core category, HUL has a brand portfolio that covers all three income groups. A case in point is the soap category in which the firm sells three major brands: at the bottom, Lifebuoy for the strivers; in the middle, Lux for the aspirers; and at the top, Dove for the affluent. HUL's 2008 (value) market share of the soap category was 51.6 percent, compared to 9.4 percent for the nearest competitor.

Innovation at HUL is not only new product development but also stretches to business processes, packaging, distribution channels, and delivery mechanisms. To develop the BOP market, HUL introduced the single-use, one rupee sachet of shampoo. The firm extended this so-called low unit price concept to other categories (e.g., detergents, tea, toothpaste). To cope with India's lack of water supply, HUL scientists developed a detergent powder (Surf Excel Quick Wash) that requires much less water than regular powders. Unilever plans to launch the brand in other markets where water scarcity is a major issue.

Diarrhea is a major disease among India's poor. Almost 20 percent of India's children suffer from diarrhea. In 2002, HUL initiated a campaign to combat this disease, which illustrates how the firm combines its business strategy with economic development. Studies had shown that washing hands with soap lowers the risk of the disease by almost half. Unfortunately, there is little awareness among India's poor of basic hygiene habits such as washing hands. To spread the message of health and hygiene to India's countryside, HUL launched the Lifebuoy Swasthya Chetana initiative in 2002.

Sources: Harish Manwani, "Winning in Developing & Emerging Markets," http://www.hul.co.in/Images/WinningInDandEMarkets_tcm114-264222 .pdf; "Hindustan Unilever Limited," Merrill Lynch India Conference Investor Presentation, February 2, 2009.

Entry Strategies for Emerging Markets

Given their volatile market environment, choosing the proper entry strategy becomes a crucial task for a successful performance in EMs. As we saw in Chapter 9, setting up an entry strategy involves many different issues. In this section we focus on two key decisions: the timing and the mode of entry.

Timing of Entry

Despite the appeal of EMs, especially the huge BRIC countries, early entry can hurt performance even for mighty brands. When the cereal industry of Western countries matured in the 1990s, it did not take long for Kellogg's to decide to enter India. A country with one billion people presents an alluring prospect for many consumer goods companies. Further, the company would have very few direct competitors. In 1994, Kellogg's ventured into India with a $65 million investment. Unfortunately, Indian consumers found the whole concept of eating breakfast cereal odd. Although initial sales were encouraging, sales never really took off. Apparently, many people bought Corn Flakes for its novelty value but then went back to more familiar breakfast entrees. Even if they liked the taste, the product was too expensive for most households.[55] Most likely, India was not yet ready for Western-style cereals, and Kellogg's entry may have been too hasty and aggressive.

There are several reasons why first movers in emerging markets can fail.[56] As the Kellogg's example shows, early entrants may not be aware of the pitfalls of newly opened emerging markets. Second, returns on investment can be low when the infrastructure is not yet fully developed. For instance, when distribution channels are dysfunctional or missing, the MNC typically needs to build up its own distribution network. Such an endeavor demands heavy investments that may be hard to recover in the short or medium term. Third, later entrants have a flatter learning curve as they can learn from the mistakes made by earlier entrants.

On the other hand, powerful arguments can also be made for early entry.[57] First, government relations are usually far more influential in EMs than in developed countries. Nurturing of these relationships could lead to favorable treatment and tangible benefits (e.g., tax holidays, licenses) that buffer the early entrant against incursions of later entrants. Second, the huge pent-up demand for previously unavailable Western brands can lead to very high initial sales. Third, early entrants can lock up access to key resources such as media access, brand endorsers, distributors, or suppliers. Such resources are often much scarcer in EMs than in developed countries. Fourth, early entrants can enjoy higher productivity of their marketing dollars. In early stages of economic development, advertising rates and competitive marketing spending are relatively low. Therefore, marketing dollars can deliver much more bang for the buck in the form of high awareness, share-of-mind, or brand preference compared to later stages. A final aspect is the potential for smaller players to outmaneuver their larger slower-moving rivals. EMs have less well-established brand preferences and higher growth rates than their developed counterparts. As a result, gaining a foothold in these markets can be much less difficult for the challengers than in more mature developed countries.

Entry Mode

An MNC that plans to enter a new EM can choose from several modes of entry (discussed in Chapter 9): exporting, licensing/franchise, joint venture, or wholly-owned subsidiary. As you may remember, the key trade-off among these choices is that between risk and control over marketing

---

[55]http://brand-failures.kuntau.net/culture-failures/kelloggs-in-india.html.

[56]Joseph Johnson and Gerard J. Tellis, "Drivers of Success for Market Entry into China and India," *Journal of Marketing* 72 (May 2008): 1–13.

[57]David J. Arnold and John A. Quelch, "New Strategies for Emerging Markets," *Sloan Management Review* 40 (Fall 1998): 7–20.

resources. Risk has both a financial (e.g., currency volatility, getting paid) and marketing (e.g., sales volume) component. In general, risk levels tend to be much higher in EMs than in developed countries. However, control can also be very critical for an MNC entering an EM. First, control protects resources from leakage, such as patent theft. Second, success in the EM often rests on strict control over scarce resources such as distribution or supply. One very important factor for the mode choice is the institutional framework in the EM. These institutions include items such as the legal framework and its enforcement, property rights protection, and regulatory regimes (e.g., antitrust). One study compared the entry choices of MNCs in four emerging economies: Vietnam, Egypt, South Africa, and India. The authors found that the stronger the institutional framework, the more likely the MNC would prefer an acquisition or greenfield entry mode over joint ventures.[58]

Given the large risks and the firm's lack of knowledge, MNCs usually first enter with a low-risk entry mode (e.g., licensing, minority JV) to minimize risks. The focus is on sales rather than marketing. There is little adaptation, as the small volumes cannot support potential adaptation costs. Over time, as sales take off, the MNC increases its commitment and shifts toward a higher-control entry mode. In case the MNC entered the market via a joint venture, it might raise its stake or even buy out the partner if the country's legal framework allows that.[59]

When developing an entry strategy, the ultimate yardstick is the firm's performance in the host country. Clearly many factors play a role in driving the entry's success or failure. One study examined the drivers of success for market entry into China and India, the two biggest emerging markets. Its main conclusions were the following:[60]

- Success is greater for entry into China than for entry into India.

- Success is greater for smaller firms than for bigger ones.

- Success is greater for entry into emerging markets with less openness and less risk and those that are economically similar to the multinational's home market.

- The greater the control of the entry mode, the larger the success.

Once the MNC has decided on an entry strategy, the firm has to develop a marketing strategy to penetrate the EM. Simply replicating strategies that served the company well in developed countries could be a recipe for disaster. In the remainder of this chapter, we discuss the different elements of the marketing mix in an EM environment.

Product Policy

Offering the right product mix is a major requirement to thrive in the EM. Scores of MNCs have failed in this regard. In what follows, we highlight three facets of the product policy: product design, branding, and packaging.

Product Innovation

Often, when first entering an EM, the multinational is reluctant to adapt its product offerings to the host market. Adaptation costs money and is time consuming. Given the high market risks, adaptation could be a gamble that the firm is not willing to make.[61] Instead, the MNC might sell a

---

[58]Klaus Meyer, Saul Estrin, Sumon Bhaumik, and Mike W. Peng, "Institutions, Resources, and Entry Strategies in Emerging Economies," *Strategic Management Journal* 30, no. 1 (2009): 61–80.

[59]*The Mirage of Global Markets*, pp. 85–90.

[60]Joseph Johnson and Gerard J. Tellis, "Drivers of Success for Market Entry into China and India," *Journal of Marketing* 72 (May 2008): 1–13.

[61]David J. Arnold and John A. Quelch, "New Strategies in Emerging Markets," *MIT Sloan Management Review* 40, no. 1 (Fall 1998): 7–20.

narrow range of existing products and position them as premium products targeted at the affluent EM customers. Still, to succeed in emerging markets, global corporations must adapt their offering to the local culture and be willing to experiment with their product development and marketing approaches. McDonald's Indonesia, for instance, sells more McChicken and McNasi combos than Big Mac meals. Also in Indonesia, LG, the Korean consumer electronics maker, has introduced microwave ovens with special settings for local dishes and launched washing machines and refrigerators with batik motifs.[62]

One approach MNCs sometimes adopt is known as **backward** or **reverse innovation**: offer a stripped-down version of the product that is sold in developed markets. Such a basic product could then be sold at a much lower price than the original product being sold in developed markets. Panasonic's so-called Emerging Markets Win (EM-WIN) products exemplify this approach. These products are mostly appliances and electronics designed in Japan, but with fewer features (e.g., fewer refrigerator doors) and modified slightly for local customers. The line targeted upper-middle income consumers (the "next rich") in fast-growing developing countries.[63]

One fallacy is the belief is that products that are at or near maturity in developed markets can act as anchors for the product policy in EMs. The underlying motivation is that the market conditions that prevailed in the developed countries when these products were first introduced are similar to the ones that exist now in the EMs. A further payoff is that the product or its stripped-down version gets an extra lease to life by selling them in the EM. While this policy may have been effective in the twentieth century, it could go badly wrong in today's cyber age. Consumers in EM often want the latest products now instead of products that have become mature or obsolete in developed countries.[64] Rapid information flows via the internet and other channels imply that EM customers are often very familiar with the latest trends in EM markets.

In recent years, companies ranging from Unilever to Siemens are pursuing a business strategy often referred to as **frugal innovation**.[65] This strategy aims to address the paradox of "doing more with less." Resource constraints are viewed not as a challenge but as an opportunity. With this business strategy, a company must come up with innovative solutions in a resource-constrained setting that deliver good quality to consumers at a price they can afford. Thus, a company starts out with finding out what consumers can afford and what their needs are. It then adjusts the product attributes and manufacturing process to come up with an offering that meets those needs below the target price. All of these conditions should be met while still generating profits for the firm. Not surprisingly, the skill set needed for frugal innovation is very different from that for conventional new product development. Typically, frugal innovation involves rethinking the entire production process and business model (e.g., ingredients and materials to be used, manufacturing process, supply chain, distribution).

A company pursuing frugal innovation must squeeze costs so that the product becomes accessible to more customers. There are three ways to cut costs.[66] The first is to contract out ever more work. Bharti Airtel, an Indian mobile phone carrier that charges some of the lowest fees in the industry, has contracted out almost everything except its core business. The second is to use existing technology in creative new ways. The third alternative is to apply mass-production approaches in new areas (e.g., heart surgery).

Unilever's Comfort One Rinse[67] range of fabric conditioners launched in South East Asia is one example of frugal innovation. Lowering water consumption around the world is a key area for

[62]"Local Brands Give Global Rivals a Run for Their Money," *Campaign Asia-Pacific* (May 2012): 70.

[63]"Panasonic Eyes Emerging Market," *Wall Street Journal Asia*, July 10–12, 2009, p. 4.

[64]"New Strategies in Emerging Markets," p. 16.

[65]Navi Radjou and Jaideep Prabhu, "Frugal Innovation: A New Business Paradigm," http://knowledge.insead.edu, accessed February 7, 2013.

[66]"The Frugal Revolution," http://blogs.reuters.com/great-debate/2012/01/17/the-frugal-revolution/, accessed January 17, 2012.

[67]In some countries (e.g., the Philippines) the brand name is Surf One Rinse.

the company. The new conditioner was designed to wash clothes using just one bucket of water instead of 3—thereby saving up to 30 liters (or nearly 8 gallons) of water per wash cycle. Launching One Rinse in South East Asia also required changing people's mindsets and old habits through seeing-is-believing product demonstrations, TV advertising, and brand ambassadors.[68] P&G's development process behind the Gillette Guard razor for Indian men offers another good illustration of frugal innovation. In this case, P&G fixed the target price at five rupees (about nine cents)—the cost of a small toothpaste tube. To save money, P&G dropped the lubrication strip and colorful handle designs for which Indian men were not willing to pay extra. P&G also found that contrary to Western men, Indians prefer lighter handles, which also cut costs.[69]

The latest trend is that several innovations originally developed for emerging markets find an audience in the West. A case in point is a range of more than 160 entry-level medical products known as SMART[70] that Siemens developed and manufactured in India and China. Siemens refers to these innovations as "good-enough" products: even though these products do not have the full functionality of more high-end ones, they offer the key benefits at an affordable price. One example is a black-and-white ultrasound scanner instead of a color model. As public healthcare budgets are squeezed in the developed world, many of these good-enough products are exported to the West. Margins for such products are still very attractive as they are made in countries with cheap labor.

Regardless of which new product development strategy a company chooses, testing the products locally is key. Gillette's experience for a new razor designed specifically for Indian men illustrates this point. Rather than testing in India, Boston-based Gillette decided to try out the new razor on Indian students at MIT. The students' positive response encouraged the company to launch it India where it flopped. Unlike much of India, the MIT students had access to running water. Lesson learned, P&G, which bought Gillette in 2005, tested Gillette Guard locally before it launched the new razor product in India in October 2010.[71]

Branding

Local brands have often humbled global brands in EMs. Assuming that consumers in EMs, even the affluent ones, will pay a premium for global brands can be a fatal mistake. Preferences for local versus global brands vary by category. One 2011 consumer survey in Indonesia found that consumers prefer global brands for luxury items. However, when it comes to personal care, sport shoes, and watches, local brands are preferred (see **Exhibit 17-6**).[72]

One McKinsey study prescribes a two-pronged branding strategy for MNCs doing business in EMs. For the wealthy segment, the MNC can pursue sophisticated, brand-building strategies. Especially among youth segments, the global brand can offer a passport to global citizenship and thereby foster a global identity.[73] However, to capture the base-of-the-pyramid market, MNCs should try to emulate their local competitors. This may involve acquiring a local brand. Focus should be on keeping the best local managers, cost reduction, operational efficiencies, and simplicity rather than product reformulations.[74] One study that compared the performance of

---

[68]http://www.unilever.com/brands-in-action, accessed February 3, 2013.

[69]"In India, Gillette Shaves Cost of Blades," *Wall Street Journal Asia*, October 4, 2010, p. 24.

[70]SMART stands for "simple, maintenance-friendly, affordable, reliable, and timely-to-market."

[71]"Can P&G Make Money in Places Where People Earn $2 a Day?" http://features.blogs.fortune.cnn.com/2011/01/06/can-pg-make-money-in-places-where-people-earn-2-a-day/, accessed January 6, 2011.

[72]"Brand Appeal," *Campaign Asia-Pacific*, May 2012): 68–69.

[73]Yuliya Strizhakova, Robin A. Coulter, and Linda L. Price, "Branded Products as a Passport to Global Citizenship: Perspectives from Developed and Developing Countries," *Journal of International Marketing*, 16, no. 4 (2008): 57–85.

[74]Gilberto Duarte de Abreu Filho, Nicola Calicchio, and Fernando Lunardini, "Brand Building in Emerging Markets," www.mckinseyquarterly.com, accessed March 29, 2009.

Exhibit 17-6
Preference for
Foreign Brands in
Indonesia (% of
Respondents)

Source: Credit Suisse Emerging Consumer Survey 2011.

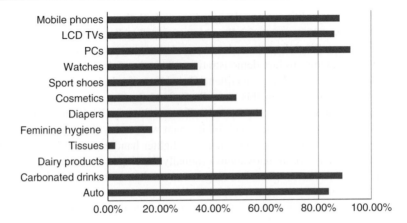

foreign and local brands in China found that the most critical elements were the brands' local advantages such as access to local resources and government support.[75]

Unilever's branding strategy in India is a good illustration of some of the tactics discussed above. The company dominates India's shampoo market with a 46.3 percent market share in 2008. It sells several of its global brands (e.g., Dove, SunSilk) as well as local brands in the category. It also reformulated its shampoos for the Indian market. Indian women often oil their hair before washing it, so Western shampoos that do not remove oil have not done well in India. Therefore, Unilever modified its shampoos for India and dropped the conditioner.[76] Unilever is also the market leader in the laundry detergent category with a 38.1 percent market share. The company's global Surf brand targets the upper crust of India's society. In response to a low-cost competitor, it launched an inexpensive brand called Wheel. The product is less refined than the premium brands but it is much cheaper. Wheel rapidly gained market share, matching the competitor's share.[77]

Packaging

MNCs operating in EMs should pay close attention to packaging. The presence of cash-strapped consumers means that global players often must offer smaller package sizes in order to make their products affordable for the mass market. For example, Colgate MaxFresh toothpaste is typically sold in 40-gram, 80-gram, and 150-gram tubes in India while it is sold in 6-oz. (170 gram) and 8-oz. (227 gram) tubes in the United States.[78] To address the needs of different segments, MNCs typically offer a variety of pack sizes at different price points. The smaller unit sizes cater toward the single-purchase buyers. The larger sizes target the bulk purchasers. Often, though, local merchants buy the family-pack size and resell it in loose form (e.g., single cigarettes from open boxes).

Because of their freshness and safety, brands sold by MNCs are often favored by local consumers. The pharmaceutical company Pfizer, for instance, benefits from the belief in much of the developing world that branded medicines are worth paying a premium for because they are safer and more effective than generics. Pfizer's prices in Venezuela, though far below U.S. prices, are still 40 to 50 percent more than generics.[79] Poor local infrastructure forces firms to

---

[75]Gerald Yong Gao, Yigan Pan, David K. Tse, and Chi Kin Yim, "Market Share Performance of Foreign and Domestic Brands in China," *Journal of International Marketing* 14, no. 2 (2006): 32–51.

[76]"The Legacy That Got Left on the Shelf," *The Economist*, February 2, 2008, pp. 66–68.

[77]"Brand Building in Emerging Markets."

[78]Sameer Mathur, "Package Sizing and Pricing in an Emerging Market," Carnegie Mellon University working paper, 2008.

[79]"Drug Firms See Poorer Nations as Cure for Sales Problems," *Wall Street Journal Asia*, July 8, 2009, pp. 14–15.

re-engineer the packaging to ensure the safety and freshness of their products. The packaging must be sturdy enough to allow shipping in suboptimal conditions to areas that are not always accessible via motorized transport. Storage facilities, such as refrigeration, that are standard in developed countries do not always exist.

Finally, MNCs should strive for sustainability regarding packaging. In many EMs, packaging materials are scarce and costly. Furthermore, waste treatment facilities are often inadequate. Therefore, packaging should ideally rely on local materials and be recyclable or biodegradable.[80]

Pricing Strategy

Not surprisingly, given the low per capita income levels in most EMs, setting the right price is an important element of the marketing strategy. In general, strategies that rely on thin margins and big volumes tend to succeed. Large volumes can make even small-ticket items that retail at one cent (e.g., gum) hugely profitable.[81] To capture sustainable sales volume, an MNC should try to saturate all price points instead of simply focusing on the upper end of the market. If it fails to do so, local competitors who cater to the mass market could achieve economies of scale and use their favorable cost position to attack the MNC in the higher-priced segment at some point in the future. In India, Unilever dominates most of the product categories in which it competes. In all of these categories, Unilever markets at least one brand in each price tier (see **Exhibit 17-7**).

To maintain or improve margins, MNCs should focus on cost innovation to improve the product's cost structure instead of continuous product innovation. By lowering fixed and variable costs, the firm can make its products affordable while still enjoying a healthy profit margin. At the same time, marketers should keep in mind that EM consumers are not always obsessed with price. Unilever's experience with Omo in Vietnam is a telling example.[82] In 1995, Unilever launched the

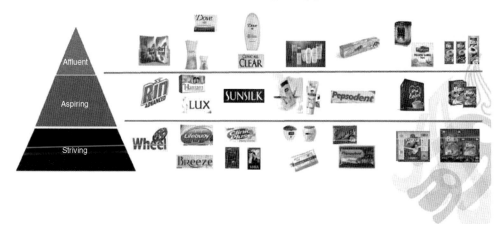

Portfolio straddling the pyramid

Exhibit 17-7 Hindustan Unilever's Brand Portfolio

Source: Hindustan Unilever Limited

---

[80]Kelly L. Weidner, Jose Antonio Rosa, and Madhubalan Viswanathan, "Marketing to Subsistence Consumers: Contemporary Methodologies and Initiatives," University of Illinois at Chicago working paper, 2008.

[81]"Rethinking Marketing Programs for Emerging Markets," p. 465.

[82]"Brands at the Starting Gate," *Media*, February 23, 2007, pp. 20–21.

laundry detergent brand Omo in Vietnam. During its first eight years, Omo was preoccupied with a bitter price war against P&G's Tide. When its market share started to slip in 2002, Unilever decided to shift its strategy for Omo from price-led to brand-led. The firm tried to create an emotional bond by weaving heritage, family, and compassion into the core of Omo's brand proposition. For instance, during the 2004 Tet New Year, it ran a commercial around the local superstition that touching the clothes of loved ones would send a message to call them back home. By 2005, Omo had become the number one recalled brand and seized category leadership in Vietnam.

The Distribution Challenge

When CEOs of multinationals are asked about the biggest hurdles of doing business in emerging markets, distribution is a common response. The lack of a suitable distribution infrastructure coupled with the sheer land size of many EMs has deterred several MNCs from early entry. Distribution in many EMs also varies enormously between urban and rural areas. In urban areas, even the small retailers carry a wide assortment of brands in spite of limited shelf space. At the same time, modern distribution formats (e.g., shopping malls, hyper/supermarkets, discount stores) are on the rise. The needs of the modern trade differ greatly from those of the traditional trade. MNCs need to develop skills in supply chain management, in-store merchandising, and key account management to cater to the needs of the modern trade. Doing this without rupturing the ties with the traditional retailers poses a big challenge.[83] Rural retailers often carry only a single brand for each category. Therefore, being first on the shelf and building a close relationship with these retailers can create a competitive edge.[84]

Compared to developed countries, distribution also tends to be much more labor intensive in EMs, especially in rural areas. In most cases, local regulations or lack of local market knowledge force the MNC to partner with a local distributor. When Philips introduced its newly developed Uday solar lantern to base-of-the-pyramid consumers in Ghana, it heavily relied on its central distributor who imported the lanterns and supplied them to local retailers. This distributor knew the right people at government level on first-name basis, was familiar with the local system of taxes and import duties, knew the regional distributors personally, and owned a training center to train the community-level retailers.[85] Middlemen in EMs often fulfill roles that elsewhere are fulfilled by the country subsidiary such as choosing target segments, setting the pricing policy, or promoting the brand.[86]

Creating Distribution Systems

If a suitable distribution infrastructure is lacking, one solution is to establish a distribution system from scratch. Some companies have come up with very innovative approaches. To reach consumers in Brazil's outlying Amazon region, the Swiss food company Nestlé dispatched a boat with 100-square meters (1,076 square feet) of supermarket space carrying over 3000 well-known Nestle brands. Named "Nestlé Até Você a Bordo"—or Nestlé Takes You Onboard—the barge journeyed to 18 small cities for nearly 3 weeks in 2010.[87] Unilever's approach to

[83]Harish Manwani, "Winning in Developing and Emerging Markets," Speech at Hindustan Unilever Limited Annual General Meeting, May 29, 2006.

[84]"Rethinking Marketing Programs for Emerging Markets," p. 469.

[85]Sofie Van den Waeyenberg and Luc Hens, "Overcoming Institutional Distance: Expansion to Base-of-the-Pyramid Markets," *Journal of Business Research* 65 (2012): 1692–1699.

[86]"New Strategies in Emerging Markets," pp. 17–18.

[87]http://www.nestle.com/Media/NewsAndFeatures/Pages/Nestle-sails-supermarket-on-the-Amazon.aspx.

distributing its products in rural India is another good example. The company's challenge was how to reach 500,000 villages in the remote areas of India. Unilever's solution, called *Project Shakti*,[88] was to tap into the growing number of women's self-help groups, of which about one million now exist across India. Unilever rolled out the project in 2001. Company representatives give presentations at self-help group meetings and invite their members to become direct-to-consumer sales distributors selling Unilever products. Unilever provides participants support with training in selling, commercial knowledge, and bookkeeping. Those who complete the training program can then choose to become *Project Shakti* entrepreneurs. Each distributor invests 10,000 to 15,000 rupees ($220–330) in stock at the outset—usually borrowed from the self-help group or micro-finance banks—and aims to get around 500 customers. Most of them generate 10,000 to 12,000 rupees sales revenues a month, which translates into a monthly profit of 700 to 1,000 rupees ($15–22).[89] As of early 2009, the project had over 45,000 distributors covering over 135,000 villages across 15 states. Unilever plans to expand the Shakti distribution model to other EM countries, including Sri Lanka, Vietnam, and Bangladesh.[90] Establishing an innovative distribution system such as Unilever's *Project Shakti* in EM countries can generate an unassailable competitive advantage.

Managing Distributor Relationships

Even when the MNC can locate distribution partners, managing the relationship is a critical task. A breakdown of the MNC/distributor partnership can often turn disastrous. Professors Arnold and Quelch identified four areas of distribution policy in which MNCs should adapt the approaches used in developed markets:[91]

1. *Distributor partner selection criteria.* In developed markets, product-market knowledge is often one of the main criteria for choosing a distributor. However, for EMs, competence in working with MNCs tends to be more promising as a selection criterion. The industry experience criterion may exclude more entrepreneurial candidates.

2. *Direct selling.* Faced with the absence of a suitable distribution infrastructure, scores of MNCs have adopted a direct selling business model in EMs. The relative low cost of labor makes such a format viable. For business-to-business (B2B) selling, EMs can also rely on the internet as a channel. Indeed, China-based Alibaba is now the world's largest B2B online global trading platform with 29.4 million registered users from over 240 countries.[92]

3. *Local autonomy.* MNCs are usually very unfamiliar with the EM's local market environment. As a result, they delegate control over many marketing tasks (e.g., pricing, promotion) to their local distributor. However, the local distributor typically focuses on short-term sales revenues instead of long-term objectives such as building up the business. To safeguard the firm's interest in the development of the business, it is better off to retain some control over some of the most critical marketing decisions.

4. *Exclusivity.* Local distributors often insist on territorial exclusivity. However, for rapid market development, having multiple distributors is often much more preferable.

---

[88]*Shakti* means "strength" in Sanskrit.

[89]http://www.hllshakti.com, accessed April 2, 2009.

[90]"Rustic Wisdom: Unilever to Take Project Shakti Global," economictimes.indiatimes.com, accessed April 6, 2009.

[91]"New Strategies in Emerging Markets," pp. 18–19.

[92]http://news.alibaba.com/specials/aboutalibaba/aligroup/index.html, accessed February 6, 2013.

Communication Strategies for Emerging Markets

Communication strategies are an important driver behind the performance of a brand in EMs. For categories that are novel to the local consumers, marketing activities must accomplish several tasks: educating consumers about the product use and benefits, raising brand awareness, and creating a brand image. A challenge for MNCs in EMs is to prioritize these tasks. In many EMs, especially those that are still in the early stage of economic development, advertising messages must be very basic. As the chief executive of one advertising agency based in Dhaka, Bangladesh, noted: "If we're launching a new Unilever soap to these communities [rural population in Bangladesh], we have to go as far as to tell people they should wash their hands after they go to the toilet and before they eat. Not only that, we have to show them how they should wash their hands."[93] Another communication-related issue for EMs is whom to target—current existing users of the product or non-users. Most MNCs concentrate on increasing demand from current users, as this is much easier to do. Still, the payoffs from converting non-users into users can be huge.[94]

Push versus Pull Activities

A recurring resource allocation dilemma that marketers face in EMs is the pull-versus-push issue: should the company focus on consumer-oriented promotions (e.g., media advertising) or trade-directed promotions instead? Getting this balance right can be a make-or-break decision for the product's success. In most EMs, the emphasis must often be on trade-directed push-type promotions. There are several reasons. First, in many of these countries, the trade has immense power, especially in rural areas. Consumers interface directly with the retailers and often rely on their brand recommendations. Second, people shop much more frequently than in the West, often on a daily basis. As a result, the opportunities to switch brands arise much more often. Therefore, in-store promotions (e.g., point-of-purchase displays, video-demonstrations) have a heavy influence on their buying decisions.

For consumer-oriented pull promotion activities, mass media like TV and radio are often ineffective, especially in a country like India with its very diverse consumer groups. Instead, targeted media are much more useful. Billboards can be used to straddle India's pyramid: they can reach the poor who do not have TVs and do not read newspapers as well as the rich who are bored being stuck in city traffic.[95] Consumers in EM countries can also process advertisements very differently from those in the West. In China, for instance, ads tend to be read literally; people want credible evidence before they believe claims made in the ads.[96] **Exhibit 17-8** provides some insights on how to communicate with consumers in rural India.

Mass Media versus Non-Traditional Marketing Approaches

In general, mass media in EMs have much less clout than in the developed world. One hurdle for mass media promotions is that the local infrastructure is often a shambles. Basic data on matters such as magazine circulation or TV viewership is often missing or highly inaccurate. Also, in rural areas, coverage by the mass media is often very poor. For instance, 500 million Indians lack TV and radio.[97] Other factors that hamper the effectiveness of mass media in countries such as India

---

[93]"Dissecting the N11," *Campaign Asia-Pacific* (February 2011): 36–38.

[94]"Rethinking Marketing Programs for Emerging Markets," p. 466.

[95]"In India, Billboard Ads Scale New Heights," *Wall Street Journal Asia*, April 26, 2007, p. 30.

[96]"One Country, Different Systems," *Media*, March 9, 2007, p. 5.

[97]Hindustan Unilever Limited, Merrill Lynch India Conference Investor Presentation, February 2, 2009.

Exhibit 17-8   Guidelines on Reaching Rural India

1. Rural India is not a consolidated entity. It is impossible to reach everybody. Due to vast cultural and language differences, common programs, even within the same state, are often not doable.
2. Mass media (e.g., TV, press, radio) are not effective as rural communities are mostly oral societies with low literacy rates. Stalls or vans parked in rural areas are much more valuable tools. They provide both brand building and sampling opportunities.
3. Opinion leaders (e.g., retailers, school teachers, *panchayats*—village heads) represent an important rural marketing channel. Such channels can be powerful brand ambassadors; consumers often trust their recommendations.
4. A key step is to identify prominent social occasions and use them to build brands. Examples include market days (*haats*) and festivals. Setting up a stall costs very little; the average turnout for a *haat* could be 5,000 people.
5. Some successful rural programs rely on local youths who sell brands in 10 to 15 villages on bicycles. Examples of brands that deployed such programs include Colgate, Heinz, and Eveready. The seller gets a small monthly stipend of around $35.
6. Product trial at a minimal charge can be very effective.

Sources: "Reaching Rural India," *Media*, May 4, 2007, p. 13; and "Countryside Competition," *Media*, June 29, 2007, p. 25.

are illiteracy and language diversity. In the urban areas, on the other hand, consumers are bombarded with TV ads for many competing brands. Given that the tastes of EM consumers tend to be very fickle, attracting and keeping them through mass media advertising tools like TV or radio often turns out to be very difficult.

Given these limitations, non-traditional communication approaches can be much more rewarding. Also, with labor being relatively cheap, people-intensive communication modes can deliver more bang for the buck. They also enable the marketer to spend more time on educating the customer and to customize the message. One approach is **grassroots marketing**, which starts from the bottom up by targeting a small group of influential people and counts on them to spread the word (off- and/or online) about your product, service, or idea. It often costs much less than mass media marketing efforts. Meguiar's would engage car clubs to organize free car-care workshops to build up its car-care brand and demonstrate how to use its products in emerging markets around the world. Many participants would post videos of the workshop on their Facebook or YouTube site that could be viewed by their friends.[98] To convince Chinese mothers in tier 2 cities that a new Kraft breakfast entrée, named Uguan-Bing, was a nutritious option for their six- to nine-year-old children, the company engaged marketing consulting firm Wildfire to organize a word-of-mouth campaign. The firm seeded the product with an army of influential moms who would start conversations about the product with their friends and give them samples. With the campaign, Kraft was able to reach over 90,000 moms with offline word-of-mouth.[99]

To reach dwellers in small towns or the countryside, event marketing can be a very potent tool. Ford Motor Co. and its agency JWT created plays based on tales of magic realism to accompany the launch of a new Ford Ranger pickup truck in Argentina. The 25-minute plays were shown in four small towns in the province of Buenos Aires. Local Ford dealers helped bring in the audience. The plays were so popular that mayors from other towns contacted Ford Motor to have them in their townships also.[100] In India, Unilever organized Mother-Daughter days in rural areas to promote its Clinic Plus shampoo brand. The events invited mother-daughter teams to display their

---

[98]Tom Muldowney, Managing Director Posh Pile, personal communication.

[99]http://www.wildfire.asia, accessed February 3, 2013.

[100]"Ford Brings Theater to Argentina's Countryside in Tales of Magic Realism," http://www.adage.com, accessed March 18, 2010.

Global Perspective 17-2

Nigeria Overtakes Ireland to Become the Second-Largest Market for Guinness Beer

In 2007, Nigeria had the distinction of overtaking Ireland as the second-largest market for Guinness, the Irish beer brand owned by Diageo (Britain is the stout's biggest market). Guinness Nigeria's success stems from several factors: development of products customized to the local market, aggressive marketing, brand heritage, and lack of strong competition. The brand thrives in Nigeria despite numerous challenges such as the logistical problems of operating in Africa, political instability, the rise of born-again Christianity, and strict enforcement of Islamic laws in Nigeria's Muslim regions.

European colonizers introduced the brand more than 200 years ago in west and central Africa. While Guinness Nigeria uses the brand's familiar harp logo, the product formulation is customized to local tastes. The main ingredient for the Nigerian brew is sorghum, a common African cereal. As a result, the Nigerian stout has a sweeter flavor. In fact, a significant share of sales comes from exports to the Nigerian diaspora in Britain. The brewer also launched Malta Guinness, a non-alcoholic beer that targets the light-beer drinking segment of the population.

Guinness Nigeria owes part of its success to the brilliant "Michael Power" campaign. The campaign centered on a fictional James Bond–like action figure. Guinness ran the campaign in Africa from 1999 to 2006. Instead of having Michael Power make a standard sales pitch, the ad agency created a series of Michael Power short films used as vehicles for Guinness product placement. As the films were free, they were very popular with many African TV stations. In 2003, Guinness took the Power campaign to a higher level with the action movie *Critical Assignment* in which the hero fights a corrupt African politician. However, given the lack of cinemas in Nigeria, the company had to spend heavily on its own screenings. It dropped the campaign in 2006 to comply with the parent company's worldwide code on marketing. The code involves cutting back on words with a potential sexual connotation, including "power." Instead, Guinness ran a new TV ad campaign that promotes the brand as "the home of greatness."

Sources: "My Goodness: Nigeria Overtakes Ireland in Guinness Sales," www.guardian.co.uk, accessed April 4, 2009; http://en.wikipedia.org/wiki/Michael_Power_(Guinness_character); and "The Power of a Campaign with a Local Flavour," *Financial Times*, February 12, 2004, p. 9.

talents in handicrafts, painting, and other popular folk arts via a talent contest. These events received a lot of media attention. The promotion strengthened the brand image in participating villages and led to an 8 percent increase in the user base.[101] **Global Perspective 17-2** discusses Diageo's marketing strategy for Guinness beer that made Nigeria the second-largest market for the brand.

SUMMARY

Scores of MNCs are salivating over the prospect of selling their goods to the billion-plus consumers located in emerging markets. Yet, emerging markets are very distinctive from developed countries. Business models that were honed in industrialized countries can fail miserably in this part of the world. The challenges faced in EMs are manifold: low incomes, lack of adequate distribution and media systems, and cultural diversity, to mention just a few. The market opportunities

---

[101]"MNCs Look to Build Real Equity in Rural Market," *Campaign Asia-Pacific* (June 2012): 22–23.

clearly do exist, but assailing these markets is not for the faint-hearted. In this chapter we covered the key characteristics of such markets. We then discussed a recent phenomenon—the rise of the so-called new champions—companies rooted in EMs that have outperformed large MNCs in their home turf. Increasingly, several of these challengers pose a threat to incumbent MNCs in the global arena.

To thrive in EMs, MNCs need to rethink their basic business models. Just focusing on the upper crust of the market while leaving the mass market to local firms can prove a fatal blunder. Instead, successful companies have been able to tap into the so-called bottom-of-the-pyramid market. Finally, we examined how the distinctive characteristics of the EM's market environment force MNCs to create new strategic marketing approaches.

QUESTIONS

1. Explain what is meant by "backward innovation." What are its pluses and minuses?

2. How can a local brand such as the Philippine fast food restaurant chain Jollibee stay on top of foreign brands like McDonald's or Wendy's?

3. What are the challenges posed by EMs in the area of distribution/communications? What are some of the solutions?

4. China-based Huawei is the world's second-largest maker of telecommunications equipment. In recent years, the company has started branching out into consumer products such as smartphones. The firm has been expanding globally since 1997. In 2000, Huawei decided to enter India. The company met several challenges in India, where the Huawei brand was little known. First, the India telecom equipment market is crowded. Huawei needed to establish a reputation as a trustworthy partner. Second, its Chinese roots worked against it. In many countries, including India, Chinese companies suffer from an image of making cheap but poor-quality goods. Huawei was seen as a low-quality, low-price manufacturer despite the fact that the firm had a respectable R&D budget. How should Huawei deal with these challenges?

5. Many companies assume that emerging markets are technology backwaters. Do you agree, or is this just a myth? Explain.

SUSTAINABLE MARKETING IN THE GLOBAL MARKETPLACE

CHAPTER OVERVIEW

1. Global corporate citizenship

2. Major areas of CSR

3. The case for sustainability

4. Challenges for sustainability strategies

5. Sustainable marketing and global consumers

6. Developing and implementing a sustainable strategy

7. Global stakeholder engagement programs

8. Sustainable marketing mix policy for the global marketplace

9. Crisis management and consumer boycotts

In the past, Dutch-based Royal DSM was known as a chemicals company. These days the company, which had a 2012 revenue of €9.1 billion, describes itself as a global materials and life sciences company active in health, nutrition, and materials. Its customers include world-class food and beverage companies and major cosmetics manufacturers. **Sustainability** has become a key driver of the company's business. The company identified three global trends that will drive its operations in the future: (1) health and wellness (ageing population, rising healthcare costs, food security), (2) global shifts (population growth, urbanization, wealth gap), and (3) climate and energy challenges (resource constraints, energy security, sustainability). It has embarked on several initiatives to meet these key challenges. For instance, as far back as 1999, DSM opened a plant in Georgia in the United States to take nylon carpets and recycle them back to their base material—"caprolactam." The recycled materials have exactly the same quality as newly made ones. Moreover, the process can be repeated many times. The technology was so astounding that Shaw Industries, the world's largest carpet maker, bought the plant in 2001, although DSM continues to run it.[1] On another front, the company pursues scores of initiatives to improve people's lives, especially in the developing world. For instance, it partnered with the United Nations World Food Program (WFP) to fight malnutrition and hidden hunger in low-income countries. The partnership, in place since 2007, has contributed to improving people's diets in developing countries such as Nepal, Kenya, and Afghanistan. One example of an innovative

---

[1]http://www.dsm.com, accessed March 13, 2013.

product marketed as part of the collaboration is NutriRice, a rice fortified with essential micronutrients that looks and tastes the same as regular rice. In some cases, the company gives products away to those who need them the most and cannot afford them.

DSM is just one example of a company that strives to be a good (or better) global corporate citizen by doing the "right thing." Very few people now believe that the sole responsibility of corporate executives is to make as much money as possible for their shareholders, as Milton Friedman famously put it in *Capitalism and Freedom*. These days, the critical question in companies' boardrooms is no longer whether to become a good corporate citizen but how. Companies realize that they must consider the impact of their decisions and policies on a wide range of stakeholders besides their shareholders. To be successful in the long term, a company must create value for its shareholders and customers but also local communities and society at large. While the idea that a company has societal obligations has been around for many decades, corporate social responsibility (CSR) has never been more prominent on the corporate agenda.[2] Many companies now dedicate an entire section on sustainability on their corporate websites. Sundry blue-chip firms (e.g., Coca-Cola, Kellogg, DuPont) have even appointed a "chief sustainability officer" (CSO) or set up sustainability committees to steer their corporate citizenship efforts. Multinationals, and global brands in particular, face tremendous challenges given the complexities of the global marketplace. In this closing chapter, we will shed light on the challenges of corporate citizenship in today's global market environment.

Global Corporate Citizenship

The relevance of ethics and corporate responsibility for marketing in the global marketplace is well accepted. Companies, especially big multinationals, can wield a lot of influence in countries where they operate. In this section, we look at the meaning and scope of corporate citizenship.

While **corporate social responsibility (CSR)** has become well-embedded as a concept, the business ethics literature and press use a range of other monikers: sustainability, corporate philanthropy, corporate citizenship, responsible business. While there may be subtle differences in the meaning of these terms, they largely overlap, and we will use them interchangeably.[3] Definitions of CSR abound. One definition of corporate social responsibility that has gained some currency in the academic literature is "the company's status and activities with respect to its perceived societal obligations."[4] The European Commission defined corporate social responsibility (CSR) as "a concept whereby companies integrate social and environmental concerns in their business operations and in their interaction with their stakeholders on a voluntary basis."[5] Besides investors, **stakeholder groups** span customers, employees, suppliers, local communities, and future generations. One element of the EC definition that we would like to emphasize is that CSR represents voluntary endeavors to benefit society.

Scope of CSR

The scope of CSR or corporate citizenship covers several domains. The **United Nations Global Compact (UNGC)** is a framework that the UN established in 2000 to help companies in adopting sustainable and socially responsible strategies. It stipulates 10 principles in the

---

[2]N. Craig Smith, "Corporate Social Responsibility: Whether or How?" *California Management Review* 45, no. 4 (2003): 52–76.

[3]For instance, sustainability typically refers to the impact of the company's activities and products on the natural environment.

[4]Tom J. Brown and Peter A. Dacin, "The Company and the Product: Corporate Associations and Consumer Product Responses," *Journal of Marketing* 61, no. 1 (1997): 68–84.

[5]http://eur-lex.europa.eu/LexUriServ/LexUriServ.do?uri = COM:2011:0681:FIN:EN:PDF, accessed March 14, 2013.

Exhibit 18-1   The UN Global Compact's Ten Principles

Human Rights

- *Principle 1*: Businesses should support and respect the protection of internationally proclaimed rights; and
- *Principle 2*: make sure that they are not complicit in human right abuses.

Labor

- *Principle 3*: Businesses should uphold the freedom of association and the effective recognition of the right to collective bargaining;
- *Principle 4*: the elimination of all forms of forced and compulsory labor;
- *Principle 5*: the effective abolition of child labor; and
- *Principle 6*: the elimination of discrimination in respect of employment and occupation.

Environment

- *Principle 7*: Businesses should support a precautionary approach to environmental challenges;
- *Principle 8*: undertake initiatives to promote greater environmental responsibility; and
- *Principle 9*: encourage the development and diffusion of environmentally friendly technologies.

Anti-Corruption

- *Principle 10*: Businesses should work against corruption in all its forms, including extortion and bribery.

Source: http://www.unglobalcompact.org, accessed March 14, 2013.

areas of human rights, labor, the environment, and anti-corruption (see **Exhibit 18-1**). In November 2010, ISO, the International Organization for Standardization, launched a standard called ISO 26000 to provide guidance for businesses and organizations to operate in a socially responsible way. The ISO 26000 standard centers around six corporate social responsibility core subjects:[6]

1. *Human rights* spanning areas such as treatment of vulnerable groups, discrimination, and cultural and political rights.

2. *Labor practices* including issues such as health and safety at work, union relationships, work conditions, and training in the workplace.

3. *The environment* with issues such as pollution prevention, eco-friendly products, sustainable resource use, climate change mitigation, protection of the environment, biodiversity, and hazardous waste management.

4. *Fair operating practices* including areas such as anti-corruption, fair competition, responsible political involvement (e.g., lobbying), respect for property rights, and promoting social responsibility in the value chain.

5. *Consumer issues* like fair marketing, protecting consumers' health and safety, sustainable consumption, customer education, consumer data protection, and privacy.

6. *Community involvement and support* covering areas that include education initiatives, employment creation and skills development, support for local culture programs, health and housing support for the poor, and social investment.

---

[6]http://www.iso.org/iso/discovering_iso_26000.pdf, accessed March 15, 2013.

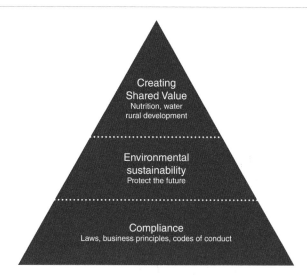

Exhibit 18-2 The Nestlé Creating-Shared-Value (CSV) Pyramid

Source: http://www.nestle .com/csv/what-is-csv/csv-explained, accessed April 15, 2013.

As you can see, the scope of CSR is very broad. A key challenge facing multinationals is to prioritize across these different CSR-related endeavors and decide the amount of resources (money, time, personnel, and intellectual capital) to dedicate to such activities.[7] The key areas to concentrate on should depend on the nature of the company's business operations and its competitive skills. Also, multinationals may often tailor their CSV priorities and allocations to the local country environment.

Nestlé, the Swiss consumer goods multinational, offers a good illustration. The company has adopted a concept for corporate responsibility that is called "Creating Shared Value" (CSV). Nestlé's framework centers on areas where the company feels it has the greatest potential to address the needs of its various stakeholders. These key areas include (see **Exhibit 18-2**):

- *Nutrition.* Help people to eat a healthier diet; improve nutrition by addressing vitamins and minerals deficiency; address obesity.

- *Water.* Reduce the impact of the company's water use; promote good water stewardship globally.

- *Rural development.* Support rural communities surrounding the company's operations.

- *Sustainability.* Offer products made in a responsible way; involve partners from supplier to consumer to improve the environmental impact.

- *Compliance.* Abide by local laws and international legislation.

Major Areas of CSR

As we noted earlier, CSR touches many diverse areas. Below we highlight five key pillars that could matter to global marketers: (1) corruption and bribery, (2) the environment, (3) supply chain management, (4) treatment of customers, and (5) community support.

Corruption/Graft

Corruption (graft) is the abuse of entrusted power by government officials for private gain. The Corruption Perceptions Index is a measure compiled each year by Transparency International

---

[7]C. B. Bhattacharya and Sankar Sen, "Doing Better at Doing Good: When, Why and How Consumers Respond to Corporate Social Initiatives," *California Management Review* 47 (Fall 2004): 9–24.

Exhibit 18-3   Corruption Perceptions Index 2012

Rank	Country	Score	Rank	Country	Score
1	Denmark, Finland & New Zealand	90	133	Comoros, Guyana, Honduras, Iran, Kazakhstan & Russia	28
4	Sweden	88	139	Azerbaijan, Kenya, Nepal, Nigeria & Pakistan	27
5	Singapore	87	144	Bangladesh, Cameroon, Central African Republic, Congo Republic, Syria & Ukraine	26
6	Switzerland	86	150	Eritrea, Guinea-Bissau, Papua New Guinea & Paraguay	25
7	Australia & Norway	85	154	Guinea & Kyrgyzstan	24
9	Canada & Netherlands	84	156	Yemen	23
11	Iceland	82	157	Angola, Cambodia & Tajikistan	22
12	Luxembourg	80	160	Democratic Republic of Congo, Laos & Libya	21
13	Germany	79	163	Equatorial Guinea & Zimbabwe	20
14	Hong Kong	77	165	Burundi, Chad, Haiti & Venezuela	19
15	Barbados	76	169	Iraq	18
16	Belgium	75	170	Turkmenistan & Uzbekistan	17
17	Japan & United Kingdom	74	172	Myanmar	15
19	United States	73	173	Sudan	13
20	Chile	72	174	Afghanistan & North Korea	8

Source: http://www.transparency.org, accessed March 25, 2013.

(TPI) showing how corrupt a country or territory is perceived to be. The index ranges between 0 and 100, where 0 means the country is seen to be highly corrupt and 100 means it is very clean. **Exhibit 18-3** shows the 20 countries that scored highest and the 20 countries at the bottom of the index in 2012. Note that even at the top, no country has a perfect score. The countries at the bottom are the usual suspects: countries plagued by conflict (war, civil strife) and/or poverty.

One of the most prominent manifestations of corruption is bribery. Most countries have stringent laws against bribery. For instance, the Foreign Corrupt Practices Act (FCPA) prohibits U.S. companies and their representatives from trying to obtain or retain business by offering improper gifts or payments to foreign government officials (see also Chapter 5). The strict interpretation of the FCPA has led several U.S. firms to complain that it places them at a competitive disadvantage vis-à-vis their foreign competitors. The FCPA's definition of a U.S. firm is very broad; it includes any company whose shares are traded on an American stock exchange (e.g., NYSE, Nasdaq). In 2008, Siemens, a German industrial conglomerate, was penalized with a $1.6 billion fine, the largest fine in modern corporate history, for bribery practices that took place in countries such as Venezuela, Iraq, and Argentina.[8]

Although anti-corruption laws are in place, enforcement can be a problem, especially in countries with weak rule of law. Many high-profile companies have developed very strict guidelines for their employees to ensure proper ethical behavior for their dealing with government authorities in host countries. For instance, Boeing has 34-page booklet on "Ethical Business Conduct Guidelines" with a summary of the company's key policies and procedures, information about business compliance issues, and a listing of resources on ethical advice.[9]

---

[8]"At Siemens, Bribery Was Just a Line Item," http://www.nytimes.com, accessed December 20, 2008.
[9]http://www.boeing.com/assets/pdf/companyoffices/aboutus/ethics/ethics_booklet.pdf, accessed March 25, 2013.

Environmental Concerns

Another prominent domain of sustainability is the environment. Environment-related issues have become a major issue for consumers around the world. The 2011 ImagePower Green Brands Survey, which collected responses from more than 9,000 consumers in 8 countries,[10] uncovered the following major trends affecting consumer behavior:[11]

- Growing concern over energy consumption. Respondents in five of the countries[12] singled out energy use as the biggest green issue.

- Emphasis on basic brand attributes. When asked which attributes are most important, consumers listed the more basic ones (e.g., good value, reliability, high quality) over greenness.

- Increased desire to buy green. A majority of respondents in Brazil, China, and India planned to spend more on green products. However, a limited assortment and access were barriers. Chinese consumers in China had one other hurdle: confusing or untrustworthy labeling. In developed countries, price and limited selection of green products are the biggest barriers.

- Interest in big-ticket green products. Consumers in all surveyed markets planned to buy more eco-friendly big ticket items (e.g., cars, technology).

- Attention to packaging. In all countries, except the United States, consumers sought out products with less packaging. In most of the countries, recyclability was the most important aspect of green packaging. Germans felt that companies should use less packaging to begin with. Chinese consumers favored packaging made from biodegradable materials.

Legions of multinationals have set lofty goals to reduce their environmental impact. Unilever, for example, announced a 10-year Sustainable Living plan in November 2010 to reduce the company's environmental footprint worldwide. The key objectives to reduce Unilever's environmental impact by 2020 include:

- Halve the greenhouse gas impact of Unilever products across the life cycle.

- Halve the water associated with the consumer use of Unilever products.

- Halve the waste associated with the disposal of the company's products.

- Source 100 percent of agricultural raw materials (e.g., palm oil sugar, cocoa) sustainably.

  Its 2011 progress report showed improvement in a number of areas such as:[13]

- Sustainable sourcing—sustainably sourced raw materials rose from 14 percent in 2010 to 24 percent.

- Renewable energy—100 percent of electricity bought in Europe came from renewable sources.

- Drinking water—since 2005, 35 million people had gained access to safe drinking water from Pureit, a relatively cheap water purifier which Unilever has introduced in India, Indonesia, Mexico, Brazil, Nigeria, and Sri Lanka (www.pureitwater.com).

Other companies have set similar lofty goals to reduce their carbon footprint through innovation and more efficient use of natural resources in their operations.

---

[10] The countries were: Australia, Brazil, China, France, Germany, India, the United Kingdom, and the United States.

[11] "Price, Packaging, and Perception. Results from the 2011 ImagePower Green Brands Survey," http://www .cohnwolfe.com/en/ideas-insights/white-papers/green-brands-survey-2011, accessed March 10, 2013.

[12] China, France, Germany, the United Kingdom, and the United States.

[13] http://www.unilever.com/sustainable-living/, accessed March 20, 2013.

Exhibit 18-4 Examples of Water Saver Initiatives

Company	Partner	Initiative	Description	Website
Unilever	LuLu Group	"Water Savers"	Educate consumers across the United Arab Emirates and offer them tools to save water.	
Nestlé		Project WET	Worldwide initiative to reach children, parents, educators, and communities with water education.	www.projectwet.org
H&M	WWF		Three-year global partnership to improve stewardship of global water supply.	www.hm.com/water
P&G		Children's Safe Drinking Water Program	Distributes water purification packets to communities in need around the globe.	http://www.csdw.org/csdw/index.shtml

Source: Based on "Brands Mark World Water Day 2013," http://www.brandchannel.com, accessed March 22, 2013.

Environmental initiatives typically center around the so-called **5Rs**—to reduce, recycle, use renewable sources, remove environmentally harmful materials, and reuse of product-related materials (e.g., packaging). Some of the environmental protection practices that PepsiCo undertook in Greater China alone in recent years include:[14]

- Construction of eco-friendly bottling plants that can save water and energy and reduce carbon emissions.

- Development with local suppliers of environmental-friendly coolers.

- Sustainable farming. With seven farms in China, PepsiCo is one of the largest agricultural enterprises in the country. Investment included advanced irrigation technology to reduce water consumption in potato cultivation.

Exhibit 18-4 lists some examples of efforts multinational firms have made to address the world's water crisis by conserving water or providing safe drinking water in poorer countries.

Environmental thinking can also heavily influence companies' global new product development efforts. For instance, PepsiCo launched the world's first 100 percent PET bottle made from fully renewable sources. **Exhibit 18-5** shows the Top 10 brands in

Exhibit 18-5 Interbrand 2012 Green Brands

Ranking	Brand Name	Country of Origin	Sector
1	Toyota	Japan	Automotive
2	Johnson & Johnson	United States	Pharmaceuticals
3	Honda	Japan	Automotive
4	Volkswagen	Germany	Automotive
5	HP	United States	Electronics
6	Panasonic	Japan	Electronics
7	Dell	United States	Electronics
8	Siemens	Germany	Diversified
9	Danone	France	FMCG
10	BMW	Germany	Automotive

Source: http://www.interbrand.com/en/best-global-brands/Best-Global-Green-Brands/2012-Report.aspx, accessed March 22, 2013.

---

[14]http://www.pepsico.com/Download/GCR_Sustainability_Report_EN_Final.pdf, accessed March 23, 2013.

Interbrand's 2012 Green Brands ranking. Note that four of these leading green brands are automotive ones.

Supply Chain Accountability

In November 2012, a fire in the Tazreen Fashion factory in Bangladesh claimed over 100 victims. Fatal fires are very common in Bangladesh's large garment manufacturing sector, due to lax safety standards and poor electrical wiring. Many of these plants have Dickensian labor conditions. Clothes account for up to 80 percent of the country's annual exports. The Tazreen facility made clothes for several major Western brands and retailers including Wal-Mart, Gap, and Tesco. However, all of these companies claimed that they did not know their goods were being made at Tazreen Fashions.[15] Apparently, the factory had been an unauthorized subcontractor for these brands.[16]

In early 2013, the horse meat crisis in Europe forced several retailers like Tesco, Aldi, and IKEA as well as food manufacturers like Nestlé to withdraw food products (e.g., lasagna, Swedish meatballs) that contained horse meat instead of beef.[17] A follow-up investigation blamed two major meat processors in France, which had been selling 750 tons of mislabeled horse meat, sourced from Romania, over a six-month period.[18] Paul Bulcke, Nestlé's CEO, commented: "Widespread fraud is being committed by a few across Europe. I understand that many consumers . . . feel misled, I feel the same. This should not happen, it is unforgivable. We have let our consumers down."[19] A global brand's supply chain is another very critical area of social responsibility and reputation for most companies. However, as the both examples show, in the global marketplace the supply chain can be extremely byzantine.

The UN Global Compact defines **supply chain sustainability** as the management of environmental, social, and economic impacts throughout the life cycles of goods and services (see **Exhibit 18-6**).[20] These days, sustainable supply chain management has become a crucial topic on many corporate agendas. Even though the supply chain usually does not fall under the responsibility of marketing managers, negative coverage in the press or allegations on social media can easily tarnish a global brand's reputation around the world. NGOs scrupulously monitor supply chain practices of multinationals and their sourcing partners. In some cases, social activists have also organized campaigns and boycotts against global brands (e.g., Nike for the use of sweatshop labor, Coca-Cola/PepsiCo for alleged depletion of water resources in India) to protest supply chain malpractices. Supply-chain–related concerns center around three main areas:

1. Environmental issues (e.g., protection of the rainforest, sustainable farming/fishing)

2. Social issues (e.g., abolition of child labor, labor union rights)

3. Economic issues (e.g., living wage, no discrimination, fair price to farmers)

---

[15]"Dhaka Bangladesh Clothes Factory Fire Kills More Than 100," http://www.bbc.co.uk/news, accessed November 25, 2012.

[16]"Bangladesh Factory Fires—The Hidden Dangers of Subcontracting," http://www.ethicalcorp.com, accessed February 5, 2013.

[17]Actually, nutrition-wise, horsemeat can be considered better than beef as it has less fat, sodium, and cholesterol. Though culturally taboo in many countries, it can be found on dinner tables around the world. It is especially popular as a dish in Russia, Belgium, China, and Italy. The main problem was that horsemeat is usually not farmed so its history cannot be traced.

[18]http://www.foodsafety.com.au/infographics/horsemeat/, accessed April 3, 2013.

[19]"Nestlé CEO Speaks Out about Sustainability, Horse Meat Scandal," http://www.brandchannel.com, accessed February 28, 2013.

[20]http://www.unglobalcompact.org, accessed March 26, 2013.

Exhibit 18-6 Steps toward Sustainable Supply Chain Management

Source: http://www .unglobalcompact.org/docs/ news_events/8.1/ Supply_Chain_Sustainability .pdf, accessed March 20, 2013.

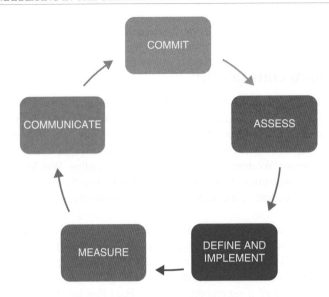

To implement sustainable supply chain management, a company should take the following steps:[21]

1. **Commit.** Develop the business case by understanding the external environment and business drivers. Benchmark against peer companies. Establish a vision and objectives for supply chain sustainability. Set sustainability expectations for the supply chain. The latter could entail preparation of a code of conduct for supply chain partners.

2. **Assess.** Determine the scope of the sustainability program. Many firms initially focus on their key suppliers. There could also be "hot spots" that are several steps removed from the firm's operations.

3. **Define and implement.** Engage with suppliers to develop a shared mindset about sustainability issues, e.g., by raising their awareness about the key trouble spots. Implement policies in supplier selection (due diligence) and engagement with existing suppliers on continuous improvement. For issues that are too challenging to tackle alone, industry collaboration or partnerships with NGOs could be useful tools.

4. **Measure.** Assess the company's performance against supply chain sustainability goals. There are a number of specialized firms that can help with the data collection.

5. **Communicate progress.** Communicate and report on the company's progress. Such a report could be useful for multiple purposes such as a source of best practice, benchmarking, self-evaluation.

Commitment toward Customers

One highly important group of stakeholders is the company's very own customers. One aspect is a company's marketing toward so-called vulnerable consumer segments such as children or low-income households. Several large food multinationals have committed themselves to **responsible marketing** of their products. PepsiCo adopted a global policy to advertise only nutritious products

---

[21]http://www.unglobalcompact.org/docs/news_events/8.1/Supply_Chain_Sustainability.pdf, accessed March 20, 2013.

toward children. It also implemented a global school-oriented program that focuses on beverage sales that foster healthy nutrition habits among students.[22]

Part of the commitment toward consumers involves developing and offering products that are beneficial for them. For instance, several global food and beverage companies such as Danone, Nestlé, and PepsiCo have focused their product innovation efforts on creating nutritious and healthy products that are affordable. In 2007, following an encounter between Danone CEO Franck Riboud and Muhammad Yunus, the 2006 Nobel Peace Prize winner, the French food giant set up a social business incubator called danone.communities. Its aim is to support and finance social businesses that will contribute to eliminating malnutrition and poverty. Examples are "1001 Fountains" in Cambodia to supply cheap, healthy drinking water to rural communities and "Laiterie du Berger" in Senegal, an enterprise that sources milk from local cattle farmers and reduces dependence on imported milk powder.[23]

Other consumer-related concerns include matters such as product labeling, product safety, and fairness. Decentralized organizations sometimes have limited ability to maintain consistent consumer-oriented CSR policies around the world. In October 2011, Wal-Mart ran into trouble in China when some of its stores in Chongqing province were accused of mislabeling ordinary pork as a more expensive organic variety.[24] Differences in pricing or customer service policies can trigger lack-of-fairness accusations in those countries where consumers feel they are on the short end of the stick. For instance, iTunes customers in the United Kingdom complained about being charged more for music downloads than users in other European Union countries. Apple argued that it always wanted to offer a fully pan-European service but that it was restricted by the content providers.[25] In March 2013, Chinese state media accused Apple of discriminating against Chinese customers with its after-sales service. One complaint was that warranties for Apple products in China were much shorter than in other countries. Another concern was Apple's use of refurbished parts for repairs. Following the attack, Apple decided to alter its warranty policy for China and also issued a formal apology on its China website.[26]

Community Support (Cause-Related Marketing)

In 2000, PepsiCo China rolled out the "Water Cellars for Mothers" program to provide safe drinking water access in rural areas of central and western China. By the end of 2010, the program had funded the construction of 1,500 water cellars. In 2008, PepsiCo China also embarked on a program with the local Red Cross Society to help improve schools for migrant children. The company also set up a program to build libraries in China's rural areas. During natural disasters such as the 2008 Sichuan earthquake, the company contributed to disaster relief efforts.[27]

A final major area of SCR is support of the local community covering aspects such as educational and housing support, donations for the local culture scene, and health policy initiatives. When these efforts are tied to a specific social issue (e.g., AIDS education, teenage pregnancy), they are often referred to as **cause-related** marketing. Whereas the previous areas primarily relate to global corporate citizenship, community support activities focus on local activities. Often such activities will involve the company's local staff. A case in point is the "Citizen Day" program created by L'Oréal. For the 2011 event, the French cosmetics company mobilized 15,600 staff in 58 countries. Initiatives included renovating an elementary school in Belgrade, helping out at a plantation in India, planting trees in Bogota.[28]

---

[22]http://www.pepsico.com/Purpose/Human-Sustainability.html, accessed April 8, 2013.

[23]http://www.danone.com/en/axes-strategiques/danone.communities.html, accessed April 8, 2013.

[24]"Mislabeling China Risk at Wal-Mart," http://online.wsj.com, accessed October 18, 2011.

[25]"EU Price Probe into Apple iTunes," http://news.bbc.co.uk, accessed April 3, 2007.

[26]"Apple Apologises for 'Arrogance' over Chinese Customer Services," *Financial Times*, April 2, 2013, p. 1.

[27]http://www.pepsico.com/Download/GCR_Sustainability_Report_EN_Final.pdf, accessed March 19, 2013.

[28]http://www.loreal.com, accessed March 20, 2013.

While philanthropy activities can be a very useful lever to establish the firm as a good local citizen, multinationals must be cautious in using them. If the firm does poorly in other CSR domains (e.g., the environment, human rights), these initiatives could raise the suspicions of being an attempt to cover up ("white-wash") the firm's poor track record. Overpromotion of community support efforts might also lead to an impression of such activities simply being publicity stints.

The Case for Sustainability

Multinationals can no longer avoid being socially responsible. Trying to be a good corporate citizen can bring valuable benefits. Below we spell out the main motivations for engaging in socially responsible endeavors.

Reputation in Consumer Markets

From a marketing perspective, probably the prime reason for pursuing CSR is that it helps building trust with consumers. A strong CSR record could contribute to the global brand's equity. People expect that global brands have a special duty to tackle issues important to society. In a 2002 survey covering 12 countries on why consumers pick global brands, "social responsibility" came out as the third-most-important element (8 percent) after "quality" (44 percent) and "global myth" (12 percent).[29] Another study that looked at 57 global brands in 10 different countries also found that CSR reinforced brand equity.[30] The playing field is not level; consumers typically set much higher standards on social issues (e.g., climate change, poverty) for multinationals than for smaller firms or domestic companies. Global brands are subject to much more scrutiny in the media and on the web. Multinationals are usually a favorite target for non-government organizations (NGOs) such as Oxfam and Greenpeace. Reputational risk coupled with greater visibility and scrutiny puts immense pressure on multinationals to engage in CSR-related activities.

One concern that multinationals face with reputation management is the so-called negativity effect: consumers place much more weight on negative publicity than on positive publicity.[31] Thus, a highly visible negative event (e.g., the BP Deepwater Horizon oil spill in the Gulf of Mexico) can easily unravel the efforts of many years to build up a positive image. In today's interconnected world, negative publicity about a brand or multinational travels fast and far beyond the place where the incident originally took place. Indeed, one study showed that a positive CSR image could work as an insurance policy by reducing the risk of damage to brand evaluation in the wake of a crisis.[32] Thus, to some extent, investing in CSR can be seen as building up a reservoir of goodwill.

Brand Loyalty

Firms with a good CSR image could also get rewarded with higher brand loyalty and the ability to charge a price premium. Ethical behavior has become an intrinsic part of the DNA for several brands such as the Body Shop, Unilever's Ben & Jerry's ice cream, or Lush, the British brand of handmade cosmetics. These brands have build up a loyal following of consumers around the world. In those industries and countries where CSR is highly valued, firms could use CSR endeavors to differentiate their brand from the competition.

---

[29]Douglas B. Holt, John A. Quelch, and Earl L. Taylor, "How Global Brands Compete," *Harvard Business Review* 82 (September 2004): 69–75.

[30]Anna Torres, Tammo H.A. Bijmolt, Joseph A. Tribó, and Peter Verhoef, "Generating Global Brand Equity through Corporate Social Responsibility to Key Stakeholders," *International Journal of Research in Marketing* 29 (2012): 13–24.

[31]See, for instance, Rohini Ahluwalia, Robert E. Burnkrant, and H. Rao Unnava, "Consumer Response to Negative Publicity: The Moderating Role of Commitment," *Journal of Marketing Research* 37 (May 2000): 203–214.

[32]Jill Klein and Niraj Dawar, "Corporate Social Responsibility and Consumers' Attributions and Brand Evaluations in a Product-Harm Crisis," *International Journal of Research in Marketing* 21 (2004): 203–217.

Some scholars also argue that consumers may be willing to pay a price premium for ethical brands.[33] Lab experiments with consumers in Brazil and other countries have shown that consumers are often willing to pay higher prices for products of companies perceived to be responsible and penalize companies perceived to be unethical by demanding a lower price for their products.[34] However, the evidence is rather mixed. Consumers may claim to be "ethical consumers" but are not necessarily willing to pay more for products with ethical claims. One example is the Fairtrade certification system that allows people to identify products that meet minimum environmental and labor standards.[35] Products that carry the Fairtrade mark can be far more expensive than comparable uncertified products. As a result, such products typically have a very small market share. Consumers' willingness to pay a price premium for products with a positive CSR image could also differ a great deal across countries.[36]

Reputation in Labor and Equity Markets

Other stakeholders who could be concerned about CSR issues are employees and investors. Many CSR activities extend to employee welfare and workplace safety. Treating employees well is an intrinsic part of being a good corporate citizen. Not surprisingly, employees often express preference working for companies with a favorable CSR image. Being perceived as a good corporate citizen can help a company in recruiting the best talent and keeping its turnover rate low.[37] Another important stakeholders group is investors. Several investor funds focus on firms that meet social responsibility criteria or divest from companies that fail to address certain issues adequately.

Besides these motivations, there could be other reasons why companies engage in CSR. Though firms often view sustainability as a costly endeavor, sometimes such efforts can lead to lower costs in the long term. CSR can also be seen as a part of the company's risk management approach. By striving to be a good local citizen (e.g., carbon emission reduction), a company could be able to preempt stricter regulations in the host country.[38]

Challenges for Sustainability Strategies

Trying to be a responsible and ethical player in the global marketplace brings a fair share of challenges. Due to cultural differences, a multinational will often experience tension between cultural values of the host market and its own corporate values or the values in the company's home market. The firm's image as a corporate citizen can often be fairly mixed. The local infrastructure to implement CSR strategies can be missing or hopelessly inadequate. Finally, while consumers may value a firm's socially responsible behavior, consumers' intentions and behaviors may not always follow suit. Below we discuss in greater detail the main obstacles a multinational might encounter on its path to a sustainable future.

---

[33]C. B. Bhattacharya and Sankar Sen, "Doing Better at Doing Good: When, Why and How Consumers Respond to Corporate Social Initiatives," *California Management Review* 47 (Fall 2004): 9–24.

[34]Remi Trudel and June Cotte, "Does It Pay to Be Good?" *MIT Sloan Management Review* 50 (Winter 2009); and Sergio W. Carvalho, Sankar Sen, Márcio de Oliveira Mota, and Renata Carneiro de Lima, "Consumer Reactions to CSR: A Brazilian Perspective," *Journal of Business Ethics* 91 (2010): 291–310.

[35]http://www.fairtrade.net, accessed March 14, 2013.

[36]Fabrice Etile and Sabrina Teyssier, "Corporate Social Responsibility and the Economics of Consumer Social Responsibility," Working Paper, Centre Nationale de la Recherche Scientifique, Ecole Polytechnique, Palaiseu Cedex, France, November 6, 2012.

[37]Geoffrey B. Sprinkle and Laureen A. Maines, "The Benefits and Costs of Corporate Social Responsibility," *Business Horizons* 53 (2010): 445–453.

[38]"The Benefits and Costs of Corporate Social Responsibility," p. 447.

Global Perspective 18-1

Google in China

When in 2006 Google launched google.cn, its search engine for China, the internet search giant agreed to comply with the Chinese government demand to censor search results related to sensitive terms such as "Tianmen Square 1989" or "Falun Gong." Many people in the West decried Google's decision and accused the company of betraying its "don't be evil" creed. Internally, Google had also been at odds over the morality of its decision to do business in China through self-censorship.

However, four years later, in March 2010, Google decided to stop self-censoring and announced that it would shut down its search service in mainland China after a two-month standoff with the Chinese government. The decision was sparked by a "sophisticated and targeted" cyber-attack on Google that originated from China. Google stated that the Gmail email accounts of Chinese human rights activists were the main target of the attack, which occurred in December 2009. Google decided to move its Chinese-language site to Hong Kong. Visitors to google.cn were redirected to google.com.hk and greeted with a message saying: "Welcome to Google search in China's new home." David Drummond, Google's chief legal officer at the time, said: "We believe this new approach of providing uncensored search in simplified Chinese from Google.com.hk is a sensible solution to the challenges we've faced. We hope the Chinese government respects our decision, though we are aware that it could at any time block access" (www.guardian.co.uk). Following the

decision, Google fans in China left flowers and other gifts outside the firm's Beijing headquarters.

Some praised Google's decision. Others noted that the search engine giant turned its back on Chinese users, its 700 employees in China, and business partners. Baidu, Google's main competitor in China, claimed that Google's decision to quit was for commercial reasons. In a blog, the chief architect of Baidu wrote: "What Google said makes me sick. If you are to quit for the sake of financial interest, then just say it." Google's Chinese revenues at the time of the withdrawal were indeed relatively small, estimated to be about $250–$300 million. However, according to one expert, they could have risen to $5–$6 billion within four years. Not surprisingly, Google's market share dropped significantly to a mere 16.7 percent by the end of 2011 (see Table A).

Table A Internet Search Market Share in China

Company	Dec. 31, 2009	Dec. 31, 2011
Baidu	58.4%	78.3%
Google	35.6%	16.7%

Source: http://www.marketwatch.com, accessed March 20, 2013.

Sources: "Google Angers China by Shifting Service to Hong Kong," http://www.guardian.co.uk, accessed March 23, 2010; "Google's Tough Call on China," http://www.ft.com, accessed March 24, 2010; "Google's Market Share Falls to 16.7%," http://www.marketwatch.com, accessed January 20, 2012.

Cultural Tensions

In early 2010 Google pulled out of mainland China after a two-month standoff over web censorship with the Chinese government. At the time, many social activists hailed the move as a heroic effort by the company to live up to its "don't be evil" credo. Other people accused the internet search giant of turning its back on its Chinese users, employees, partners, and a huge market opportunity that could have benefited Google investors (see **Global Perspective 18-1**).

Cross-border differences in cultural values and ethical conduct create an environment of moral confusion. Companies often must re-examine their assumptions about the morality of certain marketing practices (e.g., gift giving, product positioning) in the host country. As Google's experience in China illustrates, multinationals often must face tricky judgment calls. The boundaries between right and wrong in many ethical areas can be extremely murky.

There are competing attitudes to this ethical confusion. One approach is known as **cultural relativism**. Relativism states that ethical values and judgments ultimately depend upon one's culture. It is basically a variation of the "When in Rome, do as the Romans do" mindset. No culture's ethics are better or worse. There are no international rights or wrongs. If child labor in the host country is acceptable, so what? As a "guest" of the host country, the firm has no right to make moral judgments about the local norms and practices.

At the other end of the spectrum is **ethical imperialism**: the tendency of people, NGOs, and governments to impose their own norms and ethical values on other cultures.[39] One good illustration is the shark fin controversy. Many Asians see shark fin soup as an intrinsic part of Chinese cuisine, especially for special occasions such as a wedding banquet. Banning shark fin soup would infringe upon their cultural tradition. Other people, especially in the West, condemn the practice as morally repugnant given the way shark fins are "harvested" and the threat of extinction for several shark species. Several luxury hotel chains such as Shangri-La and the Peninsula decided to remove shark fin soup from their menus.[40] Likewise, in 2012 Cathay Pacific, the Hong Kong-based carrier, bowed to pressure from environmental NGOs and announced a ban of shark fin from its cargo flights.[41]

Neither ethical imperialism nor cultural relativism is desirable in shaping ethical behavior. In trying to be a good citizen, companies must balance the extremes. Thomas Donaldson, a law and ethics professor at the Wharton School, offers the following guidelines for ethical leadership in the global marketplace:[42]

1. Treat corporate values and formal standards of conduct as absolutes.

2. Design and implement conditions of engagement for suppliers and customers.

3. Allow foreign business units to help formulate ethical standards and interpret ethical issues.

4. In host countries, support efforts to decrease institutional corruption.

5. Exercise moral imagination. For instance, in the early 1990s Levi Strauss discovered that some of its suppliers in Bangladesh used child labor. Instead of simply forcing these suppliers to fire the children, it set up an arrangement where the suppliers continued to pay the children's wages while these children attended school and to offer each child a job when they graduated. Levi Strauss agreed to cover the tuition and other school-related expenses (e.g., books).

Sustainability Image

As we pointed out earlier, CSR covers many different areas, ranging from socio-economic issues to environmental concerns. Trying to excel in all these different domains is a tremendous challenge, especially in a global platform. The complexity of pursuing CSR means that companies can easily project conflicting messages. One good example is the food industry. The global "Access to Nutrition Index" is an index compiled by the Global Alliance

[39]Georges Enderle and Patrick E. Murphy, "Ethics and Corporate Social Responsibility for Marketing in the Global Marketplace," in Masaaki Kotabe and Kristiaan Helsen, eds., *The SAGE Handbook of International Marketing* (London: SAGE Publications, 2009): 504–531.

[40]"Ban on Shark Fin Soup Advances through Asia," http://online.wsj.com, accessed January 20, 2012.

[41]"Cathay Pacific Bans Shark Fin from Its Cargo Flights," http://www.scmp.com, accessed March 15, 2013.

[42]Thomas Donaldson, "Values in Tension: Ethics Away from Home," *Harvard Business Review* 74 (Sept.-Oct. 1996): 48–62.

Exhibit 18-7   Conflicting CSR Images

Ranking	Oxfam Ranking	Access-to-Nutrition Index Ranking
1	Nestlé	Danone
2	Unilever	Unilever
3	Coca-Cola	Nestlé
4	PepsiCo	PepsiCo
5	Mars	Kraft Foods
6	Danone[*]	Grupo Bimbo
7	Mondelez	ConAgra Foods
8	General Mills[**]	Heinz
9	Kellogg's	Coca-Cola
10	Associated British Foods	Kellogg's

Source: http://www.oxfam.org/en/grow/campaigns/behind-brands and http://www.accesstonutrition.org/.
[*] Danone and Mondelez were tied for the #6 spot in the Oxfam ranking.
[**] General Mills and Kellogg were tied for the #8 spot.

for Improved Nutrition, which evaluates the 25 leading global food and beverage manufacturers on their policies and practices toward obesity and malnutrition.[43] The highest-ranking brands for the first edition of the Index were Danone, Unilever, and Nestlé (see **Exhibit 18-7**). However, none of these brands did well in an Oxfam report, entitled "Behind the Brands," which focused on environmental policies and workers' rights.[44] In 2013, Oxfam also organized an online petition called "The Truth about Women and Chocolate" against Nestlé, Mondelez, and Mars, accusing these companies of ignoring the fate of female workers in the companies' cocoa supply chain.

Multinationals with a wide product portfolio can also be accused of hypocrisy when their products send out conflicting messages (e.g., electric vehicles and gas guzzlers for a car company). A case in point is the cosmetics industry. In 2006, L'Oréal took over the British beauty products retailer Body Shop, celebrated for its ethically sourced products that are not tested on animals. However, some observers pointed out that many of the cosmetics products sold by the French cosmetics giant contain ingredients that were tested on animals. Unfortunately, L'Oréal does not have much leeway. While the European Union bans the sale of all animal-tested cosmetics in its 27 member states, the situation in China is the complete opposite. China's legislation stipulates that all beauty products must be tested on animals first in order to get a license to be sold in the country. As a result, L'Oréal does not intend to launch the Body Shop in China.

A global company also faces the risk that misbehavior by one country subsidiary can easily tarnish the firm's global CSR image worldwide. This is especially the case for larger multinationals, which are often heavily scrutinized by social activists and are favorite poster children for scores of social and environmental issues. Multinationals with a decentralized setup could also be more vulnerable due to lack of oversight of local subsidiaries.

---

[43]http://www.accesstonutrition.org/about-us, accessed March 23, 2013.
[44]http://www.oxfam.org/en/grow/campaigns/behind-brands, accessed March 24, 2013.

Poor Infrastructure

Multinationals committed to sustainability are sometimes forced to scale back their aspirations due to poor infrastructure in the host country. As part of its commitment to environmental sustainability, Nestlé has set an ultimate goal of zero waste. However, in many countries the local recycling infrastructure is dysfunctional or simply missing, especially for hazardous waste. To monitor workplace conditions or supply chains, companies must often rely on third-party auditors to vet their suppliers. Unfortunately, reliable auditing systems and mechanisms are often in short supply in many developing countries, especially those with rampant corruption. In September 2012, a fire at an apparel plant in Karachi, Pakistan, killed nearly 300 workers; many of them were trapped behind locked exit doors. The plant made denim products for the German discount textile chain KiK. Shortly before the fatal fire, the plant had received a prestigious SA8000 certification, implying that the factory met international standards in nine areas, including health and safety, child labor, and minimum wages. The certificate was based on a report from two local inspectors who worked on behalf of Social Accountability International, a nonprofit group supported by large multinationals such as Gap, Gucci, Carrefour, as well as labor rights groups.[45]

Sustainable Marketing and Global Consumers

Consumer awareness about sustainability issues is growing around the world. With the rise of social media, consumers are rapidly alerted when a global brand has a harmful impact at the other end of the planet. Still, consumer behaviors do not always mirror their attitudes concerning sustainability issues such as the environment. A global survey conducted in 2010 by GfK Roper, a consumer research group, showed that 74 percent of consumers stated that it was important that companies take environmentally responsible actions. However, a mere 30 percent considered the environmental impact of their purchases.[46] GfK Roper also found that the greenest segment of global consumers, labeled "GreeninDeed," was only 15 percent (see **Exhibit 18-8**). Greendex is a

Exhibit 18-8   Gfk Roper's Global Segmentation of Environmental Consumers

Green segment	Description	Percent
GreeninDeed	• Green in their lifestyle • Advocate for others to become environmentally responsible as well	15%
GlamourGreen	• Incorporate green elements in their lifestyle but only when it is easy • Status seeking	26%
Carbon Cultured	• Live mainly in developed world • Incorporate green elements in their lifestyle, but not necessarily consciously	19%
GreeninNeed	• Have the desire, but lack the means to be environmentally responsible • Mainly in the developing world	17%
Jaded	• Exhibit least concern • Skeptical of many environmental marketing messages	22%

Based on "Environment: Long-Term Impact of Green Issues Played Down," http://www.ft.com, accessed May 18, 2011.

---

[45]"Inspectors Certified Pakistani Factory as Safe before Disaster," http://www.nytimes.com, accessed September 19, 2012.
[46]"Environment: Long-Term Impact of Green Issues Played Down," http://www.ft.com, accessed May 18, 2011.

survey run each year by National Geographic and the research consultancy GlobeScan to monitor consumer perceptions and behaviors in 65 areas (consumer goods, housing, food, transportation) that could have an impact on the environment. The 2012 survey found that environmentally friendly behavior among consumers compared to 2010 had increased in only 5 of the 17 countries surveyed. The top-scoring consumers of 2012 were in India (58.9), China (57.8), and Brazil (55.5). The lowest scorers were in industrialized countries with the Japanese (48.5), Canadians (47.9), and Americans (44.7) at the bottom of the ranking.[47]

Perceptions and trust of green messages also differ across countries. A survey run by DuPont in 2012 found that 70 percent of urban Chinese consumers expressed confidence in the environmental claims of green products. A similar survey of North American consumers, released in 2011, showed that 65 percent of Canadians and 60 percent of Americans were confident that green products are better for the environment.[48]

One factor for consumers' reluctance to follow suit is that these products (e.g., organic produce, brands with the Fair Trade label) often charge a premium price. One challenge that marketers with such products in their portfolio face is to persuade consumers to buy such products despite the higher price. One study showed that simply having a FAIR TRADE label does not suffice. Sustainable products typically entail a consumer trade-off between individual-level costs (e.g., higher prices, higher search costs due to less accessible distribution), and societal payoffs (e.g., fair wages, better working conditions). The study showed that ethical products such as goods with a FAIR TRADE label should also clearly highlight how such products have the potential to restore justice in the world.[49] An excellent example is Lipton's Rainforest Alliance tea, which sources tea from certified farms. The commercial,[50] showing footage of Unilever's tea estate in Kenya and using an upbeat soundtrack, explains how tea drinkers can make a better choice with Lipton. The message is that certified tea is better for the environment, for tea growers, and for the future.

A 2007 study of 7,751 consumers around the world conducted by McKinsey pinpointed four other barriers to sustainable buying besides the high price of green products:[51]

1. *Lack of awareness.* More than one-third of the consumers surveyed wanted to take action against climate change but did not know how to. Consumers were also confused about buying green products and understanding green product labels.

2. *Negative perceptions.* Many environmentally friendly products have a stigma problem. Consumers often believe that green products perform worse than conventional ones.

3. *Distrust.* Many consumers mistrust environmental claims by companies about their products or services.

4. *Low availability.* Consumers often find it difficult to find eco-friendly products at their local stores when they would like to purchase them.

The 2011 ImagePower Green Brands survey, which interviewed 9,000 consumers in eight countries, showed that the two biggest challenges for buying green products or services are the high price and their limited selection of items to choose from. At the same time, the study revealed some variations across the different countries as shown in **Exhibit 18-9**.

[47]http://images.nationalgeographic.com/wpf/media-content/file/NGS_2012_Final_Global_report_Jul20-cb1343059672.pdf.
[48]"Survey Reveals China's Growing Desire for Green Products," http://biosciences.dupont.com, accessed April 11, 2013.
[49]Katherine White, Rhiannon MacDonnell, and John H. Ellard, "Belief in a Just World: Consumer Intentions and Behaviors toward Ethical Products," *Journal of Marketing* 76 (January 2012): 103–118.
[50]You can view the commercial on YouTube: http://www.youtube.com/watch?v = JIxOQukeSYI.
[51]Sheila Bonini and Jeremy Oppenheim, "Cultivating the Green Consumer," http://www.ssireview.org/articles/entry/cultivating_the_green_consumer, accessed April 12, 2013.

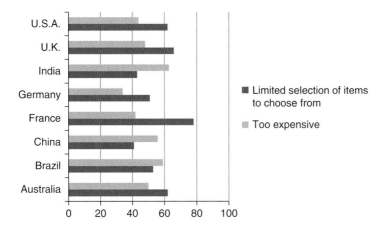

Exhibit 18-9 The Biggest Challenges to Buying Green Products/Services

Source: Based on 2011 ImagePower Green Brands Survey, http://www .cohnwolfe.com, accessed March 10, 2013.

Developing and Implementing a Sustainable Strategy

While firms with small, local brands are less vulnerable, the reputational risk can be very critical for global consumer brands and even B2B brands. Therefore, the development of a suitable CSR strategy for a global brand and its proper execution matters a great deal. The strategy could be at the corporate level. However, companies with major global brands might also develop a strategy at the individual brand level. Below, we review the key steps in devising a solid sustainable marketing strategy.

Step 1: Set Objectives and Targets

The very first step is to establish the goals and specific targets of the sustainable strategy. The firm should consider what the CSR strategy is trying to accomplish. In a global setting, these objectives could vary across countries. In most cases, the CSR strategy would include overarching objectives of sustainability worldwide. These goals would cover the minimum obligations to be met toward the different stakeholder groups—consumers, suppliers, the local community, and employees world-wide. For each of these broad objectives, the firm would spell out a set of very specific targets to be met within a certain timeline.

A good example is the Sustainable Living Plan that Unilever launched in November 2010. The plan commits the company to a 10-year journey toward sustainable growth. The 3 broad objectives of the plan are: (1) improving health and well-being, (2) reducing the environmental impact, and (3) enhancing livelihoods. The plan has over 50 specific targets that Unilever set out to realize these 3 overall objectives.[52] H&M, the Swedish fast fashion retailer, has defined 7 commitments on sustainability, namely:[53]

1. Provide fashion for sustainable-conscious customers,

2. Choose and reward responsible partners,

3. Be ethical,

4. Be climate smart,

5. Reduce, reuse, recycle,

6. Use natural resources responsibly, and

7. Strengthen communities.

---

[52]http://www.unilever.com/sustainable-living/uslp/, accessed March 26, 2013.
[53]http://about.hm.com, accessed April 11, 2013.

Exhibit 18-10   Heinz Global Sustainability Goals

Area	Goal
Energy consumption	20% reduction (per unit of finished production) through improved operational efficiency
Renewable energy	15% increase in usage of renewable energy sources, including solar, biomass, and biogas
Water	20% reduction through reuse and improved sanitation techniques
Solid waste	20% reduction through increased recycling and reuse of waste
Packaging	15% reduction by the introduction of alternative packaging materials
Agriculture	15% reduction of carbon footprint, 15% reduction of water usage and improvement of tomato, 5% improvement of tomato crop yields
Transportation	10% reduction of fuel consumption
Employees	Implementation of programs encouraging employee engagement

Source: http://www.heinz.co.uk/ourcompany/sustainability/ourvision, accessed April 10, 2013.

Exhibit 18-10 shows the specific global sustainability goals of Heinz. Compared to other business strategies, the time horizon for a sustainability strategy is often much longer given the time needed to accomplish the goals. For instance, Unilever's Sustainable Living Plan has a 10-year horizon.

Step 2: Understand the Operating Environment

Having a thorough understanding of the company's operating environment worldwide is crucial in order to formulate a sustainability strategy. That means that the company must assess how the different stages of a product's cycle—from design to sourcing to manufacturing to sale and ultimate use—could affect the various stakeholders. Unfortunately, the reality for most major multinationals is that the current global environment has become far more complex than it used to be. For instance, sustainable sourcing has become a mantra for most multinationals. But getting a complete and accurate picture of the supply chain is often an enormous task. Global brands such as Nike or Gap rely on hundreds of contract suppliers scattered around the world. Many of these often subcontract work to smaller companies. Often, the firm will work with third parties (e.g., NGOs, government agencies, university research labs) to gather information about supply chain or carbon footprint–related issues. A few years ago, Coca-Cola decided to cut the water used to make a liter of Coke from more than 3 liters to 2.5 liters. However, it overlooked the enormous amount of water it took to grow the sugar that went into Coke. It only found out about this oversight after it partnered with the World Wildlife Fund (WWF), which had the expertise to gauge the water footprint of the value chain.[54]

Step 3: Specify Strategic Sustainability Initiatives

The next step is to conceive the strategic policies the company should undertake around the world to meet its stated sustainability objectives. As a multinational typically must deal with both local and international stakeholders, it must decide as an organization how to balance efforts devoted to local and global issues. Too much focus on local concerns could result in fragmentation of a firm's sustainability activities.[55] As a result, the firm's reputation may vary a great deal across countries depending on the effectiveness of local CSR efforts. In addition, negative messages from one country could spill over to

---

[54]"Spotlight. The Sustainable Supply Chain," *Harvard Business Review* 88 (October 2010): 70–72.
[55]Michael Polonsky and Colin Jevons, "Global Branding and Strategic CSR: An Overview of Three Types of Complexity," *International Marketing Review* 26, no. 3 (2009): 327–347.

other markets and easily tarnish the company's reputation in these other countries. Overemphasis on global issues, however, could undermine a firm's engagement with domestic stakeholders. In practice, some of the efforts will be on a global basis (e.g., environment-related), while other initiatives such as those related to local communities will be customized to the host country.

A major part of the sustainability strategy formulation will involve the development of a stakeholder engagement program. To develop such a program, the firm must first identify its key stakeholders. An individual or group is considered to be a stakeholder when any of the following criteria is met:[56]

1. The individual or group could be positively or negatively affected by the organization's activities directly or indirectly.

2. The individual or group can grant or withdraw resources that are needed for the organization's activities.

3. The individual or group is valued by the company.

Once the key stakeholders have been determined, the company must conceive a strategy on how to engage them. The following drivers will impact the concrete elements of a company's sustainability strategy:

1. **Nature of the industry.** The very nature of the industries in which a company competes is a key factor. Stewardship of global water resources plays a prominent role in the sustainability strategic plans of both Coca-Cola and PepsiCo. Being among the largest corporate consumers of fresh water, both firms have a special interest in preserving water resources. IKEA, the global furniture retailer, focuses a major portion of its sustainability efforts on wood, one of the most important materials used in its products. It bans illegally logged wood and aims to increase the share of wood from responsibly managed forests. Promoting oral health worldwide is one of the hallmarks of Colgate's sustainability program. Its "Bright Smiles, Bright Futures" oral health initiative has reached 650 million children in 80 countries since 1991 and aims to reach a billion children by 2020.[57]

2. **Company heritage, mission, and values.** A solid CSR strategy should also reflect the company's heritage, mission, and core values. A sustainability strategy is most effective when it leverages the firm's competitive advantages and differentiates from the strategies employed by its competitors.

3. **Host country environment.** While some elements of the sustainability strategy could be standardized around the world, others need to be customized to the local environment. One important element is the set of local regulations. A good example is animal testing. In 2013, the European Union imposed a complete ban on the sale of cosmetics developed through animal testing, regardless of where in the world the testing took place.[58] China, however, requires personal care and cosmetics manufacturers to test their product on animals. The local culture is another critical aspect. IKEA, which has a staff of 139,000 people in 44 countries, wants 50 percent of its managers to be women by 2015.[59] In countries where there is a strong bias against women in senior management positions at the workplace, this goal could be hard to accomplish in the short- or even medium-term.[60]

---

[56]Isabelle Maignan and O. C. Ferrell, "Corporate Social Responsibility and Marketing: An Integrative Framework," *Journal of the Academy of Marketing Science* 32, no. 1 (Winter 2004): 3–19.

[57]http://www.colgate.com, accessed April 10, 2013.

[58]"EU Bans Sale of All Animal-Tested Cosmetics," http://www.bbc.co.uk/news/world-europe-21740745, accessed April 1, 2013.

[59]http://www.ikea.com/ms/en_GB/pdf/sustainability_report/ikea_group_sustainability_summary_2012.pdf, accessed April 4, 2013.

[60]In 2012, 47 percent of managers at IKEA were women.

Step 4: Implement

Once the company has conceived the key areas of its sustainability strategy, the next phase is to conceive the specific actions and programs to implement it in countries around the world. For instance, one of the pillars of Unilever's sustainable living is a strategy to improve health and well-being and to prevent disease. To carry out this strategy, Unilever focused on the following activities:[61]

1. Promote the importance and practice of hand washing with soap at the right times during the day.

2. Improve oral health. Use toothpaste and toothbrush brand and oral health improvement programs to encourage children and their parents to brush day and night.

3. Improve self-esteem, especially among girls and women. Initiatives included the Dove Self-Esteem Fund that educates and encourages young people to raise their self-esteem and the Vaseline Skin Fund to improve the lives of those affected by skin conditions.

4. Provide safe drinking water especially in countries with limited access to pressurized tap water.

5. Improve sanitation through education and raising awareness.

Exhibit 18-11 lists some of the activities that Swedish fashion retailer H&M undertook in 2012 to meets its seven sustainability commitments.

When deploying a CSR strategy on a global scale, a company is likely to encounter numerous challenges. Multinationals striving to source 100 percent of their raw materials coming from

Exhibit 18-11   Highlights of H&M's Conscious Actions in 2012

Commitment	Actions
Provide fashion for conscious customers	• Number one user of organic cotton in the world • 11.4% of all cotton used is more sustainable • H&M dresses made from conscious materials appeared on red carpets around the world • 27% of leather shoes made from certified leather
Choose and reward responsible partners	• 2,646 supplier factory audits conducted • Social dialogue project initiated in Cambodia in partnership with a Swedish trade union • Fire safety training for more than 100,000 workers and middle managers in Bangladesh
Be ethical	• 74% of managers are women • Launch of group-wide human rights policy
Be climate smart	• CO_2 emissions cut by 5% • 784,200 kwh of solar energy generated through the firm's own solar panels
Reduce, reuse, recycle	• Customers can return old clothes to stores around the world • Use of recycled polyester equivalent to 7.9 million PET bottles
Use natural resources responsibly	• Global water partnership with WWF • 450 million liters of water saved in production of water-intensive textiles like denim
Strengthen communities	• 7,402 additional jobs created • $6.3 million invested in communities • More than 3.2 million garments donated to charitable causes • Around 150,000 cotton farmers trained in better farming techniques

Source: http://about.hm.com/AboutSection/en/About/Sustainability.html, accessed April 10, 2013.

---

[61] http://www.unilever.com/sustainable-living/, accessed April 8, 2013.

agriculture or forestry must either find alternative suppliers or train existing ones to improve their farming practices and minimize their environmental impact. As more and more companies pursue sustainable sourcing, the competition for such resources will intensify. Understanding and monitoring the supply chain could also be a major hurdle because of lack of information and sheer complexity.[62] While a few companies verify their supply chain themselves, most firms engage a third party to do the monitoring and auditing of the supply chain. However, finding a reputable auditing agency can be rather difficult in some parts of the world. Drug multinationals offering cheap or even free medicine in less developed countries often face a parallel imports problem when local distributors resell these products to distributors in richer countries.

Step 5: Develop Metrics for Monitoring and Reporting

The final step is to develop metrics that allow the company to monitor its performance. Such metrics are sometimes referred to as **key performance indicators (KPIs)**. **Exhibit 18-12** lists some of the KPIs used by Colgate-Palmolive in different sustainability domains. These measures are typically a mix of quantitative performance metrics (e.g., greenhouse gas emissions, water use) and more qualitative data (e.g., job satisfaction, biodiversity). Often, some of the metrics will be established through cooperation with NGOs.

Having clearly stated targets and metrics has several advantages. First, as the saying goes: what gets measured gets done. Regular measurement and reporting keeps the firm's sustainability

Exhibit 18-12   Colgate-Palmolive's Key Performance Sustainability Indicators

People

- The number of occupational injuries and illnesses that require medical treatment per 200,000 work hours
- The number of occupational injuries and illnesses causing employees to be absent from work per 200,000 hours
- Safety notices of violation
- Safety fines paid
- Percentage minority officials and managers
- Percentage women in workforce

Performance

- Global sales
- Global charitable contributions in cash
- Global charitable contributions in kind

Planet

- Energy use efficiency (kWh × 1000/ton of product)
- Water use efficiency (cubic meters/ton of product)
- CO_2 emissions (metric tons × 1000)
- Wastewater CODs (kg/ton of product)
- Environmental incidents
- Environmental notices of violation
- Environmental fines paid

Source: http://www2.dupont.com/inclusive-innovations/en-us/gss/sustainability/performance-reporting/sustainability-reports.html, accessed April 10, 2013.

---

[62]"Is Your Supply Chain Sustainable?" *Harvard Business Review* 88 (October 2010): 74–75.

Exhibit 18-13 Starbucks Global Responsibility Plan—Goals and Progress (2011)

Goals	Progress
Ensure 100% of our coffee is ethically sourced.[*]	86% of coffee was ethically sourced under C.A.F.E. Practices (up from 84% in 2010).[**]
Invest in farmers and their communities by increasing farmer loans to $20 million.	Made nearly $14.7 million in loan commitments.
Improve farmers' access to carbon markets.	Learned from a pilot program in Indonesia and reported significant improvement with the program in Mexico.
Contribute 1 million hours community service per year.	Starbucks more than doubled community service hours from 2010.
Engage a total of 50,000 young people to innovate and take action in their communities.	Starbucks exceeded this goal.
Build all new, company-owned stores to achieve LEED certification.[***]	75% of new company-owned stores built to achieve LEED certification.
Develop comprehensive recycling solutions for paper and plastic cups by 2012.	Demonstrated viability of cup recycling solution in the U.S. and Canada. Working to bring solution to scale globally.
Implement front-of-store recycling in company-owned stores.	Brought front-of-store recycling to over 1,000 stores in the U.S. and Canada.
Serve 5 percent of beverages made in stores in personal tumblers.	Customers used personal tumblers more than 34 million times (2 percent of all beverages served worldwide).
Reduce energy consumption by 25% in company-owned stores.	Electricity use has dropped by more than 7.5% since 2008.
Purchase renewable energy equivalent to 100% of the electricity used in company-owned stores worldwide.	Bought the equivalent of more than 50% of electricity used.
Reduce water consumption by 25%.	Although water consumption had dropped more than 17% since 2008, it increased 5% in 2011 compared to 2010.

[*] Unless otherwise stated, the target year is 2015.

[**] C.A.F.E. (Coffee and Farmer Equity) Practices is a private standard established by Starbucks to ensure ethical sourcing of coffee.

[***] LEED (Leadership in Energy and Environmental Design) is a voluntary program that provides third-party verification of green buildings.

Source: http://www.starbucks.com/responsibility/global-report, accessed March 26, 2013.

activities focused around the world. Second, for some activities, metrics can also allow management to estimate the return on investment of these efforts. Third, country-level metrics allow companies to make cross-country benchmark comparisons and analyze why particular sustainability activities do well in some countries but poorly in others. **Exhibit 18-13** summarizes Starbucks's progress in 2011 on various sustainability measures. As mentioned earlier, qualitative metrics tend to be fuzzier. However, one popular set of indicators are the awards and forms of recognition granted to the firm. **Exhibit 18-14** shows the awards and honors that PepsiCo received in 2010.

Apart from tracking sustainability programs, most multinationals will also prepare annual sustainability reports and post them on their corporate websites. Such reports typically consist of three parts. The first part is forward-looking and discusses the firm's sustainability strategy and

Exhibit 18-14 Sustainability-Based Awards & Recognition Received by Pepsico (2010)

Organization/Country	Award/Honor	Ranking
Dow Jones	Sustainability World Index Food and Beverage Sector	1st
Dow Jones	Sustainability World Index	Listed for the 4th time
ENERGY STAR (United States)	Sustained Excellence	
Mexico	Social Responsibility Award	For 5th year
2010 Global Water	Environmental Contribution of the Year	
Corporate Equality Index		100 percent score
Fortune Magazine	World's Most Admired Companies	2nd
Newsweek	Green Rankings	3rd
Ethisphere	Listed as World's Most Ethical Companies	
CR Magazine	100 Best Corporate Citizens	3rd

Source: http://www.pepsico.com/purpose/environmental-sustainability.html, accessed April 9, 2013.

goals. The second part reviews activities undertaken in the current year and their impact. The final part reveals how much progress has been made in reaching the company's stated goals. According to one estimate, global reporting output per year rose from almost zero in 1992 to about 4,000 reports in 2010. In fact, some countries (e.g., France, Denmark) now require larger companies to report on CSR activities in their annual reports.[63]

Global Stakeholder Engagement Programs

Sustainability centers around the obligations the multinational has toward stakeholders around the world. As we discussed in the previous section, stakeholder engagement must be at the core of a firm's sustainability strategy. In this section, we discuss in more detail stakeholder engagement in the global marketplace.

Monitoring stakeholder priorities and perceptions is crucial, especially in the current global environment where shifts can occur very rapidly. Several problems that until recently were primarily seen as an individual's responsibility are now increasingly viewed as being part of a company's responsibility. A good example is the obesity epidemic that has become a pressing health challenge in many Western countries and is also becoming a rising threat in several emerging markets. In the past, companies in the food industry would take a defensive approach by hiding behind a few nutritious token items in their product range or on their menus or by fighting legal threats (e.g., sugar tax in France). However, a rising pressure from various stakeholders and governments has forced several of the larger food multinationals like Unilever and PepsiCo to adopt a more proactive approach by turning nutrition and health into key pillars of their sustainability programs.[64]

---

[63]Katelijne van Wensen, Wijnand Broer, Johanna Klein, and Jutta Knopf, "The State of Play in Sustainability Reporting in the European Union," http://www.businessinsociety.eu/resources/4271, accessed April 3, 2013.

[64]Jessica Davis Pluess, "The Not So Sweet Truth: Corporate Responsibility and the Obesity Epidemic," http://www.bsr.org, accessed April 10, 2013.

For each of the distinct stakeholder groups, the multinational must consider what the nature of stakeholder engagement should be. The form of stakeholder engagement that the firm adopts could involve:

- *Information provision*. Some firms view stakeholders as a valuable source of information. In early 2011, Dow Chemical entered a five-year, $10 million pact with The Nature Conservancy (TNC), a nonprofit organization, which would advise Dow and provide technical assistance on reducing the firm's carbon footprint.[65] NGOs often have a much better understanding about the relevant sustainability concerns than the company. Therefore, the company could tap into their expertise. This is especially so for matters that concern local issues in the host country.

- *Standard setting*. Firms also may use the inputs from stakeholders such as NGOs to determine the standards and targets for their sustainability activities. H&M entered a three-year global partnership with the World Wildlife Fund (WWF) to set new standards for water stewardship in the fashion industry.

- *Input on decision making*. Stakeholders could also provide decision-making input and creative assistance. One great example is an eco-friendly billboard in the Philippines that was jointly designed by the local branch of Coca-Cola and the WWF. The billboard was covered with thousands of Fukien tea plants that surrounded a Coke-bottle shaped space with the words, "This billboard absorbs air pollutants." Pots made from recycled bottles contained the plants which were expected to take over the billboard surface completely, absorbing a total of 46,800 pounds of carbon dioxide from the atmosphere during the whole process.[66]

- *Implementation*. Increasingly, firms team up with stakeholder groups to implement their sustainability programs. The collaboration between H&M and WWF mentioned earlier goes beyond simply setting sustainability standards. The two also collaborate along the entire supply chain. H&M's designers get training so that they might choose raw materials or styles that are more sustainable choices. The partnership also focuses on educating H&M employees, suppliers, and consumers on using water responsibly.[67]

- *Monitoring*. Stakeholders often play a major role in monitoring and auditing the firm's sustainability. From some stakeholders such as consumers or employees, the firm could gather feedback through surveys (e.g., customer satisfaction questionnaires) or focus group discussions. These days, many companies also listen in on discussions that run on social media or other online forums that relate to their sustainability activities. For environmental and supply chain–related audits, the firm could get help from global or local NGOs with expertise in those fields.

Stakeholder engagement is not a simple endeavor. Consider the non-profit sector, for instance. Clearly, NGOs can bring a lot to the table. With its expertise, an NGO can educate the firm and provide feedback on proposed policies. Their involvement in areas such as audits and performance measurement also lends creditability. However, the goals, priorities, and expectations of NGOs usually differ a great deal from those of the firm. Stakeholder groups may also be skittish about collaborating with companies in certain industries. Many of the large global NGOs like Oxfam, Greenpeace and WWF have to protect their global brand reputation. By embarking on a project with a company, they run the risk of tarnishing their brand image, especially if the collaboration goes wrong. This is particularly likely when the partnership involves a multinational with a tattered image (e.g., BP). Further, a partnership between the NGO and the firm could create a lot of tension. For that reason, NGOs sometimes prefer to keep a low profile and adopt a behind-the-scenes role.

---

[65]"Dow, Nature Conservancy Pledge Cooperation," http://www.businessweek.com, accessed January 24, 2011.

[66]"Coca-Cola Plant Billboard Absorbs Air Pollution," http://www.huffingtonpost.com, accessed April 10, 2013.

[67]http://about.hm.com/AboutSection/en/About/Sustainability.html, accessed April 10, 2013.

When a company decides to set up a stakeholder engagement program, it must also address a series of practical issues. The firm must decide on the scope of the collaboration. It needs to single out which representatives of stakeholder groups it should engage with. The program should also develop mechanisms (e.g., one-off versus long-term collaboration) and platforms (e.g., advisory councils) to be used.

Sustainable Marketing Mix Policy for the Global Marketplace

Sustainability provides opportunities but also creates challenges for global marketers. In this section, we discuss how marketing mix policies can support the implementation of a sustainability strategy within the global market environment.

Developing Sustainable Products and Services

As a centerpiece of their global CSR strategy, more and more multinationals have embarked on product strategies that focus on developing sustainable products or improving the sustainability of their existing items in their product portfolio. In the car industry, well-known examples that fit this pattern include Toyota's Prius line of hybrid cars and Nissan's LEAF range as well as Tesla's line of electric vehicles (EVs). Some other recent launches of sustainable products and services are the following:

- *Pureit water purifier (Unilever)*. Pureit is a range of eco-friendly water purifiers launched by Unilever. Unilever's India subsidiary launched Pureit in 2005. By 2013, it was sold in six other developing countries.[68] The benefits of Pureit are that (1) it replaces bottled water (less plastic waste) and boiling, (2) it runs without electricity (thereby saving energy), and (3) it provides protection from water-borne diseases.[69]

- *IKEA*. In 2012, IKEA launched several new home furnishing products made of more sustainable materials. These are not niche products but sold to customers around the world. Examples are "Gosa Syren" pillows that use a filling made from recycled PET bottles, "Skarpö" chairs made from 100% recycled plastic, "IKEA PS" dining tables that use bamboo, and a new lamp called VIDJA.[70]

Sustainable products or services often suffer from a poor image in the mind of customers. In terms of priorities, consumers usually attach far more weight to price, performance, and reliability than to a product's green credentials. Consumers often expect that sustainability involves sacrifices in terms of price or quality. To counter negative consumer perceptions, a company often needs to put extra effort in designing and positioning sustainable products. Toyota's Prius initially suffered from a low-power image. The carmaker redesigned the Prius by adding more horsepower and ran a campaign that positioned the vehicle as "quick, roomy, and economical." Likewise, Tesla's electric cars have a flashy design. The fact that the vehicles are popular in Hollywood and Silicon Valley adds further glamour to the brand.

To become better stewards of the environment, some big multinationals have also focused on making their product development and testing forays more sustainable. A case in point is French cosmetics giant L'Oréal. To replace animal testing, the company spent over 30 years of effort to reconstruct human skin and other biological tissues. The reproduced tissues can be used to test

---

[68]The countries are Indonesia, Mexico, Brazil, Bangladesh, Nigeria, and Sri Lanka.

[69]http://www.pureitwater.com, accessed April 11, 2013.

[70]http://www.ikea.com/ms/en_GB/about_ikea/facts_and_figures/sustainability_report/sustainability_report_2012 .html, accessed April 11, 2013.

product safety and effectiveness. In addition to a state-of-the-art facility at Gerland in France to make the reconstructed tissues, L'Oréal produces Asian skin at its research lab facilities near Shanghai.[71]

Besides devising revolutionary new green products, companies pursue lots of other product policy initiatives to make their product range more sustainable. Some steps focus on the ways products are made by striving to save energy and lower water use at manufacturing facilities. For instance, in 2009, PepsiCo opened its first overseas "green" bottling plant in Chonqing, a city in Western China. The plant was designed to use 22 percent less water and 23 percent less energy than the average PepsiCo plant in China.[72] Companies around the world also assume greater responsibility by shifting to materials and ingredients from sustainable sources. A good example is "Solidarity Sourcing," a global program of fair trade procurement that L'Oréal launched in 2010. In addition to fair pricing, it considers other dimensions such as biodiversity and support of local communities.[73]

One key finding of the 2011 ImagePower Green Brands Survey is that people worldwide agreed that most companies use too much packaging. To reduce waste, consumers seek out products with less packaging. Companies around the world increasingly push for **sustainable packaging**. Sustainable packaging initiatives focus on the three Rs of remove, reduce, and recycle. Some good examples of sustainable packaging can be found in the beauty industry. LUSH, the British brand of handmade cosmetics, uses as little packaging as possible. Many of its product items are sold without any packaging at all. LUSH bottles are made from 100 percent recycled plastic. Origins encourages its customers to bring their empty cosmetics tubes, bottles, and jars (regardless of brand) to an Origins retail store or department store counter for recycling. The program runs in North America, the United Kingdom, Taiwan, Hong Kong, Malaysia, and Singapore.[74]

Sustainable Pricing

Consumers around the globe express a desire to buy sustainable products. However, consumer surveys consistently show that price remains a hurdle for many people. Many consumers are not prepared to make such a sacrifice, especially when the economic climate is severe. One survey showed that more than a third of consumers in developed countries are not willing to pay a price premium for green products.[75] Somewhat surprisingly, consumers in developing countries seemed to be less reluctant to pay more for green products than their counterparts in the West (see **Exhibit 18-15**).

Companies realize that price can be a major obstacle for many of their customers. Increasingly, firms try to come up with sustainable solutions with prices comparable to or even less than those of conventional products. The VIDJA lamp that IKEA introduced in 2012 was a redesign of a very popular existing lamp. At the time, IKEA set out the task of developing a lamp that was easier to assemble, more sustainable, and at a low price. IKEA's designers removed redundant components (24 out of the original 33 components). The redesigned lamp had half the weight of the old one with the same performance. The lower weight also allowed IKEA to ship more lamps at once, reducing fuel usage and shipping costs. The new VIDJA lamp went on sale at a 34 percent savings on the original price.[76]

---

[71]http://www.loreal.com, accessed April 10, 2013.

[72]http://www.greenbiz.com/news/2009/06/29/pepsico-opens-green-beverage-plant-china.

[73]http://www.loreal.com, accessed April 10, 2013.

[74]"Green Is in for Fall: Beauty Brands That Recycle," http://www.huffingtonpost.ca, accessed April 10, 2013.

[75]http://www.cohnwolfe.com/en/ideas-insights/white-papers/green-brands-survey-2011, accessed April 12, 2013.

[76]"IKEA's Sustainability Strategy: Save the World, One Product at a Time," http://www.cswire.com, accessed April 13, 2013.

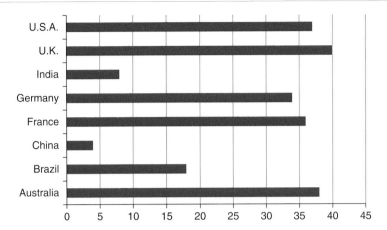

Exhibit 18-15
Percentage of
Consumers *Not*
Willing to Pay a
Price Premium for
Green Products
Source: Based on 2011
ImagePower Green Brands
Survey, http://www
.cohnwolfe.com, accessed
March 10, 2013.

One approach to dampen the sticker shock of sustainable products is to highlight to consumers the overall savings potential of such products during their lifespan. IKEA decided to sell and use only LED lights in its products, thereby cutting its customers' electricity bills by up to 30 percent.

An alternative strategy is to go for premium pricing using the high price tag as a prestige signal. Toyota's hybrid Lexus SUV and BMW's planned i-Series are two examples of prestige pricing. For fair-trade products that end up being more expensive, marketers must show how such products have the potential to restore justice.[77]

Communication and Sustainability

Communication is a critical part of a firm's sustainability strategy—both within the company (internal) as well as outside (external). Internally, there are two important tools. First, most of the larger multinationals have a **code of conduct** that sets out the core values and basic ethical rules employees must respect. Typically, a firm will post its code on the company's website. The second tool is a dedicated sustainability website that gives an overview of the firm's strategy and typically includes the firm's annual sustainability report. While useful for external audiences, a target audience of such websites also includes the company's employees. A firm may also use training workshops to educate its workforce around the world about the company's sustainability strategy and practices.

Externally, to reach out to stakeholders outside the company, marketing communication is an essential component. In what follows, we discuss the roles marketing communication can play as part of the firm's global sustainability strategy.

Inform the Public about the Firm's Sustainability Achievements

Marketing communications is often the most visible component of a firm's sustainability activities and accomplishments for the general public. While advertising and public relations are important elements, firms need to be careful. Companies have been criticized for spending more time and money on publicizing their achievements than on the initiatives themselves.[78] Too much promotion may also lead consumers to tune out.

Firms sometimes also face accusations of **greenwashing**: making exaggerated sustainability claims or using marketing communications to make products or services seem more sustainable

---

[77]Katherine White, Rhiannon MacDonnell, and John H. Ellard, "Belief in a Just World: Consumer Intentions and Behaviors toward Ethical Products," *Journal of Marketing* 76, (January 2012): 103–118.
[78]N. Craig Smith, p. 65.

than they truly are.[79] One website—www.greenwashingindex.com—names and shames advertisers that make misleading advertising claims.

Persuade

Companies introducing sustainable products often also must invest a lot of effort to persuade consumers that these products offer good value. In 2011 Unilever introduced a new fabric conditioner called One Rinse in the Asia-Pacific region.[80] With this product, consumers would only need one bucket of water for the rinse cycle instead of the standard three buckets, thereby saving up to 30 liters of water. Although the new single-rinse conditioner could save huge amounts of water, Unilever encountered consumer skepticism about the product's effectiveness. To change ingrained habits, Unilever had to demonstrate that even with just one rinse the laundry would still be as clean as with three rinses. In Vietnam Unilever organized a mass laundry event in a football stadium with thousands of participants to demonstrate the product's effectiveness. It then used footage of the event in its television advertising to show that the product really works.[81] In Indonesia, Unilever used a brand ambassador to pitch the benefits of One Rinse and to encourage people to change their laundry habits. Three years later, One Rinse accounted for one-third of the fabric conditioner market in Vietnam and 20 percent of the market in Indonesia.[82]

Educate Consumers

Marketing communications could also be an effective means to promote sustainable consumption. In India, 86 percent of consumers said that advertising helped them to make more informed decisions and understand the benefits of green products. TV ads had the greatest impact on their likelihood to buy such products.[83] Educating consumers to change their habits can go a long way toward building a more sustainable future. The challenge to change harmful consumer habits can be huge, though. A study released in 2011 by the Food and Agriculture Organization (FAO) estimated that roughly one-third of food produced for human consumption is lost or wasted globally, which amounts to 1.3 billion tons per year.[84]

A company can use marketing communication tools to help customers to understand the impact of their purchase decisions. In the United Kingdom, Kit Kat buyers could scan a QR code on the package to discover the impact of their purchase on nutrition, the environment, and society. Marketing communication can also provide guidance and educate consumers to change harmful consumption habits. In Singapore, Nestlé introduced a smartphone app called 123Recycle that provided consumers information on how to sort and dispose of their packaging.[85] To combat wasteful water habits, Unilever launched several initiatives around the globe. In the United States, the firm ran a Turn off the Tap campaign at the end of 2010 for its Suave hair care brand. The campaign communicated the environmental and economic benefits of lathering while the shower is off, showing how consumers can save millions of liters of water each day. In Turkey, where water consumption for laundry is 30 percent higher than the global average, its Omo brand created a water education campaign in partnership with WWF. The campaign encouraged consumers to do fuller loads in machine washing and avoid pre-washing.[86] In the same category, P&G ran

---

[79]Diane Martin and John Schouten, *Sustainable Marketing* (Upper Saddle River, NJ: Prentice Hall, 2012).

[80]The product was known as Surf One Rinse in the Philippines and "Comfort One Rinse" in Indonesia, Thailand, and Vietnam.

[81]http://www.youtube.com/watch?v = 8AhWD93xing.

[82]http://www.unilever.com/sustainable-living/water/consumers/, accessed March 24, 2013; the website also posts a YouTube video about the product.

[83]http://www.cohnwolfe.com/en/ideas-insights/white-papers/green-brands-survey-2011, accessed April 13, 2013.

[84]http://www.fao.org/ag/ags/ags-division/publications/publication/en/?dyna_fef%5Buid%5D=74045, accessed April 10, 2013.

[85]http://www.nestle.com/csv/environmental-sustainability, accessed April 10, 2013.

[86]http://www.unilever.com/sustainable-living/, accessed April 13, 2013.

advertising campaigns to encourage people to use cold water for their laundry, thereby saving on their utility bills and lowering energy use.

As we discussed above, marketing communications fulfill multiple roles in a firm's sustainability program. To be more effective and powerful, such campaigns must be creative and awe-inspiring. Earlier in this chapter, we mentioned the Coca-Cola/WWF billboard in the Philippines and Unilever's One Rinse promotions in South East Asia. Here are a few other examples of creative sustainability communication campaigns:

- *Volvo's One Tonne Life*. In 2011 Volvo and two other Swedish brands ran a six-month long green living experiment called One Tonne Life. The goal of the experiment was to show how a family with young children could live climate smart in a home using state-of-the-art green technology. The experiment challenged the Lindell family to lower its carbon footprint but at the same time still lead a regular life.[87] The family was able to lower its carbon dioxide emissions from 7.3 tons per year to 1.5 tons—slightly over the 1 ton goal. Unilever ran a similar experiment in the United Kingdom a few years later where it challenged 12 families to adopt a more sustainable lifestyle.

- *Volkswagen's Think Blue*. To celebrate Earth Month in April 2013, Volkswagen encouraged people around the world to Think Blu' instead of green. Using a version of the Beach Boys' "Wouldn't It Be Nice?" song, the global marketing campaign showcased the German car-maker's new natural-gas powered Eco Up! model.

- *Unilever's Putting People First in India*. Unilever's Lifebuoy is one of the leading soap brands in India. The yearlong Lifebuoy hand-washing campaign has reportedly cut by half the death rate from diarrhea amongst children. Each year millions of pilgrims flock to the Ganges River to purge their sins. The annual tradition means a huge consumption of *roti*—a flatbread that is staple of Indian diets—at local restaurants. To mark the 2013 festival, Unilever stamped the message "Did you wash your hands with Lifebuoy?" in Hindi on millions of rotis served at local eateries.[88]

- *BMW's global Born Electric tour*. To create hype for the its new range of all electric cars, BMW ran a year-long Born Electric tour making brief stops in seven cities around the world. The tour, which started in Rome June 2012,[89] allowed visitors to catch a glimpse of the all-electric BMW i3 and plug-in hybrid i8 Spyder concept vehicles.

Sustainability and Distribution Channels

Multinationals can also contribute to sustainability through their distribution channels. One target for a slew of multinationals is the carbon footprint of their channels. Tesco, a British multinational grocery retailer, adopted several initiatives to cut its carbon footprint per case of goods delivered by 25 percent by 2020. These included:[90]

- Reducing trips by maximizing the amount of goods delivered in each journey.

- Traveling fewer miles by having distribution from central locations.

- Alternative modes of transportation such as a shift from road to rail.

- Using fuel with lower carbon emissions.

Limited access to sustainable products and services has been cited as a barrier to buying such products in countries like Brazil and India. In these countries, green products can only be found in

---

[87]http://onetonnelife.com/, accessed April 2, 2013.

[88]http://www.youtube.com/watch?v = e_2tQekUDy8.

[89]The other cities on the tour were New York, Düsseldorf, Paris, London, Shanghai, and Tokyo.

[90]http://www.tescoplc.com/index.asp?pageid=152, accessed April 13, 2013.

specialty stores rather than in mainstream ones. A logical solution is broadening distribution by expanding into more mainstream channels. However, in many of these countries, distributors are often not too keen to allocate shelf space to such products.

A multinational can also promote sustainability by supporting small-scale distributors, especially in developing countries. A classic example is Project Shakti (see also Chapter 17) that Unilever established in India. The program is a door-to-door operation that provides work for a large number of low-income people, mostly women, in village communities. By 2011, 45,000 so-called Shakti ammas were selling Unilever products in 100,000 villages. In the wake of the success of Project Shakti in India, Unilever replicated the scheme in Bangladesh, Sri Lanka, and Vietnam.[91]

Crisis Management and Consumer Boycotts

China is a key market for KFC, accounting for about 40 percent of its profits. In December 2012, China's state media reported that some of KFC's suppliers misused antibiotics to fatten poultry.[92] The negative publicity led to a huge drop in KFC's sales in China. Still struggling to recover from the antibiotics scandal, a new bird flu scare badly hit KFC's sales a few months later. For most firms, crisis events like KFC's in China are not a matter of whether but of when. Any company is vulnerable to a crisis situation. A crisis can happen to both "good" and "bad" companies. It is not uncommon that a crisis affecting one brand spills over to other brands in the same product category.

A global brand's sustainability reputation, nurtured by efforts over many years, can easily be destroyed by crisis events. In many cases, the cause of such incidents is entirely beyond the multinational's control. A further complication in today's digital environment is that negative stories circulate very rapidly on social media and travel—within the country where the incident took place and in some cases also far beyond its borders. Sometimes companies must also combat negative rumor stories about their brand on the internet. Below we spell out some guidelines to cope with crises. We then focus on coping with consumer boycotts.

Crisis Management

On June 20, 1996, the managing director of Kraft Australia received a call from the local health authorities. A potential link had been identified between peanut butter sold by Kraft and an outbreak of salmonella poisoning. Kraft Australia faced the worst crisis in its 70-year history in the country. By the end of June, all Kraft-made peanut butter was removed from stores nationwide, affecting 70 percent of the category in Australia. Over one hundred cases of salmonella poisoning were reported; fortunately none of these involved fatalities. Australian media and health authorities attacked Kraft for the way it handled the crisis. Law firms launched class action suits against the firm. The distribution of all Kraft peanut butter brands was halted for four months.[93] **Global Perspective 18-2** describes another crisis—this time triggered by a viral ad of bad taste.

A crisis like this is a company's worst nightmare. Still, there are steps that a firm can take to handle a crisis—before, during, and after the event. In particular, a firm could consider the following courses of action:

- *Be prepared. Set up a crisis management team.* Setting up a crisis team of senior executives is crucial, especially in the firm's key markets. Scenario planning is vital. A well-prepared firm would develop specific scenarios and create plans to cope with each one of them. Though for many firms severe crises are unlikely "long-tail" events, preparation is essential. By being

---

[91]http://www.unilever.com/sustainable-living/, accessed April 12, 2013.

[92]"KFC Rebuilds Brand after China Antibiotics Scandal," http://www.usatoday.com, accessed February 24, 2013.

[93]Harald Van Heerde, Kristiaan Helsen, and Marnik G. Dekimpe, "The Impact of a Product-Harm Crisis on Marketing Effectiveness," *Marketing Science* 26 (March-April 2007): 230–245.

Global Perspective 18-2

Offensive Hyundai Ad Goes Viral

South Korea has an annual suicide rate of 30 per 100,000: the highest level in the OECD. Given that fact, one would expect that leading Korean companies would treat the topic with sensitivity. Unfortunately, that was not the case with a promotional video that Hyundai Motor released for its new ix35 "100 percent water emissions" car model in April 2013.

The one-minute video—made by the European division of advertising group Innocean, a sister company of Hyundai—showed a man making an attempt to kill himself in his car by breathing in carbon monoxide. But he waits in vain, finally giving up and heading back to his house. At the end of the clip, a script appeared with the tagline "the new ix35 with 100 percent water emissions" before fading to the Hyundai logo.

The makers behind the clip claimed that they had posted the video online to seek consumers' feedback on creative ideas employing hyperbole to dramatize a product advantage. Not surprisingly, the ad sparked outrage, especially among people who had family members take their own lives (some using the same approach shown in the ad). Hyundai realized its blunder and pulled the ad from YouTube. However, in the meantime, the clip had gone viral.

Even though the clip targeted the European market, the episode was very embarrassing for the Korean company. To contain the damage, Hyundai divisions around the world issued an apology. Hyundai Europe stated: "We apologize unreservedly. The video has been taken down and will not be used in any of our advertising or marketing." The carmaker's U.S. division announced: "We at Hyundai Motor America are shocked and saddened by the depiction of a suicide attempt in an inappropriate European video featuring a Hyundai. Suicide merits thoughtful discussion, not this type of treatment."

Sources: http://hyundainews.com, accessed April 30, 2013; "Sadly, Hyundai Not the First Auto Brand to Depict Suicide Attempt in an Ad," http://www.brandchannel.com, accessed April 25, 2013; and "Hyundai Pulls 'Offensive' Ad—Again," http://www.ft.com, accessed April 30, 2013.

---

ready, the firm will be able to come up with a fast response to cope with crisis situations. Just as for other aspects of a global strategy, a crisis team could leverage expertise from subsidiaries in other countries.

- *Monitor the situation.* Monitoring a crisis situation is obviously crucial. The firm should track the severity of a crisis on social media. When the crisis event relates to a product's safety (e.g., a product contamination), the firm should be prepared to implement a product recall program.

- *Handle the crisis vigorously.* A swift and vigorous response to a crisis is necessary. Hesitation will be seen by the media and the public as a sign of weakness or even guilt. In summer 2008, Maple Leaf Foods, a leading Canadian consumer packaged food company, was alerted of a possible food contamination at one of its meat processing plant. The firm responded rapidly. In the interest of public food safety, it immediately recalled all products from the affected plant. The company's chief executive took personal charge. In an interview with a Canadian newspaper, he said: "There are two advisers I've paid no attention to. The first are the lawyers, and the second are the accountants."[94]

- *Build a reputation to protect it.* As we pointed out earlier in the chapter, one advantage of sustainability programs is that they boost a firm's reputation among the general public. When a crisis happens, this reputation can help the firm to recover.

---

[94]"Responding to a Product Crisis," *Financial Times*, April 30, 2013, p. 10.

- *Communicate with stakeholders during the crisis.* Openness and rapid communication with stakeholders (e.g., the local government, consumers, distributors) is a must. Do not stonewall. Shutting down a Facebook page or removing negative comments on micro-blogging sites usually worsens the public's response. Keeping silent could be a huge mistake as it may signal an admission of guilt in the mind of consumers. One PR expert at Ogilvy China suggests that a company must make a first response within eight hours. It is also critical to speak with a single consistent message.

- *Post-crisis—rebuild the brand reputation among customers and distributors.* When a problem arises, a firm should rebuild its reputation by taking steps to prevent the problem from happening again. In its communications, the company should also showcase these steps. Yum!, the owner of KFC, launched a campaign called "Operation Thunder" to reinforce its food safety credentials in the wake of an antibiotics crisis in China. In early 2013, when a bird flu crisis threatened its core business, Yum! focused its communications on educating consumers in China that cooked chicken was safe to eat.

While a brand crisis can have devastating effects, it can also be a watershed moment that allows the strong brands to distinguish themselves from the weak ones. Brands that excel in managing a crisis situation often awe their customers and can bolster consumer loyalty in the long term.

Consumer Boycotts

One of the most fearsome and potent weapons that consumers can wield to express discontent over certain issues is the **consumer boycott**. With a boycott, consumers withold patronage to curb perceived abuses and/or increase corporate sensitivity to sustainability related issues.[95] In some cases, consumers may boycott a firm's products because of its nationality. In 2006, scores of people in the Muslim world boycotted Danish brands to protest the publication of controversial cartoons of the prophet Muhammad in a Danish newspaper. In 2012, a heated border dispute between China and Japan over a series of islands led to a damaging boycott of Japanese brands in China. Often, though, consumers start a boycott to punish controversial company practices. In that case, the aim is to put pressure on the company to change its behavior. For instance, in the 1980s–1990s, consumer activists organized a boycott against canned tuna brands to pressure the brand owners to source their tuna only from dolphin-friendly fisheries.

These days, social media such as Facebook, Twitter, or Weibo (China) offer useful and versatile tools to orchestrate consumer boycotts of global brands worldwide. Several major multinationals have been forced to make a U-turn by a boycott. One of the longest ongoing campaigns is a boycott targeting Nestlé, which began in 1977 in response to the marketing of baby milk formula in poorer countries. Nestlé is one of the most boycotted companies in the world.[96] Some consumer boycotts can have a huge negative impact on a brand's sales. For instance, a consumer boycott of Shell organized by Greenpeace in 1995 reduced Shell sales in Germany by up to 40 percent.[97]

Most often, consumer boycotts are initiated and managed by NGOs such as Oxfam or Greenpeace. These social activists tend to be very strategic in choosing issues. Often, they do not want to change the behavior of just one company but the entire industry. Therefore, they typically single out companies that are most vulnerable and most visible (e.g., KFC or McDonald's in the fast food industry to protest animal treatment) in the hope that other smaller companies will follow suit.

When a boycott happens, companies must decide whether to respond or not. One key factor is the intensity of the boycott. Consumers are more likely to participate in a boycott when:

---

[95]N. Craig Smith, *Morality and the Market: Consumer Pressure for Corporate Accountability* (London: Routledge, 1990).
[96]http://www.ethicalconsumer.org, accessed March 14, 2013.
[97]http://hbr.org/product/brent-spar-platform-controversy-b/an/IMD005-PDF-ENG, accessed March 14, 2013.

- Customers care passionately about the issue.

- The cost of participation is relatively low. This cost depends mainly on their preference for the boycotted brand as well as consumers' access to substitutes.[98]

- The underlying issues are easy to understand by the general public.

  The issue at the center of a boycott can be either one-sided (e.g., animal rights, use of sustainable materials) or two-sided (e.g., whaling, same-sex marriage). Typically, with one-sided issues, the company will make some concession or at least spell out a plan to tackle the issue. Polarized two-sided cases are more delicate as the company is forced to choose sides. If at all possible, the company should stay out of these issues.[99]

---

[98]Sankar Sen, Zeyner Gürhan-Canli, and Vicki Morwitz, "Withholding Consumption: A Social Dilemma Perspective on Consumer Boycotts," *Journal of Consumer Research* 28 (December 2001): 399–417.

[99]Daniel Diermeier, "When Do Company Boycotts Work?" http://blogs.hbr.org/cs/2012/08/when_do_company_boycotts_work.html, accessed April 17, 2013.

SUMMARY

These days most companies recognize that sustainability is here to stay. Being a responsible citizen means that the firm should pay attention to other stakeholders besides its shareholders. In today's global environment, the impact that multinationals can have on a country can be huge. A multinational aspiring to be a good responsible local player should understand its impact on the host country's economic and social conditions—both the good and the bad influences. With such insights, the company can strive to contribute to the well-being of the local country by reinforcing the good part and remedying the negative elements. At the same time, many sustainability issues also have a cross-border or even global character. To address such issues a firm could partner with other firms within the industry and/or NGOs.

Companies realize that a proactive approach is needed to address sustainability issues. Just sitting on the fence will not do. Multinationals such as Unilever, Nestlé, and Toyota are showing leadership on sustainability and being trailblazers for other firms.

In this chapter, we reviewed the multi-faceted domain of sustainability. We looked at the motivations for pursuing sustainability as well as the major challenges that multinationals encounter. We discussed the steps that a firm must take to develop a sustainable strategy. We also highlighted the contribution that global marketers can make and some of the challenges they meet in implementing a sustainable strategy. Regardless of how responsibly a firm attempts to be, sooner or later it will confront a crisis that could threaten its business within the host country. Finally, this chapter also offered guidelines on how to cope with a crisis or consumer boycott.

QUESTIONS

1. What are the reasons why multinationals increasingly engage in CSR-related activities? What are the key challenges they may encounter?

2. What is the role of a global brand manager in implementing a sustainability strategy?

3. What is the role of a stakeholder engagement program?

4. In a *Harvard Business Review* article on supply chain accountability (November 2011, pp. 88–96), Unilever's chief supply chain officer stated: "Sixty-five percent of our environment footprint is related to how consumers use our products. We have to lead beyond our own walls." Discuss how multinationals like Unilever can convince customers around the world to behave more "responsibly."

5. In a panel discussion on crisis management, Tom Grimmer, the head of communications at HSBC, pointed out the increasing threats from vocal stakeholders on social media such as Facebook or Weibo (China) have caused global brands to become hypersensitive: "The pendulum has swung too far to the right, such that brands have to respond to everything on social media."[100] Do you agree with Grimmer's observation? Why or why not?

---

[100]"Control of the Narrative," *Campaign Asia-Pacific* (December 2012): 46–47.

SUBJECT INDEX

Note: The letter(s) 'e', 'gp' following page number(s) refer to exhibit and global perspective respectively

A

Absolute advantage, 21, 22
ACE. *See* Anchor contraction effect
Acquisitions, 281–283
  expansion via, 308
  Lenovo/IBM deal, 282gp
ACTA. *See* Anti-Counterfeiting Trade
  Agreement
Activities of global marketing, 18–19
  coordination across markets, 19
  global integration, 19
  standardization efforts, 18
Ad hoc branding meetings, 496
Ad valorem duty, 473
Adaptation, 359
Adaptation to products, 327
  forces that push toward, 327
    consumer preferences, 327
    environmental conditions, 214
    managerial motivation, 285
    strong local competitors, 322
Advertising, 369–372
  advertising agency, selecting, 372–374
    conflicting accounts, 373
    creative reputation, 373
    creative talent, 373
    desirable image, 373
    market coverage, 373
    scope and quality of support services,
      373
    Size of the agency, 373
  and culture, 352–355
    cultural barriers, 354
    language barriers, 352–354
Advertising campaigns, and religion, 371
Advertising messages, content of, 370
Advertising regulations, 369–372
  Advertising Standards Authority (ASA),
    369
  advertising targeting children, 371
  China's 1995 advertising law, 369e
  comparative advertising, 370
  content of advertising messages, 370

  foreign made ads, 363, 370
  of 'vice products' and pharmaceuticals,
    370
AES. *See* Automated Export System
Aesthetics, 98–102
  car color preferences, 99–102
    China, 99, 102e
    Europe, 101e
    India, 100e
    Japan, 105
    Russia, 99e
African Regional Industrial Property
    Organization (ARIPO), 158
Agent intermediary, 439
Aggregate segmentation, 203
AGP. *See* Attitudes toward global
    products
Air freight, 420, 421
Alliances, expanding through,
    281–287. *See also* Joint ventures;
    Partnerships
  cross-border alliances, 274, 275
  strategic alliances, 254, 266
  Walgreen's tie-up with Alliance Boots,
    275gp
ALP. *See* Attitudes toward local products
Ambush marketing, 377, 378
American Challenge, The, 10gp
AMI. *See* Asia Market Intelligence
Analogy method, 187–188
Anchor contraction effect (ACE), 181
Anticipatory groups, 98
Anti-Counterfeiting Trade Agreement
    (ACTA), 159
Antidumping import duties, 473
Antidumping regulation and global
    pricing, 344–345
  minimizing risk exposure to, 344
    distribution and communication, 345
    service enhancement, 344
    trading-up, 344
Antiglobalization movement, 44gp
Antitrust laws

  of European Union, 162
    Asia-Pacific Economic Cooperation
      (APEC), 163
    Foreign Corrupt Practices Act
      (FCPA), 163
    Organization of Economic
      Cooperation and Development
      (OECD), 162–163
    U.S. Foreign Corrupt Practices Act of
      1977, 162–163
  of United States, 160
    Clayton Act of 1914, 160
    Export Trading Company legislation
      (ETC Act) in 1982, 161
    Federal Trade Commission (FTC)
      Act of 1914, 160
    Foreign Trade Antitrust
      Improvements Act of 1982, 161
    Robinson-Patman Act of 1936, 160
    Sherman Antitrust Act of 1890, 160
APEC. *See* Asia Pacific Economic
    Cooperation
Appropriability regime, 26
Arbitration, 147, 151
ARIPO. *See* African Regional Industrial
    Property Organization
Arm's length prices, 341
ASEAN. *See* Association of South East
    Asian Nations
Asia Market Intelligence (AMI), 97
Asia Pacific Economic Cooperation
    (APEC), 42, 163
Asia, marketing to rural customers in, 48,
    92–93
  language importance, 93–95
Asian financial crisis of 1997–1998,
    60–61, 74–77, 79
  and its aftermath, 74–76
  IMF in, 60–61
  mechanism of, 75e
    Southeast Asian countries (SACS), 75e
  South American financial crisis and its
    aftermath, 76

Asia-Pacific Economic Cooperation (APEC), 163
Association of South East Asian Nations (ASEAN), 48, 133
Attitudes toward global products (AGP), 218
Attitudes toward local products (ALP), 218
Automated Export System (AES), 459

B

Back-translation, 177
Backward innovation, 529
Balance of payments, 58–60
  in current account, 72–73
  direct investments, 72
  external adjustments, 73–74
  on goods, 73
  internal adjustments, 73–74
  portfolio investment, 31, 33
  on services, 71–72
  short-term capital, 72–73
  U.S. balance of payments, 1990–2011, 71e
BALS. *See* Basic Arm's Length Standard
Banner ad, 380
Barriers to marketing, 130–132
  internet marketing, 374
    cultural barriers, 296, 300, 321, 354–355
    language barriers, 352–354
    legal environment and government regulations, 147–151
    technology infrastructure, 380
  non-tariff barriers (NTBs), 41, 43, 131e
  tariff barriers, 32, 41
  trade restrictions, 132, 133
Basic Arm's Length Standard (BALS), 342
  methods to calculate, 342
    comparable/uncontrollable method, 342–343
    cost-plus method, 343
    resale price method, 342
Behavior-based segmentation, 209
Berne Convention, 158–159
Big Emerging Markets (BEMs), 37, 254
Bill of lading, 461
Black market, 388, 480gp
Bond, 33, 34, 73, 437, 472
Bottom of the pyramid (BOP), 515–516
Bottom-up budgeting, 359
Bottom-up versus top-down strategic planning, 484

BP Amoco's corporate makeover, 308
Brand architecture, 303–304
Brand equity, 319, , 338, 499
  cross-country gaps in, reasons, 299
    competitive climate, 299, 310
    cultural receptivity to brands, 300
    history, 299
    marketing support, 299
    product category penetration, 300
Brand management
  ad hoc branding meetings, 496
  brand champion, 495
  global brand manager, 495
  Global Branding Committee, 496
  informal branding meetings, 496
  organizing, 495
Branding. *See also* Global branding strategies
  approaches, types, 302
    extension branding, 302
    family (umbrella) branding, 302
    hallmark branding, 302
    solo branding, 302
  for emerging markets (EMs), 526–527
  and internet, 525
Brand-in-the-hand marketing, 379–380
Brand-name changeover strategies, 306–308
  dual branding (co-branding), 306
  factors causing change, 306
    legal rights, 306
    limited legal rights to a brand name, 306
    pruning of brand portfolio, 306
  fade-in/fade-out, 306
  summary axing, 338
  transition rules, 306–307
    BP Amoco's corporate makeover, 308gp
  transparent forewarning, 306
Brazil, Russia, India, and China (BRIC), 1, 290, 355, 505–506, 518
Bretton Woods Conference, 58
BRIC. *See* Brazil, Russia, India, and China
Bulk shipping, 420
Bulletin boards and chat groups, 184
'Bullwhip effect', 444
Business Action to Stop Counterfeiting and Piracy (BASCAP), 153
Business practices and the legal system, 148
Business-to-business (B2B), 5
  B2B e-commerce, 5–6
  B2B procurement, 431–432
Business-to-consumer (B2C), 5
  B2C e-commerce, 5–6

Buy American Act of 1933, 130
Buyer-seller relationships, differences in, 396e
Buzz marketing, 383

C

Cabotage rules in the NAFTA, 424gp
CAFTA–DR. *See* Central American–Dominican Republic Free Trade Agreement
CAPI. *See* Computer-assisted personal interviewing
Capital account, 71–72
Capitalism, 44, 126
Carrefour's operations in China, 443e
CATI. *See* Computer-assisted telephone interviewing
Cause-related marketing, 539–540
CBP. *See* Customs & Border Protection
CEM. *See* Combination export manager
Central American–Dominican Republic Free Trade Agreement (CAFTA–DR), 49
Chain ratio method, 188–189, 191
Channel configurations, 438–439
  agent intermediary, 439
  coverage, 439
  merchant intermediaries, 439
Children, advertising targeting, 371
China
  accession to WTO, 43–44, 44gp
  1995 advertising law, 369e
  advertising lynx in, 120
  China Federation of Logistics and Purchasing (CFLP), 417
  Chinese Economic Area (CEA), 37
  color TV market, price warfare in, 187–188
  cultural and human aspects of global marketing in, , 118, 177
  foreign business in, 388
    achieving salesforce effectiveness in, building pride and performance, 399gp
    sales force, importance, 399gp
  government role in promoting exports, 464–466
  guanxi code in, 98e
    rules for cracking, 98e
  guidelines for IP protection in, 313e
  joint ventures in, conflicting objectives, 277e
  Starbucks in, 292e, 314
  SWOT analysis of Carrefour's operations in, 443e

Civil law, 150
Clayton Act of 1914, 160
Climate impact on global marketing, 19–20
Clout, 103, 128, 298, 490
Cluster analysis, 168, 203, 220
  principles of, 220e
COCOM. *See* Coordinating Committee for Multilateral Controls
Code (written) law systems, 150
Code of conduct, 538, 557
Collectivism, 109, 111, 113
Combination export manager (CEM), 457
Commercial invoice, 461, 472
Commercial law, 150, 172
Commodity terms of trade, 22
Common law systems, 149–150
Common market, 19, 34, 48, 51
Communication strategies, 351–386.
      See also Advertising
  communication and cultural values, 354
      uncertainty avoidance, 354, 355
  creating advertising copy, approaches to, 364–366
      advertising with universal appeals, 365e
      export advertising, 364
      'Laissez-Faire', 364
  creative strategy, 359–360
      'standardization' versus 'adaptation' debate, 359–360
  direct marketing, 376–377
  for emerging markets, 505–509
  global advertising budget, setting, 355–357
      bottom-up budgeting, 359
      BRIC countries, 355
      competitive parity, 358
      objective-and-task method, 358
      percentage of sales method, 358
      resource allocation, 358–359
      top-down budgeting, 359
  global media decisions, 366–369
      global media landscape, recent trends in, 367–369
      media infrastructure, 199, 366
      media limitations, 366–367
      short messaging service (SMS) advertising, 511
  global public relations (PR) and publicity, 383–384
  global sponsorships, 377–379
  internet role in, 374, 376, 385
  sales promotions, 374–376
  viral marketing, 380, 383

Communication style, in sales negotiation, 407e
Communism, 67, 126
Community support (cause-related marketing), 539–540
Company costs, foreign market pricing and, 328
  setting export prices, 328
      dynamic incremental pricing, 328
      flexible cost-plus pricing, 328
      rigid cost-plus pricing, 328
Company goals, foreign market pricing and, 327–328
Comparable/uncontrollable method, 342, 343
Comparative advantage theory, 21–24
  factor endowment theory of, 23
  one person–day productivity, 22e
  production and consumption, 22e
  theory, 21–22
  at work, 22e
Comparative advertising, 355, 370
Competition, foreign market pricing and, 327
  cross-border price differentials, 329–330
  pharmaceutical industry, 330
Competitive advantage, 233
Competitive analysis, 256–257
Competitive climate, 299, 310
Competitive environment, 265, 310, 414
Competitive industry structure, 231–232
  bargaining power of buyers, 232
  bargaining power of suppliers, 232
  competitive advantage, 233
  cost leadership strategy, 233
  indirect competition, 231
  industry competitors, 231
  nature of, 231–232
  niche strategy focus, 234
  potential entrants, 231–232
  product differentiation strategy, 233
  threat of substitute products or services, 232
Competitive parity, for advertising, 358
Competitiveness of the United States, the European union, Japan, and beyond, 10gp
Competitor-focused approaches, 235
Compound duty, 473
Computer-assisted personal interviewing (CAPI), 193
Computer-assisted telephone interviewing (CATI), 193

Concept cooperation, 365
  product concept, 176, 184
Conceptual equivalence, 175
Confirmed irrevocable letter of credit, 463, 464
Confiscation, 142
Conjoint analysis for concept testing in global new product development, 168
Consumer boycotts, 560, 562
Consumer panel data, 192, 193
Consumer response to recession, 79–80
Consumers, country-of-origin (COO) influences on, 317–318
Contact method, 179
Continuous monitoring of brand sales/market share movements, 192
Contract, in sales negotiation, 407e
Control of global marketing efforts, 498
  formal (bureaucratic) control systems, 498
      analyzing and correcting deviations, 500
      establishing standards (metrics), 498–499
      measuring and evaluating performance, 499
  informal control methods, 500
      corporate culture, 500
      human resource development, 500–501
  'soft' versus 'hard' levers, 501
Convergence, 8–11
  market convergence at work in EU, 10gp
COO. *See* Country-of-origin
Cooperative exporting, 268–270
Cooperative global trade agreements, evolution of, 40–43
  antiglobalization movement, 44gp
  dispute settlement mechanism, 43–44
  Doha Development Agenda (Doha Round), 41, 43e
  Uruguay Round, 41
Cooperative joint venture, 276
Coordinating Committee for Multilateral Controls (COCOM), 146
Copyrights, 26–27, 48, 152, 155, ;157, 162
Core competencies, 426
Core components standardization, 246, 247
Core services, 435–436
Corporate (organizational) culture, 394
Corporate culture, 500

Corporate response to recession, 80–82
  increasing advertising in the region, 82
  increasing local procurement, 82
  long-term oriented solutions, 80
  looking for expansion opportunities,
    81–82
  maintaining stricter inventory, 81
  product mix, changing, 81
  product's value, emphasizing, 81
  pull-out, 80
  repackaging the goods, 81
  short-term-oriented solution, 80
Corporate social responsibility (CSR), 531
  major areas of, 533–534
    community support (cause-related
      marketing), 539–540
    corruption/graft, 533–534
    environmental concerns,
      532
    interbrand 2012 green brands, 536e
    water saver initiatives, 536e
  scope of, 531–533
Cosmopolitanism, 211, 217
Cost-based pricing, 342
Cost innovation, 515, 516
Cost leadership strategy, 233
Cost of transportation, 420
Cost-plus method, 343
Counterfeiting, 47, 153, 154
Countertrade, 134, 142
Countervailing duty, 473
Country-as-segments approach, 203
  flaws in, 203
Country-based subsidiaries, 488
Country competitiveness, 35–37
  changing, 35
  human resources and technology, 35–37
Country-of-origin (COO) effects,
    316
  COO stereotypes, coping strategies,
    318–319
    communication, 319
    distribution, 320
    pricing, 320
    product policy, 319–320
    product-country matches and
      mismatches, 319e
  influences on consumers, 317–318
    brand name familiarity, 318
    consumer demographics, 317
    culture, 318
    design versus manufacturing, 317
    emotions, 318
    product category, 318
    stability over time, 317

  willingness to pay, 317
Country risk assessment criteria, 140e
  economic risk, 140e
  financial risk, 140e
  political risk, 140e
Country risk ratings, 140e
Country screening, 199–200
Country selection, 260–262
  four-step procedure, 260–261
    compute overall score for each
      country (Step 4), 262
    determining the importance of
      country indicators (Step 2), 262
    indicator selection and data collection
      (Step 1), 268–262
    rating the countries (Step 3), 262
  logical flowchart of, 261
  prescreening market opportunities
    method, 263
  screening procedures, 260–262
Court decisions, 147
Courtesy bias, 179
Coverage, 439, 443
Creative destruction, 238
Credit risk, 458, 463
Crisis management, 560–562
Cross-border alliances, 274, 275
Cross-border price differentials, 330
Cross-country survey research, 177
Cross-cultural comparisons, 108–110
  collectivism, 109
  high- versus low-context cultures,
    108–109
  Hofstede's classification scheme, 109–110
  individualism, 109
  long termism, 110
  masculinity, 110
  uncertainty avoidance, 109
    versus power distance, 111e
  world value survey (WVS), 114e,
    113–114
Cross-cultural marketing research, survey
    methods for, 177–183
  questionnaire design, 177–178
Cross-cultural negotiations, in sales
    management, 405–409. *See also
    under* Sales management
  negotiation styles, 407e
    adapting counterpart's negotiation
      script, 408
    communication style, 407e
    context, 407e
    contract, 407e
    coordinating adjustment of both
      parties, 408

  embracing the counterpart's script,
    408
  employing agent or adviser, 406
  improvising an approach, 408
  inducing the counterpart to follow
    one's own negotiation script, 406
  involving a mediator, 406
  language, 407e
  sequence, 407e
  stages of negotiation process, 406
  strategies, 409
Cross-cultural training for expatriates, 409
Cross-licensing agreements, 270
Cross-sectional regression analysis,
    190–191
Cross-subsidization of markets, 251–252
CSR. *See* Corporate social responsibility
C-TPAT (Customers-Trade Partnership
    Against Terrorism) program,
    469gp
Cultural barriers, 296, 354
Cultural considerations, in sales,
    392–398. *See also under* Sales
    management
Cultural distance, 265
Cultural gaps bridging, in international
    joint ventures, 279
Cultural generalization, 393
Cultural references, 94
Cultural relativism, 164gp, 543
Cultural tensions, 542–543
Cultural values and legal systems, 150
Culture, 91–121. *See also* Aesthetics;
    Cross-cultural comparisons;
    Religion
  adapting to cultures, 114–116
    cross-cultural differences, managing,
      115, 116
    four-step correction mechanism, 115
    importance, 91, 110, 114
    out-group homogeneity bias, 116
    self-reference criterion (SRC), 115, 170
  and buying behavior, 92–121
  and consumption processes, stages, 91
    access, 91
    buying behavior, 91
    consumption characteristics, 91
    disposal, 91
  cultural norms and new product
    opportunities, 118
  Dentsu lifestyle survey, 107e
  distribution, 109, 111, 119
  elements of, 92–107
    language, 93–96. *See also individual
      entry*

material life, 92–93
importance from global marketing
        perspective, 95, 98
    new market opportunities, 90
    shaping company's marketing mix
        program, 90
and marketing mix, 90, 103
meaning of, 91–92
people's thought processes and, 106
pricing, 119
promotion, 120–121
social interactions, 96–97
value systems, 106–107
Currency blocs, 62–64
    Renminbi (yuan), 62
Currency floats, 61
    free (clean) float, 61
    kinds of, 61
    managed float, 61
Currency fluctuations and global pricing,
        336–339, 422
    currency gain/loss pass through,
        336–339
        local-currency price stability (LCPS),
            339
        pricing-to-market (PTM), 339
    exporter strategies under, 339e
Currency gain/loss pass through,
        336–339
Currency hedging, 68, 69, 464
Current account balance, 39, 71, 72
Customer demand, foreign market pricing
        and, 231, 241, 329
Customer-focused approaches,
        236–238
Customization
    overcustomization, 323
    standardization versus, 323
Customs, 147, 341
Customs & Border Protection (CBP),
        459
Customs receipt, 461
Customs union, 49, 51

D
Decision-making model for assessing risk
        of transfer pricing strategy, 343e
Decline stage, 25
Defining marketing, 13
Demographics, 207
Denmark, 36
Dentsu lifestyle survey, 107e
    beliefs, 107e
    concerns, 107e
    image as a nation, 107e

Design families concept, 247
Digital Millennium Copyright Act
        (DMCA), 157, 159
Direct exporting, 15, 268–270,
        458
    export department, 458
    export sales subsidiary, 458
    foreign sales branch, 458
    indirect exporting and, comparison,
        458e
Direct government subsidies, 130
Direct identification drawback, 473
Direct investments, 72
Direct marketing, 333, 374376–377
Disaggregate international consumer
        segmentation, 203
Dispute settlement mechanism, 43–44
Dissociative groups, 98
Distribution, 416–449. See also
        International distribution channels;
        Physical distribution
    challenge, for emerging markets (EMs),
        524–527
    channels, 331
    and culture, 116
    sourcing strategy, 418
Distributor relationships, managing, 525
Divergence, 9–13
    market divergence at work in EU, 10gp
DMCA. See Digital Millennium Copyright
        Act
Dodging strategy, 512
Doha Development Agenda (Doha
        Round), 41
Dollar preference scale, 318
Domestic marketing, 16, 202
    ethnocentric, 15, 16
Domestic markets saturation, 3
Domestic purchase arrangement, 430
Domestic sourcing, 429
    domestic in-house sourcing, 430
Domestication policy, 142
Donruss Playoff, 153
Dual branding (co-branding), 306
Dual-party system, 127
Dumping, 344–345
Duty-drawback, 473
Dynamic incremental pricing, 328

E
EAA. See Export Administration Act
EAPO. See Eurasian Patent Office
EAS. See European Advisory Services
E-commerce
    and logistics, 423

proliferation, 48–49
    regulations on, 150
    and retailing, 449–450
E-company, 227
Economic and financial turmoil
        worldwide, 74–78. See also
        Recession
    Asian financial crisis and its aftermath,
        74–76
    financial crises in perspective, 77
    inflation surges in emerging economies,
        78gp
    regional financial crises, responses to,
        79–82
    U.S. subprime mortgage loan crisis,
        77
Economic and Monetary Union (EMU),
        84
Economic environment, 28–54. See also
        Cooperative global trade
        agreements, evolution of;
        Emerging economies; Intertwined
        world economy; Multinational
        companies (MNCs)
    for the 21st century economy, 29
    country competitiveness, 35–37
    global competitiveness ranking,
        36e
    portfolio investment, 33–34
    second half of 1990s, 29
    world merchandise trade growth and
        GDP, 2000–2011, 29e
Economic geography impact on global
        marketing, 19–20
Economies of scale, 18, 24, 304, 306–307
Economies of scope, 24
Economist Intelligence Unit
        (E.I.U.), 139, 173
EDI. See Electronic data interchange
EDLP. See Every-day-low-pricing
Education, 104–106
EEI. See Electronic Export Information
EFTA. See European Free Trade
        Association
Electronic commerce (e-commerce),
        225–227
Electronic data interchange (EDI), 224,
        459
Electronic Export Information (EEI), 459
Electronic manufacturing services (EMS)
        companies, 432
Electronically represented intellectual
        property, 46
Embargoes, 132
EMC. See Export management company

Emerging economies, 37–40
  ASEAN, including Brunei, 38
  Big Emerging Markets (BEMs), 37
  Chinese Economic Area (CEA), 38
  Commonwealth of Independent States, 37
  India, 38
  inflation surges in, 78gp
  leading emerging economies, 39e
  smaller emerging economies, 38
  Triad regions, 37
  World's nine largest exporting countries, 38
Emerging markets (EMs), 3, 443–444, 505–509
  characteristics of, 506–509
    chronic shortage of resources, 506
    high income inequalities, 506
    huge diversity within market, 506
    low per capita incomes, 506
    technology is underdeveloped, 508
    unbranded competition, 508
    weak and highly variable infrastructure, 507
    weak distribution channels and media infrastructure, 508
  communication strategies for, 526–528
    mass media versus non-traditional marketing approaches, 526–527
    push versus pull activities, 526
    reaching rural India, guidelines on, 527e
  competing with the new champions, 509–515
  definition, 505–506
  distribution challenge, 524–525
    creating distribution systems, 524–525
  distributor relationships, managing, 525
    direct selling, 525
    distributor partner selection criteria, 525
    exclusivity, 525–526
    local autonomy, 525
  entry strategies for, 518–519
    early entry, 518
    entry mode, 518–519
    timing of entry, 518
  marketing strategies for, 505
  Myanmar's business environment, challenges in, 509e
  newcomers, competing against, 513–515

Philippines, 510
product policy, 519–523
  backward innovation, 520
  branding, 521–522
  frugal innovation, 520
  packaging, 522–523
  pricing strategy, 523–524
  product innovation, 519, 523
  reverse innovation, 520
strategic options for, 513e
success strategies, 511, 518
  business models to overcome obstacles, 511
  cheap labor and train staff in-house, 511–512
  customized offerings, 511
  investing in talent to sustain growth, 512
  latest technologies, 511
  scale up rapidly, 512
targeting/positioning strategies in, 515–516
versus G7 countries, 507e
Emic versus etic dilemma, 195
Emoticons, east west differences in, 94e
EMS. See Electronic manufacturing services
EMs. See Emerging markets
EMU. See Economic and Monetary Union
EMU. See European monetary union
Enforcement, 151
Entry decisions, 200
Entry strategies, 259–294. See also Country selection; Exit strategies
  advantages, 285e
  disadvantages, 285e
  dynamics of, 284
  exporting, 268–270
  licensing, 270–271
  mode of entry, selection, 264–268
    company objectives, 266–267
    competitive environment, 265
    cultural distance, 265
    decision criteria, 264–268
    entry modes and market development, 266e
    flexibility, 267
    government regulations (openness), 264
    internal resources, assets and capabilities, 267
    local infrastructure, 265
    need for control, 267

risk, 264
mode of, theoretical perspectives, 292–293
  institutional theory, 294
  resource-based view (RBV), 293
  transaction-cost analysis (TCA), 293
scale of entry, 263–264
  Germany, 263
  Japan, 263
  U.S. retail market, 263
timing of entry, 285–287
  near-market knowledge concept, 287
  Wal-Mart's international expansion, 286e
Environmental concerns, 535–537
  in organizational design, 485–486
EPO. See European Patent Office
Equity joint venture, 275
ERM. See Exchange Rate Mechanism
ERS. See Extreme response style
ETC. See Export Trading Company
Ethical confusion, 543
Ethical imperialism, 543
Ethnocentric domestic marketing, 15
Ethnographic research, 183gp, 183
EU. See European Union
Eurasian Patent Office (EAPO), 158
Euro area, marketing in, 82–87
  eurozone countries, 83e
  historical background, 82–84
  marketers, challenges to, 86
    adaptation of internal organizational structures, 86
    EU regulations crossing national boundaries, 86
    intensified competitive pressure, 85
    price transparency, 85
    SMEs, new opportunities for, 87
    streamlined supply chains, 86–87
  ramifications of euro for marketers, 86–87
Euromonitor, 173
European Advisory Services (EAS), 86
European Free Trade Association (EFTA), 49
European Marketing Data and Statistics, 173
European monetary union (EMU), 84
European Patent Convention, 159
European Patent Office (EPO), 158
European Union (EU) market, 9, 52
  Antitrust laws of, 162–163. See also under Antitrust laws

convergence at work in EU, 10gp
divergence at work in EU, 10gp
foreign direct investment (FDI), 10gp
major purpose of, 10gp
traditional European advantage, 10gp
Evaluation, of salespeople, 405
qualitative, 405
quantitative, 405
Event sponsorship, 377
Every-day-low-pricing (EDLP), 331
Evolution of global marketing, 13–21
defining marketing, 13
different marketing strategies, 13
domestic marketing, 16
export marketing, 16–17
global marketing, 18–19
impact of competition, 14
international marketing, 17–18
internationalization of the company, 14
marketing mix decisions, 15e
multinational marketing, 18
product planning, 15e
Exchange rate fluctuation
coping with, 66–68
forecasting, 65
Exchange Rate Mechanism (ERM), 84
Exchange rate pass-through, 69–70
Exit strategies, 287–288. *See also* Entry
strategies
guidelines, 290
reasons for exit, 288–289
difficulty in cracking the market, 288
ethical reasons, 288
intense competition, 289
premature entry, 288
resource re-allocation, 289
sustained losses, 288
volatility, 288
risks of exit, 289
damage to corporate image, 289
disposition of assets, 289
fixed costs of exit, 289
long-term opportunities, 290
signal to other markets, 290
Expatriates, 409–414
advantages of, 410
better communication, 410
development of talent, 410
difficulties of sending expatriates
abroad, 410–414
compensation, 412–413
cross-cultural training, 411
family discord, 413
motivation, 412
security risk, 413–414

generalizations about, 414
repatriation, 414
Export Administration Act (EAA) of 1979,
469gp
Export advertising, 364
Export agent, 268
Export commission house, 457
Export license, 460
requirements, 132–133
trade restrictions, reasons to be
concerned with, 133
Export management company (EMC), 269,
390–391
Export marketing, 16–17
direct exporting, 16
indirect exporting, 16
Export merchant, 268
Export regulations, 468–470
Export Trading Company (ETC) Act of
1982, 161, 162, 390–391, 468
Exporter strategies under varying currency
conditions, 337e
Export-Import Bank (Ex-Im Bank), 466–7
credit insurance, 467
repayment of loans, 467
working capital loans, 467
Exporting, entry strategies, 268–270
cooperative exporting, 269–270
direct exporting, 270
export agent, 268
export merchant, 268
indirect exporting, 268–269
piggyback exporting, 269
Exports, 453–482. *See also* Direct exporting;
Imports; Indirect exporting
export market segments, 457
export regulations, 468–470
Foreign Corrupt Practices Act of
1977, 468
Normal Trade Relations (NTR), 468
export transactions, 461
bill of lading, 461
commercial invoice, 462
customs receipt, 461
freight forwarders, 461
shipper's order bill of lading, 461
straight bill of lading, 461
terms of shipment and sale, 462
government role in promoting exports,
464–468
in China, 466
Export Enhancement Act of 1992,
465
Japan Export Information Center
(JEIC), 465

Japanese External Trade Organization
(JETRO), 465
in United States, 465
mechanics of exporting, 459–464
export license, 460
general license, 460
legality of exports, 459–461
U.S. Government Departments and
Agencies with, 462e
validated license, 460
organizing for exports, 454–460
overseas market and appropriate
segment, identification, 455
payment terms, 461, 463–464
advance payment, 463e
confirmed irrevocable letter of credit,
463e
consignment, 463e
credit risk, 463
currency hedging, 464
documents against payment (D/P), 463e
foreign exchange risk, 463
open account, 463e
political risk, 463
terms of shipment, 462e
transfer risk, 463
unconfirmed irrevocable letter of
credit, 464, 463e
research for, 454–455
tariff concessions, 467–468
American Export Trading Company,
468
foreign trade zones (FTZs), 467–468
Expropriation, 142
Extended family, 97
Extension branding, 302
External market adjustments, 74
Extreme response style (ERS), 181

F

Factor endowment theory of comparative
advantage, 23
Fade-in/fade-out strategy, 306
'Fair' price concept, 344
Family (umbrella) branding, 281, 301
Faster product diffusion, 228
Fast-track trade authority, 145
FCCP. *See* Foreign consumer culture
positioning
FCPA. *See* Foreign Corrupt Practices Act
FDI. *See* Foreign direct investment
Federal Trade Commission (FTC) Act of
1914, 160
Federation of International Trade
Associations (FITA), 381

Feng shui (wind-water), 103
Financial controls, 133
   government fiscal policies, 135
   macroeconomic policies, 134
Financial crises in perspective, 77
Financial environment, 56–88. *See also*
      Balance of payments; Economic
      and financial turmoil worldwide;
      International monetary system
   U.S. dollar, historical role of, 57–58
Finland, 36e
FIPB. *See* Foreign Investment Promotion
      Board
Firm-specific factors, in organizational
      design, 486–487
First-mover advantage vs. first-mover
      disadvantage, 234
First-to-invent principle vs.first-to-file
      principle, 155, 156gp
Fisher-Price problem, 93
FITA. *See* Federation of International
      Trade Associations
Fixed versus floating exchange rates, 61–62
Flexible cost-plus pricing, 328
Focus groups, 176, 177, 185
Foreign consumer culture positioning
      (FCCP), 218
Foreign Corrupt Practices Act (FCPA) of
      1977, 163, 534
Foreign direct investment (FDI), 10gp,
      32–33
   fluctuation of, 33
   inflows in US (1980–2011), 32e
   outward foreign direct investment
      (OFDI), 33
Foreign exchange and foreign exchange
      rates, 64–74
   Americas, 70e
   Asia-Pacific, 70e
   exchange rate fluctuation, 65
      coping with, 66–68
      forecasting, 65
   exchange rate pass-through, 69–70
   factors influencing, 66e
      fluctuations in rates, 66–67
      macroeconomic factors, 66e
      political factors, 66e
      random factors, 66e
   fluctuations, 63e
   purchasing power parity (PPP), 64–65
   spot versus forward foreign exchange,
      68–69
Foreign exchange risk, 463, 464, 481
Foreign governments role, in sales
      management, 392

Foreign Investment Promotion Board
      (FIPB), 135
Foreign made ads, 363, 370
Foreign market pricing, 326–334
   drivers of, 4Cs, 327–334
      company costs, 327
      company goals, 327–328
      competition, 330–331
      customer demand, 329
      distribution channels, 331
      government policies, 332
Foreign sales branch, 458
Foreign Trade Antitrust Improvements Act
      of 1982, 161
Foreign trade zones (FTZs), 467
Formal (bureaucratic) control systems, 498
Forward foreign exchange, spot versus,
      68–69
Forward market, 68
Franchising, 272–273
   benefits, 273
   caveats, 273
   franchisee, 272
   franchisor, 273
   international franchising, 274e
   master franchising, 273
Free (clean) currency float, 61
Free trade area, 48–50
   CAFTA–DR, 49
   common market, 51
   customs Union, 51
   EFTA, 49
   European Union, 51
   Free Trade Area of the Americas
      (FTAA), 50
   Maastricht Treaty, 51
   MERCOSUR, 50
   monetary union, 52
   NAFTA, 50–51
   RCEP, 50gp
   TPP, 50gp
Free trade zone (FTZ), 436–438
   in United States, 436, 437e
Freight forwarders, 459, 461
Frugal innovation, 520, 521
FTC. *See* Federal Trade Commission
FTZ. *See* Free trade zone
FTZs. *See* Foreign trade zones
Functional equivalence, 175, 177
Funny faces scale, 178e, 178

G
G8. *See* Group of Eight
GATT. *See* General Agreement on Tariffs
      and Trade

GCCP. *See* Global consumer culture
      positioning
GDP. *See* Gross Domestic Product
General Agreement on Tariffs and Trade
      (GATT), 28, 40, 41, 45, 145, 321
   Group of Eight (G8), 145
   Group of Eight plus Five (G8 + 5), 145
   Group of Seven (G7), 145
   Heiligendamm Process, 145
General license, 460
Geography of Thought, 106
1932 German Free Gift Act, 375
GIMC. *See* Globally integrated marketing
      communications
GlaxoSmithKline (GSK), 346gp
Global branding strategies,
      296–324. *See also* Local branding
   consumers way of valuing brands, 323
      global myth, 299
      quality signal, 299
      social responsibility, 299
   firm's global brand structure, driving
      factors, 302
      firm-based drivers, 302
      market dynamics, 303
      product-market drivers, 303
   global brand name, advantages, 298,
      300
      leverage country association for the
         product, 298
      prestige factor, 298
      scale advantage, 298–323
Global citizenship, 228
Global competition, 4–5
Global consumer culture positioning
      (GCCP), 217–218
Global cooperation, 5
Global corporate citizenship,
      531–533
Global E-commerce, 45
Global HABIT survey, 210
Global lead agency, 373
Global Leadership and Organizational
      Behavior Effectiveness (GLOBE)
      Project, 111–113
   dimensions, 111–112
Global marketing
   benefits, 239–241
      cost reduction, 240
      enhanced customer preference, 241
      improved products and program
         effectiveness, 241
      increased competitive advantage,
         241–242
      demand-side argument, 242

limits to, 242
strategies. *See* Strategies, marketing
supply-side argument, 242
Global phased rollout model.
See Waterfall model
Global pricing and antidumping
regulation, 344–345
Global pricing and currency fluctuations,
336–339. *See also*
Currency fluctuations and global
pricing, 336–339
Global reach, 12
Global strategy, 228–239
global industry, 228–231. *See also*
Industry, global
Globalization, 1–27
benefits, 1
imperative, 1–27
global marketing is imperative, reasons
for, 3–8
domestic markets saturation, 3
emerging markets, 3
global competition, 4
global cooperation, 5
internet revolution, 5–6
unfavorable domestic economy, 3–4
Globally integrated marketing
communications (GIMC),
384–385
Global-pricing contracts (GPCs),
347
pan-European price coordination, 348e
GLOBE. *See* Global Leadership and
Organizational Behavior
Effectiveness
Glocal mindset, 498
Government policies and regulations, 128–
135
direct government subsidies, 130
embargoes, 132
export license requirements,
132–133
export-active states, 129
financial controls, 133
government procurement, 130
incentives and government programs,
129
investment regulations, 134
non-tariff barriers, 130–131
ownership controls, 133–134
reasons for wanting to block trade, 128
developing new industries, 128
national security, 128
protecting declining industries, 128
sanctions, 132

state government's export promotion
activities, 129
tariff barriers, 131
trade laws, 130
Government policies, in foreign market
pricing, 332
Government procurement, 130
Government regulations (openness), 264
Government role in promoting exports,
464–470
GPCs. *See* Global-pricing contracts
GPD. *See* Global product development
Grammar, 94
Grassroots marketing, 527
Gray and black sectors of the economy,
208
Gray markets, 474–481
activities, combating, 478–479e
currency fluctuations, 475
differences in market demand, 475
legal differences, 475
opportunistic behavior, 475
segmentation strategy, 475–476
Great Depression of 1929–1932, 77
Green marketing, 149
Greenfield operations, 284
Greenwashing, 557
Gross Domestic Product (GDP), 28
Group of Eight (G8), 145
Group of Eight plus Five (G8 + 5), 145
Group of Seven (G7), 14524
GSK. *See* GlaxoSmithKline
Guanxi, 97
in China, rules for cracking, 98e

H
Hakuhodo lifestyle segmentation, 211
concerns, 211–212
seven global clusters, 211e
Hallmark branding, 302
HDI. *See* Human Development Index
Heiligendamm Process, 145
High- versus low-context cultures,
108–109
Hofstede's classification scheme,
109–110
Home country versus host country,
124–126
Human Development Index (HDI), 209
Human resource development, 500
Human resources and technology, 35–37
change in country innovativeness,
37e
Denmark, 36
Finland, 36–37

Singapore, 36
Sweden, 36–37
Switzerland, 36–37
United States, 36–37
Hypercompetition, 238
creative destruction, 238

I
IBEA. *See* Incremental break-even
analysis
ICs. *See* Innovation centers
Ideology, 126
Idioms, 94
IEEPA. *See* International Economic
Emergency Powers Act
IMC. *See* Integrated marketing
communications
IMF. *See* International Monetary Fund
Imports, 453–481. *See also* Exports; Gray
markets
buy decisions, categories, 471
modified rebuy, 471
new tasks, 471
straight buys, 471
of importer buyer behavior model, 471e
import duties, 473–474
ad valorem duty, 473
antidumping import duties, 473
compound duty, 473
countervailing duty, 473
direct identification drawback, 473
duty-drawback, 473
specific duty, 473
substitution drawback, 473
temporary importation under bond
(TIB), 473
management, 470–471
mechanics of importing, 471–474
bond, 472
documents and delivery,
472–473
Special Permit for Immediate
Delivery, 473
Income disparities, 208
Incremental approach, in international joint
ventures, 278–279
India, 38
Indirect exporting, 16, 268–269, 456–458
combination export manager (CEM),
457
export broker, 457
export commission house, 457
export merchants, 457
piggyback exporting, 458
trading company, 457, 458e

Indirect investment. *See* Portfolio investment
Individualism, 109
Industry, global, 228–231. *See also* Competitive industry structure
'city-cluster'approach to reach emerging markets, 231
ethnocentric orientation, 231
industry globalization drivers, 229
competitive forces, 230
cost forces, 230
government forces, 229–230
market forces, 229
multidomestic vs. global strategy, 230
polycentric orientation, 231
Inflation surges in emerging economies, 78gp
Inflationary environments, pricing in, 334–336
action courses, 335
adapting the product line, 336
launching new products or variants of existing products, 336
negotiating with the government, 337
predicting incidence of price controls, 337
shifting target segments or markets, 335
safeguarding against inflation, 334
components, ingredients, parts, and/or packaging materials, modifying, 334
drawing lessons from other countries, 335
including escalator clauses in long-term contracts, 335
pursuing rapid inventory turnovers, 335
quoting prices in a stable currency, 335
shortening credit terms, 335
source materials from low-cost suppliers, 334
Informal branding meetings, 496
Informal control methods, 500
Information technology (IT), 38
and the changing nature of competition, 45–50
controlling copies, 47
electronically represented intellectual property, 46
information-related products, 46
proliferation of e-commerce, 47–48
and global competition, 224–227
e-company, 227

electronic commerce (e-commerce), 225–227
faster product diffusion, ;228
global citizenship, 228
online communication, 225–227
real-time management, 224
Innovation centers (ICs), 514
Institutional Revolutionary Party (PRI), 127
Institutional theory, 294
Integrated marketing communications (IMC) program, 385
Intellectual outsourcing, 435
Intellectual property in information age, value of, 46–47
Intellectual property protection, 153–157
Business Action to Stop Counterfeiting and Piracy (BASCAP), 153
copyrights, 155, 157
counterfeiting, 153, 154
Digital Millennium Copyright Act (DMCA), 157, 159
Donruss Playoff, 153
first-to-file principle, 155
first-to-invent principle, 155
international treaties for, 157–163
Liz Claiborne, 153
patent, 155
Traceless System, 153
trade secret, 157
trademark, 157
Intellectual property rights (IPR) protection, 152, 314, 339
Intercultural considerations in sales, 388, 388e
Interdependency, 238
Interfaces among R&D, operations, and marketing, 244–249
marketing/R&D interface, 248–249
operations/ marketing interface, 246–248
core components standardization, 246–247
product design families, 247
R&D/operations interface, 244–249
universal product with all features, 247
universal product with different positioning, 247
Intermodal transportation, 421–422
Internal market adjustments, 73
Internalization/transaction cost theory, 26
International agreements, 144–146
COCOM (Coordinating Committee for Multilateral Controls), 146

Wassenaar arrangement, 146
International Bank for Reconstruction and Development, 61
International brand architecture, dimensions of, 304e
International distribution channels, 438–440
channel configurations, 438–439
agent intermediary, 439
coverage, 439
merchant intermediaries, 439–440
channel management, 439–440
International Economic Emergency Powers Act (IEEPA), 469gp
International franchising, 274
International joint ventures, 278–279
challenges, 279
drivers behind, 278–279
clear objectives, establishing, 279
cultural gaps, bridging, 279
incremental approach, 279
managerial commitment and respect, 279
right partner, selecting, 278
International law, 147–151
cultural values and legal systems, 150
jurisdiction, 151
arbitration, 151
enforcement, 151
planning ahead, 151
local legal systems and laws, 147–151. *See also individual entry*
sources, 148
court decisions, 148
customs, 150
treaties, 147
International market segmentation, 199–203
approaches, 203–204
country-as-segments approach, 203
disaggregate international consumer segmentation, 203
two-stage international segmentation, 204
bases for, 207–212
behavior-based segmentation, 209
demographics, 207
gray and black sectors of the economy, 208
income disparities, 208
lifestyle and values, 209–212
monetization of transactions within a country, 208

socioeconomic variables, 208
country screening, 199–200
entry decisions, 200
global marketing research, 200
marketing mix policy, 202–203
positioning strategy, 201
properties, 199
  accessible, 199
  actionable, 199
  identifiable, 199
  responsive, 199
  sizable, 199
  stability, 199
resource allocation, 201–202
  challenger markets, 201
  leader markets, 201
International Marketing Data and
  Statistics, 173
International marketing, 15e, 17–18
multidomestic marketing, 18
polycentric orientation, 17
International Monetary Fund (IMF), 44gp,
  59–60, 136, 173
in 1997–1998 Asian financial crisis, 60
purposes, 59
special drawing rights (SDRs), 60
International monetary system, 57–64
Bretton Woods Conference, 58–59
currency blocs, 62–64
development of today's monetary
  system, 58–64
fixed versus floating exchange rates,
  61–62
foreign exchange rate fluctuations, 63e
International Bank for Reconstruction
  and Development, 61
International Monetary Fund (IMF),
  59–60
International Organization for
  Standardization (ISO), 152–153
ISO 14000, 152–153
ISO 9000, 152–152
International personal selling, 392
International positioning strategies,
  212–217
sequence of steps, 212
uniform versus localized positioning
  strategies, 214–215
universal positioning appeals,
  215–216
International product cycle theory, 24–25
decline stage, 25
demand structure, 25e
economies of scale, 24
economies of scope, 24

growth stage, 24
innovator company marketing strategy,
  25e
international competition, 25e
introductory stage, 24
maturity stage, 25
preference similarity, 24
production, 25e
technological gap, 26
International retailing, 440–442
'bullwhip effect', 444
market information at retail level, 445
on-time retail information management,
  444–446
private-label brands
  (store brands), 442
'Push' versus 'Pull', 444
reduced inventory, 445
retailing differences across the world,
  446–447
SWOT analysis of Carrefour's
  operations in China, 443e
Wal-Mart, 441–442
International sales strategy, 388, 388e
International trade
and foreign production, 11
global reach, 12
intra-firm trade, 12
managers of, 16
versus international business, 11–12
International Trade Administration (ITA),
  129
International trade theories, 24–27
absolute advantage, 21
comparative advantage theory, 21–24
comparative advantage, 24
principles of international trade, 23
International treaties for intellectual
  property protection, 157–165
Anti-Counterfeiting Trade Agreement
  (ACTA), 159
Antitrust Laws of United States, 160
Berne Convention, 158
European Patent Convention, 158
Paris Convention, 158
Patent Cooperation Treaty (PCT), 158
Patent Law Treaty (PLT), 158
WIPO Copyright Treaty, 159
Internationalization of the company, 14
Internet
logistical revolution with, 426–427
revolution, 5–8
as a tool for global marketing research,
  184–186
  Bulletin boards and chat groups, 184

  cons of, 185e
  focus groups, 185
  Harris Poll Online Panel, 185
  online (virtual) panels, 185
  online surveys, 184
  pros of, 185e
  social media, 185
  web visitor tracking, 185
Intertwined world economy, 30–34. See
  also Foreign direct investment
  (FDI)
Intrafirm sourcing, 429, 431e
Intra-firm trade, 12
Introductory stage, 24
Inventory management, 422–425
Investment regulations, 133
IPR. See Intellectual property rights
Islamic law (Sharia) systems, 149
ISO. See International Organization for
  Standardization
IT. See Information technology
ITA. See International Trade
  Administration

J
Japan, 336
coca-cola local brands in, 311e
country managers in, job description of,
  491e
retail industry of, 445, 446
  foreign retailers and direct marketers
  entering into, 447gp
sales force importance in, 387–415
sogoshosha (general trading
  companies), 391
Joint ventures, expanding through,
  274–279. See also Alliances;
  International joint ventures;
  Partnerships
advantage of, 276
in China, 277e
cooperative joint venture, 275
equity joint venture, 276
risks, 276
synergy, 276
Jurisdiction, 151
arbitration, 151
enforcement, 151
planning ahead, 151
Just-in-time (JIT) manufacturing
  management, 27

K
Key performance indicators (KPIs), 551
KFC. See Kentucky Fried Chicken

KGFE. *See* Kraft General Foods Europe
KPC. Kuwait Petroleum Corp., 133
KPIs. *See* Key performance indicators
Kraft General Foods Europe (KGFE), 497
Kuwait Petroleum Corp. (KPC), 133

L
'Laissez-Faire', 364
Language, 93–96
  barriers in advertising, 352–354
    language-related mishaps, 352
    translating slogan, 353
    words with multiple meanings, 353
  communication aspect, 93
    silent language, 93
    spoken language, 93
  east west differences in emoticons, 94e
  facets of, bearing on marketers, 93
    diversity of languages within national
      boundaries, 93–94
    language as communication tool, 93
  how not to sell abroad, 95e
  mistranslations, 95
  non-native English speakers,
      understanding, 94
    cultural references, 94
    grammar, 94
    idioms, 94
    vocabulary, 94
  in sales negotiation, 407e
LCCP. *See* Local consumer culture
    positioning
LCPS. *See* Local-currency price stability
'Lead Market' concept, 252–254
Legal environment, 123–165
Levers, 501
Licensing, 270–271
  benefits, 271
  caveats, 271
  cross-licensing agreements, 270
  and foreign sales, 389
  licensee, 270, 271
  licensor, 270, 271
Life cycle of organizational structures,
    496–498
  Stopford-Wells staged model, 498
Lifestyle segmentation, 209
  doing well, doing good, 210
  first to crave, 210
  global HABIT survey, 210
  Hakuhodo lifestyle segmentation, 211e
  hungry climbers, 210
  invisibles, 210
  my family, my world, 210
  my life, my way, 210

stable roots, 210
Liner service, 420
Listening post, 264, 312, 491
Liz Claiborne, 153
Lobbying activities, 314, 372
Local branding, 300–324
  brand portfolio, 300, 302
  brand structure, 302, 303
  global or local branding, question of,
    301–308
  need for, 327
Local consumer culture positioning
    (LCCP), 217–219
Local culture and globalization, 9
Local-currency price stability (LCPS), 339
Local infrastructure, 265
  emerging, 265
  growth, 266
  maturing, 266
  platform, 265
Local legal systems and laws, 147–151
  business practices and legal system, 148
  civil law, 150
  code (written) law systems, 150
  commercial law, 150
  common law systems, 149
  Green marketing, 149
  Islamic law (Sharia) systems, 150
  legal issues facing the company, 148e
  regulations on e-commerce, 149
  types of legal systems, 149–150
Localized positioning strategies, 214–216
Logistics management, 416–452. *See also*
    Free trade zone (FTZ); Modes of
    Transportation
  definition of, 418
  e-commerce and logistics, 423
  logistical revolution with the internet,
    426–427
  third-party logistics (3PL) management,
    425–426
  warehousing and inventory
    management, 422–425
Long-term oriented solutions to recession,
    80
Long-term-oriented societies, 110
Low-context cultures, 108–109
  high- versus, 108–109

M
Maastricht Treaty, 52
Macroeconomic factors, 66
  influencing foreign exchange rates, 66e
    balance of payments, 66e
    economic growth, 66e

    foreign exchange reserves, 66e
    government spending, 66e
    interest rate policy, 66e
    money supply growth, 66e
    relative inflation, 66e
Macro-segmentation, 204
Managed currency float, 61
Maquiladora operation, 451–452
Market-based transfer pricing, 341, 342
Market entry options and sales force
    strategy, 389–392. *See also under*
    Sales management
Market size assessment, 186–191
  analogy method, 187
  chain ratio method, 188
  cross-sectional regression analysis,
    190–191
  trade audit, 188
Marketing mix decisions, 15e
Markets, globalization of
  convergence, 8–13
  divergence, 8–13
Masculinity, 110
Mass media versus non-traditional
    marketing approaches, 526–528
Material life, 92
Materials management, 418
Matrix structure, 492
Maturity stage, 25
MBTI. *See* Myers–Briggs type indicator
Media decisions, 366–369. *See also under*
    Communication strategies
Membership groups, 98
Merchant intermediaries, 439
MERCOSUR, 48, 49
Mergers, 281
Method of analogy. *See* Analogy method
Micro-segmentation, 204
Millions of Theoretical Operations Per
    Second (MTOPS), 469gp
Ministry of International Trade and
    Industry (MITI), 128
Mistranslations, 95
MITI. *See* Ministry of International Trade
    and Industry
MNCs. *See* Multinational companies
Mobile (brand-in-the-hand) marketing,
    379–380
Modes of transportation, 420–421
  air freight, 420
  cost of transportation, 420
  intermodal transportation, 421
  ocean shipping, 420
  perishability, 420
  value-to-volume ratio, 420

Modular approach, 366

Monetary union, 52

MTOPS. *See* Millions of Theoretical Operations Per Second

Multicountry research projects, 194
coordination of, 194–195
emic versus etic dilemma, 195

Multidomestic marketing, 17

Multi-local status, 217

Multinational companies (MNCs), 13, 52–54
and euro market, 86

Multinational enterprise theories, 21–27. *See also* International product cycle theory
absolute advantage, 21
comparative advantage theory, 21–24
internalization/transaction cost theory, 26
resource-based view and appropriability theory, 26–27

Multinational marketing, 15e, 18
regiocentric approach, 18

Multinational product lines, management, 309–339
drivers impacting, 309–310
competitive climate, 310–311
customer preferences, 309–310
history, 311–312
listening post, 312
organizational structure, 311
price spectrum, 310
Dunkin' Donuts launch of deep-fried treats in India, 310
product lines, categories, 310
product mix in host country, 309, 311

Myanmar
business environment, challenges in, 509e
preventing HIV/AIDS in, 117gp

Myers–Briggs type indicator (MBTI) of personal characteristics, 396–398, 397e
high vs. low context cultures, 397

N

NAFTA. *See* North American Free Trade Agreement

NASSCOM. *See* National Association of Software and Services Companies

National Action Party (PAN), 127

National Association of Software and Services Companies (NASSCOM), 433

National boundaries, issues transcending, 151–165. *See also* International Organization for Standardization (ISO)
cultural relativism/accommodation, 164gp
intellectual property protection, 152–157

Nationalization, 142

Near-market knowledge concept, 287

Negotiated pricing, 342

Negotiations, in sales management, 405–409
cross-cultural negotiations, 405, 408–409. *See also individual entry*

Networked organization model, 487

New champions, 510–513
emerging markets competing with, 513–515

New market information technologies, 191–193
computer-assisted personal interviewing (CAPI), 193
computer-assisted telephone interviewing (CATI), 193
consumer panel data, 193
continuous monitoring, 192
point-of-sale (POS) store scanner data, 191
scanning data, 192
shift from mass to micro marketing, 192
single-source data, 192

Newly industrialized countries (NICs), 128, 430

Next Eleven (N-11), 506

Niche strategy focus, 234

Nielsen global omnibus survey (2011), 171e

Non-governmental organizations (NGOs), 136–137
role when social pressures affect government and corporate policies, 138gp

Non-market-based pricing, 342
cost-based pricing, 342
negotiated pricing, 342

Non-native english speakers, understanding, 94

Non-tariff barriers (NTBs), 127, 131e

Normal Trade Relations (NTR), 40, 41gp, 468

North American Free Trade Agreement (NAFTA), 8, 49–50, 152, 249, 424
cabotage rules in, 424gp

Not-Invented-Here (NIH) Syndrome, 363

NPD. *See* New products development

NTBs. *See* Non-tariff barriers

NTR. *See* Normal Trade Relations

Nuclear family, 97

O

Objective-and-task method, 358

Observational research, 183

Ocean shipping, 419
bulk shipping, 420
irregular runs, 420
liner service, 420

OECD. *See* Organization for Economic Cooperation and Development

OEM. *See* Original equipment manufacturer

OFDI. *See* Outward foreign direct investment

Offshore sourcing. *See* Outsourcing

Omnibus survey, 170, 171

Online (virtual) panels, 185
Harris Poll Online Panel, 185

Online communication, 225

On-time retail information management, 444–446

Operational and marketing ability, 27

Operational hedging, 68n15

Ordinary least squares (OLS), 221

Organization for Economic Cooperation and Development (OECD), 163, 173, 455

Organizational design options, 487
country managers, new role of, 490–491490
builder, 490
cabinet member, 490
country prince, 491
representative, 490
trader, 490
geographic structure, 487
country-based subsidiaries, 488
global network solution, 493–495
global product division structure, 487–488
international division, 487
matrix organization, 487
matrix structure, 492
networked organization model, 487
product-based structure, 487
regional structures, 491
coordination, 492
pooling resources, 492
scouting, 491
signaling commitment, 492
strategic stimulation, 491

Organizational design, key criteria in, 485–486
  environmental factors, 485–486
    competitive environment, 485
    nature of customers, 486
    rate of environmental change, 485
    regional trading blocs, 485–486
  firm-specific factors, 486
    company heritage, 486
    product diversity, 486
    skills and resources within the company, 487
    strategic importance of international business, 486
Organizational structure, 311, 496
Orientation, market, 13, 17
Out-group homogeneity bias, 116
Outsourcing, 431, 431e
  intellectual outsourcing, 433
  major reasons for, 431e
  offshore subsidiary sourcing, 432
  of service activities, 432–434
  trends and issues of service offshoring, 436gp
Outward foreign direct investment (OFDI), 33
Ownership Controls, 133
Ownership strategies, 280–291. *See also* Wholly owned subsidiaries

P

Packaging, in emerging markets (EMs), 522–523
PAN. *See* National Action Party (PAN)
Parallel import. *See* Gray markets
Parallel translation, 177
Paris Convention, 158
Partner selection, in international joint ventures, 278
Partnerships, 274–275. *See also* Alliances; Joint ventures
  forms, 275
    50–50, 275
    majority, 275
    minority, 275
Patent, 155
Patent Cooperation Treaty (PCT), 158
Patent Law Treaty (PLT), 158
Percentage of sales method, 358
Perishability, 420
Personal selling process, 398–405
Personal selling, 392, 398
  international, 421
Phase-out policy, 142
Physical distribution, 418

managing, 419–420
  distance, 419
  exchange rate fluctuation, 419
  foreign intermediaries, 420
  regulation, 419
  security, 420
Piggyback exporting, 269, 457
Planned economies, 126
Planning of global marketing operations, 483–503. *See also* Strategic marketing planning
PLT. *See* Patent Law Treaty
Point-of-sale (POS) store scanner data, 191
Political economy, 123
Political environment and marketing, 123–168
  government policies and regulations, 128–135. *See also individual entry*
  home country versus host country, 124–126
    Cuban crisis in 1960s, 124
    Iranian Revolution in 1980s, 124
    Kosovo crisis, 124
    Persian Gulf War in 1990s, 124
    Soviet Union in late 1980s, 124
  individual governments, 124–135
  international agreements, 144–146
  international law and local legal environment, 147–151
  managing, 139–142
    confiscation, 142
    countertrade, 142
    country risk assessment criteria, 140e
    country risk ratings, 140e
    domestication policy, 142
    expropriation, 142
    government policy areas and instruments, 139e
    nationalization, 142
    NGOs role, 138gp
  national boundaries, issues transcending, 151–165
  social pressures and political risk, 136–142
  structure of government, 126–128. *See also individual entry*
  terrorism and the world economy, 143–144
Political factors influencing foreign exchange rates, 66e
  election year or leadership change, 66e
  exchange rate control, 66e
Political parties, 127
  dual-party system, 127
  single-party-dominant country, 127

Political risk, 463
Political union, 52
Polycentric orientation, 17
Portfolio investment, 33–34, 72
Positioning strategy, 201. *See also* Foreign consumer culture positioning (FCCP); Global consumer culture positioning (GCCP); International positioning strategies; Local consumer culture positioning (LCCP)
Power distance, 109
Preference similarity, 24
Pre-testing, 178
PRI. *See* Institutional Revolutionary Party
Price coordination, 345–347
  factors to consider, 345
    amount of product differentiation, 345
    government regulation, 347
    internal organization, 347346
    nature of channels, 345
    nature of competition, 346
    nature of customers, 345
  implementing, 349
    centralization, 349
    economic measures, 349
    formalization, 349
    informal coordination, 349
  tiered pricing, 346gp
Price escalation, 332–334
  approaches to deal with, 334
    adapting the product to escape tariffs or tax levies, 334
    assembling or manufacturing the product in foreign markets, 334
    costly features, eliminating, 334
    distribution channel, rearranging, 333
Price spectrum, 310
Price transparency, 84–85
Pricing, 315, 327–350. *See also* Currency fluctuations and global pricing; Foreign market pricing; Transfer pricing
  corridor, 348–349
  and culture, 118
  global-pricing contracts (GPCs), 347–349
  in inflationary environments, 334–336
  retail price comparison, 327e
  strategy, in emerging markets (EMs), 523–524
Pricing-to-market (PTM), 339
Primary global marketing research, 176–183

contact method, 179181
  courtesy bias, 179–180
  cross-country comparisons of survey
    response biases, 181e
  extreme response style (ERS), 181
  information collection, 179
  Nay-saying, 180
  social desirability bias, 180
  Yea-saying, 180
cross-cultural marketing research,
    survey methods for, 177–178
  back-translation, 177
  cross-country survey research, 177
  funny faces scale, 178e
  parallel translation, 177
  pre-testing, 178
  questionnaire design, 177, 186
  scalar equivalence, 177
  translation, 177
ethnographic research, 183gp, 183
focus groups, 185
house-to-house survey, 182
individualism and extreme-response
    style, 182e
observational research, 183
sampling plan, 179
shopping mall survey, 182
Principles of international trade, 23
Private-label brands (store brands),
    442–444
Probing-and-learning approach, 311
Procurement, 428–432
Product design families, 246
Product differentiation strategy, 233
Product piracy, 313–316
  strategic options against, 313–316
    communication options, 315–316
    customs, 314
    distribution, 315
    legal action, 314
    lobbying activities, 314
    pricing, 315
    product policy options, 315
Product placement, 381
Product planning, 15e
Product policy, for emerging markets
    (EMs), 519–523
Products and services, marketing,
    555–556. *See also* Country-of-
    origin (COO) effects; Global
    branding strategies; Product piracy
  issues in, 555
Project Shakti entrepreneurs, 512, 525
Promotion and culture, 120–121
Prototype standardization, 364

PTM. *See* Pricing-to-market
Public relations (PR), 373, 383
Publicity, 383–384
Pull-out strategy, 80
Purchasing power parity (PPP), 64–65,
    190, 208
Push versus pull activities, 526

Q
Qualitative evaluation of salespeople, 405
Quantitative evaluation of salespeople, 405

R
Random factors influencing foreign
    exchange rates, 66e
Rationalization, 422–423
RBV. *See* Resource-based view
RCEP. *See* Regional Comprehensive
    Economic Partnership
Real-time management, 224
Recession, 79–80. *See also* Economic and
    financial turmoil worldwide
  consumption pattern changes during, 79
    consumer response, 79
    corporate response, 80
Redundancy, 182
Reference groups, 97–98
  anticipatory groups, 98
  dissociative groups, 98
  membership groups, 98
Regiocentric approach, 18
Regional Comprehensive Economic
    Partnership (RCEP), 50gp
Regional economic arrangements, 48–50
  free trade area, 48–50
Regional financial crises, responses to, 79–
    82
Regional segments, 206
Regionalization of global marketing
    strategy, 249–257
  cross-subsidization of markets, 251–252
  emerging markets, strategies for,
    254–255–255
  'Lead Market' concept, 252–254
  regional trading blocs, favorable effects
    of, 249–250
  weak market segments, identification of,
    250, 252
Regression, 221
Relationship marketing, 394–396
  customer acquisition and customer
    retention, 395
Religion, 102–103
  advertising campaigns and, 103
  feng shui (wind-water), 103

holiday calendar, 103
women role in society, 103
Renminbi (yuan), 62–63
Repatriation, 414
Resale price method, 342
Research in global marketing, 167–197.
    See also Primary global marketing
    research; Secondary global
    marketing research
  leveraging the internet for, 184–186. *See
    also under* Internet
  online surveys, 184
  managing, 193–194
    communication skills, 194
    cost, 194
    cross-border coordination, 194
    multicountry research projects, 194
    selecting research agency, 193–194
  market size assessment, 186–191. *See
    also individual entry*
  new market information technologies,
    191–193
  primary data research, 169e
  R&D, operations, and marketing
    interfaces, 244–245. *See also*
    Interfaces among R&D, operations,
    and marketing
  research hypothesis, 169e
  research problem, 169e
  research problem formulation, 170–172
    Omnibus survey, 170, 171, 178
  scope of, 169
  secondary data research, 169e
  steps to be followed, 168
Resource allocation, 201–202
  for advertising, 358–359
  challenger markets, 201
  leader markets, 201
Resource-based view (RBV), 293
  and appropriability theory, 26
    dominant design, 26
    just-in-time (JIT) manufacturing
      management, 27
    operational and marketing ability, 27
Resources for secondary data, 172e
Retailing
  e-commerce and, 449–450
Reverse innovation, 520
RIAA. *See* Recording Industry Association
    of America
Rigid cost-plus pricing, 328
Risk, 264
Robinson-Patman Act of 1936, 160
Russia's accession to WTO, 41,
    41–42gp

S

Sales management, 387–415. *See also*
    Expatriates
buyer-seller relationships, differences in,
    396e
    Canada, 396e
    China, 396e
    France/French Belgium, 396e
    Germany/Austria, 396e
    Japan, 396
    Latin America, 396e
    Russia, 396e
    United Kingdom, 396
cross-steps in, 405
    objectives, 400
    recruitment and selection, 401–402
    strategy, 401
    supervision, 403
    training, 402–403
cultural considerations, 392–398
    corporate (organizational) culture,
        394–395
    cultural generalization, 393
    international personal selling, 392
    personal selling, 392
cultural negotiations, 405–409
culturally responsive strategies and their
    feasibility, 408e
culture impact on, and personal selling
    process, 398–405
customer salesforce structure, 400
foreign governments role, 392
high involvement approaches, 392
intercultural considerations in, 388,
    388e
international sales strategy, 388, 388e
in Japan, 391
licensing and, 391
limited involvement approaches, 391
market entry options and, 389–392
    degree of involvement and sales
        management issues, 389–390, 390e
mid-level involvement approaches, 391
Myers–Briggs type indicator of personal
    characteristics, 396–398, 397e
product salesforce structure, 400
relationship marketing, 394–395
    customer acquisition and customer
        retention, 395
sales persons, 395
    ethical perceptions in handling,
        404–405
    evaluation, 405
    management style in approaching,
        404

motivation and compensation for, 403
    territorial salesforce, 400
    in U.S., 390e, 391
    word-of-mouth referrals, 397
Sales promotions, 370, 374–375
Sanctions, 132, 145
SBUs. *See* Strategic business units
Scalar equivalence, 177
Scale economies, 361
Scale of entry, 263–264
Scanning data, 192–193
SDRs. *See* Special drawing rights
Search engine advertising, 9, 184, 542e
Secondary global marketing research,
        172–176
    Nielsen global omnibus survey (2011),
        171e
    primary data, 172
    problems with secondary data research,
        174–18
        accuracy of data, 174
        age of data, 174
        comparability of data, 175
        conceptual equivalence, 175
        functional equivalence, 175
        lumping of data, 175–176
        reliability over time, 174–175
    resources for, 172, 172e
        category-specific data, 172e
        consumer panels, 173
        country information (socioeconomic
            & political conditions), 172e
        cultural background, 172e
        international commercial law, 172e
        international trade, 172e
        syndicated datasets, 173
    secondary data, 173–174
SED. *See* Shipper's Export Declaration
Segmentation, global, 199–222. *See also*
        International market segmentation;
        Lifestyle Segmentation
    segmentation scenarios, 204–207
        antiglobalists (13.1%), 205
        civic libertarians (21.5%), 205
        global agnostics (7.6%), 205
        global citizens (10.1%), 205
        global climbers (23.3%), 205
        multinational fans (15.5%), 205
        pro-west (7.6%), 205
        regional segments, 206
        unique (diverse) segments, 206
        universal or global segments, 204
    strategy, 476
Self-reference criterion (SRC), 115
Sequence, in sales negotiation, 407e

Service activities, outsourcing of, 432–434
Services, global marketing of, 321–324
    challenges in, 321
        difficulties in customer satisfaction
            overseas measurement, 321–322
        need for geographic proximity with
            service transactions, 321
        protectionism, 321
    global Service marketing strategies,
        321–322
        add value by differentiation, 324
        capitalize on cultural forces in the
            host market, 323
        central role of information
            technologies (IT), 323–324
        establish global service networks, 323
        standardize and customize, 323
    opportunities in, 322–323–348
        deregulation of service industries, 322
        increased value consciousness,
            322–323
        increasing demand for premium
            services, 322
SES. *See* Socioeconomic strata
Sherman Antitrust Act of 1890, 160
Shift from mass to micro marketing, ;192
Shipper's Export Declaration (SED)
    information, 459
Shipper's order bill of lading, 461
Shopping mall survey, 182
Short messaging service (SMS)
    advertising, 511
Short-term capital, 72
Short-term-oriented cultures, 110
Short-term-oriented solutions to recession,
    80
Silent language, 93
    types of, 93
        agreements, 93
        friendship patterns, 93
        material possessions, 93
        space, 93
        time, 93
Singapore
    human resources and technology, 35e
Single-party-dominant country, 127
Single-source data, 192
Small and medium-sized enterprises
    (SMEs), 86
    new opportunities for, 86
SMS. *See* Short messaging service
Smuggling, 480–481gp
SNS. *See* Social networking site
Social desirability bias, 180
Social interactions, 92, 96–98

extended family, 97
individual's reference groups, 97
nuclear family, 97
Social media, 185–186
Social networking site (SNS) market, 511
Social pressures and political risk,
     136–143
   social pressures and special interests,
     136–137
   structural adjustment program, 136
Socialism, 126
Socioeconomic strata (SES) analysis, 208
Socioeconomic variables, 208–209
'Soft' versus 'hard' control levers, 501
Sogoshosha (general trading companies),
     391, 456
Solo branding, 302
SOPA. See Stop Online Piracy Act
Sourcing strategy, managing, 427–428
   comparative advantage, 428
   competitive advantage, 428
   core services, 435
   procurement, 428–432
   supplementary services, 435–436
   types of, 428–432
      domestic in-house sourcing, 430
      domestic sourcing, 429
      intrafirm sourcing, 429, 430e
      offshore sourcing, 429-
      outsourcing, 429, 431e. See also
         individual entry
South American financial crisis, 74, 76
South Korea
Southern Common Market
     (MERCOSUR), 249
Special drawing rights (SDRs), 60
Specific duty, 473
Spoken language, 93
Sponsorships, 377–379
   benefits, 376–377
   risks, 377
Spot foreign exchange
   versus forward, 68–69
SRC. See Self-reference criterion (SRC)
Stakeholder engagement programs,
     553–555
   implementation, 554
   information provision, 554
   input on decision making, 554
   monitoring, 554
   standard setting, 554
Standardization, 323, 347, 303, 360–361.
     See also Incremental break-even
     analysis (IBEA)
   barriers to, 363

advertising regulations, 363
cultural differences, 363
market maturity, 363
Not-Invented-Here (NIH) Syndrome,
     363
merits of, 361
consistent image, 361
creative talent, 362
cross-fertilization, 362
global consumer segments, 361–362
globalization of media, 361
scale economies, 361
prototype standardization, 364–365
versus 'adaptation' debate, 359–360
Stopford-Wells staged model, 497
Straight bill of lading, 461
Strategic alliances, 274, 345
Strategic business units (SBUs), 423
Strategic marketing planning, 484–485
   action plans, 484
   bottom-up versus top-down strategic
     planning, 484
   objectives and targets, 484
   pitfalls, 484–485
   situation analysis, 484
   strategies, 484
Strategies, marketing, 223–258. See also
     Emerging markets (EMs); Entry
     strategies; Global Strategy;
     Regionalization of global
     marketing strategy
   competitive analysis, 256–257
   competitor-focused approaches, 235
   creative destruction, 238
   customer-focused approaches, 235
   degree of standardizability of products
     in world markets, 244e
   emerging markets, strategies for,
     254–256
   first-mover advantage vs. first-mover
     disadvantage, 234–235
   hypercompetition, 238
   interdependency, 238
   R&D, operations, and marketing
     interfaces, 244–249. See also
        Interfaces among R&D, operations,
        and marketing
   SWOT analysis, 255–256
   value chain, 223
   variation in content and coverage of,
     239
Strengths, Weaknesses, Opportunities, and
     Threats (SWOT) analysis, 256–257
   of Carrefour's operations in China, 443e
Structural adjustment program, 136

Structure of government, 126–128
   capitalism, 126
   communism, 126
   ideology, 126
   Institutional Revolutionary Party (PRI),
     127
   National Action Party (PAN), 127
   planned economies, 126
   political parties, 127–128
   single-party-dominant country, 127
   socialism, 126
Substantive Patent Law Treaty (SPLT),
     160
Substitute products/services, threat of,
     232
Substitution drawback, 473
Summary axing, 331
Sunk costs, 306–307
Supplementary services, 435–436
Supply chain accountability, 537–538
Supply chain management, steps to be
     taken in, 538
   assess, 538
   commit, 538
   communicate progress, 538
   define and implement, 538
   measure, 538
Supply chain sustainability, 537
Sustainable marketing, 530–564. See also
     Supply chain accountability
   case for sustainability, 540–541
      brand loyalty, 540–541
      reputation in consumer markets, 541
      reputation in labor and equity
        markets, 541
   challenges for, 541–545
      cultural tensions, 542–543
      poor infrastructure, 545
      sustainability image, 543–544
   consumer boycotts, 560, 562
   crisis management, 560–563
   and global consumers, 545–546
   global corporate citizenship, 531–533
   global stakeholder engagement
     programs, 553
   ISO 26000 standard centers, 532
   marketing mix policy for global market
     place, 555–560
      communication and sustainability,
        557–559
      developing sustainable products and
        services, 555–556
      sustainability and distribution
        channels, 555–556
      sustainable pricing, 556

Sustainable marketing (*Continued*)
   sustainable strategy, developing and
      implementing, 547–553
      developing metrics for monitoring
         and reporting (Step 5), 550–553
      implementing (Step 4), 549–550–550
      setting objectives and targets (Step 1),
         389
      specifying strategic sustainability
         initiatives (Step 3), 548–549
      understanding the operating
         environment (Step 2), 548
   UNGC's ten principles, 531–532e
   United Nations Global Compact
      (UNGC), 531
Sustainable packaging, 556
Sweden, 36e
Switzerland
   human resources and technology in, 36e
SWOT. *See* Strengths, Weaknesses,
      Opportunities, and Threats
Syndicated datasets, 173

T
Tariff barriers, 130, 131e
Tariff concessions, 467
TCA. *See* Transaction-cost analysis
Technological gap, 24
Temporary Importation Under Bond (TIB),
   473
Terminology, global marketing, 1
Terrorism and the world economy,
   143–144
   fast-track trade authority, 145
   test market countries, 310e
Third-party logistics (3PL) management,
   425–426
TIB. *See* Temporary Importation Under
   Bond
Tied Aid Capital Projects Fund, 467
Tiered pricing, 346gp
Top-down budgeting, 359
Top-down strategic planning, 484
TPP. *See* Trans-Pacific Partnership
Traceless System, 153
Tracking technology, 417–418
Trade audit, 188
Trade balance, 72
Trade laws, 130, 133
Trade Related Aspects of Intellectual
      Property Rights (TRIPS), 43,
      45–46, 154
   global E-commerce, 45
Trade secret, 157
Trade shows, 380–383

Trademark, 157
Trading company, 456, 457
Transaction-cost analysis (TCA), 13n,
   436n
Transaction cost theory, 26–27
Transfer pricing, 340–343
   determinants of, 340–341
      stakeholders, 340
   influencing factors, 340–341
   MNCs's consideration criteria, 342
      cost-based pricing, 342
      joint venture partner, 341
      local market conditions, 341
      market imperfections, 341
      market-based transfer pricing, 341
      morale of local country managers,
         341
      negotiated pricing, 342
      non-market-based pricing, 342
      tax regimes, 341
   risk of transfer pricing tax audits,
      minimizing, 342–343
      decision-making model, 343e
Transfer risk, 463
Transition economies, 505
Translation, 177
Transnational organization, 493
Trans-Pacific Partnership (TPP), 50gp
Transparent forewarning, 306, 307
Treaties, 157–158
Triad regions of the world (North America,
      Western Europe, Japan), 3, 37
TRIPS. *See* Trade Related Aspects of
      Intellectual Property Rights
Two-stage international segmentation, 204
   macro-segmentation, 204
   micro-segmentation, 204

U
USP. *See* Unique selling proposition
Uncertainty avoidance, 109
   versus power distance, 111e
UNCITRAL. *See* United Nations
      Commission on International Trade
      Law
Unconfirmed irrevocable letter of credit,
   463–464
UNGC. *See* United Nations Global
      Compact
Unilateral transfers, 72, 73
Unique (diverse) segments, 206
Unique selling proposition (USP), 212
United Nations Commission on
      International Trade Law
      (UNCITRAL), 48

United Nations Conference Trade and
      Development (UNCTAD), 42gp
United Nations Global Compact (UNGC),
   531
United States, 160
   antitrust laws of, 160–162. *See also*
      under Antitrust laws
   export control in, balancing act between
      free trade and tight security, 469gp
   foreign trade zone (FTZ) in, 437e
   government role in promoting exports,
      464–481-
   U.S. dollar, historical role of, 57–58
   U.S. Foreign Corrupt Practices Act of
      1977, 162–165
   U.S. subprime mortgage loan crisis, 77
      subsequent global financial crisis,
         77
Universal or global segments, 204
Universal positioning appeals, 215–217
   levels, 215–216
   versus localized positioning strategies,
      214–215
Uruguay Round, 41

V
Validated license, 460
Value-based segmentation, 212
Value chain, 223
Value systems and culture, 106–107
Value-to-volume ratio, 420
VER. *See* Voluntary export restraints
Video game industry, 250gp
   Microsoft, 250gp
   Nintendo, 250gp
   Sony, 250gp
Viral marketing, 383–384
Virtual teamwork, guidelines, 495e
Vocabulary, 94
Voluntary export restraints (VER), 344

W
Warehousing, 418, 422–425
   inventory management, 422–425
      benefiting from tax differences, 422
      cabotage rules in the NAFTA, 424gp
      hedging against inflation and
         exchange rate fluctuations, 422
      logistical integration, 422–423
      rationalization, 422–423
Wassenaar arrangement, 146
Weak market segments, identification of,
   252
Web-based marketing of services, 9
Web visitor tracking, 185

Wholly owned subsidiaries, 280–283
   acquisitions and mergers, 281, 283
   benefits, 280
   caveats, 280–281
   greenfield operations, 280–281, 284
   routes, 280
      acquisitions, 281
      greenfield operations, 284
WIPO. *See* World Intellectual Property
      Organization

Word-of-mouse marketing, 383
Word-of-mouth referrals, 397
World Bank, 61
World Intellectual Property Organization
      (WIPO), 158–159
   WIPO Copyright Treaty, 159
World Trade Organization (WTO), 28,
      41–43, 44gp,154, 419
   China's accession to, and its
      implications, 41gp

Russia's accession to, 41gp
World Value Survey (WVS), 114e,
      113–114
   survival/self-expression dimension,
      114
   traditional/secular-rational dimension,
      113
World Wide Web, 476
WTO. *See* World Trade Organization
WVS. *See* World Value Survey

N NAME INDEX

Note: The letter 'n' following page number(s) denote notes

A

Aaker, David A., 170n, 190n, , 298n, 304n, 352n, 356n, 495n
Aaker, Jennifer I., 90n, 120n
Aboul-Fath, Mahmoud, 329n
Abramson, Neil R., 397n
Abratt, Russell, 306n
Ackelsberg, R., 342n
Adams-Florou, Athena S., 454n
Agarwal, James, 177n
Ahluwalia, Rohini, 540n
Akhter, Syed H., 341n
Akmal, Hyder S., 278n
Aksen, Gerald, 151n
Alam, Pervaiz, 341n
Albright, Madeleine K., 163n
Alden, Dana L., 217n, 375n
Aldridge, D. N., 178n, 179n, 182n, 194n
Al-Eryani, Mohammad F., 341n, 342n
Alfred, Brent, 246n
Al Janahi, Ahmed, 149n
Alvarez-Plata, Patricia, 77n
Amelio, William, 282
Amine, Lyn S., 188n, 191n
Anckar, Patrik, 340n, 463n
Andersen, Kim Viborg, 47n
Anderson, Erin, 268n
Anderson, James E., 344n
Anderson, Thomas W., 317n
Andreason, Aaron W., 414n
Anita, Kersi D., 474n, 476n
Anwar, Syed Tariq, 162n
Armstrong, Gary, 148
Armstrong, Larry, 248n
Arnold, David, 295n, 440n, 494n, 502n
Arnold, Stephen J., 402n
Arpan, Jeffrey S., 342n
Arruda, Maria Cecilia Coutinho de, 49n
Ascarelli, Silvia, 426n
Assmus, Gert, 349n
Athaide, Gerard A., 458n
Aukakh, Preet S., 157n
Aulakh, Preet S., 238n, 446n

Austin, James E., 139n
Axinn, Catherine N., 458n

B

Baack, Daniel, 9n, 233n
Bairoch, Paul, 35n
Baker, William E., 149n
Balabanis, George, 318n
Bamford, James, 279n
Bargas, Sylvia E., 13n
Barnet, Richard J., 12n
Barnevik, Percy, 494, 494n
Barney, Jay B., 26n
Baron, Steve, 184n, 185
Barr, William, 161
Barrett, Amy, 68n
Bartlett, Christopher A., 231n, 492n, 493n, 494n, 498n, 500n, 502n, 512n
Bartley, Douglas L., 142n
Bateman, Connie Rae, 342n, 343
Batra, Rajeev, 217n, 299, 300n, 356
Bauer, W., 493
Beaty, Edmund W., 250n
Beck, Ernest, 243n
Beck, Kurt, 289
Beck, Roman, 47n
Beckert, Beverly, 431n
Beise, Marian, 253n
Bello, Daniel C., 391n
Bellur, Venkatakrishna V., 335n
Benjamin, Daniel, 393n
Benson, John, 419n
Bergen, Mark, 474n, 476n
Berger, Mel, 405n
Berk, Emre, 126n
Berthon, Pierre, 379
Besson, Madeleine, 403n
Betts, Paul, 54n
Bhagat, Rabi S., 398n
Bhagwati, Jagdish, 344n
Bhattacharya, ArindamK., 510n
Bhattacharya, B., 533, 541n
Bhaumik, Sumon, 519n
Biederman, David, 45n, 455n

Biel, A. L., 299n
Bigoness, William J., 398n
Bijmolt, Tammo, H. A., 540n
Bird, Larry, 364
Bjerke, Rune, 354n
Bju'rn-Andersen, Niels, 47n
Black, J. Stewart, 410n–411n
Blackwell, Roger D., 98n
Blair, Tony, 145
Blakely, Gerald L., 398n
Bloom, Helen, 490n
Boersma, Mark, 361n
Boggs, David J., 233n
Bond, Michael H., 110n
Bonini, Sheila, 546n
Bowersox, Donald J., 418
Bowie, David, 307
Boya, U. O., 374n
Brabeck-Letmathe, Peter, 493
Briley, Donnel A., 90n, 120n
Brodowsky, Glen H., 317n
Broer, Wijnand, 553n
Brokenbaugh, Laura L., 13n
Brooks, Harvey, 26n, 245n
Brousseau, Eric, 47n
Brouthers, Keith D., 293
Brouthers, Lance Eliot, 11, 293
Brown, Shona L., 235n
Brown, Tom J., 531n
Bryan, Lowell, 3n
Buchan, Nancy R., 398n
Buckley, Peter J., 12n
Bucklin, Louis P., 422n
Bulcke, P., 493, 537
Bull, Nick, 215n
Bunduchi, Raluca, 431n
Burnkrant, Robert E., 540n
Burns, Jane, 340n
Bush, George W., 424

C

Caira, M., 493
Calantone, Roger J., 456n
Calcchio, Nicola, 521n

Campbell, Andrew, 490n, 496n
Campbell, Ian, 76n
Campbell, Scott, 474n
Cannon, Joseph P., 397n
Cantarell, L., 493
Capell, Kerry, 231n
Carpenter, Mason A., 410n
Carter, J. R., 428n
Carvalho, Sergio W., 541n
Cavarkapa, Branko, 139n
Cavusgil, S. Tamer, 14n, 16n, 19n, 188n, 191n, 228n, 328n, 333n, 341n, 456n, 465n, 479
Cerny, Michael V., 474n
Cescau, Patrick, 231
Chadwick, James, 80n, 82n
Chae, Myung-Su, 484n
Chaganti, Radharao, 335n
Chaganti, Rajeswararao, 335n
Chakravarthy, Balaj S., 14n
Chandra, Maneesh, 250n, 434n
Chandrasekaran, Deepa, 180n, 181
Chattopadhyay, Amitava, 203n, 203
Chaudhry, Peggy A., 349n
Chen, Min, 402n
Cheng, Joseph, 144n, 231n, 242n, 250n
Chintagunta, Pradeep K., 330n, 331
Chircu, Alina, 508n
Chitagunta, Pradeep K., 330, 331n
Chonko, Lawrence B., 405n
Chow, Garland, 149n
Chua, Lusan, 159n
Clague, Llewlyn, 336n
Clark, Richard T., 243n
Clark, Terry, 2n, 69n, 338n, 436n
Cleese, John, 366n
Cleff, Thomas, 253n
Closs, David J., 418n
Cobb, Charles E., Jr., 161n
Cohen, Stephen S., 430n
Collins, Thomas L., 192n
Cooper, M. Bixby, 418n
Cordell, Victor V., 318n
Corder, C. K., 178
Corstjens, Marcel, 503
Cote, Joseph A., 99n, 178n
Cotte, June, 541n
Cottarelli, Carlo, 58n
Coulter, Robin A., 521n
Coy, Peter, 68n
Craig, C. Samuel, 14n, 15, 169, 183n, 193n, 302
Cravens, David W., 398n
Crawford, Robert J., 249n
Crutsinger, Martin, 76n

Cui, Anna Shaojie, 14n
Cunningham, William H., 317n
Curry, David J., 192n
Cusumano, Michael A., 27n
Czinkota, Michael R., 17n, 129n, 249n, 465n

D
Dacin, Peter A., 531n
Dagher, Grace, 367n
Dalgic, Tevfik, 90n
D'Angelo, Paul, 2n
Darling, John R., 317n
D'Aveni, Richard, 238n
David, Kenneth, 208n
Davidson, W. H., 488n
Dawar, Niraj, 256n, 499n, 512n, 513, 540n
Dawes, Philip L., 150n
Day, George S., 170n, 190n
de Abreu Filho, 521n
Gilberto, Duarte, 521n
Dean, David L., 458n
Debanjan, Mitra, 200n, 287n
Degenholtz, Andrew, 6n
De George, Richard T., 165n
Dekimpe, Marnik G., 263n, 381n, 440n, 560n
Dell, Michael, 14, 282, 423, 496
De Lima, Renata Carneiro, 541n
De Los Santos, Gilberto, 367n
de Mooij, Marieke, 110, 120n, 213n, 243n, 307n, 355n, 369n
De Oliveira Mota, Marcio, 541n
DeNisi, Angelo S., 412n
Deshpand'e, Rohit, 205n, 320
Desiraju, Ramarao, 330, 331n
de Vries, Manfred F. R. Kets, 494n
Dhebar, Anirudh, 312n
Dholakia, Nikhilesh, 6n
Diamantopoulos, Adamantios, 317n, 318n
Diamond, Jared, 102n
Diana, Tom, 126n
Dibrell, Clay, 13n
Dickinson, Q. Todd, 156, 158n
Diermeier, Daniel, 563n
Dodd, Jonathan, 184n, 185
Doh, Jonathan P., 137n
Doke, DeeDee, 46n
Domoto, Hiroshi, 432n
Donaldson, Thomas, 398n, 543n
Doney, Patricia M., 397n, 474n, 477n
Dorfman, Peter W., 111n
Douglas, Susan P., 14n, 15, 169n, 183n, 193, 199n, 302
Doukas, John A., 54n

Doz, Yves L., 243n
Drucker, Peter F., 13n, 417n
Drummond, David, 542
Duarte, Fernanda, 151n
Dub'e, Laurette, 319n
Dubinsky, Alan J., 393n, 404n
Duhan, Dale F., 416n, 474n
Duncan, T., 362n
Dunning, John H., 24, 416n
Dutta, Shantanu, 474n, 476n

E
Eden, Lorraine, 97n
Edmonson, R. R., 459n
Edson, Lee, 156n
Eggli, Bernhard, 216
Eisenhardt, Kathleen M., 235n
Eiteman, David K., 63n, 66
Ellard, John H., 546n, 557n
El Qorchi, Mohammed, 149n
Encarnation, Dennis J., 12n
Enderle, Georges, 543n
Engel, James F., 98n
Erdem, Tülin, 300n
Erderer, Kaynak, 179n
Eremitaggio, Phyllis, 159n
Erez, Miriam, 398n
Ernst, David, 279n
Eroglu, Sevgin, 414
Eshghi, Abdolreza, 465n
Eshghi, Golpira S., 465n
Eskin, Gerry, 191n
Esserman, Susan, 44n
Estrin, Saul, 519n
Etile, Fabrice, 541n
Evansburg, Amanda R., 159n
Ewing, Jack, 163n

F
Faris, Charles W., 471n
Farley, John U., 103n
Farmer, Stacy J., 159n
Fayerweather, John, 242n
Fernie, John, 402n
Ferrell, O. C., 549n
Fiore, Mark J., 159n
Fitzgerald, Ella, 475
Flikkema, Luanne, 219n
Ford, Henry, 19
Fraedrich, John P., 342n, 343
Franois, Pierre, 379n
Frazier, Gary L., 389n
Frevert, Brad, 194n
Frick, D. P., 493

Frost, Randall, 306n
Frost, Tony, 256n, 499n, 512n, 513
Fruchter, Gila E., 395n
Fryling, Robert, 130n
Fubini, David G., 279n

G

Gaba, Vibah, 287n
Gagnon, Joseph A., 339, 339n
Gao, Gerald Yong, 13n, 522n
Gatignon, Hubert, 268n, 293n
Gelb, Betsy, 178
Gencturk, Esra F., 446n, 464
Gentry, James W., 410n
George, Mike, 226
Gerst, Martina, 431n
Ghauri, Pervez N., 278n
Ghislanzoni, Giancarlo, 494n
Ghoshal, Sumantra, 231n, 492n, 493n,
    498n, 500n, 502, 512n
Ghosn, Carlos, 512
Giannini, Curzio, 58n
Gielens, Katrijn, 263n, 440n
Gillespie, Kate, 136n, 480, 481
Gilly, Mary C., 393n, 397n
Golder, Peter N., 200n, 234n, 287n
Goold, Michael, 490n, 496n
Gopalakrishna, S., 381n
Gould, Gordon, 156
Gould, Stephen J., 382
Graham, John L., 393n, 398n, 403n,
    406n
Gregersen, Hal B., 410n
Grein, Andreas F., 385n
Greyser, Stephen, 382
Griffith, David A., 14n, 265n
Grosse, Robert, 420n
Grossfield, Rena, 336n
Grund, Martin, 159n
Grund, Michael, 159
Grunig, James E., 383n
Gu, Flora, 97n
Guile, Bruce R., 26n, 245n
Gupta, Vipin, 111n
Gürhan-Canli, Zeynep, 120n, 318n, 563n

H

Ha, Louisa, 371n
Hadjimarcou, John, 440n
Hall, Edward, 93, 108
Hamdani, Khalil, 13n
Hamel, Gary, 250n, 254n
Hamilton, Robert D., III 498n
Hanges, Paul J., 111n
Hanlon, David, 332n

Hanni, David A., 353
Haque, Mahfuzul, 60n
Harney, Alexandra, 387n
Harris, Cheryl, 185
Harris, J. J., 493
Harrison-Walker, L. Jean, 243n
Harvey, Michael G., 139n
Haspeslagh, P., 488n
Hassis, Roswitha, 170n
Hawk, Tony, 366n
Hawkins, Del I., 191n
Healey, Nigel M., 184n, 185
Heijblom, Ruud, 90n
Heinzel, Herbert, 227n
Helsen, Kristiaan, 2n, 263n, 317n, 328n,
    440n, 543n, 560n
Hemerling, Jim, 40n
Henderson, Pamela W., 99n
Henry, Clement M., 149n
Herbig, P., 381n
Hersche, Joel, 392n
Higgins, Sean, 44
Hill, C., 293n
Hill, John S., 484n
Hill, Sidney, Jr., 225n
Hise, Richard T., 465n
Hitt, Michael, 144n, 231n, 242n,
    250n
Hladik, Karen J., 278n
Ho, Rodney, 430n
Hodis, Monica, 2n
Hoegh-Krohn, Nils E. Joachim, 69n
Hoffman, Richard C., 273n
Hofstede, F. Ter, 204n
Hofstede, Geert, 91n, 109, 109n–110n,
    112, 113n, 394n
Hogna, Egil, 306n
Holt, Douglas B., 205n, 299n, 540n
Honeycutt, Earl D., Jr., 436n
Hongxin, Zhao, 243n, 293n
Horwitz, Tony, 393n
Hotchkiss, Carolyn, 163n
House, Robert J., 111n, 410n
Howell, Larry J., 246n
Hsieh, C. M., 436n
Hsu, Jamie C., 246n
Hu, Xiaorui, 243n
Huff, Lenard C., 375n
Huffman, Stephen P., 68n
Hulland, John, 319n
Hult, G. Tomas M., 453
Hung, Kineta, 97
Hunt, Todd, 383n
Hwang, P., 293n
Hyder, Akmal S., 278n

I

Ilieva, Janet, 184n, 185
Inglehart, Ronald, 114

J

Jacobs, L. W., 358n
Jagdish, Bhagwati, 344n
Jain, Subhash C., 157n
Javidan, Mansour, 111n, 410n
Jayachandran, Staish, 244n
Jevons, Colin, 548n
Jian, Yi, 364
Joachimsthaler, Erich A., 262n, 352n,
    492n
Johanson, Jan, 453n
Johansson, Johny K., 318n
Johansson, Lars Göran, 302n
Johnson, Carla, 413n
Johnson, James P., 271n
Johnson, Jean L., 178n, 419n
Johnson, Joseph, 518n, 519n
Johnson, Lester W., 455n
Jolson, Marvin A., 404n
Jordan, Michael, 364
Jun, Sunkyu, 410n
Jusko, Jill, 154n

K

Kaikati, Jack G., 447n, 448
Kalish, Shlomo, 228n
Kalliny, Morris, 367n
Kamakura, Wagner A., 199n
Kanso, Ali, 386n
Kapferer, Jean-Nöel, 18n, 296n, 306n
Karel, Jan Willem, 307n
Karunaratna, Amal R., 455n
Kashani, Kamran, 168n
Kashlak, Roger J., 456n, 499n
Katahira, Hotaka, 192n
Katsikeas, Constantine S., 440n, 455n
Kaufman, Gaye, 322n
Kaynak, Erderer, 178n
Keegan, Warren J., 17n
Kenichi, Ohmae, 33n, 244, 503
Kenny, David, 312n
Kent, John L., 355n
Kent, Muthar, 280
Keown, C. F., 358n
Kern, Horst, 170n
Kim, Ilchul, 385n
Kim, Suk H., 60n
Kim, W. Chan, 500n
Kimes, Mina, 476n
King, Julia, 224n
Kinnear, Thomas C., 176n

Kinneer, Kevin D., 414n
Kirpalani, V. H., 364n
Kitchen, Philip J., 385n
Kiyak, Tunga, 474n
Klastorin, Ted, 126n
Klein, Johanna, 553n
Klein, Jill Gabrielle, 301n
Klein, Lawrence, 74
Klein, Lisa R., 227n
Klevorick, Alvin K., 26n
Kline, Saul, 389n
Knetter, Michael M., 339, 339n
Knight, Gary A., 54n, 454n
Knoop, Carin-Isabel, 307n
Knopf, Jutta, 553n
Knudsen, Trond Riiber, 306n
Kobrin, Stephen J., 124n
Koenig, Robert, 427n
Kogut, Bruce, 428n
Koll, Jesper, 58n
Kong, Albert, 273n
Kostecki, Michel M., 344n
Kotabe, Masaaki, 2n, 12n–17n, 27, 49n, 69n, 76n, 87, 128n, 153n, 155n, 160n, 231n, 238n, 240n, 242n, 246n, 249, 250n, 254nn, 317n, 338n, 393n, 404n, 416n, 432n, 436n, 440n, 446n, 464n, 543n
Kotler, Philip H., 296n
Krasnikov, Alexander, 244n
Kreinin, Mordechai E., 24, 73n
Krell, Eric, 412n
Krugman, Paul, 37n
Kucher, Eckhard, 348n
Kumar, Nirmalya, 442n, 487n
Kurosawa, Fumiko, 428

L
Labatt-Randle, Jacquie, 209
Lanctot, Aldor, 238n
Lane, Henry W., 397n
Lang, L. H. P., 54n
Lardy, Nicholas R., 42
Laroche, Michel, 364n
Larsen, Trina L., 439n
Lasserre, Philippe, 265n, 266n, 491n
Laszlo, Tihanyi, 265
Laux, Paul A., 68n
Lawson, William V., 169
Lazzarini, Sergio G., 436n
Leal, Ricardo, 87n
Leclerc, France, 319n
LeDuc, Doug, 8n
Lee, Don Y., 150n
Lee, J. A., 115

Lee, Kam-hon, 106n
Leenders, Michiel R., 395n
Lehman, Bruce A., 157n
Lei, David, 500n
Leong, Siew Meng, 99n
Leonidou, Leonidas C., 440n, 454n, 455n
Lerman, Dawn B., 385n
Lesch, William C., 465n
Leung, Kwok, 398n
Leung, Tony, 366n
Levenstein, Margaret C., 391n
Levin, Richard C., 26n
Levitt, Theodore, 18n, 219n, 229n, 247n
Leyden, John, 149n
Li, Jiatao, 284n
Li, Shaomin, 453n
Li, Tiger, 474n, 478n
Liang, Neng, 471n
Lieberman, Martin B., 234n, 264n
Lieberthal, Kenneth, 254n
Lien-Ti Bei, 142n
Liesch, Peter W., 454n
Lilien, G. L., 380n, 381n
Lim, Chae Un, 393n, 404n
Liu, Lucy, 366n
Llosa, Mario Vargas, 9n
Loe, Terry W., 405n
Lopez, Jos'è Ignacio, 417
Lovelock, Christopher H., 323n
Low, George S., 399n
Luery, David, 500n
Lunardini, Fernando, 521n
Luo, Yadong, 33n, 278n, 293
Lusch, Robert F., 139n
Lutz, Ulrich, 346n

M
MacCormack, Alan David, 250n
Macdonnell, Rhiannon, 546n, 557n
Mackay, John, 370, 370n
Madhok, A., 293n
Mahajan, Vijay, 228n, 508n
Maheswaran, Durairaj, 120n, 317n, 318n
Mahon, John F., 274n
Maignan, Isabelle, 549n
Maines, Laureen A., 541n
Majkgård, Anders, 453n
Makadok, Richard, 234n
Makar, Stephen D., 68n
Malhotra, Naresh K., 177n, 178n
Mann, Michael A., 13n
Mansfield, Edward D., 144n
Manwani, Harish, 517, 524n
Martin, Diane, 558n
Martin, Xavier, 432n

Martinez, Ruy, 405
Martinsons, M. G., 277n, 279
Mathur, Sameer, 522n
Mauborgne, Renée A., 500n
McBeth, John, 128n
McBride, Brad, 480–481
McCann-Erickson, 370n
McCosker, Colin, 273n
McCoy, Terry L., 76n
McGuirk, Anne, 41n
McKinney, Joseph A., 321n
McLymont, Rosalind, 465n
Meier, Johannes, 276n
Menguc, Bulent, 458n
Menzies, Hugh D., 127n
Meyer, Klaus, 519n
Michael, David C., 510n
Michaels, Ronald E., 394n, 404n
Miller, Chip, 355n
Miller, Edwin L., 409n, 412n
Miller, Tom, 217
Miniard, Paul W., 98n, 294n
Minor, Michael S., 142n, 367n
Mitchell, Jennifer, 177n
Mitra, Debanjan, 200n, 287n
Mittal, Lakshmi, 256
Miyashita, Cynthia, 448
Moffett, Michael H., 63n, 66
Moinzadeh, Kamran, 126n
Mol, Michael J., 254n, 432n
Money, R. Bruce, 397n
Montgomery, David B., 176n, 234n, 244n, 264n
Moon, Hee-Cheol, 394n, 404n
Moore, Jeri, 299n, 300n
Morales, Evo, 264
Moreno, Ramon, 60n
Morita, Masataka, 387n
Morrison, Allen J., 249n
Morwitz, Vicki, 563n
Motlana, Patience, 306
Mottner, Sandra, 271n
Moyer, Reed, 25
Mullen, Michael R., 175n, 397n, 474n, 477n
Muller, Eitan, 228n,
Muller, R. E., 12
Munilla, Linda S., 152n
Murdoch, Rupert, 134
Murphy, William H., 394
Murphy, Patrick E., 543n
Murray, Edwin A., Jr., 274n
Murray, Janet Y., 13n, 254n, 432n, 436n
Myers, John G., 356n
Myers, Matthew B., 476n

N

Nachum, Lilach, 20n
Nagai, Hirohisa, 397, 397n
Nagashima, Akira, 317n
Naidu, G. M., 152n
Namakforoosh, Naghi, 183n
Narasimban, Ram, 428n
Narayandas, Das, 347n
Nathan, Ranga, 69n
Naughton, Keith, 456n
Navarro, Peter, 143n
Naylor, Thomas H., 492n
Nebenzahl, Israel D., 318n
Neelankavil, James P., 120n
Nelson, Emily, 442n
Nelson, Richard Alan, 386n
Nelson, Richard R., 26n
Neuijen, Bram, 394n
New, William, 160n
Newkirk, David, 361
Newman, Karen L., 398n
Newmann, Lawrence James, 250n
Nickerson, Jack A., 436n
Nicolaud, B., 321n
Nierop, Tom, 144n
Niiro, Katsuhiro, 149n
Nijssen, Edwin J., 302n
Nill, Alexander, 316n
Nisbett, Richard, 106, 109n
Nishimura, Kiyohiko G., 387n
Nixon, Richard, 59
Noboru, Hatakeyama, 443n
Nohria, Nitin, 498n
Nollen, Stanley D., 398n
Nomura, Hiroshi, 149n
Nye, William W., 468

O

Obama, Barack, 280
O'Boyle, Thomas F., 412n
Odgers, John F., 428n
Ohayv, Denise Daval, 394n
Ohmae, Kenichi, 33, 244
Okoroafo, Sam C., 136n, 262n
Oksenberg, Michael, 314n
O'Neill, Jim, 505, 506n
Oppenheim, Jeremy, 546n
Onkvist, Sak, 131
Onzo, Naoto, 178n, 419n
Owen, Michael, 366
Oxley, Martin, 215n

P

Palepu, Krishna G., 380, 381
Palumbo, F., 381n

Pan, Yigang, 287n, 453n
Pantzalis, Christos, 68n
Papanikolaw, Jim, 470n
Parry, Mark E., 248n,
Pascale, Richard D., 252n
Pearce, R. D., 12n
Peers, Martin, 162n
Peng, Mike W., 293n, 519n
Penttinen, Risto, 494n
Perdue, Jeanne M., 133n
Perez, Javier, 276n
Perlmutter, Howard V., 14n, 15
Peterson, Mark, 177, 177n
Peterson, Robert M., 13n, 119n
Petras, James, 44
Pett, Timothy L., 13n
Piercy, Nigel F., 398n
Pies, John, 201n
Pitt, Leyland, 379
Pluess, Jessica Davis, 553n
Polegato, Rosemary, 354n
Polonsky, Michael, 548n
Pons, Frank, 364n
Pornpitakpan, Chanthika, 393n
Porter, Lyman W., 411n
Porter, Michael E., 20n, 36, 37n, 206n,
   228n, 232, 233n, 246n, 289n, 494n
Potter, Pitman B., 314n
Powell, Bill, 42
Prahalad, C. K., 3n, 243n, 250n, 254n
Prasad, V. Kanti, 152n
Preble, John F., 273n
Presley, Elvis, 475
Price, Linda L., 521n
Probert, Jocelyn, 95n

Q

Qinghou, Zong, 259
Quelch, John A., , 205n, 209,
   227n, 299n, 312n 347n, 374n, 489n,
   490n, 518n, 519n, 540n
Quinn, John Paul, 85n

R

Rajaratnam, Daniel, 436n
Raju, P. S., 91n
Ramaprasad, J., 362n
Ramsauer, R., 493
Randall, E. James, 243n
Rao, C. P., 455n
Rapp, Stan, 192n
Reardon, James, 355n
Reardon, Kathleen K., 406n
Redding, Gordon, 490n
Reichheld, Frederick, 395n

Reitman, Valerie, 71n
Reynolds, Frank, 474n
Reynolds, Nina, 392n
Rialp, Alex, 54n
Rialp, Josep, 54n
Richards, Donald, 45n
Ricks, David A., 104n
Rijkens, Rein, 365n
Ritson, Mark, 475n
Robinson, Chris, 176n
Robinson, Patrick J., 471n
Roddick, Anita, 243
Rohm, Andrew, 380n
Roll, Martin, 1n
Romeo, Jean B., 316n, 319n
Root, Franklin R., 261, 271
Rosa, Jose Antonio, 523n
Rosenbloom, Bert, 439n
Rosenbloom, Richard S., 27n
Rosenfield, Donald B., 250n
Rosenzweig, Philip M., 398n
Roth, Kendall, 249n
Roth, Martin S., 316n, 319n
Roth, Victor J., 389n
Rouzies, Dominique, 403n
Rowley, Chris, 419n
Rugman, Alan M., 26n, 249n
Rumelt, Richard P., 252n
Russell, Craig J., 265n
Russell, Gregory R., 152n
Russow, Lloyd C., 262n, 456n
Ryans, John K., Jr., 86n
Rybina, Liza, 355n

S

Sagri, Steven, 476n
Sahay, Arvind, 238n, 446n
Sakano, Tomoaki, 178n, 419n
Sakurai, Joji, 448
Samiee, Saeed, 340n, 455n, 463n, 464n
Sampson, Peter, 212n
Sanders, Geert, 394n
Sanders, Gerard, 410n
Sano, Yoshihiro, 406n
Sashi, C. M., 474n, 477n
Saxton, Jim, 143n
Schindler, Robert M., 119n
Schmidt, Jeffrey B., 456n
Schmitt, Bernd H., 99, 101n, 103n, 319n
Schouten, John, 558n
Schroiff, Hans-Willi, 325
Schrooten, Mechthild, 77n
Schuiling, Isabelle, 18n
Schultz, Don E., 385n
Schütte, Hellmut, 95n

Schweinsberg, Christie, 461n
Seal, 366n
Sebenius, James K., 409n
Segalla, Michael, 403n
Seifert, Bruce, 438n
Sekaran, Uma, 405n
Sen, Sankar, 533n, 541n, 563n
Sequeira, I. K., 380n
Servan-Schreiber, J. J., 10
Sethi, S. Prakash, 123n
Shama, Avraham, 291n
Shang, Cian-Fong, 142n
Shankar, Venkatesh, 263n
Shanley, Mark, 234n
Shapiro, Roy D., 446n
Shar, Michael, 133n
Sharma, D. Deo, 453n
Sharma, Subhash, 317n
Sharma, Varinder M., 391n
Sharon, Ariel, 118, 301
Shaver, J. Myles, 129n
Shaw, John J., 131
Sheffet, Mary Jane, 163n, 474n
Shepherd, Dean, 234n
Shimp, Terence A., 317n
Shin, Geon-Cheol, 456n
Shiomi, Eiji, 149n
Shishkin, Philip, 162n
Shoham, Aviv, 142n
Shultz, Clifford J., II, 316n
Siders, Mark, 317n
Sigu'é, Simon P., 395n
Sikora, Ed, 479
Simintiras, A., 392n
Simkins, Betty J., 68n
Simmons, Lee C., 119n
Simon, Hermann, 348n
Simone, Joseph T., 314n
Simonin, Bernard, 233n
Simonson, Alex, 103n
Singh, Nitish, 9n, 243n
Singh, Saraswati P., 335
Sinkula, James M., 149n
Sirkin, Harold, 40n
Slater, Robert W., 500n
Slocum, John W., Jr., 500n
Smith, Jeffrey, 86n
Smith, Timothy, 436n
Soenen, Luc A., 68n
Sohi, Ravi, 392n
Sohmer, Slade, 402n
Song, X. Michael, 248nn, 249n,
Soros, George, 126n
Sowinski, Lara L., 474n
Spekman, Robert E., 406n

Speer, Lawrence J., 132n, 250n
Spencer, Aron, 143n
Sprinkle, Geoffrey B., 541n
Spich, Robert, 420n
Stafford, J., 182n
Stahl, Gunter K., 409n, 412n
Stallone, Sylvester, 382
Stam, A., 262
Steele, Henry C., 179n
Steenkamp, J-B. E. M., 180n, 181n, 182,
 197, 204n, 217n, 217n, 218n,
 299nStern, Scott, 36, 37n
Sternquist, Brenda, 441n
Stiglitz, Joseph E., 2n
Stiner, John E., 161
Stonehill, Arthur I., 63n, 66
Stopford, John M., 497
Strauss, Levi, 224, 288, 296, 298, 334,
 347, 361, 543
Stremersch, Stefan, 200n, 204n
Strizhakova, Yuliya, 521n
Stump, Rodney L., 458n
Sudharshan, D., 317n
Sugiyama, Yoshikuni, 51
Suh, Taewon, 293n
Sullivan, Sherry E., 116
Sultan, Faureena, 380, 380n
Suslow, Valerie Y., 391
Sutton, Paul, 19n
Swait, Joffre, 300n
Swaminathan, V., 318
Swan, K. Scott, 238n, 246n
Swartz, Gordon, 347
Swasy, Alecia, 90n
Swenson, Michael J., 392n
Synodinos, N. E., 358n

T
Takagi, Haruo, 397n
Takeuchi, Hirotaka, 206n, 246n
Tan, J. Justin, 317n
Tang Wei, 371
Taylor, Earl L., 205n, 299n, 540n
Taylor, James R., 176n
Taylor, Virginia A., 499
Teece, David J., 26
Teegen, Hildy J., 136n, 137n–138
Tellis, Gerard J., 180n, 181n, 234n, 518n,
 519n
Terpstra, Vern, 106, 106n, 208n
Teyssier, Sabrina, 541n
Thieme, R. Jeffrey, 249n
Thyfault, Mary E., 454n
Tihanyi, Laszlo, 265n
Toh, So Min, 412n

Toloken, Steve, 461n
Törnblom, Richard, 306n
Torres, Anna, 540n
Townes, Charles, 156
Tribo, Joseph, A., 540n
Trivisonno, Nicholas, 219
Trudel, Remi, 541n
Tse, David K., 97n, 453, 522n
Tsong, C-S, 277
Tsurumi, Hiroki, 252n
Tsurumi, Yoshi, 252n
Tu, Howard, 116
Tull, Donald S., 191n
Tuncalp, Secil, 179n
Tung, Rosalie L., 409n, 412n
Turnbull, David, 494n
Turner, Neil, 332
Turpin, Dominique, 279n

U
Ueno, Susumu, 405n
Ungson, Gerardo R., 287n
Unnava, H. Rao, 540n
Upmeyer, N., 182
Useem, Jerry, 138

V
Vachani, Sushil, 137n
Valenzuela, Ana, 300n
van Agtmael, Antoine, 505
Van den Bulte, Christophe, 381n
Vandermerwe, Sandra, 196n, 200n
Vandevert, Paulsen K., 41n
Van Heerde, Harald, 560n
Vanhonacker, Wilfried, 280n, 281n
Van Wensen, Katelijne, 553n
Verhoef, Peter, 540n
Vernon, I. R., 353
Vernon, Raymond, 24n, 53n
Vertinsky, Ilan, 106n
Vibha, Gaba, 287
Vida, Irena, 355n
Viswanathan, Madhubalan, 523n
Volkema, Roger, 405n
Vuursteen, Karel, 301

W
Wagner, Hans-Christian, 170n
Wakefield, Kirk, 405n
Walker, Chip, 208n
Walsh, Michael G., 349
Walters, Peter G. P., 455n
Warner, Malcolm, 419n
Watras, Michael, 382
Webster, Frederick E., Jr., 14n, 244n

Wedel, Michael, 199n, 204n
Weekly, James K., 336n
Weeks, William A., 405n
Wehrung, Donald A., 106n
Weidner, Kelly L., 523n
Weimer, De'Ann, 68n
Weinstein, Fannie, 243n
Weir, David, 149n
Weiss, Stephen E., 406n, 408
Weitz, Barton A., 403n
Welch, Brooke, 159n
Welch, Jack, 410
Wells, Louis T., Jr., 25, 497n
Welzel, Christian, 114
Werner, Steve, 293n
Wesberg, Nancy R., 159n
Wheiler, Kent W., 160n
White, Katherine, 546n, 557n

Wickremeratne, Lakshman Y., 463n
Wiese, Carsten, 349n
Wigand, Rolf T., 47
Wilkinson, Timothy J., 11, 13n, 129n, 153n
Williams, J. D., 380n
Williams, S. C., 175n
Williamson, Nicholas C., 391n
Williamson, Oliver E., 26n
Williamson, Peter, , 514n
Wind, Yoram, 199n, 471n
Winter, Sidney G., 26n
Witcher, Karene, 82n
Woetzel, Jonathan R., 276n
Wood, Van R., 317n

Y
Yagi, Shigeru, 192n
Yardley, Jim, 130n

Yi Chen, Cathy, 317, 318
Yim, Chi Kin, 522
Yip, George S., 205, 230, 239, 240, 323n,
You Nuo, 255n
Yu, Zhu Fang, 364
Yukl, G., 342

Z
Zadeh, Lofti A., 248
Zaklama, Loula, 329n
Zeile, William J., 13n
Zeng, Ming, 514n
Zhang, Yong, 120n
Zhao, Hongxin, 243n, 293n
Zhou, Lianxi, 364n
Zou, Shaoming, 19n, 228n
Zoubir, Yahir H., 405n
Zysman, John, 430n

Company Index

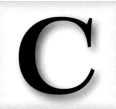

Note: The letter(s) 'e', 'gp', 'n' following page number(s) refer to exhibit, global perspective and end notes respectively

A
A. T. Kearney Inc., 433, 433n
Acer, 1, 4, 239
AchieveGlobal, 402
    omnibus survey, China, 171e
Adams, 454n
Adidas, 384e
AES Corp., 136
Ahold, 86, 303, 303n
Airbus, 133, 133n
AirTel, 520
AKI, 277
Alcatel-Lucent, 281, 281n
Alcoa, 161
Aldi, 537
Alibaba, 510, 525
Allied Domecq, 98
Amazon, 226, 425, 427, 476, 524
    e-commerce, 5–6, 45–48
    German laws and, 161
AMD, 239
American Express, 82
America Online (AOL), 236, 237gp
    in China, 237gp
    Lenovo partnering with, 237gp
Amway, 119, 255, 376–377
Apple, 539
Apple Computer, 14
    foreign expansion, 14
    iTunes, 236
Aramis, 236
Arnold, 295n, 440n, 494n
Arthur Andersen & Co., 54
Asea Brown Boveri, 490, 494,
    494n, 502
Asia Market Intelligence (AMI), 97
Associated British Foods, 544e
Assured Logistics, 427
AT&T, 156gp, 322
Autolatina, 277
Avtovaz, 134
Avis, 241
Avon, 119, 217n, 376, 410

direct-selling model, 377n
"Let's Talk" campaign, 217
Axe, 205, 331, 370

B
Baidu, 6, 542gp
Bain & Co., 395
Bajaj, 256
Bank of China, 467
Barilla, 54
Barnes and Noble, 226
Bayer, 155
BBC, 1
Ben & Jerry's ice cream, 540
Benetton, 372
BenQ, 283
Billabong, 20
BlackBerry, 253
Black & Decker, 19, 235–236
Blistex, 361
Blockbuster Video, 251, 382
BMW, 4, 9, 17, 170, 195, 339, 373, 378,
    380, 557, 559
    global manufacturing network, 17
    positioning study, 170
    website, 557, 558
Body Shop, 243, 540, 544
Boeing, 130
Boots, 275gp
Booz Allen & Hamilton, 361
Bose, 309, 395
Bossini, 319
Bottomdollar.com, 476
BP, 554
BP Deepwater Horizon oil spill, 540
British Airways, 229
British Oil (BP), 308, 308gp
BSC, 402
Buckler, 200
Burberry's, 98, 98n
Burger King, 9, 510
BuyUSA.com, 466
BYD, 511, 512

C
Cadbury, 281, 351, 352, 354
Calty Design Research, 428
Camel, 299
Campbell Soup, 310, 410
Canada Post Corp., 427
Canadian Imperial Bank of Commerce, 68
Canon, 206
    marketing programs, 206
    universal product with all features, 246,
    247
Carlsberg, 355, 379, 383, 504
    viral marketing, 383
Carrefour, 403, 441, 442, 445, 545
    outpacing Wal-Mart, 224
Cartoon Network, 118
Case, 410
Caterpillar, 267, 268
Cathay Pacific, 201, 467, 543, 543n
CCTV, 354, 371, 372
Cemex, 1, 3
Cert, 94
Cerveceria Cuauhtemoc Moctezuma, 252
Chery, 185
China Mobile, 380
Chiquita, 104
Chrysler, 4, 125, 132, 215
Cisco Systems, 5, 256
Citibank Malaysia, 322
Citigroup, 234, 486
Clan MacGregor, 81
Clinique, 236
Clover company, 306
Cnet.com, 476
CNN, 1, 223
Coach, 109
Coca-Cola, 17, 68, 93, 103, 239, 274, 280,
    330, 417, 417n, 445, 456, 554, 559
    in China, 333
    consumer segment, 456
    currency hedging by, 68
    distribution, 417
    geographic structure, 488e

Coca-Cola (*Continued*)
global advertising, 239
Huiyuan Juice and, 280
in India, 93
in Japan, 336e
local branding, 333
multinational product lines, 309
in Muslim countries, 103
Pepsi-Co and, 330
Colgate-Palmolive, 196n, 261, 551, 551e
Columbia Pictures, 79
Commerce One, Inc., 431
Compaq, 4, 239, 395, 425
Compuware Corp, 431
Converse, 316
Covisint, 431
Cummins Engines, 291
Cyrix, 239

D
Daewoo, 9, 451
Daiei, 448gp
Daihatsu, 80
Daimler, 329
DaimlerChrysler, 431
Daksh, 514
Danone, 259, 536e, 539, 544e
Clover company and, 306
Wahaha Group joint venture, 259
Danzas AEI Intercontinental, 426–427, 427n
Datacraft, 276
DDB Needham, 299
Deere & Co., 253
Delhaize, 331, 331n
Dell, 496, 536e
Dell Computer, 6, 14, 32, 82, 119–120,
226, 239, 426, 437–438, 496, 536e
direct-selling model, 377n
e-commerce and, 423–425
foreign expansion, 14
free trade zones and, 436–438
logistics, 425–427
online sales, 226
organizational structure, 501
price trimming, 82
"sell-direct" strategy, 239
Dentsu, 106, 107e, 372, 374
DHL, 230e, 421, 427, 486
Diageo, 5, 314, 314n, 528, 528gp
Diesel, 372
Disney, 91, 91n, 103, 103n, 240, 240n,
270, 299, 306
Dôme Coffees, 3
Dow Chemical, 150, 150n, 377, 489–490,
492, 554

Dow Jones, 553e
Dunkin' Donuts, 118, 272e, 310, 310n
DuPont, 423, 423n, 474, 531, 546
Durex, 186e
DSM, 530
Dymocks, 425

E
eBay, 6, 315, 315n, 317, 317n, 476
e-commerce, 6
ECA International, 412
Eddie Bauer, 448gp
Electrolux, 247, 302n, 303, 303n, 403
brand architecture guidelines, 303–304,
304e
product design families, 247
salesforce, 402, 403
Eli Lilly, 169e, 330, 426–427, 427n
logistics, 426–427
pricing, 330–331, 331n
weight loss product marketing research,
169e
EMI Group, 162, 162n
Emirates Air, 510
ENERGY STAR, 553e
Epson, 20
Ericsson, 20, 276, 276n, 488
ERX Logistics, 426
Esomar, 179–180, 180e, 184
ESPN, 368
Esprit, 81, 82n
Estée Lauder, 236–238, 238n, 456
customer-focused approach, 236–238
in Germany, 456
Ethisphere, 553e
Eunique Logistics, 427
Exxon, 137–139, 138gp, 240, 240n

F
Fabergé, 298
Federal Express, 322, 427
Ferrero Rocher, 314
Fiat, 90, 90n, 132, 356e
Fisher-Price, 93, 93n, 103, 103n
Ford, 4, 9, 19, 47, 132, 233, 253, 277,
277n, 358, 410, 417, 431, 456, 527
cost advantage, 132
design centers, 253
free trade zones and, 437
in Japan, 456
product invention, 252
Volkswagen joint venture, 277
Volvo and, 417
"1001 Fountains", 539
Fox Television, 134

Friends of the Earth, 138gp
Fuji, 251, 252n, 274, 447n
Fujitsu, 20

G
Gap, 537, 545, 548
Gateway, 274n
Geely, 233, 281, 312, 319, 417, 417n
General Electric, 162, 235, 266, 410, 444,
481gp
General Mills, 265, 270, 410, 544e
General Motors Corp, 4, 6, 9, 18, 27, 80,
95e, 134, 143, 215, 240, 245, 249,
345, 356e, 358, 410, 417, 431
in China, 215
logistics, 417
R&D at, 245–246
Thailand production plan, 80
General Nutrition Centers, 273
Gerber's, 207
GfK Roper Consulting, 545, 545e
Gillette, 97, 97n, 104, 104n, 270, 410, 521,
521n
Giordano, 319
GlaxoSmithKline (GSK), 103, 188, 330,
341, 342, 345, 346gp, 347
Internal Revenue Service, U.S. and, 341
pricing, 346gp, 347
Global Alliance, 543
GlobeScan, 546
Goldman Sachs, 256, 505, 505n, 506, 506n
Gome, 120
Goodyear, 251, 353, 410
Google, 6, 9, 154, 253, 270, 297n, 542, 542gp
Greenpeace, 138gp
Grolsch, 262, 263, 263n
Grupo Hermés, 136
Grupo Modelo, 3, 281, 281n
GTE Sylvania, 27
Gucci, 110, 545

H
H&M, 547, 550e, 554
Häagen-Dazs, 5, 329
Haier, 1, 510, 510n
Hakuhodo, 210, 210n, 211e, 374
Hamlet, 372, 372n
Heineken, 165, 200, 200n, 281, 281n, 339
marketing research, 200
pricing policy, 339
Heinz, 281, 331, 488, 489e, 514e, 544e, 548e
Henkel, 295, 345
formula adjustment, 345
local brands, 333
Herbal Essences, 363

Hermès, 136
Hershey Foods, 283
Hewlett Packard (HP), 4, 38, 82, 95, 256, 282gp, 438, 481gp
  branding committee, 495
  global equivalent name, 95
  price trimming, 82
Hindustan Lever, 256, 328
Hindustan Unilever Ltd (HUL), 517gp
Hitachi, 239, 248, 249
Hoffman-La Roche, 427
Honda, 4, 12, 12n, 24, 32, 229, 248, 248n, 277, 277n, 536e
  in United States, 228
  universal product with different positioning, 246
  "world car," 12
Honeywell International, 162
Hoya, 502
HP, 4
HSBC, 324
HTC, 271,
Huawei, 281, 281n, 511, 515, 515n, 516n
Hugo Boss, 372
Huiyuan Juice, 280, 280n
Human Rights Watch, 138gp
Hyundai, 3, 4, 319, 320n, 420, 457e, 561gp,

I

IBM, 4, 8, 109, 160n, 198, 254, 256, 276, 282gp, 352, 433, 486, 492, 496, 510, 514
  Lenovo and, 237gp, 281, 282gp, 307n
  translation errors, 352
Ikea, 81, 95e, 109, 109n, 115, 115n, 273, 285, 290, 537, 549, 555–557
  inventory, 81
  in Japan, 285
InBev, 73, 265, 267, 267n, 280, 280n, 334, 510, 510n
Information Resources (IRI), 173
Infosys Technologies, 1
Intel, 9, 232, 366
  brand awareness in China, 367
  modular advertising approach, 366
  Pentium chip, 367
Interbrand, 297, 297n, 443, 536e, 537
Intimate Brands, 448gp
Iona Technologies, PLC, 11gp
Ito-Yokado, 446, 448gp
iTunes, 539

J

Jack Daniels, 206, 315
Jaguar, 253, 253n, 378, 378n, 510

J.D. Streett & Company, 466
Johnnie Walker, 81, 203, 203n, 314, 362, 365e
  fighting product piracy, 313
  marketing schema, 202
Johnson & Johnson, 356e, 499, 536e
Jollibee Foods, 256

K

Kao, 316
Keane, Inc., 435
Kecskemeti Konzervgyar, 311
Kelkoo, 6
Kellogg Co., 265, 518, 518n, 531, 544e
  in India, 518
Kentucky Fried Chicken (KFC), 66–68
  Mexico/exchange rate fluctuations, 65–66
KFC, 560, 560n, 562
Kia Motors, 320
KiK, 545
Kimberly-Clark, 217,
Kirin Breweries, 445
K-Mart, 224
Kodak, 69, 153, 251, 252n, 299
  anti-counterfeiting system, 159
  currency hedging by, 68
Komatsu, 478e, 479e
KPMG, 276, 474
Kraft, 560
Kraft Foods, 356e
  Oreo cookies in China, 168
Kraft General Foods Europe (KGFE), 497
Krispy Kreme, 118
Kuwait Petroleum Corp. (KPC), 133

L

Labatt International, 252
Land Rover, 215, 253n, 335, 510
Lands'End, 375, 375n, 448gp
Lawson, 447
LEGO, 334, 334n
Lenovo, 1, 4, 198, 237gp, 282gp, 383, 432, 496, 510
  AOL partnering with, 237gp
  IBM and, 198, 282gp, 352, 510
Levi Strauss, 224, 347, 361, 543
  LeviLink, 224
Lifebuoy, 256, 517gp, 559
Li Ning, 512, 513, 513n
Lipton tea, 275
Listerine, 327
Liushen, 231
Liz Claiborne, 153
L'Oréal, 119n, 290, 298, 356, 358, 359e, 544, 555, 556

  resource allocation, 358, 359
Lush, 540, 556
Louis Vuitton, 110, 315, 349, 365e
Lufthansa, 137, 137n
LVMH, 320, 477

M

Magnavox, 27
Mahindra & Mahindra, 4, 253
Makita, 235
Makro, 323
Mark, 97
Marks & Spencer, 445
Marlboro, 370
Mars, 504, 544, 544e
  brand name changeover, 306, 307
  in cluster analysis, 220, 221
  in Russia, 504
Mary Kay, 377, 485
Matsushita, 444n
Mattel, 461
Maxam, 231
Maxfactor, 232
Maxim's, 8, 54
Maxtor, 239
Maytag Corp., 300
Mazda, 6, 6n, 233
McBride, 442, 480gp
McDonald's, 65, 120, 188, 188n, 218, 256, 296, 298, 301, 310e, 328, 334, 335, 364, 371, 371n, 447, 485, 485n, 494, 504, 510, 510n, 520
  advertising in India, 356e
  Big Mac Index, 65, 65e
  in Brazil, 371
  delivery service, 120
  "Hamburger University," 494, 494n
  local roots, 218
  market size assessment, 186
  multinational product lines, 309
  in Russia, 504
  strategic marketing planning, 484
McDonnell-Douglas, 130
McIlhenny, 107, 200
McKinsey, 546
McKinsey consultants, 279
Mecca Cola, 301, 301n
Mercedes-Benz, 129, 218n, 387, 456, 474
Merck, 68, 243, 243n, 402
  currency hedging, 68
  global marketing problems, 240
MetLife, 264
Metro Group, 119, 226, 448gp, 510
MGM, 73
Michelin, 86, 251, 489

Microsoft, 115, 162, 206, 225, 239, 250gp, 271, 297e, 314, 315, 315n, 433, 469gp, 511
 fighting product piracy, 313, 511
 global dominance battle, 250gp
 Nikon cross-patent agreement, 271, 271n
 online customer education, 225
 outsourcing, 469gp
 pricing, 345
 standards, 208
 Xbox, 368
Mitsubishi Heavy Industries, 391, 457
Mittal Steel, 1
Mondelez, 544, 544e
Morgan Stanley Dean Witter, 110
Motorola, 95e, 277, 395, 474, 477
Mövenpick, 9
MSN, 511
MTV, 4, 98, 368
Mysimon.com, 476
MySpace, 511

N
National Small Business United, 54
NBC, 1
Nestlé, 24, 92, 96gp, 192, 232, 265, 356e, 362, 366, 486e, 493e, 495, 524, 533, 536e, 537, 539, 544, 544e, 558, 562
 bargaining power, 232e
 brand architecture, 303
 brand champion, 495
 centralized decisions, 232
 cluster analysis, 221e
 concept cooperation advertising approach, 365–366
 General Mills joint venture, 265
 multinational product lines, 309–312
 organizational structure, 488e
 price spectrum, 310
 segmentation/positioning, 214e
 target marketing, 192
Nike, 4, 9, 23, 316, 355, 524
 "Just Do It" brand, 217
 working environment, 394
Nikon, 271
Nintendo, 250gp
Nissan's, 555
Nissan Motor Corp., 249, 356e, 360, 360gp, 431
 fuzzy logic and, 248
 shift advertising campaign, 360gp
Nokia, 20, 47, 183gp, 214, 288–289, 514
 brand forum, 212
 in China, 40

emerging market project strategy, 510
 ethnographic research, 183gp
 Japan exit strategy, 287–288
Novartis, 54, 86, 256
NutraSweet, 290

O
Omo, 523–524, 558
Oracle Corporation, 96, 433, 489
 global equivalent name, 95
Otis Elevator International, 335
Outboard Marine, 410
Oxfam, 540, 544e
Oxy, 82
OzBooks.com, 425

P
P&G, 536e, 558
Panasonic, 27, 249, 444, 520, 520n
 "Emerging Markets Win," 520
 fuzzy logic and, 248
Parker Pens, 353
Parrys, 269
Patlex Corp., 156gp
Pearl River Piano, 512
Pedigree, 306
Peninsula, 543
Pepsi Co, 260n, 516, 536–538, 539, 539n, 544e, 549, 552, 553, 556
 during Beijing Olympics, 119n
 Coca-Cola and, 330
 in Russia, 142
 Stolichnaya countertrade, 229e
Peugeot, 125
Pfizer, 47, 119, 330e, 522
Philips, 8, 27, 307, 427, 444, 460, 469gp, 492, 524
 organizational design, 486
 PROTECT system, 460
 Whirlpool and, 306–308
Pioneer Standard, 427
Pizza Hut, 3, 214, 215, 272n, 287, 382, 512
Pocari Sweat, 300
Pollo Campero, 9
Polo Ralph Lauren, 382gp
Population Services International (PSI), 116, 117gp
Prada, 327e
ProChile, 320
Proctor & Gamble, 90, 253, 287, 329, 347, 351, 354, 356e, 358, 375, 377, 441, 486
 advertising blunder, 351, 353
 advertising spending compared to Unilever, 356e

in Asia, 255
 in Australia, 298
 brand name changeover, 306
 diaper market share, 90
 every-day-low-pricing, 375
 in Japan, 442
 multinational product lines, 296, 309
 new product line, 311
 packaging, 329
 parallel imports, 346
 product piracy and, 315
 R & D of, 264
 resource allocation, 358, 359e
 in Russia, 347
PRS Group, 139
Publicis group, 11gp
Pudliszki, 301
Pureit, 535

Q
Quaker Oats, 265, 265n
Quality Express, 426
Quanta, 9, 430, 430n
Quicksilver, 20
QXL Ricardo, 6

R
Rakuten, 6, 226, 226n, 449, 449n
Raybo, 308
RCA, 27, 252
Reckitt-Benckiser, 289
Red Bull, 11gp, 378, 378n
Reebok, 379, 379n, 421
Renault, 4, 431, 512
Research in Motion (RIM), 253
ResMed, 438
Rittmuller, 512
Roche, 155
Rolex, 296, 456
Rolls Royce, 5, 312, 312n

S
Saatchi & Saatchi, 11gp
SABMiller, 206, 262n, 263n, 265, 265n, 314, 516
Safaricom, 324, 511, 515
Salem, 299
Samsonite, 98, 98n
Samsung Electronics, 1
Sanyo, 27, 153, 444
SAP, 232n, 297e, 433, 449, 469gp
Sarft, 371
Seagate Western Digital, 239
Sears, Roebuck & Co., 445

Seawind International, 470
Seibu, 448gp
Seiko, 20, 246, 476
Seiyu, 448gp
SEMATECH, 27
Semiconductor Manufacturing Technology
    (SEMATECH), 130
Sephora, 320
Service Corp. International, 322
7-Eleven, 5, 149, 229e, 445–447
7dream, 6
Seven & i Holdings Co., 5
Shangri-La, 543
Shanghai Jahwa Co., Ltd., 231, 320
Shanghai Pudong Development Bank,
    234
Sharp, 27, 252
Shell, 562
Shiseido, 299, 316
Siemens, 227, 252, 253, 383, 340, 381,
    382, 484, 492, 514, 521, 534
    fax technology, 252
    mobile trade show, 381, 382gp
Sina, 227, 510
SmithKline Beecham, 427
SM Mall of Asia, 508e
Snapple, 363
Sohu, 227, 237gp
Sony, 4, 8, 14, 27n, 146, 217, 234, 249,
    250gp, 274, 384, 422, 511
    drool campaign, 384
    first-mover advantage, 234
    fuzzy logic and, 248
    global dominance battle, 250gp
    Japan export control, 146
    microprocessor, 146
    miniaturization and, 14
    "My First Sony" brand, 217
    Playstation, 146
Southland Corporation, 446
Stanford Business School, 501
Star Alliance, One World, 324
Starbucks, 3, 79, 278e, 329, 552e
    fighting product piracy, 315
    partner criteria, 277e
    pricing, 315
    trendy customers, 79
Star TV, 223, 229, 379
Stolichnaya, 229
Strategy Research Corporation, 208
Suave, 558
Subway, 272e
Sun Microsystems, 283n
Suzuki, 135
Swatch, 298
Swedish Tobacco Co., 372

T
Taco Bell, 121, 121n, 272n, 382
TAG Heuer, 353, 353n, 365, 365n
Tata Consultancy Services, 510
Tata Motors, 253n, 357e
TelMex, 136
Tencent, 320, 510–511
Tesco, 265, 288, 442, 537, 559
Tesla's, 555
Texas Instruments, 12
The Nature Conservancy (TNC), 554
3Com, 281
3M, 474, 490, 501
Timberland, 218
Time Warner, Inc., 162, 237gp, 361
TNT, 283, 283n
Toei, 118
Toshiba, 4, 27, 94, 146, 426
Tower Records, 448gp
Toyota, 4, 8, 9, 56, 71, 77, 95e, 132, 247,
    370, 428, 428n, 494, 536e, 555, 557
    in China, 354
    General Motors joint venture, 134
    Lexus, 557
    product design families, 246
    profits, 56, 62
Toys 'R'Us, 224, 354, 445, 447gp
TTK, 270
Tupperware, 410
Twitter, 185, 491e, 562

U
UBS, 216gp, 353
Unilever, 81, 205, 207, 231, 254, 359e,
    383, 492, 499, 522–527, 535, 536e,
    544, 546, 547, 548, 555, 558–560
    Axe products, 205
    executive performance, 499
    in India, 254
    insurance companies and, 207
    local customs and, 253
    multi-local multinational, 492
    "One Unilever" plan, 231
    packaging, 99
    Project Shakti, 525, 525n
    resource allocation, 358–359
    viral marketing, 380, 383
Union Carbide, 150
Unisys, 377, 377n
United Distillers, 329
UPS, 104, 104n, 283, 421, 426–427

V
Victoria's Secret, 47
VIDJA, 555–556
Virginia Slims, 217, 372

Virgin Megastores, 448gp
Visa, 149, 355, 359, 359n, 360, 360n, 364,
    377, 495
Vodafone Group, 324, 515
Volkswagen, 125, 277, 346, 356e, 383,
    536e, 559
    competition abuses, 346
    viral marketing, 380, 383, 383n
Volvo, 132, 224, 233, 559
Von Zipper, 20

W
Wahaha Group, 259–260
Wal-Mart, 224–226, 229e, 255, 263, 442,
    445, 539, 539n
    in Argentina, 76
    Carrefour outpacing, 255
    checkouts, 449
    in China, 450
    in Europe, 443
    in Germany, 119
    international expansion timeline, 290,
        292e
    in Japan, 465, 491e
    online sales, 226
    revenues, 486
    suppliers, 489
    Trust-Mart, 255
Warner Lambert, 365e
Wasa Biscuits, 54, 54n
Watson's, 377
Weaver Popcorn Co., 8
Weight Watchers, 300
Wertkauf, 402
Weyerhaeuser, 8
Wharton School, Philadelphia, 68, 543
Whirlpool, 426, 481gp
Wipro, 514
World Peace Industrial, 427
Wrigley's, 269

X
Xerox, 86, 239, 274
Xingbake, 314

Y
Yadu Group, 314
Yahoo, 476, 511
    e-commerce, 5–6
Yamaha, 312
YouTube , 561gp
Yum! Brands, 3, 121, 272, 382, 512

Z
Zenith, 252
ZTE, 319, 511